The Legal Environment of Business, 7e

Custom Edition for UT-Chattanooga

Frank B. Cross & Roger LeRoy Miller

CENGAGE
Learning™

Australia • Brazil • Japan • Korea • Mexico • Singapore • Spain • United Kingdom • United States

CENGAGE
Learning™

The Legal Environment of Business, 7e: Custom Edition for UT-Chattanooga

Frank B. Cross & Roger LeRoy Miller

Executive Editors:
Michele Baird
Maureen Staudt
Michael Stranz

Project Development Manager:
Linda deStefano

Senior Marketing Coordinators:
Sara Mercurio
Lindsay Shapiro

Senior Production / Manufacturing Manager:
Donna M. Brown

PreMedia Services Supervisor:
Rebecca A. Walker

Rights & Permissions Specialist:
Kalina Hintz

Cover Image:
Getty Images*

* Unless otherwise noted, all cover images used by Custom Solutions, a part of Cengage Learning, have been supplied courtesy of Getty Images with the exception of the Earthview cover image, which has been supplied by the National Aeronautics and Space Administration (NASA).

ISBN-13: 978-0-324-83055-2

ISBN-10: 0-324-83055-6

Cengage Learning
5191 Natorp Boulevard
Mason, Ohio 45040
USA

Cengage Learning is a leading provider of customized learning solutions with office locations around the globe, including Singapore, the United Kingdom, Australia, Mexico, Brazil, and Japan. Locate your local office at:
international.cengage.com/region

Cengage Learning products are represented in Canada by Nelson Education, Ltd.

For your lifelong learning solutions, visit **custom.cengage.com**

Visit our corporate website at **cengage.com**

Printed in the United States of America

Brief Contents

APPENDICES

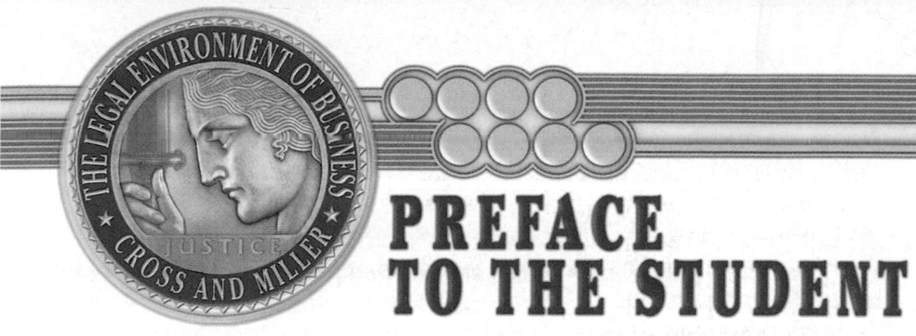

PREFACE TO THE STUDENT

Welcome to the legal environment of business. You are about to embark on the study of one of the most important topics you should master in today's changing world. A solid understanding of the legal environment of business can, of course, help you if you are going into the world of business. If you decide on a career in accounting, economics, finance, political science, or history, understanding how the legal environment works is crucial. Moreover, in your role as a consumer, you will be faced with some legal issues throughout your lifetime—renting an apartment, buying a house, obtaining a mortgage, and leasing a car, to mention only a few. In your role as an employee (if you don't go into business for yourself), you will need to know what rights you have and what rights you don't have. Even when you contemplate marriage, you will be faced with legal issues.

What You Will Find in This Text

As you will see as you thumb through the pages in this text, we have tried to make your study of the legal environment of business as efficient and enjoyable as possible. To this end, you will find the following aids:

1. **Mastering Terminology**—through ***key terms*** that are boldfaced, listed at the end of each chapter, and explained fully in the ***Glossary*** at the end of the book.
2. **Understanding Concepts**—through numerous ***Concept Summaries*** and ***Exhibits.***
3. **Observing the Law in the Context of the Real World**—through a ***Reviewing feature*** at the end of every chapter.
4. **Seeing How Legal Issues Can Arise**—through ***Video Questions*** based on Web-available short videos, many from actual Hollywood movies.
5. **Figuring Out How the Law Is Evolving**—through a feature called ***Emerging Trends.***
6. **Determining Today's Legal Controversies**—through a feature called ***Contemporary Legal Debates.***
7. **Gaining Insights into How the Law Affects or Is Affected by Other Issues**—through three new ***Insight*** features called ***Insight into E-Commerce, Insight into Ethics,*** and ***Insight into the Global Environment.***

The above list, of course, is representative only. You will understand much more of what the law is about as you read through the ***court cases*** presented in this book, including ***Extended Case excerpts,*** which will give you a feel for how the courts really decide cases, in the courts' language.

Improving Your Ability to Perform Legal Reasoning and Analysis

Although the legal environment of business may seem to be a mass of facts, your goal in taking this course should be an increased ability to use legal reasoning and analysis to figure out how legal situations will be resolved. To this end, you will find the following key learning features to assist you in mastering legal reasoning and analysis:

- **Finding and Analyzing Case Law**—In Chapter 1, you will find a section with this title that explains:
  1. Legal citations.
  2. The standard elements of a case.
  3. The different types of opinions a court can issue.
  4. How to read and understand cases.
- **Briefing a Case**—In Appendix A, you will see how to brief and analyze case problems. This explanation teaches you how to break down the elements of a case and will improve your ability to answer the ***Case Problems*** in each chapter.
- **Questions with Sample Answers**—At the end of each chapter, there is one hypothetical factual scenario that presents a legal question for which you can access a ***sample answer*** in Appendix I (and also on the text's Web site). This allows you to

practice and to see if you are answering the hypothetical problems correctly.

- **Case Problems with Sample Answers**—Each chapter has a series of chapter-ending ***Case Problems.*** You can find an answer to one problem in each chapter on this book's student companion Web site at **academic.cengage.com/blaw/cross**. You can easily compare your answer to the court's answer in the actual case.
- **Impact of This Case on Today's Law**—Each landmark classic case concludes with a short section that explains the relevance of older case law to the way courts reason today.
- **What If the Facts Were Different?**—This section, found at the end of selected cases, encourages you to think about how the outcome of a case might be different if the facts were altered.
- **The Ethical [E-Commerce, Global, or Legal Environment] Dimension**—Every case in this text concludes with two critical-thinking questions, which may include *What If the Facts Were Different?* questions, as discussed above. For this edition, we've included several new possibilities—*(The Ethical Dimension, The E-Commerce Dimension, The Global Dimension,* and *The Legal Environment Dimension.)* These questions ask you to explore the law in a variety of contexts to help you meet the specific curriculum requirements for business law students.

The Companion Student Web Site

As already mentioned, the companion student Web site at **academic.cengage.com/blaw/cross** provides you with short videos on various legal topics and with sample answers to one case problem per chapter. In addition, you will find the following:

- ***Interactive quizzes*** for every chapter.
- A ***glossary*** of terms for every chapter in the text.
- ***Flashcards*** that provide an optional study tool for reviewing the key terms in every chapter.
- ***Appendix A: How to Brief and Analyze Case Problems*** that will help you analyze cases. This useful appendix for the book is also provided on the Web site and can be downloaded.
- ***Legal reference materials*** including a "Statutes" page that offers links to the full text of selected statutes referenced in the text, a Spanish glossary, and links to other important legal resources available for free on the Web.
- ***Internet exercises*** for every chapter in the text (at least two per chapter) that introduce you to how to research the law online.
- ***Relevant Web sites*** for additional research for *Emerging Trends* features as well as links to the URLs listed in the *Law on the Web* section at the end of each chapter.
- ***Online Legal Research Guide*** that offers complete yet brief guidance to using the Internet and evaluating information obtained from the Internet. As an online resource, it now includes hyperlinks to the Web sites discussed for click-through convenience.
- ***Court case updates*** for follow-up research on topics covered in the text.
- ***Link to CengageNOW for* The Legal Environment of Business: *Interactive Assignment System*** with different types of questions related to every chapter in the text and one set of cumulative questions for each unit in the text. (Available on an instructor's request; see below.)

Interactive Assignments on the Web

Some of you may have instructors who provide assignments using our world-class interactive Web-based system, called **CengageNOW for *The Legal Environment of Business:* Interactive Assignment System.**

CengageNOW for *The Legal Environment of Business:* Interactive Assignment System allows you to improve your mastery of legal concepts and terminology, legal reasoning and analysis, and much more. Your instructor will give you further information if she or he decides to use this Web-based system.

Of course, whether or not you are using the CengageNOW system, you will wish to consider purchasing the *Study Guide,* which can help you get a better grade in your course (see the inside cover for details).

The law is all around you—and will be for the rest of your life. We hope that you begin your first course in business law and the legal environment with the same high degree of excitement that we, the authors, always have when we work on improving this text, now in its Seventh Edition. *The Legal Environment of Business* has withstood the test of time—thousands of students before you have already used and benefited by it.

Dedication

To Max,

You've come a long ways
in a few short years.
Your hard work, courage,
and mature sense of what is right
will serve you well.

R.L.M.

To my parents and sisters.

F.B.C.

UNIT ONE

The Foundations

CONTENTS

CHAPTER 1

Business and Its Legal Environment

One of the important functions of law in any society is to provide stability, predictability, and continuity so that people can be sure of how to order their affairs. If any society is to survive, its citizens must be able to determine what is legally right and legally wrong. They must know what sanctions will be imposed on them if they commit wrongful acts. If they suffer harm as a result of others' wrongful acts, they must know how they can seek redress. By setting forth the rights, obligations, and privileges of citizens, the law enables individuals to go about their business with confidence and a certain degree of predictability. The stability and predictability created by the law provide an essential framework for all civilized activities, including business activities.

What do we mean when we speak of "the law"? Although this term has had, and will continue to have, different definitions, they are all based on a general observation: at a minimum, **law** consists of *enforceable rules governing relationships among individuals and between individuals and their society.* These "enforceable rules" may consist of unwritten principles of behavior established by a nomadic tribe. They may be set forth in a law code, such as the Code of Hammurabi in ancient Babylon (c. 1780 B.C.E.) or the law code of one of today's European nations. They may consist of written laws and court decisions created by modern legislative and judicial bodies, as in the United States. Regardless of how such rules are created, they all have one thing in common: they establish rights, duties, and privileges that are consistent with the values and beliefs of their society or its ruling group.

Those who embark on a study of the legal environment will find that these broad statements leave unanswered some important questions concerning the nature of law. Part of the study of law, often referred to as **jurisprudence,** involves learning about different schools of jurisprudential thought and discovering how the approaches to law characteristic of each school can affect judicial decision making.

We open this introductory chapter with an examination of that topic. We then look at an important question for any student reading this text: How does the legal environment affect business decision making? We next describe the basic sources of American law, the common law tradition, and some general classifications of law. We conclude the chapter with sections offering practical guidance on several topics, including how to find the sources of law discussed in this chapter (and referred to throughout the text) and how to read and understand court opinions.

SECTION 1 Schools of Jurisprudential Thought

You may think that legal philosophy is far removed from the practical study of business law and the legal environment. In fact, it is not. As you will learn in the chapters of this text, how judges apply the law to specific disputes, including disputes relating to the business world, depends in part on their philosophical approaches to law.

Clearly, judges are not free to decide cases solely on the basis of their personal philosophical views or on their opinions about the issues before the court. A judge's function is not to *make* the laws—that is the function of the legislative branch of government—but to interpret and apply them. From a practical point of view, however, the courts play a significant role in defining what the law is. This is because laws enacted by legislative bodies tend to be expressed in general terms. Judges thus have some flexibility in interpreting and applying the law. It is because of this flexibility that different courts can, and often do, arrive at different conclusions in cases that involve nearly identical issues, facts, and applicable laws. This flexibility also means that each judge's unique personality, legal philosophy, set of values, and intellectual attributes necessarily frame the judicial decision-making process to some extent.

Over time several significant schools of legal, or jurisprudential, thought have evolved. We now look at some of them.

The Natural Law School

An age-old question about the nature of law has to do with the finality of a nation's laws, such as the laws of the United States at the present time. For example, what if a particular law is deemed to be a "bad" law by a substantial number of that nation's citizens? Must a citizen obey the law if it goes against his or her conscience to do so? Is there a higher or universal law to which individuals can appeal? One who adheres to the natural law tradition would answer these questions in the affirmative. **Natural law** denotes a system of moral and ethical principles that are inherent in human nature and that people can discover through the use of their natural intelligence, or reason.

The natural law tradition is one of the oldest and most significant schools of jurisprudence. It dates back to the days of the Greek philosopher Aristotle (384–322 B.C.E.), who distinguished between natural law and the laws governing a particular nation. According to Aristotle, natural law applies universally to all humankind.

The notion that people have "natural rights" stems from the natural law tradition. Those who claim that a specific foreign government is depriving certain citizens of their human rights implicitly are appealing to a higher law that has universal applicability. The question of the universality of basic human rights also comes into play in the context of international business operations. Should rights extended to workers in the United States, such as the right to be free of discrimination in the workplace, be extended to workers employed by a U.S. firm doing business in another country that does not provide for such rights? This question is rooted implicitly in a concept of universal rights that has its origins in the natural law tradition.

The Positivist School

In contrast, **positive law,** or national law (the written law of a given society at a particular point in time), applies only to the citizens of that nation or society. Those who adhere to the **positivist school** believe that there can be no higher law than a nation's positive law. According to the positivist school, there is no such thing as "natural rights." Rather, human rights exist solely because of laws. If the laws are not enforced, anarchy will result. Thus, whether a law is "bad" or "good" is irrelevant. The law is the law and must be obeyed until it is changed—in an orderly manner through a legitimate lawmaking process. A judge with positivist leanings probably would be more inclined to defer to an existing law than would a judge who adheres to the natural law tradition.

The Historical School

The **historical school** of legal thought emphasizes the evolutionary process of law by concentrating on the origin and history of the legal system. Thus, this school looks to the past to discover what the principles of contemporary law should be. The legal doctrines that have withstood the passage of time—those that have worked in the past—are deemed best suited for shaping present laws. Hence, law derives its legitimacy and authority from adhering to the standards that historical development has shown to be workable. Adherents of the historical school are more likely than those of other schools to strictly follow decisions made in past cases.

Legal Realism

In the 1920s and 1930s, a number of jurists and scholars, known as legal realists, rebelled against the historical approach to law. **Legal realism** is based on the idea that law is just one of many institutions in society and that it is shaped by social forces and needs. The law is a human enterprise, and judges should take social and economic realities into account when deciding cases. Legal realists also believe that the law can never be applied with total uniformity. Given that judges are human beings with unique personalities, value systems, and intellects, different judges will obviously bring different reasoning processes to the same case.

Legal realism strongly influenced the growth of what is sometimes called the **sociological school** of jurisprudence. This school views law as a tool for promoting justice in society. In the 1960s, for example, the justices of the United States Supreme Court played a leading role in the civil rights movement by upholding long-neglected laws calling for equal treatment for all Americans, including African Americans and other minorities. Generally, jurists who adhere to this philosophy of law are more likely to depart from past decisions than are those jurists who adhere to the other schools of legal thought. *Concept Summary 1.1* reviews the schools of jurisprudential thought.

Business Activities and the Legal Environment

As those entering the world of business will learn, laws and government regulations affect virtually all business activities—from hiring and firing decisions to workplace safety, the manufacturing and marketing of products, business financing, and more. To make good business decisions, a basic knowledge of the laws and regulations governing these activities is beneficial—if not essential. Realize also that in today's world a knowledge of "black-letter" law is not enough. Businesspersons are also pressured to make ethical decisions. Thus, the study of business law necessarily involves an ethical dimension.

Many Different Laws May Affect a Single Business Transaction

As you will note, each chapter in this text covers a specific area of the law and shows how the legal rules in that area affect business activities. Though compartmentalizing the law in this fashion promotes conceptual clarity, it does not indicate the extent to which a number of different laws may apply to just one transaction.

Consider an example. Suppose that you are the president of NetSys, Inc., a company that creates and maintains computer network systems for its clients, including business firms. NetSys also markets software for customers who require an internal computer network. One day, Hernandez, an operations officer for Southwest Distribution Corporation (SDC), contacts you by e-mail about a possible contract concerning SDC's computer network. In deciding whether to enter

CONCEPT SUMMARY 1.1
Schools of Jurisprudential Thought

School of Thought	Description
THE NATURAL LAW SCHOOL	One of the oldest and most significant schools of legal thought. Those who believe in natural law hold that there is a universal law applicable to all human beings. This law is discoverable through reason and is of a higher order than positive (national) law.
THE POSITIVIST SCHOOL	A school of legal thought centered on the assumption that there is no law higher than the laws created by the government. Laws must be obeyed, even if they are unjust, to prevent anarchy.
THE HISTORICAL SCHOOL	A school of legal thought that stresses the evolutionary nature of law and that looks to doctrines that have withstood the passage of time for guidance in shaping present laws.
LEGAL REALISM	A school of legal thought, popular during the 1920s and 1930s, that left a lasting imprint on American jurisprudence. Legal realists generally advocated a less abstract and more realistic and pragmatic approach to the law, an approach that would take into account customary practices and the circumstances in which transactions take place. Legal realism strongly influenced the growth of the *sociological school* of jurisprudence, which views law as a tool for promoting social justice.

into a contract with SDC, you should consider, among other things, the legal requirements for an enforceable contract. Are there different requirements for a contract for services and a contract for products? What are your options if SDC **breaches** (breaks, or fails to perform) the contract? The answers to these questions are part of contract law and sales law.

Other questions might concern payment under the contract. How can you guarantee that NetSys will be paid? For example, if payment is made with a check that is returned for insufficient funds, what are your options? Answers to these questions can be found in the laws that relate to negotiable instruments (such as checks) and creditors' rights. Also, a dispute may occur over the rights to NetSys's software, or there may be a question of liability if the software is defective. Questions may even be raised as to whether you and Hernandez had the authority to make the deal in the first place. A disagreement may arise from other circumstances, such as an accountant's evaluation of the contract. Resolutions of these questions may be found in areas of the law that relate to intellectual property, e-commerce, torts, product liability, agency, business organizations, or professional liability.

Finally, if any dispute cannot be resolved amicably, then the laws and the rules concerning courts and court procedures spell out the steps of a lawsuit. Exhibit 1–1 illustrates the various areas of law that may influence business decision making.

Ethics and Business Decision Making

Merely knowing the areas of law that may affect a business decision is not sufficient in today's business world. Businesspersons must also take ethics into account. As you will learn in Chapter 4, *ethics* is generally defined as the study of what constitutes right or wrong behavior. Today, business decision makers need to consider not just whether a decision is legal, but also whether it is ethical.

Throughout this text, you will learn about the relationship between the law and ethics, as well as about some of the types of ethical questions that often arise in the business context. For example, the unit-ending *Focus on Ethics* features in this text are devoted solely to the exploration of ethical questions pertaining to selected topics treated within the unit. We have also added several new features for this edition that stress

EXHIBIT 1–1 • Areas of the Law That May Affect Business Decision Making

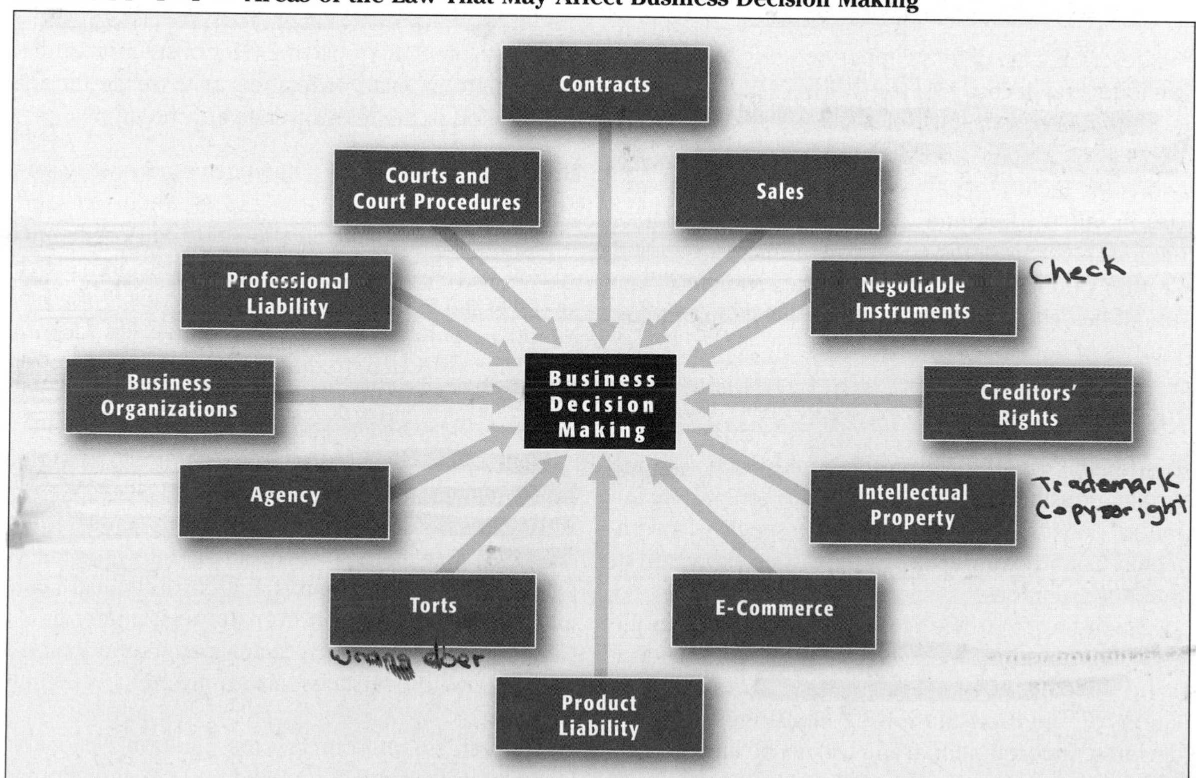

the importance of ethical considerations in today's business climate. These include the new *Ethical Dimension* questions that conclude many of the cases presented in this text and the *Insight into Ethics* features that appear in selected chapters. We have also included *A Question of Ethics* case problems at the ends of the chapters to introduce you to the ethical aspects of specific cases involving real-life situations. Additionally, Chapter 4 offers a detailed look at the importance of ethical considerations in business decision making.

Sources of American Law

There are numerous sources of American law. *Primary sources of law*, or sources that establish the law, include the following:

1. The U.S. Constitution and the constitutions of the various states.
2. Statutory law—including laws passed by Congress, state legislatures, or local governing bodies.
3. Regulations created by administrative agencies, such as the Food and Drug Administration.
4. Case law and common law doctrines.

We describe each of these important sources of law in the following pages.

Secondary sources of law are books and articles that summarize and clarify the primary sources of law. Examples include legal encyclopedias, treatises, articles in law reviews, and compilations of law, such as the *Restatements of the Law* (which will be discussed shortly). Courts often refer to secondary sources of law for guidance in interpreting and applying the primary sources of law discussed here.

Constitutional Law

The federal government and the states have separate written constitutions that set forth the general organization, powers, and limits of their respective governments. **Constitutional law** is the law as expressed in these constitutions.

According to Article VI of the U.S. Constitution, the Constitution is the supreme law of the land. As such, it is the basis of all law in the United States. A law in violation of the Constitution, if challenged, will be declared unconstitutional and will not be enforced, no matter what its source. Because of its importance in the American legal system, we present the complete text of the U.S. Constitution in Appendix B.

The Tenth Amendment to the U.S. Constitution reserves to the states all powers not granted to the federal government. Each state in the union has its own constitution. Unless it conflicts with the U.S. Constitution or a federal law, a state constitution is supreme within the state's borders.

Statutory Law

Laws enacted by legislative bodies at any level of government, such as the statutes passed by Congress or by state legislatures, make up the body of law generally referred to as **statutory law.** When a legislature passes a statute, that statute ultimately is included in the federal code of laws or the relevant state code of laws (these codes are discussed later in this chapter).

Statutory law also includes local **ordinances**—statutes (laws, rules, or orders) passed by municipal or county governing units to govern matters not covered by federal or state law. Ordinances commonly have to do with city or county land use (zoning ordinances), building and safety codes, and other matters affecting the local community.

A federal statute, of course, applies to all states. A state statute, in contrast, applies only within the state's borders. State laws thus may vary from state to state. No federal statute may violate the U.S. Constitution, and no state statute or local ordinance may violate the U.S. Constitution or the relevant state constitution.

Uniform Laws The differences among state laws were particularly notable in the 1800s, when conflicting state statutes frequently made trade and commerce among the states difficult. To counter these problems, in 1892 a group of legal scholars and lawyers formed the National Conference of Commissioners on Uniform State Laws (NCCUSL) to draft **uniform laws,** or model laws, for the states to consider adopting. The NCCUSL still exists today and continues to issue uniform laws.

Each state has the option of adopting or rejecting a uniform law. *Only if a state legislature adopts a uniform law does that law become part of the statutory law of that state.* Note that a state legislature may adopt all or part of a uniform law as it is written, or the legislature may rewrite the law however the legislature wishes. Hence, even though many states may have adopted a uniform law, those states' laws may not be entirely "uniform."

The earliest uniform law, the Uniform Negotiable Instruments Law, was completed by 1896 and adopted in every state by the early 1920s (although not all states used exactly the same wording). Over the following decades, other acts were drawn up in a similar manner. In all, more than two hundred uniform acts have been issued by the NCCUSL since its inception. The most ambitious uniform act of all, however, was the Uniform Commercial Code.

The Uniform Commercial Code The Uniform Commercial Code (UCC), which was created through the joint efforts of the NCCUSL and the American Law Institute,[1] was first issued in 1952. All fifty states,[2] the District of Columbia, and the Virgin Islands have adopted the UCC. It facilitates commerce among the states by providing a uniform, yet flexible, set of rules governing commercial transactions. The UCC assures businesspersons that their contracts, if validly entered into, normally will be enforced.

As you will read in later chapters, from time to time the NCCUSL revises the articles contained in the UCC and submits the revised versions to the states for adoption. During the 1990s, for example, four articles (Articles 3, 4, 5, and 9) were revised, and two new articles (Articles 2A and 4A) were added. Amendments to Article 1 were approved in 2001 and have now been adopted by a majority of the states. Because of its importance in the area of commercial law, we cite the UCC frequently in this text. We also present excerpts of the UCC in Appendix C.

Administrative Law

Another important source of American law is **administrative law,** which consists of the rules, orders, and decisions of administrative agencies. An **administrative agency** is a federal, state, or local government agency established to perform a specific function. Administrative law and procedures, which will be examined in detail in Chapter 6, constitute a dominant element in the regulatory environment of business. Rules issued by various administrative agencies now affect virtually every aspect of a business's operations, including its capital structure and financing, its hiring and firing procedures, its relations with employees and unions, and the way it manufactures and markets its products.

Federal Agencies At the national level, numerous **executive agencies** exist within the cabinet departments of the executive branch. The Food and Drug Administration, for example, is an agency within the Department of Health and Human Services. Executive agencies are subject to the authority of the president, who has the power to appoint and remove officers of federal agencies. There are also major **independent regulatory agencies** at the federal level, such as the Federal Trade Commission, the Securities and Exchange Commission, and the Federal Communications Commission. The president's power is less pronounced in regard to independent agencies, whose officers serve for fixed terms and cannot be removed without just cause.

State and Local Agencies There are administrative agencies at the state and local levels as well. Commonly, a state agency (such as a state pollution-control agency) is created as a parallel to a federal agency (such as the Environmental Protection Agency). Just as federal statutes take precedence over conflicting state statutes, so federal agency regulations take precedence over conflicting state regulations.

Case Law and Common Law Doctrines

The rules of law announced in court decisions constitute another basic source of American law. These rules of law include interpretations of constitutional provisions, of statutes enacted by legislatures, and of regulations created by administrative agencies. Today, this body of judge-made law is referred to as **case law.** Case law—the doctrines and principles announced in cases—governs all areas not covered by statutory law or administrative law and is part of our common law tradition. We look at the origins and characteristics of the common law tradition in some detail in the pages that follow. See *Concept Summary 1.2* on the following page for a review of the sources of American law.

The Common Law Tradition

Because of our colonial heritage, much of American law is based on the English legal system, which originated in medieval England and continued to evolve in the following centuries. Knowledge of this system is necessary to understanding the American legal system today.

1. This institute was formed in the 1920s and consists of practicing attorneys, legal scholars, and judges.

2. Louisiana has not adopted Articles 2 and 2A (covering contracts for the sale and lease of goods), however.

CONCEPT SUMMARY 1.2
Sources of American Law

Source	Description
CONSTITUTIONAL LAW	The law as expressed in the U.S. Constitution and the state constitutions. The U.S. Constitution is the supreme law of the land. State constitutions are supreme within state borders to the extent that they do not violate a clause of the U.S. Constitution or a federal law.
STATUTORY LAW	Laws (statutes and ordinances) created by federal, state, and local legislatures and governing bodies. None of these laws may violate the U.S. Constitution or the relevant state constitution. Uniform statutes, when adopted by a state, become statutory law in that state.
ADMINISTRATIVE LAW	The rules, orders, and decisions of federal, state, or local government administrative agencies.
CASE LAW AND COMMON LAW DOCTRINES	Judge-made law, including interpretations of constitutional provisions, of statutes enacted by legislatures, and of regulations created by administrative agencies.

Early English Courts

The origins of the English legal system—and thus the U.S. legal system as well—date back to 1066, when the Normans conquered England. William the Conqueror and his successors began the process of unifying the country under their rule. One of the means they used to do this was the establishment of the king's courts, or *curiae regis*. Before the Norman Conquest, disputes had been settled according to the local legal customs and traditions in various regions of the country. The king's courts sought to establish a uniform set of customs for the country as a whole. What evolved in these courts was the beginning of the **common law**—a body of general rules that applied throughout the entire English realm. Eventually, the common law tradition became part of the heritage of all nations that were once British colonies, including the United States.

Courts of Law and Remedies at Law The early English king's courts could grant only very limited kinds of **remedies** (the legal means to enforce a right or redress a wrong). If one person wronged another in some way, the king's courts could award as compensation one or more of the following: (1) land, (2) items of value, or (3) money. The courts that awarded this compensation became known as **courts of law,** and the three remedies were called **remedies at law.** (Today, the remedy at law normally takes the form of monetary **damages**—an amount given to a party whose legal interests have been injured.) Even though the system introduced uniformity in the settling of disputes, when a complaining party wanted a remedy other than economic compensation, the courts of law could do nothing, so "no remedy, no right."

Courts of Equity and Remedies in Equity Equity is a branch of law, founded on what might be described as notions of justice and fair dealing, that seeks to supply a remedy when no adequate remedy at law is available. When individuals could not obtain an adequate remedy in a court of law, they petitioned the king for relief. Most of these petitions were decided by an adviser to the king, called a **chancellor,** who had the power to grant new and unique remedies. Eventually, formal chancery courts, or **courts of equity,** were established.

The remedies granted by the equity courts became known as **remedies in equity,** or equitable remedies. These remedies include *specific performance* (ordering a party to perform an agreement as promised), an *injunction* (ordering a party to cease engaging in a specific activity or to undo some wrong or injury), and *rescission* (the cancellation of a contractual obligation). We discuss these and other equitable remedies in more detail at appropriate points in the chapters that follow, particularly in Chapter 10.

As a general rule, today's courts, like the early English courts, will not grant equitable remedies unless the remedy at law—monetary damages—is inadequate. For example, suppose that you form a contract (a legally binding agreement—see Chapter 9) to purchase a parcel of land that you think will be just perfect for your future home. Further suppose that the seller breaches this agreement. You could sue the seller for the return of any deposits or down payment you might have made on the land, but this is not the remedy you really seek. What you want is to have the court order the seller to go through with the contract. In other words, you want the court to grant the equitable remedy of specific performance because monetary damages are inadequate in this situation.

Equitable Maxims In fashioning appropriate remedies, judges often were (and continue to be) guided by so-called **equitable maxims**—propositions or general statements of equitable rules. Exhibit 1–2 lists some important equitable maxims. The last maxim listed in that exhibit—"Equity aids the vigilant, not those who rest on their rights"—merits special attention. It has become known as the equitable doctrine of **laches** (a term derived from the Latin *laxus,* meaning "lax" or "negligent"), and it can be used as a defense. A **defense** is an argument raised by the **defendant** (the party being sued) indicating why the **plaintiff** (the suing party) should not obtain the remedy sought. (Note that in equity proceedings, the party bringing a lawsuit is called the **petitioner,** and the party being sued is referred to as the **respondent.**)

The doctrine of laches arose to encourage people to bring lawsuits while the evidence was fresh. What constitutes a reasonable time, of course, varies according to the circumstances of the case. Time periods for different types of cases are now usually fixed by **statutes of limitations.** After the time allowed under a statute of limitations has expired, no action (lawsuit) can be brought, no matter how strong the case was originally.

Legal and Equitable Remedies Today

The establishment of courts of equity in medieval England resulted in two distinct court systems: courts of law and courts of equity. The systems had different sets of judges and granted different types of remedies. During the nineteenth century, however, most states in the United States adopted rules of procedure that resulted in the combining of courts of law and equity. A party now may request both legal and equitable remedies in the same action, and the trial court judge may grant either or both forms of relief.

The distinction between legal and equitable remedies remains relevant to students of business law, however, because these remedies differ. To seek the proper remedy for a wrong, one must know what remedies are available. Additionally, certain vestiges of the procedures used when there were separate courts of law and equity still exist. For example, a party has the right to demand a jury trial in an action at law, but not in an action in equity. Exhibit 1–3 on the next page summarizes the procedural differences (applicable in most states) between an action at law and an action in equity.

The Doctrine of *Stare Decisis*

One of the unique features of the common law is that it is *judge-made* law. The body of principles and doctrines that form the common law emerged over time as judges decided legal controversies.

EXHIBIT 1–2 • Equitable Maxims

1. *Whoever seeks equity must do equity.* (Anyone who wishes to be treated fairly must treat others fairly.)
2. *Where there is equal equity, the law must prevail.* (The law will determine the outcome of a controversy in which the merits of both sides are equal.)
3. *One seeking the aid of an equity court must come to the court with clean hands.* (Plaintiffs must have acted fairly and honestly.)
4. *Equity will not suffer a wrong to be without a remedy.* (Equitable relief will be awarded when there is a right to relief and there is no adequate remedy at law.)
5. *Equity regards substance rather than form.* (Equity is more concerned with fairness and justice than with legal technicalities.)
6. *Equity aids the vigilant, not those who rest on their rights.* (Equity will not help those who neglect their rights for an unreasonable period of time.)

EXHIBIT 1–3 • Procedural Differences between an Action at Law and an Action in Equity

Procedure	Action at Law	Action in Equity
Initiation of lawsuit	By filing a complaint	By filing a petition
Parties	Plaintiff and defendant	Petitioner and respondent
Decision	By jury or judge	By judge (no jury)
Result	Judgment	Decree
Remedy	Monetary damages	Specific performance, injunction, or rescission

Case Precedents and Case Reporters When possible, judges attempted to be consistent and to base their decisions on the principles suggested by earlier cases. They sought to decide similar cases in a similar way and considered new cases with care because they knew that their decisions would make new law. Each interpretation became part of the law on the subject and served as a legal **precedent**—that is, a decision that furnished an example or authority for deciding subsequent cases involving similar legal principles or facts.

In the early years of the common law, there was no single place or publication where court opinions, or written decisions, could be found. By the early fourteenth century, portions of the most important decisions of each year were being gathered together and recorded in *Year Books,* which became useful references for lawyers and judges. In the sixteenth century, the *Year Books* were discontinued, and other forms of case publication became available. Today, cases are published, or "reported," in volumes called **reporters,** or *reports.* We describe today's case reporting system in detail later in this chapter.

Stare Decisis* and the Common Law Tradition** The practice of deciding new cases with reference to former decisions, or precedents, became a cornerstone of the English and American judicial systems. The practice formed a doctrine known as ***stare decisis[3] (a Latin phrase meaning "to stand on decided cases").

Under this doctrine, judges are obligated to follow the precedents established within their jurisdictions. The term *jurisdiction* refers to an area in which a court or courts have the power to apply the law—see Chapter 2. Once a court has set forth a principle of law as being applicable to a certain set of facts, that court and courts of lower rank (within the same jurisdiction) must adhere to that principle and apply it in future cases involving similar fact patterns. Thus, *stare decisis* has two aspects: first, that decisions made by a higher court are binding on lower courts; and second, that a court should not overturn its own precedents unless there is a compelling reason to do so.

The doctrine of *stare decisis* helps the courts to be more efficient because if other courts have carefully analyzed a similar case, their legal reasoning and opinions can serve as guides. *Stare decisis* also makes the law more stable and predictable. If the law on a given subject is well settled, someone bringing a case to court can usually rely on the court to make a decision based on what the law has been in the past.

A Typical Scenario To illustrate how the doctrine of *stare decisis* works, consider an example. Suppose that the lower state courts in Georgia have reached conflicting conclusions on whether drivers are liable for accidents they cause while merging into freeway traffic. Some courts have held drivers liable even though the drivers looked and did not see any oncoming traffic and even though witnesses (passengers in their cars) testified to that effect. To settle the law on this issue, the Georgia Supreme Court decides to review a case involving this fact pattern. The court rules that, in such a situation, the driver who is merging into traffic is liable for any accidents caused by that driver's failure to yield to freeway traffic—even if that driver looked carefully and did not see an approaching vehicle.

The Georgia Supreme Court's decision on this matter is a **binding authority**—a case precedent, statute, or other source of law that a court must follow when

3. Pronounced *ster*-ay dih-*si*-ses.

deciding a case. In other words, the Georgia Supreme Court's decision will influence the outcome of all future cases on this issue brought before the Georgia state courts. Similarly, a decision on a given question by the United States Supreme Court (the nation's highest court), no matter how old, is binding on all courts.

Departures from Precedent Although courts are obligated to follow precedents, sometimes a court will depart from the rule of precedent if it decides that the precedent should no longer be followed. If a court decides that a ruling precedent is simply incorrect or that technological or social changes have rendered the precedent inapplicable, the court might rule contrary to the precedent. Cases that overturn precedent often receive a great deal of publicity.

Note that judges do have some flexibility in applying precedents. For example, a lower court may avoid applying a precedent set by a higher court in its jurisdiction by distinguishing the two cases based on their facts. When this happens, the lower court's ruling stands unless it is appealed to a higher court and that court overturns the decision.

When There Is No Precedent Occasionally, the courts must decide cases for which no precedents exist, called *cases of first impression.* For example, as you will read throughout this text, the extensive use of the Internet has presented many new and challenging issues for the courts to decide. In deciding cases of first impression, courts often look at *persuasive authorities* (precedents from other jurisdictions) for guidance. A court may also consider a number of factors, including legal principles and policies underlying previous court decisions or existing statutes, fairness, social values and customs, **public policy** (governmental policy based on widely held societal values), and data and concepts drawn from the social sciences. Which of these sources is chosen or receives the greatest emphasis depends on the nature of the case being considered and the particular judge or judges hearing the case.

Stare Decisis and Legal Reasoning

Legal reasoning is the reasoning process used by judges in deciding what law applies to a given dispute and then applying that law to the specific facts or circumstances of the case. Through the use of legal reasoning, judges harmonize their decisions with those that have been made before, as the doctrine of *stare decisis* requires.

Students of business law and the legal environment also engage in legal reasoning. For example, you may be asked to provide answers for some of the case problems that appear at the end of every chapter in this text. Each problem describes the facts of a particular dispute and the legal question at issue. If you are assigned a case problem, you will be asked to determine how a court would answer that question, and why. In other words, you will need to give legal reasons for whatever conclusion you reach.[4] We look here at the basic steps involved in legal reasoning and then describe some forms of reasoning commonly used by the courts in making their decisions.

Basic Steps in Legal Reasoning At times, the legal arguments set forth in court opinions are relatively simple and brief. At other times, the arguments are complex and lengthy. Regardless of the length of a legal argument, however, the basic steps of the legal reasoning process remain the same. These steps, which you also can follow when analyzing cases and case problems, form what is commonly referred to as the *IRAC method* of legal reasoning. IRAC is an acronym formed from the first letters of the following words: Issue, Rule, Application, and Conclusion. To apply the IRAC method, you would ask the following questions:

1. *What are the key facts and issues?* Suppose that a plaintiff comes before the court claiming *assault* (a wrongful and intentional action in which one person makes another fearful of immediate physical harm—part of a class of actions called *torts*). The plaintiff claims that the defendant threatened her while she was sleeping. Although the plaintiff was unaware that she was being threatened, her roommate heard the defendant make the threat. The legal issue, or question, raised by these facts is whether the defendant's actions constitute the tort of assault, given that the plaintiff was not aware of those actions at the time they occurred.
2. *What rules of law apply to the case?* A rule of law may be a rule stated by the courts in previous decisions, a state or federal statute, or a state or federal administrative agency regulation. In our hypothetical case, the plaintiff **alleges** (claims) that the defendant committed a tort. Therefore, the applicable law is the common law of torts—specifically, tort law governing assault (see Chapter 12 for more

4. See Appendix A for further instructions on how to analyze case problems.

detail on intentional torts). Case precedents involving similar facts and issues thus would be relevant. Often, more than one rule of law will be applicable to a case.

3. *How do the rules of law apply to the particular facts and circumstances of this case?* This step is often the most difficult because each case presents a unique set of facts, circumstances, and parties. Although cases may be similar, no two cases are ever identical in all respects. Normally, judges (and lawyers and law students) try to find **cases on point**—previously decided cases that are as similar as possible to the one under consideration. (Because of the difficulty—and importance—of this step in the legal reasoning process, we discuss it in more detail in the next subsection.)
4. *What conclusion should be drawn?* This step normally presents few problems. Usually, the conclusion is evident if the previous three steps have been followed carefully.

Forms of Legal Reasoning Judges use many types of reasoning when following the third step of the legal reasoning process—applying the law to the facts of a particular case. Three common forms of reasoning are deductive reasoning, linear reasoning, and reasoning by analogy.

Deductive Reasoning. Deductive reasoning is sometimes called *syllogistic reasoning* because it employs a **syllogism**—a logical relationship involving a major premise, a minor premise, and a conclusion. Consider the hypothetical case presented earlier, in which the plaintiff alleged that the defendant committed assault by threatening her while she was sleeping. The judge might point out that "under the common law of torts, an individual must be *aware* of a threat of danger for the threat to constitute assault" (major premise); "the plaintiff in this case was unaware of the threat at the time it occurred" (minor premise); and "therefore, the circumstances do not amount to an assault" (conclusion).

Linear Reasoning. A second important form of legal reasoning that is commonly employed might be thought of as "linear" reasoning because it proceeds from one point to another, with the final point being the conclusion. A comparison will help make this form of reasoning clear. Imagine a knotted rope, with each knot tying together separate pieces of rope to form a tightly knotted length. As a whole, the rope represents a linear progression of thought logically connecting various points, with the last point, or knot, representing the conclusion. Suppose that a tenant in an apartment building sues the landlord for damages for an injury resulting from an allegedly inadequately lit stairway. The court may engage in a reasoning process involving the following "pieces of rope":

1. The landlord, who was on the premises the evening the injury occurred, testifies that none of the other nine tenants who used the stairway that night complained about the lights.
2. The fact that none of the tenants complained is the same as if they had said the lighting was sufficient.
3. That there were no complaints does not prove that the lighting was sufficient but does prove that the landlord had no reason to believe that it was not.
4. The landlord's belief was reasonable because no one complained.
5. Therefore, the landlord acted reasonably and was not negligent with respect to the lighting in the stairway.

From this reasoning, the court concludes that the tenant is not entitled to compensation on the basis of the stairway's allegedly insufficient lighting.

Reasoning by Analogy. Another important type of reasoning that judges use in deciding cases is reasoning by *analogy*. To reason by **analogy** is to compare the facts in the case at hand to the facts in other cases and, to the extent that the patterns are similar, to apply the same rule of law to the present case. To the extent that the facts are unique, or "distinguishable," different rules may apply. For example, in case A, the court held that a driver who crossed a highway's center line was negligent. Case B involves a driver who crosses the line to avoid hitting a child. In determining whether case A's rule applies in case B, a judge would consider what the reasons were for the decision in A and whether B is sufficiently similar for those reasons to apply. If the judge holds that B's driver is not liable, that judge must indicate why case A's rule is not relevant to the facts presented in case B.

There Is No One "Right" Answer

Many persons believe that there is one "right" answer to every legal question. In most situations involving a legal controversy, however, there is no single correct result. Good arguments can often be made to support either side of a legal controversy. Quite often, a case does not involve a "good" person suing a "bad" person. In many cases, both parties have acted in good faith in some measure or in bad faith to some degree.

Additionally, each judge has her or his own personal beliefs and philosophy, which shape, at least to some extent, the process of legal reasoning. This means that the outcome of a particular lawsuit before a court cannot be predicted with absolute certainty. In fact, in some cases, even though the weight of the law would seem to favor one party's position, judges, through creative legal reasoning, have found ways to rule in favor of the other party in the interests of preventing injustice. Legal reasoning and other aspects of the common law tradition are reviewed in *Concept Summary 1.3*.

SECTION 5 The Common Law Today

Today, the common law derived from judicial decisions continues to be applied throughout the United States. Common law doctrines and principles govern all areas *not* covered by statutory or administrative law. In a dispute concerning a particular employment practice, for example, if a statute regulates that practice, the statute will apply rather than the common law doctrine that applied prior to the enactment of the statute.

The Continuing Importance of the Common Law

Because the body of statutory law has expanded greatly since the beginning of this nation, thus narrowing the applicability of common law doctrines, it might seem that the common law has dwindled in importance. This is not true, however. For one thing, even in areas governed by statutory law, there is a significant interplay between statutory law and the common law. For example, many statutes essentially codify existing common law rules, and regulations issued by various administrative agencies usually are based, at least in part, on common law principles. Additionally, the courts, in interpreting statutory law, often rely on the

CONCEPT SUMMARY 1.3
The Common Law Tradition

Aspect	Description
ORIGINS OF THE COMMON LAW	The American legal system is based on the common law tradition, which originated in medieval England. Following the conquest of England in 1066 by William the Conqueror, king's courts were established throughout England, and the common law was developed in these courts.
LEGAL AND EQUITABLE REMEDIES	The distinction between remedies at law (compensation with money or items of value, such as land) and remedies in equity (including specific performance, injunction, and rescission of a contractual obligation) originated in the early English courts of law and courts of equity, respectively.
CASE PRECEDENTS AND THE DOCTRINE OF *STARE DECISIS*	In the king's courts, judges attempted to make their decisions consistent with previous decisions, called precedents. This practice gave rise to the doctrine of *stare decisis*. This doctrine, which became a cornerstone of the common law tradition, obligates judges to abide by precedents established in their jurisdictions.
STARE DECISIS AND LEGAL REASONING	Legal reasoning refers to the reasoning process used by judges in applying the law to the facts and issues of specific cases. Legal reasoning involves becoming familiar with the key facts of a case, identifying the relevant legal rules, applying those rules to the facts, and drawing a conclusion. In applying the legal rules to the facts of a case, judges may use deductive reasoning, linear reasoning, or reasoning by analogy.

common law as a guide to what the legislators intended.

Furthermore, how the courts interpret a particular statute determines how that statute will be applied. If you wanted to learn about the coverage and applicability of a particular statute, for example, you would necessarily have to locate the statute and study it. You would also need to see how the courts in your jurisdiction have interpreted and applied the statute. In other words, you would have to learn what precedents have been established in your jurisdiction with respect to that statute. Often, the applicability of a newly enacted statute does not become clear until a body of case law develops to clarify how, when, and to whom the statute applies.

Restatements of the Law

The American Law Institute (ALI) has drafted and published compilations of the common law called *Restatements of the Law,* which generally summarize the common law rules followed by most states. There are *Restatements of the Law* in the areas of contracts, torts, agency, trusts, property, restitution, security, judgments, and conflict of laws. The *Restatements,* like other secondary sources of law, do not in themselves have the force of law, but they are an important source of legal analysis and opinion on which judges often rely in making their decisions.

Many of the *Restatements* are now in their second, third, or fourth editions. We refer to the *Restatements* frequently in subsequent chapters of this text, indicating in parentheses the edition to which we are referring. For example, we refer to the second edition of the *Restatement of the Law of Contracts* as simply the *Restatement (Second) of Contracts.*

Section 6 Classifications of Law

The substantial body of the law may be broken down according to several classification systems. For example, one classification system divides law into substantive law and procedural law. **Substantive law** consists of all laws that define, describe, regulate, and create legal rights and obligations. **Procedural law** consists of all laws that delineate the methods of enforcing the rights established by substantive law. Other classification systems divide law into federal law and state law, private law (dealing with relationships between private entities) and public law (addressing the relationship between persons and their governments), and national law and international law. Here we look at still another classification system, which divides law into civil law and criminal law, as well as at what is meant by the term *cyberlaw.*

Civil Law and Criminal Law

Civil law spells out the rights and duties that exist between persons and between persons and their governments, as well as the relief available when a person's rights are violated. Typically, in a civil case, a private party sues another private party (although the government can also sue a party for a civil law violation) to make that other party comply with a duty or pay for the damage caused by failure to comply with a duty. Much of the law that we discuss in this text is civil law. Contract law, for example, covered in Chapters 9 and 10, is civil law. The whole body of tort law (see Chapters 12 and 13) is also civil law.

Criminal law, in contrast, is concerned with wrongs committed *against the public as a whole.* Criminal acts are defined and prohibited by local, state, or federal government statutes. Criminal defendants are thus prosecuted by public officials, such as a district attorney (D.A.), on behalf of the state, not by their victims or other private parties. (See Chapter 7 for a further discussion of the distinction between civil law and criminal law.)

Cyberlaw

As mentioned, the use of the Internet to conduct business transactions has led to new types of legal issues. In response, courts have had to adapt traditional laws to situations that are unique to our age. Additionally, legislatures have created laws to deal specifically with such issues. Frequently, people use the term **cyberlaw** to refer to the emerging body of law that governs transactions conducted via the Internet. Cyberlaw is not really a classification of law, nor is it a new *type* of law. Rather, it is an informal term used to describe traditional legal principles that have been modified and adapted to fit situations that are unique to the online world. Of course, in some areas new statutes have been enacted, at both the federal and the state levels, to cover specific types of problems stemming from online communications. Throughout this book, you will read how the law in a given area is evolving to govern specific legal issues that arise in the online context.

How to Find Primary Sources of Law

This text includes numerous citations to primary sources of law—federal and state statutes, the U.S. Constitution and state constitutions, regulations issued by administrative agencies, and court cases. (A **citation** is a reference to a publication in which a legal authority—such as a statute or a court decision or other source—can be found.) In this section, we explain how you can use citations to find primary sources of law. Note that in addition to the primary sources being published in sets of books as described next, most federal and state laws and case decisions are also available online.

Finding Statutory and Administrative Law

When Congress passes laws, they are collected in a publication titled *United States Statutes at Large*. When state legislatures pass laws, they are collected in similar state publications. Most frequently, however, laws are referred to in their codified form—that is, the form in which they appear in the federal and state codes. In these codes, laws are compiled by subject.

United States Code The *United States Code* (U.S.C.) arranges all existing federal laws by broad subject. Each of the fifty subjects is given a title and a title number. For example, laws relating to commerce and trade are collected in Title 15, "Commerce and Trade." Titles are subdivided by sections. A citation to the U.S.C. includes both title and section numbers. Thus, a reference to "15 U.S.C. Section 1" means that the statute can be found in Section 1 of Title 15. ("Section" may also be designated by the symbol §, and "Sections," by §§.) In addition to the print publication of the U.S.C., the federal government also provides a searchable online database of the *United States Code* at **www.gpoaccess.gov/uscode/index.html**.

Commercial publications of federal laws and regulations are also available. For example, West Group publishes the *United States Code Annotated* (U.S.C.A.). The U.S.C.A. contains the official text of the U.S.C., plus notes (annotations) on court decisions that interpret and apply specific sections of the statutes. The U.S.C.A. also includes additional research aids, such as cross-references to related statutes, historical notes, and library references. A citation to the U.S.C.A. is similar to a citation to the U.S.C.: "15 U.S.C.A. Section 1."

State Codes State codes follow the U.S.C. pattern of arranging law by subject. They may be called codes, revisions, compilations, consolidations, general statutes, or statutes, depending on the preferences of the states. In some codes, subjects are designated by number. In others, they are designated by name. For example, "13 Pennsylvania Consolidated Statutes Section 1101" means that the statute can be found in Title 13, Section 1101, of the Pennsylvania code. "California Commercial Code Section 1101" means that the statute can be found under the subject heading "Commercial Code" of the California code in Section 1101. Abbreviations are often used. For example, "13 Pennsylvania Consolidated Statutes Section 1101" is abbreviated "13 Pa. C.S. § 1101," and "California Commercial Code Section 1101" is abbreviated "Cal. Com. Code § 1101."

Administrative Rules Rules and regulations adopted by federal administrative agencies are initially published in the *Federal Register*, a daily publication of the U.S. government. Later, they are incorporated into the *Code of Federal Regulations* (C.F.R.). Like the U.S.C., the C.F.R. is divided into fifty titles. Rules within each title are assigned section numbers. A full citation to the C.F.R. includes title and section numbers. For example, a reference to "17 C.F.R. Section 230.504" means that the rule can be found in Section 230.504 of Title 17.

Finding Case Law

Before discussing the case reporting system, we need to look briefly at the court system (which will be discussed in detail in Chapter 2). There are two types of courts in the United States, federal courts and state courts. Both the federal and state court systems consist of several levels, or tiers, of courts. *Trial courts,* in which evidence is presented and testimony given, are on the bottom tier (which also includes lower courts that handle specialized issues). Decisions from a trial court can be appealed to a higher court, which commonly is an intermediate *court of appeals,* or an *appellate court.* Decisions from these intermediate courts of appeals may be appealed to an even higher court, such as a state supreme court or the United States Supreme Court.

State Court Decisions Most state trial court decisions are not published in books (except in New

York and a few other states, which publish selected trial court opinions). Decisions from state trial courts are typically filed in the office of the clerk of the court, where the decisions are available for public inspection. Written decisions of the appellate, or reviewing, courts, however, are published and distributed (both in print and via the Internet). As you will note, most of the state court cases presented in this book are from state appellate courts. The reported appellate decisions are published in volumes called *reports* or *reporters*, which are numbered consecutively. State appellate court decisions are found in the state reporters of that particular state. Official reports are volumes that are published by the state, whereas unofficial reports are privately published.

Regional Reporters. State court opinions appear in regional units of the National Reporter System, published by West Group. Most lawyers and libraries have the West reporters because they report cases more quickly, and are distributed more widely, than the state-published reporters. In fact, many states have eliminated their own reporters in favor of West's National Reporter System. The National Reporter System divides the states into the following geographic areas: *Atlantic* (A. or A.2d), *North Eastern* (N.E. or N.E.2d), *North Western* (N.W. or N.W.2d), *Pacific* (P., P.2d, or P.3d), *South Eastern* (S.E. or S.E.2d), *South Western* (S.W., S.W.2d, or S.W.3d), and *Southern* (So. or So.2d). (The *2d* and *3d* in the preceding abbreviations refer to *Second Series* and *Third Series*, respectively.) The states included in each of these regional divisions are indicated in Exhibit 1–4, which illustrates West's National Reporter System.

Case Citations. After appellate decisions have been published, they are normally referred to (cited) by the name of the case; the volume, name, and page number of the state's official reporter (if different from West's National Reporter System); the volume, name, and page number of the National Reporter; and the volume, name, and page number of any other selected reporter. (Citing a reporter by volume number, name, and page number, in that order, is common to all citations; often, as in this book, the year the decision was issued will be included in parentheses, just after the citations to reporters.) When more than one reporter is cited for the same case, each reference is called a *parallel citation*.

Note that some states have adopted a "public domain citation system" that uses a somewhat different format for the citation. For example, in Wisconsin, a Wisconsin Supreme Court decision might be designated "2008 WI 40," meaning that the case was decided in the year 2008 by the Wisconsin Supreme Court and was the fortieth decision issued by that court during that year. Parallel citations to the *Wisconsin Reports* and West's *North Western Reporter* are still included after the public domain citation.

Consider the following case citation: *Ramirez v. Health Net of Northeast, Inc.*, 285 Conn. 1, 938 A.2d 576 (2008). We see that the opinion in this case can be found in Volume 285 of the official *Connecticut Reports*, which reports only the decisions of the Supreme Court of Connecticut, on page 1. The parallel citation is to Volume 938 of the *Atlantic Reporter, Second Series*, page 576. In presenting opinions in this text, in addition to the reporter, we give the name of the court hearing the case and the year of the court's decision. Sample citations to state court decisions are explained in Exhibit 1–5 on pages 18–20.

Federal Court Decisions Federal district (trial) court decisions are published unofficially in West's *Federal Supplement* (F.Supp. or F.Supp.2d), and opinions from the circuit courts of appeals (reviewing courts) are reported unofficially in West's *Federal Reporter* (F., F.2d, or F.3d). Cases concerning federal bankruptcy law are published unofficially in West's *Bankruptcy Reporter* (Bankr. or B.R.).

The official edition of the United States Supreme Court decisions is the *United States Reports* (U.S.), which is published by the federal government. Unofficial editions of Supreme Court cases include West's *Supreme Court Reporter* (S.Ct.) and the *Lawyers' Edition of the Supreme Court Reports* (L.Ed. or L.Ed.2d). Sample citations for federal court decisions are also listed and explained in Exhibit 1–5.

Unpublished Opinions Many court opinions that are not yet published or that are not intended for publication can be accessed through Westlaw® (abbreviated in citations as "WL"), an online legal database maintained by West Group. When no citation to a published reporter is available for cases cited in this text, we give the WL citation (see Exhibit 1–5 for an example). Can a court consider unpublished decisions as persuasive precedent? See this chapter's *Insight into E-Commerce* feature on pages 22 and 23 for a discussion of this issue.

Old Case Law On a few occasions, this text cites opinions from old, classic cases dating to the nineteenth century or earlier; some of these are from the

EXHIBIT 1–4 • West's National Reporter System—Regional/Federal

Regional Reporters	Coverage Beginning	Coverage
Atlantic Reporter (A. or A.2d)	1885	Connecticut, Delaware, District of Columbia, Maine, Maryland, New Hampshire, New Jersey, Pennsylvania, Rhode Island, and Vermont.
North Eastern Reporter (N.E. or N.E.2d)	1885	Illinois, Indiana, Massachusetts, New York, and Ohio.
North Western Reporter (N.W. or N.W.2d)	1879	Iowa, Michigan, Minnesota, Nebraska, North Dakota, South Dakota, and Wisconsin.
Pacific Reporter (P., P.2d, or P.3d)	1883	Alaska, Arizona, California, Colorado, Hawaii, Idaho, Kansas, Montana, Nevada, New Mexico, Oklahoma, Oregon, Utah, Washington, and Wyoming.
South Eastern Reporter (S.E. or S.E.2d)	1887	Georgia, North Carolina, South Carolina, Virginia, and West Virginia.
South Western Reporter (S.W., S.W.2d, or S.W.3d)	1886	Arkansas, Kentucky, Missouri, Tennessee, and Texas.
Southern Reporter (So. or So.2d)	1887	Alabama, Florida, Louisiana, and Mississippi.
Federal Reporters		
Federal Reporter (F., F.2d, or F.3d)	1880	U.S. Circuit Courts from 1880 to 1912; U.S. Commerce Court from 1911 to 1913; U.S. District Courts from 1880 to 1932; U.S. Court of Claims (now called U.S. Court of Federal Claims) from 1929 to 1932 and since 1960; U.S. Courts of Appeals since 1891; U.S. Court of Customs and Patent Appeals since 1929; U.S. Emergency Court of Appeals since 1943.
Federal Supplement (F.Supp. or F.Supp.2d)	1932	U.S. Court of Claims from 1932 to 1960; U.S. District Courts since 1932; U.S. Customs Court since 1956.
Federal Rules Decisions (F.R.D.)	1939	U.S. District Courts involving the Federal Rules of Civil Procedure since 1939 and Federal Rules of Criminal Procedure since 1946.
Supreme Court Reporter (S.Ct.)	1882	United States Supreme Court since the October term of 1882.
Bankruptcy Reporter (Bankr.)	1980	Bankruptcy decisions of U.S. Bankruptcy Courts, U.S. District Courts, U.S. Courts of Appeals, and the United States Supreme Court.
Military Justice Reporter (M.J.)	1978	U.S. Court of Military Appeals and Courts of Military Review for the Army, Navy, Air Force, and Coast Guard.

NATIONAL REPORTER SYSTEM MAP

- Pacific
- North Western
- South Western
- North Eastern
- Atlantic
- South Eastern
- Southern

EXHIBIT 1–5 • How to Read Citations

STATE COURTS

274 Neb. 796, 743 N.W.2d 632 (2008)[a]

N.W. is the abbreviation for West's publication of state court decisions rendered in the *North Western Reporter* of the National Reporter System. *2d* indicates that this case was included in the *Second Series* of that reporter. The number 743 refers to the volume number of the reporter; the number 632 refers to the page in that volume on which this case begins.

Neb. is an abbreviation for *Nebraska Reports,* Nebraska's official reports of the decisions of its highest court, the Nebraska Supreme Court.

159 Cal.App.4th 1114, 72 Cal.Rptr.3d 81 (2008)

Cal.Rptr. is the abbreviation for West's unofficial reports—titled *California Reporter*—of the decisions of California courts.

8 N.Y.3d 422, 867 N.E.2d 381, 835 N.Y.S.2d 530 (2007)

N.Y.S. is the abbreviation for West's unofficial reports—titled *New York Supplement*—of the decisions of New York courts.

N.Y. is the abbreviation for *New York Reports*, New York's official reports of the decisions of its court of appeals. The New York Court of Appeals is the state's highest court, analogous to other states' supreme courts. In New York, a supreme court is a trial court.

___ Ga.App. ___, 656 S.E.2d 222 (2008)

Ga.App. is the abbreviation for *Georgia Appeals Reports,* Georgia's official reports of the decisions of its court of appeals. The blank lines in this citation (or any other citation) will be filled in once the appropriate volume of the case reporter is printed and a page number becomes available.

FEDERAL COURTS

___ U.S. ___, 127 S.Ct. 1513, 167 L.Ed.2d 422 (2007)

L.Ed. is an abbreviation for *Lawyers' Edition of the Supreme Court Reports,* an unofficial edition of decisions of the United States Supreme Court.

S.Ct. is the abbreviation for West's unofficial reports—titled *Supreme Court Reporter*—of decisions of the United States Supreme Court.

U.S. is the abbreviation for *United States Reports*, the official edition of the decisions of the United States Supreme Court. The blank lines indicate that the volume has not yet been published and no page number is yet assigned.

a. The case names have been deleted from these citations to emphasize the publications. It should be kept in mind, however, that the name of a case is as important as the specific page numbers in the volumes in which it is found. If a citation is incorrect, the correct citation may be found in a publication's index of case names. In addition to providing a check on errors in citations, the date of a case is important because the value of a recent case as an authority is likely to be greater than that of older cases.

EXHIBIT 1–5 • How to Read Citations—Continued

FEDERAL COURTS (Continued)

512 F.3d 582 (9th Cir. 2008)

9th Cir. is an abbreviation denoting that this case was decided in the U.S. Court of Appeals for the Ninth Circuit.

478 F.Supp.2d 496 (S.D.N.Y. 2007)

S.D.N.Y. is an abbreviation indicating that the U.S. District Court for the Southern District of New York decided this case.

ENGLISH COURTS

9 Exch. 341, 156 Eng.Rep. 145 (1854)

Eng.Rep. is an abbreviation for *English Reports, Full Reprint,* a series of reports containing selected decisions made in English courts between 1378 and 1865.

Exch. is an abbreviation for *English Exchequer Reports*, which includes the original reports of cases decided in England's Court of Exchequer.

STATUTORY AND OTHER CITATIONS

18 U.S.C. Section 1961(1)(A)

U.S.C. denotes *United States Code*, the codification of *United States Statutes at Large*. The number 18 refers to the statute's U.S.C. title number and 1961 to its section number within that title. The number 1 in parentheses refers to a subsection within the section, and the letter A in parentheses to a subdivision within the subsection.

UCC 2–206(1)(b)

UCC is an abbreviation for *Uniform Commercial Code*. The first number 2 is a reference to an article of the UCC, and 206 to a section within that article. The number 1 in parentheses refers to a subsection within the section, and the letter b in parentheses to a subdivision within the subsection.

***Restatement (Second) of Torts*, Section 568**

Restatement (Second) of Torts refers to the second edition of the American Law Institute's *Restatement of the Law of Torts*. The number 568 refers to a specific section.

17 C.F.R. Section 230.505

C.F.R. is an abbreviation for *Code of Federal Regulations*, a compilation of federal administrative regulations. The number 17 designates the regulation's title number, and 230.505 designates a specific section within that title.

EXHIBIT CONTINUES

EXHIBIT 1–5 • How to Read Citations—Continued

Westlaw® Citations[b]

2008 WL 427478

WL is an abbreviation for Westlaw. The number 2008 is the year of the document that can be found with this citation in the Westlaw database. The number 427478 is a number assigned to a specific document. A higher number indicates that a document was added to the Westlaw database later in the year.

Uniform Resource Locators (URLs)

http://www.westlaw.com[c]

The suffix *com* is the top level domain (TLD) for this Web site. The TLD *com* is an abbreviation for "commercial," which usually means that a for-profit entity hosts (maintains or supports) this Web site.

westlaw is the host name—the part of the domain name selected by the organization that registered the name. In this case, West Group registered the name. This Internet site is the Westlaw database on the Web.

www is an abbreviation for "World Wide Web." The Web is a system of Internet servers that support documents formatted in *HTML* (hypertext markup language). HTML supports links to text, graphics, and audio and video files.

http://www.uscourts.gov

This is "The Federal Judiciary Home Page." The host is the Administrative Office of the U.S. Courts. The TLD *gov* is an abbreviation for "government." This Web site includes information and links from, and about, the federal courts.

http://www.law.cornell.edu/index.html

This part of a URL points to a Web page or file at a specific location within the host's domain. This page is a menu with links to documents within the domain and to other Internet resources.

This is the host name for a Web site that contains the Internet publications of the Legal Information Institute (LII), which is a part of Cornell Law School. The LII site includes a variety of legal materials and links to other legal resources on the Internet. The TLD *edu* is an abbreviation for "educational institution" (a school or a university).

http://www.ipl.org/div/news

This part of the Web site points to a static *news* page at this Web site, which provides links to online newspapers from around the world.

div is an abbreviation for "division," which is the way that the Internet Public Library tags the content on its Web site as relating to a specific topic.

ipl is an abbreviation for "Internet Public Library," which is an online service that provides reference resources and links to other information services on the Web. The IPL is supported chiefly by the School of Information at the University of Michigan. The TLD *org* is an abbreviation for "organization" (normally nonprofit).

b. Many court decisions that are not yet published or that are not intended for publication can be accessed through Westlaw®, an online legal database.
c. The basic form for a URL is "service://hostname/path." The Internet service for all of the URLs in this text is *http* (hypertext transfer protocol). Because most Web browsers add this prefix automatically when a user enters a host name or a hostname/path, we have omitted the http:// from the URLs listed in this text.

English courts. The citations to these cases may not conform to the descriptions given above because the reporters in which they were published were often known by the names of the persons who compiled the reporters and have since been replaced.

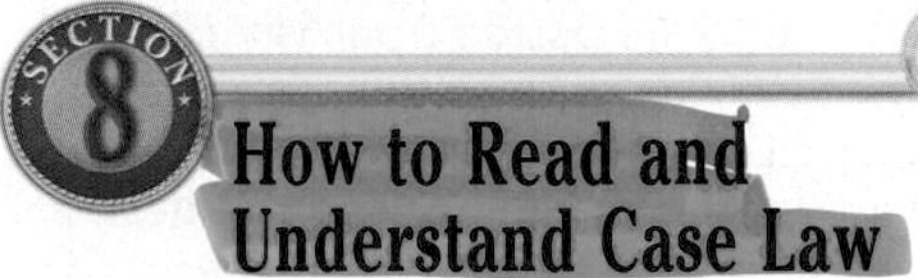

SECTION 8 How to Read and Understand Case Law

The decisions made by the courts establish the boundaries of the law as it applies to virtually all business relationships. It thus is essential that businesspersons know how to read and understand case law. The cases that we present in this text have been condensed from the full text of the courts' opinions and are presented in a special format. In approximately two-thirds of the cases, we have summarized the background and facts, as well as the court's decision and remedy, in our own words and have included only selected portions of the court's opinion ("in the language of the court"). In the remaining one-third of the cases, we have provided a longer excerpt from the court's opinion without summarizing the background and facts or decision and remedy. For those who wish to review court cases as part of research projects or to gain additional legal information, the following sections will provide useful insights into how to read and understand case law.

Case Titles

The title of a case, such as *Adams v. Jones*, indicates the names of the parties to the lawsuit. The *v.* in the case title stands for *versus*, which means "against." In the trial court, Adams was the plaintiff—the person who filed the suit. Jones was the defendant. If the case is appealed, however, the appellate court will sometimes place the name of the party appealing the decision first, so the case may be called *Jones v. Adams* if Jones is appealing. Because some appellate courts retain the trial court order of names, it is often impossible to distinguish the plaintiff from the defendant in the title of a reported appellate court decision. You must carefully read the facts of each case to identify the parties. Otherwise, the discussion by the appellate court may be difficult to understand.

Terminology

The following terms, phrases, and abbreviations are frequently encountered in court opinions and legal publications. Because it is important to understand what is meant by these terms, phrases, and abbreviations, we define and discuss them here.

Parties to Lawsuits As mentioned previously, the party initiating a lawsuit is referred to as the *plaintiff* or *petitioner*, depending on the nature of the action, and the party against whom a lawsuit is brought is the *defendant* or *respondent*. Lawsuits frequently involve more than one plaintiff and/or defendant. When a case is appealed from the original court or jurisdiction to another court or jurisdiction, the party appealing the case is called the **appellant.** The **appellee** is the party against whom the appeal is taken. (In some appellate courts, the party appealing a case is referred to as the *petitioner*, and the party against whom the suit is brought or appealed is called the *respondent*.)

Judges and Justices The terms *judge* and *justice* are usually synonymous and represent two designations given to judges in various courts. All members of the United States Supreme Court, for example, are referred to as justices, and justice is the formal title often given to judges of appellate courts, although this is not always the case. In New York, a *justice* is a judge of the trial court (which is called the Supreme Court), and a member of the Court of Appeals (the state's highest court) is called a *judge*. The term *justice* is commonly abbreviated to J., and *justices* to JJ. A Supreme Court case might refer to Justice Alito as Alito, J., or to Chief Justice Roberts as Roberts, C.J.

Decisions and Opinions Most decisions reached by reviewing, or appellate, courts are explained in written **opinions.** The opinion contains the court's reasons for its decision, the rules of law that apply, and the judgment.

Unanimous, Concurring, and Dissenting Opinions. When all judges or justices unanimously agree on an opinion, the opinion is written for the entire court and can be deemed a *unanimous opinion*. When there is not a unanimous opinion, a *majority opinion* is written; the majority opinion outlines the

INSIGHT INTO E-COMMERCE
How the Internet Is Expanding Precedent

The notion that courts should rely on precedents to decide the outcome of similar cases has long been a cornerstone of U.S. law. Nevertheless, the availability of "unpublished opinions" over the Internet is changing what the law considers to be precedent. An *unpublished opinion* is a decision made by an appellate court that is not intended for publication in a reporter (the bound books that contain court opinions).[a] Courts traditionally have not considered unpublished opinions to be "precedent," binding or persuasive, and attorneys were often not allowed to refer to these decisions in their arguments.

An Increasing Number of Decisions Are Not Published in Case Reporters but Are Available Online

The number of court decisions not published in printed books has risen dramatically in recent years. By some estimates, nearly 80 percent of the decisions of the federal appellate courts are unpublished. The number is equally high in some state court systems. California's intermediate appellate courts, for example, publish only about 7 percent of their decisions.

Even though certain decisions are not intended for publication, they are posted ("published") almost immediately on online legal databases, such as Westlaw and Lexis. With the proliferation of free legal databases and court Web sites, the general public also has almost instant access to the unpublished decisions of most courts. This situation has caused a substantial amount of debate over whether unpublished opinions should be given the same precedential effect as published opinions.

Should Unpublished Decisions Establish Precedent?

Prior to the Internet, one might have been able to justify not considering unpublished decisions to be precedent on the grounds of fairness. How could courts and lawyers be expected to consider the reasoning in unpublished decisions if they were not printed in the case reporters? Now that opinions are so readily available on the Web, however, this justification is no longer valid. Moreover, it now seems unfair not to consider these decisions as

a. Recently decided cases that are not yet published are also sometimes called *unpublished opinions,* but because these decisions will eventually be printed in reporters, we do not include them here.

view supported by the majority of the judges or justices deciding the case. If a judge agrees, or concurs, with the majority's decision, but for different reasons, that judge may write a *concurring opinion.* A *dissenting opinion* presents the views of one or more judges who disagree with the majority's decision. The dissenting opinion is important because it may form the basis of the arguments used years later in overruling the precedential majority opinion.

Other Types of Opinions. Occasionally, a court issues a *per curiam* opinion. *Per curiam* is a Latin phrase meaning "of the court." In *per curiam* opinions, there is no indication as to which judge or justice authored the opinion. This term may also be used for an announcement of a court's disposition of a case that is not accompanied by a written opinion. Some of the cases presented in this text are *en banc* decisions. When an appellate court reviews a case *en banc,* which is a French term (derived from a Latin term) for "in the bench," generally all of the judges "sitting on the bench" of that court review the case.

A Sample Court Case

To illustrate the elements in a court opinion, we present an annotated opinion in Exhibit 1–6 on pages 24–26. The opinion is from an actual case that the United States Court of Appeals for the Ninth Circuit decided in 2008.

Background of the Case The Seattle Center is an entertainment "zone" near downtown Seattle, Washington, that attracts almost ten million tourists every year. The center encompasses theaters, arenas, museums, exhibition halls, conference rooms, outdoor stadiums, and restaurants. Street performers add to the festive atmosphere. Under the authority of the city, the center's director issued rules to address safety concerns and other matters. Staff at the Seattle Center precedent to some extent because they are so publicly accessible.

Another argument against allowing unpublished decisions to be precedent concerns the quality of the legal reasoning set forth in these decisions. Staff attorneys and law clerks frequently write unpublished opinions so that judges can spend more time on the opinions intended for publication. Consequently, some claim that allowing unpublished decisions to establish precedent could result in bad precedents because the reasoning may not be up to par. If the decision is regarded merely as persuasive precedent, however, then judges who disagree with the reasoning are free to reject the conclusion.

The United States Supreme Court Changes Federal Rules on Unpublished Opinions after 2007

In spite of objections from several hundred judges and lawyers, the United States Supreme Court made history in 2006 when it announced that it would allow lawyers to refer to (cite) unpublished decisions in all federal courts. The new rule, Rule 32.1 of the Federal Rules of Appellate Procedure, states that federal courts may not prohibit or restrict the citation of federal judicial opinions that have been designated as "not for publication," "non-precedential," or "not precedent." The rule applies only to federal courts and only to unpublished opinions issued after January 1, 2007. It does not specify the effect that a court must give to one of its unpublished opinions or to an unpublished opinion from another court. Basically, the rule simply makes all the federal courts follow a uniform rule that allows attorneys to cite—and judges to consider as persuasive precedent—unpublished decisions beginning in 2007.

The impact of this new rule remains to be seen. At present, the majority of states do not allow their state courts to consider the rulings in unpublished cases as persuasive precedent, and this rule does not affect the states. The Supreme Court's decision, however, provides an example of how technology—the availability of unpublished opinions over the Internet—has affected the law.

CRITICAL THINKING

INSIGHT INTO THE SOCIAL ENVIRONMENT

Now that the Supreme Court is allowing unpublished decisions to form persuasive precedent in federal courts, should state courts follow? Why or why not?

cited one of the street performers, a balloon artist, for several rule violations. The artist filed a suit in a federal district court against the city and others, alleging that the rules violated his rights under the U.S. Constitution. The court issued a judgment in the plaintiff's favor. The city appealed to the United States Court of Appeals for the Ninth Circuit.

Editorial Practice You will note that triple asterisks (* * *) and quadruple asterisks (* * * *) frequently appear in the opinion. The triple asterisks indicate that we have deleted a few words or sentences from the opinion for the sake of readability or brevity. Quadruple asterisks mean that an entire paragraph (or more) has been omitted. Additionally, when the opinion cites another case or legal source, the citation to the case or other source has been omitted to save space and to improve the flow of the text. These editorial practices are continued in the other court opinions presented in this book. In addition, whenever we present a court opinion that includes a term or phrase that may not be readily understandable, a bracketed definition or paraphrase has been added.

Briefing Cases Knowing how to read and understand court opinions and the legal reasoning used by the courts is an essential step in undertaking accurate legal research. A further step is "briefing," or summarizing, the case. Legal researchers routinely brief cases by reducing the texts of the opinions to their essential elements. Generally, when you brief a case, you first summarize the background and facts of the case, as the authors have done for the cases presented within this text. You then indicate the issue (or issues) before the court. An important element in the case brief is, of course, the court's decision on the issue and the legal reasoning used by the court in reaching that decision. Detailed instructions on how to brief a case are given in Appendix A, which also includes a briefed version of the sample court case presented in Exhibit 1–6.

EXHIBIT 1–6 • A Sample Court Case

This section contains the citation—the name of the case, the name of the court that heard the case, the year of the decision, and the reporter in which the court's opinion can be found.

BERGER v. CITY OF SEATTLE
United States Court of Appeals,
Ninth Circuit, 2008.
512 F.3d 582.

This line provides the name of the justice (or judge) who authored the court's opinion.

O'SCANNLAIN, Circuit Judge:

We must determine the bounds of a city's authority to restrict expression in a public forum.

The court divides the opinion into several parts, headed by Roman numerals. The first part of the opinion summarizes the factual background of the case.

I

The public forum is the "Seattle Center," an entertainment zone covering roughly 80 acres of land in downtown Seattle, Washington. Each year, the Seattle Center's theaters, arenas, museums, exhibition halls, conference rooms, outdoor stadiums, and restaurants attract nearly ten million visitors. The city wields authority over this large tract of land and has delegated its power to **promulgate** rules to the Seattle Center Director ("Director"). * * * In 2002, after an open process of public comment, the Director issued a * * * set of provisions in response to specific complaints and safety concerns, which became known as the Seattle Center Campus Rules.

This litigation, originally brought by Michael Berger, a street performer, requires us to consider the validity of [the] Campus Rules. * * * Rule F.1 requires a permit for street performances and requires badges to be worn during street performances * * * . Berger mounts a **facial** attack on the **constitutionality** of these * * * restrictions.

Berger has performed in the Seattle Center since the 1980s, making balloon creations and "talk[ing] to his audience about his personal beliefs, especially the importance of reading books."

When the revised Campus Rules were enacted in 2002, Berger obtained a permit. Yet he * * * face[d] problems with the Seattle Center authorities: members of the public filed numerous complaints alleging that Berger exhibited threatening behavior and Seattle Center staff reported several rule violations. In 2003, Berger filed this **complaint** seeking damages and **injunctive relief** [alleging that the revised rules violated the Constitution]. * * * In 2005, [a federal] **district court** granted **summary judgment** to Berger, concluding that these rules facially violated the **First Amendment**.

promulgate: To formally announce or publish; to issue an order to result in a law or regulation becoming known and enforceable.

facial: The words of the rules in their apparent or obvious meaning, without any explanations, interpretations, modifications, or additions from outside sources.

constitutionality: The U.S. Constitution is the supreme law of the land. If a federal, state, or local law violates the Constitution, the law will be struck down.

complaint: A document that, when filed with a court, initiates a lawsuit.

injunctive relief: A court decree ordering a person to do or refrain from doing a certain act.

district court: A federal trial court in which a lawsuit is initiated.

summary judgment: A judgment that a court enters without beginning or continuing a trial. It can be entered only if no facts are in dispute and the only question is how the law applies.

First Amendment: The First Amendment to the Constitution guarantees, among other freedoms, the right of free speech—to express one's views without governmental restrictions.

EXHIBIT 1–6 • A Sample Court Case—Continued

A rejection or overruling of the district court's judgment.

The second major section of this opinion sets out the law that applies to the facts of the case.

The third major section of the opinion responds to the plaintiff's argument.

The city timely appeals the district court's order of summary judgment and seeks **reversal** with instructions to enter summary judgment in its favor.

II

The First Amendment states that "Congress shall make no law * * * abridging the freedom of speech, or of the press." Expression, whether oral or written or symbolized by conduct, is subject to reasonable time, place, or manner restrictions. Such restrictions * * * must be justified without reference to the content of the regulated speech, [and] they must be narrowly tailored to serve a significant governmental interest * * * .

III

* * * *

We begin with Berger's challenge to the permit requirement. Rule F.1 states that any person wishing to conduct a street performance must obtain a $5 annual permit from the Director. This rule dovetails with the badge requirement in Rule F.1, which mandates that a badge "shall be worn or displayed by the performer in plain view at all times during a performance."

* * * *

* * * The principal inquiry in determining content neutrality, in speech cases generally and in time, place, or manner cases in particular, is whether the government has adopted a regulation of speech because of disagreement with the message it conveys. A licensing statute lacks content neutrality if it burdens only certain messages or if it imposes a burden on all messages, but allows officials unchecked discretion to treat messages differently.

* * * *

* * * Contrary to Berger's argument, a rule does not discriminate based on content simply because it restricts a certain "medium" of communication. * * * We are satisfied that the rules meet * * * the test for a valid time, place, or manner restriction [on] speech.

* * * *

* * * A rule is narrowly tailored if it promotes a substantial government interest that would be achieved less effectively absent the regulation. Berger disputes the significance of the

EXHIBIT CONTINUES

EXHIBIT 1–6 • A Sample Court Case—Continued

city's interests, and also contends that the rule does not match the city's asserted aims to reduce territorial disputes among performers, deter patron harassment, and facilitate the identification and apprehension of offending performers.

As a general matter, it is clear that a State's interest in protecting the safety and convenience of persons using a public forum is a valid governmental objective. Here, * * * the Seattle Center authorities enacted the permit requirement after encountering "chronic" territorial disputes between performers and threats to public citizens by street performers. [A city employee stated that]

> Before the performer rules went into effect * * * there were approximately 3 or 4 complaints by performers against other performers per week. If Magic Mike [Berger] was here, we could expect one or more from him. * * * The general complaints by performers against other performers would be 'that is my spot and he can't be there' and/or 'that performer is doing what I am doing and they won't move.' The general complaints by the tenants against performers usually concerned too much noise or blocking access.

These complaints show that street performances posed a threat to the city's interests in maintaining order in the Seattle Center and providing harassment-free facilities. We are satisfied that the city's permit scheme was designed to further valid governmental objectives.

* * * *

In the final major section of this excerpt of the opinion, the court states its decision and gives its order.

V

In sum, [the] Rules * * * satisfy the requirements for valid restrictions on expression under the First Amendment. Such content neutral and narrowly tailored rules * * * must be upheld.

The order granting summary judgment to Berger is REVERSED. The case is **REMANDED** to the district court for further proceedings consistent with this opinion.

Sent back.

REVIEWING Business and Its Legal Environment

Suppose the California legislature passes a law that severely restricts carbon dioxide emissions from automobiles in that state. A group of automobile manufacturers files suit against the state of California to prevent the enforcement of the law. The automakers claim that a federal law already sets fuel economy standards nationwide and that fuel economy standards are essentially the same as carbon dioxide emission standards. According to the automobile manufacturers, it is unfair to allow California to impose more stringent regulations than those set by the federal law. Using the information presented in the chapter, answer the following questions.

1. Who are the parties (the plaintiffs and the defendant) in this lawsuit?
2. Are the plaintiffs seeking a legal remedy or an equitable remedy? Why?
3. What is the primary source of the law that is at issue here?
4. Where would you look to find the relevant California and federal laws?

TERMS AND CONCEPTS

administrative agency 7
administrative law 7
allege 11
analogy 12
appellant 21
appellee 21
binding authority 10
breach 5
case law 7
case on point 12
chancellor 8
citation 15
civil law 14
common law 8
constitutional law 6
court of equity 8
court of law 8
criminal law 14
cyberlaw 14
damages 8
defendant 9
defense 9
equitable maxims 9
executive agency 7
historical school 3
independent regulatory agency 7
jurisprudence 2
laches 9
law 2
legal realism 3
legal reasoning 11
natural law 3
opinion 21
ordinance 6
petitioner 9
plaintiff 9
positive law 3
positivist school 3
precedent 10
procedural law 14
public policy 11
remedy 8
remedy at law 8
remedy in equity 8
reporter 10
respondent 9
sociological school 4
***stare decisis* 10**
statute of limitations 9
statutory law 6
substantive law 14
syllogism 12
uniform law 6

QUESTIONS AND CASE PROBLEMS

1-1. How does statutory law come into existence? How does it differ from the common law? If statutory law conflicts with the common law, which law will govern?

1-2. QUESTION WITH SAMPLE ANSWER

After World War II, which ended in 1945, an international tribunal of judges convened at Nuremberg, Germany. The judges convicted several Nazis of "crimes against humanity." Assuming that the Nazi war criminals who were convicted had not disobeyed any law of their country and had merely been following their government's (Hitler's) orders, what law had they violated? Explain.

- **For a sample answer to Question 1–2, go to Appendix I at the end of this text.**

1-3. Assume that you want to read the entire court opinion in the case of *Menashe v. V Secret Catalogue, Inc.*, 409 F.Supp.2d 412 (S.D.N.Y. 2006). The case focuses on whether "SEXY LITTLE THINGS" is a suggestive or descriptive trademark and on which of the parties to the suit used the mark first in commerce. (Note that this case is presented in Chapter 14 of this text as Case 14.2.) Refer to the subsection entitled "Finding Case Law" in this chapter, and then explain specifically where you would find the court's opinion.

1-4. This chapter discussed a number of sources of American law. Which source of law takes priority in the following situations, and why?

(a) A federal statute conflicts with the U.S. Constitution.
(b) A federal statute conflicts with a state constitutional provision.
(c) A state statute conflicts with the common law of that state.
(d) A state constitutional amendment conflicts with the U.S. Constitution.

1-5. In the text of this chapter, we stated that the doctrine of *stare decisis* "became a cornerstone of the English and American judicial systems." What does *stare decisis* mean, and why has this doctrine been so fundamental to the development of our legal tradition?

1-6. What is the difference between a concurring opinion and a majority opinion? Between a concurring opinion and a dissenting opinion? Why do judges and justices write concurring and dissenting opinions, given that these opinions will not affect the outcome of the case at hand, which has already been decided by majority vote?

1-7. Courts can overturn precedents and thus change the common law. Should judges have the same authority to overrule statutory law? Explain.

1-8. "The judge's role is not to make the law but to uphold and apply the law." Do you agree or disagree with this statement? Discuss fully the reasons for your answer.

1-9. Assume that Arthur Rabe is suing Xavier Sanchez for breaching a contract in which Sanchez promised to sell Rabe a Van Gogh painting for $3 million.

(a) In this lawsuit, who is the plaintiff and who is the defendant?
(b) Suppose that Rabe wants Sanchez to perform the contract as promised. What remedy would Rabe seek from the court?
(c) Now suppose that Rabe wants to cancel the contract because Sanchez fraudulently misrepresented the painting as an original Van Gogh when in fact it is a copy. What remedy would Rabe seek?
(d) Will the remedy Rabe seeks in either situation be a remedy at law or a remedy in equity? What is the difference between legal and equitable remedies?
(e) Suppose that the trial court finds in Rabe's favor and grants one of these remedies. Sanchez then appeals the decision to a higher court. On appeal, which party will be the appellant (or petitioner), and which party will be the appellee (or respondent)?

1-10. A QUESTION OF ETHICS

*On July 5, 1884, Dudley, Stephens, and Brooks—"all able-bodied English seamen"—and a teenage English boy were cast adrift in a lifeboat following a storm at sea. They had no water with them in the boat, and all they had for sustenance were two one-pound tins of turnips. On July 24, Dudley proposed that one of the four in the lifeboat be sacrificed to save the others. Stephens agreed with Dudley, but Brooks refused to consent—and the boy was never asked for his opinion. On July 25, Dudley killed the boy, and the three men then fed on the boy's body and blood. Four days later, a passing vessel rescued the men. They were taken to England and tried for the murder of the boy. If the men had not fed on the boy's body, they would probably have died of starvation within the four-day period. The boy, who was in a much weaker condition, would likely have died before the rest. [*Regina v. Dudley and Stephens, *14 Q.B.D. (Queen's Bench Division, England) 273 (1884)]*

(a) The basic question in this case is whether the survivors should be subject to penalties under English criminal law, given the men's unusual circumstances. Were the defendants' actions necessary but unethical? Explain your reasoning. What ethical issues might be involved here?
(b) Should judges ever have the power to look beyond the written "letter of the law" in making their decisions? Why or why not?

LAW ON THE WEB

Today, business law and legal environment professors and students can go online to access information on almost every topic covered in this text. A good point of departure for online legal research is the Web site for *The Legal Environment of Business,* Seventh Edition, which can be found at **academic.cengage.com/blaw/cross**. There you will find numerous materials relevant to this text and to business law generally, including links to various legal resources on the Web. Additionally, every chapter in this text ends with a *Law on the Web* feature that contains selected Web addresses.

You can access many of the sources of law discussed in Chapter 1 at the FindLaw Web site, which is probably the most comprehensive source of free legal information on the Internet. Go to

www.findlaw.com

The Legal Information Institute (LII) at Cornell Law School, which offers extensive information about U.S. law, is also a good starting point for legal research. The URL for this site is

www.law.cornell.edu

The Library of Congress offers extensive links to state and federal government resources at

www.loc.gov

The Virtual Law Library Index, created and maintained by the Indiana University School of Law, provides an index of legal sources categorized by subject at

www.law.indiana.edu/v-lib/index.html#libdoc

Legal Research Exercises on the Web

Go to **academic.cengage.com/blaw/cross**, the Web site that accompanies this text. Select "Chapter 1" and click on "Internet Exercises." There you will find the following Internet research exercises that you can perform to learn more about some of the important sources of law discussed in Chapter 1 and other useful legal sites on the Web.

Internet Exercise 1–1: Legal Perspective
Internet Sources of Law

Internet Exercise 1–2: Management Perspective
Online Assistance from Government Agencies

Internet Exercise 1–3: Social Perspective
The Case of the Speluncean Explorers

CHAPTER 2

The Court System

Today in the United States there are fifty-two court systems—one for each of the fifty states, one for the District of Columbia, and a federal system. Keep in mind that the federal courts are not superior to the state courts; they are simply an independent system of courts, which derives its authority from Article III, Section 2, of the U.S. Constitution. By the power given to it under Article I of the U.S. Constitution, Congress has extended the federal court system beyond the boundaries of the United States to U.S. territories such as Guam, Puerto Rico, and the Virgin Islands.[1] As we shall see, the United States Supreme Court is the final controlling voice over all of these fifty-two systems, at least when questions of federal law are involved.

Every businessperson will likely face a lawsuit at some time in his or her career. Thus, anyone involved in business needs to have an understanding of the American court systems, as well as the various methods of dispute resolution that can be pursued outside the courts. In this chapter, after examining the judiciary's role in the American governmental system, we discuss some basic requirements that must be met before a party may bring a lawsuit before a particular court. We then look at the court systems of the United States in some detail and follow a hypothetical civil case through a court. We will examine some alternative methods of settling disputes in Chapter 3.

1. In Guam and the Virgin Islands, territorial courts serve as both federal courts and state courts; in Puerto Rico, they serve only as federal courts.

The Judiciary's Role in American Government

As you learned in Chapter 1, the body of American law includes the federal and state constitutions, statutes passed by legislative bodies, administrative law, and the case decisions and legal principles that form the common law. These laws would be meaningless, however, without the courts to interpret and apply them. This is the essential role of the judiciary—the courts—in the American governmental system: to interpret the laws and apply them to specific situations.

As the branch of government entrusted with interpreting the laws, the judiciary can decide, among other things, whether the laws or actions of the other two branches are constitutional. The process for making such a determination is known as **judicial review.** The power of judicial review enables the judicial branch to act as a check on the other two branches of government, in line with the system of checks and balances established by the U.S. Constitution.[2]

The power of judicial review is not mentioned in the Constitution (although many constitutional scholars conclude that the founders intended the judiciary to have this power). Rather, this power was explicitly established by the United States Supreme Court in 1803 by its decision in *Marbury v. Madison*,[3] in which the Supreme Court stated, "It is emphatically the province and duty of the Judicial Department to say

2. In a broad sense, judicial review occurs whenever a court "reviews" a case or legal proceeding—as when an appellate court reviews a lower court's decision. When referring to the judiciary's role in American government, however, the term *judicial review* is used to indicate the power of the judiciary to decide whether the actions of the other two branches of government do or do not violate the U.S. Constitution.

3. 5 U.S. (1 Cranch) 137, 2 L.Ed. 60 (1803).

what the law is. . . . If two laws conflict with each other, the courts must decide on the operation of each. . . . So if the law be in opposition to the Constitution . . . [t]he Court must determine which of these conflicting rules governs the case. This is the very essence of judicial duty." Since the *Marbury v. Madison* decision, the power of judicial review has remained unchallenged. Today, this power is exercised by both federal and state courts.

Basic Judicial Requirements

Before a lawsuit can be brought before a court, certain requirements must be met. These requirements relate to jurisdiction, venue, and standing to sue. We examine each of these important concepts here.

Jurisdiction

In Latin, *juris* means "law," and *diction* means "to speak." Thus, "the power to speak the law" is the literal meaning of the term **jurisdiction.** Before any court can hear a case, it must have jurisdiction over the person (or company) against whom the suit is brought (the defendant) or over the property involved in the suit. The court must also have jurisdiction over the subject matter of the dispute.

Jurisdiction over Persons or Property Generally, a particular court can exercise ***in personam* jurisdiction** (personal jurisdiction) over any person or business that resides in a certain geographic area. A state trial court, for example, normally has jurisdictional authority over residents (including businesses) of a particular area of the state, such as a county or district. A state's highest court (often called the state supreme court)[4] has jurisdictional authority over all residents within the state.

A court can also exercise jurisdiction over property that is located within its boundaries. This kind of jurisdiction is known as ***in rem* jurisdiction,** or "jurisdiction over the thing." For example, suppose that a dispute arises over the ownership of a boat in dry dock in Fort Lauderdale, Florida. The boat is owned by an Ohio resident, over whom a Florida court normally cannot exercise personal jurisdiction. The other party to the dispute is a resident of Nebraska. In this situation, a lawsuit concerning the boat could be brought in a Florida state court on the basis of the court's *in rem* jurisdiction.

Long Arm Statutes. Under the authority of a state **long arm statute,** a court can exercise personal jurisdiction over certain out-of-state defendants based on activities that took place within the state. Before a court can exercise jurisdiction over an out-of-state defendant under a long arm statute, though, it must be demonstrated that the defendant had sufficient contacts, or *minimum contacts,* with the state to justify the jurisdiction.[5] Generally, this means that the defendant must have enough of a connection to the state for the judge to conclude that it is fair for the state to exercise power over the defendant. For example, if an out-of-state defendant caused an automobile accident or sold defective goods within the state, a court will usually find that minimum contacts exist to exercise jurisdiction over that defendant. Similarly, a state may exercise personal jurisdiction over a nonresident defendant who is sued for breaching a contract that was formed within the state.

Corporate Contacts. Because corporations are considered legal persons, courts use the same principles to determine whether it is fair to exercise jurisdiction over a corporation.[6] A corporation normally is subject to personal jurisdiction in the state in which it is incorporated, has its principal office, and is doing business. Courts apply the minimum-contacts test to determine if they can exercise jurisdiction over out-of-state corporations.

The minimum-contacts requirement is usually met if the corporation advertises or sells its products within the state, or places its goods into the "stream of commerce" with the intent that the goods be sold in the state. For example, suppose that a business is incorporated under the laws of Maine but has a branch office and manufacturing plant in Georgia. The corporation also advertises and sells its products in Georgia. These activities would likely constitute sufficient contacts

4. As will be discussed shortly, a state's highest court is often referred to as the state supreme court, but there are exceptions. For example, in New York the supreme court is a trial court.

5. The minimum-contacts standard was first established in *International Shoe Co. v. State of Washington,* 326 U.S. 310, 66 S.Ct. 154, 90 L.Ed. 95 (1945).

6. In the eyes of the law, corporations are *legal persons*—entities that can sue and be sued. See Chapter 18.

with the state of Georgia to allow a Georgia court to exercise jurisdiction over the corporation.

Some corporations, however, do not sell or advertise products or place any goods in the stream of commerce. Determining what constitutes minimum contacts in these situations can be more difficult, as the following case—involving a resort hotel in Mexico and a hotel guest from New Jersey—illustrates.

CASE 2.1 Mastondrea v. Occidental Hotels Management S.A.

Superior Court of New Jersey, Appellate Division, 2007. 391 N.J.Super. 261, 918 A.2d 27.
lawlibrary.rutgers.edu/search.shtml[a]

• **Background and Facts** Libgo Travel, Inc., in Ramsey, New Jersey, with Allegro Resorts Management Corporation (ARMC), a marketing agency in Miami, Florida, placed an ad in the *Newark Star Ledger,* a newspaper in Newark, New Jersey, to tout vacation packages for accommodations at the Royal Hideaway Playacar, an all-inclusive resort hotel in Quintana Roo, Mexico. ARMC is part of Occidental Hotels Management, B.V., a Netherlands corporation that owns the hotel with Occidental Hoteles Management S.A., a Spanish company. In response to the ad, Amanda Mastondrea, a New Jersey resident, bought one of the packages through Liberty Travel, a chain of travel agencies in the eastern United States that Libgo owns and operates. On June 16, 2003, at the resort, Mastondrea slipped and fell on a wet staircase, breaking her ankle. She filed a suit in a New Jersey state court against the hotel, its owners, and others, alleging negligence. The defendants asked the court to dismiss the suit on the ground that it did not have personal jurisdiction over them. The court ruled in part that it had jurisdiction over the hotel. The hotel appealed this ruling to a state intermediate appellate court.

IN THE LANGUAGE OF THE COURT
***PAYNE,* J.A.D. [Judge, Appellate Division]**

* * * *

It is unquestionably true that the Hotel has no direct presence in New Jersey. * * * The Hotel's operations are located in Quintana Roo, Mexico. The Hotel is not registered, licensed or otherwise authorized to do business in New Jersey. It has no registered agent in this state for service of process, and it pays no state taxes. The Hotel maintains no business address here, it has never owned property or maintained any bank accounts in this state, and it has no employees in New Jersey.

However, * * * "Tour Operator Agreements" between the Hotel and Libgo * * * provide that the Hotel will allot a specific number of rooms at its resort to Libgo at agreed-upon rates. Libgo, as "tour operator," is then authorized by the Hotel to book those rooms on behalf of Libgo's customers. Pursuant to the contract, Libgo is required to provide the Hotel with weekly sales reports listing the number of rooms booked by Libgo and the rates at which those rooms were booked. It must also confirm all reservations in a writing sent to the Hotel.

Courts have generally sustained the exercise of personal jurisdiction over a defendant who, as a party to a contract, has had some connection with the forum state [the state in which the lawsuit is filed] or who should have anticipated that his conduct would have significant effects in that state. Here, the Hotel entered into a contract with a New Jersey entity, Libgo, which agreed to solicit business for the Hotel and derived a profit from that solicitation through sales of vacation packages. Although Libgo's business extends beyond New Jersey and throughout much of the East Coast, at least part of its customer base resides in this state. Likewise, as a result of this contract, the Hotel purposefully and successfully sought vacationers from New Jersey, and it derived a profit from them. Therefore, the Hotel should have reasonably anticipated that its conduct would have significant effects in New Jersey. [Emphasis added.]

* * * *

a. In the "SEARCH THE N.J. COURTS DECISIONS" section, type "Mastondrea" in the box, and click on "Search!" In the result, click on the case name to access the opinion. Rutgers University Law School in Camden, New Jersey, maintains this Web site.

CASE 2.1 CONTINUED

* * * Additional evidence of purposeful acts in New Jersey exists that fairly can be attributed to the Hotel and that are causally connected to plaintiff's decision to purchase the Hotel's vacation package * * *, [including] an ongoing, but undefined, relationship between the Hotel and * * * ARMC * * *. ARMC is a marketing organization that solicits business in the United States for the "Occidental Hotels & Resorts," a group of which the defendant Hotel is a part. ARMC does not have any direct contact with any of the potential customers of the various hotels that it promotes, and it does not itself sell travel or vacation packages. However, [ARMC] * * * works closely with Libgo in developing marketing strategies for the Occidental Hotels & Resorts in the New Jersey area pursuant to cooperative marketing agreements between ARMC and Libgo.

* * * *

* * * The defendant Hotel was featured, singly, [in 2003] in advertisements in the *Newark Star Ledger* on four occasions, including one in January * * *, prior to plaintiff's decision to book a vacation there.

We are satisfied * * * that * * * ARMC was operating [on behalf] of the Hotel when ARMC entered into cooperative marketing agreements with Libgo, and that ARMC's extensive contacts with Libgo in New Jersey regarding the marketing plan, together with the New Jersey fruits of that plan, can be attributed to the Hotel for jurisdictional purposes.

We are further persuaded that the *targeted advertising conducted pursuant to the cooperative marketing agreement on behalf of the Hotel provided the minimum contacts necessary to support * * * jurisdiction in this case.* [Emphasis added.]

- **Decision and Remedy** *The state intermediate appellate court affirmed the lower court's ruling. The appellate court concluded that the hotel had contacts with New Jersey, consisting of a tour operator contract and marketing activities through ARMC and Libgo, during the relevant time period and that, in response to the marketing, Mastondrea booked a vacation at the hotel. "[T]his evidence was sufficient to support the assertion of . . . personal jurisdiction over the Hotel in this State."*

- **What If the Facts Were Different?** *If Mastondrea had not seen Libgo and Allegro's ad, but had bought a Royal Hideaway vacation package on the recommendation of a Liberty Travel agent, is it likely that the result in this case would have been different? Why or why not?*

- **The Global Dimension** *What do the circumstances and the holding in this case suggest to a business firm that actively attempts to attract customers in a variety of jurisdictions?*

Jurisdiction over Subject Matter Subject-matter jurisdiction refers to the limitations on the types of cases a court can hear. Certain courts are empowered to hear certain kinds of disputes.

General and Limited Jurisdiction. In both the federal and the state court systems, there are courts of *general* (unlimited) *jurisdiction* and courts of *limited jurisdiction.* A court of general jurisdiction can decide cases involving a broad array of issues. An example of a court of general jurisdiction is a state trial court or a federal district court. An example of a state court of limited jurisdiction is a probate court. **Probate courts** are state courts that handle only matters relating to the transfer of a person's assets and obligations after that person's death, including issues relating to the custody and guardianship of children. An example of a federal court of limited subject-matter jurisdiction is a bankruptcy court. **Bankruptcy courts** handle only bankruptcy proceedings, which are governed by federal bankruptcy law (discussed in Chapter 15).

A court's jurisdiction over subject matter is usually defined in the statute or constitution creating the court. In both the federal and the state court systems, a court's subject-matter jurisdiction can be limited not only by the subject of the lawsuit but also by the sum in controversy, whether the case is a felony (a more serious type of crime) or a misdemeanor (a less serious type of crime), or whether the proceeding is a trial or an appeal.

Original and Appellate Jurisdiction. A court's subject-matter jurisdiction is also frequently limited to hearing cases at a particular stage of the dispute. Courts in which lawsuits begin, trials take place, and evidence is presented are referred to as *courts of* *original jurisdiction.* Courts having original jurisdiction are courts of the first instance, or trial courts. In the federal court system, the *district courts* are trial courts. In the various state court systems, the trial courts are known by different names, as will be discussed shortly.

Courts having appellate jurisdiction act as reviewing courts, or appellate courts. In general, cases can be brought before appellate courts only on appeal from an order or a judgment of a trial court or other lower court. In other words, the distinction between courts of original jurisdiction and courts of appellate jurisdiction normally lies in whether the case is being heard for the first time.

Jurisdiction of the Federal Courts

Because the federal government is a government of limited powers, the jurisdiction of the federal courts is limited. Federal courts have subject-matter jurisdiction in two situations.

Federal Questions. Article III of the U.S. Constitution establishes the boundaries of federal judicial power. Section 2 of Article III states that "[t]he judicial Power shall extend to all Cases, in Law and Equity, arising under this Constitution, the Laws of the United States, and Treaties made, or which shall be made, under their Authority." In effect, this clause means that whenever a plaintiff's cause of action is based, at least in part, on the U.S. Constitution, a treaty, or a federal law, a **federal question** arises. Any lawsuit involving a federal question comes under the judicial authority of the federal courts and can originate in a federal court. People who claim that their constitutional rights have been violated, for example, can begin their suits in a federal court. Note that in a case based on a federal question, a federal court will apply federal law.

Diversity of Citizenship. Federal district courts can also exercise original jurisdiction over cases involving **diversity of citizenship.** This term applies whenever a federal court has jurisdiction over a case that does not involve a question of federal law. The most common type of diversity jurisdiction has two requirements:[7] (1) the plaintiff and defendant must be residents of different states, and (2) the dollar amount in controversy must exceed $75,000. For purposes of diversity jurisdiction, a corporation is a citizen of both the state in which it is incorporated and the state in which its principal place of business is located. A case involving diversity of citizenship can be filed in the appropriate federal district court. If the case starts in a state court, it can sometimes be transferred, or "removed," to a federal court. A large percentage of the cases filed in federal courts each year are based on diversity of citizenship.

As noted, a federal court will apply federal law in cases involving federal questions. In a case based on diversity of citizenship, in contrast, a federal court will apply the relevant state law (which is often the law of the state in which the court sits).

Exclusive versus Concurrent Jurisdiction

When both federal and state courts have the power to hear a case, as is true in suits involving diversity of citizenship, **concurrent jurisdiction** exists. When cases can be tried only in federal courts or only in state courts, **exclusive jurisdiction** exists. Federal courts have exclusive jurisdiction in cases involving federal crimes, bankruptcy, and most patent and copyright claims; in suits against the United States; and in some areas of admiralty law (law governing transportation on ocean waters). State courts also have exclusive jurisdiction over certain subjects—for example, divorce and adoption. When concurrent jurisdiction exists, a party may choose to bring a suit in either a federal court or a state court.

Jurisdiction in Cyberspace

The Internet's capacity to bypass political and geographic boundaries undercuts the traditional basis on which courts assert personal jurisdiction. This basis includes a party's contacts with a court's geographic jurisdiction. As already discussed, for a court to compel a defendant to come before it, there must be at least minimum contacts—the presence of a salesperson within the state, for example. Are there sufficient minimum contacts if the only connection to a jurisdiction is an ad on a Web site originating from a remote location?

The "Sliding-Scale" Standard Gradually, the courts are developing a standard—called a "sliding-scale" standard—for determining when the exercise of personal jurisdiction over an out-of-state Internet-based defendant is proper. In developing this standard, the courts have identified three types of Internet

7. Diversity jurisdiction also exists in cases between (1) a foreign country and citizens of a state or of different states and (2) citizens of a state and citizens or subjects of a foreign country. These bases for diversity jurisdiction are less commonly used.

business contacts: (1) substantial business conducted over the Internet (with contracts and sales, for example); (2) some interactivity through a Web site; and (3) passive advertising. Jurisdiction is proper for the first category, is improper for the third, and may or may not be appropriate for the second.[8] An Internet communication is typically considered passive if people have to voluntarily access it to read the message and active if it is sent to specific individuals.

In certain situations, even a single contact can satisfy the minimum-contacts requirement. In one case, for example, a Texas resident, Connie Davis, sent an unsolicited e-mail message to numerous Mississippi residents advertising a pornographic Web site. Davis falsified the "from" header in the e-mail so that Internet Doorway appeared to be the sender. Internet Doorway filed a lawsuit against Davis in Mississippi, claiming that its reputation and goodwill in the community had been harmed. The federal court in Mississippi held that Davis's single e-mail to Mississippi residents satisfied the minimum-contacts requirement for jurisdiction. The court concluded that Davis, by sending the e-mail solicitation, should reasonably have expected that she could be "haled into court in a distant jurisdiction to answer for the ramifications."[9]

International Jurisdictional Issues Because the Internet is international in scope, international jurisdictional issues have understandingly come to the fore. The world's courts seem to be developing a standard that echoes the requirement of "minimum contacts" applied by the U.S. courts. Most courts are indicating that minimum contacts—doing business within the jurisdiction, for example—are enough to exercise jurisdiction over a defendant. The effect of this standard is that a business firm may have to comply with the laws in any jurisdiction in which it actively targets customers for its products.

To understand some of the problems created by Internet commerce, consider a French court's judgment against the U.S.-based Internet company Yahoo!, Inc. Yahoo operates an online auction site on which Nazi memorabilia have been offered for sale. In France, the display of any objects depicting symbols of Nazi ideology is illegal and leads to both criminal and civil liability. The International League against Racism and Anti-Semitism filed a suit in Paris against Yahoo for displaying Nazi memorabilia and offering them for sale via its Web site.

The French court asserted jurisdiction over Yahoo on the ground that the materials on the company's U.S.-based servers could be viewed on a Web site accessible in France. The French court ordered Yahoo to eliminate all Internet access in France to the Nazi memorabilia offered for sale through its online auctions. Yahoo then took the case to a federal district court in the United States, claiming that the French court's order violated the First Amendment to the U.S. Constitution. Although the federal district court ruled in favor of Yahoo, the U.S. Court of Appeals for the Ninth Circuit reversed. According to the appellate court, U.S. courts lacked personal jurisdiction over the French groups involved.[10] The *Yahoo* case represents the first time a U.S. court was asked to decide whether to honor a foreign judgment involving business conducted over the Internet. The federal appeals court's ruling leaves open the possibility that Yahoo, and anyone else who posts anything on the Internet, could be held answerable to the laws of any country in which the message might be received. *Concept Summary 2.1* on the following page reviews the various types of jurisdiction, including jurisdiction in cyberspace.

Venue

Jurisdiction has to do with whether a court has authority to hear a case involving specific persons, property, or subject matter. **Venue**[11] is concerned with the most appropriate location for a trial. For example, two state courts (or two federal courts) may have the authority to exercise jurisdiction over a case, but it may be more appropriate or convenient to hear the case in one court than in the other.

Basically, the concept of venue reflects the policy that a court trying a suit should be in the geographic neighborhood (usually the county) where the incident leading to the lawsuit occurred or where the parties involved in the lawsuit reside. Venue in a civil case typically is where the defendant resides, whereas venue in a criminal case is normally where the crime occurred. Pretrial publicity or other factors, though, may require a change of venue to another community, especially in criminal cases in which the defendant's right to a fair and impartial jury has been impaired.

8. For a leading case on this issue, see *Zippo Manufacturing Co. v. Zippo Dot Com, Inc.*, 952 F.Supp. 1119 (W.D.Pa. 1997).

9. *Internet Doorway, Inc. v. Parks,* 138 F.Supp.2d 773 (S.D.Miss. 2001).

10. *Yahoo! Inc. v. La Ligue Contre le Racisme et l'Antisemitisme,* 379 F.3d 1120 (9th Cir. 2004), *cert.* denied, __ U.S. __, 126 S.Ct. 2332, 164 L.Ed.2d 841 (2006).

11. Pronounced *ven-yoo.*

CONCEPT SUMMARY 2.1 Jurisdiction

Type of Jurisdiction	Description
PERSONAL	Exists when a defendant is located within the territorial boundaries within which a court has the right and power to decide cases. Jurisdiction may be exercised over out-of-state defendants under state long arm statutes. Courts have jurisdiction over corporate defendants that do business within the state, as well as corporations that advertise, sell, or place goods into the stream of commerce in the state.
PROPERTY	Exists when the property that is subject to a lawsuit is located within the territorial boundaries within which a court has the right and power to decide cases.
SUBJECT MATTER	Limits the court's jurisdictional authority to particular types of cases. 1. *Limited jurisdiction*—Exists when a court is limited to a specific subject matter, such as probate or divorce. 2. *General jurisdiction*—Exists when a court can hear cases involving a broad array of issues.
ORIGINAL	Exists with courts that have the authority to hear a case for the first time (trial courts).
APPELLATE	Exists with courts of appeal and review. Generally, appellate courts do not have original jurisdiction.
FEDERAL	1. *Federal questions*—When the plaintiff's cause of action is based at least in part on the U.S. Constitution, a treaty, or a federal law, a federal court can exercise jurisdiction. 2. *Diversity of citizenship*—In cases between citizens of different states when the amount in controversy exceeds $75,000 (or in cases between a foreign country and citizens of a state or of different states and in cases between citizens of a state and citizens or subjects of a foreign country), a federal court can exercise jurisdiction.
CONCURRENT	Exists when both federal and state courts have authority to hear the same case.
EXCLUSIVE	Exists when only state courts or only federal courts have authority to hear a case.
JURISDICTION IN CYBERSPACE	Because the Internet does not have physical boundaries, traditional jurisdictional concepts have been difficult to apply in cases involving activities conducted via the Web. Gradually, the courts are developing standards to use in determining when jurisdiction over a Web site owner or operator in another state is proper. A significant legal challenge with respect to cyberspace transactions has to do with resolving jurisdictional disputes in the international context.

Standing to Sue

In order to bring a lawsuit before a court, a party must have **standing to sue,** or a sufficient "stake" in a matter to justify seeking relief through the court system. In other words, to have standing, a party must have a legally protected and tangible interest at stake in the litigation. The party bringing the lawsuit must have suffered a harm or been threatened with a harm by the action about which she or he has complained. At times, a person can have standing to sue on behalf of another person. For example, suppose that a child suffers serious injuries as a result of a defectively manufactured toy. Because the child is a minor, another person, such as a parent or a legal guardian, can bring a lawsuit on the child's behalf.

Standing to sue also requires that the controversy at issue be a **justiciable**[12] **controversy**—a controversy that is real and substantial, as opposed to hypothetical or academic. For example, to entice DaimlerChrysler Corporation to build a $1.2 billion Jeep assembly plant in the area, the city of Toledo, Ohio, gave the company a ten-year local property tax exemption as well as a state franchise tax credit. Toledo taxpayers filed a lawsuit in state court, claiming that the tax breaks violated the commerce clause in the U.S. Constitution. The taxpayers alleged that the tax exemption and credit injured them because they would have to pay higher taxes to cover the shortfall in tax revenues. In 2006, the United States Supreme Court ruled that the taxpayers lacked standing to sue over the incentive program because their alleged injury was "conjectural or hypothetical"—that is, there was no justiciable controversy.[13]

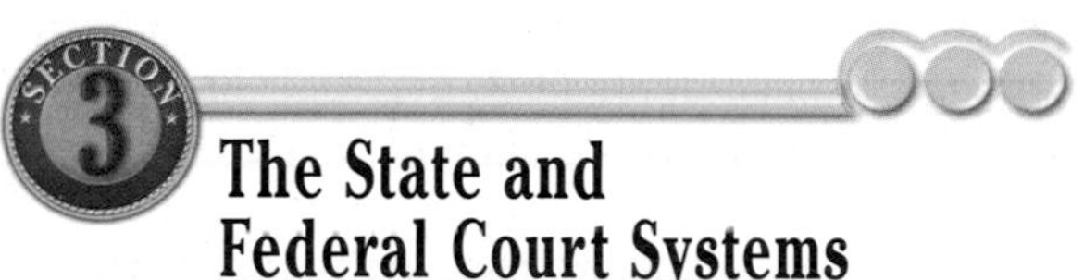

The State and Federal Court Systems

As mentioned earlier in this chapter, each state has its own court system. Additionally, there is a system of federal courts. Although no two state court systems are exactly the same, the right-hand side of Exhibit 2–1 illustrates the basic organizational framework characteristic of the court systems in many states. The exhibit also shows how the federal court system is structured. We turn now to an examination of these court systems, beginning with the state courts.

State Court Systems

Typically, a state court system includes several levels, or tiers, of courts. As indicated in Exhibit 2–1, state courts may include (1) local trial courts of limited jurisdiction, (2) state trial courts of general jurisdiction, (3) state courts of appeals (intermediate appellate courts), and (4) the state's highest court (often called the state supreme court). Generally, any person who is a party to a lawsuit has the opportunity to plead the case before a trial court and then, if he or she loses, before at least one level of appellate court. Finally, if the case involves a federal statute or federal constitutional issue, the decision of a state supreme court on that issue may be further appealed to the United States Supreme Court.

The states use various methods to select judges for their courts. Usually, voters elect judges, but in some states judges are appointed. For example, in Iowa, the governor appoints judges, and then the general population decides whether to confirm their appointment in the next general election. The states usually specify the number of years that judges will serve. In contrast, as you will read shortly, judges in the federal court system are appointed by the president of the United States

12. Pronounced jus-*tish*-a-bul.

13. *DaimlerChrysler v. Cuno,* 547 U.S. 332, 126 S.Ct.1854, 164 L.Ed.2d 589 (2006).

EXHIBIT 2–1 • The State and Federal Court Systems

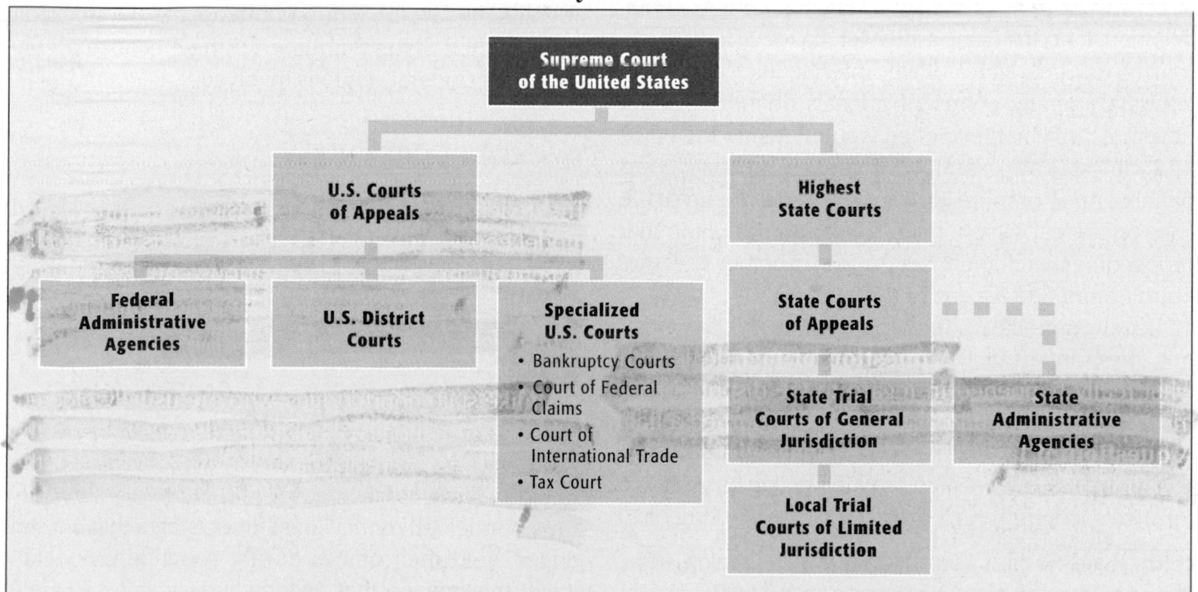

and, if they are confirmed by the Senate, hold office for life—unless they engage in blatantly illegal conduct.

Trial Courts Trial courts are exactly what their name implies—courts in which trials are held and testimony is taken. State trial courts have either general or limited jurisdiction. Trial courts that have general jurisdiction as to subject matter may be called county, district, superior, or circuit courts.[14] State trial courts of general jurisdiction have jurisdiction over a wide variety of subjects, including both civil disputes and criminal prosecutions. In some states, trial courts of general jurisdiction may hear appeals from courts of limited jurisdiction.

Courts of limited jurisdiction as to subject matter are often called special inferior trial courts or minor judiciary courts. **Small claims courts** are inferior trial courts that hear only civil cases involving claims of less than a certain amount, such as $5,000 (the amount varies from state to state). Suits brought in small claims courts are generally conducted informally, and lawyers are not required (in a few states, lawyers are not even allowed). Decisions of small claims courts and municipal courts may sometimes be appealed to a state trial court of general jurisdiction.

Other courts of limited jurisdiction include domestic relations courts, which handle primarily divorce actions and child-custody disputes; local municipal courts, which mainly deal with traffic cases; and probate courts, as mentioned earlier.

Appellate, or Reviewing, Courts Every state has at least one court of appeals (appellate court, or reviewing court), which may be an intermediate appellate court or the state's highest court. About three-fourths of the states have intermediate appellate courts. Generally, courts of appeals do not conduct new trials, in which evidence is submitted to the court and witnesses are examined. Rather, an appellate court panel of three or more judges reviews the record of the case on appeal, which includes a transcript of the trial proceedings, and then determines whether the trial court committed an error.

Usually, appellate courts focus on questions of law, not questions of fact. A **question of fact** deals with what really happened in regard to the dispute being tried—such as whether a party actually burned a flag. A **question of law** concerns the application or interpretation of the law—such as whether flag-burning is a form of speech protected by the First Amendment to the Constitution. Only a judge, not a jury, can rule on questions of law. Appellate courts normally defer to the trial court's findings on questions of fact because the trial court judge and jury were in a better position to evaluate testimony—by directly observing witnesses' gestures, demeanor, and other nonverbal behavior during the trial. At the appellate level, the judges review the written transcript of the trial, which does not include these nonverbal elements. Thus, an appellate court will not tamper with a trial court's finding of fact unless it is clearly erroneous (contrary to the evidence presented at trial) or when there is no evidence to support the finding.

Highest State Courts The highest appellate court in a state is usually called the supreme court but may be designated by some other name. For example, in both New York and Maryland, the highest state court is called the Court of Appeals. In Maine and Massachusetts, the highest court is labeled the Supreme Judicial Court. In West Virginia, the highest state court is the Supreme Court of Appeals.

The decisions of each state's highest court on all questions of state law are final. Only when issues of federal law are involved can the United States Supreme Court overrule a decision made by a state's highest court. For example, suppose that a city ordinance prohibits citizens from engaging in door-to-door advocacy without first registering with the mayor's office and receiving a permit. Further suppose that a religious group sues the city, arguing that the law violates the freedoms of speech and religion guaranteed by the First Amendment. If the state supreme court upholds the law, the group could appeal the decision to the United States Supreme Court—because a constitutional (federal) issue is involved.

The Federal Court System

The federal court system is basically a three-tiered model consisting of (1) U.S. district courts (trial courts of general jurisdiction) and various courts of limited jurisdiction, (2) U.S. courts of appeals (intermediate courts of appeals), and (3) the United States Supreme Court.

Unlike state court judges, who are usually elected, federal court judges—including the justices of the Supreme Court—are appointed by the president of the United States, subject to confirmation by the U.S. Senate. Article III of the Constitution states that federal judges "hold their offices during good Behaviour." In effect, this means that federal judges have lifetime

14. The name in Ohio and Pennsylvania is Court of Common Pleas; the name in New York is Supreme Court, Trial Division.

appointments. Although they can be impeached (removed from office) for misconduct, this is rarely done. In the entire history of the United States, only seven federal judges have been removed from office through impeachment proceedings.

U.S. District Courts At the federal level, the equivalent of a state trial court of general jurisdiction is the district court. U.S. district courts have original jurisdiction in federal matters, and federal cases typically originate in district courts. There are other federal courts with original, but special (or limited), jurisdiction, such as the federal bankruptcy courts and others shown earlier in Exhibit 2–1 on page 37.

There is at least one federal district court in every state. The number of judicial districts can vary over time, primarily owing to population changes and corresponding changes in caseloads. Currently, there are ninety-four federal judicial districts. Exhibit 2–2 shows the boundaries of the U.S. district courts, as well as the U.S. courts of appeals (discussed next).

U.S. Courts of Appeals In the federal court system, there are thirteen U.S. courts of appeals—referred to as U.S. circuit courts of appeals. Twelve of the federal courts of appeals (including the Court of Appeals for the D.C. Circuit) hear appeals from the federal district courts located within their respective judicial circuits, or geographic boundaries (shown in Exhibit 2–2).[15] The Court of Appeals for the Thirteenth Circuit, called the Federal Circuit, has national appellate jurisdiction over certain types of cases, such as those involving patent law and those in which the U.S. government is a defendant. The decisions of a circuit court of appeals are binding on all courts within the circuit court's jurisdiction and are final in most cases, but appeal to the United States Supreme Court is possible.

United States Supreme Court At the highest level in the three-tiered federal court system is the United States Supreme Court. According to the language of Article III of the U.S. Constitution, there is only one national Supreme Court. All other courts in the federal system are considered "inferior." Congress is empowered to create other inferior courts as it deems necessary. The inferior courts that Congress

15. Historically, judges were required to "ride the circuit" and hear appeals in different courts around the country, which is at the origin of the name "circuit court."

EXHIBIT 2–2 • Geographic Boundaries of the U.S. Courts of Appeals and U.S. District Courts

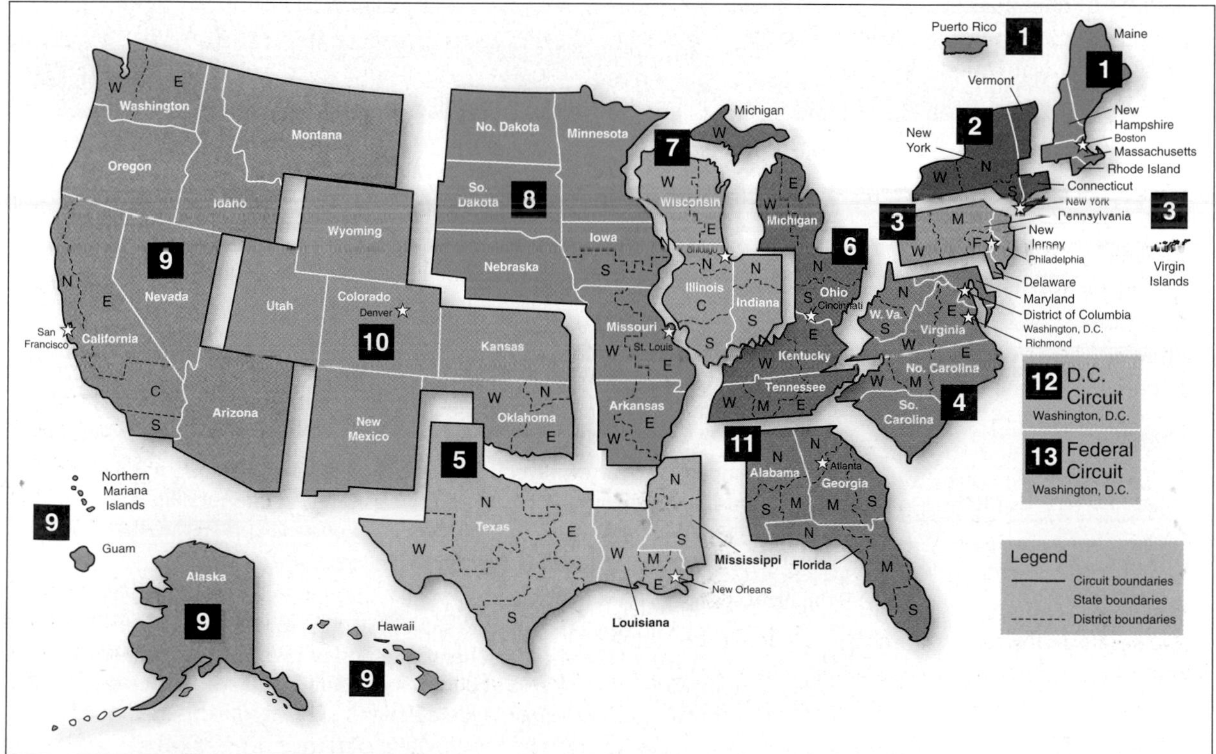

Source: Administrative Office of the United States Courts.

has created include the second tier in our model—the U.S. circuit courts of appeals—as well as the district courts and the various federal courts of limited, or specialized, jurisdiction.

The United States Supreme Court consists of nine justices. Although the Supreme Court has original, or trial, jurisdiction in rare instances (set forth in Article III, Sections 1 and 2), most of its work is as an appeals court. The Supreme Court can review any case decided by any of the federal courts of appeals, and it also has appellate authority over cases involving federal questions that have been decided in the state courts. The Supreme Court is the final arbiter of the Constitution and federal law.

Appeals to the Supreme Court. To bring a case before the Supreme Court, a party requests the Court to issue a writ of *certiorari*.[16] A **writ of *certiorari*** is an order issued by the Supreme Court to a lower court requiring the latter to send it the record of the case for review. The Court will not issue a writ unless at least four of the nine justices approve of it. This is called the **rule of four.** Whether the Court will issue a writ of *certiorari* is entirely within its discretion, and most petitions for writs are denied. (Thousands of cases are filed with the Supreme Court each year, yet it hears, on average, fewer than one hundred of these cases.[17]) A denial is not a decision on the merits of a case, nor does it indicate agreement with the lower court's opinion. Also, denial of the writ has no value as a precedent. Denial simply means that the lower court's decision remains the law in that jurisdiction.

Petitions Granted by the Court. Typically, the Court grants petitions in cases that raise important constitutional questions or when the lower courts have issued conflicting decisions on a significant issue. The justices, however, never explain their reasons for hearing certain cases and not others, so it is difficult to predict which type of case the Court might select. (See *Concept Summary 2.2* to review the various types of courts in the federal and state court systems.)

16. Pronounced sur-shee-uh-*rah*-ree.

17. From the mid-1950s through the early 1990s, the Supreme Court reviewed more cases per year than it has since then. In the Court's 1982–1983 term, for example, the Court issued written opinions in 151 cases. In contrast, during the Court's 2006–2007 term, the Court issued written opinions in only 75 cases.

CONCEPT SUMMARY 2.2 Types of Courts

Court	Description
TRIAL COURTS	Trial courts are courts of original jurisdiction in which actions are initiated. 1. *State courts*—Courts of general jurisdiction can hear any case that has not been specifically designated for another court; courts of limited jurisdiction include, among others, domestic relations courts, probate courts, municipal courts, and small claims courts. 2. *Federal courts*—The federal district court is the equivalent of the state trial court. Federal courts of limited jurisdiction include the bankruptcy courts and others shown in Exhibit 2–1 on page 37.
INTERMEDIATE APPELLATE COURTS	Courts of appeals are reviewing courts; generally, appellate courts do not have original jurisdiction. About three-fourths of the states have intermediate appellate courts; in the federal court system, the U.S. circuit courts of appeals are the intermediate appellate courts.
SUPREME COURT	The highest state court is that state's supreme court, although it may be called by some other name. Appeal from state supreme courts to the United States Supreme Court is possible only if a federal question is involved. The United States Supreme Court is the highest court in the federal court system and the final arbiter of the Constitution and federal law.

Judicial Procedures: Following a Case through the Court

American and English courts follow the *adversarial system of justice*. Although clients are allowed to represent themselves in court (called *pro se* representation),[18] most parties to lawsuits hire attorneys to represent them. Each lawyer acts as his or her client's advocate, presenting the client's version of the facts in such a way as to convince the judge (or the judge and jury, in a jury trial) that this version is correct.

Most of the judicial procedures that you will read about in the following pages are rooted in the adversarial framework of the American legal system. In this section, after a brief overview of judicial procedures, we illustrate the steps involved in a lawsuit with a hypothetical civil case (criminal procedures will be discussed in Chapter 7).

Procedural Rules

The parties to a lawsuit must comply with the procedural rules of the court in which the lawsuit is filed. Although most people, when considering the outcome of a case, think of matters of substantive law, procedural law can have a significant impact on one's ability to assert a legal claim. Procedural rules provide a framework for every dispute and specify what must be done at each stage of the litigation process. All civil trials held in federal district courts are governed by the **Federal Rules of Civil Procedure (FRCP)**.[19] Each state also has rules of civil procedure that apply to all courts within that state. In addition, each court has its own local rules of procedure that supplement the federal or state rules.

Broadly speaking, the litigation process has three phases: pretrial, trial, and posttrial. Each phase involves specific procedures. Although civil lawsuits may vary greatly in terms of complexity, cost, and detail, they typically progress through the specific stages charted in Exhibit 2–3 on the next page.

To illustrate the procedures involved in a civil lawsuit, we will use a simple hypothetical case. The case arose from an automobile accident, which occurred when a car driven by Antonio Carvello, a resident of New Jersey, collided with a car driven by Jill Kirby, a resident of New York. The accident took place at an intersection in New York City. Kirby suffered personal injuries, which caused her to incur medical and hospital expenses as well as lost wages for four months. In all, she calculated that the cost to her of the accident was $100,000.[20] Carvello and Kirby have been unable to agree on a settlement, and Kirby now must decide whether to sue Carvello for the $100,000 compensation she feels she deserves.

Consulting with an Attorney

As mentioned, rules of procedure often affect the outcome of a dispute—a fact that highlights the importance of obtaining the advice of counsel. The first step taken by virtually anyone contemplating a lawsuit is to seek the guidance of a qualified attorney. In the hypothetical Kirby-Carvello case, assume that Kirby consults with a lawyer. The attorney will advise her regarding what she can expect in a lawsuit, her probability of success at trial, and the procedures that will be involved. If more than one court would have jurisdiction over the matter, the attorney will also discuss the advantages and disadvantages of filing in a particular court. Depending on the court hearing the case, the attorney will give Kirby an idea of how much time it will take to resolve the dispute through litigation and provide an estimate of the costs involved.

The attorney will also inform Kirby of the legal fees that she will have to pay in an attempt to collect damages from the defendant, Carvello. Attorneys base their fees on such factors as the difficulty of a matter, the amount of time involved, the experience and skill of the attorney in the particular area of the law, and the cost of doing business. In the United States, legal fees range from $125 to $600 per hour or even higher (the average fee per hour is between $175 and $300). In addition, the client is also responsible for paying various expenses related to the case (called "out-of-pocket" costs), including court filing fees, travel expenses, and the cost of expert witnesses and investigators, for example.

---

18. This right was definitively established in *Faretta v. California*, 422 U.S. 806, 95 S.Ct. 2525, 45 L.Ed.2d 562 (1975).

19. The United States Supreme Court has authority to set forth these rules, as spelled out in 28 U.S.C. Sections 2071–2077. Generally, though, the federal judiciary appoints committees that make recommendations to the Supreme Court. The Court then publishes any proposed changes in the rules and allows for public comment before finalizing the rules.

20. In this example, we are ignoring damages for pain and suffering or for permanent disabilities. Often, plaintiffs in personal-injury cases seek such damages.

EXHIBIT 2–3 • Stages in a Typical Lawsuit

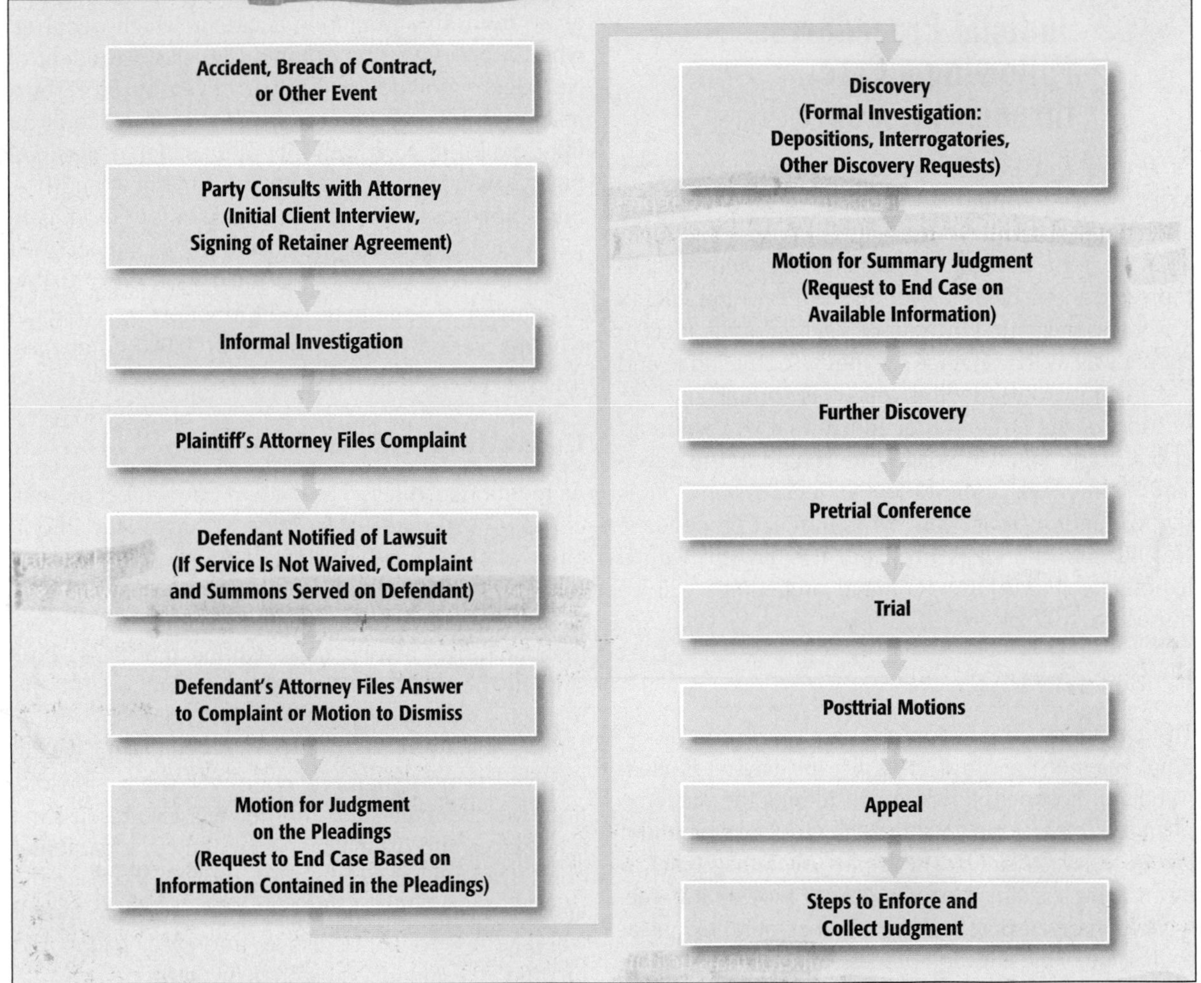

Types of Attorneys' Fees For a particular legal matter, an attorney may charge one type of fee or a combination of several types. *Fixed fees* may be charged for the performance of such services as drafting a simple will. *Hourly fees* may be computed for matters that will involve an indeterminate period of time. Any case brought to trial, for example, may involve an expenditure of time that cannot be precisely estimated in advance. *Contingency fees* are fixed as a percentage (usually between 25 and 40 percent) of a client's recovery in certain types of lawsuits, such as a personal-injury lawsuit.[21] If the lawsuit is unsuccessful, the attorney receives no fee, but the client will have to reimburse the attorney for any out-of-pocket costs incurred. Because Kirby's claim involves a personal injury, her lawyer will likely take the case on a contingency-fee basis, but she may have to pay an amount up front to cover the court costs.

In some cases, the winning party may be able to recover at least some portion of her or his attorneys' fees from the losing party. Many state and federal statutes provide for an award of attorneys' fees in certain legal actions, such as probate matters (settling a person's estate after death). In these situations, the judge sets the amount of the fee, which may be specified by statute or based on other factors, such as the fee customarily charged for similar services in the area. An attorney will advise the client as to whether

21. Note that attorneys may charge a contingency fee in only certain types of cases and are typically prohibited from entering into this type of fee arrangement in criminal cases, divorce cases, and cases involving the distribution of assets after death.

she or he would be entitled to recover some or all of the attorneys' fees in a case.

Settlement Considerations Once an attorney has been retained, the attorney is required to pursue a resolution of the matter on the client's behalf. Nevertheless, the amount of energy an attorney will spend on a given case is also determined by how much time and funds the client wishes to devote to the process. If the client is willing to pay for a lengthy trial and one or more appeals, the attorney may pursue those actions. Often, however, once a client learns the substantial costs involved in litigation, he or she may decide to pursue a settlement of the claim. Attempts to settle the case may be ongoing throughout the litigation process.

Another important factor in deciding whether to pursue litigation is the defendant's ability to pay the damages sought. Even if Kirby is awarded damages, it may be difficult to enforce the court's judgment if, for example, the amount exceeds the limits of Carvello's automobile insurance policy. (We will discuss the problems involved in enforcing a judgment later in this chapter.)

Pretrial Procedures

The pretrial litigation process involves the filing of the *pleadings,* the gathering of evidence (called *discovery*), and possibly other procedures, such as a pretrial conference and jury selection.

The Pleadings The *complaint* and *answer* (and other legal documents discussed below), taken together, are known as the **pleadings.** The pleadings inform each party of the other's claims and specify the issues (disputed questions) involved in the case. Because the rules of procedure vary depending on the jurisdiction of the court, the style and form of the pleadings may be different from those shown in this chapter.

The Plaintiff's Complaint. Kirby's action against Carvello will commence when her lawyer files a **complaint**[22] with the clerk of the appropriate court. The complaint contains a statement alleging (1) the facts showing that the court has jurisdiction, (2) the facts establishing the plaintiff's basis for relief, and (3) the remedy the plaintiff is seeking. Complaints can be lengthy or brief, depending on the complexity of the case and the rules of the jurisdiction.

Exhibit 2–4 on the following page illustrates how a complaint in the Kirby-Carvello case might appear. The complaint asserts facts indicating that the federal district court has jurisdiction because of diversity of citizenship. It then gives a brief statement of the facts of the accident and alleges that Carvello negligently drove his vehicle through a red light, striking Kirby's car and causing serious personal injury and property damage. The complaint goes on to state that Kirby is seeking $100,000 in damages, although in some state civil actions the plaintiff need not specify the amount of damages sought.

Service of Process. Before the court can exercise jurisdiction over the defendant (Carvello)—in effect, before the lawsuit can begin—the court must have proof that the defendant was notified of the lawsuit. Formally notifying the defendant of a lawsuit is called **service of process.** The plaintiff must deliver, or serve, a copy of the complaint and a **summons** (a notice requiring the defendant to appear in court and answer the complaint) to the defendant. The summons notifies Carvello that he must file an answer to the complaint within a specified time period (twenty days in the federal courts) or suffer a default judgment against him. A **default judgment** in Kirby's favor would mean that she would be awarded the damages alleged in her complaint because Carvello failed to respond to the allegations. A typical summons is shown in Exhibit 2–5 on page 45.

Method of Service. How service of process occurs depends on the rules of the court or jurisdiction in which the lawsuit is brought. Under the Federal Rules of Civil Procedure, anyone who is at least eighteen years of age and is not a party to the lawsuit can serve process in federal court cases. In state courts, the process server is often a county sheriff or an employee of an independent company that provides process service in the local area. Usually, the server hands the summons and complaint to the defendant personally or leaves it at the defendant's residence or place of business. In some states, process can be served by mail if the defendant consents (accepts service). When the defendant cannot be reached, special rules provide for alternative means of service, such as publishing a

22. Sometimes, the document filed with the court is called a *petition* or a *declaration* instead of a complaint.

EXHIBIT 2–4 • A Typical Complaint

IN THE UNITED STATES DISTRICT COURT
FOR THE SOUTHERN DISTRICT OF NEW YORK

CIVIL NO. 09-1047

JILL KIRBY
Plaintiff,
v.
ANTONIO CARVELLO
Defendant.

COMPLAINT

The plaintiff brings this cause of action against the defendant, alleging as follows:

1. This action is between the plaintiff, who is a resident of the State of New York, and the defendant, who is a resident of the State of New Jersey. There is diversity of citizenship between the parties.
2. The amount in controversy, exclusive of interest and costs, exceeds the sum of $75,000.
3. On September 10th, 2008, the plaintiff, Jill Kirby, was exercising good driving habits and reasonable care in driving her car through the intersection of Boardwalk and Pennsylvania Avenue, New York City, New York, when the defendant, Antonio Carvello, negligently drove his vehicle through a red light at the intersection and collided with the plaintiff's vehicle.
4. As a result of the collision, the plaintiff suffered severe physical injury, which prevented her from working, and property damage to her car.

WHEREFORE, the plaintiff demands judgment against the defendant for the sum of $100,000 plus interest at the maximum legal rate and the costs of this action.

By Joseph Roe

Joseph Roe
Attorney for Plaintiff
100 Main Street
New York, New York

1/2/09

notice in the local newspaper. In some situations, such as when the parties are in other countries or no other alternative is available, courts have even allowed service of process via e-mail, provided that it is reasonably calculated to provide notice and an opportunity to respond.

In cases involving corporate defendants, the summons and complaint may be served on an officer or on a *registered agent* (representative) of the corporation. The name of a corporation's registered agent can usually be obtained from the secretary of state's office in the state where the company incorporated its business (and, frequently, from the secretary of state's office in any state where the corporation does business).

Did the plaintiff in the following case effect proper service of the summons and the complaint on an out-of-state corporation?

EXHIBIT 2–5 • A Typical Summons

UNITED STATES DISTRICT COURT
FOR THE SOUTHERN DISTRICT OF NEW YORK

CIVIL ACTION, FILE NO. 09-1047

JILL KIRBY

Plaintiff,

v.

SUMMONS

ANTONIO CARVELLO

Defendant.

To the above-named Defendant:

You are hereby summoned and required to serve upon Joseph Roe, plaintiff's attorney, whose address is 100 Main Street, New York, NY, an answer to the complaint which is herewith served upon you, within 20 days after service of this summons upon you, exclusive of the day of service. If you fail to do so, judgment by default will be taken against you for the relief demanded in the complaint.

C. H. Hynek
CLERK

January 2, 2009
DATE

John Dolan
BY DEPUTY CLERK

EXTENDED CASE 2.2 **Cruz v. Fagor America, Inc.**

California Court of Appeal, Fourth District, Division 1, 2007
52 Cal.Rptr.3d 862, 146 Cal.App.4th 488.

***AARON,* J. [Judge]**

* * * *

[Alan] Cruz's parents purchased a pressure cooker from a vendor at the San Diego County Fair [in California] in the summer of 2001. On September 10, 2001, Cruz, who was 16 years old at the time, suffered burns on the left side of his torso and thigh when he attempted to take the lid off of the pressure cooker. Fagor [America, Inc.] is the American distributor of the pressure cooker.

On the date of the incident involving the pressure cooker, Cruz's parents sent an e-mail to Fagor to alert the company about what had occurred.

On June 2, 2003, [Fagor] notified Cruz that it was denying liability.

* * * *

Cruz filed a complaint [in a California state court] against Fagor on December 1, 2004, alleging causes of action for negligence and product liability. On December 14, 2004, Cruz, through his attorney, mailed the summons and complaint to Fagor by certified mail, return receipt requested. The

CASE 2.2 CONTINUED

CASE 2.2 CONTINUED

envelope was addressed to "Patricio Barriga, Chairman of the Board, FAGOR AMERICA, INC., A Delaware Corporation, 1099 Wall Street, Lyndhurst, NJ 07071-3678."

The return receipt indicates that it was signed by an individual named Tina Hayes on December 22. Fagor did not file an answer.

* * * *

A default judgment [a judgment entered against a defendant who fails to answer or respond to the plaintiff's complaint] in the amount of $259,114.50 was entered against Fagor on May 31, 2005.

Fagor did not make an appearance in the matter until November 29, 2005, when Fagor's attorneys * * * [filed] a motion to set aside the entry of default and default judgment.

* * * *

* * * On February 1, the trial court granted the motion. Cruz [appealed to a state intermediate appellate court] on February 16.

* * * *

* * * The trial court found that service was not effected because there was no proof that the summons and complaint (1) were served on Fagor's designated agent for service; (2) were delivered to the president or other officer, manager, or person authorized to receive service in accordance with [California Civil Procedure Code Section] 416.10; or (3) were served in accordance with [California] Corporations Code [S]ection 2110, which provides for service on a foreign corporation by hand delivery to an officer or designated agent for service of process.

* * * [But] the proofs of service demonstrate that Cruz served Fagor, an out-of-state corporation, in accordance with [California Civil Procedure Code Section] 415.40. Section 415.40 provides in pertinent part:

> A summons may be served on a person outside this state in any manner provided by this article or by sending a copy of the summons and of the complaint to the person to be served by first-class mail, postage prepaid, requiring a return receipt.

Because Fagor is a corporate entity, Cruz was also required to comply with the mandates of [S]ection 416.10. That section details how a plaintiff is to serve a summons on a corporate defendant and provides in relevant part:

> A summons may be served on a corporation by delivering a copy of the summons and of the complaint: * * * To the president or other head of the corporation, a vice president, a secretary or assistant secretary, a treasurer or assistant treasurer, a general manager, or a person authorized by the corporation to receive service of process.

* * * *

A number of documents in the record establish that Cruz properly served Fagor with process pursuant to California's statutory requirements. The first is a Judicial Counsel of California proof of service form, completed and signed by Cruz's attorney, Harold Thompson. In that form, Thompson states that the summons and complaint were addressed and mailed to Patricio Barriga, the president of Fagor, at 1099 Wall Street, Lyndhurst, New Jersey 07071-3678, which is the address Fagor listed in 2003 with the New York State Department of State—Division of Corporations as its "service of process address."

* * * *Thompson's declaration was properly executed because it shows that Cruz addressed the summons and complaint to a person to be served, as listed under [S]ection 416.10.* [Emphasis added.]

Cruz also submitted a signed return receipt to establish the fact of actual delivery. A return receipt attached to the proof of service form shows that the envelope was accepted at the Lyndhurst address. The receipt was signed by Hayes.

* * * *

* * * Cruz submitted the declaration of his attorney, Harold Thompson, in which Thompson states that he confirmed with a representative of the United States Postal Service in Lyndhurst, New Jersey, that Hayes regularly receives mail on behalf of Fagor at its Lyndhurst office. This is * * * sufficient to establish that an agent authorized to receive mail on the defendant's behalf received the summons and complaint.

* * * *

CASE 2.2 CONTINUED

* * * *By virtue of her authority to accept mail on Fagor's behalf, Hayes's notice of the action is imputed to Fagor and its officers. Barriga's statement that he did not receive the summons and complaint does not establish that service of process was invalid.* Barriga had constructive knowledge of the existence of the action, and of the summons and complaint, once an individual authorized to receive corporate mail acknowledged service. To hold otherwise would be to ignore the realities of corporate life, in which the duty to sign for mail received often resides with a designated mailroom employee, a receptionist, a secretary, or an assistant. A plaintiff who has provided evidence that a person authorized to receive mail on behalf of a corporation in fact received an item that was mailed to an officer of the corporation should not be held responsible for any failure on the part of the corporate defendant to effectively distribute that mail. [Emphasis added.]

* * * Cruz has * * * satisfied all of the elements necessary to establish effective service.

* * * *

The order of the trial court is reversed.

QUESTIONS

1. Suppose that Cruz had misaddressed the envelope but the summons had still reached Hayes and Cruz could prove it. Would this have been sufficient to establish valid service? Explain.
2. Should a plaintiff be required to serve a defendant with a summons and a copy of a complaint more than once? Why or why not?

Waiver of Formal Service of Process. In many instances, the defendant is already aware that a lawsuit is being filed and is willing to waive (give up) her or his right to be served personally. The Federal Rules of Civil Procedure (FRCP) and many states' rules allow defendants to waive formal service of process, provided that certain procedures are followed. Kirby's attorney, for example, could mail to defendant Carvello a copy of the complaint, along with "Waiver of Service of Summons" forms for Carvello to sign. If Carvello signs and returns the forms within thirty days, formal service of process is waived. Moreover, under the FRCP, defendants who agree to waive formal service of process receive additional time to respond to the complaint (sixty days, instead of twenty days). Some states provide similar incentives to encourage defendants to waive formal service of process and thereby reduce associated costs and foster cooperation between the parties.

The Defendant's Response. Typically, the defendant's response to the complaint takes the form of an **answer.** In an answer, the defendant either admits or denies each of the allegations in the plaintiff's complaint and may also set forth defenses to those allegations. Under the federal rules, any allegations that are not denied by the defendant will be deemed by the court to have been admitted. If Carvello admits to all of Kirby's allegations in his answer, a judgment will be entered for Kirby. If Carvello denies Kirby's allegations, the matter will proceed further.

Affirmative Defenses. Carvello can also admit the truth of Kirby's complaint but raise new facts to show that he should not be held liable for Kirby's damages. This is called raising an **affirmative defense.** As will be discussed in subsequent chapters, defendants in both civil and criminal cases can raise affirmative defenses. For example, Carvello could assert Kirby's own negligence as a defense by alleging that Kirby was driving negligently at the time of the accident. In some states, a plaintiff's contributory negligence operates as a complete defense. In most states, however, the plaintiff's own negligence constitutes only a partial defense (see Chapter 12).

Counterclaims. Carvello could also deny Kirby's allegations and set forth his own claim that the accident occurred as a result of Kirby's negligence and that therefore she owes Carvello for damage to his car. This is appropriately called a **counterclaim.** If Carvello files a counterclaim, Kirby will have to submit an answer to the counterclaim.

Dismissals and Judgments before Trial Many actions for which pleadings have been filed never come to trial. The parties may, for example, negotiate a settlement of the dispute at any stage of the litigation process. There are also numerous procedural avenues for disposing of a case without a trial. Many of them involve one or the other party's attempts to get the case dismissed through the use of various motions.

A **motion** is a procedural request submitted to the court by an attorney on behalf of her or his client. When one party files a motion with the court, that party must also send to, or serve on, the opposing party a *notice of motion.* The notice of motion informs the opposing party that the motion has been filed. **Pretrial motions** include the motion to dismiss, the motion for judgment on the pleadings, and the motion for summary judgment, as well as the other motions listed in Exhibit 2–6.

Motion to Dismiss. Either party can file a **motion to dismiss** requesting the court to dismiss the case for the reasons stated in the motion, although normally it is the defendant who requests dismissal. A defendant could file a motion to dismiss if the plaintiff's complaint fails to state a claim for which relief (a remedy) can be granted. Such a motion asserts that even if the facts alleged in the complaint are true, they do not give rise to any legal claim against the defendant. For example, if the allegations in Kirby's complaint do not constitute negligence on Carvello's part, Carvello could move to dismiss the case for failure to state a claim. Defendant Carvello could also file a motion to dismiss on the grounds that he was not properly served, that the court lacked jurisdiction, or that the venue was improper.

If the judge grants the motion to dismiss, the plaintiff generally is given time to file an amended complaint. If the judge denies the motion, the suit will go forward, and the defendant must then file an answer. Note that if Carvello wishes to discontinue the suit because, for example, an out-of-court settlement has been reached, he can likewise move for dismissal. The court can also dismiss a case on its own motion.

EXHIBIT 2–6 • **Pretrial Motions**

MOTION TO DISMISS

A motion normally filed by the defendant in which the defendant asks the court to dismiss the case for a specified reason, such as improper service, lack of personal jurisdiction, or the plaintiff's failure to state a claim for which relief can be granted.

MOTION TO STRIKE

A motion filed by the defendant in which the defendant asks the court to strike (delete) from the complaint certain paragraphs contained in the complaint. Motions to strike help to clarify the underlying issues that form the basis for the complaint by removing paragraphs that are redundant or irrelevant to the action.

MOTION TO MAKE MORE DEFINITE AND CERTAIN

A motion filed by the defendant to compel the plaintiff to clarify the basis of the plaintiff's cause of action. The motion is filed when the defendant believes that the complaint is too vague or ambiguous for the defendant to respond to it in a meaningful way.

MOTION FOR JUDGMENT ON THE PLEADINGS

A motion that may be filed by either party in which the party asks the court to enter a judgment in his or her favor based on information contained in the pleadings. A judgment on the pleadings will be made only if there are no facts in dispute and the only question is how the law applies to a set of undisputed facts.

MOTION TO COMPEL DISCOVERY

A motion that may be filed by either party in which the party asks the court to compel the other party to comply with a discovery request. If a party refuses to allow the opponent to inspect and copy certain documents, for example, the party requesting the documents may make a motion to compel production of those documents.

MOTION FOR SUMMARY JUDGMENT

A motion that may be filed by either party in which the party asks the court to enter judgment in his or her favor without a trial. Unlike a motion for judgment on the pleadings, a motion for summary judgment can be supported by evidence outside the pleadings, such as witnesses' affidavits, answers to interrogatories, and other evidence obtained prior to or during discovery.

Motion for Judgment on the Pleadings. At the close of the pleadings, either party may make a **motion for judgment on the pleadings,** which asks the court to decide the issue solely on the pleadings without proceeding to trial. The judge will grant the motion only when there is no dispute over the facts of the case and the sole issue to be resolved is a question of law. For example, in the Kirby-Carvello case, if Carvello had admitted to all of Kirby's allegations in his answer and had raised no affirmative defenses, Kirby could file a motion for judgment on the pleadings.

In deciding a motion for judgment on the pleadings, the judge may consider only the evidence contained in the pleadings. In contrast, in a motion for summary judgment, discussed next, the court may consider evidence outside the pleadings, such as sworn statements and other materials that would be admissible as evidence at trial.

Motion for Summary Judgment. Either party can file a **motion for summary judgment,** which asks the court to grant a judgment in that party's favor without a trial. As with a motion for judgment on the pleadings, a court will grant a motion for summary judgment only if it determines that no facts are in dispute and the only question is how the law applies to the facts. A motion for summary judgment can be made before or during a trial, but it will be granted only if, when the evidence is viewed in the light most favorable to the other party, there clearly are no factual disputes in contention.

To support a motion for summary judgment, one party can submit evidence obtained at any point prior to trial that refutes the other party's factual claim. The evidence may consist of **affidavits** (sworn statements by parties or witnesses) or documents, such as a contract. Of course, the evidence must be *admissible* evidence—that is, evidence that the court would allow to be presented during the trial. As mentioned, the use of additional evidence is one feature that distinguishes the motion for summary judgment from the motion to dismiss and the motion for judgment on the pleadings.

Discovery Before a trial begins, the parties can use a number of procedural devices to obtain information and gather evidence about the case. Kirby, for example, will want to know how fast Carvello was driving, whether he had been drinking or was under the influence of any medication, and whether he was wearing corrective lenses if he was required by law to do so while driving. The process of obtaining information from the opposing party or from witnesses prior to trial is known as **discovery.** Discovery includes gaining access to witnesses, documents, records, and other types of evidence. In federal courts, the parties are required to make initial disclosures of relevant evidence to the opposing party.

The FRCP and similar state rules set forth the guidelines for discovery activity. Generally, discovery is allowed regarding any matter that is relevant to the claim or defense of any party. Discovery rules also attempt to protect witnesses and parties from undue harassment, and to safeguard privileged or confidential material from being disclosed. Only information that is relevant to the case at hand—or likely to lead to the discovery of relevant information—is discoverable. If a discovery request involves privileged or confidential business information, a court can deny the request and can limit the scope of discovery in a number of ways. For example, a court can require the party to submit the materials to the judge in a sealed envelope so that the judge can decide if they should be disclosed to the opposing party.

Discovery prevents surprises at trial by giving both parties access to evidence that might otherwise be hidden. This allows the litigants to learn as much as they can about what to expect at a trial before they reach the courtroom. Discovery also serves to narrow the issues so that trial time is spent on the main questions in the case.

Depositions and Interrogatories. Discovery can involve the use of depositions or interrogatories, or both. A **deposition** is sworn testimony by a party to the lawsuit or by any witness, recorded by an authorized court official. The person deposed gives testimony and answers questions asked by the attorneys from both sides. The questions and answers are recorded, sworn to, and signed. These answers, of course, will help the attorneys prepare their cases. Depositions also give attorneys the opportunity to evaluate how their witnesses will conduct themselves at trial. In addition, depositions can be employed in court to *impeach* (challenge the credibility of) a party or a witness who changes testimony at the trial. A deposition can also be used as testimony if the witness is not available at trial.

Interrogatories are written questions for which written answers are prepared and then signed under oath. The main difference between interrogatories and written depositions is that interrogatories are directed to a party to the lawsuit (the plaintiff or the defendant), not to a witness, and the party can prepare answers with the aid of an attorney. Whereas depositions are useful for eliciting candid responses from a party and answers not prepared in advance, interrogatories are designed to obtain accurate information about specific topics, such as, for example, how many contracts were signed and when. The scope of interrogatories is also broader because parties are obligated to answer questions, even if that means disclosing information from their records and files.

Requests for Admissions. One party can serve the other party with a written request for an admission of the truth of matters relating to the trial. Any fact admitted under such a request is conclusively established as true for the trial. For example, Kirby can ask Carvello to admit that his driver's license was suspended at the time of the accident. A request for admission shortens the trial because the parties will not have to spend time proving facts on which they already agree.

Requests for Documents, Objects, and Entry upon Land. A party can gain access to documents and other items not in her or his possession in order to inspect and examine them. Carvello, for example, can gain permission to inspect and copy Kirby's car repair bills. Likewise, a party can gain "entry upon land" to inspect the premises.

Request for Examinations. When the physical or mental condition of one party is in question, the opposing party can ask the court to order a physical or mental examination by an independent examiner. If the court agrees to make the order, the opposing party can obtain the results of the examination. Note that the court will make such an order only when the need for the information outweighs the right to privacy of the person to be examined.

Electronic Discovery. Any relevant material, including information stored electronically, can be the object of a discovery request. The federal rules and most state rules (as well as court decisions) now specifically allow individuals to obtain discovery of electronic "data compilations." Electronic evidence, or **e-evidence,** consists of all computer-generated or electronically recorded information, such as e-mail, voice mail, spreadsheets, word-processing documents, and other data. E-evidence can reveal significant facts that are not discoverable by other means. For example, computers automatically record certain information about files—such as who created the file and when, and who accessed, modified, or transmitted it—on their hard drives. This information can only be obtained from the file in its electronic format—not from printed-out versions.

Amendments to the FRCP that took effect in December 2006 deal specifically with the preservation, retrieval, and production of electronic data. Although traditional means, such as interrogatories and depositions, are still used to find out whether e-evidence exists, a party must usually hire an expert to retrieve the evidence in its electronic format. The expert uses software to reconstruct e-mail exchanges to establish who knew what and when they knew it. The expert can even recover files from a computer that the user thought had been deleted. Reviewing back-up copies of documents and e-mail can provide useful—and often quite damaging—information about how a particular matter progressed over several weeks or months.

Electronic discovery has significant advantages over paper discovery, but it is also time consuming and expensive. These costs are amplified when the parties involved in the lawsuit are large corporations with many offices and employees. Who should pay the costs associated with electronic discovery? For a discussion of how the courts are handling this issue, see this chapter's *Emerging Trends* feature on pages 52 and 53.

Pretrial Conference After discovery has taken place and before the trial begins, the attorneys may meet with the trial judge in a **pretrial conference,** or hearing. Usually, the hearing consists of an informal discussion between the judge and the opposing attorneys after discovery has taken place. The purpose of the hearing is to explore the possibility of a settlement without trial and, if this is not possible, to identify the matters that are in dispute and to plan the course of the trial. In particular, the parties may attempt to establish ground rules to restrict the number of expert witnesses or discuss the admissibility or costs of certain types of evidence.

The Right to a Jury Trial The Seventh Amendment to the U.S. Constitution guarantees the right to a jury trial for cases at law in *federal* courts when the amount in controversy exceeds $20. Most states have similar guarantees in their own constitutions (although the threshold dollar amount is higher than $20). The right to a trial by jury need not be exercised, and many cases are tried without a jury. In most states and in federal courts, one of the parties must request a jury, or the judge presumes the parties waive this right. If there is no jury, the judge determines the truth of the facts alleged in the case.

Jury Selection Before a jury trial commences, a panel of jurors must be selected. Although some types of trials require twelve-person juries, most civil matters can be heard by six-person juries. The jury selection process is known as ***voir dire.***[23] During *voir dire* in most jurisdictions, attorneys for the plaintiff and the defendant ask prospective jurors oral questions to determine whether a potential jury member is biased or has any connection with a party to the action or with a prospective witness. In some jurisdictions, the judge may do all or part of the questioning based on written questions submitted by counsel for the parties.

During *voir dire,* a party may challenge a certain number of prospective jurors *peremptorily*—that is, ask that an individual not be sworn in as a juror without providing any reason. Alternatively, a party may challenge a prospective juror *for cause*—that is, provide a reason why an individual should not be sworn in as a juror. If the judge grants the challenge, the individual will be asked to step down. A prospective juror, however, may not be excluded by the use of discriminatory challenges, such as those based on racial criteria or gender. (See *Concept Summary 2.3* for a review of pretrial procedures.)

23. Pronounced *vwahr deehr.* These old French verbs mean "to speak the truth." In legal language, the phrase refers to the process of questioning jurors to learn about their backgrounds, attitudes, and similar attributes.

CONCEPT SUMMARY 2.3
Pretrial Procedures

Procedure	Description
PLEADINGS	1. *The plaintiff's complaint*—The plaintiff's statement of the cause of action and the parties involved, filed with the court by the plaintiff's attorney. After the filing, the defendant is notified of the suit through service of process. 2. *The defendant's response*—The defendant's response to the plaintiff's complaint may take the form of an answer, in which the defendant admits or denies the plaintiff's allegations. The defendant may raise an affirmative defense and/or assert a counterclaim.
PRETRIAL MOTIONS	1. *Motion to dismiss*—A motion requesting the judge to dismiss the case for reasons that are provided in the motion (such as failure to state a claim for which relief can be granted). 2. *Motion for judgment on the pleadings*—May be made by either party; will be granted only if no facts are in dispute and only questions of law are at issue. 3. *Motion for summary judgment*—May be made by either party; will be granted only if no facts are in dispute and only questions of law are at issue. Unlike the motion for judgment on the pleadings, the motion for summary judgment may be supported by evidence outside the pleadings, such as testimony and other evidence obtained during the discovery phase of litigation.
DISCOVERY	The process of gathering evidence concerning the case; involves (1) *depositions* (sworn testimony by either party or any witness); (2) *interrogatories* (in which parties to the action write answers to questions with the aid of their attorneys); and (3) requests for admissions, documents, examinations, or other information relating to the case. Discovery may also involve electronically recorded information, such as e-mail, voice mail, and other data.
PRETRIAL CONFERENCE	A pretrial hearing, at the request of either party or the court, to identify the matters in dispute after discovery has taken place and to explore the possibility of settling the dispute without a trial. If no settlement is possible, the parties plan the course of the trial.
JURY SELECTION	In a jury trial, the selection of members of the jury from a pool of prospective jurors. During a process known as *voir dire,* the attorneys for both sides may challenge prospective jurors either for cause or peremptorily (for no cause).

EMERGING TRENDS IN THE LEGAL ENVIRONMENT OF BUSINESS
E-Discovery and Cost-Shifting

Before the computer age, discovery involved searching through paper records—physical evidence. Today, less than 0.5 percent of new information is created on paper. Instead of sending letters and memos, for example, people send e-mails—almost 600 billion of them annually in the United States. The all-inclusive nature of electronic information means that electronic discovery (e-discovery) now plays an important role in almost every business lawsuit.

Changes in the Federal Rules of Civil Procedure

As e-discovery has become ubiquitous, the Federal Rules of Civil Procedure (FRCP) have changed to encompass it. Amended Section 26(f) of the FRCP, for example, requires that the parties confer about "preserving discoverable information" and discuss "any issues relating to . . . discovery of electronically stored information, including the electronic forms in which it should be produced."

The most recent amendment to Section 34(a) of the FRCP expressly permits one party to a lawsuit to request that the other produce "electronically stored information—including . . . data compilation stored in any medium from which information can be obtained." The new rule has put in place a two-tiered process for discovery of electronically stored information. Relevant and nonprivileged information that is reasonably accessible is discoverable as a matter of right. Discovery of less accessible—and therefore more costly to obtain—electronic data may or may not be allowed by the court. The problem of the costs of e-discovery is discussed further below.

The *Ameriwood* Three-Step Process

The new federal rules were applied in *Ameriwood Industries, Inc. v. Liberman,* a major case involving e-discovery in which the court developed a three-step procedure for obtaining electronic data.[a] In the first step, *imaging,* mirror images of a party's hard drives can be required. The second step involves *recovering* available word-processing documents, e-mails, PowerPoint presentations, spreadsheets, and other files. The final step is *full disclosure* in which a party sends the other party all responsive and nonprivileged documents and information obtained in the previous two steps.

Limitations on E-Discovery and Cost-Shifting

Complying with requests for electronically discoverable information can cost hundreds of thousands, if not millions, of dollars, especially if a party is a large corporation with thousands of employees creating millions of electronic documents. Consequently, there is a trend toward limiting e-discovery. Under the FRCP, a court can limit electronic discovery (1) when it would be unreasonably cumulative or duplicative, (2) when the requesting party has already had ample opportunity during discovery to obtain the information, or (3) when the burden or expense outweighs the likely benefit.

a. 2007 WL 685623 (E.D.Mo. 2007).

The Trial

Various rules and procedures govern the trial phase of the litigation process. There are rules governing what kind of evidence will or will not be admitted during the trial, as well as specific procedures that the participants in the lawsuit must follow.

Opening Statements At the beginning of the trial, both attorneys are allowed to make **opening statements** setting forth the facts that they expect to prove during the trial. The opening statement provides an opportunity for each lawyer to give a brief version of the facts and the supporting evidence that will be used during the trial. Then the plaintiff's case is presented. In our hypothetical case, Kirby's lawyer would introduce evidence (relevant documents, exhibits, and the testimony of witnesses) to support Kirby's position.

Rules of Evidence Whether evidence will be admitted in court is determined by the **rules of evidence**—a series of rules that have been created by the courts to ensure that any evidence presented during a trial is fair and reliable. The Federal Rules of Evidence govern the admissibility of evidence in federal courts.

Evidence Must Be Relevant to the Issues. Evidence will not be admitted in court unless it is relevant to the matter in question. **Relevant evidence** is evidence that tends to prove or disprove a fact in question or to establish the degree of probability of a fact or action. For example, evidence that a suspect's gun was in the home of another person when a victim was shot would be relevant—because it would tend to prove that the suspect did not shoot the victim.

Many courts are allowing responding parties to object to e-discovery requests on the ground that complying with the request would cause an undue financial burden. In a suit between E*Trade and Deutsche Bank, for example, the court denied E*Trade's request that the defendant produce its hard drives because doing so would create an undue burden.[b]

In addition, sometimes when a court finds that producing the requested information would create an undue financial burden, the court orders the party to comply but shifts the cost to the requesting party (usually the plaintiff). A major case in this area involved Rowe Entertainment and the William Morris Agency. When the e-discovery costs were estimated to be as high as $9 million, the court determined that cost-shifting was warranted.[c] In deciding whether to order cost-shifting, courts increasingly take into account the amount in controversy and each party's ability to pay. Sometimes, a court may require the responding party to restore and produce representative documents from a small sample of the requested medium to verify the relevance of the data before the party incurs significant expenses.[d]

b. *E*Trade Securities, LLC v. Deutsche Bank A.G.*, 230 F.R.D. 582 (D.Minn. 2005). This is a *Federal Rules Decision* not designated for publication in the *Federal Supplement*, citing *Zubulake v. UBS Warburg, LLC*, 2003 WL 21087884 (S.D.N.Y. 2003).

c. *Rowe Entertainment, Inc. v. William Morris Agency, Inc.*, 2002 WL 975713 (S.D.N.Y. 2002).

d. See, for example, *Quinby v. West LBAG*, 2006 WL 2597900 (S.D.N.Y. 2006).

IMPLICATIONS FOR THE BUSINESSPERSON

1. Whenever there is a "reasonable anticipation of litigation," all the relevant documents must be preserved. Preserving data can be a challenge, particularly for large corporations that have electronic data scattered across multiple networks, servers, desktops, laptops, handheld devices, and even home computers.
2. Even though an e-mail is deleted, it is not necessarily eliminated from one's hard drive, unless it is completely overwritten by new data. Thus, businesspersons should be aware that their hard drives can contain information they presumed no longer existed.

FOR CRITICAL ANALYSIS

1. How might a large corporation protect itself from allegations that it intentionally failed to preserve electronic data?
2. Given the significant and often burdensome costs associated with electronic discovery, should courts consider cost-shifting in every case involving electronic discovery? Why or why not?

RELEVANT WEB SITES

To locate information on the Web concerning the issues discussed in this feature, go to this text's Web site at **academic.cengage.com/blaw/cross**, select "Chapter 2," and click on "Emerging Trends."

Even relevant evidence may not be admitted in court if its reliability is questionable or if its probative (proving) value is substantially outweighed by other important considerations of the court. For example, a video or a photograph that shows in detail the severity of a victim's injuries would be relevant evidence, but the court might exclude this evidence on the ground that it would emotionally inflame the jurors.

Hearsay Evidence Not Admissible. Generally, hearsay is not admissible as evidence. **Hearsay** is defined as any testimony given in court about a statement made by someone else who was not under oath at the time of the statement. Literally, it is what someone heard someone else say. For example, if a witness in the Kirby-Carvello case testified in court concerning what he or she heard another observer say about the accident, that testimony would be hearsay, or secondhand knowledge. Admitting hearsay into evidence carries many risks because, even though it may be relevant, there is no way to test its reliability.

Examination of Witnesses Because Kirby is the plaintiff, she has the burden of proving that her allegations are true. Her attorney begins the presentation of Kirby's case by calling the first witness for the plaintiff and examining, or questioning, the witness. (For both attorneys, the types of questions and the manner of asking them are governed by the rules of evidence.) This questioning is called **direct examination.** After Kirby's attorney is finished, the witness is subject to **cross-examination** by Carvello's attorney. Then Kirby's attorney has another opportunity to question the witness in *redirect examination,* and Carvello's attorney may follow the redirect examination with a *recross-examination*. When both attorneys have finished with the first witness, Kirby's attorney calls the succeeding witnesses in the plaintiff's case, each of whom is subject to examination by the attorneys in the manner just described.

Potential Motion and Judgment. At the conclusion of the plaintiff's case, the defendant's attorney has the opportunity to ask the judge to direct a verdict for the defendant on the ground that the plaintiff has presented no evidence to support her or his claim. This is called a **motion for a judgment as a matter of law** (or a **motion for a directed verdict** in state courts). In considering the motion, the judge looks at the evidence in the light most favorable to the plaintiff and grants the motion only if there is insufficient evidence to raise an issue of fact. (Motions for directed verdicts at this stage of a trial are seldom granted.)

Defendant's Evidence. The defendant's attorney then presents the evidence and witnesses for the defendant's case. Witnesses are called and examined by the defendant's attorney. The plaintiff's attorney has the right to cross-examine them, and there may be a redirect examination and possibly a recross-examination. At the end of the defendant's case, either attorney can move for a directed verdict, and the test again is whether the jury can, through any reasonable interpretation of the evidence, find for the party against whom the motion has been made. After the defendant's attorney has finished introducing evidence, the plaintiff's attorney can present a **rebuttal,** which includes additional evidence to refute the defendant's case. The defendant's attorney can, in turn, refute that evidence in a **rejoinder.**

Closing Arguments, Jury Instructions, and Verdict After both sides have rested their cases, each attorney presents a closing argument. In the **closing argument,** each attorney summarizes the facts and evidence presented during the trial and indicates why the facts and evidence support his or her client's claim. In addition to generally urging a verdict in favor of the client, the closing arguments typically reveal the shortcomings of the points made by the opposing party during the trial.

Attorneys generally present closing arguments whether or not the trial was heard by a jury. If it was a jury trial, the judge then instructs the jury in the law that applies to the case (these instructions are often called *charges*), and the jury retires to the jury room to deliberate a verdict. In most civil cases, the standard of proof is a *preponderance of the evidence.*[24] In other words, the plaintiff (Kirby in our hypothetical case) need only show that her factual claim is more likely to be true than the defendant's. (As you will read in Chapter 7, in a criminal trial the prosecution has a higher standard of proof to meet—it must prove its case *beyond a reasonable doubt.*)

Once the jury has reached a decision, it issues a **verdict** in favor of one party; the verdict specifies the jury's factual findings. In some cases, the jury also decides on the amount of the *award* (the compensation to be paid to the prevailing party). After the announcement of the verdict, which marks the end of the trial itself, the jurors are dismissed. (See *Concept Summary 2.4* for a review of trial procedures.)

Posttrial Motions

After the jury has rendered its verdict, either party may make a posttrial motion. The prevailing party usually requests that the court enter a judgment in accordance with the verdict. The nonprevailing party frequently files one of the motions discussed next.

Motion for a New Trial At the end of the trial, a motion can be made to set aside an adverse verdict and any judgment and to hold a new trial. The **motion for a new trial** will be granted only if the judge is convinced, after looking at all the evidence, that the jury was in error, but does not feel it is appropriate to grant judgment for the other side. This will usually occur when the jury verdict is obviously the result of a misapplication of the law or a misunderstanding of the evidence presented at trial. A new trial can also be granted on the grounds of newly discovered evidence, misconduct by the participants during the trial (such as when an attorney has made prejudicial and inflammatory remarks), or error by the judge.

Motion for Judgment *N.O.V.* If Kirby wins, and if Carvello's attorney has previously moved for a directed verdict, then Carvello's attorney can now make a **motion for judgment *n.o.v.***—from the Latin *non obstante veredicto,* meaning "notwithstanding the

24. Note that some civil claims must be proved by "clear and convincing evidence," meaning that the evidence must show that the truth of the party's claim is highly probable. This standard is often applied in situations that present a particular danger of deception, such as allegations of fraud.

verdict." (Federal courts use the term *judgment as a matter of law* instead of *judgment n.o.v.*) Such a motion will be granted only if the jury's verdict was unreasonable and erroneous. If the judge grants the motion, then the jury's verdict will be set aside, and a judgment will be entered in favor of the opposing party (Carvello). If the motion is denied, Carvello may then appeal the case. (Kirby may also appeal the case, even though she won at trial. She might appeal, for example, if she received a smaller monetary award than she had sought.)

The Appeal

Either party may appeal not only the jury's verdict but also the judge's ruling on any pretrial or posttrial motion. Many of the appellate court cases that appear in this text involve appeals of motions for summary judgment or other motions that were denied or granted by trial court judges. Note that a party must have legitimate grounds to file an appeal (some legal error) and that few trial court decisions are reversed on appeal. Moreover, the expenses associated with an appeal can be considerable.

Filing the Appeal If Carvello decides to appeal the verdict in Kirby's favor, then his attorney must file a *notice of appeal* with the clerk of the trial court within a prescribed period of time. Carvello then becomes the *appellant* or *petitioner.* The clerk of the trial court sends to the reviewing court (usually an intermediate court of appeals) the *record on appeal.* The record contains all the pleadings, motions, and other documents filed with the court and a complete written transcript of the proceedings, including testimony, arguments, jury instructions, and judicial rulings.

Carvello's attorney will file an appellate *brief* with the reviewing court. The **brief** is a formal legal document outlining the facts and issues of the case, the judge's rulings or jury's findings that should be reversed or modified, the applicable law, and arguments on Carvello's behalf (citing applicable statutes and relevant cases as precedents). The attorney for the *appellee* (Kirby, in our hypothetical case) usually files an answering brief. Carvello's attorney can file a reply, although it is not required. The reviewing court then considers the case.

Appellate Review A court of appeals does not hear any evidence. Rather, it reviews the record for errors of law. Its decision concerning a case is based

CONCEPT SUMMARY 2.4
Trial Procedures

Procedure	Description
OPENING STATEMENTS	Each party's attorney is allowed to present an opening statement indicating what the attorney will attempt to prove during the course of the trial.
EXAMINATION OF WITNESSES	1. Plaintiff's introduction and direct examination of witnesses, cross-examination by defendant's attorney, possible redirect examination by plaintiff's attorney, and possible recross-examination by defendant's attorney. 2. At the close of the plaintiff's case, the defendant may make a motion for a directed verdict (or judgment as a matter of law), which, if granted by the court, will end the trial before the defendant presents witnesses. 3. Defendant's introduction and direct examination of witnesses, cross-examination by plaintiff's attorney, possible redirect examination by defendant's attorney, and possible recross-examination by plaintiff's attorney. 4. Possible rebuttal of defendant's argument by plaintiff's attorney, who presents more evidence. 5. Possible rejoinder by defendant's attorney to meet that evidence.
CLOSING ARGUMENTS, JURY INSTRUCTIONS, AND VERDICT	Each party's attorney argues in favor of a verdict for his or her client. The judge instructs (or charges) the jury as to how the law applies to the issue, and the jury retires to deliberate. When the jury renders its verdict, this brings the trial to an end.

on the record on appeal and the briefs and arguments. The attorneys present oral arguments, after which the case is taken under advisement. The court then issues a written opinion. In general, appellate courts do not reverse findings of fact unless the findings are unsupported or contradicted by the evidence.

An appellate court has the following options after reviewing a case:

1. The court can *affirm* the trial court's decision.
2. The court can *reverse* the trial court's judgment if it concludes that the trial court erred or that the jury did not receive proper instructions.
3. The appellate court can *remand* (send back) the case to the trial court for further proceedings consistent with its opinion on the matter.
4. The court might also affirm or reverse a decision *in part.* For example, the court might affirm the jury's finding that Carvello was negligent but remand the case for further proceedings on another issue (such as the extent of Kirby's damages).
5. An appellate court can also *modify* a lower court's decision. If the appellate court decides that the jury awarded an excessive amount in damages, for example, the court might reduce the award to a more appropriate, or fairer, amount.

Appellate courts apply different standards of review depending on the type of issue involved and the lower court's rulings. Generally, these standards require the reviewing court to give a certain amount of deference, or weight, to the findings of lower courts on specific issues. The following case illustrates the importance of standards of review as a means of exercising judicial restraint.

CASE 2.3 Evans v. Eaton Corp. Long Term Disability Plan

United States Court of Appeals, Fourth Circuit, 2008. 514 F.3d 315.

• **Background and Facts** Eaton Corporation is a multinational manufacturing company that funds and administers a long-term disability benefits plan for its employees. Brenda Evans was an employee at Eaton. In 1998, due to severe rheumatoid arthritis, Brenda Evans quit her job at Eaton and filed for disability benefits. Eaton paid disability benefits to Evans without controversy prior to 2003, but that year, Evans's disability status became questionable. Her physician had prescribed a new medication that had dramatically improved Evans's arthritis. In addition, Evans had injured her spine in a car accident in 2002, and was claiming to be disabled by continuing back problems as well as arthritis. But diagnostic exams during that period indicated that the injuries to Evans's back were not severe, and she could cook, shop, do laundry, wash dishes, and drive about seven miles a day. By 2004, several physicians that reviewed Evans's file had determined that she could work and was no longer totally disabled, and Eaton terminated Evans's disability benefits. Evans filed a complaint in the U.S. District Court for South Carolina alleging violations of the Employee Retirement Income Security Act of 1974 (ERISA is a federal law regulating pension plans that will be discussed in Chapter 20). The district court examined the evidence in great detail and concluded that Eaton's termination of Evans's benefits was an abuse of discretion because the physicians who testified in Evans's favor were more believable than the reviewing physicians. Eaton appealed to the U.S. Court of Appeals for the Fourth Circuit.

IN THE LANGUAGE OF THE COURT
***WILKINSON*, Circuit Judge.**

* * * *

This case turns on a faithful application of the abuse of discretion standard of review, and so we begin with what is most crucial: a clear understanding of what that standard is, and what such standards are for.

The purpose of standards of review is to focus reviewing courts upon their proper role when passing on the conduct of other decision-makers. Standards of review are thus an elemental expression of judicial restraint, which, in their deferential varieties, safeguard the superior vantage points of those entrusted with primary decisional responsibility. * * * The clear error standard, for example, protects district courts' primacy as triers of fact. * * * Rational basis review protects the political choices of our government's elected branches. And trust law, to which ERISA is so intimately linked, uses the abuse of discretion standard to protect a fiduciary's [one whose relationship is based on trust] decisions concerning the trust funds in his care. [Emphasis added.]

CASE 2.3 CONTINUED

The precise definitions of these various standards, the nuances separating them from one another,"cannot be imprisoned within any forms of words" * * *. But what these and other such standards share is the designation of a primary decision-maker other than the reviewing court, and the instrument, deference, with which that primacy is to be maintained.

* * * In [this] case, the Plan's language giving Eaton "discretionary authority to determine eligibility for benefits" and "the power and discretion to determine all questions of fact * * * arising in connection with the administration, interpretation and application of the Plan" is unambiguous, and Evans does not dispute the standard it requires. Thus the district court functions in this context as a deferential reviewing court with respect to the ERISA fiduciary's decision.

* * * *

At its immovable core, the abuse of discretion standard requires a reviewing court to show enough deference to a primary decision-maker's judgment that the court does not reverse merely because it would have come to a different result * * *. The trial judge has discretion in those cases where his ruling will not be reversed simply because an appellate court disagrees. [Emphasis added.]

* * * *

Under no formulation, however, may a court, faced with discretionary language like that in the plan instrument in this case, forget its duty of deference and its secondary rather than primary role in determining a claimant's right to benefits. The abuse of discretion standard in ERISA cases protects important values: the plan administrator's greater experience and familiarity with plan terms and provisions; the enhanced prospects of achieving consistent application of those terms and provisions that results; the desire of those who establish ERISA plans to preserve at least some role in their administration; and the importance of ensuring that funds which are not unlimited go to those who, according to the terms of the plan, are truly deserving.

* * * *

* * * Where an ERISA administrator rejects a claim to benefits on the strength of substantial evidence, careful and coherent reasoning, faithful adherence to the letter of ERISA and the language in the plan, and a fair and searching process, there can be no abuse of discretion—even if another, and arguably a better, decision-maker might have come to a different, and arguably a better, result.

* * * *

So standards of review do matter, for in every context they keep judges within the limits of their role and preserve other decision-makers' functions against judicial intrusion.

• **Decision and Remedy** *The U.S. Court of Appeals for the Fourth Circuit reversed the district court's award of benefits to Evans and remanded the case with instructions that the district court enter a judgment in favor of Eaton. The district court incorrectly applied the abuse of discretion standard when reviewing Eaton's termination of Evans's benefits.*

• **What If the Facts Were Different?** *Suppose that the district court had concluded that Eaton Corporation's termination of Evans's benefits was not an abuse of discretion, and Evans had appealed. In that situation, would Evans have had any grounds for appealing the district court's decision? Explain.*

• **The Ethical Dimension** *The appellate court noted in this case that the district court's decision—which granted benefits to Evans—may arguably have been a better decision under these facts. If the court believes the district court's conclusion was right, then why did it reverse the decision? What does this tell you about the standards for review that judges use?*

Higher Appellate Courts If the reviewing court is an intermediate appellate court, the losing party may decide to appeal the decision to the state's highest court, usually called its supreme court. Although the losing party has a right to ask (petition) a higher court to review the case, the party does not have a right to have the case heard by the higher appellate court. Appellate courts normally have discretionary power and can accept or reject an appeal. As with the United States Supreme Court, getting a case heard in most state supreme courts is unlikely. If the petition is granted, new briefs must be filed before the state supreme court, and the attorneys may be allowed or requested to present oral arguments. Like the intermediate appellate courts, the supreme court can reverse or affirm the lower appellate court's decision or remand the case. At this point, the case typically has reached its end (unless a federal question is at issue and one of the parties has legitimate grounds to seek review by a federal appellate court). (*Concept Summary 2.5* reviews the options that the parties may pursue after the trial.)

Enforcing the Judgment

The uncertainties of the litigation process are compounded by the lack of guarantees that any judgment will be enforceable. Even if the jury awards Kirby the full amount of damages requested ($100,000), for example, Carvello's auto insurance coverage might have lapsed, in which event the company would not pay any of the damages. Alternatively, Carvello's insurance policy might be limited to $50,000, meaning that Carvello personally would have to pay the remaining $50,000.

Requesting Court Assistance in Collecting the Judgment If the defendant does not have the funds available to pay the judgment, the plaintiff can go back to the court and request that the court issue a *writ of execution.* A **writ of execution** is an order directing the sheriff to seize and sell the defendant's nonexempt assets, or property (certain assets are exempted by law from creditors' actions). The proceeds of the sale would then be used to pay the damages owed, and any excess proceeds would be returned to the defendant. Alternatively, the nonexempt property itself could be transferred to the plaintiff in lieu of an outright payment. (Creditors' remedies, including those of judgment creditors, as well as exempt and nonexempt property, will be discussed in more detail in Chapter 15.)

CONCEPT SUMMARY 2.5
Posttrial Options

Procedure	Description
POSTTRIAL MOTIONS	1. *Motion for a new trial*—If the judge believes that the jury was in error but is not convinced that the losing party should have won, the motion normally will be granted. It can also be granted on the basis of newly discovered evidence, misconduct by the participants during the trial, or error by the judge. 2. *Motion for judgment n.o.v. ("notwithstanding the verdict")*—The party making the motion must have filed a motion for a directed verdict at the close of the presentation of evidence during the trial; the motion will be granted if the judge is convinced that the jury was in error.
APPEAL	Either party can appeal the trial court's judgment to an appropriate court of appeals. 1. *Filing the appeal*—The appealing party must file a notice of appeal with the clerk of the trial court, who forwards the record on appeal to the appellate court. Attorneys file appellate briefs. 2. *Appellate review*—The appellate court does not hear evidence but bases its opinion, which it issues in writing, on the record on appeal and the attorneys' briefs and oral arguments. The court may affirm or reverse all (or part) of the trial court's judgment and/or remand the case for further proceedings consistent with its opinion. Most decisions are affirmed on appeal. 3. *Further review*—In some cases, further review may be sought from a higher appellate court, such as a state supreme court. If a federal question is involved, the case may ultimately be appealed to the United States Supreme Court.

Availability of Assets The problem of collecting a judgment is less pronounced, of course, when a party is seeking to satisfy a judgment against a defendant with substantial assets that can be easily located, such as a major corporation. Usually, one of the factors considered by the plaintiff and his or her attorney before a lawsuit is initiated is whether the defendant has sufficient assets to cover the amount of damages sought. In addition, during the discovery process, attorneys routinely seek information about the location of the defendant's assets that might potentially be used to satisfy a judgment.

REVIEWING The Court System

Stan Garner resides in Illinois and promotes boxing matches for SuperSports, Inc., an Illinois corporation. Garner created the concept of "Ages" promotion—a three-fight series of boxing matches pitting an older fighter (George Foreman) against a younger fighter, such as John Ruiz or Riddick Bowe. The concept included titles for each of the three fights ("Challenge of the Ages," "Battle of the Ages," and "Fight of the Ages"), as well as promotional epithets to characterize the two fighters ("the Foreman Factor"). Garner contacted George Foreman and his manager, who both reside in Texas, to sell the idea, and they arranged a meeting at Caesar's Palace in Las Vegas, Nevada. At some point in the negotiations, Foreman's manager signed a nondisclosure agreement prohibiting him from disclosing Garner's promotional concepts unless the parties signed a contract. Nevertheless, after negotiations between Garner and Foreman fell through, Foreman used Garner's "Battle of the Ages" concept to promote a subsequent fight. Garner filed a suit against Foreman and his manager in a federal district court located in Illinois, alleging breach of contract. Using the information presented in the chapter, answer the following questions.

1. On what basis might the federal district court in Illinois exercise jurisdiction in this case?
2. Does the federal district court have original or appellate jurisdiction?
3. Suppose that Garner had filed his action in an Illinois state court. Could an Illinois state court exercise personal jurisdiction over Foreman or his manager? Why or why not?
4. Assume that Garner had filed his action in a Nevada state court. Would that court have personal jurisdiction over Foreman or his manager? Explain.

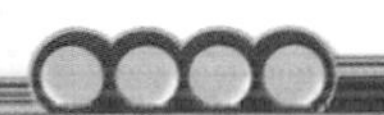

TERMS AND CONCEPTS

affidavit 49
affirmative defense 47
answer 47
bankruptcy court 33
brief 55
closing argument 54
complaint 43
concurrent jurisdiction 34
counterclaim 47
cross-examination 53
default judgment 43
deposition 49
direct examination 53
discovery 49
diversity of citizenship 34
e-evidence 50
exclusive jurisdiction 34
federal question 34
Federal Rules of Civil Procedure (FRCP) 41
hearsay 53
***in personam* jurisdiction 31**
***in rem* jurisdiction 31**
interrogatories 49
judicial review 30
jurisdiction 31
justiciable controversy 37
long arm statute 31
motion 48
motion for a directed verdict 54
motion for a judgment as a matter of law 54
motion for a new trial 54
motion for judgment *n.o.v.* 54
motion for judgment on the pleadings 49

motion for summary judgment 49
motion to dismiss 48
opening statement 52
pleadings 43
pretrial conference 50
pretrial motion 48
probate court 33
question of fact 38
question of law 38
rebuttal 54
rejoinder 54
relevant evidence 52
rule of four 40
rules of evidence 52
service of process 43
small claims court 38
standing to sue 36
summons 43
venue 35
verdict 54
***voir dire* 51**
writ of *certiorari* 40
writ of execution 58

QUESTIONS AND CASE PROBLEMS

2-1. When and for what purpose is each of the following motions made? Which of them would be appropriate if a defendant claimed that the only issue between the parties was a question of law and that the law was favorable to the defendant's position?

(a) A motion for judgment on the pleadings.
(b) A motion for a directed verdict.
(c) A motion for summary judgment.
(d) A motion for judgment *n.o.v.*

2-2. QUESTION WITH SAMPLE ANSWER

The defendant in a lawsuit is appealing the trial court's decision in favor of the plaintiff. On appeal, the defendant claims that the evidence presented at trial to support the plaintiff's claim was so scanty that no reasonable jury could have found for the plaintiff. Therefore, argues the defendant, the appellate court should reverse the trial court's decision. Will an appellate court ever reverse a trial court's findings with respect to questions of fact? Discuss fully.

- **For a sample answer to Question 2–2, go to Appendix I at the end of this text.**

2-3. Washoe Medical Center, Inc., admitted Shirley Swisher for the treatment of a fractured pelvis. During her stay, Swisher suffered a fatal fall from her hospital bed. Gerald Parodi, the administrator of her estate, and others filed an action against Washoe seeking damages for the alleged lack of care in treating Swisher. During *voir dire*, when the plaintiffs' attorney returned a few minutes late from a break, the trial judge led the prospective jurors in a standing ovation. The judge joked with one of the prospective jurors, whom he had known in college, about his fitness to serve as a judge and personally endorsed another prospective juror's business. After the trial, the jury returned a verdict in favor of Washoe. The plaintiffs moved for a new trial, but the judge denied the motion. The plaintiffs then appealed, arguing that the tone set by the judge during *voir dire* prejudiced their right to a fair trial. Should the appellate court agree? Why or why not?

2-4. Advance Technology Consultants, Inc. (ATC), contracted with RoadTrac, L.L.C., to provide software and client software systems for the products of global positioning satellite (GPS) technology being developed by RoadTrac. RoadTrac agreed to provide ATC with hardware with which ATC's software would interface. Problems soon arose, however. ATC claimed that RoadTrac's hardware was defective, making it difficult to develop the software. RoadTrac contended that its hardware was fully functional and that ATC had simply failed to provide supporting software. ATC told RoadTrac that it considered their contract terminated. RoadTrac filed a suit in a Georgia state court against ATC alleging breach of contract. During discovery, RoadTrac requested ATC's customer lists and marketing procedures. ATC objected to providing this information because RoadTrac and ATC had become competitors in the GPS industry. Should a party to a lawsuit have to hand over its confidential business secrets as part of a discovery request? Why or why not? What limitations might a court consider imposing before requiring ATC to produce this material?

2-5. Service of Process. To establish a Web site, a person must have an Internet service provider or hosting company, register a domain name, and acquire domain name servicing. Pfizer, Inc., Pfizer Ireland Pharmaceuticals, and Warner-Lambert Co. (collectively, Pfizer) filed a suit in a federal district court against Domains By Proxy, Inc., and other persons alleged to be behind two Web sites—genericlipitors.com and econopetcare.com. Among the defendants were an individual and a company that, according to Pfizer, were located in a foreign country. Without investigating other means of serving these two defendants, Pfizer asked the court for permission to accomplish service of process via e-mail. Under what circumstances is service via e-mail proper? Would it be appropriate in this case? Explain. [*Pfizer, Inc. v. Domains By Proxy*, ___ F.Supp.2d ___ (D.Conn. 2004)]

2-6. Standing to Sue. Michael and Karla Covington live in Jefferson County, Idaho. When they bought their home, a gravel pit was across the street. In 1995, the county converted the pit to a landfill. Under the county's operation, the landfill accepted major appliances, household garbage, spilled grain, grass clippings, straw, manure, animal carcasses, containers with hazardous content warnings, leaking car batteries, and waste oil, among other things. The deposits were often left uncovered, attracting insects and other scavengers and contaminating the groundwater. Fires broke out, including at least one started by an intruder who entered the property through an unlocked gate. The Covingtons complained to the state, which inspected the landfill, but no changes were made to address their concerns. Finally, the Covingtons filed a suit in a federal district court against the county and the state, charging violations of federal environmental laws. Those laws were designed to minimize the risks of injuries from fires, scavengers, groundwater contamination, and other pollution dangers. Did the Covingtons have standing to sue? What principles apply? Explain. [*Covington v. Jefferson County*, 358 F.3d 626 (9th Cir. 2004)]

2-7. CASE PROBLEM WITH SAMPLE ANSWER

Xcentric Ventures, LLC, is an Arizona firm that operates the Web sites RipOffReport.com and BadBusinessBureau.com. Visitors to the sites can buy a copy of a book titled *Do-It-Yourself Guide: How to Get Rip-Off Revenge*. The price ($21.95) includes shipping to anywhere in the United States, including Illinois, to which thirteen copies have been shipped. The sites accept donations and feature postings by individuals who claim to have been "ripped off." Some visitors posted comments about George S. May International Co., a management consulting firm. The postings alleged fraud, larceny, possession of child pornography, and possession of controlled substances (illegal drugs). May filed a suit in a federal district court in Illinois against Xcentric and others, charging, among other things, "false descriptions and representations." The defendants filed a motion to dismiss for lack of jurisdiction. What is the standard for exercising jurisdiction over a party whose only connection to a jurisdiction is over the Web? How would that standard apply in this case? Explain. [*George S. May International Co. v. Xcentric Ventures, LLC*, 409 F.Supp.2d 1052 (N.D.Ill. 2006)]

- **To view a sample answer for Problem 2–7, go to this book's Web site at academic.cengage.com/blaw/cross, select "Chapter 2," and click on "Case Problem with Sample Answer."**

2-8. Jurisdiction. In 2001, Raul Leal, the owner and operator of Texas Labor Contractors in East Texas, contacted Poverty Point Produce, Inc., which operates a sweet potato farm in West Carroll Parish, Louisiana, and offered to provide field workers. Poverty Point accepted the offer. Jeffrey Brown, an owner of, and field manager for, the farm, told Leal the number of workers needed and gave him forms for them to fill out and sign. Leal placed an ad in a newspaper in Brownsville, Texas. Job applicants were directed to Leal's car dealership in Weslaco, Texas, where they were told the details of the work. Leal recruited, among others, Elias Moreno, who lives in the Rio Grande Valley in Texas, and transported Moreno and the others to Poverty Point's farm. At the farm, Leal's brother Jesse oversaw the work with instructions from Brown, lived with the workers in the on-site housing, and gave them their paychecks. When the job was done, the workers were returned to Texas. Moreno and others filed a suit in a federal district court against Poverty Point and others, alleging, in part, violations of Texas state law related to the work. Poverty Point filed a motion to dismiss the suit on the ground that the court did not have personal jurisdiction. All of the meetings between Poverty Point and the Leals occurred in Louisiana. All of the farmwork was done in Louisiana. Poverty Point has no offices, bank accounts, or phone listings in Texas. It does not advertise or solicit business in Texas. Despite these facts, can the court exercise personal jurisdiction? Explain. [*Moreno v. Poverty Point Produce, Inc.*, 243 F.R.D. 275 (S.D.Tex. 2007)]

2-9. A QUESTION OF ETHICS

*Narnia Investments, Ltd., filed a suit in a Texas state court against several defendants, including Harvestons Securities, Inc., a securities dealer. (Securities are documents evidencing the ownership of a corporation, in the form of stock, or debts owed by it, in the form of bonds.) Harvestons is registered with the state of Texas and thus may be served with a summons and a copy of a complaint by serving the Texas Securities Commissioner. In this case, the return of service indicated that process was served on the commissioner "by delivering to JoAnn Kocerek defendant, in person, a true copy of this [summons] together with the accompanying copy(ies) of the [complaint]." Harvestons did not file an answer, and Narnia obtained a default judgment against the defendant for $365,000, plus attorneys' fees and interest. Five months after this judgment, Harvestons filed a motion for a new trial, which the court denied. Harvestons appealed to a state intermediate appellate court, claiming that it had not been served in strict compliance with the rules governing service of process. [*Harvestons Securities, Inc. v. Narnia Investments, Ltd.,* *218 S.W.3d 126, (Tex.App.—Houston [14 Dist.] 2007)]*

(a) Harvestons asserted that Narnia's service was invalid in part because "the return of service states that process was delivered to 'JoAnn Kocerek'" and did not show that she "had the authority to accept process on behalf of Harvestons or the Texas Securities Commissioner." Should such a detail, if it is required, be strictly construed and applied? Should it apply in this case? Explain.

(b) Whose responsibility is it to see that service of process is accomplished properly? Was it accomplished properly in this case? Why or why not?

2–10. SPECIAL CASE ANALYSIS

Go to Case 2.2, *Cruz v. Fagor America, Inc.*, 52 Cal.Rptr.3d 862, 146 Cal.App.4th 488 (4 Dist. Div. 1 2007), on pages 45–47. Read the excerpt and answer the following questions.

(a) **Issue:** What was the main issue in this case?
(b) **Rule of Law:** What rule of law did the court apply?
(c) **Applying the Rule of Law:** Describe how the court applied the rule of law to the facts of this case.
(d) **Conclusion:** What was the court's conclusion in this case?

2–11. VIDEO QUESTION

Go to this text's Web site at **academic.cengage.com/blaw/cross** and select "Chapter 2." Click on "Video Questions" and view the video titled *Jurisdiction in Cyberspace.* Then answer the following questions.

(a) What standard would a court apply to determine whether it has jurisdiction over the out-of-state computer firm in the video?
(b) What factors is a court likely to consider in assessing whether sufficient contacts existed when the only connection to the jurisdiction is through a Web site?
(c) How do you think the court would resolve the issue in this case?

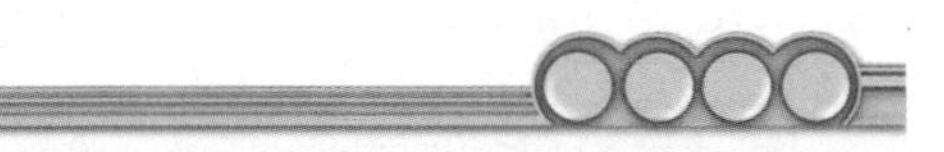

LAW ON THE WEB

For updated links to resources available on the Web, as well as a variety of other materials, visit this text's Web site at

academic.cengage.com/blaw/cross

For the decisions of the United States Supreme Court, as well as information about the Supreme Court and its justices, go to either

www.supremecourtus.gov

or

www.oyez.org

The Web site for the federal courts offers information on the federal court system and links to all federal courts at

www.uscourts.gov

The National Center for State Courts (NCSC) offers links to the Web pages of all state courts. Go to

www.ncsconline.org

If you are interested in learning more about the Federal Rules of Civil Procedure (FRCP) and the Federal Rules of Evidence (FRE), you can access them via the Internet at the following Web site:

www.law.cornell.edu

Legal Research Exercises on the Web

Go to **academic.cengage.com/blaw/cross**, the Web site that accompanies this text. Select "Chapter 2" and click on "Internet Exercises." There you will find the following Internet research exercises that you can perform to learn more about the topics covered in this chapter.

Internet Exercise 2–1: Legal Perspective
Civil Procedure

Internet Exercise 2–2: Technological Perspective
Virtual Courtrooms

Internet Exercise 2–3: Historical Perspective
The Judiciary's Role in American Government

CHAPTER 3

Alternative and Online Dispute Resolution

Trials are costly and time consuming. It has been said that this is the result of "too many lawyers, too many lawsuits, and too many laws." In fact, since 1960, the number of lawyers has tripled, the number of lawsuits has tripled, and the number of laws has multiplied, while the numbers of judges and courts have not kept pace.

Although it is true that the number of lawsuits filed has grown rapidly, only 5 to 10 percent of lawsuits filed actually go to trial. Most cases are settled or dismissed long before the parties enter a courtroom. Moreover, the number of cases that are litigated does not appear to be growing any faster than the population. When compared with the large number of transactions that occur in our highly complex economy, the rate of litigation appears low to some.

Nevertheless, in any individual case, it may be months before a hearing can even be scheduled. Depending on the complexity of the case, the extent of discovery proceedings required, the delaying tactics of the opposing party, and the backlog of cases pending in the particular court, several years may pass before a case is actually tried. Even in the best of situations, the civil procedures discussed in Chapter 2 all require much time and expense, particularly when electronic discovery is involved. As the cost and complexity of litigation have grown, businesspersons and other individuals have asked, "Is there a more appropriate way to resolve disputes?"

The Search for Alternatives to Litigation

A number of solutions have been proposed, and some have been implemented, to reduce the congestion in our court system and to reduce the litigation costs facing all members of society. The enforcement of arbitration clauses, the use of court-referred arbitration and mediation, and the emergence of an increasing number of private forums for dispute resolution have all helped to reduce the caseload of the courts.

Another solution to the problem involves putting caps on damage awards, particularly for pain and suffering. (We will discuss some of the proposals to reform tort law in a *Contemporary Legal Debates* feature in Chapter 12.) Without the probability of obtaining multimillion-dollar judgments for pain and suffering, some potential litigants will be deterred from undertaking lawsuits to obtain damages. Another avenue of attack is to penalize those who bring frivolous lawsuits. Rule 11 of the Federal Rules of Civil Procedure allows for disciplinary sanctions against lawyers and litigants who bring frivolous lawsuits in federal courts.

Many courts require *mediation* or *arbitration* before a case goes to trial. There are proposals to further reduce delay and expenses in federal civil cases, and proposals are being considered by the states as well. Some of the proposals can be viewed as case-management plans. One proposal, for example, would require each federal district court to implement procedures for placing cases on different tracks, with simple cases being handled more quickly than complex ones.

Politics and Law

Because reforms of any system affect individuals and groups differently, they seldom are accomplished easily and quickly. Reform of the court system is a prime example. At the federal level, members of Congress long have been concerned with bringing court costs and delay under control. These concerns led to legislation that required the federal courts to develop a plan to cut costs and reduce delay within the federal judicial system.

New Methods and Arrangements

The search for alternative means to resolve disputes has produced several distinct methods and arrangements. These range from neighbors sitting down over a cup of coffee to work out their differences to huge multinational corporations agreeing to resolve a dispute through a formal hearing before a panel of experts. All of these alternatives to traditional litigation make up what is broadly termed **alternative dispute resolution (ADR).**

ADR describes any procedure or device for resolving disputes outside the traditional judicial process. ADR is normally a less expensive and less time-consuming process than formal litigation. In some instances, it also has the advantage of being more private. Except in disputes involving court-annexed arbitration (discussed later in this chapter), no public record of ADR proceedings is created; only the parties directly involved are privy to the information presented during the process. This is a particularly important consideration in many business disputes, because such cases may involve sensitive commercial information. As you will read later in this chapter, today ADR also includes online methods of resolving disputes.

The great advantage of ADR is its flexibility. Normally, the parties themselves can control how the dispute will be settled, what procedures will be used, whether a neutral third party will be present or make a decision, and whether that decision will be legally binding or nonbinding. ADR also offers more privacy than court proceedings and allows disputes to be resolved relatively quickly.

Negotiation and Mediation

Alternative dispute resolution methods differ in the degree of formality involved and the extent to which third parties participate in the process. Generally, negotiation is the least formal method and involves no third parties. Mediation may be similarly informal but does involve the participation of a third party.

Negotiation

The simplest form of ADR is **negotiation.** In the process of negotiation, the parties come together informally, with or without attorneys to represent them. Within this informal setting, the parties air their differences and try to reach a settlement or resolution without the involvement of independent third parties. Because no third parties are involved and because of the informal setting, negotiation is the simplest form of ADR. Even if a lawsuit has been initiated, the parties may continue to negotiate their differences at any time during the litigation process and attempt to settle their dispute. Less than 10 percent of all corporate lawsuits, for example, end up in trial—the rest are settled beforehand.

Preparation for Negotiation In spite of the informality of negotiation, each party must carefully prepare his or her side of the case. The elements of the dispute should be considered, documents and other evidence should be collected, and witnesses should be prepared to testify. Negotiating from a well-prepared position improves the odds of obtaining a favorable result. Even if a dispute is not resolved through negotiation, preparation for negotiation will reduce the effort required to prepare for the next step in the dispute-resolution process.

Assisted Negotiation To facilitate negotiation, various forms of what might be called "assisted negotiation" have emerged in recent years. Assisted negotation, as the term implies, involves the assistance of a third party. Forms of ADR associated with the negotation process include mini-trials, early neutral case evaluation, and facilitation. Another form of assisted negotiation—the summary jury trial—will be discussed later in this chapter.

A **mini-trial** is a private proceeding in which each party's attorney briefly argues the party's case before the other party. Typically, a neutral third party, who acts as an adviser and an expert in the area being disputed, is also present. If the parties fail to reach an agreement, the adviser renders an opinion as to how a court would likely decide the issue. The proceeding assists the parties in determining whether they should negotiate a settlement of the dispute or take it to court.

In **early neutral case evaluation,** the parties select a neutral third party (generally an expert in the subject matter of the dispute) to evaluate their respective positions. The parties explain their positions to the case evaluator however they wish. The evaluator then assesses the strengths and weaknesses of the parties' positions, and this evaluation forms the basis for negotiating a settlement.

Disputes may also be resolved in a friendly, nonadversarial manner through **facilitation,** in which a third party assists parties to a dispute in reconciling their differences. The facilitator helps to schedule negotiating sessions and carries offers back and forth between the parties when they refuse to face each other in direct negotiations. Technically, facilitators are not to recommend solutions. In practice, however, they often do. In contrast, a mediator is expected to propose solutions.

Mediation

One of the oldest forms of ADR is mediation. In **mediation,** a neutral third party acts as a **mediator** and works with both sides in the dispute to facilitate a resolution. The mediator normally talks with the parties separately as well as jointly, emphasizes points of agreement, and helps the parties to evaluate their options. Although the mediator may propose a solution (called a mediator's proposal), he or she does not make a decision resolving the matter. The mediator, who need not be a lawyer, usually charges a fee for his or her services (which can be split between the parties). States that require parties to undergo ADR before trial often offer mediation as one of the ADR options or (as in Florida) the only option.

Mediation is essentially a form of assisted negotiation. We treat it separately here because traditionally it has been viewed as an alternative to negotiation. Additionally, a mediator usually plays a more active role than the neutral third parties in negotiation-associated forms of ADR.

Advantages of Mediation Few procedural rules are involved in the mediation process—far fewer than in a courtroom setting. The proceedings can be tailored to fit the needs of the parties—the mediator can be told to maintain a diplomatic role or be asked to express an opinion about the dispute, lawyers can be excluded from the proceedings, and the exchange of a few documents can replace the more expensive and time-consuming process of pretrial discovery. Disputes are often settled far more quickly in mediation than in formal litigation.

One of the biggest advantages of mediation is that it is not as adversarial in nature as litigation. In mediation, the mediator takes an active role and attempts to bring the parties together so that they can come to a mutually satisfactory resolution. The mediation process tends to reduce the antagonism between the disputants, allowing them to resume their former relationship while minimizing hostility. For this reason, mediation is often the preferred form of ADR for disputes involving business partners, employers and employees, or other parties involved in long-term relationships.

Today, characteristics of mediation are being combined with those of arbitration (to be discussed next). In *binding mediation,* for example, the parties agree that if they cannot resolve the dispute, the mediator can make a legally binding decision on the issue. In *mediation-arbitration,* or "med-arb," the parties first attempt to settle their dispute through mediation. If no settlement is reached, the dispute will be arbitrated.

Another important benefit of mediation is that the mediator is selected by the parties. In litigation, the parties have no control over the selection of a judge. In mediation, the parties may select a mediator on the basis of expertise in a particular field as well as for fairness and impartiality. To the degree that the mediator has these attributes, he or she will more effectively aid the parties in reaching an agreement over their dispute.

Disadvantages of Mediation Mediation is not without disadvantages. A mediator is likely to charge a fee. (This can be split between the parties, though, and thus may represent less expense than would both sides' hiring lawyers.)

Informality and the absence of a third party referee can also be disadvantageous. (Remember that a mediator can only help the parties reach a decision, not make a decision for them.) Without a deadline hanging over the parties' heads, and without the threat of sanctions if they fail to negotiate in good faith, they may be less willing to make concessions or otherwise strive honestly and diligently to reach a settlement. This can slow the process or even cause it to fail.

Arbitration

A more formal method of ADR is **arbitration,** in which an **arbitrator** (a neutral third party or a panel of experts) hears a dispute and imposes a resolution on the parties. Arbitration differs from other forms of ADR in that the third party hearing the dispute makes a decision for the parties. Exhibit 3–1 on page 66 outlines the basic differences among the three traditional forms of

EXHIBIT 3–1 • Basic Differences in the Traditional Forms of ADR

Type of ADR	Description	Neutral Third Party Present	Who Decides the Resolution
Negotiation	Parties meet informally with or without their attorneys and attempt to agree on a resolution.	No.	The parties themselves reach a resolution.
Mediation	A neutral third party meets with the parties and emphasizes points of agreement to bring them toward resolution of their dispute.	Yes.	The parties, but the mediator may suggest or propose a resolution.
Arbitration	The parties present their arguments and evidence before an arbitrator at a hearing, and the arbitrator renders a decision resolving the parties' dispute.	Yes.	The arbitrator imposes a resolution on the parties that may be either binding or nonbinding.

ADR. The key difference between arbitration and the forms of ADR just discussed is that in arbitration, the third party's decision may be legally binding on the parties. Usually the parties in arbitration agree that the third party's decision will be *legally binding*, although the parties can also agree to *nonbinding* arbitration.

When a dispute arises, the parties can agree to settle their differences informally through arbitration rather than formally through the court system. Alternatively, the parties may agree ahead of time that, if a dispute should arise, they will submit to arbitration rather than bring a lawsuit. If the parties agree that the arbitrator's decision will be legally binding, they are obligated to abide by the arbitrator's decision regardless of whether or not they agree with it. (See this chapter's *Insight into Ethics* feature on pages 70 and 71 for a discussion of some potential ethical implications of the use of arbitration.)

The federal government and many state governments favor arbitration over litigation. The federal policy favoring arbitration is embodied in the Federal Arbitration Act (FAA) of 1925.[1] The FAA requires that courts give deference to all voluntary arbitration agreements in cases governed by federal law. Virtually any dispute can be the subject of arbitration. A voluntary agreement to arbitrate a dispute normally will be enforced by the courts if the agreement does not compel an illegal act or contravene public policy.

The Federal Arbitration Act

The Federal Arbitration Act does not establish a set arbitration procedure. The parties themselves must agree on the manner of resolving their dispute. The FAA provides the means for enforcing the arbitration procedure that the parties have established for themselves.

Section 4 allows a party to petition a federal district court for an order compelling arbitration under an agreement to arbitrate a dispute. If the judge is "satisfied that the making of the agreement for arbitration or the failure to comply therewith is not in issue, the court shall make an order directing the parties to proceed with arbitration in accordance with the terms of the agreement."

Under Section 9 of the FAA, the parties to the arbitration may agree to have the arbitrator's decision confirmed in a federal district court. Through confirmation, one party obtains a court order directing another party to comply with the terms of the arbitrator's decision. Section 10 establishes the grounds by which the arbitrator's decision may be set aside (canceled). The grounds for setting aside a decision are limited to misconduct, fraud, corruption, or abuse of power in the arbitration process itself; a court will not review the merits of the dispute or the arbitrator's judgment.

The FAA covers any arbitration clause in a contract that involves interstate commerce. Business activities that have even remote connections or minimal effects on commerce between two or more states are considered to be included. Thus, arbitration agreements involving transactions only slightly connected to the flow of interstate commerce may fall under the FAA, even if the parties, at the time of contracting, did not expect their arbitration agreement to involve interstate commerce.

1. 9 U.S.C. Sections 1–15.

The question in the following case was whether a court or an arbitrator should consider a claim that an entire contract, including its arbitration clause, is rendered void by the alleged illegality of a separate provision in the contract.

CASE 3.1 Buckeye Check Cashing, Inc. v. Cardegna

Supreme Court of the United States, 2006. 546 U.S. 440, 126 S.Ct. 1204, 163 L.Ed.2d 1038.
www.law.cornell.edu/supct/index.html[a]

• **Background and Facts** Buckeye Check Cashing, Inc., cashes personal checks for consumers in Florida. Buckeye agrees to delay submitting a check for payment in exchange for a consumer's payment of a "finance charge." For each transaction, the consumer signs a "Deferred Deposit and Disclosure Agreement," which states, "By signing this Agreement, you agree that i[f] a dispute of any kind arises out of this Agreement * * * th[e]n either you or we or third-parties involved can choose to have that dispute resolved by binding arbitration." John Cardegna and others filed a suit in a Florida state court against Buckeye, alleging that the "finance charge" represented an illegally high interest rate in violation of Florida state laws, rendering the agreement "criminal on its face." Buckeye filed a motion to compel arbitration. The court denied the motion. On Buckeye's appeal, a state intermediate appellate court reversed this denial, but on the plaintiffs' appeal, the Florida Supreme Court reversed the lower appellate court's decision. Buckeye appealed to the United States Supreme Court.

IN THE LANGUAGE OF THE COURT
Justice *SCALIA* delivered the opinion of the Court.

* * * *

* * * Section 2 [of the Federal Arbitration Act (FAA)] embodies the national policy favoring arbitration and places arbitration agreements on equal footing with all other contracts:

> A written provision in * * * a contract * * * to settle by arbitration a controversy thereafter arising out of such contract * * * shall be valid, irrevocable, and enforceable, save upon such grounds as exist at law or in equity for the revocation of any contract.

* * * The crux of the [respondents'] complaint is that the contract as a whole (including its arbitration provision) is rendered invalid by the * * * finance charge.

* * * *

* * * [Our holdings in previous cases] answer the question presented here by establishing three propositions. First, as a matter of substantive federal arbitration law, *an arbitration provision is severable [capable of being legally separated] from the remainder of the contract.* Second, unless the challenge is to the arbitration clause itself, *the issue of the contract's validity is considered by the arbitrator in the first instance.* Third, *this arbitration law applies in state as well as federal courts.* * * * Applying [those holdings] to this case, we conclude that because respondents [Cardegna and others] challenge the Agreement, but not specifically its arbitration provisions, those provisions are enforceable apart from the remainder of the contract. The challenge should therefore be considered by an arbitrator, not a court. [Emphasis added.]

* * * *

* * * Since, respondents argue, the only arbitration agreements to which [Section] 2 applies are those involving a "contract," and since an agreement void *ab initio* [from the beginning] under state law is not a "contract," there is no "written provision" in or "controversy arising out of" a "contract," to which [Section] 2 can apply. * * * We do not read "contract" so narrowly. The word appears four times in [Section] 2. Its last appearance is in the final clause, which allows a challenge to an arbitration provision "upon such grounds as exist at law or in equity for the revocation of any contract." There can be no doubt that "contract" as used this last time must include contracts that

a. In the "Supreme Court Collection" menu at the top of the page, click on "Search." When that page opens, in the "Search for:" box, type "Buckeye Check," choose "All decisions" in the accompanying list, and click on "Search." In the result, scroll to the name of the case and click on the appropriate link to access the opinion.

CASE CONTINUES

CASE 3.1 CONTINUED

later prove to be void. Otherwise, the grounds for revocation would be limited to those that rendered a contract voidable—which would mean (implausibly) that an arbitration agreement could be challenged as voidable but not as void. Because the sentence's final use of "contract" so obviously includes putative [alleged] contracts, we will not read the same word earlier in the same sentence to have a more narrow meaning.

• **Decision and Remedy** *The United States Supreme Court reversed the judgment of the Florida Supreme Court and remanded the case for further proceedings. The United States Supreme Court ruled that a challenge to the validity of a contract as a whole, and not specifically to an arbitration clause contained in the contract, must be resolved by an arbitrator.*

• **The Ethical Dimension** *Does the holding in this case permit a court to enforce an arbitration agreement in a contract that the arbitrator later finds to be void? Is this fair? Why or why not?*

• **The Legal Environment Dimension** *As indicated in the parties' arguments and the Court's reasoning in this case, into what categories can contracts be classified with respect to their enforceability?*

State Arbitration Statutes

Virtually all states follow the federal approach to voluntary arbitration. Most of the states and the District of Columbia have adopted the Uniform Arbitration Act, which was drafted by the National Conference of Commissioners on Uniform State Laws in 1955. Those states that have not adopted the uniform act nonetheless follow many of the practices specified in it.

Under the uniform act, the basic approach is to give full effect to voluntary agreements to arbitrate disputes between private parties. The act supplements private arbitration agreements by providing explicit procedures and remedies for enforcing arbitration agreements. The uniform act does not, however, dictate the terms of the agreement. Moreover, under both federal and state statutes, the parties are afforded considerable latitude in deciding the subject matter of the arbitration and the methods for conducting the arbitration process. In the absence of a controlling statute, the rights and duties of the parties are established and limited by their agreement.

The Arbitration Process

The arbitration process begins with a *submission.* **Submission** is the act of referring a dispute to an arbitrator. The next step is the *hearing,* in which evidence and arguments are presented to the arbitrator. The process culminates in an *award,* which is the decision of the arbitrator.

The right to appeal the award to a court of law is limited. If the award was made under a voluntary arbitration agreement, a court normally will not set it aside even if it was the result of an erroneous determination of fact or an incorrect interpretation of law by the arbitrator.

This limitation is based on at least two grounds. First, if an award is not treated as final, then rather than speeding up the dispute-resolution process, arbitration would merely add one more layer to the process of litigation. Second, the basis of arbitration—the freedom of parties to agree among themselves how to settle a controversy—supports treating an award as final. Having had the opportunity to frame the issues and to set out the manner for resolving the dispute, one party should not complain if the result was not what that party had hoped it would be.

Submission The parties may agree to submit questions of fact, questions of law, or both to the arbitrator. The parties may even agree to leave the interpretation of the arbitration agreement to the arbitrator. In the case of an existing agreement to arbitrate, the clause itself is the submission to arbitration.

The submission typically states the identities of the parties, the nature of the dispute to be resolved, the monetary amounts involved in the controversy, the location at which the arbitration is to take place, and the intention of the parties to be bound by the arbitrator's award. Exhibit 3–2 contains a sample submission form.

Most states require that an agreement to submit a dispute to arbitration be in writing. Moreover, because the goal of arbitration is speed and efficiency in

EXHIBIT 3–2 • Sample Submission Form

American Arbitration Association

SUBMISSION TO DISPUTE RESOLUTION

The named parties hereby submit the following dispute for resolution, under the rules of the American Arbitration Association:

Rules Selected: ☐ Commercial ☐ Construction
☐ Other ______________________ (describe)

Procedure Selected: ☐ Binding arbitration ☐ Mediation
☐ Other ______________________ (describe)

Nature of the Dispute (attach additional sheets if necessary):

Amount of Monetary Claim or Nature of Non-Monetary Claim:

Type of Business: Claimant ______________ Respondent ______________

Place of Hearing: ______________________

We agree that, if arbitration is selected, we will abide by and perform any award rendered hereunder and that a judgment may be entered on the award.

To be completed and signed by all parties
(attach additional sheets if necessary, please remember to obtain signatures)

Name of Party	Name of Party
Address	Address
City, State, and Zip Code	City, State, and Zip Code
(____) Telephone Fax	(____) Telephone Fax
Name of the Party's Attorney or Representative	Name of the Party's Attorney or Representative
Name of Firm (if applicable)	Name of Firm (if applicable)
Address	Address
City, State, and Zip Code	City, State, and Zip Code
(____) Telephone Fax	(____) Telephone Fax
Signed† (may be signed by a representative) Title	Signed† (may be signed by a representative) Title
Date: ____________	Date: ____________

Please file two signed copies and the non-refundable filing fee with the AAA.
For additional information, please visit our Web site at www.adr.org

† *Signatures of all parties are required.*

Form G1A-3/03

INSIGHT INTO ETHICS
Implications of an Increasingly Private Justice System

Downtown Houston boasts a relatively new courthouse with thirty-nine courtrooms, but more and more often, many of those courtrooms often stand empty. Has litigation in Texas slowed down? Indeed, it has not—the courtrooms are empty because fewer civil lawsuits are going to trial. A similar situation is occurring in the federal courts. In the northern district of Florida, for example, the four federal judges presided over only a dozen civil trials in 2007. In 1984, more than 12,000 civil trials were heard in our federal courts. Today, only about 3,500 federal civil trials take place annually. University of Wisconsin law professor Mark Galanter has labeled this trend the "vanishing trial." Two developments in particular are contributing to the disappearance of civil trials—arbitration and private judges.

Arbitration Is One Cause

Since the 1980s, corporations have been eschewing the public court system and taking cases to arbitration instead. Every day millions of Americans sign arbitration agreements, often unknowingly committing themselves to allow private arbitrators to solve their disputes with employers and the corporations with which they do business, such as cell phone service providers.

This trend raises some troublesome ethical issues, however. For one thing, arbitration agreements may force consumers to travel long distances to participate in these private forums. Perhaps more disturbing is that the supposedly neutral arbitrators may actually be captive to the industries they serve. Arbitrators are paid handsomely and typically would like to serve again. Thus, they may be reluctant to rule against a company that is involved in a dispute. After all, the company may well need arbitrators to resolve a subsequent dispute, whereas the other party—a consumer or employee—is unlikely to need the arbitrators again.

Private Judges Are Another Cause

Another reason for the decline in the number of civil trials in our public courts is the growing use of private judges. A private judge, who is usually a retired judge, has the power to conduct trials and grant legal resolutions of disputes. Private judges increasingly are being used to resolve commercial disputes, as well as divorces and custody battles, for two reasons. One reason is that a case can be heard by a private judge much sooner than it would be heard in a public court. The other reason is that proceedings before a private judge can be kept secret.

resolving controversies, most states require that matters be submitted within a definite period of time, generally six months from the date on which the dispute arises.

The Hearing Because the parties are free to construct the method by which they want their dispute resolved, they must state the issues that will be submitted and the powers that the arbitrator will exercise. The arbitrator may be given power at the outset of the process to establish rules that will govern the proceedings. Typically, these rules are much less restrictive than those governing formal litigation. Regardless of who establishes the rules, the arbitrator will apply them during the course of the hearing.

Restrictions on the kind of evidence and the manner in which it is presented may be less rigid in arbitration, partly because the arbitrator is likely to be an expert in the subject matter involved in the controversy. Restrictions may also be less stringent because there is less fear that the arbitrator will be swayed by improper evidence. In contrast, evidence in a jury trial must sometimes be presented twice: once to the judge, outside the presence of the jury, to determine if the evidence may be heard by the jury, and—depending on the judge's ruling—again, to the jury.

In the typical hearing format, the parties begin as they would at trial by presenting opening arguments to the arbitrator and stating what remedies should or should not be granted. After the opening statements have been made, evidence is presented. Witnesses may be called and examined by both sides. After all the evidence has been presented, the parties give their closing arguments. On completion of the closing arguments, the arbitrator closes the hearing.

The Award After each side has had an opportunity to present evidence and to argue its case, the arbitrator reaches a decision. The final decision of the arbitrator is referred to as an **award,** even if no money is conferred on a party as a result of the proceedings. Under most statutes, the arbitrator must render an award within thirty days of the close of the hearing.

In most states, the award need not state the arbitrator's findings regarding factual questions in the case. Nor must the award state the conclusions that the arbi-

In Ohio, for example, a state statute allows the parties to any civil action to have their dispute tried by a retired judge of their choosing who will make a decision in the matter.[a] Recently, though, private judging came under criticism in that state because private judges were conducting jury trials in county courtrooms at taxpayers' expense. A public judge, Nancy Margaret Russo, refused to give up jurisdiction over one case on the ground that private judges are not authorized to conduct jury trials. The Ohio Supreme Court agreed. As the state's highest court noted, private judging raises significant public-policy issues that the legislature needs to consider.[b]

One issue is that private judges charge relatively large fees. This means that litigants who are willing and able to pay the extra cost can have their case heard by a private judge long before they would be able to set a trial date in a regular court. Is it fair that those who cannot afford private judges should have to wait longer for justice? Similarly, is it ethical to allow parties to pay extra for secret proceedings before a private judge and thereby avoid the public scrutiny of a regular trial? Some even suggest that the use of private judges is leading to two different systems of justice.

a. See Ohio Revised Code Section 2701.10.

b. *State ex rel. Russo v. McDonnell,* 110 Ohio St.3d 144, 852 N.E.2d 145 (2006). (The term *ex rel.* is Latin for *ex relatione.* This phrase refers to an action brought on behalf of the state, by the attorney general, at the instigation of an individual who has a private interest in the matter.)

A Threat to the Common Law System?

The decline in the number of civil trials may also be leading to the erosion of this country's common law system. As discussed in Chapter 1, courts are obligated to consider precedents—the decisions rendered in previous cases with similar facts and issues—when deciding the outcome of a dispute. If fewer disputes go to trial because they are arbitrated or heard by a private judge, then they will never become part of the body of cases and appeals that form the case law on that subject. With fewer precedents on which to draw, individuals and businesses will have less information about what constitutes appropriate business behavior in today's world. Furthermore, private dispute resolution does not allow our case law to keep up with new issues related to areas such as biotechnology and the online world. Thus, the long-term effects of the decline of public justice could be a weakening of the common law itself.

CRITICAL THINKING

INSIGHT INTO THE SOCIAL ENVIRONMENT

If wealthier individuals increasingly use private judges, how will our justice system be affected in the long run?

trator reached on any questions of law that may have been presented. All that is required for the award to be valid is that it completely resolve the controversy.

Most states do, however, require that the award be in writing, regardless of whether any conclusions of law or findings of fact are included. If the arbitrator does state his or her legal conclusions and factual findings, then a letter or an opinion will be drafted containing the basis for the award. Even when there is no statutory requirement that the arbitrator state the factual and legal basis for the award, the parties may impose the requirement in their submission or in their predispute agreement to arbitrate.

Enforcement of Agreements to Submit to Arbitration

The role of the courts in the arbitration process is limited. One important role is played at the prearbitration stage. A court may be called on to order one party to an arbitration agreement to submit to arbitration under the terms of the agreement. The court in this role is essentially interpreting a contract. The court must determine what the parties have committed themselves to before ordering that they submit to arbitration.

The Issue of Arbitrability When a dispute arises as to whether or not the parties have agreed in an arbitration clause to submit a particular matter to arbitration, one party may file suit to compel arbitration. The court before which the suit is brought will not decide the basic controversy but must decide the issue of arbitrability—that is, whether the issue is one that must be resolved through arbitration. If the court finds that the subject matter in controversy is covered by the agreement to arbitrate, then a party may be compelled to arbitrate the dispute involuntarily.

Although the parties may agree to submit the issue of arbitrability to an arbitrator, the agreement must be explicit; a court will never *infer* an agreement to arbitrate. Unless a court finds an *explicit* agreement to have the arbitrator decide whether a dispute is arbitrable, the court will decide the issue. This is an important initial determination, because no party will be ordered to submit to arbitration unless the court is convinced that the party has consented to do so.

The terms of an arbitration agreement can limit the types of disputes that the parties agree to arbitrate. When the parties do not specify limits, however, disputes can arise as to whether the particular matter is covered by the arbitration agreement, and it is up to the court to resolve the issue of arbitrability. In the following case, the parties had previously agreed to arbitrate disputes involving their contract to develop software, but the dispute involved claims of copyright infringement (see Chapter 14). The question was whether the copyright infringement claims were beyond the scope of the arbitration clause.

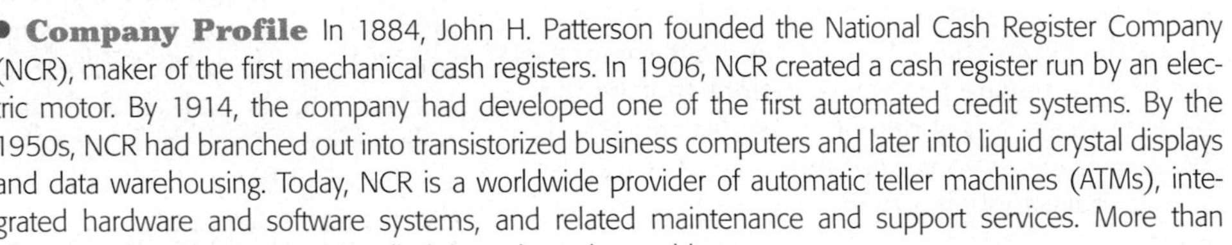

CASE 3.2 NCR Corp. v. Korala Associates, Ltd.

United States Court of Appeals, Sixth Circuit, 2008. 512 F.3d 807.
www.ca6.uscourts.gov[a]

• **Company Profile** In 1884, John H. Patterson founded the National Cash Register Company (NCR), maker of the first mechanical cash registers. In 1906, NCR created a cash register run by an electric motor. By 1914, the company had developed one of the first automated credit systems. By the 1950s, NCR had branched out into transistorized business computers and later into liquid crystal displays and data warehousing. Today, NCR is a worldwide provider of automatic teller machines (ATMs), integrated hardware and software systems, and related maintenance and support services. More than 300,000 of NCR's ATMs are installed throughout the world.

• **Background and Facts** In response to a need to upgrade the security of its ATMs, NCR developed a software solution to install in all of its machines. At the same time, Korala Associates, Ltd. (KAL) claimed to have developed a similar security upgrade for NCR's ATMs. Indeed, KAL had entered into a contract with NRC in 1998 (the "1998 Agreement") to develop such software. In order to do so, NCR loaned to KAL a proprietary ATM that contained copyrighted software called "APTRA XFS." NCR alleged that KAL "obtained access to, made unauthorized use of, and engaged in unauthorized copying of the APTRA XFS software." By so doing, KAL developed its own version of a security upgrade for NCR's ATMs. When NCR brought a suit against KAL, the latter moved to compel arbitration under the terms of the 1998 Agreement between the two companies. At trial, KAL prevailed. NCR appealed the order compelling arbitration to the U.S. Court of Appeals for the Sixth Circuit.

IN THE LANGUAGE OF THE COURT
Chief Justice *BATCHELDER* delivered the opinion of the Court.

* * * *

The arbitration clause contained within the 1998 Agreement provides that:

> Any controversy or claim arising out of or relating to this contract, or breach thereof, shall be settled by arbitration and judgment upon the award rendered by the arbitrator may be entered in any court having jurisdiction thereof. The arbitrator shall be appointed upon the mutual agreement of both parties failing which both parties will agree to be subject to any arbitrator that shall be chosen by the President of the Law Society.

The parties do not dispute that a valid agreement to arbitrate exists; rather the issue of contention is whether NCR's claims fall within the substantive scope of the agreement.

As a matter of federal law, any doubts concerning the scope of arbitrable issues should be resolved in favor of arbitration. Despite this strong presumption in favor of arbitration, "arbitration is a matter of contract between the parties, and one cannot be required to submit to arbitration a dispute which it has not agreed to submit to arbitration." *When faced with a broad arbitration clause, such as one covering any dispute arising out of an agreement, a court should follow the presumption of arbitration and resolve doubts in favor of arbitration. Indeed, in such a case, only an express provision excluding a specific dispute, or the most forceful evidence of a purpose to exclude the claim from arbitration, will remove the dispute from consideration by the arbitrators.* [Emphasis added.]

a. Click on "Opinions Search" and then on "Short Title;" and type "NCR." Next, click on the opinion link in the first column of the row corresponding to the name of this case.

CASE 3.2 CONTINUED

* * * *

* * * It is sufficient that a court would have to reference the 1998 Agreement for part of NCR's direct [copyright] infringement claim. Under these circumstances, we find that the copyright infringement claim as to APTRA XFS falls within the scope of the arbitration agreement.

• **Decision and Remedy** *The U.S. Court of Appeals for the Sixth Circuit affirmed part of the district court's decision. Specifically, it affirmed the judgment compelling arbitration as to NCR's claims relating to direct copyright infringement of the APTRA XFS software.*

• **The Ethical Dimension** *Could NCR have a claim that KAL engaged in unfair competition because KAL had engaged in unethical business practices? (Hint: Unfair competition may occur when one party deceives the public into believing that his or her goods are the goods of another.) Why or why not?*

• **The Legal Environment Dimension** *Why do you think that NCR did not want its alleged claims decided by arbitration?*

Mandatory Arbitration in the Employment Context A significant question in the last several years has concerned mandatory arbitration clauses in employment contracts. Many claim that employees' rights are not sufficiently protected when they are forced, as a condition of being hired, to agree to arbitrate all disputes and thus waive their rights under statutes specifically designed to protect employees. The United States Supreme Court, however, has held that mandatory arbitration clauses in employment contracts are generally enforceable.[2]

Compulsory arbitration agreements often spell out the rules for a mandatory proceeding. For example, an agreement may address in detail the amount and payment of filing fees and other expenses. Some courts have overturned provisions in employment-related agreements that require the parties to split the costs when an individual worker lacks the ability to pay. The court in the following case took this reasoning a step further.

2. For a landmark decision on this issue, see *Gilmer v. Interstate/Johnson Lane Corp.*, 500 U.S. 20, 111 S.Ct. 1647, 114 L.Ed.2d 26 (1991).

EXTENDED CASE 3.3

Morrison v. Circuit City Stores, Inc.

United States Court of Appeals, Sixth Circuit, 2003. 317 F.3d 646.
www.ca6.uscourts.gov/internet/index.htm[a]

KAREN NELSON MOORE, **Circuit Judge.**

* * * *

* * * Plaintiff-Appellant Morrison, an African-American female with a bachelor's degree in engineering from the U.S. Air Force Academy and a master's degree in administration from Central Michigan University, submitted an application for a managerial position at a Circuit City store in Cincinnati, Ohio. As part of the application process, Morrison was required to sign a * * * "Dispute Resolution Agreement." This document contained an arbitration clause that required resolution of all disputes or controversies arising out of employment with Circuit City in an arbitral forum. * * * Circuit City would not consider any application for employment unless the arbitration agreement was signed * * * .

* * * *

a. This is a page within the Web site of the U.S. Court of Appeals for the Sixth Circuit. In the left-hand column, click on "Opinions Search." In the "Short Title contains" box, type "Morrison" and click "Submit Query." In the "Opinion" box corresponding to the name of the case, click on the number to access the opinion.

CASE CONTINUES

CASE 3.3 CONTINUED

Pursuant to [the agreement] each party is required to pay one-half of the costs of arbitration following the issuance of an arbitration award * * * . In addition, * * * if an employee is able to pay her share of the arbitration costs within [ninety days], her costs (not including attorney fees) are then limited to the greater of either five hundred dollars or three percent of her most recent annual compensation.

* * * *

* * * Morrison began her employment at Circuit City on or about December 1, 1995. Two years later, on December 12, 1997, she was terminated. Morrison alleges that her termination was the result of race and sex discrimination.[b] She filed this lawsuit * * * in Ohio state court, alleging federal and state claims of race and sex discrimination * * * . Circuit City removed the case to federal court and then moved to compel arbitration and to dismiss Morrison's claims. The district court granted Circuit City's motion * * * .

* * * Morrison's appeal followed.

* * * *

We hold that *potential litigants must be given an opportunity, prior to arbitration on the merits, to demonstrate that the potential costs of arbitration are great enough to deter them and similarly situated individuals from seeking to vindicate [assert] their federal statutory rights in the arbitral forum.* * * * Thus, in order to protect the statutory rights at issue, the reviewing court must look to more than just the interests and conduct of a particular plaintiff. * * * A court considering whether a cost-splitting provision is enforceable should consider similarly situated potential litigants, for whom costs will loom as a larger concern, because it is, in large part, their presence in the system that will deter discriminatory practices. [Emphasis added.]

For this reason, *if the reviewing court finds that the cost-splitting provision would deter a substantial number of similarly situated potential litigants, it should refuse to enforce the cost-splitting provision in order to serve the underlying functions of the federal statute.* [Emphasis added.]

* * * *

This analysis will yield different results in different cases. It will find, in many cases, that high-level managerial employees and others with substantial means can afford the costs of arbitration, thus making cost-splitting provisions in such cases enforceable. In the case of other employees, however, this standard will render cost-splitting provisions unenforceable in many, if not most, cases.

* * * Circuit City argues that Morrison could have avoided having to pay half of the cost of the arbitration * * * if she could have arranged to pay the greater of $500 or 3 percent of her annual salary (in this case, 3 percent of $54,060, or $1,622) within ninety days of the arbitrator's award.

In the abstract, this sum may not appear prohibitive, but it must be considered from the vantage point of the potential litigant in a case such as this. Recently terminated, the potential litigant must continue to pay for housing, utilities, transportation, food, and the other necessities of life in contemporary society despite losing her primary, and most likely only, source of income.

The provision reducing the (former) employee's exposure to the greater of $500 or three percent of her annual compensation presents a closer issue. However, a potential litigant considering arbitration would still have to arrange to pay three percent of her most recent salary, in this case, $1,622, within a three-month period, or risk incurring her full half of the costs * * * . Faced with this choice—which really boils down to risking one's scarce resources in the hopes of an uncertain benefit—it appears to us that a substantial number of similarly situated persons would be deterred from seeking to vindicate their statutory rights under these circumstances.[c]

Based on this reasoning, we hold that Morrison has satisfied her burden in the present case in demonstrating that * * * the cost-splitting provision in the agreement was unenforceable with respect to her claims.

b. Employment discrimination will be discussed in detail in Chapter 21.

c. The court also concluded that the provision could be severed from the agreement, which meant that the rest of the agreement could be enforced. Because the arbitration in this case had already occurred, and Morrison had not been required to pay any share of the costs, the court affirmed the lower court's order compelling arbitration, "on these different grounds."

CASE 3.3 CONTINUED

QUESTIONS

1. On what argument did Morrison base her appeal of the court's order to arbitrate her employment-discrimination claims?
2. Why did the U.S. Court of Appeals for the Sixth Circuit hold in Morrison's case that the arbitration agreement's cost-splitting provision was unenforceable?

Setting Aside an Arbitration Award

After the arbitration has been concluded, the losing party may appeal the arbitrator's award to a court, or the winning party may seek a court order compelling the other party to comply with the award. The scope of review in either situation is much more restricted than in an appellate court's review of a trial court decision. The court does not look at the merits of the underlying dispute, and the court will not add to or subtract from the remedies provided by the award. The court's role is limited to determining whether there exists a valid award. If so, the court will order the parties to comply with the terms. The general view is that because the parties were free to frame the issues and set the powers of the arbitrator at the outset, they cannot complain about the result.

Fact Findings and Legal Conclusions The arbitrator's fact findings and legal conclusions are normally final. That the arbitrator may have erred in a ruling during the hearing or made an erroneous fact finding is normally no basis for setting aside an award: the parties agreed that the arbitrator would be the judge of the facts. Similarly, no matter how obviously the arbitrator was mistaken in a conclusion of law, the award is normally nonetheless binding: the parties agreed to accept the arbitrator's interpretation of the law. A court will not look at the merits of the dispute, the sufficiency of the evidence presented, or the arbitrator's reasoning in reaching a particular decision.

This approach is consistent with the underlying view of all voluntary arbitration—that its basis is really contract law. If the parties freely contract with one another, courts will not interfere simply because one side feels that it received a bad bargain. Any party challenging an award must face the presumption that a final award is valid. But is an award final or binding if the parties did not agree that it would be?

Public Policy and Illegality In keeping with contract law principles, no award will be enforced if compliance with the award would result in the commission of a crime or would conflict with some greater social policy mandated by statute. A court will not overturn an award, however, simply because the arbitrator was called on to resolve a dispute involving a matter of significant public concern. For an award to be set aside, it must call for some action on the part of the parties that would conflict with or in some way undermine public policy.

Defects in the Arbitration Process There are some bases for setting aside an award when there is a defect in the arbitration process. These bases are typified by those set forth in the Federal Arbitration Act. Section 10 of the act provides four grounds on which an arbitration award may be set aside:

1. The award was the result of corruption, fraud, or other "undue means."
2. The arbitrator exhibited bias or corruption.
3. The arbitrator refused to postpone the hearing despite sufficient cause, refused to hear evidence pertinent and material to the dispute, or otherwise acted to substantially prejudice the rights of one of the parties.
4. The arbitrator exceeded his or her powers or failed to use them to make a mutual, final, and definite award.

The first three bases for setting aside the award include actions or decisions that are more than simply mistakes in judgment. Each requires some "bad faith" on the part of the arbitrator. Bad faith actions or decisions are ones that affect the integrity of the arbitration process. The honesty and impartiality, rather than the judgment, of the arbitrator are called into question.

Sometimes it is difficult to make the distinction between honest mistakes in judgment and actions or decisions made in bad faith. A bribe is clearly the kind of "undue means" included in the first basis for setting aside an award. Letting only one side argue its case is likewise a clear violation of the second basis.

Meetings between the arbitrator and one party outside the presence of the other party also taint the arbitration process. Although meetings might not involve the kind of corruption that results from taking a bribe, they do affect the integrity of the process; the third basis for setting aside an award is meant to protect against this.

Not every refusal by an arbitrator to admit certain evidence is grounds for setting aside an award under the third basis. As noted, to provide a basis for overturning an award, the arbitrator's decision must be more than an error in judgment, no matter how obviously incorrect that judgment might appear to another observer. The decision must be so obviously wrong or unfair as to imply bias or corruption. Otherwise, the decision normally cannot be a basis for setting aside an award.

The fourth basis for setting aside an award is that the arbitrator exceeded his or her powers in arbitrating the dispute. This issue involves the question of arbitrability. An arbitrator exceeds his or her powers and authority by attempting to resolve an issue that is not covered by the agreement to submit to arbitration.[3]

Waiver Although a defect in the arbitration process is sufficient grounds for setting aside an award, a party sometimes forfeits the right to challenge an award by failing to object to the defect in a timely manner. The party must object when he or she learns of the problem. After making the objection, the party can still proceed with the arbitration process and still challenge the award in court after the arbitration proceedings have concluded. If, however, a party makes no objection and proceeds with the arbitration process, then a later court challenge to the award may be denied on the ground that the party *waived* the right to challenge the award on the basis of the defect.

Frequently, this occurs when a party fails to object that an arbitrator is exceeding his or her powers in resolving a dispute because the subject matter is not arbitrable or because the party did not agree to arbitrate the dispute. The question of arbitrability is one for the courts to decide. If a party does not object on this issue at the first demand for arbitration, however, a court may consider the objection waived.

Conflicts of Law Parties are afforded wide latitude in establishing the manner in which their disputes will be resolved. Nevertheless, an agreement to arbitrate may be governed by the Federal Arbitration Act (FAA) or one of the many state arbitration acts, even though the parties do not refer to a statute in their agreement. Recall that the FAA covers any arbitration clause in a contract that involves interstate commerce. Frequently, however, transactions involving interstate commerce also have substantial connections to particular states, which may in turn have their own arbitration acts. In such situations, unless the FAA and state arbitration law are nearly identical, the acts may conflict. How are these conflicts to be resolved?

As a general principle, the supremacy clause and the commerce clause of the U.S. Constitution are the bases for giving federal law preeminence; when there is a conflict, state law is preempted by federal law. Thus, in cases of arbitration, the strong federal policy favoring arbitration can override a state's laws that might be more favorable to normal litigation.

Choice of Law Notwithstanding federal preemption of conflicting state laws, the Federal Arbitration Act has been interpreted as allowing the parties to choose a particular state law to govern their arbitration agreement. The parties may choose to have the laws of a specific state govern their agreement by including in the agreement a *choice-of-law clause*. The FAA does not mandate any particular set of rules that parties must follow in arbitration; the parties are free to agree on the manner best suited to their needs. Consistent with this view that arbitration is at heart a contractual matter between private parties, the United States Supreme Court has upheld arbitration agreements containing choice-of-law provisions.

Disadvantages of Arbitration

Arbitration has some disadvantages. The result in any particular dispute can be unpredictable, in part because arbitrators do not need to follow any previous cases in rendering their decisions. Unlike judges, arbitrators do not have to issue written opinions or facilitate a participant's appeal to a court. Arbitrators must decide disputes according to whatever rules have been provided by the parties, regardless of how unfair those rules may be. In some cases, arbitration can be nearly as expensive as litigation. In part, this is because both sides must prepare their cases for presentation before a third party decision maker, just as they would have to do to appear in court. Discovery is usually not available in arbitration, however, which means that during the hearing the parties must take the time to question witnesses whom, in a lawsuit, they would not need to call.

3. See, for example, *Major League Baseball Players Association v. Garvey*, 532 U.S. 1015, 121 S.Ct. 1724, 149 L.Ed.2d 740 (2001).

The Integration of ADR and Formal Court Procedures

Increasingly, courts are requiring that parties attempt to settle their differences through some form of ADR before proceeding to trial. For example, several federal district courts encourage nonbinding arbitration for cases involving amounts less than $100,000. Less than 10 percent of the cases referred for arbitration ever go to trial. About half of all federal courts have adopted formal rules regarding the use of ADR, and many other courts without such rules use ADR procedures.

Most states have adopted programs that allow them to refer certain types of cases for negotiation, mediation, or arbitration. Typically—as in California and Hawaii—court systems have adopted mandatory mediation or nonbinding arbitration programs for certain types of disputes, usually involving less than a specified threshold dollar amount. Only if the parties fail to reach an agreement, or if one of the parties disagrees with the decision of a third party mediating or arbitrating the dispute, will the case be heard by a court. South Carolina was the first state to institute a voluntary arbitration program at the appellate court level. In the South Carolina system, litigants must waive a court hearing when requesting arbitration. All decisions by the arbitrators are final and binding.

Court-Annexed Arbitration

Court-annexed arbitration differs significantly from the voluntary arbitration process discussed above. There are some disputes that courts will not allow to go to arbitration. Most states, for example, do not allow court-annexed arbitration in disputes involving title to real estate or in cases in which a court's equity powers are involved.

A Fundamental Difference The fundamental difference between voluntary arbitration and court-annexed arbitration is the finality and reviewability of the award. With respect to court-annexed arbitration, either party may reject the award for any reason. In the event that one of the parties does reject the award, the case will proceed to trial, and the court will hear the case *de novo*—that is, the court will reconsider all the evidence and legal questions as though no arbitration had occurred.

Everyone who has a recognizable cause of action or against whom such an action is brought is entitled to have the issue decided in a court of law. Because court-annexed arbitration is not voluntary, there must be some safeguard against using it in a way that denies an individual his or her day in court. This safeguard is provided by permitting either side to reject the award regardless of the reason for so doing.

The party rejecting the award may be penalized, however. Many statutes providing for court-annexed arbitration impose court costs and fees on a party who rejects an arbitration award but does not improve his or her position by going to trial. Thus, for example, if a party rejects an arbitration award, and the award turns out to be more favorable to that party than the subsequent jury verdict, the party may be compelled to pay the costs of the arbitration or some fee for the costs of the trial.

In court-annexed arbitration, discovery of evidence occurs before the hearing. After the hearing has commenced, a party seeking to discover new evidence must usually secure approval from the court that mandated the arbitration. This is intended to prevent the parties from using arbitration as a means of previewing each other's cases and then rejecting the arbitrator's award.

The Role of the Arbitrator Notwithstanding the differences between voluntary and court-annexed arbitration, the role of the arbitrator is essentially the same in both types of proceedings. The arbitrator determines issues of both fact and law. The arbitrator also makes all decisions concerning applications of the rules of procedure and evidence during the hearing.

Which Rules Apply Regarding the rules of evidence, there are differences among the states. Most states impose the same rules of evidence on an arbitration hearing as on a trial. Other states allow all evidence relevant to the dispute regardless of whether the evidence would be admissible at trial. Still other jurisdictions leave it to the arbitrator to decide what evidence is admissible.

Waiver Once a court directs that a dispute is to be submitted to court-annexed arbitration, the parties must proceed to arbitration. As noted above, either side may reject the award that results from the arbitration for any reason. If a party fails to appear at, or participate in, the arbitration proceeding as directed by the court, however, that failure constitutes a waiver of the right to reject the award.

Court-Related Mediation

Mediation is proving to be more popular than arbitration as a court-related method of ADR, and mediation programs continue to increase in number in both federal and state courts. Today, more court systems offer or require mediation, rather than arbitration, as an alternative to litigation.

Mediation is often used in disputes relating to employment law, environmental law, product liability, and franchises. One of the most important business advantages of mediation is its lower cost, which can be 25 percent (or less) of the expense of litigation. Another advantage is the speed with which a dispute can go through mediation (possibly one or two days) compared with arbitration (possibly months) or litigation (possibly years).

Part of the popularity of mediation is that its goal, unlike that of litigation and some other forms of ADR, is for opponents to work out a resolution that benefits both sides. The rate of participants' satisfaction with the outcomes in mediated disputes is high.

Summary Jury Trials

Another means by which the courts have integrated alternative dispute-resolution methods into the traditional court process is through the use of summary jury trials. A **summary jury trial** is a mock trial that occurs in a courtroom before a judge and jury. Evidence is presented in an abbreviated form, along with each side's major contentions. The jury then presents a verdict.

The fundamental difference between a traditional trial and a summary jury trial is that in the latter, the jury's verdict is only advisory. A summary jury trial's goal is to give each side an idea of how it would fare in a full-blown jury trial with a more elaborate and detailed presentation of evidence and arguments. At the end of the summary jury trial, the presiding judge meets with the parties and may encourage them to settle their dispute without going through a standard jury trial.

ADR Forums and Services

Services facilitating dispute resolution outside the courtroom are provided by both government agencies and private organizations.

Nonprofit Organizations

The major source of private arbitration services is the American Arbitration Association (AAA). Most of the largest law firms in the nation are members of this association. Founded in 1926, the AAA now settles more than 200,000 disputes a year and has offices in every state. Cases brought before the AAA are heard by an expert or a panel of experts—of whom usually about half are lawyers—in the area relating to the dispute. To cover its costs, this nonprofit organization charges a fee, paid by the party filing the claim. In addition, each party to the dispute pays a price for each hearing day, as well as a special additional fee in cases involving personal injuries or property loss.

In addition to the AAA, hundreds of other state and local nonprofit organizations provide arbitration services. For example, the Arbitration Association of Florida provides ADR services in that state. The Better Business Bureau offers ADR programs to aid in the resolution of certain types of disagreements. Many industries—including the insurance, automobile, and securities industries—also now have mediation or arbitration programs to facilitate timely and inexpensive settlement of claims.

For-Profit Organizations

Those who seek to settle their disputes quickly can turn to private, for-profit organizations to act as mediators or arbitrators. The leading firm in this private system of justice is JAMS/Endispute, which is based in California. The private system of justice includes hundreds of firms throughout the country offering dispute-resolution services by hired judges.

Procedures in these private courts are fashioned to meet the desires of the clients seeking their services. For example, the parties might decide on the date of the hearing, the presiding judge, whether the judge's decision will be legally binding, and the site of the hearing—which could be a conference room, a law school office, or a leased courtroom complete with the American flag and Bible. The judges may follow procedures similar to those of the federal courts and use similar rules. Each party to the dispute may pay a filing fee and a designated fee for a half-day hearing session or a special, one-hour settlement conference.

Online Dispute Resolution

An increasing number of companies and organizations are offering dispute-resolution services using the Internet. The settlement of disputes in these online forums is known as **online dispute resolution (ODR).** To date, the disputes resolved in these forums have most commonly involved disagreements over the rights to domain names (Web site addresses—see Chapter 14) and disagreements over the quality of goods sold via the Internet, including goods sold through Internet auction sites.

Currently, ODR may be best for resolving small- to medium-sized business liability claims, which may not be worth the expense of litigation or even traditional methods of alternative dispute resolution. Rules being developed in online forums, however, may ultimately become a code of conduct for everyone who does business in cyberspace. Most online forums do not automatically apply the law of any specific jurisdiction. Instead, results are often based on general, more universal legal principles. As with traditional offline methods of dispute resolution, any party may appeal to a court at any time.

Negotiation and Mediation Services

The online negotiation of a dispute is generally simpler and more practical than litigation. Typically, one party files a complaint, and the other party is notified by e-mail. Password-protected access is possible twenty-four hours a day, seven days a week. Fees are generally low (often 2 to 4 percent, or less, of the disputed amount).

CyberSettle.com, National Arbitration and Mediation (NAM), and other Web-based firms offer online forums for negotiating monetary settlements. Even the Better Business Bureau now provides online dispute settlement.[4] The parties to a dispute may agree to submit offers; if the offers fall within a previously agreed-on range, they will end the dispute. Special software keeps secret any offers that are not within the range. If there is no agreed-on range, typically an offer includes a deadline when the offer will expire, and the other party must respond before then. The parties can drop the negotiations at any time.

Mediation providers have also tried resolving disputes online. SquareTrade, for example, provides mediation services for the online auction site eBay as well as other parties. It has resolved more than 2 million disputes between merchants and consumers in 120 countries. SquareTrade uses Web-based software that walks participants through a five-step e-resolution process. Disputing parties first attempt to negotiate directly on a secure page within SquareTrade's Web site. There is no fee for negotiation. If the parties cannot reach an agreement, they can consult with a mediator. The entire process takes as little as ten to fourteen days.

Arbitration Programs

A number of organizations, including the American Arbitration Association, offer online arbitration programs. The Internet Corporation for Assigned Names and Numbers (ICANN), a nonprofit corporation that the federal government set up to oversee the distribution of domain names, has issued special rules for the resolution of domain name disputes.[5] ICANN has also authorized several organizations to arbitrate domain name disputes in accordance with ICANN's rules.

Resolution Forum, Inc. (RFI), a nonprofit organization associated with the Center for Legal Responsibility at South Texas College of Law, offers arbitration services through its CAN-WIN conferencing system. Using standard browser software and an RFI password, the parties to a dispute can access an online conference room.

The Virtual Magistrate (VMAG) is a program provided through Chicago-Kent College of Law. VMAG offers arbitration for disputes involving online activities, including torts such as spamming and defamation (discussed in Chapter 12), wrongful messages and postings, and online contract or property disputes. VMAG attempts to resolve a dispute quickly (within seventy-two hours) and inexpensively. A VMAG arbitrator's decision is issued in a written opinion and may be appealed to a court.

International Dispute Resolution

Businesspersons who engage in international business transactions normally take special precautions to protect themselves in the event that a party with whom they are dealing in another country breaches an agreement. Often, parties to international contracts include special clauses in their contracts providing for how any disputes arising under the contracts will be resolved.

4. You can find the Better Business Bureau Online Program at **www.bbbonline.org**.

5. ICANN's Rules for Uniform Domain Name Dispute Resolution Policy are online at **www.icann.org/dndr/udrp/uniform-rules.htm**. Domain names will be discussed in more detail in Chapter 14, in the context of trademark law.

Forum-Selection and Choice-of-Law Clauses

Parties to international contracts often include *forum-selection clauses.* These clauses designate the jurisdiction (court or country) in which any dispute arising under the contract will be litigated and the nation's law that will be applied. Choice-of-law clauses, which were discussed earlier in this chapter, are also frequently included in international contracts. If no forum and choice-of-law clauses have been included in an international contract, however, legal proceedings will be more complex and attended by much more uncertainty. For example, litigation may take place in two or more countries, with each country applying its own national law to the particular transactions.

Furthermore, even if a plaintiff wins a favorable judgment in a lawsuit litigated in the plaintiff's country, there is no guarantee that the court's judgment will be enforced by judicial bodies in the defendant's country. As will be discussed in Chapter 8, for reasons of courtesy, the judgment may be enforced in the defendant's country, particularly if the defendant's country is the United States and the foreign court's decision is consistent with U.S. national law and policy. Other nations, however, may not be as accommodating as the United States, and the plaintiff may be left empty-handed.

Arbitration Clauses

In an attempt to prevent such problems, parties to international contracts often include arbitration clauses in their contracts, requiring that any contract disputes be decided by a neutral third party. In international arbitration proceedings, the third party may be a neutral entity (such as the International Chamber of Commerce), a panel of individuals representing both parties' interests, or some other group or organization. The United Nations Convention on the Recognition and Enforcement of Foreign Arbitral Awards[6]—which has been implemented in more than fifty countries, including the United States—assists in the enforcement of arbitration clauses, as do provisions in specific treaties among nations. The American Arbitration Association provides arbitration services for international as well as domestic disputes.

6. June 10, 1958, 21 U.S.T. 2517, T.I.A.S. No. 6997 (the "New York Convention").

REVIEWING Alternative and Online Dispute Resolution

Adrian Reese, a resident of New York, owned a strip mall located in Ohio, which he leased out to different businesses. The tenants in the building had complained that the two public restrooms were substandard and in need of repair. Reese therefore contracted with Lyle Copeland, a licensed contractor in Ohio, to remodel the bathrooms and fix the outdated plumbing. Copeland began the work on the date promised but progressed very slowly. Then, while ripping out the existing pipes, Copeland accidentally broke the main pipe, which caused flooding and water damage to the building. Several of the tenants immediately vacated the property after the incident. Reese claimed that Copeland was legally responsible for $300,000 in property damage because his actions were reckless and incompetent. Copeland maintained that it was an accident and refused to pay for the damage. Using the information presented in the chapter, answer the following questions.

1. What types of assisted negotiation might the parties use to settle this dispute?
2. Does the fact that the parties reside in different jurisdictions have any effect on whether they might try mediation or negotiation? Why or why not?
3. Why would the parties wish to use some method of alternative dispute resolution (ADR) rather than filing a traditional lawsuit?
4. Suppose that one of the parties rejects any attempt at using ADR and instead files a lawsuit in a federal district court. That court happens to require that this dispute be arbitrated prior to any trial on the matter. Explain whether this arbitration is likely to be legally binding on the parties.

TERMS AND CONCEPTS

alternative dispute resolution (ADR) 64
arbitration 65
arbitrator 65
award 70
early neutral case evaluation 64
facilitation 65
mediation 65
mediator 65
mini-trial 64
negotiation 64
online dispute resolution (ODR) 78
submission 68
summary jury trial 78

QUESTIONS AND CASE PROBLEMS

3-1. In an arbitration proceeding, the arbitrator need not be a judge or even a lawyer. How, then, can the arbitrator's decision have the force of law and be binding on the parties involved?

3-2. QUESTION WITH SAMPLE ANSWER

Two private U.S. corporations enter into a joint-venture agreement to conduct mining operations in the newly formed Middle Eastern nation of Euphratia. As part of the agreement, the companies include an arbitration clause and a choice-of-law provision. The first states that any controversy arising out of the performance of the agreement will be settled by arbitration. The second states that the agreement is to be governed by the laws of the location of the venture, Euphratia. A dispute arises, and the parties discontinue operations. One of the parties claims sole ownership to the Euphratian mines and orders the other party to remove its equipment from the mines. The other party disputes the claim of sole ownership and seeks an order from a U.S. federal court compelling the parties to submit to arbitration over the ownership issue and alleged breaches of the joint-venture agreement. How should the court rule if the laws of Euphratia state that, whereas arbitration agreements are to be enforced generally, matters of ownership of natural resources can only be resolved in a Euphratian court of law? Does it matter that two U.S. companies engaged in international commerce would be governed by the Federal Arbitration Act?

- **For a sample answer to Question 3–2, go to Appendix I at the end of this text.**

3-3. Two brothers, both of whom are certified public accountants (CPAs), form a professional association to provide tax-accounting services to the public. They also agree, in writing, that any disputes that arise between them over matters concerning the association will be submitted to an independent arbitrator, whom they designate to be their father, who is also a CPA. A dispute arises, and the matter is submitted to the father for arbitration. During the course of arbitration, which occurs over several weeks, the father asks the older brother, who is visiting one evening, to explain a certain entry in the brothers' association accounts. The younger brother learns of the discussion at the next meeting for arbitration; he says nothing about it, however. The arbitration is concluded in favor of the older brother, who seeks a court order compelling the younger brother to comply with the award. The younger brother seeks to set aside the award, claiming that the arbitration process was tainted by bias because "Dad always liked my older brother best." The younger brother also seeks to have the award set aside on the basis of improper conduct in that matters subject to arbitration were discussed between the father and older brother without the younger brother's being present. Should a court confirm the award or set it aside? Why?

3-4. After resolving their dispute, the two brothers encountered in Question 3–3 decide to resume their tax-accounting practice according to the terms of their original agreement. Again a dispute arises, and again it is decided by the father (now retired except for numerous occasions on which he acts as an arbitrator) in favor of the older brother. The older brother files a petition to enforce the award. The younger brother seeks to set aside the award and offers evidence that the father, as arbitrator, made a gross error in calculating the accounts that were material to the dispute being arbitrated. If the court is convinced that the father erred in the calculations, should the award be set aside? Why?

3-5. Arbitrator's Authority. In 1999, Michael Steinmetz agreed to buy espresso equipment and the training to use it from Malted Mousse, Inc. (MM), in Tacoma, Washington. Steinmetz gave MM a $5,000 deposit, but later believing that MM misrepresented the condition of the equipment and the extent of the training, he stopped payment on the check. MM filed a suit in a Washington state court against Steinmetz to recover the amount of the deposit. Under the rules of the court, the parties submitted their dispute to arbitration. The arbitrator issued an award in favor of Steinmetz, who asked for attorneys' fees on the basis of a state statute that required their award in cases involving less than $10,000. The arbitrator declared that the statute was unconstitutional and denied Steinmetz's request. Steinmetz appealed this denial to the court, arguing that the arbitrator exceeded his authority. Should the court reverse the arbitrator's award on the issue of the fees? Explain. [*Malted Mousse, Inc. v. Steinmetz,* 113 Wash.App. 157, 52 P.3d 555 (Div. 2, 2002)]

3–6. Arbitration. Alexander Little worked for Auto Stiegler, Inc., an automobile dealership in Los Angeles County, California, eventually becoming the service manager. While employed, Little signed an arbitration agreement that required the submission of all employment-related disputes to arbitration. The agreement also provided that any award more than $50,000 could be appealed to a second arbitrator. Little was later demoted and terminated. Alleging that these actions were in retaliation for investigating and reporting warranty fraud and thus were in violation of public policy, Little filed a suit in a California state court against Auto Stiegler. The defendant filed a motion with the court to compel arbitration. Little responded that the arbitration agreement should not be enforced in part because the appeal provision was unfairly one sided. Is this provision enforceable? Should the court grant Auto Stiegler's motion? Why or why not? [*Little v. Auto Stiegler, Inc.*, 29 Cal.4th 1064, 63 P.3d 979, 130 Cal.Rptr.2d 892 (2003)]

3–7. CASE PROBLEM WITH SAMPLE ANSWER

Licensed real estate brokers in Colorado who belong to the Denver Metropolitan Commercial Association of Realtors (DMCAR) agree, as a condition of membership, to submit all disputes about real estate transactions to binding arbitration in accordance with procedures of the National Association of Realtors. Some realtors challenged the arbitration agreement, contending it was invalid because the parties did not execute arbitration agreements with each other and because membership in DMCAR is voluntary, so it does not create a binding obligation to arbitration if a member resigns from the association. Would such a condition of membership be valid and binding on members in the event a dispute arose? [*Lane v. Urgitus,* 145 P.3d 672 (Colo.Sup.Ct. 2006)]

- **To view a sample answer for Problem 3–7, go to this book's Web site at academic.cengage.com/blaw/cross, select "Chapter 3," and click on "Case Problem with Sample Answer."**

3–8. Arbitration. Kathleen Lowden sued cellular phone company T-Mobile, claiming that its service agreements were not enforceable under Washington state law. Lowden sued to create a class action suit, contending her claims would extend to similarly affected customers. She contended that T-Mobile had improperly charged her fees beyond the advertised price of service and charged her for roaming calls that should not have been classified as roaming. T-Mobile moved to force arbitration in accord with the arbitration provision in the service agreement. The arbitration provision was clearly explained in the service agreement. The agreement also specified that no class action suit could be brought, so T-Mobile requested the court to dismiss the class action request. Was T-Mobile correct that Lowden's only course of action would be to file arbitration personally? [*Lowden v. T-Mobile USA, Inc.*, 512 F.3d 1213 (9th Cir. 2008)]

3–9. Arbitration. Thomas Baker and others who bought new homes from Osborne Development Corp. sued for multiple defects in the houses they purchased. When Osborne sold the homes, it paid for them to be in a new home warranty program administered by Home Buyers Warranty (HBW). When the company enrolled a home with HBW, it paid a fee and filled out a form that stated the following: "By signing below, you acknowledge that you . . . CONSENT TO THE TERMS OF THESE DOCUMENTS INCLUDING THE BINDING ARBITRATION PROVISION contained therein." HBW then issued warranty booklets to the new homeowners that stated: "Any and all claims, disputes and controversies by or between the Homeowner, the Builder, the Warranty Insurer and/or HBW . . . shall be submitted to arbitration." Would the new homeowners be bound by the arbitration agreement or could they sue the builder, Osborne, in court? [*Baker v. Osborne Development Corp.*, 159 Cal.App.4th 884, 71 Cal.Rptr.3d 854 (2008)]

3–10. A QUESTION OF ETHICS

*Nellie Lumpkin, who suffered from various illnesses, including dementia, was admitted to the Picayune Convalescent Center, a nursing home. Because of her mental condition, her daughter, Beverly McDaniel, filled out the admissions paperwork and signed the admissions agreement. It included a clause requiring parties to submit to arbitration any disputes that arose. After Lumpkin left the center two years later, she sued, through her husband, for negligent treatment and malpractice during her stay. The center moved to force the matter to arbitration. The trial court held that the arbitration agreement was not enforceable. The center appealed. [*Covenant Health & Rehabilitation of Picayune, LP v. Lumpkin, ___ *So.2d* ___ *(Miss. App. 2008)]*

(a) Should a dispute involving medical malpractice be forced into arbitration? This is a claim of negligent care, not a breach of a commercial contract. Is it ethical for medical facilities to impose such a requirement? Is there really any bargaining over such terms?

(b) Should a person with limited mental capacity be held to the arbitration clause agreed to by the next-of-kin who signed on behalf of that person?

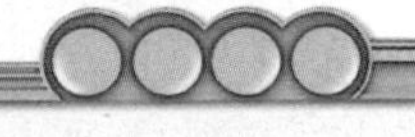

LAW ON THE WEB

For updated links to resources available on the Web, as well as a variety of other materials, visit this text's Web site at

academic.cengage.com/blaw/cross

For information on alternative dispute resolution, go to the American Arbitration Association's Web site at

www.adr.org

To learn more about online dispute resolution, go to the following Web sites:

www.mediate.com

cybersettle.com

SquareTrade.com

Legal Research Exercises on the Web

Go to **academic.cengage.com/blaw/cross**, the Web site that accompanies this text. Select "Chapter 3" and click on "Internet Exercises." There you will find the following Internet research exercises that you can perform to learn more about the topics covered in this chapter.

Internet Exercise 3–1: Legal Perspective
Alternative Dispute Resolution

Internet Exercise 3–2: Management Perspective
Resolve a Dispute Online

CHAPTER 4

Ethics and Business Decision Making

All of the following businesspersons have been in the news recently:

- Dennis Kozlowski (former chairman and chief executive officer of Tyco International).
- Mark H. Swartz (former chief financial officer of Tyco International).
- Jeffrey Skilling (former chief executive officer of Enron Corporation).
- Bernard Ebbers (former chief executive officer of WorldCom).

What do these individuals have in common? They are all in prison, and some may stay there until they die. They were all convicted of various crimes ranging from overseeing revenue exaggeration in order to increase stock prices to personal use of millions of dollars of public company funds. Not only did they break the law, but they also clearly violated even the minimum ethical principles that a civil society expects to be followed. Other officers and directors of the companies mentioned in the preceding list cost shareholders billions of dollars. In the case of those companies that had to enter bankruptcy, such as Enron Corporation, tens of thousands of employees lost their jobs.

Acting ethically in a business context is not child's play; it can mean billions of dollars—up or down—for corporations, shareholders, and employees. In the wake of the recent scandals, Congress attempted to prevent similar unethical business behavior in the future by passing stricter legislation in the form of the Sarbanes-Oxley Act of 2002, which will be explained in detail in Chapter 28. This act generally imposed more reporting requirements on corporations in an effort to deter unethical behavior and encourage accountability.

Business Ethics

As you might imagine, business ethics is derived from the concept of ethics. **Ethics** can be defined as the study of what constitutes right or wrong behavior. It is a branch of philosophy focusing on morality and the way moral principles are derived. Ethics has to do with the fairness, justness, rightness, or wrongness of an action.

What Is Business Ethics?

Business ethics focuses on what is right and wrong behavior in the business world. It has to do with how businesses apply moral and ethical principles to situations that arise in the workplace. Because business decision makers must often address more complex ethical issues in the workplace than they face in their personal lives, business ethics is more complicated than personal ethics.

Why Is Business Ethics Important?

For an answer to the question of why business ethics is so important, reread the list at the beginning of this chapter. All of the individuals who are sitting behind bars could have avoided their fates. Had they engaged in ethical decision making throughout their business careers, they would never have followed their different paths to criminal behavior. The corporations, shareholders, and employees who suffered because of those individuals' unethical and criminal behavior certainly paid a high price. Thus, an in-depth understanding of business ethics is important to the long-run viability of any corporation today. It is also important to the well-being of individual officers and directors and to the firm's employees. Finally, unethical corporate decision making can negatively affect suppliers, consumers, the community, and society as a whole.

At the end of every unit in this book, you will be exposed to a series of ethical issues in features called *Focus on Ethics.* In each of these unit-ending features, we expand on the concepts of business ethics that we present in this chapter.

Common Reasons Why Ethical Problems Occur

Not that many years ago, the popular painkiller Vioxx was recalled because its long-term use increased the risk of heart attack and stroke. Little by little, evidence surfaced that the drug's maker, Merck & Company, knew about these dangers yet allowed Vioxx to remain on the market. Merck's failure to recall the drug earlier could potentially have adversely affected the health of thousands of patients. In addition, Merck has undergone investigations by both Congress and the U.S. Department of Justice. Merck was facing thousands of lawsuits, years of litigation, and millions of dollars in attorneys' fees and settlements when it agreed, in November 2007, to settle all outstanding cases concerning Vioxx for $4.85 billion. How did a major corporation manage to make so many missteps? The answer is simply that certain officers and employees of Merck felt that it was not necessary to reveal the results of studies that might have decreased sales of Vioxx.

In other words, the common thread among the ethical problems that occur in business is the desire to increase sales (or not lose them), thereby increasing profits and, for the corporation, increasing market value. In most situations, though, ethically wrong behavior by a corporation turns out to be costly to everyone concerned. Just ask the shareholders of Merck (and, of course, Enron, WorldCom, and Tyco).

Short-Run Profit Maximization Some people argue that a corporation's only goal should be profit maximization, which will be reflected in a higher market value. When all firms strictly adhere to the goal of profit maximization, resources tend to flow to where they are most highly valued by society. Ultimately, profit maximization, in theory, leads to the most efficient allocation of scarce resources.

Corporate executives and employees have to distinguish, though, between *short-run* and *long-run* profit maximization. In the short run, the employees of Merck & Company may have increased profits because of the continuing sales of Vioxx. In the long run, though, because of lawsuits, large settlements, and bad publicity, profits have suffered. Thus, business ethics is consistent only with long-run profit maximization.

Determining Society's Rules—The Role of Corporate Influence Another possible cause of bad business ethics has to do with corporations' role in influencing the law. Corporations may use lobbyists to persuade government agencies not to institute new regulations that would increase the corporations' costs and reduce their profits. Once regulatory rules are promulgated, corporations may undertake actions to reduce their impact. One way to do this is to make it known that members of regulatory agencies will always have jobs waiting for them when they leave the agencies. This revolving door, as it is commonly called, has existed as long as there have been regulatory agencies at the state and federal levels of government.

The Importance of Ethical Leadership

Talking about ethical business decision making is meaningless if management does not set standards. Furthermore, managers must apply the same standards to themselves as they do to the employees of the company.

Attitude of Top Management One of the most important ways to create and maintain an ethical workplace is for top management to demonstrate its commitment to ethical decision making. A manager who is not totally committed to an ethical workplace rarely succeeds in creating one. Management's behavior, more than anything else, sets the ethical tone of a firm. Employees take their cues from management. For example, an employee who observes a manager cheating on her expense account quickly learns that such behavior is acceptable.

Managers who set unrealistic production or sales goals increase the probability that employees will act unethically. If a sales quota can be met only through high-pressure, unethical sales tactics, employees will try to act "in the best interest of the company" and will continue to behave unethically.

A manager who looks the other way when she or he knows about an employee's unethical behavior also sets an example—one indicating that ethical transgressions will be accepted. Managers have found that discharging even one employee for ethical reasons has a tremendous impact as a deterrent to unethical behavior in the workplace.

Behavior of Owners and Managers Business owners and managers sometimes take more active roles in fostering unethical and illegal conduct. This may indicate to their co-owners, co-managers, employees, and others that unethical business behavior will be tolerated. The following case illustrates how business owners' misbehavior can have negative consequences for themselves and their business. Not only can a court sanction the business owners and managers, but it can also issue an injunction that prevents them from engaging in similar patterns of conduct in the future.

EXTENDED CASE 4.1 Baum v. Blue Moon Ventures, LLC

United States Court of Appeals, Fifth Circuit, 2008. 513 F.3d 181.

***DeMOSS*, Circuit Judge:**

* * * *

Douglas Baum purports to run an asset recovery business. He researches various unclaimed funds, tries to locate the rightful owner, and then gets paid either with a finder's fee or by taking an assignment [a right to payment of some or all of the funds]. * * * Douglas Baum acts in concert with his brother, Brian Baum, and his father, Sheldon Baum ("the Baums").

In September 2002, the Baums [became involved in] a federal district court case * * * by recruiting investors—through misrepresentation—to sue a receiver [a court-appointed person who oversees a business firm's affairs], the receiver's attorney, other investors, and those investors' attorneys. The district court * * * determined that the Baums' pleadings were "gratuitous, malicious attacks with legal propositions that were wholly disconnected from the facts of the defendants' behavior." The district court admonished the Baums for wrongfully interfering in the case, wrongfully holding themselves out to be attorneys licensed to practice in Texas, lying to the parties and the court, and for generally abusing the judicial system. The district court stated:

> This case is an example of guerilla warfare through litigation. The Baums brought this suit to satisfy their illusion of hidden funds or to extort deals for their other clients. These claims were fraudulent. Once instituted, the Baums maintained them with singular ineptitude. When asked to explain their case—or anything else—Brian and Sheldon Baum did not tell the truth.
>
> The Baums have wasted the time and money of the defendants and the scarce resources that the taxpayers entrust to the judiciary. They have flouted the authority of this court—an authority they invoked. They have no concept of the purpose and function of the courts.

The district court sanctioned both Brian and Sheldon Baum to ten days in jail and ordered them to pay $100,000 in attorney's fees to the defendants. The court also issued a permanent * * * injunction against all three Baums [to prohibit them from filing claims related to the same case in Texas state courts without the permission of Judge Lynn Hughes, the district court judge].

* * * *

* * * In June 2005, the Baums entered an appearance in another bankruptcy case [a proceeding to ensure equitable treatment to creditors competing for a debtor's assets]. * * * Danny Hilal owned and operated several limited liability companies, including Appellee, Blue Moon Ventures, L.L.C. Blue Moon's primary business was purchasing real property at foreclosure sales and leasing those properties to residential tenants.

Sheldon Baum claimed to be a * * * creditor in the Hilal case, but he would not identify his claim. Brian Baum was again misleading the parties and the court as to being a licensed attorney in Texas, and Douglas Baum participated in the scheme by posting a fake notice [that the Internal Revenue Service might foreclose on Hilal's property to collect unpaid taxes].

* * * *

* * * [The bankruptcy court concluded that this was] a continuation of a pattern of conduct identified by [the district court that was] materially misleading to creditors and parties in interest in this case. * * * [The bankruptcy court forwarded a memo on the case to the district court that had imposed the sanctions on the Baums.]

* * * *

CASE 4.1 CONTINUED

The [district] court conducted two three-hour hearings in which the Baums all testified, as well as counsel for the Appellees (collectively referred to as "Blue Moon"). The court concluded that the Baums had continued in their abusive * * * practices, and thus a modification of the * * * injunction was necessary. [The court expanded the injunction to include the filing of any claim in any federal or state court or agency in Texas.]

Douglas refused to agree to any modification of the * * * injunction on the grounds that it would impede his business. * * * Douglas Baum filed a timely notice of appeal [to the U.S. Court of Appeals for the Fifth Circuit].

* * * *

* * * Douglas Baum argues that the district court lacked jurisdiction to * * * modify the pre-filing injunction. We disagree.

A district court has jurisdiction to impose a pre-filing injunction to deter vexatious [intended to annoy], abusive, and harassing litigation.

* * * *

* * * *Federal courts have both the inherent power and the constitutional obligation to protect their jurisdiction from conduct [that] impairs their ability to carry out [their] functions.* If such power did not exist, or if its exercise were somehow dependent upon the actions of another branch of government or upon the entitlement of a private party to injunctive relief, the independence and constitutional role of [the] courts would be endangered. Because the district court has jurisdiction to * * * impose a pre-filing injunction to deter vexatious filings, it also has jurisdiction to * * * modify an existing permanent injunction to accomplish the same goal. [Emphasis added.]

* * * *

* * * Modification of an injunction is appropriate when the legal or factual circumstances justifying the injunction have changed.

Federal courts have the power to enjoin [prevent] plaintiffs from future filings when those plaintiffs consistently abuse the court system and harass their opponents. * * * [Emphasis added.]

* * * *

The district court could consider Baum's conduct in the state court proceedings in determining whether his conduct before the bankruptcy court was undertaken in bad faith or for an improper motive. Limiting the injunction to any particular defendants did not stop Baum from repeating his pattern of abusive litigation practices; therefore, the district court did not abuse its discretion in determining that a broader injunction is necessary to protect both the court and future parties.

* * * *

* * * Baum argues that the district court abused its discretion in extending the injunction to prohibit Baum from filing any claims in state courts or agencies.

* * * *

* * * A district court's pre-filing injunction may extend to filings in lower federal courts within the circuit that the issuing court is located, * * * a district court's pre-filing injunction may not extend to filings in any federal appellate court, and * * * a district court's pre-filing injunction may not extend to filings in any state court. Based on the facts of this case, we find that the district court abused its discretion in extending the pre-filing injunction to filings in state courts, state agencies, and this Court. * * * Those courts or agencies are capable of taking appropriate action on their own. We uphold those provisions of the pre-filing injunction that prevent Douglas Baum from filing claims in federal bankruptcy courts, federal district courts, and federal agencies in the state of Texas without the express written permission of Judge Hughes.

QUESTIONS

1. Would there by any way in which the Baums could have operated their business ethically? Explain.
2. Are there situations in which a business owner's conduct would be more reprehensible than the Baums' behavior in this case? Explain.

Approaches to Ethical Reasoning

Each individual, when faced with a particular ethical dilemma, engages in **ethical reasoning**—that is, a reasoning process in which the individual examines the situation at hand in light of his or her moral convictions or ethical standards. Businesspersons do likewise when making decisions with ethical implications.

How do business decision makers decide whether a given action is the "right" one for their firms? What ethical standards should be applied? Broadly speaking, ethical reasoning relating to business traditionally has been characterized by two fundamental approaches. One approach defines ethical behavior in terms of duty, which also implies certain rights. The other approach determines what is ethical in terms of the consequences, or outcome, of any given action. We examine each of these approaches here.

In addition to the two basic ethical approaches, a few theories have been developed that specifically address the social responsibility of corporations. Because these theories also influence today's business decision makers, we conclude this section with a short discussion of the different views of corporate social responsibility.

Duty-Based Ethics

Duty-based ethical standards often are derived from revealed truths, such as religious precepts. They can also be derived through philosophical reasoning.

Religious Ethical Standards In the Judeo-Christian tradition, which is the dominant religious tradition in the United States, the Ten Commandments of the Old Testament establish fundamental rules for moral action. Other religions have their own sources of revealed truth. Religious rules generally are absolute with respect to the behavior of their adherents. For example, the commandment "Thou shalt not steal" is an absolute mandate for a person who believes that the Ten Commandments reflect revealed truth. Even a benevolent motive for stealing (such as Robin Hood's) cannot justify the act because the act itself is inherently immoral and thus wrong.

Kantian Ethics Duty-based ethical standards may also be derived solely from philosophical reasoning. The German philosopher Immanuel Kant (1724–1804), for example, identified some general guiding principles for moral behavior based on what he believed to be the fundamental nature of human beings. Kant believed that human beings are qualitatively different from other physical objects and are endowed with moral integrity and the capacity to reason and conduct their affairs rationally. Therefore, a person's thoughts and actions should be respected. When human beings are treated merely as a means to an end, they are being treated as the equivalent of objects and are being denied their basic humanity.

A central theme in Kantian ethics is that individuals should evaluate their actions in light of the consequences that would follow if *everyone* in society acted in the same way. This **categorical imperative** can be applied to any action. For example, suppose that you are deciding whether to cheat on an examination. If you have adopted Kant's categorical imperative, you will decide *not* to cheat because if everyone cheated, the examination (and the entire education system) would be meaningless.

The Principle of Rights Because a duty cannot exist without a corresponding right, duty-based ethical standards imply that human beings have basic rights. The principle that human beings have certain fundamental rights (to life, freedom, and the pursuit of happiness, for example) is deeply embedded in Western culture. As discussed in Chapter 1, the natural law tradition embraces the concept that certain actions (such as killing another person) are morally wrong because they are contrary to nature (the natural desire to continue living). Those who adhere to this **principle of rights,** or "rights theory," believe that a key factor in determining whether a business decision is ethical is how that decision affects the rights of others. These others include the firm's owners, its employees, the consumers of its products or services, its suppliers, the community in which it does business, and society as a whole.

A potential dilemma for those who support rights theory, however, is that they may disagree on which rights are most important. When considering all those affected by a business decision, for example, how much weight should be given to employees relative to shareholders, customers relative to the community, or employees relative to society as a whole?

In general, rights theorists believe that whichever right is stronger in a particular circumstance takes precedence. Suppose that a firm can either keep a plant open, saving the jobs of twelve workers, or shut the plant down and avoid contaminating a river with pollutants that would endanger the health of thousands of people. In this situation, a rights theorist can easily choose which group to favor. (Not all choices are so clear-cut, however.)

Outcome-Based Ethics: Utilitarianism

"The greatest good for the greatest number" is a paraphrase of the major premise of the utilitarian approach to ethics. **Utilitarianism** is a philosophical theory developed by Jeremy Bentham (1748–1832) and modified by John Stuart Mill (1806–1873)—both British philosophers. In contrast to duty-based ethics, utilitarianism is outcome oriented. It focuses on the consequences of an action, not on the nature of the action itself or on any set of preestablished moral values or religious beliefs.

Under a utilitarian model of ethics, an action is morally correct, or "right," when, among the people it affects, it produces the greatest amount of good for the greatest number. When an action affects the majority adversely, it is morally wrong. Applying the utilitarian theory thus requires (1) a determination of which individuals will be affected by the action in question; (2) a **cost-benefit analysis,** which involves an assessment of the negative and positive effects of alternative actions on these individuals; and (3) a choice among alternative actions that will produce maximum societal utility (the greatest positive net benefits for the greatest number of individuals).

Corporate Social Responsibility

For many years, groups concerned with civil rights, employee safety and welfare, consumer protection, environmental preservation, and other causes have pressured corporate America to behave in a responsible manner with respect to these causes. Thus was born the concept of **corporate social responsibility**—the idea that those who run corporations can and should act ethically and be accountable to society for their actions. Just what constitutes corporate social responsibility has been debated for some time, however, and there are a number of different theories today.

Stakeholder Approach One view of corporate social responsibility stresses that corporations have a duty not just to shareholders, but also to other groups affected by corporate decisions ("stakeholders"). Under this approach, a corporation would consider the impact of its decision on the firm's employees, customers, creditors, suppliers, and the community in which the corporation operates. The reasoning behind this "stakeholder view" is that in some circumstances, one or more of these other groups may have a greater stake in company decisions than the shareholders do. Although this may be true, it is often difficult to decide which group's interests should receive greater weight if the interests conflict (see the discussion of the principle of rights on the facing page).

Corporate Citizenship Another theory of social responsibility argues that corporations should behave as good citizens by promoting goals that society deems worthwhile and taking positive steps toward solving social problems. The idea is that because business controls so much of the wealth and power of this country, business in turn has a responsibility to society to use that wealth and power in socially beneficial ways. Under a corporate citizenship view, companies are judged on how much they donate to social causes, as well as how they conduct their operations with respect to employment discrimination, human rights, environmental concerns, and similar issues.

In the following case, a corporation's board of directors did not seem to doubt the priority of the firm's responsibilities. Focused solely on the profits delivered into the hands of the shareholders, the board failed to check the actions of the firm's chief executive officer (CEO) and, in fact, appeared to condone the CEO's misconduct. If the board had applied a different set of priorities, the shareholders might have been in a better financial position, however. A regulatory agency soon found the situation "troubling" and imposed a restriction on the firm. The board protested. The protest reminded the court of "the old saw about the child who murders his parents and then asks for mercy because he is an orphan."

CASE 4.2 Fog Cutter Capital Group, Inc. v. Securities and Exchange Commission

United States Court of Appeals, District of Columbia Circuit, 2007. 474 F.3d 822.

• **Background and Facts** The National Association of Securities Dealers (NASD) operates the Nasdaq, an electronic securities exchange, on which Fog Cutter Capital Group was listed.[a] Andrew

a. Securities (stocks and bonds) can be bought and sold through national exchanges. Whether a security is listed on an exchange is subject to the discretion of the organization that operates it. The Securities and Exchange Commission oversees the securities exchanges (see Chapter 28).

CASE CONTINUES

CASE 4.2 CONTINUED

Wiederhorn had founded Fog Cutter in 1997 to manage a restaurant chain and make other investments. With family members, Wiederhorn controlled more than 50 percent of Fog Cutter's stock. The firm agreed that if Wiederhorn was terminated "for cause," he was entitled only to his salary through the date of termination. If terminated "without cause," he would be owed three times his $350,000 annual salary, three times his largest annual bonus from the previous three years, and any unpaid salary and bonus. "Cause" included the conviction of a felony. In 2001, Wiederhorn became the target of an investigation into the collapse of Capital Consultants, LLC. Fog Cutter then redefined "cause" in his termination agreement to cover only a felony involving Fog Cutter. In June 2004, Wiederhorn agreed to plead guilty to two felonies, serve eighteen months in prison, pay a $25,000 fine, and pay $2 million to Capital Consultants. The day before he entered his plea, Fog Cutter agreed that while he was in prison, he would keep his title, responsibilities, salary, bonuses, and other benefits. It also agreed to a $2 million "leave of absence payment." In July, the NASD delisted Fog Cutter from the Nasdaq. Fog Cutter appealed this decision to the Securities and Exchange Commission (SEC), which dismissed the appeal. Fog Cutter petitioned the U.S. Court of Appeals for the District of Columbia Circuit for review.

IN THE LANGUAGE OF THE COURT
***RANDOLPH,* Circuit Judge.**

* * * *

Fog Cutter's main complaint is that the Commission failed to take into account the company's sound business reasons for acting as it did. The decision to enter into the leave-of-absence agreement was, Fog Cutter argues, in the best interest of its shareholders. The company tells us that Wiederhorn's continuing commitment to the company and his return to an active role in the company after his incarceration were essential to preserving Fog Cutter's core business units.

* * * *

* * * Fog Cutter made a deal with Wiederhorn that cost the company $4.75 million in a year in which it reported a $3.93 million net loss. We know as well that Fog Cutter handed Wiederhorn a $2 million bonus right before he went off to prison, a bonus stemming directly from the consequences of Wiederhorn's criminal activity.

* * * *

Here there was ample evidence supporting the NASD's grounds for taking action against Fog Cutter: Wiederhorn's guilty plea, the leave-of-absence deal and its cost to the company, the Board's determination that Wiederhorn should retain his positions with Fog Cutter, and the concern that Wiederhorn would continue to exert influence on company affairs even while he was in prison. *The decision was in accordance with NASD rules giving the organization broad discretion to determine whether the public interest requires delisting securities in light of events at a company. That rule is obviously consistent with the [law], and NASD's decision did not burden competition.* [Emphasis added.]

Fog Cutter claims that it had to pay Wiederhorn and retain him because if it fired him in light of his guilty plea, it would have owed him $6 million. This scarcely speaks well for the company's case. The potential obligation is a result of an amendment the Board granted Wiederhorn in 2003 while he was under investigation. * * * Before the amendment to Wiederhorn's employment agreement in 2003, termination "for cause" included the conviction of any felony other than a traffic offense. In the 2003 amendment, the relevant provision allowed the Board to terminate Wiederhorn "for cause" upon conviction of a felony involving Fog Cutter. The Board had known about the investigation of Wiederhorn in connection with Capital Consultants for more than two years when it agreed to this amendment.

Fog Cutter thinks NASD's action was "unfair." But it was the company that bowed to Wiederhorn's demand for an amendment to his employment agreement, knowing full well that it was dramatically increasing the cost of firing him. Now it argues that terminating Wiederhorn would have been too expensive. One is reminded of the old saw about the child who murders his parents and then asks for mercy because he is an orphan. The makeup of Fog Cutter's Board was virtually unchanged between the time it amended the employment agreement and entered into the leave-of-absence agreement. It was, to say the least, not arbitrary or capricious for the Commission to find that Wiederhorn exercised thorough control over the Board, and to find this troubling. We agree that the Board provided little or no check on Wiederhorn's conduct, and that the Board's actions only aggravated the concerns Wiederhorn's conviction and imprisonment raised.

That Fog Cutter did not itself violate the [law] and that it disclosed the relevant events does not demonstrate any error in the delisting decision. The NASD's rules state that it may apply criteria

CASE 4.2 CONTINUED more stringent than the minimum [legal] standards for listing. Fog Cutter's disclosure of its arrangements with Wiederhorn did not change the nature of those arrangements, which is what led the NASD to find that the company's actions were contrary to the public interest and a threat to public confidence in the Nasdaq exchange.

• **Decision and Remedy** *The U.S. Court of Appeals for the District of Columbia Circuit denied Fog Cutter's petition for review of the SEC's decision. The NASD was concerned with "the integrity and the public's perception of the Nasdaq exchange" in light of Wiederhorn's legal troubles and the Fog Cutter board's acquiescence to his demands. The SEC "amply supported these concerns and was well within its authority to dismiss Fog Cutter's" appeal.*

• **The Ethical Dimension** *Should more consideration have been given to the fact that Fog Cutter was not convicted of a violation of the law? Why or why not?*

• **The Global Dimension** *What does the decision in this case suggest to foreign investors who may be considering investments in securities listed on U.S. exchanges?*

Creating Ethical Codes of Conduct

One of the most effective ways to set a tone of ethical behavior within an organization is to create an ethical code of conduct. A well-written code of ethics explicitly states a company's ethical priorities and demonstrates the company's commitment to ethical behavior. The code should set forth guidelines for ethical conduct, establish procedures that employees can follow if they have questions or complaints, and inform employees why these ethics policies are important to the company. A well-written code might also provide appropriate examples to clarify what the company considers to be acceptable and unacceptable conduct.

Providing Ethics Training to Employees

For an ethical code to be effective, its provisions must be clearly communicated to employees. Most large companies have implemented ethics training programs in which management discusses with employees on a face-to-face basis the firm's policies and the importance of ethical conduct. Some firms hold periodic ethics seminars during which employees can openly discuss any ethical problems that they may be experiencing and learn how the firm's ethical policies apply to those specific problems. Smaller firms should also offer some form of ethics training to employees, because this is one factor that courts will consider if the firm is later accused of an ethics violation.

The Sarbanes-Oxley Act and Web-Based Reporting Systems The Sarbanes-Oxley Act of 2002[1] requires that companies set up confidential systems so that employees and others can "raise red flags" about suspected illegal or unethical auditing and accounting practices. The act required publicly traded companies to have such systems in place by April 2003.

Some companies have created online reporting systems to accomplish this goal. In one such system, employees can click on an icon on their computers that anonymously links them with Ethicspoint, an organization based in Portland, Oregon. Through Ethicspoint, employees can report suspicious accounting practices, sexual harassment, and other possibly unethical behavior. Ethicspoint, in turn, alerts management personnel or the audit committee at the designated company to the potential problem. Those who have used the system say that it is less inhibiting than calling a company's toll-free number.

SECTION 3

How the Law Influences Business Ethics

Although business ethics and the law are closely related, they are not always identical. Here, we examine some situations in which what is legal and what is ethical may not be the same.

The Moral Minimum

Compliance with the law is normally regarded as the **moral minimum**—the minimum acceptable standard for ethical business behavior. In many corporate scandals, had most of the businesspersons involved simply followed the law, they would not have gotten into trouble. Note, though, that in the

1. Public Company Accounting Reform and Investor Protection Act (Sarbanes-Oxley Act of 2002), Pub. L. No. 107-204, 116 Stat. 745 (July 30, 2002). This act will be discussed in Chapter 28.

interest of preserving personal freedom, as well as for practical reasons, the law does not—and cannot—codify all ethical requirements. As they make business decisions, businesspersons must remember that just because an action is legal does not necessarily make it ethical. Look at Exhibit 4–1. Here, you see that there is an intersection between what is ethical and what is legal. Businesspersons should attempt to operate in the area where what is legal and what is ethical intersect.

Excessive Executive Pay As just mentioned, business behavior that is legal may still be unethical. Consider executive pay. There is no law that specifies what public corporations can pay their officers. Consequently, "executive-pay scandals" do not have to do with executives breaking the law. Rather, such scandals have to do with the ethical underpinnings of executive-pay scales that can exceed millions of dollars. Such high pay for executives may appear unethical when their companies are not making very high profits (or are even suffering losses) and their share prices are falling.

Even this subject, though, does not lend itself to a black-and-white ethical analysis. As with many other things, there is a market for executives that operates according to supply and demand. Sometimes, corporate boards decide to offer executives very large compensation packages in order either to entice them to come to work for the company or to keep them from leaving for another corporation. There is no simple formula for determining the ethical level of compensation for a given executive in a given company. If a law were passed that limited executive compensation to, say, twenty times the salary of the lowest-paid worker in the company, there would be fewer individuals willing to undergo the stress and long hours associated with running major companies.

EXHIBIT 4–1 • The Intersection of What Is Legal and What Is Ethical

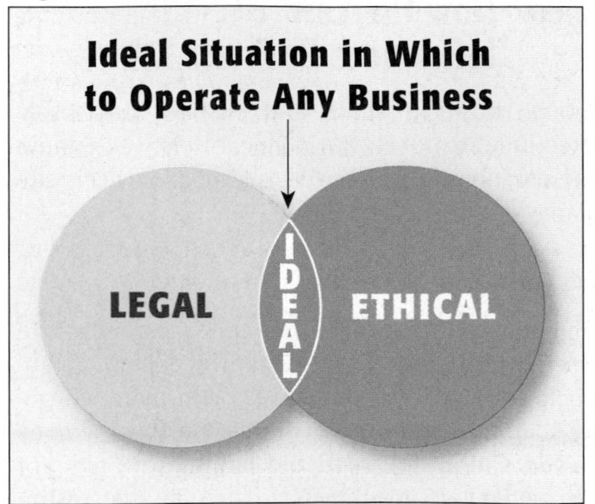

Determining the Legality of a Given Action It may seem that determining the legality of a given action should be simple. Either something is legal or it is not. In fact, one of the major challenges businesspersons face is that the legality of a particular action is not always clear. In part, this is because there are so many laws regulating business that it is increasingly possible to violate one of them without realizing it. The law also contains numerous "gray areas," making it difficult to predict with certainty how a court will apply a given law to a particular action.

Determining whether a planned action is legal thus requires that decision makers keep abreast of the law. Normally, large business firms have attorneys on their staffs to assist them in making key decisions. Small firms must also seek legal advice before making important business decisions because the consequences of just one violation of a regulatory rule may be costly.

Ignorance of the law will not excuse a business owner or manager from liability for violating a statute or regulation. In one case, for example, the court imposed criminal fines, as well as imprisonment, on a company's supervisory employee for violating a federal environmental act—even though the employee was completely unaware of what was required under the provisions of that act.[2]

The Law Cannot Control All Business Behavior

Congress, the regulatory agencies, and state and local governments do not have perfect knowledge. Often they only discover the negative impact of corporate activities after the fact. The same can be true of corporate executives. They do not always know the full impact of their actions. When asbestos was used for insulation, for example, the corporations that supplied it did not know that it was capable of causing a rare type of cancer.

At other times, though, the law is not ambiguous. Nevertheless, it may still be unable to control business behavior—at least initially.

2. *United States v. Hanousek*, 176 F.3d 1116 (9th Cir. 1999).

Breaking the Law—Backdating Stock Options Stock options are a device that potentially rewards hard work. Publicly held corporations offer stock options to employees at the current price of the company's stock on the day that the options are granted. If at a later time the market price of the stock has gone up, an employee can exercise the stock options and reap the difference between the price of the options and the current market price.

In 2006 and 2007, it was revealed that a number of large corporations had backdated stock options. If stock options are granted and the price of the company's stock subsequently falls or does not rise very much, the value of the stock options is essentially zero. One way around this problem is to go back and change the date on which the stock options were granted to the employee. In other words, the date of the stock options is simply moved back to a day when the stock had a lower price than it has currently, thereby making the options valuable again.

Backdating is illegal if companies do not follow proper accounting procedures and SEC disclosure rules. It is also illegal if the company misrepresents the authorization for, or falsifies records relating to, the backdating. For example, in February 2007, the former chief executive officer of Brocade Communications Systems, Inc., Gregory L. Reyes, Jr., was sentenced to twenty-one months in prison, plus a $15 million fine for "tampering" with records of stock option grants. At least a dozen other business executives faced similar charges.

The backdating scandal is another example of unethical behavior resulting in long-run profit reduction. As of 2008, at least 252 public companies had disclosed that they had undertaken internal investigations to discover if backdating had occurred without following proper procedures. The companies involved face more than 125 shareholder lawsuits and as many SEC investigations, plus fifty-eight Department of Justice investigations and even six criminal cases.

Misleading Regulators—The Case of OxyContin In 1996, the pharmaceutical company Purdue Pharma, LP, started marketing a "wonder" narcotic painkiller called OxyContin. This powerful, long-lasting drug provides pain relief for twelve hours. Just a few years after its introduction, Purdue Pharma's annual sales of the drug reached $1 billion.

The company's executives initially contended that OxyContin, because of its time-release formulation, posed no risk for serious abuse or addiction. Quickly, though, experienced drug abusers and even teenagers discovered that chewing on an OxyContin tablet or crushing one and snorting the powder produced a powerful high, comparable to that of heroin. By 2000, large parts of the United States were experiencing increases in addiction and crime related to OxyContin.

In reality, the company and three of its executives had fraudulently marketed OxyContin for over six years as a drug unlikely to lead to abuse. Internal company documents showed that even before OxyContin was marketed, executives recognized that if physicians knew that the drug could be abused and become addictive, they would be less likely to prescribe it. Consequently, the company simply kept the information secret.

On May 10, 2007, Purdue Pharma and three former executives pleaded guilty to criminal charges that they had misled regulators, patients, and physicians about OxyContin's risks of addiction. Purdue Pharma agreed to pay $600 million in fines and other payments. The three ex-executives agreed to pay $34.5 million in fines. Once again, company executives engaged in unethical reasoning because they wanted to maximize profits in the short run, rather than engaging in behavior that would lead to profit maximization in the long run.

"Gray Areas" in the Law

In many situations, business firms can predict with a fair amount of certainty whether a given action is legal. For instance, firing an employee solely because of that person's race or gender clearly violates federal laws prohibiting employment discrimination. In some situations, though, the legality of a particular action may be less clear.

Suppose that a firm decides to launch a new advertising campaign. How far can the firm go in making claims for its products or services? Federal and state laws prohibit firms from engaging in "deceptive advertising." At the federal level, the test for deceptive advertising normally used by the Federal Trade Commission is whether an advertising claim would deceive a "reasonable consumer."[3] At what point, though, would a reasonable consumer be deceived by a particular ad?

In addition, many rules of law require a court to determine what is "foreseeable" or "reasonable" in a particular situation. Because a business has no way of

3. See Chapter 23 for a discussion of the Federal Trade Commission's role in regulating deceptive trade practices, including misleading advertising.

predicting how a specific court will decide these issues, decision makers need to proceed with caution and evaluate an action and its consequences from an ethical perspective. The same problem often occurs in cases involving the Internet because it is often unclear how a court will apply existing laws in the context of cyberspace. Generally, if a company can demonstrate that it acted in good faith and responsibly in the circumstances, it has a better chance of successfully defending its action in court or before an administrative law judge.

The following case shows that businesses and their customers have different expectations with respect to the standard of care regarding the handling of personal information. The case also illustrates that the legal standards in this area may be inconsistent and vague.

CASE 4.3 Guin v. Brazos Higher Education Service Corp.

United States District Court, District of Minnesota, 2006. __ F.Supp.2d __.

● **Background and Facts** Brazos Higher Education Service Corporation, which is based in Waco, Texas, makes and services student loans. Brazos issued a laptop computer to its employee John Wright, who worked from an office in his home in Silver Spring, Maryland, analyzing loan information. Wright used the laptop to store borrowers' personal information. In September 2004, Wright's home was burglarized and the laptop was stolen. Based on Federal Trade Commission (FTC) guidelines and California state law (which requires notice to all resident borrowers), Brazos sent a letter to all of its 550,000 customers. The letter stated that "some personal information associated with your student loan, including your name, address, Social Security number and loan balance, may have been inappropriately accessed by [a] third party." The letter urged borrowers to place "a free 90-day security alert" on their credit bureau files and review FTC consumer assistance materials. Brazos set up a call center to answer further questions and track any reports of identity theft. Stacy Guin, a Brazos customer, filed a suit in a federal district court against Brazos, alleging negligence. Brazos filed a motion for summary judgment.

IN THE LANGUAGE OF THE COURT

KYLE, J. [Judge]

* * * *

* * * *Negligence [is] the failure to exercise due or reasonable care. In order to prevail on a claim for negligence, a plaintiff must prove [among other things] the existence of a duty of care [and] a breach of that duty* * * * . [Emphasis added.]

* * * *

Guin argues that the Gramm-Leach-Bliley Act (the "GLB Act") establishes a statutory-based duty for Brazos to protect the security and confidentiality of customers' nonpublic personal information. * * * Brazos concedes that the GLB Act applies to these circumstances and establishes a duty of care. The GLB Act was created "to protect against unauthorized access to or use of such records which could result in substantial harm or inconvenience to any customer [of a financial institution]." Under the GLB Act, a financial institution must comply with several objectives, including:

> Develop, implement, and maintain a comprehensive written information security program that is written in one or more readily accessible parts and contains administrative, technical, and physical safeguards that are appropriate to your size and complexity, the nature and scope of your activities, and the sensitivity of any customer information at issue * * * .

Guin argues that Brazos breached the duty imposed by the GLB Act by (1) "providing Wright with [personal information] that he did not need for the task at hand," (2) "permitting Wright to continue keeping [personal information] in an unattended, insecure personal residence," and (3) "allowing Wright to keep [personal information] on his laptop unencrypted."

The Court concludes that Guin has not presented sufficient evidence from which a fact finder could determine that Brazos failed to comply with the GLB Act. In September 2004, when Wright's home was burglarized and the laptop was stolen, Brazos had written security policies, current risk assessment reports, and proper safeguards for its customers' personal information as required by

CASE 4.3 CONTINUED

the GLB Act. Brazos authorized Wright to have access to customers' personal information because Wright needed the information to analyze loan portfolios * * * . Thus, his access to the personal information was within "the nature and scope of [Brazos's] activities." Furthermore, the GLB Act does not prohibit someone from working with sensitive data on a laptop computer in a home office. Despite Guin's persistent argument that any nonpublic personal information stored on a laptop computer should be encrypted, the GLB Act does not contain any such requirement. Accordingly, Guin has not presented any evidence showing that Brazos violated the GLB Act requirements.

- **Decision and Remedy** *The court granted the defendant's motion for summary judgment and dismissed the case. Brazos may have owed Guin a duty of care under the GLB Act, but neither Brazos nor Wright breached that duty. Wright had followed Brazos's written security procedures, which was all that the GLB Act required.*

- **What If the Facts Were Different?** *Suppose that Wright had not been a financial analyst and his duties for Brazos had not included reviewing confidential loan data. How might the opinion of the court have been different?*

- **The Ethical Dimension** *Do businesses have an ethical duty to use enhanced security measures to protect confidential customer information? Why or why not? Does the fact that Brazos allowed its employees to store customers' unencrypted personal information on a laptop outside the office violate any ethical duty?*

Section 4 Making Ethical Business Decisions

As Dean Krehmeyer, executive director of the Business Roundtable's Institute for Corporate Ethics, once said, "Evidence strongly suggests being ethical—doing the right thing—pays." Instilling ethical business decision making into the fabric of a business organization is no small task, even if ethics "pays." The job is to get people to understand that they have to think more broadly about how their decisions will affect employees, shareholders, customers, and even the community. Great companies, such as Enron and the accounting firm Arthur Andersen, were brought down by the unethical behavior of a few. A two-hundred-year-old British investment banking firm, Barings Bank, was destroyed by the actions of one employee and a few of his friends. Clearly, ensuring that all employees get on the ethical business decision-making "bandwagon" is crucial in today's fast-paced world.

The George S. May International Company has provided six basic guidelines to help corporate employees judge their actions. Each employee—no matter what his or her level in the organization—should evaluate his or her actions using the following six guidelines:

1. *The law.* Is the action you are considering legal? If you do not know the laws governing the action, then find out. Ignorance of the law is no excuse.
2. *Rules and procedures.* Are you following the internal rules and procedures that have already been laid out by your company? They have been developed to avoid problems. Is what you are planning to do consistent with your company's policies and procedures? If not, stop.
3. *Values.* Laws and internal company policies reinforce society's values. You might wish to ask yourself whether you are attempting to find a loophole in the law or in your company's policies. Next, you have to ask yourself whether you are following the "spirit" of the law as well as the letter of the law or the internal policy.
4. *Conscience.* If you have any feeling of guilt, let your conscience be your guide. Alternatively, ask yourself whether you would be happy to be interviewed by a national news magazine about the actions you are going to take.
5. *Promises.* Every business organization is based on trust. Your customers believe that your company will do what it is supposed to do. The same is true for your suppliers and employees. Will your actions live up to the commitments you have made to others, both inside the business and outside?

6. *Heroes.* We all have heroes who are role models for us. Is what you are planning on doing an action that your hero would take? If not, how would your hero act? That is how you should be acting.

Business Ethics on a Global Level

Given the various cultures and religions throughout the world, conflicts in ethics frequently arise between foreign and U.S. businesspersons. For example, in certain countries the consumption of alcohol and specific foods is forbidden for religious reasons. Under such circumstances, it would be thoughtless and imprudent for a U.S. businessperson to invite a local business contact out for a drink.

The role played by women in other countries may also present some difficult ethical problems for firms doing business internationally. Equal employment opportunity is a fundamental public policy in the United States, and Title VII of the Civil Rights Act of 1964 prohibits discrimination against women in the employment context (see Chapter 21). Some other countries, however, offer little protection for women against gender discrimination in the workplace, including sexual harassment.

We look here at how the employment practices that affect workers in other countries, particularly developing countries, have created some especially difficult ethical problems for U.S. sellers of goods manufactured in foreign nations. We also examine some of the ethical ramifications of laws prohibiting bribery and the expansion of ethics programs in the global community.

Monitoring the Employment Practices of Foreign Suppliers

Many U.S. businesses now contract with companies in developing nations to produce goods, such as shoes and clothing, because the wage rates in those nations are significantly lower than those in the United States. Yet what if a foreign company hires women and children at below-minimum-wage rates, for example, or requires its employees to work long hours in a workplace full of health hazards? What if the company's supervisors routinely engage in workplace conduct that is offensive to women?

Given today's global communications network, few companies can assume that their actions in other nations will go unnoticed by "corporate watch" groups that discover and publicize unethical corporate behavior. As a result, U.S. businesses today usually take steps to avoid such adverse publicity—either by refusing to deal with certain suppliers or by arranging to monitor their suppliers' workplaces to make sure that the employees are not being mistreated.

The Foreign Corrupt Practices Act

Another ethical problem in international business dealings has to do with the legitimacy of certain side payments to government officials. In the United States, the majority of contracts are formed within the private sector. In many foreign countries, however, government officials make the decisions on most major construction and manufacturing contracts because of extensive government regulation and control over trade and industry. Side payments to government officials in exchange for favorable business contracts are not unusual in such countries, nor are they considered to be unethical. In the past, U.S. corporations doing business in these nations largely followed the dictum, "When in Rome, do as the Romans do."

In the 1970s, however, the U.S. press uncovered a number of business scandals involving large side payments by U.S. corporations to foreign representatives for the purpose of securing advantageous international trade contracts. In response to this unethical behavior, in 1977 Congress passed the Foreign Corrupt Practices Act (FCPA), which prohibits U.S. businesspersons from bribing foreign officials to secure beneficial contracts. (For a discussion of how a German corporation ran afoul of Germany's antibribery laws, see this chapter's *Insight into the Global Environment* feature.)

Prohibition against the Bribery of Foreign Officials The first part of the FCPA applies to all U.S. companies and their directors, officers, shareholders, employees, and agents. This part prohibits the bribery of most officials of foreign governments if the purpose of the payment is to get the official to act in his or her official capacity to provide business opportunities.

The FCPA does not prohibit payment of substantial sums to minor officials whose duties are ministerial. These payments are often referred to as "grease," or facilitating payments. They are meant to accelerate the performance of administrative services that might otherwise be carried out at a slow pace. Thus, for example,

INSIGHT INTO THE GLOBAL ENVIRONMENT

Breach of Trust Issues Hit Major German Corporations

Whether you call it immoral, unethical, illegal, or a breach of trust, bribery by any name is wrong. In recent years, officers and managing directors at several major German corporations have been investigated, arrested, and fined for bribery. One German firm that has faced numerous charges is Siemens, a venerable corporation that was founded in 1847. Siemens built the first long-distance telegraph line in Europe from Berlin to Frankfurt in 1849. Today, the company, which its almost 500,000 workers like to call the House of Siemens, has operations in communications, radar, traffic control, and cell phones.

Corruption Charges Are Not New

When global competition intensified in the 1980s and 1990s, Siemens began to face fierce competition from multinational giants such as General Electric. To maintain the company's cash flow and sales dominance, some of Siemens managers started bribing potential clients—usually government agencies—to generate new business. In the early 1990s, the German government investigated Siemens's activities and convicted nine of the company's managers on bribery charges. The judge in the case wondered why the managers kept referring to the company as the "House of Siemens"—a name that, in the judge's view, implies "that the firm rises above the muck of ordinary business; it conveys a sense of moral exemption and entitlement." Of course, part of Siemens's problem may have been the somewhat ambiguous approach to bribery taken by German law. Bribes paid to foreign officials were tax deductible in Germany until 1999.

Unethical Actions Continue

Apparently, Siemens did not learn its lesson, for complaints about its behavior continued. In the early 2000s, Swiss authorities began an investigation that continued for a year and a half. The allegations of corruption did not trouble Heinrich von Pierer, Siemens's chair, however, or spur him to look into his managers' behavior. Instead, he stated simply, "I'm aware that our organization is hard to understand for outsiders. The job of board members is primarily strategic. Going over the books is the responsibility of others."

Several years later, the company finally disclosed that about $600 million in "suspicious transactions" (read "bribes") had been discovered. By 2007, von Pierer had resigned, and the chief executive officer decided not to ask for a new contract. In the meantime, a German court had convicted two former Siemens executives of bribery and fined the company about $50 million.

Once again, ambiguities in German law entered the case. One former Siemens executive told the court that he did indeed authorize millions of dollars of bribes to win contracts from an Italian electric company. He insisted, though, that he did not break any laws and that the payments were not illegal because German law only forbids payments to "civil servants." The executive contended that the payments he made to the Italian company's managers were made to representatives of a private-sector company, not to "civil servants." German prosecutors had to admit that the legal definition of what constitutes a civil servant allows room for interpretation.

Bribing the Union

Siemens executives may not have restricted their activities to bribing "civil servants" or private-sector managers. One Siemens executive, Johannes Feldmayer, has been arrested on a special type of bribery charge. He has been accused of bribing the head of a workers' organization, a type of independent labor union. Apparently, Siemens wanted a counterweight to IG Metall, the most powerful German union, and Feldmayer allegedly oversaw the transfer of some $45 million to the independent union to facilitate this. Earlier, another major German corporation, Volkswagen (VW), faced similar charges of making illegal payments to the head of its workers council. Peter Harz, formerly VW's head of labor relations, pleaded guilty to the charges and paid a fine of about $750,000.

CRITICAL THINKING

INSIGHT INTO CULTURE

Clearly, the corporate culture at Siemens, at least in the last few decades, did not distinguish among actions that were both ethical and legal, actions that were unethical but perhaps legal, and actions that were both unethical and illegal. What could top management at that company have done to instill a different corporate culture that would have resulted in a different outcome?

if a firm makes a payment to a minor official to speed up an import licensing process, the firm has not violated the FCPA. Generally, the act, as amended, permits payments to foreign officials if such payments are lawful within the foreign country. The act also does not prohibit payments to private foreign companies or other third parties unless the U.S. firm knows that the payments will be passed on to a foreign government in violation of the FCPA.

Accounting Requirements In the past, bribes were often concealed in corporate financial records. Thus, the second part of the FCPA is directed toward accountants. All companies must keep detailed records that "accurately and fairly" reflect their financial activities. In addition, all companies must have accounting systems that provide "reasonable assurance" that all transactions entered into by the companies are accounted for and legal. These requirements assist in detecting illegal bribes. The FCPA further prohibits any person from making false statements to accountants or false entries in any record or account.

Penalties for Violations In 1988, the FCPA was amended to provide that business firms that violate the act may be fined up to $2 million. Individual officers or directors who violate the FCPA may be fined up to $100,000 (the fine cannot be paid by the company) and may be imprisoned for up to five years.

REVIEWING Ethics and Business Decision Making

Isabel Arnett was promoted to chief executive officer (CEO) of Tamik, Inc., a pharmaceutical company that manufactures a vaccine called Kafluk, which supposedly provides some defense against bird flu. The company began marketing Kafluk throughout Asia. After numerous media reports that bird flu could soon become a worldwide epidemic, the demand for Kafluk increased, sales soared, and Tamik earned record profits. Tamik's CEO, Arnett, then began receiving disturbing reports from Southeast Asia that in some patients, Kafluk had caused psychiatric disturbances, including severe hallucinations, and heart and lung problems. Arnett was informed that six children in Japan had committed suicide by jumping out of windows after receiving the vaccine. To cover up the story and prevent negative publicity, Arnett instructed Tamik's partners in Asia to offer cash to the Japanese families whose children had died in exchange for their silence. Arnett also refused to authorize additional research within the company to study the potential side effects of Kafluk. Using the information presented in the chapter, answer the following questions.

1. This scenario illustrates one of the main reasons why ethical problems occur in business. What is that reason?
2. Would a person who adheres to the principle of rights consider it ethical for Arnett not to disclose potential safety concerns and to refuse to perform additional research on Kafluk? Why or why not?
3. If Kafluk prevented fifty Asian people who were infected with bird flu from dying, would Arnett's conduct in this situation be ethical under a utilitarian model of ethics? Why or why not?
4. Did Tamik or Arnett violate the Foreign Corrupt Practices Act in this scenario? Why or why not?

TERMS AND CONCEPTS

business ethics 84
categorical imperative 88
corporate social responsibility 89
cost-benefit analysis 89
ethical reasoning 88
ethics 84
moral minimum 91
principle of rights 88
utilitarianism 89

QUESTIONS AND CASE PROBLEMS

4–1. Some business ethicists maintain that whereas personal ethics has to do with "right" or "wrong" behavior, business ethics is concerned with "appropriate" behavior. In other words, ethical behavior in business has less to do with moral principles than with what society deems to be appropriate behavior in the business context. Do you agree with this distinction? Do personal and business ethics ever overlap? Should personal ethics play any role in business ethical decision making?

4–2. QUESTION WITH SAMPLE ANSWER

If a firm engages in "ethical" behavior solely for the purpose of gaining profits from the goodwill it generates, the "ethical" behavior is essentially a means toward a self-serving end (profits and the accumulation of wealth). In this situation, is the firm acting unethically in any way? Should motive or conduct carry greater weight on the ethical scales in this situation?

- **For a sample answer to Question 4–2, go to Appendix I at the end of this text.**

4–3. Susan Whitehead serves on the city planning commission. The city is planning to build a new subway system, and Susan's brother-in-law, Jerry, who owns the Custom Transportation Co., has submitted the lowest bid for the system. Susan knows that Jerry could complete the job for the estimated amount, but she also knows that once Jerry finishes this job, he will probably sell his company and retire. Susan is concerned that Custom Transportation's subsequent management might not be as easy to work with if revisions need to be made on the subway system after its completion. She is torn as to whether she should tell the city about the potential changes in Custom Transportation's management. If the city knew about the instability of Custom Transportation, it might prefer to give the contract to one of Jerry's competitors, whose bid was only slightly higher than Jerry's. Does Susan have an ethical obligation to disclose the information about Jerry to the city planning commission? How would you apply duty-based ethical standards to this question? What might be the outcome of a utilitarian analysis? Discuss fully.

4–4. Assume that you are a high-level manager for a shoe manufacturer. You know that your firm could increase its profit margin by producing shoes in Indonesia, where you could hire women for $40 a month to assemble them. You also know, however, that human rights advocates recently accused a competing shoe manufacturer of engaging in exploitative labor practices because the manufacturer sold shoes made by Indonesian women working for similarly low wages. You personally do not believe that paying $40 a month to Indonesian women is unethical because you know that in their impoverished country, $40 a month is a better-than-average wage rate. Assuming that the decision is yours to make, should you have the shoes manufactured in Indonesia and make higher profits for your company? Or should you avoid the risk of negative publicity and the consequences of that publicity for the firm's reputation and subsequent profits? Are there other alternatives? Discuss fully.

4–5. Shokun Steel Co. owns many steel plants. One of its plants is much older than the others. Equipment at the old plant is outdated and inefficient, and the costs of production at that plant are now twice as high as at any of Shokun's other plants. Shokun cannot increase the price of its steel because of competition, both domestic and international. The plant employs more than a thousand workers; it is located in Twin Firs, Pennsylvania, which has a population of about forty-five thousand. Shokun is contemplating whether to close the plant. What factors should the firm consider in making its decision? Will the firm violate any ethical duties if it closes the plant? Analyze these questions from the two basic perspectives on ethical reasoning discussed in this chapter.

4–6. CASE PROBLEM WITH SAMPLE ANSWER

Eden Electrical, Ltd., owned twenty-five appliance stores throughout Israel, at least some of which sold refrigerators made by Amana Co. Eden bought the appliances from Amana's Israeli distributor, Pan El A/Yesh Shem, which approached Eden about taking over the distributorship. Eden representatives met with Amana executives. The executives made assurances about Amana's good faith, its hope of having a long-term business relationship with Eden, and its willingness to have Eden become its exclusive distributor in Israel. Eden signed a distributorship agreement and paid Amana $2.4 million. Amana failed to deliver this amount in inventory to Eden, continued selling refrigerators to other entities for the Israeli market, and represented to others that it was still looking for a long-term distributor. Less than three months after signing the agreement with Eden, Amana terminated it, without explanation. Eden filed a suit in a federal district court against Amana, alleging fraud. The court awarded Eden $12.1 million in damages. Is this amount warranted? Why or why not? How does this case illustrate why business ethics is important? [*Eden Electrical, Ltd. v. Amana Co.*, 370 F.3d 824 (8th Cir. 2004)]

- **To view a sample answer for Problem 4–6, go to this book's Web site at academic.cengage.com/blaw/cross, select "Chapter 4," and click on "Case Problem with Sample Answer."**

4–7. Ethical Conduct. Richard Fraser was an "exclusive career insurance agent" under a contract with Nationwide Mutual Insurance Co. Fraser leased computer hardware and software from Nationwide for his business. During a dispute between Nationwide and the Nationwide Insurance Independent Contractors Association, an organization representing Fraser and other exclusive career agents, Fraser prepared a letter to Nationwide's competitors asking whether they were interested in acquiring the represented agents' policyholders. Nationwide obtained a copy of the letter and searched its electronic file server for e-mail indicating that the letter had been sent. It found a stored e-mail that Fraser had sent to a co-worker indicating that the letter had been sent to at least one competitor. The e-mail was retrieved from the co-worker's file of already received and discarded messages stored on the server. When Nationwide canceled its contract with Fraser, he filed a suit in a federal district court against the firm, alleging, among other things, violations of various federal laws that prohibit the interception of electronic communications during transmission. In whose favor should the court rule, and why? Did Nationwide act ethically in retrieving the e-mail? Explain. [*Fraser v. Nationwide Mutual Insurance Co.*, 352 F.3d 107 (3d Cir. 2004)]

4–8. Ethical Conduct. Unable to pay more than $1.2 billion in debt, Big Rivers Electric Corp. filed a petition to declare bankruptcy in a federal bankruptcy court in September 1996. Big Rivers' creditors included Bank of New York (BONY), Chase Manhattan Bank, Mapco Equities, and others. The court appointed J. Baxter Schilling to work as a "disinterested" (neutral) party with Big Rivers and the creditors to resolve their disputes and set an hourly fee as Schilling's compensation. Schilling told Chase, BONY, and Mapco that he wanted them to pay him an additional percentage fee based on the "success" he attained in finding "new value" to pay Big Rivers' debts. Without such a deal, he told them, he would not perform his mediation duties. Chase agreed; the others disputed the deal, but no one told the court. In October 1998, Schilling asked the court for nearly $4.5 million in compensation, including the hourly fees, which totaled about $531,000, and the percentage fees. Big Rivers and others asked the court to deny Schilling any fees on the basis that he had improperly negotiated "secret side agreements." How did Schilling violate his duties as a "disinterested" party? Should he be denied compensation? Why or why not? [*In re Big Rivers Electric Corp.*, 355 F.3d 415 (6th Cir. 2004)]

4–9. Ethical Conduct. Ernest Price suffered from sickle-cell anemia. In 1997, Price asked Dr. Ann Houston, his physician, to prescribe OxyContin, a strong narcotic, for the pain. Over the next several years, Price saw at least ten different physicians at ten different clinics in two cities, and used seven pharmacies in three cities, to obtain and fill simultaneous prescriptions for OxyContin. In March 2001, when Houston learned of these activities, she refused to write more prescriptions for Price. As other physicians became aware of Price's actions, they also stopped writing his prescriptions. Price filed a suit in a Mississippi state court against Purdue Pharma Co. and other producers and distributors of OxyContin, as well as his physicians and the pharmacies that had filled the prescriptions. Price alleged negligence, among other things, claiming that OxyContin's addictive nature caused him injury and that this was the defendants' fault. The defendants argued that Price's claim should be dismissed because it arose from his own wrongdoing. Who should be held *legally* liable? Should any of the parties be considered *ethically* responsible? Why or why not? [*Price v. Purdue Pharma Co.*, 920 So.2d 479 (Miss. 2006)]

4–10. Ethical Leadership. In 1999, Andrew Fastow, chief financial officer of Enron Corp., asked Merrill Lynch, an investment firm, to participate in a bogus sale of three barges so that Enron could record earnings of $12.5 million from the sale. Through a third entity, Fastow bought the barges back within six months and paid Merrill for its participation. Five Merrill employees were convicted of conspiracy to commit wire fraud, in part, on an "honest services" theory. Under this theory, an employee deprives his or her employer of "honest services" when the employee promotes his or her own interests, rather than the interests of the employer. Four of the employees appealed to the U.S. Court of Appeals for the Fifth Circuit, arguing that this charge did not apply to the conduct in which they engaged. The court agreed, reasoning that the barge deal was conducted to benefit Enron, not to enrich the Merrill employees at Enron's expense. Meanwhile, Kevin Howard, chief financial officer of Enron Broadband Services (EBS), engaged in "Project Braveheart," which enabled EBS to show earnings of $111 million in 2000 and 2001. Braveheart involved the sale of an interest in the future revenue of a video-on-demand venture to nCube, a small technology firm, which was paid for its help when EBS bought the interest back. Howard was convicted of wire fraud, in part, on the "honest services" theory. He filed a motion to vacate his conviction on the same basis that the Merrill employees had argued. Did Howard act unethically? Explain. Should the court grant his motion? Discuss. [*United States v. Howard*, 471 F.Supp.2d 772 (S.D.Tex. 2007)]

4–11. A QUESTION OF ETHICS

Steven Soderbergh is the Academy Award–winning director of Erin Brockovich, Traffic, *and many other films. CleanFlicks, LLC, filed a suit in a federal district court against Soderbergh, fifteen other directors, and the Directors Guild of America. The plaintiff asked the court to rule that it had the right to sell DVDs of the defendants' films altered without the defendants' consent to delete scenes of "sex, nudity, profanity and gory violence." CleanFlicks sold or rented the edited DVDs under the slogan "It's About Choice" to consumers, sometimes indirectly through retailers. It would not sell to retailers that made unauthorized copies of the edited films. The defendants, with DreamWorks, LLC and seven other movie studios that own the copyrights to the films, filed a counterclaim against CleanFlicks and others engaged in the same business, alleging copyright infringement. Those filing the counterclaim asked the court to enjoin (prevent) CleanFlicks and the others from making and marketing altered versions of the films. [*CleanFlicks of Colorado, LLC v. Soderbergh, *433 F.Supp.2d 1236 (D.Colo. 2006)]*

(a) Movie studios often edit their films to conform to content and other standards and sell the edited versions to network television and other commercial buyers. In this case, however, the studios objected when CleanFlicks edited the films and sold the altered versions directly to consumers. Similarly, CleanFlicks made unauthorized copies of the studios' DVDs to edit the films, but objected to others' making unauthorized copies of the altered versions. Is there anything unethical about these apparently contradictory positions? Why or why not?

(b) CleanFlicks and its competitors asserted, among other things, that they were making "fair use" of the studios' copyrighted works. They argued that by their actions "they are criticizing the objectionable content commonly found in current movies and that they are providing more socially acceptable alternatives to enable families to view the films together, without exposing children to the presumed harmful effects emanating from the objectionable content." If you were the judge, how would you view this argument? Is a court the appropriate forum for making determinations of public or social policy? Explain.

4-12. VIDEO QUESTION

Go to this text's Web site at **academic.cengage.com/blaw/cross** and select "Chapter 4." Click on "Video Questions" and view the video titled *Ethics: Business Ethics an Oxymoron?* Then answer the following questions.

(a) According to the instructor in the video, what is the primary reason that businesses act ethically?

(b) Which of the two approaches to ethical reasoning that were discussed in the chapter seems to have had more influence on the instructor in the discussion of how business activities are related to societies? Explain your answer.

(c) The instructor asserts that "[i]n the end, it is the unethical behavior that becomes costly, and conversely ethical behavior creates its own competitive advantage." Do you agree with this statement? Why or why not?

LAW ON THE WEB

For updated links to resources available on the Web, as well as a variety of other materials, visit this text's Web site at

academic.cengage.com/blaw/cross

South-Western Legal Studies in Business at Cengage Learning offers an in-depth "Inside Look" at the Enron debacle at

insidelook.westbuslaw.com

You can find articles on issues relating to shareholders and corporate accountability at the Corporate Governance Web site. Go to

www.corpgov.net

For an example of an online group that focuses on corporate activities from the perspective of corporate social responsibility, go to

www.corpwatch.org

Global Exchange offers information on global business activities, including some of the ethical issues stemming from those activities, at

www.globalexchange.org

Legal Research Exercises on the Web

Go to **academic.cengage.com/blaw/cross**, the Web site that accompanies this text. Select "Chapter 4" and click on "Internet Exercises." There you will find the following Internet research exercises that you can perform to learn more about the topics covered in this chapter.

Internet Exercise 4–1: Legal Perspective
Ethics in Business

Internet Exercise 4–2: Management Perspective
Environmental Self-Audits

UNIT ONE · FOCUS ON ETHICS

Ethics and the Foundations

In Chapter 4, we examined the importance of ethical standards in the business context. We also offered suggestions on how business decision makers can create an ethical workplace. Certainly, it is not wrong for a businessperson to try to increase his or her firm's profits. But there are limits, both ethical and legal, to how far businesspersons can go. In preparing for a career in business, you will find that a background in business ethics and a commitment to ethical behavior are just as important as a knowledge of the specific laws that are covered in this text. Of course, no textbook can give an answer to each and every ethical question that arises in the business environment. Nor can it anticipate the types of ethical questions that will arise in the future, as technology and globalization continue to transform the workplace and business relationships.

The most we can do is examine the types of ethical issues that businesspersons have faced in the past and that they are facing today. In the *Focus on Ethics* sections in this book, we provide examples of specific ethical issues that have arisen in various areas of business activity.

In this initial *Focus on Ethics* feature, we look first at the relationship between business ethics and the legal environment. We then examine various obstacles to ethical behavior in the business context. We conclude the feature by exploring the parameters of corporate social responsibility through a discussion of whether corporations have an ethical duty to the community or society at large.

Business Ethics and the Legal Environment

Business ethics and the legal environment are closely intertwined because ultimately the law rests on social beliefs about right and wrong behavior in the business world. Thus, businesspersons, by complying with the law, are acting ethically. Mere legal compliance (the "moral minimum" in terms of business ethics), however, is often not enough. This is because the law does not—and cannot—provide the answers for all ethical questions.

In the business world, numerous actions may be unethical but not necessarily illegal. Consider an example. Suppose that a pharmaceutical company is banned from marketing a particular drug in the United States because of the drug's possible adverse side effects. Yet no law prohibits the company from selling the drug in foreign markets—even though some consumers in those markets may suffer serious health problems as a result of using the drug. At issue here is not whether it would be legal to market the drug in other countries but whether it would be *ethical* to do so. In other words, the law has its limits—it cannot make all ethical decisions for us. Rather, the law assumes that those in business will behave ethically in their day-to-day dealings. If they do not, the courts will not come to their assistance.

Obstacles to Ethical Business Behavior

People sometimes behave unethically in the business context, just as they do in their private lives. Some businesspersons knowingly engage in unethical behavior because they think that they can "get away with it"—that no one will ever learn of their unethical actions. Examples of this kind of unethical behavior include padding expense accounts, casting doubts on the integrity of a rival co-worker to gain a job promotion, and stealing company supplies or equipment. Obviously, these acts are unethical, and some of them are illegal as well. In some situations, however, businesspersons who would choose to act ethically may be deterred from doing so because of situational circumstances or external pressures.

Ethics and the Corporate Environment Individuals in their personal lives normally are free to decide ethical issues as they wish and to follow through on those decisions. In the business world, and particularly in the corporate environment, rarely is such a decision made by *one* person. If you are an officer or a manager of a large company, for example, you will find that the decision as to what is right or wrong for the company is not totally yours to make. Your input may weigh in the decision, but ultimately a corporate decision is a collective undertaking.

Additionally, collective decision making, because it places emphasis on consensus and unity of opinion, tends to hinder individual ethical assertiveness. Suppose that a director has ethical concerns about a planned corporate venture that promises to be highly profitable. If the other directors have no such misgivings, the director who does may be swayed by the others' enthusiasm for the project and downplay her or his own criticisms.

Furthermore, just as no one person makes a collective decision, so no one person (normally) is held accountable for the decision. The corporate enterprise thus tends to shield corporate

FOCUS *on* ETHICS

personnel from both individual exposure to the consequences of their decisions (such as direct experience with someone who suffers harm from a corporate product) and personal accountability for those decisions.

Ethics and Management Much unethical business behavior occurs simply because management does not always make clear what ethical standards and behaviors are expected of the firm's employees. Although most firms now issue ethical policies or codes of conduct, these policies and codes are not always effective in creating an ethical workplace. At times, this is because the firm's ethical policies are not communicated clearly to employees or do not bear on the real ethical issues confronting decision makers. Additionally, particularly in a large corporation, unethical behavior in one corporate department may simply escape the attention of the officers in control of the corporation or those responsible for implementing and monitoring the company's ethics program.

Unethical behavior may also occur when corporate management, by its own conduct, indicates that ethical considerations take a back seat. If management makes no attempt to deter unethical behavior—through reprimands or employment terminations, for example—it will be obvious to employees that management is not all that serious about ethics. Likewise, if a company gives promotions or salary increases to those who clearly use unethical tactics to increase the firm's profits, then employees who do not resort to such tactics will be at a disadvantage. An employee in this situation may decide that because "everyone else does it," he or she might as well do it, too.

Of course, an even stronger encouragement to unethical behavior occurs when employers engage in blatantly unethical or illegal conduct and expect their employees to do so as well. An employee in this situation faces two options, neither of which is satisfactory: participate in the conduct or "blow the whistle" on (inform authorities of) the employer's actions—and, of course, risk being fired. (See Chapter 21 for a more detailed discussion of this ethical dilemma and its consequences for employees.)

Corporate Social Responsibility

As discussed in Chapter 4, just what constitutes corporate social responsibility has been debated for some time. In particular, questions arise concerning a corporation's ethical obligations to its community and to society as a whole.

A Corporation's Duty to the Community In some circumstances, the community in which a business enterprise is located is greatly affected by corporate decisions and therefore may be considered a stakeholder. Assume, for example, that a company employs two thousand workers at one of its plants. If the company decides that it would be profitable to close the plant, the employees—and the community—would suffer as a result. To be considered ethical in that situation (and, in some circumstances, to comply with laws governing plant shutdowns), a corporation must take both employees' needs and community needs into consideration when making such a decision.

Another ethical question sometimes arises when a firm moves into a community. Does the company have an obligation to evaluate first how its presence will affect that community (even though the community is not a stakeholder yet)? This question has surfaced in regard to the expansion of Wal-Mart Stores, Inc., into smaller communities. Generally, most people in such communities welcome the lower prices and wider array of goods that Wal-Mart offers relative to other, smaller stores in the area. A vocal minority of people in some communities, however, claim that smaller stores often find it impossible to compete with Wal-Mart's prices and thus are forced to go out of business. Many of these smaller stores have existed for years and, according to Wal-Mart's critics, enhance the quality of community life. These critics claim that it is unethical of Wal-Mart to disregard a town's interest in the quality and character of its community life.

In addition to expanding, Wal-Mart has been consolidating some of its smaller stores into large "superstores." As it consolidates, Wal-Mart is closing stores in some of the very towns in which it drove its smaller competitors out of business. This development raises yet another ethical question: Does a store such as Wal-Mart have an obligation to continue operations in a community once it has driven its competitors out of business?

A Corporation's Duty to Society Perhaps the most disputed area of corporate social responsibility is the nature of a corporation's duty to society at large. Those who contend that corporations should first and foremost attend to the goal of profit

(Continued)

UNIT ONE FOCUS ON ETHICS

maximization would argue that it is by generating profits that a firm can best contribute to society. Society benefits by profit-making activities because profits can only be realized when a firm markets products or services that are desired by society. These products and services enhance the standard of living, and the profits accumulated by successful business firms generate national wealth. Our laws and court decisions promoting trade and commerce reflect the public policy that the fruits of commerce (wealth) are desirable and good. Because our society values wealth as an ethical goal, corporations, by contributing to that wealth, automatically are acting ethically.

Those arguing for profit maximization as a corporate goal also point out that it would be inappropriate to use the power of the corporate business world to further society's goals by promoting social causes. Determinations as to what exactly is in society's best interest involve questions that are essentially political, and therefore the public, through the political process, should have a say in making those determinations. Thus, the legislature—not the corporate boardroom—is the appropriate forum for such decisions.

Critics of the profit-maximization view believe that corporations should become actively engaged in seeking and furthering solutions to social problems. Because so much of the wealth and power of this country is controlled by business, business in turn has a responsibility to society to use that wealth and power in socially beneficial ways. Corporations should therefore promote human rights, strive for equal treatment of minorities and women in the workplace, take steps to preserve the environment, and generally not profit from activities that society has deemed unethical. The critics also point out that it is ethically irresponsible to leave decisions concerning social welfare up to the government, because many social needs are not being met sufficiently through the political process.

It Pays to Be Ethical

Most corporations today have learned that it pays to be ethically responsible—even if this means less profit in the short run (and it often does). Today's corporations are subject to more intensive scrutiny—by both government agencies and the public—than corporations of the past. "Corporate watch" groups monitor the activities of U.S. corporations, including activities conducted in foreign countries. Through the Internet, complaints about a corporation's practices can easily be disseminated to a worldwide audience. Similarly, dissatisfied customers and employees can voice their complaints about corporate policies, products, or services in Internet chat rooms and other online forums. Thus, if a corporation fails to conduct its operations ethically or to respond quickly to an ethical crisis, its goodwill and reputation (and future profits) will likely suffer as a result.

There are other reasons as well for a corporation to behave ethically. For example, companies that demonstrate a commitment to ethical behavior—by implementing ethical programs, complying with environmental regulations, and promptly investigating product complaints, for example—often receive more lenient treatment from government agencies and the courts. Additionally, investors may shy away from a corporation's stock if the corporation is perceived to be socially irresponsible. Finally, unethical (and/or illegal) corporate behavior may result in government action, such as new laws imposing further requirements on corporate entities.

DISCUSSION QUESTIONS

1. What might be some other deterrents to ethical behavior in the business context, besides those discussed in this *Focus on Ethics* feature?
2. Can you think of a situation in which a business firm may be acting ethically but not in a socially responsible manner? Explain.
3. Why are consumers and the public generally more concerned with ethical and socially responsible business behavior today than they were, say, fifty years ago?
4. Suppose that an automobile manufacturing company has to choose between two alternatives: contributing $1 million annually to the United Way or reinvesting the $1 million in the company. In terms of ethics and social responsibility, which is the "better" choice?
5. Have Internet chat rooms and online forums affected corporate decision makers' willingness to consider the community and public interest when making choices? Are corporate decision makers more apt to make ethical choices in the cyber age? Explain.

UNIT TWO

The Public and International Environment

CONTENTS

CHAPTER 5

Constitutional Law

The U.S. Constitution is the supreme law in this country.[1] As mentioned in Chapter 1, neither Congress nor any state may pass a law that conflicts with the Constitution. Laws that govern business have their origin in the lawmaking authority granted by this document.

In this chapter, we examine some basic constitutional concepts and clauses and their significance for businesspersons. We then look at certain freedoms guaranteed by the first ten amendments to the Constitution—the Bill of Rights—and discuss how these freedoms affect business activities.

1. See Appendix B for the full text of the U.S. Constitution.

The Constitutional Powers of Government

Following the Revolutionary War, the states—through the Articles of Confederation—created a *confederal form of government* in which the states had the authority to govern themselves and the national government could exercise only limited powers. When problems arose because the nation was facing an economic crisis and state laws interfered with the free flow of commerce, a national convention was called, and the delegates drafted the U.S. Constitution. This document, after its ratification by the states in 1789, became the basis for an entirely new form of government.

A Federal Form of Government

The new government created by the Constitution reflected a series of compromises made by the convention delegates on various issues. Some delegates wanted sovereign power to remain with the states; others wanted the national government alone to exercise sovereign power. The end result was a compromise—a **federal form of government** in which the national government and the states *share* sovereign power.

The Constitution sets forth specific powers that can be exercised by the national government and provides that the national government has the implied power to undertake actions necessary to carry out its expressly designated powers (or *enumerated powers*). All other powers are expressly "reserved" to the states under the Tenth Amendment to the Constitution.

The Regulatory Powers of the States As part of their inherent sovereignty, state governments have the authority to regulate affairs within their borders. As mentioned, this authority stems, in part, from the Tenth Amendment to the Constitution, which reserves all powers not delegated to the national government to the states or to the people. State regulatory powers are often referred to as **police powers.** The term does not relate solely to criminal law enforcement but rather refers to the broad right of state governments to regulate private activities to protect or promote the public order, health, safety, morals, and general welfare. Fire and building codes, antidiscrimination laws, parking regulations, zoning restrictions, licensing requirements, and thousands of other state statutes covering virtually every aspect of life have been enacted pursuant to states' police powers. Local governments, including cities, also exercise police powers.[2] Generally, state laws enacted pursuant to a state's police powers carry a strong presumption of validity.

Delineating State and National Powers The broad language of the Constitution has left much room for debate over the specific nature and scope of the respective powers of the states and the national government. Generally, it has been the task of the courts to determine where the boundary line between state and national powers should lie—and that line shifts over time, moving first one way and then the other like a pendulum. During certain periods, the national government has met with little resistance from the courts when extending its regulatory authority over broad areas of social and economic life. During other periods, in contrast, the courts, and particularly the United States Supreme Court, have tended to interpret the Constitution in such a way as to curb the national government's regulatory powers.

Relations among the States

The Constitution also includes provisions concerning relations among the states in our federal system. Particularly important are the privileges and immunities clause and the full faith and credit clause.

The Privileges and Immunities Clause Article IV, Section 2, of the Constitution provides that the "Citizens of each State shall be entitled to all Privileges and Immunities of Citizens in the several States." This clause is often referred to as the **interstate privileges and immunities clause.**[3] It prevents a state from imposing unreasonable burdens on citizens of another state—particularly with regard to means of livelihood or doing business. When a citizen of one state engages in basic and essential activities in another state (the "foreign state"), the foreign state must have a *substantial reason* for treating the nonresident differently from its own residents. Basic activities include transferring property, seeking employment, or accessing the court system. The foreign state must also establish that its reason for the discrimination is *substantially related* to the state's ultimate purpose in adopting the legislation or activity.[4]

In general, the idea is to prevent any state (including municipalities within the state) from discriminating against citizens of other states in favor of its own. The clause does not prohibit all discrimination. It applies only to discrimination for which the state cannot demonstrate a substantial reason significantly related to its objective. For example, giving hiring preferences to state or city residents has been found to violate the privileges and immunities clause.[5] In contrast, requiring nonresidents to pay more for hunting licenses or tuition at state universities has been found *not* to violate the clause because the state articulated a substantial reason for the difference.[6]

The Full Faith and Credit Clause Article IV, Section 1, of the Constitution provides that "Full Faith and Credit shall be given in each State to the public Acts, Records, and judicial Proceedings of every other State." This clause, which is referred to as the **full faith and credit clause,** applies only to civil matters. It ensures that rights established under deeds, wills, contracts, and similar instruments in one state will be honored by other states. It also ensures that any judicial decision with respect to such property rights will be honored and enforced in all states.

The full faith and credit clause was originally included in the Articles of Confederation to promote mutual friendship among the people of the various states. In fact, it has contributed to the unity of American citizens because it protects their legal rights as they move about from state to state. It also protects the rights of those to whom they owe obligations, such as a person who is awarded monetary damages by a court. The ability to enforce such rights is extremely important for the conduct of business in a country with a very mobile citizenry.

2. Local governments derive their authority to regulate their communities from the state because they are creatures of the state. In other words, they cannot come into existence unless authorized by the state to do so.

3. Interpretations of this clause commonly use the terms *privilege* and *immunity* synonymously. Generally, the terms refer to certain rights, benefits, or advantages enjoyed by individuals.

4. This test was first announced in *Supreme Court of New Hampshire v. Piper,* 470 U.S. 274, 105 S.Ct. 1272, 84 L.Ed.2d 205 (1985). For another example, see *Lee v. Miner,* 369 F.Supp.2d 527 (D.Del. 2005).

5. *United Building and Construction Trades Council of Camden County and Vicinity v. Mayor and Council of City of Camden,* 465 U.S. 208, 104 S.Ct. 1020, 79 L.Ed.2d 249 (1984). See also *Council of Insurance Agents + Brokers v. Viken,* 408 F.Supp.2d 836 (D.S.Dak. 2005).

6. *Baldwin v. Fish and Game Commission of Montana,* 436 U.S. 371, 98 S.Ct. 1852, 56 L.Ed.2d 354 (1978); and *Saenz v. Roe,* 526 U.S. 489, 119 S.Ct. 1518, 143 L.Ed.2d 689 (1999).

The Separation of the National Government's Powers

To prevent the possibility that the national government might use its power arbitrarily, the Constitution provided for three branches of government. The legislative branch makes the laws, the executive branch enforces the laws, and the judicial branch interprets the laws. Each branch performs a separate function, and no branch may exercise the authority of another branch.

Additionally, a system of **checks and balances** allows each branch to limit the actions of the other two branches, thus preventing any one branch from exercising too much power. Some examples of these checks and balances include the following:

1. The legislative branch (Congress) can enact a law, but the executive branch (the president) has the constitutional authority to veto that law.
2. The executive branch is responsible for foreign affairs, but treaties with foreign governments require the advice and consent of the Senate.
3. Congress determines the jurisdiction of the federal courts and the president appoints federal judges, with the advice and consent of the Senate, but the judicial branch has the power to hold actions of the other two branches unconstitutional.[7]

The Commerce Clause

To prevent states from establishing laws and regulations that would interfere with trade and commerce among the states, the Constitution expressly delegated to the national government the power to regulate interstate commerce. Article I, Section 8, of the Constitution explicitly permits Congress "[t]o regulate Commerce with foreign Nations, and among the several States, and with the Indian Tribes." This clause, referred to as the **commerce clause,** has had a greater impact on business than any other provision in the Constitution. The commerce clause provides the basis for the national government's extensive regulation of state and even local affairs.

One of the early questions raised by the commerce clause was whether the word *among* in the phrase "among the several States" meant *between* the states or *between and within* the states. For some time, the courts interpreted the commerce clause to apply only to commerce between the states (*interstate* commerce) and not commerce within the states (*intrastate* commerce). In 1824, however, the United States Supreme Court decided the landmark case of *Gibbons v. Ogden.*[8] The Court ruled that commerce within the states could also be regulated by the national government as long as the commerce *substantially affected* commerce involving more than one state.

The Expansion of National Powers under the Commerce Clause In *Gibbons v. Ogden,* the Supreme Court expanded the commerce clause to cover activities that "substantially affect interstate commerce." As the nation grew and faced new kinds of problems, the commerce clause became a vehicle for the additional expansion of the national government's regulatory powers. Even activities that seemed purely local in nature came under the regulatory reach of the national government if those activities were deemed to substantially affect interstate commerce.

In 1942, for example, the Supreme Court held that wheat production by an individual farmer intended wholly for consumption on his own farm was subject to federal regulation.[9] In *Heart of Atlanta Motel v. United States,*[10] a landmark case decided in 1964, the Supreme Court upheld the federal government's authority to prohibit racial discrimination nationwide in public facilities, including local motels, based on its powers under the commerce clause. The Court noted that "if it is interstate commerce that feels the pinch, it does not matter how local the operation that applies the squeeze."

The Commerce Power Today Today, the national government continues to rely on the commerce clause for its constitutional authority to regulate business activities in the United States. The breadth of the commerce clause permits the national government to legislate in areas in which Congress has not explicitly been granted power. In the last fifteen years, however, the Supreme Court has begun to curb somewhat the national government's regulatory authority under the commerce clause. In 1995, the Court held—for the first time in sixty years—that Congress had exceeded its regulatory authority under the commerce clause. The Court struck down an act that banned the possession of guns within one thousand

7. As discussed in Chapter 2, the power of judicial review was established by the United States Supreme Court in *Marbury v. Madison,* 5 U.S. (1 Cranch) 137, 2 L.Ed. 60 (1803).

8. 22 U.S. (9 Wheat.) 1, 6 L.Ed. 23 (1824).

9. *Wickard v. Filburn,* 317 U.S. 111, 63 S.Ct. 82, 87 L.Ed. 122 (1942).

10. 379 U.S. 241, 85 S.Ct. 348, 13 L.Ed.2d 258 (1964).

feet of any school because the act attempted to regulate an area that had "nothing to do with commerce."[11] Subsequently, the Court invalidated key portions of two other federal acts on the ground that they exceeded Congress's commerce clause authority.[12]

Medical Marijuana and the Commerce Clause In one notable case, however, the Supreme Court did allow the federal government to regulate noncommercial activities taking place wholly within a state's borders. Eleven states, including California, have adopted "medical marijuana" laws, which legalize marijuana for medical purposes. Marijuana possession, however, is illegal under the federal Controlled Substances Act (CSA).[13] After the federal government seized the marijuana that two seriously ill California women were using on the advice of their physicians, the women filed a lawsuit. They argued that it was unconstitutional for the federal statute to prohibit them from using marijuana for medical purposes that were legal within the state. In 2003, the U.S. Court of Appeals for the Ninth Circuit agreed, reasoning that the marijuana in this situation would never enter the stream of commerce. In 2005, however, the United States Supreme Court held that Congress has the authority to prohibit the *intra*state possession and noncommercial cultivation of marijuana as part of a larger regulatory scheme (the CSA).[14] In other words, state laws that allow the use of medical marijuana do not insulate the users from federal prosecution.

State Actions and the "Dormant" Commerce Clause The United States Supreme Court has interpreted the commerce clause to mean that the national government has the *exclusive* authority to regulate commerce that substantially affects trade and commerce among the states. This express grant of authority to the national government, which is often referred to as the "positive" aspect of the commerce clause, implies a negative aspect—that the states do *not* have the authority to regulate interstate commerce. This negative aspect of the commerce clause is often referred to as the "dormant" (implied) commerce clause.

The dormant commerce clause comes into play when state regulations impinge on interstate commerce. In this situation, the courts weigh the state's interest in regulating a certain matter against the burden that the state's regulation places on interstate commerce. For example, the Supreme Court invalidated state regulations that, in the interest of promoting traffic safety, limited the length of trucks traveling on the state's highways. The Court concluded that the regulations imposed a "substantial burden on interstate commerce" yet failed to "make more than the most speculative contribution to highway safety."[15] Because courts balance the interests involved, it is difficult to predict the outcome in a particular case. For a discussion of how state regulations pertaining to Internet prescriptions might violate the dormant commerce clause, see this chapter's *Contemporary Legal Debates* feature on pages 110–111.

At one time, many states regulated the sale of alcoholic beverages, including wine, through a "three-tier" system. This system required separate licenses for producers, wholesalers, and retailers, subject to a complex set of overlapping regulations that effectively banned direct sales to many consumers from out-of-state wineries. In-state wineries, in contrast, could obtain a license for direct sales to consumers. The United States Supreme Court ruled that these laws did violate the dormant commerce clause.

The Supremacy Clause and Federal Preemption

Article VI of the U.S. Constitution, commonly referred to as the **supremacy clause,** provides that the Constitution, laws, and treaties of the United States are "the supreme Law of the Land." When there is a direct conflict between a federal law and a state law, the state law is rendered invalid. Because some powers are *concurrent* (shared by the federal government and the states), however, it is necessary to determine which law governs in a particular circumstance.

Preemption of State Laws **Preemption** occurs when Congress chooses to act exclusively in an area in which the federal government and the states have concurrent powers. A valid federal statute or regulation will take precedence over a conflicting state or local law or regulation on the same general subject.

11. The Court held the Gun-Free School Zones Act of 1990 to be unconstitutional in *United States v. Lopez,* 514 U.S. 549, 115 S.Ct. 1624, 131 L.Ed.2d 626 (1995).

12. *Printz v. United States,* 521 U.S. 898, 117 S.Ct. 2365, 138 L.Ed.2d 914 (1997), involving the Brady Handgun Violence Prevention Act of 1993; and *United States v. Morrison,* 529 U.S. 598, 120 S.Ct. 1740, 146 L.Ed.2d 658 (2000), concerning the federal Violence Against Women Act of 1994.

13. 21 U.S.C. Sections 801 *et seq.*

14. *Gonzales v. Raich,* 545 U.S. 1, 125 S.Ct. 2195, 162 L.Ed.2d 1 (2005).

15. *Raymond Motor Transportation, Inc. v. Rice,* 434 U.S. 429, 98 S.Ct. 787, 54 L.Ed.2d 664 (1978).

CONTEMPORARY LEGAL DEBATES

Does State Regulation of Internet Prescription Transactions Violate the Dormant Commerce Clause?

Every year, about 30 percent of American households purchase some prescription drugs online. As such transactions become more common, questions are being raised about who has the authority to regulate them. As explained in the text, under the Tenth Amendment to the U.S. Constitution, the states have the authority to regulate activities affecting the safety and welfare of their citizens. In the late 1800s, the states used this authority to begin regulating the dispensing of prescription medicines—physicians were granted the exclusive right to prescribe drugs, and pharmacists were given the exclusive right to dispense them. The courts routinely upheld these state laws.[a]

All states have continued to use their police powers to regulate the licensing of pharmacists and physicians, as well as the prescribing and dispensing of drugs. But does this authority extend to out-of-state physicians and pharmacists who prescribe drugs and fill prescriptions via the Internet?

The States Attempt to Regulate Internet Prescriptions

About 40 percent of the states have attempted to regulate Internet prescription transactions by changing their licensing laws to require a "safe" consulting relationship between the prescribing physician and the pharmacist who dispenses the prescription drugs. Some states, for example, require an electronic diagnosis before a prescription can be filled—the patient completes an online questionnaire that is "approved" by a physician who then transmits the prescription to a pharmacist. Other states, however, specifically prohibit a physician from creating a prescription unless he or she has physical contact with the patient. Another approach is to try to regulate Internet pharmacies. In Nevada, for example, residents cannot obtain a prescription from an Internet pharmacy unless it is licensed and certified under the laws of that state.

Recently, the New York State Bureau of Narcotic Enforcement took an additional regulatory step and began investigating all companies in New Jersey and Mississippi that had supplied prescription medicines to New York residents via Internet transactions. None of the companies under investigation has offices in New York State. Furthermore, the authority to enforce regulations involving prescription drugs and their distributors generally belongs to the federal Food and Drug Administration.

Are the States Violating the Dormant Commerce Clause?

As explained in the text, the courts have held that the dormant commerce clause prohibits the states from regulating interstate commerce. Hence, the states may not institute regulations that impose an undue burden on interstate commerce. In the past, the courts have used the dormant commerce clause in

a. See, for example, *Dent v. West Virginia,* 129 U.S. 114, 9 S.Ct. 231, 32 L.Ed. 623 (1889).

Often, it is not clear whether Congress, in passing a law, intended to preempt an entire subject area against state regulation, and it is left to the courts to determine whether Congress intended to exercise exclusive power over a given area. No single factor is decisive as to whether a court will find preemption. Generally, congressional intent to preempt will be found if a federal law regulating an activity is so pervasive, comprehensive, or detailed that the states have no room to regulate in that area. Also, when a federal statute creates an agency to enforce the law, matters that may come within the agency's jurisdiction will likely preempt state laws.

Preemption and State Regulation Aimed at Global Warming A question of preemption was raised in 2006, when California governor Arnold Schwarzenegger signed into law the first state statute attempting to limit the amount of greenhouse-gas emissions from automobiles within the state.[16] Under federal law, the Environmental Protection Agency (EPA) is the agency that regulates and sets standards for air pollution and tailpipe emissions across the country (see Chapter 24). Normally, because EPA regu-

16. The law amends California Health and Safety Code Section 43018.5.

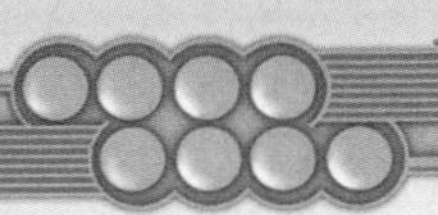

evaluating state regulations that affected out-of-state pharmacies involved in activities such as mail-order prescriptions.[b]

Today, the question is whether state laws that attempt to regulate Internet prescription transactions, such as those described above, violate the dormant commerce clause. To date, no court has ruled directly on this issue, but there have been cases involving similar state efforts to regulate other out-of-state Internet activities. A number of courts have accepted the argument that under the dormant commerce clause, the federal government can assume full regulatory power over any firms conducting business over the Internet because they are engaged in interstate commerce.[c]

Other courts, however, have taken the opposing view and found that state regulation of Internet activities does *not* always violate the dormant commerce clause. In one case, a court upheld a New York law that banned the sale of cigarettes to New York residents over the Internet on the ground that the state had an interest in protecting the health of its citizens.[d] In another case, a Texas statute that prohibited automobile manufacturers from selling vehicles on their Web sites was upheld on similar grounds.[e]

Whether the reasoning in these cases will be extended to cases involving Internet prescriptions remains to be seen. Some laws seem likely to be upheld. The Nevada law mentioned earlier that requires Internet pharmacies to be licensed in the state is an example. Because this law applies equally to in-state pharmacies and out-of-state Internet pharmacies, it is nondiscriminatory. In addition, the requirement that an Internet pharmacy obtain a license before doing business in the state would probably *not* be considered an undue burden on interstate commerce.

b. See, for example, *Pharmaceutical Manufacturers' Association v. New Mexico Board of Pharmacy,* 86 N.M. 571, 525 P.2d 931 (N.M.App. 1974); and *State v. Rasmussen,* 213 N.W.2d 661 (Iowa 1973).

c. See, for example, *American Libraries Association v. Pataki,* 969 F.Supp. 160 (S.D.N.Y. 1997).

d. *Brown & Williamson Tobacco Corp. v. Pataki,* 320 F.3d 200 (2d Cir. 2003).

e. *Ford Motor Co. v. Texas Department of Transportation,* 264 F.3d 493 (5th Cir. 2001).

WHERE DO YOU STAND?

Clearly, there are two sides to this debate. Many states contend that they must regulate the provision of prescription drugs via the Internet in order to ensure the safety and well-being of their citizens. In some instances, however, the states may be imposing such regulations at the behest of traditional pharmacies, which do not like online competition.

What is your stand on whether state regulation of Internet prescription drug transactions violates the dormant commerce clause of the Constitution? Realize that if you agree that it does, then you probably favor less state regulation. If you believe that it does not, then you probably favor more state regulation.

lations are comprehensive and detailed, they preempt state statutes attempting to regulate the same topic. California is in a different position from other states, though, because it has been given special permission to regulate air pollution in the past. Nevertheless, the Bush administration and the EPA have opposed this most recent legislation and claim that it is preempted by the federal standards. Although Californians might want to enact more stringent standards for emissions due to the number of vehicles operated within the state, it remains to be seen whether the courts will find that the legislation has been preempted. (We will discuss an important 2007 ruling from the United States Supreme Court on the topic of global warming in Chapter 24.)

The Taxing and Spending Powers

Article I, Section 8, provides that Congress has the "Power to lay and collect Taxes, Duties, Imposts, and Excises." Section 8 further requires uniformity in taxation among the states, and thus Congress may not tax some states while exempting others. Traditionally, if Congress attempted to regulate indirectly, by taxation, an area over which it had no authority, the courts would invalidate the tax. Today, however, if a tax measure is reasonable, it is generally held to be within the national taxing power. Moreover, the expansive interpretation of the commerce clause almost always provides a basis for sustaining a federal tax.

Article I, Section 8, also gives Congress its spending power—the power "to pay the Debts and provide for the common Defence and general Welfare of the United States." Congress can spend revenues not only to carry out its expressed powers but also to promote any objective it deems worthwhile, so long as it does not violate the Bill of Rights. The spending power necessarily involves policy choices, with which taxpayers may disagree.

Business and the Bill of Rights

The importance of a written declaration of the rights of individuals eventually caused the first Congress of the United States to submit twelve amendments to the U.S. Constitution to the states for approval. The first ten of these amendments, commonly known as the **Bill of Rights,** were adopted in 1791 and embody a series of protections for the individual against various types of interference by the federal government.[17] The protections guaranteed by these ten amendments are summarized in Exhibit 5–1.[18] Some of these constitutional protections apply to business entities as well. For example, corporations exist as separate legal entities, or *legal persons,* and enjoy many of the same rights and privileges as *natural persons* do.

Limits on Both Federal and State Governmental Actions

As originally intended, the Bill of Rights limited only the powers of the national government. Over time, however, the United States Supreme Court "incorporated" most of these rights into the protections against state actions afforded by the Fourteenth Amendment to the Constitution. That amendment, passed in 1868 after the Civil War, provides in part that "[n]o State shall . . . deprive any person of life, liberty, or property, without due process of law." Starting in 1925, the Supreme Court began to define various rights and liberties guaranteed in the U.S. Constitution as constituting "due process of law," which was required of state governments under the Fourteenth Amendment. Today, most of the rights and liberties set forth in the Bill of Rights apply to state governments as well as the national government. In other words, neither the federal government nor state governments can deprive persons of those rights and liberties.

The rights secured by the Bill of Rights are not absolute. As you can see in Exhibit 5–1, many of the rights guaranteed by the first ten amendments are described in very general terms. For example, the Fourth Amendment prohibits *unreasonable* searches and seizures, but it does not define what constitutes an unreasonable search or seizure. Similarly, the Eighth Amendment prohibits excessive bail or fines, but no definition of *excessive* is contained in that amendment. Ultimately, it is the United States Supreme Court, as the final interpreter of the Constitution, that defines our rights and determines their boundaries.

Freedom of Speech

A democratic form of government cannot survive unless people can freely voice their political opinions and criticize government actions or policies. Freedom of speech, particularly political speech, is thus a prized right, and traditionally the courts have protected this right to the fullest extent possible.

Symbolic speech—gestures, movements, articles of clothing, and other forms of expressive conduct—is also given substantial protection by the courts. For example, in 1989 the United States Supreme Court ruled that the burning of the American flag as part of a peaceful protest is a constitutionally protected form of expression.[19] Similarly, participating in a hunger strike, holding signs at an antiwar protest, or wearing a black armband would be protected as symbolic speech.

Reasonable Restrictions Expression—oral, written, or symbolized by conduct—is subject to reasonable restrictions. A balance must be struck between a government's obligation to protect its citizens and those citizens' exercise of their rights. Reasonableness is analyzed on a case-by-case basis. If a restriction imposed by the government is content neutral, then a court may allow it. To be content neutral, the restriction must be aimed at combating some

17. Another of these proposed amendments was ratified 203 years later (in 1992) and became the Twenty-seventh Amendment to the Constitution. See Appendix B.

18. See the Constitution in Appendix B for the complete text of each amendment.

19. *Texas v. Johnson,* 491 U.S. 397, 109 S.Ct. 2533, 105 L.Ed.2d 342 (1989).

EXHIBIT 5–1 • Protections Guaranteed by the Bill of Rights

First Amendment: Guarantees the freedoms of religion, speech, and the press and the rights to assemble peaceably and to petition the government.

Second Amendment: States that the right of the people to keep and bear arms shall not be infringed.

Third Amendment: Prohibits, in peacetime, the lodging of soldiers in any house without the owner's consent.

Fourth Amendment: Prohibits unreasonable searches and seizures of persons or property.

Fifth Amendment: Guarantees the rights to indictment by grand jury, to due process of law, and to fair payment when private property is taken for public use; prohibits compulsory self-incrimination and double jeopardy (being tried again for an alleged crime for which one has already stood trial).

Sixth Amendment: Guarantees the accused in a criminal case the right to a speedy and public trial by an impartial jury and with counsel. The accused has the right to cross-examine witnesses against him or her and to solicit testimony from witnesses in his or her favor.

Seventh Amendment: Guarantees the right to a trial by jury in a civil case involving at least twenty dollars.[a]

Eighth Amendment: Prohibits excessive bail and fines, as well as cruel and unusual punishment.

Ninth Amendment: Establishes that the people have rights in addition to those specified in the Constitution.

Tenth Amendment: Establishes that those powers neither delegated to the federal government nor denied to the states are reserved to the states and to the people.

a. Twenty dollars was forty days' pay for the average person when the Bill of Rights was written.

societal problem, such as crime, and not be aimed at suppressing the expressive conduct or its message. For example, courts have often protected nude dancing as a form of symbolic expression but have also allowed content-neutral laws that ban all public nudity, not just erotic dancing.[20]

The United States Supreme Court has also held that schools may restrict students' free speech rights at school events. In 2007, for example, the Court heard a case involving a high school student who had held up a banner saying "Bong Hits 4 Jesus" at an off-campus but school-sanctioned event. In a split decision, the majority of the Court ruled that school officials did not violate the student's free speech rights when they confiscated the banner and suspended the student for ten days. Because the banner could reasonably be interpreted as promoting the use of marijuana, and because the school had a written policy against illegal drugs, the majority concluded that the school's actions were justified. Several justices disagreed, however, noting that the majority's holding creates a special exception that will allow schools to censor any student speech that mentions drugs.[21]

20. See, for example, *Rameses, Inc. v. County of Orange,* 481 F.Supp.2d 1305 (M.D.Fla. 2007) and *City of Erie v. Pap's A.M.,* 529 U.S. 277, 120 S.Ct. 1382, 146 L.Ed.2d 265 (2000).

21. *Morse v. Frederick,* ___ U.S.___, 127 S.Ct. 2618, 168 L.Ed.2d 290 (2007).

Corporate Political Speech Political speech by corporations also falls within the protection of the First Amendment. For example, many years ago the United States Supreme Court ruled that a Massachusetts statute, which prohibited corporations from making political contributions or expenditures that individuals were permitted to make, was unconstitutional.[22] Similarly, the Court has held that a law forbidding a corporation from placing inserts in its billing to express its views on controversial issues violates the First Amendment.[23] Although the Supreme Court has reversed this trend somewhat,[24] corporate political speech continues to be given significant protection under the First Amendment. For example, in 2003 and again in 2007 the Supreme Court struck down some portions of bipartisan campaign-finance reform laws as unconstitutional restraints on corporate political speech.[25]

22. *First National Bank of Boston v. Bellotti,* 435 U.S. 765, 98 S.Ct. 1407, 55 L.Ed.2d 707 (1978).

23. *Consolidated Edison Co. v. Public Service Commission,* 447 U.S. 530, 100 S.Ct. 2326, 65 L.Ed.2d 319 (1980).

24. See *Austin v. Michigan Chamber of Commerce,* 494 U.S. 652, 110 S.Ct. 1391, 108 L.Ed.2d 652 (1990), in which the Supreme Court upheld a state law prohibiting corporations from using general corporate funds for independent expenditures in state political campaigns.

25. *McConnell v. Federal Election Commission,* 540 U.S. 93, 124 S.Ct. 619, 157 L.Ed.2d 491 (2003); and *Federal Election Commission v. Wisconsin Right to Life, Inc.,* ___U.S. ___, 127 S.Ct. 2652, 168 L.Ed.2d 329 (2007).

Commercial Speech The courts also give substantial protection to *commercial speech,* which consists of communications—primarily advertising and marketing—made by business firms that involve only their commercial interests. The protection given to commercial speech under the First Amendment is not as extensive as that afforded to noncommercial speech, however. A state may restrict certain kinds of advertising, for example, in the interest of preventing consumers from being misled by the advertising practices. States also have a legitimate interest in the beautification of roadsides, and this interest allows states to place restraints on billboard advertising. For example, in one Florida case, the court found that a law preventing a nude dancing establishment from billboard advertising was constitutionally permissible because it directly advanced a substantial government interest in highway beautification and safety.[26]

Generally, a restriction on commercial speech will be considered valid as long as it meets three criteria: (1) it must seek to implement a substantial government interest, (2) it must directly advance that interest, and (3) it must go no further than necessary to accomplish its objective. At issue in the following case was whether a government agency had unconstitutionally restricted commercial speech when it prohibited the inclusion of a certain illustration on beer labels.

26. *Café Erotica v. Florida Department of Transportation,* 830 So.2d 181 (Fla.App. 1 Dist. 2002); review denied by *Café Erotica/We Dare to Bare v. Florida Department of Transportation,* 845 So.2d 888 (Fla. 2003).

CASE 5.1 Bad Frog Brewery, Inc. v. New York State Liquor Authority

United States Court of Appeals, Second Circuit, 1998. 134 F.3d 87.
www.findlaw.com/casecode/index.html[a]

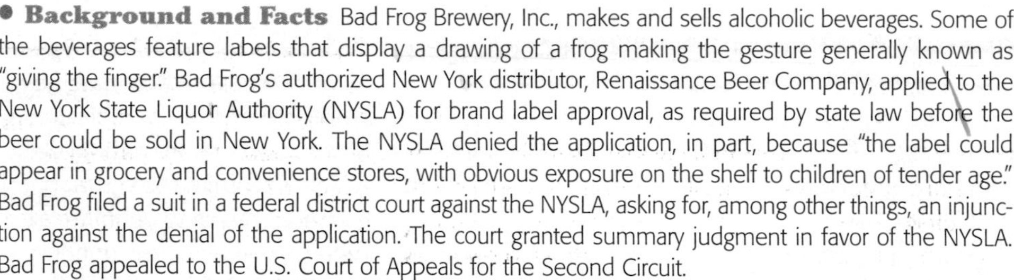

• **Background and Facts** Bad Frog Brewery, Inc., makes and sells alcoholic beverages. Some of the beverages feature labels that display a drawing of a frog making the gesture generally known as "giving the finger." Bad Frog's authorized New York distributor, Renaissance Beer Company, applied to the New York State Liquor Authority (NYSLA) for brand label approval, as required by state law before the beer could be sold in New York. The NYSLA denied the application, in part, because "the label could appear in grocery and convenience stores, with obvious exposure on the shelf to children of tender age." Bad Frog filed a suit in a federal district court against the NYSLA, asking for, among other things, an injunction against the denial of the application. The court granted summary judgment in favor of the NYSLA. Bad Frog appealed to the U.S. Court of Appeals for the Second Circuit.

IN THE LANGUAGE OF THE COURT
***JON O. NEWMAN,* Circuit Judge:**

* * * *

* * * To support its asserted power to ban Bad Frog's labels [NYSLA advances] * * * the State's interest in "protecting children from vulgar and profane advertising" * * * .

[This interest is] substantial * * * . *States have a compelling interest in protecting the physical and psychological well-being of minors* * * * . [Emphasis added.]

* * * *

* * * NYSLA endeavors to advance the state interest in preventing exposure of children to vulgar displays by taking only the limited step of barring such displays from the labels of alcoholic beverages. *In view of the wide currency of vulgar displays throughout contemporary society, including comic books targeted directly at children, barring such displays from labels for alcoholic beverages cannot realistically be expected to reduce children's exposure to such displays to any significant degree.* [Emphasis added.]

* * * If New York decides to make a substantial effort to insulate children from vulgar displays in some significant sphere of activity, at least with respect to materials likely to be seen by children, NYSLA's label prohibition might well be found to make a justifiable contribution to the material advancement of such an effort, but its currently isolated response to the perceived problem, applicable only to labels on a product that children cannot purchase, does not suffice. * * *

a. Under the heading "US Court of Appeals," click on "2nd." Enter "Bad Frog Brewery" in the "Party Name Search" box and click on "Search." On the resulting page, click on the case name to access the opinion.

CASE 5.1 CONTINUED

A state must demonstrate that its commercial speech limitation is part of a substantial effort to advance a valid state interest, not merely the removal of a few grains of offensive sand from a beach of vulgarity.

* * * *

* * * Even if we were to assume that the state materially advances its asserted interest by shielding children from viewing the Bad Frog labels, it is plainly excessive to prohibit the labels from all use, including placement on bottles displayed in bars and taverns where parental supervision of children is to be expected. Moreover, to whatever extent NYSLA is concerned that children will be harmfully exposed to the Bad Frog labels when wandering without parental supervision around grocery and convenience stores where beer is sold, that concern could be less intrusively dealt with by placing restrictions on the permissible locations where the appellant's products may be displayed within such stores.

- **Decision and Remedy** *The U.S. Court of Appeals for the Second Circuit reversed the judgment of the district court and remanded the case for the entry of a judgment in favor of Bad Frog. The NYSLA's ban on the use of the labels lacked a "reasonable fit" with the state's interest in shielding minors from vulgarity, and the NYSLA did not adequately consider alternatives to the ban.*

- **What If the Facts Were Different?** *If Bad Frog had sought to use the offensive label to market toys instead of beer, would the court's ruling likely have been the same? Why or why not?*

- **The Legal Environment Dimension** *Whose interests are advanced by the banning of certain types of advertising?*

Unprotected Speech The United States Supreme Court has made it clear that certain types of speech will not be protected under the First Amendment. Speech that violates criminal laws (threatening speech and pornography, for example) is not constitutionally protected. Other unprotected speech includes "fighting words" (speech that is likely to incite others to respond violently).

Speech that harms the good reputation of another, or defamatory speech (see Chapter 12), also is not protected under the First Amendment. To constitute defamation and thus have no First Amendment protection, the speech in question must be an assertion of fact and not merely an opinion. Unlike an opinion, a statement of purported fact can be verified and may require proof in a lawsuit claiming that the statement is defamatory.

In the following case, the issue was whether a certain statement was an unprotected factual assertion.

EXTENDED CASE 5.2 Lott v. Levitt

United States District Court, Northern District of Illinois, Eastern Division, 2007. 469 F.Supp.2d 575.

***RUBEN CASTILLO*, United States District Court Judge.**

In 2005, well-known economist Steven Levitt ("Levitt") and journalist Stephen J. Dubner ("Dubner") coauthored the best-selling book *Freakonomics,* which was published by * * * HarperCollins Publishers, Inc. ("HarperCollins"). This Court, like many other individuals, has completed a cover-to-cover reading of the book. In the book, Levitt and Dubner spend one paragraph discussing the theory for which fellow economist, * * * John R. Lott, Jr. ("Lott"), is known[:] * * * that laws permitting individuals to carry concealed weapons result in a statistically significant and provable reduction in serious crime rates. Lott filed the instant lawsuit against Levitt and [others] * * * . Lott claims [in part] that an email written by Levitt to another economist * * * constitutes defamation * * * . [Levitt filed a motion to dismiss this claim.]

* * * *

Lott is discussed in the following single paragraph in Chapter 4 of *Freakonomics,* entitled "Where Have All the Criminals Gone?":

CASE CONTINUES

CASE 5.2 CONTINUED

> * * * There is an * * * argument—that we need more guns on the street, but in the hands of the right people * * * . The economist John R. Lott Jr. is the main champion of this idea. His calling card is the book *More Guns, Less Crime,* in which he argues that violent crime has decreased in areas where law-abiding citizens are allowed to carry concealed weapons. His theory might be surprising, but it is sensible. If a criminal thinks his potential victim may be armed, he may be deterred from committing the crime. Handgun opponents call Lott a pro-gun ideologue * * * . There was the troubling allegation that Lott actually invented some of the survey data that support his more-guns/less-crime theory. Regardless of whether the data were faked, Lott's admittedly intriguing hypothesis doesn't seem to be true. When other scholars have tried to replicate his results, they found that right-to-carry laws simply don't bring down crime.

On May 24 or May 25, 2005, John McCall ("McCall"), described by Lott as an economist residing in Texas, sent Levitt an email regarding the above passage, stating:

> I * * * found the following citations—have not read any of them yet, but it appears they all replicate Lott's research. [McCall referred to a "Special Issue" of *The Journal of Law and Economics* published in October 2001 that contained a collection of articles delivered at an academic conference co-sponsored by the Center for Law, Economics, and Public Policy at Yale Law School and the American Enterprise Institute, where Lott had recently been a resident scholar.] *The Journal of Law and Economics* is not chopped liver.

That same day, Levitt responded:

> It was not a peer refereed edition of the *Journal.* For $15,000 he was able to buy an issue and put in only work that supported him. My best friend was the editor and was outraged the press let Lott do this.

* * * *

A statement is considered defamatory if it tends to cause such harm to the reputation of another that it lowers that person in the eyes of the community or deters third persons from associating with that person. [Emphasis added.]

* * * *

* * * Lott contends that the statements about him in * * * the email * * * imply that his results were falsified or that his theories lack merit, and thus impute a lack of ability and integrity in his profession as an economist, academic, and researcher. Indeed, a claim that an academic or economist falsified his results and could only publish his theories by buying an issue of a journal and avoiding peer review would surely impute a lack of ability and prejudice that person in his profession.

* * * *

* * * *The First Amendment protects statements that cannot be reasonably interpreted as stating actual facts.* [Emphasis added.]

The test for whether a statement is a factual assertion is whether the statement is precise, readily understood, and susceptible of being verified as true or false. This test * * * is a reasonableness standard; whether a reasonable reader would understand the defendant to be informing him of a fact or opinion. Language that is loose, figurative, or hyperbolic negates the impression that a statement is asserting actual facts. Accordingly, *vague, unprovable statements and statements of opinion do not give rise to a defamation claim.* If it is plain that the speaker is expressing a subjective view, an interpretation, a theory, conjecture, or surmise, rather than claiming to be in possession of objectively verifiable facts, the statement is not actionable. [Emphasis added.]

In this case, however, Levitt's email sounds as if he was in possession of objectively verifiable facts. * * * First, it would be unreasonable to interpret Levitt's unqualified statement that the *Journal* edition was not "peer refereed" as Levitt [argues that he was] merely giving his opinion on the "peers" chosen to review, or referee, the Special Issue. Indeed, the editor of the *Journal* might be able to verify the truth or falsity of whether the Special Issue was reviewed by peers. Furthermore, while Levitt argues that one person's " 'peer' in the academic realm may be another person's 'hack'," this distinction is not reasonable when discussing the review process at a top university's academic journal. Second, a reasonable reader would not interpret Levitt's assertion that "For $15,000 [Lott] was able to buy an issue and put in only work that supported him" as simply a statement of Levitt's opinion. Levitt's email appears to state objectively verifiable facts: that Lott paid $15,000 to control the content of the Special Issue. The editor of the *Journal* again might be the source to verify the truth or falsity of this statement. Third, the same editor could verify whether he was "outraged" by

CASE 5.2 CONTINUED

the acts described in the foregoing statements. Therefore, the defamatory statements in Levitt's email to McCall are objectively verifiable * * * .

* * * *

* * * In his email to McCall, * * * Levitt made a string of defamatory assertions about Lott's involvement in the publication of the Special Issue of the *Journal* that—no matter how rash or short-sighted Levitt was when he made them—cannot be reasonably interpreted as innocent or mere opinion.

* * * Levitt's motion to dismiss [this part of Lott's] Complaint is denied.

QUESTIONS

1. Did the statements about Lott in *Freakonomics* constitute unprotected speech? Explain.
2. Should the First Amendment protect all speech? Discuss.

Obscene Speech. The Supreme Court has also held that the First Amendment does not protect obscene speech. Establishing an objective definition of obscene speech has proved difficult, however, and the Court has grappled from time to time with this problem. In a 1973 case, *Miller v. California*,[27] the Supreme Court created a test for legal obscenity, including a set of requirements that must be met for material to be legally obscene. Under this test, material is obscene if (1) the average person finds that it violates contemporary community standards; (2) the work taken as a whole appeals to a prurient (arousing or obsessive) interest in sex; (3) the work shows patently offensive sexual conduct; and (4) the work lacks serious redeeming literary, artistic, political, or scientific merit.

Because community standards vary widely, the *Miller* test has had inconsistent applications, and obscenity remains a constitutionally unsettled issue. Numerous state and federal statutes make it a crime to disseminate obscene materials, and the Supreme Court has often upheld such laws, including laws prohibiting the sale and possession of child pornography.[28]

Online Obscenity. A significant problem facing the courts and lawmakers today is how to control the dissemination of obscenity and child pornography via the Internet. Congress first attempted to protect minors from pornographic materials on the Internet by passing the Communications Decency Act (CDA) of 1996. The CDA declared it a crime to make available to minors online any "obscene or indecent" message that "depicts or describes, in terms patently offensive as measured by contemporary community standards, sexual or excretory activities or organs."[29] Civil rights groups challenged the act, and ultimately the Supreme Court ruled that portions of the act were unconstitutional. The Court held that the terms *indecent* and *patently offensive* covered large amounts of nonpornographic material with serious educational or other value.[30]

Subsequent Attempts to Regulate Online Obscenity. Congress's second attempt to protect children from online obscenity, the Child Online Protection Act (COPA) of 1998,[31] met with a similar fate. Although the COPA was more narrowly tailored than its predecessor, the CDA, it still used "contemporary community standards" to define which material was obscene and harmful to minors. Ultimately, in 2004 the Supreme Court concluded that it was likely that the COPA did violate the right to free speech and prevented enforcement of the act.[32]

In 2000, Congress enacted the Children's Internet Protection Act (CIPA),[33] which requires public schools and libraries to install **filtering software** to keep children from accessing adult content. Such software is

27. 413 U.S. 15, 93 S.Ct. 2607, 37 L.Ed.2d 419 (1973).
28. For example, see *Osborne v. Ohio*, 495 U.S. 103, 110 S.Ct. 1691, 109 L.Ed.2d 98 (1990).
29. 47 U.S.C. Section 223(a)(1)(B)(ii).
30. *Reno v. American Civil Liberties Union*, 521 U.S. 844, 117 S.Ct. 2329, 138 L.Ed.2d 874 (1997).
31. 47 U.S.C. Section 231.
32. *American Civil Liberties Union v. Ashcroft*, 542 U.S. 646, 124 S.Ct. 2783, 159 L.Ed.2d 690 (2004). See also *Ashcroft v. American Civil Liberties Union*, 535 U.S. 564, 122 S.Ct. 1700, 152 L.Ed.2d 771 (2002); and *American Civil Liberties Union v. Ashcroft*, 322 F.3d 240 (3d Cir. 2003).
33. 17 U.S.C. Sections 1701–1741.

designed to prevent persons from viewing certain Web sites based on a site's Internet address or its **meta tags,** or key words. The CIPA was also challenged on constitutional grounds, but in 2003 the Supreme Court held that the act does not violate the First Amendment. The Court concluded that because libraries can disable the filters for any patrons who ask, the system is reasonably flexible and does not burden free speech to an unconstitutional extent.[34]

Because of the difficulties of policing the Internet as well as the constitutional complexities of prohibiting online obscenity through legislation, it remains a continuing problem in the United States (and worldwide).

Freedom of Religion

The First Amendment states that the government may neither establish any religion nor prohibit the free exercise of religious practices. The first part of this constitutional provision, which is referred to as the **establishment clause,** has to do with the separation of church and state. The second part of the provision is known as the **free exercise clause.**

The Establishment Clause The establishment clause prohibits the government from establishing a state-sponsored religion, as well as from passing laws that promote (aid or endorse) religion or that show a preference for one religion over another. Establishment clause issues often involve such matters as the legality of allowing or requiring school prayers, using state-issued school vouchers to pay for tuition at religious schools, teaching evolutionary versus creationist theory, and giving state and local government aid to religious organizations and schools.

Federal or state laws that do not promote or place a significant burden on religion are constitutional even if they have some impact on religion. "Sunday closing laws," for example, make the performance of some commercial activities on Sunday illegal. These statutes, also known as "blue laws" (from the color of the paper on which an early Sunday law was written), have been upheld on the ground that it is a legitimate function of government to provide a day of rest to promote the health and welfare of workers. Even though closing laws admittedly make it easier for Christians to attend religious services, the courts have viewed this effect as an incidental, not a primary, purpose of Sunday closing laws.

The Free Exercise Clause The free exercise clause guarantees that no person can be compelled to do something that is contrary to his or her religious beliefs. For this reason, if a law or policy is contrary to a person's religious beliefs, exemptions are often made to accommodate those beliefs.

When religious practices work against public policy and the public welfare, though, the government can act. For example, regardless of a child's or parent's religious beliefs, the government can require certain types of vaccinations in the interest of public welfare. The government's interest must be sufficiently compelling, however. The United States Supreme Court ruled in 2006 that the government had failed to demonstrate a sufficiently compelling interest in barring a church from the sacramental use of an illegal controlled substance. (The church members used hoasca tea, which is brewed from plants native to the Amazon rain forest and contains a hallucinogenic drug, in the practice of a sincerely held religious belief.)[35]

For business firms, an important issue involves the accommodation that businesses must make for the religious beliefs of their employees. Generally, if an employee's religion prohibits her or him from working on a certain day of the week or at a certain type of job, the employer must make a reasonable attempt to accommodate these religious requirements. The only requirement is that the belief be religious in nature and sincerely held by the employee.[36] (See Chapter 21 for a further discussion of religious freedom in the employment context.)

Searches and Seizures

The Fourth Amendment protects the "right of the people to be secure in their persons, houses, papers, and effects." Before searching or seizing private property, law enforcement officers must usually obtain a **search warrant**—an order from a judge or other public official authorizing the search or seizure.

Search Warrants and Probable Cause To obtain a search warrant, law enforcement officers must convince a judge that they have reasonable grounds, or probable cause, to believe a search will reveal evidence of a specific illegality. To establish **probable cause,** the officers must have trustworthy evidence that would convince a reasonable person

34. *United States v. American Library Association,* 539 U.S. 194, 123 S.Ct. 2297, 156 L.Ed.2d 221 (2003).

35. *Gonzales v. O Centro Espirita Beneficiente Uniao Do Vegtal,* 546 U.S. 418, 126 S.Ct. 1211, 163 L.Ed.2d 1017 (2006).

36. *Frazee v. Illinois Department of Employment Security,* 489 U.S. 829, 109 S.Ct. 1514, 103 L.Ed.2d 914 (1989).

that the proposed search or seizure is more likely justified than not. Furthermore, the Fourth Amendment prohibits *general* warrants. It requires a particular description of whatever is to be searched or seized. General searches through a person's belongings are impermissible. The search cannot extend beyond what is described in the warrant.

The requirement for a search warrant has several exceptions. One exception applies when the items sought are likely to be removed before a warrant can be obtained. For example, if a police officer has probable cause to believe that an automobile contains evidence of a crime and that the vehicle will likely be unavailable by the time a warrant is obtained, the officer can search the vehicle without a warrant.

Searches and Seizures in the Business Context Constitutional protection against unreasonable searches and seizures is important to businesses and professionals. Equally important is the government's interest in ensuring compliance with federal and state regulations, especially rules meant to protect the safety of employees and the public.

Because of the strong governmental interest in protecting the public, a warrant normally is not required for the seizure of spoiled or contaminated food. In addition, warrants are not required for searches of businesses in such highly regulated industries as liquor, guns, and strip mining. General manufacturing is not considered to be one of these highly regulated industries, however.

Generally, government inspectors do not have the right to search business premises without a warrant, although the standard of probable cause is not the same as that required in nonbusiness contexts. The existence of a general and neutral enforcement plan normally will justify issuance of the warrant. Lawyers and accountants frequently possess the business records of their clients, and inspecting these documents while they are out of the hands of their true owners also requires a warrant.

In the following case, after receiving a report of suspected health-care fraud, state officials entered and searched the office of a licensed physician without obtaining a warrant. The physician claimed that the search was unreasonable and improper.

CASE 5.3 U.S. v. Moon

United States Court of Appeals, Sixth Circuit, 2008. 513 F.3d 527.
www.ca6.uscourts.gov[a]

• **Background and Facts** Young Moon was a licensed physician, specializing in oncology and hematology. Moon operated a medical practice in Crossville, Tennessee. As part of her practice, Moon contracted with the state of Tennessee to provide medical treatment to patients pursuant to a state and federally funded health benefit program for the uninsured known as "TennCare." Moon routinely utilized chemotherapy medications in her treatment of cancer patients insured under the program. In March 2001, the Tennessee Bureau of Investigation (TBI) received a complaint from one of Moon's employees alleging that she had administered partial doses of chemotherapy medication while billing the insurance program for full doses. In January 2002, investigating agents conducted an on-site review at Moon's office. The agents identified themselves, informed Moon of a general complaint against her, and requested permission to "scan" particular patient records. Moon agreed. She also provided agents with a location where they could scan the requested files. Later, Moon attempted to suppress the evidence, arguing that it was obtained without a search warrant. The federal district court sentenced Moon to 188 months in prison, followed by two years of supervised release. She was also ordered to pay restitution of $432,000. She appealed her conviction and sentence to the U.S. Court of Appeals for the Sixth Circuit.

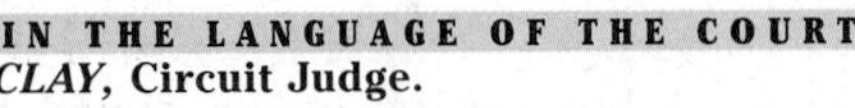

IN THE LANGUAGE OF THE COURT
CLAY, Circuit Judge.

* * * *

The Fourth Amendment bars the government from conducting unreasonable searches and seizures. This prohibition extends to both private homes and commercial premises. Additionally, searches pursuant to criminal as well as administrative investigations must comport

a. Click on "Opinions Search" and in the "Short Title contains" box, type in "Moon." Click on Submit Query. Under "Published Opinions," select the link to "0820031p.06" to access the opinion.

CASE CONTINUES

CASE 5.3 CONTINUED to the strictures of the Fourth Amendment. Under the Fourth Amendment, searches "conducted without a warrant issued upon probable cause [are] per se unreasonable * * * subject only to a few specifically established and well-delineated exceptions."

*The well-delineated exception at issue here is consent. If an officer obtains consent to search, a warrantless search does not offend the Constitution. * * * Consent is voluntary when it is "unequivocal, specific and intelligently given, uncontaminated by any duress or coercion."* [Emphasis added.]

* * * *

We find that the district court's denial of the motion to suppress was not clearly erroneous inasmuch as Defendant voluntarily consented to the search of her office. The only evidence on the question of verbal consent was provided in the form of testimony by Agent Andy Corbitt of TBI at the suppression hearing. Agent Corbitt testified that three members of the TBI investigative team entered Defendant's office dressed in "business professional" attire, with weapons concealed. Agents identified themselves to Defendant, explained that there was an ongoing investigation and requested access to particular patient files. Defendant inquired about the nature of the investigation but was not informed of the specific nature of the allegations. Following this conversation, Defendant stated it would be "fine" for agents to access requested files and that they "could scan whatever [they] needed to." Further, Defendant provided agents with a space where they could scan the requested files.

Defendant, however, claims that the verbal consent was not voluntary as she merely acquiesced to a claim of lawful authority.

* * * Based on the totality of the circumstances, we find that Defendant voluntarily consented to the search of her office and therefore the motion to suppress was properly denied.

- **Decision and Remedy** *The U.S. Court of Appeals for the Sixth Circuit affirmed the district court's decision. Because Dr. Moon voluntarily allowed the agents to examine her files and to scan them, the resulting evidence did not need to be suppressed. A search warrant was not necessary.*

- **What If the Facts Were Different?** *Assume that Dr. Moon had proved that using partial doses of the chemotherapy drugs did not affect the "cure" rate for her cancer patients. Would the court have ruled differently? Why or why not?*

- **The Legal Environment Dimension** *Does the length of Dr. Moon's prison sentence seem appropriate here? Why or why not?*

Border Searches of Computers Warrantless border searches have long been upheld by the courts as means to prevent persons from physically bringing drugs, contraband, and illegal aliens into the United States. In recent years, the courts have also started allowing border guards to search through the temporary files stored on laptop computers and to use the history of Web pages viewed as criminal evidence.

Consider, for example, a 2006 case involving Stuart Romm, a suspended lawyer from Massachusetts who traveled to British Columbia on business. A border agent asked to see Romm's laptop computer and briefly examined the Internet cache, or temporary folder showing the history of Web sites that Romm had visited. The border guards discovered that Romm had looked at some child pornography Web sites and detained him while a forensic computer specialist analyzed the hard drive. Analysis confirmed that Romm had viewed ten images of child pornography and then deleted (or at least attempted to delete) the images from his computer. Romm was convicted and sentenced to serve ten to fifteen years in prison. A federal appellate court upheld his conviction.[37] The holding in this case could be applied to any type of illegal material found on a laptop computer during a border search, including unauthorized images of copyrighted materials or confidential business data (see Chapter 14).

Self-Incrimination

The Fifth Amendment guarantees that no person "shall be compelled in any criminal case to be a witness against himself." Thus, in any federal or state (because the due process clause extends the protection to state courts) proceeding, an accused person cannot be forced to give testimony that might subject him or her to any criminal prosecution.

37. *United States v. Romm*, 455 F.3d 990 (9th Cir. 2006).

The Fifth Amendment's guarantee against self-incrimination extends only to natural persons. Therefore, neither corporations nor partnerships receive Fifth Amendment protection. When a partnership is required to produce business records, it must do so even if the information provided incriminates the individual partners of the firm. In contrast, sole proprietors and sole practitioners (those who fully own their businesses) cannot be compelled to produce their business records. These individuals have full protection against self-incrimination because they function in only one capacity; there is no separate business entity.

Due Process and Equal Protection

Other constitutional guarantees of great significance to Americans are mandated by the *due process clauses* of the Fifth and Fourteenth Amendments and the *equal protection clause* of the Fourteenth Amendment.

Due Process

Both the Fifth and Fourteenth Amendments provide that no person shall be deprived "of life, liberty, or property, without due process of law." The **due process clause** of these constitutional amendments has two aspects—procedural and substantive. Note that the due process clause applies to "legal persons" (that is, corporations), as well as to individuals.

Procedural Due Process *Procedural* due process requires that any government decision to take life, liberty, or property must be made equitably; that is, the government must give a person proper notice and an opportunity to be heard. Fair procedures must be used in determining whether a person will be subjected to punishment or have some burden imposed on her or him. Fair procedure has been interpreted as requiring that the person have at least an opportunity to object to a proposed action before an impartial, neutral decision maker (which need not be a judge). Thus, for example, if a driver's license is construed as a property interest, the state must provide some sort of opportunity for the driver to object before suspending or terminating the license.

Substantive Due Process Substantive due process protects an individual's life, liberty, or property against certain government actions regardless of the fairness of the procedures used to implement them. Substantive due process limits what the government may do in its legislative and executive capacities.[38] Legislation must be fair and reasonable in content and must further a legitimate governmental objective. Only when state conduct is arbitrary, or shocks the conscience, however, will it rise to the level of violating substantive due process.[39]

If a law or other governmental action limits a fundamental right, the state must have a legitimate and compelling interest to justify its action. Fundamental rights include interstate travel, privacy, voting, marriage and family, and all First Amendment rights. Thus, a state must have substantial reason for taking any action that infringes on a person's free speech rights. In situations not involving fundamental rights, a law or action does not violate substantive due process if it rationally relates to any legitimate government purpose. Under this test, virtually any business regulation will be upheld as reasonable.

Equal Protection

Under the Fourteenth Amendment, a state may not "deny to any person within its jurisdiction the equal protection of the laws." The United States Supreme Court has interpreted the due process clause of the Fifth Amendment to make the **equal protection clause** applicable to the federal government as well. Equal protection means that the government cannot enact laws that treat similarly situated individuals differently.

Both substantive due process and equal protection require review of the substance of the law or other governmental action rather than review of the procedures used. When a law or action limits the liberty of all persons to do something, it may violate substantive due process; when a law or action limits the liberty of some persons but not others, it may violate the equal protection clause. Thus, for example, if a law prohibits all advertising on the sides of trucks, it raises a substantive due process question; if it makes an exception to allow truck owners to advertise their own businesses, it raises an equal protection issue.

In an equal protection inquiry, when a law or action distinguishes between or among individuals, the basis for the distinction, or classification, is examined.

38. *County of Sacramento v. Lewis,* 523 U.S. 833, 118 S.Ct. 1708, 140 L.Ed.2d 1043 (1998).

39. See, for example, *Breen v. Texas A&M University*, 485 F.3d 325 (5th Cir. 2007); *Hart v. City of Little Rock,* 432 F.3d 801 (8th Cir. 2005); *County of Sacramento v. Lewis,* 523 U.S. 833, 118 S.Ct. 1708, 140 L.Ed.2d 1043 (1998); and *United States v. Salerno,* 481 U.S. 739, 107 S.Ct. 2095, 95 L.Ed.2d 697 (1987).

Depending on the classification, the courts apply different levels of scrutiny, or "tests," to determine whether the law or action violates the equal protection clause. The courts use one of three standards: strict scrutiny, intermediate scrutiny, or the "rational basis" test.

Strict Scrutiny The most difficult standard to meet is that of *strict scrutiny.* Under strict scrutiny, the classification must be necessary to promote a *compelling state interest.* Generally, few laws or actions survive strict-scrutiny analysis by the courts.

Strict scrutiny is applied when a law or action prohibits some persons from exercising a fundamental right or classifies individuals based on a *suspect trait*—such as race, national origin, or citizenship status. For example, to prevent violence caused by racial gangs in prisons, corrections officials in California segregated prisoners by race for up to sixty days after they entered (or transferred to) a correctional facility. A prisoner challenged that policy. Ultimately, the United States Supreme Court held that all racial classifications, because they are based on a suspect trait, must be analyzed under strict scrutiny.[40]

Intermediate Scrutiny Another standard, that of *intermediate scrutiny,* is applied in cases involving discrimination based on gender or legitimacy. Laws using these classifications must be *substantially related to important government objectives.* For example, an important government objective is preventing illegitimate teenage pregnancies. Therefore, because males and females are not similarly situated in this regard—only females can become pregnant—a law that punishes men but not women for statutory rape will be upheld, even though it treats men and women unequally.

The state also has an important objective in establishing time limits (called *statutes of limitation*) for how long after an event a particular type of action can be brought. Such limits prevent persons from bringing fraudulent and stale (outdated) claims. Nevertheless, the limitation period must be substantially related to the important objective. Suppose that a state law requires illegitimate children to file a paternity action within six years of their birth in order to seek support from their biological fathers. This law will fail if legitimate children can seek support from their fathers at any time because distinguishing between support claims on the basis of legitimacy has no relation to the objective of preventing fraudulent or stale claims.

The "Rational Basis" Test In matters of economic or social welfare, a classification will be considered valid if there is any conceivable *rational basis* on which the classification might relate to a legitimate government interest. It is almost impossible for a law or action to fail the rational basis test. Thus, for example, a city ordinance that in effect prohibits all pushcart vendors, except a specific few, from operating in a particular area of the city will be upheld if the city provides a rational basis—such as reducing the traffic in the particular area—for the ordinance. In contrast, a law that provides unemployment benefits only to people over six feet tall would clearly fail the rational basis test because it could not further any legitimate government objective.

Privacy Rights

The U.S. Constitution does not explicitly mention a general right to privacy. In a 1928 Supreme Court case, *Olmstead v. United States,*[41] Justice Louis Brandeis stated in his dissent that the right to privacy is "the most comprehensive of rights and the right most valued by civilized men." The majority of the justices at that time did not agree, and it was not until the 1960s that a majority on the Supreme Court endorsed the view that the Constitution protects individual privacy rights. In a landmark 1965 case, *Griswold v. Connecticut,*[42] the Supreme Court held that a constitutional right to privacy was implied by the First, Third, Fourth, Fifth, and Ninth Amendments.

Federal Statutes Affecting Privacy Rights

In the last several decades, Congress has enacted a number of statutes that protect the privacy of individuals in various areas of concern. In the 1960s, Americans were sufficiently alarmed by the accumulation of personal information in government files that they pressured Congress to pass laws permitting individuals to access their files. Congress responded in 1966 with the Freedom of Information Act, which allows any person to request copies of any information on her or him contained in federal government files. In 1974, Congress passed the Privacy Act, which also gives persons the right to access such information. Since then, Congress has passed numerous other

40. *Johnson v. California,* 543 U.S. 499, 125 S.Ct. 1141, 160 L.Ed.2d 949 (2005).

41. 277 U.S. 438, 48 S.Ct. 564, 72 L.Ed. 944 (1928).

42. 381 U.S. 479, 85 S.Ct. 1678, 14 L.Ed.2d 510 (1965).

laws protecting individuals' privacy rights with respect to financial transactions, electronic communications, and other activities in which personal information may be gathered and stored by organizations.

Medical Information Responding to the growing need to protect the privacy of individuals' health records—particularly computerized records—Congress passed the Health Insurance Portability and Accountability Act (HIPAA) of 1996.[43] This act, which took effect on April 14, 2003, defines and limits the circumstances in which an individual's "protected health information" may be used or disclosed.

The HIPAA requires health-care providers and health-care plans, including certain employers who sponsor health plans, to inform patients of their privacy rights and of how their personal medical information may be used. The act also states that a person's medical records generally may not be used for purposes unrelated to health care—such as marketing, for example—or disclosed to others without the individual's permission. Covered entities must formulate written privacy policies, designate privacy officials, limit access to computerized health data, physically secure medical records with lock and key, train employees and volunteers on their privacy policies, and sanction those who violate the policies. These protections are intended to assure individuals that their health information, including genetic information, will be properly protected and not used for purposes that the patient did not know about or authorize.

The Patriot Act In the wake of the terrorist attacks of September 11, 2001, Congress passed legislation often referred to as the USA Patriot Act.[44] The Patriot Act has given government officials increased authority to monitor Internet activities (such as e-mail and Web site visits) and to gain access to personal financial information and student information. Law enforcement officials can now track a person's telephone and e-mail communications to find out the identity of the other party or parties. The government must certify that the information likely to be obtained by such monitoring is relevant to an ongoing criminal investigation but does not need to provide proof of any wrongdoing to gain access to this information.[45] Privacy advocates argue that this law adversely affects the constitutional rights of all Americans, and it has been widely criticized in the media, fueling a public debate over how to secure privacy rights in an electronic age.

Other Laws Affecting Privacy

State constitutions and statutes also protect individuals' privacy rights, often to a significant degree. Privacy rights are also protected under tort law (see Chapter 12). Additionally, the Federal Trade Commission has played an active role in protecting the privacy rights of online consumers (see Chapter 23). The protection of employees' privacy rights, particularly with respect to electronic monitoring practices, is an area of growing concern (see Chapter 20).

43. The HIPAA was enacted as Pub. L. No. 104-191 (1996) and is codified in 29 U.S.C.A. Sections 1181 *et seq.*

44. The Uniting and Strengthening America by Providing Appropriate Tools Required to Intercept and Obstruct Terrorism Act of 2001, also known as the USA Patriot Act, was enacted as Pub. L. No. 107-56 (2001) and extended in early 2006 by Pub. L. No. 109-173 (2006).

45. See, for example, a case in which a federal appeals court upheld the government's warrantless monitoring of electronic communications. *American Civil Liberties Union v. National Security Agency*, 493 F.3d 644 (6th Cir. 2007).

REVIEWING Constitutional Law

A state legislature enacted a statute that required any motorcycle operator or passenger on the state's highways to wear a protective helmet. Jim Alderman, a licensed motorcycle operator, sued the state to block enforcement of the law. Alderman asserted that the statute violated the equal protection clause because it placed requirements on motorcyclists that were not imposed on other motorists. Using the information presented in the chapter, answer the following questions.

1. Why does this statute raise equal protection issues instead of substantive due process concerns?
2. What are the three levels of scrutiny that the courts use in determining whether a law violates the equal protection clause?
3. Which standard of scrutiny, or test, would apply to this situation? Why?
4. Applying this standard, or test, is the helmet statute constitutional? Why or why not?

TERMS AND CONCEPTS

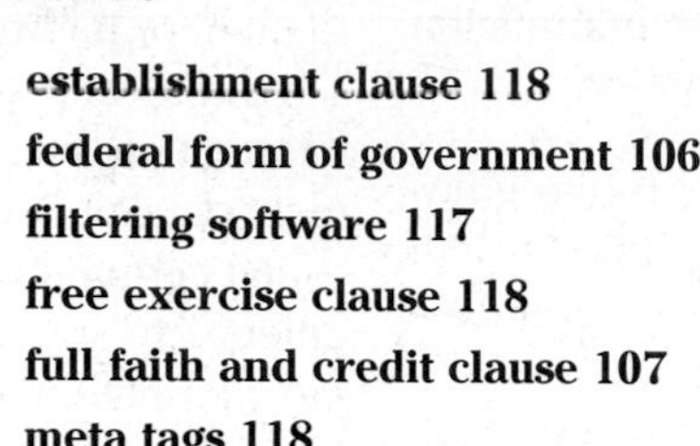

Bill of Rights 112
checks and balances 108
commerce clause 108
due process clause 121
equal protection clause 121
establishment clause 118
federal form of government 106
filtering software 117
free exercise clause 118
full faith and credit clause 107
meta tags 118
police powers 106
preemption 109
privileges and immunities clause 107
probable cause 118
search warrant 118
supremacy clause 109
symbolic speech 112

QUESTIONS AND CASE PROBLEMS

5-1. A Georgia state law requires the use of contoured rear-fender mudguards on trucks and trailers operating within Georgia state lines. The statute further makes it illegal for trucks and trailers to use straight mudguards. In approximately thirty-five other states, straight mudguards are legal. Moreover, in Florida, straight mudguards are explicitly required by law. There is some evidence suggesting that contoured mudguards might be a little safer than straight mudguards. Discuss whether this Georgia statute violates any constitutional provisions.

5-2. QUESTION WITH SAMPLE ANSWER

Thomas worked in the nonmilitary operations of a large firm that produced both military and nonmilitary goods. When the company discontinued the production of nonmilitary goods, Thomas was transferred to a plant producing military equipment. Thomas left his job, claiming that it violated his religious principles to participate in the manufacture of goods to be used in destroying life. In effect, he argued, the transfer to the military equipment plant forced him to quit his job. He was denied unemployment compensation by the state because he had not been effectively "discharged" by the employer but had voluntarily terminated his employment. Did the state's denial of unemployment benefits to Thomas violate the free exercise clause of the First Amendment? Explain.

- **For a sample answer to Question 5–2, go to Appendix I at the end of this text.**

5-3. A business has a backlog of orders, and to meet its deadlines, management decides to run the firm seven days a week, eight hours a day. One of the employees, Abe Placer, refuses to work on Saturday on religious grounds. His refusal to work means that the firm may not meet its production deadlines and may therefore suffer a loss of future business. The firm fires Placer and replaces him with an employee who is willing to work seven days a week. Placer claims that by terminating his employment, his employer has violated his constitutional right to the free exercise of his religion. Do you agree? Why or why not?

5-4. The framers of the U.S. Constitution feared the twin evils of tyranny and anarchy. Discuss how specific provisions of the Constitution and the Bill of Rights reflect these fears and protect against both of these extremes.

5-5. Freedom of Speech. Henry Mishkoff is a Web designer whose firm does business as "Webfeats." When Taubman Co. began building a mall called "The Shops at Willow Bend" near Mishkoff's home, Mishkoff registered the domain name "shopsatwillowbend.com" and created a Web site with that address. The site featured information about the mall, a disclaimer indicating that Mishkoff's site was unofficial, and a link to the mall's official site. Taubman discovered Mishkoff's site and filed a suit in a federal district court against him. Mishkoff then registered other various names, including "taubmansucks.com," with links to a site documenting his battle with Taubman. (A Web name with a "sucks.com" moniker attached to it is known as a *complaint name,* and the process of registering and using such names is known as *cybergriping.*) Taubman asked the court to order Mishkoff to stop using all of these names. Should the court grant Taubman's request? On what basis might the court protect Mishkoff's use of the names? [*Taubman Co. v. Webfeats,* 319 F.3d 770 (6th Cir. 2003)]

5-6. CASE PROBLEM WITH SAMPLE ANSWER

To protect the privacy of individuals identified in information systems maintained by federal agencies, the Privacy Act of 1974 regulates the use of the information. The statute provides for a minimum award of $1,000 for "actual damages sustained" caused by "intentional or willful actions" to the "person entitled to recovery." Buck Doe filed for certain disability benefits with an office of the U.S. Department of Labor (DOL). The application form asked for Doe's Social Security number, which the DOL used to identify his claim on documents sent to groups of claimants, their employers, and the lawyers involved in their cases. This disclosed Doe's Social Security number beyond the limits set by the Privacy Act. Doe filed a suit in a federal district court against the DOL, alleging that he was "torn . . . all to pieces" and "greatly concerned and worried" because of the disclosure of his Social Security number and its potentially "devastating" consequences. He did not offer any proof of actual injury, however. Should damages be awarded in such circumstances solely on the basis of the agency's conduct, or should proof of some actual injury be required? Why? [*Doe v. Chao,* 540 U.S. 614, 124 S.Ct. 1204, 157 L.Ed.2d 1122 (2004)]

- **To view a sample answer for Problem 5–6, go to this book's Web site at academic.cengage.com/blaw/cross, select "Chapter 5," and click on "Case Problem with Sample Answer."**

5–7. Due Process. In 1994, the Board of County Commissioners of Yellowstone County, Montana, created Zoning District 17 in a rural area of the county and a planning and zoning commission for the district. The commission adopted zoning regulations, which provided, among other things, that "dwelling units" could be built only through "on-site construction." Later, county officials were unable to identify any health or safety concerns that were addressed by requiring on-site construction. There was no evidence that homes built off-site would negatively affect property values or cause harm to any other general welfare interest of the community. In December 1999, Francis and Anita Yurczyk bought two forty-acre tracts in District 17. The Yurczyks also bought a modular home and moved it onto the property the following spring. Within days, the county advised the Yurczyks that the home violated the on-site construction regulation and would have to be removed. The Yurczyks filed a suit in a Montana state court against the county, alleging, among other things, that the zoning regulation violated their due process rights. Does the Yurczyks' claim relate to procedural or substantive due process rights? What standard would the court apply to determine whether the regulation is constitutional? How should the court rule? Explain. [*Yurczyk v. Yellowstone County*, 2004 MT 3, 319 Mont. 169, 83 P.3d 266 (2004)]

5–8. Supremacy Clause. The Federal Communications Act of 1934 grants the right to govern all *interstate* telecommunications to the Federal Communications Commission (FCC) and the right to regulate all *intrastate* telecommunications to the states. The federal Telephone Consumer Protection Act of 1991, the Junk Fax Protection Act of 2005, and FCC rules permit a party to send unsolicited fax ads to recipients with whom the party has an "established business relationship" if those ads include an "opt-out" alternative. Section 17538.43 of California's Business and Professions Code (known as "SB 833") was enacted in 2005 to provide the citizens of California with greater protection than that afforded under federal law. SB 833 omits the "established business relationship" exception and requires a sender to obtain a recipient's express consent (an "opt-in" provision) before faxing an ad to that party into or out of California. The Chamber of Commerce of the United States filed a suit against Bill Lockyer, California's state attorney general, seeking to block the enforcement of SB 833. What principles support the plaintiff's position? How should the court resolve the issue? Explain. [*Chamber of Commerce of the United States v. Lockyer,* 463 F.3d 1076 (E.D.Cal. 2006)]

5–9. Freedom of Speech. For decades, New York City has had to deal with the vandalism and defacement of public property caused by unauthorized graffiti. Among other attempts to stop the damage, in December 2005 the city banned the sale of aerosol spray-paint cans and broad-tipped indelible markers to persons under twenty-one years of age and prohibited them from possessing such items on property other than their own. By May 1, 2006, five people—all under age twenty-one—had been cited for violations of these regulations, while 871 individuals had been arrested for actually making graffiti. Artists who wished to create graffiti on legal surfaces, such as canvas, wood, and clothing, included college student Lindsey Vincenty, who was studying visual arts. Unable to buy her supplies in the city or to carry them in the city if she bought them elsewhere, Vincenty and others filed a suit in a federal district court on behalf of themselves and other young artists against Michael Bloomberg, the city's mayor, and others. The plaintiffs claimed that, among other things, the new rules violated their right to freedom of speech. They asked the court to enjoin the enforcement of the rules. Should the court grant this request? Why or why not? [*Vincenty v. Bloomberg,* 476 F.3d 74 (2d Cir. 2007)]

5–10. A QUESTION OF ETHICS

Aric Toll owns and manages the Balboa Island Village Inn, a restaurant and bar in Newport Beach, California. Anne Lemen owns the "Island Cottage," a residence across an alley from the Inn. Lemen often complained to the authorities about excessive noise and the behavior of the Inn's customers, whom she called "drunks" and "whores." Lemen referred to Theresa Toll, Aric's wife, as "Madam Whore." Lemen told the Inn's bartender Ewa Cook that Cook "worked for Satan," was "Satan's wife," and was "going to have Satan's children." She told the Inn's neighbors that it was "a whorehouse" with "prostitution going on inside" and that it sold illegal drugs, sold alcohol to minors, made "sex videos," was involved in child pornography, had "Mafia connections," encouraged "lesbian activity," and stayed open until 6:00 A.M. Lemen also voiced her complaints to potential customers, and the Inn's sales dropped more than

*20 percent. The Inn filed a suit in a California state court against Lemen, asserting defamation and other claims. [*Balboa Island Village Inn, Inc. v. Lemen, *40 Cal.4th 1141, 156 P.3d 339 (2007)]*

(a) Are Lemen's statements about the Inn's owners, customers, and activities protected by the U.S. Constitution? Should such statements be protected? In whose favor should the court rule? Why?

(b) Did Lemen behave unethically in the circumstances of this case? Explain.

5-11. SPECIAL CASE ANALYSIS

Go to Case 5.2, *Lott v. Levitt,* 469 F.Supp.2d 575 (N.D.Ill. 2007), on pages 115–117. Read the excerpt and answer the following questions.

(a) **Issue:** What was the main issue in this case?

(b) **Rule of Law:** What rule of law did the court apply?

(c) **Applying the Rule of Law:** Describe how the court applied the rule of law to the facts of this case.

(d) **Conclusion:** What was the court's conclusion in this case?

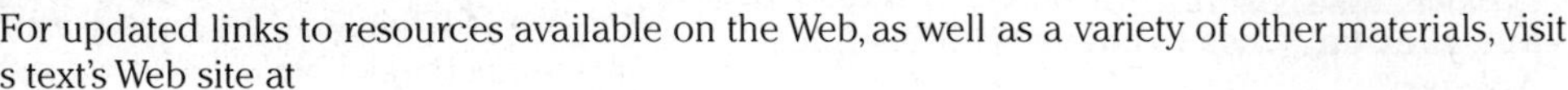

LAW ON THE WEB

For updated links to resources available on the Web, as well as a variety of other materials, visit this text's Web site at

academic.cengage.com/blaw/cross

For an online version of the Constitution that provides hypertext links to amendments and other changes, as well as the history of the document, go to

www.constitutioncenter.org

An ongoing debate in the United States is whether the national government exercises too much regulatory control over intrastate affairs. To find current articles on this topic, go to

www.vote-smart.org/issues/FEDERALISM_STATES_RIGHTS

For discussions of current issues involving the rights and liberties contained in the Bill of Rights, go to the Web site of the American Civil Liberties Union at

www.aclu.org

For a menu of selected constitutional law decisions by the United States Supreme Court, go to the Web site of Cornell Law School's Legal Information Institute at

www.law.cornell.edu/supct/cases/conlaw.htm

Legal Research Exercises on the Web

Go to **academic.cengage.com/blaw/cross**, the Web site that accompanies this text. Select "Chapter 5" and click on "Internet Exercises." There you will find the following Internet research exercises that you can perform to learn more about the topics covered in this chapter.

Internet Exercise 5–1: Legal Perspective
Commercial Speech

Internet Exercise 5–2: Management Perspective
Privacy Rights in Cyberspace

CHAPTER 6

Administrative Law

Government agencies established to administer the law have a great impact on the day-to-day operations of the government and the economy. Administrative agencies issue rules covering virtually every aspect of a business's activities. At the federal level, the Securities and Exchange Commission regulates a firm's capital structure and financing, as well as its financial reporting. The National Labor Relations Board oversees relations between a firm and any unions with which it may deal. The Equal Employment Opportunity Commission also regulates employer-employee relationships. The Environmental Protection Agency and the Occupational Safety and Health Administration affect the way a firm manufactures its products, and the Federal Trade Commission influences the way it markets those products.

Added to this layer of federal regulation is a second layer of state regulation that, when not preempted, may cover many of the same activities as federal regulation or regulate independently the activities that federal regulation does not cover. Finally, agency regulations at the county or municipal level also affect certain types of business activities.

The rules, orders, and decisions of administrative agencies make up the body of *administrative law*. You were introduced briefly to some of the main principles of administrative law in Chapter 1. In the following pages, we look at these principles in much greater detail.

The Practical Significance of Administrative Law

Unlike statutory law, administrative law is created by administrative agencies, not by legislatures, but it is nevertheless of paramount significance for businesses. When Congress—or a state legislature—enacts legislation, it typically adopts a rather general statute and leaves its implementation to an administrative agency, which then creates the detailed rules and regulations necessary to carry out the statute. The administrative agency, with its specialized personnel, has the time, resources, and expertise to make the detailed decisions required for regulation. For example, when Congress enacted the Clean Air Act, it provided only general directions for the prevention of air pollution. The specific pollution-control requirements imposed on business are almost entirely the product of decisions made by the Environmental Protection Agency (EPA).

Legislation and regulations have great benefits—in the example of the Clean Air Act, a much cleaner environment than existed in decades past. At the same time, these benefits entail costs for business. The EPA has estimated the costs of compliance with the Clean Air Act at tens of billions of dollars yearly. Although the agency has calculated that the overall benefits of its regulations often exceed their costs, the burden on business is substantial. The Small Business Administration has estimated the costs of regulation to business, by size of business, and produced the figures shown in Exhibit 6–1 on page 128.[1] These costs are averages and vary considerably by type of business (for example, retail or manufacturing). The costs are proportionately higher for small businesses because

1. W. Mark Crain, "The Impact of Regulatory Costs on Small Firms," Small Business Research Summary No. 264, September 2005.

EXHIBIT 6–1 • Costs of Regulation to Businesses

Type of Regulation	Cost per Employee (<20 Employees)	Cost per Employee (500+ Employees)
All federal regulations	$7,647	$5,282
Environmental	$3,296	$ 710
Economic	$2,127	$2,952
Workplace	$ 920	$ 841
Tax compliance	$1,304	$ 780

they cannot take advantage of the economies of scale available to larger operations. Clearly, the costs of regulation to business are considerable—and are significantly higher today than they were in 2005.

Given the costs that regulation entails, business has a strong incentive to try to influence the regulatory environment. Whenever new regulations are proposed, as happens constantly, companies may lobby the agency to try to persuade it not to adopt a particular regulation or to adopt one that is more cost-effective. These lobbying efforts consist mainly of providing information to regulators about the costs and problems that the rule may pose for business. At the same time, public-interest groups may be lobbying in favor of more stringent regulation. The rulemaking process, including these lobbying efforts, is governed by administrative law. If persuasion fails, administrative law also provides a tool by which businesses or other groups may challenge the legality of the new regulation.

SECTION 2

Agency Creation and Powers

To create an administrative agency, Congress passes **enabling legislation,** which specifies the name, purposes, functions, and powers of the agency being created. Federal administrative agencies may exercise only those powers that Congress has delegated to them in enabling legislation. Through similar enabling acts, state legislatures create state administrative agencies, which commonly parallel federal agencies.

An agency's enabling statute defines its legal authority. An agency cannot regulate beyond the powers granted by the statute, and it may be required to take some regulatory action by the terms of that statute.

Enabling Legislation—An Example

Consider the enabling legislation for the Federal Trade Commission (FTC). The enabling statute for this agency is the Federal Trade Commission Act of 1914.[2] The act prohibits unfair methods of competition and deceptive trade practices. It also describes the procedures that the FTC must follow to charge persons or organizations with violations of the act, and it provides for judicial review of agency orders. The act grants the FTC the power to do the following:

1. Create "rules and regulations for the purpose of carrying out the Act."
2. Conduct investigations of business practices.
3. Obtain reports from interstate corporations concerning their business practices.
4. Investigate possible violations of federal antitrust statutes.[3]
5. Publish findings of its investigations.
6. Recommend new legislation.
7. Hold trial-like hearings to resolve certain kinds of trade disputes that involve FTC regulations or federal antitrust laws.

The authorizing statute for the FTC allows it to prevent the use of "unfair methods of competition," but does not define *unfairness.* Congress delegated that authority to the commission, thereby providing it with considerable discretion in regulating competition.

When regulated groups oppose a rule adopted by an agency, they often bring a lawsuit arguing that the rule was not authorized by the enabling statute and is therefore void. Conversely, a group may file a suit claiming that an agency has illegally *failed* to pursue regulation required by the enabling statute.

2. 15 U.S.C. Sections 41–58.
3. The FTC shares enforcement of the Clayton Act with the Antitrust Division of the U.S. Department of Justice.

Types of Agencies

As discussed in Chapter 1, there are two basic types of administrative agencies: executive agencies and independent regulatory agencies. Federal *executive agencies* include the cabinet departments of the executive branch, which were formed to assist the president in carrying out executive functions, and the subagencies within the cabinet departments. The Occupational Safety and Health Administration, for example, is a subagency within the U.S. Department of Labor. Exhibit 6–2 on page 132 lists the cabinet departments and some of their most important subagencies.

All administrative agencies are part of the executive branch of government, but *independent regulatory agencies* are outside the major executive departments. The Federal Trade Commission and the Securities and Exchange Commission are examples of independent regulatory agencies. These and other selected independent regulatory agencies, as well as their principal functions, are listed in Exhibit 6–3 on page 133.

The accountability of the regulators is the most significant difference between the two types of agencies. Agencies that are considered part of the executive branch are subject to the authority of the president, who has the power to appoint and remove federal officers. The president could give orders to the head of an executive agency and fire him or her for failing to carry them out. This power is less pronounced in regard to independent agencies, whose officers serve for fixed terms and cannot be removed without just cause. In practice, however, the president's ability to exert influence over independent regulatory agencies is often considerable because the president has the authority to appoint the members of the agencies.

All three branches of government exercise certain controls over agency powers and functions, as will be discussed later in this chapter, but in many ways administrative agencies function independently. None of the other branches, including the presidency, has the time and resources necessary to monitor the multitude of administrative actions constantly under way. For this reason, administrative agencies, which constitute the **bureaucracy,** are sometimes referred to as the "fourth branch" of the U.S. government.

SECTION 3 The Administrative Procedure Act

All federal agencies must follow specific procedural requirements in their rulemaking, adjudication, and other functions. Sometimes, Congress specifies certain procedural requirements in an agency's enabling legislation. In the absence of any directives from Congress concerning a particular agency procedure, the Administrative Procedure Act (APA) of 1946[4] applies.

The Arbitrary and Capricious Test

One of Congress's goals in enacting the APA was to provide for more judicial control over administrative agencies, which had assumed greater powers during the expansion of government that had taken place as a result of the Great Depression of the 1930s and World War II (1939–1945). To that end, the APA provides that courts should "hold unlawful and set aside" agency actions found to be "arbitrary, capricious, an abuse of discretion, or otherwise not in accordance with law."[5] Under this standard, parties can challenge regulations as contrary to law or so irrational as to be arbitrary and capricious.

The definition of what makes a rule arbitrary and capricious is a vague one, but it includes factors such as whether the agency has done any of the following:

1. Failed to provide a rational explanation for its decision.
2. Changed its prior policy without justification.
3. Considered legally inappropriate factors.
4. Entirely failed to consider a relevant factor.
5. Rendered a decision plainly contrary to the evidence.

The following case considers the application of the arbitrary and capricious standard.

4. 5 U.S.C. Sections 551–706.
5. 5 U.S.C. Section 706(2)(A).

EXTENDED CASE 6.1 **Fox Television Stations, Inc. v. Federal Communications Commission**

United States Court of Appeals, Second Circuit, 2007. 489 F.3d 444.

POOLER, **Circuit Judge.**

* * * *

CASE CONTINUES

CASE 6.1 CONTINUED

The [Federal Communications Commission's (FCC's)] policing of "indecent" speech stems from 18 U.S.C. [Section] 1464, which provides that "[w]hoever utters any obscene, indecent, or profane language by means of radio communication shall be fined * * * or imprisoned not more than two years, or both." * * * The FCC first exercised its statutory authority to sanction indecent (but non-obscene) speech in 1975, when it found Pacifica Foundation's radio broadcast of comedian George Carlin's "Filthy Words" monologue indecent * * * .

* * * *

* * * Under the Commission's definition, "indecent speech is language that describes, in terms patently offensive as measured by contemporary community standards for the broadcast medium, sexual or excretory activities and organs.

* * * *

* * * During [a] January 19, 2003, live broadcast of the Golden Globe Awards, musician Bono stated in his acceptance speech "this is really, really, f***ing brilliant. Really, really, great."

* * * [On a complaint about the broadcast by individuals associated with the Parents Television Council, the] FCC held that any use of any variant of "the F-Word" inherently has sexual connotation and therefore falls within the scope of the indecency definition. * * * The Commission found the fleeting and isolated use of the word irrelevant and overruled all prior decisions in which fleeting use of an expletive was held not indecent.

* * * *

On February 21, 2006, * * * the Commission found * * * [Fox Television Stations, Inc.'s] broadcast of the 2002 Billboard Music Awards [and] Fox's broadcast of the 2003 Billboard Music Awards * * * indecent and profane. * * * [On the 2002 broadcast] Cher stated: "People have been telling me I'm on the way out every year, right? So f*** 'em." * * * [On the 2003 broadcast] Nicole Richie * * * stated: "Have you ever tried to get cow shit out of a Prada purse? It's not so f***ing simple."

Fox * * * filed a petition for review of the [FCC's] Order in [the U.S. Court of Appeals for the Second Circuit].

* * * *

Agencies are of course free to revise their rules and policies. Such a change, however, must provide a reasoned analysis for departing from prior precedent. *When an agency reverses its course, a court must satisfy itself that the agency knows it is changing course, has given sound reasons for the change, and has shown that the rule is consistent with the law that gives the agency its authority to act.* In addition, the agency must consider reasonably obvious alternatives and, if it rejects those alternatives, it must give reasons for the rejection * * * . *The agency must explain why the original reasons for adopting the rule or policy are no longer dispositive* [a deciding factor]. * * * [Emphasis added.]

* * * The primary reason for the crackdown on fleeting expletives advanced by the FCC is the so-called "first blow" theory * * * . Indecent material on the airwaves enters into the privacy of the home uninvited and without warning. * * * To say that one may avoid further offense by turning off the [television or] radio when he hears indecent language is like saying that the remedy for an assault is to run away after the first blow.

We cannot accept this argument as a reasoned basis justifying the Commission's new rule. First, the Commission provides no reasonable explanation for why it has changed its perception that a fleeting expletive was not a harmful "first blow" for the nearly thirty years between [the decisions in Pacifica's case] and Golden Globes. More problematic, however, is that the "first blow" theory bears no rational connection to the Commission's actual policy regarding fleeting expletives. * * * A re-broadcast of precisely the same offending clips from the two Billboard Music Award programs for the purpose of providing background information on this case would not result in any action by the FCC * * * .

The * * * Order makes passing reference to other reasons that purportedly support its change in policy, none of which we find sufficient. For instance, the Commission states that even non-literal uses of expletives fall within its indecency definition because it is "difficult (if not impossible) to distinguish whether a word is being used as an expletive or as a literal description of sexual or excretory functions." This defies any commonsense understanding of these words, which, as the general public well knows, are often used in everyday conversation without any "sexual or excretory" meaning. * * * Even the top leaders of our government have used variants of

CASE 6.1 CONTINUED

these expletives in a manner that no reasonable person would believe referenced "sexual or excretory organs or activities." [The court proceeded to recount examples of when President Bush and Vice President Cheney had used the questionable words in public.]

* * * *

Accordingly, we find that the FCC's new policy regarding "fleeting expletives" fails to provide a reasoned analysis justifying its departure from the agency's established practice. For this reason, Fox's petition for review is granted, the * * * Order is vacated, and the matter is remanded to the FCC for further proceedings consistent with this opinion.

QUESTIONS

1. According to the court's opinion in this case, is an administrative agency locked into its first interpretation of a statute? Why or why not?
2. Were the agency's reasons for its actions rejected in this case because the court disagreed with those reasons? Explain.

Rulemaking Procedures

Today, the major function of an administrative agency is **rulemaking**—the formulation of new regulations, or rules, as they are often called. The APA defines a *rule* as "an agency statement of general or particular applicability and future effect designed to implement, interpret, or prescribe law and policy."[6] Regulations are sometimes said to be *quasi-legislative* because, like statutes, they have a binding effect. Like those who violate statutes, violators of agency rules may be punished. Because agency rules have such great legal force, the APA established procedures for agencies to follow in creating rules. Many rules must be adopted using the APA's *notice-and-comment rulemaking* procedure.

Notice-and-comment rulemaking involves three basic steps: notice of the proposed rulemaking, a comment period, and the final rule. The APA recognizes some limited exceptions to these procedural requirements, but they are seldom invoked. If the required procedures are violated, the resulting rule may be invalid. The impetus for rulemaking may come from various sources, including Congress, the agency itself, or private parties who may petition an agency to begin a rulemaking (or repeal a rule). For example, environmental groups have petitioned for stricter pollution controls to combat global warming.

Notice of the Proposed Rulemaking When a federal agency decides to create a new rule, the agency publishes a notice of the proposed rulemaking proceedings in the *Federal Register*, a daily publication of the executive branch that prints government orders, rules, and regulations. The notice states where and when the proceedings will be held, the agency's legal authority for making the rule (usually its enabling legislation), and the terms or subject matter of the proposed rule. Courts have ruled that the APA requires an agency to make available to the public certain information, such as the key scientific data underlying the proposal.

Comment Period Following the publication of the notice of the proposed rulemaking proceedings, the agency must allow ample time for persons to comment in writing on the proposed rule. The purpose of this comment period is to give interested parties the opportunity to express their views on the proposed rule in an effort to influence agency policy. The comments may be in writing or, if a hearing is held, may be given orally.

The agency need not respond to all comments, but it must respond to any significant comments that bear directly on the proposed rule. The agency responds by either modifying its final rule or explaining, in a statement accompanying the final rule, why it did not make any changes. In some circumstances, particularly when the procedure being used in a specific instance is less formal, an agency may accept comments after the comment period is closed. The agency should summarize these *ex parte*[7] (private, "off-the-record") comments in the record for possible review.

6. 5 U.S.C. Section 551(4).

7. In Latin, *ex parte* means "from the part." In the law, it refers to one of the parties taking some action on his or her own, such as communicating with a judge or bringing a motion, without notifying the other party or giving the other party a chance to respond.

EXHIBIT 6-2 • Executive Departments and Important Subagencies

Department and Date Formed	Selected Subagencies
State (1789)	Passport Office; Bureau of Diplomatic Security; Foreign Service; Bureau of Human Rights and Humanitarian Affairs; Bureau of Consular Affairs; Bureau of Intelligence and Research
Treasury (1789)	Internal Revenue Service; U.S. Mint
Interior (1849)	U.S. Fish and Wildlife Service; National Park Service; Bureau of Indian Affairs; Bureau of Land Management
Justice (1870)[a]	Federal Bureau of Investigation; Drug Enforcement Administration; Bureau of Prisons; U.S. Marshals Service
Agriculture (1889)	Soil Conservation Service; Agricultural Research Service; Food Safety and Inspection Service; Forest Service
Commerce (1913)[b]	Bureau of the Census; Bureau of Economic Analysis; Minority Business Development Agency; U.S. Patent and Trademark Office; National Oceanic and Atmospheric Administration
Labor (1913)[b]	Occupational Safety and Health Administration; Bureau of Labor Statistics; Employment Standards Administration; Office of Labor-Management Standards; Employment and Training Administration
Defense (1949)[c]	National Security Agency; Joint Chiefs of Staff; Departments of the Air Force, Navy, Army; service academies
Housing and Urban Development (1965)	Office of Community Planning and Development; Government National Mortgage Association; Office of Fair Housing and Equal Opportunity
Transportation (1967)	Federal Aviation Administration; Federal Highway Administration; National Highway Traffic Safety Administration; Federal Transit Administration
Energy (1977)	Office of Civilian Radioactive Waste Management; Office of Nuclear Energy; Energy Information Administration
Health and Human Services (1980)[d]	Food and Drug Administration; Centers for Medicare and Medicaid Services; Centers for Disease Control and Prevention; National Institutes of Health
Education (1980)[d]	Office of Special Education and Rehabilitation Services; Office of Elementary and Secondary Education; Office of Postsecondary Education; Office of Vocational and Adult Education
Veterans Affairs (1989)	Veterans Health Administration; Veterans Benefits Administration; National Cemetery System
Homeland Security (2002)	U.S. Citizenship and Immigration Services; U. S. Customs and Border Protection; Transportation Security Administration; U.S. Coast Guard; Federal Emergency Management Agency

a. Formed from the Office of the Attorney General (created in 1789).
b. Formed from the Department of Commerce and Labor (created in 1903).
c. Formed from the Department of War (created in 1789) and the Department of the Navy (created in 1798).
d. Formed from the Department of Health, Education, and Welfare (created in 1953).

EXHIBIT 6–3 • Selected Independent Regulatory Agencies

Name and Date Formed	Principal Duties
Federal Reserve System Board of Governors (Fed) (1913)	Determines policy with respect to interest rates, credit availability, and the money supply.
Federal Trade Commission (FTC) (1914)	Prevents businesses from engaging in unfair trade practices; stops the formation of monopolies in the business sector; protects consumer rights.
Securities and Exchange Commission (SEC) (1934)	Regulates the nation's stock exchanges, in which shares of stock are bought and sold; enforces the securities laws, which require full disclosure of the financial profiles of companies that wish to sell stock and bonds to the public.
Federal Communications Commission (FCC) (1934)	Regulates all communications by telegraph, cable, telephone, radio, satellite, and television.
National Labor Relations Board (NLRB) (1935)	Protects employees' rights to join unions and bargain collectively with employers; attempts to prevent unfair labor practices by both employers and unions.
Equal Employment Opportunity Commission (EEOC) (1964)	Works to eliminate discrimination in employment based on religion, gender, race, color, disability, national origin, or age; investigates claims of discrimination.
Environmental Protection Agency (EPA) (1970)	Undertakes programs aimed at reducing air and water pollution; works with state and local agencies to help fight environmental hazards.
Nuclear Regulatory Commission (NRC) (1975)	Ensures that electricity-generating nuclear reactors in the United States are built and operated safely; regularly inspects operations of such reactors.

The Final Rule After the agency reviews the comments, it drafts the final rule and publishes it in the *Federal Register*. Such a final rule must contain a "concise general statement of . . . basis and purpose" that describes the reasoning behind the rule.[8] The final rule may change the terms of the proposed rule, in light of the public comments, but cannot change the proposal too radically, or a new proposal and a new opportunity for comment are required. The final rule is later compiled along with the rules and regulations of other federal administrative agencies in the *Code of Federal Regulations* (C.F.R.). Final rules have binding legal effect unless the courts later overturn them. For this reason, they are often referred to as legislative rules. *Legislative rules* are substantive in that they affect legal rights, whereas *interpretive rules* issued by agencies simply declare policy and do not affect legal rights or obligations (see the discussion of informal agency actions later in this chapter).

The court in the following case considered whether to enforce rules that were issued outside the rulemaking procedure.

8. 5 U.S.C. Section 555(c).

CASE 6.2 Hemp Industries Association v. Drug Enforcement Administration

United States Court of Appeals, Ninth Circuit, 2004. 357 F.3d 1012.

• **Background and Facts** The members of the Hemp Industries Association (HIA) import and distribute sterilized hemp seed and oil and cake derived from hemp seed. They also make and sell food and cosmetic products made from hemp seed and oil. These products contain only nonpsychoactive

CASE CONTINUES

CASE 6.2 CONTINUED

trace amounts of tetrahydrocannabinols (THC).[a] On October 9, 2001, the U.S. Drug Enforcement Administration (DEA) published an interpretive rule declaring that "any product that contains any amount of THC is a Schedule I controlled substance."[b] On the same day, the DEA proposed two legislative rules. One rule—DEA-205F—amended the listing of THC in Schedule I to include natural, as well as synthetic, THC. The second rule—DEA-206F—exempted from control nonpsychoactive hemp products that contain trace amounts of THC not intended to enter the human body. On March 21, 2003, without following formal rulemaking procedures, the DEA declared that these rules were final. This effectively banned the possession and sale of the food products of the HIA's members. The HIA petitioned the U.S. Court of Appeals for the Ninth Circuit to review the rules, asserting that they should not be enforced.

IN THE LANGUAGE OF THE COURT

***BETTY B. FLETCHER*, Circuit Judge.**

* * * *

* * * Appellants * * * argue that DEA-205F is a scheduling action—placing nonpsychoactive hemp in Schedule I for the first time—that fails to follow the procedures for such actions required by the Controlled Substances Act ("CSA").

* * * *

Under 21 U.S.C. [Section] 811(a) [of the CSA]:

> the Attorney General may by rule—
> (1) add to * * * a schedule * * * any drug or other substance if he—
> * * *
> (B) makes with respect to such drug or other substance the findings prescribed by subsection (b) of [S]ection 812 of this title * * * .

Rules of the Attorney General under this subsection shall be made on the record after opportunity for a hearing pursuant to the rulemaking procedures prescribed by [the Administrative Procedure Act (APA)].

* * * *Formal rulemaking requires hearings on the record, and [the APA] invites parties to submit proposed findings and oppose the stated bases of tentative agency decisions, and requires the agency to issue formal rulings on each finding, conclusion, or exception on the record.* We will not reproduce the entirety of the [APA] here; it suffices to say that the DEA did not and does not claim to have followed formal rulemaking procedures. [Emphasis added.]

In addition, the DEA did not comply with [Section] 811(a)(1)(B), because the findings required by [Section] 812(b) were not made. Section 812(b) states:

> (b) Placement on schedules; findings required. * * * A drug or other substance may not be placed in any schedule unless the findings required for such schedule are made with respect to such drug or other substance.

* * * *

The DEA does not purport to have met the requirements for placement of nonpsychoactive hemp on Schedule I * * * . Instead, the DEA argues that naturally occurring THC in those parts of the hemp plant excluded from the definition of "marijuana" have always been included under the listing for "THC" * * * .

* * * *

Two CSA provisions are relevant to determining whether Appellants' hemp products were banned before [DEA-205F and DEA-206F]: the definition of THC and the definition of marijuana. Both are unambiguous * * * : Appellants' products do not contain the "synthetic" "substances or derivatives" that are covered by the definition of THC, and nonpsychoactive hemp is explicitly excluded from the definition of marijuana.

* * * *

---

a. A *nonpsychoactive substance* is one that does not affect a person's mind or behavior. Nonpsychoactive hemp is derived from industrial hemp plants grown in Canada and in Europe, the flowers of which contain only a trace amount of the THC contained in marijuana varieties grown for psychoactive use.

b. A *controlled substance* is a drug whose availability is restricted by law.

CASE 6.2 CONTINUED

Under 21 U.S.C. [Section] 802(16) [of the CSA]:

> The term "marihuana" means all parts of the plant Cannabis sativa L. * * * .Such term does not include the mature stalks of such plant, fiber produced from such stalks, oil or cake made from the seeds of such plant, any other compound, manufacture, salt, derivative, mixture, or preparation of such mature stalks (except the resin extracted therefrom), fiber, oil, or cake, or the sterilized seed of such plant which is incapable of germination.

The nonpsychoactive hemp in Appellants' products is derived from the "mature stalks" or is "oil and cake made from the seeds" of the *Cannabis* plant, and therefore fits within the plainly stated exception to the CSA definition of marijuana.

* * * Congress knew what it was doing, and its intent to exclude nonpsychoactive hemp from regulation is entirely clear.

• **Decision and Remedy** *The U.S. Court of Appeals for the Ninth Circuit held that DEA-205F and DEA-206F "are inconsistent with the unambiguous meaning of the CSA definitions of marijuana and THC," and that the DEA did not follow the proper administrative procedures required to add a substance to Schedule I. The court issued an injunction against the enforcement of the rules with respect to nonpsychoactive hemp or products containing it.*

• **What If the Facts Were Different?** *Suppose that the statutory definitions of THC and marijuana covered naturally occurring THC and nonpsychoactive hemp. Would the result in this case have been different? Explain.*

• **The E-Commerce Dimension** *How might the Internet expedite formal rulemaking procedures such as those required by the U.S. Court of Appeals for the Ninth Circuit in this case? Discuss.*

Informal Agency Actions

Rather than take the time to conduct notice-and-comment rulemaking, agencies have increasingly been using more informal methods of policymaking. These include issuing *interpretive rules,* which are specifically exempted from the APA's requirements. Such rules simply declare the agency's interpretation of its enabling statute's meaning, and they impose no direct and legally binding obligations on regulated parties. In addition, agencies issue various other materials, such as "guidance documents," that advise the public on the agencies' legal and policy positions.

Such informal actions are exempt from the APA's requirements because they do not establish legal rights—a party cannot be directly prosecuted for violating an interpretive rule or a guidance document. Nevertheless, an agency's informal action can be of practical importance because it warns regulated entities that the agency may engage in formal rulemaking if they fail to heed the positions taken informally by the agency.

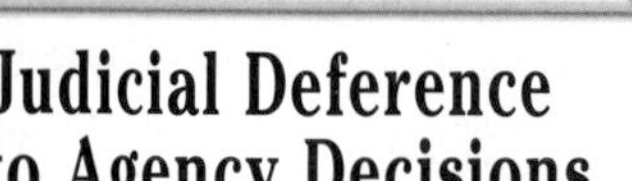

Judicial Deference to Agency Decisions

When asked to review agency decisions, courts historically granted some deference (significant weight) to the agency's judgment, often citing the agency's great expertise in the subject area of the regulation. This deference seems especially appropriate when applied to an agency's analysis of factual questions, but should it also extend to an agency's interpretation of its own legal authority? In *Chevron U.S.A., Inc. v. Natural Resources Defense Council, Inc.,*[9] the United States Supreme Court held that it should, thereby creating a standard of broadened deference to agencies on questions of legal interpretation.

The Holding of the *Chevron* Case

At issue in the *Chevron* case was whether the courts should defer to an agency's interpretation of a statute

9. 467 U.S. 837, 104 S.Ct. 2778, 81 L.Ed.2d 694 (1984).

giving it authority to act. The Environmental Protection Agency (EPA) had interpreted the phrase "stationary source" in the Clean Air Act as referring to an entire manufacturing plant, and not to each facility within a plant. The agency's interpretation enabled it to adopt the so-called bubble policy that allowed companies to offset increases in emissions in part of a plant with decreases elsewhere in the plant—an interpretation that reduced the pollution-control compliance costs faced by manufacturers. An environmental group challenged the legality of the EPA's interpretation.

The Supreme Court held that the courts should defer to an agency's interpretation of *law* as well as fact. The Court found that the agency's interpretation of the statute was reasonable and upheld the bubble policy. The Court's decision in the *Chevron* case created a new standard for courts to use when reviewing agency interpretations of law, which involves the following two questions:

1. Did Congress directly address the issue in dispute in the statute? If so, the statutory language prevails.
2. If the statute is silent or ambiguous, is the agency's interpretation "reasonable"? If it is, a court should uphold the agency's interpretation even if the court would have interpreted the law differently.

When Courts Will Give *Chevron* Deference to Agency Interpretation

The notion that courts should defer to agencies on matters of law was controversial. Under the holding of the *Chevron* case, when the meaning of a particular statute's language is unclear and an agency interprets it, the court must follow the agency's interpretation as long as it is reasonable. This led to considerable discussion and litigation to test the boundaries of the *Chevron* holding. For instance, are courts required to give deference to all agency interpretations or only to those interpretations that result from adjudication or formal rulemaking procedures? The United States Supreme Court has held that in order for agency interpretations to be assured of *Chevron* deference, they must meet the formal legal standards for notice-and-comment rulemaking.[10] Nevertheless, there are still gray areas and many agency interpretations are challenged in court.

In the case that follows, an environmental organization brought an action challenging the U.S. Forest Service's decision to issue a special use permit to a business that conducts helicopter-skiing operations in two national forests. As you will read in Chapter 24, the National Environmental Policy Act requires federal agencies to prepare an *environmental impact statement* (EIS) that considers every significant aspect of the environmental impact of a proposed action. Although the Forest Service prepared an EIS before issuing the use permit to the helicopter-skiing operation, environmental groups claimed that the EIS did not sufficiently analyze increasing recreational pressures in the forests. The groups sought to have the court invalidate the permit.

10. *United States v. Mead Corp.*, 533 U.S. 218, 121 S.Ct. 2164, 150 L.Ed.2d 292 (2001).

CASE 6.3 Citizens' Committee to Save Our Canyons v. Krueger

United States Court of Appeals, Tenth Circuit, 2008. 513 F.3d 1169.

• **Background and Facts** Under the National Forest Management Act (NFMA), the U.S. Forest Service manages national forests pursuant to forest plans periodically developed for each forest. The plans for two national forests—the Wasatch-Cache and Uinta forests—were initially adopted in 1985 and revised in 2003. The Forest Service interpreted the 1985 forest plans as requiring the forests to allow helicopter skiing, and the plans expressly recognized helicopter skiing as a legitimate use of the national forests. Wasatch Powderbird Guides (WPG) has continuously operated a guided helicopter-skiing business in the Wasatch-Cache and Uinta national forests since 1973. It operates pursuant to special use permits periodically issued by the Forest Service. Citizens' Committee to Save Our Canyons and Utah Environmental Congress (referred to collectively as SOC) are nonprofit organizations comprised of members who use the areas in which WPG operates for nonmotorized uses such as backcountry skiing, snowshoeing, hiking, and camping. They claim that their recreational opportunities and experiences are diminished by WPG's operations and argue that the Forest Service failed to comply with relevant laws when issuing WPG's most recent permit. The district court upheld the Forest Service permit, and SOC appealed to the U.S. Court of Appeals for the Tenth Circuit.

CASE 6.3 CONTINUED

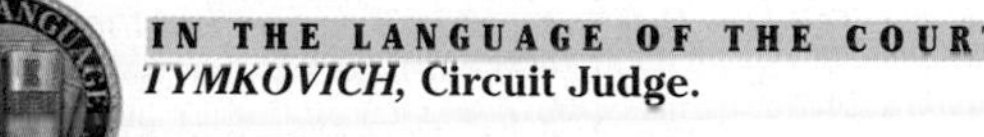

IN THE LANGUAGE OF THE COURT
TYMKOVICH, **Circuit Judge.**

In this appeal we consider the United States Forest Service's decision to issue a special use permit to Wasatch Powderbird Guides (WPG) to conduct helicopter skiing operations in two national forests. Citizens' Committee to Save Our Canyons and Utah Environmental Congress argue the decision violated the National Forest Management Act and the National Environmental Policy Act.

Under the Administrative Procedure Act ("APA"), which governs judicial review of agency actions, * * * we set aside the agency's action * * * if it is "arbitrary, capricious, an abuse of discretion, or otherwise not in accordance with law." We will also set aside an agency action if the agency has failed to follow required procedures.

Our review is highly deferential [respectful of the agency's reasoning]. The duty of a court reviewing agency action under the "arbitrary or capricious" standard is to ascertain whether the agency examined the relevant data and articulated a rational connection between the facts found and the decision made. Furthermore, in reviewing the agency's explanation, the reviewing court must determine whether the agency considered all relevant factors and whether there has been a clear error of judgment. A presumption of validity attaches to the agency action and the burden of proof rests with the appellants who challenge such action. [Emphasis added.]

* * * *

NFMA requires the Forest Service to "develop, maintain, and, as appropriate, revise land and resource management plans for units of the National Forest System." All permits the Forest Service issues "for the use and occupancy of National Forest System lands shall be consistent with the land management plans."

* * * The EIS examined various options and concluded an acceptable balance between helicopter skiing and other uses could be reached by imposing certain restrictions on WPG's operations. These restrictions reflect no special consideration for WPG's economic viability beyond the goal of providing "a range of diverse, recreational opportunities" including helicopter skiing. The EIS thoroughly explains the Forest Service's approach, and the 2005 permit includes a number of reasonable restrictions on WPG with the goal of allowing both helicopter skiers and other backcountry users to enjoy the national forests. In the end, the Forest Service's permit reflected the "type and level" of heli-skiing it thought appropriately balanced the competing recreational uses in the forests.

Taking the interpretation of the forest plans represented by the EIS as a whole, the EIS and the ultimate permitting decision comply with the Forest Service's interpretation of its forest plans. The Forest Service properly considered how particular options would affect the range of recreational opportunities available in the forests and balanced interests in a way it believed promoted multiple forest uses.

* * * *

In sum, the Forest Service's EIS fully disclosed and considered the impact of its decision to issue a special use permit to WPG. *Our objective is not to "fly speck" the [EIS], but rather, to make a pragmatic judgment whether the [EIS]'s form, content and preparation foster both informed decision-making and informed public participation.* The NEPA process in this case, including extensive public comment, considered a variety of options and yielded a number of reasonable restrictions on WPG's operations designed to minimize conflict among forest users. This is all NEPA requires. [Emphasis added.]

• **Decision and Remedy** *The U.S. Court of Appeals for the Tenth Circuit affirmed the district court's decision that upheld the Forest Service permit allowing WPG to conduct helicopter-skiing operations in two national forests. The Forest Service's EIS properly considered all relevant factors and allowed for public comment. Because the Forest Service's interpretation of the NFMA and NEPA was reasonable, the court found that the permit complied with federal laws.*

CASE CONTINUES

CASE 6.3 CONTINUED

• **What If the Facts Were Different?** *Suppose that the Forest Service had granted WPG a permit for its helicopter-skiing operations on national forest land without preparing an EIS or soliciting public comment. How might that have changed the court's ruling in this case?*

• **The Ethical Dimension** *If it turned out that the helicopter-skiing operation had paid a substantial sum to the Forest Service official who prepared the EIS to influence its findings, would the court have been able to consider this fact and invalidate the permit? Why or why not?*

Section 5 Agency Enforcement and Adjudication

Although rulemaking is the most prominent agency activity, enforcement of the rules is also critical. Often, an agency itself enforces its rules. It identifies alleged violators and pursues civil remedies against them in a proceeding held by the agency rather than in federal court, although the agency's determinations are reviewable in court.

Investigation

After final rules are issued, agencies conduct investigations to monitor compliance with those rules or the terms of the enabling statute. A typical agency investigation of this kind might begin when a citizen reports a possible violation to the agency. Many agency rules also require considerable compliance reporting from regulated entities, and such a report may trigger an enforcement investigation. For example, environmental regulators often require reporting of emissions, and the Occupational Safety and Health Administration (OSHA) requires companies to report any work-related deaths.

Inspections Many agencies gather information through on-site inspections. Sometimes, inspecting an office, a factory, or some other business facility is the only way to obtain the evidence needed to prove a regulatory violation. Administrative inspections and tests cover a wide range of activities, including safety inspections of underground coal mines, safety tests of commercial equipment and automobiles, and environmental monitoring of factory emissions. An agency may also ask a firm or individual to submit certain documents or records to the agency for examination. For example, the Federal Trade Commission often asks to inspect corporate records for compliance.

Normally, business firms comply with agency requests to inspect facilities or business records because it is in any firm's interest to maintain a good relationship with regulatory bodies. In some instances, however, such as when a firm thinks an agency's request is unreasonable and may be detrimental to the firm's interest, the firm may refuse to comply with the request. In such situations, an agency may resort to the use of a subpoena or a search warrant.

Subpoenas There are two basic types of subpoenas. The subpoena *ad testificandum* ("to testify") is an ordinary subpoena. It is a writ, or order, compelling a witness to appear at an agency hearing. The subpoena *duces tecum*[11] ("bring it with you") compels an individual or organization to hand over books, papers, records, or documents to the agency. An administrative agency may use either type of subpoena to obtain testimony or documents.

There are limits on the information that an agency can demand. To determine whether an agency is abusing its discretion in its pursuit of information as part of an investigation, a court may consider such factors as the following:

1. *The purpose of the investigation.* An investigation must have a legitimate purpose. Harassment is an example of an improper purpose. An agency may not issue an administrative subpoena to inspect business records if the agency's motive is to harass or pressure the business into settling an unrelated matter.
2. *The relevance of the information being sought.* Information is relevant if it reveals that the law is being violated or if it assures the agency that the law is not being violated.
3. *The specificity of the demand for testimony or documents.* A subpoena must, for example, adequately describe the material being sought.

11. Pronounced *doo*-cheez *tee*-kum.

4. *The burden of the demand on the party from whom the information is sought.* In responding to a request for information, a party must bear the costs of, for example, copying the documents that must be handed over; a business is generally protected from revealing such information as trade secrets, however.

Searches during Site Inspections As mentioned, agency investigations often involve on-site inspections. The Environmental Protection Agency (EPA) frequently conducts inspections to enforce environmental laws. For example, the EPA may inspect a site to determine if hazardous wastes are being stored properly or to sample a facility's wastewater to ensure that it complies with the Clean Water Act. Usually, companies do not resist such inspections, although in some circumstances they may do so.

The Fourth Amendment protects against unreasonable searches and seizures by requiring that in most instances a physical search for evidence must be conducted under the authority of a search warrant. An agency's search warrant is an order directing law enforcement officials to search a specific place for a specific item and present it to the agency. Although it was once thought that administrative inspections were exempt from the warrant requirement, the United States Supreme Court held in *Marshall v. Barlow's, Inc.*,[12] that the requirement does apply to the administrative process.

Agencies can conduct warrantless searches in several situations. Warrants are not required to conduct searches in highly regulated industries. Firms that sell firearms or liquor, for example, are automatically subject to inspections without warrants. Sometimes, a statute permits warrantless searches of certain types of hazardous operations, such as coal mines. Also, a warrantless inspection in an emergency situation is normally considered reasonable.

Adjudication

After conducting an investigation of a suspected rule violation, an agency may begin to take administrative action against an individual or organization. Most administrative actions are resolved through negotiated settlements at their initial stages, without the need for formal **adjudication** (the process of resolving a dispute by presenting evidence and arguments before a neutral third party decision maker).

12. 436 U.S. 307, 98 S.Ct. 1816, 56 L.Ed.2d 305 (1978).

Negotiated Settlements Depending on the agency, negotiations may take the form of a simple conversation or a series of informal conferences. Whatever form the negotiations take, their purpose is to rectify the problem to the agency's satisfaction and eliminate the need for additional proceedings.

Settlement is an appealing option to firms for two reasons: to avoid appearing uncooperative and to avoid the expense involved in formal adjudication proceedings and in possible later appeals. Settlement is also an attractive option for agencies. To conserve their own resources and avoid formal actions, administrative agencies devote a great deal of effort to giving advice and negotiating solutions to problems.

Formal Complaints If a settlement cannot be reached, the agency may issue a formal complaint against the suspected violator. If the EPA, for example, finds that a factory is polluting groundwater in violation of federal pollution laws, the EPA will issue a complaint against the violator in an effort to bring the plant into compliance with federal regulations. This complaint is a public document, and a press release may accompany it. The factory charged in the complaint will respond by filing an answer to the EPA's allegations. If the factory and the EPA cannot agree on a settlement, the case will be adjudicated.

Agency adjudication may involve a trial-like arbitration procedure before an **administrative law judge (ALJ).** The Administrative Procedure Act (APA) requires that before the hearing takes place, the agency must issue a notice that includes the facts and law on which the complaint is based, the legal authority for the hearing, and its time and place. The administrative adjudication process is described below and illustrated graphically in Exhibit 6–4 on the following page.

The Role of the Administrative Law Judge The ALJ presides over the hearing and has the power to administer oaths, take testimony, rule on questions of evidence, and make determinations of fact. Although technically, the ALJ is not an independent judge and works for the agency prosecuting the case (in our example, the EPA), the law requires an ALJ to be an unbiased adjudicator (judge).

Certain safeguards prevent bias on the part of the ALJ and promote fairness in the proceedings. For example, the APA requires that the ALJ be separate from an agency's investigative and prosecutorial staff. The APA also prohibits *ex parte* (private) communications

EXHIBIT 6–4 • The Process of Formal Administrative Adjudication

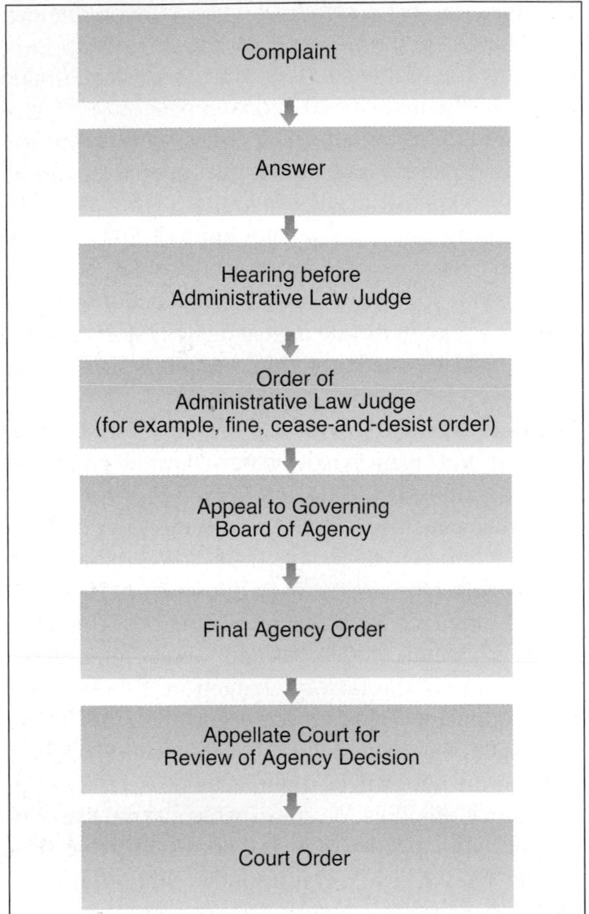

between the ALJ and any party to an agency proceeding, such as the EPA or the factory. Finally, provisions of the APA protect the ALJ from agency disciplinary actions unless the agency can show good cause for such an action.

Hearing Procedures Hearing procedures vary widely from agency to agency. Administrative agencies generally exercise substantial discretion over the type of procedure that will be used. Frequently, disputes are resolved through informal adjudication proceedings. For example, the parties, their counsel, and the ALJ may simply meet at a table in a conference room to attempt to settle the dispute.

A formal adjudicatory hearing, in contrast, resembles a trial in many respects. Prior to the hearing, the parties are permitted to undertake discovery—involving depositions, interrogatories, and requests for documents or other information, as described in Chapter 2—although the discovery process is not quite as extensive as it would be in a court proceeding. The hearing itself must comply with the procedural requirements of the APA and must also meet the constitutional standards of due process. During the hearing, the parties may give testimony, present other evidence, and cross-examine adverse witnesses. A significant difference between a trial and an administrative agency hearing, though, is that normally much more information, including hearsay (secondhand information), can be introduced as evidence during an administrative hearing. The burden of proof in an enforcement proceeding is placed on the agency.

Agency Orders Following a hearing, the ALJ renders an **initial order,** or decision, on the case. Either party can appeal the ALJ's decision to the board or commission that governs the agency. If the factory in the previous example is dissatisfied with the ALJ's decision, it can appeal the decision to the EPA. If the factory is dissatisfied with the commission's decision, it can appeal the decision to a federal court of appeals. If no party appeals the case, the ALJ's decision becomes the **final order** of the agency. The ALJ's decision also becomes final if a party appeals and the commission and the court decline to review the case. If a party appeals and the case is reviewed, the final order comes from the commission's decision or (if that decision is appealed to a federal appellate court) that of the court.

Limitations on Agency Powers

Combining the functions normally divided among the three branches of government into an administrative agency concentrates considerable power in a single organization. Because of this concentration of authority, one of the major policy objectives of the government is to control the risks of arbitrariness and overreaching by administrative agencies without hindering the effective use of agency power to deal with particular problem areas, as Congress intends.

The judicial branch of the government exercises control over agency powers through the courts' review of agency actions. The executive and legislative branches of government also exercise control over agency authority.

Judicial Controls

As described earlier, the Administrative Procedure Act provides for judicial review of most agency decisions. Agency actions are not automatically subject to judicial review, however. Procedural doctrines such as exhaustion and ripeness may limit the opportunity of judicial review.

The Exhaustion Doctrine The *exhaustion doctrine* requires that a regulated party use all of its potential administrative remedies before going to court, even though the party might prefer to go straight to the independent federal courts, rather than going through the administrative adjudication process. Requiring the administrative process first allows the agency to evaluate the argument and enables a court to take advantage of the agency's own fact-finding capabilities before ruling. The exhaustion of administrative remedies is not required, though, if the party can demonstrate that those remedies are inadequate to address its challenge.

In the classic exhaustion case, a company was served with a complaint from the National Labor Relations Board (NLRB) alleging that it had engaged in unfair labor practices.[13] The company argued that because it was not operating in interstate commerce, the NLRB had no jurisdiction. The United States Supreme Court rejected this argument and held that the company was required to first use administrative procedures to challenge the complaint.

The Ripeness Doctrine Under what is known as the *ripeness doctrine*, a court will not review an administrative agency's decision until the case is "ripe for review." Generally, a case is ripe for review if the parties can demonstrate that they have met certain requirements. The party bringing the action must have *standing to sue* the agency (the party must have a direct stake in the outcome of the judicial proceeding), and there must be an *actual controversy* at issue. Recall from Chapter 2 that these are basic judicial requirements that must be met before any court will hear a case.

Standing requires that a plaintiff have an actual injury, that the injury be causally connected with the challenged action, and that the injury be one that can be successfully redressed by a judicial resolution of the case. The rationale for this doctrine is to prevent courts from entangling themselves in abstract disagreements over administrative policies. The doctrine also protects agencies from judicial interference until an administrative decision has been formalized and its effects are clear. The court can then evaluate both the appropriateness of an issue for judicial resolution and the hardship that the plaintiff will suffer if the court refuses to hear the case.

Executive Controls

The executive branch of government exercises control over agencies both through the president's power to appoint federal officers and through the president's veto power. The president may veto enabling legislation presented by Congress or congressional attempts to modify an existing agency's authority. In addition, the president has created a process whereby the Office of Information and Regulatory Affairs (OIRA) of the Office of Management and Budget reviews the cost-effectiveness of agency rules. The OIRA also reviews agencies' compliance with the Paperwork Reduction Act,[14] which requires agencies to minimize the paperwork burden on regulated entities. These reviews provide regulated entities with a pathway to challenge rules, through lobbying, even after the rules have been adopted. The reviews are not subject to the requirements of the Administrative Procedure Act.

Legislative Controls

Congress also exercises authority over agency powers. Through enabling legislation, Congress gives power to an agency. Of course, an agency may not exceed the power that Congress has delegated to it. Through subsequent legislation, Congress can take away that power or even abolish an agency altogether. Legislative authority is required to fund an agency, and enabling legislation usually sets certain time and monetary limits on the funding of particular programs. Congress can always revise these limits.

In addition to its power to create and fund agencies, Congress has the authority to investigate the implementation of its laws and the agencies that it has created. Individual legislators may also affect agency policy through their "casework" activities, which

13. *Myers v. Bethlehem Shipbuilding Corp.*, 303 U.S. 41, 58 S.Ct. 459, 82 L.Ed. 638 (1938).

14. Pub. L. No. 104-13, May 22, 1995, 109 Stat. 163, amending 44 U.S.C. Sections 3501 *et seq.*

involve attempts to help their constituents deal with agencies.

Congress also has the power to "freeze" the enforcement of most federal regulations before the regulations take effect. Under the Small Business Regulatory Enforcement Fairness Act of 1996,[15] all federal agencies must submit final rules to Congress before the rules become effective. If, within sixty days, Congress passes a joint resolution disapproving of a rule, its enforcement is frozen while the rule is reviewed by congressional committees.

Another legislative check on agency actions is the Administrative Procedure Act, discussed earlier in this chapter. Additionally, the laws discussed in the next section provide certain checks on the actions of administrative agencies.

Public Accountability

As a result of growing public concern over the powers exercised by administrative agencies, Congress passed several laws to make agencies more accountable through public scrutiny. We discuss here the most significant of these laws.

Freedom of Information Act

Enacted in 1966, the Freedom of Information Act (FOIA)[16] requires the federal government to disclose certain records to any person or entity on written request. The FOIA exempts certain types of records, such as those pertaining to national security, and records containing information that is confidential or personal.

A request that complies with the FOIA procedures need only contain a reasonably specific description of the information sought. Many agencies now accept requests via e-mail, as well as by fax. The agency has twenty working days to answer a request and must notify the individual if the information sought is being withheld and which exemptions apply. The agency typically charges the person requesting the information a fee for research, copying, and other services.

An agency's failure to comply with an FOIA request may be challenged in a federal district court. The media, industry trade associations, public-interest groups, and even companies seeking information about competitors rely on these FOIA provisions to obtain information from government agencies.

Under a 1996 amendment to the FOIA, all federal government agencies must make their records available electronically on the Internet, on CD-ROMs, and in other electronic formats. Any document an agency creates must be accessible by computer within a year after its creation. Agencies must also provide a clear index to all of their documents.

Government in the Sunshine Act

Congress passed the Government in the Sunshine Act,[17] or open meeting law, in 1976. It requires that "every portion of every meeting of an agency" be open to "public observation." The act also requires the establishment of procedures to ensure that the public is provided with adequate advance notice of scheduled meetings and agendas. Like the FOIA, the Sunshine Act contains certain exceptions. Closed meetings are permitted when (1) the subject of the meeting concerns accusing any person of a crime, (2) an open meeting would frustrate the implementation of agency actions, or (3) the subject of the meeting involves matters relating to future litigation or rulemaking. Courts interpret these exceptions to allow open access whenever possible.

Regulatory Flexibility Act

Concern over the effects of regulation on the efficiency of businesses, particularly smaller ones, led Congress to pass the Regulatory Flexibility Act[18] in 1980. Under this act, whenever a new regulation will have a "significant impact upon a substantial number of small entities," the agency must conduct a regulatory flexibility analysis. The analysis must measure the cost that the rule would impose on small businesses and must consider less burdensome alternatives. The act also contains provisions to alert small businesses—through advertising in trade journals, for example—about forthcoming regulations. The act reduces some record-keeping burdens for small businesses, especially with regard to hazardous waste management.

Small Business Regulatory Enforcement Fairness Act

As mentioned earlier, the Small Business Regulatory Enforcement Fairness Act (SBREFA) of 1996 allows

15. 5 U.S.C. Sections 801–808.
16. 5 U.S.C. Section 552.
17. 5 U.S.C. Section 552b.
18. 5 U.S.C. Sections 601–612.

Congress to review new federal regulations for at least sixty days before they take effect. This period gives opponents of the rules time to present their arguments to Congress.

The SBREFA also authorizes the courts to enforce the Regulatory Flexibility Act. This helps to ensure that federal agencies, such as the Internal Revenue Service, will consider ways to reduce the economic impact of new regulations on small businesses. Federal agencies are required to prepare guides that explain in "plain English" how small businesses can comply with federal regulations.

The SBREFA also set up the National Enforcement Ombudsman at the Small Business Administration to receive comments from small businesses about their dealings with federal agencies. Based on these comments, Regional Small Business Fairness Boards rate the agencies and publicize their findings.

Finally, the SBREFA allows small businesses to recover their expenses and legal fees from the government when an agency makes demands for fines or penalties that a court considers excessive.

REVIEWING Administrative Law

Assume that the Securities and Exchange Commission (SEC) has a rule that it will enforce statutory provisions prohibiting insider trading only when the insiders make monetary profits for themselves. Then the SEC makes a new rule, declaring that it will now bring enforcement actions against individuals for insider trading even if the individuals did not personally profit from the transactions. In making the new rule, the SEC does not conduct a rulemaking procedure but simply announces its decision. A stockbrokerage firm objects and says that the new rule was unlawfully developed without opportunity for public comment. The brokerage firm challenges the rule in an action that ultimately is reviewed by a federal appellate court. Using the information presented in the chapter, answer the following questions.

1. Is the SEC an executive agency or an independent regulatory agency? Does it matter to the outcome of this dispute? Explain.
2. Suppose that the SEC asserts that it has always had the statutory authority to pursue persons for insider trading regardless of whether they personally profited from the transaction. This is the only argument the SEC makes to justify changing its enforcement rules. Would a court be likely to find that the SEC's action was arbitrary and capricious under the Administrative Procedure Act (APA)? Why or why not?
3. Would a court be likely to give *Chevron* deference to the SEC's interpretation of the law on insider trading? Why or why not?
4. Now assume that a court finds that the new rule is merely "interpretive." What effect would this determination have on whether the SEC had to follow the APA's rulemaking procedures?

TERMS AND CONCEPTS

adjudication 139
administrative law judge (ALJ) 139
bureaucracy 129
enabling legislation 128
final order 140
initial order 140
notice-and-comment rulemaking 131
rulemaking 131

QUESTIONS AND CASE PROBLEMS

6–1. For decades, the Federal Trade Commission (FTC) resolved fair trade and advertising disputes through individual adjudications. In the 1960s, the FTC began promulgating rules that defined fair and unfair trade practices. In cases involving violations of these rules, the due process rights of participants were more limited and did not include cross-examination. Although anyone found violating a rule would receive a full adjudication, the legitimacy of the rule itself could not be challenged in the adjudication. Any party charged with violating a rule was almost certain to lose the adjudication. Affected parties complained to a court, arguing that their rights before the FTC were unduly limited by the new rules. What will the court examine to determine whether to uphold the new rules?

6–2. QUESTION WITH SAMPLE ANSWER

Assume that the Food and Drug Administration (FDA), using proper procedures, adopts a rule describing its future investigations. This new rule covers all future circumstances in which the FDA wants to regulate food additives. Under the new rule, the FDA is not to regulate food additives without giving food companies an opportunity to cross-examine witnesses. At a subsequent time, the FDA wants to regulate methylisocyanate, a food additive. The FDA undertakes an informal rulemaking procedure, without cross-examination, and regulates methylisocyanate. Producers protest, saying that the FDA promised them the opportunity for cross-examination. The FDA responds that the Administrative Procedure Act does not require such cross-examination and that it is free to withdraw the promise made in its new rule. If the producers challenge the FDA in court, on what basis would the court rule in their favor?

- **For a sample answer to Question 6–2, go to Appendix I at the end of this text.**

6–3. Rulemaking. The Occupational Safety and Health Administration (OSHA) is part of the U.S. Department of Labor. OSHA issued a "Directive" under which each employer in selected industries was to be inspected unless it adopted a "Comprehensive Compliance Program (CCP)"—a safety and health program designed to meet standards that in some respects exceeded those otherwise required by law. The Chamber of Commerce of the United States objected to the Directive and filed a petition for review with the U.S. Court of Appeals for the District of Columbia Circuit. The Chamber claimed, in part, that OSHA did not use proper rulemaking procedures in issuing the Directive. OSHA argued that it was not required to follow those procedures because the Directive itself was a "rule of procedure." OSHA claimed that the rule did not "alter the rights or interests of parties, although it may alter the manner in which the parties present themselves or their viewpoints to the agency." What are the steps of the most commonly used rulemaking procedure? Which steps are missing in this case? In whose favor should the court rule and why? [*Chamber of Commerce of the United States v. U.S. Department of Labor,* 174 F.3d 206 (D.C.Cir. 1999)]

6–4. Arbitrary and Capricious Test. Lion Raisins, Inc., is a family-owned, family-operated business that grows raisins and markets them to private enterprises. In the 1990s, Lion also successfully bid on more than fifteen contracts awarded by the U.S. Department of Agriculture (USDA). In May 1999, a USDA investigation reported that Lion appeared to have falsified inspectors' signatures, given false moisture content, and changed the grade of raisins on three USDA raisin certificates issued between 1996 and 1998. Lion was subsequently awarded five more USDA contracts. Then, in November 2000, the company was the low bidder on two new USDA contracts for school lunch programs. In January 2001, however, the USDA awarded these contracts to other bidders and, on the basis of the May 1999 report, suspended Lion from participating in government contracts for one year. Lion filed a suit in the U.S. Court of Federal Claims against the USDA, seeking, in part, lost profits on the school lunch contracts on the ground that the USDA's suspension was arbitrary and capricious. What reasoning might the court employ to grant a summary judgment in Lion's favor? [*Lion Raisins, Inc. v. United States,* 51 Fed.Cl. 238 (2001)]

6–5. Investigation. Maureen Droge began working for United Air Lines, Inc. (UAL), as a flight attendant in 1990. In 1995, she was assigned to Paris, France, where she became pregnant. Because UAL does not allow its flight attendants to fly during their third trimester of pregnancy, Droge was placed on involuntary leave. She applied for temporary disability benefits through the French social security system, but her request was denied because UAL does not contribute to the French system on behalf of its U.S.-based flight attendants. Droge filed a charge of discrimination with the U.S. Equal Employment Opportunity Commission (EEOC), alleging that UAL had discriminated against her and other Americans. The EEOC issued a subpoena, asking UAL to detail all benefits received by all UAL employees living outside the United States. UAL refused to provide the information, in part, on the grounds that it was irrelevant and compliance would be unduly burdensome. The EEOC filed a suit in a federal district court against UAL. Should the court enforce the subpoena? Why or why not? [*Equal Employment Opportunity Commission v. United Air Lines, Inc.,* 287 F.3d 643 (7th Cir. 2002)]

6–6. Judicial Controls. Under federal law, when accepting bids on a contract, an agency must hold "discussions" with all offerors. An agency may ask a single offeror for "clarification" of its proposal, however, without holding "discussions" with the others.

Regulations define *clarifications* as "limited exchanges." In March 2001, the U.S. Air Force asked for bids on a contract. The winning contractor would examine, assess, and develop means of integrating national intelligence assets with the U.S. Department of Defense space systems, to enhance the capabilities of the Air Force's Space Warfare Center. Among the bidders were Information Technology and Applications Corp. (ITAC) and RS Information Systems, Inc. (RSIS). The Air Force asked the parties for more information on their subcontractors but did not allow them to change their proposals. Determining that there were weaknesses in ITAC's bid, the Air Force awarded the contract to RSIS. ITAC filed a suit in the U.S. Court of Federal Claims against the government, contending that the postproposal requests to RSIS, and its responses, were improper "discussions." Should the court rule in ITAC's favor? Why or why not? [*Information Technology & Applications Corp. v. United States,* 316 F.3d 1312 (Fed.Cir. 2003)].

6–7. CASE PROBLEM WITH SAMPLE ANSWER

Riverdale Mills Corp. makes plastic-coated steel wire products in Northbridge, Massachusetts. Riverdale uses a water-based cleaning process that generates acidic and alkaline wastewater. To meet federal clean-water requirements, Riverdale has a system within its plant to treat the water. It then flows through a pipe that opens into a manhole-covered test pit outside the plant in full view of Riverdale's employees. Three hundred feet away, the pipe merges into the public sewer system. In October 1997, the U.S. Environmental Protection Agency (EPA) sent Justin Pimpare and Daniel Granz to inspect the plant. Without a search warrant and without Riverdale's express consent, the agents took samples from the test pit. Based on the samples, Riverdale and James Knott, the company's owner, were charged with criminal violations of the federal Clean Water Act. The defendants filed a suit in a federal district court against the EPA agents and others, alleging violations of the Fourth Amendment. What right does the Fourth Amendment provide in this context? This right is based on a "reasonable expectation of privacy." Should the agents be held liable? Why or why not? [*Riverdale Mills Corp. v. Pimpare,* 392 F.3d 55 (1st Cir. 2004)]

- **To view a sample answer for Problem 6–7, go to this book's Web site at academic.cengage.com/blaw/cross, select "Chapter 6," and click on "Case Problem with Sample Answer."**

6–8. Rulemaking. The Investment Company Act of 1940 prohibits a mutual fund from engaging in certain transactions in which there may be a conflict of interest between the manager of the fund and its shareholders. Under rules issued by the Securities and Exchange Commission (SEC), however, a fund that meets certain conditions may engage in an otherwise prohibited transaction. In June 2004, the SEC added two new conditions. A year later, the SEC reconsidered the new conditions in terms of the costs that they would impose on the funds. Within eight days, and without asking for public input, the SEC readopted the conditions. The Chamber of Commerce of the United States—which is both a mutual fund shareholder and an association with mutual fund managers among its members—asked the U.S. Court of Appeals for the Second Circuit to review the new rules. The Chamber charged, in part, that in readopting the rules, the SEC relied on materials not in the "rulemaking record" without providing an opportunity for public comment. The SEC countered that the information was otherwise "publicly available." In adopting a rule, should an agency consider information that is not part of the rulemaking record? Why or why not? [*Chamber of Commerce of the United States v. Securities and Exchange Commission,* 443 F.3d 890 (D.C.Cir. 2006)]

6–9. Agency Powers. A well-documented rise in global temperatures has coincided with a significant increase in the concentration of carbon dioxide in the atmosphere. Some scientists believe that the two trends are related, because when carbon dioxide is released into the atmosphere, it produces a greenhouse effect, trapping solar heat. Under the Clean Air Act (CAA) of 1963, the Environmental Protection Agency (EPA) is authorized to regulate "any" air pollutants "emitted into . . . the ambient air" that in its "judgment cause, or contribute to, air pollution." Calling global warming "the most pressing environmental challenge of our time," a group of private organizations asked the EPA to regulate carbon dioxide and other "greenhouse gas" emissions from new motor vehicles. The EPA refused, stating, among other things, that Congress last amended the CAA in 1990 without authorizing new, binding auto emissions limits. The petitioners—nineteen states, including Massachusetts, and others—asked the U.S. Court of Appeals for the District of Columbia Circuit to review the EPA's denial. Did the EPA have the authority to regulate greenhouse gas emissions from new motor vehicles? If so, was its stated reason for refusing to do so consistent with that authority? Discuss. [*Massachusetts v. Environmental Protection Agency,* __ U.S. __, 127 S.Ct. 1438, 167 L.Ed.2d 248 (2007)]

6–10. A QUESTION OF ETHICS

To ensure highway safety and protect driver health, Congress charged federal agencies with regulating the hours of service of commercial motor vehicle operators. Between 1940 and 2003, the regulations that applied to long-haul truck drivers were mostly unchanged. (Long-haul drivers are those who operate beyond a 150-mile radius of their base.) In 2003, the Federal Motor Carrier Safety Administration (FMSCA) revised the regulations significantly, increasing the number of daily and weekly hours that drivers could work. The agency had not considered the impact of the changes on the health of the drivers, however, and the revisions were overturned. The FMSCA then issued a notice that it would reconsider the revisions and opened them up for public comment. The agency analyzed the costs to the industry and the crash risks due to driver fatigue under different options and concluded that the safety benefits of not increasing the hours did not outweigh the economic costs. In 2005, the agency issued a rule that was nearly identical to the 2003 version. Public Citizen, Inc., and others, including the Owner-Operator Independent Drivers Association, asked the U.S. Court of Appeals for the District of Columbia Circuit to review the 2005 rule as it applied to long-haul drivers. [Owner-Operator Independent Drivers Association, Inc. v. Federal Motor Carrier Safety Administration, *494 F.3d 188 (D.C. Cir. 2007)*]

(a) The agency's cost-benefit analysis included new methods that were not disclosed to the public in time for comments. Was this unethical? Should the agency have disclosed the new methodology sooner? Why or why not?

(b) The agency created a graph to show the risk of a crash as a function of the time a driver spent on the job. The graph plotted the first twelve hours of a day individually, but the rest of the time was depicted with an aggregate figure at the seventeenth hour. This made the risk at those hours appear to be lower. Is it unethical for an agency to manipulate data? Explain.

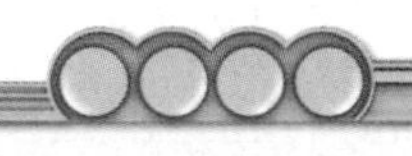

LAW ON THE WEB

For updated links to resources available on the Web, as well as a variety of other materials, visit this text's Web site at

academic.cengage.com/blaw/cross

To view the text of the Administrative Procedure Act of 1946, go to

www.oalj.dol.gov/libapa.htm

For information on the Freedom of Information Act and sample request letters, go to

www.nist.gov/admin/foia/foia.htm

The U.S. Government Printing Office provides a searchable online database of the *Code of Federal Regulations* at

www.gpoaccess.gov/cfr/index.html

Legal Research Exercises on the Web

Go to **academic.cengage.com/blaw/cross**, the Web site that accompanies this text. Select "Chapter 6" and click on "Internet Exercises." There you will find the following Internet research exercises that you can perform to learn more about the topics covered in this chapter.

Internet Exercise 6–1: Legal Perspective
The Freedom of Information Act

Internet Exercise 6–2: Management Perspective
Agency Inspections

CHAPTER 7

Criminal Law and Cyber Crime

The law imposes various sanctions in attempting to ensure that individuals engaging in business in our society can compete and flourish. These sanctions include those imposed by civil law, such as damages for various types of tortious conduct (discussed in Chapter 12); damages for breach of contract (to be discussed in Chapter 10); and the equitable remedies discussed in Chapters 1 and 10. Additional sanctions are imposed under criminal law. Indeed, many statutes regulating business provide for criminal as well as civil penalties. Therefore, criminal law joins civil law as an important element in the legal environment of business.

In this chapter, after explaining some essential differences between criminal law and civil law, we look at how crimes are classified and at the elements that must be present for criminal liability to exist. We then examine the various categories of crimes, the defenses that can be raised to avoid criminal liability, and the rules of criminal procedure. We conclude the chapter with a discussion of crimes that occur in cyberspace, which are often referred to as *cyber crime.* Generally, cyber crime refers more to the way in which particular crimes are committed than to a new category of crimes.

Civil Law and Criminal Law

Recall from Chapter 1 that *civil law* pertains to the duties that exist between persons or between persons and their governments. Criminal law, in contrast, has to do with crime. A **crime** can be defined as a wrong against society proclaimed in a statute and punishable by a fine and/or imprisonment—or, in some cases, death. As mentioned in Chapter 1, because crimes are *offenses against society as a whole,* they are prosecuted by a public official, such as a district attorney (D.A.) or an attorney general (A.G.), not by the victims. Once a crime has been reported, the D.A. typically has the discretion to decide whether to file criminal charges and also determines to what extent to pursue the prosecution or carry out additional investigation.

Major Differences between Civil Law and Criminal Law

Because the state has extensive resources at its disposal when prosecuting criminal cases, there are numerous procedural safeguards to protect the rights of defendants. We look here at one of these safeguards—the higher burden of proof that applies in a criminal case—as well as the harsher sanctions for criminal acts compared with civil wrongs. Exhibit 7–1 on the following page summarizes these and other key differences between civil law and criminal law.

Burden of Proof In a civil case, the plaintiff usually must prove his or her case by a *preponderance of the evidence.* Under this standard, the plaintiff must convince the court that based on the evidence presented by both parties, it is more likely than not that the plaintiff's allegation is true.

In a criminal case, in contrast, the state must prove its case **beyond a reasonable doubt.** If the jury views the evidence in the case as reasonably permitting either a guilty or a not guilty verdict, then the jury's verdict must be not guilty. In other words, the government (prosecutor) must prove beyond a reasonable doubt that the defendant has committed every essential element of the offense with which she or he is charged. If the jurors are not convinced of the defendant's guilt beyond a reasonable doubt, they must find the defendant not guilty. Note also that in a criminal

EXHIBIT 7–1 • Key Differences between Civil Law and Criminal Law

Issue	Civil Law	Criminal Law
Party who brings suit	Person who suffered harm	The state
Wrongful act	Causing harm to a person or to a person's property	Violating a statute that prohibits some type of activity
Burden of proof	Preponderance of the evidence	Beyond a reasonable doubt
Verdict	Three-fourths majority (typically)	Unanimous
Remedy	Damages to compensate for the harm or a decree to achieve an equitable result	Punishment (fine, imprisonment, or death)

case, the jury's verdict normally must be unanimous—agreed to by all members of the jury—to convict the defendant. (In a civil trial by jury, in contrast, typically only three-fourths of the jurors need to agree.)

Criminal Sanctions The sanctions imposed on criminal wrongdoers are also harsher than those that are applied in civil cases. As you will read in Chapter 12, the purpose of tort law is to enable a person harmed by the wrongful act of another to obtain compensation from the wrongdoer, rather than to punish the wrongdoer. In contrast, criminal sanctions are designed to punish those who commit crimes and to deter others from committing similar acts in the future. Criminal sanctions include fines as well as the much harsher penalty of the loss of one's liberty by incarceration in a jail or prison. Most criminal sanctions also involve probation and sometimes require performance of community service, completion of an educational or treatment program, or payment of restitution. The harshest criminal sanction is, of course, the death penalty.

Civil Liability for Criminal Acts

Some torts, such as assault and battery, provide a basis for a criminal prosecution as well as a civil action in tort. For example, suppose that Jonas is walking down the street, minding his own business, when a person attacks him. In the ensuing struggle, the attacker stabs Jonas several times, seriously injuring him. A police officer restrains and arrests the wrongdoer. In this situation, the attacker may be subject both to criminal prosecution by the state and to a tort lawsuit brought by Jonas to obtain compensation for his injuries. Exhibit 7–2 illustrates how the same wrongful act can result in both a civil (tort) action and a criminal action against the wrongdoer.

Classification of Crimes

Depending on their degree of seriousness, crimes are classified as felonies or misdemeanors.

Felonies

Felonies are serious crimes punishable by death or by imprisonment in a federal or state penitentiary for one year or longer.[1] The Model Penal Code[2] provides for four degrees of felony:

1. Capital offenses, for which the maximum penalty is death.
2. First degree felonies, punishable by a maximum penalty of life imprisonment.
3. Second degree felonies, punishable by a maximum of ten years' imprisonment.
4. Third degree felonies, punishable by up to five years' imprisonment.

Although criminal laws vary from state to state, some general rules apply when grading crimes by

1. Some states, such as North Carolina, consider felonies to be punishable by incarceration for at least two years.

2. The American Law Institute issued the Official Draft of the Model Penal Code in 1962. The Model Penal Code contains four parts: (1) general provisions, (2) definitions of special crimes, (3) provisions concerning treatment and corrections, and (4) provisions on the organization of corrections. The Model Penal Code is not a uniform code, however. Because of our federal structure of government, each state has developed its own set of laws governing criminal acts. Thus, types of crimes and prescribed punishments may differ from one jurisdiction to another.

EXHIBIT 7–2 • Civil (Tort) Lawsuit and Criminal Prosecution for the Same Act

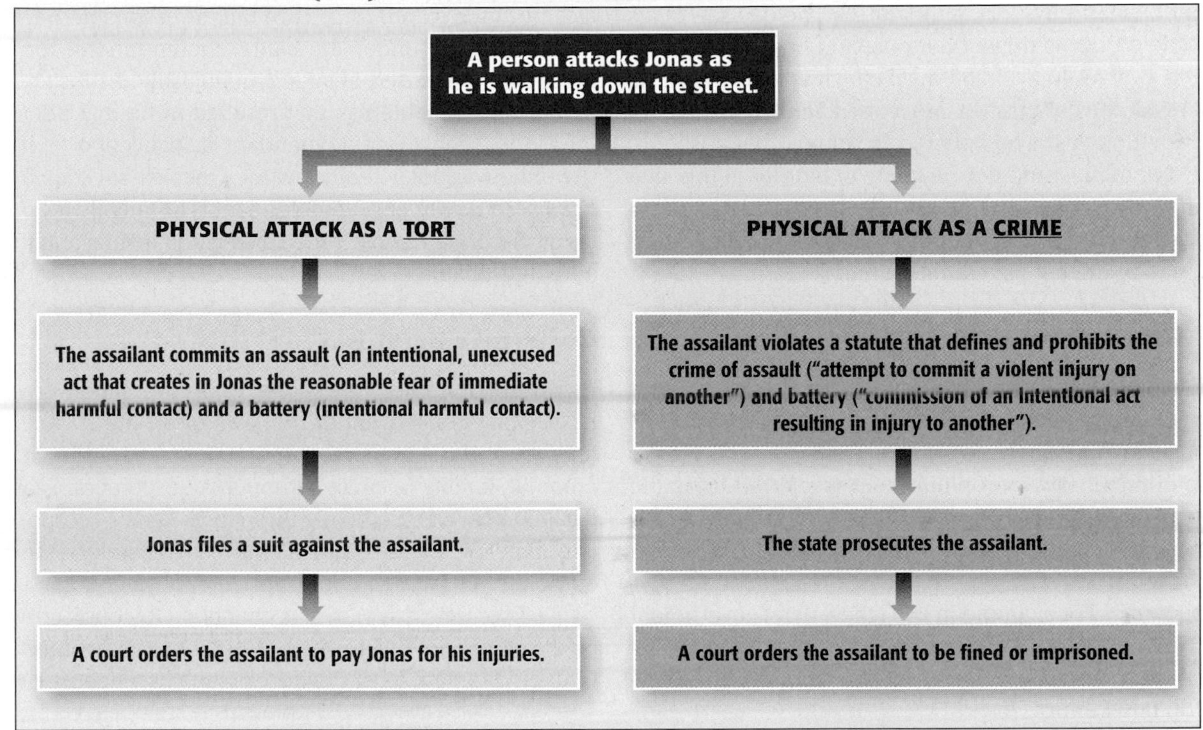

degree. For example, most jurisdictions punish a burglary that involves a forced entry into a home at night more harshly than a burglary that takes place during the day and involves a nonresidential building or structure. A homicide—the taking of another's life—is classified according to the degree of intent involved.

For example, first degree murder requires that the homicide be premeditated and deliberate, as opposed to a spontaneous act of violence. When no premeditation or deliberation is present but the offender acts with *malice aforethought* (that is, with wanton disregard for the consequences of his or her actions for the victim), the homicide is classified as second degree murder. A homicide that is committed without malice toward the victim is known as *manslaughter. Voluntary manslaughter* occurs when the intent to kill may be present, as in a crime committed in the heat of passion, but malice is lacking. A homicide is classified as *involuntary manslaughter* when it results from an act of negligence (such as when a drunk driver causes the death of another person) and there is no intent to kill.

Misdemeanors and Petty Offenses

Under federal law as well as under the law of most states, any crime that is not a felony is considered a **misdemeanor.** Misdemeanors are less serious crimes punishable by a fine or by incarceration for up to one year. Disorderly conduct and trespass are common misdemeanors. In most jurisdictions, **petty offenses** are considered to be a subset of misdemeanors. Petty offenses are minor violations, such as disturbing the peace and violating building codes. Even for petty offenses, however, a guilty party can be put in jail for a few days, fined, or both, depending on state law.

Whether a crime is a felony or a misdemeanor can determine in which court the case is tried and, in some states, whether the defendant has a right to a jury trial. Many states have several classes of misdemeanors. For example, in Illinois, misdemeanors are either Class A (confinement for up to a year), Class B (not more than six months), or Class C (not more than thirty days).

Criminal Liability

Two elements must exist for a person to be convicted of a crime: (1) the performance of a prohibited act and (2) a specified state of mind, or intent, on the part of the actor. Additionally, to establish criminal liability, there must be a *concurrence* between the act and the intent. In other words, these two elements must occur together.

For example, suppose that a woman intends to kill her husband by poisoning him. On the day she plans to do so, she is driving her husband home from work and swerves to avoid hitting a cat crossing the road. As a result, the car crashes into a tree, killing her husband. Even though she had planned to murder her husband, the woman would not be guilty of murder in this situation because the two elements did not occur together. The woman had not intended to kill her husband by driving the car into a tree.

The Criminal Act

Every criminal statute prohibits certain behavior. Most crimes require an act of *commission*—that is, a person must *do* something in order to be accused of a crime. In criminal law, a prohibited act is referred to as the ***actus reus,***[3] or guilty act. In some instances, an act of omission can be a crime, but only when a person has a legal duty to perform the omitted act, such as filing a tax return. For example, in 2005 the federal government criminally prosecuted a former winner of the reality TV show *Survivor* for failing to report more than $1 million in winnings.

The *guilty act* requirement is based on one of the premises of criminal law—that a person should be punished for harm done to society. For a crime to exist, the guilty act must cause some harm to a person or to property. Thinking about killing someone or about stealing a car may be morally wrong, but the thoughts do no harm until they are translated into action. Of course, a person can be punished for *attempting* murder or robbery, but normally only if substantial steps toward the criminal objective have been taken.

State of Mind

A wrongful mental state (***mens rea***)[4] is also typically required to establish criminal liability. The required mental state, or intent, is indicated in the applicable statute or law. Murder, for example, involves the guilty act of killing another human being, and the guilty mental state is the desire, or intent, to take another's life. For theft, the guilty act is the taking of another person's property, and the mental state involves both the awareness that the property belongs to another and the desire to deprive the owner of it.

A guilty mental state can be attributed to acts of negligence or recklessness as well. *Criminal negligence* involves the mental state in which the defendant deviates from the standard of care that a reasonable person would use under the same circumstances. The defendant is accused of taking an unjustified, substantial, and foreseeable risk that resulted in harm. Under the Model Penal Code, a defendant is negligent even if she or he was not actually aware of the risk but *should have been aware* of it.[5] A defendant is criminally reckless if he or she consciously disregards a substantial and unjustifiable risk.

Corporate Criminal Liability

As will be discussed in Chapter 18, a corporation is a legal entity created under the laws of a state. At one time, it was thought that a corporation could not incur criminal liability because, although a corporation is a legal person, it can act only through its agents (corporate directors, officers, and employees). Therefore, the corporate entity itself could not "intend" to commit a crime. Over time, this view has changed. Obviously, corporations cannot be imprisoned, but they can be fined or denied certain legal privileges (such as a license).

Liability of the Corporate Entity Today, corporations are normally liable for the crimes committed by their agents and employees within the course and scope of their employment.[6] For such criminal liability to be imposed, the prosecutor normally must show that the corporation could have prevented the act or that there was authorized consent to, or knowledge of, the act by persons in supervisory positions within the corporation. In addition, corporations can be criminally liable for failing to perform specific duties imposed by law (such as duties under environmental laws or securities laws).

Liability of Corporate Officers and Directors Corporate directors and officers are personally liable for the crimes they commit, regardless of whether the crimes were committed for their private benefit or on the corporation's behalf. Additionally, corporate directors and officers may be held liable for the actions of employees under their supervision. Under the *responsible corporate officer* doctrine, a court may impose criminal liability on a corporate officer regardless of whether he or she participated in, directed, or even knew about a given criminal violation.

3. Pronounced *ak*-tuhs *ray*-uhs.
4. Pronounced *mehns ray*-uh.
5. Model Penal Code Section 2.02(2)(d).
6. See Model Penal Code Section 2.07.

Types of Crimes

Numerous actions are designated as criminal. Federal, state, and local laws provide for the classification and punishment of hundreds of thousands of different criminal acts. Generally, though, criminal acts can be grouped into five broad categories: violent crime (crimes against persons), property crime, public order crime, white-collar crime, and organized crime. Cyber crime—which consists of crimes committed in cyberspace with the use of computers—is, as mentioned earlier in this chapter, less a category of crime than a new way to commit crime. We will examine cyber crime later in this chapter.

Violent Crime

Certain crimes are called *violent crimes*, or crimes against persons, because they cause others to suffer harm or death. Murder is a violent crime. So is sexual assault, or rape. Assault and battery, which will be discussed in Chapter 12 in the context of tort law, are also classified as violent crimes. **Robbery**—defined as the taking of money, personal property, or any other article of value from a person by means of force or fear—is also a violent crime. Typically, states have more severe penalties for *aggravated robbery*—robbery with the use of a deadly weapon.

Each of these violent crimes is further classified by degree, depending on the circumstances surrounding the criminal act. These circumstances include the intent of the person committing the crime, whether a weapon was used, and (for crimes other than murder) the level of pain and suffering experienced by the victim.

Property Crime

The most common type of criminal activity is property crime, or those crimes in which the goal of the offender is some form of economic gain or the damaging of property. Robbery is a form of property crime, as well as a violent crime, because the offender seeks to gain the property of another. We look here at a number of other crimes that fall within the general category of property crime.

Burglary Traditionally, **burglary** was defined as breaking and entering the dwelling of another at night with the intent to commit a felony. Originally, the definition was aimed at protecting an individual's home and its occupants. Most state statutes have eliminated some of the requirements found in the common law definition. The time of day at which the breaking and entering occurs, for example, is usually immaterial. State statutes frequently omit the element of breaking, and some states do not require that the building be a dwelling. When a deadly weapon is used in a burglary, the perpetrator can be charged with *aggravated burglary* and punished more severely.

Larceny Under the common law, the crime of **larceny** involved the unlawful taking and carrying away of someone else's personal property with the intent to permanently deprive the owner of possession. Put simply, larceny is stealing or theft. Whereas robbery involves force or fear, larceny does not. Therefore, picking pockets is larceny, not robbery. Similarly, taking company products and supplies home for personal use, if one is not authorized to do so, is larceny. (Note that a person who commits larceny generally can also be sued under tort law because the act of taking possession of another's property involves a trespass to personal property.)

Most states have expanded the definition of property that is subject to larceny statutes. Stealing computer programs may constitute larceny even though the "property" consists of magnetic impulses. Stealing computer time may also be considered larceny. So, too, may the theft of natural gas or Internet and television cable service. Trade secrets can be subject to larceny statutes.

The common law distinguishes between grand and petit larceny depending on the value of the property taken. Many states have abolished this distinction, but in those that have not, grand larceny (or theft of an item worth above a certain amount) is a felony and petit larceny is a misdemeanor.

Arson The willful and malicious burning of a building (and, in some states, personal property) owned by another is the crime of **arson.** At common law, arson applied only to burning down another person's house. The law was designed to protect human life. Today, arson statutes have been extended to cover the destruction of any building, regardless of ownership, by fire or explosion.

Every state has a special statute that covers the act of burning a building for the purpose of collecting insurance. If Shaw owns an insured apartment building that is falling apart and sets fire to it himself or pays someone else to do so, he is guilty not only of arson but also of defrauding the insurer, which is an attempted larceny. Of course, the insurer need not pay the claim when insurance fraud is proved.

Receiving Stolen Goods It is a crime to receive stolen goods. The recipient of such goods need not know the true identity of the owner or the thief. All that is necessary is that the recipient knows or should know that the goods are stolen, which implies an intent to deprive the owner of those goods.

Forgery The fraudulent making or altering of any writing (including electronic records) in a way that changes the legal rights and liabilities of another is **forgery.** If, without authorization, Severson signs Bennett's name to the back of a check made out to Bennett, Severson is committing forgery. Forgery also includes changing trademarks, falsifying public records, counterfeiting, and altering a legal document.

Obtaining Goods by False Pretenses It is a criminal act to obtain goods by false pretenses, such as buying groceries with a check knowing that one has insufficient funds to cover it. Using another's credit-card number to obtain goods is an additional example of obtaining goods by false pretenses. Statutes dealing with such illegal activities vary widely from state to state.

Public Order Crime

Historically, societies have always outlawed activities that are considered contrary to public values and morals. Today, the most common public order crimes include public drunkenness, prostitution, gambling, and illegal drug use. These crimes are sometimes referred to as *victimless crimes* because they normally harm only the offender. From a broader perspective, however, they are deemed detrimental to society as a whole because they may create an environment that gives rise to property and violent crimes.

White-Collar Crime

Crimes occurring in the business context are popularly referred to as white-collar crimes. Although there is no official definition of **white-collar crime,** the term is commonly used to mean an illegal act or series of acts committed by an individual or business entity using some nonviolent means to obtain a personal or business advantage. Usually, this kind of crime takes place in the course of a legitimate business occupation. Corporate crimes fall into this category. Certain property crimes, such as larceny and forgery, may also be white-collar crimes if they occur within the business context. The crimes discussed next normally occur only in the business environment.

Embezzlement When a person entrusted with another person's property or funds fraudulently appropriates that property or those funds, the crime of **embezzlement** occurs. Typically, embezzlement is carried out by an employee who steals funds. Banks are particularly prone to this problem, but embezzlement can occur in any firm. In a number of businesses, corporate officers or accountants have fraudulently converted funds for their own benefit and then "jimmied" the books to cover up their crime. Embezzlement is not larceny because the wrongdoer does not *physically* take the property from the possession of another, and it is not robbery because no force or fear is used.

It does not matter whether the accused takes the funds from the victim or from a third person. If the financial officer of a large corporation pockets a certain number of checks from third parties that were given to her to deposit into the corporate account, she is embezzling. Frequently, an embezzler takes a relatively small amount at one time but does so repeatedly over a long period. This might be done by underreporting income or deposits and embezzling the remaining amount, for example, or by creating fictitious persons or accounts and writing checks to them from the corporate account.

Practically speaking, an embezzler who returns what has been taken may not be prosecuted because the owner is unwilling to take the time to make a complaint, cooperate with the state's investigative efforts, and appear in court. Also, the owner may not want the crime to become public knowledge. Nevertheless, the intent to return the embezzled property is not a defense to the crime of embezzlement.

When an employer collects withholding taxes from his or her employees yet fails to remit these funds to the state, does such an action constitute a form of embezzlement? This was the primary issue in the following case.

CASE 7.1 George v. Commonwealth of Virginia

Court of Appeals of Virginia, 2008. 51 Va.App. 137, 655 S.E.2d 43.
www.courts.state.va.us/wpcap.htm[a]

● **Background and Facts** Dr. Francis H. George owned and operated a medical practice in Luray, Virginia. From 2001 to 2004, George employed numerous individuals, including nursing assistants, nurse practitioners, and a pediatrician. George withheld funds from his employees' salaries, funds that represented state income taxes owed to the commonwealth[b] of Virginia. George placed these funds in the same banking account that he used to pay his personal and business expenses. During this period, George failed to file withholding tax returns required by state law. Moreover, he did not remit the withheld funds to the state. At trial, a jury convicted George on four counts of embezzlement. George appealed to the state intermediate appellate court claiming, among other things, that the evidence was insufficient to sustain the convictions because the state did not prove that he was entrusted with the property of another.

IN THE LANGUAGE OF THE COURT
***FITZPATRICK,* S.J. [Senior Judge]**

* * * *

Appellant [George] * * * argues that the Commonwealth's evidence was insufficient to prove him guilty of violating [Virginia] Code Section 18.2-111, which provides:

> If any person wrongfully and fraudulently use, dispose of, conceal or embezzle any money, bill, note, check, order, draft, bond, receipt, bill of lading or any other personal property, tangible or intangible, which he shall have received for another or for his employer, principal or bailor [someone entrusting another with goods], or by virtue of his office, trust, or employment, or which shall have been entrusted or delivered to him by another or by any court, corporation or company, he shall be guilty of embezzlement.

To sustain a conviction of embezzlement, the Commonwealth must prove that the accused wrongfully appropriated to his or her own benefit property entrusted or delivered to the accused with the intent to deprive the owner thereof. Although the Commonwealth need not establish the existence of a formal fiduciary relationship [one based on trust], it must prove that the defendant was entrusted with the property of another. [Emphasis added.]

Appellant contends the evidence was insufficient to prove embezzlement because the funds he withheld from his employees' paychecks were not owned or entrusted to him by the Commonwealth. The money in appellant's bank account contained fees paid to him and his business for medical services rendered, as well as the withheld funds. Appellant argues that because the withheld funds amounted to nothing more than a debt he owed the Commonwealth, he did not commit embezzlement.

* * * *

However, while appellant at all relevant times remained responsible for paying the Commonwealth the funds he had withheld from his employees' paychecks, the Commonwealth was not merely his creditor. By operation of statute, the funds appellant retained for withholding taxes were maintained in his possession in trust for the Commonwealth. [Virginia] Code Section 58.1-474 provides:

> Every employer who fails to withhold or pay to the Tax Commissioner any sums required by this article to be withheld and paid shall be personally and individually liable therefor. Any sum or sums withheld in accordance with the provisions of this article shall be deemed to be held in trust for the Commonwealth.

* * * *

Despite the obligations of the fiduciary relationship [one based on trust] created by [Virginia] Code Section 58.1-474, appellant [George] neither remitted the withheld funds to the

a. Scroll down and click on case "0332064" for January 15, 2008 to access this opinion.

b. In addition to Virginia, three other states designate themselves as commonwealths—Kentucky, Massachusetts, and Pennsylvania. The term *commonwealth* dates to the fifteenth century when it meant "common well-being."

CASE CONTINUES

CASE 7.1 CONTINUED

Commonwealth nor maintained them for its benefit. In fact, appellant continued to use the money as though it were his own. "A person entrusted with possession of another's personalty [personal property] who converts such property to his own use or benefit is guilty of the statutory offense of embezzlement."

• **Decision and Remedy** *The Court of Appeals of Virginia ruled that the evidence clearly established that Dr. George used for his own benefit funds that he held in trust for the state. Thus, he was guilty of embezzlement and his appeal to set aside his conviction was denied.*

• **What If the Facts Were Different?** *Assume that Dr. George had actually kept a separate account for taxes withheld from his employees' salaries, but he simply failed to remit them to the state. Would the court have ruled differently? If so, in what way?*

• **The Ethical Dimension** *Does an employer ever have a valid reason for failing to remit withholding taxes to the state? Why or why not?*

Mail and Wire Fraud One of the most potent weapons against white-collar criminals is the Mail Fraud Act of 1990.[7] Under this act, it is a federal crime to use the mails to defraud the public. Illegal use of the mails must involve (1) mailing or causing someone else to mail a writing—something written, printed, or photocopied—for the purpose of executing a scheme to defraud and (2) contemplating or organizing a scheme to defraud by false pretenses. If, for example, Johnson advertises by mail the sale of a cure for cancer that he knows to be fraudulent because it has no medical validity, he can be prosecuted for fraudulent use of the mails.

7. 18 U.S.C. Sections 1341–1342.

Federal law also makes it a crime (wire fraud) to use wire, radio, or television transmissions to defraud.[8] Violators may be fined up to $1,000, imprisoned for up to twenty years, or both. If the violation affects a financial institution, the violator may be fined up to $1 million, imprisoned for up to thirty years, or both.

The following case involved charges of mail fraud stemming from the use of telemarketing to solicit funds that were misrepresented as going to support charities. The question for the court was whether the prosecution could offer proof of the telemarketers' commission rate when no one had lied about it.

8. 18 U.S.C. Section 1343.

CASE 7.2 United States v. Lyons

United States Court of Appeals, Ninth Circuit, 2007. 472 F.3d 1055.

• **Background and Facts** In 1994, in California, Gabriel Sanchez formed the First Church of Life (FCL), which had no congregation, services, or place of worship. Timothy Lyons, Sanchez's friend, formed a fund-raising company called North American Acquisitions (NAA). Through FCL, Sanchez and Lyons set up six charities—AIDS Research Association, Children's Assistance Foundation, Cops and Sheriffs of America, Handicapped Youth Services, U.S. Firefighters, and U.S. Veterans League. NAA hired telemarketers to solicit donations on the charities' behalf. Over time, more than $6 million was raised, of which less than $5,000 was actually spent on charitable causes. The telemarketers kept 80 percent of the donated funds as commissions, and NAA took 10 percent. Most of the rest of the funds went to Sanchez, who spent it on himself. In 2002, Lyons and Sanchez were charged in a federal district court with mail fraud and other crimes. Throughout the trial, the prosecution referred to the high commissions paid to the telemarketers. The defendants were convicted, and each was sentenced to fifteen years in prison. They asked the U.S. Court of Appeals for the Ninth Circuit to overturn their convictions, asserting that the prosecution had used the high cost of fund-raising as evidence of fraud even though the defendants had not lied about the cost.

CASE 7.2 CONTINUED

IN THE LANGUAGE OF THE COURT
***McKEOWN*, Circuit Judge.**

* * * *

Rare is the person who relishes getting calls from those great patrons of the telephone, telemarketers. Yet many charities, especially small, obscure or unpopular ones, could not fund their operations without telemarketers. Some professional telemarketers take the lion's share of solicited donations, sometimes requiring and receiving commission rates of up to 85%. Most donors would probably be shocked or surprised to learn that most of their contributions were going to for-profit telemarketers instead of charitable activities. *But * * * under the First Amendment, the bare failure to disclose these high costs to donors cannot, by itself, support a fraud conviction. Evidence of high fundraising costs may, nonetheless, support a fraud prosecution when nondisclosure is accompanied by intentionally misleading statements designed to deceive the listener.* [Emphasis added.]

* * * Timothy Lyons and Gabriel Sanchez challenge their convictions for mail fraud and money laundering on the basis that they never lied, and never asked the telemarketers in their employ to lie, about the fact that around 80% of donations to their charities were earmarked for telemarketing commissions.

Lyons and Sanchez did, however, misrepresent to donors how they spent contributions net of telemarketer commissions. Their undoing was not that the commissions were large but that their charitable web was a scam. Donors were told their contributions went to specific charitable activities when, in reality, almost no money did.

* * * *

* * * A rule in criminal prosecutions for fraud involving telemarketing [is that] the bare failure to disclose the high cost of fundraising directly to potential donors does not suffice to establish fraud. That is, the mere fact that a telemarketer keeps 85% of contributions it solicits cannot be the basis of a fraud conviction, and neither can the fact that a telemarketer fails to volunteer this information to would-be donors.

* * * [But] when nondisclosure is accompanied by intentionally misleading statements designed to deceive the listener, the high cost of fundraising may be introduced as evidence of fraud in a criminal case. * * * *The State may vigorously enforce its antifraud laws to prohibit professional fundraisers from obtaining money on false pretenses or by making false statements.* [Emphasis added.]

* * * Lyons and Sanchez urge that unless the government could show that they lied to donors about how much the telemarketers would receive, the government was barred from introducing evidence of the high commissions paid to telemarketers.

* * * *

* * * The government both alleged in its indictment and offered evidence at trial of specific misrepresentations and omissions [that Lyons and Sanchez] made regarding the use of donated funds. Specifically, the government's evidence underscored the fact that virtually none of the money that ended up in the bank accounts of the six FCL charities went to any charitable activities at all, let alone the specific charitable activities mentioned in the telemarketers' calls or promotional pamphlets.

* * * [A]dmission of evidence regarding the fundraising costs was essential to understanding the overall scheme and the shell game of the multiple charities. The government did not violate Lyons' or Sanchez's * * * rights by introducing evidence that third-party telemarketers received 80% of funds donated to the various FCL charities because the government had also shown that Lyons and Sanchez, through their respective organizations, had made fraudulent misrepresentations regarding disposition of the charitable funds.

• **Decision and Remedy** *The U.S. Court of Appeals for the Ninth Circuit upheld the convictions. Evidence of the commissions paid to the telemarketers could be introduced even though no one lied to the would-be donors about the commissions. The defendants' "undoing was not that the commissions were large but that their charitable web was a scam."*

CASE CONTINUES

CASE 7.2 CONTINUED

- **The Ethical Dimension** *It may have been legal in this case, but was it ethical for the prosecution to repeatedly emphasize the size of the telemarketers' commissions? Why or why not?*

- **The Legal Environment Dimension** *In what circumstance would the prosecution be prevented from introducing evidence of high fund-raising costs? Why?*

Bribery The crime of bribery involves offering to give something of value to a person in an attempt to influence that person, who is usually, but not always, a public official, to act in a way that serves a private interest. Three types of bribery are considered crimes: bribery of public officials, commercial bribery, and bribery of foreign officials. As an element of the crime of bribery, intent must be present and proved. The bribe itself can be anything the recipient considers to be valuable. Realize that the *crime of bribery occurs when the bribe is offered*—it is not required that the bribe be accepted. *Accepting a bribe* is a separate crime.

Commercial bribery involves corrupt dealings between private persons or businesses. Typically, people make commercial bribes to obtain proprietary information, cover up an inferior product, or secure new business. Industrial espionage sometimes involves commercial bribes. For example, a person in one firm may offer an employee in a competing firm some type of payoff in exchange for trade secrets or pricing schedules. So-called kickbacks, or payoffs for special favors or services, are a form of commercial bribery in some situations.

Bribing foreign officials to obtain favorable business contracts is a crime. This crime was discussed in detail in Chapter 4, along with the Foreign Corrupt Practices Act of 1977, which was passed to curb the use of bribery by U.S. businesspersons in securing foreign contracts.

Bankruptcy Fraud Federal bankruptcy law (see Chapter 15) allows individuals and businesses to be relieved of oppressive debt through bankruptcy proceedings. Numerous white-collar crimes may be committed during the many phases of a bankruptcy action. A creditor, for example, may file a false claim against the debtor, which is a crime. Also, a debtor may fraudulently transfer assets to favored parties before or after the petition for bankruptcy is filed. For instance, a company-owned automobile may be "sold" at a bargain price to a trusted friend or relative. Closely related to the crime of fraudulent transfer of property is the crime of fraudulent concealment of property, such as the hiding of gold coins.

Insider Trading An individual who obtains "inside information" about the plans of a publicly listed corporation can often make stock-trading profits by purchasing or selling corporate securities based on this information. *Insider trading* is a violation of securities law and will be considered more fully in Chapter 28. Basically, securities law prohibits a person who possesses inside information and has a duty not to disclose it to outsiders from trading on that information. He or she may not profit from the purchase or sale of securities based on inside information until the information is made available to the public.

The Theft of Trade Secrets As will be discussed in Chapter 14, trade secrets constitute a form of intellectual property that for many businesses can be extremely valuable. The Economic Espionage Act of 1996[9] makes the theft of trade secrets a federal crime. The act also makes it a federal crime to buy or possess another person's trade secrets, knowing that the trade secrets were stolen or otherwise acquired without the owner's authorization.

Violations of the act can result in steep penalties. The act provides that an individual who violates the act can be imprisoned for up to ten years and fined up to $500,000. If a corporation or other organization violates the act, it can be fined up to $5 million. Additionally, the law provides that any property acquired as a result of the violation, such as airplanes and automobiles, and any property used in the commission of the violation, such as computers and other electronic devices, is subject to criminal forfeiture—meaning that the government can take the property. A theft of trade secrets conducted via the Internet, for example, could result in the forfeiture of every computer or other device used to commit or facilitate the violation as well as any assets gained.

Organized Crime

White-collar crime takes place within the confines of the legitimate business world. Organized crime, in contrast, operates *illegitimately* by, among other things, providing illegal goods and services. Traditionally, the

9. 18 U.S.C. Sections 1831–1839.

preferred markets for organized crime have been gambling, prostitution, illegal narcotics, and loan sharking (lending funds at higher-than-legal interest rates), along with more recent ventures into counterfeiting and credit-card scams.

Money Laundering The profits from organized crime and illegal activities amount to billions of dollars a year, particularly the profits from illegal drug transactions and, to a lesser extent, from racketeering, prostitution, and gambling. Under federal law, banks, savings and loan associations, and other financial institutions are required to report currency transactions involving more than $10,000. Consequently, those who engage in illegal activities face difficulties in depositing their cash profits from illegal transactions.

As an alternative to storing cash from illegal transactions in a safe-deposit box, wrongdoers and racketeers have invented ways to launder "dirty" money to make it "clean." This **money laundering** is done through legitimate businesses. For example, suppose that Harris, a successful drug dealer, becomes a partner with a restaurateur. Little by little, the restaurant shows increasing profits. As a partner in the restaurant, Harris is able to report the "profits" of the restaurant as legitimate income on which he pays federal and state taxes. He can then spend those funds without worrying that his lifestyle may exceed the level possible with his reported income.

RICO In 1970, in an effort to curb the entry of organized crime into the legitimate business world, Congress passed the Racketeer Influenced and Corrupt Organizations Act (RICO) as part of the Organized Crime Control Act.[10] The statute makes it a federal crime to (1) use income obtained from racketeering activity to purchase any interest in an enterprise, (2) acquire or maintain an interest in an enterprise through racketeering activity, (3) conduct or participate in the affairs of an enterprise through racketeering activity, or (4) conspire to do any of the preceding activities.

The broad language of RICO has allowed it to be applied in cases that have little or nothing to do with organized crime. In fact, today the statute is used to attack white-collar crimes more often than organized crime. In addition, RICO creates civil as well as criminal liability.

Criminal Provisions RICO incorporates by reference twenty-six separate types of federal crimes and nine types of state felonies—including many business-related crimes, such as bribery, embezzlement, forgery, mail and wire fraud, and securities fraud.[11] For purposes of RICO, a "pattern of racketeering activity" requires a person to commit at least two of these offenses. Any individual who is found guilty is subject to a fine of up to $25,000 per violation, imprisonment for up to twenty years, or both. Additionally, the statute provides that those who violate RICO may be required to forfeit (give up) any assets, in the form of property or cash, that were acquired as a result of the illegal activity or that were "involved in" or an "instrumentality of" the activity.

Civil Liability In the event of a RICO violation, the government can seek civil penalties, including the divestiture of a defendant's interest in a business (called forfeiture) or the dissolution of the business. Moreover, in some cases, the statute allows private individuals to sue violators and potentially recover three times their actual losses (treble damages), plus attorneys' fees, for business injuries caused by a violation of the statute. This is perhaps the most controversial aspect of RICO and one that continues to cause debate in the nation's federal courts.

The prospect of receiving treble damages in civil RICO lawsuits has given plaintiffs financial incentive to pursue businesses and employers for violations. For example, Mohawk Industries, Inc., one of the largest carpeting manufacturers in the United States, was sued by a group of its employees for RICO violations. The employees claimed Mohawk conspired with recruiting agencies to hire and harbor illegal immigrants in an effort to keep labor costs low. The employees argued that Mohawk's pattern of illegal hiring expanded Mohawk's hourly workforce and resulted in lower wages for the plaintiffs. Mohawk filed a motion to dismiss, arguing that its conduct had not violated RICO. In 2006, however, a federal appellate court ruled that the plaintiffs had presented sufficient evidence of racketeering activity and remanded the case for a trial.[12] (See *Concept Summary 7.1* on the next page for a review of the different types of crimes.)

10. 18 U.S.C. Sections 1961–1968.

11. See 18 U.S.C. Section 1961(1)(A). The crimes listed in this section include murder, kidnapping, gambling, arson, robbery, bribery, extortion, money laundering, securities fraud, counterfeiting, dealing in obscene matter, dealing in controlled substances (illegal drugs), and a number of others.

12. *Williams v. Mohawk Industries, Inc.*, 465 F.3d 1277 (11th Cir. 2006); *cert.* denied, ___ U.S. ___, 127 S.Ct. 1381, 167 L.Ed.2d 174 (2007). See also *Trollinger v. Tyson Foods, Inc.*, 2007 WL 1574275 (E.D.Tenn. 2007) presented as Case 22.1 on page 552.

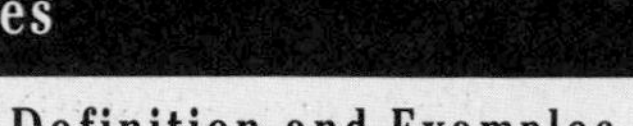

CONCEPT SUMMARY 7.1
Types of Crimes

Crime Category	Definition and Examples
VIOLENT CRIME	*Definition*: Crime that causes others to suffer harm or death. *Examples*: Murder, assault and battery, sexual assault (rape), and robbery.
PROPERTY CRIME	*Definition*: Crime in which the goal of the offender is some form of economic gain or the damaging of property; the most common form of crime. *Examples*: Burglary, larceny, arson, receiving stolen goods, forgery, and obtaining goods by false pretenses.
PUBLIC ORDER CRIME	*Definition*: Crime that is contrary to public values and morals. *Examples*: Public drunkenness, prostitution, gambling, and illegal drug use.
WHITE-COLLAR CRIME	*Definition*: An illegal act or series of acts committed by an individual or business entity using some nonviolent means to obtain a personal or business advantage; usually committed in the course of a legitimate occupation. *Examples*: Embezzlement, mail and wire fraud, bribery, bankruptcy fraud, insider trading, and the theft of trade secrets.
ORGANIZED CRIME	*Definition*: A form of crime conducted by groups operating illegitimately to satisfy the public's demand for illegal goods and services (such as gambling and illegal narcotics). *Examples*: 1. *Money laundering*—The establishment of legitimate enterprises through which "dirty" money (obtained through criminal activities, such as illegal drug trafficking) can be "laundered" (made to appear to be legitimate income). 2. *RICO*—The Racketeer Influenced and Corrupt Organizations Act (RICO) of 1970 makes it a federal crime to (a) use income obtained from racketeering activity to purchase any interest in an enterprise, (b) acquire or maintain an interest in an enterprise through racketeering activity, (c) conduct or participate in the affairs of an enterprise through racketeering activity, or (d) conspire to do any of the preceding activities. RICO provides for both civil and criminal liability.

Defenses to Criminal Liability

In certain circumstances, the law may allow a person to be excused from criminal liability because she or he lacks the required mental state. Criminal defendants may also be relieved of criminal liability if they can show that their criminal actions were justified, given the circumstances. Among the most important defenses to criminal liability are infancy, intoxication, insanity, mistake, consent, duress, justifiable use of force, necessity, entrapment, and the statute of limitations. Additionally, in some cases defendants are given *immunity* from prosecution and thus are relieved, at least in part, of criminal liability for their actions. We look next at each of these defenses.

Note that procedural violations (such as obtaining evidence without a valid search warrant) may also operate as defenses. Evidence obtained in violation of a defendant's constitutional rights may not be admitted in court. If the evidence is suppressed, then there may be no basis for prosecuting the defendant.

Infancy

The term *infant*, as used in the law, refers to any person who has not yet reached the age of majority (see Chapter 9). At common law, children under the age of seven could not commit a crime, and it was presumed that children between the ages of seven and fourteen were incapable of committing crimes because of their incapacity to appreciate right and wrong. Today, most state courts no longer presume that children are incapable of criminal conduct, but may evaluate the particular child's state of mind. In all states, certain courts handle cases involving children who allegedly have violated the law. Courts that handle juvenile cases may also have jurisdiction over additional matters. In most states, a child may be treated as an adult and tried in a regular court if she or he is above a certain age (usually fourteen) and is charged with a felony, such as rape or murder.

Intoxication

The law recognizes two types of intoxication, whether from drugs or from alcohol: involuntary and voluntary. *Involuntary intoxication* occurs when a person either is physically forced to ingest or inject an intoxicating substance or is unaware that such a substance contains drugs or alcohol. Involuntary intoxication is a defense to a crime if its effect was to make a person incapable of understanding that the act committed was wrong or incapable of obeying the law. Voluntary intoxication is rarely a defense, but it may be effective in cases in which the defendant was so *extremely* intoxicated as to negate the state of mind that a crime requires.

Insanity

Just as a child may be incapable of the state of mind required to commit a crime, so also may a person who suffers from a mental illness. Thus, insanity may be a defense to a criminal charge. The courts have had difficulty deciding what the test for legal insanity should be, however, and psychiatrists as well as lawyers are critical of the tests used. Almost all federal courts and some states use the relatively liberal standard set forth in the Model Penal Code:

> A person is not responsible for criminal conduct if at the time of such conduct as a result of mental disease or defect he or she lacks substantial capacity either to appreciate the wrongfulness of his [or her] conduct or to conform his [or her] conduct to the requirements of the law.

Some states use the *M'Naghten* test,[13] under which a criminal defendant is not responsible if, at the time of the offense, he or she did not know the nature and quality of the act or did not know that the act was wrong. Other states use the irresistible-impulse test. A person operating under an irresistible impulse may know an act is wrong but cannot refrain from doing it. Under any of these tests, proving insanity is extremely difficult. For this reason, the insanity defense is rarely used and usually is not successful.

13. A rule derived from *M'Naghten's* Case, 8 Eng.Rep. 718 (1843).

Mistake

Everyone has heard the saying "Ignorance of the law is no excuse." Ordinarily, ignorance of the law or a mistaken idea about what the law requires is not a valid defense. In some states, however, that rule has been modified. People who claim that they honestly did not know that they were breaking a law may have a valid defense if (1) the law was not published or reasonably made known to the public or (2) the people relied on an official statement of the law that was erroneous.

A *mistake of fact,* as opposed to a *mistake of law*, operates as a defense if it negates the mental state necessary to commit a crime. If, for example, Oliver Wheaton mistakenly walks off with Julie Tyson's briefcase because he thinks it is his, there is no theft. Theft requires knowledge that the property belongs to another. (If Wheaton's act causes Tyson to incur damages, however, Wheaton may be subject to liability for trespass to personal property or conversion, torts that will be discussed in Chapter 12.)

Consent

What if a victim consents to a crime or even encourages the person intending a criminal act to commit it? **Consent** is not a defense to most crimes. The law forbids murder, prostitution, and drug use whether the victim consents or not. Consent may serve as a defense, however, in certain situations when it negates an element of the alleged criminal offense. Because crimes against property, such as burglary and larceny, usually require that the defendant intended to take someone else's property, the fact that the owner gave the defendant permission to take it will operate as a defense. Consent or forgiveness given after a crime has been committed is never a defense, although it can affect the likelihood of prosecution.

Duress

Duress exists when the *wrongful threat* of one person induces another person to perform an act that he or she would not otherwise have performed. In such a situation, duress is said to negate the mental state necessary to commit a crime because the defendant was forced or compelled to commit the act. Duress can be used as a defense to most crimes except murder.

Duress excuses a crime only when another's unlawful threat of serious bodily injury or death reasonably causes the defendant to do a criminal act. In addition, there must have been no opportunity for the

EMERGING TRENDS IN THE LEGAL ENVIRONMENT OF BUSINESS

Stand-Your-Ground Laws

Traditionally, the justifiable use of force, or self-defense, doctrine required prosecutors to distinguish between deadly and nondeadly force. In general, state laws have allowed individuals to use the amount of nondeadly force that is necessary to protect themselves, their dwellings, or other property, or to prevent the commission of a crime.

The Duty-to-Retreat Doctrine

In the past, most states allowed deadly force to be used in self-defense only if the individual reasonably believed that imminent death or bodily harm would otherwise result. Additionally, the attacker had to be using unlawful force, and the defender had to have no other possible response or alternative way out of the life-threatening situation.[a] Today, many states, particularly in the Northeast, still have "duty-to-retreat" laws on their statute books. Under these laws, when a person's home is invaded or an assailant approaches, the person is required to retreat unless her or his life is in danger. Juries have sometimes been reluctant to apply the duty-to-retreat doctrine, however. In a famous case in the 1980s, Bernard Goetz shot and injured four young men who asked him for money while he was riding the subway in New York City. The jury found that Goetz had reasonably believed that he was in danger of being physically attacked.[b]

Stand-Your-Ground Legislation on the Increase

Whereas the duty-to-retreat doctrine attempts to reduce the likelihood that deadly—or even nondeadly—force will be used in defense of one's person or home, today several states are taking a very different approach and expanding the occasions when deadly force can be used in self-defense. Because such laws allow or even encourage the defender to stay and use force, they are known as "stand-your-ground" laws.

On October 1, 2005, for example, Florida enacted a statute that allows the use of deadly force to prevent the commission of a "forcible felony," including not only murder but also such crimes as robbery, carjacking, and sexual battery.[c] The law applies to both homes and vehicles. Under this statute, Floridians may use deadly force without having to prove that they feared for their safety. In other words, a Florida resident now has the right to shoot an intruder in his or her home or a would-be carjacker even if there is no physical threat to the owner's safety. The law prohibits the arrest, detention, or prosecution of individuals covered by the law and also prohibits civil suits against them.

Since the Florida statute was enacted, Alabama, Alaska, Arizona, Georgia, Indiana, Kentucky, Louisiana, Michigan, Mississippi, Missouri,

a. *State v. Sandoval,* 342 Or. 506, 156 P.3d 60 (2007).

b. *People v. Goetz,* 506 N.Y.S.2d 18, 497 N.E.2d 41 (1986). See also *People v. Douglas,* 29 A.D.3d 47, 809 N.Y.S.2d 36 (2006); and *State v. Augustin,* 101 Haw. 127, 63 P.3d 1097 (2002).

c. Florida Statutes Section 776.012.

defendant to escape or avoid the threatened danger.[14] Essentially, to successfully assert duress as a defense, the defendant must reasonably believe in the immediate danger, and the jury (or judge) must conclude that the defendant's belief was reasonable.

Justifiable Use of Force

Probably the best-known defense to criminal liability is **self-defense.** Other situations, however, also justify the use of force: the defense of one's dwelling, the defense of other property, and the prevention of a crime. In all of these situations, it is important to distinguish between deadly and nondeadly force. *Deadly force* is likely to result in death or serious bodily harm. *Nondeadly force* is force that reasonably appears necessary to prevent the imminent use of criminal force.

Generally speaking, people can use the amount of nondeadly force that seems necessary to protect themselves, their dwellings, or other property, or to prevent the commission of a crime. Deadly force can be used in self-defense only when the defender *reasonably believes* that imminent death or grievous bodily harm will otherwise result and has no other means of escaping or avoiding the situation. Deadly force normally can be used to defend a dwelling only if the unlawful entry is violent and the person believes deadly force is necessary to prevent imminent death or great bodily harm. In some jurisdictions, however, deadly force can also be used if the person believes it is necessary to prevent the commission of a felony in the dwelling. Many states are expanding the situations in which the use of deadly force can be justified—see this chapter's *Emerging Trends* feature for a discussion of this trend.

Necessity

Sometimes, criminal defendants can be relieved of liability by showing that a criminal act was necessary to prevent an even greater harm. According to the Model

14. See, for example, *State v. Heinemann,* 282 Conn. 281, 920 A.2d 278 (2007).

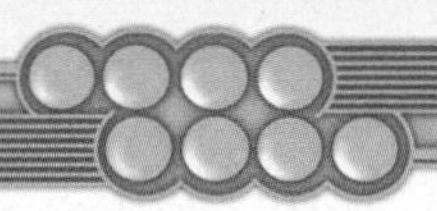

Montana, Oklahoma, Pennsylvania, South Dakota, Washington, and Wyoming have passed or are considering passing similar laws. Utah already had a "stand-your-ground" law.[d] Louisiana's statute, which mimics the Florida statute, was passed after Hurricane Katrina devastated New Orleans. In Louisiana, there is now a presumption of innocence for anyone who uses deadly force when threatened with violence in his or her home, car, or place of business.

North Carolina's stand-your-ground statute is typical. It states that "(a) A lawful occupant within a home or other place of residence is justified in using any degree of force that the occupant reasonably believes is necessary, including deadly force, against an intruder to prevent a forcible entry into the home or residence or to terminate the intruder's unlawful entry (i) if the occupant reasonably apprehends that the intruder may kill or inflict serious bodily harm to the occupant or others in the home or residence, or (ii) if the occupant reasonably believes that the intruder intends to commit a felony in the home or residence. (b) A lawful occupant within a home or other place of residence does not have a duty to retreat from an intruder in the circumstances described in this section."[e]

Although the media sometimes describe stand-your-ground laws as "new," these statutes are actually based on a centuries-old precedent. The laws are a throwback to the "castle" doctrine, which was derived from English common law in the 1700s, when a person's home was considered to be his or her castle.[f]

IMPLICATIONS FOR THE BUSINESSPERSON

1. States that have enacted stand-your-ground laws often include places of business as well as homes and vehicles. Consequently, businesspersons in those states can be less concerned about the duty-to-retreat doctrine.
2. Presumably, business liability insurance will eventually be less costly in stand-your-ground states.

FOR CRITICAL ANALYSIS

1. Those who oppose stand-your-ground laws argue that they encourage vigilantism and preemptive shootings. Do you agree? Explain.
2. "A person's home is his or her castle." Does this traditional saying justify the use of deadly force against an intruder under all circumstances? Why or why not?

RELEVANT WEB SITES

To locate information on the Web concerning the issues discussed in this feature, go to this text's Web site at **academic.cengage.com/blaw/cross**, select "Chapter 7," and click on "Emerging Trends."

d. Utah Code Ann. 76-2-402 and 76-2-407.

e. North Carolina General Statutes Ann. 14–51.1

f. One reference to the castle doctrine can be found in William Blackstone, *Commentaries on the Laws of England,* Book 4, Chapter 16.

Penal Code, the defense of **necessity** is justifiable if "the harm or evil sought to be avoided by such conduct is greater than that sought to be prevented by the law defining the offense charged."[15] For example, in one case a convicted felon was threatened by an acquaintance with a gun. The felon grabbed the gun and fled the scene, but subsequently he was arrested under a statute that prohibits convicted felons from possessing firearms. In this situation, the necessity defense succeeded because the defendant's crime avoided a "greater evil."[16]

Entrapment

Entrapment is a defense designed to prevent police officers or other government agents from enticing persons to commit crimes in order to later prosecute them for criminal acts. In the typical entrapment case, an undercover agent *suggests* that a crime be committed and somehow pressures or induces an individual to commit it. The agent then arrests the individual for the crime. For entrapment to be considered a defense, both the suggestion and the inducement must take place. The defense is not intended to prevent law enforcement agents from setting a trap for an unwary criminal; rather, the intent is to prevent them from pushing the individual into it. The crucial issue is whether the person who committed a crime was predisposed to commit the illegal act or did so because the agent induced it.

Statute of Limitations

With some exceptions, such as the crime of murder, statutes of limitations apply to crimes just as they do to civil wrongs. In other words, the state must initiate criminal prosecution within a certain number of years. If a criminal action is brought after the statutory time period has expired, the accused person can raise the statute of limitations as a defense. The running of the

15. Model Penal Code Section 3.02.

16. *United States v. Paolello,* 951 F.2d 537 (3d Cir. 1991).

time period in a statute of limitations may be tolled—that is, suspended or stopped temporarily—if the defendant is a minor or is not in the jurisdiction. When the defendant reaches the age of majority or returns to the jurisdiction, the statute revives—that is, its time period begins to run or to run again.

Immunity

At times, the state may wish to obtain information from a person accused of a crime. Accused persons are understandably reluctant to give information if it will be used to prosecute them, and they cannot be forced to do so. The privilege against self-incrimination is guaranteed by the Fifth Amendment to the U.S. Constitution, which reads, in part, "nor shall [any person] be compelled in any criminal case to be a witness against himself." In cases in which the state wishes to obtain information from a person accused of a crime, the state can grant *immunity* from prosecution or agree to prosecute for a less serious offense in exchange for the information. Once immunity is given, the person now has an absolute privilege against self-incrimination and therefore can no longer refuse to testify on Fifth Amendment grounds.

Often, a grant of immunity from prosecution for a serious crime is part of the **plea bargaining** between the defending and prosecuting attorneys. The defendant may be convicted of a lesser offense, while the state uses the defendant's testimony to prosecute accomplices for serious crimes carrying heavy penalties.

Criminal Procedures

Criminal law brings the force of the state, with all of its resources, to bear against the individual. Criminal procedures are designed to protect the constitutional rights of individuals and to prevent the arbitrary use of power on the part of the government.

The U.S. Constitution provides specific safeguards for those accused of crimes. The United States Supreme Court has ruled that most of these safeguards apply not only in federal court but also in state courts by virtue of the due process clause of the Fourteenth Amendment. These protections include the following:

1. The Fourth Amendment protection from unreasonable searches and seizures.
2. The Fourth Amendment requirement that no warrant for a search or an arrest be issued without probable cause.
3. The Fifth Amendment requirement that no one be deprived of "life, liberty, or property without due process of law."
4. The Fifth Amendment prohibition against **double jeopardy** (trying someone twice for the same criminal offense).[17]
5. The Fifth Amendment requirement that no person be required to be a witness against (incriminate) himself or herself.
6. The Sixth Amendment guarantees of a speedy trial, a trial by jury, a public trial, the right to confront witnesses, and the right to a lawyer at various stages in some proceedings.
7. The Eighth Amendment prohibitions against excessive bail and fines and cruel and unusual punishment.

The Exclusionary Rule

Under what is known as the **exclusionary rule,** all evidence obtained in violation of the constitutional rights spelled out in the Fourth, Fifth, and Sixth Amendments generally is not admissible at trial. All evidence derived from the illegally obtained evidence is known as the "fruit of the poisonous tree," and such evidence normally must also be excluded from the trial proceedings. For example, if a confession is obtained after an illegal arrest, the arrest is the "poisonous tree," and the confession, if "tainted" by the arrest, is the "fruit."

As you will read shortly, under the *Miranda* rule, suspects must be advised of certain constitutional rights when they are arrested. For example, the Sixth Amendment right to counsel is one of the rights of which a suspect must be advised when she or he is arrested. In many cases, a statement that a criminal suspect makes in the absence of counsel is not admissible at trial unless the suspect has knowingly and voluntarily waived this right. In the following case, the United States Supreme Court considered at what point a suspect's right to counsel is triggered during criminal proceedings.

17. The prohibition against double jeopardy means that once a criminal defendant is found not guilty of a particular crime, the government may not reindict the person and retry him or her for the same crime. The prohibition does not preclude a *civil* lawsuit against the same person by the crime victim to recover damages. For example, a person found not guilty of assault and battery in a criminal case may be sued by the victim in a civil tort case for damages. Additionally, a state's prosecution of a crime will not prevent a separate federal prosecution of the same crime, and vice versa. For example, a defendant found not guilty of violating a state law can be tried in federal court for the same act, if the act is also defined as a crime under federal law.

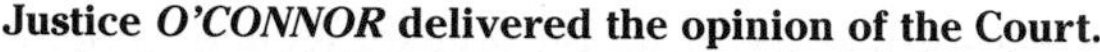

EXTENDED CASE 7.3 Fellers v. United States

Supreme Court of the United States, 2004. 540 U.S. 519, 124 S.Ct. 1019, 157 L.Ed.2d 1016.

Justice *O'CONNOR* delivered the opinion of the Court.

* * * *

On February 24, 2000, after a grand jury indicted petitioner [John J. Fellers] for conspiracy to distribute methamphetamine, Lincoln Police Sergeant Michael Garnett and Lancaster County Deputy Sheriff Jeff Bliemeister went to petitioner's home in Lincoln, Nebraska, to arrest him. The officers knocked on petitioner's door and, when petitioner answered, identified themselves and asked if they could come in. Petitioner invited the officers into his living room.

The officers advised petitioner they had come to discuss his involvement in methamphetamine distribution. They informed petitioner that they had a federal warrant for his arrest and that a grand jury had indicted him for conspiracy to distribute methamphetamine. The officers told petitioner that the indictment referred to his involvement with certain individuals, four of whom they named. Petitioner then told the officers that he knew the four people and had used methamphetamine during his association with them.

After spending about 15 minutes in petitioner's home, the officers transported petitioner to the Lancaster County jail. There, the officers advised petitioner for the first time of his [right to counsel under the Sixth Amendment]. Petitioner and the two officers signed a * * * waiver form, and petitioner then reiterated the inculpatory [incriminating] statements he had made earlier, admitted to having associated with other individuals implicated in the charged conspiracy, and admitted to having loaned money to one of them even though he suspected that she was involved in drug transactions.

Before trial, petitioner moved to suppress the inculpatory statements he made at his home and at the county jail.

The District Court suppressed the "unwarned" statements petitioner made at his house but admitted petitioner's jailhouse statements * * * , concluding petitioner had knowingly and voluntarily waived his * * * rights before making the statements.

Following a jury trial at which petitioner's jailhouse statements were admitted into evidence, petitioner was convicted of conspiring to possess with intent to distribute methamphetamine. Petitioner appealed, arguing that his jailhouse statements should have been suppressed as fruits of the statements obtained at his home in violation of the Sixth Amendment. The [U.S.] Court of Appeals [for the Eighth Circuit] affirmed. * * * The Court of Appeals stated:" * * * The officers did not interrogate [the petitioner] at his home." * * * [Fellers appealed to the United States Supreme Court.]

* * * *

*The Sixth Amendment right to counsel is triggered at or after the time that judicial proceedings have been initiated * * * whether by way of formal charge, preliminary hearing, indictment, information, or arraignment.* We have held that an accused is denied the basic protections of the Sixth Amendment when there is used against him at his trial evidence of his own incriminating words, which federal agents * * * deliberately elicited from him after he had been indicted and in the absence of his counsel. [Emphasis added.]

We have consistently applied the *deliberate-elicitation standard* in * * * Sixth Amendment cases * * * . [Emphasis added.]

The Court of Appeals erred in holding that the absence of an "interrogation" foreclosed petitioner's claim that the jailhouse statements should have been suppressed as fruits of the statements taken from petitioner [Fellers] at his home. First, there is no question that the officers in this case deliberately elicited information from petitioner. Indeed, the officers, upon arriving at petitioner's house, informed him that their purpose in coming was to discuss his involvement in the distribution of methamphetamine and his association with certain charged co-conspirators. Because the ensuing discussion took place after petitioner had been indicted, outside the presence of counsel, and in the absence of any waiver of petitioner's Sixth Amendment rights, the Court of Appeals erred in holding that the officers' actions did not violate the Sixth Amendment standards * * * .

CASE CONTINUES

CASE 7.3 CONTINUED

Second, because of its erroneous determination that petitioner was not questioned in violation of Sixth Amendment standards, the Court of Appeals improperly conducted its "fruits" analysis * * * . Specifically, it * * * [held] that the admissibility of the jailhouse statements turns solely on whether the statements were knowingly and voluntarily made. The Court of Appeals did not reach the question whether the Sixth Amendment requires suppression of petitioner's jailhouse statements on the ground that they were the fruits of previous questioning conducted in violation of the Sixth Amendment deliberate-elicitation standard. We have not had occasion to decide whether [such statements should be excluded from trial] when a suspect makes incriminating statements after a knowing and voluntary waiver of his right to counsel notwithstanding earlier police questioning in violation of Sixth Amendment standards. We therefore remand to the Court of Appeals to address this issue in the first instance.

Accordingly, the judgment of the Court of Appeals is reversed, and the case is remanded for further proceedings consistent with this opinion.

It is so ordered.

QUESTIONS

1. Why did Fellers argue on appeal that his "jailhouse statements" should have been excluded from his trial?
2. Should Fellers's "jailhouse statements" have been excluded from his trial? Why or why not?

Purpose of the Exclusionary Rule The purpose of the exclusionary rule is to deter police from conducting warrantless searches and from engaging in other misconduct. The rule is sometimes criticized because it can lead to injustice. Many a defendant has "gotten off on a technicality" because law enforcement personnel failed to observe procedural requirements based on the above-mentioned constitutional amendments. Even though a defendant may be obviously guilty, if the evidence of that guilt was obtained improperly (without a valid search warrant, for example), it cannot be used against the defendant in court.

Exceptions to the Exclusionary Rule Over the last several decades, the United States Supreme Court has diminished the scope of the exclusionary rule by creating some exceptions to its applicability. For example, if illegally obtained evidence would have been discovered "inevitably" and obtained by the police using lawful means, the evidence will be admissible at trial.[18] The Court has also created a "good faith" exception to the exclusionary rule.[19] Under this exception, if the police officer who used a technically incorrect search warrant form to obtain evidence was acting in good faith, the evidence will be admissible. Additionally, the courts can exercise a certain amount of discretion in determining whether evidence has been obtained improperly—a possibility that somewhat balances the scales.

18. *Nix v. Williams,* 467 U.S. 431, 104 S.Ct. 2501, 81 L.Ed.2d 377 (1984).

19. *Massachusetts v. Sheppard,* 468 U.S. 981, 104 S.Ct. 3424, 82 L.Ed.2d 737 (1984).

The *Miranda* Rule

In regard to criminal procedure, one of the questions many courts faced in the 1950s and 1960s was not whether suspects had constitutional rights—that was not in doubt—but how and when those rights could be exercised. Could the right to be silent (under the Fifth Amendment's prohibition against self-incrimination) be exercised during pretrial interrogation proceedings or only during the trial? Were confessions obtained from suspects admissible in court if the suspects had not been advised of their right to remain silent and other constitutional rights?

To clarify these issues, the United States Supreme Court issued a landmark decision in 1966 in *Miranda v. Arizona,* which we present here. Today, the procedural rights required by the Court in this case are familiar to virtually every American.

CASE 7.4 Miranda v. Arizona

Supreme Court of the United States, 1966. 384 U.S. 436, 86 S.Ct. 1602, 16 L.Ed.2d 694.

• **Background and Facts** On March 13, 1963, Ernesto Miranda was arrested at his home for the kidnapping and rape of an eighteen-year-old woman. Miranda was taken to a Phoenix, Arizona, police station and questioned by two officers. Two hours later, the officers emerged from the interrogation room with a written confession signed by Miranda. A paragraph at the top of the confession stated that the confession had been made voluntarily, without threats or promises of immunity, and "with full knowledge of my legal rights, understanding any statement I make may be used against me." Miranda was at no time advised that he had a right to remain silent and a right to have a lawyer present. The confession was admitted into evidence at the trial, and Miranda was convicted and sentenced to prison for twenty to thirty years. Miranda appealed the decision, claiming that he had not been informed of his constitutional rights. The Supreme Court of Arizona held that Miranda's constitutional rights had not been violated and affirmed his conviction. The *Miranda* case was subsequently reviewed by the United States Supreme Court.

IN THE LANGUAGE OF THE COURT

Mr. Chief Justice *WARREN* delivered the opinion of the Court.

The cases before us raise questions which go to the roots of our concepts of American criminal jurisprudence; the restraints society must observe consistent with the Federal Constitution in prosecuting individuals for crime.

* * * *

At the outset, if a person in custody is to be subjected to interrogation, he must first be informed in clear and unequivocal terms that he has the right to remain silent.

* * * *

The warning of the right to remain silent must be accompanied by the explanation that anything said can and will be used against the individual in court. This warning is needed in order to make him aware not only of the privilege, *but also of the consequences of forgoing it.* [Emphasis added.]

The circumstances surrounding in-custody interrogation can operate very quickly to overbear the will of one merely made aware of his privilege by his interrogators. Therefore the right to have counsel present at the interrogation is indispensable to the protection of the Fifth Amendment privilege under the system we delineate today.

* * * *

In order fully to apprise a person interrogated of the extent of his rights under this system then, it is necessary to warn him not only that he has the right to consult with an attorney, but also that if he is indigent [without funds] a lawyer will be appointed to represent him. * * * The warning of a right to counsel would be hollow if not couched in terms that would convey to the indigent—the person most often subjected to interrogation—the knowledge that he too has a right to have counsel present.

• **Decision and Remedy** *The United States Supreme Court held that Miranda could not be convicted of the crime on the basis of his confession because his confession was inadmissible as evidence. For any statement made by a defendant to be admissible, the defendant must be informed of certain constitutional rights prior to police interrogation. If the accused waives his or her rights to remain silent and to have counsel present, the government must demonstrate that the waiver was made knowingly, voluntarily, and intelligently.*

• **Impact of This Case on Today's Law** *Police officers routinely advise suspects of their "Miranda rights" on arrest. When Ernesto Miranda himself was later murdered, the suspected murderer was "read his* Miranda *rights." Despite significant criticisms and later attempts to overrule the* Miranda *decision through legislation, the requirements stated in this case continue to provide the benchmark by which criminal procedures are judged today.*

CASE CONTINUES

CASE 7.4 CONTINUED

• **International Considerations** **The Right to Remain Silent in Great Britain** *The right to remain silent has long been a legal hallmark in Great Britain as well as in the United States. In 1994, however, the British Parliament passed an act that provides that a criminal defendant's silence may be interpreted as evidence of the defendant's guilt. British police officers are now required, when making an arrest, to inform the suspect, "You do not have to say anything. But if you do not mention now something which you later use in your defense, the court may decide that your failure to mention it now strengthens the case against you. A record will be made of everything you say, and it may be given in evidence if you are brought to trial."*

Congress's Response to the *Miranda* Ruling The Supreme Court's *Miranda* decision was controversial, and two years later Congress attempted to overrule it by enacting Section 3501 of the Omnibus Crime Control and Safe Streets Act of 1968.[20] Essentially, Section 3501 reinstated the rule that had been in effect for 180 years before the *Miranda* ruling—namely, that statements by defendants can be used against them as long as the statements are made voluntarily. The U.S. Department of Justice immediately refused to enforce Section 3501, however. Although the U.S. Court of Appeals for the Fourth Circuit attempted to enforce the provision in 1999, the United States Supreme Court reversed its decision in 2000. The Supreme Court held that the *Miranda* rights enunciated by the Court in the 1966 case were constitutionally based and thus could not be overruled by a legislative act.[21]

Exceptions to the *Miranda* Rule As part of a continuing attempt to balance the rights of accused persons against the rights of society, the Supreme Court has made a number of exceptions to the *Miranda* ruling. For example, the Court has recognized a "public safety" exception, holding that certain statements—such as statements concerning the location of a weapon—are admissible even if the defendant was not given *Miranda* warnings.[22] The Court has also clarified that, in certain circumstances, a defendant's confession need not be excluded as evidence even if the police failed to inform the defendant of his or her *Miranda* rights.[23] If other, legally obtained evidence admitted at trial is strong enough to justify the conviction without the confession, then the fact that the confession was obtained illegally can, in effect, be ignored.[24]

The Supreme Court has also ruled that a suspect must unequivocally and assertively request to exercise her or his right to counsel in order to stop police questioning. Saying, "Maybe I should talk to a lawyer" during an interrogation after being taken into custody is not enough. The Court held that police officers are not required to decipher the suspect's intentions in such situations.[25]

Criminal Process

As mentioned earlier in this chapter, a criminal prosecution differs significantly from a civil case in several respects. These differences reflect the desire to safeguard the rights of the individual against the state. Exhibit 7–3 summarizes the major steps in processing a criminal case. We now discuss three phases of the criminal process—arrest, indictment or information, and trial—in more detail.

Arrest Before a warrant for arrest can be issued, there must be probable cause for believing that the individual in question has committed a crime. As discussed in Chapter 5, *probable cause* can be defined as a substantial likelihood that the person has committed or is about to commit a crime. Note that probable cause involves a likelihood, not just a possibility. Arrests can be made without a warrant if there is no time to get one, but the action of the arresting officer is still judged by the standard of probable cause.

Indictment or Information Individuals must be formally charged with having committed specific crimes before they can be brought to trial. If issued by

20. 42 U.S.C. Section 3789d.
21. *Dickerson v. United States,* 530 U.S. 428, 120 S.Ct. 2326, 147 L.Ed.2d 405 (2000).
22. *New York v. Quarles,* 467 U.S. 649, 104 S.Ct. 2626, 81 L.Ed.2d 550 (1984).
23. *Moran v. Burbine,* 475 U.S. 412, 106 S.Ct. 1135, 89 L.Ed.2d 410 (1986).
24. *Arizona v. Fulminante,* 499 U.S. 279, 111 S.Ct. 1246, 113 L.Ed.2d 302 (1991).
25. *Davis v. United States,* 512 U.S. 452, 114 S.Ct. 2350, 129 L.Ed.2d 362 (1994).

EXHIBIT 7–3 • Major Procedural Steps in a Criminal Case

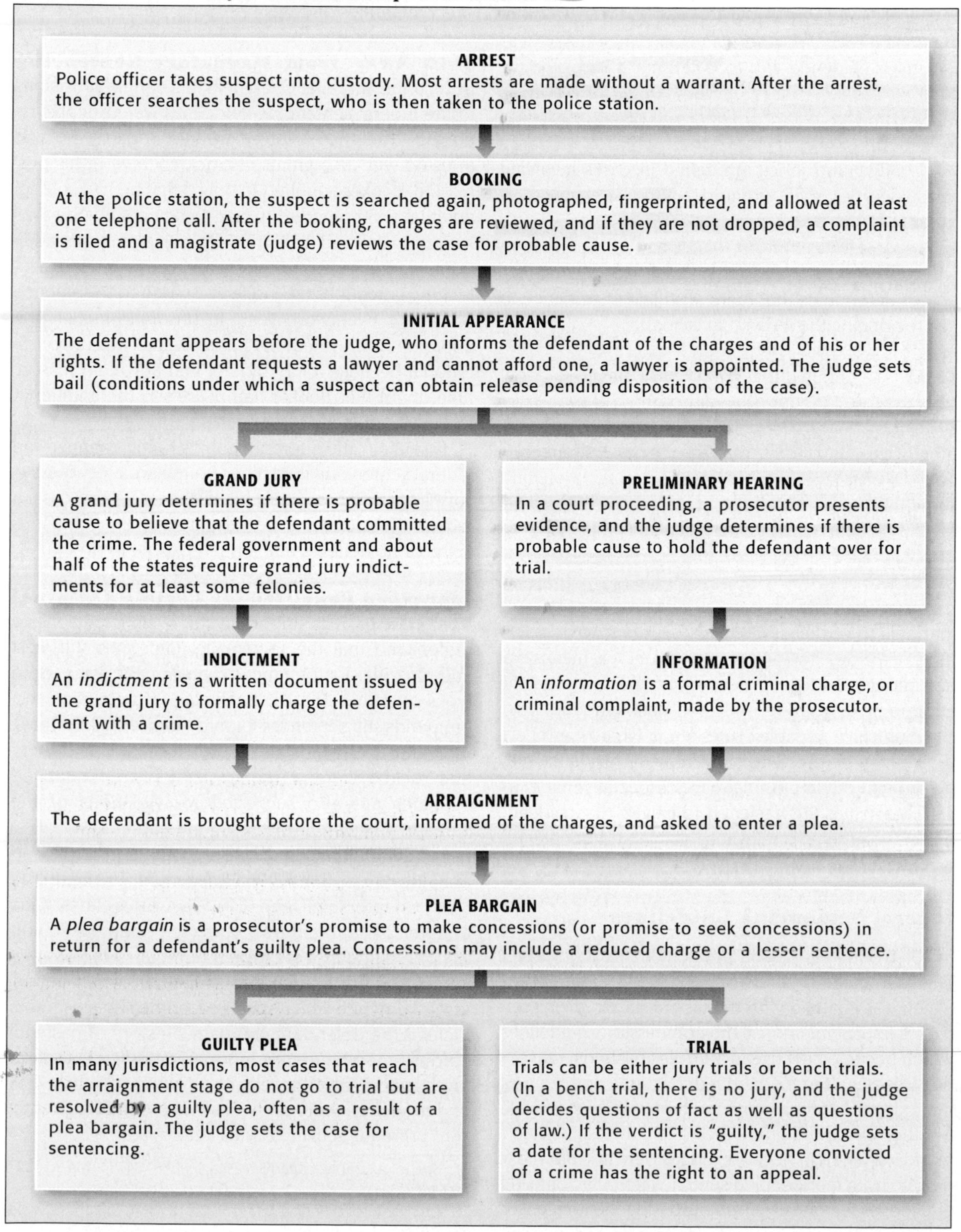

ARREST
Police officer takes suspect into custody. Most arrests are made without a warrant. After the arrest, the officer searches the suspect, who is then taken to the police station.

BOOKING
At the police station, the suspect is searched again, photographed, fingerprinted, and allowed at least one telephone call. After the booking, charges are reviewed, and if they are not dropped, a complaint is filed and a magistrate (judge) reviews the case for probable cause.

INITIAL APPEARANCE
The defendant appears before the judge, who informs the defendant of the charges and of his or her rights. If the defendant requests a lawyer and cannot afford one, a lawyer is appointed. The judge sets bail (conditions under which a suspect can obtain release pending disposition of the case).

GRAND JURY
A grand jury determines if there is probable cause to believe that the defendant committed the crime. The federal government and about half of the states require grand jury indictments for at least some felonies.

INDICTMENT
An *indictment* is a written document issued by the grand jury to formally charge the defendant with a crime.

PRELIMINARY HEARING
In a court proceeding, a prosecutor presents evidence, and the judge determines if there is probable cause to hold the defendant over for trial.

INFORMATION
An *information* is a formal criminal charge, or criminal complaint, made by the prosecutor.

ARRAIGNMENT
The defendant is brought before the court, informed of the charges, and asked to enter a plea.

PLEA BARGAIN
A *plea bargain* is a prosecutor's promise to make concessions (or promise to seek concessions) in return for a defendant's guilty plea. Concessions may include a reduced charge or a lesser sentence.

GUILTY PLEA
In many jurisdictions, most cases that reach the arraignment stage do not go to trial but are resolved by a guilty plea, often as a result of a plea bargain. The judge sets the case for sentencing.

TRIAL
Trials can be either jury trials or bench trials. (In a bench trial, there is no jury, and the judge decides questions of fact as well as questions of law.) If the verdict is "guilty," the judge sets a date for the sentencing. Everyone convicted of a crime has the right to an appeal.

a grand jury, such a charge is called an **indictment.**[26] A **grand jury** does not determine the guilt or innocence of an accused party; rather, its function is to hear the state's evidence and to determine whether a reasonable basis (probable cause) exists for believing that a crime has been committed and that a trial ought to be held.

Usually, grand juries are called in cases involving serious crimes, such as murder. For lesser crimes, an individual may be formally charged with a crime by an **information,** or criminal complaint. An information will be issued by a government prosecutor if the prosecutor determines that there is sufficient evidence to justify bringing the individual to trial.

Trial At a criminal trial, the accused person does not have to prove anything; the entire burden of proof is on the prosecutor (the state). As discussed at the beginning of this chapter, the burden of proof is higher in a criminal case than in a civil case. The prosecution must show that, based on all the evidence, the defendant's guilt is established *beyond a reasonable doubt.* If there is reasonable doubt as to whether a criminal defendant did, in fact, commit the crime with which she or he has been charged, then the verdict must be "not guilty." Note that giving a verdict of "not guilty" is not the same as stating that the defendant is innocent; it merely means that not enough evidence was properly presented to the court to prove guilt beyond a reasonable doubt.

Courts have complex rules about what types of evidence may be presented and how the evidence may be brought out in criminal cases, especially in jury trials. These rules are designed to ensure that evidence presented at trials is relevant, reliable, and not prejudicial toward the defendant.

Federal Sentencing Guidelines

In 1984, Congress passed the Sentencing Reform Act. This act created the U.S. Sentencing Commission, which was charged with the task of standardizing sentences for *federal* crimes. The commission's guidelines, which became effective in 1987, established a range of possible penalties for each federal crime and required the judge to select a sentence from within that range. In other words, the guidelines originally established a mandatory system because judges were not allowed to deviate from the specified sentencing range. Some federal judges felt uneasy about imposing the long prison sentences required by the guidelines on certain criminal defendants, particularly first-time offenders and those convicted in illegal substances cases involving small quantities of drugs.[27]

Shift Away from Mandatory Sentencing In 2005, the Supreme Court held that certain provisions of the federal sentencing guidelines were unconstitutional.[28] The case involved Freddie Booker, who was arrested with 92.5 grams of crack cocaine in his possession. Booker admitted to police that he had sold an additional 566 grams of crack cocaine, but he was never charged with, or tried for, possessing this additional quantity. Nevertheless, under the federal sentencing guidelines the judge was required to sentence Booker to twenty-two years in prison. Ultimately, the Supreme Court ruled that this sentence was unconstitutional because a jury did not find beyond a reasonable doubt that Booker had possessed the additional 566 grams of crack.

Essentially, the Supreme Court's ruling changed the federal sentencing guidelines from mandatory to advisory. Depending on the circumstances of the case, a federal trial judge may now depart from the guidelines if she or he believes that it is reasonable to do so.

Increased Penalties for Certain Criminal Violations It is important for businesspersons to understand that the sentencing guidelines still exist and provide for enhanced punishment for certain types of crimes. The U.S. Sentencing Commission recommends stiff sentences for many white-collar crimes, including mail and wire fraud, commercial bribery and kickbacks, and money laundering. Enhanced penalties are also suggested for violations of the Sarbanes-Oxley Act (discussed in Chapter 4).[29]

In addition, the commission recommends increased penalties for criminal violations of employment laws (see Chapters 21 and 22), securities laws (see Chapter 28), and antitrust laws (see Chapters 26 and 27). The guidelines set forth a number of factors that judges should take into consideration when imposing a sentence for a specified crime. These factors include the defendant company's history of past violations, management's cooperation with federal investigators, and the extent to which the firm has undertaken specific programs and procedures to prevent criminal activities by its employees.

26. Pronounced in-*dyte*-ment.

27. See, for example, *United States v. Angelos,* 347 F.Supp.2d 1227 (D. Utah 2004).

28. *United States v. Booker,* 543 U.S. 220, 125 S.Ct. 738, 160 L.Ed.2d 621 (2005).

29. As required by the Sarbanes-Oxley Act of 2002, the U.S. Sentencing Commission revised its guidelines in 2003 to impose stiffer penalties for corporate securities fraud—see Chapter 28.

Cyber Crime

Some years ago, the American Bar Association defined **computer crime** as any act that is directed against computers and computer parts, that uses computers as instruments of crime, or that involves computers and constitutes abuse. Today, because much of the crime committed with the use of computers occurs in cyberspace, many computer crimes fall under the broad label of **cyber crime.** Here we look at several types of activity that constitute cyber crimes against persons or property. Other cyber crimes will be discussed in later chapters as they relate to particular topics, such as banking or consumer law.

Cyber Theft

In cyberspace, thieves are not subject to the physical limitations of the "real" world. A thief can steal data stored in a networked computer with Internet access from anywhere on the globe. Only the speed of the connection and the thief's computer equipment limit the quantity of data that can be stolen.

Financial Crimes Computer networks also provide opportunities for employees to commit crimes that can involve serious economic losses. For example, employees of a company's accounting department can transfer funds among accounts with little effort and often with less risk than would be involved in transactions evidenced by paperwork.

Generally, the dependence of businesses on computer operations has left firms vulnerable to sabotage, fraud, embezzlement, and the theft of proprietary data, such as trade secrets or other intellectual property. As will be mentioned in Chapter 14, the piracy of intellectual property via the Internet is one of the most serious legal challenges facing lawmakers and the courts today.

Identity Theft A form of cyber theft that has become particularly troublesome in recent years is **identity theft.** Identity theft occurs when the wrongdoer steals a form of identification—such as a name, date of birth, or Social Security number—and uses the information to access the victim's financial resources. This crime existed to a certain extent before the widespread use of the Internet. Thieves would "steal" calling-card numbers by watching people using public telephones, or they would rifle through garbage to find bank account or credit-card numbers. The identity thieves would then use the calling-card or credit-card numbers or would withdraw funds from the victims' accounts. The Internet, however, has turned identity theft into perhaps the fastest-growing financial crime in the United States. The Internet provides those who steal information offline with an easy medium for using items such as stolen credit-card numbers while remaining protected by anonymity.

Three federal statutes deal specifically with identity theft. The Identity Theft and Assumption Deterrence Act of 1998[30] made identity theft a federal crime and directed the U.S. Sentencing Commission to incorporate the crime into its sentencing guidelines. The Fair and Accurate Credit Transactions Act of 2003[31] gives victims of identity theft certain rights in working with creditors and credit bureaus to remove negative information from their credit reports. This act will be discussed in detail in Chapter 23 in the context of consumer law. The Identity Theft Penalty Enhancement Act of 2004[32] authorized more severe penalties in aggravated cases in which the identity theft was committed in connection with the thief's employment or with other serious crimes (such as terrorism or firearms or immigration offenses).

Hacking

Persons who use one computer to break into another are sometimes referred to as **hackers.** Hackers who break into computers without authorization often commit cyber theft. Sometimes, however, their principal aim is to prove how smart they are by gaining access to others' password-protected computers and causing random data errors or making toll telephone calls for free.[33]

Cyberterrorism Hackers who, rather than trying to gain attention, strive to remain undetected so that they can exploit computers for a serious impact are called **cyberterrorists.** Just as "real" terrorists destroyed the World Trade Center towers and a portion of the Pentagon on September 11, 2001, cyberterrorists might explode "logic bombs" to shut down central computers. Such activities obviously can pose a danger to national security.

---

30. 18 U.S.C. Section 1028.
31. 15 U.S.C. Sections 1681 *et seq.*
32. 18 U.S.C. Section 1028A.
33. The total cost of crime on the Internet is estimated to be several billion dollars annually, but two-thirds of that total is said to consist of unpaid-for long-distance calls.

The Threat to Business Activities Any business may be targeted by cyberterrorists as well as hackers. The goals of a hacking operation might include a wholesale theft of data, such as a merchant's customer files, or the monitoring of a computer to discover a business firm's plans and transactions. A cyberterrorist might also want to insert false codes or data. For example, the processing control system of a food manufacturer could be changed to alter the levels of ingredients so that consumers of the food would become ill.

A cyberterrorist attack on a major financial institution, such as the New York Stock Exchange or a large bank, could leave securities or money markets in flux and seriously affect the daily lives of millions of citizens. Similarly, any prolonged disruption of computer, cable, satellite, or telecommunications systems due to the actions of expert hackers would have serious repercussions on business operations—and national security—on a global level. Computer viruses are another tool that can be used by cyberterrorists to cripple communications networks.

Spam

As we will discuss in Chapter 12, *spamming* (sending bulk unsolicited e-mail) has become a major problem for businesses. A few states, such as Maryland and Virginia, have passed laws that make spamming a crime.[34] Under the Virginia statute, it is a crime against property to use a computer or computer network "with the intent to falsify or forge electronic mail transmission information or other routing information in any manner." Attempting to send spam to more than 2,500 recipients in a twenty-four-hour period is a felony. The Virginia law also includes provisions authorizing the forfeiture of assets obtained through an illegal spamming operation. The Maryland law is similar in that it prohibits spamming that falsely identifies the sender, the routing information, or the subject. Under the Maryland law, however, the number of spam messages required to convict a person of the offense is much lower. Sending only ten illegal messages in twenty-four hours violates the statute, and the more spam sent, the more severe the punishment will be, up to a maximum of ten years in prison and a $25,000 fine.

In 2006, a Virginia appellate court upheld the first felony conviction for criminal spamming in the United States against Jeremy Jaynes, who until his arrest was the eighth most prolific spammer in the world. Jaynes, a resident of North Carolina, had sent more than ten thousand junk messages a day using sixteen Internet connections and a number of aliases (such as Gaven Stubberfield). Because he had sent some of the messages through servers in Virginia, the court found that Virginia had jurisdiction over Jaynes. He was convicted of three counts of felony spamming and sentenced to nine years in prison.

34. See, for example, Maryland Code, Criminal Law, Section 3-805.1, and Virginia Code Ann. Sections 18.2–152.3:1.

Prosecuting Cyber Crime

The "location" of cyber crime (cyberspace) has raised new issues in the investigation of crimes and the prosecution of offenders. A threshold issue is, of course, jurisdiction. A person who commits an act against a business in California, where the act is a cyber crime, might never have set foot in California but might instead reside in New York, or even in Canada, where the act may not be a crime. If the crime was committed via e-mail, the question arises as to whether the e-mail would constitute sufficient "minimum contacts" (see Chapter 2) for the victim's state to exercise jurisdiction over the perpetrator.

Identifying the wrongdoer can also be difficult. Cyber criminals do not leave physical traces, such as fingerprints or DNA samples, as evidence of their crimes. Even electronic "footprints" can be hard to find and follow. For example, e-mail may be sent through a remailer, an online service that guarantees that a message cannot be traced to its source.

For these reasons, laws written to protect physical property often are difficult to apply in cyberspace. Nonetheless, governments at both the state and the federal level have taken significant steps toward controlling cyber crime, both by applying existing criminal statutes and by enacting new laws that specifically address wrongs committed in cyberspace.

The Computer Fraud and Abuse Act

Perhaps the most significant federal statute specifically addressing cyber crime is the Counterfeit Access Device and Computer Fraud and Abuse Act of 1984 (commonly known as the Computer Fraud and Abuse Act, or CFAA).[35] Among other things, this act provides that a person who accesses a computer online, without authority, to obtain classified, restricted, or protected data (or attempts to do so) is subject to criminal prosecution. Such data could include financial and

35. 18 U.S.C. Section 1030.

credit records, medical records, legal files, military and national security files, and other confidential information in government or private computers. The crime has two elements: accessing a computer without authority and taking the data.

This theft is a felony if it is committed for a commercial purpose or for private financial gain, or if the value of the stolen data (or computer time) exceeds $5,000. Penalties include fines and imprisonment for up to twenty years. A victim of computer theft can also bring a civil suit against the violator to obtain damages, an injunction, and other relief.

REVIEWING Criminal Law and Cyber Crime

Edward Hanousek worked for Pacific & Arctic Railway and Navigation Company (P&A) as a roadmaster of the White Pass & Yukon Railroad in Alaska. Hanousek was responsible "for every detail of the safe and efficient maintenance and construction of track, structures and marine facilities of the entire railroad," including special projects. One project was a rock quarry, known as "6-mile," above the Skagway River. Next to the quarry, and just beneath the surface, ran a high-pressure oil pipeline owned by Pacific & Arctic Pipeline, Inc., P&A's sister company. When the quarry's backhoe operator punctured the pipeline, an estimated 1,000 to 5,000 gallons of oil were discharged into the river. Hanousek was charged with negligently discharging a harmful quantity of oil into a navigable water of the United States in violation of the criminal provisions of the Clean Water Act (CWA). Using the information presented in the chapter, answer the following questions.

1. Did Hanousek have the required mental state (*mens rea*) to be convicted of a crime? Why or why not?
2. Which theory discussed in the chapter would enable a court to hold Hanousek criminally liable for violating the statute regardless of whether he participated in, directed, or even knew about the specific violation?
3. Could the quarry's backhoe operator who punctured the pipeline also be charged with a crime in this situation? Explain.
4. Suppose that at trial, Hanousek argued that he could not be convicted because he was not aware of the requirements of the CWA. Would this defense be successful? Why or why not?

TERMS AND CONCEPTS

actus reus 150
arson 151
beyond a reasonable doubt 147
burglary 151
computer crime 169
consent 159
crime 147
cyber crime 169
cyberterrorist 169
double jeopardy 162
duress 159
embezzlement 152
entrapment 161
exclusionary rule 162
felony 148
forgery 152
grand jury 168
hacker 169
identity theft 169
indictment 168
information 168
larceny 151
mens rea 150
misdemeanor 149
money laundering 157
necessity 161
petty offense 149
plea bargaining 162
robbery 151
self-defense 160
white-collar crime 152

QUESTIONS AND CASE PROBLEMS

7-1. The following situations are similar (in all of them, Juanita's laptop computer is stolen), yet three different crimes are described. Identify the three crimes, noting the differences among them.

(a) While passing Juanita's house one night, Sarah sees a laptop computer left unattended on Juanita's lawn. Sarah takes the laptop, carries it home, and tells everyone she owns it.
(b) While passing Juanita's house one night, Sarah sees Juanita outside with a laptop computer. Holding Juanita at gunpoint, Sarah forces her to give up the computer. Then Sarah runs away with it.
(c) While passing Juanita's house one night, Sarah sees a laptop computer on a desk inside. Sarah breaks the front-door lock, enters, and leaves with the computer.

7-2. Which, if any, of the following crimes necessarily involves illegal activity on the part of more than one person?

(a) Bribery.
(b) Forgery.
(c) Embezzlement.
(d) Larceny.
(e) Receiving stolen property.

7-3. QUESTION WITH SAMPLE ANSWER

Armington, while robbing a drugstore, shot and seriously injured a drugstore clerk, Jennings. Subsequently, in a criminal trial, Armington was convicted of armed robbery and assault and battery. Jennings later brought a civil tort suit against Armington for damages. Armington contended that he could not be tried again for the same crime, as that would constitute double jeopardy, which is prohibited by the Fifth Amendment to the Constitution. Is Armington correct? Explain.

- **For a sample answer to Question 7–3, go to Appendix I at the end of this text.**

7-4. Rafael stops Laura on a busy street and offers to sell her an expensive wristwatch for a fraction of its value. After some questioning by Laura, Rafael admits that the watch is stolen property, although he says he was not the thief. Laura pays for and receives the wristwatch. Has Laura committed any crime? Has Rafael? Explain.

7-5. Theft of Trade Secrets. Four Pillars Enterprise Co. is a Taiwanese company owned by Pin Yen Yang. Avery Dennison, Inc., a U.S. corporation, is one of Four Pillars' chief competitors in the manufacture of adhesives. In 1989, Victor Lee, an Avery employee, met Yang and Yang's daughter Hwei Chen. They agreed to pay Lee $25,000 a year to serve as a consultant to Four Pillars. Over the next eight years, Lee supplied the Yangs with confidential Avery reports, including information that Four Pillars used to make a new adhesive that had been developed by Avery. The Federal Bureau of Investigation (FBI) confronted Lee, and he agreed to cooperate in an operation to catch the Yangs. When Lee next met the Yangs, he showed them documents provided by the FBI. The documents bore "confidential" stamps, and Lee said that they were Avery's confidential property. The FBI arrested the Yangs with the documents in their possession. The Yangs and Four Pillars were charged with, among other crimes, the attempted theft of trade secrets. The defendants argued in part that it was impossible for them to have committed this crime because the documents were not actually trade secrets. Should the court acquit them? Why or why not? [*United States v. Yang*, 281 F.3d 534 (6th Cir. 2002)]

7-6. CASE PROBLEM WITH SAMPLE ANSWER

The Sixth Amendment secures to a defendant who faces possible imprisonment the right to counsel at all critical stages of the criminal process, including the arraignment and the trial. In 1996, Felipe Tovar, a twenty-one-year-old college student, was arrested in Ames, Iowa, for operating a motor vehicle while under the influence of alcohol (OWI). Tovar was informed of his right to apply for court-appointed counsel and waived it. At his arraignment, he pleaded guilty. Six weeks later, he appeared for sentencing, again waived his right to counsel, and was sentenced to two days' imprisonment. In 1998, Tovar was convicted of OWI again, and in 2000, he was charged with OWI for a third time. In Iowa, a third OWI offense is a felony. Tovar asked the court not to use his first OWI conviction to enhance the third OWI charge. He argued that his 1996 waiver of counsel was not "intelligent" because the court did not make him aware of "the dangers and disadvantages of self-representation." What determines whether a person's choice in any situation is "intelligent"? What should determine whether a defendant's waiver of counsel is "intelligent" at critical stages of a criminal proceeding? [*Iowa v. Tovar*, 541 U.S. 77, 124 S.Ct. 1379, 158 L.Ed.2d 209 (2004)]

- **To view a sample answer for Problem 7–6, go to this book's Web site at academic.cengage.com/blaw/cross, select "Chapter 7," and click on "Case Problem with Sample Answer."**

7-7. Larceny. In February 2001, a homeowner hired Jimmy Smith, a contractor claiming to employ a crew of thirty workers, to build a garage. The homeowner paid Smith $7,950 and agreed to make additional payments as needed to complete the project, up to $15,900. Smith promised to start the next day and finish within eight weeks. Nearly a month passed with no work, while Smith lied to the homeowner that materials were on "back order." During a second month, footings were created for the foundation, and a subcontractor poured the concrete slab, but Smith did not return the homeowner's phone calls. After eight weeks, the homeowner confronted Smith, who promised to complete the job, worked on the site that day until lunch, and never returned. Three months later, the homeowner again confronted Smith, who promised to "pay [him] off" later that day but did not do so. In March 2002, the state of Georgia filed criminal charges against Smith. While his trial was pending, he promised to pay the homeowner "next week" but again failed to refund any of the funds paid. The value of the labor performed before Smith abandoned the project was between $800 and $1,000, the value of the materials was $367, and the subcontractor was paid $2,270. Did Smith commit larceny? Explain. [*Smith v. State of Georgia,* 592 S.E.2d 871 (Ga.App. 2004)]

7–8. Trial. Robert Michels met Allison Formal through an online dating Web site in 2002. Michels represented himself as the retired chief executive officer of a large company that he had sold for millions of dollars. In January 2003, Michels proposed that he and Formal create a *limited liability company* (a special form of business organization discussed in Chapter 17)—Formal Properties Trust, LLC—to "channel their investments in real estate." Formal agreed to contribute $100,000 to the company and wrote two $50,000 checks to "Michels and Associates, LLC." Six months later, Michels told Formal that their LLC had been formed in Delaware. Later, Formal asked Michels about her investments. He responded evasively, and she demanded that an independent accountant review the firm's records. Michels refused. Formal contacted the police. Michels was charged in a Virginia state court with obtaining funds by false pretenses. The Delaware secretary of state verified, in two certified documents, that "Formal Properties Trust, L.L.C." and "Michels and Associates, L.L.C." did not exist in Delaware. Did the admission of the Delaware secretary of state's certified documents at Michels's trial violate his rights under the Sixth Amendment? Why or why not? [*Michels v. Commonwealth of Virginia,* 47 Va.App. 461, 624 S.E.2d 675 (2006)]

7–9. White-Collar Crime. Helm Instruction Co. in Maumee, Ohio, makes custom electrical control systems. Helm hired Patrick Walsh in September 1998 to work as comptroller. Walsh soon developed a close relationship with Richard Wilhelm, Helm's president, who granted Walsh's request to hire Shari Price as Walsh's assistant. Wilhelm was not aware that Walsh and Price were engaged in an extramarital affair. Over the next five years, Walsh and Price spent more than $200,000 of Helm's money on themselves. Among other things, Walsh drew unauthorized checks on Helm's accounts to pay his personal credit cards and issued to Price and himself unauthorized salary increases, overtime payments, and tuition reimbursement payments, altering Helm's records to hide the payments. After an investigation, Helm officials confronted Walsh. He denied the affair with Price, claimed that his unauthorized use of Helm's funds was an "interest-free loan," and argued that it was less of a burden on the company to pay his credit cards than to give him the salary increases to which he felt he was entitled. Did Walsh commit a crime? If so, what crime did he commit? Discuss. [*State v. Walsh,* 113 Ohio App.3d 1515, 866 N.E.2d 513 (6 Dist. 2007)]

7–10. A QUESTION OF ETHICS

*A troublesome issue concerning the constitutional privilege against self-incrimination is the extent to which law enforcement officers may use trickery during an interrogation to induce a suspect to incriminate himself or herself. For example, in one case two officers questioned Charles McFarland, who was incarcerated in a state prison, about his connection to a handgun that had been used to shoot two other officers. McFarland was advised of his rights but was not asked whether he was willing to waive those rights. Instead, to induce McFarland to speak, the officers deceived him into believing that "[n]obody is going to give you charges." McFarland made incriminating admissions and was indicted for possessing a handgun as a convicted felon. [*United States v. McFarland, *424 F.Supp.2d 427 (N.D.N.Y. 2006)]*

(a) Review Case 7.4, *Miranda v. Arizona,* on pages 165–166 in this chapter. Should McFarland's statements be suppressed—that is, not be treated as admissible evidence at trial—because he was not asked whether he was willing to waive his rights prior to making his self-incriminating statements? Does the *Miranda* rule apply to McFarland's situation?
(b) Do you think that it is fair for the police to resort to trickery and deception to bring those who have committed crimes to justice? Why or why not? What rights or public policies must be balanced in deciding this issue?

7–11. VIDEO QUESTION

Go to this text's Web site at **academic.cengage.com/blaw/cross** and select "Chapter 7." Click on "Video Questions" and view the video titled *Casino.* Then answer the following questions.

(a) In the video, a casino manager, Ace (Robert DeNiro), discusses how politicians "won their 'comp life' when they got elected." "Comps" are the free gifts that casinos give to high-stakes gamblers to keep their business. If an elected official accepts comps, is he or she committing a crime? If so, what type of crime? Explain your answers.
(b) Assume that Ace committed a crime by giving politicians comps. Can the casino, Tangiers Corp., be held liable for that crime? Why or why not? How could a court punish the corporation?

(c) Suppose that the Federal Bureau of Investigation wants to search the premises of Tangiers for evidence of criminal activity. If casino management refuses to consent to the search, what constitutional safeguards and criminal procedures, if any, protect Tangiers?

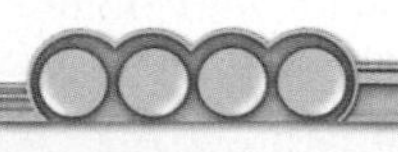

LAW ON THE WEB

For updated links to resources available on the Web, as well as a variety of other materials, visit this text's Web site at

academic.cengage.com/blaw/cross

The Bureau of Justice Statistics in the U.S. Department of Justice offers an impressive collection of statistics on crime at the following Web site:

ojp.usdoj.gov/bjs

For summaries of famous criminal cases and documents relating to these trials, go to Court TV's Web site at

www.courttv.com/sitemap/index.html

Many state criminal codes are now online. To find your state's code, go to the following home page and select "States" under the link to "Cases & Codes":

www.findlaw.com

You can learn about some of the constitutional questions raised by various criminal laws and procedures by going to the Web site of the American Civil Liberties Union at

www.aclu.org

The following Web site, which is maintained by the U.S. Department of Justice, offers information ranging from the various types of cyber crime to a description of how computers and the Internet are being used to prosecute cyber crime:

www.cybercrime.gov

Legal Research Exercises on the Web

Go to **academic.cengage.com/blaw/cross**, the Web site that accompanies this text. Select "Chapter 7" and click on "Internet Exercises." There you will find the following Internet research exercises that you can perform to learn more about the topics covered in this chapter.

Internet Exercise 7–1: Legal Perspective
Revisiting *Miranda*

Internet Exercise 7–2: Management Perspective
Hackers

Internet Exercise 7–3: International Perspective
Fighting Cyber Crime Worldwide

CHAPTER 8

International Law in a Global Economy

International business transactions are not unique to the modern world. What is new in our day is the dramatic growth in world trade and the emergence of a global business community. Because the exchange of goods, services, and ideas (intellectual property) on a worldwide level is now routine, students of business law and the legal environment should be familiar with the laws pertaining to international business transactions.

Laws affecting the international legal environment of business include both international law and national law. **International law** can be defined as a body of law—formed as a result of international customs, treaties, and organizations—that governs relations among or between nations. International law may be public, creating standards for the nations themselves; or it may be private, establishing international standards for private transactions that cross national borders. **National law** is the law of a particular nation, such as Brazil, Germany, Japan, or the United States. In this chapter, we examine how both international law and national law frame business operations in the international context.

Section 1 International Law

The major difference between international law and national law is that government authorities can enforce national law What government, however, can enforce international law? By definition, a *nation* is a sovereign entity—which means that there is no higher authority to which that nation must submit. If a nation violates an international law and persuasive tactics fail, other countries or international organizations have no recourse except to take coercive actions—from severance of diplomatic relations and boycotts to, as a last resort, war—against the violating nation.

In essence, international law is the result of centuries-old attempts to reconcile the traditional need of each country to be the final authority over its own affairs with the desire of nations to benefit economically from trade and harmonious relations with one another. Sovereign nations can, and do, voluntarily agree to be governed in certain respects by international law for the purpose of facilitating international trade and commerce, as well as civilized discourse. As a result, a body of international law has evolved. In this section, we examine the primary sources and characteristics of that body of law, as well as some important legal principles and doctrines that have been developed over time to facilitate dealings among nations.

Sources of International Law

Basically, there are three sources of international law: international customs, treaties and international agreements, and international organizations and conferences. We look at each of these sources here.

International Customs One important source of international law consists of the international customs that have evolved among nations in their relations with one another. Article 38(1) of the Statute of the International Court of Justice refers to an international custom as "evidence of a general practice accepted as law." The legal principles and doctrines that you will read about shortly are rooted in international customs and traditions that have evolved over time in the international arena.

Treaties and International Agreements Treaties and other explicit agreements between or among foreign nations provide another important source of international law. A **treaty** is an agreement or contract between two or more nations that must be authorized and ratified by the supreme power of each nation. Under Article II, Section 2, of the U.S. Constitution, the president has the power "by and with the Advice and Consent of the Senate, to make Treaties, provided two-thirds of the Senators present concur."

A *bilateral* agreement, as the term implies, is an agreement formed by two nations to govern their commercial exchanges or other relations with one another. A *multilateral* agreement is formed by several nations. For example, regional trade associations such as the European Union (EU, which is discussed later in this chapter) are the result of multilateral trade agreements. Other regional trade associations that have been created through multilateral agreements include the Association of Southeast Asian Nations (ASEAN) and the Andean Common Market (ANCOM).

International Organizations In international law, the term **international organization** generally refers to an organization composed mainly of officials of member nations and usually established by treaty. The United States is a member of more than one hundred multilateral and bilateral organizations, including at least twenty through the United Nations. These organizations adopt resolutions, declarations, and other types of standards that often require nations to behave in a particular manner. The General Assembly of the United Nations, for example, has adopted numerous nonbinding resolutions and declarations that embody principles of international law. Disputes with respect to these resolutions and declarations may be brought before the International Court of Justice. That court, however, normally has authority to settle legal disputes only when nations voluntarily submit to its jurisdiction.

The United Nations Commission on International Trade Law has made considerable progress in establishing uniformity in international law as it relates to trade and commerce. One of the commission's most significant creations to date is the 1980 Convention on Contracts for the International Sale of Goods (CISG). The CISG is similar to Article 2 of the Uniform Commercial Code in that it is designed to settle disputes between parties to sales contracts (see Chapter 11). It spells out the duties of international buyers and sellers that will apply if the parties have not agreed otherwise in their contracts. The CISG governs only sales contracts between trading partners in nations that have ratified the CISG, however.

Common Law and Civil Law Systems

Companies operating in foreign nations are subject to the laws of those nations. In addition, international disputes often are resolved through the court systems of foreign nations. Therefore, businesspersons should understand that legal systems around the globe generally are divided into *common law* and *civil law* systems. As discussed in Chapter 1, in a common law system, the courts independently develop the rules governing certain areas of law, such as torts and contracts. These common law rules apply to all areas not covered by statutory law. Although the common law doctrine of *stare decisis* obligates judges to follow precedential decisions in their jurisdictions, courts may modify or even overturn precedents when deemed necessary.

In contrast to common law countries, most of the European nations, as well as nations in Latin America, Africa, and Asia, base their legal systems on Roman civil law, or "code law." The term *civil law,* as used here, refers not to civil as opposed to criminal law but to *codified* law—an ordered grouping of legal principles enacted into law by a legislature or other governing body. In a **civil law system,** the only official source of law is a statutory code. Courts interpret the code and apply the rules to individual cases, but courts may not depart from the code and develop their own laws. In theory, the law code sets forth all of the principles needed for the legal system. Trial procedures also differ in civil law systems. Unlike judges in common law systems, judges in civil systems often actively question witnesses. Exhibit 8–1 lists examples of the nations that use civil law systems and examples that use common law systems.

International Principles and Doctrines

Over time, a number of legal principles and doctrines have evolved and have been employed—to a greater or lesser extent—by the courts of various nations to resolve or reduce conflicts that involve a foreign element. The three important legal principles discussed next are based primarily on courtesy and respect, and

EXHIBIT 8–1 • The Legal Systems of Selected Nations

Civil Law		Common Law	
Argentina	Indonesia	Australia	Nigeria
Austria	Iran	Bangladesh	Singapore
Brazil	Italy	Canada	United Kingdom
Chile	Japan	Ghana	United States
China	Mexico	India	Zambia
Egypt	Poland	Israel	
Finland	South Korea	Jamaica	
France	Sweden	Kenya	
Germany	Tunisia	Malaysia	
Greece	Venezuela	New Zealand	

are applied in the interests of maintaining harmonious relations among nations.

The Principle of Comity Under what is known as the principle of **comity,** one nation will defer and give effect to the laws and judicial decrees of another country, as long as they are consistent with the law and public policy of the accommodating nation. For example, a Swedish seller and a U.S. buyer have formed a contract, which the buyer breaches. The seller sues the buyer in a Swedish court, which awards damages. The buyer's assets, however, are in the United States and cannot be reached unless the judgment is enforced by a U.S. court. In this situation, if a U.S. court determines that the procedures and laws applied in the Swedish court are consistent with U.S. national law and policy, the U.S. court will likely defer to, and enforce, the foreign court's judgment.

One way to understand the principle of comity (and the *act of state doctrine,* which will be discussed shortly) is to consider the relationships among the states in our federal form of government. Each state honors (gives "full faith and credit" to) the contracts, property deeds, wills, and other legal obligations formed in other states, as well as judicial decisions with respect to such obligations. On a worldwide basis, nations similarly attempt to honor judgments rendered in other countries when it is feasible to do so. Of course, in the United States the states are constitutionally required to honor other states' actions, whereas, internationally, nations are not *required* to honor the actions of other nations.

The Act of State Doctrine The **act of state doctrine** is a judicially created doctrine that provides that the judicial branch of one country will not examine the validity of public acts committed by a recognized foreign government within the latter's own territory. This doctrine is premised on the theory that the judicial branch should not pass judgment on the validity of foreign acts when to do so would upset the harmony of our international relations with that foreign nation.

When a Foreign Government Takes Private Property. The act of state doctrine can have important consequences for individuals and firms doing business with, and investing in, other countries. This doctrine is frequently employed in cases involving **expropriation,** which occurs when a government seizes a privately owned business or privately owned goods for a proper public purpose and awards just compensation. When a government seizes private property for an illegal purpose and without just compensation, the taking is referred to as a **confiscation.** The line between these two forms of taking is sometimes blurred because of differing interpretations of what is illegal and what constitutes just compensation.

For example, Flaherty, Inc., a U.S. company, owns a mine in Brazil. The government of Brazil seizes the mine for public use and claims that the profits Flaherty has already realized from the mine constitute just compensation. Flaherty disagrees, but the act of state doctrine may prevent that company's recovery in a U.S. court. Note that in a case alleging that a foreign government has wrongfully taken the plaintiff's property, the defendant government has the burden of proving that the taking was an expropriation, not a confiscation.

Doctrine May Immunize a Foreign Government's Actions. When applicable, both the act of state doctrine and the doctrine of *sovereign immunity,* which we discuss next, tend to shield foreign nations from the jurisdiction of U.S. courts. As a result, firms or individuals who own property overseas generally have little legal protection against government actions in the countries where they operate.

The Doctrine of Sovereign Immunity When certain conditions are satisfied, the doctrine of **sovereign immunity** exempts foreign nations from the jurisdiction of the U.S. courts. In 1976, Congress codified this rule in the Foreign Sovereign Immunities Act (FSIA).[1] The FSIA exclusively governs the circumstances in which an action may be brought in the United States against a foreign nation, including attempts to attach a foreign nation's property. Because the law is jurisdictional in nature, a plaintiff generally has the burden of showing that a defendant is not entitled to sovereign immunity.

Section 1605 of the FSIA sets forth the major exceptions to the jurisdictional immunity of a foreign state. A foreign state is not immune from the jurisdiction of U.S. courts in the following situations:

1. When the foreign state has waived its immunity either explicitly or by implication.
2. When the foreign state has engaged in commercial activity within the United States or in commercial activity outside the United States that has "a direct effect in the United States."[2]
3. When the foreign state has committed a tort in the United States or has violated certain international laws.

In applying the FSIA, questions frequently arise as to whether an entity is a "foreign state" and what constitutes a "commercial activity." Under Section 1603 of the FSIA, a *foreign state* includes both a political subdivision of a foreign state and an instrumentality (department or agency of any branch of a government) of a foreign state. Section 1603 broadly defines a *commercial activity* as a commercial activity that is carried out by a foreign state within the United States, but it does not describe the particulars of what constitutes a commercial activity. Thus, the courts are left to decide whether a particular activity is governmental or commercial in nature.

1. 28 U.S.C. Sections 1602–1611.

2. See, for example, *Keller v. Central Bank of Nigeria,* 277 F.3d 811 (6th Cir. 2002), in which the court held that failure to pay promised funds to an account in a bank in Cleveland, Ohio, was an action having a direct effect in the United States.

Doing Business Internationally

A U.S. domestic firm can engage in international business transactions in a number of ways. The simplest way is to seek out foreign markets for domestically produced products or services. In other words, U.S. firms can **export** their goods and services to markets abroad. Alternatively, a U.S. firm can establish foreign production facilities to be closer to the foreign market or markets in which its products are sold. The advantages may include lower labor costs, fewer government regulations, and lower taxes and trade barriers. A domestic firm can also obtain revenues by licensing its technology to an existing foreign company or by selling franchises to overseas entities.

Exporting

Exporting can take two forms: direct exporting and indirect exporting. In *direct exporting,* a U.S. company signs a sales contract with a foreign purchaser that provides for the conditions of shipment and payment for the goods. If sufficient business develops in a foreign country, a U.S. company may establish a specialized marketing organization there by appointing a foreign agent or a foreign distributor. This is called *indirect exporting.*

When a U.S. firm wishes to limit its involvement in an international market, it will typically establish an agency relationship with a foreign firm. Recall that in an agency relationship, one person (the agent) agrees to act on behalf of, or instead of, another (the principal) (see Chapter 19). The foreign agent is empowered to enter into contracts in the agent's country on behalf of the U.S. principal.

When a foreign country represents a substantial market, a U.S. firm may wish to appoint a distributor located in that country. The U.S. firm and the distributor enter into a **distribution agreement**—a contract setting out the terms and conditions of the distributorship, such as price, currency of payment, guarantee of supply availability, and method of payment. Disputes concerning distribution agreements may involve jurisdictional or other issues, as well as contract law, however.

Manufacturing Abroad

An alternative to direct or indirect exporting is the establishment of foreign manufacturing facilities.

Typically, U.S. firms establish manufacturing plants abroad when they believe that by doing so they will reduce costs—particularly for labor, shipping, and raw materials—and thereby be able to compete more effectively in foreign markets. Foreign firms have done the same in the United States. Sony, Nissan, and other Japanese manufacturers have established U.S. plants to avoid import duties that the U.S. Congress may impose on Japanese products entering this country.

A U.S. firm can conduct manufacturing operations in other countries in several ways. Two of these ways are through licensing and franchising.

Licensing A U.S. firm can obtain business abroad by licensing a foreign manufacturing company to use its copyrighted, patented, or trademarked intellectual property or trade secrets. Like any other licensing agreement (see Chapters 11 and 14), a licensing agreement with a foreign-based firm calls for a payment of royalties on some basis—such as so many cents per unit produced or a certain percentage of profits from units sold in a particular geographic territory. For example, the Coca-Cola Bottling Company licenses firms worldwide to use (and keep confidential) its secret formula for the syrup used in its soft drink; in return, the company receives a percentage of the income gained from the sale of Coca-Cola by those firms.

The licensing of intellectual property rights benefits all parties to the transaction. The firm that receives the license can take advantage of an established reputation for quality. The firm that grants the license receives income from the foreign sales of its products and also establishes a global reputation. Also, once a firm's trademark is known worldwide, the demand for other products manufactured or sold by that firm may increase—obviously, an important consideration.

Franchising Franchising is a well-known form of licensing. A *franchise* is an arrangement by which the owner of a trademark, trade name, or copyright (the franchisor) licenses another (the franchisee) to use the trademark, trade name, or copyright, under certain conditions or limitations, in the selling of goods or services. In return, the franchisee pays a fee, which is usually based on a percentage of gross or net sales (see Chapter 16). Examples of international franchises include Holiday Inn and Hertz.

Regulation of Specific Business Activities

Doing business abroad can affect the economies, foreign policies, domestic politics, and other national interests of the countries involved. For this reason, nations impose laws to restrict or facilitate international business. Controls may also be imposed by international agreements.

Investing

Firms that invest in foreign nations face the risk that the foreign government may expropriate the investment property. Expropriation, as mentioned earlier in this chapter, occurs when property is taken and the owner is paid just compensation for what is taken. This does not violate generally observed principles of international law. Confiscating property without compensation (or without adequate compensation), however, normally violates these principles. Few remedies are available for confiscation of property by a foreign government. Claims are often resolved by lump-sum settlements after negotiations between the United States and the taking nation.

To counter the deterrent effect that the possibility of confiscation may have on potential investors, many countries guarantee compensation to foreign investors if property is taken. A guaranty can be in the form of national constitutional or statutory laws or provisions in international treaties. As further protection for foreign investments, some countries provide insurance for their citizens' investments abroad.

Export Controls

The U.S. Constitution provides in Article I, Section 9, that "No Tax or Duty shall be laid on Articles exported from any State." Thus, Congress cannot impose any export taxes. Congress can, however, use a variety of other devices to restrict or encourage exports. Congress may set export quotas on various items, such as grain being sold abroad. Under the Export Administration Act of 1979,[3] the flow of technologically advanced products and technical data can be restricted. In recent years, the U.S. Department of Commerce has made a controversial attempt to restrict the export of encryption software.

3. 50 U.S.C. Sections 2401–2420.

While restricting certain exports, the United States (and other nations) also use incentives and subsidies to stimulate other exports and thereby aid domestic businesses. The Revenue Act of 1971,[4] for instance, promoted exports by exempting from taxes the income earned by firms marketing their products overseas through certain foreign sales corporations. Under the Export Trading Company Act of 1982,[5] U.S. banks are encouraged to invest in export trading companies, which are formed when exporting firms join together to export a line of goods.

Import Controls

All nations have restrictions on imports, and the United States is no exception. Restrictions include strict prohibitions, quotas, and tariffs. Under the Trading with the Enemy Act of 1917,[6] for example, no goods may be imported from nations that have been designated enemies of the United States. Other laws prohibit the importation of illegal drugs, books that urge insurrection against the United States, and agricultural products that pose dangers to domestic crops or animals.

Importing goods that infringe U.S. patents is also prohibited. The International Trade Commission is an independent agency of the U.S. government that, among other duties, investigates allegations that imported goods infringe U.S. patents and imposes penalties if necessary. In the following case, the court considered an appeal from a party fined more than $13.5 million for importing certain disposable cameras.

4. 26 U.S.C. Sections 991–994.
5. 15 U.S.C. Sections 4001, 4003.
6. 12 U.S.C. Section 95a.

CASE 8.1 Fuji Photo Film Co. v. International Trade Commission

United States Court of Appeals, Federal Circuit, 2007. 474 F.3d 1281.

• **Background and Facts** Fuji Photo Film Company owns fifteen patents for "lens-fitted film packages" (LFFPs), popularly known as disposable cameras. An LFFP consists of a plastic shell preloaded with film. To develop the film, a consumer gives the LFFP to a film processor and receives back the negatives and prints, but not the shell. Fuji makes and sells LFFPs. Jazz Photo Corporation collected used LFFP shells in the United States, shipped them abroad to insert new film, and imported refurbished shells back into the United States for sale. The International Trade Commission (ITC) determined that Jazz's resale of shells originally sold outside the United States infringed Fuji's patents. In 1999, the ITC issued a cease-and-desist order to stop the imports. While the order was being disputed at the ITC and in the courts, between August 2001 and December 2003 Jazz imported and sold 27 million refurbished LFFPs. Fuji complained to the ITC, which fined Jazz more than $13.5 million. Jack Benun, Jazz's chief operating officer, appealed to the U.S. Court of Appeals for the Federal Circuit.

IN THE LANGUAGE OF THE COURT
***DYK*, Circuit Judge.**

* * * *

* * * The Commission concluded that 40% of the LFFPs in issue were first sold abroad * * * . This conclusion was supported by substantial evidence. It was based on * * * the identifying numbers printed on the LFFPs and Fuji's production and shipping databases to determine where samples of Fuji-type LFFPs with Jazz packaging (i.e., ones that were refurbished by Jazz) were first sold.

Benun urges that the Commission's decision in this respect was not supported by substantial evidence, primarily arguing that Jazz's so-called informed compliance program required a finding in Jazz's favor. Benun asserts that this program tracked shells from collection through the refurbishment process to sale and insured that only shells collected from the United States were refurbished for sale here. The Commission rejected this argument for two reasons. First, it concluded that the program was too disorganized and incomplete to provide credible evidence that Jazz only refurbished shells collected from the United States. Second, the Commission concluded that at most the program could insure that Jazz only refurbished LFFPs collected from the United States, not LFFPs that were first sold here.

CASE 8.1 CONTINUED

Responding to the second ground, Benun urges that proof that Jazz limited its activities to shells collected in the United States was sufficient * * * because Fuji "infected the pool" of camera shells collected in the United States by taking actions that made it difficult for Jazz and Benun to insure that these shells were from LFFPs first sold here. These actions allegedly included allowing [one company] to import cameras with Japanese writing on them for sale in the United States; allowing [that company] to import spent shells into the United States for recycling; and allowing tourists to bring cameras first sold abroad into the United States for personal use. Under these circumstances, Benun argues that a presumption should arise that shells collected in the United States were first sold here. However, the Commission found that the number of shells falling into these categories was insignificant, and that finding was supported by substantial evidence. Moreover, there was evidence that Jazz treated substantial numbers of its own shells collected in the United States * * * as having been sold in the United States even though it knew that 90% of these shells were first sold abroad * * * .

In any event, the Commission's first ground—that the program was too incomplete and disorganized to be credible—was supported by substantial evidence. Since there was no suggestion that the incomplete and disorganized nature of the program was due to Fuji's actions, this ground alone was sufficient to justify a conclusion that Benun had not carried his burden to prove [the refurbished LFFPs had been sold first in the United States].

- **Decision and Remedy** *The U.S. Court of Appeals for the Federal Circuit held that Jazz had violated the cease-and-desist order, affirming this part of the ITC's decision. The court concluded, among other things, that "substantial evidence supports the finding that the majority of the cameras were first sold abroad."*

- **What If the Facts Were Different?** *Suppose that, after this decision, Jazz fully compensated Fuji for the infringing sales of LFFPs. Would Jazz have acquired the right to refurbish those LFFPs in the future? Explain.*

- **The Global Dimension** *How does prohibiting the importing of goods that infringe U.S. patents protect those patents outside the United States?*

Quotas and Tariffs Limits on the amounts of goods that can be imported are known as **quotas.** At one time, the United States had legal quotas on the number of automobiles that could be imported from Japan. Today, Japan "voluntarily" restricts the number of automobiles exported to the United States. **Tariffs** are taxes on imports. A tariff is usually a percentage of the value of the import, but it can be a flat rate per unit (such as per barrel of oil). Tariffs raise the prices of imported goods, causing some consumers to purchase more domestically manufactured goods.

Antidumping Duties The United States has specific laws directed at what it sees as unfair international trade practices. **Dumping,** for example, is the sale of imported goods at "less than fair value." *Fair value* is usually determined by the price of those goods in the exporting country. Foreign firms that engage in dumping in the United States hope to undersell U.S. businesses to obtain a larger share of the U.S. market. To prevent this, an extra tariff—known as an *antidumping duty*—may be assessed on the imports.

The procedure for imposing antidumping duties involves two U.S. government agencies: the International Trade Commission (ITC) and the International Trade Administration (ITA). The ITC assesses the effects of dumping on domestic businesses and then makes recommendations to the president concerning temporary import restrictions. The ITA, which is part of the Department of Commerce, decides whether imports were sold at less than fair value. The ITA's determination establishes the amount of antidumping duties, which are set to equal the difference between the price charged in the United States and the price charged in the exporting country. A duty may be retroactive to cover past dumping.

Minimizing Trade Barriers through Trade Agreements

Restrictions on imports are also known as *trade barriers.* The elimination of trade barriers is sometimes seen as essential to the world's economic well-being.

Most of the world's leading trading nations are members of the World Trade Organization (WTO), which was established in 1995. To minimize trade barriers among nations, each member country of the WTO is required to grant **normal trade relations (NTR) status** (formerly known as *most-favored-nation status*) to other member countries. This means that each member is obligated to treat other members at least as well as it treats the country that receives its most favorable treatment with regard to imports or exports. Various regional trade agreements and associations also help to minimize trade barriers between nations.

The European Union (EU) The European Union (EU) arose out of the 1957 Treaty of Rome, which created the Common Market, a free trade zone comprising the nations of Belgium, France, Italy, Luxembourg, the Netherlands, and West Germany. Today, the EU is a single integrated trading unit made up of twenty-seven European nations.

The EU has its own governing authorities. These include the Council of Ministers, which coordinates economic policies and includes one representative from each nation; a commission, which proposes regulations to the council; and an elected assembly, which oversees the commission. The EU also has its own court, the European Court of Justice, which can review each nation's judicial decisions and is the ultimate authority on EU law.

The EU has gone a long way toward creating a new body of law to govern all of the member nations—although some of its efforts to create uniform laws have been confounded by nationalism. The council and the commission issue regulations, or directives, that define EU law in various areas, and these requirements normally are binding on all member countries. EU directives govern such issues as environmental law, product liability, anticompetitive practices, and laws governing corporations. The EU directive on product liability, for example, states that a "producer of an article shall be liable for damages caused by a defect in the article, whether or not he [or she] knew or could have known of the defect." Liability extends to anyone who puts a trademark or other identifying feature on an article, and liability may not be excluded, even by contract.

The North American Free Trade Agreement (NAFTA) The North American Free Trade Agreement (NAFTA), which became effective on January 1, 1994, created a regional trading unit consisting of Canada, Mexico, and the United States. The goal of NAFTA was to eliminate tariffs among these three nations on substantially all goods by reducing the tariffs incrementally over a period of time. NAFTA gives the three countries a competitive advantage by retaining tariffs on goods imported from countries outside the NAFTA trading unit. Additionally, NAFTA provided for the elimination of barriers that traditionally have prevented the cross-border movement of services, such as financial and transportation services. NAFTA also attempts to eliminate citizenship requirements for the licensing of accountants, attorneys, physicians, and other professionals.

The Central America–Dominican Republic–United States Free Trade Agreement (CAFTA-DR) A more recent trade agreement, the Central America–Dominican Republic–United States Free Trade Agreement (CAFTA-DR), was signed into law by President George W. Bush in 2005. This agreement was formed by Costa Rica, the Dominican Republic, El Salvador, Guatemala, Honduras, Nicaragua, and the United States. Its purpose was to reduce trade tariffs and improve market access among all of the signatory nations, including the United States. As of 2008, legislatures from all seven countries had approved the CAFTA-DR, despite significant opposition in certain nations, including Costa Rica, where nationwide strikes erupted in response to legislation adopting the treaty.

U.S. Laws in a Global Context

The internationalization of business raises questions about the extraterritorial application of a nation's laws—that is, the effect of the country's laws outside its boundaries. To what extent do U.S. domestic laws apply to other nations' businesses? To what extent do U.S. domestic laws apply to U.S. firms doing business abroad? Here, we discuss the extraterritorial application of certain U.S. laws, including the Sarbanes-Oxley Act and laws prohibiting employment discrimination.

The Sarbanes-Oxley Act

The Sarbanes-Oxley Act of 2002, which was discussed in Chapter 4, is designed to improve the quality and clarity of financial reporting and auditing of public companies. The act prescribes the issuance of codes of ethics, increases the criminal penalties for securities fraud, and utilizes other means to hold public companies to higher reporting standards.

Three provisions protect whistleblowers. One section requires public companies to adopt procedures that encourage employees to expose "questionable" accounting. Another section imposes criminal sanctions for retaliation against anyone who reports the commission of any federal offense to law enforcement officers.

A third section—18 U.S.C. Section 1514A—creates an administrative complaint procedure and a federal civil cause of action for employees who report violations of the federal laws relating to fraud against the shareholders of public companies. The extraterritorial application of this section was at issue in the following case.

CASE 8.2 Carnero v. Boston Scientific Corp.

United States Court of Appeals, First Circuit, 2006. 433 F.3d 1.
www.ca1.uscourts.gov[a]

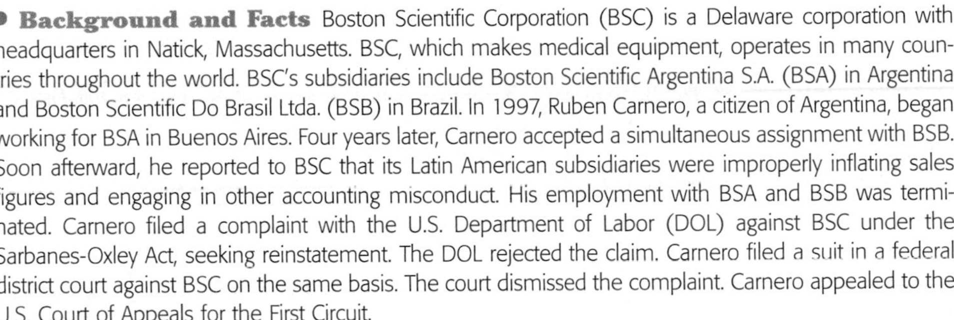

● **Background and Facts** Boston Scientific Corporation (BSC) is a Delaware corporation with headquarters in Natick, Massachusetts. BSC, which makes medical equipment, operates in many countries throughout the world. BSC's subsidiaries include Boston Scientific Argentina S.A. (BSA) in Argentina and Boston Scientific Do Brasil Ltda. (BSB) in Brazil. In 1997, Ruben Carnero, a citizen of Argentina, began working for BSA in Buenos Aires. Four years later, Carnero accepted a simultaneous assignment with BSB. Soon afterward, he reported to BSC that its Latin American subsidiaries were improperly inflating sales figures and engaging in other accounting misconduct. His employment with BSA and BSB was terminated. Carnero filed a complaint with the U.S. Department of Labor (DOL) against BSC under the Sarbanes-Oxley Act, seeking reinstatement. The DOL rejected the claim. Carnero filed a suit in a federal district court against BSC on the same basis. The court dismissed the complaint. Carnero appealed to the U.S. Court of Appeals for the First Circuit.

IN THE LANGUAGE OF THE COURT
***LEVIN H. CAMPBELL*, Senior Circuit Judge.**

* * * *

Carnero argues that [18 U.S.C. Section 1514A] should be given extraterritorial effect, so as to allow him to pursue in federal court his whistleblower claim brought under its provisions. He says his claim not only fits within the literal language of the statute but that to limit the operation of the statute to purely domestic conduct in the United States would improperly insulate the foreign operations of covered companies. This, he says, would frustrate the basic purpose of the Sarbanes-Oxley Act of which the whistleblower protection statute at issue is a part, to protect both the investors in U.S. securities markets and the integrity of those markets.

While Carnero's argument has some force, it faces a high and we think insurmountable hurdle in the well-established presumption against the extraterritorial application of Congressional statutes. Where, as here, a statute is silent as to its territorial reach, and no contrary congressional intent clearly appears, there is generally a presumption against its extraterritorial application.

* * * *

The presumption serves at least two purposes. It protects against unintended clashes between our laws and those of other nations which could result in international discord, and it reflects the notion that when Congress legislates, it is primarily concerned with domestic conditions. [Emphasis added.]

* * * *

* * * Pertinent factors run strongly counter to finding an extraterritorial legislative intent. These contrary *indicia* [signs, or indications] prevent our determining that Congress has evidenced its "clear intent" for extraterritorial application. Not only is the text of 18 U.S.C. Section 1514A silent

a. In the right-hand column, click on "Opinions." When that page opens, in the "Short Title *contains*" box, type "Carnero" and click on "Submit Search." In the result, in the "Click for Opinion" column, click on one of the numbers to access the opinion.

CASE CONTINUES

CASE 8.2 CONTINUED

as to any intent to apply it abroad, the statute's legislative history indicates that Congress gave no consideration to either the possibility or the problems of overseas application. In sharp contrast with this silence, Congress has provided expressly elsewhere in the Sarbanes-Oxley Act for extraterritorial enforcement of a different, criminal, whistleblower statute. By so providing, Congress demonstrated that it was well able to call for extraterritorial application when it so desired. Also in the Act, Congress has provided expressly for the extraterritorial application of certain other unrelated statutes, tailoring these so as to cope with problems of sovereignty and the like—again demonstrating Congress's ability to provide for foreign application when it wished. Here, however, while placing the whistleblower provision's enforcement in the hands of the DOL, a domestic agency, Congress has made no provision for possible problems arising when that agency seeks to regulate employment relationships in foreign nations, nor has Congress provided the DOL with special powers and resources to conduct investigations abroad. Furthermore, judicial venue provisions written into the whistleblower protection statute were made expressly applicable only to whistleblower violations within the United States and to complainants residing here on the date of violation, with no corresponding basis being provided for venue as to foreign complainants claiming violations in foreign countries.

These factors * * * not only fail to imply a clear congressional intent for extraterritorial application, but indicate that Congress never expected such application.

- **Decision and Remedy** *The U.S. Court of Appeals for the First Circuit affirmed the lower court's dismissal of Carnero's complaint under 18 U.S.C. Section 1514A. Congress "made no reference to [the statute's] application abroad and tailored the * * * statute to purely domestic application." This section of the act "does not reflect the necessary clear expression of congressional intent to extend its reach beyond our nation's borders."*

- **What If the Facts Were Different?** *Suppose that Carnero had been an American working for BSA and BSB. Would the result in this case have been the same? Discuss.*

- **The Legal Environment Dimension** *How might the court's decision in this case frustrate the basic purpose of the Sarbanes-Oxley Act, which is to protect investors in U.S. securities markets and the integrity of those markets?*

Antidiscrimination Laws

As will be explained in Chapter 21, federal laws in the United States prohibit discrimination on the basis of race, color, national origin, religion, gender, age, and disability. These laws, as they affect employment relationships, generally apply extraterritorially. Since 1984, for example, the Age Discrimination in Employment Act of 1967 has covered U.S. employees working abroad for U.S. employers. The Americans with Disabilities Act of 1990, which requires employers to accommodate the needs of workers with disabilities, also applies to U.S. nationals working abroad for U.S. firms.

For some time, it was uncertain whether the major U.S. law regulating discriminatory practices in the workplace, Title VII of the Civil Rights Act of 1964, applied extraterritorially. The Civil Rights Act of 1991 addressed this issue. The act provides that Title VII applies extraterritorially to all U.S. employees working for U.S. employers abroad. Generally, U.S. employers must abide by U.S. discrimination laws unless to do so would violate the laws of the country where their workplaces are located. This "foreign laws exception" allows employers to avoid being subjected to conflicting laws.

International Tort Claims

The international application of tort liability is growing in significance and controversy. An increasing number of U.S. plaintiffs are suing foreign (or U.S.) entities for torts that these entities have allegedly committed overseas. Often, these cases involve human rights violations by foreign governments. The Alien Tort Claims Act (ATCA),[7] adopted in 1789, allows even foreign citizens to bring civil suits in U.S. courts for injuries caused by violations of the law of nations or a treaty of the United States.

Since 1980, plaintiffs have increasingly used the ATCA to bring actions against companies operating in other countries. ATCA actions have been brought against companies doing business in nations such as

7. 28 U.S.C. Section 1350.

Colombia, Ecuador, Egypt, Guatemala, India, Indonesia, Nigeria, and Saudi Arabia. Some of these cases have involved alleged environmental destruction. In addition, mineral companies in Southeast Asia have been sued for collaborating with oppressive government regimes.

The following case involved claims against "hundreds" of corporations that allegedly "aided and abetted" the government of South Africa in maintaining its apartheid (racially discriminatory) regime.

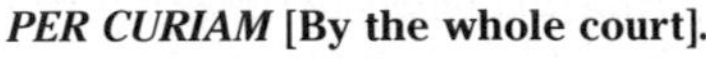

EXTENDED CASE 8.3

Khulumani v. Barclay National Bank, Ltd.

United States Court of Appeals, Second Circuit, 2007. 504 F.3d 254.

***PER CURIAM* [By the whole court].**

* * * *

The plaintiffs in this action bring claims under the Alien Tort Claims Act ("ATCA") against approximately fifty corporate defendants and hundreds of "corporate Does" [including Bank of America, N.A.; Barclay National Bank, Ltd.; Citigroup, Inc.; Credit Suisse Group; Deutsche Bank A.G.; General Electric Company; IBM Corporation; and Shell Oil Company]. The plaintiffs argue that these defendants actively and willingly collaborated with the government of South Africa in maintaining a repressive, racially based system known as "apartheid," which restricted the majority black African population in all areas of life while providing benefits for the minority white population.

Three groups of plaintiffs filed ten separate actions in multiple federal district courts asserting these apartheid-related claims. One group, the Khulumani Plaintiffs, filed a complaint against twenty-three domestic and foreign corporations, charging them with various violations of international law. The other two groups, the Ntsebeza and Digwamaje Plaintiffs, brought class action claims on behalf of the "victims of the apartheid related atrocities, human rights' violations, crimes against humanity and unfair [and] discriminatory forced labor practices."

* * *. All of the actions [were transferred to a federal district court in] the Southern District of New York * * * . Thirty-one of the fifty-five defendants in the Ntsebeza and Digwamaje actions * * * [and] eighteen of the twenty-three defendants in [the Khulumani] action * * * filed * * * motion[s] to dismiss.

* * * *

Ruling on the defendants' motions to dismiss, the district court held that the plaintiffs failed to establish subject matter jurisdiction under the ATCA. * * * The district court therefore dismissed the plaintiffs' complaints in their entirety. * * * The plaintiffs filed timely notices of appeal [with the U.S. Court of Appeals for the Second Circuit].

* * * *

* * * [This court] vacate[s] the district court's dismissal of the plaintiffs' ATCA claims because the district court erred in holding that aiding and abetting violations of customary international law cannot provide a basis for ATCA jurisdiction. *We hold that * * * a plaintiff may plead a theory of aiding and abetting liability under the ATCA.* * * * [The majority of the judges on the panel that heard this case agreed on the result but differed on the reasons, which were presented in two concurring opinions. One judge believed that liability on these facts is "well established in international law," citing such examples as the Rome Statute of the International Criminal Court. Another judge stated that grounds existed in such resources of U.S. law as Section 876(b) of the *Restatement (Second) of Torts,* under which liability could be assessed in part for "facilitating the commission of human rights violations by providing the principal tortfeasor with the tools, instrumentalities, or services to commit those violations."] [Emphasis added.]

* * * *

* * * We decline to affirm the dismissal of plaintiffs' ATCA claims on the basis of the prudential concerns[a] raised by the defendants. * * * [T]he Supreme Court [has] identified two

a. The term *prudential concerns* refers to the defendants' arguments that the plaintiffs do not have standing to pursue their case in a U.S. court. Here, *prudential* means that the arguments are based on judicially (or legislatively) created principles rather than on the constitutionally based requirements set forth in Article III of the U.S. Constitution (the case or controversy clause).

CASE CONTINUES

CASE 8.3 CONTINUED

different respects in which courts should consider prudential concerns [exercise great caution and carefully evaluate international norms and potential adverse foreign policy consequences] in deciding whether to hear claims brought under the ATCA.[b] First, * * * courts should consider prudential concerns in the context of determining whether to recognize a cause of action under the ATCA. Specifically, * * * the determination whether a norm is sufficiently definite to support a cause of action should (and, indeed, inevitably must) involve an element of judgment about the practical consequences of making that cause available to litigants in the federal courts. Second, * * * in certain cases, other prudential principles might operate to limit the availability of relief in the federal courts for violations of customary international law.

* * * *

One such principle * * * [is] a policy of case-specific deference to the political branches [of the U.S. government]. *This policy of judicial deference to the Executive Branch on questions of foreign policy has long been established under the prudential justiciability [appropriate for a court to resolve] doctrine known as the political question doctrine. Another prudential doctrine that the defendants raise in this case is international comity.* This doctrine * * * asks whether adjudication of the case by a United States court would offend amicable working relationships with a foreign country. [Emphasis added.]

* * * *

We decline to address these case-specific prudential doctrines now and instead remand to the district court to allow it to engage in the first instance in the careful "case-by-case" analysis that questions of this type require.

* * * *

* * * We VACATE the district court's dismissal of the plaintiffs' ATCA claims * * * and REMAND for further proceedings consistent with this opinion.

QUESTIONS

1. What are the ramifications for the defendants of the ruling in this case?
2. How might such "prudential concerns" as the principle of comity affect the eventual outcome?

b. The court is referring to the decision of the United States Supreme Court in *Sosa v. Alvarez-Machain,* 542 U.S. 692, 124 S.Ct. 2739, 159 L.Ed.2d 718 (2004). In the *Sosa* case, the Supreme Court outlined the need for caution in deciding actions under the Alien Tort Claims Act and said that the "potential implications for the foreign relations of the United States of recognizing such causes should make courts particularly wary of impinging [encroaching] on the discretion of the Legislative and Executive Branches in managing foreign affairs."

REVIEWING International Law in a Global Economy

Robco, Inc., was a Florida arms dealer. The armed forces of Honduras contracted to purchase weapons from Robco over a six-year period. After the government was replaced and a democracy installed, the Honduran government sought to reduce the size of its military, and its relationship with Robco deteriorated. Honduras refused to honor the contract and purchase the inventory of arms, which Robco could sell only at a much lower price. Robco filed a suit in a federal district court in the United States to recover damages for this breach of contract by the government of Honduras. Using the information presented in the chapter, answer the following questions.

1. Should the Foreign Sovereign Immunities Act (FSIA) preclude this lawsuit? Why or why not?
2. Does the act of state doctrine bar Robco from seeking to enforce the contract? Explain.

REVIEWING International Law in a Global Economy, Continued

3. Suppose that prior to this lawsuit, the new government of Honduras had enacted a law making it illegal to purchase weapons from foreign arms dealers. What doctrine of deference might lead a U.S. court to dismiss Robco's case in that situation?
4. Now suppose that the U.S. court hears the case and awards damages to Robco, but the government of Honduras has no assets in the United States that can be used to satisfy the judgment. Under which doctrine might Robco be able to collect the damages by asking another nation's court to enforce the U.S. judgment?

TERMS AND CONCEPTS

act of state doctrine 177
civil law system 176
comity 177
confiscation 177
distribution agreement 178
dumping 181
export 178
expropriation 177
international law 175
international organization 176
national law 175
normal trade relations (NTR) status 182
quota 181
sovereign immunity 178
tariff 181
treaty 176

QUESTIONS AND CASE PROBLEMS

8–1. In 1995, France implemented a law making the use of the French language mandatory in certain legal documents. Documents relating to securities offerings, such as prospectuses, for example, must be written in French. So must instruction manuals and warranties for goods and services offered for sale in France. Additionally, all agreements entered into with French state or local authorities, with entities controlled by state or local authorities, and with private entities carrying out a public service (such as providing utilities) must be written in French. What kinds of problems might this law pose for U.S. businesspersons who wish to form contracts with French individuals or business firms?

8–2. QUESTION WITH SAMPLE ANSWER

As China and formerly Communist nations move toward free enterprise, they must develop a new set of business laws. If you could start from scratch, what kind of business law system would you adopt, a civil law system or a common law system? What kind of business regulations would you impose?

- **For a sample answer to Question 8–2, go to Appendix I at the end of this text.**

8–3. Sovereign Immunity. Tonoga, Ltd., doing business as Taconic Plastics, Ltd., is a manufacturer incorporated in Ireland with its principal place of business in New York. In 1997, Taconic entered into a contract with a German construction company to supply special material for a tent project designed to shelter religious pilgrims visiting holy sites in Saudi Arabia. Most of the material was made in, and shipped from, New York. The company did not pay Taconic and eventually filed for bankruptcy. Another German firm, Werner Voss Architects and Engineers, acting as an agent for the government of Saudi Arabia, guaranteed the payments due Taconic to induce it to complete the project. When Taconic received all but the final payment, the firm filed a suit in a federal district court against the government of Saudi Arabia, claiming a breach of the guaranty and seeking to collect, in part, about $3 million. The defendant filed a motion to dismiss based on the doctrine of sovereign immunity, among other things. Under what circumstances does this doctrine apply? What are its exceptions? Should this suit be dismissed under the "commercial activity" exception? Explain. [*Tonoga, Ltd. v. Ministry of Public Works and Housing of Kingdom of Saudi Arabia,* 135 F.Supp.2d 350 (N.D.N.Y. 2001)]

8–4. Import Controls. DaimlerChrysler Corp. made and marketed motor vehicles. DaimlerChrysler assembled the 1993 and 1994 model years of its trucks at plants in Mexico. Assembly involved sheet metal components sent from the United States. DaimlerChrysler subjected some of the parts to a complicated treatment process, which included the application of coats of paint to prevent corrosion, impart color, and protect the finish. Under federal law, goods that are assembled abroad using U.S.-made parts can be imported tariff free. A federal statute provides that painting is "incidental" to assembly and does not affect the status of the goods. A federal regulation states that "painting primarily intended to enhance the appearance of an article or to impart distinctive features or characteristics" is not incidental. The U.S. Customs Service levied a tariff on the trucks. DaimlerChrysler filed a suit in the U.S. Court of International Trade, challenging the levy. Should the court rule in DaimlerChrysler's favor? Why or why not? [*DaimlerChrysler Corp. v. United States,* 361 F.3d 1378 (Fed.Cir. 2004)]

8–5. Comity. E&L Consulting, Ltd., is a U.S. corporation that sells lumber products in New Jersey, New York, and Pennsylvania. Doman Industries, Ltd., is a Canadian corporation that also sells lumber products, including green hem-fir, a durable product used for home building. Doman supplies more than 95 percent of the green hem-fir for sale in the northeastern United States. In 1990, Doman contracted to sell green hem-fir through E&L, which received monthly payments plus commissions. In 1998, Sherwood Lumber Corp., a New York firm and an E&L competitor, approached E&L about a merger. The negotiations were unsuccessful. According to E&L, Sherwood and Doman then conspired to monopolize the green hem-fir market in the United States. When Doman terminated its contract with E&L, the latter filed a suit in a federal district court against Doman, alleging violations of U.S. antitrust law. Doman filed for bankruptcy in a Canadian court and asked the U.S. court to dismiss E&L's suit, in part, under the principle of comity. What is the "principle of comity"? On what basis would it apply in this case? What would be the likely result? Discuss. [*E&L Consulting, Ltd. v. Doman Industries, Ltd.,* 360 F.Supp.2d 465 (E.D.N.Y. 2005)]

8–6. Dumping. A newspaper printing press system is more than a hundred feet long, stands four or five stories tall, and weighs 2 million pounds. Only about ten of the systems are sold each year in the United States. Because of the size and cost, a newspaper may update its system, rather than replace it, by buying "additions." By the 1990s, Goss International Corp. was the only domestic maker of the equipment in the United States and represented the entire U.S. market. Tokyo Kikai Seisakusho (TKSC), a Japanese corporation, makes the systems in Japan. In the 1990s, TKSC began to compete in the U.S. market, forcing Goss to cut its prices below cost. TKSC's tactics included offering its customers "secret" rebates on prices that were ultimately substantially less than the products' actual market value in Japan. According to TKSC office memos, the goal was to "win completely this survival game" against Goss, the "enemy." Goss filed a suit in a federal district court against TKSC and others, alleging illegal dumping. At what point does a foreign firm's attempt to compete with a domestic manufacturer in the United States become illegal dumping? Was that point reached in this case? Discuss. [*Goss International Corp. v. Man Roland Druckmaschinen Aktiengesellschaft,* 434 F.3d 1081 (8th Cir. 2006)]

8–7. CASE PROBLEM WITH SAMPLE ANSWER

Jan Voda, M.D., a resident of Oklahoma City, Oklahoma, owns three U.S. patents related to guiding catheters for use in interventional cardiology, as well as corresponding foreign patents issued by the European Patent Office, Canada, France, Germany, and Great Britain. Voda filed a suit in a federal district court against Cordis Corp., a U.S. firm, alleging infringement of the U.S. patents under U.S. patent law and of the corresponding foreign patents under the patent law of the various foreign countries. Cordis admitted, "[T]he XB catheters have been sold domestically and internationally since 1994. The XB catheters were manufactured in Miami Lakes, from 1993 to 2001 and have been manufactured in Juarez, Mexico, since 2001." Cordis argued, however, that Voda could not assert infringement claims under foreign patent law because the court did not have jurisdiction over such claims. Which of the important international legal principles discussed in this chapter would be most likely to apply in this case? How should the court apply it? Explain. [*Voda v. Cordis Corp.,* 476 F.3d 887 (Fed.Cir. 2007)]

- **To view a sample answer for Problem 8–7, go to this book's Web site at academic.cengage.com/blaw/cross, select "Chapter 8," and click on "Case Problem with Sample Answer."**

8–8. SPECIAL CASE ANALYSIS

Go to Case 8.3, *Khulumani v. Barclay National Bank, Ltd.,* 504 F.3d 254 (2d Cir. 2007), on pages 185–186. Read the excerpt and answer the following questions.

(a) **Issue:** What was the main issue in this case?
(b) **Rule of Law:** What rule of law did the court apply?
(c) **Applying the Rule of Law:** Describe how the court applied the rule of law to the facts of this case.
(d) **Conclusion:** What was the court's conclusion in this case?

8–9. A QUESTION OF ETHICS

On December 21, 1988, Pan Am Flight 103 exploded 31,000 feet in the air over Lockerbie, Scotland, killing all 259 passengers and crew on board and 11 people on the ground. Among those killed was Roger Hurst, a U.S. citizen. An investigation determined that a portable radio-cassette player packed in a brown Samsonite suitcase smuggled onto the plane was the source of the explosion. The explosive device was constructed with a digital timer specially made for, and bought by, Libya. Abdel Basset Ali Al-Megrahi, a Libyan government official and an employee of the Libyan Arab Airline (LAA), was convicted by the Scottish High Court of Justiciary on criminal charges that he planned and executed the bombing in association with members of the Jamahiriya Security Organization (JSO) (an agency of the Libyan government that performs security and intelligence functions) or the Libyan military. Members of the victims' families filed a suit in a U.S. federal district court against the JSO, the LAA, Al-Megrahi, and others. The plaintiffs claimed violations of U.S. federal law, including the Anti-Terrorism Act, and state law, including the intentional infliction of emotional distress. [Hurst v. Socialist People's Libyan Arab Jamahiriya, *474 F.Supp.2d 19 (D.D.C. 2007)]*

(a) Under what doctrine, codified in which federal statute, might the defendants claim to be immune from the jurisdiction of a U.S. court? Should this law include an exception for "state-sponsored terrorism"? Why or why not?

(b) The defendants agreed to pay $2.7 billion, or $10 million per victim, to settle all claims for "compensatory death damages." The families of eleven victims, including Hurst, were excluded from the settlement because they were "not wrongful death beneficiaries under applicable state law." These plaintiffs continued the suit. The defendants filed a motion to dismiss. Should the motion be granted on the ground that the settlement bars the plaintiffs' claims? Explain.

LAW ON THE WEB

For updated links to resources available on the Web, as well as a variety of other materials, visit this text's Web site at

academic.cengage.com/blaw/cross

FindLaw, which is now a part of West Group, includes an extensive array of links to international doctrines and treaties, as well as to the laws of other nations, on its Web site. Go to

www.findlaw.com/12international

For information on the legal requirements of doing business internationally, a good source is the Internet Law Library's collection of laws of other countries. You can access this source at

www.lawguru.com/ilawlib/?id=52

Legal Research Exercises on the Web

Go to **academic.cengage.com/blaw/cross**, the Web site that accompanies this text. Select "Chapter 8" and click on "Internet Exercises." There you will find the following Internet research exercises that you can perform to learn more about the topics covered in this chapter.

Internet Exercise 8–1: Legal Perspective
The World Trade Organization

Internet Exercise 8–2: Management Perspective
Overseas Business Opportunities

UNIT TWO FOCUS ON ETHICS

Ethics and the Public and International Environment

No other areas of law are as dynamic and engender as much controversy as those relating to the public and international environment. All areas of law touch on ethical considerations. But many laws have as their basis practical necessity or commercial need. The law of the public environment, however, concerns issues such as the protection of freedom of speech, the promotion of racial equality, and government regulation of behavior for the public welfare versus individual rights.

The law in the international environment involves such questions as the influence of foreign and international laws, the impact of divergent cultures, and the effect of different legal, political, and economic systems. These issues are in large measure purely ethical in nature. In resolving them, one must rely on basic notions of fairness and justice. Yet conceptions of fairness, justice, and equality differ among individuals and change over time.

Ethical and legal concepts are often closely intertwined. This is because the common law, as it evolved in England and then in America, reflects society's values and customs. This connection between law and ethics is clearly evident in the area of criminal law, which is founded on concepts of right and wrong behavior—although common law concepts governing criminal acts are now expressed in, or replaced by, federal, state, and local criminal statutes. The number of crimes has continued to expand as new ways to commit wrongs have been discovered. In this *Focus on Ethics* feature, we look at the ethical dimensions of selected topics discussed in the preceding chapters, including some issues that are unique to the cyber age.

Free Speech and the Corporation

Free speech is regarded as one of the basic rights of a democratic society. Yet it has never been considered an absolute right. The right of free speech must be balanced against other important rights and the advancement of other important social goals. In that sense, the proper extent of freedom of speech, in its many forms, involves ethical considerations.

Because freedom of speech is not absolute, not all forms of expression are protected. Pornography, for example, is not protected by the First Amendment. Nor are utterances protected that would induce an immediate threat of violence or injury. Even within the context of protected speech, the Supreme Court has historically looked to the nature of the speech involved in determining the extent of the protection afforded.

As mentioned in Chapter 5, for example, commercial speech is afforded less protection from government restriction than is noncommercial speech. The lesser degree of protection means in practical terms that it is easier for government to show that the interest it seeks to promote by regulating the speech is more important than protecting the right of speech. But in balancing such conflicting rights and goals, value judgments must be made. For instance, should it make a difference that the speaker is a corporation? Or should the only issue be whether the speech is of a political nature? Is it fair to allow corporations to use their superior economic resources and marketing skills to influence politics? Although it is legal, some argue that it is unethical, particularly when a corporation's decision to allocate funds and influence legislation is motivated by self-interest (profit maximization) rather than by a concern for public welfare.

Global Companies and Censorship Issues—Google China

Doing business on a global level can sometimes involve serious ethical challenges. Consider the ethical firestorm that erupted when Google, Inc., decided to market "Google China." This version of Google's widely used search engine was especially tailored to the Chinese government's censorship requirements. To date, the Chinese government has maintained strict control over the flow of information in that country. The government's goal is to stop the flow of what it considers to be "harmful information." Web sites that offer pornography, criticism of the government, or information on sensitive topics, such as the Tiananmen Square massacre in 1989, are censored—that is, they cannot be accessed by Web users. Government agencies enforce the censorship and encourage citizens to inform on one another. Thousands of Web sites are shut down each year, and the sites' operators are subject to potential imprisonment.

Google's code of conduct opens with the company's informal motto: "Don't be evil." Yet critics question whether Google is following this motto.

Human rights groups have come out strongly against Google's decision, maintaining that the company is seeking profits in a lucrative marketplace at the expense of assisting the Chinese Communist Party in suppressing free speech. In February 2006, Tom Lantos, the only Holocaust survivor serving in Congress, stated that the "sickening collaboration" of Google and three other Web companies (Cisco Systems, Microsoft Corporation, and Yahoo!, Inc.) with the Chinese government was "decapitating the voice of dissidents" in that nation.[1]

Focus on Ethics

Google's Response

Google defends its actions by pointing out that its Chinese search engine at least lets users know which sites are being censored. Google China includes the links to censored sites, but when a user tries to access a link, the program states that it is not accessible. Google claims that its approach is essentially the "lesser of two evils": if U.S. companies did not cooperate with the Chinese government, Chinese residents would have less user-friendly Internet access. Moreover, Google asserts that providing Internet access, even if censored, is a step toward more open access in the future because technology is, in itself, a revolutionary force.

The Chinese Government's Defense

The Chinese government insists that in restricting access to certain Web sites, it is merely following the lead of other national governments, which also impose controls on information access. As an example, it cites France, which bans access to any Web sites selling or portraying Nazi paraphernalia. The United States itself prohibits the dissemination of certain types of materials, such as child pornography, over the Internet. Furthermore, the U.S. government monitors Web sites and e-mail communications to protect against terrorist threats. How, ask Chinese officials, can other nations point their fingers at China for engaging in a common international practice?

Ethics and the Administrative Process

In Chapter 5, we noted some of the other constitutional protections that apply in the context of business. We looked in Chapter 6 at how some of those protections apply in the administrative process. As noted in Chapter 6, effective governmental regulation necessitates the gathering of relevant information. Often that information can be obtained only by an on-site inspection of business premises or a firsthand examination of business records. When regulatory needs conflict with constitutional principles, not only are legal issues raised, but ethical ones as well.

Recall that the Fourth Amendment protection from unreasonable searches and seizures applies in the context of business. Within the context of administrative law, this protection has been interpreted as requiring that information sought by a regulatory agency be relevant to the matter under scrutiny. Furthermore, any demand for information must be reasonably specific and not unduly burdensome to the business providing the information.

Regulation and Privacy Rights Despite acceptance of the need for regulators to gather information, an inherent conflict exists between the regulatory need for information and the individual's right of privacy. Specifically, how much latitude should be afforded to regulators in gathering information and overseeing private activities?

The United States Supreme Court has attempted to resolve the conflict by balancing the regulators' need to know against individual and corporate expectations of freedom from excessive government prying. An important consideration in resolving the conflict is the less intrusive nature of regulatory searches of businesses: most people simply do not have the same degree of concern about protecting places of business as they do about protecting the family dwelling. As a result, the standards for conducting regulatory investigations and searches are different from those that apply when ordinary police investigations and searches are conducted. For example, even though there may be no suspicion of a regulatory violation, an agency may conduct an investigation or search the premises of a business merely to be assured that no violation is occurring. Within industries subject to a history of extensive regulation, searches may be made even without a warrant. Still, though, as noted in Chapter 6, government is restricted in obtaining private information for regulatory purposes only.

1. As quoted in Tom Ziller, Jr., "Web Firms Questioned on Dealings in China," *The New York Times*, February 16, 2006.

(Continued)

UNIT TWO FOCUS ON ETHICS

The Ethics of Legal Avoidance In the face of an agency investigation, a business may prevent or delay agency efforts by asserting legal challenges to the nature or manner of the investigation. There remains, however, the question of whether—in an ethical rather than legal sense—a business should challenge any such investigation. We would be expected to challenge an unreasonable search of our homes. Regulatory investigations may be somehow different, though.

Most regulatory investigations have as their objective ensuring compliance with existing regulatory schemes or gathering information for future ones. Such schemes are designed to promote the public welfare. Though individuals may disagree about the effectiveness of the scheme or the individual motives of the regulators, society generally accepts the underlying purpose of the regulation—the promotion of public welfare. In such instances, businesses may have an ethical duty not to use legal means to avoid agency action. Indeed, they may have an ethical duty to aid in regulation by compliance, even though they may have a legal right to delay or avoid it.

Ethics and International Transactions

Conducting business internationally involves unique challenges, including, at times, ethical challenges. This is understandable, given that laws and cultures vary from one country to another. Consider the role of women. In the United States, equal employment opportunity is a fundamental public policy. This policy is clearly expressed in Title VII of the Civil Rights Act of 1964 (discussed in Chapter 21), which prohibits discrimination against women in the employment context. Some other countries, however, largely reject any professional role for women, which may cause difficulties for American women conducting business transactions in those countries. For example, when the World Bank sent a delegation that included women to negotiate with the Central Bank of Korea, the Koreans were surprised and offended. They thought that the presence of women meant that the Koreans were not being taken seriously.

There are also some important ethical differences among nations. In Islamic countries, for example, the consumption of alcohol and certain foods is forbidden by the Islamic religion. Thus, it would be thoughtless and imprudent to invite a Saudi Arabian business contact out for a drink. Additionally, in many foreign nations, gift giving is a common practice between contracting companies or between companies and government officials. To Americans, such gift giving may look suspiciously like an unethical (and possibly illegal) bribe. This has been an important source of friction in international business, particularly after the U.S. Congress passed the Foreign Corrupt Practices Act in 1977 (discussed in Chapters 4 and 7). This act prohibits U.S. business firms from offering certain side payments to foreign officials to secure favorable contracts.

DISCUSSION QUESTIONS

1. Do companies, such as Google, that do business on a global level have an ethical duty to foreign citizens not to suppress free speech, or is it acceptable to censor the information that they provide in other nations at the request of a foreign government?
2. The United States banned the pesticide DDT, primarily because of its adverse effects on wildlife. In Asia, however, DDT has been a critical component of the mosquito control necessary to combat malaria. Should the ban in the United States prevent U.S. firms from manufacturing DDT and shipping it to an Asian country, where it could be used to save lives? Why or why not?
3. What are some of the ethical implications for businesspersons doing business internationally? Should a company refuse to send its women employees to represent the company in nations that reject professional roles for women? Should businesspersons traveling abroad always observe the cultural and religious customs of that location? Why or why not?

UNIT THREE

The Commercial Environment

CONTENTS

CHAPTER 9

Contract Formation

The noted legal scholar Roscoe Pound once said that "[t]he social order rests upon the stability and predictability of conduct, of which keeping promises is a large item."[1] Contract law deals with, among other things, the formation and keeping of promises. A **promise** is a person's assurance that the person will or will not do something.

Like other types of law, contract law reflects our social values, interests, and expectations at a given point in time. It shows, for example, to what extent our society allows people to make promises or commitments that are legally binding. It distinguishes between promises that create only *moral* obligations (such as a promise to take a friend to lunch) and promises that are legally binding (such as a promise to pay for merchandise purchased). Contract law also demonstrates what excuses our society accepts for breaking certain types of promises. In addition, it indicates what promises are considered to be contrary to public policy—against the interests of society as a whole—and therefore legally invalid. When the person making a promise is a child or is mentally incompetent, for example, a question will arise as to whether the promise should be enforced. Resolving such questions is the essence of contract law. The common law governs all contracts except when it has been modified or replaced by statutory law, such as the Uniform Commercial Code (UCC),[2] or by administrative agency regulations. Contracts relating to services, real estate, employment, and insurance, for example, generally are governed by the common law of contracts.

Contracts for the sale and lease of goods, however, are governed by the UCC—to the extent that the UCC has modified general contract law. The relationship between general contract law and the law governing sales and leases of goods will be explored in detail in Chapter 11. In the discussion of general contract law that follows, we indicate in footnotes the areas in which the UCC has significantly altered common law contract principles.

1. R. Pound, *Jurisprudence*, Vol. 3 (St. Paul: West Publishing Co., 1959), p. 162.

2. See Chapters 1 and 11 for further discussions of the significance and coverage of the UCC. Excerpts from the UCC are presented in Appendix C at the end of this book.

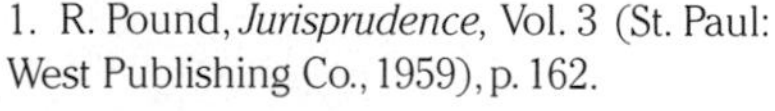

The Function and Definition of Contract Law

The law encourages competent parties to form contracts for lawful objectives. Indeed, no aspect of modern life is entirely free of contractual relationships. Even the ordinary consumer in his or her daily activities acquires rights and obligations based on contract law. You acquire rights and obligations, for example, when you purchase an iPod or when you borrow funds to buy a house. Contract law is designed to provide stability and predictability, as well as certainty, for both buyers and sellers in the marketplace.

Contract law deals with, among other things, the formation and enforcement of agreements between parties (in Latin, *pacta sunt servanda*—"agreements shall be kept"). By supplying procedures for enforcing private contractual agreements, contract law provides an essential condition for the existence of a market economy. Without a legal framework of reasonably assured expectations within which to plan and venture, businesspersons would be able to rely only on the good faith of others. Duty and good faith are usually sufficient to obtain compliance with a promise, but when price changes or adverse economic factors make compliance costly, these elements may not be enough. Contract law is necessary to ensure compliance with a promise or to entitle the innocent party to some form of relief.

Definition of a Contract

A **contract** is "a promise or a set of promises for the breach of which the law gives a remedy, or the performance of which the law in some way recognizes as a duty."[3] Put simply, a contract is a legally binding agreement between two or more parties who agree to perform or to refrain from performing some act now or in the future. Generally, contract disputes arise when there is a promise of future performance. If the contractual promise is not fulfilled, the party who made it is subject to the sanctions of a court (see Chapter 10). That party may be required to pay damages for failing to perform the contractual promise; in limited instances, the party may be required to perform the promised act.

The Objective Theory of Contracts

In determining whether a contract has been formed, the element of intent is of prime importance. In contract law, intent is determined by what is called the *objective theory of contracts,* not by the personal or subjective intent, or belief, of a party. The theory is that a party's intention to enter into a legally binding agreement, or contract, is judged by outward, objective facts as interpreted by a *reasonable* person, rather than by the party's own secret, subjective intentions. Objective facts include (1) what the party said when entering into the contract, (2) how the party acted or appeared (intent may be manifested by conduct as well as by oral or written words), and (3) the circumstances surrounding the transaction. We will look further at the objective theory of contracts later in this chapter, in the context of contract formation.

3. *Restatement (Second) of Contracts.* The *Restatement of the Law of Contracts* is a nonstatutory, authoritative exposition of the common law of contracts compiled by the American Law Institute in 1932. The Restatement, which is now in its second edition (a third edition is being drafted), will be referred to throughout this chapter on contract law.

Elements of a Contract

The many topics that will be discussed in this and the following chapter on contract law require an understanding of the basic elements of a valid contract and the way in which a contract is created. These topics also require an understanding of the types of circumstances in which even legally valid contracts will not be enforced.

Requirements of a Valid Contract

The following list briefly describes the four requirements that must be met before a valid contract exists. If any of these elements is lacking, no contract will have been formed. (Each requirement will be explained more fully later in this chapter.)

1. *Agreement.* An agreement to form a contract includes an *offer* and an *acceptance.* One party must offer to enter into a legal agreement, and another party must accept the terms of the offer.
2. *Consideration.* Any promises made by the parties to the contract must be supported by legally sufficient and bargained-for *consideration* (something of value received or promised, such as money, to convince a person to make a deal).
3. *Contractual capacity.* Both parties entering into the contract must have the contractual *capacity* to do so; the law must recognize them as possessing characteristics that qualify them as competent parties.
4. *Legality.* The contract's purpose must be to accomplish some goal that is legal and not against public policy.

Defenses to the Enforceability of a Contract

Even if all of the above-listed requirements are satisfied, a contract may be unenforceable if the following requirements are not met. These requirements typically are raised as *defenses* to the enforceability of an otherwise valid contract.

1. *Genuineness of assent, or voluntary consent.* The apparent consent of both parties must be genuine, or voluntary. For example, if a contract was formed as a result of fraud, undue influence, mistake, or duress, the contract may not be enforceable.
2. *Form.* The contract must be in whatever form the law requires; for example, some contracts must be in writing to be enforceable.

Types of Contracts

There are many types of contracts. In this section, you will learn that contracts can be categorized based on legal distinctions as to formation, performance, and enforceability.

Contract Formation

As you can see in Exhibit 9–1, three classifications, or categories, of contracts are based on how and when a contract is formed. We explain each of these types of contracts in the following subsections.

Bilateral versus Unilateral Contracts

Every contract involves at least two parties. The *offeror* is the party making the offer. The *offeree* is the party to whom the offer is made. Whether the contract is classified as *unilateral* or *bilateral* depends on what the offeree must do to accept the offer and to bind the offeror to a contract.

Bilateral Contracts. If to accept the offer the offeree must only promise to perform, the contract is a *bilateral contract.* Hence, a bilateral contract is a "promise for a promise." No performance, such as payment of money or delivery of goods, need take place for a bilateral contract to be formed. The contract comes into existence at the moment the promises are exchanged.

For example, Javier offers to buy Ann's digital camcorder for $200. Javier tells Ann that he will give her the funds for the camera next Friday when he gets paid. Ann accepts Javier's offer and promises to give him the camcorder when he pays her on Friday. Javier and Ann have formed a bilateral contract.

Unilateral Contracts. If the offer is phrased so that the offeree can accept the offer only by completing the contract performance, the contract is a *unilateral contract.* Hence, a unilateral contract is a "promise for an act."[4] In other words, the time of contract formation in a unilateral contract is not at the moment when promises are exchanged but when the contract is *performed.* A classic example of a unilateral contract is as follows: O'Malley says to Parker, "If you carry this package across the Brooklyn Bridge, I'll give you $20." Only on Parker's complete crossing with the package does she fully accept O'Malley's offer to pay $20. If she chooses not to undertake the walk, there are no legal consequences.

Contests, lotteries, and other competitions involving prizes are examples of offers to form unilateral contracts. If a person complies with the rules of the contest—such as by submitting the right lottery number at the right place and time—a unilateral contract is formed, binding the organization offering the prize to a contract to perform as promised in the offer.

A Problem with Unilateral Contracts. A problem arises in unilateral contracts when the *promisor* (the one making the promise) attempts to *revoke* (cancel) the offer after the *promisee* (the one to whom the promise was made) has begun performance but before the act has been completed. The promisee can accept the offer only on full performance, and under

4. Clearly, a contract cannot be "one sided," because by definition, an agreement implies the existence of two or more parties. Therefore, the phrase *unilateral contract,* if read literally, is a contradiction in terms. As traditionally used in contract law, however, the phrase refers to the kind of contract that results when only one promise is being made (the promise made by the offeror in return for the offeree's performance).

EXHIBIT 9–1 • Classifications Based on Contract Formation

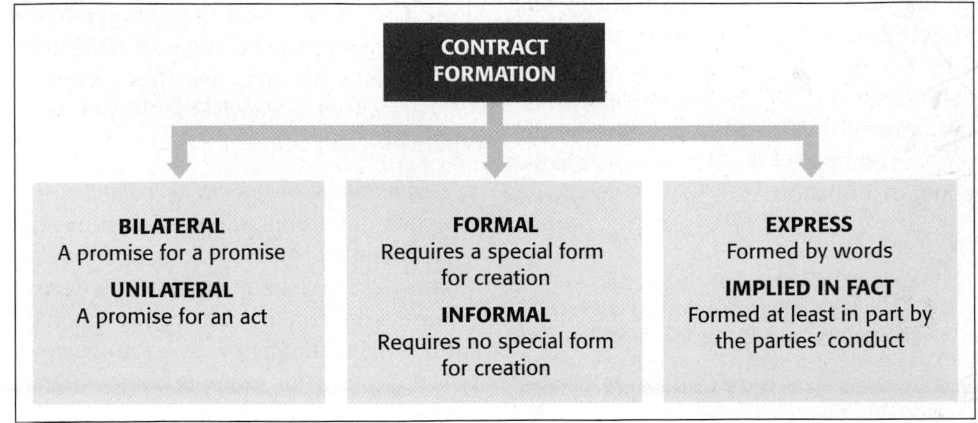

traditional contract principles, an offer may be revoked at any time before the offer is accepted. The present-day view, however, is that an offer to form a unilateral contract becomes irrevocable—cannot be revoked—once performance has begun. Thus, even though the offer has not yet been accepted, the offeror is prohibited from revoking it for a reasonable time period.

For instance, in the earlier example involving the Brooklyn Bridge, suppose that Parker is walking across the bridge and has only three yards to go when O'Malley calls out to her, "I revoke my offer." Under traditional contract law, O'Malley's revocation would terminate the offer. Under the modern view of unilateral contracts, however, O'Malley will not be able to revoke his offer because Parker has undertaken performance and walked all but three yards of the bridge. In these circumstances, Parker can finish crossing the bridge and bind O'Malley to the contract.

Formal versus Informal Contracts Another classification system divides contracts into formal contracts and informal contracts. *Formal contracts* are contracts that require a special form or method of creation (formation) to be enforceable. *Contracts under seal* are a type of formal contract that involves a formalized writing with a special seal attached.[5] In the past, the seals were often made of wax and impressed on the paper document. Today, the significance of the seal in contract law has lessened, though standard-form contracts still sometimes include a place for a seal next to the signature lines. *Letters of credit,* which are frequently used in international sales contracts, are another type of formal contract. As will be discussed in Chapter 11, letters of credit are agreements to pay contingent on the purchaser's receipt of invoices and bills of lading (documents evidencing receipt of, and title to, goods shipped).

Informal contracts (also called *simple contracts*) include all other contracts. No special form is required (except for certain types of contracts that must be in writing), as the contracts are usually based on their substance rather than their form. Typically, businesspersons put their contracts in writing to ensure that there is some proof of a contract's existence should problems arise.

5. The contract under seal has been almost entirely abolished under such provisions as UCC 2–203 (Section 2–203 of the UCC). In sales of real estate, however, it is still common to use a seal (or an acceptable substitute).

Express versus Implied-in-Fact Contracts Contracts may also be categorized as *express* or *implied* by the conduct of the parties. We look here at the differences between these two types of contracts.

Express Contracts. In an **express contract,** the terms of the agreement are fully and explicitly stated in words, oral or written. A signed lease for an apartment or a house is an express written contract. If a classmate calls you on the phone and agrees to buy your textbook from last semester for $45, an express oral contract has been made.

Implied-in-Fact Contracts. A contract that is implied from the conduct of the parties is called an **implied-in-fact contract** or an *implied contract.* This type of contract differs from an express contract in that the conduct of the parties, rather than their words, creates and defines the terms of the contract. (Note that a contract may be a mixture of an express contract and an implied-in-fact contract. In other words, a contract may contain some express terms, while others are implied.)

Requirements for Implied-in-Fact Contracts. For an implied-in-fact contract to arise, certain requirements must be met. Normally, if the following conditions exist, a court will hold that an implied contract was formed:

1. The plaintiff furnished some service or property.
2. The plaintiff expected to be paid for that service or property, and the defendant knew or should have known that payment was expected.
3. The defendant had a chance to reject the services or property and did not.

For example, suppose that you need an accountant to complete your tax return this year. You look through the Yellow Pages and find an accountant at an office in your neighborhood, so you drop by to see her. You go into the accountant's office and explain your problem, and she tells you what her fees are. The next day you return and give her administrative assistant all the necessary information and documents—canceled checks, W-2 forms, and so on. You then walk out the door without saying anything expressly to the assistant. In this situation, you have entered into an implied-in-fact contract to pay the accountant the usual and reasonable fees for her services. The contract is implied by your conduct and by hers. She expects to be paid for completing your tax return, and by bringing in the records she will need to do the work, you have implied an intent to pay her.

Contract Performance

Contracts are also classified according to the degree to which they have been performed. A contract that has been fully performed on both sides is called an *executed contract.* A contract that has not been fully performed by the parties is called an *executory contract.* If one party has fully performed but the other has not, the contract is said to be executed on the one side and executory on the other, but the contract is still classified as executory.

Assume that you agree to buy ten tons of coal from the Northern Coal Company. Further assume that Northern has delivered the coal to your steel mill, where it is now being burned. At this point, the contract is executed on the part of Northern and executory on your part. After you pay Northern for the coal, the contract will be executed on both sides.

Contract Enforceability

A *valid contract* has the elements necessary to entitle at least one of the parties to enforce it in court. Those elements, as mentioned earlier, consist of (1) an agreement consisting of an offer and an acceptance of that offer, (2) supported by legally sufficient consideration, (3) made by parties who have the legal capacity to enter into the contract, and (4) made for a legal purpose. As you can see in Exhibit 9–2, valid contracts may be enforceable, voidable, or unenforceable. Additionally, a contract may be referred to as a *void contract.* We look next at the meaning of the terms *voidable, unenforceable,* and *void* in relation to contract enforceability.

Voidable Contracts A *voidable contract* is a valid contract but one that can be avoided at the option of one or both of the parties. The party having the option can elect either to avoid any duty to perform or to *ratify* (make valid) the contract. If the contract is avoided, both parties are released from it. If it is ratified, both parties must fully perform their respective legal obligations.

As a general rule, but subject to exceptions, contracts made by minors are voidable at the option of the minor. Contracts entered into under fraudulent conditions are voidable at the option of the defrauded party. In addition, contracts entered into under duress or undue influence are voidable.

Unenforceable Contracts An *unenforceable contract* is one that cannot be enforced because of certain legal defenses against it. It is not unenforceable because a party failed to satisfy a legal requirement of the contract; rather, it is a valid contract rendered unenforceable by some statute or law. For example, certain contracts must be in writing, and if they are not, they will not be enforceable except in certain exceptional circumstances.

Void Contracts A *void contract* is no contract at all. The terms *void* and *contract* are contradictory. A void contract produces no legal obligations on any of the parties. For example, a contract can be void

EXHIBIT 9–2 • Enforceable, Voidable, Unenforceable, and Void Contracts

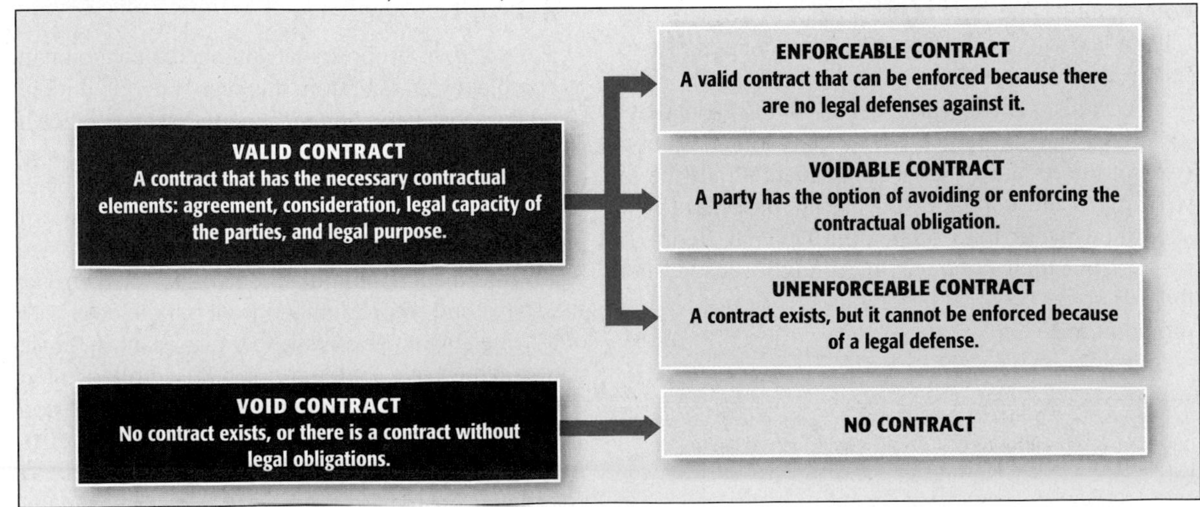

because one of the parties was adjudged by a court to be legally insane (and thus lacked the legal capacity to enter into a contract) or because the purpose of the contract was illegal. To review the various types of contracts, see *Concept Summary 9.1.*

Agreement

An essential element for contract formation is **agreement**—that is, the parties must agree on the terms of the contract and manifest their **mutual assent** (agreement) to the same bargain. Ordinarily, agreement is evidenced by two events: an *offer* and an *acceptance.* One party offers a certain bargain to another party, who then accepts that bargain. The agreement does not necessarily have to be in writing. Both parties, however, must manifest their assent to the same bargain. Once an agreement is reached, if the other elements of a contract are present (consideration, capacity, and legality, which will be discussed later in this chapter), a valid contract is formed, generally creating enforceable rights and duties between the parties.

Note that not all agreements are contracts. John and Kevin may agree to play golf on a certain day, but a court would not hold that their agreement is an enforceable contract. A *contractual* agreement arises only when the terms of the agreement impose legally enforceable obligations on the parties.

In today's world, contracts are frequently formed via the Internet. Online offers and acceptances will be discussed in Chapter 11, in the context of electronic contracts, or e-contracts.

Requirements of the Offer

The parties to a contract are the *offeror,* the one who makes an offer or proposal to another party, and the *offeree,* the one to whom the offer or proposal is made. An **offer** is a promise or commitment to do or refrain from doing some specified thing in the future. Under the common law, three elements are necessary for an offer to be effective:

CONCEPT SUMMARY 9.1
Types of Contracts

Aspect	Definition
FORMATION	1. *Bilateral*—A promise for a promise. 2. *Unilateral*—A promise for an act (acceptance is the completed performance of the act). 3. *Formal*—Requires a special form for creation. 4. *Informal*—Requires no special form for creation. 5. *Express*—Formed by words (oral, written, or a combination). 6. *Implied in fact*—Formed by the conduct of the parties.
PERFORMANCE	1. *Executed*—A fully performed contract. 2. *Executory*—A contract not fully performed.
ENFORCEABILITY	1. *Valid*—The contract has the necessary contractual elements: agreement (offer and acceptance), consideration, legal capacity of the parties, and legal purpose. 2. *Voidable*—One party has the option of avoiding or enforcing the contractual obligation. 3. *Unenforceable*—A contract exists, but it cannot be enforced because of a legal defense. 4. *Void*—No contract exists, or there is a contract without legal obligations.

1. The offeror must have a serious intention to become bound by the offer.
2. The terms of the offer must be reasonably certain, or definite, so that the parties and the court can ascertain the terms of the contract.
3. The offer must be communicated by the offeror to the offeree, resulting in the offeree's knowledge of the offer.

Once an effective offer has been made, the offeree has the power to accept the offer. If the offeree accepts, an agreement is formed (and thus a contract arises, if other essential elements are present).

Intention The first requirement for an effective offer is a serious intent on the part of the offeror. Serious intent is not determined by the *subjective* intentions, beliefs, and assumptions of the offeror. As discussed in Section 1, courts generally adhere to the *objective theory of contracts* in determining whether a contract has been formed. Under this theory, a party's words and conduct are held to mean whatever a reasonable person in the offeree's position would think they meant.

Offers made in obvious anger, jest, or undue excitement do not meet the intent test because a reasonable person would realize that a serious offer was not being made. Because these offers are not effective, an offeree's acceptance does not create an agreement. For example, suppose that you and three classmates ride to school each day in Davina's new automobile, which has a market value of $20,000. One cold morning, the four of you get into the car, but Davina cannot get the car started. She yells in anger, "I'll sell this car to anyone for $500!" You drop $500 in her lap. Given these facts, a reasonable person, taking into consideration Davina's frustration and the obvious difference in worth between the market value of the car and the proposed purchase price, would declare that her offer was not made with serious intent and that you did not have an agreement.

The concept of intention can be further clarified through an examination of the types of expressions and statements that are *not* offers. We look at these expressions and statements in the subsections that follow. In the classic case of *Lucy v. Zehmer,* presented below, the court considered whether an offer made "after a few drinks" met the serious-intent requirement.

CASE 9.1 Lucy v. Zehmer

Supreme Court of Appeals of Virginia, 1954. 196 Va. 493, 84 S.E.2d 516.

• **Background and Facts** W. O. Lucy and J. C. Lucy, the plaintiffs, filed a suit against A. H. Zehmer and Ida Zehmer, the defendants, to compel the Zehmers to transfer title of their property, known as the Ferguson Farm, to the Lucys for $50,000, as the Zehmers had allegedly agreed to do. Lucy had known Zehmer for fifteen or twenty years and for the last eight years or so had been anxious to buy the Ferguson Farm from Zehmer. One night, Lucy stopped in to visit the Zehmers in the combination restaurant, filling station, and motor court they operated. While there, Lucy tried to buy the Ferguson Farm once again. This time he tried a new approach. According to the trial court transcript, Lucy said to Zehmer, "I bet you wouldn't take $50,000 for that place." Zehmer replied, "Yes, I would too; you wouldn't give fifty." Throughout the evening, the conversation returned to the sale of the Ferguson Farm for $50,000. At the same time, the parties continued to drink whiskey and engage in light conversation. Eventually, Lucy enticed Zehmer to write up an agreement to the effect that Zehmer would sell to Lucy the Ferguson Farm for $50,000. Later, Lucy sued Zehmer to compel him to go through with the sale. Zehmer argued that he had been drunk and that the offer had been made in jest and hence was unenforceable. The trial court agreed with Zehmer, and Lucy appealed.

IN THE LANGUAGE OF THE COURT
***BUCHANAN,* J. [Justice] delivered the opinion of the court.**

* * * *

In his testimony, Zehmer claimed that he "was high as a Georgia pine," and that the transaction "was just a bunch of two doggoned drunks bluffing to see who could talk the biggest and say the most." That claim is inconsistent with his attempt to testify in great detail as to what was said and what was done.

CASE 9.1 CONTINUED

* * * *

The appearance of the contract, the fact that it was under discussion for forty minutes or more before it was signed; Lucy's objection to the first draft because it was written in the singular, and he wanted Mrs. Zehmer to sign it also; the rewriting to meet that objection and the signing by Mrs. Zehmer; the discussion of what was to be included in the sale, the provision for the examination of the title, the completeness of the instrument that was executed, the taking possession of it by Lucy with no request or suggestion by either of the defendants that he give it back, are facts which furnish persuasive evidence that the execution of the contract was a serious business transaction rather than a casual, jesting matter as defendants now contend.

* * * *

In the field of contracts, as generally elsewhere, *[w]e must look to the outward expression of a person as manifesting his intention rather than to his secret and unexpressed intention.* The law imputes to a person an intention corresponding to the reasonable meaning of his words and acts. [Emphasis added.]

* * * *

Whether the writing signed by the defendants and now sought to be enforced by the complainants was the result of a serious offer by Lucy and a serious acceptance by the defendants, or was a serious offer by Lucy and an acceptance in secret jest by the defendants, in either event it constituted a binding contract of sale between the parties.

• **Decision and Remedy** *The Supreme Court of Virginia determined that the writing was an enforceable contract and reversed the ruling of the lower court. The Zehmers were required by court order to follow through with the sale of the Ferguson Farm to the Lucys.*

• **Impact of This Case on Today's Law** *This is a classic case in contract law because it illustrates so clearly the objective theory of contracts with respect to determining whether a serious offer was intended. Today, the courts continue to apply the objective theory of contracts and routinely cite* Lucy v. Zehmer *as a significant precedent in this area.*

• **What If the Facts Were Different?** *Suppose that the day after Lucy signed the purchase agreement for the farm, he decided that he didn't want it after all, and Zehmer sued Lucy to perform the contract. Would this change in the facts alter the court's decision that Lucy and Zehmer had created an enforceable contract? Why or why not?*

Expressions of Opinion. An expression of opinion is not an offer. It does not evidence an intention to enter into a binding agreement. Consider an example. Hawkins took his son to McGee, a physician, and asked McGee to operate on the son's hand. McGee said that the boy would be in the hospital three or four days and that the hand would *probably* heal a few days later. The son's hand did not heal for a month, but the father did not win a suit for breach of contract. The court held that McGee had not made an offer to heal the son's hand in a few days. He had merely expressed an opinion as to when the hand would heal.[6]

Statements of Future Intent. If Arif says, "I *plan* to sell my stock in Novation, Inc., for $150 per share," a contract is not created if John "accepts" and tenders the $150 per share for the stock. Arif has merely expressed his intention to enter into a future contract for the sale of the stock. If John accepts and tenders the $150 per share, no contract is formed because a reasonable person would conclude that Arif was only *thinking about* selling his stock, not *promising* to sell it.

Preliminary Negotiations. A request or invitation to negotiate is not an offer. It only expresses a willingness to discuss the possibility of entering into a contract. Included are statements such as "Will you sell Blythe Estate?" or "I wouldn't sell my car for less than $5,000." A reasonable person in the offeree's position would not conclude that these statements evidenced an intention to enter into a binding obligation. Likewise, when the government or private firms require construction work, they invite contractors to submit bids. The *invitation* to submit bids is not an offer, and a contractor does not bind the government or private firm by submitting a bid. (The bids that the contractors submit are offers, however, and the government or private firm can bind the contractor by accepting the bid.)

6. *Hawkins v. McGee,* 84 N.H. 114, 146 A. 641 (1929).

Agreements to Agree. During preliminary negotiations, the parties may form an agreement to agree to a material term of a contract at some future date. Traditionally, such "agreements to agree" were not considered to be binding contracts. The modern view, however, is that agreements to agree may be enforceable agreements (contracts) if it is clear that the parties intended to be bound by the agreements. In other words, under the modern view the emphasis is on the parties' intent rather than on form.

For example, after a person was injured and nearly drowned on a water ride at Six Flags Amusement Park, Six Flags, Inc., filed a lawsuit against the manufacturer that designed the particular ride. The defendant manufacturer claimed that there was no binding contract between the parties, only preliminary negotiations that were never formalized into a construction contract. The court, however, held that a faxed document specifying the details of the water ride, along with the parties' subsequent actions (beginning construction and handwriting notes on the fax), was sufficient to show an intent to be bound. Because of the court's finding, the manufacturer was required to provide insurance for the water ride at Six Flags, and its insurer was required to defend Six Flags in the personal-injury lawsuit that arose out of the incident.[7]

7. *Six Flags, Inc. v. Steadfast Insurance Co.*, 474 F.Supp.2d 201 (D.Mass. 2007).

Increasingly, the courts are holding that a preliminary agreement constitutes a binding contract if the parties have agreed on all essential terms and no disputed issues remain to be resolved.[8] In contrast, if the parties agree on certain major terms but leave other terms open for further negotiation, a preliminary agreement is binding only in the sense that the parties have committed themselves to negotiate the undecided terms in good faith in an effort to reach a final agreement.[9]

In the following case, the dispute was over an agreement to settle a case during a trial. One party claimed that the agreement formed via e-mail was binding, and the other party claimed it was merely an agreement to agree or an agreement to work out the terms of a settlement in the future. Can an exchange of e-mails create a complete and unambiguous agreement?

8. See, for example, *Tractebel Energy Marketing, Inc. v. AEP Power Marketing, Inc.*, 487 F.3d 89 (2d Cir. 2007); and *Florine On Call, Ltd. v. Fluorogas Limited*, No. 01-CV-186 (W.D.Tex. 2002), contract issue affirmed on appeal at 380 F.3d 849 (5th Cir. 2004).

9. See, for example, *MBH, Inc. v. John Otte Oil & Propane, Inc.*, 727 N.W.2d 238 (Neb.App. 2007); and *Barrand v. Whataburger, Inc.*, 214 S.W.3d 122 (Tex.App.—Corpus Christi 2006).

CASE 9.2 Basis Technology Corp. v. Amazon.com, Inc.

Appeals Court of Massachusetts, 2008. 71 Mass.App.Ct. 29, 878 N.E.2d 952.
www.malawyersweekly.com/macoa.cfm[a]

• Background and Facts Basis Technology created software and provided technical services for Amazon's Japanese language Web site. The agreement between the two companies allowed for separately negotiated contracts for additional services that Basis might provide Amazon. At the end of 1999, Basis and Amazon entered into stock-purchase agreements. Later, Amazon objected to certain actions related to the securities that Basis sold. Basis sued Amazon for various claims involving these securities and for nonpayment of services performed by Basis that were not included in the original agreement. During the trial, the two parties appeared to reach an agreement to settle out of court via a series of e-mail exchanges outlining the settlement. When Amazon reneged, Basis served a motion to enforce the proposed settlement. The trial judge entered judgment against Amazon, which appealed.

IN THE LANGUAGE OF THE COURT
***SIKORA*, J. [Judge]**

* * * *

* * * On the evening of March 23, after the third day of evidence and after settlement discussions, Basis counsel sent an e-mail with the following text to Amazon counsel:

a. In the search box on the right, enter "71 Mass.App.Ct. 29" and click on "Search." On the resulting page, click on the case name.

CASE 9.2 CONTINUED

> [Amazon counsel]—This e-mail confirms the essential business terms of the settlement between our respective clients * * *. Basis and Amazon agree that they promptly will take all reasonable steps to memorialize in a written agreement, to be signed by individuals authorized by each party, the terms set forth below, as well as such other terms that are reasonably necessary to make these terms effective.
>
> * * * *
>
> [Amazon counsel], please contact me first thing tomorrow morning if this e-mail does not accurately summarize the settlement terms reached earlier this evening.
>
> See you tomorrow morning when we report this matter settled to the Court.

At 7:26 A.M. on March 24, Amazon counsel sent an e-mail with a one-word reply: "correct." Later in the morning, in open court and on the record, both counsel reported the result of a settlement without specification of the terms.

On March 25, Amazon's counsel sent a facsimile of the first draft of a settlement agreement to Basis's counsel. The draft comported with all the terms of the e-mail exchange, and added some implementing and boilerplate [standard contract provisions] terms.

* * * *

[Within a few days, though,] the parties were deadlocked. On April 21, Basis served its motion to enforce the settlement agreement. Amazon opposed. * * * The motion and opposition presented the issues whether the e-mail terms were sufficiently complete and definite to form an agreement and whether Amazon had intended to be bound by them.

* * * *

We examine the text of the terms for the incompleteness and indefiniteness charged by Amazon. *Provisions are not ambiguous simply because the parties have developed different interpretations of them.* [Emphasis added.]

* * * *

We must interpret the document as a whole. In the preface to the enumerated terms, Basis counsel stated that the "e-mail confirms the essential business terms of the settlement between our respective clients," and that the parties "agree that they promptly will take all reasonable steps to memorialize" those terms. Amazon counsel concisely responded, "correct." Thus the "essential business terms" were resolved. The parties were proceeding to "memorialize" or record the settlement terms, not to create them.

* * * *

To ascertain intent, a court considers the words used by the parties, the agreement taken as a whole, and surrounding facts and circumstances. The essential circumstance of this disputed agreement is that it concluded a trial.

* * * As the trial judge explained in her memorandum of decision, she "terminated" the trial; she did not suspend it for exploratory negotiations. She did so in reliance upon the parties' report of an accomplished agreement for the settlement of their dispute.

* * * *

In sum, the deliberateness and the gravity attributable to a report of a settlement, especially during the progress of a trial, weigh heavily as circumstantial evidence of the intention of a party such as Amazon to be bound by its communication to the opposing party and to the court.

● **Decision and Remedy** *The Appeals Court of Massachusetts affirmed the trial court's finding that Amazon intended to be bound by the terms of the March 23 e-mail. That e-mail constituted a complete and unambiguous statement of the parties' desire to be bound by the settlement terms.*

● **What If the Facts Were Different?** *Assume that the attorneys for both sides had simply had a phone conversation that included all of the terms they actually agreed on in their e-mail exchanges. Would the court have ruled differently? Why or why not?*

● **The Ethical Dimension** *Under what circumstances could Amazon justify its "about face" after having agreed in an e-mail to the settlement terms?*

Advertisements. In general, advertisements—including representations made in mail-order catalogues, price lists, and circulars—are treated not as offers to contract but as invitations to negotiate. Suppose that Loeser advertises a used paving machine. The ad is mailed to hundreds of firms and reads, "Used Loeser Construction Co. paving machine. Builds curbs and finishes cement work all in one process. Price: $42,350." If Star Paving calls Loeser and says, "We accept your offer," no contract is formed. Any reasonable person would conclude that Loeser was not promising to sell the paving machine but rather was soliciting offers to buy it. If such an ad were held to constitute a legal offer, and fifty people accepted the offer, there would be no way for Loeser to perform all fifty of the resulting contracts. He would have to breach forty-nine contracts. Obviously, the law seeks to avoid such unfairness.

Price lists are another form of invitation to negotiate or trade. A seller's price list is not an offer to sell at that price; it merely invites the buyer to offer to buy at that price. In fact, the seller usually puts "prices subject to change" on the price list. Only in rare circumstances will a price quotation be construed as an offer.

Although most advertisements and the like are treated as invitations to negotiate, this does not mean that an advertisement can never be an offer. On some occasions, courts have construed advertisements to be offers because the ads contained definite terms that invited acceptance (such as an ad offering a reward for the return of a lost dog).

Definiteness of Terms The second requirement for an effective offer involves the definiteness of its terms. An offer must have terms that are reasonably definite so that, if it is accepted and a contract formed, a court can determine if a breach has occurred and can provide an appropriate remedy. The specific terms required depend, of course, on the type of contract. Generally, a contract must include the following terms, either expressed in the contract or capable of being reasonably inferred from it:

1. The identification of the parties.
2. The identification of the object or subject matter of the contract (also the quantity, when appropriate), including the work to be performed, with specific identification of such items as goods, services, and land.
3. The consideration to be paid.
4. The time of payment, delivery, or performance.

An offer may invite an acceptance to be worded in such specific terms that the contract is made definite. Suppose that Marcus Business Machines contacts your corporation and offers to sell "from one to ten MacCool copying machines for $1,600 each; state number desired in acceptance." Your corporation agrees to buy two copiers. Because the quantity is specified in the acceptance, the terms are definite, and the contract is enforceable.

Courts sometimes are willing to supply a missing term in a contract when the parties have clearly manifested an intent to form a contract. If, in contrast, the parties have attempted to deal with a particular term of the contract but their expression of intent is too vague or uncertain to be given any precise meaning, the court will not supply a "reasonable" term because to do so might conflict with the intent of the parties. In other words, the court will not rewrite the contract.[10] The following case illustrates this point.

10. See Chapter 11 and UCC 2–204. Article 2 of the UCC specifies different rules relating to the definiteness of terms used in a contract for the sale of goods. In essence, Article 2 modifies general contract law by requiring less specificity.

EXTENDED CASE 9.3 Baer v. Chase

United States Court of Appeals, Third Circuit, 2004. 392 F.3d 609.

***GREENBERG,* Circuit Judge.**

* * * *

[David] Chase, who originally was from New Jersey, but relocated to Los Angeles in 1971, is the creator, producer, writer and director of *The Sopranos.* Chase has numerous credits for other television productions as well. * * * Chase had worked on a number of projects involving organized crime activities based in New Jersey, including a script for "a mob boss in therapy," a concept that, in part, would become the basis for *The Sopranos.*

In 1995, Chase was producing and directing a *Rockford Files* "movie-of-the-week" when he met Joseph Urbancyk who was working on the set as a camera operator and temporary director of photography.

CASE 9.3 CONTINUED

[Through Urbancyk, Chase met Robert] Baer, * * * a New Jersey attorney [who] recently had left his employment in the Union County Prosecutor's Office in Elizabeth, New Jersey, where he had worked for the previous six years.

* * * *

Chase, Urbancyk, and Baer met for lunch on June 20, 1995 * * * , with Baer describing his experience as a prosecutor. Baer also pitched the idea to shoot "a film or television shows about the New Jersey Mafia." At that time Baer was unaware of Chase's previous work involving mob activity premised in New Jersey. At the lunch there was no reference to any payment that Chase might make to Baer for the latter's services * * * .

In October 1995, Chase visited New Jersey for three days. During this "research visit" Baer arranged meetings for Chase with Detective Thomas Koczur, Detective Robert A. Jones, and Tony Spirito who provided Chase with information, material, and personal stories about their experiences with organized crime. * * * Baer does not dispute that virtually all of the ideas and locations that he "contributed" to Chase existed in the public record.

After returning to Los Angeles, Chase sent Baer a copy of a draft of a *Sopranos* screenplay that he had written, which was dated December 20, 1995. Baer asserts that after he read it he called Chase and made various comments with regard to it. Baer claims that the two spoke at least four times during the following year and that he sent a letter to Chase dated February 10, 1997, discussing *The Sopranos* script.

* * * *

Baer asserts that he and Chase orally agreed on three separate occasions that if the show became a success, Chase would "take care of" Baer, and "remunerate Baer in a manner commensurate to the true value of his services."

Baer claims that on each of these occasions the parties had the same conversation in which Chase offered to pay Baer, stating "you help me; I pay you." Baer always rejected Chase's offer, reasoning that Chase would be unable to pay him "for the true value of the services Baer was rendering." Each time Baer rejected Chase's offer he did so with a counteroffer, "that I would perform the services while assuming the risk that if the show failed Chase would owe me nothing. If, however, the show succeeded he would remunerate me in a manner commensurate to the true value of my services." Baer acknowledges that this counteroffer * * * always was oral and did not include any fixed term of duration or price. * * * In fact, Chase has not paid Baer for his services.

On or about May 15, 2002, Baer filed a * * * complaint against Chase in [a federal] district court * * * [claiming among other things] * * * breach of implied contract. Eventually Chase brought a motion for summary judgment * * * . Chase claimed that the alleged contract * * * [was] too vague, ambiguous and lacking in essential terms to be enforced * * * . The district court granted Chase's motion * * * .

* * * *

Baer predicates [bases] his contract claim on this appeal on an implied-in-fact contract * * * . The issue with respect to the implied-in-fact contract claim concerns whether Chase and Baer entered into an enforceable contract for services Baer rendered that aided in the creation and production of *The Sopranos*.

* * * *

* * * A contract arises from offer and acceptance, and must be sufficiently definite so that the performance to be rendered by each party can be ascertained with reasonable certainty. Therefore parties create an enforceable contract when they agree on its essential terms and manifest an intent that the terms bind them. *If parties to an agreement do not agree on one or more essential terms of the purported agreement, courts generally hold it to be unenforceable.* [Emphasis added.]

* * * *

* * * [The] law deems the price term, i.e., the amount of compensation, an essential term of any contract. An agreement lacking definiteness of price, however, is not unenforceable if the parties specify a practicable method by which they can determine the amount. However, *in the absence of an agreement as to the manner or method of determining compensation the purported agreement is invalid.* Additionally, *the duration of the contract is deemed an essential term and*

CASE CONTINUES

CASE 9.3 CONTINUED *therefore any agreement must be sufficiently definitive to allow a court to determine the agreed upon length of the contractual relationship.* [Emphasis added.]

* * * *

The * * * question with respect to Baer's contract claim, therefore, is whether his contract is enforceable in light of the traditional requirement of definitiveness * * * . A contract may be expressed in writing, or orally, or in acts, or partly in one of these ways and partly in others. There is a point, however, at which interpretation becomes alteration. In this case, even when all of the parties' verbal and non-verbal actions are aggregated and viewed most favorably to Baer, we cannot find a contract that is distinct and definitive enough to be enforceable.

Nothing in the record indicates that the parties agreed on how, how much, where, or for what period Chase would compensate Baer. The parties did not discuss who would determine the "true value" of Baer's services, when the "true value" would be calculated, or what variables would go into such a calculation. There was no discussion or agreement as to the meaning of "success" of *The Sopranos*. There was no discussion how "profits" were to be defined. There was no contemplation of dates of commencement or termination of the contract. And again, nothing in Baer's or Chase's conduct, or the surrounding circumstances of the relationship, shed light on, or answers, any of these questions. The district court was correct in its description of the contract between the parties: "The contract as articulated by the Plaintiff lacks essential terms, and is vague, indefinite and uncertain; no version of the alleged agreement contains sufficiently precise terms to constitute an enforceable contract." We therefore will affirm the district court's rejection of Baer's claim to recover under a theory of implied-in-fact contract.

QUESTIONS

1. **Why must the terms of a contract be "sufficiently definite" before a court will enforce the contract?**
2. **What might a court consider when looking for a "sufficiently definite meaning" to make a contract term enforceable?**

Communication A third requirement for an effective offer is communication of the offer to the offeree, resulting in the offeree's knowledge of the offer. Ordinarily, one cannot agree to a bargain without knowing that it exists. Suppose that Estrich advertises a reward for the return of his lost dog. Hoban, not knowing of the reward, finds the dog and returns it to Estrich. Hoban cannot recover the reward, because she did not know it had been offered.[11]

Termination of the Offer

The communication of an effective offer to an offeree gives the offeree the power to transform the offer into a binding, legal obligation (a contract) by an acceptance. This power of acceptance, however, does not continue forever. It can be terminated either by the action of the parties or by operation of law.

Termination by Action of the Parties An offer can be terminated by the action of the parties in any of three ways: by revocation, by rejection, or by counteroffer.

Revocation of the Offer by the Offeror. The offeror's act of withdrawing (revoking) an offer is known as **revocation.** Unless an offer is irrevocable (irrevocable offers will be discussed shortly), the offeror usually can revoke the offer (even if he or she has promised to keep it open) as long as the revocation is communicated to the offeree before the offeree accepts. Revocation may be accomplished by express repudiation of the offer (for example, with a statement such as "I withdraw my previous offer of October 17") or by performance of acts that are inconsistent with the existence of the offer and are made known to the offeree.

11. A few states allow recovery of the reward, but not on contract principles. Because Estrich wanted his dog to be returned and Hoban returned it, these few states would allow Hoban to recover on the basis that it would be unfair to deny her the reward just because she did not know it had been offered.

The general rule followed by most states is that a revocation becomes effective when the offeree or the offeree's agent (a person acting on behalf of the offeree) actually receives it. Therefore, a letter of revocation mailed on April 1 and delivered at the offeree's residence or place of business on April 3 becomes effective on April 3.

An offer made to the general public can be revoked in the same manner that the offer was originally communicated. Suppose that a department store offers a $10,000 reward to anyone providing information leading to the apprehension of the persons who burglarized the store's downtown branch. The offer is published in three local papers and four papers in neighboring communities. To revoke the offer, the store must publish the revocation in all of the seven papers in which it published the offer. The revocation is then accessible to the general public, even if some particular offeree does not know about it.

Irrevocable Offers. Although most offers are revocable, some can be made irrevocable—that is, they cannot be revoked, or canceled. An option contract involves one type of irrevocable offer. Increasingly, courts also refuse to allow an offeror to revoke an offer when the offeree has changed position because of justifiable reliance on the offer. (An offer for the sale of goods may also be considered irrevocable if the merchant-offeror gives assurances in a signed writing that the offer will remain open—see the discussion of the "merchant's firm offer" in Chapter 11.)

An *option contract* is created when an offeror promises to hold an offer open for a specified period of time in return for a payment (consideration) given by the offeree. An option contract takes away the offeror's power to revoke the offer for the period of time specified in the option. If no time is specified, then a reasonable period of time is implied. For example, suppose that you are in the business of writing movie scripts. Your agent contacts the head of development at New Line Cinema and offers to sell New Line your latest movie script. New Line likes your script and agrees to pay you $25,000 for a six-month option. In this situation, you (through your agent) are the offeror, and New Line is the offeree. You cannot revoke your offer to sell New Line your script for the next six months. If after six months no contract has been formed, however, New Line loses the $25,000, and you are free to sell the script to another movie studio.

When the offeree justifiably relies on an offer to her or his detriment, the court may hold that this *detrimental reliance* makes the offer irrevocable. For example, assume that Angela has rented commercial property from Jake for the past thirty-three years under a series of five-year leases. Under business conditions existing as their seventh lease nears its end, the rental property market is more favorable for tenants than for landlords. Angela tells Jake that she is going to look at other, less expensive properties as possible sites for her business. Wanting Angela to remain a tenant, Jake promises to reduce the rent in their next lease. In reliance on the promise, Angela continues to occupy and do business on Jake's property and does not look at other sites. When they sit down to negotiate a new lease, however, Jake says he has changed his mind and will increase the rent. Can he effectively revoke his promise?

Normally he cannot, because Angela has been relying on his promise to reduce the rent. Had the promise not been made, she would have relocated her business. This is a case of detrimental reliance on a promise, which therefore cannot be revoked. In this situation, the doctrine of **promissory estoppel** comes into play. To **estop** means to bar, impede, or preclude someone from doing something. Thus, promissory estoppel means that the promisor (the offeror) is barred from revoking the offer, in this case because the offeree has already changed her actions in reliance on the offer.

Rejection of the Offer by the Offeree. The offer may be rejected by the offeree, in which case the offer is terminated. Any subsequent attempt by the offeree to accept will be construed as a new offer, giving the original offeror (now the offeree) the power of acceptance. A rejection is ordinarily accomplished by words or conduct evidencing an intent not to accept the offer. As with revocation, rejection of an offer is effective only when it is actually received by the offeror or the offeror's agent.

Merely inquiring about an offer does not constitute rejection. Suppose that a friend offers to buy your PlayStation 3 for $300, and you respond, "Is that your best offer?" or "Will you pay me $375 for it?" A reasonable person would conclude that you had not rejected the offer but had merely made an inquiry for further consideration of the offer. You can still accept and bind your friend to the $300 purchase price. When the offeree merely inquires as to the firmness of the offer, there is no reason to presume that he or she intends to reject it.

Counteroffer by the Offeree. A **counteroffer** occurs when the offeree rejects the original offer and simultaneously makes a new offer. Suppose that Duffy offers to sell her Picasso lithograph to Wong for $4,500. Wong responds, "Your price is too high. I'll offer to purchase your lithograph for $4,000." Wong's response is a counteroffer, because it terminates Duffy's offer to sell at $4,500 and creates a new offer by Wong to purchase at $4,000.

At common law, the **mirror image rule** requires the offeree's acceptance to match the offeror's offer exactly—to mirror the offer. Any change in, or addition to, the terms of the original offer automatically terminates that offer and substitutes the counteroffer. The counteroffer, of course, need not be accepted; but if the original offeror does accept the terms of the counteroffer, a valid contract is created.[12]

Termination by Operation of Law The power of the offeree to transform the offer into a binding, legal obligation can be terminated by operation of law through the occurrence of any of the following events:

1. Lapse of time.
2. Destruction of the specific subject matter of the offer.
3. Death or incompetence of the offeror or the offeree.
4. Supervening illegality of the proposed contract.

An offer terminates automatically by law when the period of time specified in the offer has passed. For example, suppose Alejandro offers to sell his camper to Kelly if she accepts within twenty days. Kelly must accept within the twenty-day period or the offer will lapse (terminate). The time period specified in an offer normally begins to run when the offer is actually received by the offeree, not when it is sent or drawn up. When the offer is delayed (through the misdelivery of mail, for example), the period begins to run from the date the offeree would have received the offer, but only if the offeree knows or should know that the offer is delayed.

If the offer does not specify a time for acceptance, the offer terminates at the end of a *reasonable* period of time. What constitutes a reasonable period of time depends on the subject matter of the contract, business and market conditions, and other relevant circumstances. An offer to sell farm produce, for example, will terminate sooner than an offer to sell farm equipment because farm produce is perishable and subject to greater fluctuations in market value. *Concept Summary 9.2* provides a review of the ways in which an offer can be terminated.

Acceptance

Acceptance is a voluntary act (either words or conduct) by the offeree that shows assent (agreement) to the terms of an offer. The acceptance must be unequivocal and must be communicated to the offeror.

Unequivocal Acceptance To exercise the power of acceptance effectively, the offeree must accept unequivocally. This is the *mirror image rule* previously discussed. If the acceptance is subject to new conditions or if the terms of the acceptance change the original offer, the acceptance may be deemed a counteroffer that implicitly rejects the original offer. An acceptance may be unequivocal even though the offeree expresses dissatisfaction with the contract. For example, "I accept the offer, but I wish I could have gotten a better price" is an effective acceptance. So, too, is "I accept, but can you shave the price?" In contrast, the statement "I accept the offer but only if I can pay on ninety days' credit" is not an unequivocal acceptance and operates as a counteroffer, rejecting the original offer.

Certain terms, when added to an acceptance, will not qualify the acceptance sufficiently to constitute rejection of the offer. Suppose that in response to an offer to sell a piano, the offeree replies, "I accept; please send a written contract." The offeree is requesting a written contract but is not making it a condition for acceptance. Therefore, the acceptance is effective without the written contract. If the offeree replies, "I accept if you send a written contract," however, the acceptance is expressly conditioned on the request for a writing, and the statement is not an acceptance but a counteroffer. (Notice how important each word is!)[13]

Silence as Acceptance Ordinarily, silence cannot constitute acceptance, even if the offeror states, "By your silence and inaction, you will be deemed to have accepted this offer." This general rule applies because

12. The mirror image rule has been greatly modified in regard to sales contracts. Section 2–207 of the UCC provides that a contract is formed if the offeree makes a definite expression of acceptance (such as signing the form in the appropriate location), even though the terms of the acceptance modify or add to the terms of the original offer.

13. In regard to sales contracts, the UCC provides that an acceptance may still be valid even if some terms are added. The new terms are simply treated as proposed additions to the contract.

CONCEPT SUMMARY 9.2
Methods by Which an Offer Can Be Terminated

BY ACTION OF THE PARTIES

1. *Revocation*—Unless the offer is irrevocable, it can be revoked at any time before acceptance without liability. Revocation is not effective until received by the offeree or the offeree's agent. Some offers, such as a merchant's firm offer and option contracts, are irrevocable. Also, in some situations, an offeree's detrimental reliance will cause a court to rule that the offeror cannot revoke the offer.
2. *Rejection*—Accomplished by words or actions that demonstrate a clear intent not to accept the offer; not effective until received by the offeror or the offeror's agent.
3. *Counteroffer*—A rejection of the original offer and the making of a new offer.

BY OPERATION OF LAW

1. *Lapse of time*—The offer terminates (a) at the end of the time period specified in the offer or (b) if no time period is stated in the offer, at the end of a reasonable time period.
2. *Destruction of the subject matter*—When the specific subject matter of the offer is destroyed before the offer is accepted, the offer automatically terminates.
3. *Death or incompetence of the offeror or offeree*—If the offeror or offeree dies or becomes incompetent, this terminates the offer (unless the offer is irrevocable).
4. *Supervening illegality*—When a statute or court decision makes the proposed contract illegal, the offer automatically terminates.

an offeree should not be obligated to act affirmatively to reject an offer when no consideration has passed to the offeree to impose such a duty.

In some instances, however, the offeree does have a duty to speak, in which case her or his silence or inaction will operate as an acceptance. For example, silence may be an acceptance when an offeree takes the benefit of offered services even though he or she had an opportunity to reject them and knew that they were offered with the expectation of compensation. Suppose that Sayre watches while a stranger rakes his leaves, even though the stranger has not been asked to rake the yard. Sayre knows the stranger expects to be paid and does nothing to stop her. Here, his silence constitutes an acceptance, and an implied-in-fact contract is created. He is bound to pay a reasonable value for the stranger's work. This rule normally applies only when the offeree has received a benefit from the goods or services rendered.

Silence can also operate as acceptance when the offeree has had prior dealings with the offeror. Suppose that a merchant routinely receives shipments from a certain supplier and always notifies that supplier when defective goods are rejected. In this situation, silence regarding a shipment will constitute acceptance.

Communication of Acceptance Whether the offeror must be notified of the acceptance depends on the nature of the contract. In a bilateral contract, communication of acceptance is necessary because acceptance is in the form of a promise (not performance) and the contract is formed when the promise is made (rather than when the act is performed). The offeree must communicate the acceptance to the offeror. Communication of acceptance is not necessary, however, if the offer dispenses with the requirement. Additionally, if the offer can be accepted by silence, no communication is necessary.

Because a unilateral contract calls for the full performance of some act, acceptance is usually evident, and notification is therefore unnecessary. Nevertheless, exceptions do exist, such as when the offeror requests notice of acceptance or has no adequate means of determining whether the requested act has been performed. In addition, sometimes the law requires notice of acceptance, and thus notice is necessary.

Mode and Timeliness of Acceptance In bilateral contracts, acceptance must be timely. The general rule is that acceptance in a bilateral contract is timely if it is made before the offer is terminated.

Problems may arise, though, when the parties involved are not dealing face to face. In such situations, the offeree should use an authorized mode of communication.

Acceptance takes effect, thus completing formation of the contract, at the time the offeree sends or delivers the communication via the mode expressly or impliedly authorized by the offeror. This is the so-called **mailbox rule,** which the majority of courts follow. Under this rule, if the authorized mode of communication is the mail, then an acceptance becomes valid when it is dispatched (placed in the control of the U.S. Postal Service)—*not* when it is received by the offeror.

The mailbox rule was created to prevent the confusion that arises when an offeror sends a letter of revocation but, before it arrives, the offeree sends a letter of acceptance. Thus, whereas a revocation becomes effective only when it is *received* by the offeree, an acceptance becomes effective on *dispatch* (when sent, even if it is never received), provided that an *authorized* means of communication is used.

The mailbox rule does not apply to instantaneous forms of communication, such as when the parties are dealing face to face, by telephone, or by fax. There is still some uncertainty in the courts as to whether e-mail should be considered an instantaneous form of communication to which the mailbox rule does not apply. If the parties have agreed to conduct transactions electronically and if the Uniform Electronic Transactions Act (to be discussed in Chapter 11) applies, then e-mail is considered sent when it either leaves control of the sender or is received by the recipient. This rule takes the place of the mailbox rule when the Uniform Electronic Transactions Act applies but essentially allows an e-mail acceptance to become effective when sent (as it would if sent by U.S. mail).

Authorized Means of Acceptance A means of communicating acceptance can be expressly authorized—that is, expressly stipulated in the offer—or impliedly authorized by the facts and circumstances surrounding the situation or by law.[14] An acceptance sent by means not expressly or impliedly authorized normally is not effective until it is received by the offeror.

When an offeror specifies how acceptance should be made (for example, by overnight delivery), *express authorization* is said to exist, and the contract is not formed unless the offeree uses that specified mode of acceptance. Moreover, both offeror and offeree are bound in contract the moment this means of acceptance is employed. For example, Shaylee & Perkins, a Massachusetts firm, offers to sell a container of antique furniture to Leaham's Antiques in Colorado. The offer states that Leaham's must accept the offer via FedEx overnight delivery. The acceptance is effective (and a binding contract is formed) the moment that Leaham's gives the overnight envelope containing the acceptance to the FedEx driver.

When the Preferred Means of Acceptance Is Not Indicated. Most offerors do not expressly specify the means by which the offeree is to accept. When the offeror does not specify expressly that the offeree is to accept by a certain means, or that the acceptance will be effective only when received, acceptance of an offer may be made by any medium that is *reasonable under the circumstances.*[15]

Whether a mode of acceptance is reasonable depends on what would reasonably be expected by parties in the position of the contracting parties. Courts look at prevailing business usages and other surrounding circumstances such as the method of communication the parties have used in the past and the means that were used to convey the offer. The offeror's choice of a particular means in making the offer implies that the offeree is authorized to use the same *or a faster* means for acceptance. Suppose that two parties have been negotiating a deal via fax and then the offeror sends a formal contract offer by priority mail without specifying the means of acceptance. In that situation, the offeree's acceptance by priority mail or by fax is impliedly authorized.

When the Authorized Means of Acceptance Is Not Used. An acceptance sent by means not expressly or impliedly authorized normally is not effective *until it is received by the offeror.* For example, suppose that Frank Cochran is interested in buying a house from Ray Nunez. Cochran faxes an offer to Nunez that clearly specifies acceptance by fax. Nunez has to be out of town for a few days, however, and doesn't

14. *Restatement (Second) of Contracts,* Section 30, provides that an offer invites acceptance "by any medium reasonable in the circumstances," unless the offer is specific about the means of acceptance. Under Section 65, a medium is reasonable if it is one used by the offeror or one customary in similar transactions, unless the offeree knows of circumstances that would argue against the reasonableness of a particular medium (the need for speed because of rapid price changes, for example).

15. *Restatement (Second) of Contracts,* Section 30. This is also the rule under UCC 2–206(1)(a).

have access to a fax machine. Therefore, Nunez sends his acceptance to Cochran via FedEx instead of by fax. In this situation, the acceptance is not effective (and no contract is formed) until Cochran receives the FedEx delivery. The use of an alternative method does not render the acceptance ineffective if the substituted method performs the same function or serves the same purpose as the authorized method.[16]

Exceptions The following are three basic exceptions to the rule that a contract is formed when an acceptance is sent by authorized means:

1. If the offeree's acceptance is not properly dispatched, in most states it will not be effective until it is received by the offeror. For example, if an offeree types in the recipient's e-mail address incorrectly when accepting an offer via e-mail, or if the offeree faxes an acceptance to the wrong telephone number, it will not be effective until received by the offeror. If U.S. mail is the authorized means for acceptance, the offeree's letter must be properly addressed and have the correct postage. Nonetheless, if the acceptance is timely sent and timely received, despite the offeree's carelessness in sending it, it may still be considered to have been effective on dispatch.[17]

16. See, for example, *Osprey, L.L.C. v. Kelly Moore Paint Co.*, 984 P.2d 194 (Okla. 1999).

17. *Restatement (Second) of Contracts*, Section 67.

2. If the offer stipulates when acceptance will be effective, then the offer will not be effective until the time specified. The offeror has the power to control the offer and can stipulate both the means by which the offer is accepted and the precise time that an acceptance will be effective. For example, an offer might state that acceptance will not be effective until it is received by the offeror, or it might make acceptance effective twenty-four hours after being shipped via DHL delivery.
3. Sometimes, an offeree sends a rejection first, then later changes his or her mind and sends an acceptance. Obviously, this chain of events could cause confusion and even detriment to the offeror, depending on whether the rejection or the acceptance arrived first. In such situations, the law cancels the rule of acceptance on dispatch, and the first communication received by the offeror determines whether a contract is formed. If the rejection arrives first, there is no contract.[18]

For a review of the effective time of acceptance, see *Concept Summary 9.3*.

Consideration

The fact that a promise has been made does not mean the promise can or will be enforced. Under Roman law, a promise was not enforceable without

18. *Restatement (Second) of Contracts*, Section 40.

CONCEPT SUMMARY 9.3
Effective Time of Acceptance

Acceptance	Time Effective
BY AUTHORIZED MEANS OF COMMUNICATION	Effective at the time communication is sent (deposited in a mailbox or delivered to a courier service) via the mode expressly or impliedly authorized by the offeror (mailbox rule).
	Exceptions: 1. If the acceptance is not properly dispatched, it will not be effective until received by the offeror. 2. If the offeror specifically conditioned the offer on receipt of acceptance, it will not be effective until received by the offeror. 3. If acceptance is sent after rejection, whichever is received first is given effect.
BY UNAUTHORIZED MEANS OF COMMUNICATION	Effective on receipt of acceptance by the offeror (if timely received, it is considered to have been effective on dispatch).

some sort of *causa*—that is, a reason for making the promise that was also deemed to be a sufficient reason for enforcing it. Under the common law, a primary basis for the enforcement of promises is consideration. **Consideration** is usually defined as the value (such as cash) given in return for a promise (such as the promise to sell a stamp collection on receipt of payment) or in return for a performance.

Often, consideration is broken down into two parts: (1) something of *legally sufficient value* must be given in exchange for the promise; and (2) usually, there must be a *bargained-for* exchange.

Legal Value

The "something of legally sufficient value" may consist of (1) a promise to do something that one has no prior legal duty to do, (2) the performance of an action that one is otherwise not obligated to undertake, or (3) the refraining from an action that one has a legal right to undertake (called a *forbearance*). Consideration in bilateral contracts normally consists of a promise in return for a promise, as explained earlier. For example, suppose that in a contract for the sale of goods, the seller promises to ship specific goods to the buyer, and the buyer promises to pay for those goods when they are received. Each of these promises constitutes consideration for the contract.

In contrast, unilateral contracts involve a promise in return for a performance. Suppose that Anita says to her neighbor, "When you finish painting the garage, I will pay you $100." Anita's neighbor paints the garage. The act of painting the garage is the consideration that creates Anita's contractual obligation to pay her neighbor $100.

What if, in return for a promise to pay, a person refrains from pursuing harmful habits (a forbearance), such as the use of tobacco and alcohol? Does such forbearance constitute legally sufficient consideration? In most situations, the answer is yes. Generally, a waiver of any legal right at the request of another party is a sufficient consideration for a promise.[19]

Bargained-For Exchange

The second element of consideration is that it must provide the basis for the bargain struck between the contracting parties. The promise given by the promisor (offeror) must induce the promisee (offeree) to offer a return promise, a performance, or a forbearance, and the promisee's promise, performance, or forbearance must induce the promisor to make the promise.

This element of bargained-for exchange distinguishes contracts from gifts. Suppose that Arlene says to her son, "In consideration of the fact that you are not as wealthy as your brothers, I will pay you $5,000." The fact that the word *consideration* is used does not, by itself, mean that consideration has been given. Indeed, this is not an enforceable promise because the son need not do anything in order to receive the promised $5,000.[20] The son need not give Arlene something of legal value in return for her promise, and the promised $5,000 does not involve a bargained-for exchange. Rather, Arlene has simply stated her motive for giving her son a gift.

Adequacy of Consideration

Legal sufficiency of consideration involves the requirement that consideration be something of legally sufficient value in the eyes of the law. Adequacy of consideration involves "how much" consideration is given. Essentially, adequacy of consideration concerns the fairness of the bargain. On the surface, fairness would appear to be an issue when the items exchanged are of unequal value. In general, however, a court will not question the adequacy of consideration if the consideration is legally sufficient. Under the doctrine of freedom of contract, parties are normally free to bargain as they wish. If people could sue merely because they had entered into an unwise contract, the courts would be overloaded with frivolous suits.

In extreme cases, a court may consider the adequacy of consideration in terms of its amount or worth because inadequate consideration may indicate that fraud, duress, or undue influence was involved or that the element of bargained-for exchange was lacking. It may also reflect a party's incompetence (for example, an individual might have been too intoxicated or simply too young to make a contract). Suppose that Dylan has a house worth $180,000 and sells it for $90,000. A $90,000 sale could indicate that the buyer unduly pressured Dylan into selling the house at that price or that Dylan was defrauded into selling the house at far below market value. (Of course, it might also indicate that Dylan was in a hurry to sell and that the amount was legally sufficient.)

19. For a classic case in which the court held that refraining from smoking, drinking, swearing, and playing cards or billiards for cash constituted legally sufficient consideration, see *Hamer v. Sidway*, 124 N.Y. 538, 27 N.E. 256 (1891).

20. See *Fink v. Cox*, 18 Johns. 145, 9 Am.Dec. 191 (N.Y. 1820).

Agreements That Lack Consideration

Sometimes, one of the parties (or both parties) to an agreement may think that consideration has been exchanged when in fact it has not. Here, we look at some situations in which the parties' promises or actions do not qualify as contractual consideration.

Preexisting Duty Under most circumstances, a promise to do what one already has a legal duty to do does not constitute legally sufficient consideration. The preexisting legal duty may be imposed by law or may arise out of a previous contract. A sheriff, for example, cannot collect a reward for providing information leading to the capture of a criminal if the sheriff already has a legal duty to capture the criminal.

Likewise, if a party is already bound by contract to perform a certain duty, that duty cannot serve as consideration for a second contract. For example, suppose that Bauman-Bache, Inc., begins construction on a seven-story office building and after three months demands an extra $75,000 on its contract. If the extra $75,000 is not paid, Bauman-Bache will stop working. The owner of the land, finding no one else to complete the construction, agrees to pay the extra $75,000. The agreement is unenforceable because it is not supported by legally sufficient consideration; Bauman-Bache was under a preexisting contract to complete the building.

Unforeseen Difficulties The rule regarding preexisting duty is meant to prevent extortion and the so-called holdup game. What happens, though, when an honest contractor who has contracted with a landowner to construct a building runs into extraordinary difficulties that were totally unforeseen at the time the contract was formed? In the interests of fairness and equity, the courts sometimes allow exceptions to the preexisting duty rule. In the example just mentioned, if the landowner agrees to pay extra compensation to the contractor for overcoming unforeseen difficulties, the court may refrain from applying the preexisting duty rule and enforce the agreement. When the "unforeseen difficulties" that give rise to a contract modification involve the types of risks ordinarily assumed in business, however, the courts will usually assert the preexisting duty rule.

Rescission and New Contract The law recognizes that two parties can mutually agree to rescind, or cancel, their contract, at least to the extent that it is executory (still to be carried out). *Rescission* is the unmaking of a contract so as to return the parties to the positions they occupied before the contract was made. When rescission and the making of a new contract take place at the same time, but the duties of both parties remain the same as in their rescinded contract, the courts frequently are given a choice of applying the preexisting duty rule or allowing rescission and letting the new contract stand.

Past Consideration Promises made in return for actions or events that have already taken place are unenforceable. These promises lack consideration in that the element of bargained-for exchange is missing. In short, you can bargain for something to take place now or in the future but not for something that has already taken place. **Past consideration** is no consideration.

Suppose that Blackmon became friends with Iverson when Iverson was a high school student who showed tremendous promise as an athlete. One evening, Blackmon suggested that Iverson use "The Answer" as a nickname in the summer league basketball tournaments. Blackmon said that Iverson would be "The Answer" to all of the National Basketball Association's woes. Later that night, Iverson said that he would give Blackmon 25 percent of any proceeds from the merchandising of products that used "The Answer" as a logo or a slogan. Because Iverson's promise was made in return for past consideration, it is unenforceable; in effect, Iverson stated his intention to give Blackmon a gift.[21] *Concept Summary 9.4* on page 214 provides a summary of the main aspects of consideration.

Promissory Estoppel

Under the doctrine of *promissory estoppel* (also called *detrimental reliance*), a person who has reasonably and substantially relied on the promise of another may be able to obtain some measure of recovery. This doctrine is applied in a wide variety of contexts in which a promise is otherwise unenforceable, such as when a promise is not supported by consideration. Under this doctrine, a court may enforce an otherwise unenforceable promise to avoid the injustice that would otherwise result. For the doctrine to be applied, the following elements are required:

1. There must be a clear and definite promise.
2. The promisee must justifiably rely on the promise.

21. *Blackmon v. Iverson*, 324 F.Supp.2d 602 (E.D.Pa. 2003).

CONCEPT SUMMARY 9.4
Consideration

Elements of Consideration	Consideration is the value given in exchange for a promise. A contract cannot be formed without sufficient consideration. Consideration is often broken down into two elements: 1. *Legal value*—Something of legally sufficient value must be given in exchange for a promise. This may consist of a promise, a performance, or a forbearance. 2. *Bargained-for exchange*—There must be a bargained-for exchange.
Adequacy of Consideration	Adequacy of consideration relates to how much consideration is given and whether a fair bargain was reached. Courts will inquire into the adequacy of consideration (if the consideration is legally sufficient) only when fraud, undue influence, duress, or the lack of a bargained-for exchange may be involved.
Agreements That Lack Consideration	Consideration is lacking in the following situations: 1. *Preexisting duty*—Consideration is not legally sufficient if one is either by law or by contract under a *preexisting duty* to perform the action being offered as consideration for a new contract. 2. *Past consideration*—Actions or events that have already taken place do not constitute legally sufficient consideration.

3. The reliance normally must be of a substantial and definite character.
4. Justice will be better served by enforcement of the promise.

If these requirements are met, a promise may be enforced even though it is not supported by consideration. In essence, the promisor will be *estopped* (prevented) from asserting the lack of consideration as a defense. For example, suppose that your uncle tells you, "I'll pay you $350 a week so you won't have to work anymore." In reliance on your uncle's promise, you quit your job, but your uncle refuses to pay you. Under the doctrine of promissory estoppel, you may be able to enforce such a promise.[22]

Capacity

In addition to agreement and consideration, for a contract to be deemed valid the parties to the contract must have *contractual capacity*—the legal ability to enter into a contractual relationship. Courts generally presume the existence of contractual capacity, but there are some situations in which capacity is lacking or may be questionable. For example, in many situations, a minor has the capacity to enter into a contract but also has the right to avoid liability under it.

Historically, the law has given special protection to those who bargain with the inexperience of youth or those who lack the degree of mental competence required by law. If a court has determined a person to be mentally incompetent, for example, that person cannot form a legally binding contract with another party. In other situations, a party may have the capacity to enter into a valid contract but also have the right to avoid liability under it. For example, minors—or *infants*, as they are commonly referred to in legal terminology—usually are not legally bound by contracts. In this section, we look at the effect of youth, intoxication, and mental incompetence on contractual capacity.

Minors

Today, in virtually all states, the *age of majority* (when a person is no longer a minor) for contractual purposes is eighteen years.[23] In addition, some states provide for the termination of minority on marriage. Minority status may also be terminated by a minor's *emancipation*, which occurs when a child's parent or legal guardian relinquishes the legal right to exercise control over the child. Normally, a minor who leaves home to support himself or herself is considered emancipated. Several

22. *Ricketts v. Scothorn*, 57 Neb. 51, 77 N.W. 365 (1898).

23. The age of majority may still be twenty-one for other purposes, such as the purchase and consumption of alcohol.

jurisdictions permit minors to petition a court for emancipation themselves. For business purposes, a minor may petition a court to be treated as an adult.

The general rule is that a minor can enter into any contract that an adult can, provided that the contract is not one prohibited by law for minors (for example, the sale of tobacco or alcoholic beverages). A contract entered into by a minor, however, is voidable at the option of that minor, subject to certain exceptions. To exercise the option to avoid a contract, a minor need only manifest an intention not to be bound by it. The minor "avoids" the contract by disaffirming it.

Disaffirmance is the legal avoidance, or setting aside, of a contractual obligation. To disaffirm, a minor must express his or her intent, through words or conduct, not to be bound to the contract. The minor must disaffirm the entire contract, not merely a portion of it. For example, the minor cannot decide to keep part of the goods purchased under a contract and return the remaining goods.

Intoxication

Intoxication is a condition in which a person's normal capacity to act or think is inhibited by alcohol or some other drug. A contract entered into by an intoxicated person can be either voidable or valid (and thus enforceable). If the person was sufficiently intoxicated to lack mental capacity, then the transaction may be voidable at the option of the intoxicated person even if the intoxication was purely voluntary. For the contract to be voidable, the person must prove that the intoxication impaired her or his reason and judgment so severely that she or he did not comprehend the legal consequences of entering into the contract.

Mental Incompetence

If a court has previously determined that a person is mentally incompetent and has appointed a guardian to represent the individual, any contract made by the mentally incompetent person is *void*—no contract exists. Only the guardian can enter into binding legal obligations on the incompetent person's behalf.

Legality

For a contract to be valid and enforceable, it must be formed for a legal purpose. A contract to do something that is prohibited by federal or state statutory law is illegal and, as such, void from the outset and thus unenforceable. Also, a contract that calls for a tortious act or an action contrary to public policy is illegal and unenforceable. It is important to note that a contract or a clause in a contract may be illegal even in the absence of a specific statute prohibiting the action promised by the contract.

Contracts Contrary to Statute

Statutes often prescribe the terms of contracts. We now examine several ways in which contracts may be contrary to statute and thus illegal.

Contracts to Commit a Crime Any contract to commit a crime is a contract in violation of a statute. Thus, a contract to sell an illegal drug (the sale of which is prohibited by statute) is not enforceable, and a contract to provide inside information regarding the sale of securities is unenforceable (violations of securities laws will be discussed in Chapter 28). Should the object or performance of the contract be rendered illegal by statute *after* the contract has been entered into, the contract is considered to be discharged by law. (See the discussion of impossibility or impracticability of performance in Chapter 10.)

Usury Virtually every state has a statute that sets the maximum rate of interest that can be charged for different types of transactions, including ordinary loans. A lender who makes a loan at an interest rate above the lawful maximum commits *usury*. The maximum rate of interest varies from state to state, as do the consequences for lenders who make usurious loans. Some states allow the lender to recover only the principal of a loan along with interest up to the legal maximum. In effect, the lender is denied recovery of the excess interest. In other states, the lender can recover the principal amount of the loan but no interest.

Although usury statutes place a ceiling on allowable rates of interest, exceptions have been made to facilitate business transactions. For example, many states exempt corporate loans from the usury laws, and nearly all states allow higher-interest-rate loans for borrowers who could not otherwise obtain funds.

Gambling All states have statutes that regulate gambling—defined as any scheme that involves a distribution of property by chance among persons who have paid a valuable consideration for the opportunity (chance) to receive the property. Gambling is the creation of risk for the purpose of assuming it. Traditionally, state statutes have deemed gambling contracts to be illegal and thus void.

CONTEMPORARY LEGAL DEBATES

Are Online Fantasy Sports Gambling?

As many as 20 million adults in the United States play some form of fantasy sports via the Internet. A fantasy sport is a game in which participants, often called owners, build teams composed of real-life players from different real-life teams. A fantasy team then competes against the fantasy teams belonging to other "owners." At the end of each week, the statistical performances of all the real-life players are translated into points, and the points of all the players on an owner's fantasy team are totaled. Although a wide variety of fantasy games are available, most participants play fantasy football. On many fantasy sports sites, participants pay a fee in order to play and use the site's facilities, such as statistical tracking and message boards; at the end of the season, prizes ranging from T-shirts to flat-screen televisions are awarded to the winners.

In other instances, the participants in fantasy sports gamble directly on the outcome. In a fantasy football league, for example, each participant-owner adds a given amount to the pot and then "drafts" his or her fantasy team from actual National Football League players. At the end of the football season, each owner's points are totaled, and the owner with the most points wins the pot.

Congress Weighs In

As online gambling has expanded, Congress has attempted to regulate it. In late 2006, a federal law went into effect that makes it illegal for credit-card companies and banks to engage in transactions with Internet gambling companies.[a] Although the law does not prohibit individuals from placing online bets, in effect it makes it almost impossible for them to do so by preventing them from obtaining financing for online gambling. At first glance, the legislation appears comprehensive, but it specifically exempts Internet wagers on horse racing, state lotteries, and fantasy sports. Hence, one could argue that Congress has determined that fantasy sports do not constitute a prohibited Internet gambling activity.

Testing the Gambling Aspect in Court

Thus far, the courts have had the opportunity to rule only on whether the pay-to-play fantasy sports sites that charge an entrance fee and offer prizes to the winners are running gambling operations. Charles Humphrey brought a lawsuit against Viacom, ESPN, *The Sporting News,* and other hosts of such fantasy sports sites under a New Jersey statute that allows the recovery of gambling losses. Humphrey claimed that the fantasy sports leagues were games of chance, not games of skill, because events beyond the participants' control could determine the

a. Security and Accountability for Every Port Act, Public L. No. 109-347, Sections 5361–5367, 120 Stat. 1884 (2006). (A version of the Unlawful Internet Gambling Enforcement Act of 2006 was incorporated into this statute as Title VIII.)

In several states, however, including Louisiana, Michigan, Nevada, and New Jersey, casino gambling is lawful. In other states, certain forms of gambling are legal. California, for example, has not defined draw poker as a crime, although criminal statutes prohibit numerous other types of gambling games. A number of states allow gambling at horse races, and the majority of the states have legalized state-operated lotteries, as well as lotteries (such as bingo) conducted for charitable purposes. Many states also allow gambling on Indian reservations.

A significant issue today is how gambling laws can be applied in the Internet context. Because state laws pertaining to gambling differ, online gambling raises a number of unique issues. For example, if a state does not allow casino gambling or offtrack betting, what can the state government do if its residents place bets online? Also, where does the actual act of gambling occur? Suppose that a resident of New York places bets via the Internet at a gambling site located in Antigua. Is the actual act of "gambling" taking place in New York or in Antigua? According to a New York court in one case, "if the person engaged in gambling is located in New York, then New York is the location where the gambling occurred."[24] Other states' courts may take a different view, however.

Another issue is whether entering into contracts that involve gambling on sports teams that do not really exist—fantasy sports—is a form of gambling. For a discussion of this issue, see this chapter's *Contemporary Legal Debates* feature.

24. *United States v. Cohen,* 260 F.3d. 68 (2d Cir. 2001).

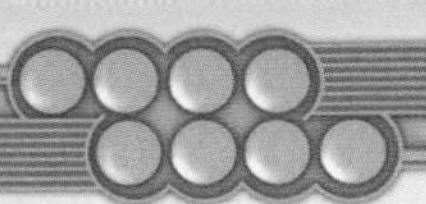

outcome—for example, a star quarterback might be injured. He also pointed out that in the offline world, federal law prohibits any games of chance, such as sweepstakes or drawings, that require entrants to submit consideration in order to play. *Consideration* has been defined as the purchase of a product or the payment of money. For these reasons, he argued, the entrance fees constituted gambling losses that could be recovered.

The federal district court that heard the case ruled against Humphrey, mostly on procedural grounds, but the court did conclude that as a matter of law the entrance fees did not constitute "bets" or "wagers" because the fees are paid unconditionally, the prizes offered are for a fixed amount and certain to be awarded, and the defendants do not compete for the prizes.[b] The court also observed that if a combination of entrance fees and prizes constituted gambling, a host of contests ranging from golf tournaments to track meets to spelling bees and beauty contests would be gambling operations—a conclusion that the court deemed "patently absurd."[c] Note, however, that the case involved only pay-to-play sites. The court did not have to address the question of whether fantasy sports sites that enable participants to contibute to a pot in the hopes of winning it at the end of the season constitute gambling sites.

b. *Humphrey v. Viacom, Inc.*, 2007 WL 1797648 (D.N.J. 2007).

c. In reaching this conclusion, the federal district court cited portions of an Arizona Supreme Court ruling, *State v. American Holiday Association, Inc.*, 151 Ariz. 312, 727 P.2d 807 (1986).

WHERE DO YOU STAND?

Determining what is and what is not gambling does not always lend itself to an easy answer. If you buy a mutual fund that consists of a broad array of stocks and your purpose is to enhance your standard of living during your retirement, no one considers that gambling. In contrast, if you are a day trader—buying and selling stocks during a one-day period—you are clearly "betting" that the stocks you buy in the morning and then sell in the evening will have gone up in value. Should day trading be deemed gambling and therefore illegal? Where do you draw the line between what is and what is not gambling in our society?

Licensing Statutes All states require that members of certain professions or occupations obtain licenses allowing them to practice. Physicians, lawyers, real estate brokers, architects, electricians, and stockbrokers are but a few of the people who must be licensed. Some licenses are obtained only after extensive schooling and examinations, which indicate to the public that a special skill has been acquired. Others require only that the particular person be of good moral character and pay a fee.

Generally, business licenses provide a means of regulating and taxing certain enterprises and protecting the public against actions that could threaten the general welfare. For example, in nearly all states, a stockbroker must be licensed and must file a bond with the state to protect the public from fraudulent stock transactions. Similarly, a plumber must be licensed and bonded to protect the public against incompetent plumbers and to protect the public health. Only persons or businesses possessing the qualifications and complying with the conditions required by statute are entitled to licenses.

When a person enters into a contract with an unlicensed individual, the contract may still be enforceable, depending on the nature of the licensing statute. Some states expressly provide that the lack of a license in certain occupations bars the enforcement of work-related contracts. If the statute does not expressly declare this, one must look to the underlying purpose of the licensing requirements for a particular occupation. If the purpose is to protect the public from unauthorized practitioners, a contract involving an unlicensed individual normally is illegal and unenforceable. If the underlying purpose of the statute is to raise government revenues, however, a contract entered into with an unlicensed practitioner generally is enforceable—although the unlicensed person is usually fined.

Contracts Contrary to Public Policy

Although contracts involve private parties, some are not enforceable because of the negative impact they would have on society. Examples include a contract to commit an immoral act, such as selling a child, and a contract that prohibits marriage. We look here at certain types of business contracts that are often said to be *contrary to public policy.*

Contracts in Restraint of Trade Contracts in restraint of trade (anticompetitive agreements) usually adversely affect the public policy that favors competition in the economy. Typically, such contracts also violate one or more federal or state statutes.[25] An exception is recognized when the restraint is reasonable and is contained in an ancillary (secondary, or subordinate) clause in a contract. Many such exceptions involve a type of restraint called a **covenant not to compete,** or a *restrictive covenant.*

Covenants Not to Compete and the Sale of an Ongoing Business. Covenants (promises) not to compete are often contained as ancillary clauses in contracts concerning the sale of an ongoing business. A covenant not to compete is created when a seller agrees not to open a new store in a certain geographic area surrounding the existing store. Such agreements enable the seller to sell, and the purchaser to buy, the goodwill and reputation of an ongoing business. If, for example, a well-known merchant sells her store and opens a competing business a block away, many customers will likely do business at the merchant's new store. This, in turn, renders less valuable the good name and reputation purchased for a price by the new owner of the old store. If a covenant not to compete is not ancillary to a sales agreement, however, it is void, because it unreasonably restrains trade and is contrary to public policy.

Covenants Not to Compete in Employment Contracts. Agreements not to compete (sometimes referred to as *noncompete agreements*) can also be contained in employment contracts. People in middle- or upper-level management positions commonly agree not to work for competitors or not to start competing businesses for a specified period of time after termination of employment. Such agreements are legal in most states so long as the specified period of time (of restraint) is not excessive in duration and the geographic restriction is reasonable. What constitutes a reasonable time period may be shorter in the online environment than in conventional employment contracts because the restrictions apply worldwide.

To be reasonable, a restriction on competition must protect a legitimate business interest and must not be any greater than necessary to protect that interest.[26] In the following case, the court had to decide whether it was reasonable for an employer's noncompete agreement to restrict a former employee from competing "in any area of business" in which the employer was engaged.

25. Federal statutes include the Sherman Antitrust Act, the Clayton Act, and the Federal Trade Commission Act (see Chapter 26).

26. See, for example, *Gould & Lamb, LLC v. D'Alusio,* 949 So.2d 1212 (Fla.App. 2007). See also *Moore v. Midwest Distribution, Inc.,* 76 Ark.App. 397, 65 S.W.3d 490 (2002).

CASE 9.4 Stultz v. Safety and Compliance Management, Inc.

Court of Appeals of Georgia, 2007. 285 Ga.App. 799, 648 S.E.2d 129.

• **Background and Facts** Safety and Compliance Management, Inc. (S & C), in Rossville, Georgia, provides alcohol- and drug-testing services in multiple states. In February 2002, S & C hired Angela Burgess. Her job duties included providing customer service, ensuring that specimens were properly retrieved from clients and transported to the testing lab, contacting clients, and managing the office. Burgess signed a covenant not to compete "in any area of business conducted by Safety and Compliance Management . . . for a two-year period . . . beginning at the termination of employment." In May 2004, Burgess quit her job to work at Rossville Medical Center (RMC) as a medical assistant. RMC provides medical services, including occupational medicine, medical physicals, and workers' compensation injury treatment. RMC also offers alcohol- and drug-testing services. Burgess's duties included setting

CASE 9.4 CONTINUED

patient appointments, taking patient medical histories, checking vital signs, performing urinalysis testing, administering injections, conducting alcohol breath tests, and collecting specimens for drug testing. S & C filed a suit in a Georgia state court against Burgess and others (including a defendant named Stultz), alleging, among other things, that she had violated the noncompete agreement. The court issued a summary judgment in S & C's favor. Burgess appealed to a state intermediate appellate court.

IN THE LANGUAGE OF THE COURT
***BERNES*, Judge.**

* * * *

Restrictive covenants that are ancillary to an employment contract are subject to strict scrutiny and will be voided by Georgia courts if they impose an unreasonable restraint on trade. Whether the restraint imposed by the employment contract is reasonable is a question of law for determination by the court, which considers the nature and extent of the trade or business, the situation of the parties, and all the other circumstances. *A three-element test of duration, territorial coverage, and scope of activity has evolved as a helpful tool in examining the reasonableness of the particular factual setting to which it is applied.* * * * [Emphasis added.]

* * * Burgess contends that the trial court erred in concluding that the non-competition agreement was reasonable as to the scope of the activity prohibited.

The non-competition agreement provides that Burgess "will not compete * * * in any area of business conducted by [S & C]." Although the next sentence of the agreement provides some particularity by referring to the solicitation of existing accounts, the agreement, when read as a whole, plainly is intended to prevent any type of competing activity whatsoever, with the reference to solicitation merely being illustrative of one type of activity that is prohibited. * * * Thus, when properly construed, the non-competition agreement prohibits, without qualification, Burgess from competing in any area of business conducted by S & C.

Such a prohibition clearly is unreasonable * * * . A non-competition covenant which prohibits an employee from working for a competitor in any capacity, that is, *a covenant which fails to specify with particularity the activities which the employee is prohibited from performing, is too broad and indefinite to be enforceable.* And, Georgia courts have interpreted contractual language similar to that found in the present case as essentially prohibiting an employee from working for a competitor in any capacity whatsoever. * * * In light of this case law, we conclude that the non-competition agreement imposes a greater limitation upon Burgess than is necessary for the protection of S & C and therefore is unenforceable. [Emphasis added.]

It is true, as S & C maintains, that there are factual circumstances where an otherwise questionable restrictive covenant that prohibits working for a competitor will be upheld as reasonable. More specifically, a suspect restriction upon the scope of activity may nevertheless be upheld when the underlying facts reflect that the contracting party was the very heart and soul of the business whose departure effectively brought the business to a standstill. Moreover, the "heart and soul" exception is applicable only where the restrictive covenant otherwise applies to a very restricted territory and for a short period of time.

S & C, however, has failed to allege or present evidence showing that Burgess was the heart and soul of its alcohol and drug testing business. Although Burgess was a major player in S & C's business, she was, when all is said and done, an employee. Her departure may have hurt S & C; but it did not bring the business to a halt. It cannot be said, therefore, that Burgess was the heart and soul of the business.

● **Decision and Remedy** *The Court of Appeals of Georgia reversed the judgment of the lower court. The state intermediate appellate court concluded that the covenant not to compete that Burgess signed "is unreasonable as to the scope of the activity prohibited" because "it is overly broad and indefinite." Thus, the covenant was not enforceable.*

● **The Ethical Dimension** *To determine the enforceability of a covenant not to compete, the courts balance the rights of an employer against those of a former employee. What are these rights? How did S & C's covenant not to compete tip the balance in the employer's favor?*

CASE CONTINUES

CASE 9.4 CONTINUED • **The Global Dimension** *Should an employer be permitted to restrict a former employee from engaging in a competing business on a global level? Why or why not?*

Enforcement Problems. The laws governing the enforceability of covenants not to compete vary significantly from state to state. In some states, such as Texas, such a covenant will not be enforced unless the employee has received some benefit in return for signing the noncompete agreement. This is true even if the covenant is reasonable as to time and area. If the employee receives no benefit, the covenant will be deemed void. California prohibits the enforcement of covenants not to compete altogether.

If a covenant is found to be unreasonable in time or geographic area, courts in some jurisdictions may convert the terms into reasonable ones and then enforce the reformed covenant. A court normally will engage in this kind of rewriting of the terms only in rare situations, however, when it is necessary to prevent undue burdens or hardships.

Unconscionable Contracts or Clauses Ordinarily, a court does not look at the fairness or equity of a contract. For example, the courts generally do not inquire into the adequacy of consideration (as discussed earlier). Persons are assumed to be reasonably intelligent, and the courts will not come to their aid just because they have made an unwise or foolish bargain. In certain circumstances, however, bargains are so oppressive that the courts relieve innocent parties of part or all of their duties. Such bargains are deemed **unconscionable** because they are so unscrupulous or grossly unfair as to be "void of conscience."[27] A contract can be unconscionable on either procedural or substantive grounds.

Procedural Unconscionability. *Procedural* unconscionability has to do with how a term becomes part of a contract and involves factors that make it difficult for a party to know or understand the contract terms—for example, inconspicuous print, unintelligible language ("legalese"), or the lack of an opportunity to read the contract or to ask questions about its meaning. Procedural unconscionability may also occur when there is such disparity in bargaining power between the two parties that the weaker party's consent is not voluntary. Contracts entered into because of one party's vastly superior bargaining power may be deemed unconscionable. These situations often involve an **adhesion contract,** which is a contract written exclusively by one party (the dominant party, usually the seller or creditor) and presented to the other (the adhering party, usually the buyer or borrower) on a take-it-or-leave-it basis. In other words, the adhering party has no opportunity to negotiate the terms of the contract. Standard-form contracts are often adhesion contracts.

Substantive Unconscionability. *Substantive* unconscionability characterizes those contracts, or portions of contracts, that are oppressive or overly harsh. Courts generally focus on provisions that deprive one party of the benefits of the agreement or leave that party without a remedy for nonperformance by the other. For example, suppose that a person with little income and with only a fourth-grade education agrees to purchase a refrigerator for $4,000 and signs a two-year installment contract. The same type of refrigerator usually sells for $900 on the market. Some courts have held this type of contract to be unconscionable because the contract terms are so oppressive as to "shock the conscience" of the court.[28]

Substantive unconscionability can arise in a wide variety of business contexts. For example, a contract clause that gives the business entity free access to the courts but requires the other party to arbitrate any dispute with the firm may be unconscionable.[29] Similarly, an arbitration clause in a credit-card agreement that prevents credit cardholders from obtaining relief for abusive debt-collection practices under consumer law may be unconscionable.[30] Contracts drafted by insur-

27. The Uniform Commercial Code incorporated the concept of unconscionability in Sections 2–302 and 2A–108. These provisions, which apply to contracts for the sale or lease of goods, will be discussed in Chapter 11.

28. See, for example, *Jones v. Star Credit Corp.,* 59 Misc.2d 189, 298 N.Y.S.2d 264 (1969).

29. See, for example, *Wisconsin Auto Loans, Inc. v. Jones,* 290 Wis.2d 514, 714 N.W.2d 155 (2006).

30. See, for example, *Coady v. Cross County Bank,* 2007 WI App 26, 299 Wis.2d 420, 729 N.W.2d 732 (2007).

ance companies and cell phone providers have been struck down as substantively unconscionable when they included provisions that were overly harsh or one sided.[31]

Exculpatory Clauses Closely related to the concept of unconscionability are **exculpatory clauses**—clauses that release a party from liability in the event of monetary or physical injury *no matter who is at fault.* Indeed, courts sometimes refuse to enforce such clauses on the ground that they are unconscionable.

Although courts view exculpatory clauses with disfavor, they do enforce such clauses when they do not contravene public policy, are not ambiguous, and do not claim to protect parties from liability for intentional misconduct. Businesses such as health clubs, racetracks, amusement parks, skiing facilities, horse-rental operations, golf-cart concessions, and skydiving organizations frequently use exculpatory clauses to limit their liability for patrons' injuries. Because these services are not essential, the firms offering them are sometimes considered to have no relative advantage in bargaining strength, and anyone contracting for their services is considered to do so voluntarily.

31. See, for example, *Gatton v. T-Mobile USA, Inc.*, 152 Cal.App.4th 571, 61 Cal.Rptr.3d 344 (2007); *Kinkel v. Cingular Wireless, LLC*, 223 Ill.2d 1, 857 N.E.2d 250, 306 Ill.Dec. 157 (2006); and *Aul v. Golden Rule Insurance Co.*, 2007 WI App 165, 737 N.W.2d 24 (2007).

Voluntary Consent

A contract has been entered into by two parties, each with full legal capacity and for a legal purpose. The contract is also supported by consideration. The contract thus meets the four requirements for a valid contract that were specified previously. Nonetheless, the contract may be unenforceable if the parties have not genuinely assented to its terms. Lack of *voluntary consent* can be used as a defense to the contract's enforceability. Genuineness of assent, or **voluntary consent,** may be lacking because of a mistake, misrepresentation, undue influence, or duress—in other words, because there is no true "meeting of the minds." In this section, we examine problems relating to voluntary consent.

Mistakes

We all make mistakes, and it is therefore not surprising that mistakes are made when contracts are formed. It is important to distinguish between *mistakes of fact* and *mistakes of value or quality.* Only a mistake of fact makes a contract voidable.

Mistakes of Fact Mistakes of fact occur in two forms—*bilateral* and *unilateral.* A bilateral, or mutual, mistake is made by both of the contracting parties. A unilateral mistake is made by only one of the parties. We look next at these two types of mistakes and illustrate them graphically in Exhibit 9–3.

EXHIBIT 9–3 • Mistakes of Fact

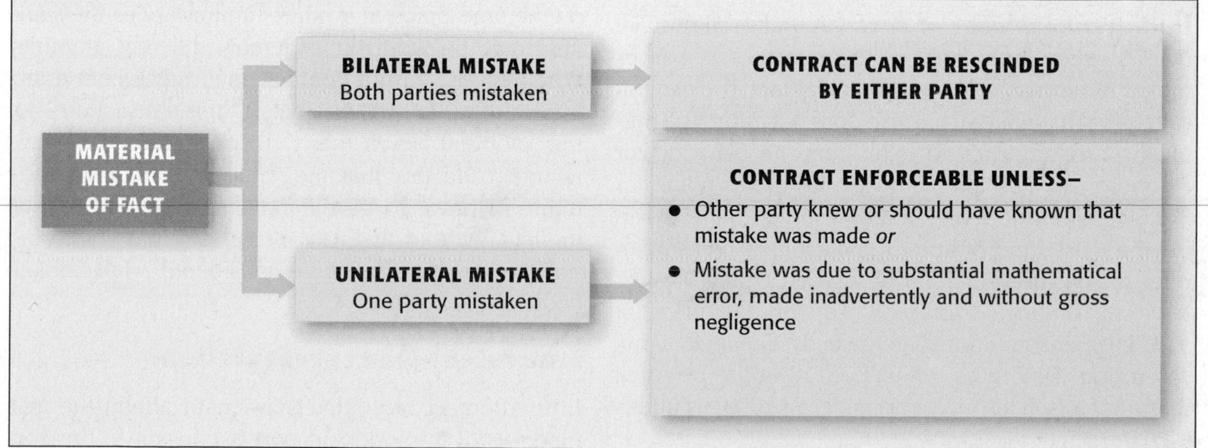

Bilateral (Mutual) Mistakes of Fact. A bilateral, or mutual, mistake occurs when both parties are mistaken as to some *material fact*—that is, a fact important to the subject matter of the contract. When a bilateral mistake occurs, the contract can be rescinded, or canceled, by either party. For example, Keeley buys a landscape painting from Umberto's art gallery. Both Umberto and Keeley believe that the painting is by the artist Vincent van Gogh. Later, Keeley discovers that the painting is a very clever fake. Because neither Umberto nor Keeley was aware of this material fact when they made their deal, Keeley can rescind the contract and recover the purchase price of the painting.

A word or term in a contract may be subject to more than one reasonable interpretation. In that situation, if the parties to the contract attach materially different meanings to the term, their mutual mistake of fact may allow the contract to be rescinded because there has been no "meeting of the minds," or true assent, which is required for a contract to arise.

The classic case on bilateral mistake is *Raffles v. Wichelhaus,*[32] which was decided by an English court in 1864. The defendant, Wichelhaus, paid for a shipment of Surat cotton from the plaintiff, Raffles, "to arrive 'Peerless' from Bombay." Wichelhaus expected the goods to be shipped on the *Peerless,* a ship sailing from Bombay, India, in October. Raffles expected to ship the goods on a different *Peerless,* which sailed from Bombay in December. When the goods arrived and Raffles tried to deliver them, Wichelhaus refused to accept them. The court held for Wichelhaus, concluding that no mutual assent existed because the parties had attached materially different meanings to an essential term of the written contract (the ship that was to transport the goods).

Unilateral Mistakes of Fact. A unilateral mistake occurs when only one of the contracting parties makes a mistake as to some material fact. The general rule is that a unilateral mistake does not afford the mistaken party any right to relief from the contract. For example, DeVinck intends to sell his motor home for $32,500. When he learns that Benson is interested in buying a used motor home, DeVinck faxes Benson an offer to sell the vehicle to him. When typing the fax, however, DeVinck mistakenly keys in the price of $23,700. Benson immediately sends DeVinck a fax accepting DeVinck's offer. Even though DeVinck intended to sell his motor home for $32,500, his unilateral mistake falls on him. He is bound in contract to sell the motor home to Benson for $23,700.

There are at least two exceptions to this general rule. First, if the *other* party to the contract knows or should have known that a mistake of fact was made, the contract may not be enforceable. In the above example, if Benson knew that DeVinck intended to sell his motor home for $32,500, then DeVinck's unilateral mistake (stating $23,700 in his offer) may render the resulting contract unenforceable. The second exception arises when a unilateral mistake of fact was due to a mathematical mistake in addition, subtraction, division, or multiplication and was made inadvertently and without gross (extreme) negligence. If a contractor's bid was significantly low because he or she made a mistake in addition when totaling the estimated costs, any contract resulting from the bid may be rescinded, or canceled. Of course, in both situations, the mistake must still involve some material fact.

Mistakes of Value If a mistake concerns the future market value or quality of the object of the contract, the mistake is one of *value,* and either party can normally enforce the contract. Mistakes of value can be bilateral or unilateral; but either way, they do not serve as a basis for avoiding a contract. Suppose that Chi buys a violin from Bev for $250. Although the violin is very old, neither party believes that it is extremely valuable. An antiques dealer later informs the parties, however, that the violin is rare and worth thousands of dollars. Although a mutual mistake has been made, the mistake is not a mistake of *fact* that warrants contract rescission. Similarly, a unilateral mistake of value will not serve as the basis for avoiding a contract.

The reason that mistakes of value or quality have no legal significance is that value is variable. Depending on the time, place, and other circumstances, the same item may be worth considerably different amounts. When parties form a contract, their agreement establishes the value of the object of their transaction—for the moment. Each party is considered to have assumed the risk that the value will change in the future or prove to be different from what he or she thought. Without this rule, almost any party who did not receive what she or he considered a fair bargain could argue mistake.

Fraudulent Misrepresentation

In the context of contract law, fraud affects the genuineness of the innocent party's consent to the contract. Thus, the transaction is not voluntary in the sense

32. 159 Eng.Rep. 375 (1864).

of involving "mutual assent." When an innocent party is fraudulently induced to enter into a contract, the contract normally can be avoided because that party has not *voluntarily* consented to its terms. Normally, the innocent party can either rescind (cancel) the contract and be restored to his or her original position or enforce the contract and seek damages for any injuries resulting from the fraud.

The word *fraudulent* means many things in the law. Generally, fraudulent misrepresentation refers only to misrepresentation that is consciously false and is intended to mislead another. The perpetrator of the fraudulent misrepresentation knows or believes that the assertion is false or knows that she or he does not have a basis (stated or implied) for the assertion. Typically, fraudulent misrepresentation consists of the following elements:

1. A misrepresentation of a material fact must occur.
2. There must be an intent to deceive.
3. The innocent party must justifiably rely on the misrepresentation.

To collect damages, a party must also have been injured. To obtain rescission of a contract, or to defend against the enforcement of a contract on the basis of fraudulent misrepresentation, in most states a party need not have suffered an injury.

For a person to recover damages caused by fraud, proof of an injury is universally required. The measure of damages is ordinarily equal to the property's value had it been delivered as represented, less the actual price paid for the property. In actions based on fraud, courts often award *punitive damages,* or *exemplary damages,* which are granted to a plaintiff over and above the proved, actual compensation for the loss. As will be discussed in Chapter 12, punitive damages are based on the public-policy consideration of punishing the defendant or setting an example to deter similar wrongdoing by others.

Nonfraudulent Misrepresentation

If a plaintiff seeks to rescind a contract on the ground of *fraudulent* misrepresentation, the plaintiff must prove that the defendant had the intent to deceive. Most courts also allow rescission in cases involving *nonfraudulent* misrepresentation—that is, innocent or negligent misrepresentation—if all of the other elements of misrepresentation exist.

Innocent Misrepresentation If a person makes a statement that he or she believes to be true but that actually misrepresents material facts, the person is guilty only of an *innocent misrepresentation,* not of fraud. If an innocent misrepresentation occurs, the aggrieved party can rescind the contract but usually cannot seek damages. For example, Parris tells Roberta that a tract contains 250 acres. Parris is mistaken—the tract of land contains only 215 acres—but Parris does not know that. Roberta is induced by the statement to make a contract to buy the land. Even though the misrepresentation is innocent, Roberta can avoid the contract if the misrepresentation is material.

Negligent Misrepresentation Sometimes a party will make a misrepresentation through carelessness, believing the statement is true. This misrepresentation is negligent if the person fails to exercise reasonable care in uncovering or disclosing the facts or does not use the skill and competence that her or his business or profession requires. For example, an operator of a weight scale certifies the weight of Sneed's commodity, even though the scale's accuracy has not been checked in more than a year. In this situation, the scale operator's lack of action could constitute *negligent misrepresentation.*

In virtually all states, such negligent misrepresentation is equal to *scienter,* or knowingly making a misrepresentation. In effect, negligent misrepresentation is treated as fraudulent misrepresentation, even though the misrepresentation was not purposeful. In negligent misrepresentation, culpable ignorance of the truth supplies the intention to mislead, even if the defendant can claim, "I didn't know."

Undue Influence

Undue influence arises from special kinds of relationships in which one party can greatly influence another party, thus overcoming that party's free will. A contract entered into under excessive or undue influence lacks genuine assent and is therefore voidable. Minors and elderly people, for example, are often under the influence of guardians (persons who are legally responsible for another). If a guardian induces a young or elderly ward (the person whom the guardian looks after) to enter into a contract that benefits the guardian, undue influence may have been exerted. Undue influence can arise from a number of confidential or fiduciary relationships: attorney-client, physician-patient, guardian-ward, parent-child, husband-wife, or trustee-beneficiary.

The essential feature of undue influence is that the party being taken advantage of does not, in reality, exercise free will in entering into a contract. Just because a person is elderly or suffers from some physical or mental impairment does not mean that he or she was the victim of undue influence. There must be clear and convincing evidence that the person did not act out of her or his free will.

Duress

Consent to the terms of a contract is not voluntary if one of the parties is *forced* into the agreement. Forcing a party to do something, including entering into a contract, through fear created by threats is legally defined as *duress*. In addition, blackmail or extortion to induce consent to a contract constitutes duress. Duress is both a defense to the enforcement of a contract and a ground for the rescission of a contract.

To establish duress, there must be proof of a threat to do something that the threatening party has no right to do. The threatened act must be legally or morally wrongful and must render the person incapable of exercising free will. Suppose that Joan accidentally drives into Olin's car at a stoplight. Joan has no automobile insurance, but she has substantial assets. At the scene, Olin claims to have suffered whiplash and tells Joan he will agree not to file a lawsuit against her if she pays him $5,000. Joan initially refuses, but after an argument, Olin says, "If you don't pay me $5,000 right now, I'm going to sue you for $25,000." Joan then gives Olin a check for $5,000 to avoid the lawsuit. The next day, Joan stops payment on the check. When Olin later sues to enforce their oral settlement agreement for $5,000, Joan claims duress as a defense to its enforcement. In this situation, because Olin had a right to sue Joan, threatening to sue her will not constitute duress. A court would not consider the threat of a civil suit to constitute duress.

Economic need generally is not sufficient to constitute duress, even when one party exacts a very high price for an item that the other party needs. If the party exacting the price also creates the need, however, *economic duress* may be found.

The Statute of Frauds

At early common law, parties to a contract were not allowed to testify. This led to the practice of hiring third party witnesses. As early as the seventeenth century, the English recognized the many problems presented by this practice and enacted a statute to help deal with it. The statute, passed by the English Parliament in 1677, was known as "An Act for the Prevention of Frauds and Perjuries." The act established that certain types of contracts, to be enforceable, had to be evidenced by a writing and signed by the party against whom enforcement was sought.

Modern Statutes of Frauds

Today, every state has a statute, modeled after the English act, that stipulates what types of contracts must be in writing. Although the statutes vary slightly from state to state, all states require certain types of contracts to be in writing or evidenced by a written (or electronic) memorandum signed by the party against whom enforcement is sought, unless certain exceptions apply. In this text, we refer to these statutes collectively as the **Statute of Frauds.** The actual name of the Statute of Frauds is misleading because it neither applies to fraud nor invalidates any type of contract. Rather, it denies *enforceability* to certain contracts that do not comply with its requirements. The following types of contracts are said to fall "within" or "under" the Statute of Frauds and therefore require a writing:

1. Contracts involving interests in land.
2. Contracts that cannot by their terms be performed within one year from the date of formation.
3. Collateral, or secondary, contracts, such as promises to answer for the debt or duty of another and promises by the administrator or executor of an estate to pay a debt of the estate personally—that is, out of his or her own pocket.
4. Promises made in consideration of marriage.
5. Under the UCC, contracts for the sale of goods priced at $500 or more.

Promissory Estoppel and the Statute of Frauds

In some states, an oral contract that would otherwise be unenforceable under the Statute of Frauds may be enforced under the doctrine of promissory estoppel, based on detrimental reliance. Section 139 of the *Restatement (Second) of Contracts* provides that in these circumstances, an oral promise can be enforceable notwithstanding the Statute of Frauds if the reliance was foreseeable to the person making the promise and if injustice can be avoided only by enforcing the promise.

Third Party Rights

Once it has been determined that a valid and legally enforceable contract exists, attention can turn to the rights and duties of the parties to the contract. A contract is a private agreement between the parties who have entered into it, and traditionally these parties alone have rights and liabilities under the contract. This principle is referred to as *privity of contract.* A *third party*—one who is not a direct party to a particular contract—normally does not have rights under that contract.

There are exceptions to the rule of privity of contract. One exception allows a party to a contract to transfer the rights or duties arising from the contract to another person through an *assignment* (of rights) or a *delegation* (of duties). Another exception involves a *third party beneficiary contract*—a contract in which the parties to the contract intend that the contract benefit a third party.

Assignments

In a bilateral contract, the two parties have corresponding rights and duties. One party has a *right* to require the other to perform some task, and the other has a *duty* to perform it. The transfer of contractual *rights* to a third party is known as an **assignment.** When rights under a contract are assigned unconditionally, the rights of the *assignor* (the party making the assignment) are extinguished. The third party (the *assignee,* or party receiving the assignment) has a right to demand performance from the other original party to the contract. The assignee takes only those rights that the assignor originally had.

As a general rule, all rights can be assigned. Exceptions are made, however, in some circumstances. If a statute expressly prohibits assignment of a particular right, that right cannot be assigned. When a contract is *personal* in nature, the rights under the contract cannot be assigned unless all that remains is a money payment. A right cannot be assigned if assignment will materially increase or alter the risk or duties of the obligor (the other original party owing performance under the contract).[33] If a contract stipulates that a right cannot be assigned, then *ordinarily* the right cannot be assigned.

There are several exceptions to the rule that a contract can, by its terms, prohibit any assignment of the contract. These exceptions are as follows:

1. A contract cannot prevent an assignment of the right to receive money. This exception exists to encourage the free flow of money and credit in modern business settings.
2. The assignment of rights in real estate often cannot be prohibited, because such a prohibition is contrary to public policy. Prohibitions of this kind are called restraints against *alienation* (transfer of land ownership).
3. The assignment of *negotiable instruments* (which include checks and promissory notes) cannot be prohibited.
4. In a contract for the sale of goods, the right to receive damages for breach of contract or for payment of an account owed may be assigned even though the sales contract prohibits such assignment.

Delegations

Just as a party can transfer rights through an assignment, a party can also transfer duties. The transfer of contractual *duties* to a third party is known as a **delegation.** Normally, a delegation of duties does not relieve the party making the delegation (the *delegator*) of the obligation to perform in the event that the party to whom the duty has been delegated (the *delegatee*) fails to perform. No special form is required to create a valid delegation of duties. As long as the delegator expresses an intention to make the delegation, it is effective; the delegator need not even use the word *delegate.*

As a general rule, any duty can be delegated. Delegation is prohibited, however, in the following circumstances:

1. When special trust has been placed in the obligor.
2. When performance depends on the personal skill or talents of the *obligor* (the person contractually obligated to perform).
3. When performance by a third party will vary materially from that expected by the *obligee* (the one to whom performance is owed) under the contract.
4. When the contract expressly prohibits delegation.

If a delegation of duties is enforceable, the *obligee* (the one to whom performance is owed) must accept performance from the *delegatee* (the one to whom the duties have been delegated). The obligee can legally refuse performance from the delegatee only if the duty is one that cannot be delegated.

A valid delegation of duties does not relieve the delegator of obligations under the contract. Thus, if the

33. Section 2–210(2) of the Uniform Commercial Code.

delegatee fails to perform, the delegator is still liable to the obligee.

Third Party Beneficiaries

Another exception to the doctrine of privity of contract exists when the original parties to the contract intend at the time of contracting that the contract performance directly benefit a third person. In this situation, the third person becomes a **third party beneficiary** of the contract. As an **intended beneficiary** of the contract, the third party has legal rights and can sue the promisor directly for breach of the contract.

The benefit that an **incidental beneficiary** receives from a contract between two parties is unintentional. Because the benefit is *unintentional,* an incidental beneficiary cannot sue to enforce the contract. For example, suppose that Bollow contracts with Coolidge to build a recreational facility on Coolidge's land. Once the facility is constructed, it will greatly enhance the property values in the neighborhood. If Bollow subsequently refuses to build the facility, Tran, Coolidge's neighbor, cannot enforce the contract against Bollow, because Tran is an incidental beneficiary.

REVIEWING Contract Formation

Grant Borman, who was engaged in a construction project, leased a crane from Allied Equipment and hired Crosstown Trucking Co. to deliver the crane to the construction site. Crosstown, while the crane was in its possession and without permission from either Borman or Allied Equipment, used the crane to install a transformer for a utility company, which paid Crosstown for the job. Crosstown then delivered the crane to Borman's construction site at the appointed time of delivery. When Allied Equipment learned of the unauthorized use of the crane by Crosstown, it sued Crosstown for damages, seeking to recover the rental value of Crosstown's use of the crane. Using the information presented in the chapter, answer the following questions.

1. What are the four requirements of a valid contract?
2. Did Crosstown have a valid contract with Borman concerning the use of the crane? If so, was it a bilateral or a unilateral contract? Explain.
3. What are the requirements of an implied-in-fact contract? Can Allied Equipment obtain damages from Crosstown based on an implied-in-fact contract? Explain.
4. Does the Statute of Frauds apply to this contractual situation? Why or why not?

TERMS AND CONCEPTS

acceptance 208
adhesion contract 220
agreement 199
assignment 225
consideration 212
contract 195
counteroffer 208
covenant not to compete 218
delegation 225
estop 207
exculpatory clause 221
express contract 197
implied-in-fact contract 197
incidental beneficiary 226
intended beneficiary 226
mailbox rule 210
mirror image rule 208
mutual assent 199
offer 199
past consideration 213
promise 194
promissory estoppel 207
revocation 206
Statute of Frauds 224
third party beneficiary 226
unconscionable 220
voluntary consent (genuineness of assent) 221

QUESTIONS AND CASE PROBLEMS

9–1. Suppose that Everett McCleskey, a local businessperson, is a good friend of Al Miller, the owner of a local candy store. Every day on his lunch hour, McCleskey goes into Miller's candy store and spends about five minutes looking at the candy. After examining Miller's candy and talking with Miller, McCleskey usually buys one or two candy bars. One afternoon, McCleskey goes into Miller's candy shop, looks at the candy, and picks up a $1 candy bar. Seeing that Miller is very busy, he catches Miller's eye, waves the candy bar at Miller without saying a word, and walks out. Is there a contract? If so, classify it within the categories presented in this chapter.

9–2. QUESTION WITH SAMPLE ANSWER

Janine was hospitalized with severe abdominal pain and placed in an intensive care unit. Her doctor told the hospital personnel to order around-the-clock nursing care for Janine. At the hospital's request, a nursing services firm, Nursing Services Unlimited, provided two weeks of in-hospital care and, after Janine was sent home, an additional two weeks of at-home care. During the at-home period of care, Janine was fully aware that she was receiving the benefit of the nursing services. Nursing Services later billed Janine $4,000 for the nursing care, but Janine refused to pay on the ground that she had never contracted for the services, either orally or in writing. In view of the fact that no express contract was ever formed, can Nursing Services recover the $4,000 from Janine? If so, under what legal theory? Discuss.

- **For a sample answer to Question 9–2, go to Appendix I at the end of this text.**

9–3. Ball writes Sullivan and inquires how much Sullivan is asking for a specific forty-acre tract of land Sullivan owns. In a letter received by Ball, Sullivan states, "I will not take less than $60,000 for the forty-acre tract as specified." Ball immediately sends Sullivan a telegram stating, "I accept your offer for $60,000 for the forty-acre tract as specified." Discuss whether Ball can hold Sullivan to a contract for the sale of the land.

9–4. After Kira had had several drinks one night, she sold Charlotte a diamond necklace worth thousands of dollars for just $100. The next day, Kira offered the $100 to Charlotte and requested the return of her necklace. Charlotte refused to accept the $100 or return the necklace, claiming that there was a valid contract of sale. Kira explained that she had been intoxicated at the time the bargain was made and thus the contract was voidable at her option. Was Kira correct? Explain.

9–5. Intention. Music that is distributed on compact discs and similar media generates income in the form of "mechanical" royalties. Music that is publicly performed, such as when a song is played on a radio, used in a movie or commercial, or sampled in another song, produces "performance" royalties. Each of these types of royalties is divided between the songwriter and the song's publisher. Vincent Cusano is a musician and songwriter who performed under the name "Vinnie Vincent" as a guitarist with the group KISS in the early 1980s. Cusano co-wrote three songs—entitled "Killer," "I Love It Loud," and "I Still Love You"—that KISS recorded and released in 1982 on an album titled *Creatures of the Night.* Cusano left KISS in 1984. Eight years later, Cusano sold to Horipro Entertainment Group "one hundred (100%) percent undivided interest" of his rights in the songs "other than Songwriter's share of performance income." Later, Cusano filed a suit in a federal district court against Horipro, claiming in part that he never intended to sell the writer's share of the mechanical royalties. Horipro filed a motion for summary judgment. Should the court grant the motion? Explain. [*Cusano v. Horipro Entertainment Group,* 301 F.Supp.2d 272 (S.D.N.Y. 2004)]

9–6. CASE PROBLEM WITH SAMPLE ANSWER

As a child, Martha Carr once visited her mother's 108-acre tract of unimproved land in Richland County, South Carolina. In 1968, Betty and Raymond Campbell leased the land. Carr, a resident of New York, was diagnosed as having schizophrenia and depression in 1986, was hospitalized five or six times, and subsequently took prescription drugs for the illnesses. In 1996, Carr inherited the Richland property and, two years later, contacted the Campbells about selling the land to them. Carr asked Betty about the value of the land, and Betty said that the county tax assessor had determined that the land's *agricultural value* was $54,000. The Campbells knew at the time that the county had assessed the total property value at $103,700 for tax purposes. A real estate appraiser found that the *real market value* of the property was $162,000. On August 6, Carr signed a contract to sell the land to the Campbells for $54,000. Believing the price to be unfair, however, Carr did not deliver the deed. The Campbells filed a suit in a South Carolina state court against Carr, seeking specific performance of the contract. At trial, an expert real estate appraiser testified that the real market value of the property was $162,000 at the time of the contract. Under what circumstances will a court examine the adequacy of consideration? Are those circumstances present in this case? Should the court enforce the contract between Carr and the Campbells? Explain. [*Campbell v. Carr,* 361 S.C. 258, 603 S.E.2d 625 (App. 2004)]

- **To view a sample answer for Problem 9–6, go to this book's Web site at academic.cengage.com/blaw/cross, select "Chapter 9," and click on "Case Problem with Sample Answer."**

9–7. Requirements of the Offer. The Pittsburgh Board of Public Education in Pittsburgh, Pennsylvania, as required by state law, keeps lists of eligible teachers in order of their rank or standing. According to an "Eligibility List" form made available to applicants, no one may be hired to teach whose name is not within the top 10 percent of the names on the list. In 1996, Anna Reed was in the top 10 percent. She was not hired that year, although four other applicants who placed lower on the list—and not within the top 10 percent—were hired. In 1997 and 1998, Reed was again in the top 10 percent, but she was not hired until 1999. Reed filed a suit in a federal district court against the board and others. She argued in part that the state's requirement that the board keep a list constituted an offer, which she accepted by participating in the process to be placed on that list. She claimed that the board breached this contract by hiring applicants who ranked lower than she did. The case was transferred to a Pennsylvania state court. What are the requirements of an offer? Do the circumstances in this case meet those requirements? Why or why not? [*Reed v. Pittsburgh Board of Public Education,* 862 A.2d 131 (Pa.Cmwlth. 2004)]

9–8. Agreement. In 2000, David and Sandra Harless leased 2.3 acres of real property at 2801 River Road S.E. in Winnabow, North Carolina, to their son-in-law and daughter, Tony and Jeanie Connor. The Connors planned to operate a "general store/variety store" on the premises. They agreed to lease the property for sixty months with an option to renew for an additional sixty months. The lease included an option to buy the property for "fair market value at the time of such purchase (based on at least two appraisals)." In March 2003, Tony told David that the Connors wanted to buy the property. In May, Tony gave David an appraisal that estimated the property's value at $140,000. In July, the Connors presented a second appraisal that determined the value to be $160,000. The Connors offered $150,000. The Harlesses replied that "under no circumstances would they ever agree to sell their old store building and approximately 2.5 acres to their daughter . . . and their son-in-law." The Connors filed a suit in a North Carolina state court against the Harlesses, alleging breach of contract. Did these parties have a contract to sell the property? If so, what were its terms? If not, why not? [*Connor v. Harless,* 176 N.C.App. 402, 626 S.E.2d 755 (2006)]

9–9. Offer. In August 2000, in California, Terry Reigelsperger sought treatment for pain in his lower back from chiropractor James Siller. Reigelsperger felt better after the treatment and did not intend to return for more, although he did not mention this to Siller. Before leaving the office, Reigelsperger signed an "informed consent" form that read, in part, "I intend this consent form to cover the entire course of treatment for my present condition and for any future condition(s) for which I seek treatment." He also signed an agreement that required the parties to submit to arbitration "any dispute as to medical malpractice. . . . This agreement is intended to bind the patient and the health care provider . . . who now or in the future treat[s] the patient." Two years later, Reigelsperger sought treatment from Siller for a different condition relating to his cervical spine and shoulder. Claiming malpractice with respect to the second treatment, Reigelsperger filed a suit in a California state court against Siller. Siller asked the court to order the dispute to be submitted to arbitration. Did Reigelsperger's lack of intent to return to Siller after his first treatment affect the enforceability of the arbitration agreement and consent form? Why or why not? [*Reigelsperger v. Siller,* 40 Cal.4th 574, 150 P.3d 764, 53 Cal.Rptr.3d 887 (2007)]

9–10. Fraudulent Misrepresentation. According to the student handbook at Cleveland Chiropractic College (CCC) in Missouri, *academic misconduct* includes "selling . . . any copy of any material intended to be used as an instrument of academic evaluation in advance of its initial administration." Leonard Verni was enrolled at CCC in Dr. Aleksandr Makarov's dermatology class. Before the first examination, Verni was reported to be selling copies of the test. CCC investigated and concluded that Verni had committed academic misconduct. He was dismissed from CCC, which informed him of his right to an appeal. According to the handbook, at the hearing on appeal a student could have an attorney or other adviser, present witnesses' testimony and other evidence, and "question any testimony . . . against him/her." At his hearing, however, Verni did not bring his attorney, present evidence on his behalf, or question any adverse witnesses. When the dismissal was upheld, Verni filed a suit in a Missouri state court against CCC and others, claiming, in part, fraudulent misrepresentation. Verni argued that because he "relied" on the handbook's "representation" that CCC would follow its appeal procedure, he was unable to properly refute the charges against him. Can Verni succeed with this argument? Explain. [*Verni v. Cleveland Chiropractic College,* 212 S.W.3d 150 (Mo. 2007)]

9–11. A QUESTION OF ETHICS

Dow AgroSciences, LLC (DAS), makes and sells agricultural seed products. In 2000, Timothy Glenn, a DAS sales manager, signed a covenant not to compete. He agreed that for two years from the date of his termination, he would not "engage in or contribute my knowledge to any work or activity involving an area of technology or business that is then competitive with a technology or business with respect to which I had access to Confidential Information during the five years immediately prior to such termination." Working with DAS business, operations, and research and development personnel, and being a member of high-level teams, Glenn had access to confidential DAS information, including agreements with DAS's business partners, marketing plans, litigation details, product secrets, new product development, future plans, and pricing strategies. In 2006, Glenn *resigned to work for Pioneer Hi-Bred International, Inc., a DAS competitor. DAS filed a suit in an Indiana state court against Glenn, asking that he be enjoined from accepting any "position that would call on him to use confidential DAS information." [*Glenn v. Dow AgroSciences, LLC*, 861 N.E.2d 1 (Ind.App. 2007)]*

(a) Generally, what interests are served by enforcing covenants not to compete? What interests are served by refusing to enforce them?
(b) What argument could be made in support of reforming (and then enforcing) illegal covenants not to compete? What argument could be made against this practice?
(c) How should the court rule in this case? Why?

9-12. VIDEO QUESTION

Go to this text's Web site at **academic.cengage.com/blaw/cross** and select "Chapter 9." Click on "Video Questions" and view the video titled *Mistake*. Then answer the following questions.

(a) What kind of mistake is involved in the dispute shown in the video (mutual or unilateral, mistake of fact or mistake of value)?
(b) According to the chapter, in what two situations would the supermarket be able to rescind a contract to sell peppers to Melnick at the incorrectly advertised price?
(c) Does it matter if the price that was advertised was a reasonable price for the peppers? Why or why not?

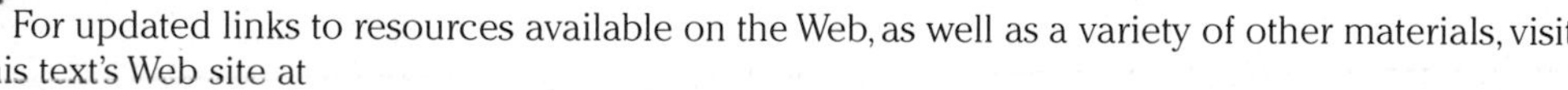

LAW ON THE WEB

For updated links to resources available on the Web, as well as a variety of other materials, visit this text's Web site at

academic.cengage.com/blaw/cross

The 'Lectric Law Library provides information on contract law, including a definition of a contract, the elements required for a contract, and so on. Go to

www.lectlaw.com/lay.html

A good way to learn more about how the courts decide such issues as whether consideration was lacking for a particular contract is to look at relevant case law. To find recent cases on contract law decided by the United States Supreme Court and the federal appellate courts, access Cornell University's School of Law site at

www.law.cornell.edu/topics/contracts.html

The *New Hampshire Consumer's Sourcebook* provides information on contract law, including consideration, from a consumer's perspective. You can access this site at

www.doj.nh.gov/consumer/sourcebook

Legal Research Exercises on the Web

Go to **academic.cengage.com/blaw/cross**, the Web site that accompanies this text. Select "Chapter 9" and click on "Internet Exercises." There you will find the following Internet research exercises that you can perform to learn more about the topics covered in this chapter.

Internet Exercise 9–1: Historical Perspective
Contracts in Ancient Mesopotamia

Internet Exercise 9–2: Ethical Perspective
Offers and Advertisements

Internet Exercise 9–3: Social Perspective
Online Gambling

CHAPTER 10

Contract Performance, Breach, and Remedies

Just as rules are necessary to determine when a legally enforceable contract exists, so also are they required to determine when one of the parties can justifiably say, "I have fully performed, so I am now discharged from my obligations under this contract." The legal environment of business requires the identification of some point at which the parties can reasonably know that their duties are at an end. Additionally, the parties to a contract need to know what remedies are available to them if the contract is breached.

Performance and Discharge

The most common way to **discharge,** or terminate, one's contractual duties is by the **performance** of those duties. For example, a buyer and seller have a contract for the sale of a 2009 Lexus for $39,000. This contract will be discharged on the performance by the parties of their obligations under the contract—the buyer's payment of $39,000 to the seller and the seller's transfer of possession of the Lexus to the buyer.

The duty to perform under a contract may be *conditioned* on the occurrence or nonoccurrence of a certain event, or the duty may be *absolute*. In the first part of this section, we look at conditions of performance and the degree of performance required. We then examine some other ways in which a contract can be discharged, including discharge by agreement of the parties and discharge by operation of law.

Conditions

In most contracts, promises of performance are not expressly conditioned or qualified. Instead, they are *absolute promises.* They must be performed, or the parties promising the acts will be in breach of contract. For example, Jerome contracts to sell Alfonso a painting for $10,000. The parties' promises—Jerome's transfer of the painting to Alfonso and Alfonso's payment of $10,000 to Jerome—are unconditional. The payment does not have to be made if the painting is not transferred.

In some situations, however, performance is contingent on the occurrence or nonoccurrence of a certain event. A **condition** is a possible future event, the occurrence or nonoccurrence of which will trigger the performance of a legal obligation or terminate an existing obligation under a contract.[1] If this condition is not satisfied, the obligations of the parties are discharged. Suppose that Alfonso, in the previous example, offers to purchase Jerome's painting only if an independent appraisal indicates that it is worth at least $10,000. Jerome accepts Alfonso's offer. Their obligations (promises) are conditioned on the outcome of the appraisal. Should the condition not be satisfied (for example, if the appraiser deems the value of the painting to be only $5,000), the parties' obligations to each other are discharged and cannot be enforced.

Discharge by Performance

The great majority of contracts are discharged by performance. The contract comes to an end when both parties fulfill their respective duties by performing the acts they have promised. Performance can also be

1. The *Restatement (Second) of Contracts,* Section 224, defines a *condition* as "an event, not certain to occur, which must occur, unless its nonoccurrence is excused, before performance under a contract becomes due."

accomplished by *tender*. **Tender** is an unconditional offer to perform by a person who is ready, willing, and able to do so. Therefore, a seller who places goods at the disposal of a buyer has tendered delivery and can demand payment. A buyer who offers to pay for goods has tendered payment and can demand delivery of the goods. Once performance has been tendered, the party making the tender has done everything possible to carry out the terms of the contract. If the other party then refuses to perform, the party making the tender can sue for breach of contract.

There are two basic types of performance—*complete performance* and *substantial performance*. A contract may stipulate that performance must meet the personal satisfaction of either the contracting party or a third party. Such a provision must be considered in determining whether the performance rendered satisfies the contract.

Complete Performance When a party performs exactly as agreed, there is no question as to whether the contract has been performed. When a party's performance is perfect, it is said to be complete.

Normally, conditions expressly stated in a contract must be fully satisfied for complete performance to take place. For example, most construction contracts require the builder to meet certain specifications. If the specifications are conditions, complete performance is required to avoid material breach (*material breach* will be discussed shortly). If the conditions are met, the other party to the contract must then fulfill her or his obligation to pay the builder. If the specifications are not conditions and if the builder, without the other party's permission, fails to comply with the specifications, performance is not complete. What effect does such a failure have on the other party's obligation to pay? The answer is part of the doctrine of *substantial performance*.

Substantial Performance A party who in good faith performs substantially all of the terms of a contract can enforce the contract against the other party under the doctrine of substantial performance. Note that good faith is required. Intentionally failing to comply with the terms is a breach of the contract.

Confers Most Benefits Promised in the Contract. Generally, to qualify as substantial, the performance must not vary greatly from the performance promised in the contract, and it must create substantially the same benefits as those promised in the contract. If the omission, variance, or defect in performance is unimportant and can easily be compensated for by awarding damages, a court is likely to hold that the contract has been substantially performed.

Courts decide whether the performance was substantial on a case-by-case basis, examining all of the facts of the particular situation. For example, in a construction contract, a court would look at the intended purpose of the structure and the expense required to bring the structure into complete compliance with the contract. Thus, the exact point at which performance is considered substantial varies.

Entitles Other Party to Damages. Because substantial performance is not perfect, the other party is entitled to damages to compensate for the failure to comply with the contract. The measure of the damages is the cost to bring the object of the contract into compliance with its terms, if that cost is reasonable under the circumstances. If the cost is unreasonable, the measure of damages is the difference in value between the performance that was rendered and the performance that would have been rendered if the contract had been performed completely. The following classic case emphasizes that there is no exact formula for deciding when a contract has been substantially performed.

EXTENDED CASE 10.1 Jacob & Youngs v. Kent

Court of Appeals of New York, 1921. 230 N.Y. 239, 129 N.E. 889.

CARDOZO, J. **[Judge]**

The plaintiff built a country residence for the defendant at a cost of upwards of $77,000, and now sues to recover a balance of $3,483.46, remaining unpaid. The work of construction ceased in June, 1914, and the defendant then began to occupy the dwelling. There was no complaint of defective performance until March, 1915. One of the specifications for the plumbing work provides that—

> All wrought-iron pipe must be well galvanized, lap welded pipe of the grade known as "standard pipe" of Reading manufacture.

CASE CONTINUES

CASE 10.1 CONTINUED

The defendant learned in March, 1915, that some of the pipe, instead of being made in Reading, was the product of other factories. The plaintiff was accordingly directed by the architect to do the work anew. The plumbing was then encased within the walls except in a few places where it had to be exposed. Obedience to the order meant more than the substitution of other pipe. It meant the demolition at great expense of substantial parts of the completed structure. The plaintiff left the work untouched, and asked for a certificate that the final payment was due. Refusal of the certificate was followed by this suit [in a New York state court].

The evidence sustains a finding that the omission of the prescribed brand of pipe was neither fraudulent nor willful. It was the result of the oversight and inattention of the plaintiff's subcontractor. Reading pipe is distinguished from Cohoes pipe and other brands only by the name of the manufacturer stamped upon it at intervals of between six and seven feet. Even the defendant's architect, though he inspected the pipe upon arrival, failed to notice the discrepancy. The plaintiff tried to show that the brands installed, though made by other manufacturers, were the same in quality, in appearance, in market value, and in cost as the brand stated in the contract—that they were, indeed, the same thing, though manufactured in another place. The evidence was excluded, and a verdict directed for the defendant. The [state intermediate appellate court] reversed, and granted a new trial.

We think the evidence, if admitted, would have supplied some basis for the inference that the defect was insignificant in its relation to the project. The courts never say that one who makes a contract fills the measure of his duty by less than full performance. They do say, however, that *an omission, both trivial and innocent, will sometimes be atoned for by allowance of the resulting damage, and will not always be the breach of a condition* * * * . [Emphasis added.]

* * * Where the line is to be drawn between the important and the trivial cannot be settled by a formula. In the nature of the case precise boundaries are impossible. The same omission may take on one aspect or another according to its setting. Substitution of equivalents may not have the same significance in fields of art on the one side and in those of mere utility on the other. Nowhere will change be tolerated, however, if it is so dominant or pervasive as in any real or substantial measure to frustrate the purpose of the contract. There is no general license to install whatever, in the builder's judgment, may be regarded as "just as good." The question is one of degree, to be answered, if there is doubt, by the triers of the facts, and, if the inferences are certain, by the judges of the law. *We must weigh the purpose to be served, the desire to be gratified, the excuse for deviation from the letter, the cruelty of enforced adherence. Then only can we tell whether literal fulfillment is to be implied by law as a condition.* [Emphasis added.]

In the circumstances of this case, we think the measure of the allowance is not the cost of replacement, which would be great, but the difference in value, which would be either nominal or nothing. Some of the exposed sections might perhaps have been replaced at moderate expense. The defendant did not limit his demand to them, but treated the plumbing as a unit to be corrected from cellar to roof. In point of fact, the plaintiff never reached the stage at which evidence of the extent of the allowance became necessary. The trial court had excluded evidence that the defect was unsubstantial, and in view of that ruling there was no occasion for the plaintiff to go farther with an offer of proof. We think, however, that the offer, if it had been made, would not of necessity have been defective because directed to difference in value. It is true that in most cases the cost of replacement is the measure. The owner is entitled to the money which will permit him to complete, unless the cost of completion is grossly and unfairly out of proportion to the good to be attained. When that is true, the measure is the difference in value. * * * The rule that gives a remedy in cases of substantial performance with compensation for defects of trivial or inappreciable importance has been developed by the courts as an instrument of justice. The measure of the allowance must be shaped to the same end.

The order should be affirmed, and judgment absolute directed in favor of the plaintiff upon the stipulation, with costs in all courts.

QUESTIONS

1. The New York Court of Appeals found that Jacob & Youngs had substantially performed the contract. To what, if any, remedy is Kent entitled?

CASE 10.1 CONTINUED

2. A requirement of substantial performance is good faith. Do you think that Jacob & Youngs substantially performed all of the terms of the contract in good faith? Why or why not?

• **Impact of This Case on Today's Law** *At the time of the* Jacob & Youngs *case, some courts did not apply the doctrine of substantial performance to disputes involving breaches of contract. This landmark decision contributed to a developing trend toward equity and fairness in those circumstances. Today, an unintentional and trivial omission or deviation from the terms of a contract will not prevent its enforcement but will permit an adjustment in the value of its performance.*

Performance to the Satisfaction of Another Contracts often state that completed work must personally satisfy one of the parties or a third person. The question then is whether this satisfaction becomes a condition precedent, requiring actual personal satisfaction or approval for discharge, or whether the test of satisfaction is an absolute promise requiring such performance as would satisfy a *reasonable person* (substantial performance).

When the subject matter of the contract is *personal*, a contract to be performed to the satisfaction of one of the parties is conditioned, and performance must actually satisfy that party. For example, contracts for portraits, works of art, and tailoring are considered personal. Therefore, only the personal satisfaction of the party fulfills the condition—unless a court finds the party is expressing dissatisfaction only to avoid payment or otherwise is not acting in good faith.

Most other contracts need to be performed only to the satisfaction of a reasonable person unless they *expressly state otherwise*. When such contracts require performance to the satisfaction of a third party (for example, "to the satisfaction of Robert Ames, the supervising engineer"), the courts are divided. A majority of courts require the work to be satisfactory to a reasonable person, but some courts hold that the personal satisfaction of the third party designated in the contract (Robert Ames, in this example) must be met. Again, the personal judgment must be made honestly, or the condition will be excused.

Material Breach of Contract

A **breach of contract** is the nonperformance of a contractual duty. The breach is *material* when performance is not at least substantial.[2] If there is a material breach, then the nonbreaching party is excused from the performance of contractual duties and can sue for damages resulting from the breach. If the breach is *minor* (not material), the nonbreaching party's duty to perform can sometimes be suspended until the breach has been remedied, but the duty to perform is not entirely excused. Once the minor breach has been cured, the nonbreaching party must resume performance of the contractual obligations undertaken.

Any breach entitles the nonbreaching party to sue for damages, but only a material breach discharges the nonbreaching party from the contract. The policy underlying these rules allows contracts to go forward when only minor problems occur but allows them to be terminated if major difficulties arise.

Anticipatory Repudiation

Before either party to a contract has a duty to perform, one of the parties may refuse to carry out his or her contractual obligations. This is called **anticipatory repudiation**[3] of the contract. When anticipatory repudiation occurs, it is treated as a material breach of contract, and the nonbreaching party is permitted to bring an action for damages immediately, even though the scheduled time for performance under the contract may still be in the future. Until the nonbreaching party treats an early repudiation as a breach, however, the repudiating party can retract her or his anticipatory repudiation by proper notice and restore the parties to their original obligations.[4]

An anticipatory repudiation is treated as a present, material breach for two reasons. First, the nonbreaching party should not be required to remain ready and willing to perform when the other party has already repudiated the contract. Second, the nonbreaching party should have the opportunity to seek a similar

2. *Restatement (Second) of Contracts*, Section 241.

3. *Restatement (Second) of Contracts*, Section 253; Section 2–610 of the Uniform Commercial Code (UCC).

4. See UCC 2–611.

contract elsewhere and may have a duty to do so to minimize his or her loss.[5]

Time for Performance If no time for performance is stated in the contract, a *reasonable time* is implied.[6] If a specific time is stated, the parties must usually perform by that time. Unless time is expressly stated to be vital, however, a delay in performance will not destroy the performing party's right to payment.[7] When time is expressly stated to be "of the essence" or vital, the parties normally must perform within the stated time period because the time element becomes a condition.

Discharge by Agreement

Any contract can be discharged by agreement of the parties. The agreement can be contained in the original contract, or the parties can form a new contract for the express purpose of discharging the original contract.

Discharge by Rescission As mentioned in previous chapters, *rescission* is the process by which a contract is canceled or terminated and the parties are returned to the positions they occupied prior to forming it. For **mutual rescission** to take place, the parties must make another agreement that also satisfies the legal requirements for a contract. There must be an *offer,* an *acceptance,* and *consideration.* Ordinarily, if the parties agree to rescind the original contract, their promises not to perform the acts stipulated in the original contract will be legal consideration for the second contract (the rescission).

Agreements to rescind executory contracts (in which neither party has performed) are generally enforceable, even if the agreement is made orally and even if the original agreement was in writing. An exception applies under the Uniform Commercial Code (UCC) to agreements rescinding a contract for the sale of goods, regardless of price, when the contract requires a written rescission. Also, agreements to rescind contracts involving transfers of realty must be evidenced by a writing.

5. The doctrine of anticipatory repudiation first arose in the landmark case of *Hochster v. De La Tour,* 2 Ellis and Blackburn Reports 678 (1853), when an English court recognized the delay and expense inherent in a rule requiring a nonbreaching party to wait until the time of performance before suing on an anticipatory repudiation.

6. See UCC 2–204.

7. See, for example, *Manganaro Corp. v. Hitt Contracting, Inc.,* 193 F.Supp.2d 88 (D.D.C. 2002).

When one party has fully performed, an agreement to cancel the original contract normally will not be enforceable. Because the performing party has received no consideration for the promise to call off the original bargain, additional consideration is necessary.

Discharge by Novation A contractual obligation may also be discharged through novation. A **novation** occurs when both of the parties to a contract agree to substitute a third party for one of the original parties. The requirements of a novation are as follows:

1. A previous valid obligation.
2. An agreement by all the parties to a new contract.
3. The extinguishing of the old obligation (discharge of the prior party).
4. A new contract that is valid.

For example, suppose that Union Corporation contracts to sell its pharmaceutical division to British Pharmaceuticals, Ltd. Before the transfer is completed, Union, British Pharmaceuticals, and a third company, Otis Chemicals, execute a new agreement to transfer all of British Pharmaceuticals' rights and duties in the transaction to Otis Chemicals. As long as the new contract is supported by consideration, the novation will discharge the original contract (between Union and British Pharmaceuticals) and replace it with the new contract (between Union and Otis Chemicals).

A novation expressly or impliedly revokes and discharges a prior contract. The parties involved may expressly state in the new contract that the old contract is now discharged. If the parties do not expressly discharge the old contract, it will be impliedly discharged if the new contract's terms are inconsistent with the old contract's terms.

Discharge by Substituted Agreement A *compromise,* or settlement agreement, that arises out of a genuine dispute over the obligations under an existing contract will be recognized at law. Such an agreement will be substituted as a new contract, and it will either expressly or impliedly revoke and discharge the obligations under any prior contract. In contrast to a novation, a substituted agreement does not involve a third party. Rather, the two original parties to the contract form a different agreement to substitute for the original one.

Discharge by Accord and Satisfaction For a contract to be discharged by accord and satisfaction, the parties must agree to accept performance that is different from the performance originally promised. An *accord* is a contract to perform some act to satisfy an existing contractual duty. The duty has not yet been discharged. A *satisfaction* is the performance of the accord agreement. An accord and its satisfaction discharge the original contractual obligation.

Once the accord has been made, the original obligation is merely suspended. The obligor (the one owing the obligation) can discharge the obligation by performing either the obligation agreed to in the accord or the original obligation. If the obligor refuses to perform the accord, the obligee (the one to whom performance is owed) can bring action on the original obligation or seek a decree compelling specific performance on the accord.

Suppose that Frazer has a judgment against Ling for $8,000. Later, both parties agree that the judgment can be satisfied by Ling's transfer of his automobile to Frazer. This agreement to accept the auto in lieu of $8,000 in cash is the accord. If Ling transfers the car to Frazer, the accord is fully performed, and the debt is discharged. If Ling refuses to transfer the car, the accord is breached. Because the original obligation is merely suspended, Frazer can sue Ling to enforce the original judgment for $8,000 in cash or bring an action for breach of the accord.

Discharge by Operation of Law

Under certain circumstances, contractual duties may be discharged by operation of law. These circumstances include material alteration of the contract, the running of the statute of limitations, bankruptcy, and the impossibility or impracticability of performance.

Alteration of the Contract To discourage parties from altering written contracts, the law operates to allow an innocent party to be discharged when the other party has materially altered a written contract without consent. For example, contract terms such as quantity or price might be changed without the knowledge or consent of all parties. If so, the party who was not involved in the alteration can treat the contract as discharged or terminated.[8]

8. The contract is voidable, and the innocent party can also treat the contract as in effect, either on the original terms or on the terms as altered. For example, a buyer who discovers that a seller altered the quantity of goods in a sales contract from 100 to 1,000 by secretly inserting a zero can purchase either 100 or 1,000 of the items.

Statutes of Limitations As mentioned earlier in this text, statutes of limitations restrict the period during which a party can sue on a particular cause of action. After the applicable limitations period has passed, a suit can no longer be brought. For example, the limitations period for bringing suits for breach of oral contracts is usually two to three years; for written contracts, four to five years; and for recovery of amounts awarded in judgments, ten to twenty years, depending on state law. Lawsuits for breach of a contract for the sale of goods generally must be brought within four years after the breach occurs. By their original agreement, the parties can reduce this four-year period to not less than one year, but they cannot agree to extend it.

Bankruptcy A proceeding in bankruptcy attempts to allocate the assets the debtor owns to the creditors in a fair and equitable fashion. Once the assets have been allocated, the debtor receives a *discharge in bankruptcy.* A discharge in bankruptcy will ordinarily bar enforcement of most of the debtor's contracts by the creditors. Partial payment of a debt after discharge in bankruptcy will not revive the debt. (Bankruptcy will be discussed in detail in Chapter 15.)

Impossibility or Impracticability of Performance

After a contract has been made, supervening events (such as a fire) may make performance impossible in an objective sense. This is known as **impossibility of performance** and can discharge a contract.[9] Performance may also become so difficult or costly due to some unforeseen event that a court will consider it commercially unfeasible, or impracticable.

Objective Impossibility of Performance *Objective impossibility* ("It can't be done") must be distinguished from *subjective impossibility* ("I'm sorry, I simply can't do it"). For example, subjective impossibility occurs when a party cannot deliver goods on time because of freight car shortages or cannot make payment on time because the bank is closed. In effect, in each of these situations the party is saying, "It is impossible for *me* to perform," not "It is impossible for *anyone* to perform." Accordingly, such excuses do not discharge a contract, and the nonperforming party is normally held in breach of contract.

9. *Restatement (Second) of Contracts,* Section 261.

Note that to justify not performing the contract, the supervening event must have been unforeseeable at the time of the contract. Parties are supposed to consider foreseeable events, such as floods in a flood zone, at the time of contracting and allocate those risks accordingly through insurance and other means. Three basic types of situations, however, may qualify as grounds for the discharge of contractual obligations based on impossibility of performance:[10]

1. *When one of the parties to a personal contract dies or becomes incapacitated prior to performance.* For example, Fred, a famous dancer, contracts with Ethereal Dancing Guild to play a leading role in its new ballet. Before the ballet can be performed, Fred becomes ill and dies. His personal performance was essential to the completion of the contract. Thus, his death discharges the contract and his estate's liability for his nonperformance.
2. *When the specific subject matter of the contract is destroyed.* For example, A-1 Farm Equipment agrees to sell Gudgel the green tractor on its lot and promises to have it ready for Gudgel to pick up on Saturday. On Friday night, however, a truck veers off the nearby highway and smashes into the tractor, destroying it beyond repair. Because the contract was for this specific tractor, A-1's performance is rendered impossible owing to the accident.
3. *When a change in law renders performance illegal.* For example, a contract to build an apartment building becomes impossible to perform when the zoning laws are changed to prohibit the construction of residential rental property at the planned location. A contract to paint a bridge using lead paint becomes impossible when the government passes new regulations forbidding the use of lead paint on bridges.[11]

Temporary Impossibility An occurrence or event that makes performance temporarily impossible operates to suspend performance until the impossibility ceases. Then, ordinarily, the parties must perform the contract as originally planned. If, however, the lapse of time and the change in circumstances surrounding the contract make it substantially more burdensome for the parties to perform the promised acts, the contract is discharged.

The leading case on the subject, *Autry v. Republic Productions,*[12] involved an actor (Gene Autry) who was drafted into the army in 1942. Being drafted rendered the actor's contract temporarily impossible to perform, and it was suspended until the end of the war. When the actor got out of the army, the purchasing power of the dollar had so diminished that performance of the contract would have been substantially burdensome to him. Therefore, the contract was discharged.

A more recent example involves a contract entered into shortly before Hurricane Katrina hit Louisiana. On August 22, 2005, Keefe Hurwitz contracted to sell his home in Madisonville, Louisiana, to Wesley and Gwendolyn Payne for a price of $241,500. On August 26—just four days after the parties signed the contract—Hurricane Katrina made landfall and caused extensive property damage to the house. The cost of repairs was estimated at $60,000 and Hurwitz would have to make the repairs before the *closing date* (see Chapter 25). Hurwitz did not have the funds and refused to pay $60,000 for the repairs only to sell the property to the Paynes for the previously agreed-on price of $241,500. The Paynes filed a lawsuit to enforce the contract. Hurwitz claimed that Hurricane Katrina had made it impossible for him to perform and had discharged his duties under the contract. The court, however, ruled that Hurricane Katrina had only caused a temporary impossibility. Hurwitz was required to pay for the necessary repairs and to perform the contract as written. In other words, he could not obtain a higher purchase price to offset the cost of the repairs.[13]

Commercial Impracticability When a supervening event does not render performance objectively impossible, but does make it much more difficult or expensive to perform, the courts may excuse the parties' obligations under the contract. For someone to invoke the doctrine of **commercial impracticability** successfully, however, the anticipated performance must become significantly more difficult or costly than originally contemplated at the time the contract was formed.[14]

The added burden of performing not only must be extreme but also *must not have been known by the parties when the contract was made.* In one case, for example, the court allowed a party to rescind a con-

10. *Restatement (Second) of Contracts,* Sections 262–266; UCC 2–615.
11. *M. J. Paquet, Inc. v. New Jersey Department of Transportation,* 171 N.J. 378, 794 A.2d 141 (2002).
12. 30 Cal.2d 144, 180 P.2d 888 (1947).
13. *Payne v. Hurwitz,* ___ So.2d ___ (La.App. 2008).
14. *Restatement (Second) of Contracts,* Section 264.

tract for the sale of land because of a potential problem with contaminated groundwater under the land. The court found that "the potential for substantial and unbargained-for" liability made contract performance economically impracticable. Interestingly, the court in that case also noted that the possibility of "environmental degradation with consequences extending well beyond the parties' land sale" was just as important to its decision as the economic considerations.[15]

The contract dispute in the following case arose out of the cancellation of a wedding reception due to a power failure. Is a power failure sufficient to invoke the doctrine of commercial impracticability?

15. *Cape-France Enterprises v. Estate of Peed*, 305 Mont. 513, 29 P.3d 1011 (2001).

CASE 10.2 Facto v. Pantagis

Superior Court of New Jersey, Appellate Division, 2007. 390 N.J.Super. 227, 915 A.2d 59.
lawlibrary.rutgers.edu/search.shtml[a]

• **Background and Facts** Leo and Elizabeth Facto contracted with Snuffy Pantagis Enterprises, Inc., for the use of Pantagis Renaissance, a banquet hall in Scotch Plains, New Jersey, for a wedding reception in August 2002. The Factos paid the $10,578 price in advance. The contract excused Pantagis from performance "if it is prevented from doing so by an act of God (for example, flood, power failure, etc.), or other unforeseen events or circumstances." Soon after the reception began, there was a power failure. The lights and the air-conditioning shut off. The band hired for the reception refused to play without electricity to power their instruments, and the lack of lighting prevented the photographer and videographer from taking pictures. The temperature was in the 90s, the humidity was high, and the guests quickly became uncomfortable. Three hours later, after a fight between a guest and a Pantagis employee, the emergency lights began to fade, and the police evacuated the hall. The Factos filed a suit in a New Jersey state court against Pantagis, alleging breach of contract, among other things. The Factos sought to recover their prepayment, plus amounts paid to the band, the photographer, and the videographer. The court concluded that Pantagis did not breach the contract and dismissed the complaint. The Factos appealed to a state intermediate appellate court.

IN THE LANGUAGE OF THE COURT
***SKILLMAN*, P. J.A.D. [Presiding Judge, Appellate Division]**

* * * *

Even if a contract does not expressly provide that a party will be relieved of the duty to perform if an unforeseen condition arises that makes performance impracticable, a court may relieve him of that duty if performance has unexpectedly become impracticable as a result of a supervening event. *In deciding whether a party should be relieved of the duty to perform a contract, a court must determine whether the existence of a specific thing is necessary for the performance of a duty and its * * * destruction or * * * deterioration * * * makes performance impracticable.* * * * A power failure is the kind of unexpected occurrence that may relieve a party of the duty to perform if the availability of electricity is essential for satisfactory performance. [Emphasis added.]

* * * *

The * * * Pantagis Renaissance contract provided: "Snuffy's will be excused from performance under this contract if it is prevented from doing so by an act of God (e.g., flood, power failure, etc.), or other unforeseen events or circumstances." Thus, the contract specifically identified a "power failure" as one of the circumstances that would excuse the Pantagis Renaissance's performance. We do not attribute any significance to the fact the * * * clause refers to a power failure as an example of an "act of God." *This term has been construed to refer not just to natural events such as storms but to comprehend all misfortunes and accidents arising from inevitable necessity which human prudence could not foresee or prevent.* Furthermore, the * * * clause in the

a. In the "Search by party name" section, select the "Appellate Division," type "Pantagis" in the "First Name:" box, and click on "Submit Form." In the result, click on the "click here to get this case" link to access the opinion. The Rutgers University School of Law in Camden, New Jersey, maintains this Web site.

CASE CONTINUES

CASE 10.2 CONTINUED Pantagis Renaissance contract excuses performance not only for "acts of God" but also "other unforeseen events or circumstances." Consequently, even if a power failure caused by circumstances other than a natural event were not considered to be an "act of God," it still would constitute an unforeseen event or circumstance that would excuse performance. [Emphasis added.]

The fact that a power failure is not absolutely unforeseeable during the hot summer months does not preclude relief from the obligation to perform. * * * *Absolute unforeseeability of a condition is not a prerequisite to the defense of impracticability.* The party seeking to be relieved of the duty to perform only needs to show that the destruction, or * * * deterioration of a specific thing necessary for the performance of the contract makes performance impracticable. In this case, the Pantagis Renaissance sought to eliminate any possible doubt that the availability of electricity was a specific thing necessary for the wedding reception by specifically referring to a "power failure" as an example of an "act of God" that would excuse performance. [Emphasis added.]

It is also clear that the Pantagis Renaissance was "prevented from" substantial performance of the contract. The power failure began less than forty-five minutes after the start of the reception and continued until after it was scheduled to end. The lack of electricity prevented the band from playing, impeded the taking of pictures by the photographer and videographer and made it difficult for guests to see inside the banquet hall. Most significantly, the shutdown of the air conditioning system made it unbearably hot shortly after the power failure began. It is also undisputed that the power failure was an area-wide event that was beyond the Pantagis Renaissance's control. These are precisely the kind of circumstances under which the parties agreed * * * [in their contract] that the Pantagis Renaissance would be excused from performance.

* * * Where one party to a contract is excused from performance as a result of an unforeseen event that makes performance impracticable, the other party is also generally excused from performance.

* * * Therefore, the power failure that relieved the Pantagis Renaissance of the obligation to furnish plaintiffs with a wedding reception also relieved plaintiffs of the obligation to pay the contract price for the reception.

Nevertheless, since the Pantagis Renaissance partially performed the contract by starting the reception before the power failure, it is entitled * * * to recover the value of the services it provided to plaintiffs.

• **Decision and Remedy** *The state intermediate appellate court agreed that the power failure relieved Pantagis of its contractual obligation, but held that Pantagis's inability to perform also relieved the Factos of their obligation. The court reversed the dismissal and remanded the case for an award to the Factos of the amount of their prepayment less the value of the services they received.*

• **The Ethical Dimension** *Should Pantagis have offered to reschedule the reception? Would this have absolved Pantagis of the obligation to refund the Factos' prepayment? Explain.*

• **The Legal Environment Dimension** *Does a power failure always constitute the kind of unexpected occurrence that relieves a party of the duty to perform a contract? In what circumstances might a power failure have no effect on a contract? (Hint: Is electricity always necessary for the performance of a contract?)*

Frustration of Purpose A theory closely allied with the doctrine of commercial impracticability is the doctrine of **frustration of purpose.** In principle, a contract will be discharged if supervening circumstances make it impossible to attain the purpose both parties had in mind when making the contract. As with commercial impracticability and impossibility, the supervening event must not have been reasonably foreseeable at the time of the contracting. In contrast to impracticability, which usually involves an event that increases the cost or difficulty of performance, frustration of purpose typically involves an event that decreases the value of what a party receives under the contract.

Because many problems are foreseeable by contracting parties and value is subjective, courts rarely excuse contract performance on this basis. For example, in one case, New Beginnings was searching for a new location for its drug rehabilitation center. After receiving preliminary approval for the use of a particular building from the city zoning official, New Beginnings signed a three-year lease on the property. Then opposition from the community developed, and the city denied New Beginnings a permit to use the property for a rehab center. New Beginnings appealed the decision and eventually received a permit from the city, but by then the state was threatening to rescind all state contracts with New Beginnings if it moved into that location. Because New Beginnings would lose its funding if it actually moved onto the property, the value of the leased building was practically worthless. Nevertheless, the court refused to excuse New Beginnings from the lease contract on the ground of frustration of purpose because the situation was reasonably foreseeable.[16]

See Exhibit 10–1 for an illustration of the ways in which a contract may be discharged.

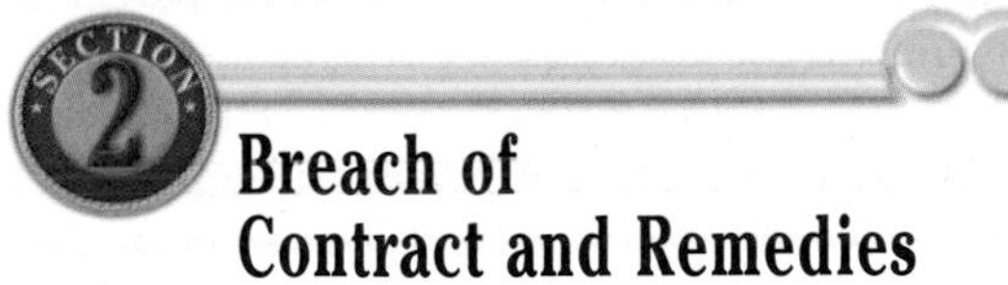

Breach of Contract and Remedies

When one party breaches a contract, the other party—the nonbreaching party—can choose one or more of several remedies. A *remedy* is the relief provided for an innocent party when the other party has breached the contract. It is the means employed to enforce a right or to redress an injury.

The most common remedies available to a nonbreaching party include damages, rescission and restitution, specific performance, and reformation. As discussed in Chapter 1, a distinction is made between *remedies at law* and *remedies in equity*. Today, the remedy at law is normally monetary damages, which are discussed in the first part of this section. Equitable remedies include rescission and restitution, specific performance, and reformation, all of which will be examined later in this section. Usually, a court will not award an equitable remedy unless the remedy at law is inadequate. Special legal doctrines and concepts relating to remedies will be discussed in the final pages of this chapter.

Damages

A breach of contract entitles the nonbreaching party to sue for monetary damages. Damages are designed to compensate a party for harm suffered as a result of another's wrongful act. In the context of contract law, damages compensate the nonbreaching party for the loss of the bargain. Often, courts say that innocent parties are to be placed in the position they would have occupied had the contract been fully performed.[17]

16. *Adbar, L.C. v. New Beginnings C-Star*, 103 S.W.3d 799 (Mo.App. 2003).

17. *Restatement (Second) of Contracts*, Section 347; Section 1–106(1) of the Uniform Commercial Code (UCC).

EXHIBIT 10–1 • Contract Discharge

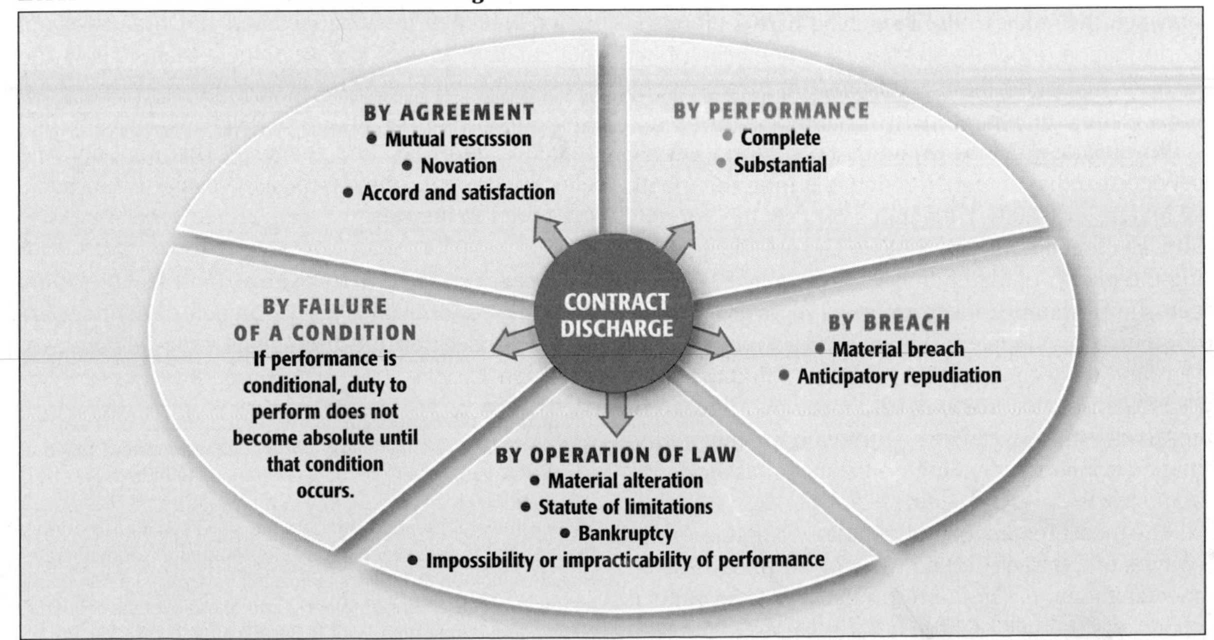

Realize at the outset, though, that to collect damages through a court judgment means litigation, which can be expensive and time consuming. Also keep in mind that court judgments are often difficult to enforce, particularly if the breaching party does not have sufficient assets to pay the damages awarded (as discussed in Chapter 2). For these reasons, the majority of actions for damages (or other remedies) are settled by the parties before trial.

Types of Damages There are basically four broad categories of damages:

1. Compensatory (to cover direct losses and costs).
2. Consequential (to cover indirect and foreseeable losses).
3. Punitive (to punish and deter wrongdoing).
4. Nominal (to recognize wrongdoing when no monetary loss is shown).

We look here at compensatory and consequential damages.

Compensatory Damages Damages compensating the nonbreaching party for the *loss of the bargain* are known as *compensatory damages.* These damages compensate the injured party only for damages actually sustained and proved to have arisen directly from the loss of the bargain caused by the breach of contract. They simply replace what was lost because of the wrong or damage. The standard measure of compensatory damages is the difference between the value of the breaching party's promised performance under the contract and the value of her or his actual performance. This amount is reduced by any loss that the injured party has avoided, however.

To illustrate: Wilcox contracts to perform certain services exclusively for Hernandez during the month of March for $4,000. Hernandez cancels the contract and is in breach. Wilcox is able to find another job during the month of March but can earn only $3,000. He can sue Hernandez for breach and recover $1,000 as compensatory damages. Wilcox can also recover from Hernandez the amount that he spent to find the other job. Expenses that are caused directly by a breach of contract—such as those incurred to obtain performance from another source—are known as *incidental damages.*

The measurement of compensatory damages varies by type of contract. Certain types of contracts deserve special mention. They are contracts for the sale of goods and the sale of land.

Sale of Goods. In a contract for the sale of goods, the usual measure of compensatory damages is an amount equal to the difference between the contract price and the market price.[18] Suppose that Chrylon Corporation contracts to buy ten model UTS network servers from an XEXO Corporation dealer for $8,000 each. The dealer, however, fails to deliver the ten servers to Chrylon. The market price of the servers at the time the buyer learns of the breach is $8,150. Chrylon's measure of damages is therefore $1,500 (10 × $150) plus any incidental damages (expenses) caused by the breach. In a situation in which the buyer breaches and the seller has not yet produced the goods, compensatory damages normally equal lost profits on the sale, not the difference between the contract price and the market price.

Sale of Land. Ordinarily, because each parcel of land is unique, the remedy for a seller's breach of a contract for a sale of real estate is specific performance—that is, the buyer is awarded the parcel of property for which she or he bargained (specific performance will be discussed more fully later in this chapter). When this remedy is unavailable (for example, when the seller has sold the property to someone else), or when the breach is on the part of the buyer, the measure of damages is ordinarily the same as in contracts for the sale of goods—that is, the difference between the contract price and the market price of the land. The majority of states follow this rule.

A minority of states follow a different rule when the seller breaches the contract and the breach is not deliberate.[19] In this situation, these states allow the prospective purchaser to recover any down payment plus any expenses incurred (such as fees for title searches, attorneys, and escrows). This minority rule effectively places purchasers in the position they occupied prior to the sale.

Consequential Damages Foreseeable damages that result from a party's breach of contract are called **consequential damages,** or *special damages.*

18. In other words, the amount is the difference between the contract price and the market price at the time and place at which the goods were to be delivered or tendered. See UCC 2–708 and 2–713.

19. "Deliberate" breaches include the seller's failure to convey the land because the market price has gone up. "Nondeliberate" breaches include the seller's failure to convey the land because an unknown easement (another's right of use over the property) has rendered title unmarketable. See Chapter 25.

They differ from compensatory damages in that they are caused by special circumstances beyond the contract itself. They flow from the consequences, or results, of a breach.

For example, if a seller fails to deliver goods, and the seller knows that a buyer is planning to resell these goods immediately, consequential damages will be awarded for the loss of profit from the planned resale. The buyer will also recover compensatory damages for the difference between the contract price and the market price of the goods.

To recover consequential damages, the breaching party must know (or have reason to know) that special circumstances will cause the nonbreaching party to suffer an additional loss. This rule was enunciated in the classic case of *Hadley v. Baxendale,* which is presented next. In reading this decision, it is helpful to understand that it was customary in the mid-1800s in England for large flour mills to have more than one crankshaft in the event that the main crankshaft broke and had to be repaired. Also, in those days it was common knowledge that flour mills did indeed have spare crankshafts. It is against this background that the parties in the case presented here argued their respective positions on whether the damages resulting from the loss of profits while the crankshaft was repaired were reasonably foreseeable.

CASE 10.3 Hadley v. Baxendale

Court of Exchequer, 1854. 156 Eng.Rep. 145.

• **Background and Facts** The Hadleys (the plaintiffs) ran a flour mill in Gloucester. The crankshaft attached to the steam engine in the mill broke, causing the mill to shut down. The shaft had to be sent to a foundry located in Greenwich so that the new shaft could be made to fit the other parts of the engine. Baxendale, the defendant, was a common carrier that transported the shaft from Gloucester to Greenwich. The freight charges were collected in advance, and Baxendale promised to deliver the shaft the following day. It was not delivered for a number of days, however. As a consequence, the mill was closed for several days. The Hadleys sued to recover the profits lost during that time. Baxendale contended that the loss of profits was "too remote" to be recoverable. The court held for the plaintiffs, and the jury was allowed to take into consideration the lost profits. The defendant appealed.

IN THE LANGUAGE OF THE COURT
***ALDERSON,* B. [Baron]**

* * * *

* * * Where two parties have made a contract which one of them has broken, the damages which the other party ought to receive in respect of such breach of contract should be such as may fairly and reasonably be considered either arising naturally, *i.e.*, according to the usual course of things, from such breach of contract itself, or such as may reasonably be supposed to have been in the contemplation of both parties, at the time they made the contract, as the probable result of the breach of it. Now, if the special circumstances under which the contract was actually made were communicated by the plaintiffs to the defendants, and thus known to both parties, the damages resulting from the breach of such a contract, *which they would reasonably contemplate,* would be the amount of injury which would ordinarily follow from a breach of contract under these special circumstances so known and communicated. * * * Now, in the present case, if we are to apply the principles above laid down, we find that the only circumstances here communicated by the plaintiffs to the defendants at the time the contract was made, were, that the article to be carried was the broken shaft of a mill, and that the plaintiffs were the millers of that mill. * * * Special circumstances were here never communicated by the plaintiffs to the defendants. It follows, therefore, that the loss of profits here cannot reasonably be considered such a consequence of the breach of contract as could have been fairly and reasonably contemplated by both the parties when they made this contract. [Emphasis added.]

CASE CONTINUES

CASE 10.3 CONTINUED

• **Decision and Remedy** *The Court of Exchequer ordered a new trial. According to the court, to collect consequential damages, the plaintiffs would have to have given express notice of the special circumstances that caused the loss of profits.*

• **Impact of This Case on Today's Law** *This case established the rule that when damages are awarded, compensation is given only for those injuries that the defendant could reasonably have foreseen as a probable result of the usual course of events following a breach. Today, the rule enunciated by the court in this case still applies. To recover consequential damages, the plaintiff must show that the defendant had reason to know or foresee that a particular loss or injury would occur.*

• **The E-Commerce Dimension** *If a Web merchant loses business due to a computer system's failure that can be attributed to malfunctioning software, can the merchant recover the lost profits from the software maker? Explain.*

Mitigation of Damages In most situations, when a breach of contract occurs, the innocent injured party is held to a duty to mitigate, or reduce, the damages that he or she suffers. Under this doctrine of **mitigation of damages,** the duty owed depends on the nature of the contract.

For example, some states require a landlord to use reasonable means to find a new tenant if a tenant abandons the premises and fails to pay rent. If an acceptable tenant is found, the landlord is required to lease the premises to this tenant to mitigate the damages recoverable from the former tenant. The former tenant is still liable for the difference between the amount of the rent under the original lease and the rent received from the new tenant. If the landlord has not used the reasonable means necessary to find a new tenant, presumably a court can reduce the award made by the amount of rent the landlord could have received had such reasonable means been used.

In the majority of states, persons whose employment has been wrongfully terminated owe a duty to mitigate damages suffered because of their employers' breach of the employment contract. In other words, wrongfully terminated employees have a duty to take similar jobs if they are available. If the employees fail to do this, the damages they are awarded will be equivalent to their salaries less the incomes they would have received in similar jobs obtained by reasonable means. The employer has the burden of proving that such a job existed and that the employee could have been hired. Normally, the employee is under no duty to take a job of a different type and rank, however.

Liquidated Damages Provisions

A **liquidated damages** provision in a contract specifies that a certain dollar amount is to be paid in the event of a *future* default or breach of contract. (*Liquidated* means determined, settled, or fixed.) For example, a provision requiring a construction contractor to pay $300 for every day he or she is late in completing the project is a liquidated damages provision. Liquidated damages provisions are frequently used in construction contracts because it is difficult to estimate the amount of damages that would be caused by a delay in completion. They are also common in contracts for the sale of goods.[20]

Liquidated damages differ from penalties. A **penalty** specifies a certain amount to be paid in the event of a default or breach of contract and is designed to penalize the breaching party. Liquidated damages provisions normally are enforceable. In contrast, if a court finds that a provision calls for a penalty, the agreement as to the amount will not be enforced, and recovery will be limited to actual damages. To determine if a particular provision is for liquidated damages or for a penalty, the court asks two questions:

1. When the contract was entered into, was it apparent that damages would be difficult to estimate in the event of a breach?
2. Was the amount set as damages a reasonable estimate and not excessive?[21]

If the answers to both questions are yes, the provision normally will be enforced. If either answer is no, the provision normally will not be enforced. For example, in a case involving a sophisticated business contract to lease computer equipment, the court held that a liquidated damages provision that valued computer equipment at more than four times its market value was a

20. Section 2–718(1) of the UCC specifically authorizes the use of liquidated damages provisions.
21. *Restatement (Second) of Contracts,* Section 356(1).

reasonable estimate. According to the court, the amount of actual damages was difficult to ascertain at the time the contract was formed because of the "speculative nature of the value of computers at termination of lease schedules."[22]

Rescission and Restitution

As discussed earlier in this chapter, rescission is essentially an action to undo, or terminate, a contract—to return the contracting parties to the positions they occupied prior to the transaction.[23] When fraud, a mistake, duress, undue influence, misrepresentation, or lack of capacity to contract is present, unilateral rescission is available. Rescission may also be available by statute.[24] The failure of one party to perform entitles the other party to rescind the contract. The rescinding party must give prompt notice to the breaching party.

Restitution Generally, to rescind a contract, both parties must make **restitution** to each other by returning goods, property, or funds previously conveyed.[25] If the physical property or goods can be returned, they must be. If the goods or property have been consumed, restitution must be made in an equivalent amount of cash.

Essentially, restitution refers to the plaintiff's recapture of a benefit conferred on the defendant through which the defendant has been unjustly enriched. For example, Katie pays $10,000 to Bob in return for Bob's promise to design a house for her. The next day Bob calls Katie and tells her that he has taken a position with a large architectural firm in another state and cannot design the house. Katie decides to hire another architect that afternoon. Katie can obtain restitution of the $10,000.

Restitution Is Not Limited to Rescission Cases Restitution may be appropriate when a contract is rescinded, but the right to restitution is not limited to rescission cases. Restitution may be sought in actions for breach of contract, tort actions, and other actions at law or in equity. Usually, restitution can be obtained when funds or property has been transferred by mistake or because of fraud. An award in a case may include restitution of funds or property obtained through embezzlement, conversion, theft, copyright infringement, or misconduct by a party in a confidential or other special relationship.

Specific Performance

The equitable remedy of **specific performance** calls for the performance of the act promised in the contract. This remedy is quite attractive to the nonbreaching party for three reasons:

1. The nonbreaching party need not worry about collecting the monetary damages awarded by a court (see the discussion in Chapter 2 of some of the difficulties that may arise when trying to enforce court judgments).
2. The nonbreaching party need not spend time seeking an alternative contract.
3. The performance is more valuable than the monetary damages.

Normally, however, specific performance will not be granted unless the party's legal remedy (monetary damages) is inadequate.[26] For this reason, contracts for the sale of goods rarely qualify for specific performance. The legal remedy—monetary damages—is ordinarily adequate in such situations because substantially identical goods can be bought or sold in the market. Only if the goods are unique will a court grant specific performance. For example, paintings, sculptures, or rare books or coins are so unique that monetary damages will not enable a buyer to obtain substantially identical substitutes in the market.

Sale of Land Specific performance is granted to a buyer in a contract for the sale of land. The legal remedy for breach of a land sales contract is inadequate because every parcel of land is considered to be unique. Monetary damages will not compensate a buyer adequately because the same land in the same location obviously cannot be obtained elsewhere. Only when specific performance is unavailable (for example, when the seller has sold the property to someone else) will monetary damages be awarded instead.

22. *Winthrop Resources Corp. v. Eaton Hydraulics, Inc.*, 361 F.3d 465 (8th Cir. 2004).

23. The rescission discussed here is *unilateral* rescission, in which only one party wants to undo the contract. In mutual rescission, both parties agree to undo the contract. Mutual rescission discharges the contract; unilateral rescission is generally available as a remedy for breach of contract.

24. The Federal Trade Commission and many states have rules or statutes allowing consumers to unilaterally rescind contracts made at home with door-to-door salespersons. Rescission is allowed within three days for any reason or for no reason at all. See, for example, California Civil Code Section 1689.5.

25. *Restatement (Second) of Contracts*, Section 370.

26. *Restatement (Second) of Contracts*, Section 359.

Is specific performance warranted when one of the parties has substantially—but not *fully*—performed under the contract? That was the question in the following case.

CASE 10.4 Stainbrook v. Low

Court of Appeals of Indiana, 2006. 842 N.E.2d 386.

• **Background and Facts** In April 2004, Howard Stainbrook agreed to sell to Trent Low forty acres of land in Jennings County, Indiana, for $45,000. Thirty-two of the acres were wooded and eight were tillable. Under the agreement, Low was to pay for a survey of the property and other costs, including a tax payment due in November. Low gave Stainbrook a check for $1,000 to show his intent to fulfill the contract. They agreed to close the deal on May 11, and Low made financial arrangements to meet his obligations. On May 8, a tractor rolled over on Stainbrook, and he died. Howard's son David became the executor of Stainbrook's estate. David asked Low to withdraw his offer to buy the forty acres. Low refused and filed a suit against David in an Indiana state court, seeking to enforce the contract. The court ordered specific performance. David appealed to a state intermediate appellate court, arguing, among other things, that his father's contract with Low was "ambiguous and inequitable."

IN THE LANGUAGE OF THE COURT
***VAIDIK*, Judge.**

* * * *

The Estate [David] * * * contends that Low failed to preserve the remedy of specific performance here because he failed to perform sufficiently under the Agreement. * * * The Estate argues that "[i]n order to be entitled to specific performance, the claimant has the burden to prove *full and complete performance* on their part of the contract." Low * * * argues that specific performance was appropriate because he either *substantially performed* his obligations under the Agreement or offered to do so, and this, rather than full and complete performance, is all that is required to preserve a claim for specific performance.

We agree with Low. Because Low offered to perform his obligations under the Agreement, specific performance was a proper remedy. * * * The Estate argues that Low is not entitled to the remedy of specific performance because he did not pay the November 2004 property taxes. Low, however, * * * offered to make the tax payment and the Estate refused his offer.

The Estate also contends * * * that specific performance was inappropriate because Low failed to tender the purchase price listed in the Agreement and arrange for a survey of the land before the closing date. * * * The Estate's argument assumes that a party may not be granted specific performance unless that party has fully and completely performed under the terms of the contract. *On the contrary, * * * specific performance is an appropriate remedy to a party who has* substantially *performed under the terms of the contract.* Regarding Low's payment of the purchase price, we note that Low * * * had obtained financing before the closing date, and there is nothing * * * to indicate that he was not prepared to meet his financial obligations at that time. Further, * * * shortly after Stainbrook's death, the Executor of the Estate requested that Low withdraw his offer, and Low declined to do so, indicating that he was prepared to go forward. Regarding Low's failure to order a land survey, the Estate presents no evidence to suggest that this matter, particularly in isolation, reaches the level of failure to perform under the Agreement, and we decline to sanction such a rule. [Emphasis added.]

* * * *

The Estate finally argues that the trial court should not have awarded specific performance here because the Agreement between Low and Stainbrook was unfair. * * * Since Low was twenty-two years old and Stainbrook was eighty-nine at the time of contract, and because the combined estimates of property and timber values was as high as $121,000.00 and Low and Stainbrook had agreed to a $45,000.00 purchase price, the Estate argues that the trial court should have found the contract to be unfair or unconscionable and to have found that Low would be unjustly enriched by its execution.

* * * The Estate stipulated at trial that Stainbrook was competent at the time of contract, and evidence was presented that Stainbrook consulted a lawyer regarding the Agreement and

CASE 10.4 CONTINUED that he insisted upon several handwritten changes to the contract that benefited his own interests. We find no support for the Estate's contention that Stainbrook was anything less than a party entirely capable of entering into this Agreement, nor for its contention that the Agreement was unfair.

• **Decision and Remedy** *The state intermediate appellate court held that specific performance was an appropriate remedy in this case and affirmed the lower court's order. The appellate court explained that a contracting party's substantial performance is sufficient to support a court's order for specific performance. Here, "Low both offered to perform and substantially performed his contractual obligations."*

• **The Ethical Dimension** *Should a party who seeks specific performance of a contract be required to prove that he or she has performed, substantially performed, or offered to perform his or her contract obligations? Why or why not?*

• **The Global Dimension** *Suppose that Stainbrook and Low had been citizens and residents of other countries. Would the location of the land that was the subject of their contract have been sufficient to support the Indiana state court's jurisdiction and award in this case? Discuss.*

Contracts for Personal Services

Personal-service contracts require one party to work personally for another party. Courts normally refuse to grant specific performance of personal-service contracts because to order a party to perform personal services against his or her will amounts to a type of involuntary servitude.[27]

Moreover, the courts do not want to have to monitor a service contract if supervision would be difficult—as it would be if the contract required the exercise of personal judgment or talent. For example, if you contracted with a brain surgeon to perform brain surgery on you and the surgeon refused to perform, the court would not compel (and you certainly would not want) the surgeon to perform under those circumstances. A court cannot assure meaningful performance in such a situation.[28] If a contract is not deemed personal, the remedy at law of monetary damages may be adequate if substantially identical service (for example, lawn mowing) is available from other persons.

Reformation

Reformation is an equitable remedy used when the parties have *imperfectly* expressed their agreement in writing. Reformation allows a court to rewrite the contract to reflect the parties' true intentions.

When Fraud or Mutual Mistake Is Present Reformation occurs most often when fraud or mutual mistake (for example, a clerical error) is present. It is almost always sought so that some other remedy may then be pursued. For example, if Keshan contracts to buy a certain parcel of land from Malboa but their contract mistakenly refers to a parcel of land different from the one being sold, the contract does not reflect the parties' intentions. Accordingly, a court can reform the contract so that it conforms to the parties' intentions and accurately refers to the parcel of land being sold. Keshan can then, if necessary, show that Malboa has breached the contract as reformed. She can at that time request an order for specific performance.

Oral Contracts and Covenants Not to Compete There are two other situations in which the courts frequently reform contracts. The first involves two parties who have made a binding oral contract. They further agree to put the oral contract in writing, but in doing so, they make an error in stating the terms. Normally, the courts will allow into evidence the correct terms of the oral contract, thereby reforming the written contract.

The second situation is when the parties have executed a written covenant not to compete (discussed in Chapter 9). If the covenant is for a valid and legitimate purpose (such as the sale of a business) but the area or time restraints of the covenant are unreasonable, some courts will reform the restraints by making them reasonable and will enforce the entire contract as

27. Involuntary servitude, or slavery, is contrary to the public policy expressed in the Thirteenth Amendment to the U.S. Constitution. A court can, however, enter an order (injunction) prohibiting a person who breached a personal-service contract from engaging in similar contracts for a period of time in the future.

28. Similarly, courts often refuse to order specific performance of construction contracts because courts are not set up to operate as construction supervisors or engineers.

reformed. Other courts, however, will throw out the entire restrictive covenant as illegal.

Exhibit 10–2 graphically summarizes the remedies, including reformation, that are available to the nonbreaching party. *Concept Summary 10.1* reviews all the equitable remedies.

Election of Remedies

In many cases, a nonbreaching party has several remedies available. When the remedies are inconsistent with one another, the common law of contracts requires the party to choose which remedy to pursue. This is called *election of remedies.*

The Purpose of the Doctrine The purpose of the doctrine of election of remedies is to prevent double recovery. Suppose, for example, that McCarthy agrees in writing to sell his land to Tally. Then McCarthy changes his mind and repudiates the contract. Tally can sue for compensatory damages or for specific performance. If Tally could seek compensatory damages in addition to specific performance, she would recover twice for the same breach of contract. The doctrine of election of remedies requires Tally to choose the remedy she wants, and it eliminates any possibility of double recovery. In other words, the election doctrine represents the legal embodiment of the adage "You can't have your cake and eat it, too."

The doctrine has often been applied in a rigid and technical manner, leading to some harsh results. Suppose that Beacham is fraudulently induced to buy a parcel of land for $150,000. He spends an additional $10,000 moving onto the land and then discovers the fraud. Instead of suing for damages, Beacham sues to rescind the contract. The court allows Beacham to recover only the purchase price of $150,000 in restitution, but not the additional $10,000 in moving expenses (because the seller did not receive these funds, he or she will not be required to return them). So Beacham suffers a net loss of $10,000 on the transaction. If Beacham had elected to sue for damages instead of seeking the remedy of rescission and restitution, he could have recovered the $10,000 as well as the $150,000.

The UCC's Rejection of the Doctrine Because of the many problems associated with the doctrine of election of remedies, the UCC expressly rejects it.[29] As will be discussed in Chapter 11, remedies under the UCC are not exclusive but cumulative in nature and include all the available remedies for breach of contract.

Pleading in the Alternative Although the parties must ultimately elect which remedy to pursue, modern court procedures do allow plaintiffs to plead their cases "in the alternative" (pleadings were discussed in Chapter 2). In other words, when the plaintiff originally files a lawsuit, he or she can ask the court to order either rescission (and restitution) or damages, for example. Then, as the case progresses to trial, the parties can elect which remedy is most beneficial or appropriate, or the judge can order one remedy and not another. This process still prevents double recovery because the party can only be awarded one of the remedies that was requested.

Waiver of Breach

Under certain circumstances, a nonbreaching party may be willing to accept a defective performance of the contract. This knowing relinquishment of a legal right (that is, the right to require satisfactory and full performance) is called a **waiver.**

29. See UCC 2–703 and 2–711.

EXHIBIT 10–2 • Remedies for Breach of Contract

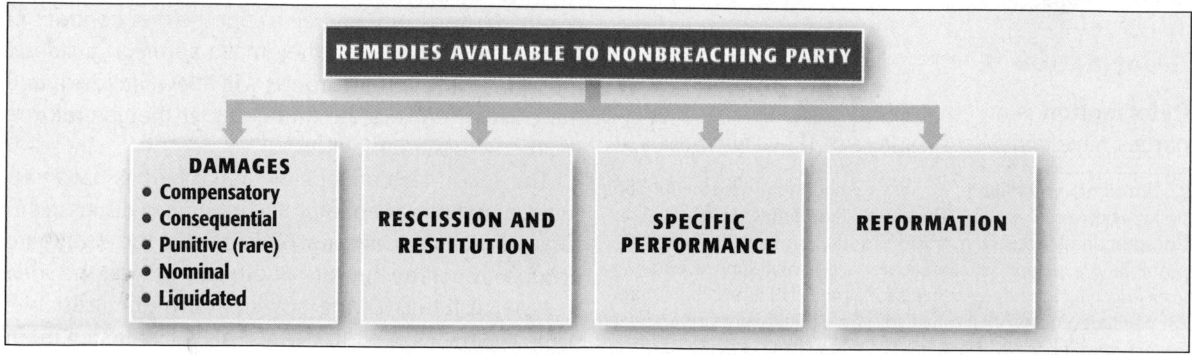

CONCEPT SUMMARY 10.1 Equitable Remedies

Remedy	Description
RESCISSION AND RESTITUTION	1. *Rescission*—A remedy whereby a contract is canceled and the parties are restored to the original positions that they occupied prior to the transaction. 2. *Restitution*—When a contract is rescinded, both parties must make restitution to each other by returning the goods, property, or funds previously conveyed.
SPECIFIC PERFORMANCE	An equitable remedy calling for the performance of the act promised in the contract. Only available when monetary damages would be inadequate—such as in contracts for the sale of land or unique goods—and never available in personal-service contracts.
REFORMATION	An equitable remedy allowing a contract to be "reformed," or rewritten, to reflect the parties' true intentions. Available when an agreement is imperfectly expressed in writing, such as when a mutual mistake has occurred.

Consequences of a Waiver of Breach When a waiver of a breach of contract occurs, the party waiving the breach cannot take any later action on it. In effect, the waiver erases the past breach; the contract continues as if the breach had never occurred. Of course, the waiver of breach of contract extends only to the matter waived and not to the whole contract.

Reasons for Waiving a Breach Businesspersons often waive breaches of contract to get whatever benefit is still possible out of the contract. For example, a seller contracts with a buyer to deliver to the buyer ten thousand tons of coal on or before November 1. The contract calls for the buyer to pay by November 10 for coal delivered. Because of a coal miners' strike, coal is hard to find. The seller breaches the contract by not tendering delivery until November 5. The buyer may be well advised to waive the seller's breach, accept delivery of the coal, and pay as contracted.

Waiver of Breach and Subsequent Breaches Ordinarily, the waiver by a contracting party will not operate to waive subsequent, additional, or future breaches of contract. This is always true when the subsequent breaches are unrelated to the first breach. For example, an owner who waives the right to sue for late completion of a stage of construction does not waive the right to sue for failure to comply with engineering specifications on the same job. A waiver will be extended to subsequent defective performance, however, if a reasonable person would conclude that similar defective performance in the future will be acceptable. Therefore, a *pattern of conduct* that waives a number of successive breaches will operate as a continued waiver. To change this result, the nonbreaching party should give notice to the breaching party that full performance will be required in the future.

The party who has rendered defective or less-than-full performance remains liable for the damages caused by the breach of contract. In effect, the waiver operates to keep the contract going. The waiver prevents the nonbreaching party from calling the contract to an end or rescinding the contract. The contract continues, but the nonbreaching party can recover damages caused by defective or less-than-full performance.

Contract Provisions Limiting Remedies

A contract may include provisions stating that no damages can be recovered for certain types of breaches or that damages must be limited to a maximum amount. The contract may also provide that the only remedy for breach is replacement, repair, or refund of the purchase price. Provisions stating that no damages can be recovered are called *exculpatory clauses*. Provisions that affect the availability of certain remedies are called *limitation-of-liability clauses*.

Whether these contract provisions and clauses will be enforced depends on the type of breach that is excused by the provision. For example, a provision excluding liability for fraudulent or intentional injury will not be enforced. Likewise, a clause excluding liability for illegal acts or violations of law will not be enforced. A clause excluding liability for negligence may be enforced in certain cases, however. When an exculpatory clause for negligence is contained in a contract made between parties who have roughly equal bargaining positions, the clause usually will be enforced.

REVIEWING Contract Performance, Breach, and Remedies

Val's Foods signs a contract to buy 1,500 pounds of basil from Sun Farms, a small organic herb grower, as long as an independent organization inspects and certifies that the crop contains no pesticide or herbicide residue. Val's has a number of contracts with different restaurant chains to supply pesto and intends to use Sun Farms' basil in its pesto to fulfill these contracts. While Sun Farms is preparing to harvest the basil, an unexpected hailstorm destroys half the crop. Sun Farms attempts to purchase additional basil from other farms, but it is late in the season and the price is twice the normal market price. Sun Farms is too small to absorb this cost and immediately notifies Val's that it will not fulfill the contract. Using the information presented in the chapter, answer the following questions.

1. Suppose that the basil does not pass the chemical-residue inspection. Which concept discussed in the chapter might allow Val's to refuse to perform the contract in this situation?
2. Under which legal theory or theories might Sun Farms claim that its obligation under the contract has been discharged by operation of law? Discuss fully.
3. Suppose that Sun Farms contacts every basil grower in the country and buys the last remaining chemical-free basil anywhere. Nevertheless, Sun Farms is only able to ship 1,475 pounds to Val's. Would this fulfill Sun Farms' obligations to Val's? Why or why not?
4. Now suppose that Sun Farms sells its operations to Happy Valley Farms. As a part of the sale, all three parties agree that Happy Valley will provide the basil as stated under the original contract. What is this type of agreement called? Does it discharge the obligations of any of the parties? Explain.

TERMS AND CONCEPTS

anticipatory repudiation 233
breach of contract 233
commercial impracticability 236
condition 230
consequential damages 240
discharge 230
frustration of purpose 238
impossibility of performance 235
liquidated damages 242
mitigation of damages 242
mutual rescission 234
novation 234
penalty 242
performance 230
reformation 245
restitution 243
specific performance 243
tender 231
waiver 246

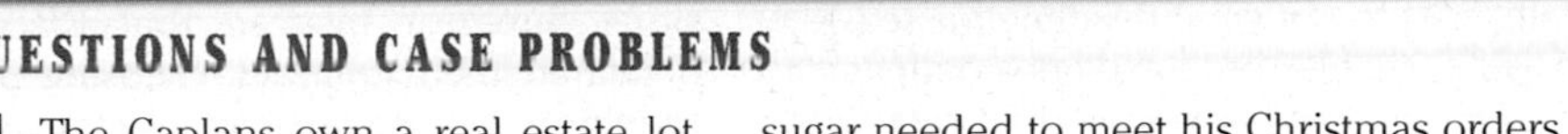

QUESTIONS AND CASE PROBLEMS

10–1. The Caplans own a real estate lot, and they contract with Faithful Construction, Inc., to build a house on it for $360,000. The specifications list "all plumbing bowls and fixtures . . . to be Crane brand." The Caplans leave on vacation, and during their absence Faithful is unable to buy and install Crane plumbing fixtures. Instead, Faithful installs Kohler brand fixtures, an equivalent in the industry. On completion of the building contract, the Caplans inspect the work, discover the substitution, and refuse to accept the house, claiming Faithful has breached the conditions set forth in the specifications. Discuss fully the Caplans' claim.

10–2. QUESTION WITH SAMPLE ANSWER

Junior owes creditor Iba $1,000, which is due and payable on June 1. Junior has been in a car accident, has missed a great deal of work, and consequently will not have the funds on June 1. Junior's father, Fred, offers to pay Iba $1,100 in four equal installments if Iba will discharge Junior from any further liability on the debt. Iba accepts. Is this transaction a novation or an accord and satisfaction? Explain.

- **For a sample answer to Question 10–2, go to Appendix I at the end of this text.**

10–3. In the following situations, certain events take place after the formation of contracts. Discuss which of these contracts are discharged because the events render the contracts impossible to perform.

(a) Jimenez, a famous singer, contracts to perform in your nightclub. He dies prior to performance.
(b) Raglione contracts to sell you her land. Just before title is to be transferred, she dies.
(c) Oppenheim contracts to sell you one thousand bushels of apples from her orchard in the state of Washington. Because of a severe frost, she is unable to deliver the apples.
(d) Maxwell contracts to lease a service station for ten years. His principal income is from the sale of gasoline. Because of an oil embargo by foreign oil-producing nations, gasoline is rationed, cutting sharply into Maxwell's gasoline sales. He cannot make his lease payments.

10–4. Ken owns and operates a famous candy store and makes most of the candy sold in the store. Business is particularly heavy during the Christmas season. Ken contracts with Sweet, Inc., to purchase ten thousand pounds of sugar to be delivered on or before November 15. Ken has informed Sweet that this particular order is to be used for the Christmas season business. Because of problems at the refinery, the sugar is not tendered to Ken until December 10, at which time Ken refuses it as being too late. Ken has been unable to purchase the quantity of sugar needed to meet his Christmas orders and has had to turn down numerous regular customers, some of whom have indicated that they will purchase candy elsewhere in the future. What sugar Ken has been able to purchase has cost him 10 cents per pound above the price contracted for with Sweet. Ken sues Sweet for breach of contract, claiming as damages the higher price paid for sugar from others, lost profits from this year's lost Christmas sales, future lost profits from customers who have indicated that they will discontinue doing business with him, and punitive damages for failure to meet the contracted delivery date. Sweet claims Ken is limited to compensatory damages only. Discuss who is correct, and why.

10–5. CASE PROBLEM WITH SAMPLE ANSWER

Train operators and other railroad personnel use signaling systems to ensure safe train travel. Reading Blue Mountain & Northern Railroad Co. (RBMN) and Norfolk Southern Railway Co. entered into a contract for the maintenance of a signaling system that serviced a stretch of track near Jim Thorpe, Pennsylvania. The system included a series of poles, similar to telephone poles, suspending wires above the tracks. The contract provided that "the intent of the parties is to maintain the existing . . . facilities" and split the cost equally. In December 2002, a severe storm severed the wires and destroyed most of the poles. RBMN and Norfolk discussed replacing the old system, which they agreed was antiquated, inefficient, dangerous to rebuild, and expensive, but they could not agree on an alternative. Norfolk installed an entirely new system and filed a suit in a federal district court against RBMN to recover half of the cost. RBMN filed a motion for summary judgment, asserting in part the doctrine of frustration of purpose. What is this doctrine? Does it apply in this case? How should the court rule on RBMN's motion? Explain. [*Norfolk Southern Railway Co. v. Reading Blue Mountain & Northern Railroad Co.*, 364 F.Supp.2d 270 (M.D.Pa. 2004)]

- **To view a sample answer for Problem 10–5, go to this book's Web site at academic.cengage.com/blaw/cross, select "Chapter 10," and click on "Case Problem with Sample Answer."**

10–6. Waiver of Breach. In May 1998, RDP Royal Palm Hotel, L.P., contracted with Clark Construction Group, Inc., to build the Royal Palms Crowne Plaza Resort in Miami Beach, Florida. The deadline for "substantial completion" was February 28, 2000, but RDP could ask for changes, and the date would be adjusted accordingly. During construction, Clark faced many setbacks, including a buried seawall, contaminated soil, the unforeseen deterioration of the existing hotel, and RDP's issue of hundreds of change orders. Clark requested extensions of the deadline, and RDP agreed, but the parties never specified a date. After the original deadline passed, RDP continued to issue change orders, Clark continued to perform, and RDP accepted the work. In March 2002, when the resort was substantially complete, RDP stopped paying Clark. Clark stopped working. RDP hired another contractor to finish the resort, which opened in May. RDP filed a suit in a federal district court against Clark, alleging, among other things, breach of contract for the two-year delay in the resort's completion. In whose favor should the court rule, and why? Discuss. [*RDP Royal Palm Hotel, L.P. v. Clark Construction Group, Inc.*, __ F.3d __ (11th Cir. 2006)]

10–7. Remedies. On July 7, 2000, Frances Morelli agreed to sell to Judith Bucklin a house at 126 Lakedell Drive in Warwick, Rhode Island, for $77,000. Bucklin made a deposit on the house. The closing at which the parties would exchange the deed for the price was scheduled for September 1. The agreement did not state that "time is of the essence," but it did provide, in "Paragraph 10," that "[i]f Seller is unable to [convey good, clear, insurable, and marketable title], Buyer shall have the option to: (a) accept such title as Seller is able to convey without abatement or reduction of the Purchase Price, or (b) cancel this Agreement and receive a return of all Deposits." An examination of the public records revealed that the house did not have marketable title. Wishing to be flexible, Bucklin offered Morelli time to resolve the problem, and the closing did not occur as scheduled. Morelli decided "the deal is over" and offered to return the deposit. Bucklin refused and, in mid-October, decided to exercise her option under Paragraph 10(a). She notified Morelli, who did not respond. Bucklin filed a suit in a Rhode Island state court against Morelli. In whose favor should the court rule? Should damages be awarded? If not, what is the appropriate remedy? Why? [*Bucklin v. Morelli*, 912 A.2d 931 (R.I. 2007)]

10–8. Material Breach. Kermit Johnson formed FB&I Building Products, Inc., in Watertown, South Dakota, to sell building materials. In December 1998, FB&I contracted with Superior Truss & Components in Minneota, Minnesota, "to exclusively sell Superior's open-faced wall panels, floor panels, roof trusses and other miscellaneous products." In March 2000, FB&I agreed to exclusively sell Component Manufacturing Co.'s building products in Colorado. Two months later, Superior learned of FB&I's deal with Component and terminated its contract with FB&I. That contract provided that on cancellation, "FB&I will be entitled to retain the customers that they continue to sell and service with Superior products." Superior refused to honor this provision. Between the cancellation of FB&I's contract and 2004, Superior made $2,327,528 in sales to FB&I customers without paying a commission. FB&I filed a suit in a South Dakota state court against Superior, alleging, in part, breach of contract and seeking the unpaid commissions. Superior insisted that FB&I had materially breached their contract, excusing Superior from performing. In whose favor should the court rule and why? [*FB&I Building Products, Inc. v. Superior Truss & Components, a Division of Banks Lumber, Inc.*, 2007 SD 13, 727 N.W.2d 474 (2007)]

10–9. A QUESTION OF ETHICS

*King County, Washington, hired Frank Coluccio Construction Co. (FCCC) to act as general contractor for a public works project involving the construction of a small utility tunnel under the Duwamish Waterway. FCCC hired Donald B. Murphy Contractors, Inc. (DBM), as a subcontractor. DBM was responsible for constructing an access shaft at the eastern end of the tunnel. Problems arose during construction, including a "blow-in" of the access shaft that caused it to fill with water, soil, and debris. FCCC and DBM incurred substantial expenses from the repairs and delays. Under the project contract, King County was supposed to buy an insurance policy to "insure against physical loss or damage by perils included under an 'All-Risk' Builder's Risk policy." Any claim under this policy was to be filed through the insured. King County, which had general property damage insurance, did not obtain an all-risk builder's risk policy. For the losses attributable to the blow-in, FCCC and DBM submitted builder's risk claims, which the county denied. FCCC filed a suit in a Washington state court against King County, alleging, among other claims, breach of contract. [*Frank Coluccio Construction Co. v. King County, *136 Wash.App. 751, 150 P.3d 1147 (Div. 1 2007)]*

(a) King County's property damage policy specifically excluded, at the county's request, coverage of tunnels. The county drafted its contract with FCCC to require the all-risk builder's risk policy and authorize itself to "sponsor" claims. When FCCC and DBM filed their claims, the county secretly colluded with its property damage insurer to deny payment. What do these facts indicate about the county's ethics and legal liability in this situation?

(b) Could DBM, as a third party to the contract between King County and FCCC, maintain an action on the contract against King County? Discuss.

(c) All-risk insurance is a promise to pay on the "fortuitous" happening of a loss or damage from any cause except those that are specifically excluded. Payment usually is not made on a loss that, at the time the insurance was obtained, the claimant subjectively knew would occur. If a loss results from faulty workmanship on the part of a contractor, should the obligation to pay under an all-risk policy be discharged? Explain.

10-10. VIDEO QUESTION

Go to this text's Web site at **academic.cengage.com/blaw/cross** and select "Chapter 10." Click on "Video Questions" and view the video titled *Midnight Run*. Then answer the following questions.

(a) In the video, Eddie (Joe Pantoliano) and Jack (Robert DeNiro) negotiate a contract for Jack to find the Duke, a mob accountant who embezzled funds, and bring him back for trial. Assume that the contract is valid. If Jack breaches the contract by failing to bring in the Duke, what kinds of remedies, if any, can Eddie seek? Explain your answer.

(b) Would the equitable remedy of specific performance be available to either Jack or Eddie in the event of a breach? Why or why not?

(c) Now assume that the contract between Eddie and Jack is unenforceable. Nevertheless, Jack performs his side of the bargain (brings in the Duke). Does Jack have any legal recourse in this situation? Why or why not?

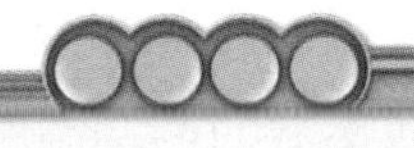

LAW ON THE WEB

For updated links to resources available on the Web, as well as a variety of other materials, visit this text's Web site at

academic.cengage.com/blaw/cross

For a summary of how contracts may be discharged and other principles of contract law, go to

www.rnoon.com/law_for_laymen/contracts/performance.html

Legal Research Exercises on the Web

Go to **academic.cengage.com/blaw/cross**, the Web site that accompanies this text. Select "Chapter 10" and click on "Internet Exercises." There you will find the following Internet research exercises that you can perform to learn more about the topics covered in this chapter.

Internet Exercise 10–1: Legal Perspective
Anticipatory Repudiation

Internet Exercise 10–2: Management Perspective
Commercial Impracticability

Internet Exercise 10–3: Management Perspective
The Duty to Mitigate

CHAPTER 11

Sales, Leases, and E-Contracts

When we turn to contracts for the sale and lease of goods, we move away from common law principles and into the area of statutory law. State statutory law governing sales and lease transactions is based on the Uniform Commercial Code (UCC), which, as mentioned in Chapter 1, has been adopted as law by all states.[1] Relevant sections of the UCC are noted in the following discussion of sales and lease contracts and Article 2 is included in Appendix C at the back of this book.

We open this chapter with a look at the scope of Article 2 and Article 2A. Article 2 of the UCC sets out the requirements of sales contracts and how they are formed. It also addresses the sometimes sticky concept of when title passes and who bears the risk of loss for goods in the process of being sold—for example, goods en route from the seller to the buyer—along with the concept of insurable interest. Article 2 regulates performance and obligations required under sales contracts. It also delineates when a breach by either the buyer or the seller occurs and what remedies normally may be sought. A sale of goods usually carries with it at least one type of warranty; sales warranties, express and implied, likewise are governed by the UCC. Article 2A covers similar issues for lease contracts.

In the final section of this chapter, we look at how traditional laws are being applied to contracts formed online. We also examine some new laws that have been created to apply in situations in which traditional laws governing contracts have sometimes been thought inadequate. For example, traditional laws governing signature and writing requirements are not easily adapted to contracts formed in the online environment. Thus, new laws have been created to address these issues.

1. Louisiana has not adopted Articles 2 and 2A, however. In addition, no state has adopted the amendments to Article 2 (on sales) and 2A (on leases) that were approved by the National Conference of Commissioners on Uniform State Laws in 2003.

The Scope of Article 2—The Sale of Goods

Article 2 of the UCC governs **sales contracts,** or contracts for the sale of goods. To facilitate commercial transactions, Article 2 modifies some of the common law contract requirements that were discussed in the previous chapters. To the extent that it has not been modified by the UCC, however, the common law of contracts also applies to sales contracts. For example, the common law requirements for a valid contract—agreement (offer and acceptance), consideration, capacity, and legality—that were discussed in Chapter 9 are also applicable to sales contracts. Thus, you should reexamine these common law principles when studying the law of sales.

In general, the rule is that whenever there is a conflict between a common law contract rule and the UCC, the UCC controls. In other words, when a UCC provision addresses a certain issue, the UCC governs; when the UCC is silent, the common law governs.

In regard to Article 2, you should keep two points in mind. First, Article 2 deals with the sale of goods; it does not deal with real property (real estate), services, or intangible property such as stocks and bonds. Thus, if the subject matter of a dispute is goods, the UCC governs. If it is real estate or services, the common law applies. Second, in some cases, the rules may vary quite a bit, depending on whether the buyer or the seller is a *merchant*. We look now at how the UCC defines a *sale, goods,* and *merchant status.*

What Is a Sale?

Section 2–102 of the UCC states that Article 2 "applies to transactions in goods." This implies a broad scope—covering gifts, bailments (temporary deliveries of personal property), and purchases of goods. In this chapter, however, we treat Article 2 as being applicable only to an actual sale (as would most authorities and courts). The UCC defines a **sale** as "the passing of title from the seller to the buyer for a price," where *title* refers to the formal right of ownership of property [UCC 2–106(1)]. The price may be payable in money or in other goods, services, or realty (real estate).

What Are Goods?

To be characterized as a *good,* an item of property must be *tangible,* and it must be *movable.* **Tangible property** has physical existence—it can be touched or seen. Intangible property—such as corporate stocks and bonds, patents and copyrights, and ordinary contract rights—has only conceptual existence and thus does not come under Article 2. A *movable* item can be carried from place to place. Hence, real estate is excluded from Article 2.

Who Is a Merchant?

Article 2 governs the sale of goods in general. It applies to sales transactions between all buyers and sellers. In a limited number of instances, however, the UCC presumes that in certain phases of sales transactions involving merchants, special business standards ought to be imposed because of the merchants' relatively high degree of commercial expertise.[2] Such standards do not apply to the casual or inexperienced seller or buyer ("consumer").

In general, a person is a **merchant** when he or she, acting in a mercantile capacity, possesses or uses an expertise specifically related to the goods being sold. This basic distinction is not always clear-cut. For example, courts in some states have determined that farmers may be merchants, while courts in other states have determined that the drafters of the UCC did not intend to include farmers as merchants.

2. The provisions that apply only to merchants deal principally with the Statute of Frauds, firm offers, confirmatory memoranda, warranties, and contract modification. These special rules reflect expedient business practices commonly known to merchants in the commercial setting. They will be discussed later in this chapter.

The Scope of Article 2A—Leases

In the past few decades, leases of personal property (goods) have become increasingly common. Consumers and business firms lease automobiles, industrial equipment, items for use in the home (such as floor polishers), and many other types of goods. Until Article 2A was added to the UCC, no specific body of law addressed the legal problems that arose when goods were leased, rather than sold. In cases involving leased goods, the courts generally applied a combination of common law rules, real estate law, and principles expressed in Article 2 of the UCC.

Article 2A of the UCC was created to fill the need for uniform guidelines in this area. Article 2A covers any transaction that creates a lease of goods, as well as subleases of goods [UCC 2A–102, 2A–103(k)]. Article 2A is essentially a repetition of Article 2, except that it applies to leases of goods, rather than sales of goods, and thus varies to reflect differences between sales and lease transactions.

Article 2A defines a **lease agreement** as the bargain between the lessor and lessee, as found in their language and as implied by other circumstances [UCC 2A–103(k)]. A **lessor** is one who sells the right to the possession and use of goods under a lease [UCC 2A–103(p)]. A **lessee** is one who acquires the right to the possession and use of goods under a lease [UCC 2A–103(o)]. Article 2A applies to all types of leases of goods, including commercial leases and consumer leases.

The Formation of Sales and Lease Contracts

In regard to the formation of sales and lease contracts, the UCC modifies the common law of contracts in several ways. We look here at how Article 2 and Article 2A of the UCC modify common law contract rules.

Remember that parties to sales contracts are free to establish whatever terms they wish. The UCC comes into play when the parties have not, in their contract, provided for a contingency that later gives rise to a dispute. The UCC makes this very clear time and again by its use of such phrases as "unless the parties otherwise agree" and "absent a contrary agreement by the parties."

Offer

In general contract law, the moment a definite offer is met by an unqualified acceptance, a binding contract is formed. In commercial sales transactions, the verbal exchanges, the correspondence, and the actions of the parties may not reveal exactly when a binding contractual obligation arises. The UCC states that an agreement sufficient to constitute a contract can exist even if the moment of its making is undetermined [UCC 2–204(2), 2A–204(2)].

Open Terms According to contract law, an offer must be definite enough for the parties (and the courts) to ascertain its essential terms when it is accepted. The UCC states that a sales or lease contract will not fail for indefiniteness even if one or more terms are left open as long as (1) the parties intended to make a contract and (2) there is a reasonably certain basis for the court to grant an appropriate remedy [UCC 2–204(3), 2A–204(3)].

Although the UCC has radically lessened the requirement of definiteness of terms, keep in mind that if too many terms are left open, a court may find that the parties did not intend to form a contract.

The appendix that follows this chapter shows an actual sales contract used by Starbucks Coffee Company. The contract illustrates many of the terms and clauses that are typically contained in contracts for the sale of goods.

Open Price Term. If the parties have not agreed on a price, the court will determine a "reasonable price at the time for delivery" [UCC 2–305(1)]. If either the buyer or the seller is to determine the price, the price is to be fixed in good faith [UCC 2–305(2)]. Under the UCC, *good faith* means honesty in fact and the observance of reasonable commercial standards of fair dealing in the trade [UCC 2–103(1)(b)]. The concepts of *good faith* and *commercial reasonableness* permeate the UCC.

Sometimes the price fails to be fixed through the fault of one of the parties. In that case, the other party can treat the contract as canceled or fix a reasonable price. For example, Perez and Merrick enter into a contract for the sale of goods and agree that Perez will fix the price. Perez refuses to fix the price. Merrick can either treat the contract as canceled or set a reasonable price [UCC 2–305(3)].

Open Payment Term. When parties do not specify payment terms, payment is due at the time and place at which the buyer is to receive the goods [UCC 2–310(a)]. The buyer can tender payment using any commercially normal or acceptable means, such as a check or credit card. If the seller demands payment in cash, however, the buyer must be given a reasonable time to obtain it [UCC 2–511(2)]. This is especially important when the contract states a definite and final time for performance.

Open Delivery Term. When no delivery terms are specified, the buyer normally takes delivery at the seller's place of business [UCC 2–308(a)]. If the seller has no place of business, the seller's residence is used. When goods are located in some other place and both parties know it, delivery is made there. If the time for shipment or delivery is not clearly specified in the sales contract, then the court will infer a "reasonable" time for performance [UCC 2–309(1)].

Open Quantity Term. Normally, if the parties do not specify a quantity, a court will have no basis for determining a remedy. The UCC recognizes two exceptions in requirements and output contracts [UCC 2–306(1)].

In a **requirements contract,** the buyer agrees to purchase—and the seller agrees to sell—all or up to a stated amount of what the buyer *needs* or *requires.* There is implicit consideration in a requirements contract, for the buyer gives up the right to buy from any other seller, and this forfeited right creates a legal detriment. Requirements contracts are common in the business world and are normally enforceable. If, however, the buyer promises to purchase only if the buyer *wishes* to do so, or if the buyer reserves the right to buy the goods from someone other than the seller, the promise is illusory (without consideration) and unenforceable by either party.

In an **output contract,** the seller agrees to sell and the buyer agrees to buy all or up to a stated amount of what the seller *produces.* Again, because the seller essentially forfeits the right to sell goods to another buyer, there is implicit consideration in an output contract.

The UCC imposes a *good faith limitation* on requirements and output contracts. The quantity under such contracts is the amount of requirements or the amount of output that occurs during a *normal* production year. The actual quantity purchased or sold cannot be unreasonably disproportionate to normal or comparable prior requirements or output [UCC 2–306].

Merchant's Firm Offer Under regular contract principles (discussed in Chapter 9), an offer can be revoked at any time before acceptance. The major common law exception is an *option contract,* in which the offeree pays consideration for the offeror's irrevocable promise to keep the offer open for a stated period. The UCC creates a second exception, which applies only to firm offers for the sale or lease of goods made by a merchant (regardless of whether or not the offeree is a merchant). A **firm offer** arises when a merchant-offeror gives assurances *in a signed writing* that the offer will remain open. The merchant's firm offer is irrevocable without the necessity of consideration[3] for the stated period or, if no definite period is stated, a reasonable period (neither to exceed three months) [UCC 2–205, 2A–205].

Acceptance

Acceptance of an offer to buy, sell, or lease goods generally may be made in any reasonable manner and by any reasonable means. The UCC generally takes the position that if the offeree's response indicates a *definite* acceptance of the offer, a contract is formed, even if the acceptance includes terms additional to, or different from, those contained in the offer [UCC 2–207(1)].

Promise to Ship or Prompt Shipment The UCC permits acceptance of an offer to buy goods "either by a prompt promise to ship or by the prompt or current shipment of conforming or nonconforming goods" [UCC 2–206(1)(b)]. Conforming goods accord with the contract's terms; nonconforming goods do not. The prompt shipment of *nonconforming goods* constitutes both an *acceptance,* which creates a contract, and a *breach* of that contract. This rule does not apply if the seller **seasonably** (within a reasonable amount of time) notifies the buyer that the nonconforming shipment is offered only as an *accommodation,* or as a favor. The notice of accommodation must clearly indicate to the buyer that the shipment does not constitute an acceptance and that, therefore, no contract has been formed.

Communication of Acceptance Under the common law, because a unilateral offer invites acceptance by a performance, the offeree need not notify the offeror of performance unless the offeror would not otherwise know about it. The UCC is more stringent than the common law in this regard. Under the UCC, if the offeror is not notified that the offeree has accepted the contract by beginning performance, then the offeror can treat the offer as having lapsed before acceptance [UCC 2–206(2), 2A–206(2)].

Additional Terms If the acceptance includes terms additional to, or different from, those contained in the offer and one (or both) of the parties is a *nonmerchant,* the contract is formed according to the terms of the original offer submitted by the original offeror and not according to the additional terms of the acceptance [UCC 2–207(2)]. The drafters of the UCC created a special rule for merchants that is designed to avoid the "battle of the forms," which occurs when two merchants exchange standard forms containing different contract terms. Under UCC 2–207(2), in contracts *between merchants,* the additional terms *automatically* become part of the contract *unless:*

1. The original offer expressly limited acceptance to its terms,
2. The new or changed terms materially alter the contract, or
3. The offeror objects to the new or changed terms within a reasonable period of time.

What constitutes a material alteration of the contract is usually a question of fact that only a court (or a jury, in a jury trial) can decide. Generally, if the modification involves no unreasonable element of surprise or hardship for the offeror, a court is likely to hold that the modification did not materially alter the contract.

In the following case, the court explains the "revolutionary change in contract law" caused by the UCC's principles on additional terms.

3. If the offeree pays consideration, then an option contract (not a merchant's firm offer) is formed.

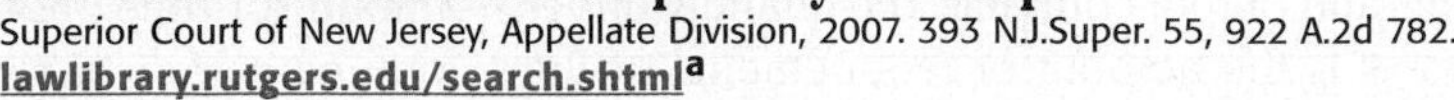

CASE 11.1 Sun Coast Merchandise Corp. v. Myron Corp.

Superior Court of New Jersey, Appellate Division, 2007. 393 N.J.Super. 55, 922 A.2d 782.
lawlibrary.rutgers.edu/search.shtml[a]

• **Background and Facts** Sun Coast Merchandise Corporation, a California firm, designs and sells products that businesses distribute as promotional items. Myron Corporation, a New Jersey firm, asked Sun about a flip-top calculator on which Myron could engrave the names of its customers. In December 2000, Myron began to submit purchase orders for about 400,000 of what the parties referred to as "Version I" calculators. In April 2001, Sun redesigned the flip-top. Over the next few weeks, the parties discussed terms for the making and shipping of 4 million of the "Version II" calculators before the Christmas season. By May 27, Myron had faxed four orders with specific delivery dates. Two days later, Sun announced a delayed schedule and asked Myron to submit revised orders. Unwilling to agree to the new dates, Myron did not honor this request. The parties attempted to negotiate the issue but were unsuccessful. Finally, Sun filed a suit in a New Jersey state court against Myron, claiming, among other things, breach of contract. The court entered a judgment in Sun's favor. On appeal to a state intermediate appellate court, Myron argued, among other things, that the judge's instruction to the jury regarding Sun's claim was inadequate.

IN THE LANGUAGE OF THE COURT
***FISHER,* J.A.D. [Judge, Appellate Division]**

* * * *

The era when a valid, binding contract could only come into existence when a party's acceptance mirrored the other party's offer ended with the adoption of the Uniform Commercial Code (UCC).The UCC altered the common law approach, finding it to be inconsistent with the modern realities of commerce. * * * Article 2 of the UCC radically altered sales law and expanded our conception of a contract.The heart of this revolutionary change in contract law can be found in [New Jersey Statutes Annotated (N.J.S.A.)] 12A:2-207(1) [New Jersey's version of UCC 2–207(1)], which declares that "[a] definite and seasonable expression of acceptance or a written confirmation which is sent within a reasonable time operates as an acceptance even though it states terms additional to or different from those offered or agreed upon, unless acceptance is expressly made conditional on assent to the additional or different terms." *No longer are communicating parties left to debate whether an acceptance perfectly meets the terms of an offer, but instead the existence of a binding contract may be based on words or conduct, which need not mirror an offer, so long as they reveal the parties' intention to be bound.* [Emphasis added.]

Considering that the UCC permits the formation of a contract by way of conduct that reveals the parties' understanding that a contract exists, and notwithstanding the suggestion of additional or even non-conforming terms, the complex of communications between [Sun and Myron] demonstrates that neither can the formation of a contract be confirmed or foreclosed without a resolution of the existing factual disputes and the weighing of the significance of the parties' convoluted communications.

* * * *

In short, it is conceivable—and the jury could find—that the parties' inability to agree on certain terms reveals the lack of an intent to be bound; in other words, that their communications constituted mere negotiations that never ripened into a contract. By the same token, the jury could find that a contract was formed despite a failure or an inability to agree on all terms. N.J.S.A. 12A:2-207(2) provides that an acceptance coupled with the proposal of new or different terms does not necessarily preclude the formation of a contract. *In such a circumstance, * * * the new or different terms proposed by the offeree [could] become part of the contract * * * .* [Emphasis added.]

All these questions required that the factfinder analyze the meaning and significance of the parties' communications based upon the legal framework provided by the UCC.

* * * *

a. In the "SEARCH THE N.J. COURTS DECISIONS" section, type "Sun Coast" in the box, and click on "Search!" In the result, click on the case name to access the opinion.

CASE 11.1 CONTINUED

* * * The trial judge correctly determined that the [contentions about] contract formation * * * raised fact questions to be decided by the jury * * * .

* * * *

In describing for the jury what it takes for the parties to form a binding contract, the judge stated:

> A proposal to accept an offer on any different terms is not an acceptance of the original offer. If any new or different terms are proposed in response to the offer, the response is not an acceptance, but rather a counteroffer. A counteroffer is a new offer by the party making that proposal. The new offer must in turn be agreed to by the party who made the original offer for there to be an acceptance.

As we have already explained, the UCC does not require that a party's response mirror an offer to result in a binding contract. The offeree may propose additional or different terms without necessarily having the response viewed as a non-binding counteroffer. Instead, an offeree's proposal of additional or conflicting terms may be found to constitute an acceptance, and the other or different terms viewed as mere proposals to modify the contract thus formed.

The judge's misstatement in this regard was hardly harmless * * * . In describing when the law recognizes that a contract was formed, the judge provided the jury with erroneous instructions that struck directly at the heart of the case.

• **Decision and Remedy** *The state intermediate appellate court concluded that the judge's instruction to the jury with respect to the question of whether Sun and Myron had formed a contract was "fundamentally flawed" and "provided insufficient guidance for the jury's resolution of the issues." On this basis, the court reversed the lower court's judgment and remanded the case for a new trial.*

• **The Ethical Dimension** *How does the UCC's obligation of good faith relate to the application of the principles concerning additional terms?*

• **The Legal Environment Dimension** *Applying the correct principles to the facts in this case, how would you have decided the issue? Explain.*

Additional Terms May Be Stricken. The UCC provides yet another option for dealing with conflicting terms in the parties' writings. Section 2–207(3) states that conduct by both parties that recognizes the existence of a contract is sufficient to establish a contract for sale even though the writings of the parties do not otherwise establish a contract. In this situation, "the terms of the particular contract will consist of those terms on which the writings of the parties agree, together with any supplementary terms incorporated under any other provisions of this Act." In a dispute over contract terms, this provision allows a court simply to strike from the contract those terms on which the parties do not agree.

Suppose that SMT Marketing orders goods over the phone from Brigg Sales, Inc., which ships the goods with an acknowledgment form (confirming the order) to SMT. SMT accepts and pays for the goods. The parties' writings do not establish a contract, but there is no question that a contract exists. If a dispute arises over the terms, such as the extent of any warranties, UCC 2–207(3) provides the governing rule.

As noted previously, the fact that a merchant's acceptance frequently contains additional terms or even terms that conflict with those of the offer is often referred to as the "battle of the forms." Although the UCC tries to eliminate this battle, the problem of differing contract terms still arises in commercial settings, particularly when contracts are based on the merchants' standard forms, such as order forms and confirmation forms.

Consideration

The common law rule that a contract requires consideration also applies to sales and lease contracts. Unlike the common law, however, the UCC does not require a contract modification to be supported by new consideration. The UCC states that an agreement modifying a contract for the sale or lease of goods "needs no consideration to be binding" [UCC 2–209(1), 2A–208(1)].

Of course, any contract modification must be made in good faith [UCC 1–203]. For example, Jim agrees to lease certain goods to Louise for a stated price.

Subsequently, a sudden shift in the market makes it difficult for Jim to lease the items to Louise at the given price without suffering a loss. Jim tells Louise of the situation, and Louise agrees to pay an additional sum for leasing the goods. Later, Louise reconsiders and refuses to pay more than the original lease price. Under the UCC, Louise's promise to modify the contract needs no consideration to be binding. Hence, Louise is bound by the modified contract.

In this example, a shift in the market is a *good faith* reason for contract modification. What if there really was no shift in the market, however, and Jim knew that Louise needed the goods immediately but refused to deliver them unless Louise agreed to pay an additional sum? This sort of extortion of a modification without a legitimate commercial reason would be ineffective, because it would violate the duty of good faith. Jim would not be permitted to enforce the higher price.

The Statute of Frauds

As discussed in Chapter 9, the Statute of Frauds requires that certain types of contracts, to be enforceable, must be in writing or evidenced by a writing. The UCC contains Statute of Frauds provisions covering sales and lease contracts. Under these provisions, sales contracts for goods priced at $500 or more and lease contracts requiring total payments of $1,000 or more must be in writing to be enforceable [UCC 2–201(1), 2A–201(1)]. (Note that these low threshold amounts may eventually be raised.)

Sufficiency of the Writing

The UCC has greatly relaxed the requirements for the sufficiency of a writing to satisfy the Statute of Frauds. A writing or a memorandum will be sufficient as long as it indicates that the parties intended to form a contract and as long as it is signed by the party (or agent of the party) against whom enforcement is sought. The contract normally will not be enforceable beyond the quantity of goods shown in the writing, however. All other terms can be proved in court by oral testimony. For leases, the writing must reasonably identify and describe the goods leased and the lease term.

Special Rules for Contracts between Merchants

Once again, the UCC provides a special rule for merchants. The rule, however, applies only to sales (under Article 2); there is no corresponding rule that applies to leases (under Article 2A).[4] Merchants can satisfy the requirements of a writing for the Statute of Frauds if, after the parties have agreed orally, one of the merchants sends a signed written confirmation to the other merchant. The communication must indicate the terms of the agreement, and the merchant receiving the confirmation must have reason to know of its contents. Unless the merchant who receives the confirmation gives written notice of objection to its contents within ten days after receipt, the writing is sufficient against the receiving merchant, even though he or she has not signed anything [UCC 2–201(2)].

Exceptions

The UCC defines three exceptions to the writing requirements of the Statute of Frauds. An oral contract for the sale of goods priced at $500 or more or the lease of goods involving total payments of $1,000 or more will be enforceable despite the absence of a writing in the circumstances described in the following subsections [UCC 2–201(3), 2A–201(4)]. These exceptions and other ways in which sales law differs from general contract law are summarized in Exhibit 11–1.

Specially Manufactured Goods An oral contract is enforceable if (1) it is for goods that are specially manufactured for a particular buyer or specially manufactured or obtained for a particular lessee, (2) these goods are not suitable for resale or lease to others in the ordinary course of the seller's or lessor's business, and (3) the seller or lessor has substantially started to manufacture the goods or has made commitments for the manufacture or procurement of the goods. In these situations, once the seller or lessor has taken action, the buyer or lessee cannot repudiate the agreement claiming the Statute of Frauds as a defense.

Admissions An oral contract for the sale or lease of goods is enforceable if the party against whom enforcement is sought admits in pleadings, testimony, or other court proceedings that a sales or lease contract was made. In this situation, the contract will be enforceable even though it was oral, but enforceability will be limited to the quantity of goods admitted.

4. According to the comments accompanying UCC 2A–201 (Article 2A's Statute of Frauds), the "between merchants" provision was not included because "the number of such transactions involving leases, as opposed to sales, was thought to be modest."

EXHIBIT 11–1 • Major Differences between Contract Law and Sales Law

	Contract Law	Sales Law
Contract Terms	Contract must contain all material terms.	Open terms are acceptable if parties intended to form a contract, but contract is not enforceable beyond quantity term.
Acceptance	Mirror image rule applies. If additional terms are added in acceptance, counteroffer is created.	Additional terms will not negate acceptance unless acceptance is expressly conditioned on assent to the additional terms.
Contract Modification	Modification requires consideration.	Modification does not require consideration.
Irrevocable Offers	Option contracts (with consideration).	Merchants' firm offers (without consideration).
Statute of Frauds Requirements	All material terms must be included in the writing.	Writing is required only for sale of goods of $500 or more, but contract is not enforceable beyond quantity specified. Merchants can satisfy the writing requirement by a confirmatory memorandum evidencing their agreement. *Exceptions:* 1. Specially manufactured goods. 2. Admissions by party against whom enforcement is sought. 3. Partial performance.

Partial Performance An oral contract for the sale or lease of goods is enforceable if payment has been made and accepted or goods have been received and accepted. This is the "partial performance" exception. The oral contract will be enforced at least to the extent that performance *actually* took place.

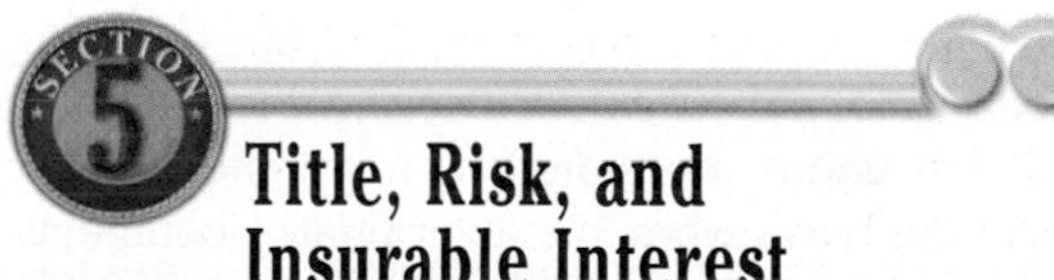

Section 5 Title, Risk, and Insurable Interest

Before the creation of the UCC, *title*—the right of ownership—was the central concept in sales law, controlling all issues of rights and remedies of the parties to a sales contract. There were numerous problems with this concept. For example, frequently it was difficult to determine when title actually passed from seller to buyer, and therefore it was also difficult to predict which party a court would decide had title at the time of a loss. Because of such problems, the UCC divorced the question of title as completely as possible from the question of the rights and obligations of buyers, sellers, and third parties (such as subsequent purchasers, creditors, or the tax collector).

In some situations, title is still relevant under the UCC, and the UCC has special rules for locating title. In most situations, however, the UCC has replaced the concept of title with three other concepts: (1) identification, (2) risk of loss, and (3) insurable interest.

In lease contracts, of course, title to the goods is retained by the lessor-owner of the goods. Hence, the UCC's provisions relating to passage of title do not apply to leased goods. Other concepts discussed in this chapter, though, including *identification, risk of loss,* and *insurable interest,* relate to lease contracts as well as to sales contracts.

Identification

Before any interest in specific goods can pass from the seller or lessor to the buyer or lessee, two conditions must prevail:

1. The goods must be in existence.
2. They must be identified as the specific goods designated in the contract.

Identification takes place when the goods are designated as the subject matter of a sales or lease contract. Title and risk of loss cannot pass to the buyer from the seller unless the goods are identified to the contract [UCC 2–105(2)]. (As mentioned, title to leased goods remains with the lessor—or, if the owner is a third party, with that party. The lessee does not acquire title to leased goods.) Identification is significant because it gives the buyer or lessee the right to insure (or obtain an insurable interest in) the goods and the right to recover from third parties who damage the goods.

Once the goods are in existence, the parties can agree in their contract on when identification will take place. If they do not so specify, however, and if the contract calls for the sale or lease of specific and ascertained goods that are already in existence, identification takes place at the time the contract is made [UCC 2–501(1), 2A–217].

Existing Goods If the contract calls for the sale or lease of specific and ascertained goods that are already in existence, identification takes place at the time the contract is made. For example, you contract to purchase or lease a fleet of five cars by the vehicle identification numbers of the cars.

Goods that are part of a larger mass are identified when the goods are marked, shipped, or somehow designated by the seller or lessor as the particular goods to pass under the contract. Suppose that a buyer orders one thousand cases of beans from a lot of ten thousand cases. Until the seller separates the one thousand cases of beans from the ten-thousand-case lot, title and risk of loss remain with the seller.

Future Goods If a sale or lease involves unborn animals to be born within twelve months after contracting, identification takes place when the animals are conceived. If a sale involves crops that are to be harvested within twelve months (or the next harvest season occurring after contracting, whichever is longer), identification takes place when the crops are planted; otherwise, identification takes place when the crops begin to grow. In a sale or lease of any other future goods, identification occurs when the goods are shipped, marked, or otherwise designated by the seller or lessor as the goods to which the contract refers.

When Title Passes

Once goods exist and are identified, the provisions of UCC 2–401 apply to the passage of title. Unless an agreement is explicitly made,[5] title passes to the buyer at the time and the place the seller performs the *physical delivery* of the goods [UCC 2–401(2)].

Shipment and Destination Contracts In the absence of agreement, delivery arrangements can determine when title passes from the seller to the buyer. In a **shipment contract,** the seller is required or authorized to ship goods by carrier, such as a trucking company. Under a shipment contract, the seller is required only to deliver the goods into the hands of a carrier, and title passes to the buyer at the time and place of shipment [UCC 2–401(2)(a)]. *Generally, all contracts are assumed to be shipment contracts if nothing to the contrary is stated in the contract.*

In a **destination contract,** the seller is required to deliver the goods to a particular destination, usually directly to the buyer, although sometimes the buyer designates that the goods should be delivered to another party. Title passes to the buyer when the goods are *tendered* at that destination [UCC 2–401(2)(b)]. A *tender of delivery* is the seller's placing or holding of conforming goods at the buyer's disposition (with any necessary notice), enabling the buyer to take delivery [UCC 2–503(1)].

Delivery without Movement of the Goods When the contract of sale does not call for the seller's shipment or delivery of the goods (when the buyer is to pick up the goods), the passage of title depends on whether the seller must deliver a *document of title,* such as a bill of lading or a warehouse receipt, to the buyer. A *bill of lading* is a receipt for goods that is signed by a carrier and that serves as a contract for the transportation of the goods. A *warehouse receipt* is a receipt issued by a warehouser for goods stored in a warehouse.

When a document of title is required, title passes to the buyer *when and where the document is delivered.* Thus, if the goods are stored in a warehouse, title passes to the buyer when the appropriate documents are delivered to the buyer. The goods never move. In fact, the buyer can choose to leave the goods at the same warehouse for a period of time, and the buyer's title to those goods will be unaffected.

When no documents of title are required, and delivery is made without moving the goods, title passes at

5. In many sections of the UCC, the words "unless otherwise explicitly agreed" appear, meaning that any explicit agreement between the buyer and the seller determines the rights, duties, and liabilities of the parties, including when title passes.

the time and place the sales contract is made, if the goods have already been identified. If the goods have not been identified, title does not pass until identification occurs. Consider an example. Rogers sells lumber to Bodan. It is agreed that Bodan will pick up the lumber at the yard. If the lumber has been identified (segregated, marked, or in any other way distinguished from all other lumber), title passes to Bodan when the contract is signed. If the lumber is still in general storage bins at the mill, title does not pass to Bodan until the particular pieces of lumber to be sold under this contract are identified [UCC 2–401(3)].

The Entrustment Rule According to UCC 2–403(2), entrusting goods to a merchant *who deals in goods of that kind* gives the merchant the power to transfer all rights to *a buyer in the ordinary course of business.* This is known as the *entrustment rule.* A buyer in the ordinary course of business is a person who—in good faith and without knowledge that the sale violates the rights of another party—buys goods in the ordinary course from a merchant (other than a pawnbroker) in the business of selling goods of that kind [UCC 1–201(9)].

In Sales Contracts. The entrustment rule basically allows innocent buyers to obtain title to goods purchased from merchants even if the merchants do not have good title. Consider an example. Jan leaves her watch with a jeweler to be repaired. The jeweler sells both new and used watches. The jeweler sells Jan's watch to Kim, a customer who does not know that the jeweler has no right to sell it. Kim, as a good faith buyer, gets good title against Jan's claim of ownership.[6]

Note, however, that Kim obtains only those rights held by the person entrusting the goods (here, Jan). Suppose instead that in this example, Jan had stolen the watch from Greg and then left it with the jeweler to be repaired. The jeweler then sold it to Kim. Kim would obtain good title against Jan, who entrusted the watch to the jeweler, but not against Greg (the real owner), who neither entrusted the watch to Jan nor authorized Jan to entrust it.

Red Elvis, an artwork by Andy Warhol, was at the center of the dispute over title in the following case.

6. Jan, of course, can sue the jeweler for the tort of conversion (or trespass to personal property) to obtain damages equivalent to the cash value of the watch (see Chapter 12).

CASE 11.2 Lindholm v. Brant

Supreme Court of Connecticut, 2007. 283 Conn. 65, 925 A.2d 1048.

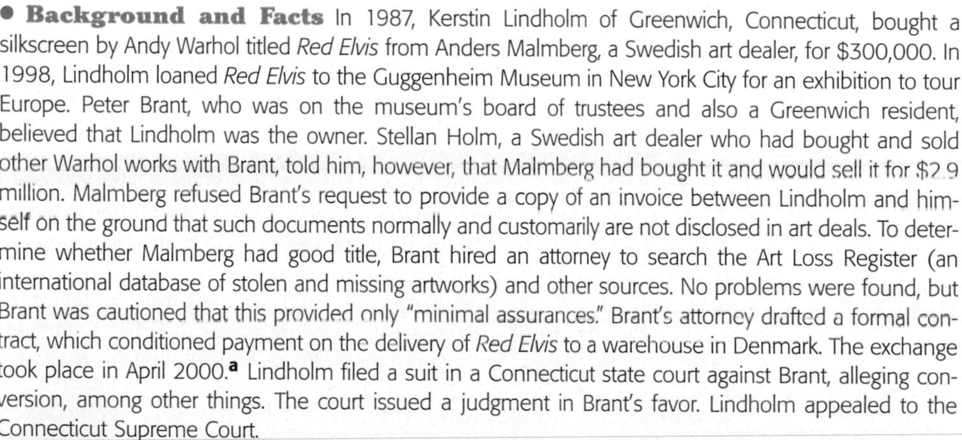

• Background and Facts In 1987, Kerstin Lindholm of Greenwich, Connecticut, bought a silkscreen by Andy Warhol titled *Red Elvis* from Anders Malmberg, a Swedish art dealer, for $300,000. In 1998, Lindholm loaned *Red Elvis* to the Guggenheim Museum in New York City for an exhibition to tour Europe. Peter Brant, who was on the museum's board of trustees and also a Greenwich resident, believed that Lindholm was the owner. Stellan Holm, a Swedish art dealer who had bought and sold other Warhol works with Brant, told him, however, that Malmberg had bought it and would sell it for $2.9 million. Malmberg refused Brant's request to provide a copy of an invoice between Lindholm and himself on the ground that such documents normally and customarily are not disclosed in art deals. To determine whether Malmberg had good title, Brant hired an attorney to search the Art Loss Register (an international database of stolen and missing artworks) and other sources. No problems were found, but Brant was cautioned that this provided only "minimal assurances." Brant's attorney drafted a formal contract, which conditioned payment on the delivery of *Red Elvis* to a warehouse in Denmark. The exchange took place in April 2000.[a] Lindholm filed a suit in a Connecticut state court against Brant, alleging conversion, among other things. The court issued a judgment in Brant's favor. Lindholm appealed to the Connecticut Supreme Court.

IN THE LANGUAGE OF THE COURT
***SULLIVAN,* J. [Justice]**

* * * *

* * * "A person buys goods in the ordinary course if the sale to the person comports with the usual or customary practices in the kind of business in which the seller is engaged

a. Unaware of this deal, Lindholm accepted a Japanese buyer's offer of $4.6 million for *Red Elvis.* The funds were wired to Malmberg, who kept them. Lindholm filed a criminal complaint against Malmberg in Sweden. In 2003, a Swedish court convicted Malmberg of "gross fraud embezzlement." The court awarded Lindholm $4.6 million and other relief.

CASE CONTINUES

CASE 11.2 CONTINUED or with the seller's own usual or customary practices * * *" [according to Connecticut General Statutes Annotated Section 42a-1-201(9), Connecticut's version of UCC 1–201(9)]. *A person buys goods in good faith if there is "honesty in fact and the observance of reasonable commercial standards of fair dealing" in the conduct or transaction concerned [under Section 42a-1-201(20)].* [Emphasis added.]

We are required, therefore, to determine whether the defendant followed the usual or customary practices and observed reasonable commercial standards of fair dealing in the art industry in his dealings with Malmberg. * * * The defendant presented expert testimony that the vast majority of art transactions, in which the buyer has no reason for concern about the seller's ability to convey good title, are "completed on a handshake and an exchange of an invoice." It is not customary for sophisticated buyers and sellers to obtain a signed invoice from the original seller to the dealer prior to a transaction, nor is it an ordinary or customary practice to request the underlying invoice or corroborating information as to a dealer's authority to convey title. Moreover, it is not customary to approach the owner of an artwork if the owner regularly worked with a particular art dealer because any inquiries about an art transaction customarily are presented to the art dealer rather than directly to the [owner]. *It is customary to rely upon representations made by respected dealers regarding their authority to sell works of art.* A dealer customarily is not required to present an invoice establishing when and from whom he bought the artwork or the conditions of the purchase. [Emphasis added.]

We are compelled to conclude, however, that the sale from Malmberg to the defendant was unlike the vast majority of art transactions. * * * Under such circumstances, a handshake and an exchange of invoice is not sufficient to confer status as a buyer in the ordinary course.

* * * *

* * * A merchant buyer has a heightened duty of inquiry when a reasonable merchant would have doubts or questions regarding the seller's authority to sell. * * * In the present case, the defendant had concerns about Malmberg's ability to convey good title to *Red Elvis* because he believed that Lindholm might have had a claim to the painting. The defendant also was concerned that Malmberg had not yet acquired title to the painting * * * .

Because of his concern that Lindholm might make a claim to *Red Elvis*, the defendant took the extraordinary step of hiring counsel to conduct an investigation and to negotiate a formal contract of sale on his behalf. * * * Such searches typically are not conducted during the course of a normal art transaction and, therefore, provided the defendant with at least some assurance that Lindholm had no claims to the painting.

Moreover, * * * both Malmberg and Holm had reputations as honest, reliable, and trustworthy art dealers. * * * The defendant had little reason to doubt Malmberg's claim that he was the owner of *Red Elvis*, and any doubts that he did have reasonably were allayed [dispelled] by relying on Holm's assurances that Malmberg had bought the painting from the plaintiff * * * .

The defendant's concerns were further allayed when Malmberg delivered *Red Elvis* to a * * * warehouse in Denmark, the delivery location the parties had agreed to in the contract of sale. At the time of the sale, the painting was on loan to the Guggenheim, whose policy it was to release a painting on loan only to the true owner, or to someone the true owner had authorized to take possession. * * * We conclude that these steps were sufficient to conform to reasonable commercial standards for the sale of artwork under the circumstances and, therefore, that the defendant had status as a buyer in the ordinary course of business.

• **Decision and Remedy** *The Connecticut Supreme Court affirmed the judgment of the lower court. The state supreme court concluded, "on the basis of all the circumstances surrounding this sale," that Brant was a buyer in the ordinary course of business and, therefore, took all rights to* Red Elvis *under UCC 2–403(2).*

• **The Ethical Dimension** *How did the "usual and customary" methods of dealing in the art business help Malmberg deceive the other parties in this case? What additional steps might those parties have taken to thwart this deceit?*

• **The Global Dimension** *Considering the international locales in this case, why was Lindholm able to bring an action against Brant in Connecticut?*

In Lease Contracts. Article 2A provides a similar rule for leased goods. If a lessor entrusts goods to a lessee-merchant who deals in goods of that kind, and the merchant transfers the goods to a buyer or sublessee in the ordinary course of business, the buyer or sublessee acquires all of the rights that the lessor had in the goods [UCC 2A–305(2)].

Risk of Loss

Under the UCC, risk of loss does not necessarily pass with title. When risk of loss passes from a seller or lessor to a buyer or lessee is generally determined by the contract between the parties. Sometimes, the contract states expressly when the risk of loss passes. At other times, it does not, and a court must interpret the existing terms to ascertain whether the risk has passed.

Delivery with Movement of the Goods

When there is no specification in the agreement, the following rules apply to cases involving movement of the goods (so-called carrier cases). In a shipment contract, if the seller or lessor is required or authorized to ship goods by carrier (but not required to deliver them to a particular destination), risk of loss passes to the buyer or lessee when the goods are duly delivered to the carrier [UCC 2–509(1)(a), 2A–219(2)(a)]. In a destination contract, the risk of loss passes to the buyer or lessee when the goods are tendered to the buyer or lessee at the specified destination [UCC 2–509(1)(b), 2A–219(2)(b)].

Specific terms in the contract help determine when risk of loss passes to the buyer. These terms, which are listed and defined in Exhibit 11–2, relate generally to the determination of which party will bear the costs of delivery, as well as which party will bear the risk of loss.

Shipment Contracts. As noted, in a shipment contract, risk of loss passes to the buyer or lessee when the goods are duly delivered to the carrier [UCC 2–509(1)(a), 2A–219(2)(a)]. For example, a seller in Texas sells five hundred cases of grapefruit to a buyer in New York, F.O.B. Houston (free on board in Houston, which means that the buyer pays the transportation charges from Houston—see Exhibit 11–2). The contract authorizes shipment by carrier; it does not require that the seller tender the grapefruit in New York. Risk passes to the buyer when conforming goods are properly placed in the possession of the carrier. If the goods are damaged in transit, the loss is the buyer's. (Actually, buyers have recourse against carriers, subject to certain limitations, and they may insure the goods from the time the goods leave the seller.)

Destination Contracts. As stated above, in a destination contract, the risk of loss passes to the buyer or lessee when the goods are tendered to the buyer or lessee at the specified destination [UCC 2–509(1)(b), 2A–219(2)(b)]. In the preceding example, if the contract had been a destination contract, F.O.B. New York (see Exhibit 11–2), risk of loss during transit to New

EXHIBIT 11–2 • Contract Terms—Definitions

The contract terms listed and defined in this exhibit help to determine which party will bear the costs of delivery and when risk of loss will pass from the seller to the buyer

F.O.B. (free on board)—Indicates that the selling price of goods includes transportation costs to the specific F.O.B. place named in the contract. The seller pays the expenses and carries the risk of loss to the F.O.B. place named [UCC 2–319(1)]. If the named place is the place from which the goods are shipped (for example, the seller's city or place of business), the contract is a shipment contract. If the named place is the place to which the goods are to be shipped (for example, the buyer's city or place of business), the contract is a destination contract.

F.A.S. (free alongside)—Requires that the seller, at his or her own expense and risk, deliver the goods alongside the carrier before risk passes to the buyer [UCC 2–319(2)].

C.I.F. or **C.&F.** (cost, insurance, and freight or just cost and freight)—Requires, among other things, that the seller "put the goods in possession of a carrier" before risk passes to the buyer [UCC 2–320(2)]. (These are basically pricing terms, and the contracts remain shipment contracts, not destination contracts.)

Delivery ex-ship (delivery from the carrying vessel)—Means that risk of loss does not pass to the buyer until the goods are properly unloaded from the ship or other carrier [UCC 2–322].

York would have been the seller's and would not have passed to the buyer until the carrier tendered the goods to the buyer in New York.

Delivery without Movement of the Goods The UCC also addresses situations in which the seller or lessor is required neither to ship nor to deliver the goods. Frequently, the buyer or lessee is to pick up the goods from the seller or lessor, or the goods are to be held by a bailee. A *bailment* is a temporary delivery of personal property, without passage of title, into the care of another, called a *bailee*. Under the UCC, a bailee is a party who—by a bill of lading, warehouse receipt, or other document of title—acknowledges possession of goods and contracts to deliver them. A warehousing company, for example, or a trucking company that normally issues documents of title for the goods it receives is a bailee.

Goods Held by the Seller. If the goods are held by the seller, a document of title usually is not used. If the seller is not a merchant, the risk of loss to goods held by the seller passes to the buyer on *tender of delivery* [UCC 2–509(3)]. If the seller is a merchant, risk of loss to goods held by the seller passes to the buyer when the buyer *actually takes physical possession of the goods* [UCC 2–509(3)]. For example, Henry Ganno purchases lumber at a lumberyard, and an employee at the lumberyard loads it onto Ganno's truck with a forklift. Once the truck is loaded, the risk of loss passes to Ganno because he has taken physical possession of the goods. In the event that Ganno suffers a loss driving away from the lumberyard, he—not the lumberyard—will bear the burden of that loss.[7]

In respect to leases, the risk of loss passes to the lessee on the lessee's receipt of the goods if the lessor is a merchant. Otherwise, the risk passes to the lessee on tender of delivery [UCC 2A–219(c)]. For example, Erikson Crane leases a helicopter from Jevis, Ltd., which is in the business of renting aircraft. While Erikson's pilot is on the way to Idaho to pick up the particular helicopter, the helicopter is damaged during an unexpected storm. In this situation, Jevis is a merchant-lessor, so it would bear the risk of loss to the leased helicopter until Erikson took possession of the helicopter.

Goods Held by a Bailee. When a bailee is holding goods for a person who has contracted to sell them and the goods are to be delivered without being moved, the goods are usually represented by a negotiable or nonnegotiable document of title (a bill of lading or a warehouse receipt). Risk of loss passes to the buyer when (1) the buyer receives a negotiable document of title for the goods, (2) the bailee acknowledges the buyer's right to possess the goods, or (3) the buyer receives a nonnegotiable document of title or a writing (record) directing the bailee *and* has had a *reasonable time* to present the document to the bailee and demand the goods. Obviously, if the bailee refuses to honor the document, the risk of loss remains with the seller [UCC 2–503(4)(b), 2–509(2)].

With respect to leases, if goods held by a bailee are to be delivered without being moved, the risk of loss passes to the lessee on acknowledgment by the bailee of the lessee's right to possession of the goods [UCC 2A–219(2)(b)].

Conditional Sales Buyers and sellers sometimes form sales contracts that are conditioned either on the buyer's approval of the goods or on the buyer's resale of the goods. Under such contracts, the buyer is in possession of the goods. Sometimes, however, problems arise as to whether the buyer or seller should bear the loss if, for example, the goods are damaged or stolen while in the possession of the buyer.

Sale or Return. A **sale or return** (sometimes called a *sale and return*) is a type of contract by which the buyer purchases the goods but has a conditional right to return the goods (undo the sale) within a specified time period. When the buyer receives possession at the time of sale, title and risk of loss pass to the buyer. Title and risk of loss remain with the buyer until the buyer returns the goods to the seller within the time period specified. If the buyer fails to return the goods within this time period, the sale is finalized. The return of the goods is made at the buyer's risk and expense. Goods held under a sale-or-return contract are subject to the claims of the buyer's creditors while they are in the buyer's possession.

The UCC treats a **consignment** as a sale or return. Under a consignment, the owner of goods (the *consignor*) delivers them to another (the *consignee*) for the consignee to sell or to keep. If the consignee sells the goods, the consignee must pay the consignor for them. If the consignee does not sell or keep the goods, they may simply be returned to the consignor. While the goods are in the possession of the consignee, the consignee holds title to them, and creditors

7. *Ganno v. Lanoga Corp.*, 119 Wash.App. 310, 80 P.3d 180 (2003).

of the consignee will prevail over the consignor in any action to repossess the goods [UCC 2–326(3)].

Sale on Approval. Usually, when a seller offers to sell goods to a buyer and permits the buyer to take the goods on a trial basis, a **sale on approval** is made. The term *sale* here is a misnomer, as only an *offer* to sell has been made, along with a bailment created by the buyer's possession.

Therefore, title and risk of loss (from causes beyond the buyer's control) remain with the seller until the buyer accepts (approves) the offer. Acceptance can be made expressly, by any act inconsistent with the *trial* purpose or the seller's ownership, or by the buyer's election not to return the goods within the trial period. If the buyer does not wish to accept, the buyer may notify the seller of that fact within the trial period, and the return is made at the seller's expense and risk [UCC 2–327(1)]. Goods held on approval are not subject to the claims of the buyer's creditors until acceptance.

Risk of Loss When a Sales or Lease Contract Is Breached There are many ways to breach a sales or lease contract, and the transfer of risk operates differently depending on which party breaches. Generally, the party in breach bears the risk of loss.

When the Seller or Lessor Breaches. If the goods are so nonconforming that the buyer has the right to reject them, the risk of loss does not pass to the buyer until the defects are *cured* (that is, until the goods are repaired, replaced, or discounted in price by the seller) or until the buyer accepts the goods in spite of their defects (thus waiving the right to reject). For example, a buyer orders blue file cabinets from a seller, F.O.B. seller's plant. The seller ships black file cabinets instead. The black cabinets (nonconforming goods) are damaged in transit. The risk of loss falls on the seller. Had the seller shipped blue cabinets (conforming goods) instead, the risk would have fallen on the buyer [UCC 2–510(2)].

If a buyer accepts a shipment of goods and later discovers a defect, acceptance can be revoked. Revocation allows the buyer to pass the risk of loss back to the seller, at least to the extent that the buyer's insurance does not cover the loss [UCC 2–510(2)].

In regard to leases, Article 2A states a similar rule. If the lessor or supplier tenders goods that are so nonconforming that the lessee has the right to reject them, the risk of loss remains with the lessor or the supplier until cure or acceptance [UCC 2A–220(1)(a)]. If the lessee, after acceptance, revokes his or her acceptance of nonconforming goods, the revocation passes the risk of loss back to the seller or supplier, to the extent that the lessee's insurance does not cover the loss [UCC 2A–220(1)(b)].

When the Buyer or Lessee Breaches. The general rule is that when a buyer or lessee breaches a contract, the risk of loss *immediately* shifts to the buyer or lessee. There are three important limitations to this rule [UCC 2–510(3), 2A–220(2)]:

1. The seller or lessor must already have identified the contract goods.
2. The buyer or lessee bears the risk for only a *commercially reasonable time* after the seller or lessor has learned of the breach.
3. The buyer or lessee is liable only to the extent of any deficiency in the seller's or lessor's insurance coverage.

Insurable Interest

Parties to sales and lease contracts often obtain insurance coverage to protect against damage, loss, or destruction of goods. Any party purchasing insurance, however, must have a sufficient interest in the insured item to obtain a valid policy. Insurance laws—not the UCC—determine sufficiency. The UCC is helpful, however, because it contains certain rules regarding insurable interests in goods.

A buyer or lessee has an **insurable interest** in identified goods. The moment the contract goods are *identified* by the seller or lessor, the buyer or lessee has a special property interest that allows the buyer or lessee to obtain necessary insurance coverage for those goods even before the risk of loss has passed [UCC 2–501(1), 2A–218(1)].

A seller has an insurable interest in goods as long as he or she retains title to the goods. Even after title passes to a buyer, however, a seller who has a security interest in the goods, which is a legal right to secure payment, still has an insurable interest and can insure the goods [UCC 2–501(2)]. Hence, both a buyer and a seller can have an insurable interest in identical goods at the same time. Of course, the buyer or seller must sustain an actual loss to have the right to recover from an insurance company. In regard to leases, the lessor retains an insurable interest in leased goods until an option to buy has been exercised by the lessee and the risk of loss has passed to the lessee [UCC 2A–218(3)].

Performance of Sales and Lease Contracts

To understand the obligations of the parties under a sales or lease contract, it is necessary to know the duties and obligations each party has assumed under the terms of the contract. Keep in mind that "duties and obligations" under the terms of the contract include those specified by the agreement, by custom, and by the UCC.

In the performance of a sales or lease contract, the basic obligation of the seller or lessor is to *transfer and deliver conforming goods.* The basic obligation of the buyer or lessee is to *accept and pay for conforming goods* in accordance with the contract [UCC 2–301, 2A–516(1)]. Overall performance of a sales or lease contract is controlled by the agreement between the parties. When the contract is unclear and disputes arise, the courts look to the UCC.

The Good Faith Requirement

The obligations of good faith and commercial reasonableness underlie every sales and lease contract within the UCC. These obligations can form the basis for a suit for breach of contract later on. The UCC's good faith provision, which can never be disclaimed, reads as follows: "Every contract or duty within this Act imposes an obligation of good faith in its performance or enforcement" [UCC 1–203]. Good faith means honesty in fact. In the case of a merchant, it means honesty in fact and the observance of reasonable commercial standards of fair dealing in the trade [UCC 2–103(1)(b)]. In other words, merchants are held to a higher standard of performance or duty than nonmerchants.

Obligations of the Seller or Lessor

The major obligation of the seller or lessor under a sales or lease contract is to tender conforming goods to the buyer or lessee. **Tender of delivery** requires that the seller or lessor have and hold *conforming goods* at the disposal of the buyer or lessee and give the buyer or lessee whatever notification is reasonably necessary to enable the buyer or lessee to take delivery [UCC 2–503(1), 2A–508(1)]. **Conforming goods** are goods that conform exactly to the description of the goods in the contract.

Tender must occur at a *reasonable hour* and in a *reasonable manner.* For example, a seller cannot call the buyer at 2:00 A.M. and say, "The goods are ready. I'll give you twenty minutes to get them." Unless the parties have agreed otherwise, the goods must be tendered for delivery at a reasonable hour and kept available for a reasonable period of time to enable the buyer to take possession of them [UCC 2–503(1)(a)].

All goods called for by a contract must be tendered in a single delivery unless the parties agree otherwise [UCC 2–612, 2A–510] or the circumstances are such that either party can rightfully request delivery in lots [UCC 2–307].

Place of Delivery If the contract does not designate the place of delivery for the goods, and the buyer is expected to pick them up, the place of delivery is the *seller's place of business* or, if the seller has none, the *seller's residence* [UCC 2–308]. If the contract involves the sale of *identified goods,* and the parties know when they enter into the contract that these goods are located somewhere other than at the seller's place of business (such as at a warehouse), then the *location of the goods* is the place for their delivery [UCC 2–308].

The Perfect Tender Rule As previously noted, the seller or lessor has an obligation to ship or tender *conforming goods,* and this entitles the buyer or lessee to accept and pay for the goods according to the terms of the contract. Under the common law, the seller was obligated to deliver goods in conformity with the terms of the contract in every detail. This was called the **perfect tender rule.** The UCC preserves the perfect tender doctrine by stating that if goods or tender of delivery fail *in any respect* to conform to the contract, the buyer or lessee has the right to accept the goods, reject the entire shipment, or accept part and reject part [UCC 2–601, 2A–509].

Exceptions to the Perfect Tender Rule Because of the rigidity of the perfect tender rule, several exceptions to the rule have been created, some of which we discuss here.

Agreement of the Parties. Exceptions to the perfect tender rule may be established by agreement. If the parties have agreed, for example, that defective goods or parts will not be rejected if the seller or lessor is able to repair or replace them within a reasonable period of time, the perfect tender rule does not apply.

Cure. The UCC does not specifically define the term **cure,** but it refers to the right of the seller or lessor to repair, adjust, or replace defective or nonconforming goods [UCC 2–508, 2A–513]. When any tender of delivery is rejected because of nonconforming goods and the time for performance has not yet expired, the seller or lessor can promptly notify the buyer or lessee of the intention to cure and can then do so *within the contract time for performance* [UCC 2–508(1), 2A–513(1)]. Once the time for performance under the contract has expired, the seller or lessor can still exercise the right to cure if he or she has *reasonable grounds to believe that the nonconforming tender will be acceptable to the buyer or lessee* [UCC 2–508(2), 2A–513(2)].

The right to cure substantially restricts the right of the buyer or lessee to reject goods. For example, if a lessee refuses a tender of goods as nonconforming but does not disclose the nature of the defect to the lessor, the lessee cannot later assert the defect as a defense if the defect is one that the lessor could have cured. Generally, buyers and lessees must act in good faith and state specific reasons for refusing to accept goods [UCC 2–605, 2A–514].

Substitution of Carriers. When an agreed-on manner of delivery (such as the use of a particular carrier to transport the goods) becomes impracticable or unavailable through no fault of either party, but a commercially reasonable substitute is available, this substitute performance is sufficient tender to the buyer and must be used [UCC 2–614(1)].

Commercial Impracticability. Occurrences unforeseen by either party when a contract was made may make performance commercially impracticable. When this occurs, the rule of perfect tender no longer holds. According to UCC 2–615(a) and 2A–405(a), delay in delivery or nondelivery in whole or in part is not a breach when performance has been made impracticable "by the occurrence of a contingency the nonoccurrence of which was a basic assumption on which the contract was made." The seller or lessor must, however, notify the buyer or lessee as soon as practicable that there will be a delay or nondelivery.

Destruction of Identified Goods. Sometimes, an unexpected event, such as a fire, totally destroys goods through no fault of either party and before risk passes to the buyer or lessee. In such a situation, if the *goods were identified at the time the contract was formed,* the parties are excused from performance [UCC 2–613, 2A–221]. If the goods are only partially destroyed, however, the buyer or lessee can inspect them and either treat the contract as void or accept the damaged goods with a reduction of the contract price.

Cooperation and Assurance. Two other exceptions to the perfect tender doctrine apply equally to parties to sales and lease contracts: the duty of cooperation and the right of assurance.

Sometimes the performance of one party depends on the cooperation of the other. The UCC provides that when such cooperation is not forthcoming, the other party can either suspend his or her own performance without liability and hold the uncooperative party in breach or proceed to perform the contract in any reasonable manner [see UCC 2–311(3)(b)].

The UCC provides that if one of the parties to a contract has "reasonable grounds" to believe that the other party will not perform as contracted, he or she may in *writing* "demand adequate assurance of due performance" from the other party. Until such assurance is received, he or she may "suspend" further performance without liability. What constitutes "reasonable grounds" is determined by commercial standards. If such assurances are not forthcoming within a reasonable time (not to exceed thirty days), the failure to respond may be treated as a *repudiation* of the contract [UCC 2–609, 2A–401].

Obligations of the Buyer or Lessee

Once the seller or lessor has adequately tendered delivery, the buyer or lessee is obligated to accept the goods and pay for them according to the terms of the contract.

Payment In the absence of any specific agreements, the buyer or lessee must make payment at the time and place the buyer or lessee *receives* the goods [UCC 2–310(a), 2A–516(1)]. When a sale is made on credit, the buyer is obliged to pay according to the specified credit terms (for example, 60, 90, or 120 days), not when the goods are received. The credit period usually begins on the *date of shipment* [UCC 2–310(d)]. Under a lease contract, a lessee must make the lease payment specified in the contract [UCC 2A–516(1)].

Payment can be made by any means agreed on between the parties—cash or any other method generally acceptable in the commercial world. If the seller demands cash when the buyer offers a check, credit card, or the like, the seller must permit the buyer reasonable time to obtain legal tender [UCC 2–511].

Acceptance A buyer or lessee can manifest assent to the delivered goods in the following ways, each of which constitutes acceptance:

1. There is an acceptance if the buyer or lessee, after having had a reasonable opportunity to inspect the goods, signifies agreement to the seller or lessor that the goods are either conforming or are acceptable in spite of their nonconformity [UCC 2–606(1)(a), 2A–515(1)(a)].
2. Acceptance is presumed if the buyer or lessee has had a reasonable opportunity to inspect the goods and has failed to reject them within a reasonable period of time [UCC 2–602(1), 2–606(1)(b), 2A–515(1)(b)].
3. In sales contracts, the buyer will be deemed to have accepted the goods if he or she performs any act inconsistent with the seller's ownership. For example, any use or resale of the goods generally constitutes an acceptance. Limited use for the sole purpose of testing or inspecting the goods is not an acceptance, however [UCC 2–606(1)(c)].

If some of the goods delivered do not conform to the contract and the seller or lessor has failed to cure, the buyer or lessee can make a *partial* acceptance [UCC 2–601(c), 2A–509(1)]. The same is true if the nonconformity was not reasonably discoverable before acceptance. A buyer or lessee cannot accept less than a single commercial unit, however. A *commercial unit* is defined by the UCC as a unit of goods that, by commercial usage, is viewed as a "single whole" for purposes of sale, division of which would materially impair the character of the unit, its market value, or its use [UCC 2–105(6), 2A–103(c)]. A commercial unit can be a single article (such as a machine), a set of articles (such as a suite of furniture or an assortment of sizes), a quantity (such as a bale, a gross, or a carload), or any other unit treated in the trade as a single whole.

Anticipatory Repudiation

What if, before the time for contract performance, one party clearly communicates to the other the intention not to perform? Such an action is a breach of the contract by *anticipatory repudiation*. When anticipatory repudiation occurs, the nonbreaching party has a choice of two responses. One option is to treat the repudiation as a final breach by pursuing a remedy; the other is to wait and hope that the repudiating party will decide to honor the obligations required by the contract despite the avowed intention to renege [UCC 2–610, 2A–402]. (In either situation, the nonbreaching party may suspend performance.)

Should the second option be pursued, the UCC permits the breaching party (subject to some limitations) to "retract" his or her repudiation. This can be done by any method that clearly indicates an intent to perform. Once retraction is made, the rights of the repudiating party under the contract are reinstated [UCC 2–611, 2A–403].

Remedies for Breach of Sales and Lease Contracts

Sometimes, circumstances make it difficult for a person to carry out the performance promised in a contract, in which case the contract may be breached. When a breach occurs, the aggrieved party looks for remedies. These remedies range from retaining the goods to requiring the breaching party's performance under the contract. The general purpose of these remedies is to put the aggrieved party "in as good a position as if the other party had fully performed." Remedies under the UCC are *cumulative* in nature. In other words, an innocent party to a breached sales or lease contract is not limited to one, exclusive remedy. (Of course, a party still may not recover twice for the same harm.)

Remedies of the Seller or Lessor

A buyer or lessee breaches a sales or lease contract by any of the following actions: (1) wrongfully rejecting tender of the goods; (2) wrongfully revoking acceptance of the goods; (3) failing to make payment on or before delivery of the goods; or (4) repudiating the contract. On the buyer's or lessee's breach, the seller or lessor is afforded several distinct remedies under the UCC, including those discussed here.

The Right to Withhold Delivery In general, sellers and lessors can withhold or discontinue performance of their obligations under sales or lease contracts when the buyers or lessees are in breach. If a buyer or lessee has wrongfully rejected or revoked acceptance of contract goods (rejection and revocation of acceptance will be discussed shortly), failed to make proper and timely payment, or repudiated a part of the contract, the seller or lessor can withhold delivery of the goods in question [UCC 2–703(a), 2A–523(1)(c)]. If the breach results from the buyer's or lessee's insolvency (inability to pay debts as they become due), the seller or lessor can refuse to deliver the goods unless the buyer or lessee pays in cash [UCC 2–702(1), 2A–525(1)].

The Right to Resell or Dispose of the Goods When a buyer or lessee breaches or repudiates the contract while the seller or lessor is still in possession of the goods, the seller or lessor can resell or dispose of the goods, holding the buyer or lessee liable for any loss [UCC 2–703(d), 2–706(1), 2A–523(1)(e), 2A–527(1)].

The Right to Recover the Purchase Price or Lease Payments Due Under the UCC, an unpaid seller or lessor who is unable to resell or dispose of the goods can bring an action to recover the purchase price or the payments due under the lease contract, plus incidental damages, but only under one of the following circumstances:

1. When the buyer or lessee has accepted the goods and has not revoked acceptance.
2. When conforming goods have been lost or damaged after the risk of loss has passed to the buyer or lessee.
3. When the buyer or lessee has breached after the goods have been identified to the contract and the seller or lessor is unable to resell or otherwise dispose of the goods [UCC 2–709(1), 2A–529(1)].

If a seller or lessor sues under these circumstances, the goods must be held for the buyer or lessee. The seller or lessor can resell or dispose of the goods at any time prior to collection of the judgment from the buyer or lessee, but in that situation the net proceeds from the sale must be credited to the buyer or lessee. This is an example of the duty to mitigate damages.

The Right to Recover Damages If a buyer or lessee repudiates a contract or wrongfully refuses to accept the goods, a seller or lessor can maintain an action to recover the damages sustained. Ordinarily, the amount of damages equals the difference between the contract price (or lease payments) and the market price (or lease payments) at the time and place of tender of the goods, plus incidental damages [UCC 2–708(1), 2A–528(1)]. The time and place of tender are frequently given by such terms as F.O.B., F.A.S., C.I.F., and the like (see Exhibit 11–2 on page 263), which determine whether there is a shipment or a destination contract.

If the difference between the contract price (or payments due under the lease contract) and the market price (or payments due under the lease contract) is too small to place the seller or lessor in the position that he or she would have been in if the buyer or lessee had fully performed, the proper measure of damages is the lost profits of the seller or lessor, including a reasonable allowance for overhead and other expenses [UCC 2–708(2), 2A–528(2)].

Remedies of the Buyer or Lessee

A seller or lessor breaches a sales or lease contract by failing to deliver conforming goods or repudiating the contract prior to delivery. On the breach, the buyer or lessee has a choice of several remedies under the UCC, including those discussed here.

The Right of Cover In certain situations, buyers and lessees can protect themselves by obtaining **cover**—that is, by buying or leasing substitute goods for those that were due under the contract. This option is available when the seller or lessor repudiates the contract or fails to deliver the goods. It is also available to a buyer or lessee who has rightfully rejected goods or revoked acceptance. Rejection and revocation of acceptance will be discussed shortly.

In obtaining cover, the buyer or lessee must act in good faith and without unreasonable delay [UCC 2–712, 2A–518]. After purchasing or leasing substitute goods, the buyer or lessee can recover from the seller or lessor the difference between the cost of cover and the contract price (or lease payments), plus incidental and consequential damages, less the expenses (such as delivery costs) that were saved as a result of the breach [UCC 2–712, 2–715, 2A–518]. Consequential damages are any losses suffered by the buyer or lessee that the seller or lessor could have foreseen (had reason to know about) at the time of contract formation and any injury to the buyer's or lessee's person or property proximately resulting from the contract's breach [UCC 2–715(2), 2A–520(2)].

Buyers and lessees are not required to cover, and failure to do so will not bar them from using any other remedies available under the UCC. A buyer or lessee who fails to cover, however, risks not being able to collect consequential damages—a situation that could have been avoided had he or she purchased or leased substitute goods.

The Right to Obtain Specific Performance A buyer or lessee can obtain specific performance when the goods are unique or when the remedy at law is inadequate [UCC 2–716(1), 2A–521(1)]. Ordinarily, an award of monetary damages is sufficient to place a buyer or lessee in the position he or she would have occupied if the seller or lessor had fully performed. When the contract is for the purchase of a particular work of art or a similarly unique item, however, monetary damages may not be sufficient. Under these circumstances, equity will require that the seller or lessor perform exactly by delivering the particular goods identified to the contract (a remedy of specific performance).

The Right to Recover Damages If a seller or lessor repudiates the sales contract or fails to deliver the goods, or if the buyer is justified in rejecting goods that the seller or lessor tenders, then the buyer or lessee has several options under the UCC. The buyer or lessee may cancel the contract and recover as much of the price as has been paid to the seller or lessor. Following cancellation, the buyer or lessee may either (1) cover by obtaining goods from another seller or lessor and seeking reimbursement for the extra costs incurred or (2) recover damages for breach of the contract.

If the buyer or lessee elects to sue for damages, the measure of recovery is the difference between the contract price (or lease payments) and the market price of the goods (or lease payments that could be obtained for the goods) at the time the buyer (or lessee) *learned* of the breach. The market price or market lease payments are determined at the place where the seller or lessor was supposed to deliver the goods. The buyer or lessee can also recover incidental and consequential damages less the expenses that were saved as a result of the breach [UCC 2–713, 2A–519].

Consider an example. Schilling orders 10,000 bushels of wheat from Valdone for $25.00 per bushel, with delivery due on June 14 and payment due on June 20. Valdone does not deliver on June 14. On June 14, the market price of wheat is $25.50 per bushel. Schilling chooses to do without the wheat. He sues Valdone for damages for nondelivery. Schilling can recover $0.50 × 10,000, or $5,000, plus any expenses the breach has caused him. The measure of damages is the market price on the day Schilling was to have received delivery less the contract price. (Any expenses Schilling saved by the breach would be deducted from the damages.)

The Right to Reject the Goods If either the goods or the tender of the goods by the seller or lessor fails to conform to the contract in any respect, the buyer or lessee can reject the goods. If some of the goods conform to the contract, the buyer or lessee can keep the conforming goods and reject the rest [UCC 2–601, 2A–509]. The buyer or lessee must reject the goods within a reasonable amount of time after delivery or tender of delivery, and the seller or lessor must be notified *seasonably*—that is, in a timely fashion or at the proper time [UCC 2–602(1), 2A–509(2)].

If a *merchant buyer* or *lessee* rightfully rejects goods, and the seller or lessor has no agent or business at the place of rejection, the buyer or lessee is required to follow any reasonable instructions received from the seller or lessor with respect to the goods controlled by the buyer or lessee. The buyer or lessee is entitled to reimbursement for the care and cost entailed in following the instructions [UCC 2–603, 2A–511]. The same requirements hold if the buyer or lessee rightfully revokes his or her acceptance of the goods at some later time [UCC 2–608(3), 2A–517(5)].

If no instructions are forthcoming and the goods are perishable or threaten to decline in value quickly, the buyer or lessee can resell the goods in good faith, taking appropriate reimbursement and a selling commission (not to exceed 10 percent of the gross proceeds) from the proceeds [UCC 2–603(1), (2); 2A–511(1)]. If the goods are not perishable, the buyer or lessee may store them for the seller or lessor or reship them to the seller or lessor [UCC 2–604, 2A–512].

The Right to Recover Damages for Accepted Goods A buyer or lessee who has accepted nonconforming goods may also keep the goods and recover for any loss "resulting in the ordinary course of events . . . as determined in any manner which is reasonable" [UCC 2–714(1), 2A–519(3)]. The buyer or lessee, however, must notify the seller or lessor of the breach within a reasonable time after the defect was or should have been discovered.

When the goods delivered are not as warranted, the measure of damages equals the difference between the value of the goods as accepted and their value if they had been delivered as warranted unless special circumstances show proximately caused damages of a different amount, plus incidental and consequential damages [UCC 2–714, 2A–519].

Revocation of Acceptance Acceptance of the goods precludes the buyer or lessee from exercising the right of rejection, but it does not necessarily preclude the buyer or lessee from pursuing other remedies. Additionally, in certain circumstances, a buyer or lessee is permitted to *revoke* his or her acceptance of the goods. Acceptance of a lot or a commercial unit can be revoked if the nonconformity *substantially* impairs the value of the lot or unit and if one of the following factors is present:

1. Acceptance was predicated on the reasonable assumption that the nonconformity would be cured, and it has not been cured within a reasonable period of time [UCC 2–608(1)(a), 2A–517(1)(a)].
2. The buyer or lessee did not discover the nonconformity before acceptance, either because it was difficult to discover before acceptance or because assurances made by the seller or lessor that the goods were conforming kept the buyer or lessee from inspecting the goods [UCC 2–608(1)(b), 2A–517(1)(b)].

Revocation of acceptance is not effective until notice is given to the seller or lessor. Notice must occur within a reasonable time after the buyer or lessee either discovers or *should have discovered* the grounds for revocation. Additionally, revocation must occur before the goods have undergone any substantial change (such as spoilage) not caused by their own defects [UCC 2–608(2), 2A–517(4)]. Once acceptance is revoked, the buyer or lessee can pursue remedies, just as if the goods had been rejected.

Is two years after a sale of goods a reasonable time period in which to discover a defect in those goods and notify the seller or lessor of a breach? That was the question in the following case.

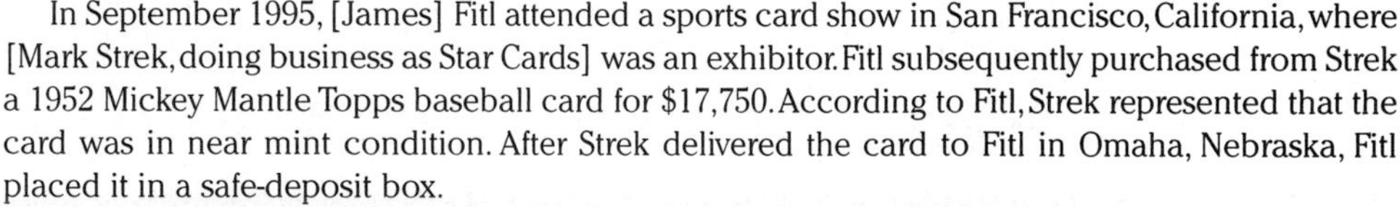

EXTENDED CASE 11.3 Fitl v. Strek

Supreme Court of Nebraska, 2005. 269 Neb. 51, 690 N.W.2d 605.

***WRIGHT,* J. [Judge]**

* * * *

In September 1995, [James] Fitl attended a sports card show in San Francisco, California, where [Mark Strek, doing business as Star Cards] was an exhibitor. Fitl subsequently purchased from Strek a 1952 Mickey Mantle Topps baseball card for $17,750. According to Fitl, Strek represented that the card was in near mint condition. After Strek delivered the card to Fitl in Omaha, Nebraska, Fitl placed it in a safe-deposit box.

In May 1997, Fitl sent the baseball card to Professional Sports Authenticators (PSA), a grading service for sports cards that is located in Newport Beach, California. PSA reported to Fitl that the baseball card was ungradable because it had been discolored and doctored.

On May 29, 1997, Fitl wrote to Strek * * * . Strek replied that Fitl should have initiated a return of the baseball card in a timely fashion so that Strek could have confronted his source and remedied the situation. Strek asserted that a typical grace period for the unconditional return of a card was from 7 days to 1 month.

* * * *

* * * Fitl sued Strek [in a Nebraska state court, which entered a judgment for Fitl. Strek appealed to the Nebraska Supreme Court.]

* * * *

Strek claims that the [trial] court erred in determining that notification of the defective condition of the baseball card 2 years after the date of purchase was timely pursuant to [UCC] 2–607(3)(a).

* * * The [trial] court found that Fitl had notified Strek within a reasonable time after discovery of the breach. Therefore, our review is whether the [trial] court's finding as to the reasonableness of the notice was clearly erroneous.

CASE CONTINUES

CASE 11.3 CONTINUED

Section 2–607(3)(a) states:"Where a tender has been accepted * * * the buyer must within a reasonable time after he discovers or should have discovered any breach notify the seller of breach or be barred from any remedy." [Under UCC 1–204(2)] *"[w]hat is a reasonable time for taking any action depends on the nature, purpose and circumstances of such action."* [Emphasis added.]

The notice requirement set forth in Section 2–607(3)(a) serves three purposes. * * * The most important one is to enable the seller to make efforts to cure the breach by making adjustments or replacements in order to minimize the buyer's damages and the seller's liability. A second policy is to provide the seller a reasonable opportunity to learn the facts so that he may adequately prepare for negotiation and defend himself in a suit. A third policy * * * is the same as the policy behind statutes of limitation: to provide a seller with a terminal point in time for liability.

* * * *A party is justified in relying upon a representation made to the party as a positive statement of fact when an investigation would be required to ascertain its falsity.* In order for Fitl to have determined that the baseball card had been altered, he would have been required to conduct an investigation. We find that he was not required to do so. Once Fitl learned that the baseball card had been altered, he gave notice to Strek. [Emphasis added.]

* * * One of the most important policies behind the notice requirement * * * is to allow the seller to cure the breach by making adjustments or replacements to minimize the buyer's damages and the seller's liability. However, even if Fitl had learned immediately upon taking possession of the baseball card that it was not authentic and had notified Strek at that time, there is no evidence that Strek could have made any adjustment or taken any action that would have minimized his liability. In its altered condition, the baseball card was worthless.

* * * Earlier notification would not have helped Strek prepare for negotiation or defend himself in a suit because the damage to Fitl could not be repaired. Thus, the policies behind the notice requirement, to allow the seller to correct a defect, to prepare for negotiation and litigation, and to protect against stale claims at a time beyond which an investigation can be completed, were not unfairly prejudiced by the lack of an earlier notice to Strek. Any problem Strek may have had with the party from whom he obtained the baseball card was a separate matter from his transaction with Fitl, and an investigation into the source of the altered card would not have minimized Fitl's damages.

* * * *

The judgment of the district court is affirmed.

QUESTIONS

1. **Suppose that Fitl and Strek had included in their deal a clause requiring Fitl to give notice of any defect in the card within "7 days to 1 month" of its receipt. Would the result have been different? Why or why not?**
2. **What might a buyer who prevails in a dispute such as the one in this case be awarded?**

Contractual Provisions Affecting Remedies

The parties to a sales or lease contract can vary their respective rights and obligations by contractual agreement. For example, a seller and buyer can expressly provide for remedies in addition to those provided in the UCC. They can also specifiy remedies in lieu of those provided in the UCC, or they can change the measure of damages. The seller can stipulate that the buyer's only remedy on the seller's breach be repair or replacement of the item, or the seller can limit the buyer's remedy to return of the goods and refund of the purchase price. In sales and lease contracts, an agreed-on remedy is in addition to those provided in the UCC unless the parties expressly agree that the remedy is exclusive of all others [UCC 2–719(1), 2A–503(1)].

If the parties state that a remedy is exclusive, then it is the sole remedy. When circumstances cause an exclusive remedy to fail in its essential purpose, however, it is no longer exclusive [UCC 2–719(2), 2A–503(2)]. For example, a sales contract that limits the buyer's remedy to repair or replacement fails in its essential purpose if the item cannot be repaired and no replacements are available.

Sales and Lease Warranties

Warranty is an age-old concept. In sales and lease law, a warranty is an assurance by one party of the existence of a fact on which the other party can rely. Article 2 and Article 2A of the UCC designate several types of warranties that can arise in a sales or lease contract. These warranties include warranties of title, express warranties, and implied warranties.

Because a warranty imposes a duty on the seller or lessor, a breach of warranty is a breach of the seller's or lessor's promise. If the parties have not agreed to limit or modify the remedies available to the buyer or lessee and if the seller or lessor breaches a warranty, the buyer or lessee can sue to recover damages from the seller or lessor. Under some circumstances, a breach can allow the buyer or lessee to rescind (cancel) the agreement.[8]

Warranty of Title

Title warranty arises automatically in most sales contracts. UCC 2–312 imposes three types of warranties of title.

Good Title In most cases, sellers warrant that they have good and valid title to the goods sold and that transfer of the title is rightful [UCC 2–312(1)(a)].

No Liens or Infringements A second warranty of title provided by the UCC protects buyers who are unaware of any encumbrances (claims, charges, or liabilities—usually called *liens*[9]) against goods at the time the contract is made [UCC 2–312(1)(b)]. This warranty protects buyers who, for example, unknowingly purchase goods that are subject to a creditor's security interest (see Chapter 15). If a creditor legally repossesses the goods from a buyer *who had no actual knowledge of the security interest*, the buyer can recover from the seller for breach of warranty. (The buyer who has *actual knowledge of a security interest* has no recourse against a seller.) Article 2A affords similar protection for lessees. Section 2A–211(1) provides that during the term of the lease, no claim of any third party will interfere with the lessee's enjoyment of the leasehold interest.

A merchant seller is also deemed to warrant that the goods delivered are free from any copyright, trademark, or patent claims of a third person [UCC 2–312(3), 2A–211(2)].

Disclaimer of Title Warranty In an ordinary sales transaction, the title warranty can be disclaimed or modified only by *specific language* in a contract. For example, sellers may assert that they are transferring only such rights, title, and interest as they have in the goods. In a lease transaction, the disclaimer must "be specific, be by a writing, and be conspicuous" [UCC 2A–214(4)]. In certain cases, the circumstances surrounding the sale are sufficient to indicate clearly to a buyer that no assurances as to title are being made. The classic example is a sheriff's sale, when buyers know that the goods have been seized to satisfy debts and the sheriff cannot guarantee title [UCC 2–312(2)].

Express Warranties

A seller or lessor can create an **express warranty** by making representations concerning the quality, condition, description, or performance potential of the goods. Under UCC 2–313 and 2A–210, express warranties arise when a seller or lessor indicates any of the following:

1. That the goods conform to any *affirmation or promise of fact* that the seller or lessor makes to the buyer or lessee about the goods. Such affirmations or promises are usually made during the bargaining process. Statements such as "these drill bits will *easily* penetrate stainless steel—and without dulling" are express warranties.
2. That the goods conform to any *description* of them. For example, a label that reads "Crate contains one 150-horsepower diesel engine" or a contract that calls for the delivery of a "wool coat" creates an express warranty that the content of the goods sold conforms to the description.
3. That the goods conform to any *sample or model* of the goods shown to the buyer or lessee.

8. *Rescission* restores the parties to the positions they were in before the contract was made.

9. Pronounced *leens*. Liens will be discussed in detail in Chapter 15.

Express warranties can be found in a seller's or lessor's advertisement, brochure, or promotional materials, in addition to being made orally or in an express warranty provision in a sales or lease contract. To create an express warranty, a seller or lessor does not have to use formal words such as *warrant* or *guarantee*. It is only necessary that a reasonable buyer or lessee would regard the representation as part of the basis of the bargain [UCC 2–313(2), 2A–210(2)].

Basis of the Bargain The UCC requires that for an express warranty to be created, the affirmation, promise, description, or sample must become part of the "basis of the bargain" [UCC 2–313(1), 2A–210(1)]. Just what constitutes the basis of the bargain is difficult to say. The UCC does not define the concept, and it is a question of fact in each case whether a representation was made at such a time and in such a way that it induced the buyer or lessee to enter into the contract. Therefore, if an express warranty is not intended, the marketing agent or salesperson should not promise too much.

Statements of Opinion and Value If the seller or lessor merely makes a statement that relates to the value or worth of the goods, or makes a statement of opinion or recommendation about the goods, the seller or lessor is not creating an express warranty [UCC 2–313(2), 2A–210(2)].

For example, a seller claims that "this is the best used car to come along in years; it has four new tires and a 150-horsepower engine just rebuilt this year." The seller has made several *affirmations of fact* that can create a warranty: the automobile has an engine; it has a 150-horsepower engine; the engine was rebuilt this year; there are four tires on the automobile; and the tires are new. The seller's *opinion* that the vehicle is "the best used car to come along in years," however, is known as *puffery* and creates no warranty. (**Puffery** is an expression of opinion by a seller or lessor that is not made as a representation of fact.) A statement relating to the value of the goods, such as "it's worth a fortune" or "anywhere else you'd pay $10,000 for it," usually does not create a warranty.

An Exception: Statements of Opinion by Experts. Although an ordinary seller or lessor can give an opinion that is not a warranty, if the seller or lessor is an expert and gives an opinion as an expert to a layperson, then a warranty may be created. For example, Saul is an art dealer and an expert in seventeenth-century paintings. If Saul states to Lauren, a purchaser, that in his opinion a particular painting is a Rembrandt, Saul has warranted the accuracy of his opinion.

Puffery versus Express Warranties. It is not always easy to determine what constitutes an express warranty and what constitutes puffery. The reasonableness of the buyer's or lessee's reliance appears to be the controlling criterion in many cases. For example, a salesperson's statements that a ladder will "never break" and will "last a lifetime" are so clearly improbable that no reasonable buyer should rely on them. Additionally, the context in which a statement is made may be relevant in determining the reasonableness of a buyer's or lessee's reliance. For example, a reasonable person is more likely to rely on a written statement made in an advertisement than on a statement made orally by a salesperson.

Implied Warranties

An **implied warranty** is one that *the law derives* by inference from the nature of the transaction or the relative situations or circumstances of the parties. Under the UCC, merchants impliedly warrant that the goods they sell or lease are merchantable and, in certain circumstances, fit for a particular purpose. In addition, an implied warranty may arise from a course of dealing or usage of trade. We examine these three types of implied warranties in the following subsections.

Implied Warranty of Merchantability An **implied warranty of merchantability** automatically arises in every sale or lease of goods made *by a merchant* who deals in goods of the kind sold or leased [UCC 2–314, 2A–212]. Thus, a merchant who is in the business of selling ski equipment makes an implied warranty of merchantability every time the merchant sells a pair of skis, but a neighbor selling his or her skis at a garage sale does not.

To be *merchantable,* goods must be "reasonably fit for the ordinary purposes for which such goods are used." They must be of at least average, fair, or medium-grade quality. The quality must be comparable to quality that will pass without objection in the trade or market for goods of the same description. To be merchantable, the goods must also be adequately packaged and labeled as provided by the agreement, and they must conform to the promises or affirmations of fact made on the container or label, if any.

It makes no difference whether the merchant knew of, or could have discovered, that a product was defective (not merchantable). Of course, merchants are not absolute insurers against *all* accidents arising in connection with the goods. For example, a bar of soap is not unmerchantable merely because a user could slip and fall by stepping on it.

The UCC recognizes the serving of food or drink to be consumed on or off the premises as a sale of goods subject to the implied warranty of merchantability [UCC 2–314(1)]. *Merchantable food* is food that is fit to eat on the basis of consumer expectations. In the following classic case, the court had to determine whether one should reasonably expect to find a fish bone in fish chowder.

CASE 11.4 Webster v. Blue Ship Tea Room, Inc.

Supreme Judicial Court of Massachusetts, 1964. 347 Mass. 421, 198 N.E.2d 309.

• **Background and Facts** Blue Ship Tea Room, Inc., was located in Boston in an old building overlooking the ocean. Webster, who had been born and raised in New England, went to the restaurant and ordered fish chowder. The chowder was milky in color. After three or four spoonfuls, she felt something lodged in her throat. As a result, she underwent two esophagoscopies; in the second esophagoscopy, a fish bone was found and removed. Webster filed a suit against the restaurant in a Massachusetts state court for breach of the implied warranty of merchantability. The jury rendered a verdict for Webster, and the restaurant appealed to the state's highest court.

IN THE LANGUAGE OF THE COURT

***REARDON*, Justice.**

[The plaintiff] ordered a cup of fish chowder. Presently, there was set before her "a small bowl of fish chowder." * * * After 3 or 4 [spoonfuls] she was aware that something had lodged in her throat because she "couldn't swallow and couldn't clear her throat by gulping and she could feel it." This misadventure led to two esophagoscopies [procedures in which a telescope-like instrument is used to look into the throat] at the Massachusetts General Hospital, in the second of which, on April 27, 1959, a fish bone was found and removed. The sequence of events produced injury to the plaintiff which was not insubstantial.

We must decide whether a fish bone lurking in a fish chowder, about the ingredients of which there is no other complaint, constitutes a breach of implied warranty under applicable provisions of the Uniform Commercial Code * * * . As the judge put it in his charge [jury instruction], "Was the fish chowder fit to be eaten and wholesome? * * * Nobody is claiming that the fish itself wasn't wholesome. * * * But the bone of contention here—I don't mean that for a pun—but was this fish bone a foreign substance that made the fish chowder unwholesome or not fit to be eaten?"

* * * *

[We think that it] is not too much to say that a person sitting down in New England to consume a good New England fish chowder embarks on a gustatory [taste-related] adventure which may entail the removal of some fish bones from his bowl as he proceeds. We are not inclined to tamper with age-old recipes by any amendment reflecting the plaintiff's view of the effect of the Uniform Commercial Code upon them. We are aware of the heavy body of case law involving foreign substances in food, but we sense a strong distinction between them and those relative to unwholesomeness of the food itself [such as] tainted mackerel, and a fish bone in a fish chowder. * * * We consider that the joys of life in New England include the ready availability of fresh fish chowder. We should be prepared to cope with the hazards of fish bones, the occasional presence of which in chowders is, it seems to us, to be anticipated, and which, in the light of a hallowed tradition, do not impair their fitness or merchantability.

• **Decision and Remedy** *The Supreme Judicial Court of Massachusetts "sympathized with a plaintiff who has suffered a peculiarly New England injury" but entered a judgment for the defendant, Blue Ship Tea Room. A fish bone in fish chowder is not a breach of the implied warranty of merchantability.*

CASE CONTINUES

CASE 11.4 CONTINUED • **Impact of This Case on Today's Law** *This classic case, phrased in memorable language, was an early application of the UCC's implied warranty of merchantability to food products. The case established the rule that consumers should expect to find, on occasion, elements of food products that are natural to the product (such as fish bones in fish chowder). Courts today still apply this rule.*

• **The E-Commerce Dimension** *If Webster had made the chowder herself from a recipe that she had found on the Internet, could she have successfully brought an action against its author for a breach of the implied warranty of merchantability? Explain.*

Implied Warranty of Fitness for a Particular Purpose The **implied warranty of fitness for a particular purpose** arises when any *seller or lessor* (merchant or nonmerchant) knows the particular purpose for which a buyer or lessee will use the goods *and* knows that the buyer or lessee is relying on the skill and judgment of the seller or lessor to select suitable goods [UCC 2–315, 2A–213].

A "particular purpose" of the buyer or lessee differs from the "ordinary purpose for which goods are used" (merchantability). Goods can be merchantable but unfit for a particular purpose. For example, suppose that you need a gallon of paint to match the color of your living room walls—a light shade somewhere between coral and peach. You take a sample to your local hardware store and request a gallon of paint of that color. Instead, you are given a gallon of bright blue paint. Here, the salesperson has not breached any warranty of implied merchantability—the bright blue paint is of high quality and suitable for interior walls—but he or she has breached an implied warranty of fitness for a particular purpose.

A seller or lessor does not need to have actual knowledge of the buyer's or lessee's particular purpose. It is sufficient if a seller or lessor "has reason to know" the purpose. The buyer or lessee, however, must have *relied* on the skill or judgment of the seller or lessor in selecting or furnishing suitable goods for an implied warranty to be created.

For example, Bloomberg leases a computer from Future Tech, a lessor of technical business equipment. Bloomberg tells the clerk that she wants a computer that will run a complicated new engineering graphics program at a realistic speed. Future Tech leases Bloomberg an Architex One computer with a CPU speed of only 2.4 gigahertz, even though a speed of at least 3.8 gigahertz would be required to run Bloomberg's graphics program at a "realistic speed." Bloomberg, after realizing that it takes her forever to run her program, wants a refund. Here, because Future Tech has breached the implied warranty of fitness for a particular purpose, Bloomberg normally will be able to recover. The clerk knew specifically that Bloomberg wanted a computer with enough speed to run certain software. Furthermore, Bloomberg relied on the clerk to furnish a computer that would fulfill this purpose. Because Future Tech did not do so, the warranty was breached.

Implied Warranty Arising from Course of Dealing or Trade Usage Implied warranties can also arise (or be excluded or modified) as a result of a course of dealing or usage of trade [UCC 2–314(3), 2A–212(3)]. In the absence of evidence to the contrary, when both parties to a sales or lease contract have knowledge of a well-recognized trade custom, the courts will infer that both parties intended for that custom to apply to their contract. For example, if it is an industry-wide custom to lubricate a new car before it is delivered and a dealer fails to do so, the dealer can be held liable to a buyer for damages resulting from the breach of an implied warranty. (This, of course, would also be negligence on the part of the dealer.)

Warranty Disclaimers Because each type of warranty is created in a special way, the manner in which warranties can be disclaimed or qualified by a seller or lessor varies with the type of warranty.

Express Warranties. As already stated, any affirmation of fact or promise, description of the goods, or use of samples or models by a seller or lessor creates an express warranty. Obviously, then, express warranties can be excluded if the seller or lessor carefully refrains from making any promise or affirmation of fact relating to the goods, describing the goods, or using a sample or model.

The UCC does permit express warranties to be negated or limited by specific and unambiguous language, provided that this is done in a manner that protects the buyer or lessee from surprise. Therefore, a written disclaimer in language that is clear and conspicuous, and called to a buyer's or lessee's attention, could negate all oral express warranties not included in the written sales or lease contract [UCC 2–316(1), 2A–214(1)]. This allows the seller or lessor to avoid false allegations that oral warranties were made, and it ensures that only representations made by properly authorized individuals are included in the bargain.

Implied Warranties. Generally speaking, unless circumstances indicate otherwise, the implied warranties of merchantability and fitness are disclaimed by the expressions "as is," "with all faults," and other similar expressions that in common understanding for *both* parties call the buyer's or lessee's attention to the fact that there are no implied warranties [UCC 2–316(3)(a), 2A–214(3)(a)].

The UCC also permits a seller or lessor to specifically disclaim an implied warranty either of fitness or of merchantability [UCC 2–316(2), 2A–214(2)]. To disclaim an implied warranty of fitness for a particular purpose, the disclaimer must be in writing and be conspicuous. The word *fitness* does not have to be mentioned in the writing; it is sufficient if, for example, the disclaimer states, "THERE ARE NO WARRANTIES THAT EXTEND BEYOND THE DESCRIPTION ON THE FACE HEREOF."

A merchantability disclaimer must be more specific; it must mention *merchantability*. It need not be written; but if it is, the writing must be conspicuous [UCC 2–316(2), 2A–214(4)].

E-Contracts

The basic principles of contract law evolved over a long period of time. Certainly, they were formed long before cyberspace and electronic contracting became realities. Therefore, new legal theories, new adaptations of existing laws, and new laws are needed to govern **e-contracts,** or contracts entered into electronically. To date, however, most courts have adapted traditional contract law principles and, when applicable, provisions of the UCC to cases involving e-contract disputes.

Online Contract Formation

Today, numerous contracts are being formed online. Although the medium through which these contracts are generated has changed, the age-old problems attending contract formation have not. Disputes concerning contracts formed online continue to center around contract terms and whether the parties voluntarily assented to those terms.

Note that online contracts may be formed not only for the sale of goods and services but also for the purpose of *licensing*. The "sale" of software generally involves a license, or a right to use the software, rather than the passage of title (ownership rights) from the seller to the buyer. For example, Galynn wants to obtain software that will allow her to work on spreadsheets on her BlackBerry. She goes online and purchases GridMagic. During the transaction, she has to click on several on-screen "I agree" boxes to indicate that she understands that she is purchasing only the right to use the software and will not obtain any ownership rights. After she agrees to these terms (the licensing agreement), she can download the software to her BlackBerry. Although in this chapter we typically refer to the offeror and offeree as a *seller* and a *buyer*, in many transactions these parties would be more accurately described as a *licensor* and a *licensee*.

Online Offers Sellers doing business via the Internet can protect themselves against contract disputes and legal liability by creating offers that clearly spell out the terms that will govern their transactions if the offers are accepted. Significant terms should be conspicuous and easy to view.

Displaying the Offer. The seller's Web site should include a hypertext link to a page containing the full contract so that potential buyers are made aware of the terms to which they are assenting. The contract generally must be displayed online in a readable format such as a twelve-point typeface. For example, suppose that Netquip sells a variety of heavy equipment, such as trucks and trailers, online at its Web site. Netquip must include its full pricing schedule on the Web site with explanations of all complex provisions. In addition, the terms of the sale (such as any warranties and Netquip's refund policy) must be fully disclosed.

Is an online contract enforceable if the offeror requires an offeree to scroll down or print the contract to read its terms, which are otherwise readily accessible and clear? That was the question in the following case.

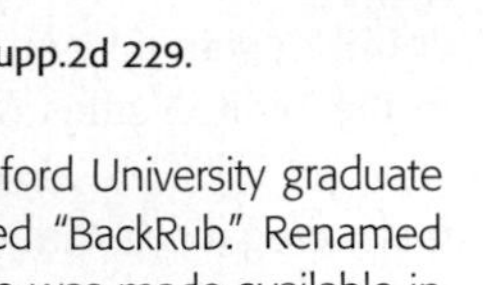

CASE 11.5 Feldman v. Google, Inc.

United States District Court, Eastern District of Pennsylvania, 2007. 513 F.Supp.2d 229.

• **Company Profile** In the mid-1990s, Larry Page and Sergey Brin, Stanford University graduate students in computer science, began work on an Internet search engine called "BackRub." Renamed "Google" after the mathematical term for a 1 followed by 100 zeros, the engine was made available in 1998. In less than a year, the service was acquiring major clients, receiving achievement awards, being included on many "Top Web Site" lists, and handling millions of queries per day. By 2000, Google had become the world's largest search engine. According to Google, Inc.'s Web site at **www.google.com**, its mission is to organize the world's information and make it universally accessible and useful. The company's revenue derives from keyword-targeted advertising.

• **Background and Facts** In Google, Inc.'s AdWords program, when an Internet user searches on **www.google.com** using key words that an advertiser has identified, an ad appears. If the user clicks on it, Google charges the advertiser. Google requires an advertiser to agree to certain terms before placing an ad. These terms—set out in a preamble and seven paragraphs—are displayed online in a window with a scroll bar. A link to a printer-friendly version of the terms is at the top of the window. At the bottom of the page, viewable without scrolling, are the words, "Yes, I agree to the above terms and conditions," and a box on which an advertiser must click to proceed. Among the terms, a forum-selection clause provides that any dispute over the program is to be "adjudicated in Santa Clara County, California." Lawrence Feldman, a lawyer, participated in the program by selecting key words, including "Vioxx," "Bextra," and "Celebrex," to trigger a showing of his ad to potential clients. In a subsequent suit between Feldman and Google in a federal district court in Pennsylvania, Feldman claimed that at least 20 percent of the clicks for which he was charged $100,000 between January 2003 and January 2006 were fraudulent.[a] Feldman filed a motion for summary judgment. Google asked the court to transfer the case to a court in Santa Clara County, California.

IN THE LANGUAGE OF THE COURT
GILES, J. [Judge]

* * * *

The type of contract at issue here is commonly referred to as a "clickwrap" agreement. A clickwrap agreement appears on an Internet web page and requires that a user consent to any terms or conditions by clicking on a dialog box on the screen in order to proceed with the Internet transaction. *Even though they are electronic, clickwrap agreements are considered to be writings because they are printable and storable.* [Emphasis added.]

To determine whether a clickwrap agreement is enforceable, courts presented with the issue apply traditional principles of contract law and focus on whether the plaintiffs had reasonable notice of and manifested assent to the clickwrap agreement. *Absent a showing of fraud, failure to read an enforceable clickwrap agreement, as with any binding contract, will not excuse compliance with its terms.* [Emphasis added.]

* * * *

Plaintiff [Feldman] claims he did not have notice or knowledge of the forum selection clause, and therefore that there was no "meeting of the minds" required for contract formation.

* * * *

* * * In order to activate an AdWords account, the user had to visit a Web page which displayed the Agreement in a scrollable text box. * * * The user did not have to scroll down to a submerged screen or click on a series of hyperlinks to view the Agreement. Instead, text of the AdWords Agreement was immediately visible to the user, as was a prominent admonition in boldface to read the terms and conditions carefully, and with instruction to indicate assent if the user agreed to the terms.

a. Feldman was alleging that *click fraud* had taken place. Click fraud occurs when someone, such as a competitor or a prankster with no interest in an advertiser's goods or services, clicks repeatedly on an ad, driving up the ad's cost to the advertiser without generating a sale.

CASE 11.5 CONTINUED

That the user would have to scroll through the text box of the Agreement to read it in its entirety does not defeat notice because there was sufficient notice of the Agreement itself and clicking "Yes" constituted assent to all of the terms. The preamble, which was immediately visible, also made clear that assent to the terms was binding. The Agreement was presented in readable 12-point font. It was only seven paragraphs long—not so long so as to render scrolling down to view all of the terms inconvenient or impossible. A printer-friendly, full-screen version was made readily available. The user had ample time to review the document.

* * * The user * * * had to take affirmative action and click the "Yes, I agree to the above terms and conditions" button in order to proceed to the next step. Clicking "Continue" without clicking the "Yes" button would have returned the user to the same Web page. If the user did not agree to all of the terms, he could not have activated his account, placed ads, or incurred charges.

* * * *

A reasonably prudent Internet user would have known of the existence of terms in the AdWords Agreement. Plaintiff had to have had reasonable notice of the terms. By clicking on "Yes, I agree to the above terms and conditions" button, Plaintiff indicated assent to the terms.

• **Decision and Remedy** *The court held that "the requirements of an express contract for reasonable notice of terms and mutual assent are satisfied." Feldman and Google were bound to the terms. The court denied Feldman's motion for summary judgment and granted Google's motion to transfer the case.*

• **The Ethical Dimension** *With respect to click fraud, which was the heart of Feldman's claim in this case, what circumstances might suggest unethical behavior by Google?*

• **The E-Commerce Dimension** *Under what different facts might the court have held that the plaintiff did not have reasonable notice of the terms of the agreement and thus did not assent to them?*

Provisions to Include. An important rule to keep in mind is that the offeror controls the offer and thus the resulting contract. Therefore, the seller should anticipate the terms that he or she wants to include in a contract and provide for them in the offer. At a minimum, an online offer should include the following provisions:

1. A clause that clearly indicates what constitutes the buyer's agreement to the terms of the offer, such as a box containing the words "I accept" that the buyer can click on to indicate acceptance. (Mechanisms for accepting online offers are discussed in detail later in the chapter.)
2. A provision specifying how payment for the goods and of any applicable taxes must be made.
3. A statement of the seller's refund and return policies.
4. Disclaimers of liability for certain uses of the goods. For example, an online seller of business forms may add a disclaimer that the seller does not accept responsibility for the buyer's reliance on the forms rather than on an attorney's advice.
5. A provision specifying the remedies available to the buyer if the goods are found to be defective or if the contract is otherwise breached. Any limitation of remedies should be clearly spelled out.
6. A statement indicating how the seller will use the information gathered about the buyer.
7. Provisions relating to dispute settlement, such as an arbitration clause or a *forum-selection clause* (discussed next).

Dispute-Settlement Provisions. Online offers frequently include provisions relating to dispute settlement. An arbitration clause might be included, indicating that any dispute arising under the contract will be arbitrated in a specified forum. Many online contracts also contain a **forum-selection clause,** which indicates the forum, or place (such as the court or jurisdiction), for the resolution of any dispute arising under the contract. These clauses can help online sellers avoid having to appear in court in many distant jurisdictions when customers are dissatisfied with their purchases.

Online Acceptances Section 2–204 of the UCC, the law governing sales contracts, provides that any contract for the sale of goods "may be made in any manner sufficient to show agreement, including conduct by both parties which recognizes the existence of such a contract." The *Restatement (Second) of Contracts,* a compilation of common law contract principles, has a similar provision. It states that parties may agree to a contract "by written or spoken words or by other action or by failure to act."[10]

Click-On Agreements. The courts have used the provisions just discussed to conclude that a binding contract can be created by conduct, including conduct accepting an online offer by clicking on a box indicating "I agree" or "I accept." The agreement resulting from such an acceptance is often called a **click-on agreement.**

Generally, the law governing contracts, including sales and lease contracts under the UCC, does not require that all of the terms in a contract must actually have been read by all of the parties to be effective. Therefore, clicking on a button or box that states "I agree" to certain terms can be enough.[11]

Browse-Wrap Terms. Like the terms of a click-on agreement, **browse-wrap terms** can occur in a transaction conducted over the Internet. Unlike a click-on agreement, however, browse-wrap terms do not require an Internet user to assent to the terms before, say, downloading or using certain software. In other words, a person can install the software without clicking "I agree" to the terms of a license. Offerors of browse-wrap terms generally assert that the terms are binding without the user's active consent.

Critics contend that browse-wrap terms are not enforceable because they do not satisfy the basic elements of contract formation. It has been suggested that to form a valid contract online, a user must at least be presented with the terms before indicating assent.[12] With a browse-wrap term, this would require that a user navigate past it and agree to it before being able to obtain whatever is being granted.

10. *Restatement (Second) of Contracts,* Section 19.
11. See, for example, *i.LANSystems, Inc. v. NetScout Service Level Corp.,* 183 F.Supp.2d 838 (D.Mass. 2002).
12. American Bar Association Committee on the Law of Cyberspace, "Click-Through Agreements: Strategies for Avoiding Disputes on the Validity of Assent" (document presented at the annual American Bar Association meeting in August 2001).

E-Signatures

In many instances, a contract cannot be enforced unless it is signed by the party against whom enforcement is sought. A significant issue in the context of e-commerce has to do with how electronic signatures, or **e-signatures,** can be created and verified on e-contracts.

E-Signature Technologies Today, numerous technologies allow electronic documents to be signed. The most prevalent e-signature technology is the *asymmetric cryptosystem,* which creates a digital signature using two different (asymmetric) cryptographic "keys," one private and one public. With this system, a person attaches a digital signature to a document using a private key, or code. The key has a publicly available counterpart. Anyone with the appropriate software can use the public key to verify that the digital signature was made using the private key. A *cybernotary,* or legally recognized certification authority, issues the key pair, identifies the owner of the keys, and certifies the validity of the public key. The cybernotary also serves as a repository for public keys. Cybernotaries already are available.

State Laws Governing E-Signatures Most states have laws governing e-signatures. The problem is that state e-signature laws are not uniform. Some states—California is a notable example—prohibit many types of documents from being signed with e-signatures, whereas other states are more permissive.

In an attempt to create more uniformity among the states, in 1999 the National Conference of Commissioners on Uniform State Laws and the American Law Institute promulgated the Uniform Electronic Transactions Act (UETA). To date, the UETA has been adopted, at least in part, by forty-eight states. Among other things, the UETA states that a signature may not be denied legal effect or enforceability solely because it is in electronic form.[13] (We will look more closely at the UETA shortly.)

Federal Law Governing E-Signatures and E-Documents In 2000, Congress enacted the Electronic Signatures in Global and National Commerce Act (E-SIGN Act),[14] which provides that no

13. Most states have also included a similar provision in their version of the UCC.
14. 15 U.S.C. Sections 7001 *et seq.*

contract, record, or signature may be "denied legal effect" solely because it is in an electronic form. In other words, under this law, an e-signature is as valid as a signature on paper, and an e-document can be as enforceable as a paper one.

For an e-signature to be enforceable, the contracting parties must have agreed to use electronic signatures. For an electronic document to be valid, it must be in a form that can be retained and accurately reproduced.

The E-SIGN Act does not apply to all types of documents, however. Contracts and documents that are exempt include court papers, divorce decrees, evictions, foreclosures, health-insurance terminations, prenuptial agreements, and wills. Also, the only agreements governed by the UCC that fall under this law are those covered by Articles 2 and 2A and UCC 1–107 and 1–206.

The E-SIGN Act refers explicitly to the UETA and provides that if a state has enacted the uniform version of the UETA, that law is not preempted by the E-SIGN Act. In other words, if the state has enacted the UETA without modification, state law will govern. The problem is that many states have enacted nonuniform (modified) versions of the UETA, largely for the purpose of excluding other areas of state law from the UETA's terms. The E-SIGN Act specifies that those exclusions will be preempted to the extent that they are inconsistent with the E-SIGN Act's provisions.

The Uniform Electronic Transactions Act

As noted earlier, the UETA, promulgated in 1999, represents one of the first comprehensive efforts to create uniformity and introduce certainty in state laws pertaining to e-commerce. The primary purpose of the UETA is to remove barriers to e-commerce by giving the same legal effect to electronic records and signatures as is currently given to paper documents and signatures. The UETA broadly defines an e-signature as "an electronic sound, symbol, or process attached to or logically associated with a record and executed or adopted by a person with the intent to sign the record."[15] A *record* is defined as "information that is inscribed on a tangible medium or that is stored in an electronic or other medium and is retrievable in perceivable [visual] form."[16]

The UETA does not apply to all writings and signatures but only to electronic records and electronic signatures *relating to a transaction.* A *transaction* is defined as an interaction between two or more people relating to business, commercial, or governmental activities.[17] The act specifically does not apply to laws governing wills or testamentary trusts or the UCC (other than Articles 2 and 2A).[18] In addition, the provisions of the UETA allow the states to exclude its application to other areas of law.

15. UETA 102(8).
16. UETA 102(15).
17. UETA 2(12) and 3.
18. UETA 3(b).

REVIEWING Sales, Leases, and E-Contracts

GFI, Inc., a Hong Kong company, makes audio decoder chips, one of the essential components used in the manufacture of MP3 players. Egan Electronics contracts with GFI to buy 2,500 chips F.O.B. Hong Kong via Air Express. At the time for the delivery, GFI delivers only 2,400 chips but explains to Egan that while the shipment is less than 5 percent short, the chips are of a higher quality than those specified in the contract and are worth 5 percent more than the contract price. Egan accepts the shipment and pays GFI the contract price. Two months later, Egan and GFI form another contract, under which GFI is to ship 2,000 more chips to Egan, again F.O.B. Hong Kong via Air Express. Just after the contract is formed, GFI's major manufacturing plant burns down, and its entire inventory of chips is destroyed. GFI, however, is able to ship Egan 1,000 chips that it had stored in its office at a separate location. While the 1,000 chips are in transit, they are destroyed. Nearly a year later, GFI notifies Egan that the plant has been rebuilt, it is back in business, and it can again supply Egan with chips if Egan is interested. Egan responds with an offer to purchase 2,000 chips, with the same delivery terms,

REVIEWING CONTINUES

REVIEWING Sales, Leases, and E-Contracts, Continued

and GFI accepts the offer. Two months later, Egan has neither received the shipment nor heard anything further from GFI. Using the information presented in the chapter, answer the following questions.

1. Suppose that Egan refused to pay for the first shipment and sued GFI for breach of contract. Had GFI breached the contract? What would be GFI's best defense against this claim?
2. Assume that the second shipment of chips had not been destroyed in transit. In this situation, would GFI be in breach of contract because it only shipped 1,000 chips, not the contracted-for quantity (2,000 chips)?
3. With respect to the 1,000 chips that were destroyed in transit, which party must bear the loss? Why?
4. Regarding the final contract, does Egan have a right to ask GFI about its intentions to perform the contract? If so, does GFI have an obligation to respond? Explain.

TERMS AND CONCEPTS

browse-wrap term 280
click-on agreement 280
conforming goods 266
consignment 264
cover 269
cure 267
destination contract 260
e-contract 277
e-signature 280
express warranty 273
firm offer 255
forum-selection clause 279
identification 260
implied warranty 274
implied warranty of fitness for a particular purpose 276
implied warranty of merchantability 274
insurable interest 265
lease agreement 253
lessee 253
lessor 253
merchant 253
output contract 254
perfect tender rule 266
puffery 274
requirements contract 254
sale 253
sale on approval 265
sale or return 264
sales contract 252
seasonably 255
shipment contract 260
tangible property 253
tender of delivery 266

QUESTIONS AND CASE PROBLEMS

11-1. A. B. Zook, Inc., is a manufacturer of washing machines. Over the telephone, Zook offers to sell Radar Appliances one hundred model Z washers at a price of $150 per unit. Zook agrees to keep this offer open for ninety days. Radar tells Zook that the offer appears to be a good one and that it will let Zook know of its acceptance within the next two to three weeks. One week later, Zook sends, and Radar receives, notice that Zook has withdrawn its offer. Radar immediately thereafter telephones Zook and accepts the $150-per-unit offer. Zook claims, first, that no sales contract was ever formed between it and Radar and, second, that if there is a contract, the contract is unenforceable. Discuss Zook's contentions.

11-2. QUESTION WITH SAMPLE ANSWER

Anne is a reporter for *Daily Business Journal*, a print publication consulted by investors and other businesspersons. She often uses the Internet to conduct research for the articles that she writes for the publication. While visiting the Web site of Cyberspace Investments Corp., Anne reads a pop-up window that states, "Our business newsletter, *E-Commerce Weekly*, is available at a one-year subscription rate of $5 per issue. To subscribe, enter your e-mail address below and click 'SUBSCRIBE.' By subscribing, you agree to the terms of the subscriber's agreement. To read this agreement, click 'AGREEMENT.' " Anne enters her e-mail address, but does not click on "AGREEMENT" to read the terms. Has Anne entered into an enforceable contract to pay for *E-Commerce Weekly?* Explain.

- **For a sample answer to Question 11-2, go to Appendix I at the end of this text.**

11-3. On May 1, Sikora goes into Carson's retail clothing store to purchase a suit. Sikora finds a suit he likes for $190 and buys it. The suit needs alteration. Sikora is to pick up the altered suit at Carson's store on May 10. Consider the following separate sets of circumstances:

(a) One of Carson's major creditors obtains a judgment on the debt Carson owes and has the court issue a *writ of execution* (a court order to seize a debtor's property to satisfy a debt) to collect on that judgment all clothing in Carson's possession. Discuss Sikora's rights in the suit under these circumstances.
(b) On May 9, through no fault of Carson's, the store burns down, and all contents are a total loss. Between Carson and Sikora, who suffers the loss of the suit destroyed by fire? Explain.

11-4. McDonald has contracted to purchase five hundred pairs of shoes from Vetter. Vetter manufactures the shoes and tenders delivery to McDonald. McDonald accepts the shipment. Later, on inspection, McDonald discovers that ten pairs of the shoes are poorly made and will have to be sold to customers as seconds. If McDonald decides to keep all five hundred pairs of shoes, what remedies are available to her? Discuss.

11-5. Kirk has contracted to deliver to Doolittle one thousand cases of Wonder brand beans on or before October 1. Doolittle is to specify the means of transportation twenty days prior to the date of shipment. Payment for the beans is to be made by Doolittle on tender of delivery. On September 10, Kirk prepares the one thousand cases for shipment. Kirk asks Doolittle how he would like the goods to be shipped, but Doolittle does not respond. On September 21, Kirk, in writing, demands assurance that Doolittle will be able to pay on tender of the beans. Kirk asks that the money be placed in escrow prior to October 1 in a bank in Doolittle's city named by Kirk. Doolittle does not respond to any of Kirk's requests, but on October 5 he wants to file suit against Kirk for breach of contract for failure to deliver the beans as agreed. Discuss Kirk's liability for failure to tender delivery on October 1.

11-6. CASE PROBLEM WITH SAMPLE ANSWER

In 1998, Johnson Controls, Inc. (JCI), began buying auto parts from Q.C. Onics Ventures, LP. For each part, JCI would inform Onics of its need and ask the price. Onics would analyze the specifications, contact its suppliers, and respond with a formal quotation. A quote listed a part's number and description, the price per unit, and an estimate of units available for a given year. A quote did not state payment terms, an acceptance date, timing of performance, warranties, or quantities. JCI would select a supplier and issue a purchase order for a part. The purchase order required the seller to supply all of JCI's requirements for the part but gave the buyer the right to end the deal at any time. Using this procedure, JCI issued hundreds of purchase orders. In July 2001, JCI terminated its relationship with Onics and began buying parts through another supplier. Onics filed a suit in a federal district court against Johnson, alleging breach of contract. Which documents—the price quotations or the purchase orders—constituted offers? Which were acceptances? What effect would the answers to these questions have on the result in this case? Explain. [*Q.C. Onics Ventures, LP v. Johnson Controls, Inc.*, __ F.Supp.2d __ (N.D.Ind. 2006)]

- **To view a sample answer for Problem 11-6, go to this book's Web site at academic.cengage.com/blaw/cross, select "Chapter 11," and click on "Case Problem with Sample Answer."**

11-7. Shipment and Destination Contracts. In 2003, Karen Pearson and Steve and Tara Carlson agreed to buy a 2004 Dynasty recreational vehicle (RV) from DeMartini's RV Sales in Grass Valley, California. On September 29, Pearson, the Carlsons, and DeMartini's signed a contract providing that "seller agrees to deliver the vehicle to you on the date this contract is signed." The buyers made a payment of $145,000 on the total price of $356,416 the next day, when they also signed a form acknowledging that the RV had been inspected and accepted. They agreed to return later to have the RV transported out of state for delivery (to avoid paying state sales tax on the purchase). On October 7, Steve Carlson returned to DeMartini's to ride with the seller's driver to Nevada to consummate the out-of-state delivery. When the RV developed problems, Pearson and the Carlsons filed a suit in a federal district court against the RV's manufacturer, Monaco Coach Corp., alleging, in part, breach of warranty under state law. The applicable statute is expressly limited to goods sold in California. Monaco argued that this RV had been sold in Nevada. How does the Uniform Commercial Code (UCC) define a sale? What does the UCC provide with respect to the passage of title? How do these provisions apply here? Discuss. [*Carlson v. Monaco Coach Corp.*, 486 F.Supp.2d 1127 (E.D.Cal. 2007)]

11-8. Online Acceptances. Internet Archive (IA) is devoted to preserving a record of resources on the Internet for future generations. IA uses the "Wayback Machine" to automatically browse Web sites and reproduce their contents in an archive. IA does not ask the owners' permission before copying their material but will remove it on request. Suzanne Shell, a resident of Colorado, owns **www.profane-justice.org**, which is dedicated to providing information to individuals accused of child abuse or neglect. The site warns, "IF YOU COPY OR DISTRIBUTE ANYTHING ON THIS SITE YOU ARE ENTERING INTO A

CONTRACT." The terms, which can be accessed only by clicking on a link, include, among other charges, a fee of $5,000 for each page copied "in advance of printing." Neither the warning nor the terms require a user to indicate assent. When Shell discovered that the Wayback Machine had copied the contents of her site—approximately eighty-seven times between May 1999 and October 2004—she asked IA to remove the copies from its archive and pay her $100,000. IA removed the copies and filed a suit in a federal district court against Shell, who responded, in part, with a counterclaim for breach of contract. IA filed a motion to dismiss this claim. Did IA contract with Shell? Explain. [*Internet Archive v. Shell,* 505 F.Supp.2d 755 (D.Colo. 2007)]

11–9. Additional Provisions Affecting Remedies. Nomo Agroindustrial Sa De CV is a farm company based in Mexico that grows tomatoes, cucumbers, and other vegetables to sell in the United States. In the early 2000s, Nomo had problems when its tomato plants contracted a disease: tomato spotted wilt virus (TSWV). To obtain a crop that was resistant to TSWV, Nomo contacted Enza Zaden North America, Inc., an international corporation that manufactures seeds. Enza's brochures advertised—and Enza told Nomo—that its Caiman variety was resistant to TSWV. Based on these assurances, Nomo bought Caiman seeds. The invoice, which Nomo's representative signed, limited any damages to the purchase price of the seeds. The plants germinated from the Caiman seeds contracted TSWV, destroying Nomo's entire tomato crop. Nomo filed a suit in a federal district court against Enza, seeking to recover for the loss. Enza argued, in part, that any damages were limited to the price of the seeds. Can parties agree to limit their remedies under the UCC? If so, what are Nomo's best arguments against the enforcement of the limitations clause in Enza's invoice? What should the court rule on this issue? Why? [*Nomo Agroindustrial Sa De CV v. Enza Zaden North America, Inc.,* 492 F.Supp.2d 1175 (D.Ariz. 2007)]

11–10. SPECIAL CASE ANALYSIS

Go to Case 11.3, *Fitl v. Strek,* 269 Neb. 51, 690 N.W.2d 605 (2005), on pages 271 and 272. Read the excerpt and answer the following questions.

(a) **Issue:** What was the main issue in this case?
(b) **Rule of Law:** What rule of law did the court apply?
(c) **Applying the Rule of Law:** Describe how the court applied the rule of law to the facts of this case.
(d) **Conclusion:** What was the court's conclusion in this case?

11–11. A QUESTION OF ETHICS

Scotwood Industries, Inc., sells calcium chloride flake for use in ice melt products. Between July and September 2004, Scotwood delivered thirty-seven shipments of flake to Frank Miller & Sons, Inc. After each delivery, Scotwood billed Miller, which paid thirty-five of the invoices and processed 30 to 50 percent of the flake. In August, Miller began complaining about the quality. Scotwood assured Miller that it would remedy the situation. Finally, in October, Miller told Scotwood, "[T]his is totally unacceptable. We are willing to discuss Scotwood picking up the material." Miller claimed that the flake was substantially defective because it was chunked. Calcium chloride maintains its purity for up to five years but chunks if it is exposed to and absorbs moisture, making it unusable. In response to Scotwood's suit to collect payment on the unpaid invoices, Miller filed a counterclaim in a federal district court for breach of contract, seeking to recover based on revocation of acceptance, among other things. [Scotwood Industries, Inc. v. Frank Miller & Sons, Inc., *435 F.Supp.2d 1160 (D.Kan. 2006)]*

(a) What is revocation of acceptance? How does a buyer effectively exercise this option? Do the facts in this case support this theory as a ground for Miller to recover damages? Why or why not?
(b) Is there an ethical basis for allowing a buyer to revoke acceptance of goods and recover damages? If so, is there an ethical limit to this right? Discuss.

11–12. VIDEO QUESTION

Go to this text's Web site at **academic.cengage.com/blaw/cross** and select "Chapter 11." Click on "Video Questions" and view the video titled *E-Contracts: Agreeing Online.* Then answer the following questions.

(a) According to the instructor in the video, what is the key factor in determining whether a particular term in an online agreement is enforceable?
(b) Suppose that you click on "I accept" in order to download software from the Internet. You do not read the terms of the agreement before accepting it, even though you know that such agreements often contain forum-selection and arbitration clauses. The software later causes irreparable harm to your computer system, and you want to sue. When you go to the Web site and view the agreement, however, you discover that a choice-of-law clause in the contract specifies that the law of Nigeria controls. Is this term enforceable? Is it a term that should be reasonably expected in an online contract?
(c) Does it matter what the term actually says if it is a type of term that one could reasonably expect to be in the contract? What arguments can be made for and against enforcing a choice-of-law clause in an online contract?

LAW ON THE WEB

For updated links to resources available on the Web, as well as a variety of other materials, visit this text's Web site at

academic.cengage.com/blaw/cross

For information about the National Conference of Commissioners on Uniform State Laws (NCCUSL) and links to online uniform acts, go to

www.nccusl.org

For more information on shipment and destination contracts and a list of related commercial law Web links, go to

www.legalmatch.com/law-library/article/merchandise-risk-of-loss.html

Cornell University's Legal Information Institute offers online access to the UCC, as well as to UCC articles as enacted by particular states and proposed revisions to articles, at

www.law.cornell.edu/ucc/index.html

Legal Research Exercises on the Web

Go to **academic.cengage.com/blaw/cross**, the Web site that accompanies this text. Select "Chapter 11" and click on "Internet Exercises." There you will find the following Internet research exercises that you can perform to learn more about the topics covered in this chapter.

Internet Exercise 11–1: Legal Perspective
E-Contract Formation

Internet Exercise 11–2: Management Perspective
A Checklist for Sales Contracts

An Example of a Contract for the International Sale of Coffee

1 OVERLAND COFFEE IMPORT CONTRACT
OF THE
GREEN COFFEE ASSOCIATION
OF
NEW YORK CITY, INC.*

Contract Seller's No.: 504617
Buyer's No.: P9264
Date: 10/11/09

2 SOLD BY: XYZ Co.
TO: Starbucks

3 QUANTITY: Five Hundred (500) Bags Tons of Mexican coffee
weighing about 152.117 lbs. per bag.

4 PACKAGING: Coffee must be packed in clean sound bags of uniform size made of sisal, henequen, jute, burlap, or similar woven material, without inner lining or outer covering of any material properly sewn by hand and/or machine.
Bulk shipments are allowed if agreed by mutual consent of Buyer and Seller.

5 DESCRIPTION: High grown Mexican Altura

6 PRICE: At Ten/$10.00 dollars U.S. Currency, per lb. net, (U.S. Funds)
Upon delivery in Bonded Public Warehouse at Laredo, TX (City and State)

7 PAYMENT: Cash against warehouse receipts

Bill and tender to DATE when all import requirements and governmental regulations have been satisfied, and coffee delivered or discharged (as per contract terms). Seller is obliged to give the Buyer two (2) calendar days free time in Bonded Public Warehouse following but not including date of tender.

8 ARRIVAL: During December (Period) via truck (Method of Transportation)
from Mexico (Country of Exportation) for arrival at Laredo, TX, USA (Country of Importation)
Partial shipments permitted.

9 ADVICE OF ARRIVAL: Advice of arrival with warehouse name and location, together with the quantity, description, marks and place of entry, must be transmitted directly, or through Seller's Agent/Broker, to the Buyer or his Agent/Broker. Advice will be given as soon as known but not later than the fifth business day following arrival at the named warehouse. Such advice may be given verbally with written confirmation to be sent the same day.

10 WEIGHTS: (1) DELIVERED WEIGHTS: Coffee covered by this contract is to be weighed at location named in tender. Actual tare to be allowed.
(2) SHIPPING WEIGHTS: Coffee covered by this contract is sold on shipping weights. Any loss in weight exceeding 1/2 percent at location named in tender is for account of Seller at contract price.
(3) Coffee is to be weighed within fifteen (15) calendar days after tender. Weighing expenses, if any, for account of Seller (Seller or Buyer)

11 MARKINGS: Bags to be branded in English with the name of Country of Origin and otherwise to comply with laws and regulations of the Country of Importation, in effect at the time of entry, governing marking of import merchandise. Any expense incurred by failure to comply with these regulations to be borne by Exporter/Seller.

12 RULINGS: The "Rulings on Coffee Contracts" of the Green Coffee Association of New York City, Inc., in effect on the date this contract is made, is incorporated for all purposes as a part of this agreement, and together herewith, constitute the entire contract. No variation or addition hereto shall be valid unless signed by the parties to the contract.
Seller guarantees that the terms printed on the reverse hereof, which by reference are made a part hereof, are identical with the terms as printed in By-Laws and Rules of the Green Coffee Association of New York City, Inc., heretofore adopted.
Exceptions to this guarantee are:

ACCEPTED:
XYZ Co. Seller
BY DM Agent

Starbucks Buyer
BY Agent

COMMISSION TO BE PAID BY: Seller

ABC Brokerage
13 Broker(s)

When this contract is executed by a person acting for another, such person hereby represents that he is fully authorized to commit his principal.

* Reprinted with permission of The Green Coffee Association of New York City, Inc.

1 This is a contract for a sale of coffee to be *imported* internationally. If the parties have their principal places of business located in different countries, the contract may be subject to the United Nations Convention on Contracts for the International Sale of Goods (CISG). If the parties' principal places of business are located in the United States, the contract may be subject to the Uniform Commercial Code (UCC).

2 Quantity is one of the most important terms to include in a contract. Without it, a court may not be able to enforce the contract. See Chapter 11.

3 Weight per unit (bag) can be exactly stated or approximately stated. If it is not so stated, usage of trade in international contracts determines standards of weight.

4 Packaging requirements can be conditions for acceptance and payment. See Chapter 10. Bulk shipments are not permitted without the consent of the buyer.

5 A description of the coffee and the "Markings" constitute express warranties. Warranties in contracts for domestic sales of goods are discussed generally in Chapter 11. International contracts rely more heavily on descriptions and models or samples.

6 Under the UCC, parties may enter into a valid contract even though the price is not set. See Chapter 11. Under the CISG, a contract must provide for an exact determination of the price.

7 The terms of payment may take one of two forms: credit or cash. Credit terms can be complicated. A cash term can be simple, and payment can be made by any means acceptable in the ordinary course of business (for example, a personal check or a letter of credit). If the seller insists on actual cash, the buyer must be given a reasonable time to get it. See Chapter 11.

8 *Tender* means the seller has placed goods that conform to the contract at the buyer's disposition. What constitutes a valid tender is explained in Chapter 11. This contract requires that the coffee meet all import regulations and that it be ready for pickup by the buyer at a "Bonded Public Warehouse." (A *bonded warehouse* is a place in which goods can be stored without paying taxes until the goods are removed.)

9 The delivery date is significant because, if it is not met, the buyer may hold the seller in breach of the contract. Under this contract, the seller can be given a "period" within which to deliver the goods, instead of a specific day, which could otherwise present problems. The seller is also given some time to rectify goods that do not pass inspection (see the "Guarantee" clause on page two of the contract). For a discussion of the remedies of the buyer and seller, see Chapter 11.

10 As part of a proper tender, the seller (or its agent) must inform the buyer (or its agent) when the goods have arrived at their destination. The responsibilities of agents are set out in Chapter 19.

11 In some contracts, delivered and shipped weights can be important. During shipping, some loss can be attributed to the type of goods (spoilage of fresh produce, for example) or to the transportation itself. A seller and buyer can agree on the extent to which either of them will bear such losses. See Chapter 11 for a discussion of the liability of common carriers for loss during shipment.

12 Documents are often incorporated in a contract by reference, because including them word for word can make a contract difficult to read. If the document is later revised, the entire contract might have to be reworked. Documents that are typically incorporated by reference include detailed payment and delivery terms; special provisions; and sets of rules, codes, and standards.

13 In international sales transactions, and for domestic deals involving certain products, brokers are used to form the contracts. When so used, the brokers are entitled to a commission. See Chapter 19.

(Continued)

TERMS AND CONDITIONS

14

ARBITRATION: All controversies relating to, in connection with, or arising out of this contract, its modification, making or the authority or obligations of the signatories hereto, and whether involving the principals, agents, brokers, or others who actually subscribe hereto, shall be settled by arbitration in accordance with the "Rules of Arbitration" of the Green Coffee Association of New York City, Inc., as they exist at the time of the arbitration (including provisions as to payment of fees and expenses). Arbitration is the sole remedy hereunder, and it shall be held in accordance with the law of New York State, and judgment of any award may be entered in the courts of that State, or in any other court of competent jurisdiction. All notices or judicial service in reference to arbitration or enforcement shall be deemed given if transmitted as required by the aforesaid rules.

15

GUARANTEE: (a) If all or any of the coffee is refused admission into the country of importation by reason of any violation of governmental laws or acts, which violation existed at the time the coffee arrived at Bonded-Public Warehouse, seller is required, as to the amount not admitted and as soon as possible, to deliver replacement coffee in conformity to all terms and conditions of this contract, excepting only the Arrival terms, but not later than thirty (30) days after the date of the violation notice. Any payment made and expenses incurred for any coffee denied entry shall be refunded within ten (10) calendar days of denial of entry, and payment shall be made for the replacement delivery in accordance with the terms of this contract. Consequently, if Buyer removes the coffee from the Bonded Public Warehouse, Seller's responsibility as to such portion hereunder ceases.

16

(b) Contracts containing the overstamp "No Pass-No Sale" on the face of the contract shall be interpreted to mean: If any or all of the coffee is not admitted into the country of Importation in its original condition by reason of failure to meet requirements of the government's laws or Acts, the contract shall be deemed null and void as to that portion of the coffee which is not admitted in its original condition. Any payment made and expenses incurred for any coffee denied entry shall be refunded within ten (10) calendar days of denial of entry.

CONTINGENCY: This contract is not contingent upon any other contract.

CLAIMS: Coffee shall be considered accepted as to quality unless within *fifteen* (15) calendar days after delivery at Bonded Public Warehouse or within *fifteen* (15) calendar days after all Government clearances have been received, whichever is later, either:

(a) Claims are settled by the parties hereto, or,

17

(b) Arbitration proceedings have been filed by one of the parties in accordance with the provisions hereof.

(c) If neither (a) nor (b) has been done in the stated period or if any portion of the coffee has been removed from the Bonded Public Warehouse before representative sealed samples have been drawn by the Green Coffee Association of New York City, Inc., in accordance with its rules, Seller's responsibility for quality claims ceases for that portion so removed.

(d) Any question of quality submitted to arbitration shall be a matter of allowance only, unless otherwise provided in the contract.

18

DELIVERY: (a) No more than three (3) chops may be tendered for each lot of 250 bags.

(b) Each chop of coffee tendered is to be uniform in grade and appearance. All expense necessary to make coffee uniform shall be for account of seller.

(c) Notice of arrival and/or sampling order constitutes a tender, and must be given not later than the fifth business day following arrival at Bonded Public Warehouse stated on the contract.

INSURANCE: Seller is responsible for any loss or damage, or both, until Delivery and Discharge of coffee at the Bonded Public Warehouse in the Country of Importation.

All Insurance Risks, costs and responsibility are for Seller's Account until Delivery and Discharge of coffee at the Bonded Public Warehouse in the Country of Importation.

19

Buyer's insurance responsibility begins from the day of importation or from the day of tender, whichever is later.

20

FREIGHT: Seller to provide and pay for all transportation and related expenses to the Bonded Public Warehouse in the Country of Importation.

EXPORT DUTIES/TAXES: Exporter is to pay all Export taxes, duties or other fees or charges, if any, levied because of exportation.

21

IMPORT DUTIES/TAXES: Any Duty or Tax whatsoever, imposed by the government or any authority of the Country of Importation, shall be borne by the Importer/Buyer.

INSOLVENCY OR FINANCIAL FAILURE OF BUYER OR SELLER: If, at any time before the contract is fully executed, either party hereto shall meet with creditors because of inability generally to make payment of obligations when due, or shall suspend such payments, fail to meet his general trade obligations in the regular course of business, shall file a petition in bankruptcy or, for an arrangement, shall become insolvent, or commit an act of bankruptcy, then the other party may at his option, expressed in writing, declare the aforesaid to constitute a breach and default of this contract, and may, in addition to other remedies, decline to deliver further or make payment or may sell or purchase for the defaulter's account, and may collect damage for any injury or loss, or shall account for the profit, if any, occasioned by such sale or purchase.

22

This clause is subject to the provisions of (11 USC 365 (e) 1) if invoked.

23

BREACH OR DEFAULT OF CONTRACT: In the event either party hereto fails to perform, or breaches or repudiates this agreement, the other party shall subject to the specific provisions of this contract be entitled to the remedies and relief provided for by the Uniform Commercial Code of the State of New York. The computation and ascertainment of damages, or the determination of any other dispute as to relief, shall be made by the arbitrators in accordance with the Arbitration Clause herein.

Consequential damages shall not, however, be allowed.

14 Arbitration is the settling of a dispute by submitting it to a disinterested party (other than a court) that renders a decision. The procedures and costs can be provided for in an arbitration clause or incorporated through other documents. To enforce an award rendered in an arbitration, the winning party can "enter" (submit) the award in a court "of competent jurisdiction." For a general discussion of arbitration and other forms of dispute resolution (other than courts), see Chapter 3.

15 When goods are imported internationally, they must meet certain import requirements before being released to the buyer. Because of this, buyers frequently want a guaranty clause that covers the goods not admitted into the country and that either requires the seller to replace the goods within a stated time or allows the contract for those goods not admitted to be void. See Chapter 10.

16 In the "Claims" clause, the parties agree that the buyer has a certain time within which to reject the goods. The right to reject is a right by law and does not need to be stated in a contract. If the buyer does not exercise the right within the time specified in the contract, the goods will be considered accepted. See Chapter 11.

17 Many international contracts include definitions of terms so that the parties understand what they mean. Some terms are used in a particular industry in a specific way. Here, the word *chop* refers to a unit of like-grade coffee bean. The buyer has a right to inspect ("sample") the coffee. If the coffee does not conform to the contract, the seller must correct the nonconformity. See Chapter 11.

18 The "Delivery," "Insurance," and "Freight" clauses, with the "Arrival" clause on page one of the contract, indicate that this is a destination contract. The seller has the obligation to deliver the goods to the destination, not simply deliver them into the hands of a carrier. Under this contract, the destination is a "Bonded Public Warehouse" in a specific location. The seller bears the risk of loss until the goods are delivered at their destination. Typically, the seller will have bought insurance to cover the risk. See Chapter 11 for a discussion of delivery terms and the risk of loss.

19 Delivery terms are commonly placed in all sales contracts. Such terms determine who pays freight and other costs and, in the absence of an agreement specifying otherwise, who bears the risk of loss. International contracts may use these delivery terms or they may use INCOTERMS, which are published by the International Chamber of Commerce. For example, the INCOTERM DDP (delivered duty paid) requires the seller to arrange shipment, obtain and pay for import or export permits, and get the goods through customs to a named destination.

20 Exported and imported goods are subject to duties, taxes, and other charges imposed by the governments of the countries involved. International contracts spell out who is responsible for these charges.

21 This clause protects a party if the other party should become financially unable to fulfill the obligations under the contract. Thus, if the seller cannot afford to deliver, or the buyer cannot afford to pay, for the stated reasons, the other party can consider the contract breached. This right is subject to "11 USC 365(e)(1)," which refers to a specific provision of the U.S. Bankruptcy Code dealing with executory contracts. Bankruptcy provisions are covered in Chapter 15.

22 In the "Breach or Default of Contract" clause, the parties agreed that the remedies under this contract are the remedies (except for consequential damages) provided by the UCC, as in effect in the state of New York. The amount and "ascertainment" of damages, as well as other disputes about relief, are to be determined by arbitration. Breach of contract and contractual remedies in general are explained in Chapter 11. Arbitration is discussed in Chapter 3.

23 Three clauses frequently included in international contracts are omitted here. There is no choice-of-language clause designating the official language to be used in interpreting the contract terms. There is no choice-of-forum clause designating the place in which disputes will be litigated, except for arbitration (law of New York State). Finally, there is no *force majeure* clause relieving the sellers or buyers from nonperformance due to events beyond their control.

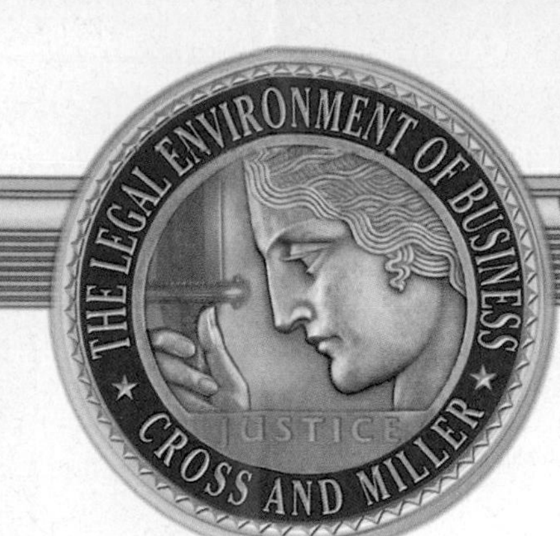

CHAPTER 12

Torts and Cyber Torts

Part of doing business today—and, indeed, part of everyday life—is the risk of being involved in a lawsuit. The list of circumstances in which businesspersons can be sued is long and varied. A customer who is injured by a security guard at a business establishment, for example, may attempt to sue the business owner, claiming that the security guard's conduct was wrongful. Any time that one party's allegedly wrongful conduct causes injury to another, an action may arise under the law of **torts** (the word *tort* is French for "wrong"). Through tort law, society compensates those who have suffered injuries as a result of the wrongful conduct of others.

Many of the lawsuits brought by or against business firms are based on the tort theories discussed in this chapter, which covers intentional torts, and unintentional torts. *Intentional torts* arise from intentional acts, whereas *unintentional torts* often result from carelessness (as when an employee at a store knocks over a display case, injuring a customer). In addition, this chapter discusses how tort law applies to wrongful actions in the online environment. Tort theories also come into play in the context of product liability (liability for defective products), which will be discussed in detail in Chapter 13.

The Basis of Tort Law

Two notions serve as the basis of all torts: wrongs and compensation. Tort law is designed to compensate those who have suffered a loss or injury due to another person's wrongful act. In a tort action, one person or group brings a lawsuit against another person or group to obtain compensation (monetary damages) or other relief for the harm suffered.

The Purpose of Tort Law

The basic purpose of tort law is to provide remedies for the invasion of various *protected interests*. Society recognizes an interest in personal physical safety, and tort law provides remedies for acts that cause physical injury or that interfere with physical security and freedom of movement. Society recognizes an interest in protecting property, and tort law provides remedies for acts that cause destruction or damage to property. Society also recognizes an interest in protecting certain intangible interests, such as personal privacy, family relations, reputation, and dignity, and tort law provides remedies for violation of these interests.

Damages Available in Tort Actions

Because the purpose of tort law is to compensate the injured party for the damage suffered, you need to have an understanding of the types of damages that plaintiffs seek in tort actions. The high cost to society of sizable damages awards in tort cases has fueled the tort reform movement, which is discussed in this chapter's *Contemporary Legal Debates* feature on pages 292 and 293.

Compensatory Damages **Compensatory damages** are intended to compensate or reimburse a plaintiff for actual losses—to make the plaintiff whole and put her or him in the same position that she or he would have been had the tort not occurred. Compensatory damages awards are often broken down into special damages and general damages. *Special damages* compensate the plaintiff for quantifiable monetary losses, such as medical expenses, lost wages and benefits (now and in the future), extra costs, the loss of irreplaceable items, and the costs of repairing or replacing damaged property. *General damages* compensate individuals (not companies) for the nonmonetary aspects of the harm suffered, such as pain and suffering. A court might award general damages for physical or emotional pain and suffering, loss of companionship, loss of consortium (losing the emotional and physical benefits of a spousal relationship), disfigurement, loss of reputation, or loss or impairment of mental or physical capacity.

Punitive Damages Occasionally, the courts may also award **punitive damages** in tort cases to punish the wrongdoer and deter others from similar wrongdoing. Punitive damages are appropriate only when the defendant's conduct was particularly egregious or reprehensible. Usually, this means that punitive damages are available mainly in intentional tort actions and only rarely in negligence lawsuits (*negligence* actions will be discussed later in this chapter). They may be awarded, however, in suits involving *gross negligence,* which can be defined as an intentional failure to perform a manifest duty in reckless disregard of the consequences of such a failure for the life or property of another.

Courts exercise great restraint in granting punitive damages to plaintiffs in tort actions because punitive damages are subject to the limitations imposed by the due process clause of the U.S. Constitution (discussed in Chapter 2). In *State Farm Mutual Automobile Insurance Co. v. Campbell,*[1] the United States Supreme Court held that to the extent an award of punitive damages is grossly excessive, it furthers no legitimate purpose and violates due process requirements. Although this case dealt with intentional torts (fraud and intentional infliction of emotional distress), the Court's holding applies equally to punitive damages awards in gross negligence cases (as well as to product liability cases, which will be discussed in Chapter 13).

Intentional Torts against Persons

An **intentional tort,** as the term implies, requires intent. The **tortfeasor** (the one committing the tort) must intend to commit an act, the consequences of which interfere with the personal or business interests of another in a way not permitted by law. An evil or harmful motive is not required—in fact, the actor may even have a beneficial motive for committing what turns out to be a tortious act. In tort law, *intent* means only that the actor intended the consequences of his or her act or knew with substantial certainty that specific consequences would result from the act. The law generally assumes that individuals intend the *normal* consequences of their actions. Thus, forcefully pushing another—even if done in jest and without any evil motive—is an intentional tort (if injury results), because the object of a strong push can ordinarily be expected to be abruptly displaced.

Intentional torts against persons include assault and battery, false imprisonment, infliction of emotional distress, defamation, invasion of privacy, appropriation, fraudulent misrepresentation, and torts related to misuse of litigation. We discuss these torts in the following subsections.

Assault and Battery

Any intentional, unexcused act that creates in another person a reasonable apprehension of immediate harmful or offensive contact is an **assault.** Note that apprehension is not the same as fear. If a contact is such that a reasonable person would want to avoid it, and if there is a reasonable basis for believing that the contact will occur, then the plaintiff suffers apprehension whether or not she or he is afraid. The interest protected by tort law concerning assault is the freedom from having to expect harmful or offensive contact. The arousal of apprehension is enough to justify compensation.

The *completion* of the act that caused the apprehension, if it results in harm to the plaintiff, is a **battery,** which is defined as an unexcused and harmful or offensive physical contact *intentionally* performed. For example, Ivan threatens Jean with a gun, then shoots her. The pointing of the gun at Jean is an assault; the firing of the gun (if the bullet hits Jean) is a battery. The interest protected by tort law concerning battery is the right to personal security and safety. The contact can be harmful, or it can be merely offensive (such as an unwelcome kiss). Physical injury need not occur. The contact can involve any part of the body or anything attached to it—for example, a hat or other item of clothing, a purse, or a chair or an automobile in which one is sitting. Whether the contact is offensive is

1. 538 U.S. 408, 123 S.Ct. 1513, 155 L.Ed.2d 585 (2003).

CONTEMPORARY LEGAL DEBATES

Tort Reform

The question of whether our tort law system is in need of reform has aroused heated debate. While some argue that the current system imposes excessive costs on society, others contend that the system protects consumers from unsafe products and practices.

"End the Tort Tax and Frivolous Lawsuits," Say the Critics

Critics of the current tort law system contend that it encourages too many frivolous lawsuits, which clog the courts, and is unnecessarily costly. In particular, they say, damages awards are often excessive and bear little relationship to the actual damage suffered. Such large awards encourage plaintiffs to bring frivolous suits, hoping that they will "hit the jackpot." Trial lawyers, in turn, are eager to bring the suits because they are paid on a contingency-fee basis, meaning that they receive a percentage of the damages awarded.

The result, in the critics' view, is a system that disproportionately rewards a few lucky plaintiffs while imposing enormous costs on business and society as a whole. They refer to the economic burden that the tort system imposes on society as the "tort tax." According to one recent study, more than $300 billion per year is expended on tort litigation, including plaintiffs' and defendants' attorneys' fees, damages awards, and other costs. Most of the costs are from class-action lawsuits involving product liability or medical malpractice.[a] (A *class action* is a lawsuit in which a single person or a small group of people represents the interests of a larger group.) Although even the critics would not contend that the tort tax encompasses the entire $300 billion, they believe that it includes a sizable portion of that amount. Furthermore, they say, the tax appears in other ways. Because physicians, hospitals, and pharmaceutical companies are worried about medical malpractice suits, they have changed their behavior. Physicians, for example, engage in defensive medicine by ordering more tests than necessary. PricewaterhouseCoopers has calculated that the practice of defensive medicine increases health-care costs by more than $100 billion per year.

To solve the problems they perceive, critics want to reduce both the number of tort cases brought each year and the amount of damages awards. They advocate the following tort reform measures: (1) limit the amount of punitive damages that can be awarded; (2) limit the amount of general noneconomic damages that can be awarded (for example, for pain and suffering); (3) limit the amount that attorneys can collect in contingency fees; and (4) to discourage the filing of meritless suits, require the losing party to pay both the plaintiff's and the defendant's expenses.

"The Current System Promotes Fairness and Safefy," Say Their Opponents

Others are not so sure that the current system needs such drastic reform. They say that the prospect of tort lawsuits encourages companies to produce safer products and deters them from putting dangerous products on the market. In the health-care industry,

a. Lawrence J. McQuillan, Hovannes Abramyan, and Anthony P. Archie, *Jackpot Justice: The True Cost of America's Tort System* (San Francisco: Pacific Research Institute, 2007).

determined by the *reasonable person standard*.[2] The contact can be made by the defendant or by some force the defendant sets in motion—for example, a rock thrown, food poisoned, or a stick swung.

Compensation If the plaintiff shows that there was contact, and the jury (or judge, if there is no jury) agrees that the contact was offensive, then the plaintiff has a right to compensation. There is no need to establish that the defendant acted out of malice. The underlying motive does not matter, only the intent to bring about the harmful or offensive contact to the plaintiff. In fact, proving a motive is never necessary. A plaintiff may be compensated for the emotional harm or loss of reputation resulting from a battery, as well as for physical harm.

Defenses to Assault and Battery A defendant who is sued for assault, battery, or both can raise any of the following legally recognized defenses:

2. The *reasonable person standard* is an "objective" test of how a reasonable person would have acted under the same circumstances. See the subsection entitled "The Duty of Care and Its Breach" later in this chapter on page 305.

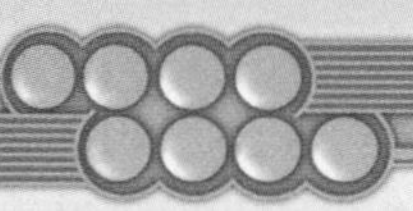

the potential for medical malpractice suits has led to safer and more effective medical practices.

Imposing limits on the amount of punitive and general noneconomic damages would be unfair, say the system's defenders, and would reduce efficiency in our legal and economic system. After all, corporations conduct cost-benefit analyses when they decide how much safety to build into their products. Any limitation on potential damages would mean that corporations would have less incentive to build safer products. Indeed, Professor Stephen Teret of the Johns Hopkins University School of Public Health says that tort litigation is an important tool for preventing injuries because it forces manufacturers to opt for more safety in their products rather than less.[b] Limiting contingency fees would also be unfair, say those in favor of the current system, because low-income consumers who have been injured could not afford to pay an attorney to take a case on an hourly fee basis—and an attorney would not expend the time needed to pursue a case without the prospect of a large reward in the form of a contingency fee.

Tort Reform in Reality

While the debate continues, the federal government and a number of states have begun to take some steps toward tort reform. At the federal level, the Class Action Fairness Act (CAFA) of 2005[c] shifted jurisdiction over large interstate tort and product liability class-action lawsuits from the state courts to the federal courts. The intent was to prevent plaintiffs' attorneys from shopping around for a state court that might be predisposed to be sympathetic to their clients' cause and to award large damages in class-action suits.

At the state level, more than twenty states have placed caps ranging from $250,000 to $750,000 on noneconomic damages, especially in medical malpractice suits. More than thirty states have limited punitive damages, with some imposing outright bans.

WHERE DO YOU STAND?

Large damages awards in tort litigation have to be paid by someone. If the defendant is insured, then insurance companies foot the bill. Ultimately, though, high insurance rates are passed on to consumers of goods and services in the United States. Consequently, tort reform that reduces the size and number of damages awards ultimately will mean lower costs of goods and services to consumers. The downside of these lower costs, though, might be higher risks of medical malpractice and dangerous products. Do you believe that this trade-off is real? Why or why not?

b. "Litigation Is an Important Tool for Injury and Gun Violence Prevention," Johns Hopkins University Center for Gun Policy and Research, July 15, 2006.

c. 28 U.S.C.A. Sections 1711–1715, 1453.

1. *Consent.* When a person consents to the act that is allegedly tortious, there may be a complete or partial defense to liability.
2. *Self-defense.* An individual who is defending her or his life or physical well-being can claim self-defense. In a situation of either *real* or *apparent* danger, a person may normally use whatever force is *reasonably* necessary to prevent harmful contact (see Chapter 7 for a more detailed discussion of self-defense).
3. *Defense of others.* An individual can act in a reasonable manner to protect others who are in real or apparent danger.
4. *Defense of property.* Reasonable force may be used in attempting to remove intruders from one's home, although force that is likely to cause death or great bodily injury normally cannot be used just to protect property.

False Imprisonment

False imprisonment is defined as the intentional confinement or restraint of another person's activities without justification. It involves interference with the freedom to move without restriction. The confinement can be accomplished through the use of physical barriers, physical restraint, or threats of physical force. Moral pressure does not constitute false imprisonment. Furthermore, it is essential that the person being restrained not agree to the restraint.

Businesspersons often face suits for false imprisonment after they have attempted to confine a suspected shoplifter for questioning. Under the laws of most states, merchants may detain persons suspected of shoplifting and hold them for the police. Although laws vary from state to state, normally only a merchant's security personnel—not salesclerks or other employees—have the right to detain suspects. Reasonable or probable cause must exist to believe that the person being detained has committed a theft. Additionally, most states require that any detention be conducted in a *reasonable* manner and for only a *reasonable* length of time. Tackling a customer suspected of theft in the parking lot would be considered unreasonable in many jurisdictions.

Intentional Infliction of Emotional Distress

The tort of *intentional infliction of emotional distress* can be defined as an intentional act that amounts to extreme and outrageous conduct resulting in severe emotional distress to another. To be **actionable** (capable of serving as the ground for a lawsuit), the act must be extreme and outrageous to the point that it exceeds the bounds of decency accepted by society. For example, a prankster telephones a pregnant woman and says that her husband and two sons have just been killed in a horrible accident (although they have not). As a result, the woman suffers intense mental pain and has a miscarriage. In that situation, the woman would be able to sue for intentional infliction of emotional distress.

Courts in most jurisdictions are wary of emotional distress claims and confine them to situations involving truly outrageous behavior. Acts that cause indignity or annoyance alone usually are not sufficient. Many times, however, repeated annoyances (such as those experienced by a person who is being stalked), coupled with threats, are enough.

Note that when the outrageous conduct consists of speech about a public figure, the First Amendment's guarantee of freedom of speech also limits emotional distress claims. For example, *Hustler* magazine once printed a fake advertisement that showed a picture of Reverend Jerry Falwell and described him as having lost his virginity to his mother in an outhouse while he was drunk. Falwell sued the magazine for intentional infliction of emotional distress and won, but the United States Supreme Court overturned the decision. The Court held that creators of parodies of public figures are protected under the First Amendment from intentional infliction of emotional distress claims. (The Court used the same standards that apply to public figures in defamation lawsuits, discussed next.)[3]

Defamation

As discussed in Chapter 5, the freedom of speech guaranteed by the First Amendment is not absolute. In interpreting the First Amendment, the courts must balance the vital guarantee of free speech against other pervasive and strong social interests, including society's interest in preventing and redressing attacks on reputation.

Defamation of character involves wrongfully hurting a person's good reputation. The law imposes a general duty on all persons to refrain from making false, defamatory *statements of fact* about others. Breaching this duty in writing or other permanent form (such as an electronic recording) involves the tort of **libel.** Breaching this duty orally involves the tort of **slander.** The tort of defamation also arises when a false statement of fact is made about a person's product, business, or legal ownership rights.

Note that generally only false statements that represent something as a fact (such as "Vladik cheats on his taxes") constitute defamation. Expressions of personal opinion (such as "Vladik is a jerk") are protected by the First Amendment and normally cannot lead to tort liability.

The Publication Requirement The basis of the tort of defamation is the publication of a statement or statements that hold an individual up to contempt, ridicule, or hatred. *Publication* here means that the defamatory statements are communicated (either intentionally or accidentally) to persons other than the defamed party. If Thompson writes Andrews a private letter falsely accusing him of embezzling funds, the action does not constitute libel. If Peters falsely

3. *Hustler Magazine, Inc. v. Falwell,* 485 U.S. 46, 108 S.Ct. 876, 99 L.Ed.2d 41 (1988). For another example of how the courts protect parody, see *Busch v. Viacom International, Inc.,* 477 F.Supp.2d 764 (N.D.Tex. 2007), involving a fake endorsement of televangelist Pat Robertson's diet shake.

states that Gordon is dishonest and incompetent when no one else is around, the action does not constitute slander. In neither case was the message communicated to a third party.

The courts have generally held that even dictating a letter to a secretary constitutes publication, although the publication may be privileged (a concept that will be explained shortly). Moreover, if a third party merely overhears defamatory statements by chance, the courts usually hold that this also constitutes publication. Defamatory statements made via the Internet are actionable as well. Note also that any individual who repeats or republishes defamatory statements normally is liable even if that person reveals the source of the statements.

Damages for Libel Once a defendant's liability for libel is established, *general damages* are presumed as a matter of law. General damages are designed to compensate the plaintiff for nonspecific harms such as disgrace or dishonor in the eyes of the community, humiliation, injured reputation, and emotional distress—harms that are difficult to measure. In other words, to recover damages in a libel case, the plaintiff need not prove that he or she was actually injured in any way as a result of the libelous statement.

Damages for Slander In contrast to cases alleging libel, in a case alleging slander, the plaintiff must prove *special damages* to establish the defendant's liability. The plaintiff must show that the slanderous statement caused her or him to suffer actual economic or monetary losses. Unless this initial hurdle of proving special damages is overcome, a plaintiff alleging slander normally cannot go forward with the suit and recover any damages. This requirement is imposed in slander cases because oral statements have a temporary quality. In contrast, a libelous (written) statement has the quality of permanence, can be circulated widely, and usually results from some degree of deliberation on the part of the author.

Exceptions to the burden of proving special damages in cases alleging slander are made for certain types of slanderous statements. If a false statement constitutes "slander *per se*," no proof of special damages is required for it to be actionable. In most states, the following four types of utterances are considered to be slander *per se:*

1. A statement that another has a loathsome disease (historically, leprosy and sexually transmitted diseases, but now also including allegations of mental illness).
2. A statement that another has committed improprieties while engaging in a profession or trade.
3. A statement that another has committed or has been imprisoned for a serious crime.
4. A statement that a person (usually only an unmarried person and sometimes only a woman) is unchaste or has engaged in serious sexual misconduct.

Defenses to Defamation Truth is normally an absolute defense against a defamation charge. In other words, if a defendant in a defamation case can prove that the allegedly defamatory statements of fact were true, normally no tort has been committed. Other defenses to defamation may exist if the speech is *privileged* or concerns a public figure. Note that the majority of defamation actions are filed in state courts, and state laws differ somewhat in the defenses they allow, such as privilege (discussed next).

Privileged Speech. In some circumstances, a person will not be liable for defamatory statements because she or he enjoys a **privilege,** or immunity. With respect to defamation, privileged communications are of two types: absolute and qualified.[4] Only in judicial proceedings and certain government proceedings is an *absolute privilege* granted. For example, statements made by attorneys and judges in the courtroom during a trial are absolutely privileged. So are statements made by government officials during legislative debate, even if the legislators make such statements maliciously—that is, knowing them to be untrue. An absolute privilege is granted in these situations because judicial and government personnel deal with matters that are so much in the public interest that the parties involved should be able to speak out fully and freely and without restriction.

In other situations, a person will not be liable for defamatory statements because he or she has a *qualified,* or *conditional, privilege.* An employer's statements in written evaluations of employees are an example of a qualified privilege. Generally, if the statements are made in good faith and the publication is limited to those who have a legitimate interest in the communication, the statements fall within the area of qualified privilege. The concept of conditional privilege rests on the common law assumption that in some situations, the right to know or speak is equal in importance

4. Note that the term *privileged communication* in this context is not the same as privileged communication between a professional, such as an attorney, and his or her client.

to the right not to be defamed. If a communication is conditionally privileged, to recover damages, the plaintiff must show that the privilege was abused.

Public Figures. Public officials who exercise substantial governmental power and any persons in the public limelight are considered *public figures.* In general, public figures are considered "fair game," and false and defamatory statements about them that are published in the press will not constitute defamation unless the statements are made with **actual malice.** To be made with actual malice, a statement must be made *with either knowledge of its falsity or a reckless disregard of the truth.*[5]

Statements made about public figures, especially when they are communicated via a public medium, are usually related to matters of general public interest; they refer to people who substantially affect all of us. Furthermore, public figures generally have some access to a public medium for answering disparaging falsehoods about themselves; private individuals do not. For these reasons, public figures have a greater burden of proof in defamation cases (they must prove actual malice) than do private individuals.

Invasion of Privacy

A person has a right to solitude and freedom from prying public eyes—in other words, to privacy. As mentioned in Chapter 5, the courts have held that certain amendments to the U.S. Constitution imply a right to privacy. Some state constitutions explicitly provide for privacy rights, as do a number of federal and state statutes. Tort law also safeguards these rights through the tort of *invasion of privacy.* Four acts qualify as invasions of privacy:

1. *Appropriation of identity.* Under the common law, using a person's name, picture, or other likeness for commercial purposes without permission is a tortious invasion of privacy. Most states today have also enacted statutes prohibiting *appropriation* (discussed further in the next subsection).
2. *Intrusion into an individual's affairs or seclusion.* For example, invading someone's home or searching someone's personal computer without authorization is an invasion of privacy. This tort has been held to extend to eavesdropping by wiretap, unauthorized scanning of a bank account, compulsory blood testing, and window peeping.
3. *False light.* The publication of information that places a person in a false light is another category of invasion of privacy. This could be a story attributing to someone ideas not held or actions not taken by that person. (The publication of such a story could involve the tort of defamation as well.)
4. *Public disclosure of private facts.* This type of invasion of privacy occurs when a person publicly discloses private facts about an individual that an ordinary person would find objectionable or embarrassing. A newspaper account of a private citizen's sex life or financial affairs could be an actionable invasion of privacy, even if the information revealed is true, because it is not of public concern.

The following case included an allegation of an intrusion into an individual's affairs or seclusion.

5. *New York Times Co. v. Sullivan,* 376 U.S. 254, 84 S.Ct. 710, 11 L.Ed.2d 686 (1964). As mentioned earlier, the First Amendment protects the creator of a parody from liability for defamation of a public figure.

CASE 12.1 Anderson v. Mergenhagen

Court of Appeals of Georgia, 2007. 283 Ga.App. 546, 642 S.E.2d 105.

• **Background and Facts** After Dick and Karyn Anderson's marriage collapsed and they divorced, Karyn harassed Dick's new wife, Maureen, until Maureen obtained a warrant for Karyn's arrest. According to Maureen, Karyn's new boyfriend, Paul Mergenhagen, then began following Maureen. On more than a dozen occasions between mid-2003 and mid-2005, Paul took photos of, and made obscene gestures to, Maureen as she was driving in her car or walking with her children. Frightened and upset, Maureen called the police several times. Paul admitted that he had followed Maureen at least four times and had taken at least forty photos of her car. The security guard at the entrance to the Andersons' subdivision corroborated Maureen's account that Paul often lay in wait for her and that she was "visibly shaken and upset, almost to the point of tears," at least once. Maureen filed a suit in a Georgia state court against Paul, alleging, among other things, invasion of privacy. The court issued a summary judgment in Paul's favor on this charge. Maureen appealed to a state intermediate appellate court.

CASE 12.1 CONTINUED

IN THE LANGUAGE OF THE COURT
***BARNES,* Chief Judge.**

* * * *

* * * The right of privacy, or the right of the individual to be let alone, is a personal right * * * . It is the complement of the right to the immunity of one's person. The individual has always been entitled to be protected in the exclusive use and enjoyment of that which is his own. *The common law regarded his person and property as inviolate, and he has the absolute right to be let alone. The principle is fundamental, and essential in organized society, that every one, in exercising a personal right and in the use of his property, shall respect the rights and properties of others.* * * * The right of privacy is embraced within the absolute rights of personal security and personal liberty, "to be let alone," to live a life of seclusion or to be free of unwarranted interference by the public about matters [with] which the public is not necessarily concerned, or to be protected from any wrongful intrusion into an individual's private life which would outrage or cause mental suffering, shame or humiliation to a person of ordinary sensibilities. [Emphasis added.]

With regard to the tort of intrusion upon seclusion or solitude, which is the claim made here, * * * the "unreasonable intrusion" aspect involves a prying or intrusion, which would be offensive or objectionable to a reasonable person, into a person's private concerns.

* * * *

* * * Traditionally, watching or observing a person in a public place is not an intrusion upon one's privacy. However, Georgia courts have held that surveillance of an individual on public thoroughfares, where such surveillance aims to frighten or torment a person, is an unreasonable intrusion upon a person's privacy.

In cases holding that public surveillance did not establish a privacy violation, we have found that the surveillance was reasonable in light of the situation. For example, reasonable surveillance of a residence from a public road to investigate a husband's disability claim constituted no intrusion upon his wife's seclusion or solitude, or into her private affairs. The surveillance of the husband at his house and on public roads also did not establish a privacy violation. Reasonable surveillance is recognized as a common method to obtain evidence to defend a lawsuit. It is only when such is conducted in a vicious or malicious manner not reasonably limited and designated to obtain information needed for the defense of a lawsuit or deliberately calculated to frighten or torment the plaintiff, that the courts will not countenance it.

In this case, [Maureen] Anderson alleges that her privacy was violated when [Paul] Mergenhagen followed her repeatedly in the car and took numerous photographs of her and her car. While * * * a driver may have no cause of action for mere observation or even for having her photograph taken, a relatively harmless activity can become tortious with repetition * * * . Repeatedly following a woman, who was pregnant for part of that time and was frequently alone or with her small children, photographing her at least 40 times, repeatedly causing her to become frightened and upset, to flee to her home, and to call the police seeking help, creates a jury question as to whether the defendant's actions amounted to a course of hounding the plaintiff that intruded upon her privacy.

• **Decision and Remedy** *The state intermediate appellate court reversed the grant of summary judgment to Paul on Maureen's invasion of privacy claim. The court remanded the case for trial on the issue of whether the defendant followed and photographed the plaintiff so frequently as to amount to an intrusion into her privacy.*

• **What If the Facts Were Different?** *Suppose that Dick and Karyn had two children and Dick had been awarded custody of them. If Paul had been watching Maureen to determine her fitness to care for the children, would the result in this case have been different? Explain.*

• **The Legal Environment Dimension** *To succeed on a claim of intrusion into an individual's affairs or seclusion, should a plaintiff have to prove a physical intrusion? Why or why not?*

Appropriation

The use of another person's name, likeness, or other identifying characteristic, without permission and for the benefit of the user, constitutes the tort of **appropriation** (sometimes referred to as the *right of publicity*). Under the law, normally an individual's right to privacy includes the right to the exclusive use of his or her identity. For example, in one early case, Vanna White, the hostess of the popular *Wheel of Fortune* game show, brought a case against Samsung Electronics America, Inc. Without permission, Samsung had included in an advertisement a robotic image dressed in a wig, gown, and jewelry, in a setting that resembled the *Wheel of Fortune* set, in a stance for which White is famous. The court ruled in White's favor, holding that the tort of appropriation does not require the use of a celebrity's name or actual likeness. The court stated that Samsung's robot ad left "little doubt" as to the identity of the celebrity that the ad was meant to depict.[6]

Degree of Likeness In recent cases, courts have reached different conclusions as to the degree of likeness that is required to impose liability for the tort of appropriation. In one case, a former professional hockey player, Anthony "Tony" Twist, who had a reputation for fighting, sued the publishers of the comic book *Spawn,* which included an evil character named Anthony Tony Twist Twistelli. The Missouri Supreme Court held that the use of Tony Twist's name alone was sufficient proof of likeness to support a misappropriation claim.[7] Ultimately, the hockey player was awarded $15 million in damages.[8]

In California, in contrast, Keirin Kirby, the lead singer in a 1990s funk band called Deee-Lite, lost her appropriation claim against the makers of the video game *Space Channel 5.* Although the video game's character "Ulala" had some of Kirby's distinctive traits—hot pink hair, short skirt, platform shoes, and dance moves—there were not enough similarities, according to the state appellate court, to constitute misappropriation.[9]

Right of Publicity as a Property Right As mentioned, the common law tort of appropriation in many states has become known as the right of publicity.[10] Rather than being aimed at protecting a person's right to be left alone (privacy), this right aims to protect an individual's pecuniary (financial) interest in the commercial exploitation of his or her identity. In other words, it gives public figures, celebrities, and entertainers a right to sue anyone who uses their images for commercial benefit without their permission. Cases involving the right of publicity generally turn on whether the use was commercial. For instance, if a television news program reports on a celebrity and shows an image of the person, the use likely would not be classified as commercial; in contrast, including the celebrity's image on a poster without his or her permission would be a commercial use.

Because the right of publicity is similar to a property right, most states have concluded that the right is inheritable and survives the death of the person who held the right. Normally, though, the person must provide for the passage of the right to another in her or his will. In 2007, for example, a court held that because Marilyn Monroe's will did not specifically state a desire to pass the right to publicity to her heirs, the beneficiaries under her will did not have a right to prevent a company from marketing T-shirts and other merchandise using Monroe's name, picture, and likeness.[11]

Fraudulent Misrepresentation

A misrepresentation leads another to believe in a condition that is different from the condition that actually exists. This is often accomplished through a false or an incorrect statement. Although persons sometimes make misrepresentations accidentally because they are unaware of the existing facts, the tort of **fraudulent misrepresentation,** or *fraud,* involves *intentional* deceit for personal gain. The tort includes several elements:

1. A misrepresentation of material facts or conditions with knowledge that they are false or with reckless disregard for the truth.
2. An intent to induce another party to rely on the misrepresentation.
3. A justifiable reliance on the misrepresentation by the deceived party.

---

6. *White v. Samsung Electronics America, Inc.,* 971 F.2d 1395 (9th Cir. 1992).
7. *Doe v. TCI Cablevision,* 110 S.W.3d 363 (Mo. 2003).
8. The amount of damages was appealed and subsequently affirmed. See *Doe v. McFarlane,* 207 S.W.3d 52 (Mo.App. 2006).
9. *Kirby v. Sega of America, Inc.,* 144 Cal.App.4th 47, 50 Cal.Rptr.3d 607 (2006).
10. See, for example, California Civil Code Sections 3344 and 3344.1.
11. *Shaw Family Archives, Ltd. v. CMG Worldwide, Inc.,* 486 F.Supp.2d 309 (S.D.N.Y. 2007).

4. Damages suffered as a result of that reliance.
5. A causal connection between the misrepresentation and the injury suffered.

Fact versus Opinion For fraud to occur, more than mere *puffery,* or *seller's talk,* must be involved. Fraud exists only when a person represents as a fact something he or she knows is untrue. For example, it is fraud to claim that the roof of a building does not leak when one knows that it does. Facts are objectively ascertainable, whereas seller's talk—such as "I am the best accountant in town"—is not, because the speaker is representing a subjective view.

Normally, the tort of fraudulent misrepresentation occurs only when there is reliance on a *statement of fact.* Sometimes, however, reliance on a *statement of opinion* may involve the tort of fraudulent misrepresentation if the individual making the statement of opinion has superior knowledge of the subject matter. For example, when a lawyer makes a statement of opinion about the law in a state in which the lawyer is licensed to practice, a court would construe reliance on such a statement to be equivalent to reliance on a statement of fact.

Negligent Misrepresentation Sometimes, a tort action can arise from misrepresentations that are made negligently rather than intentionally. The key difference between intentional and negligent misrepresentation is whether the person making the misrepresentation had actual knowledge of its falsity. Negligent misrepresentation only requires that the person making the statement or omission did not have a reasonable basis for believing its truthfulness. Liability for negligent misrepresentation usually arises when the defendant who made the misrepresentation owed a duty of care to the particular plaintiff to supply correct information. Statements or omissions made by attorneys and accountants to their clients, for example, can lead to liability for negligent misrepresentation.

In the following case, a commercial tenant claimed that the landlord made negligent misrepresentations about the size of the leased space.

CASE 12.2 McClain v. Octagon Plaza, LLC

Court of Appeal of California, Second District, Division 4, 2008.
159 Cal.App.4th 784, 71 Cal.Rptr.3d 885.
www.courtinfo.ca.gov/courts/courtsofappeal[a]

• **Background and Facts** Kelly McClain operates a business known as A+ Teaching Supplies. Ted and Wanda Charanian, who are married, are the principals of Octagon Plaza, LLC, which owns and manages a shopping center in Valencia. In February 2003, McClain agreed to lease commercial space within the shopping center. The lease described the size of the unit leased by McClain as "approximately 2,624 square feet," and attached to the lease was a diagram of the shopping center that represented the size of the unit as 2,624 square feet. Because the base rent in the shopping center was $1.45 per square foot per month, McClain's total base rent was $3,804 per month. Moreover, because the unit presumably occupied 23 percent of the shopping center, McClain was responsible for this share of the common expenses. McClain claimed that the Charanians knew that the representations were materially inaccurate. As a result of Octagon's misrepresentations, McClain was induced to enter into a lease that obliged her to pay excess rent. At trial, the Charanians prevailed. McClain appealed.

IN THE LANGUAGE OF THE COURT
MANELLA, J. [Judge]

* * * *

McClain contends that the [first amended claim at trial] adequately alleges a claim for fraud in the inducement, that is, misrepresentation involving a contract in which "the promisor knows what he or she is signing but consent is induced by fraud." We agree. *Generally, "[t]he elements of fraud, which give rise to the tort action for deceit, are (a) misrepresentation (false representation, concealment, or nondisclosure); (b) knowledge of falsity (or* 'scienter'*); (c) intent to*

a. Click on "2nd District" and then click on "recent Published Opinions." Then find January 31, 2008, and click on the case name.

CASE CONTINUES

CASE 12.2 CONTINUED *defraud, i.e., to induce reliance; (d) justifiable reliance; and (e) resulting damage.*" Claims for negligent misrepresentation deviate from this set of elements. "*The tort of negligent misrepresentation does not require* scienter *or intent to defraud.* It encompasses '[t]he assertion, as a fact, of that which is not true, by one who has no reasonable ground for believing it to be true', and '[t]he positive assertion, in a manner not warranted by the information of the person making it, of that which is not true, though he believes it to be true.'" [Emphasis added.]

* * * *

It is well established that the kind of disclaimer in Paragraph 2.4 [of the commercial lease], which asserts that McClain had an adequate opportunity to examine the leased unit, does not insulate Octagon from liability for fraud or prevent McClain from demonstrating justified reliance on the Charanians' representations.

* * * *

Here, McClain alleges that the Charanians exaggerated the size of her unit by 186 square feet, or 7.6 percent of its actual size, and increased her share of the common expenses by 4 percent through a calculation that understated the size of the shopping center by 965 square feet, or 8.1 percent of its actual size. [These discrepancies] operated to increase the rental payments incurred by McClain's retail business by more than $90,000 over the term of the lease.

• **Decision and Remedy** *The Court of Appeal of the State of California, Second Appellate District, reversed the trial court's judgment with respect to McClain's claim for misrepresentation.*

• **The Ethical Dimension** *At what point do the misrepresentations about the size of the leased space become unethical—at 1 percent, 2 percent, or more?*

• **The Legal Environment Dimension** *What defense could the shopping center owners raise to counter McClain's claim?*

Abusive or Frivolous Litigation

Persons or businesses generally have a right to sue when they have been injured. In recent years, however, an increasing number of meritless lawsuits have been filed—sometimes simply to harass the defendant. Defending oneself in any legal proceeding can be costly, time consuming, and emotionally draining. Tort law recognizes that people have a right not to be sued without a legally just and proper reason. It therefore protects individuals from the misuse of litigation. Torts related to abusive litigation include malicious prosecution and abuse of process.

If the party that initiated a lawsuit did so out of malice and without probable cause (a legitimate legal reason), and ended up losing that suit, the party can be sued for *malicious prosecution.* In some states, the plaintiff (who was the defendant in the first proceeding) must also prove injury other than the normal costs of litigation, such as lost profits. *Abuse of process* can apply to any person using a legal process against another in an improper manner or to accomplish a purpose for which the process was not designed. The key difference between the torts of abuse of process and malicious prosecution is the level of proof. Abuse of process does not require the plaintiff to prove malice or show that the defendant (who was previously the plaintiff) lost in a prior legal proceeding.[12] Abuse of process is also not limited to prior litigation. It can be based on the wrongful use of subpoenas, court orders to attach or seize real property, or other types of formal legal process. *Concept Summary 12.1* reviews intentional torts against persons.

Business Torts

Most torts can occur in any context, but a few torts, referred to as **business torts,** apply only to wrongful interferences with the business rights of others. Business torts generally fall into two categories—interference with a contractual relationship and interference with a business relationship.

12. *Bernhard-Thomas Building Systems, LLC v. Duncan,* 918 A.2d 889 (Conn.App. 2007); and *Hewitt v. Rice,* 154 P.3d 408 (Colo. 2007).

CONCEPT SUMMARY 12.1
Intentional Torts against Persons

Name of Tort	Description
ASSAULT AND BATTERY	Any unexcused and intentional act that causes another person to be apprehensive of immediate harm is an assault. An assault resulting in physical contact is battery.
FALSE IMPRISONMENT	An intentional confinement or restraint of another person's movement without justification.
INTENTIONAL INFLICTION OF EMOTIONAL DISTRESS	An intentional act that amounts to extreme and outrageous conduct resulting in severe emotional distress to another.
DEFAMATION (LIBEL OR SLANDER)	A false statement of fact, not made under privilege, that is communicated to a third person and that causes damage to a person's reputation. For public figures, the plaintiff must also prove that the statement was made with actual malice.
INVASION OF PRIVACY	Publishing or otherwise making known or using information relating to a person's private life and affairs, with which the public has no legitimate concern, without that person's permission or approval.
APPROPRIATION	The use of another person's name, likeness, or other identifying characteristic without permission and for the benefit of the user.
FRAUDULENT MISREPRESENTATION (FRAUD)	A false representation made by one party, through misstatement of facts or through conduct, with the intention of deceiving another and on which the other reasonably relies to his or her detriment.
ABUSIVE LITIGATION	The filing of a lawsuit without legitimate grounds and with malice or the use of a legal process in an improper manner.

Wrongful Interference with a Contractual Relationship

The body of tort law relating to *wrongful interference with a contractual relationship* has increased greatly in recent years. A landmark case in this area involved an opera singer, Joanna Wagner, who was under contract to sing for a man named Lumley for a specified period of years. A man named Gye, who knew of this contract, nonetheless "enticed" Wagner to refuse to carry out the agreement, and Wagner began to sing for Gye. Gye's action constituted a tort because it interfered with the contractual relationship between Wagner and Lumley. (Of course, Wagner's refusal to carry out the agreement also entitled Lumley to sue Wagner for breach of contract.)[13]

Three elements are necessary for wrongful interference with a contractual relationship to occur:

1. A valid, enforceable contract must exist between two parties.
2. A third party must know that this contract exists.
3. This third party must *intentionally induce* a party to the contract to breach the contract.

In principle, any lawful contract can be the basis for an action of this type. The contract could be between a firm and its employees or a firm and its customers. Sometimes, a competitor of a firm draws away one of the firm's key employees. Only if the original employer can show that the competitor knew of the contract's existence, and intentionally induced the breach, can damages be recovered from the competitor.

Wrongful Interference with a Business Relationship

Businesspersons devise countless schemes to attract customers, but they are prohibited from unreasonably interfering with another's business in their attempts to gain a greater share of the market. There is a difference between *competitive practices* and *predatory behavior*—actions undertaken with the intention of unlawfully driving competitors completely out of the market.

13. *Lumley v. Gye*, 118 Eng.Rep. 749 (1853).

Attempting to attract customers in general is a legitimate business practice, whereas specifically targeting the customers of a competitor is more likely to be predatory. For example, the mall contains two athletic shoe stores: Joe's and Sprint. Joe's cannot station an employee at the entrance of Sprint to divert customers to Joe's and tell them that Joe's will beat Sprint's prices. Doing this would constitute the tort of wrongful interference with a business relationship because it would interfere with a prospective (economic) advantage; such behavior is commonly considered to be an unfair trade practice. If this type of activity were permitted, Joe's would reap the benefits of Sprint's advertising.

Although state laws vary on wrongful interference with a business relationship, generally a plaintiff must prove that the defendant used predatory methods to intentionally harm an established business relationship or prospective economic advantage. The plaintiff must also prove that the defendant's interference caused the plaintiff to suffer economic harm.

Defenses to Wrongful Interference

A person will not be liable for the tort of wrongful interference with a contractual or business relationship if it can be shown that the interference was justified, or permissible. Bona fide competitive behavior is a permissible interference even if it results in the breaking of a contract.

For example, if Jerrod's Meats advertises so effectively that it induces Sam's Restaurant to break its contract with Burke's Meat Company, Burke's Meat Company will be unable to recover against Jerrod's Meats on a wrongful interference theory. After all, the public policy that favors free competition through advertising outweighs any possible instability that such competitive activity might cause in contractual relations. Although luring customers away from a competitor through aggressive marketing and advertising strategies obviously interferes with the competitor's relationship with its customers, courts typically allow such activities in the spirit of competition.

Section 4 Intentional Torts against Property

Intentional torts against property include trespass to land, trespass to personal property, conversion, and disparagement of property. These torts are wrongful actions that interfere with individuals' legally recognized rights with regard to their land or personal property. The law distinguishes real property from personal property (see Chapter 25). *Real property* is land and things permanently attached to the land. *Personal property* consists of all other items, which are basically movable. Thus, a house and lot are real property, whereas the furniture inside a house is personal property. Cash and securities are also personal property.

Trespass to Land

The tort of **trespass to land** occurs any time a person, without permission, enters onto, above, or below the surface of land that is owned by another; causes anything to enter onto the land; or remains on the land or permits anything to remain on it. Actual harm to the land is not an essential element of this tort because the tort is designed to protect the right of an owner to exclusive possession. Common types of trespass to land include walking or driving on another's land; shooting a gun over another's land; throwing rocks at or spraying water on a building that belongs to someone else; building a dam across a river, thereby causing water to back up on someone else's land; and constructing one's building so that it extends onto an adjoining landowner's property.

Trespass Criteria, Rights, and Duties Before a person can be a trespasser, the real property owner (or other person in actual and exclusive possession of the property, such as a person who is leasing the property) must establish that person as a trespasser. For example, "posted" trespass signs expressly establish as a trespasser a person who ignores these signs and enters onto the property. Any person who enters onto another's property to commit an illegal act (such as a thief entering a lumberyard at night to steal lumber) is established impliedly as a trespasser, without posted signs.

At common law, a trespasser is liable for damages caused to the property and generally cannot hold the owner liable for injuries that the trespasser sustains on the premises. This common law rule is being abandoned in many jurisdictions, however, in favor of a "reasonable duty" rule that varies depending on the status of the parties. For example, a landowner may have a duty to post a notice that the property is patrolled by guard dogs. Also, under the "attractive nuisance" doctrine, a landowner may be held liable for injuries sustained by young children on the landowner's property if the children were attracted to the premises by some object, such as a swimming pool or an abandoned building. Finally, an owner can remove a trespasser from the premises—or detain a trespasser on the premises for a reasonable time—through the use of reasonable force without being liable for assault, battery, or false imprisonment.

Defenses against Trespass to Land Trespass to land involves wrongful interference with another person's real property rights. If it can be shown that the trespass was warranted, however, as when a trespasser enters to assist someone in danger, a defense exists. Another defense exists when the trespasser can show that he or she had a license to come onto the land. A *licensee* is one who is invited (or allowed to enter) onto the property of another for the licensee's benefit. A person who enters another's property to read an electric meter, for example, is a licensee. When you purchase a ticket to attend a movie or sporting event, you are licensed to go onto the property of another to view that movie or event. Note that licenses to enter onto another's property are *revocable* by the property owner. If a property owner asks a meter reader to leave and the meter reader refuses to do so, the meter reader at that point becomes a trespasser.

Trespass to Personal Property

Whenever any individual, without consent, takes or harms the personal property of another or otherwise interferes with the lawful owner's possession and enjoyment of personal property, **trespass to personal property** occurs. This tort may also be called *trespass to chattels* or *trespass to personalty.* In this context, harm means not only destruction of the property, but also anything that diminishes its value, condition, or quality. Trespass to personal property involves intentional meddling with a possessory interest (an interest arising from possession), including barring an owner's access to personal property. If Kelly takes Ryan's business law book as a practical joke and hides it so that Ryan is unable to find it for several days prior to the final examination, Kelly has engaged in a trespass to personal property.

If it can be shown that trespass to personal property was warranted, then a complete defense exists. Most states, for example, allow automobile repair shops to hold a customer's car (under what is called an *artisan's lien,* discussed in Chapter 15) when the customer refuses to pay for repairs already completed.

Conversion

Whenever a person wrongfully possesses or uses the personal property of another as if the property belonged to her or him, the tort of **conversion** occurs. Any act that deprives an owner of personal property of the use of that property without that owner's permission and without just cause can be conversion. Often, when conversion occurs, a trespass to personal property also occurs because the original taking of the personal property from the owner was a trespass, and wrongfully retaining it is conversion. Conversion requires a more serious interference with the personal property than trespass, in terms of the duration and extensiveness of use.

Conversion is the civil side of crimes related to theft, but it is not limited to theft. Even when the rightful owner consented to the initial taking of the property so there was no theft or trespass, a failure to return the personal property may still be conversion. For example, Chen borrows Marik's iPod to use while traveling home from school for the holidays. When Chen returns to school, Marik asks for his iPod back, but Chen says that he gave it to his little brother for Christmas. In this situation, Marik can sue Chen for conversion, and Chen will have to either return the iPod or pay damages equal to its value.

Similarly, even if a person mistakenly believed that she or he was entitled to the goods, a tort of conversion may still have occurred. In other words, good intentions are not a defense against conversion; in fact, conversion can be an entirely innocent act. Someone who buys stolen goods, for example, has committed the tort of conversion even if he or she did not know the goods were stolen. Note that even the taking of electronic records and data may form the basis of a common law conversion claim.[14] So can the wrongful taking of a domain name or the misappropriation of a net tax loss that harms a company.[15] Thus, the personal property need not be tangible (physical) property.

Disparagement of Property

Disparagement of property occurs when economically injurious falsehoods are made about another's product or property rather than about another's reputation (as in the tort of defamation). *Disparagement of property* is a general term for torts that can be more specifically referred to as *slander of quality* or *slander of title.*

14. See *Thyroff v. Nationwide Mutual Insurance Co.,* 8 N.Y.3d 283, 864 N.E.2d 1272 (2007).

15. See *Kremen v. Cohen,* 325 F.3d 1035 (9th Cir. 2003); and *Fremont Indemnity Co. v. Fremont General Corp.,* 148 Cal.App.4th 97, 55 Cal.Rptr.3d 621 (2d Dist. 2007).

Slander of Quality Publishing false information about another's product, alleging it is not what its seller claims, constitutes the tort of **slander of quality,** or **trade libel.** The plaintiff must prove that actual damages proximately resulted from the slander of quality. In other words, the plaintiff must show not only that a third person refrained from dealing with the plaintiff because of the improper publication but also that the plaintiff suffered damages because the third person refrained from dealing with him or her. The economic calculation of such damages—they are, after all, conjectural—is often extremely difficult.

An improper publication may be both a slander of quality and a defamation of character. For example, a statement that disparages the quality of a product may also, by implication, disparage the character of a person who would sell such a product.

Slander of Title When a publication falsely denies or casts doubt on another's legal ownership of property, resulting in financial loss to the property's owner, the tort of **slander of title** occurs. Usually, this is an intentional tort in which someone knowingly publishes an untrue statement about another's ownership of certain property with the intent of discouraging a third person from dealing with the person slandered. For example, it would be difficult for a car dealer to attract customers after competitors published a notice that the dealer's stock consisted of stolen autos. See *Concept Summary 12.2* for a review of intentional torts against property.

Negligence

In contrast to intentional torts, in torts involving **negligence,** the tortfeasor neither wishes to bring about the consequences of the act nor believes that they will occur. The actor's conduct merely creates a risk of such consequences. If no risk is created, there is no negligence. Moreover, the risk must be foreseeable; that is, it must be such that a reasonable person engaging in the same activity would anticipate the risk and guard against it. In determining what is reasonable conduct, courts consider the nature of the possible harm. Creating a very slight risk of a dangerous explosion might be unreasonable, whereas creating a distinct possibility of someone's burning his or her fingers on a stove might be reasonable.

As discussed earlier, many of the actions on intentional torts constitute negligence if the element of intent is missing (or cannot be proved). Suppose that Juarez walks up to Natsuyo and intentionally shoves her. Natsuyo falls and breaks her arm as a result. In this situation, Juarez has committed an intentional tort (battery). If Juarez carelessly bumps into Natsuyo, however, and she falls and breaks her arm as a result, Juarez's action constitutes negligence. In either situation, Juarez has committed a tort.

To succeed in a negligence action, the plaintiff must prove each of the following:

1. That the defendant owed a duty of care to the plaintiff.

CONCEPT SUMMARY 12.2
Intentional Torts against Property

Name of Tort	Description
TRESPASS TO LAND	The invasion of another's real property without consent or privilege. Once a person is expressly or impliedly established as a trespasser, the property owner has specific rights, which may include the right to detain or remove the trespasser.
TRESPASS TO PERSONAL PROPERTY	The intentional interference with an owner's right to use, possess, or enjoy his or her personal property without the owner's consent.
CONVERSION	The wrongful possession or use of another person's personal property without just cause.
DISPARAGEMENT OF PROPERTY	Any economically injurious falsehood that is made about another's product or property; an inclusive term for the torts of *slander of quality* and *slander of title.*

2. That the defendant breached that duty.
3. That the plaintiff suffered a legally recognizable injury.
4. That the defendant's breach caused the plaintiff's injury.

We discuss here each of these four elements of negligence.

The Duty of Care and Its Breach

Central to the tort of negligence is the concept of a **duty of care.** This concept arises from the notion that if we are to live in society with other people, some actions can be tolerated and some cannot, and some actions are reasonable and some are not. The basic principle underlying the duty of care is that people are free to act as they please so long as their actions do not infringe on the interests of others.

When someone fails to comply with the duty to exercise reasonable care, a potentially tortious act may have been committed. Failure to live up to a standard of care may be an act (setting fire to a building) or an omission (neglecting to put out a campfire). It may be a careless act or a carefully performed but nevertheless dangerous act that results in injury. Courts consider the nature of the act (whether it is outrageous or commonplace), the manner in which the act is performed (heedlessly versus cautiously), and the nature of the injury (whether it is serious or slight) in determining whether the duty of care has been breached.

The Reasonable Person Standard Tort law measures duty by the **reasonable person standard.** In determining whether a duty of care has been breached, for example, the courts ask how a reasonable person would have acted in the same circumstances. The reasonable person standard is said to be (though in an absolute sense it cannot be) objective. It is not necessarily how a particular person *would* act. It is society's judgment of how an ordinarily prudent person *should* act. If the so-called reasonable person existed, he or she would be careful, conscientious, even tempered, and honest. That individuals are required to exercise a reasonable standard of care in their activities is a pervasive concept in business law, and many of the issues discussed in subsequent chapters of this text have to do with this duty.

In negligence cases, the degree of care to be exercised varies, depending on the defendant's occupation or profession, her or his relationship with the plaintiff, and other factors. Generally, whether an action constitutes a breach of the duty of care is determined on a case-by-case basis. The outcome depends on how the judge (or jury, if it is a jury trial) decides a reasonable person in the position of the defendant would act in the particular circumstances of the case. In the following subsections, we examine the degree of care typically expected of landowners and professionals.

Duty of Landowners Landowners are expected to exercise reasonable care to protect individuals coming onto their property from harm. In some jurisdictions, landowners may even have a duty to protect trespassers against certain risks. Landowners who rent or lease premises to tenants are expected to exercise reasonable care to ensure that the tenants and their guests are not harmed in common areas, such as stairways, entryways, and laundry rooms (see Chapter 25).

Duty to Warn Business Invitees of Risks. Retailers and other firms that explicitly or implicitly invite persons to come onto their premises are usually charged with a duty to exercise reasonable care to protect these **business invitees.** For example, if you entered a supermarket, slipped on a wet floor, and sustained injuries as a result, the owner of the supermarket would be liable for damages if, when you slipped, there was no sign warning that the floor was wet. A court would hold that the business owner was negligent because the owner failed to exercise a reasonable degree of care in protecting the store's customers against foreseeable risks about which the owner knew or *should have known.* That a patron might slip on the wet floor and be injured as a result was a foreseeable risk, and the owner should have taken care to avoid this risk or warn the customer of it.[16]

Obvious Risks Provide an Exception. Some risks, of course, are so obvious that an owner need not warn of them. For example, a business owner does not need to warn customers to open a door before attempting to walk through it. Other risks, however, even though they may seem obvious to a business owner, may not be so in the eyes of another, such as a child. For example, a hardware store owner may not think it is necessary to warn customers that, if climbed, a stepladder leaning against the back wall of the store could fall down and harm them. It is possible, though, that a child could tip

16. A business owner can warn of a risk in a number of ways; for example, to warn of a hole in the business's parking lot, the owner could place a sign, traffic cone, sawhorse, board, or the like near the hole.

the ladder over while climbing it and be hurt as a result.

Duty of Professionals If an individual has knowledge or skill superior to that of an ordinary person, the individual's conduct must be consistent with that status. Professionals—including physicians, dentists, architects, engineers, accountants, and lawyers, among others—are required to have a standard minimum level of special knowledge and ability. Therefore, in determining what constitutes reasonable care in the case of professionals, the court takes their training and expertise into account. In other words, an accountant cannot defend against a lawsuit for negligence by stating, "But I was not familiar with that general principle of accounting."

If a professional violates his or her duty of care toward a client, the client may bring a suit against the professional, alleging **malpractice,** which is essentially professional negligence. For example, a patient might sue a physician for *medical malpractice.* A client might sue an attorney for *legal malpractice.*

No Duty to Rescue Although the law requires individuals to act reasonably and responsibly in their relations with one another, if a person fails to come to the aid of a stranger in peril, that person will not be considered negligent under tort law. For example, assume that you are walking down a city street and see a pedestrian about to step directly in front of an oncoming bus. You realize that the person has not seen the bus and is unaware of the danger. Do you have a legal duty to warn that individual? No. Although most people would probably concede that, in this situation, the observer has an *ethical* duty to warn the other, tort law does not impose a general duty to rescue others in peril. Duties may be imposed in regard to certain types of peril, however. For example, most states require a motorist involved in an automobile accident to stop and render aid. Failure to do so is both a tort and a crime.

The Injury Requirement and Damages

To recover damages (receive compensation), the plaintiff in a tort lawsuit must prove that she or he suffered a *legally recognizable* injury. In other words, the plaintiff must have suffered some loss, harm, wrong, or invasion of a protected interest. This is true in lawsuits for intentional torts as well as lawsuits for negligence. Essentially, the purpose of tort law is to compensate for legally recognized harms and injuries resulting from wrongful acts. If no harm or injury results from a given negligent action, there is nothing to compensate—and no tort exists.

For example, if you carelessly bump into a passerby, who stumbles and falls as a result, you may be liable in tort if the passerby is injured in the fall. If the person is unharmed, however, there normally can be no suit for damages because no injury was suffered. Although the passerby might be angry and suffer emotional distress, few courts recognize negligently inflicted emotional distress as a tort unless it results in some physical disturbance or dysfunction.

Compensatory damages are the norm in negligence cases. Occasionally, though, a court will award punitive damages if the defendant's conduct was grossly negligent, meaning that the defendant intentionally failed to perform a duty with reckless disregard of the consequences to others.

Causation

Another element necessary to the tort of negligence—and intentional torts as well—is *causation.* If a person breaches a duty of care and someone suffers injury, the wrongful activity must have caused the harm for a tort to have been committed.

Causation in Fact and Proximate Cause In deciding whether the requirement of causation is met, the court must address two questions:

1. *Is there causation in fact?* Did the injury occur because of the defendant's act, or would it have occurred anyway? If an injury would not have occurred without the defendant's act, then there is causation in fact. **Causation in fact** can usually be determined by use of the *but for* test: "but for" the wrongful act, the injury would not have occurred. This test determines whether there was an actual cause-and-effect relationship between the act and the injury suffered. In theory, causation in fact is limitless. One could claim, for example, that "but for" the creation of the world, a particular injury would not have occurred. Thus, as a practical matter, the law has to establish limits, and it does so through the concept of proximate cause.
2. *Was the act the proximate, or legal, cause of the injury?* **Proximate cause,** or *legal cause,* exists when the connection between an act and an injury is strong enough to justify imposing liability. Consider an example. Ackerman carelessly leaves a

campfire burning. The fire not only burns down the forest but also sets off an explosion in a nearby chemical plant that spills chemicals into a river, killing all the fish for a hundred miles downstream and ruining the economy of a tourist resort. Should Ackerman be liable to the resort owners? To the tourists whose vacations were ruined? These are questions of proximate cause that a court must decide.

Both questions must be answered in the affirmative for liability in tort to arise. If a defendant's action constitutes causation in fact but a court decides that the action is not the proximate cause of the plaintiff's injury the causation requirement has not been met—and the defendant normally will not be liable to the plaintiff.

Foreseeability Questions of proximate cause are linked to the concept of foreseeability because it would be unfair to impose liability on a defendant unless the defendant's actions created a foreseeable risk of injury. Probably the most cited case on the concept of foreseeability and proximate cause is the *Palsgraf* case. The question before the court was as follows: Does the defendant's duty of care extend only to those who may be injured as a result of a foreseeable risk, or does it extend also to persons whose injuries could not reasonably be foreseen?

CASE 12.3 Palsgraf v. Long Island Railroad Co.

Court of Appeals of New York, 1928. 248 N.Y. 339, 162 N.E. 99.

• **Background and Facts** The plaintiff, Helen Palsgraf, was waiting for a train on a station platform. A man carrying a package was rushing to catch a train that was moving away from a platform across the tracks from Palsgraf. As the man attempted to jump aboard the moving train, he seemed unsteady and about to fall. A railroad guard on the car reached forward to grab him, and another guard on the platform pushed him from behind to help him board the train. In the process, the man's package, which (unknown to the railroad guards) contained fireworks, fell on the railroad tracks and exploded. There was nothing about the package to indicate its contents. The repercussions of the explosion caused scales at the other end of the train platform to fall on Palsgraf, causing injuries for which she sued the railroad company. At the trial, the jury found that the railroad guards had been negligent in their conduct. The railroad company appealed. The appellate court affirmed the trial court's judgment, and the railroad company appealed to New York's highest state court.

IN THE LANGUAGE OF THE COURT

CARDOZO, C.J. [Chief Justice]

* * * *

The conduct of the defendant's guard, if a wrong in its relation to the holder of the package, was not a wrong in its relation to the plaintiff, standing far away. Relatively to her it was not negligence at all. * * *

* * * *

* * * What the plaintiff must show is "a wrong" to herself; i.e., a violation of her own right, and not merely a wrong to someone else[.] * * * *The risk reasonably to be perceived defines the duty to be obeyed[.]* * * * Here, by concession, there was nothing in the situation to suggest to the most cautious mind that the parcel wrapped in newspaper would spread wreckage through the station. If the guard had thrown it down knowingly and willfully, he would not have threatened the plaintiff's safety, so far as appearances could warn him. His conduct would not have involved, even then, an unreasonable probability of invasion of her bodily security. Liability can be no greater where the act is inadvertent. [Emphasis added.]

* * * One who seeks redress at law does not make out a cause of action by showing without more that there has been damage to his person. If the harm was not willful, he must show that the act as to him had possibilities of danger so many and apparent as to entitle him to be protected against the doing of it though the harm was unintended. * * * The victim does not sue * * *

CASE CONTINUES

CASE 12.3 CONTINUED

to vindicate an interest invaded in the person of another. * * * He sues for breach of a duty owing to himself.

* * * [To rule otherwise] would entail liability for any and all consequences, however novel or extraordinary.

• **Decision and Remedy** *Palsgraf's complaint was dismissed. The railroad had not been negligent toward her because injury to her was not foreseeable. Had the owner of the fireworks been harmed, and had he filed a suit, there could well have been a different result.*

• **Impact of This Case on Today's Law** *The* Palsgraf *case established foreseeability as the test for proximate cause. Today, the courts continue to apply this test in determining proximate cause—and thus tort liability for injuries. Generally, if the victim of a harm or the consequences of a harm done are unforeseeable, there is no proximate cause.*

• **International Considerations** **Differing Standards of Proximate Cause** *The concept of proximate cause is common among nations around the globe, but its application differs from country to country. French law uses the phrase "adequate cause." An event breaks the chain of adequate cause if the event is both unforeseeable and irresistible. England has a "nearest cause" rule that attributes liability based on which event was nearest in time and space. Mexico bases proximate cause on the foreseeability of the harm but does not require that an event be reasonably foreseeable.*

• **The Global Dimension** *What would be the advantages and disadvantages of a universal principle of proximate cause applied everywhere by all courts in all relevant cases? Discuss.*

SECTION 6 Defenses to Negligence

The basic defenses to liability in negligence cases are (1) assumption of risk, (2) superseding cause, and (3) contributory and comparative negligence. Additionally, defendants often defend against negligence claims by asserting that the plaintiffs failed to prove the existence of one or more of the required elements for negligence.

Assumption of Risk

A plaintiff who voluntarily enters into a risky situation, knowing the risk involved, will not be allowed to recover. This is the defense of **assumption of risk.** The requirements of this defense are (1) knowledge of the risk and (2) voluntary assumption of the risk. This defense is frequently asserted when the plaintiff is injured during recreational activities that involve known risk, such as skiing and parachuting.

The risk can be assumed by express agreement, or the assumption of risk can be implied by the plaintiff's knowledge of the risk and subsequent conduct. For example, a driver entering an automobile race knows there is a risk of being injured or killed in a crash. The driver has assumed the risk of injury. Of course, the plaintiff does not assume a risk different from or greater than the risk normally carried by the activity. In our example, the race driver assumes the risk of being injured in the race but not the risk that the banking in the curves of the racetrack will give way during the race because of a construction defect.

Risks are not deemed to be assumed in situations involving emergencies. Neither are they assumed when a statute protects a class of people from harm and a member of the class is injured by the harm. For example, courts have generally held that an employee cannot assume the risk of an employer's violation of safety statutes passed for the benefit of employees.

In the following case, a ball kicked by a player practicing on a nearby field injured a man who was attending his son's soccer tournament. The question before the court was whether a bystander who was not watching a soccer match at the time of injury had nevertheless assumed the risk of being struck by a wayward ball.

EXTENDED CASE 12.4 Sutton v. Eastern New York Youth Soccer Association, Inc.

New York Supreme Court, Appellate Division, Third Department, 2004.
8 A.D.3d 855, 779 N.Y.S.2d 149.

***SPAIN*, J. [Justice]**

* * * *

While attending a soccer tournament in which his son was a participant, plaintiff D. James Sutton (hereinafter plaintiff) was struck by a soccer ball kicked by a 16-year-old boy practicing on one of the soccer fields between games. Thereafter, plaintiff and his wife * * * commenced this personal injury action [in a New York state court] against organizations and teams sponsoring and/or participating in the tournament, as well as the boy who kicked the ball, seeking to recover damages for injuries he sustained to his knee as a result of the accident. [The] Court granted summary judgment to all defendants, finding that plaintiff had assumed the risk of being struck by a soccer ball, and dismissed the complaint.

According to plaintiff, May 30, 1999 was a sunny, exceedingly hot day and his son, a member of defendant Latham Circle Soccer Club, was participating in a Highland Soccer Club Tournament at Maalyck Park in the Town of Glenville, Schenectady County [in New York]. Plaintiff attended as a spectator and had just finished watching his son's second game of the day from one of the sidelines when he walked to the end of the field to a tent which had been erected by his son's team some 30 to 40 yards behind the goal line in order to provide shade for the players while they were not engaged on the field. While walking past the field, plaintiff noticed six or seven players from defendant Guilderland Soccer Club on the field "hacking around" and warming up for the next game. Once under the tent, plaintiff was in the process of removing a sandwich from his son's cooler when he was struck in the chest and knocked off his feet by a soccer ball kicked from the field by a Guilderland player, defendant Ian Goss.

The first argument raised on appeal is that plaintiff was not a voluntary spectator of the soccer match at the point in time when he was injured; accordingly, plaintiffs argue, he cannot be found to have assumed the risk of injury. In support of this contention, plaintiffs point to the fact that a game was not in progress on the field and that, when injured, he was standing some 30 to 40 yards away from the field of play. We are unpersuaded. *The doctrine of assumption of risk can apply not only to participants of sporting events, but to spectators and bystanders who are not actively engaged in watching the event at the time of their injury.* Indeed, the spectator at a sporting event, no less than the participant, accepts the dangers that inhere in it so far as they are obvious and necessary, just as a fencer accepts the risk of a thrust by his antagonist or a spectator at a ball game the * * * chance of contact with the ball * * * . The timorous [nervous] may stay at home. Here, plaintiff admitted that he was at the tournament as a spectator and was aware that players were practicing on the field when he walked past them. Furthermore, although plaintiff's son's team had just finished a game, the tournament involved hundreds of players with teams playing at various times on at least five fields and plaintiff had been at the tournament all morning, surrounded by this activity. Under these circumstances, we find that plaintiff's presence at the tournament rendered him a voluntary spectator to the soccer play in progress throughout the day. [Emphasis added.]

Next, plaintiffs contend that the placement of the tent behind the goal line of one of the soccer fields enhanced the risk to spectators at the game, thereby undermining the argument that plaintiff assumed the risk of getting struck by a ball. Plaintiffs rely on evidence * * * that spectators at soccer games should, for their safety, observe the game from the sidelines and that standing behind the goal line increases the chance of being struck by a kicked ball. This Court has not previously had occasion to address directly the duty of care owed to spectators at a soccer match. Existing jurisprudence surrounding the duty owed to spectators at a baseball game, though not controlling given the differences in the games of baseball and soccer, is nonetheless helpful to our analysis.

* * * Taking into consideration the independence of spectators who might want to watch a [baseball] game from an unprotected vantage point, and recognizing that even after the exercise of reasonable care, some risk of being struck by a ball will continue to exist, * * * the

CASE CONTINUES

CASE 12.4 CONTINUED

proprietor of a ball park need only provide screening for the area of the field behind home plate where the danger of being struck by a ball is the greatest. * * * [T]he municipal owner of a baseball park which has provided adequate space for spectators to view the game from behind the backstop [does] not owe a duty to install screens or netting above a fence running along the first baseline to protect spectators walking in the area between the fence and bathrooms against the risk of being struck by foul balls.

Unlike baseball parks, outdoor soccer fields typically have no protective screening or fencing for spectators, presumably because the ball is larger and moves slower, enabling the spectator who observes a ball coming his or her way to avoid being struck. Indeed, plaintiffs do not suggest that, in the exercise of reasonable care, defendants had a duty to provide any protective measures along the sidelines. Instead, plaintiffs assert that defendants unreasonably enhanced the risk of injury to plaintiff by essentially inviting him to stand at the end of the field through their placement of the team tent. Although we agree that a factual question has been presented as to whether the risk of being struck by a soccer ball is enhanced when a spectator is standing behind the goal line, we find that question immaterial to the disposition of this action. There is no suggestion that there was not adequate room for the spectators to remain along the sidelines; in fact, plaintiff was seated along the sidelines prior to moving to the tent to get a sandwich. Accordingly, just as the owner of a baseball park is not responsible for the spectator who leaves his or her seat and walks through a potentially more hazardous zone to reach a bathroom or concession stand, thereby assuming the open and obvious risk of being hit by a ball, *defendants here cannot be held responsible for the risk assumed by plaintiff when he, aware that players were active on the field, left the sidelines and stood in the tent positioned in the arguably more dangerous zone behind the goal line.* [Emphasis added.]

We also reject plaintiffs' contention that the risk of being struck while some 40 yards away from a field upon which no formal game was in progress was not open and obvious. *In the context of a sporting event, where the risks are fully comprehended or perfectly obvious, a participant will be deemed to have consented to such risk.* As discussed, plaintiff had been in attendance for hours at a tournament where soccer games were almost continuously in progress and had actual knowledge that players were kicking the ball around on the field when he opted to move to the tent behind the goal line. Further, he was familiar with the game of soccer having admittedly been a frequent spectator of the game for over 14 years. Under these circumstances, we hold that plaintiff should have appreciated the risk of being hit by an errant [stray] soccer ball when he opted to enter the tent in the area behind the goal. [Emphasis added.]

ORDERED that the order is affirmed * * * .

QUESTIONS

1. What is the basis underlying the defense of assumption of risk, and how does that basis support the court's decision in the *Sutton* case?
2. Had the plaintiffs prevailed, how might the sites for soccer matches be different today?

Superseding Cause

An unforeseeable intervening event may break the causal connection between a wrongful act and an injury to another. If so, the intervening event acts as a *superseding cause*—that is, it relieves a defendant of liability for injuries caused by the intervening event. For example, suppose that Derrick, while riding his bicycle, negligently hits Julie, who is walking on the sidewalk. As a result of the impact, Julie falls and fractures her hip. While she is waiting for help to arrive, a small aircraft crashes nearby and explodes, and some of the fiery debris hits her, causing her to sustain severe burns. Derrick will be liable for the damages caused by Julie's fractured hip, but normally he will not be liable for the injuries caused by the plane crash—because the risk of a plane crashing nearby and injuring Julie was not foreseeable.

Contributory and Comparative Negligence

All individuals are expected to exercise a reasonable degree of care in looking out for themselves. In the past, under the common law doctrine of **contributory negligence,** a plaintiff who was also negligent (failed to exercise a reasonable degree of care) could not recover anything from the defendant. Under this rule, no matter how insignificant the plaintiff's negligence was relative to the defendant's negligence, the plaintiff would be precluded from recovering any damages. Today, only a few jurisdictions still hold to this doctrine.

In the majority of states, the doctrine of contributory negligence has been replaced by a **comparative negligence** standard. The comparative negligence standard enables both the plaintiff's and the defendant's negligence to be computed and the liability for damages distributed accordingly. Some jurisdictions have adopted a "pure" form of comparative negligence that allows the plaintiff to recover damages even if her or his fault is greater than that of the defendant. Many states' comparative negligence statutes, however, contain a "50 percent" rule, under which the plaintiff recovers nothing if she or he was more than 50 percent at fault. Under this rule, a plaintiff who is 35 percent at fault could recover 65 percent of his or her damages, but a plaintiff who is 65 percent (more than 50 percent) at fault could recover nothing.

Special Negligence Doctrines and Statutes

A number of special doctrines and statutes relating to negligence are also important. We examine a few of them here.

Res Ipsa Loquitur

Generally, in lawsuits involving negligence, the plaintiff has the burden of proving that the defendant was negligent. In certain situations, however, the courts may presume that negligence has occurred, in which case the burden of proof rests on the defendant—that is, the defendant must prove that he or she was *not* negligent. The presumption of the defendant's negligence is known as the doctrine of ***res ipsa loquitur,***[17] which translates as "the facts speak for themselves."

This doctrine is applied only when the event creating the damage or injury is one that ordinarily does not occur in the absence of negligence. For example, suppose that a person undergoes abdominal surgery and following the surgery has nerve damage in her spine near the area of the operation. In this situation, the person can sue the surgeon under a theory of *res ipsa loquitur,* because the injury would not have occurred in the absence of the surgeon's negligence.[18] For the doctrine of *res ipsa loquitur* to apply, the event must have been within the defendant's power to control, and it must not have been due to any voluntary action or contribution on the part of the plaintiff.

Negligence *Per Se*

Certain conduct, whether it consists of an action or a failure to act, may be treated as **negligence *per se*** ("in or of itself"). Negligence *per se* may occur if an individual violates a statute or an ordinance providing for a criminal penalty and that violation causes another to be injured. The injured person must prove (1) that the statute clearly sets out what standard of conduct is expected, when and where it is expected, and of whom it is expected; (2) that he or she is in the class intended to be protected by the statute; and (3) that the statute was designed to prevent the type of injury that he or she suffered. The standard of conduct required by the statute is the duty that the defendant owes to the plaintiff, and a violation of the statute is the breach of that duty.

For example, a statute provides that anyone who operates a motor vehicle on a public highway and fails to give full time and attention to the operation of that vehicle is guilty of inattentive driving. After an accident involving two motor vehicles, one of the drivers is cited for and later found guilty of violating the inattentive driver statute. If the other driver was injured and subsequently files a lawsuit, a court could consider the violation of the statute to constitute negligence *per se.* The statute set forth a standard of attentive driving specifically to protect the safety of the traveling public.[19]

"Danger Invites Rescue" Doctrine

Under the "danger invites rescue" doctrine, a person who is injured while going to someone else's rescue can sue the person who caused the dangerous situation. The original wrongdoer is liable not only for the injuries to the person who was placed in danger, but also for injuries to an individual attempting a rescue. The idea is that the rescuer should not be held liable for any damages because he or she did not cause the

17. Pronounced *rihz ihp*-suh *low*-kwuh-duhr.

18. See, for example, *Gubbins v. Hurson,* 885 A.2d 269 (D.C. 2005).
19. See, for example, *Wright v. Moore,* 931 A.2d 405 (Del.Supr. 2007).

danger and because danger invites rescue. For example, Ludlam, while driving down a street, fails to see a stop sign because he is trying to end a squabble between his two young children in the car's backseat. Salter, on the curb near the stop sign, realizes that Ludlam is about to hit a pedestrian walking across the street at the intersection. Salter runs into the street to push the pedestrian out of the way, and Ludlam's vehicle hits Salter instead. Ludlam will be liable for Salter's injury as the rescuer, as well as for any injuries the other pedestrian (or any bystanders) may have sustained.

Special Negligence Statutes

A number of states have enacted statutes prescribing duties and responsibilities in certain circumstances. For example, most states now have what are called **Good Samaritan statutes.**[20] Under these statutes, persons who are aided voluntarily by others cannot turn around and sue the "Good Samaritans" for negligence. These laws were passed largely to protect physicians and other medical personnel who volunteer their services for free in emergency situations to those in need, such as individuals hurt in car accidents.[21]

Many states have also passed **dram shop acts,**[22] under which a tavern owner or bartender may be held liable for injuries caused by a person who became intoxicated while drinking at the bar or who was already intoxicated when served by the bartender. Some states' statutes also impose liability on *social hosts* (persons hosting parties) for injuries caused by guests who became intoxicated at the hosts' homes. Under these statutes, it is unnecessary to prove that the tavern owner, bartender, or social host was negligent. Sometimes, the definition of a "social host" is broadly fashioned. For example, in a New York case, the court held that the father of a minor who hosted a "bring-your-own-keg" party could be held liable for injuries caused by an intoxicated guest.[23]

20. These laws derive their name from the Good Samaritan story in the Bible. In the story, a traveler who had been robbed and beaten lay along the roadside, ignored by those passing by. Eventually, a man from the region of Samaria (the "Good Samaritan") stopped to render assistance to the injured person.

21. See, for example, the discussions of various state statutes in *Chamley v. Khokha,* 730 N.W.2d 864 (N.D. 2007), and *Mueller v. McMillian Warner Insurance Co.,* 2006 WI 54, 290 Wis.2d 571, 714 N.W.2d 183 (2006).

22. Historically, a dram was a small unit of liquid, and spirits were sold in drams. Thus, a dram shop was a place where liquor was sold in drams.

23. *Rust v. Reyer,* 91 N.Y.2d 355, 693 N.E.2d 1074, 670 N.Y.S.2d 822 (1998).

Cyber Torts

Torts can also be committed in the online environment. Torts committed via the Internet are often called **cyber torts.** Over the years, the courts have had to decide how to apply traditional tort law to torts committed in cyberspace. Consider, for example, issues of proof. How can it be proved that an online defamatory remark was "published" (which requires that a third party see or hear it)? How can the identity of the person who made the remark be discovered? Can an Internet service provider (ISP), such as America Online, Inc. (AOL), be forced to reveal the source of an anonymous comment? We explore some of these questions in this section, as well as some legal issues that have arisen with respect to bulk e-mail advertising.

Defamation Online

Recall from the discussion of defamation earlier in this chapter that one who repeats or otherwise republishes a defamatory statement is subject to liability as if he or she had originally published it. Thus, publishers generally can be held liable for defamatory contents in the books and periodicals that they publish. Now consider online message forums. These forums allow anyone—customers, employees, or crackpots—to complain about a business firm's personnel, policies, practices, or products. Regardless of whether the complaint is justified and whether it is true, it might have an impact on the firm's business. One of the early questions in the online legal arena was whether the providers of such forums could be held liable, as publishers, for defamatory statements made in those forums.

Immunity of Internet Service Providers

Newspapers, magazines, and television and radio stations may be held liable for defamatory remarks that they disseminate, even if those remarks are prepared or created by others. Prior to the passage of the Communications Decency Act (CDA) of 1996, the courts grappled on several occasions with the question of whether ISPs should be regarded as publishers and thus be held liable for defamatory messages made by users of their services. The CDA resolved the issue by stating that "[n]o provider or user of an interactive computer service shall be treated as the publisher or speaker of any information provided by another information content provider."[24] In other words, Internet

24. 47 U.S.C. Section 230.

publishers are treated differently from publishers in print, television, and radio, and are not liable for publishing defamatory statements, provided that the material came from a third party.

In a leading case on this issue, decided the year after the CDA was enacted, America Online, Inc. (AOL, now part of Time Warner, Inc.), was not held liable even though it failed to promptly remove defamatory messages of which it had been made aware. In upholding a district court's ruling in AOL's favor, a federal appellate court stated that the CDA "plainly immunizes computer service providers like AOL from liability for information that originates with third parties." The court explained that the purpose of the statute is "to maintain the robust nature of Internet communication and, accordingly, to keep government interference in the medium to a minimum."[25] The courts have reached similar conclusions in subsequent cases, extending the CDA's immunity to Web message boards, online auction houses, Internet dating services, and any business that provides e-mail and Web browsing services.[26]

In the following case, the court considered the scope of immunity that could be accorded to an online roommate-matching service under the CDA.

25. *Zeran v. America Online, Inc.*, 129 F.3d 327 (4th Cir. 1997); *cert.* denied, 524 U.S. 937, 118 S.Ct. 2341, 141 L.Ed.2d 712 (1998).

26. See *Universal Communications Systems, Inc. v. Lycos, Inc.*, 478 F.3d 413 (1st Cir. 2007); *Barrett v. Rosenthal*, 40 Cal.4th 33, 51 Cal.Rptr.3d 55 (2006); *Delfino v. Agilent Technologies, Inc.*, 145 Cal.App. 4th 790, 52 Cal.Rptr.3d 376 (N.D.Cal. 2006); *Noah v. AOL Time Warner, Inc.*, 261 F.Supp.2d 532 (E.D.Va. 2003); and *Carafano v. Metrosplash.com, Inc.*, 339 F.3d 1119 (9th Cir. 2003).

CASE 12.5 Fair Housing Council of San Fernando Valley v. Roommate.com, LLC

United States Court of Appeals, Ninth Circuit, 2007. 489 F.3d 921.

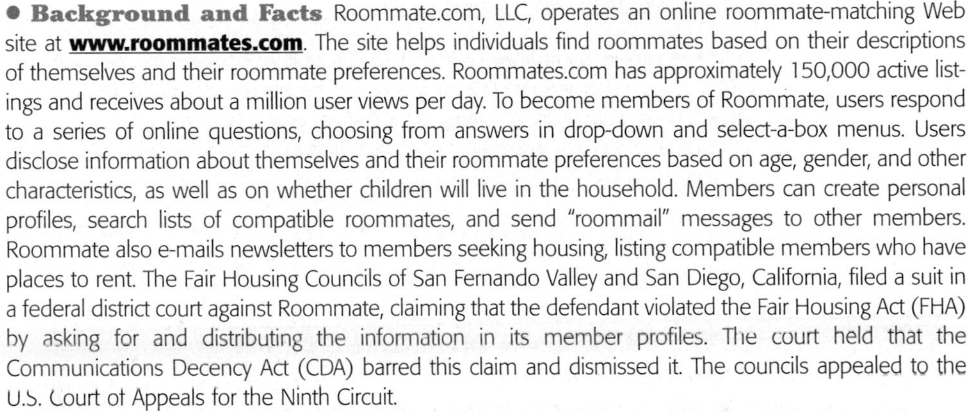

• Background and Facts Roommate.com, LLC, operates an online roommate-matching Web site at **www.roommates.com**. The site helps individuals find roommates based on their descriptions of themselves and their roommate preferences. Roommates.com has approximately 150,000 active listings and receives about a million user views per day. To become members of Roommate, users respond to a series of online questions, choosing from answers in drop-down and select-a-box menus. Users disclose information about themselves and their roommate preferences based on age, gender, and other characteristics, as well as on whether children will live in the household. Members can create personal profiles, search lists of compatible roommates, and send "roommail" messages to other members. Roommate also e-mails newsletters to members seeking housing, listing compatible members who have places to rent. The Fair Housing Councils of San Fernando Valley and San Diego, California, filed a suit in a federal district court against Roommate, claiming that the defendant violated the Fair Housing Act (FHA) by asking for and distributing the information in its member profiles. The court held that the Communications Decency Act (CDA) barred this claim and dismissed it. The councils appealed to the U.S. Court of Appeals for the Ninth Circuit.

IN THE LANGUAGE OF THE COURT

KOZINSKI, **Circuit Judge.**

* * * *

The touchstone of [the CDA] is that providers of interactive computer services are immune from liability for content created by third parties. *The immunity applies to a defendant who is the "provider * * * of an interactive computer service" and is being sued "as the publisher or speaker of any information provided by" someone else.* Reviewing courts have treated [this] immunity as quite robust. [Emphasis added.]

The Councils do not dispute that Roommate is a provider of an interactive computer service. As such, Roommate is immune so long as it merely publishes information provided by its members. However, Roommate is not immune for publishing materials as to which it is an "information content provider." [Under the CDA, a] content provider is "any person or entity that is responsible, in whole or in part, for the creation or development of information provided through the Internet." In other words, if Roommate passively publishes information provided by others, the CDA protects

CASE CONTINUES

CASE 12.5 CONTINUED

it from liability that would otherwise attach under state or federal law as a result of such publication. But if it is responsible, in whole or in part, for creating or developing the information, it becomes a content provider and is not entitled to CDA immunity.

* * * *

* * * Roommate is "responsible" for [the] questionnaires [that it requires users to fill out to register with the service] because it "creat[ed] or develop[ed]" the forms and answer choices. As a result, Roommate is a content provider of these questionnaires and does not qualify for CDA immunity for their publication.

* * * *

We now turn to the more difficult question of whether the CDA exempts Roommate from liability for publishing and distributing its members' profiles, which it generates from their answers to the form questionnaires.

* * * *

* * * Roommate does more than merely publish information it solicits from its members. Roommate also channels the information based on members' answers to various questions, as well as the answers of other members. Thus, Roommate allows members to search only the profiles of members with compatible preferences. For example, a female room-seeker who is living with a child can only search profiles of room-providers who have indicated they are willing to live with women and children. Roommate also sends room-seekers e-mail notifications that exclude listings incompatible with their profiles. Thus, Roommate will not notify our female about room-providers who say they will not live with women or children.

While Roommate provides a useful service, its search mechanism and e-mail notifications mean that it is neither a passive pass-through of information provided by others nor merely a facilitator of expression by individuals. By categorizing, channeling and limiting the distribution of users' profiles, Roommate provides an additional layer of information that it is responsible at least in part for creating or developing.

• **Decision and Remedy** *The U.S. Court of Appeals for the Ninth Circuit concluded that the CDA does not immunize Roommate for all of the content on its Web site and in its e-mail newsletters. The appellate court reversed the lower court's summary judgment and remanded the case for "a determination of whether [Roommate's] non-immune publication and distribution of information violates the FHA [Fair Housing Act]."*

• **The Ethical Dimension** *Do Internet service providers (ISPs) have an ethical duty to advise their users if the information that the users provide for distribution through the ISPs might violate the law? Explain.*

• **The E-Commerce Dimension** *Should the courts continue to regard the CDA's grant of immunity to ISPs as "quite robust"? Why or why not?*

Piercing the Veil of Anonymity A threshold barrier to anyone who seeks to bring an action for online defamation is discovering the identity of the person who posted the defamatory message online. ISPs can disclose personal information about their customers only when ordered to do so by a court. Consequently, businesses and individuals often resort to filing lawsuits against "John Does" (John Doe is a fictitious name that is used when the name of the particular person is not known). Then, using the authority of the courts, they attempt to obtain from the ISPs the identities of the persons responsible for the messages. This strategy has worked in some cases,[27] but not in others.[28] Courts typically are reluctant to deter those who would potentially post messages on the Internet from exercising their First Amendment right to speak anonymously. After all, speaking anonymously is part of the nature of the Internet and helps to make it a useful forum for public discussion.

27. *Does v. Hvide,* 770 So.2d 1237 (Fla.App.3d 2000).

28. See, for example, *Doe v. Cahill,* 884 A.2d 451 (Del.Supr. 2005); and *Dendrite International, Inc. v. Doe No. 3,* 342 N.J.Super. 134, 775 A.2d 756 (2001).

Spam

Bulk, unsolicited e-mail ("junk" e-mail) sent to all of the users on a particular e-mailing list or all of the members of a newsgroup is often called **spam.**[29] Typically, spam consists of product ads. Spam can waste user time and network bandwidth (the amount of data that can be transmitted within a certain time). It also imposes a burden on an ISP's equipment as well as on an e-mail recipient's computer system.[30] Because of the problems associated with spam, the majority of states now have laws regulating its transmission. In 2003, the U.S. Congress also enacted a law to regulate the use of spam, although the volume of spam has actually increased since the law was enacted.

Statutory Regulation of Spam In an attempt to combat spam, thirty-six states have enacted laws that prohibit or regulate its use. Many state laws regulating spam require the senders of e-mail ads to instruct the recipients on how they can "opt out" of further e-mail ads from the same sources. For instance, in some states an unsolicited e-mail ad must include a toll-free phone number or return e-mail address through which the recipient can contact the sender to request that no more ads be e-mailed. The most stringent state law is California's antispam law, which went into effect on January 1, 2004. That law follows the "opt-in" model favored by consumer groups and antispam advocates. In other words, the law prohibits any person or business from sending e-mail ads to or from any e-mail address in California unless the recipient has expressly agreed to receive e-mails from the sender. An exemption is made for e-mail sent to consumers with whom the advertiser has a "preexisting or current business relationship."

The Federal CAN-SPAM Act In 2003, Congress enacted the Controlling the Assault of Non-Solicited Pornography and Marketing (CAN-SPAM) Act, which took effect on January 1, 2004. The legislation applies to any "commercial electronic mail messages" that are sent to promote a commercial product or service. Significantly, the statute preempts state antispam laws except for those provisions in state laws that prohibit false and deceptive e-mailing practices.

Generally, the act permits the use of unsolicited commercial e-mail but prohibits certain types of spamming activities, including the use of a false return address and the use of false, misleading, or deceptive information when sending e-mail. The statute also prohibits the use of "dictionary attacks"—sending messages to randomly generated e-mail addresses—and the "harvesting" of e-mail addresses from Web sites through the use of specialized software. Notwithstanding the requirements of the federal act, the reality is that the problem of spam is difficult to address because much of it is funneled through foreign servers.

29. The term *spam* is said to come from a Monty Python song with the lyrics, "Spam spam spam spam, spam spam spam spam, lovely spam, wonderful spam." Like these lyrics, spam online is often considered to be a repetition of worthless text.

30. For an early case in which a court found that spam constituted a trespass to personal property because of the burden on the ISP's equipment, see *CompuServe, Inc. v. Cyber Promotions, Inc.*, 962 F.Supp. 1015 (S.D.Ohio 1997).

REVIEWING Torts and Cyber Torts

Two sisters, Darla and Irene, are partners in an import business located in a small town in Rhode Island. Irene is married to a well-known real estate developer and is campaigning to be the mayor of their town. Darla is in her mid-thirties and has never been married. Both sisters travel to other countries to purchase the goods they sell at their retail store. Irene buys Indonesian goods, and Darla buys goods from Africa. After a tsunami (tidal wave) destroys many of the cities in Indonesia to which Irene usually travels, she phones one of her contacts there and asks him to procure some items and ship them to her. He informs her that it will be impossible to buy these items now because the townspeople are being evacuated due to a water shortage. Irene is angry and tells the man that if he cannot purchase the goods, he should just take them without paying for them after the town has been

REVIEWING CONTINUES

REVIEWING Torts and Cyber Torts, Continued

evacuated. Darla overhears her sister's instructions and is outraged. They have a falling-out, and Darla decides that she no longer wishes to be in business with her sister. Using the information presented in the chapter, answer the following questions.

1. Suppose that Darla tells several of her friends about Irene's instructing the man to take goods without paying for them after the tsunami disaster. Under which intentional tort theory discussed in this chapter might Irene attempt to sue Darla? Would Irene's suit be successful? Why or why not?
2. Now suppose that Irene wins the election and becomes the city's mayor. Darla then writes a letter to the editor of the local newspaper disclosing Irene's misconduct. What intentional tort might Irene accuse Darla of committing? What defenses could Darla assert?
3. If Irene accepts goods shipped from Indonesia that were wrongfully obtained, has she committed an intentional tort against property? Explain.
4. Suppose now that Irene, who is angry with her sister for disclosing her business improprieties, writes a letter to the editor falsely accusing Darla of having sexual relations with her neighbor's thirteen-year-old son. For what intentional tort or torts could Darla sue Irene in this situation?

TERMS AND CONCEPTS

actionable 294
actual malice 296
appropriation 298
assault 291
assumption of risk 308
battery 291
business invitee 305
business tort 300
causation in fact 306
comparative negligence 311
compensatory damages 290
contributory negligence 310
conversion 303
cyber tort 312
defamation 294
disparagement of property 303
dram shop act 312
duty of care 305
fraudulent misrepresentation 298
Good Samaritan statute 312
intentional tort 291
libel 294
malpractice 306
negligence 304
negligence *per se* 311
privilege 295
proximate cause 306
punitive damages 291
reasonable person standard 305
res ipsa loquitur 311
slander 294
slander of quality 304
slander of title 304
spam 315
tort 290
tortfeasor 291
trade libel 304
trespass to land 302
trespass to personal property 303

QUESTIONS AND CASE PROBLEMS

12-1. Shannon's physician gives her some pain medication and tells her not to drive after she takes it, as the medication induces drowsiness. In spite of the doctor's warning, Shannon decides to drive to the store while on the medication. Owing to her lack of alertness, she fails to stop at a traffic light and crashes into another vehicle, causing a passenger in that vehicle to be injured. Is Shannon liable for the tort of negligence? Explain fully.

12-2. QUESTION WITH SAMPLE ANSWER

Lothar owns a bakery. He has been trying to obtain a long-term contract with the owner of

Martha's Tea Salons for some time. Lothar starts a local advertising campaign on radio and television and in the newspaper. This advertising campaign is so persuasive that Martha decides to break the contract she has had with Harley's Bakery so that she can patronize Lothar's bakery. Is Lothar liable to Harley's Bakery for the tort of wrongful interference with a contractual relationship? Is Martha liable for this tort?

- **For a sample answer to Question 12–2, go to Appendix I at the end of this text.**

12–3. Gerrit is a former employee of ABC Auto Repair Co. He enters ABC's repair shop, claiming that the company owes him $800 in back wages. Gerrit argues with ABC's general manager, Steward, and Steward orders him off the property. Gerrit refuses to leave, and Steward tells two mechanics to throw him off the property. Gerrit runs to his truck, but on the way, he grabs some tools valued at $800; then he drives away. Gerrit refuses to return the tools.

(a) Discuss whether Gerrit has committed any torts.
(b) If the mechanics had thrown Gerrit off the property, would ABC be guilty of assault and battery? Explain.

12–4. A North Carolina Department of Transportation regulation prohibits the placement of telephone booths within public rights-of-way. Despite this regulation, GTE South, Inc., placed a booth in the right-of-way near the intersection of Hillsborough and Sparger Roads in Durham County. A pedestrian, Laura Baldwin, was using the booth when an accident at the intersection caused a dump truck to cross the right-of-way and smash into the booth. Was Baldwin within the class of persons protected by the regulation? If so, did GTE's placement of the booth constitute negligence *per se?* Explain.

12–5. Intentional Torts against Property. In 1994, Gary Kremen registered the domain name "sex.com" with Network Solutions, Inc., to the name of Kremen's business, Online Classifieds. Later, Stephen Cohen sent Network Solutions a letter that he claimed to have received from Online Classifieds. It stated that "we have no objections to your use of the domain name sex.com and this letter shall serve as our authorization to the Internet registrar to transfer sex.com to your corporation." Without contacting Kremen, Network Solutions transferred the name to Cohen, who subsequently turned sex.com into a lucrative business. Kremen filed a suit in a federal district court against Cohen and others, seeking the name and Cohen's profits. The court ordered Cohen to return the name to Kremen and pay $65 million in damages. Cohen ignored the order and disappeared. Against what other parties might Kremen attempt to obtain relief? Under which theory of intentional torts against property might Kremen be able to file an action? What is the likely result, and why? [*Kremen v. Cohen,* 337 F.3d 1024 (9th Cir. 2003)]

12–6. Defamation. Lydia Hagberg went to her bank, California Federal Bank, FSB, to cash a check made out to her by Smith Barney (SB), an investment services firm. Nolene Showalter, a bank employee, suspected that the check was counterfeit. Showalter called SB and was told that the check was not valid. As she phoned the police, Gary Wood, a bank security officer, contacted SB again and was informed that its earlier statement was "erroneous" and that the check was valid. Meanwhile, a police officer arrived, drew Hagberg away from the teller's window, spread her legs, patted her down, and handcuffed her. The officer searched her purse, asked her whether she had any weapons or stolen property and whether she was driving a stolen vehicle, and arrested her. Hagberg filed a suit in a California state court against the bank and others, alleging, among other things, slander. Should the absolute privilege for communications made in judicial or other official proceedings apply to statements made when a citizen contacts the police to report suspected criminal activity? Why or why not? [*Hagberg v. California Federal Bank,* FSB, 32 Cal.4th 350, 81 P.3d 244, 7 Cal.Rptr.3d 803 (2004)]

12–7. CASE PROBLEM WITH SAMPLE ANSWER

Between 1996 and 1998, Donna Swanson received several anonymous, handwritten letters that, among other things, accused her husband, Alan, of infidelity. In 1998, John Grisham, Jr., the author of *The Firm* and many other best-selling novels, received an anonymous letter that appeared to have been written by the same person. Grisham and the Swansons suspected Katherine Almy, who soon filed a suit in a Virginia state court against them, alleging, among other things, intentional infliction of emotional distress. According to Almy, Grisham intended to have her "really, really, suffer" for writing the letters, and the three devised a scheme to falsely accuse her. They gave David Liebman, a handwriting analyst, samples of Almy's handwriting. These included copies of confidential documents from her children's files at St. Anne's–Belfield School in Charlottesville, Virginia, where Alan taught and Grisham served on the board of directors. In Almy's view, Grisham influenced Liebman to report that Almy might have written the letters and misrepresented this report as conclusive, which led the police to confront Almy. She claimed that she then suffered severe emotional distress and depression, causing "a complete disintegration of virtually every aspect of her life" and requiring her "to undergo extensive therapy." In response, the defendants asked the court to dismiss the complaint for failure to state a claim. Should the court grant this request? Explain. [*Almy v. Grisham,* 273 Va. 68, 639 S.E.2d 182 (2007)]

- **To view a sample answer for Problem 12–7, go to this book's Web site at academic.cengage.com/blaw/cross, select "Chapter 12," and click on "Case Problem with Sample Answer."**

12–8. Negligence. In July 2004, Emellie Anderson hired Kenneth Whitten, a licensed building contractor, to construct a two-story addition to her home. The bottom floor was to be a garage and the second floor a home office. In

August, the parties signed a second contract under which Whitten agreed to rebuild a deck and railing attached to the house and to further improve the office. A later inspection revealed gaps in the siding on the new garage, nails protruding from incomplete framing, improper support for a stairway to the office, and gaps in its plywood flooring. One post supporting the deck was cracked; another was too short. Concrete had not been poured underneath the old posts. A section of railing was missing, and what was installed was warped, with gaps at the joints. Anderson filed a suit in a Connecticut state court against Whitten, alleging that his work was "substandard, not to code, unsafe and not done in a [workmanlike] manner." Anderson claimed that she would have to pay someone else to repair all of the work. Does Whitten's "work" satisfy the requirements for a claim grounded in negligence? Should Anderson's complaint be dismissed, or should she be awarded damages? Explain. [*Anderson v. Whitten,* 100 Conn.App. 730, 918 A.2d 1056 (2007)]

12–9. Defenses to Negligence. Neal Peterson's entire family skied, and Peterson started skiing at the age of two. In 2000, at the age of eleven, Peterson was in his fourth year as a member of a ski race team. After a race one morning in February, Peterson continued to practice his skills through the afternoon. Coming down a slope very fast, at a point at which his skis were not touching the ground, Peterson collided with David Donahue. Donahue, a forty-three-year-old advanced skier, was skating (skiing slowly) across the slope toward the parking lot. Peterson and Donahue knew that falls or collisions and accidents and injuries were possible with skiing. Donahue saw Peterson "split seconds" before the impact, which knocked Donahue out of his skis and down the slope ten or twelve feet. When Donahue saw Peterson lying motionless nearby, he immediately sought help. To recover for his injuries, Peterson filed a suit in a Minnesota state court against Donahue, alleging negligence. Based on these facts, which defense to a claim of negligence is Donahue most likely to assert? How is the court likely to apply that defense and rule on Peterson's claim? Why? [*Peterson ex rel. Peterson v. Donahue,* 733 N.W.2d 790 (Minn.App. 2007)]

12–10. SPECIAL CASE ANALYSIS

Go to Case 12.4, *Sutton v. Eastern New York Youth Soccer Association, Inc.*, 8 A.D.3d 855, 779 N.Y.S.2d 149 (3 Dept. 2004), on pages 309–310. Read the excerpt and answer the following questions.

(a) **Issue:** What was the main issue in this case?
(b) **Rule of Law:** What rule of law did the court apply?
(c) **Applying the Rule of Law:** Describe how the court applied the rule of law to the facts of this case.
(d) **Conclusion:** What was the court's conclusion in this case?

12–11. A QUESTION OF ETHICS

*White Plains Coat & Apron Co. is a New York–based linen rental business. Cintas Corp. is a nationwide business that rents similar products. White Plains had five-year exclusive contracts with some of its customers. As a result of Cintas's soliciting of business, dozens of White Plains' customers breached their contracts and entered into rental agreements with Cintas. White Plains demanded that Cintas stop its solicitation of White Plains' customers. Cintas refused. White Plains filed a suit in a federal district court against Cintas, alleging wrongful interference with existing contracts. Cintas argued that it had no knowledge of any contracts with White Plains and had not induced any breach. The court dismissed the suit, ruling that Cintas had a legitimate interest as a competitor to solicit business and make a profit. White Plains appealed to the U.S. Court of Appeals for the Second Circuit. [*White Plains Coat & Apron Co. v. Cintas Corp.*, 8 N.Y.3d 422, 867 N.E.2d 381 (2007)]*

(a) What are the two important policy interests at odds in wrongful interference cases? When there is an existing contract, which of these interests should be accorded priority?
(b) The U.S. Court of Appeals for the Second Circuit asked the New York Court of Appeals to answer a question: Is a general interest in soliciting business for profit a sufficient defense to a claim of wrongful interference with a contractual relationship? What do you think? Why?

12–12. VIDEO QUESTION

Go to this text's Web site at **academic.cengage.com/blaw/cross**, and select "Chapter 12." Click on "Video Questions" and view the video titled *Jaws.* Then answer the following questions.

(a) In the video, the mayor (Murray Hamilton) and a few other men try to persuade Chief Brody (Roy Scheider) not to close the town's beaches. If Brody keeps the beaches open and a swimmer is injured or killed because he failed to warn swimmers about the potential shark danger, has Brody committed the tort of negligence? Explain.
(b) Can Chief Brody be held liable for any injuries or deaths to swimmers under any intentional tort theories? Why or why not?
(c) Suppose that Chief Brody goes against the mayor's instructions and warns townspeople to stay off the beach. Nevertheless, several swimmers do not heed his warning and are injured as a result. What defense or defenses could Brody raise under these circumstances if he is sued for negligence?

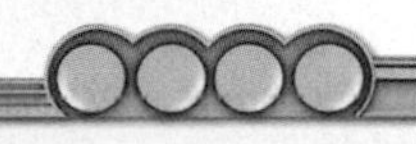

LAW ON THE WEB

For updated links to resources available on the Web, as well as a variety of other materials, visit this text's Web site at

academic.cengage.com/blaw/cross

You can find cases and articles on torts, including business torts, in the tort law library at the Internet Law Library's Web site. Go to

www.lawguru.com/ilawlib

Legal Research Exercises on the Web

Go to **academic.cengage.com/blaw/cross**, the Web site that accompanies this text. Select "Chapter 12" and click on "Internet Exercises." There you will find the following Internet research exercises that you can perform to learn more about the topics covered in this chapter.

Internet Exercise 12–1: Legal Perspective
Online Defamation

Internet Exercise 12–2: Management Perspective
Legal and Illegal Uses of Spam

Internet Exercise 12–3: Legal Perspective
Negligence and the *Titanic*

CHAPTER 13

Strict Liability and Product Liability

The intentional torts and torts of negligence discussed in Chapter 12 involve acts that depart from a reasonable standard of care and cause injuries. In this chapter, we look at another category of tort—**strict liability,** or *liability without fault.* Under the doctrine of strict liability, a person who engages in certain activities can be held responsible for any harm that results to others even if the person used the utmost care.

We open this chapter with an examination of this doctrine. We then look at an area of tort law of particular importance to businesspersons—product liability. **Product liability** refers to the liability incurred by manufacturers and sellers of products when product defects cause injury or property damage to consumers, users, or **bystanders** (people in the vicinity of the product).

Strict Liability

The modern concept of strict liability traces its origins, in part, to the 1868 English case of *Rylands v. Fletcher.*[1] In the coal-mining area of Lancashire, England, the Rylands, who were mill owners, had constructed a reservoir on their land. Water from the reservoir broke through a filled-in shaft of an abandoned coal mine nearby and flooded the connecting passageways in an active coal mine owned by Fletcher. Fletcher sued the Rylands, and the court held that the defendants (the Rylands) were liable, even though the circumstances did not fit within existing tort liability theories. The court held that a "person who for his own purposes brings on his land and collects and keeps there anything likely to do mischief if it escapes ... is *prima facie* [on initial examination] answerable for all the damage which is the natural consequence of its escape."

British courts liberally applied the doctrine that emerged from the *Rylands v. Fletcher* case. Initially, few U.S. courts accepted this doctrine, presumably because the courts were worried about its effect on the expansion of American business. Today, however, the doctrine of strict liability is the norm rather than the exception.

1. 3 L.R.–E & I App. [Law Reports, English & Irish Appeal Cases] (H.L. [House of Lords] 1868).

Abnormally Dangerous Activities

Strict liability for damages proximately caused by an abnormally dangerous, or ultrahazardous, activity is one application of strict liability. Courts apply the doctrine of strict liability in these situations because of the extreme risk of the activity. Abnormally dangerous activities are those that involve a high risk of serious harm to persons or property that cannot be completely guarded against by the exercise of reasonable care—activities such as blasting or storing explosives. Even if blasting with dynamite is performed with all reasonable care, there is still a risk of injury. Balancing that risk against the potential for harm, it seems reasonable to ask the person engaged in the activity to pay for injuries caused by that activity. Although there is no fault, there is still responsibility because of the dangerous nature of the undertaking.

Other Applications of Strict Liability

Persons who keep wild animals are strictly liable for any harm inflicted by the animals. The basis for applying strict liability is that wild animals, should they escape from confinement, pose a serious risk of harm to persons in the vicinity. An owner of domestic animals (such as dogs, cats, cows, or sheep) may be strictly liable for harm caused by those animals if the owner knew, or should have known, that the animals were dangerous or had a propensity to harm others.

A significant application of strict liability is in the area of product liability—liability of manufacturers and sellers for harmful or defective products. Liability here is a matter of social policy and is based on two factors: (1) the manufacturing company can better bear the cost of injury because it can spread the cost throughout society by increasing prices of goods, and (2) the manufacturing company is making a profit from its activities and therefore should bear the cost of injury as an operating expense. We discuss product liability in greater detail throughout the remainder of this chapter.

SECTION 2 Product Liability

Those who make, sell, or lease goods can be held liable for physical harm or property damage caused by those goods to a consumer, user, or bystander. This is called product liability. Because one particular product may cause harm to a number of consumers, product liability actions are sometimes filed by a group of plaintiffs acting together. (For a discussion of a law that requires claims filed by a large group of plaintiffs to be heard in federal courts, see this chapter's *Emerging Trends* feature on pages 324 and 325.)

Product liability may be based on the theories of negligence, misrepresentation, and strict liability. We look here at product liability based on negligence and on misrepresentation.

Product Liability Based on Negligence

In Chapter 12, *negligence* was defined as the failure to exercise the degree of care that a reasonable, prudent person would have exercised under the circumstances. If a manufacturer fails to exercise "due care" to make a product safe, a person who is injured by the product may sue the manufacturer for negligence.

Due Care Must Be Exercised Due care must be exercised in designing the product, selecting the materials, using the appropriate production process, assembling and testing the product, and placing adequate warnings on the label informing the user of dangers of which an ordinary person might not be aware. The duty of care also extends to the inspection and testing of any purchased components that are used in the product sold by the manufacturer.

To succeed in a product liability suit against a manufacturer based on negligence, does a plaintiff have to prove the specific defect that caused the plaintiff's injury? That was the question in the following case.

CASE 13.1 Jarvis v. Ford Motor Co.

United States Court of Appeals, Second Circuit, 2002. 283 F.3d 33.

• **Company Profile** Henry Ford founded the Ford Motor Company (**www.ford.com**) in Dearborn, Michigan, in 1903 to design and make a mass-produced automobile. Five years later, Ford introduced the Model T, which was made affordable by the company's efficient use of assembly lines. By 1920, 60 percent of all of the vehicles on the road were made by Ford. Today, Ford is the world's largest maker of pickup trucks and the second-largest producer of cars. Ford brand names include Aston Martin, Jaguar, Lincoln, Mercury, and Volvo. Its most popular models are Ford Taurus cars and F-Series pickup trucks. Ford also makes the Aerostar minivan.

• **Background and Facts** In 1991, Kathleen Jarvis bought a new Aerostar. Six days later, she started the van in the driveway of her home in Woodstock, New York. After she turned on the ignition, the engine suddenly revved and the vehicle took off. Jarvis pumped the brake with both feet, but the van would not stop. She steered to avoid people walking in the road before the van entered a ditch and turned over. As a result of the accident, Jarvis suffered a head injury and could not return to her job. She filed a suit in a federal district court against Ford, asserting product liability based, in part, on negligence.

CASE CONTINUES

CASE 13.1 CONTINUED Jarvis alleged that a defect in the van had caused the sudden acceleration. Her proof included her testimony, the testimony of other Aerostar owners who had experienced similar problems, and evidence that hundreds of additional Aerostar owners had experienced sudden acceleration. She also presented an expert who theorized that the van's cruise control had malfunctioned and who proposed an inexpensive remedy for this problem. Ford argued that Jarvis had failed to prove the defect that caused the cruise control to malfunction. A jury issued a verdict in Jarvis's favor, but the court granted Ford's motion for judgment as a matter of law. Jarvis appealed to the U.S. Court of Appeals for the Second Circuit.

IN THE LANGUAGE OF THE COURT
***SOTOMAYOR,* Circuit Judge.**

* * * *

* * * A plaintiff's failure to prove why a product malfunctioned does not necessarily prevent a plaintiff from showing that the product was defective. * * * While the burden is upon the plaintiff to prove that the product was defective and that the defect existed while the product was in the manufacturer's possession, [the] plaintiff is not required to prove the specific defect, especially where the product is complicated in nature. *Proof of necessary facts may be circumstantial. Though the happening of the accident is not proof of a defective condition, a defect may be inferred from proof that the product did not perform as intended by the manufacturer* * * *. [Emphasis added.]

* * * *

The district court erred in requiring proof of a specific defect in the Aerostar's cruise control and in not considering Jarvis's circumstantial evidence of a defect. The malfunction in the design of the Aerostar that Jarvis has alleged is that it suddenly accelerated, opening full throttle without Jarvis depressing the accelerator pedal, and that her efforts to stop the vehicle by pumping the brakes were unavailing. If Jarvis's six-day-old Aerostar performed in this manner, a jury could reasonably conclude that it was defective when put on the market by Ford, and that the defect made it reasonably certain that the vehicle would be dangerous when put to normal use, as required [in a cause of action based on] negligent design. Although Ford argued that the accident was caused instead by driver error, this theory would have been rejected if the jury had believed Jarvis's testimony that she had her feet on the brake and not on the accelerator, as Ford claimed. * * * Construing the evidence in Jarvis's favor and crediting her version of events, a reasonable jury could find that Ford breached its duty of care. Even accepting as true that sudden acceleration in the 1991 Aerostar would occur, at most, very infrequently when measured against all Aerostar ignition starts [as Ford claimed], the consequences of sudden acceleration could easily be catastrophic, the design of which Jarvis complains has no particular utility to balance its potential for harm, and, according to Jarvis's expert, the malfunction in the cruise control could be avoided by an inexpensive switch that would shut off power to the cruise control when not in use.

• **Decision and Remedy** *The U.S. Court of Appeals for the Second Circuit vacated (set aside, voided) the judgment of the lower court and remanded the case with instructions to reinstate the jury's verdict that Ford was negligent in the design of the cruise control mechanism in the 1991 Aerostar. A plaintiff in a product liability action based on negligence is not required to prove a specific defect when a defect may be inferred from proof that the product did not perform as the manufacturer intended.*[a]

• **The Legal Environment Dimension** *If plaintiffs were required to prove the specific defect that caused their injury, as the trial court in this case had ruled, what impact would this have on product liability claims based on negligence? Would there be more or fewer of these types of lawsuits filed?*

• **The Global Dimension** *Assume that other nations do not have laws concerning product liability based on negligence. Can a U.S. manufacturer sell a negligently designed product in a foreign market without risk of liability? Should it? Why or why not?*

a. This is also the principle in a strict product liability action, according to the *Restatement (Third) of Torts: Products Liability*, which will be discussed later in this chapter.

Privity of Contract Not Required A product liability action based on negligence does not require the injured plaintiff and the negligent defendant-manufacturer to be in **privity of contract.** In other words, the plaintiff and the defendant need not be directly involved in a contractual relationship (that is, in privity). Thus, any person who is injured by a product may bring a negligence suit even though he or she was not the one who actually purchased the product. A manufacturer, seller, or lessor is liable for failure to exercise due care to *any person* who sustains an injury proximately caused by a negligently made (defective) product. Relative to the long history of the common law, this exception to the privity requirement is a fairly recent development, dating to the early part of the twentieth century.[2]

Product Liability Based on Misrepresentation

When a fraudulent misrepresentation has been made to a user or consumer and that misrepresentation ultimately results in an injury, the basis of liability may be the tort of fraud. In this situation, the misrepresentation must have been made knowingly or with reckless disregard for the facts. For example, the intentional mislabeling of packaged cosmetics and the intentional concealment of a product's defects would constitute fraudulent misrepresentation. The misrepresentation must be of a material fact, and the seller must have had the intent to induce the buyer's reliance on the misrepresentation. Misrepresentation on a label or advertisement is enough to show an intent to induce the reliance of anyone who may use the product. In addition, the buyer must have relied on the misrepresentation.

Section 3 Strict Product Liability

Under the doctrine of *strict liability* (discussed previously), people may be liable for the results of their acts regardless of their intentions or their exercise of reasonable care. In addition, liability does not depend on privity of contract. The injured party does not have to be the buyer or a third party beneficiary (see page 226), as required under contract warranty theory. In the 1960s, courts applied the doctrine of strict liability in several landmark cases involving manufactured goods, and it has since become a common method of holding manufacturers liable.

Strict Product Liability and Public Policy

The law imposes strict product liability as a matter of public policy. This public policy rests on the threefold assumption that (1) consumers should be protected against unsafe products; (2) manufacturers and distributors should not escape liability for faulty products simply because they are not in privity of contract with the ultimate user of those products; and (3) manufacturers, sellers, and lessors of products are in a better position to bear the costs associated with injuries caused by their products—costs that they can ultimately pass on to all consumers in the form of higher prices.

California was the first state to impose strict product liability in tort on manufacturers. In a landmark 1962 decision, *Greenman v. Yuba Power Products, Inc.*,[3] the California Supreme Court set out the reason for applying tort law rather than contract law (including laws governing warranties) in cases involving consumers who were injured by defective products. According to the *Greenman* court, the "purpose of such liability is to [e]nsure that the costs of injuries resulting from defective products are borne by the manufacturers . . . rather than by the injured persons who are powerless to protect themselves." Today, the majority of states recognize strict product liability, although some state courts limit its application to situations involving personal injuries (rather than property damage).

The Requirements for Strict Product Liability

The courts often look to the *Restatements of the Law* for guidance, even though the *Restatements* are not binding authorities. Section 402A of the *Restatement (Second) of Torts,* which was originally issued in 1964, has become a widely accepted statement of the liabilities of sellers of goods (including manufacturers, processors, assemblers, packagers, bottlers, wholesalers, distributors, retailers, and lessors).

The bases for an action in strict liability, which are set forth in Section 402A of the *Restatement (Second) of Torts* and commonly applied by the courts, can be summarized as a series of six requirements, which are listed here. Depending on the jurisdiction, if these requirements are met, a manufacturer's liability to an injured party can be virtually unlimited.

2. A landmark case in this respect is *MacPherson v. Buick Motor Co.*, 217 N.Y. 382, 111 N.E. 1050 (1916).

3. 59 Cal.2d 57, 377 P.2d 897, 27 Cal.Rptr. 697 (1962).

EMERGING TRENDS IN THE LEGAL ENVIRONMENT OF BUSINESS
Removing Class-Action Lawsuits to the Federal Courts

Many product liability actions are class actions. A *class action* is a lawsuit in which a single person or a small group of people represents the interests of a larger group. Women allegedly injured by silicone breast implants, for example, sued the manufacturers as a class, as did many of those allegedly injured by asbestos and tobacco. The idea behind class actions is that an individual consumer who has been injured by a product is unlikely to have the financial means to pursue complex litigation against a large corporation. A class action allows all those injured by a product to pool their resources and obtain competent legal counsel to bring a single lawsuit on their behalf.

Federal courts have always had specific requirements for class actions. For example, the class (the group of plaintiffs) must be so large that individual suits would be impracticable, and the case must involve legal or factual issues common to all members of the class. Until 2005, however, any state or federal court could hear class actions.

The Class Action Fairness Act of 2005

The Class Action Fairness Act (CAFA) of 2005[a] significantly changed the way class actions are tried. Though it affects all class actions, the CAFA was primarily designed to shift large, interstate product liability and tort class-action suits from the state courts to the federal courts. Under the act, federal district courts now have original (trial) jurisdiction over any civil action in which there are one hundred plaintiffs from multiple states and the damages sought exceed $5 million.

Under the CAFA, a state court can retain jurisdiction over a case *only* if more than two-thirds of the plaintiffs and at least one principal defendant are citizens of the state and the injuries were incurred in that state. If more than one-third but less than two-thirds of the plaintiffs live in a state, the act allows a federal judge to decide (based on specified considerations) whether the trial should be held in state or federal court.

In addition, the act makes it easier for a defendant to remove (transfer) a case from a state court to a federal court, even if the defendant is a citizen of the state where the action was filed. In cases involving multiple defendants, the CAFA also allows one defendant to remove the case to federal court without the consent of all the defendants (as was previously required). In sum, the act encourages all class actions to be heard in federal courts, which have historically been less sympathetic to consumers' product liability claims than state courts have been.

Goals of the Act

One of the main goals of the CAFA was to prevent plaintiffs' lawyers from "forum shopping," or looking for the state court that is most likely to be sympathetic to their claims. Corporate lawyers and business groups have long complained that class actions are often brought in states and counties where the judges and juries have a reputation for awarding large verdicts against corporate defendants. Sometimes, cases are even brought in states where only a small number of the plaintiffs reside. According to these critics, the CAFA will prevent such practices and help cut down on frivolous lawsuits. Not only will the business community benefit, but consumers will gain as well because businesses will no longer have to bear the costs of frivolous suits and will therefore be able to lower prices. President George W. Bush said that the act marks a critical step toward ending the "lawsuit culture in our country."[b]

Critics of the act contend, however, that class actions are the only way that individual consumers

a. Pub. L. No. 109-2, 119 St. 4 (February 18, 2005), codified at 28 U.S.C. Sections 1711 *et seq.*

b. Presidential press release, "President Signs Class-Action Fairness Act of 2005," February 18, 2005.

1. The product must be in a *defective condition* when the defendant sells it.
2. The defendant must normally be engaged in the *business of selling* (or otherwise distributing) that product.
3. The product must be *unreasonably dangerous* to the user or consumer because of its defective condition (in most states).
4. The plaintiff must incur *physical harm* to self or property by use or consumption of the product.
5. The defective condition must be the *proximate cause* of the injury or damage.
6. The goods *must not have been substantially changed* from the time the product was sold to the time the injury was sustained.

Proving a Defective Condition Under these requirements, in any action against a manufacturer, seller, or lessor the plaintiff need not show why or in what manner the product became defective. The plain-

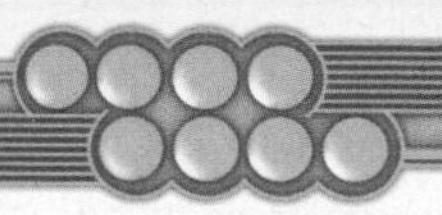

can obtain redress for injuries suffered from defective products. They say that by making it more difficult to pursue class actions, the CAFA is making it harder for injured parties to hold large corporations accountable for their wrongful acts and harmful products.

Even with the CAFA, Removing a Class Action to Federal Court Is Not Always Easy

The CAFA contains numerous ambiguities that the courts are still interpreting as they try to establish the new "rules of engagement" under the act. PepsiCo, Inc., found this out when it tried to remove a class-action suit from a New Jersey state court to a federal district court under the CAFA. The plaintiff had brought the suit against PepsiCo "for herself and on behalf of all persons in New Jersey who, within the past four years, purchased beverages with the tendency to contain benzene." The federal court held, however, that the case did not meet the CAFA's requirement that the amount in controversy exceed $5 million.[c]

Alabama Power Company suffered a similar fate when it also tried to remove a class action to a federal district court. When it appealed to the U.S. Court of Appeals for the Eleventh Circuit, the court denied the company's request in a seventy-seven-page ruling that addressed not only the $5 million threshold requirement but a number of other unresolved issues raised by the CAFA as well.[d]

In essence, the Eleventh Circuit raised the burden of proof for defendants seeking to remove cases to federal court. To do so, defendants must now prove that the amount-in-controversy requirement is a legal certainty. Prior to this ruling, the tradition was the use of a "preponderance of the evidence" standard.

IMPLICATIONS FOR THE BUSINESSPERSON

1. Product liability actions may still be tried in state courts. The CAFA applies only to class actions in which the plaintiffs seek damages of more than $5 million.
2. Businesspersons should be aware that even though a law appears to change only procedural rules, such as where and how a dispute is litigated, it may have consequences that affect substantive rights, including a party's ability to litigate.

FOR CRITICAL ANALYSIS

1. Do you agree that the CAFA will be effective in curtailing frivolous lawsuits? What other methods can you suggest to stop plaintiffs from filing suits that have no merit?
2. Critics of the CAFA argue that this legislation deprives Americans of "their day in court" when they are wronged by powerful corporations. Under what circumstances could this criticism be justified?

RELEVANT WEB SITES

To locate information on the Web concerning the issues discussed in this feature, go to this text's Web site at **academic.cengage.com/blaw/cross**, select "Chapter 13, and click on "Emerging Trends."

c. *Lamond v. PepsiCo, Inc.*, 2007 WL 1695401 (D.N.J. 2007).

d. *Lowery v. Alabama Power Co.*, 483 F.3d 1184 (11th Cir. 2007).

tiff does, however, have to prove that the product was defective at the time it left the hands of the seller or lessor and that this defective condition makes it "unreasonably dangerous" to the user or consumer. Unless evidence can be presented to support the conclusion that the product was defective when it was sold or leased, the plaintiff will not succeed. If the product was delivered in a safe condition and subsequent mishandling made it harmful to the user, the seller or lessor is normally not strictly liable.

Unreasonably Dangerous Products The *Restatement* recognizes that many products cannot be made entirely safe for all uses; thus, sellers or lessors are liable only for products that are *unreasonably* dangerous. A court could consider a product so defective as to be an **unreasonably dangerous product** in either of the following situations:

1. The product was dangerous beyond the expectation of the ordinary consumer.

2. A less dangerous alternative was *economically* feasible for the manufacturer, but the manufacturer failed to produce it.

As will be discussed next, a product may be unreasonably dangerous due to a flaw in the manufacturing process, a design defect, or an inadequate warning.

Product Defects

Because Section 402A of the *Restatement (Second) of Torts* did not clearly define such terms as *defective* and *unreasonably dangerous,* these terms have been subject to different interpretations by different courts. In 1997, to address these concerns, the American Law Institute (ALI) issued the *Restatement (Third) of Torts: Products Liability.* This *Restatement* defines the three types of product defects that have traditionally been recognized in product liability law—manufacturing defects, design defects, and inadequate warnings.

Manufacturing Defects According to Section 2(a) of the *Restatement (Third) of Torts,* a product "contains a manufacturing defect when the product departs from its intended design even though all possible care was exercised in the preparation and marketing of the product." Basically, a manufacturing defect is a departure from a product's design specifications. A glass bottle that is made too thin and explodes in a consumer's face is an example of a manufacturing defect. Liability is imposed on the manufacturer (and on the wholesaler and retailer) regardless of whether the manufacturer's quality control efforts were "reasonable." The idea behind holding defendants strictly liable for manufacturing defects is to encourage greater investment in product safety and stringent quality control standards. Cases involving allegations of a manufacturing defect are often decided based on the opinions and testimony of experts.[4]

Design Defects Unlike a product with a manufacturing defect, a product with a design defect is made in conformity with the manufacturer's design specifications but nevertheless results in injury to the user because the design itself was improper. The product's design creates an unreasonable risk to the user. A product "is defective in design when the foreseeable risks of harm posed by the product could have been reduced or avoided by the adoption of a reasonable alternative design by the seller or other distributor, or a predecessor in the commercial chain of distribution, and the omission of the alternative design renders the product not reasonably safe."[5]

Test for Design Defects. To successfully assert a design defect, a plaintiff has to show that a reasonable alternative design was available and that the defendant's failure to adopt the alternative design rendered the product not reasonably safe. In other words, a manufacturer or other defendant is liable only when the harm was reasonably preventable. In one case, for example, Gillespie, who cut off several of his fingers while operating a table saw, alleged that the blade guards on the saw were defectively designed. At the trial, however, an expert testified that the alternative design for blade guards used for table saws could not have been used for the particular cut that Gillespie was performing at the time he was injured. The court found that Gillespie's claim that the blade guards were defective failed because there was no proof that a guard with a "better" design would have prevented his injury.[6]

Factors to Be Considered. According to the *Restatement,* a court can consider a broad range of factors, including the magnitude and probability of the foreseeable risks, and the relative advantages and disadvantages of the product as it was designed and as it could have been designed. Basically, most courts engage in a risk-utility analysis, determining whether the risk of harm from the product as designed outweighs its utility to the user and to the public.

For example, suppose that a nine-year-old child finds rat poison in a cupboard at the local boys' club and eats it, thinking that it is candy. The child dies, and his parents file a suit against the manufacturer alleging that the rat poison was defectively designed because it looked like candy and was supposed to be placed in cupboards. In this situation, a court would probably consider factors such as the foreseeability that a child would think the rat poison was candy, the gravity of the potential harm from consumption, the availability of an alternative design, and the usefulness of the product. If the parents could offer sufficient evidence for a reasonable person to conclude that the harm was reasonably preventable, then the manufacturer could be held liable.

4. See, for example, *Derienzo v. Trek Bicycle Corp.,* 376 F.Supp.2d 537 (S.D.N.Y. 2005).

5. *Restatement (Third) of Torts: Products Liability,* Section 2(b).

6. *Gillespie v. Sears, Roebuck & Co.,* 386 F.3d 21 (1st Cir. 2004).

In the following case, a smoker who developed lung cancer sued a cigarette manufacturer claiming, among other things, that there was a defect in the design of its cigarettes. The jury instruction given by the trial court and quoted by the appellate court shows the numerous factors that judges and juries consider in determining design defects.

CASE 13.2 Bullock v. Philip Morris USA, Inc.

Court of Appeal of California, Second District, Division 3, 2008.
159 Cal.App. 4th 655, 71 Cal.Rptr 3d 775.
www.courtinfo.ca.gov/courts/courtsofappeal[a]

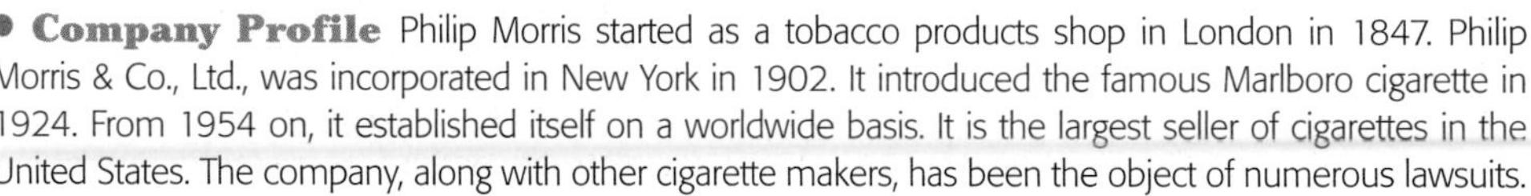

• **Company Profile** Philip Morris started as a tobacco products shop in London in 1847. Philip Morris & Co., Ltd., was incorporated in New York in 1902. It introduced the famous Marlboro cigarette in 1924. From 1954 on, it established itself on a worldwide basis. It is the largest seller of cigarettes in the United States. The company, along with other cigarette makers, has been the object of numerous lawsuits.

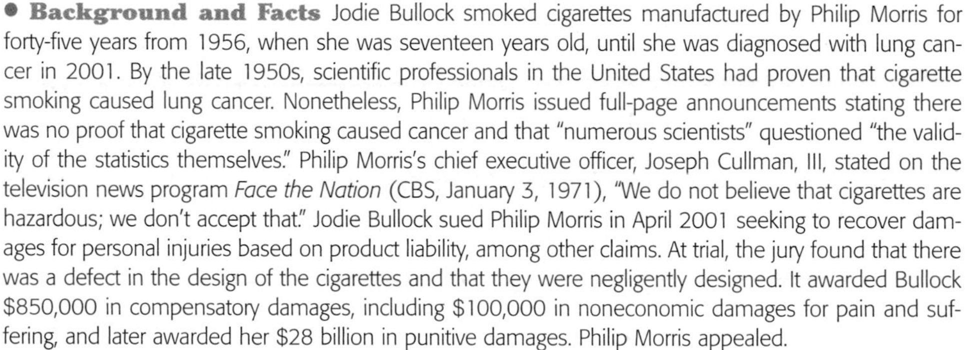

• **Background and Facts** Jodie Bullock smoked cigarettes manufactured by Philip Morris for forty-five years from 1956, when she was seventeen years old, until she was diagnosed with lung cancer in 2001. By the late 1950s, scientific professionals in the United States had proven that cigarette smoking caused lung cancer. Nonetheless, Philip Morris issued full-page announcements stating there was no proof that cigarette smoking caused cancer and that "numerous scientists" questioned "the validity of the statistics themselves." Philip Morris's chief executive officer, Joseph Cullman, III, stated on the television news program *Face the Nation* (CBS, January 3, 1971), "We do not believe that cigarettes are hazardous; we don't accept that." Jodie Bullock sued Philip Morris in April 2001 seeking to recover damages for personal injuries based on product liability, among other claims. At trial, the jury found that there was a defect in the design of the cigarettes and that they were negligently designed. It awarded Bullock $850,000 in compensatory damages, including $100,000 in noneconomic damages for pain and suffering, and later awarded her $28 billion in punitive damages. Philip Morris appealed.

IN THE LANGUAGE OF THE COURT
***CROSKEY,* J. [Judge]**

* * * *

Philip Morris heavily advertised its cigarettes on television in the 1950's and 1960's, until the federal government banned cigarette advertising on television in 1970. Television advertising had a particularly strong influence on youths under the age of 18, for whom there was a positive correlation between television viewing time and the incidence of smoking. Philip Morris's print advertisements for Marlboro and other cigarette brands in 1956, when Bullock began smoking at the age of 17, and generally in the years from 1954 to 1969, depicted handsome men and glamorous young women. Some advertisements featured slogans such as "Loved for Gentleness" and "'The <u>gentlest</u> cigarette you can smoke.'"

* * * *

Philip Morris contends (1) the evidence failed to establish a design defect under the risk-benefit test because there is no substantial evidence that a safer alternative cigarette design was available, that the failure to use a safer design was a cause of Bullock's lung cancer, or that Bullock would have smoked a safer cigarette if it were available; (2) the evidence failed to establish a design defect under the consumer expectations test or liability based on a failure to warn because there is no substantial evidence that the ordinary consumer was unaware of the dangers of cigarette smoking.

* * * *

A product is defective in design for purposes of tort liability if the benefits of the design do not outweigh the risk of danger inherent in the design, or if the product, used in an intended or

a. To access this court opinion, click on "Opinions 2nd District" and then click on recent "Published Opinions." Go to "January 30, 2008" and click on the name of the case.

CASE CONTINUES

CASE 13.2 CONTINUED *reasonably foreseeable manner, has failed to perform as safely as an ordinary consumer would expect.* [Emphasis added.]

Philip Morris challenges the finding of liability for design defect based on a risk-benefit theory by challenging the sufficiency of the evidence that a safer alternative design existed and the sufficiency of the evidence that its failure to use a safer alternative design caused Bullock's injuries. Philip Morris's argument is based on the premise that a plaintiff alleging a design defect based on a risk-benefit theory must prove that the defendant could have used a safer alternative design. The jury, however, was not so instructed. The court instructed the jury to determine whether the benefits of the design outweighed the risks by considering several factors, but did not instruct that any single factor was essential:

"In determining whether the benefits of the design outweigh its risks, you should consider, among other things, the gravity of the danger posed by the design, the likelihood that the danger would cause damage, the existence or nonexistence of warnings, the time of the manufacture, the financial cost of an improved design, and the adverse consequences to the product and the consumer that would result from an alternate design."

* * * We review the sufficiency of the evidence to support a verdict under the law stated in the instructions given, rather than under some other law on which the jury was not instructed. * * * Accordingly, we conclude that Philip Morris has shown no error with respect to the finding of liability for a design defect based on the risk-benefit test.

- **Decision and Remedy** *The Court of Appeal of California for the Second District affirmed the trial court's judgment as to the finding of liability. Philip Morris failed to show any error with respect to its liability for product liability based on a design defect.*

- **What If the Facts Were Different?** *Assume that Philip Morris had never publicly denied the scientific link between smoking and lung cancer. In other words, the company simply sold cigarettes without saying anything about the medical consequences of smoking. Do you think the jury award would have been the same? If yes, how?*

- **The Ethical Dimension** *Under what circumstances, if any, could Philip Morris have justified its continuing campaign to discredit the scientific arguments that linked smoking with lung cancer?*

Inadequate Warnings A product may also be deemed defective because of inadequate instructions or warnings. A product will be considered defective "when the foreseeable risks of harm posed by the product could have been reduced or avoided by the provision of reasonable instructions or warnings by the seller or other distributor, or a predecessor in the commercial chain of distribution, and the omission of the instructions or warnings renders the product not reasonably safe."[7]

Important factors for a court to consider include the risks of a product, the "content and comprehensibility" and "intensity of expression" of warnings and instructions, and the "characteristics of expected user groups."[8] A "reasonableness" test applies to determine if the warnings adequately alert consumers to the product's risks. For example, children would likely respond readily to bright, bold, simple warning labels, whereas educated adults might need more detailed information.

If a warning is provided with a product, can its manufacturer or seller assume that the warning will be read and obeyed? That was a question in the following case.

7. *Restatement (Third) of Torts: Products Liability,* Section 2(c).

8. *Restatement (Third) of Torts: Products Liability,* Section 2, Comment h.

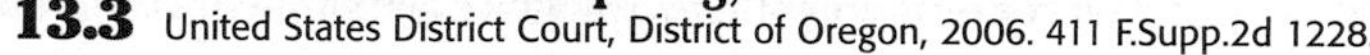
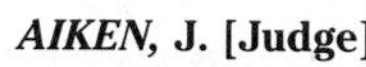

EXTENDED CASE 13.3 Crosswhite v. Jumpking, Inc.

United States District Court, District of Oregon, 2006. 411 F.Supp.2d 1228.

***AIKEN,* J. [Judge]**

* * * *

On May 11, 2002, plaintiff, Gary Crosswhite, was jumping on a trampoline with another boy. The trampoline was owned by Jack and Misty Urbach * * * . The 14-foot round-shaped "backyard" trampoline was manufactured by defendant * * * , Jumpking [Inc.], and purchased by the Urbachs from Costco, Inc. sometime in 1999.

While on the trampoline, plaintiff attempted to execute a back-flip and accidentally landed on his head and neck. The force of the fall caused a fracture in plaintiff's cervical spine resulting in paraplegia. Plaintiff was sixteen years old at the time of his injury. Plaintiff alleges that his injuries were caused by * * * inadequate warnings and instructions [among other things]. Plaintiff brings this lawsuit [in a federal district court] against Jumpking alleging * * * strict liability [and other product liability claims].

Plaintiff, represented by counsel, filed this lawsuit on September 1, 2004. Over one year later, on November 10, 2005, defendant filed the summary judgment motion at bar.

* * * *

* * * *A product is not in a defective condition when it is safe for normal handling.* * * * *If the injury results from abnormal handling* * * * *the seller is not liable. Where, however, the seller has reason to anticipate that danger may result from a particular use,* * * * *the seller may be required to give adequate warning of the danger* * * * *and a product sold without such warning is in a defective condition.* [Emphasis added.]

* * * To prevent the product from being unreasonably dangerous, the seller may be required to give directions or warning, on the container, as to its use. However, where warning is given, the seller may reasonably assume that it will be read and heeded; and a product bearing such a warning is not in a defective condition, nor is it unreasonably dangerous.

Defendant's trampoline is manufactured with nine warning labels that are affixed to various trampoline components. In addition to these nine warning labels, defendant also provides a large laminated warning placard that is designed to be attached by the consumer to the metal frame near the ladder upon which jumpers mount the trampoline. Defendant further provides consumers with a detailed *User Manual* and a videotape that instructs both users and supervisors about safe and responsible trampoline use.

Uniform trampoline safety standards are published by the American Society for Testing and Materials (ASTM). The ASTM standard sets forth specific warning language to accompany trampolines. The record supports defendant's allegation that the trampoline at issue, including the warning that accompanied it, complied with all ASTM standards relevant at the time. Moreover, the ASTM standards at that time did not require warnings against users performing somersaults (flips) and/or jumping with multiple people to appear on the trampoline itself, however, defendant did affix those warnings to the trampoline as well as on a large warning placard attached to the trampoline at the point of entry or mounting. Specifically, one warning attached to the trampoline frame leg stated:

! WARNING
Do not land on head or neck.
Paralysis or death can result, even if you
land in the middle of the trampoline mat (bed).
To reduce the chance of landing on your head or neck, do not do flips.

Accompanying these warning labels is a "stick-figure" drawing of an individual landing on his head. The drawing is located above the warning language and is enclosed in a circular "x-ed" or "crossed-out" notation, commonly understood to mean that the conduct described should be avoided.

Another pair of warning labels affixed to the trampoline legs read:

CASE CONTINUES

CASE 13.3 CONTINUED

! WARNING
Only one person at a time on the trampoline. Multiple jumpers increase the chances of loss of control, collision, and falling off. This can result in broken head, neck, back or leg.

Accompanying these warnings and placed above the warning language is a drawing of two individuals jumping on a single trampoline, which is also enclosed in a "crossed-out" or "x-ed" notation. These same warning labels warning users against performing flips or somersaults and against jumping with multiple people were also on the trampoline frame pad, the large 8" × 11" warning placard framed by the colors orange and yellow and attached to the trampoline frame at the point of entry, and in various places throughout the *User Manual.* The court notes that these warnings went beyond what was required by the ASTM safety standards.

Further, Jack Urbach testified that the warning placard, which specifically warns against both multiple jumping and performing flips or somersaults and the risk of paralysis, was included in the trampoline he purchased, and that he attached the placard to the trampoline upon its initial assembly. Urbach further testified that he had his entire family watch the safety video provided by defendant prior to assembling and using the trampoline.

* * * [D]efendant is entitled to assume that its many warnings will be read, watched and heeded. *The fact that plaintiff may not have seen the many warnings defendant provided prior to his accident does not create a material issue of fact as to whether the warnings rendered the trampoline defective and unreasonably dangerous.* Defendant's summary judgment motion is granted as to plaintiff's claim that the trampoline's warnings were inadequate. I find that defendant's warnings were adequate as a matter of law. [Emphasis added.]

* * * *

IT IS SO ORDERED.

QUESTIONS

1. If Crosswhite had proved that he had not seen, before his accident, the warnings that Jumpking provided, would the court have considered the trampoline defective or unreasonably dangerous? Why or why not?
2. Is the danger from jumping on a trampoline so obvious that even if Jumpking's product had lacked warnings, the manufacturer should not be held liable for a user's injuries? Explain.

Obvious Risks. There is no duty to warn about risks that are obvious or commonly known. Warnings about such risks do not add to the safety of a product and could even detract from it by making other warnings seem less significant. As will be discussed later in the chapter, the obviousness of a risk and a user's decision to proceed in the face of that risk may be a defense in a product liability suit based on an inadequate warning. Nevertheless, risks that may seem obvious to some users will not be obvious to all users, especially when the users are likely to be children. For example, suppose that an eleven-year-old child dives into a shallow, above-ground pool, hits the bottom, and is paralyzed as a result. She later sues the pool maker. The manufacturer cannot escape liability for failing to warn about the hazards of diving into a pool simply by claiming that the risk was obvious.[9]

9. *Bunch v. Hoffinger Industries, Inc.*, 123 Cal.App.4th 1278, 20 Cal.Rptr.3d 780 (2004).

Foreseeable Misuses. Generally, a seller must warn those who purchase its product of the harm that can result from the foreseeable misuse of the product as well. The key is the foreseeability of the misuse. Sellers are not required to take precautions against every conceivable misuse of a product, just those that are foreseeable.

Market-Share Liability

Ordinarily, in all product liability claims, a plaintiff must prove that the defective product that caused his or her injury was the product of a specific defendant. In a few situations, however, courts have dropped this requirement when plaintiffs could not prove which of many distributors of a harmful product supplied the particular product that caused the injuries. For example, in one case a plaintiff who was a hemophiliac received injections of a blood protein known as antihemophiliac factor (AHF) concentrate. The plaintiff later tested positive for the AIDS (acquired immune deficiency syndrome) virus. Because it was not known which manufacturer was responsible for the particular AHF received by the plaintiff, the court held that all of the manufacturers of AHF could be held liable under the theory of **market-share liability.**[10]

Courts in many jurisdictions do not recognize this theory of liability, believing that it deviates too significantly from traditional legal principles.[11] In jurisdictions that do recognize market-share liability, it is usually applied in cases involving drugs or chemicals, when it is difficult or impossible to determine which company made a particular product.

Other Applications of Strict Product Liability

Virtually all courts extend the strict liability of manufacturers and other sellers to injured bystanders. Thus, if a defective forklift that will not go into reverse injures a passerby, that individual can sue the manufacturer for product liability (and possibly bring a negligence action against the forklift operator as well).

Strict product liability also applies to suppliers of component parts. Suppose that General Motors buys brake pads from a subcontractor and puts them in Chevrolets without changing their composition. If those pads are defective, both the supplier of the brake pads and General Motors will be held strictly liable for the damages caused by the defects.

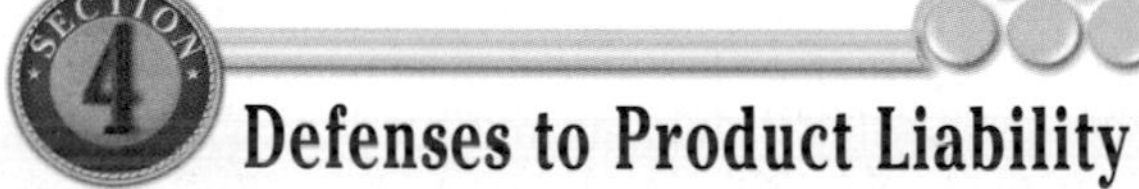

SECTION 4 Defenses to Product Liability

Defendants in product liability suits can raise a number of defenses. One defense, of course, is to show that there is no basis for the plaintiff's claim. For example, in a product liability case based on negligence, if a defendant can show that the plaintiff has *not* met the requirements (such as causation) for an action in negligence, generally the defendant will not be liable. In regard to strict product liability, a defendant can claim that the plaintiff failed to meet one of the requirements for an action in strict liability. For example, if the defendant establishes that the goods have been subsequently altered, normally the defendant will not be held liable.[12] Defendants may also assert the defenses discussed next.

Assumption of Risk

Assumption of risk can sometimes be used as a defense in a product liability action. To establish such a defense, the defendant must show that (1) the plaintiff knew and appreciated the risk created by the product defect and (2) the plaintiff voluntarily assumed the risk, even though it was unreasonable to do so. For example, if a buyer failed to heed a seller's product recall, the buyer may be deemed to have assumed the risk of the product defect that the seller offered to cure. (See Chapter 12 for a more detailed discussion of assumption of risk.)

Product Misuse

Similar to the defense of voluntary assumption of risk is that of **product misuse,** which occurs when a product is used for a purpose for which it was not intended. Here, in contrast to assumption of risk, the injured party *does not know that the product is dangerous for a particular use.* The courts have severely limited this defense, however. Even if the injured party does not know about the inherent danger of using the product in a wrong way, if the misuse is reasonably foreseeable, the seller must take measures to guard against it.

Comparative Negligence (Fault)

Developments in the area of comparative negligence, or fault (discussed in Chapter 12), have also affected the doctrine of strict liability. In the past, the plaintiff's conduct was never a defense to liability for a defective product. Today, courts in many jurisdictions will consider the negligent or intentional actions of both the plaintiff and the defendant when apportioning liability and damages.[13] This means that a defendant may be able to limit at least some of its liability if it can show that the plaintiff's misuse of the product contributed to his or her injuries. When proved,

10. *Smith v. Cutter Biological, Inc.,* 72 Haw. 416, 823 P.2d 717 (1991); *Sutowski v. Eli Lilly & Co.,* 82 Ohio St.3d 347, 696 N.E.2d 187 (1998); and *In re Methyl Tertiary Butyl Ether ("MTBE") Products Liability Litigation,* 447 F.Supp.2d 289 (S.D.N.Y. 2006).

11. For the Illinois Supreme Court's position on market-share liability, see *Smith v. Eli Lilly & Co.,* 137 Ill.2d 222, 560 N.E.2d 324 (1990). Pennsylvania law also does not recognize market-share liability. See *Bortell v. Eli Lilly & Co.,* 406 F.Supp.2d 1 (D.D.C. 2005).

12. See, for example, *Edmondson v. Macclesfield L-P Gas Co.,* 642 S.E.2d 265 (N.C.App. 2007); and *Pichardo v. C. S. Brown Co.,* 35 A.D.3d 303, 827 N.Y.S.2d 131 (N.Y.App. 2006).

13. See, for example, *State Farm Insurance Companies v. Premier Manufactured Systems, Inc.,* 213 Ariz. 419, 142 P.3d 1232 (2006); and *Ready v. United/Goedecke Services, Inc.,* 367 Ill.App.3d 272, 854 N.E.2d 758 (2006).

comparative negligence does not completely absolve the defendant of liability (as do other defenses), but it can reduce the total amount of damages that will be awarded to the plaintiff.

Note that some jurisdictions allow only intentional conduct to affect a plaintiff's recovery, whereas other states allow ordinary negligence to be used as a defense to product liability. For example, Dan Smith, a mechanic in Alaska, was not wearing a hard hat at work when he was asked to start the diesel engine of an air compressor. Because the compressor was an older model, he had to prop open a door to start it. When he got the engine started, the door fell from its position and hit Smith's head. The injury caused him to suffer from seizures and epilepsy. Smith sued the manufacturer, claiming that the engine was defectively designed. The manufacturer contended that Smith had been negligent by failing to wear a hard hat and propping open the door in an unsafe manner. Smith's attorney argued that ordinary negligence could not be used as a defense in product liability cases. The Alaska Supreme Court ruled that defendants in product liability actions can raise the plaintiff's ordinary negligence to reduce their liability proportionately.[14]

Commonly Known Dangers

The dangers associated with certain products (such as matches and sharp knives) are so commonly known that, as already mentioned, manufacturers need not warn users of those dangers. If a defendant succeeds in convincing the court that a plaintiff's injury resulted from a *commonly known danger,* the defendant will not be liable.

A classic case on this issue involved a plaintiff who was injured when an elastic exercise rope she had purchased slipped off her foot and struck her in the eye, causing a detachment of the retina. The plaintiff claimed that the manufacturer should be liable because it had failed to warn users that the exerciser might slip off a foot in such a manner. The court stated that to hold the manufacturer liable in these circumstances "would go beyond the reasonable dictates of justice in fixing the liabilities of manufacturers." After all, stated the court, "[a]lmost every physical object can be inherently dangerous or potentially dangerous in a sense. . . . A manufacturer cannot manufacture a knife that will not cut or a hammer that will not mash a thumb or a stove that will not burn a finger. The law does not require [manufacturers] to warn of such common dangers."[15]

Knowledgeable User

A related defense is the *knowledgeable user* defense. If a particular danger (such as electrical shock) is or should be commonly known by particular users of a product (such as electricians), the manufacturer need not warn these users of the danger.

In one case, for example, the parents of a group of teenagers who had become overweight and developed health problems filed a product liability suit against McDonald's. The teenagers claimed that the well-known fast-food chain should be held liable for failing to warn customers of the adverse health effects of eating its food products. The court rejected this claim, however, based on the *knowledgeable user defense.* The court found that it is well known that the food at McDonald's contains high levels of cholesterol, fat, salt, and sugar and is therefore unhealthful. The court's opinion, which thwarted future lawsuits against fast-food restaurants, stated: "If consumers know (or reasonably should know) the potential ill health effects of eating at McDonald's, they cannot blame McDonald's if they, nonetheless, choose to satiate their appetite with a surfeit [excess] of supersized McDonald's products."[16]

Statutes of Limitations and Repose

As previously discussed, statutes of limitations restrict the time within which an action may be brought. The statute of limitations for product liability cases varies according to state law, and unlike warranty claims, product liability claims are not subject to the UCC's limitation period. Usually, the injured party must bring a product liability claim within two to four years. Often, the running of the prescribed period is *tolled* (that is, suspended) until the party suffering an injury has discovered it or should have discovered it. To ensure that sellers and manufacturers will not be left vulnerable to lawsuits indefinitely, many states have passed laws, called **statutes of repose,** that place *outer* time limits on product liability actions. For example, a statute of repose may require that claims be brought within twelve years from the date of sale or manufacture of the defective product. If the plaintiff does not bring an action before the prescribed period expires, the seller cannot be held liable.

14. *Smith v. Ingersoll-Rand Co.,* 14 P.3d 990 (Alaska 2000).

15. *Jamieson v. Woodward & Lothrop,* 247 F.2d 23 (D.C. Cir. 1957).

16. *Pelman v. McDonald's Corp.,* 237 F.Supp.2d 512 (S.D.N.Y. 2003).

REVIEWING Strict Liability and Product Liability

Shalene Kolchek bought a Great Lakes spa from Val Porter, a dealer who was selling spas at the state fair. Kolchek signed an installment contract; then Porter and Kolchek arranged for the spa to be delivered and installed for her the next day. Three months later, Kolchek left her six-year-old daughter, Litisha, alone in the spa. While exploring the spa's hydromassage jets, Litisha stuck her index finger into one of the jet holes and was unable to remove her finger from the jet. Litisha yanked hard, injuring her finger, then panicked and screamed for help. Kolchek was unable to remove Litisha's finger, and the local police and rescue team were called to assist. After a three-hour operation that included draining the spa, sawing out a section of the spa's plastic molding, and slicing the jet casing, Litisha's finger was freed. Following this procedure, the spa was no longer functional. Litisha was taken to the local emergency room, where she was told that a bone in her finger was broken in two places. Using the information presented in the chapter, answer the following questions.

1. Under which theory or theories of product liability can Kolchek sue to recover for Litisha's injuries? Could Kolchek sue Porter or Great Lakes?
2. Would privity of contract be required for Kolchek to succeed in a product liability action against Great Lakes?
3. For an action in strict product liability against Great Lakes, what six requirements must Kolchek meet?
4. What defenses to product liability might Porter or Great Lakes be able to assert?

TERMS AND CONCEPTS

bystanders 320
market-share liability 331
privity of contract 323
product liability 320
product misuse 331
statute of repose 332
strict liability 320
unreasonably dangerous product 325

QUESTIONS AND CASE PROBLEMS

13-1. Chen buys a television set manufactured by Quality TV Appliance, Inc. She is going on vacation, so she takes the set to her mother's house for her mother to use. Because the set is defective, it explodes, causing her mother to be seriously injured. Chen's mother sues Quality to obtain compensation for her injury and for the damage to her house. Under what theory or theories discussed in this chapter might Chen's mother recover damages from Quality?

13-2. QUESTION WITH SAMPLE ANSWER

Colt manufactures a new pistol. The firing of the pistol depends on an enclosed high-pressure device. The pistol has been thoroughly tested in two laboratories in the Midwest, and its design and manufacture are in accord with current technology. Wayne purchases one of the new pistols from Hardy's Gun and Rifle Emporium. When he uses the pistol in the high altitude of the Rockies, the difference in pressure causes the pistol to misfire, resulting in serious injury to Wayne. Colt can prove that all due care was used in the manufacturing process, and it refuses to pay for Wayne's injuries. Discuss Colt's liability in tort.

- **For a sample answer to Question 13-2, go to Appendix I at the end of this text.**

13-3. A water pipe burst, flooding a company's switchboard and tripping the switchboard circuit breakers. Company employees assigned to reactivate the switchboard included an electrical technician with twelve years of on-the-job training, a licensed electrician, and an electrical engineer who had studied power engineering in college and had twenty years of experience. The employees attempted to switch one of the circuit breakers back on without testing for short circuits, which they later admitted they knew how to do and should have done. The circuit breaker failed to engage but ignited an explosive fire. The company sued the supplier of the circuit breakers for damages, alleging that the supplier had failed to give adequate warnings and instructions regarding the circuit breakers. How might the supplier defend against this claim? Discuss.

13–4. Gina is standing on a street corner waiting for a ride to work. Gomez has just purchased a new car manufactured by Optimal Motors. He is driving down the street when suddenly the steering mechanism breaks, causing him to run over Gina. Gina suffers permanent injuries. Gomez's total income per year has never exceeded $15,000. Thus, instead of suing Gomez, Gina files suit against Optimal under the theory of strict liability in tort. Optimal claims that it is not liable because (1) due care was used in the manufacture of the car, (2) Optimal is not the manufacturer of the steering mechanism (Smith is), and (3) strict product liability applies only to users or consumers, and Gina is neither. Discuss the validity of the defenses claimed by Optimal.

13–5. Baxter manufactures electric hair dryers. Julie purchases a Baxter dryer from her local Ace Drugstore. Cox, a friend and guest in Julie's home, has taken a shower and wants to dry her hair. Julie tells Cox to use the new Baxter hair dryer that she has just purchased. As Cox plugs in the dryer, sparks fly out from the motor, and sparks continue to fly as she operates it. Despite this, Cox begins drying her hair. Suddenly, the entire dryer ignites into flames, severely burning Cox's scalp. Cox sues Baxter on the basis of negligence and strict liability in tort. Baxter admits that the dryer was defective but denies liability, particularly because Cox was not the person who purchased the dryer. In other words, Cox had no contractual relationship with Baxter. Discuss the validity of Baxter's defense. Are there any other defenses that Baxter might assert to avoid liability? Discuss fully.

13–6. Liability to Third Parties. Lee Stegemoller was a union member who insulated large machinery between 1947 and 1988. During his career, he worked for a number of different companies. Stegemoller primarily worked with asbestos insulation, which was used on industrial boilers, engines, furnaces, and turbines. After he left a work site, some of the asbestos dust always remained on his clothing. His wife, Ramona, who laundered his work clothes, was also exposed to the dust on a daily basis. Allegedly, as a result of this contact, she was diagnosed with colon cancer, pulmonary fibrosis, and pleural thickening in April 1998. The Stegemollers filed a suit in an Indiana state court against ACandS, Inc., and thirty-three others, contending among other things that the asbestos originated from products attributable to some of the defendants and from the premises of other defendants. Several defendants filed a motion to dismiss the complaint, asserting that Ramona was not a "user or consumer" of asbestos because she was not in the vicinity of the product when it was used. Should the court dismiss the suit on this basis? Explain. [*Stegemoller v. ACandS, Inc.*, 767 N.E.2d 974 (Ind. 2002)]

13–7. Product Liability. In January 1999, John Clark of Clarksdale, Mississippi, bought a paintball gun. Clark practiced with the gun and knew how to screw in the carbon dioxide cartridge, pump the gun, and use its safety and trigger. He hunted and had taken a course in hunter safety education. He knew that protective eyewear was available for purchase, but he chose not to buy it. Clark also understood that it was "common sense" not to shoot anyone in the face. Chris Rico, another Clarksdale resident, owned a paintball gun made by Brass Eagle, Inc. Rico was similarly familiar with the gun's use and its risks. At that time and place, Clark, Rico, and their friends played a game that involved shooting paintballs at cars whose occupants also had the guns. One night, while Clark and Rico were cruising with their guns, Rico shot at Clark's car but hit Clark in the eye. Clark filed a suit in a Mississippi state court against Brass Eagle to recover for the injury, alleging, among other things, that its gun was defectively designed. During the trial, Rico testified that his gun "never malfunctioned." In whose favor should the court rule? Why? [*Clark v. Brass Eagle, Inc.*, 866 So.2d 456 (Miss. 2004)]

13–8. CASE PROBLEM WITH SAMPLE ANSWER

Mary Jane Boerner began smoking in 1945 at the age of fifteen. For a short time, she smoked Lucky Strikes (a brand of cigarettes) before switching to the Pall Mall brand, which she smoked until she quit altogether in 1981. Pall Malls had higher levels of carcinogenic tar than other cigarettes and lacked effective filters, which would have reduced the amount of tar inhaled into the lungs. In 1996, Mary Jane developed lung cancer. She and her husband, Henry Boerner, filed a suit in a federal district court against Brown & Williamson Tobacco Co., the maker of Pall Malls. The Boerners claimed, among other things, that Pall Malls contained a design defect. Mary Jane died in 1999. According to Dr. Peter Marvin, her treating physician, she died from the effects of cigarette smoke. Henry continued the suit, offering evidence that Pall Malls featured a filter that actually increased the amount of tar taken into the body. When is a product defective in design? Does this product meet the requirements? Why or why not? [*Boerner v. Brown & Williamson Tobacco Co.*, 394 F.3d 594 (8th Cir. 2005)]

- **To view a sample answer for Problem 13–8, go to this book's Web site at academic.cengage.com/blaw/cross, select "Chapter 13," and click on "Case Problem with Sample Answer."**

13–9. Product Liability. Bret D'Auguste was an experienced skier when he rented equipment to ski at Hunter Mountain Ski Bowl, Inc., owned by Shanty Hollow Corp., in New York. The adjustable retention/release value for the bindings on the rented equipment was set at a level that, according to skiing industry standards, was too low—meaning that the skis would be released too easily—given D'Auguste's height, weight, and ability. When D'Auguste entered a "double black diamond," or extremely difficult, trail, he noticed immediately that the surface consisted of ice and virtually no snow. He tried to exit the steeply declining trail by making a sharp right turn, but in the attempt, his left ski snapped off. D'Auguste lost his balance, fell, and slid down the mountain, striking his face and head against a fence along the trail. According to a report by a rental shop employee, one of the bindings on D'Auguste's skis had a "cracked heel housing." D'Auguste filed a suit in a New York state court against Shanty Hollow and others, including the bindings' manufacturer, on a theory of strict product liability. The manufacturer filed a motion for summary judgment. On what basis might the court *grant* the motion? On what basis might the court *deny* the motion? How should the court rule? Explain. [*D'Auguste v. Shanty Hollow Corp.*, 26 A.D.3d 403, 809 N.Y.S.2d 555 (2 Dept. 2006)]

13-10. A QUESTION OF ETHICS

Susan Calles lived with her four daughters, Amanda, age 11, Victoria, age 5, and Jenna and Jillian, age 3. In March 1998, Calles bought an Aim N Flame utility lighter, which she stored on the top shelf of her kitchen cabinet. A trigger can ignite the Aim N Flame after an "ON/OFF" switch is slid to the "on" position. On the night of March 31, Calles and Victoria left to get videos. Jenna and Jillian were in bed, and Amanda was watching television. Calles returned to find fire trucks and emergency vehicles around her home. Robert Finn, a fire investigator, determined that Jenna had started a fire using the lighter. Jillian suffered smoke inhalation, was hospitalized, and died on April 21. Calles filed a suit in an Illinois state court against Scripto-Tokai Corp., which distributed the Aim N Flame, and others. In her suit, which was grounded, in part, in strict liability claims, Calles alleged that the lighter was an "unreasonably dangerous product." Scripto filed a motion for summary judgment. [Calles v. Scripto-Tokai Corp., *224 Ill.2d 247, 864 N.E.2d 249, 309 Ill.Dec. 383 (2007)]*

(a) A product is "unreasonably dangerous" when it is dangerous beyond the expectation of the ordinary consumer. Whose expectation—Calles's or Jenna's—applies here? Why? Does the lighter pass this test? Explain.

(b) A product is also "unreasonably dangerous" when a less dangerous alternative was economically feasible for its maker, who failed to produce it. Scripto contended that because its product was "simple" and the danger was "obvious," it should be excepted from this test. Do you agree? Why or why not?

(c) Calles presented evidence as to the likelihood and seriousness of injury from lighters that do not have child-safety devices. Scripto argued that the Aim N Flame is a useful, inexpensive, alternative source of fire and is safer than a match. Calles admitted that she was aware of the dangers presented by lighters in the hands of children. Scripto admitted that it had been a defendant in at least twenty-five suits for injuries that occurred under similar circumstances. With these factors in mind, how should the court rule? Why?

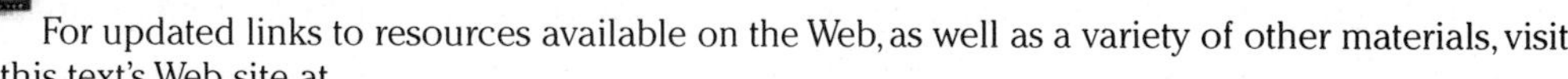

LAW ON THE WEB

For updated links to resources available on the Web, as well as a variety of other materials, visit this text's Web site at

academic.cengage.com/blaw/cross

The Federal Trade Commission posts *A Businessperson's Guide to Federal Warranty Law* at

www.ftc.gov/bcp/conline/pubs/buspubs/warranty.htm

For information on product liability suits against tobacco companies, go to the Web site of the Library & Center for Knowledge Management, which is maintained by the University of California–San Francisco, at

library.ucsf.edu/tobacco/litigation

Legal Research Exercises on the Web

Go to **academic.cengage.com/blaw/cross**, the Web site that accompanies this text. Select "Chapter 13" and click on "Internet Exercises." There you will find the following Internet research exercises that you can perform to learn more about the topics covered in this chapter.

Internet Exercise 13–1: Legal Perspective
Product Liability Litigation

Internet Exercise 13–2: Management Perspective
The Duty to Warn

CHAPTER 14

Intellectual Property and Internet Law

Most people think of wealth in terms of houses, land, cars, stocks, and bonds. Wealth, however, also includes **intellectual property,** which consists of the products that result from intellectual, creative processes. Although it is an abstract term for an abstract concept, intellectual property is nonetheless wholly familiar to virtually everyone. *Trademarks, service marks, copyrights,* and *patents* are all forms of intellectual property. The book you are reading is copyrighted. The software you use, the movies you see, and the music you listen to are all forms of intellectual property. We provide a comprehensive synopsis of these forms of intellectual property, as well as intellectual property that consists of *trade secrets,* in *Concept Summary 14.1* on page 358. In this chapter, we examine each of these forms in some detail.

Intellectual property has taken on increasing significance globally as well as in the United States. Today, the value of the world's intellectual property probably exceeds the value of physical property, such as machines and houses. For many U.S. companies, ownership rights in intangible intellectual property are more important to their prosperity than are their tangible assets. As you will read in this chapter, a pressing issue for businesspersons today is how to protect these valuable rights in the online world.

The need to protect creative works was voiced by the framers of the U.S. Constitution over two hundred years ago: Article I, Section 8, of the U.S. Constitution authorized Congress "[t]o promote the Progress of Science and useful Arts, by securing for limited Times to Authors and Inventors the exclusive Right to their respective Writings and Discoveries." Laws protecting patents, trademarks, and copyrights are explicitly designed to protect and reward inventive and artistic creativity. Although intellectual property law limits the economic freedom of some individuals, it does so to protect the freedom of others to enjoy the fruits of their labors—in the form of profits.

Trademarks and Related Property

A **trademark** is a distinctive mark, motto, device, or implement that a manufacturer stamps, prints, or otherwise affixes to the goods it produces so that they can be identified on the market and their origins made known. In other words, a trademark is a source indicator. At common law, the person who used a symbol or mark to identify a business or product was protected in the use of that trademark. Clearly, by using another's trademark, a business could lead consumers to believe that its goods were made by the other business. The law seeks to avoid this kind of confusion. In this section, we examine various aspects of the law governing trademarks.

In the following classic case concerning Coca-Cola, the defendants argued that the Coca-Cola trademark was entitled to no protection under the law because the term did not accurately represent the product.

CASE 14.1 The Coca-Cola Co. v. The Koke Co. of America

Supreme Court of the United States, 1920. 254 U.S. 143, 41 S.Ct. 113, 65 L.Ed. 189.
www.findlaw.com/casecode/supreme.html[a]

• **Company Profile** John Pemberton, an Atlanta pharmacist, invented a caramel-colored, carbonated soft drink in 1886. His bookkeeper, Frank Robinson, named the beverage Coca-Cola after two of the ingredients, coca leaves and kola nuts. Asa Candler bought the Coca-Cola Company (**www.cocacolacompany.com**) in 1891, and within seven years, he made the soft drink available in all of the United States, as well as in parts of Canada and Mexico. Candler continued to sell Coke aggressively and to open up new markets, reaching Europe before 1910. In doing so, however, he attracted numerous competitors, some of which tried to capitalize directly on the Coke name.

• **Background and Facts** The Coca-Cola Company sought to enjoin (prevent) the Koke Company of America and other beverage companies from, among other things, using the word *Koke* for their products. The Koke Company of America and other beverage companies contended that the Coca-Cola trademark was a fraudulent representation and that Coca-Cola was therefore not entitled to any help from the courts. The Koke Company and the other defendants alleged that the Coca-Cola Company, by its use of the Coca-Cola name, represented that the beverage contained cocaine (from coca leaves), which it no longer did. The trial court granted the injunction against the Koke Company, but the appellate court reversed the lower court's ruling. Coca-Cola then appealed to the United States Supreme Court.

IN THE LANGUAGE OF THE COURT
Mr. Justice *HOLMES* delivered the opinion of the Court.

* * * *

* * * Before 1900 the beginning of [Coca-Cola's] good will was more or less helped by the presence of cocaine, a drug that, like alcohol or caffeine or opium, may be described as a deadly poison or as a valuable [pharmaceutical item, depending on the speaker's purposes]. The amount seems to have been very small,[b] but it may have been enough to begin a bad habit and after the Food and Drug Act of June 30, 1906, if not earlier, long before this suit was brought, it was eliminated from the plaintiff's compound.

* * * Since 1900 the sales have increased at a very great rate corresponding to a like increase in advertising. The name now characterizes a beverage to be had at almost any soda fountain. It means a single thing coming from a single source, and well known to the community. It hardly would be too much to say that the drink characterizes the name as much as the name the drink. In other words *Coca-Cola probably means to most persons the plaintiff's familiar product to be had everywhere rather than a compound of particular substances.* * * * Before this suit was brought the plaintiff had advertised to the public that it must not expect and would not find cocaine, and had eliminated everything tending to suggest cocaine effects except the name and the picture of [coca] leaves and nuts, which probably conveyed little or nothing to most who saw it. It appears to us that it would be going too far to deny the plaintiff relief against a palpable [readily evident] fraud because possibly here and there an ignorant person might call for the drink with the hope for incipient cocaine intoxication. The plaintiff's position must be judged by the facts as they were when the suit was begun, not by the facts of a different condition and an earlier time. [Emphasis added.]

• **Decision and Remedy** *The district court's injunction was allowed to stand. The competing beverage companies were enjoined from calling their products Koke.*

---

a. This is the "U.S. Supreme Court Opinions" page within the Web site of the "FindLaw Internet Legal Resources" database. This page provides several options for accessing an opinion. Because you know the citation for this case, you can go to the "Citation Search" box, type in the appropriate volume and page numbers for the *United States Reports* ("254" and "143," respectively, for the *Coca-Cola* case), and click on "get it."

b. In reality, until 1903 the amount of active cocaine in each bottle of Coke was equivalent to one "line" of cocaine.

CASE CONTINUES

CASE 14.1 CONTINUED

- **Impact of This Case on Today's Law** *In this early case, the United States Supreme Court made it clear that trademarks and trade names (and nicknames for those marks and names, such as the nickname "Coke" for "Coca-Cola") that are in common use receive protection under the common law. This holding is significant historically because it is the predecessor to the federal statute later passed to protect trademark rights—the Lanham Act of 1946, to be discussed next. In many ways, this act represented a codification of common law principles governing trademarks.*

- **What If the Facts Were Different?** *Suppose that Coca-Cola had been trying to make the public believe that its product contained cocaine. Would the result in this case likely have been different? Why or why not?*

Statutory Protection of Trademarks

Statutory protection of trademarks and related property is provided at the federal level by the Lanham Act of 1946.[1] The Lanham Act was enacted, in part, to protect manufacturers from losing business to rival companies that used confusingly similar trademarks. The Lanham Act incorporates the common law of trademarks and provides remedies for owners of trademarks who wish to enforce their claims in federal court. Many states also have trademark statutes.

Trademark Dilution In 1995, Congress amended the Lanham Act by passing the Federal Trademark Dilution Act,[2] which extended the protection available to trademark owners by allowing them to bring a suit in federal court for trademark **dilution**. Until the passage of this amendment, federal trademark law prohibited only the unauthorized use of the same mark on competing—or on noncompeting but "related"—goods or services when such use would likely confuse consumers as to the origin of those goods and services. Trademark dilution laws protect "distinctive" or "famous" trademarks (such as Jergens, McDonald's, Dell, and Apple) from certain unauthorized uses even when the use is on noncompeting goods or is unlikely to confuse. More than half of the states have also enacted trademark dilution laws.

Use of a Similar Mark May Constitute Trademark Dilution A famous mark may be diluted not only by the use of an *identical* mark but also by the use of a *similar* mark. In 2003, however, the United States Supreme Court ruled that to constitute dilution, the similar mark must reduce the value of the famous mark or lessen its ability to identify goods and services. Therefore, lingerie maker Victoria's Secret could not establish a dilution claim against a small adult store named "Victor's Little Secret" because there was not enough evidence that Victoria's Secret's mark would be diminished in value.[3]

A similar mark is more likely to lessen the value of a famous mark when the companies using the marks provide related goods or compete against each other in the same market. For example, a woman was operating a coffee shop under the name "Sambuck's Coffeehouse" in Astoria, Oregon, even though she knew that "Starbucks" is one of the largest coffee chains in the nation. When Starbucks Corporation filed a dilution lawsuit, the federal court ruled that use of the "Sambuck's" mark constituted trademark dilution because it created confusion for consumers. Not only was there a "high degree" of similarity between the marks, but also both companies provided coffee-related services and marketed their services through "stand-alone" retail stores. Therefore, the use of the similar mark (Sambuck's) reduced the value of the famous mark (Starbucks).[4]

Trademark Registration

Trademarks may be registered with the state or with the federal government. To register for protection under federal trademark law, a person must file an application with the U.S. Patent and Trademark Office in Washington, D.C. Under current law, a mark can be registered (1) if it is currently in commerce or (2) if the applicant intends to put it into commerce within six months.

In special circumstances, the six-month period can be extended by thirty months, giving the applicant a total of three years from the date of notice of trademark approval to make use of the mark and file the required use statement. Registration is postponed until the mark is actually used. Nonetheless, during this waiting period, any applicant can legally protect his or her

1. 15 U.S.C. Sections 1051–1128.
2. 15 U.S.C. Section 1125.
3. *Moseley v. V Secret Catalogue, Inc.*, 537 U.S. 418, 123 S.Ct. 1115, 155 L.Ed.2d 1 (2003). (A different case involving Victoria's Secret's trademark is presented as Case 14.2 on pages 339–341.)
4. *Starbucks Corp. v. Lundberg*, 2005 WL 3183858 (D.Or. 2005).

trademark against a third party who previously has neither used the mark nor filed an application for it. Registration is renewable between the fifth and sixth years after the initial registration and every ten years thereafter (every twenty years for those trademarks registered before 1990).

Trademark Infringement

Registration of a trademark with the U.S. Patent and Trademark Office gives notice on a nationwide basis that the trademark belongs exclusively to the registrant. The registrant is also allowed to use the symbol ® to indicate that the mark has been registered. Whenever that trademark is copied to a substantial degree or used in its entirety by another, intentionally or unintentionally, the trademark has been *infringed* (used without authorization). When a trademark has been infringed, the owner of the mark has a cause of action against the infringer. To sue for trademark infringement, a person need not have registered the trademark, but registration does furnish proof of the date of inception of the trademark's use.

A central objective of the Lanham Act is to reduce the likelihood that consumers will be confused by similar marks. For that reason, only those trademarks that are deemed sufficiently distinctive from all competing trademarks will be protected.

Distinctiveness of Mark

A trademark must be sufficiently distinct to enable consumers to identify the manufacturer of the goods easily and to distinguish between those goods and competing products.

Strong Marks Fanciful, arbitrary, or suggestive trademarks are generally considered to be the most distinctive (strongest) trademarks. Marks that are fanciful, arbitrary, or suggestive are protected as inherently distinctive without demonstrating secondary meaning. These marks receive automatic protection because they serve to identify a particular product's source, as opposed to describing the product itself.

Fanciful trademarks include invented words, such as "Xerox" for one manufacturer's copiers and "Kodak" for another company's photographic products. Arbitrary trademarks are those that use common words in an uncommon way that is nondescriptive, such as "English Leather" used as a name for an after-shave lotion (and not for leather processed in England). Suggestive trademarks imply something about a product without describing the product directly. For example, the trademark "Dairy Queen" suggests an association between the products and milk, but it does not directly describe ice cream.

Secondary Meaning Descriptive terms, geographic terms, and personal names are not inherently distinctive and do not receive protection under the law until they acquire a secondary meaning. A secondary meaning may arise when customers begin to associate a specific term or phrase (such as London Fog) with specific trademarked items (coats with "London Fog" labels). Whether a secondary meaning becomes attached to a term or name usually depends on how extensively the product is advertised, the market for the product, the number of sales, and other factors.

Once a secondary meaning is attached to a term or name, a trademark is considered distinctive and is protected. The United States Supreme Court has held that even a color can qualify for trademark protection, once customers associate that color with the product.[5] In 2006, a federal court held that trademark law protects the particular color schemes used by the sports teams of four state universities, including Ohio State University and Louisiana State University.[6]

At issue in the following case was whether a certain mark was suggestive or descriptive.

5. *Qualitex Co. v. Jacobson Products Co.*, 514 U.S. 159, 115 S.Ct. 1300, 131 L.Ed.2d 248 (1995).

6. *Board of Supervisors of Louisiana State University v. Smack Apparel Co.*, 438 F.Supp.2d 653 (E.D.La.2006).

CASE 14.2 Menashe v. V Secret Catalogue, Inc.

United States District Court, Southern District of New York, 2006. 409 F.Supp.2d 412.

• **Background and Facts** In autumn 2002, Victoria's Secret Stores, Inc., and its affiliated companies, including V Secret Catalogue, Inc., began to develop a panty collection to be named "SEXY LITTLE THINGS." In spring 2004, Ronit Menashe, a publicist, and Audrey Quock, a fashion model and actress, began to plan a line of women's underwear also called "SEXY LITTLE THINGS." Menashe and

CASE CONTINUES

CASE 14.2 CONTINUED Quock designed their line, negotiated for its manufacture, registered the domain name **www.sexylittlethings.com**, and filed an intent-to-use (ITU) application with the U.S. Patent and Trademark Office (USPTO). In July, Victoria's Secret's collection appeared in its stores in Ohio, Michigan, and California, and, in less than three months, was prominently displayed in all its stores, in its catalogues, and on its Web site. By mid-November, more than 13 million units of the line had been sold, accounting for 4 percent of the company's sales for the year. When the firm applied to register "SEXY LITTLE THINGS" with the USPTO, it learned of Menashe and Quock's ITU application. The firm warned the pair that their use of the phrase constituted trademark infringement. Menashe and Quock filed a suit in a federal district court against V Secret Catalogue and others, asking the court to, among other things, declare "non-infringement of the trademark."

IN THE LANGUAGE OF THE COURT
***BAER*, District Judge.**

* * * *

Plaintiffs claim that Victoria's Secret has no right of priority in the Mark because "SEXY LITTLE THINGS" for lingerie is a descriptive term that had not attained secondary meaning by the time Plaintiffs filed their ITU application. Consequently, Plaintiffs assert that they have priority based on * * * their ITU application on September 13, 2004. Victoria's Secret counters that the Mark is suggestive and thus qualifies for trademark protection without proof of secondary meaning. Therefore, Victoria's Secret has priority by virtue of its *bona fide* use of the Mark in commerce beginning July 28, 2004.

* * * *

To merit trademark protection, a mark must be capable of distinguishing the products it marks from those of others. * * * A descriptive term * * * conveys an immediate idea of the ingredients, qualities or characteristics of the goods. In contrast, a suggestive term requires imagination, thought and perception to reach a conclusion as to the nature of the goods. *Suggestive marks are automatically protected because they are inherently distinctive, i.e., their intrinsic nature serves to identify a particular source of a product.* Descriptive marks are not inherently distinctive and may only be protected on a showing of secondary meaning, i.e., that the purchasing public associates the mark with a particular source. [Emphasis added.]

* * * To distinguish suggestive from descriptive marks [a court considers] whether the purchaser must use some imagination to connect the mark to some characteristic of the product * * * and * * * whether the proposed use would deprive competitors of a way to describe their goods.

* * * I find "SEXY LITTLE THINGS" to be suggestive. First, while the term describes the erotically stimulating quality of the trademarked lingerie, it also calls to mind the phrase "sexy little thing" popularly used to refer to attractive lithe young women. Hence, the Mark prompts the purchaser to mentally associate the lingerie with its targeted twenty- to thirty-year-old consumers. *Courts have classified marks that both describe the product and evoke other associations as inherently distinctive.* * * * [Also] it is hard to believe that Victoria's Secret's use of the Mark will deprive competitors of ways to describe their lingerie products. Indeed, Victoria's Secret's own descriptions of its lingerie in its catalogues and Web site illustrate that there are numerous ways to describe provocative underwear. [Emphasis added.]

* * * *

* * * Victoria's Secret used "SEXY LITTLE THINGS" as a trademark in commerce beginning on July 28, 2004. Commencing on that date, the prominent use of the Mark in four stores * * * satisfies the "use in commerce" requirement * * * . Similarly, Victoria's Secret's prominent use of the Mark in its catalogues beginning on September 4, 2004, and on its Web site beginning on or about September 9, 2004, together with pictures and descriptions of the goods meets the * * * test * * * . I find that because Victoria's Secret made *bona fide* trademark use of "SEXY LITTLE THINGS" in commerce before Plaintiffs filed their ITU application, and has continued to use that Mark in commerce, Victoria's Secret has acquired priority in the Mark.

• **Decision and Remedy** *The district court ruled that Menashe and Quock were not entitled to a judgment of "non-infringement" and dismissed their complaint. The court concluded that "SEXY*

CASE 14.2 CONTINUED *LITTLE THINGS" was a suggestive mark and that Victoria's Secret had used it in commerce before the plaintiffs filed their ITU application. For this reason, Victoria's Secret had "priority in the Mark."*

- **The E-Commerce Dimension** *Under the reasoning of the court in this case, would the use of a purported trademark solely on a Web site satisfy the "use in commerce" requirement? Explain.*

- **The Legal Environment Dimension** *Why is it important to allow those who have applied for trademark protection—in this case, ITU applicants Menashe and Quock—to defend preemptively against the use of the mark by another party? (Hint: Why were Menashe and Quock seeking a court declaration of "non-infringement of a trademark"?)*

Generic Terms Generic terms that refer to an entire class of products, such as *bicycle* and *computer,* receive no protection, even if they acquire secondary meanings. A particularly thorny problem arises when a trademark acquires generic use. For example, *aspirin* and *thermos* were originally the names of trademarked products, but today the words are used generically. Other examples are *escalator, trampoline, raisin bran, dry ice, lanolin, linoleum, nylon,* and *corn flakes.*

Sometimes, a company's use of a particular phrase becomes so closely associated with that company that the firm claims it should be protected under trademark law. In one case, for example, America Online, Inc. (AOL), sued AT&T Corporation, claiming that AT&T's use of "You Have Mail" on its WorldNet Service infringed AOL's trademark rights in the same phrase. The court ruled, however, that because each of the three words in the phrase was a generic term, the phrase as a whole was generic. Although the phrase had become widely associated with AOL's e-mail notification service, and thus might have acquired a secondary meaning, this issue was of no significance in the case. The court stated that it would not consider whether the mark had acquired any secondary meaning because "generic marks with secondary meaning are still not entitled to protection."[7]

Trade Dress

The term **trade dress** refers to the image and overall appearance of a product. Trade dress is a broad concept and can include either all or part of the total image or overall impression created by a product or its packaging. For example, the distinctive decor, menu, layout, and style of service of a particular restaurant may be regarded as trade dress. Trade dress can also include the layout and appearance of a catalogue, the use of a lighthouse as part of the design of a golf hole, the fish shape of a cracker, or the G-shaped design of a Gucci watch.

Basically, trade dress is subject to the same protection as trademarks. In cases involving trade dress infringement, as in trademark infringement cases, a major consideration is whether consumers are likely to be confused by the allegedly infringing use.

Service, Certification, and Collective Marks

A **service mark** is essentially a trademark that is used to distinguish the *services* (rather than the products) of one person or company from those of another. For example, each airline has a particular mark or symbol associated with its name. Titles and character names used in radio and television are frequently registered as service marks.

Other marks protected by law include certification marks and collective marks. A **certification mark** is used by one or more persons, other than the owner, to certify the region, materials, mode of manufacture, quality, or other characteristic of specific goods or services. When used by members of a cooperative, association, or other organization, it is referred to as a **collective mark.** Examples of certification marks are the phrases "Good Housekeeping Seal of Approval" and "UL Tested." Collective marks appear at the ends of motion picture credits to indicate the various associations and organizations that participated in the making of the films. The union marks found on the tags of certain products are also collective marks.

Counterfeit Goods

Counterfeit goods copy or otherwise imitate trademarked goods but are not genuine. The importation of goods that bear a counterfeit (fake) trademark poses a growing problem for U.S. businesses, consumers, and law enforcement. In addition to having

7. *America Online, Inc. v. AT&T Corp.,* 243 F.3d 812 (4th Cir. 2001).

negative financial effects on legitimate businesses, sales of certain counterfeit goods, such as pharmaceuticals and nutritional supplements, can present serious public health risks. It is estimated that nearly 7 percent of the goods imported into the United States from abroad are counterfeit.

Stop Counterfeiting in Manufactured Goods Act In 2006, Congress enacted the Stop Counterfeiting in Manufactured Goods Act[8] (SCMGA) to combat the growing problem of counterfeit goods. The act makes it a crime to intentionally traffic in or attempt to traffic in counterfeit goods or services, or to knowingly use a counterfeit mark on or in connection with goods or services. Prior to this act, the law did not prohibit the creation or shipment of counterfeit labels that were not attached to any product.[9] Therefore, counterfeiters would make labels and packaging bearing another's trademark, ship the labels to another location, and then affix them to an inferior product to deceive buyers. The SCMGA has closed this loophole by making it a crime to knowingly traffic in or attempt to traffic in counterfeit labels, stickers, packaging, and the like, regardless of whether the item is attached to any goods.

Penalties for Counterfeiting Persons found guilty of violating the SCMGA may be fined up to $2 million or imprisoned for up to ten years (or more if they are repeat offenders). If a court finds that the statute was violated, it must order the defendant to forfeit the counterfeit products (which are then destroyed), as well as any property used in the commission of the crime. The defendant must also pay restitution to the trademark holder or victim in an amount equal to the victim's actual loss. For example, in one case the defendant pleaded guilty to conspiring with others to import cigarette-rolling papers from Mexico that were falsely marked as "Zig-Zags" and sell them in the United States. The court sentenced the defendant to prison and ordered him to pay $566,267 in restitution. On appeal, the court affirmed the prison sentence but reversed the restitution because the amount exceeded the amount of actual loss suffered by the legitimate sellers of Zig-Zag rolling papers.[10]

8. Pub. L. No. 109-181 (2006), which amended 18 U.S.C. Sections 2318–2320.

9. See, for example, *United States v. Giles,* 213 F.3d 1247 (10th Cir. 2000).

10. For a case discussing the appropriate measure of restitution, see *United States v. Beydoun,* 469 F.3d 102 (5th Cir. 2006).

Trade Names

Trademarks apply to *products.* The term **trade name** is used to indicate part or all of a business's name, whether the business is a sole proprietorship, a partnership, or a corporation. Generally, a trade name is directly related to a business and its goodwill. A trade name may be protected as a trademark if the trade name is also the name of the company's trademarked product—for example, Coca-Cola. Unless also used as a trademark or service mark, a trade name cannot be registered with the federal government. Trade names are protected under the common law, but only if they are unusual or fancifully used. The word *Safeway,* for example, was sufficiently fanciful to obtain protection as a trade name for a grocery chain.[11]

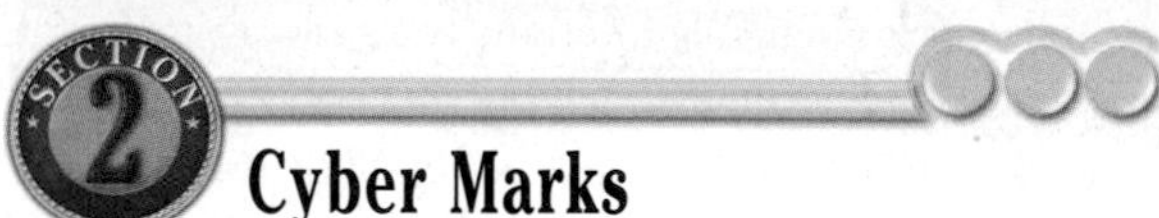

Cyber Marks

In cyberspace, trademarks are sometimes referred to as **cyber marks.** We turn now to a discussion of various trademark issues that are unique to cyberspace, such as domain names and cybersquatting, and how new laws and the courts are addressing these issues.

Domain Names

Conflicts over rights to domain names first emerged as e-commerce expanded on a worldwide scale and have reemerged in the last ten years. By using the same, or a similar, domain name, parties have attempted to profit from the goodwill of a competitor, sell pornography, offer for sale another party's domain name, and otherwise infringe on others' trademarks. A **domain name** is the core part of an Internet address—for example, "westlaw.com." It includes at least two parts. Every domain name ends with a generic top level domain (TLD), which is the part of the name to the right of the period. The TLD typically indicates the type of entity that operates the site. For example, *com* is an abbreviation for *commercial,* and *edu* is short for *education.* Although originally there were only six possible TLDs, several more generic TLDs are now available, some of which are not restricted to a particular type of entity (see Exhibit 14–1 for a list of generic TLDs and their uses).

The second level domain (SLD), which is the part of the name to the left of the period, is chosen by the

11. *Safeway Stores v. Suburban Foods,* 130 F.Supp. 249 (E.D.Va. 1955).

EXHIBIT 14–1 • Existing Generic Top Level Domain Names

.aero	Reserved for members of the air-transportation industry.
.asia	Restricted to the Pan-Asia and Asia Pacific community.
.biz	For businesses.
.cat	Reserved for the Catalan linguistic and cultural community.
.com	Originally intended for commercial organizations, but is now unrestricted in the United States.
.coop	Restricted to cooperative associations.
.edu	For postsecondary educational establishments.
.gov	Reserved for government agencies in the United States.
.info	For informational sites, but is unrestricted.
.int	Reserved for international organizations established by treaty.
.jobs	Reserved for human resource managers.
.mil	For the U.S. military.
.mobi	Reserved for consumers and providers of mobile products and services.
.museum	Reserved for museums.
.name	Reserved for individuals and families.
.net	Originally intended for network infrastructures, but is now unrestricted.
.org	Originally intended for noncommercial organizations, but is now unrestricted.
.pro	Restricted to certain credentialed professionals.
.tel	For business services involving connections between a telephone network and the Internet.
.travel	Reserved for the travel industry.

business entity or individual registering the domain name. Competition among firms with similar names and products for SLDs has caused numerous disputes over domain name rights. The Internet Corporation for Assigned Names and Numbers (ICANN), a nonprofit corporation, oversees the distribution of domain names. ICANN also facilitates the settlement of domain name disputes and operates an online arbitration system. In recent years, however, ICANN has been criticized for failing to keep up with the sheer volume of complaints involving domain names and accusations of cybersquatting. **Cybersquatting** occurs when a person registers a domain name that is the same as, or confusingly similar to, the trademark of another and then offers to sell the domain name back to the trademark owner.

Anticybersquatting Legislation

During the 1990s, cybersquatting led to so much litigation that Congress passed the Anticybersquatting Consumer Protection Act of 1999[12] (ACPA), which amended the Lanham Act—the federal law protecting trademarks discussed earlier. The ACPA makes it illegal for a person to "register, traffic in, or use" a domain name (1) if the name is identical or confusingly similar to the trademark of another and (2) if the one registering, trafficking in, or using the domain name has a "bad faith intent" to profit from that trademark.

The act does not define what constitutes bad faith. Instead, it lists several factors that courts can consider in deciding whether bad faith exists. For example, courts focus on the trademark rights of the other person and whether the alleged cybersquatter intended to divert consumers in a way that could harm the goodwill represented by the trademark. Courts also consider whether the alleged cybersquatter offered to transfer or sell the domain name to the trademark owner, or intended to use the domain name to offer goods and services.

The Ongoing Problem of Cybersquatting

The ACPA was intended to stamp out cybersquatting, but it continues to present a problem for businesses today, largely because, as mentioned, more TLDs are available and many more companies are registering domain names. Indeed, domain name registrars have proliferated. These companies charge a fee to businesses and individuals to register new names and to renew annual registrations (often through automated software). Many of these companies also buy and sell expired domain names. Although all domain name registrars are supposed to relay information about these transactions to ICANN and the other companies that keep a master list of domain names, this does not

12. 15 U.S.C. Section 1129.

always occur. The speed at which domain names change hands and the difficulty in tracking mass automated registrations have created an environment in which cybersquatting can flourish.

Cybersquatters have also developed new tactics, such as typosquatting, or registering a name that is a misspelling of a popular brand, such as hotmai.com or myspac.com. Because many Internet users are not perfect typists, Web pages using these misspelled names get a lot of traffic. More traffic generally means increased profit (advertisers often pay Web sites based on the number of unique visits, or hits), which in turn provides incentive for more cybersquatters. Also, if the misspelling is significant, the trademark owner may have difficulty proving that the name is identical or confusingly similar to the trademark of another, as the ACPA requires.

Cybersquatting is costly for businesses, which must attempt to register all variations of a name to protect their domain name rights from would-be cybersquatters. Large corporations may have to register thousands of domain names across the globe just to protect their basic brands and trademarks.

Applicability of the ACPA and Sanctions under the Act The ACPA applies to all domain name registrations. Successful plaintiffs in suits brought under the act can collect actual damages and profits, or they can elect to receive statutory damages ranging from $1,000 to $100,000.

Although some companies have been successful suing under the ACPA, there are roadblocks to succeeding in such lawsuits. Some domain name registrars offer privacy services that hide the true owners of Web sites, making it difficult for trademark owners to identify cybersquatters. Thus, before a trademark owner can bring a suit, he or she has to ask the court for a subpoena to discover the identity of the owner of the infringing Web site. Because of the high costs of court proceedings, discovery, and even arbitration, many disputes over cybersquatting are settled out of court. Some companies have found that simply purchasing the domain name from the cybersquatter is the least expensive solution.

Meta Tags

Search engines compile their results by looking through a Web site's key-word field. **Meta tags,** or key words, may be inserted into this field to increase the likelihood that a site will be included in search engine results, even though the site may have nothing to do with the inserted words. Using this same technique, one site may appropriate the key words of other sites with more frequent hits so that the appropriating site will appear in the same search engine results as the more popular sites. Using another's trademark in a meta tag without the owner's permission, however, normally constitutes trademark infringement.

Some uses of another's trademark as a meta tag may be permissible if the use is reasonably necessary and does not suggest that the owner authorized or sponsored the use. For example, Terri Welles, a former model who had been "Playmate of the Year" in *Playboy* magazine, established a Web site that used the terms *Playboy* and *Playmate* as meta tags. Playboy Enterprises, Inc. (PEI), which publishes *Playboy,* filed a suit seeking to prevent Welles from using these meta tags. The court determined that Welles's use of PEI's meta tags to direct users to her Web site was permissible because it did not suggest sponsorship and there were no descriptive substitutes for the terms *Playboy* and *Playmate.*[13]

Dilution in the Online World

As discussed earlier, trademark *dilution* occurs when a trademark is used, without authorization, in a way that diminishes the distinctive quality of the mark. Unlike trademark infringement, a claim of dilution does not require proof that consumers are likely to be confused by a connection between the unauthorized use and the mark. For this reason, the products involved need not be similar. In the first case alleging dilution on the Web, a court precluded the use of "candyland.com" as the URL for an adult site. The successful lawsuit was brought by the company that manufactures the "Candyland" children's game and owns the "Candyland" mark.[14]

Licensing

One way to make use of another's trademark or other form of intellectual property, while avoiding litigation, is to obtain a license to do so. A license in this context is essentially an agreement, or contract, permitting the use of a trademark, copyright, patent, or trade secret for certain purposes. The party that owns the intellectual property rights and issues the license is the *licensor,* and the party obtaining the license is the *licensee.* A

13. *Playboy Enterprises, Inc. v. Welles,* 279 F.3d 796 (9th Cir. 2002). See also *Rhino Sports, Inc. v. Sport Court, Inc.,* ___ F.Supp.2d ___ (D.Ariz. 2007).

14. *Hasbro, Inc. v. Internet Entertainment Group, Ltd.,* 1996 WL 84853 (W.D.Wash. 1996).

licensor might, for example, allow the licensee to use the trademark as part of its company name, or as part of its domain name, but not otherwise use the mark on any products or services. Often, selling a license to an infringer is an inexpensive solution to the problem, at least when compared with the costs associated with litigation.

Note, however, that under modern law a licensor of trademarks has a duty to maintain some form of control over the nature and quality of goods or services sold under the mark. If the license does not include any provisions to protect the quality of goods or services provided under the trademark, then the courts may conclude that the licensor has abandoned the trademark and lost her or his trademark rights.[15] To avoid such problems, licensing agreements normally include detailed provisions that protect the trademark owners' rights.

Patents

A **patent** is a grant from the government that gives an inventor the right to exclude others from making, using, and selling an invention for a period of twenty years from the date of filing the application for a patent. Patents for designs, as opposed to inventions, are given for a fourteen-year period. The applicant must demonstrate to the satisfaction of the U.S. Patent and Trademark Office that the invention, discovery, process, or design is novel, useful, and not obvious in light of current technology.

In contrast to patent law in many other countries, in the United States the first person to invent a product or process gets the patent rights rather than the first person to file for a patent on that product or process. Because it can be difficult to prove who invented an item first, however, the first person to file an application is often deemed the first to invent (unless the inventor has detailed prior research notes or other evidence). An inventor can publish the invention or offer it for sale prior to filing a patent application but must apply for a patent within one year of doing so or forfeit the patent rights. The period of patent protection begins on the date the patent application is filed, rather than when the patent is issued, which may sometimes be years later. After the patent period ends (either fourteen or twenty years later), the product or process enters the public domain, and anyone can make, sell, or use the invention without paying the patent holder.

Searchable Patent Databases

A significant development relating to patents is the availability online of the world's patent databases. The Web site of the U.S. Patent and Trademark Office (see the *Law on the Web* section at the end of this chapter for its URL) provides searchable databases covering U.S. patents granted since 1976. The Web site of the European Patent Office (its URL is also in the *Law on the Web* section) provides online access to 50 million patent documents in more than seventy nations through a searchable network of databases. Businesses use these searchable databases in many ways. Because patents are valuable assets, businesses may need to perform patent searches to list or inventory their assets. Patent searches may also be conducted to study trends and patterns in a specific technology or to gather information about competitors in the industry. In addition, a business might search patent databases to develop a business strategy in a particular market or to evaluate a job applicant's contributions to a technology. Although online databases are accessible to anyone, businesspersons might consider hiring a specialist to perform advanced patent searches.

What Is Patentable?

Under federal law, "[w]hoever invents or discovers any new and useful process, machine, manufacture, or composition of matter, or any new and useful improvement thereof, may obtain a patent therefor, subject to the conditions and requirements of this title."[16] Thus, to be patentable, the item must be novel and not obvious.

In sum, almost anything is patentable, except (1) the laws of nature,[17] (2) natural phenomena, and

15. This is referred to as a *naked license,* and a trademark owner who fails to exercise adequate control over the mark is estopped, or prevented, from asserting his or her rights. See, for example, *Barcamerica International USA Trust v. Tyfield Importers, Inc.*, 289 F.3d 589 (9th Cir. 2002); and *Exxon Corp. v. Oxxford Clothes, Inc.*, 109 F.3d 1070 (5th Cir. 1997).

16. 35 U.S.C. 101.

17. Note that in 2006, several justices of the United States Supreme Court indicated that they believed a process to diagnose vitamin deficiencies should not be patentable, because allowing a patent would improperly give a monopoly over a scientific relationship, or law of nature. Nevertheless, the majority of the Supreme Court allowed the patent to stand. *Laboratory Corporation of America Holdings v. Metabolite Laboratories, Inc.*, 548 U.S. 124, 126 S.Ct. 2921, 165 L.Ed.2d 399 (2006).

(3) abstract ideas (including algorithms[18]). Even artistic methods, certain works of art, and the structure of storylines are patentable, provided that they are novel and not obvious. Plants that are reproduced asexually (by means other than from seed), such as hybrid or genetically engineered plants, are patentable in the United States, as are genetically engineered (or cloned) microorganisms and animals.

In the following case, the focus was on the application of the test for proving whether a patent claim is "obvious."

18. An *algorithm* is a step-by-step procedure, formula, or set of instructions for accomplishing a specific task—such as the set of rules used by a search engine to rank the listings contained within its index in response to a particular query.

EXTENDED CASE 14.3 KSR International Co. v. Teleflex, Inc.

Supreme Court of the United States, 2007. __ U.S. __, 127 S.Ct. 1727, 167 L.Ed.2d 705.

Justice *KENNEDY* delivered the opinion of the Court.

Teleflex Incorporated * * * sued KSR International Company [in a federal district court] for patent infringement. The patent at issue is entitled "Adjustable Pedal Assembly With Electronic Throttle Control." The patentee is Steven J. Engelgau, and the patent is referred to as "the Engelgau patent." Teleflex holds the exclusive license to the patent.

Claim 4 of the Engelgau patent describes a mechanism for combining an electronic sensor with an adjustable automobile pedal so the pedal's position can be transmitted to a computer that controls the throttle in the vehicle's engine. [KSR designed a pedal assembly for General Motors Corporation (GMC) to use in its Chevrolet and GMC light trucks.] When Teleflex accused KSR of infringing the Engelgau patent * * *, KSR countered that claim 4 was invalid * * * because its subject matter was obvious.

* * * *

Seeking to resolve the question of obviousness with * * * uniformity and consistency, [the courts have] employed an approach referred to by the parties as the "teaching, suggestion, or motivation" test (TSM test), under which a patent claim is only proved obvious if some motivation or suggestion to combine the prior art teachings can be found in the prior art, the nature of the problem, or the knowledge of a person having ordinary skill in the art. KSR challenges that test, or at least its application in this case.

* * * *

* * * Important for this case are two adjustable pedals disclosed in [other patents]. The Asano patent reveals a support structure that houses the pedal so that even when the pedal location is adjusted relative to the driver, one of the pedal's pivot points stays fixed. * * * The Redding patent reveals a different, sliding mechanism where both the pedal and the pivot point are adjusted.

[Also important for this case are two] patents involving electronic pedal sensors for computer-controlled throttles. These inventions * * * taught that it was preferable to detect the pedal's position in the pedal assembly, not in the engine. The [Smith] patent disclosed a pedal with an electronic sensor on a pivot point in the pedal assembly.

* * * *

* * * The [Rixon patent] discloses an adjustable pedal assembly with an electronic sensor for detecting the pedal's position.

* * * *

The District Court granted summary judgment in KSR's favor.

* * * *

* * * The court compared the teachings of the prior art to the claims of Engelgau. It found "little difference." [The] Asano [patent] taught everything contained in claim 4 except the use of a sensor to detect the pedal's position and transmit it to the computer controlling the throttle. That additional aspect was revealed in sources such as * * * sensors [previously] used by Chevrolet.

CASE 14.3 CONTINUED

* * * The District Court [also] held KSR had satisfied the [TSM] test. It reasoned (1) the state of the industry would lead inevitably to combinations of electronic sensors and adjustable pedals, (2) Rixon provided the basis for these developments, and (3) Smith taught a solution to the wire chafing problems in Rixon, namely locating the sensor on the fixed structure of the pedal.

* * * *

* * * [The U.S.] Court of Appeals [for the Federal Circuit] reversed. It ruled the District Court had not been strict enough in applying the [TSM] test, having failed to make "finding[s] as to the specific understanding or principle within the knowledge of a skilled artisan that would have motivated one with no knowledge of [the] invention * * * to attach an electronic control to the support bracket of the Asano assembly."

Here, the Court of Appeals found, the Asano pedal was designed to solve the "constant ratio problem"—that is, to ensure that the force required to depress the pedal is the same no matter how the pedal is adjusted—whereas Engelgau sought to provide a simpler, smaller, cheaper adjustable electronic pedal. As for Rixon, the court explained, that pedal suffered from the problem of wire chafing but was not designed to solve it. In the court's view Rixon did not teach anything helpful to Engelgau's purpose. Smith, in turn, did not relate to adjustable pedals and did not "necessarily go to the issue of motivation to attach the electronic control on the support bracket of the pedal assembly."

* * * *

We begin by rejecting the rigid approach of the Court of Appeals. Throughout this Court's engagement with the question of obviousness, our cases have set forth an expansive and flexible approach inconsistent with the way the Court of Appeals applied its TSM test here.

* * * *For over a half century, the Court has held that a patent for a combination which only unites old elements with no change in their respective functions * * * obviously withdraws what is already known into the field of its monopoly and diminishes the resources available to skillful [persons].* [Emphasis added.]

* * * *

* * * If a technique has been used to improve one device, and a person of ordinary skill in the art would recognize that it would improve similar devices in the same way, using the technique is obvious unless its actual application is beyond his or her skill.

* * * *

The first error of the Court of Appeals in this case was to * * * [hold] that courts and patent examiners should look only to the problem the patentee was trying to solve.

The second error of the Court of Appeals lay in its assumption that a person of ordinary skill attempting to solve a problem will be led only to those elements of prior art designed to solve the same problem.

* * * *

When we apply the standards we have explained to the instant facts, claim 4 must be found obvious. * * * We see little difference between the teachings of Asano and Smith and the adjustable electronic pedal disclosed in claim 4 of the Engelgau patent. A person having ordinary skill in the art could have combined Asano with a pedal position sensor in a fashion encompassed by claim 4, and would have seen the benefits of doing so.

* * * *

* * * The judgment of the Court of Appeals is reversed, and the case remanded for further proceedings consistent with this opinion.

QUESTIONS

1. **If a person of ordinary skill can implement a predictable variation of another's patented invention, does the Court's opinion indicate that the item is likely not to be patentable?**
2. **Based on the Court's reasoning, what other factors should be considered when determining the obviousness of a patent?**

Patents for Software At one time, it was difficult for developers and manufacturers of software to obtain patent protection because many software products simply automate procedures that can be performed manually. In other words, it was thought that computer programs did not meet the "novel" and "not obvious" requirements previously mentioned. Also, the basis for software is often a mathematical equation or formula, which is not patentable. In 1981, however, the United States Supreme Court held that it is possible to obtain a patent for a *process* that incorporates a computer program—providing, of course, that the process itself is patentable.[19] Subsequently, many patents have been issued for software-related inventions.

Patents for Business Processes In 1998, in a landmark case, *State Street Bank & Trust Co. v. Signature Financial Group, Inc.*,[20] the U.S. Court of Appeals for the Federal Circuit ruled that business processes were patentable. After this decision, numerous technology firms applied for business process patents. Walker Digital applied for a business process patent for its "Dutch auction" system, which allowed consumers to make offers for airline tickets on the Internet and led to the creation of Priceline.com. Amazon.com obtained a business process patent for its "one-click" ordering system, a method of processing credit-card orders securely. Indeed, since the *State Street* decision, the number of Internet-related patents issued by the U.S. Patent and Trademark Office has increased dramatically.

Patent Infringement

If a firm makes, uses, or sells another's patented design, product, or process without the patent owner's permission, the tort of patent infringement occurs. Patent infringement may arise even though the patent owner has not put the patented product into commerce. Patent infringement may also occur even though not all features or parts of a product are identical to those used in the patented invention, provided that the features are equivalent. (With respect to a patented process, however, all steps or their equivalent must be copied for infringement to exist.)

Note that, as a general rule, under U.S. law no patent infringement occurs when a patented product is made and sold in another country. In 2007, this issue came before the United States Supreme Court in a patent infringement case that AT&T Corporation had brought against Microsoft Corporation. AT&T holds a patent on a device used to digitally encode, compress, and process recorded speech. Microsoft's Windows operating system, as Microsoft admitted, incorporated software code that infringed on AT&T's patent. The only question before the Supreme Court was whether Microsoft's liability extended to computers made in another country. The Court held that it did not. Microsoft was liable only for infringement in the United States and not for the Windows-based computers sold in foreign locations. The Court reasoned that Microsoft had not "supplied" the software for the computers but had only electronically transmitted a master copy, which the foreign manufacturers then copied and loaded onto the computers.[21]

Remedies for Patent Infringement

If a patent is infringed, the patent holder may sue for relief in federal court. The patent holder can seek an injunction against the infringer and can also request damages for royalties and lost profits. In some cases, the court may grant the winning party reimbursement for attorneys' fees and costs. If the court determines that the infringement was willful, the court can triple the amount of damages awarded (treble damages).

In the past, permanent injunctions were routinely granted to prevent future infringement. In 2006, however, the United States Supreme Court ruled that patent holders are not automatically entitled to a permanent injunction against future infringing activities—the courts have discretion to decide whether equity requires it. According to the Supreme Court, a patent holder must prove that it has suffered irreparable injury and that the public interest would not be disserved by a permanent injunction.[22]

This decision gives courts discretion to decide what is equitable in the circumstances and allows them to consider what is in the public interest rather than just the interests of the parties. For example, in the first case applying this rule, a court found that although Microsoft had infringed on the patent of a small software company, the latter was not entitled to

19. *Diamond v. Diehr,* 450 U.S. 175, 101 S.Ct. 1048, 67 L.Ed.2d 155 (1981).
20. 149 F.3d 1368 (Fed.Cir. 1998).
21. *Microsoft Corp. v. AT&T Corp.,* ___ U.S. ___, 127 S.Ct. 1746, 167 L.Ed.2d 737 (2007).
22. *eBay, Inc. v. MercExchange, LLC,* 547 U.S. 388, 126 S.Ct. 1837, 164 L.Ed.2d 641 (2006).

an injunction. According to the court, the small company was not irreparably harmed and could be adequately compensated by damages. Also, the public might suffer negative effects from an injunction because the infringement involved part of Microsoft's widely used Office suite software.[23]

Copyrights

A **copyright** is an intangible property right granted by federal statute to the author or originator of a literary or artistic production of a specified type. Today, copyrights are governed by the Copyright Act of 1976,[24] as amended. Works created after January 1, 1978, are automatically given statutory copyright protection for the life of the author plus 70 years. For copyrights owned by publishing houses, the copyright expires 95 years from the date of publication or 120 years from the date of creation, whichever is first. For works by more than one author, the copyright expires 70 years after the death of the last surviving author.

These time periods reflect the extensions of the length of copyright protection enacted by Congress in the Copyright Term Extension Act of 1998.[25] Critics challenged this act as overstepping the bounds of Congress's power and violating the constitutional requirement that copyrights endure for only a limited time. In 2003, however, the United States Supreme Court upheld the act in *Eldred v. Ashcroft.*[26] This holding obviously favored copyright holders by preventing copyrighted works from the 1920s and 1930s from losing protection and falling into the public domain for an additional two decades.

Copyrights can be registered with the U.S. Copyright Office in Washington, D.C. A copyright owner no longer needs to place the symbol © or the term *Copr.* or *Copyright* on the work to have the work protected against infringement. Chances are that if somebody created it, somebody owns it.

What Is Protected Expression?

Works that are copyrightable include books, records, films, artworks, architectural plans, menus, music videos, product packaging, and computer software. To be protected, a work must be "fixed in a durable medium" from which it can be perceived, reproduced, or communicated. Protection is automatic. Registration is not required.

To obtain protection under the Copyright Act, a work must be original and fall into one of the following categories:

1. Literary works (including newspaper and magazine articles, computer and training manuals, catalogues, brochures, and print advertisements).
2. Musical works and accompanying words (including advertising jingles).
3. Dramatic works and accompanying music.
4. Pantomimes and choreographic works (including ballets and other forms of dance).
5. Pictorial, graphic, and sculptural works (including cartoons, maps, posters, statues, and even stuffed animals).
6. Motion pictures and other audiovisual works (including multimedia works).
7. Sound recordings.
8. Architectural works.

Section 102 Exclusions Section 102 of the Copyright Act specifically excludes copyright protection for any "idea, procedure, process, system, method of operation, concept, principle, or discovery, regardless of the form in which it is described, explained, illustrated, or embodied." Note that it is not possible to copyright an *idea*. The underlying ideas embodied in a work may be freely used by others. What is copyrightable is the particular way in which an idea is expressed. Whenever an idea and an expression are inseparable, the expression cannot be copyrighted. Generally, anything that is not an original expression will not qualify for copyright protection. Facts widely known to the public are not copyrightable. Page numbers are not copyrightable because they follow a sequence known to everyone. Mathematical calculations are not copyrightable.

Compilations of Facts Unlike ideas, *compilations* of facts are copyrightable. Under Section 103 of the Copyright Act a compilation is "a work formed by the collection and assembling of preexisting materials or data that are selected, coordinated, or arranged in such a way that the resulting work as a whole constitutes an original work of authorship." The key requirement in the copyrightability of a compilation is originality. If the facts are selected, coordinated, or arranged in an original way, they can qualify for copyright protection.

23. *Z4 Technologies, Inc. v. Microsoft Corp.*, 434 F.Supp.2d 437 (E.D.Tex. 2006).
24. 17 U.S.C. Sections 101 *et seq.*
25. 17 U.S.C. Section 302.
26. 537 U.S. 186, 123 S.Ct. 769, 154 L.Ed.2d 683 (2003).

Therefore, the white pages of a telephone directory do not qualify for copyright protection because the facts (names, addresses, and telephone numbers) are listed in alphabetical order rather than being selected, coordinated, or arranged in an original way.[27] The Yellow Pages of a telephone directory, in contrast, can qualify for copyright protection.[28] Similarly, a compilation of information about yachts listed for sale may qualify for copyright protection.[29]

Copyright Infringement

Whenever the form or expression of an idea is copied, an infringement of copyright has occurred. The reproduction does not have to be exactly the same as the original, nor does it have to reproduce the original in its entirety. If a substantial part of the original is reproduced, the copyright has been infringed.

Damages for Copyright Infringement Those who infringe copyrights may be liable for damages or criminal penalties. These range from actual damages or statutory damages, imposed at the court's discretion, to criminal proceedings for willful violations. Actual damages are based on the harm caused to the copyright holder by the infringement, while statutory damages, not to exceed $150,000, are provided for under the Copyright Act. Criminal proceedings may result in fines and/or imprisonment.

The "Fair Use" Exception An exception to liability for copyright infringement is made under the "fair use" doctrine. In certain circumstances, a person or organization can reproduce copyrighted material without paying royalties (fees paid to the copyright holder for the privilege of reproducing the copyrighted material). Section 107 of the Copyright Act provides as follows:

> [T]he fair use of a copyrighted work, including such use by reproduction in copies or phonorecords or by any other means specified by [Section 106 of the Copyright Act], for purposes such as criticism, comment, news reporting, teaching (including multiple copies for classroom use), scholarship, or research, is not an infringement of copyright. In determining whether the use made of a work in any particular case is a fair use the factors to be considered shall include–
>
> (1) the purpose and character of the use, including whether such use is of a commercial nature or is for nonprofit educational purposes;
> (2) the nature of the copyrighted work;
> (3) the amount and substantiality of the portion used in relation to the copyrighted work as a whole; and
> (4) the effect of the use upon the potential market for or value of the copyrighted work.

Because these guidelines are very broad, the courts determine whether a particular use is fair on a case-by-case basis. Thus, anyone reproducing copyrighted material may still be committing a violation. In determining whether a use is fair, courts have often considered the fourth factor to be the most important.

In the following case, the owner of copyrighted music had issued a license to the manufacturer of karaoke devices to reproduce the sound recordings, but had not given its permission to reprint the song lyrics. The issue was whether the manufacturer should pay additional fees to display the lyrics at the same time as the music was playing. The manufacturer claimed, in part, that its use of the lyrics was educational and therefore did not constitute copyright infringement under the fair use exception.

27. *Feist Publications, Inc. v. Rural Telephone Service Co.*, 499 U.S. 340, 111 S.Ct. 1282, 113 L.Ed.2d 358 (1991).
28. *Bellsouth Advertising & Publishing Corp. v. Donnelley Information Publishing, Inc.*, 999 F.2d 1436 (11th Cir. 1993).
29. *BUC International Corp. v. International Yacht Council, Ltd.*, 489 F.3d 1129 (11th Cir. 2007).

CASE 14.4 Leadsinger, Inc. v. BMG Music Publishing

United States Court of Appeals, Ninth Circuit, 2008. 512 F.3d 522.
www.ca9.uscourts.gov[a]

• **Background and Facts** Leadsinger, Inc., manufactures and sells karaoke devices. Specifically, it sells a microphone that has a chip inside with embedded songs and lyrics that appear at the bottom of a TV screen. This device is similar to those in which compact discs and DVDs are inserted to display lyrics on a TV monitor. All karaoke devices necessarily involve copyrighted works. BMG Music Publishing owns and administers copyrights for such music. BMG had issued to Leadsinger the appropriate licenses to copyrighted musical compositions under Section 115 of the Copyright Act. Leadsinger sought a declaration that it be entitled to print or display song lyrics in real time with song recordings without paying any additional fees. In contrast, BMG demanded that Leadsinger and other karaoke companies pay a "lyric

a. Click on "Opinions" and then scroll down to "01/02/08." Find the case name and click on it to access the opinion.

CASE 14.1 CONTINUED

reprint" fee and a "synchronization" fee. Leadsinger refused to pay, filing for a declaratory judgment to resolve whether it had the right to display song lyrics in real time with sound recordings without paying any additional fees. The district court concluded that a Section 115 license did not grant Leadsinger the right to display visual images *and* lyrics in real time with music. Leadsinger appealed to the U.S. Court of Appeals for the Ninth Circuit.

IN THE LANGUAGE OF THE COURT
***SMITH, M.D.,* C.J. [Circuit Judge]**

* * * *

In deciding whether the district court properly dismissed Leadsinger's complaint, we are guided by the language of the Copyright Act. Section 102 of the Copyright Act extends copyright protection to, among other original works of authorship, literary works, musical works (including any accompanying words), and sound recordings. Though Section 106 grants copyright owners the exclusive right to reproduce copyrighted works "in copies or phonorecords" and to "distribute copies or phonorecords of the copyrighted work to the public by sale," [Section 115] limits copyright owners' exclusive rights with respect to phonorecords.

* * * *

* * * Though it is not explicit in the Copyright Act, courts have recognized a copyright holder's right to control the synchronization of musical compositions with the content of audiovisual works and have required parties to obtain synchronization licenses from copyright holders. * * * Song lyrics are copyrightable as a literary work and, therefore, enjoy separate protection under the Copyright Act.

* * * *

The district court reasoned that Leadsinger's device falls outside of the definition of phonorecord because the device contains more than sounds. * * * While it is true that the microchip in Leadsinger's device stores visual images and visual representations of lyrics in addition to sounds, the plain language of the Copyright Act does not expressly preclude a finding that devices on which sounds *and* visual images are fixed fall within the definition of phonorecords. The definition of phonorecords is explicit, however, that audiovisual works are not phonorecords and are excluded from Section 115's compulsory licensing scheme. We need not settle upon a precise interpretation of Section 101's definition of phonorecords in this case because Leadsinger's karaoke device meets each element of the statutory definition of audiovisual works and, therefore, cannot be a phonorecord.

* * * *

We hold that Leadsinger's device falls within the definition of an audiovisual work. As a result, in addition to any Section 115 compulsory licenses necessary to make and distribute phonorecords and reprint licenses necessary to reprint song lyrics, Leadsinger is also required to secure synchronization licenses to display images of song lyrics in timed relation with recorded music. [Emphasis added.]

* * * *

The Copyright Act does not grant a copyright holder exclusive rights to reproduce his or her work. Section 107 of the Copyright Act explains that "the fair use of a copyrighted work . . . for purposes such as criticism, comment, news reporting, teaching . . . , scholarship, or research, is not an infringement of copyright."

* * * *

* * * While Leadsinger argued on appeal that karaoke teaches singing, that allegation is not set forth in its complaint. Even if the court could infer that a karaoke device has the potential to teach singing because the device allows consumers to sing along with recorded music, it is not reasonable to infer that teaching is actually the purpose of Leadsinger's use of the copyrighted lyrics.

* * * *

* * * Leadsinger's basic purpose remains a commercial one—to sell its karaoke device for profit. And *commercial use of copyrighted material is "presumptively an unfair exploitation of the monopoly privilege that belongs to the owner of the copyright."* [Emphasis added.]

* * * *

CASE CONTINUES

CASE 14.4 CONTINUED

We have * * * concluded that Leadsinger's use is intended for commercial gain, and it is well accepted that when "the intended use is for commercial gain," the likelihood of market harm "may be presumed." We have not hesitated to apply this presumption in the past, and we are not reluctant to apply it here. Moreover, "the importance of [the market effect] factor [varies], not only with the amount of harm, but also with the relative strength of the showing on the other factors." The showing on all other factors under Section 107 is strong: the purpose and character of Leadsinger's use is commercial; song lyrics fall within the core of copyright protection; and Leadsinger uses song lyrics in their entirety. On this basis, we affirm the district court's dismissal of Leadsinger's request for a declaration based on the fair use doctrine.

- **Decision and Remedy** *The U.S. Court of Appeals for the Ninth Circuit affirmed the district court's decision to dismiss Leadsinger's complaint without the possibility of amending its complaint.*

- **The Global Dimension** *Could Leadsinger have attempted to show that its karaoke programs were used extensively abroad to help others learn English? If successful in this line of reasoning, might Leadsinger have prevailed on appeal? Explain your answer.*

- **The Legal Environment Dimension** *What was the underlying basis of Leadsinger's attempt to avoid paying additional licensing fees to BMG?*

Copyright Protection for Software

In 1980, Congress passed the Computer Software Copyright Act, which amended the Copyright Act of 1976 to include computer programs in the list of creative works protected by federal copyright law.[30] The 1980 statute, which classifies computer programs as "literary works," defines a computer program as a "set of statements or instructions to be used directly or indirectly in a computer in order to bring about a certain result."

The unique nature of computer programs, however, has created problems for the courts in applying and interpreting the 1980 act. Generally, the courts have held that copyright protection extends not only to those parts of a computer program that can be read by humans, such as the "high-level" language of a source code, but also to the binary-language object code, which is readable only by the computer.[31] Additionally, such elements as the overall structure, sequence, and organization of a program have been deemed copyrightable, but generally not the "look and feel" of computer programs.[32] The "look and feel" of computer programs refers to their general appearance, command structure, video images, menus, windows, and other screen displays.

30. Pub. L. No. 96-517 (1980), amending 17 U.S.C. Sections 101, 117.

31. See *Stern Electronics, Inc. v. Kaufman*, 669 F.2d 852 (2d Cir. 1982); and *Apple Computer, Inc. v. Franklin Computer Corp.*, 714 F.2d 1240 (3d Cir. 1983).

32. *Whelan Associates, Inc. v. Jaslow Dental Laboratory, Inc.*, 797 F.2d 1222 (3d Cir. 1986).

Copyrights in Digital Information

Copyright law is probably the most important form of intellectual property protection on the Internet. This is because much of the material on the Internet consists of works of authorship (including multimedia presentations, software, and database information), which are the traditional focus of copyright law. Copyright law is also important because the nature of the Internet requires that data be "copied" to be transferred online. Traditionally, many of the controversies arising in this area of the law have involved copies.

The Copyright Act of 1976

When Congress drafted the principal U.S. law governing copyrights, the Copyright Act of 1976, cyberspace did not exist for most of us. At that time, the primary threat to copyright owners was from persons making unauthorized *tangible* copies of works. Because of the nature of cyberspace, however, one of the early controversies was determining at what point an intangible, electronic "copy" of a work has been made. The courts have held that loading a file or program into a computer's random access memory, or RAM, constitutes the making of a "copy" for purposes of copyright law.[33] RAM is a portion of a computer's memory into which a file, for example, is loaded so that it can be accessed. Thus, a copyright is infringed when a party downloads software into RAM without owning the software or otherwise having a right to download it.[34] Today, technology has vastly increased the potential for copyright infringement. For a discussion of whether search engines that use thumbnail images of copyrighted materials are liable for infringement, see this chapter's *Insight into E-Commerce* feature on pages 354 and 355.

Further Developments in Copyright Law

In the last fifteen years, Congress has enacted legislation designed specifically to protect copyright holders in a digital age. Particularly significant are the No Electronic Theft Act of 1997[35] and the Digital Millennium Copyright Act of 1998.[36]

The No Electronic Theft Act Prior to 1997, criminal penalties could be imposed under copyright law only if unauthorized copies were exchanged for financial gain. Yet much piracy of copyrighted materials was "altruistic" in nature; that is, unauthorized copies were made and distributed not for financial gain but simply for reasons of generosity—to share the copies with others. To combat altruistic piracy and for other reasons, Congress passed the No Electronic Theft (NET) Act of 1997.

NET extended criminal liability for the piracy of copyrighted materials to persons who exchange unauthorized copies of copyrighted works, such as software, even though they realize no profit from the exchange. The act also altered the traditional "fair use" doctrine by imposing penalties on those who make unauthorized electronic copies of books, magazines, movies, or music for *personal* use. The criminal penalties for violating the act are relatively severe; they include fines as high as $250,000 and incarceration for up to five years.

The Digital Millennium Copyright Act of 1998 The passage of the Digital Millennium Copyright Act (DMCA) of 1998 gave significant protection to owners of copyrights in digital information.[37] Among other things, the act established civil and criminal penalties for anyone who circumvents (bypasses, or gets around—by using a special decryption program, for example) encryption software or other technological antipiracy protection. Also prohibited are the manufacture, import, sale, and distribution of devices or services for circumvention.

The DMCA provides for exceptions to fit the needs of libraries, scientists, universities, and others. In general, the law does not restrict the "fair use" of circumvention methods for educational and other noncommercial purposes. For example, circumvention is allowed to test computer security, to conduct encryption research, to protect personal privacy, and to enable parents to monitor their children's use of the Internet. The exceptions are to be reconsidered every three years.

The DMCA also limits the liability of Internet service providers (ISPs). Under the act, an ISP is not liable for any copyright infringement by its customer *unless* the ISP is aware of the subscriber's violation. An ISP may be held liable only if it fails to take action to shut the subscriber down after learning of the violation. A copyright holder must act promptly, however, by pursuing a claim in court, or the subscriber has the right to be restored to online access.

MP3 and File-Sharing Technology

Soon after the Internet became popular, a few enterprising programmers created software to compress large data files, particularly those associated with music. The reduced file sizes make transmitting music over the Internet feasible. The most widely known compression and decompression system is MP3, which enables music fans to download songs or entire CDs onto their computers or onto portable listening devices, such as Rio or iPod. The MP3 system also made it possible for music fans to access other music fans' files by engaging in file-sharing via the Internet.

Peer-to-Peer (P2P) Networking File-sharing via the Internet is accomplished through what is called **peer-to-peer (P2P) networking.** The concept is simple. Rather than going through a central Web server,

33. *MAI Systems Corp. v. Peak Computer, Inc.*, 991 F.2d 511 (9th Cir. 1993).
34. *DSC Communications Corp. v. Pulse Communications, Inc.*, 170 F.3d 1354 (Fed.Cir. 1999).
35. Pub. L. No. 105-147 (1997). Codified at 17 U.S.C. Sections 101, 506; 18 U.S.C. Sections 2311, 2319, 2319A, 2320; and 28 U.S.C. Sections 994 and 1498.
36. 17 U.S.C. Sections 512, 1201–1205, 1301–1332; and 28 U.S.C. Section 4001.
37. This act implemented the World Intellectual Property Organization Copyright Treaty of 1996, which will be discussed later in this chapter.

INSIGHT INTO E-COMMERCE
Search Engines versus Copyright Owners

Since their humble beginnings more than a decade ago, search engines have become ubiquitous in the e-commerce world. Every day, millions of consumers use search engines to locate various products on the Web. A major legal question arises, however, when the results of a search include copyrighted intellectual property, such as books, downloadable software, movies and other videos, and images. Can the owner of the search engine that returned these results be held liable for copyright infringement?

The Betamax Doctrine

The basic rule that has governed issues relating to the application of new technology for uses that might include copyright infringement was set out more than two decades ago by the United States Supreme Court in the landmark case *Sony Corporation of America v. Universal City Studios.*[a] The case involved the then-new technology of the videocassette recorder (VCR), which was available in two formats—VHS and Betamax. Owners of copyrighted television programs, concerned that VCR owners were using the equipment to copy TV programs, brought a suit against a VCR manufacturer, claiming that it was liable for its customers' copyright infringement. The Supreme Court, however, in what became known as the *Betamax doctrine,* held that the manufacturer was not liable for creating a technology that certain customers might use for copyright infringing purposes, as long as that technology was capable of substantial noninfringing uses. Legal scholars believe that the Betamax doctrine has allowed for the development of many other technologies that are capable of both infringing and noninfringing uses—including CD-ROM burners, DVRs, TiVo, Apple's iPod, and even the personal computer.

As discussed later in the text, twenty years after the *Sony* case, organizations and companies in the music and film industries brought a copyright infringement suit against Grokster, Morpheus, and KaZaA, the makers of file-sharing software that allowed millions of individuals to copy copyrighted music. In that case, the United States Supreme Court did find that there was ample evidence that the software makers had taken steps to promote copyright infringement, but significantly the Court did not overturn the Betamax doctrine. The Court did not specify what steps are necessary to impose liability on the provider of a technology, however.[b]

Does Providing Thumbnail Images Violate Copyright Law?

Just as VCRs and file-sharing technology raised new issues of copyright infringement, so does today's search engine technology. In response to a search

a. 464 U.S. 417, 104 S.Ct. 774, 78 L.Ed.2d 574 (1984).

b. *Metro-Goldwyn-Mayer Studios, Inc. v. Grokster, Ltd.,* 545 U.S. 913, 125 S.Ct. 2764, 162 L.Ed.2d 781 (2005).

P2P uses numerous personal computers (PCs) that are connected to the Internet. Files stored on one PC can be accessed by others who are members of the same network. Sometimes this is called a **distributed network** because parts of the network are distributed all over the country or the world. File-sharing offers an unlimited number of uses for distributed networks. For example, thousands of researchers allow their home computers' computing power to be simultaneously accessed through file-sharing software so that very large mathematical problems can be solved quickly. Additionally, persons scattered throughout the country or the world can work together on the same project by using file-sharing programs.

Sharing Stored Music Files When file-sharing is used to download others' stored music files, copyright issues arise. Recording artists and their labels stand to lose large amounts of royalties and revenues if relatively few CDs are purchased and then made available on distributed networks, from which everyone can get them for free. The issue of file-sharing infringement has been the subject of an ongoing debate for some time.

For example, in the highly publicized case of *A&M Records, Inc. v. Napster, Inc.,*[38] several firms in the recording industry sued Napster, Inc., the owner of the then popular Napster Web site. The Napster site provided registered users with free software that enabled them to transfer exact copies of the contents of MP3 files from one computer to another via the Internet. Napster also maintained centralized search indices so that users could locate specific titles or artists' recordings on the computers of other members. The firms

38. 239 F.3d 1004 (9th Cir. 2001).

request, numerous search engines show thumbnail images of books, album covers, and copyrighted photographs. Arriba Soft Corporation (now ditto.com), for example, operated a search engine that displayed its results in the form of thumbnail pictures. It obtained its database of photographs by copying images from other Web sites. When professional photographer Leslie Kelly discovered that his copyrighted photographs were part of Arriba's database, he brought a suit for copyright infringement. Arriba prevailed, as the Ninth Circuit Court of Appeals ruled that its thumbnails were a fair use under the Copyright Act.[c]

A recent innovation enables search engines to search specifically for images. Google Image Search, for example, stores thumbnail images of its search results on Google's servers. The thumbnail images are reduced, lower-resolution versions of full-size images stored on third party computers. In 2005, *Perfect 10,* a men's magazine that features high-resolution photographs of topless and nude women, brought a suit to enjoin Google from caching and displaying its photographs as thumbnails. *Perfect 10* argued that because Google "created the audience" for its sites and indexes, Google should be liable for whatever infringements occurred on those sites. The magazine also contended that Google had directly infringed *Perfect 10*'s copyrights by in-line linking and framing images published on other sites. (The case was combined with a similar suit brought against Amazon.com for its A9 search engine.) Once again, however, as in its *Arriba* decision, the Ninth Circuit Court of Appeals held that the thumbnails constituted a fair use. Pointing out the public benefit that search engines provide, the court said that until *Perfect 10* gave Google specific URLs for infringing images, Google had no duty to act and could not be held liable. The court further held that Google could not "supervise or control" the third party Web sites linked to its search results.[d] In sum, the court refused to hold the creators of image search technology liable for users' infringement because the technology is capable of both infringing and noninfringing uses—just as the Betamax doctrine protected VCR manufacturers from liability for users' infringement.

CRITICAL THINKING

INSIGHT INTO TECHNOLOGY

What has changed in the world of technology since the Betamax doctrine was enunciated? Does the fact that more and more intellectual property is being digitized and made available online alter the reasoning underlying the Betamax doctrine?

c. *Kelly v. Arriba Soft Corporation,* 336 F.3d 811 (9th Cir. 2003).

d. *Perfect 10, Inc. v. Amazon.com, Inc.,* 487 F.3d 701 (9th Cir. 2007).

argued that Napster should be liable for contributory and vicarious[39] (indirect) copyright infringement because it assisted others in obtaining copies of copyrighted music without the copyright owners' permission. The federal district court agreed, and the U.S. Court of Appeals for the Ninth Circuit affirmed, holding Napster liable for violating copyright laws. The court reasoned that Napster was liable for its users' infringement because the technology that Napster had used was centralized and gave it "the ability to locate infringing material listed on its search indices and the right to terminate users' access to the system."

After the *Napster* decision, the recording industry filed and won numerous lawsuits against companies that distribute online file-sharing software. The courts held these companies liable based on two theories: contributory infringement, which applies if the company had reason to know about a user's infringement and failed to stop it, and vicarious liability, which exists if the company was able to control the users' activities and stood to benefit financially from their infringement.

Evolution of File-Sharing Technologies

In the wake of the *Napster* decision, other companies developed new technologies that allow P2P network users to share stored music files, without paying a fee, more quickly and efficiently than ever. Software such as Morpheus, KaZaA, and LimeWire, for example, provides users with an interface that is similar to a Web

39. *Vicarious (indirect) liability* exists when one person is subject to liability for another's actions. A common example occurs in the employment context, when an employer is held vicariously liable by third parties for torts committed by employees in the course of their employment.

browser.[40] Companies need not locate songs for users on other members' computers. Instead, the software automatically annotates files with descriptive information so that the music can easily be categorized and cross-referenced (by artist and title, for instance). When a user performs a search, the software is able to locate a list of peers that have the file available for downloading. Also, to expedite the P2P transfer, the software distributes the download task over the entire list of peers simultaneously. By downloading even one file, the user becomes a point of distribution for that file, which is then automatically shared with others on the network.

Because the file-sharing software was decentralized and did not use search indices that would enable the companies to locate infringing material, they had no ability to supervise or control which music (or other media files) their users exchanged. In addition, it was difficult for courts to apply the traditional doctrines of contributory and vicarious liability to these new technologies.

The Supreme Court's *Grokster* Decision

In 2005, the United States Supreme Court expanded the liability of file-sharing companies in its decision in *Metro-Goldwyn-Mayer Studios, Inc. v. Grokster, Ltd.*[41] In that case, organizations in the music and film industry (the plaintiffs) sued several companies that distribute file-sharing software used in P2P networks, including Grokster, Ltd., and StreamCast Networks, Inc. (the defendants). The plaintiffs claimed that the defendants were contributorily and vicariously liable for the infringement of their end users. The Supreme Court held that "one who distributes a device [software] with the object of promoting its use to infringe the copyright, as shown by clear expression or other affirmative steps taken to foster infringement, is liable for the resulting acts of infringement by third parties."

Although the Supreme Court did not specify what kind of affirmative steps are necessary to establish liability, it did note that there was ample evidence that the defendants had acted with the intent to cause copyright violations. (Grokster, Ltd., later settled this dispute out of court and stopped distributing its software.) Essentially, this means that file-sharing companies that have taken affirmative steps to promote copyright infringement can be held secondarily liable for millions of infringing acts that their users commit daily. Because the Court did not define exactly what is necessary to impose liability, however, a substantial amount of legal uncertainty remains concerning this issue. Although some file-sharing companies have been shut down, illegal file-sharing—and lawsuits against file-sharing companies and the individuals who use them—has continued in the years since this decision.

Trade Secrets

The law of trade secrets protects some business processes and information that are not, or cannot be, patented, copyrighted, or trademarked against appropriation by competitors. **Trade secrets** include customer lists, plans, research and development, pricing information, marketing methods, production techniques, and generally anything that makes an individual company unique and that would have value to a competitor.

Unlike copyright and trademark protection, protection of trade secrets extends both to ideas and to their expression. (For this reason, and because a trade secret involves no registration or filing requirements, trade secret protection may be well suited for software.) Of course, the secret formula, method, or other information must be disclosed to some persons, particularly to key employees. Businesses generally attempt to protect their trade secrets by having all employees who use the process or information agree in their contracts, or in confidentiality agreements, never to divulge it.

State and Federal Law on Trade Secrets

Under Section 757 of the *Restatement of Torts*, "One who discloses or uses another's trade secret, without a privilege to do so, is liable to the other if (1) he [or she] discovered the secret by improper means, or (2) his [or her] disclosure or use constitutes a breach of confidence reposed in him [or her] by the other in disclosing the secret to him [or her]." The theft of confidential business data by industrial espionage, as when a business taps into a competitor's computer, is a theft of trade secrets without any contractual violation and is actionable in itself.

Until thirty years ago, virtually all law with respect to trade secrets was common law. In an effort to reduce the unpredictability of the common law in this area, a

40. Note that in 2005, KaZaA entered a settlement agreement with four major music companies that had alleged copyright infringement. KaZaA agreed to offer only legitimate, fee-based music downloads in the future.

41. 545 U.S. 913, 125 S.Ct. 2764, 162 L.Ed.2d 781 (2005).

model act, the Uniform Trade Secrets Act, was presented to the states for adoption in 1979. Parts of the act have been adopted in more than thirty states. Typically, a state that has adopted parts of the act has adopted only those parts that encompass its own existing common law. Additionally, in 1996 Congress passed the Economic Espionage Act,[42] which made the theft of trade secrets a federal crime. We examined the provisions and significance of this act in Chapter 7, in the context of crimes related to business.

Trade Secrets in Cyberspace

New computer technology is undercutting a business firm's ability to protect its confidential information, including trade secrets.[43] For example, a dishonest employee could e-mail trade secrets in a company's computer to a competitor or a future employer. If e-mail is not an option, the employee might walk out with the information on a flash pen drive.

International Protection for Intellectual Property

For many years, the United States has been a party to various international agreements relating to intellectual property rights. For example, the Paris Convention of 1883, to which about 170 countries are signatory, allows parties in one country to file for patent and trademark protection in any of the other member countries. Other international agreements in this area include the Berne Convention, the TRIPS agreement, and the Madrid Protocol.

The Berne Convention

Under the Berne Convention (an international copyright agreement) of 1886, as amended, if an American writes a book, every country that has signed the convention must recognize the American author's copyright in the book. Also, if a citizen of a country that has not signed the convention first publishes a book in one of the 170 countries that have signed, all other countries that have signed the convention must recognize that author's copyright. Copyright notice is not needed to gain protection under the Berne Convention for works published after March 1, 1989.

The laws of many countries, as well as international laws, are being updated to reflect changes in technology and the expansion of the Internet. Copyright holders and other owners of intellectual property generally agree that changes in the law are needed to stop the increasing international piracy of their property. The World Intellectual Property Organization (WIPO) Copyright Treaty of 1996, a special agreement under the Berne Convention, attempts to update international law governing copyright protection to include more safeguards against copyright infringement via the Internet. The United States signed the WIPO treaty in 1996 and implemented its terms in the Digital Millennium Copyright Act of 1998, which was discussed earlier in this chapter.

The Berne Convention and other international agreements have given some protection to intellectual property on a global level. Another significant worldwide agreement to increase such protection is the Trade-Related Aspects of Intellectual Property Rights agreement—or, more simply, the TRIPS agreement.

The TRIPS Agreement

Representatives from more than one hundred nations signed the TRIPS agreement in 1994. It was one of several documents that were annexed to the agreement that created the World Trade Organization, or WTO, in 1995. The TRIPS agreement established, for the first time, standards for the international protection of intellectual property rights, including patents, trademarks, and copyrights for movies, computer programs, books, and music. The TRIPS agreement provides that each member country must include in its domestic laws broad intellectual property rights and effective remedies (including civil and criminal penalties) for violations of those rights.

Members Cannot Discriminate against Foreign Intellectual Property Owners Generally, the TRIPS agreement forbids member nations from discriminating against foreign owners of intellectual property rights (in the administration, regulation, or adjudication of such rights). In other words, a member nation cannot give its own nationals (citizens) favorable treatment without offering the same treatment to nationals of all member countries. For instance, if a U.S. software manufacturer brings a suit for the infringement of intellectual property rights under a member nation's national laws, the U.S. manufacturer is entitled to receive the same treatment as a domestic manufacturer. Each member

---

42. 18 U.S.C. Sections 1831–1839.

43. Note that in at least one case, a court has held that customers' e-mail addresses may constitute trade secrets. See *T-N-T Motorsports, Inc. v. Hennessey Motorsports, Inc.*, 965 S.W.2d 18 (Tex.App.—Houston [1 Dist.] 1998); rehearing overruled (1998); petition dismissed (1998).

CONCEPT SUMMARY 14.1 Forms of Intellectual Property

	Definition	How Acquired	Duration	Remedy for Infringement
Patent	A grant from the government that gives an inventor exclusive rights to an invention.	By filing a patent application with the U.S. Patent and Trademark Office and receiving its approval.	Twenty years from the date of the application; for design patents, fourteen years.	Monetary damages, including royalties and lost profits, *plus* attorneys' fees. Damages may be tripled for intentional infringements.
Copyright	The right of an author or originator of a literary or artistic work, or other production that falls within a specified category, to have the exclusive use of that work for a given period of time.	Automatic (once the work or creation is fixed in a durable medium). Only the *expression* of an idea (and not the idea itself) can be protected by copyright.	For authors: the life of the author plus 70 years. For publishers: 95 years after the date of publication or 120 years after creation.	Actual damages plus profits received by the party who infringed or statutory damages under the Copyright Act, *plus* costs and attorneys' fees in either situation.
Trademark (Service Mark and Trade Dress)	Any distinctive word, name, symbol, or device (image or appearance), or combination thereof, that an entity uses to distinguish its goods or services from those of others. The owner has the exclusive right to use that mark or trade dress.	1. At common law, ownership created by use of the mark. 2. Registration with the appropriate federal or state office gives notice and is permitted if the mark is currently in use or will be within the next six months.	Unlimited, as long as it is in use. To continue notice by registration, the owner must renew by filing between the fifth and sixth years, and thereafter, every ten years.	1. Injunction prohibiting the future use of the mark. 2. Actual damages plus profits received by the party who infringed (can be increased under the Lanham Act). 3. Destruction of articles that infringed. 4. *Plus* costs and attorneys' fees.
Trade Secret	Any information that a business possesses and that gives the business an advantage over competitors (including formulas, lists, patterns, plans, processes, and programs).	Through the originality and development of the information and processes that constitute the business secret and are unknown to others.	Unlimited, so long as not revealed to others. Once revealed to others, it is no longer a trade secret.	Monetary damages for misappropriation (the Uniform Trade Secrets Act also permits punitive damages if willful), *plus* costs and attorneys' fees.

nation must also ensure that legal procedures are available for parties who wish to bring actions for infringement of intellectual property rights. Additionally, a related document established a mechanism for settling disputes among member nations.

Covers All Types of Intellectual Property Particular provisions of the TRIPS agreement relate to patent, trademark, and copyright protection for intellectual property. The agreement specifically provides copyright protection for computer programs by stating that compilations of data, databases, and other materials are "intellectual creations" and are to be protected as copyrightable works. Other provisions relate to trade secrets and the rental of computer programs and cinematographic works.

The Madrid Protocol

In the past, one of the difficulties in protecting U.S. trademarks internationally was the time and expense involved in applying for trademark registration in foreign countries. The filing fees and procedures for trademark registration vary significantly among individual countries. The Madrid Protocol, which President George W. Bush signed into law in 2003, may help to resolve these problems. The Madrid Protocol is an international treaty that has been signed by seventy-three countries. Under its provisions, a U.S. company wishing to register its trademark abroad can submit a single application and designate other member countries in which the U.S. company would like to register its mark. The treaty is designed to reduce the costs of international trademark protection by more than 60 percent, according to proponents.

Although the Madrid Protocol may simplify and reduce the cost of trademark registration in foreign countries, it remains to be seen whether it will provide significant benefits to trademark owners. Even assuming that the registration process will be easier, there is still the issue of whether member countries will enforce the law and protect the mark.

REVIEWING Intellectual Property and Internet Law

Two computer science majors, Trent and Xavier, have an idea for a new video game, which they propose to call "Hallowed." They form a business and begin developing their idea. Several months later, Trent and Xavier run into a problem with their design and consult with a friend, Brad, who is an expert in designing computer source codes. After the software is completed but before Hallowed is marketed, a video game called "Halo 2" is released for both the Xbox and Game Cube systems. Halo 2 uses source codes similar to those of Hallowed and imitates Hallowed's overall look and feel, although not all the features are alike. Using the information presented in the chapter, answer the following questions.

1. Would the name "Hallowed" receive protection as a trademark or as trade dress?
2. If Trent and Xavier had obtained a business process patent on Hallowed, would the release of Halo 2 infringe on their patent? Why or why not?
3. Based only on the facts described above, could Trent and Xavier sue the makers of Halo 2 for copyright infringement? Why or why not?
4. Suppose that Trent and Xavier discover that Brad took the idea of Hallowed and sold it to the company that produced Halo 2. Which type of intellectual property issue does this raise?

TERMS AND CONCEPTS

certification mark 341
collective mark 341
copyright 349
cyber mark 342
cybersquatting 343
dilution 338
distributed network 354
domain name 342
intellectual property 336
meta tag 344
patent 345
peer-to-peer (P2P) networking 353
service mark 341
trade dress 341
trade name 342
trade secret 356
trademark 336

QUESTIONS AND CASE PROBLEMS

14–1. Professor Wise is teaching a summer seminar in business torts at State University. Several times during the course, he makes copies of relevant sections from business law texts and distributes them to his students. Wise does not realize that the daughter of one of the textbook authors is a member of his seminar. She tells her father about Wise's copying activities, which have taken place without her father's or his publisher's permission. Her father sues Wise for copyright infringement. Wise claims protection under the fair use doctrine. Who will prevail? Explain.

14–2. QUESTION WITH SAMPLE ANSWER

In which of the following situations would a court likely hold Ursula liable for copyright infringement?

(a) Ursula goes to the library and photocopies ten pages from a scholarly journal relating to a topic on which she is writing a term paper.
(b) Ursula makes blouses, dresses, and other clothes and sells them in her small shop. She advertises some of the outfits as Guest items, hoping that customers might mistakenly assume that they were made by Guess, the well-known clothing manufacturer.
(c) Ursula teaches Latin American history at a small university. She has a DVR (digital video recorder) and frequently records television programs relating to Latin America. She then copies the programs to a DVD and brings them to her classroom so that her students can watch them.

- **For a sample answer to Question 14–2, go to Appendix I at the end of this text.**

14–3. Domain Name Disputes. In 1999, Steve and Pierce Thumann and their father, Fred, created Spider Webs, Ltd., a partnership, to, according to Steve, "develop Internet address names." Spider Webs registered nearly two thousand Internet domain names at an average cost of $70 each, including the names of cities, the names of buildings, names related to a business or trade (such as air-conditioning or plumbing), and the names of famous companies. It offered many of the names for sale on its Web site and through eBay.com. Spider Webs registered the domain name "ERNESTANDJULIOGALLO.COM" in Spider Webs' name. E. & J. Gallo Winery filed a suit against Spider Webs, alleging, in part, violations of the Anticybersquatting Consumer Protection Act (ACPA). Gallo asked the court for, among other things, statutory damages. Gallo also sought to have the domain name at issue transferred to Gallo. During the suit, Spider Webs published anticorporate articles and negative opinions about Gallo, as well as discussions of the suit and of the risks associated with alcohol use, at the URL ERNESTANDJULIOGALLO.COM. Should the court rule in Gallo's favor? Why or why not? [*E. & J. Gallo Winery v. Spider Webs, Ltd.*, 129 F.Supp.2d 1033 (S.D.Tex. 2001)]

14–4. CASE PROBLEM WITH SAMPLE ANSWER

Gateway, Inc., sells computers, computer products, computer peripherals, and computer accessories throughout the world. By 1988, Gateway had begun its first national advertising campaign using black-and-white cows and black-and-white cow spots. By 1991, black-and-white cows and spots had become Gateway's symbol. The next year, Gateway registered a black-and-white cow-spots design in association with computers and computer peripherals as its trademark. Companion Products, Inc. (CPI), sells stuffed animals trademarked as "Stretch Pets." Stretch Pets have an animal's head and an elastic body that can wrap around the edges of computer monitors, computer cases, or televisions. CPI produces sixteen Stretch Pets, including a polar bear, a moose, several dogs, and a penguin. One of CPI's top-selling products is a black-and-white cow that CPI identifies as "Cody Cow," which was first sold in 1999. Gateway filed a suit in a federal district court against CPI, alleging trade dress infringement and related claims. What is trade dress? What is the major factor in cases involving trade dress infringement? Does that factor exist in this case? Explain. [*Gateway, Inc. v. Companion Products, Inc.*, 384 F.3d 503 (8th Cir. 2004)]

- **To view a sample answer for Problem 14–4, go to this book's Web site at academic.cengage.com/blaw/cross, select "Chapter 14," and click on "Case Problem with Sample Answer."**

14–5. Patent Infringement. As a cattle rancher in Nebraska, Gerald Gohl used handheld searchlights to find and help calving animals (animals giving birth) in harsh blizzard conditions. Gohl thought that it would be more helpful to have a portable searchlight mounted on the outside of a vehicle and remotely controlled. He and Al Gebhardt developed and patented practical applications of this idea—the Golight and the wireless, remote-controlled Radio Ray, which could rotate 360 degrees—and formed Golight, Inc., to make and market these products. In 1997, Wal-Mart Stores, Inc., began selling a portable, wireless, remote-controlled searchlight that was identical to the Radio Ray except for a stop piece that prevented the light from rotating more than 351 degrees. Golight sent Wal-Mart a letter claiming that its device infringed Golight's patent. Wal-Mart sold its remaining inventory of the devices and stopped carrying the product. Golight filed a suit in a federal district court against Wal-Mart, alleging patent infringement. How should the court rule? Explain. [*Golight, Inc. v. Wal-Mart Stores, Inc.*, 355 F.3d 1327 (Fed.Cir. 2004)]

14–6. Copyright Infringement. Bridgeport Music, Inc., is in the business of publishing music and exploiting musical composition copyrights. Westbound Records, Inc., is in the business of recording and distributing sound recordings. Bridgeport and Westbound own the composition and recording copyrights to "Get Off Your Ass and Jam" by George Clinton, Jr., and the Funkadelics. The recording "Get Off" opens with a three-note solo guitar riff that lasts four seconds. The rap song "100 Miles and Runnin" contains a two-second sample from the guitar solo, at a lower pitch, looped and extended to sixteen beats, in five places in the song, with each looped segment lasting about seven seconds. "100 Miles" was included in the sound track of the movie *I Got the Hook Up,* which was distributed by No Limit Films. Bridgeport, Westbound, and others filed a suit in a federal district court against No Limit and others, alleging copyright infringement. Does a musician commit copyright infringement when he or she copies any part—even as little as two seconds—of a copyrighted sound recording without the permission of the copyright's owner? If so, how can an artist legally incorporate a riff from another's work in his or her own recording? Discuss. [*Bridgeport Music, Inc. v. Dimension Films,* 410 F.3d 792 (6th Cir. 2005)]

14–7. Trade Secrets. Briefing.com offers Internet-based analyses of investment opportunities to investors. Richard Green is the company's president. One of Briefing.com's competitors is StreetAccount, LLC (limited liability company), whose owners include Gregory Jones and Cynthia Dietzmann. Jones worked for Briefing.com for six years until he quit in March 2003 and was a member of its board of directors until April 2003. Dietzmann worked for Briefing.com for seven years until she quit in March 2003. As Briefing.com employees, Jones and Dietzmann had access to confidential business data. For instance, Dietzmann developed a list of contacts through which Briefing.com obtained market information to display online. When Dietzmann quit, however, she did not return all of the contact information to the company. Briefing.com and Green filed a suit in a federal district court against Jones, Dietzmann, and StreetAccount, alleging that they appropriated these data and other "trade secrets" to form a competing business. What are trade secrets? Why are they protected? Under what circumstances is a party liable at common law for their appropriation? How should these principles apply in this case? [*Briefing.com v. Jones,* 2006 WY 16, 126 P.3d 928 (2006)]

14–8. Trademarks. In 1969, Jack Masquelier, a professor of pharmacology, discovered a chemical antioxidant made from the bark of a French pine tree. The substance supposedly assists in nutritional distribution and blood circulation. Horphag Research, Ltd., began to sell the product under the name Pycnogenol, which Horphag registered as a trademark in 1993. Pycnogenol became one of the fifteen best-selling herbal supplements in the United States. In 1999, through the Web site **healthierlife.com**, Larry Garcia began to sell Masquelier's Original OPCs, a supplement derived from grape pits. Claiming that this product was the "true Pycnogenol," Garcia used the mark as a meta tag and a generic term, attributing the results of research on Horphag's product to Masquelier's and altering quotations from scientific literature to substitute the name of Masquelier's product for Horphag's. Customers who purchased Garcia's product contacted Horphag about it, only to learn that they had not bought Horphag's product. Others called Horphag to ask whether Garcia "was selling . . . real Pycnogenol." Horphag filed a suit in a federal district court against Garcia, alleging, among other things, that he was diluting Horphag's mark. What is trademark dilution? Did it occur here? Explain. [*Horphag Research, Ltd. v. Garcia,* 475 F.3d 1029 (9th Cir. 2007)]

14–9. A QUESTION OF ETHICS

*Custom Copies, Inc., in Gainesville, Florida, is a copy shop that, on request, reproduces and distributes, for profit, material published and owned by others. One of the copy shop's primary activities is the preparation and sale of coursepacks, which contain compilations of readings for college courses. For a particular coursepack, a teacher selects the readings and delivers a syllabus to the copy shop, which obtains the materials from a library, copies them, and then binds and sells the copies. Blackwell Publishing, Inc., in Malden, Massachusetts, publishes books and journals in medicine and other fields and owns the copyrights to these publications. Blackwell and others filed a suit in a federal district court against Custom Copies, alleging copyright infringement for its "routine and systematic reproduction of materials from plaintiffs' publications, without seeking permission," to compile coursepacks for classes at the University of Florida. The plaintiffs asked the court to issue an injunction and award them damages, as well the profit from the infringement. The defendant filed a motion to dismiss the complaint. [*Blackwell Publishing, Inc. v. Custom Copies, Inc., ___ F.Supp.2d ___ (N.D.Fla. 2006)]*

(a) Custom Copies argued in part that it did not "distribute" the coursepacks. Does a copy shop violate copyright law if it only copies materials for coursepacks? Does the copying fall under the "fair use" exception? Should the court grant the defendant's motion? Why or why not?

(b) What is the potential impact of creating and selling copies of a book or journal without the permission of, and the payment of royalties or a fee to, the copyright owner? Explain.

14–10. VIDEO QUESTION

Go to this text's Web site at **academic.cengage.com/blaw/cross** and select "Chapter 14." Click on "Video Questions" and view the video titled *The Jerk.* Then answer the following questions.

(a) In the video, Navin (Steve Martin) creates a special handle for Mr. Fox's (Bill Macy's) glasses. Can Navin obtain a patent or a copyright protecting his invention? Explain your answer.

(b) Suppose that after Navin legally protects his idea, Fox steals it and decides to develop it for himself, without Navin's permission. Has Fox committed infringement? If so, what kind—trademark, patent, or copyright?

(c) Suppose that after Navin legally protects his idea, he realizes he doesn't have the funds to mass-produce the glasses' special handle. Navin therefore agrees to allow Fox to manufacture the product. Has Navin granted Fox a license? Explain.

(d) Assume that Navin is able to manufacture his invention. What might Navin do to ensure that his product is identifiable and can be distinguished from other products on the market?

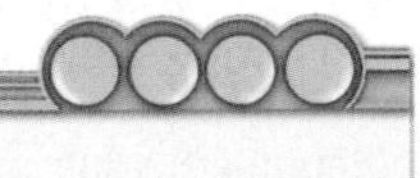

LAW ON THE WEB

For updated links to resources available on the Web, as well as a variety of other materials, visit this text's Web site at

academic.cengage.com/blaw/cross

An excellent overview of the laws governing various forms of intellectual property is available at FindLaw's Web site. Go to

profs.lp.findlaw.com

You can find answers to frequently asked questions (FAQs) about patents, trademarks, and copyrights—and links to registration forms, statutes, international patent and trademark offices, and numerous other resources—at the Web site of the U.S. Patent and Trademark Office. Go to

www.uspto.gov

To perform patent searches and to access information on the patenting process, go to

www.bustpatents.com

You can also access the European Patent Office's Web site at

www.epo.org

For information on copyrights, go to the U.S. Copyright Office at

www.copyright/gov

You can find extensive information on copyright law—including United States Supreme Court decisions in this area and the texts of the Berne Convention and other international treaties on copyright issues—at the Web site of the Legal Information Institute at Cornell University's School of Law. Go to

www.law.cornell.edu/wex/index.php/Copyright

Legal Research Exercises on the Web

Go to **academic.cengage.com/blaw/cross**, the Web site that accompanies this text. Select "Chapter 14" and click on "Internet Exercises." There you will find the following Internet research exercises that you can perform to learn more about the topics covered in this chapter.

Internet Exercise 14–1: Legal Perspective
Unwarranted Legal Threats

Internet Exercise 14–2: Management Perspective
Protecting Intellectual Property across Borders

Internet Exercise 14–3: Technological Perspective
File-Sharing

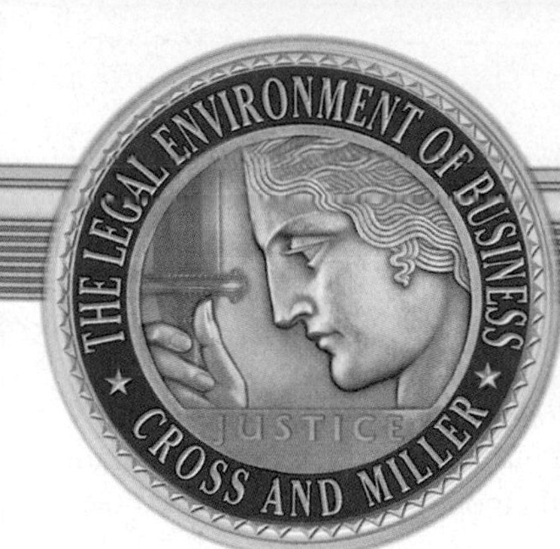

CHAPTER 15

Creditor-Debtor Relations and Bankruptcy

Normally, creditors have no problem collecting the debts owed to them. When disputes arise over the amount owed, however, or when the debtor simply cannot or will not pay, what happens? What remedies are available to creditors when a debtor **defaults** (fails to pay as promised)? In this chapter, we focus first on some basic laws that assist the debtor and creditor in resolving their dispute. We then examine the process of bankruptcy as a last resort in resolving debtor-creditor problems. Throughout the discussion of bankruptcy, we have incorporated the changes that resulted from the 2005 Bankruptcy Reform Act.[1]

1. The full title of the act is the Bankruptcy Abuse Prevention and Consumer Protection Act of 2005, Pub. L. No. 109-8, 119 Stat. 23 (April 20, 2005). The bulk of the act became effective in October 2005.

Laws Assisting Creditors

Both the common law and statutory laws create various rights and remedies for creditors. We discuss here some of these rights and remedies, including liens, garnishment, creditors' composition agreements, and mortgage foreclosure.

Liens

A **lien** is a claim against a debtor's property that must be satisfied before the property (or its proceeds) is available to satisfy the claims of other creditors. As mentioned, liens may arise under the common law or under statutory law. Statutory liens include *mechanic's liens,* whereas *artisan's liens* were recognized at common law. *Judicial liens* are those that represent a creditor's efforts to collect on a debt before or after a judgment is entered by a court. Liens are a very important tool for creditors because they generally take priority over other claims against the same property.

Mechanic's Liens When a person contracts for labor, services, or materials to be furnished for the purpose of making improvements on real property but does not immediately pay for the improvements, the creditor can place a **mechanic's lien** on the property. This creates a special type of debtor-creditor relationship in which the real estate itself becomes security for the debt.

For example, a painter agrees to paint a house for a homeowner for an agreed-on price to cover labor and materials. If the homeowner cannot pay or pays only a portion of the charges, a mechanic's lien against the property can be created. The painter is the lienholder, and the real property is encumbered (burdened) with the mechanic's lien for the amount owed. If the homeowner does not pay the lien, the property can be sold to satisfy the debt. Notice of the *foreclosure* (the enforcement of the lien) must be given to the debtor in advance, however.

Note that state law governs the procedures that must be followed to create a mechanic's lien. Generally, the lienholder has to file a written notice of lien against the particular property involved. The notice of lien must be filed within a specific time period, measured from the last date on which materials or labor was provided (usually within 60 to 120 days). If the property owner fails to pay the debt, the lienholder is entitled to foreclose on the real estate on which the improvements were made and to sell it to satisfy the amount of the debt. Of course, as mentioned, the lienholder is required by statute to give notice to the owner of the property prior to foreclosure and sale. The sale proceeds are used to pay the debt and the costs of the legal proceedings; the surplus, if any, is paid to the former owner.

Artisan's Liens An **artisan's lien** is a device created at common law through which a creditor can recover payment from a debtor for labor and materials furnished in the repair of personal property. In contrast to a mechanic's lien, an artisan's lien is *possessory*. This means that the lienholder ordinarily must have retained possession of the property and have expressly or impliedly agreed to provide the services on a cash, not a credit, basis. The lien remains in existence as long as the lienholder maintains possession, and the lien is terminated once possession is voluntarily surrendered—unless the surrender is only temporary.

For example, Whitney leaves her diamond ring at the jewelry shop to be repaired and to have her initials engraved on the band. In the absence of an agreement, the jeweler can keep the ring until Whitney pays for the services that the jeweler provides. Should Whitney fail to pay, the jeweler has a lien on Whitney's ring for the amount of the bill and can sell the ring in satisfaction of the lien.

Modern statutes permit the holder of an artisan's lien to foreclose and sell the property subject to the lien to satisfy payment of the debt. As with a mechanic's lien, the lienholder is required to give notice to the owner of the property prior to foreclosure and sale. The sale proceeds are used to pay the debt and the costs of the legal proceedings, and the surplus, if any, is paid to the former owner.

Judicial Liens When a debt is past due, a creditor can bring a legal action against the debtor to collect the debt. If the creditor is successful in the action, the court awards the creditor a judgment against the debtor (usually for the amount of the debt plus any interest and legal costs incurred in obtaining the judgment). Frequently, however, the creditor is unable to collect the awarded amount.

To ensure that a judgment in the creditor's favor will be collectible, the creditor is permitted to request that certain nonexempt property of the debtor be seized to satisfy the debt. (As will be discussed later in this chapter, under state or federal statutes, some kinds of property are exempt from attachment by creditors.) If the court orders the debtor's property to be seized prior to a judgment in the creditor's favor, the court's order is referred to as a *writ of attachment*. If the court orders the debtor's property to be seized following a judgment in the creditor's favor, the court's order is referred to as a *writ of execution*.

Writ of Attachment. In the context of judicial liens, **attachment** refers to a court-ordered seizure and taking into custody of property prior to the securing of a judgment for a past-due debt. Normally, attachment is a *prejudgment* remedy, occurring either at the time a lawsuit is filed or immediately thereafter. In order to attach *before* a judgment, a creditor must comply with the specific state's statutory restrictions. The due process clause of the Fourteenth Amendment to the U.S. Constitution also applies and requires that the debtor be given notice and an opportunity to be heard (see Chapter 5).

The creditor must have an enforceable right to payment of the debt under law and must follow certain procedures. Otherwise, the creditor can be liable for damages for wrongful attachment. Typically, the creditor must file with the court an *affidavit* (a written or printed statement, made under oath or sworn to) stating that the debtor has failed to pay and delineating the statutory grounds under which attachment is sought. The creditor must also post a bond to cover at least the court costs, the value of the property attached, and the value of the loss of use of that property suffered by the debtor. When the court is satisfied that all the requirements have been met, it issues a **writ of attachment,** which directs the sheriff or other officer to seize nonexempt property. If the creditor prevails at trial, the seized property can be sold to satisfy the judgment.

Writ of Execution. If a creditor obtains a judgment against the debtor and the debtor will not or cannot pay the judgment, the creditor is entitled to go back to the court and request a writ of execution. A **writ of execution** is an order that directs the sheriff to seize (levy) and sell any of the debtor's nonexempt real or personal property that is within the court's geographic jurisdiction (usually the county in which the courthouse is located). The proceeds of the sale are used to pay the judgment, accrued interest, and the costs of the sale. Any excess is paid to the debtor. The debtor can pay the judgment and redeem the nonexempt property at any time before the sale takes place. (Because of exemption laws and bankruptcy laws, however, many judgments are virtually uncollectible.)

Garnishment

An order for **garnishment** permits a creditor to collect a debt by seizing property of the debtor that is being held by a third party. In a garnishment proceeding, the third party—the person or entity on whom the garnishment judgment is served—is called the *garnishee*. Typically, the garnishee is the debtor's employer, and the creditor is seeking a judgment so that part of the debtor's usual paycheck will be paid to the creditor. In some situations, however, the garnishee is a third party that holds funds belonging to the debtor (such as a bank) or who has possession of, or exercises control over, funds or other types of property belonging to the debtor. Almost all types of property can be garnished, including tax refunds, pensions, and trust funds—so long as the property is not exempt from garnishment and is in the possession of a third party.

Garnishment Proceedings State law governs garnishment actions, so the specific procedures vary from state to state. According to the laws in many states, the judgment creditor needs to obtain only one order of garnishment, which will then apply continuously to the judgment debtor's weekly wages until the entire debt is paid. Garnishment can be a prejudgment remedy, requiring a hearing before a court, or a postjudgment remedy.

Laws Limiting the Amount of Wages Subject to Garnishment Both federal and state laws limit the amount that can be taken from a debtor's weekly take-home pay through garnishment proceedings.[2] Federal law provides a minimal framework to protect debtors from losing all their income to pay judgment debts.[3] State laws also provide dollar exemptions, and these amounts are often larger than those provided by federal law. Under federal law, an employer cannot dismiss an employee because his or her wages are being garnished.

The question in the following case was whether payments to an independent contractor for services performed could be garnished.

2. A few states (for example, Texas) do not permit garnishment of wages by private parties except under a child-support order.

3. For example, the federal Consumer Credit Protection Act, 15 U.S.C. Sections 1601–1693r, provides that a debtor can retain either 75 percent of his or her disposable earnings per week or an amount equivalent to thirty hours of work paid at federal minimum wage rates, whichever is greater.

CASE 15.1 Indiana Surgical Specialists v. Griffin

Court of Appeals of Indiana, 2007. 867 N.E.2d 260.

• **Background and Facts** Helen Griffin owed Indiana Surgical Services a certain amount. When the debt was not paid, Indiana Surgical filed a suit in an Indiana small claims court against Griffin. Griffin did not answer the complaint. In 2001, the court issued a default judgment against her. Four years later, Indiana Surgical learned that Griffin worked for MDS Courier Services. On Indiana Surgical's request, the court issued a garnishment order against MDS to "withhold from the earnings of" Griffin the appropriate amount until her debt was paid. MDS responded,

> MDS Courier Services, Inc. employs drivers on a "contract" basis, therefore, drivers are not actual employees, but rather "contracted" to do a particular job. Because of this, we are not responsible for any payroll deductions including garnishments.

Indiana Surgical asked the court to hold MDS in contempt. Dawn Klingenberger, an MDS manager, testified that Griffin was a subcontractor of MDS, called as needed, compensated per job at "thirty-five percent of whatever she does," and paid on a biweekly basis. The court ruled that "the judgment debtor is a subcontractor, and not an employee," and that her earnings could not be garnished. Indiana Surgical appealed to a state intermediate appellate court.

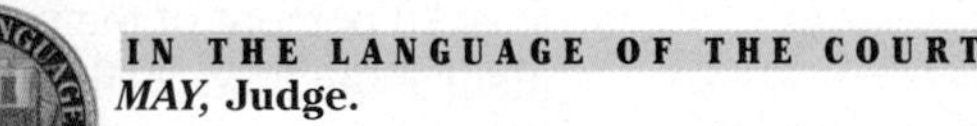

IN THE LANGUAGE OF THE COURT

***MAY,* Judge.**

* * * *

Indiana Surgical argues the trial court erred by declining to enforce the garnishment order issued to MDS on the ground Griffin was a "subcontractor" and not an employee of MDS. Indiana Surgical asserts the trial court's "distinction between wages subject to withholding and other earnings" is not supported in law. Under the facts of this case, we agree.

Garnishment refers to "any legal or equitable proceedings through which the earnings of an individual are required to be withheld by a garnishee, by the individual debtor, or by any other person for the payment of a judgment" [under Indiana Code Section 24-4.5-5-105(1)(b)].

CASE CONTINUES

CASE 15.1 CONTINUED Earnings are [defined in Indiana Code Section 24-4.5-1-301(9) as] "compensation paid or payable for personal services, whether denominated as wages, salary, commission, bonus, or otherwise, and includes periodic payments under a pension or retirement program."[a] In discussing the [provision in the Consumer Credit Protection Act that is the] federal counterpart to the Indiana statute, the [United States] Supreme Court stated: "*There is every indication that Congress, in an effort to avoid the necessity of bankruptcy, sought to regulate garnishment in its usual sense as a levy on periodic payments of compensation needed to support the wage earner and his family on a week-to-week, month-to-month basis.*" [Emphasis added.]

Griffin received "periodic payments of compensation" for her personal services as a courier. These payments were earnings that could be garnished through a garnishment order. The trial court erred to the extent it held otherwise. We reverse and remand for further proceedings including, but not limited to, a determination of MDS's liability for payments made to Griffin after Indiana Surgical acquired an equitable lien upon service of process in [garnishment proceedings]. In light of our holding, the trial court should also determine whether MDS should be held in contempt of the garnishment order.

• **Decision and Remedy** *The state intermediate appellate court held that payments for the services of an independent contractor fall within the applicable definition of "earnings" and thus Griffin's earnings as an independent contractor could be garnished. The court reversed the decision of the lower court and remanded the case.*

• **The Ethical Dimension** *Should some persons be exempt from garnishment orders? Explain.*

• **The Legal Environment Dimension** *Building contractors and subcontractors are typically classified as independent contractors. Could payments to these parties also fall within the definition of "earnings" applied in this case? Discuss.*

a. Indiana's definition of earnings is included in the part of the Indiana Code known as the Uniform Consumer Credit Code, which was derived from the federal Consumer Credit Protection Act. The federal provision defining earnings is identical.

Creditors' Composition Agreements

Creditors may contract with the debtor for discharge of the debtor's liquidated debts (debts that are definite, or fixed, in amount) on payment of a sum less than that owed. These agreements are referred to as *composition agreements* or **creditors' composition agreements** and are usually held to be enforceable unless they are formed under duress.

Mortgages

A **mortgage** is a written instrument giving a creditor an interest in (lien on) the debtor's real property as security for the payment of a debt. Financial institutions grant mortgage loans for the purchase of property—usually a dwelling (real property will be discussed in Chapter 25). Given the relatively large sums that many individuals borrow to purchase a home, defaults are not uncommon. In fact, during 2007 and 2008 the number of defaults on mortgages increased dramatically. (For a discussion of the so-called subprime mortgage crisis, see the *Focus on Ethics* feature at the end of Unit 6.) Mortgages are recorded with the county in the state where the property is located. Recording ensures that the creditor is officially on record as holding an interest in the property. As a further precaution, most creditors require mortgage life insurance for debtors who do not pay at least 20 percent of the purchase price as a down payment at the time of the transaction.

Mortgage Foreclosure In the event of a debtor's default, the entire mortgage debt becomes due and payable. If the debtor cannot pay, the mortgage holder has the right to foreclose on the mortgaged property. The usual method of foreclosure is by judicial sale of the property, although the statutory methods of foreclosure vary from state to state. If the proceeds of the foreclosure sale are sufficient to cover both the costs of the foreclosure and the mortgage debt, any surplus goes to the debtor. If the sale proceeds are insufficient to cover the foreclosure costs and the mortgage debt, however, the **mortgagee** (the creditor-lender) can seek to recover the difference from the **mortgagor** (the debtor) by obtaining a *deficiency judgment.*

The mortgagee obtains a deficiency judgment in a separate legal action that is pursued subsequent to the foreclosure action. The deficiency judgment entitles the creditor to recover from other property owned by the debtor. Some states do not permit deficiency judgments for certain types of real estate interests.

Redemption Rights Before the foreclosure sale, a defaulting mortgagor can redeem the property by paying the full amount of the debt, plus any interest and costs that have accrued. This is known as the **right of redemption.** Some states even allow a mortgagor to redeem the property within a certain period of time after the foreclosure sale—called a *statutory period of redemption.* In states that allow redemption after the sale, the deed to the property usually is not delivered to the purchaser until the statutory period has expired. *Concept Summary 15.1* provides a synopsis of the remedies available to creditors.

Section 2 Suretyship and Guaranty

When a third person promises to pay a debt owed by another in the event that the debtor does not pay, either a *suretyship* or a *guaranty* relationship is created. Exhibit 15–1 on the following page illustrates these relationships. The third person's credit becomes the security for the debt owed. At common law, there were significant differences in the liability of a surety and a guarantor, as will be discussed in the following subsections. Today, however, the distinctions outlined here have been abolished in some states.

Suretyship

A contract of **suretyship** is a promise made by a third person to be responsible for the debtor's obligation. It is an express contract between the **surety** (the third party) and the creditor. In the strictest sense, the surety is primarily liable for the debt of the principal. This means that the creditor can demand payment from the surety from the moment the debt is due and that the creditor need not exhaust all legal remedies against the principal debtor before holding the surety responsible for payment. Thus, a suretyship contract is

CONCEPT SUMMARY 15.1 Remedies Available to Creditors

Remedy	Description
LIENS	1. *Mechanic's lien*—A lien placed on an owner's real estate for labor, services, or materials furnished for improvements made to the realty. 2. *Artisan's lien*—A lien placed on an owner's personal property for labor performed or value added to that property. 3. *Judicial liens*— a. Writ of attachment—A court-ordered seizure of property prior to a court's final determination of the creditor's rights to the property. Creditors must strictly comply with applicable state statutes to obtain a writ of attachment. b. Writ of execution—A court order directing the sheriff to seize (levy) and sell a debtor's nonexempt real or personal property to satisfy a court's judgment in the creditor's favor.
GARNISHMENT	A collection remedy that allows the creditor to attach a debtor's funds (such as wages owed or bank accounts) and property that are held by a third person.
CREDITORS' COMPOSITION AGREEMENT	A contract between a debtor and her or his creditors by which the debtor's debts are discharged by payment of a sum less than the sum that is actually owed.
MORTGAGE FORECLOSURE	On the debtor's default, the entire mortgage debt is due and payable, allowing the creditor to foreclose on the realty by selling it to satisfy the debt.

EXHIBIT 15–1 • Suretyship and Guaranty Parties

In a suretyship or guaranty arrangement, a third party promises to be responsible for a debtor's obligations. A third party who agrees to be responsible for the debt even if the primary debtor does not default is known as a surety; a third party who agrees to be *secondarily* responsible for the debt—that is, responsible only if the primary debtor defaults—is known as a guarantor. Normally, a promise of guaranty (a collateral, or secondary, promise) must be in writing to be enforceable.

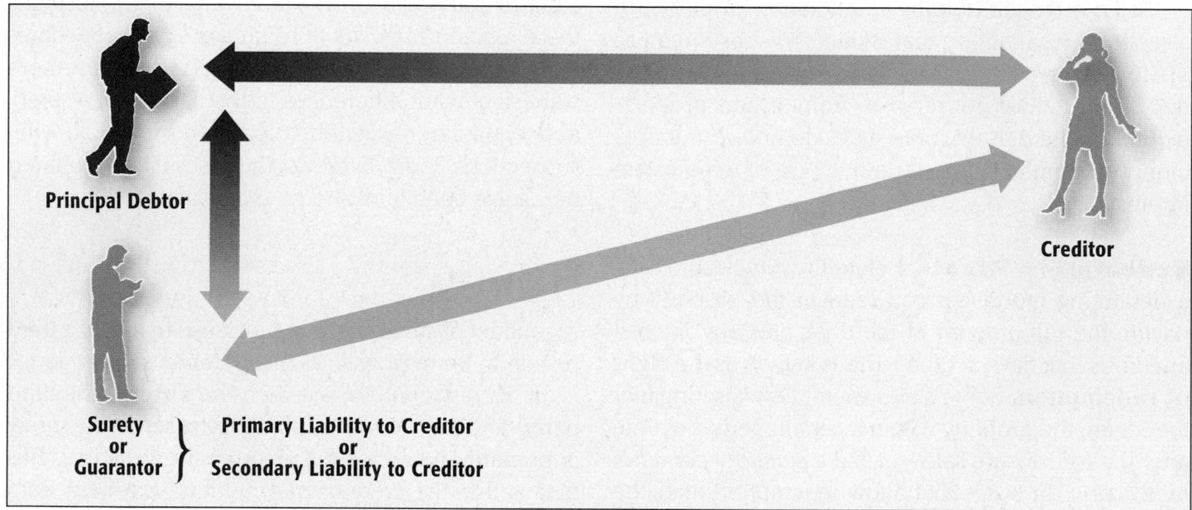

not a form of indemnity; that is, it is not merely a promise to make good any loss that a creditor may incur as a result of the debtor's failure to pay. Moreover, a surety agreement does not have to be in writing to be enforceable, although usually such agreements are in writing.

For example, Jason Oller wants to borrow funds from the bank to buy a used car. Because Jason is still in college, the bank will not lend him the funds unless his father, Stuart Oller, who has dealt with the bank before, will cosign the note (add his signature to the note, thereby becoming jointly liable for payment of the debt). When Mr. Oller cosigns the note, he becomes primarily liable to the bank. On the note's due date, the bank can seek payment from Jason Oller, Stuart Oller, or both jointly.

Guaranty

A guaranty contract is similar to a suretyship contract in that it includes a promise to answer for the debt or default of another. There are some significant differences between these two types of contracts, however.

Suretyship versus Guaranty With a suretyship arrangement, the surety is *primarily* liable for the debtor's obligation. With a guaranty arrangement, the **guarantor**—the third person making the guaranty—is *secondarily* liable. The guarantor can be required to pay the obligation only after the principal debtor defaults, and usually only after the creditor has made an attempt to collect from the debtor.

For example, a corporation, BX Enterprises, needs to borrow to meet its payroll. The bank is skeptical about the creditworthiness of BX and requires Dawson, its president, who is a wealthy businessperson and owner of 70 percent of BX Enterprises, to sign an agreement making herself personally liable for payment if BX does not pay off the loan. As a guarantor of the loan, Dawson cannot be held liable until BX Enterprises is in default.

Under the Statute of Frauds, a guaranty contract between the guarantor and the creditor must be in writing to be enforceable unless the *main purpose* exception applies.[4] A suretyship agreement, by contrast, need not be in writing to be enforceable. In other words, surety agreements can be oral, whereas guaranty contracts must be written.

The Extent and Time of the Guarantor's Liability The guaranty contract terms determine the extent and time of the guarantor's liability. For

4. Briefly, the main purpose exception provides that if the main purpose of the guaranty agreement is to benefit the guarantor, then the contract need not be in writing to be enforceable.

example, the guaranty can be *continuing*, designed to cover a series of transactions by the debtor. Also, the guaranty can be *unlimited* or *limited* as to time and amount. In addition, the guaranty can be *absolute* or *conditional*. When a guaranty is absolute, the guarantor becomes liable immediately on the debtor's default. With a conditional guaranty, the guarantor becomes liable only on the happening of a certain event. For example, Days Inns of America, Inc., entered into a contract that licensed P&N Enterprises, Inc., to operate a guest lodging facility in Connecticut. The president of P&N Enterprises, Paul Yeh, signed the licensing contract and also signed a guaranty contract, in his individual capacity. Yeh personally guaranteed P&N's obligations under the license agreement, "provided that P&N's tangible net worth was less than $1,000,000 at the time of payment or performance." The condition of that promise (the guaranty) was the tangible net worth requirement.[5]

Defenses of the Surety and the Guarantor

The defenses of the surety and the guarantor are basically the same. Therefore, the following discussion applies to both, although it refers only to the surety.

Actions Releasing the Surety Certain actions will release the surety from the obligation. If the principal obligation is paid by the debtor or by another person on behalf of the debtor, the surety is discharged from the obligation. Similarly, if valid tender of payment is made, and the creditor for some reason rejects it with knowledge of the surety's existence, then the surety is released from any obligation on the debt.

In addition, if a creditor surrenders the collateral to the debtor or impairs the collateral while knowing of the surety and without the surety's consent, the surety is released to the extent of any loss suffered as a result of the creditor's actions. The primary reason for this requirement is to protect a surety who agreed to become obligated only because the debtor's collateral was in the possession of the creditor.

Finally, making any material modification in the terms of the original contract between the principal debtor and the creditor can operate to discharge a surety's obligations. For example, a gratuitous surety will be completely discharged if the principal debtor and the creditor materially modify the contract without first obtaining the surety's consent. (A *gratuitous surety* is one who receives no consideration in return for acting as a surety, such as a father who agrees to assume responsibility for his daughter's debt obligation.) A surety who is compensated (such as a venture capitalist who will profit from a loan made to the principal debtor) will be discharged from the contract only if the modification is actually or potentially detrimental to the surety.

Defenses of the Principal Debtor Generally, the surety can use any defenses available to the principal debtor to avoid liability on the obligation to the creditor. The ability of the surety to assert any defenses the debtor may have against the creditor is the most important concept in suretyship. It means that most of the defenses available to the debtor are also those of the surety. A few exceptions do exist, however. The surety cannot assert the principal debtor's incapacity or bankruptcy as a defense, nor can the surety assert the statute of limitations as a defense.

Obviously, a surety may also have his or her own defenses—for example, incapacity or bankruptcy. If the creditor fraudulently induced the surety to guarantee the debt, the surety can assert fraud as a defense. In most states, the creditor has a legal duty to inform the surety, prior to the formation of the suretyship contract, of material facts known by the creditor that would substantially increase the surety's risk. Failure to so inform is fraud and makes the suretyship obligation voidable.

Rights of the Surety and the Guarantor

Generally, when the surety or guarantor pays the debt owed to the creditor, the surety or guarantor is entitled to certain rights. Because the rights of the surety and the guarantor are basically the same, the following discussion applies to both.

The Right of Subrogation First, the surety has the legal **right of subrogation.** Simply stated, this means that any right the creditor had against the debtor now becomes the right of the surety. Included are creditor rights in bankruptcy and rights to judgments obtained by the creditor. In short, the surety now stands in the shoes of the creditor and may pursue any remedies that were available to the creditor against the debtor.

5. *Days Inns of America, Inc. v. P&N Enterprises, Inc.*, 2006 WL 2801248 (D.Conn. 2006). For another example of a conditional guaranty, see *Express Recovery Services, Inc. v. Rice*, 2005 UT App 495, 125 P.3d 108 (2005).

The Right of Reimbursement Second, the surety has a **right of reimbursement** from the debtor. Basically, the surety is entitled to receive from the debtor all outlays made on behalf of the suretyship arrangement. Such outlays can include expenses incurred as well as the actual amount of the debt paid to the creditor.

The Right of Contribution Third, in the situation of **co-sureties** (two or more sureties on the same obligation owed by the debtor), a surety who pays more than her or his proportionate share on a debtor's default is entitled to recover from the co-sureties the amount paid above the surety's obligation. This is the **right of contribution.** Generally, a co-surety's liability either is determined by agreement or, in the absence of agreement, is set at the maximum liability under the suretyship contract.

Suppose that two co-sureties are obligated under a suretyship contract to guarantee the debt of a debtor. Together, the sureties' maximum liability is $25,000. Surety A's maximum liability is $15,000, and surety B's is $10,000. The debtor owes $10,000 and is in default. Surety A pays the creditor the entire $10,000. In the absence of agreement, surety A can recover $4,000 from surety B ($10,000/$25,000 × $10,000 = $4,000, surety B's obligation).

Protection for Debtors

The law protects debtors as well as creditors. Certain property of the debtor, for example, is exempt under state law from creditors' actions. Consumer protection statutes (see Chapter 23) also protect debtors' rights. Of course, bankruptcy laws, which will be discussed shortly, are designed specifically to assist debtors in need of help.

In most states, certain types of real and personal property are exempt from execution or attachment. State exemption statutes usually include both real and personal property.

Exempted Real Property

Probably the most familiar exemption is the **homestead exemption.** Each state permits the debtor to retain the family home, either in its entirety or up to a specified dollar amount, free from the claims of unsecured creditors or trustees in bankruptcy. (Note that federal bankruptcy laws after 2005 place a cap of $125,000 for debtors in bankruptcy who have recently moved and are seeking to use state homestead exemptions.)

Suppose that Beere owes Veltman $40,000. The debt is the subject of a lawsuit, and the court awards Veltman a judgment of $40,000 against Beere. Beere's homestead is valued at $50,000, and the homestead exemption is $25,000. There are no outstanding mortgages or other liens on his homestead. To satisfy the judgment debt, Beere's family home is sold at public auction for $45,000. The proceeds of the sale are distributed as follows:

1. Beere is given $25,000 as his homestead exemption.
2. Veltman is paid $20,000 toward the judgment debt, leaving a $20,000 deficiency judgment (that is, "leftover debt") that can be satisfied from any other nonexempt property (personal or real) that Beere may own, if permitted by state law.

In a few states, statutes allow the homestead exemption only if the judgment debtor has a family. If a judgment debtor does not have a family, a creditor may be entitled to collect the full amount realized from the sale of the debtor's home.

Exempted Personal Property

Personal property that is most often exempt from satisfaction of judgment debts includes the following:

1. Household furniture up to a specified dollar amount.
2. Clothing and certain personal possessions, such as family pictures or a Bible.
3. A vehicle (or vehicles) for transportation (at least up to a specified dollar amount).
4. Certain classified animals, usually livestock but including pets.
5. Equipment that the debtor uses in a business or trade, such as tools or professional instruments, up to a specified dollar amount.

Bankruptcy and Reorganization

We look now at another significant right of debtors: the right to petition for bankruptcy relief under federal law. Article I, Section 8, of the U.S. Constitution gave Congress the power to establish "uniform Laws on the subject of Bankruptcies throughout the United States."

Bankruptcy law in the United States has two goals—to protect a debtor by giving him or her a fresh start, free from creditors' claims, and to ensure equitable treatment to creditors who are competing for a debtor's assets. Federal bankruptcy legislation was first enacted in 1898 and has undergone several modifications since that time, most recently in 2005 as a result of the 2005 Bankruptcy Reform Act. The 2005 act significantly overhauled certain provisions of the Bankruptcy Code for the first time in twenty-five years.

Bankruptcy Proceedings

Bankruptcy proceedings are held in federal bankruptcy courts, which are under the authority of the U.S. district courts, and rulings from bankruptcy courts can be appealed to the district courts. Although bankruptcy law is federal law, state laws on secured transactions, liens, judgments, and exemptions also play a role in federal bankruptcy proceedings.

Essentially, a bankruptcy court fulfills the role of an administrative court for the federal district court concerning matters in bankruptcy. The bankruptcy court holds proceedings dealing with the procedures required to administer the estate of the debtor in bankruptcy (the *estate* consists of the debtor's assets, as will be discussed shortly). A bankruptcy court can conduct a jury trial if the appropriate district court has authorized it and the parties to the bankruptcy consent.

Types of Bankruptcy Relief

Title 11 of the *United States Code* encompasses the Bankruptcy Code, which has eight chapters. Chapters 1, 3, and 5 of the Code contain general definitional provisions, as well as provisions governing case administration, creditors, the debtor, and the estate. These three chapters normally apply to all kinds of bankruptcies. The next five chapters of the Code set forth the different types of relief that debtors may seek. Chapter 7 provides for **liquidation** proceedings (the selling of all nonexempt assets and the distribution of the proceeds to the debtor's creditors). Chapter 9 governs the adjustment of a municipality's debts. Chapter 11 governs reorganizations. Chapters 12 and 13 provide for the adjustment of debts by parties with regular incomes (family farmers and family fishermen under Chapter 12 and individuals under Chapter 13).[6] A debtor (except for a municipality) does not have to be insolvent[7] to file for bankruptcy relief under any chapter of the Bankruptcy Code. Anyone obligated to a creditor can declare bankruptcy.

Special Treatment of Consumer-Debtors

To ensure that consumer-debtors are fully informed of the various types of relief available, the Code requires that the clerk of the bankruptcy court provide certain information to all consumer-debtors before they file for bankruptcy. A **consumer-debtor** is a debtor whose debts result primarily from the purchase of goods for personal, family, or household use. First, the clerk must give consumer-debtors written notice of the general purpose, benefits, and costs of each chapter of the Bankruptcy Code under which they might proceed. Second, the clerk must provide consumer-debtors with informational materials on the types of services available from credit counseling agencies.

Liquidation Proceedings

Liquidation under Chapter 7 of the Bankruptcy Code is generally the most familiar type of bankruptcy proceeding and is often referred to as an *ordinary*, or *straight, bankruptcy*. Put simply, a debtor in a liquidation bankruptcy turns all assets over to a **trustee.** The trustee sells the nonexempt assets and distributes the proceeds to creditors. With certain exceptions, the remaining debts are then **discharged** (extinguished), and the debtor is relieved of the obligation to pay the debts.

Any "person"—defined as including individuals, partnerships, and corporations[8]—may be a debtor in a liquidation proceeding. Railroads, insurance companies, banks, savings and loan associations, investment companies licensed by the Small Business Administration, and credit unions cannot be debtors in a liquidation bankruptcy, however. Other chapters of the Bankruptcy Code or other federal or state statutes apply to them. A husband and wife may file jointly for bankruptcy under a single petition.

6. There are no Chapters 2, 4, 6, 8, or 10 in Title 11. Such "gaps" are not uncommon in the *United States Code*. This is because chapter numbers (or other subdivisional unit numbers) are sometimes reserved for future use when a statute is enacted. (A gap may also appear if a law has been repealed.)

7. The inability to pay debts as they become due is known as *equitable* insolvency. A *balance sheet* insolvency, which exists when a debtor's liabilities exceed assets, is not the test. Thus, it is possible for debtors to petition for bankruptcy voluntarily or to be forced into involuntary bankruptcy even though their assets far exceed their liabilities. This may occur when a debtor's cash flow problems become severe.

8. The definition of *corporation* includes unincorporated companies and associations. It also covers labor unions.

A straight bankruptcy may be commenced by the filing of either a voluntary or an involuntary **petition in bankruptcy**—the document that is filed with a bankruptcy court to initiate bankruptcy proceedings. If a debtor files the petition, it is a voluntary bankruptcy. If one or more creditors file a petition to force the debtor into bankruptcy, it is called an involuntary bankruptcy. We discuss both voluntary and involuntary bankruptcy proceedings under Chapter 7 in the following subsections.

Voluntary Bankruptcy

To bring a voluntary petition in bankruptcy, the debtor files official forms designated for that purpose in the bankruptcy court. Under the Bankruptcy Reform Act of 2005, before debtors can file a petition, they must receive credit counseling from an approved nonprofit agency within the 180-day period preceding the date of filing. The act outlined detailed criteria for the **U.S. trustee** (a government official who performs appointment and other administrative tasks that a bankruptcy judge would otherwise have to perform) to approve nonprofit budget and counseling agencies and required the U.S. trustee to make the list of approved agencies publicly available. A debtor filing a Chapter 7 petition must include a certificate proving that he or she received individual or group briefing from an approved counseling agency within the last 180 days (roughly six months).

The Code requires a consumer-debtor who has opted for liquidation bankruptcy proceedings to confirm the accuracy of the petition's contents. The debtor must also state in the petition, at the time of filing, that he or she understands the relief available under other chapters of the Code and has chosen to proceed under Chapter 7. If an attorney is representing the consumer-debtor, the attorney must file an affidavit stating that she or he has informed the debtor of the relief available under each chapter of the Bankruptcy Code. In addition, the Code requires the attorney to reasonably attempt to verify the accuracy of the consumer-debtor's petition and schedules (described below). Failure to do so is considered perjury.

Chapter 7 Schedules The voluntary petition must contain the following schedules:

1. A list of both secured and unsecured creditors, their addresses, and the amount of debt owed to each.
2. A statement of the financial affairs of the debtor.
3. A list of all property owned by the debtor, including property that the debtor claims is exempt.
4. A list of current income and expenses.
5. A certificate of credit counseling (as discussed previously).
6. Proof of payments received from employers within sixty days prior to the filing of the petition.
7. A statement of the amount of monthly income, itemized to show how the amount is calculated.
8. A copy of the debtor's federal income tax return for the most recent year ending immediately before the filing of the petition.

As previously noted, the official forms must be completed accurately, sworn to under oath, and signed by the debtor. To conceal assets or knowingly supply false information on these schedules is a crime under the bankruptcy laws.

With the exception of tax returns, failure to file the required schedules within forty-five days after the filing of the petition (unless an extension of up to forty-five days is granted) will result in an automatic dismissal of the petition. The debtor has up to seven days before the date of the first creditors' meeting to provide a copy of the most recent tax returns to the trustee.

Additional Information May Be Required At the request of the court, the trustee, or any party in interest, the debtor must file tax returns at the end of each tax year while the case is pending and provide copies to the court. This requirement also applies to Chapter 11 and 13 bankruptcies (discussed later in this chapter). Also, if requested by the trustee, the debtor must provide a photo document establishing his or her identity (such as a driver's license or passport) or other such personal identifying information.

Substantial Abuse Prior to 2005, a bankruptcy court could dismiss a Chapter 7 petition for relief (discharge of debts) if the use of Chapter 7 would constitute a "substantial abuse" of that chapter. The Bankruptcy Reform Act of 2005 established a new system of "means testing" (the debtor's income) to determine whether a debtor's petition is presumed to be a "substantial abuse" of Chapter 7.

When Abuse Will Be Presumed. If the debtor's family income is greater than the median family income in the state in which the petition is filed, the trustee or any party in interest (such as a creditor) can bring a motion to dismiss the Chapter 7 petition. State median incomes vary from state to state and are calculated and reported by the U.S. Bureau of the Census.

The debtor's current monthly income is calculated using the last six months' average income, less certain "allowed expenses" reflecting the basic needs of the debtor. The monthly amount is then multiplied by twelve. If the resulting income exceeds the state median income by $6,000 or more,[9] abuse is presumed, and the trustee or any creditor can file a motion to dismiss the petition. A debtor can rebut (refute) the presumption of abuse "by demonstrating special circumstances that justify additional expenses or adjustments of current monthly income for which there is no reasonable alternative." (An example might be anticipated medical costs not covered by health insurance.) These additional expenses or adjustments must be itemized and their accuracy attested to under oath by the debtor.

9. This amount ($6,000) is the equivalent of $100 per month for five years, indicating that the debtor could pay at least $100 per month under a Chapter 13 five-year repayment plan.

When Abuse Will Not Be Presumed. If the debtor's income is below the state median (or if the debtor has successfully refuted the means-test presumption), abuse will not be presumed. In these situations, the court may still find substantial abuse, but the creditors will not have standing (see Chapter 2) to file a motion to dismiss. Basically, this leaves intact the prior law on substantial abuse, allowing the court to consider such factors as the debtor's bad faith or circumstances indicating substantial abuse.

Can a debtor seeking relief under Chapter 7 exclude voluntary contributions to a retirement plan as a reasonably necessary expense in calculating her income? The Code does not disallow the contributions, but whether their exclusion constitutes substantial abuse requires a review of the debtor's circumstances, as in the following case.

EXTENDED CASE 15.2 Hebbring v. U.S. Trustee

United States Court of Appeals, Ninth Circuit, 2006. 463 F.3d 902.

***WARDLAW*, Circuit Judge.**

* * * *

Lisa Hebbring filed a Chapter 7 bankruptcy petition in the United States Bankruptcy Court for the District of Nevada on June 5, 2003, seeking relief from $11,124 in consumer credit card debt. Her petition and accompanying schedules show that Hebbring owns a single-family home in Reno, Nevada valued at $160,000, on which she owes $154,103; a 2001 Volkswagen Beetle valued at $14,000, on which she owes $18,839; and miscellaneous personal property valued at $1,775. Hebbring earns approximately $49,000 per year as a customer service representative for SBC Nevada. Her petition reports monthly net income of $2,813 and monthly expenditures of $2,897, for a monthly deficit of $84. In calculating her income, Hebbring excluded a $232 monthly pre-tax deduction for a 401(k) plan and an $81 monthly after-tax deduction for a retirement savings bond. When she filed for bankruptcy Hebbring was thirty-three years old and had accumulated $6,289 in retirement savings.

The United States Trustee ("Trustee") moved to dismiss Hebbring's petition for substantial abuse, see 11 U.S.C. [Section] 707(b), arguing that she should not be allowed to deduct voluntary retirement contributions from her income and that her recent paystubs showed that her gross income was higher than she had claimed. As a result, the Trustee contended, Hebbring's monthly net income was actually $3,512, leaving her $615 per month in disposable income, sufficient to repay 100% of her unsecured debt over three years.

* * * *

The bankruptcy court granted the Trustee's motion to dismiss * * * [and ultimately Hebbring appealed the dismissal to the U.S. Court of Appeals for the Ninth Circuit].

* * * *

* * * In determining whether a petition constitutes a substantial abuse of Chapter 7, we examine the totality of the circumstances, focusing principally on whether the debtor will have sufficient future disposable income to fund a Chapter 13 plan that would pay a substantial portion of his unsecured debt. To calculate a debtor's disposable income, we begin with current monthly income and subtract amounts reasonably necessary to be expended * * * for the maintenance or support of the debtor or a dependent of the debtor.

* * * [Some] courts * * * have adopted a case-by-case approach, under which contributions to a retirement plan may be found reasonably necessary depending on the debtor's circumstances.

CASE CONTINUES

CASE 15.2 CONTINUED

We believe this * * * approach better comports [is consistent] with Congress's intent, as expressed in the language, purpose, and structure of the Bankruptcy Code. By not defining the phrase "reasonably necessary" or providing any examples of expenses that categorically are or are not reasonably necessary, the Code suggests courts should examine each debtor's specific circumstances to determine whether a claimed expense is reasonably necessary for that debtor's maintenance or support. We find no evidence that Congress intended courts to employ a *per se* rule against retirement contributions, which may be crucial for debtors' support upon retirement, particularly for older debtors who have little or no savings. Where Congress intended courts to use a *per se* rule rather than a case-by-case approach in classifying financial interests or obligations under the Bankruptcy Code, it has explicitly communicated its intent. *Congress's decision not to categorically exclude any specific expense, including retirement contributions, from being considered reasonably necessary is probative* [an indication] *of its intent.* [Emphasis added.]

Requiring a fact-specific analysis to determine whether an expense is reasonably necessary is sound policy because it comports with the Code's approach to identifying substantial abuse of the Chapter 7 relief provisions. * * * Congress chose [not] to define "substantial abuse" * * * . Congress thus left a flexible standard enabling courts to address each petition on its own merit. That Congress granted courts the discretion to identify substantial abuse necessarily suggests it intended courts to have the discretion to answer the subsidiary question of whether particular expenses are reasonably necessary.

In light of these considerations, and in the absence of any indication that Congress sought to prohibit debtors from voluntarily contributing to retirement plans *per se,* we conclude that bankruptcy courts have discretion to determine whether retirement contributions are a reasonably necessary expense for a particular debtor based on the facts of each individual case. In making this fact-intensive determination, courts should consider a number of factors, including but not limited to: the debtor's age, income, overall budget, expected date of retirement, existing retirement savings, and amount of contributions; the likelihood that stopping contributions will jeopardize the debtor's fresh start by forcing the debtor to make up lost contributions after emerging from bankruptcy; and the needs of the debtor's dependents. *Courts must allow debtors to seek bankruptcy protection while voluntarily saving for retirement if such savings appear reasonably necessary for the maintenance or support of the debtor or the debtor's dependents.* [Emphasis added.]

* * * *

Here, the bankruptcy court * * * found * * * that Hebbring's retirement contributions are not a reasonably necessary expense based on her age and specific financial circumstances. * * * When she filed her bankruptcy petition, Hebbring was only thirty-three years old and was contributing approximately 8% of her gross income toward her retirement. Although Hebbring had accumulated only $6,289 in retirement savings, she was earning $49,000 per year and making mortgage payments on a house. In light of these circumstances, the bankruptcy court's conclusion that Hebbring's retirement contributions are not a reasonably necessary expense is not clearly erroneous.

* * * *

For the foregoing reasons, the district court's order affirming the bankruptcy court's order dismissing this case is AFFIRMED.

QUESTIONS

1. Is it fair for the court to treat retirement contributions differently depending on a person's age?
2. Is it likely to have made a difference to the result in this case that the debtor's retirement contributions were automatically and electronically deducted from her pay? Explain.

Additional Grounds for Dismissal As noted, a debtor's voluntary petition for Chapter 7 relief may be dismissed for substantial abuse or for failing to provide the necessary documents (such as schedules and tax returns) within the specified time. In addition, a motion to dismiss a Chapter 7 filing might be granted in two other situations under the Bankruptcy Reform Act of 2005. First, if the debtor has been convicted of a violent crime or a drug-trafficking offense, the victim can file a motion to dismiss the voluntary petition.[10] Second, if the debtor fails to pay postpetition domestic-support obligations (which include child and spousal support), the court may dismiss the debtor's Chapter 7 petition.

Order for Relief If the voluntary petition for bankruptcy is found to be proper, the filing of the petition will itself constitute an **order for relief.** (An order for relief is a court's grant of assistance to a petitioner.) Once a consumer-debtor's voluntary petition has been filed, the clerk of the court or other appointee must give the trustee and creditors notice of the order for relief by mail not more than twenty days after entry of the order.

Involuntary Bankruptcy

An involuntary bankruptcy occurs when the debtor's creditors force the debtor into bankruptcy proceedings. An involuntary case cannot be commenced against a farmer[11] or a charitable institution. For an involuntary action to be filed against other debtors, the following requirements must be met: If the debtor has twelve or more creditors, three or more of these creditors having unsecured claims totaling at least $13,475 must join in the petition. If a debtor has fewer than twelve creditors, one or more creditors having a claim of $13,475 may file.

If the debtor challenges the involuntary petition, a hearing will be held, and the bankruptcy court will enter an order for relief if it finds either of the following:

1. The debtor is generally not paying debts as they become due.
2. A general receiver, assignee, or custodian took possession of, or was appointed to take charge of, substantially all of the debtor's property within 120 days before the filing of the petition.

If the court grants an order for relief, the debtor will be required to supply the same information in the bankruptcy schedules as in a voluntary bankruptcy.

An involuntary petition should not be used as an everyday debt-collection device, and the Code provides penalties for the filing of frivolous petitions against debtors. Judgment may be granted against the petitioning creditors for the costs and attorneys' fees incurred by the debtor in defending against an involuntary petition that is dismissed by the court. If the petition is filed in bad faith, damages can be awarded for injury to the debtor's reputation. Punitive damages may also be awarded.

Automatic Stay

The moment a petition, either voluntary or involuntary, is filed, an **automatic stay,** or suspension, of virtually all actions by creditors against the debtor or the debtor's property normally goes into effect. In other words, once a petition has been filed, creditors cannot contact the debtor by phone or mail or start any legal proceedings to recover debts or to repossess property. A secured creditor or other party in interest, however, may petition the bankruptcy court for relief from the automatic stay. The Code provides that if a creditor knowingly violates the automatic stay (a willful violation), any injured party, including the debtor, is entitled to recover actual damages, costs, and attorneys' fees, and may be awarded punitive damages as well.

Underlying the Code's automatic-stay provision for a secured creditor is a concept known as *adequate protection.* The **adequate protection doctrine,** among other things, protects secured creditors from losing their security as a result of the automatic stay. The bankruptcy court can provide adequate protection by requiring the debtor or trustee to make periodic cash payments or a one-time cash payment (or to provide additional collateral or replacement liens) to the extent that the stay may actually cause the value of the property to decrease.

Exceptions to the Automatic Stay There are several exceptions to the automatic stay. The 2005 Bankruptcy Reform Act created a new exception for domestic-support obligations, which include any debt owed to or recoverable by a spouse, former spouse, or child of the debtor; a child's parent or guardian; or a governmental unit. In addition, proceedings against the debtor related to divorce, child custody or visitation, domestic violence, and support enforcement are not stayed. Also excepted are investigations by a securities regulatory agency, the creation or perfection of statutory liens for property

10. Note that the court may not dismiss a case on this ground if the debtor's bankruptcy is necessary to satisfy a claim for a domestic-support obligation.

11. The definition of *farmer* includes persons who receive more than 50 percent of their gross income from farming operations, such as tilling the soil, dairy farming, ranching, or the production or raising of crops, poultry, or livestock. Corporations and partnerships may qualify under certain conditions.

taxes or special assessments on real property, eviction actions on judgments obtained prior to filing the petition, and withholding from the debtor's wages for repayment of a retirement account loan.

Limitations on the Automatic Stay Under the Code, if a creditor or other party in interest requests relief from the stay, the stay will automatically terminate sixty days after the request, unless the court grants an extension[12] or the parties agree otherwise. Also, the automatic stay on secured debts will terminate thirty days after the petition is filed if the debtor had filed a bankruptcy petition that was dismissed within the prior year. Any party in interest can request the court to extend the stay by showing that the filing is in good faith.

If two or more bankruptcy petitions were dismissed during the prior year, the Code presumes bad faith, and the automatic stay does not go into effect until the court determines that the filing was made in good faith. In addition, if the petition is subsequently dismissed because the debtor failed to file the required documents within thirty days of filing, for example, the stay is terminated. Finally, the automatic stay on secured property terminates forty-five days after the creditors' meeting (to be discussed shortly) unless the debtor redeems or reaffirms certain debts (*reaffirmation* is discussed later in this chapter). In other words, the debtor cannot keep the secured property (such as a financed automobile), even if she or he continues to make payments on it, without reinstating the rights of the secured party to collect on the debt.

Property of the Estate

On the commencement of a liquidation proceeding under Chapter 7, an *estate in property* is created. The estate consists of all the debtor's legal and equitable interests in property currently held, wherever located, together with community property (property jointly owned by a husband and wife in certain states—see Chapter 25), property transferred in a transaction voidable by the trustee, proceeds and profits from the property of the estate, and certain after-acquired property. Interests in certain property—such as gifts, inheritances, property settlements (from divorce), and life insurance death proceeds—to which the debtor becomes entitled *within 180 days after filing* may also become part of the estate. Withholdings for employee benefit plan contributions are excluded from the estate. Generally, though, the filing of a bankruptcy petition fixes a dividing line: property acquired prior to the filing of the petition becomes property of the estate, and property acquired after the filing of the petition, except as just noted, remains the debtor's.

Creditors' Meeting and Claims

Within a reasonable time after the order for relief has been granted (not less than twenty days or more than forty days), the trustee must call a meeting of the creditors listed in the schedules filed by the debtor. The bankruptcy judge does not attend this meeting, but the debtor is required to attend and to submit to examination under oath by the creditors and the trustee. At the meeting, the trustee ensures that the debtor is aware of the potential consequences of bankruptcy and of his or her ability to file for bankruptcy under a different chapter of the Bankruptcy Code.

To be entitled to receive a portion of the debtor's estate, each creditor normally files a *proof of claim* with the bankruptcy court clerk within ninety days of the creditors' meeting.[13] The proof of claim lists the creditor's name and address, as well as the amount that the creditor asserts is owed to the creditor by the debtor. A proof of claim is necessary if there is any dispute concerning the claim. Generally, any legal obligation of the debtor is a claim (except claims for breach of employment contracts or real estate leases for terms longer than one year).

Exemptions

The trustee takes control over the debtor's property, but an individual debtor is entitled to exempt certain property from the bankruptcy. The Bankruptcy Code exempts the following property:[14]

1. Up to $20,200 in equity in the debtor's residence and burial plot (the homestead exemption).
2. Interest in a motor vehicle up to $3,225.
3. Interest, up to $525 for a particular item, in household goods and furnishings, wearing apparel, appliances, books, animals, crops, and musical

12. The court might grant an extension, for example, on a motion by the trustee that the property is of value to the estate.

13. This ninety-day rule applies in Chapter 12 and Chapter 13 bankruptcies as well.

14. The dollar amounts stated in the Bankruptcy Code are adjusted automatically every three years on April 1 based on changes in the Consumer Price Index. The adjusted amounts are rounded to the nearest $25. The amounts stated in this chapter are in accordance with those computed on April 1, 2007.

instruments (the aggregate total of all items is limited, however, to $10,775).[15]

4. Interest in jewelry up to $1,350.
5. Interest in any other property up to $1,075, plus any unused part of the $20,200 homestead exemption up to $10,125.
6. Interest in any tools of the debtor's trade up to $2,025.
7. Life insurance contracts owned by the debtor.
8. Certain interests in accrued dividends and interest under life insurance contracts owned by the debtor, not to exceed $10,775.
9. Professionally prescribed health aids.
10. The right to receive Social Security and certain welfare benefits, alimony and support, certain retirement funds and pensions, and education savings accounts held for specific periods of time.
11. The right to receive certain personal-injury and other awards up to $20,200.

Individual states have the power to pass legislation precluding debtors from using the federal exemptions within the state; a majority of the states have done this. In those states, debtors may use only state, not federal, exemptions. In the rest of the states, an individual debtor (or a husband and wife filing jointly) may choose either the exemptions provided under state law or the federal exemptions.

The Homestead Exemption

The 2005 Bankruptcy Reform Act significantly changed the law for those debtors seeking to use state homestead exemption statutes. Under prior law, the homestead exemptions of six states, including Florida and Texas, allowed debtors petitioning for bankruptcy to shield *unlimited* amounts of equity in their homes from creditors. The Code now places limits on the amount that can be claimed as exempt in bankruptcy. Also, a debtor must have lived in a state for two years prior to filing the petition to be able to use the state homestead exemption (the prior law required only six months).

In general, if the debtor acquired the homestead within three and a half years preceding the date of filing, the maximum equity exempted is $136,875, even if state law would permit a higher amount. Moreover, the debtor may not claim the homestead exemption if he or she has committed any criminal act, intentional tort, or willful or reckless misconduct that caused serious physical injury or death to another individual in the preceding five years. Similarly, a debtor who has been convicted of a felony may not be able to claim the exemption.

The Trustee

Promptly after the order for relief in the liquidation proceeding has been entered, a trustee is appointed. The basic duty of the trustee is to collect the debtor's available estate and reduce it to cash for distribution, preserving the interests of both the debtor and unsecured creditors. This requires that the trustee be accountable for administering the debtor's estate. To enable the trustee to accomplish this duty, the Code gives the trustee certain powers, stated in both general and specific terms. These powers must be exercised within two years of the order for relief.

The trustee has additional duties with regard to means testing debtors and protecting domestic-support creditors. The trustee is required to promptly review all materials filed by the debtor to determine if there is substantial abuse. Within ten days after the first meeting of the creditors, the trustee must file a statement indicating whether the case is presumed to be an abuse under the means test. The trustee must provide all creditors with a copy of this statement. When there is a presumption of abuse, the trustee must either file a motion to dismiss the petition (or convert it to a Chapter 13 case) or file a statement setting forth the reasons why a motion would not be appropriate. If the debtor owes a domestic-support obligation (such as child support), the trustee is required to provide written notice of the bankruptcy to the claim holder (a former spouse, for example).

The Trustee's Powers The trustee occupies a position *equivalent* in rights to that of certain other parties. For example, the trustee has the same rights as a creditor who could have obtained a judicial lien or levy execution on the debtor's property. This means that a trustee has priority over an unperfected secured party as to the debtor's property.[16] This right of a

15. The 2005 Bankruptcy Reform Act clarified that "household goods and furnishings" includes, for example, one computer, one radio, one television, and one videocassette recorder. Other items, such as works of art, electronic entertainment equipment with a fair market value of more than $500, and antiques and jewelry (except wedding rings) valued at more than $500, are not included.

16. Nevertheless, in most states a creditor with an unperfected purchase-money security interest may prevail against a trustee if the creditor perfects (files) within twenty days of the debtor's receipt of the collateral. This is normally true even if the debtor files a bankruptcy petition before the creditor perfects.

trustee, which is equivalent to that of a lien creditor, is known as the *strong-arm power.* A trustee also has power equivalent to that of a *bona fide purchaser* of real property from the debtor.

The Right to Possession of the Debtor's Property The trustee has the power to require persons holding the debtor's property at the time the petition is filed to deliver the property to the trustee. (Usually, though, the trustee takes constructive, rather than actual, possession of the debtor's property. For example, to obtain control of a debtor's business inventory, a trustee might change the locks on the doors to the business and hire a security guard.)

Avoidance Powers The trustee also has specific powers of *avoidance*—that is, the trustee can set aside a sale or other transfer of the debtor's property, taking it back as a part of the debtor's estate. These powers include any voidable rights available to the debtor, preferences, certain statutory liens, and fraudulent transfers by the debtor. Each of these powers is discussed in more detail below. Note that under the 2005 act, the trustee no longer has the power to avoid any transfer that was a bona fide payment of a domestic-support debt.

The debtor shares most of the trustee's avoidance powers. Thus, if the trustee does not take action to enforce one of the rights mentioned above, the debtor in a liquidation bankruptcy can still enforce that right.[17]

Voidable Rights A trustee steps into the shoes of the debtor. Thus, any reason that a debtor can use to obtain the return of her or his property can be used by the trustee as well. These grounds include fraud, duress, incapacity, and mutual mistake.

For example, Ben sells his boat to Tara. Tara gives Ben a check, knowing that she has insufficient funds in her bank account to cover the check. Tara has committed fraud. Ben has the right to avoid that transfer and recover the boat from Tara. Once an order for relief under Chapter 7 of the Code has been entered for Ben, the trustee can exercise the same right to recover the boat from Tara, and the boat becomes a part of the debtor's estate.

17. Under a Chapter 11 bankruptcy (to be discussed later), for which no trustee other than the debtor generally exists, the debtor has the same avoidance powers as a trustee under Chapter 7. Under Chapters 12 and 13 (also to be discussed later), a trustee must be appointed.

Preferences A debtor is not permitted to transfer property or to make a payment that favors—or gives a **preference** to—one creditor over others. The trustee is allowed to recover payments made both voluntarily and involuntarily to one creditor in preference over another. If a **preferred creditor** (one who has received a preferential transfer from the debtor) has sold the property to an innocent third party, the trustee cannot recover the property from the innocent party. The preferred creditor, however, generally can be held accountable for the value of the property.

To have made a preferential payment that can be recovered, an *insolvent* debtor generally must have transferred property, for a *preexisting* debt, within *ninety days* prior to the filing of the bankruptcy petition. The transfer must have given the creditor more than the creditor would have received as a result of the bankruptcy proceedings. The trustee need not prove insolvency, as the Code presumes that the debtor is insolvent during this ninety-day period.

Preferences to Insiders. Sometimes, the creditor receiving the preference is an **insider**—an individual, a partner, a partnership, a corporation, or an officer or a director of a corporation (or a relative of one of these) who has a close relationship with the debtor. In this situation, the avoidance power of the trustee is extended to transfers made within *one year* before filing; however, the *presumption* of insolvency is confined to the ninety-day period. Therefore, the trustee must prove that the debtor was insolvent at the time of a transfer that occurred prior to the ninety-day period.

Transfers That Do Not Constitute Preferences. Not all transfers are preferences. To be a preference, the transfer must be made for something other than current consideration. Most courts generally assume that payment for services rendered within fifteen days prior to the payment is not a preference. If a creditor receives payment in the ordinary course of business from an individual or business debtor, such as payment of last month's telephone bill, the trustee in bankruptcy cannot recover the payment. To be recoverable, a preference must be a transfer for an antecedent (preexisting) debt, such as a year-old printing bill. In addition, the Code permits a consumer-debtor to transfer any property to a creditor up to a total value of $5,475, without the transfer's constituting a preference (this amount was increased from $600 to $5,000 by the 2005 act and is increased periodically under the law). Payment of domestic-support debts does not constitute a preference.

Liens on Debtor's Property The trustee has the power to avoid certain statutory liens against the debtor's property, such as a landlord's lien for unpaid rent. The trustee can avoid statutory liens that first became effective against the debtor when the bankruptcy petition was filed or when the debtor became insolvent. The trustee can also avoid any lien against a good faith purchaser that was not perfected or enforceable on the date of the bankruptcy filing.

Fraudulent Transfers The trustee may avoid fraudulent transfers or obligations if they were made within two years of the filing of the petition or if they were made with actual intent to hinder, delay, or defraud a creditor. Transfers made for less than a reasonably equivalent consideration are also vulnerable if by making them, the debtor became insolvent or intended to incur debts that he or she could not pay. Similarly, a transfer that left a debtor engaged in business with an unreasonably small amount of capital may be considered fraudulent. When a fraudulent transfer is made outside the Code's two-year limit, creditors may seek alternative relief under state laws. Some state laws often allow creditors to recover for transfers made up to three years prior to the filing of a petition.

Distribution of Property

The Code provides specific rules for the distribution of the debtor's property to secured and unsecured creditors. (We will examine these distributions shortly.) Anything remaining after the priority classes of creditors have been satisfied is turned over to the debtor. Exhibit 15–2 illustrates the collection and distribution of property in most voluntary bankruptcies.

In a bankruptcy case in which the debtor has no assets (called "no-asset cases"), creditors are notified of the debtor's petition for bankruptcy but are instructed not to file a claim. In no-asset cases, the unsecured creditors will receive no payment, and most, if not all, of these debts will be discharged.

Distribution to Secured Creditors The Code provides that a consumer-debtor must file with the clerk a statement of intention with respect to the secured collateral. The statement must be filed within thirty days of filing a liquidation petition or before the date of the first meeting of the creditors (whichever is first). The statement must indicate whether the debtor will redeem the collateral (make a single payment equal to the current value of the property), reaffirm the debt (continue making payments on the debt), or surrender the property to the secured party.[18] The trustee is obligated to enforce the debtor's statement within forty-five days after the meeting of the creditors. As noted previously, failure of the debtor to redeem or reaffirm within forty-five days terminates the automatic stay.

18. Also, if applicable, the debtor must specify whether the collateral will be claimed as exempt property.

EXHIBIT 15–2 • Collection and Distribution of Property in Most Voluntary Bankruptcies

This exhibit illustrates the property that might be collected in a debtor's voluntary bankruptcy and how it might be distributed to creditors. Involuntary bankruptcies and some voluntary bankruptcies could include additional types of property and other creditors.

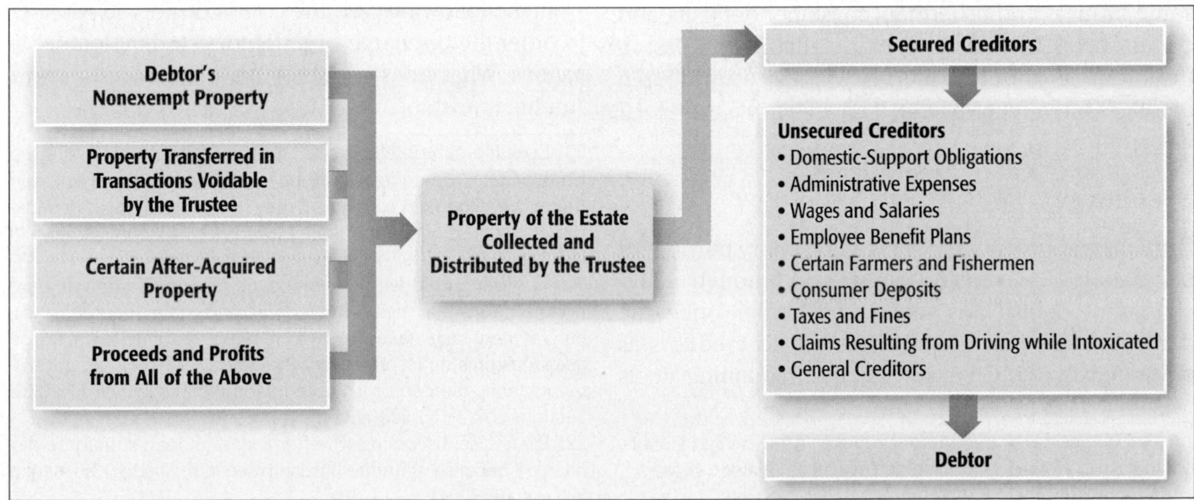

If the collateral is surrendered to the perfected secured party, the secured creditor can either accept the property in full satisfaction of the debt or foreclose on the collateral and use the proceeds to pay off the debt. Thus, the perfected secured party has priority over unsecured parties as to the proceeds from the disposition of the collateral. When the proceeds from sale of the collateral exceed the amount of the perfected secured party's claim, the secured party also has priority to an amount that will cover the reasonable fees and costs incurred. Any excess over this amount is returned to the trustee and used to satisfy the claims of unsecured creditors. If the collateral is insufficient to cover the secured debt owed, the secured creditor becomes an unsecured creditor for the difference.

Distribution to Unsecured Creditors Bankruptcy law establishes an order of priority for classes of debts owed to *unsecured* creditors, and they are paid in the order of their priority. Each class must be fully paid before the next class is entitled to any of the remaining proceeds. If there are insufficient proceeds to pay fully all the creditors in a class, the proceeds are distributed *proportionately* to the creditors in that class, and classes lower in priority receive nothing.

The 2005 act elevated domestic-support (mainly child-support) obligations to the highest priority of unsecured claims—so these are the first debts to be paid. After that, administrative expenses related to the bankruptcy (such as court costs, trustee fees, and attorneys' fees) are paid; next come any expenses that a debtor in an involuntary bankruptcy incurs in the ordinary course of business. Unpaid wages, salaries, and commissions earned within ninety days prior to the petition are paid next, followed by certain claims for contributions to employee benefit plans, claims by some farmers and fishermen, consumer deposits, and certain taxes. Claims of general creditors rank last in the order of priority, which is why these unsecured creditors often receive little, if anything, in a Chapter 7 bankruptcy.

Discharge

From the debtor's point of view, the primary purpose of liquidation is to obtain a fresh start through a discharge of debts.[19] As mentioned earlier, once the debtor's assets have been distributed to creditors as permitted by the Code, the debtor's remaining debts are then discharged, meaning that the debtor is not obligated to pay them. Any judgments on the debts are voided, and creditors are enjoined (prevented) from bringing any actions to collect them. A discharge does not affect the liability of a co-debtor.

Certain debts, however, are not dischargeable in bankruptcy. Also, certain debtors may not qualify to have all debts discharged in bankruptcy. These situations are discussed next.

Exceptions to Discharge Discharge of a debt may be denied because of the nature of the claim or the conduct of the debtor. A court will not discharge claims that are based on a debtor's willful or malicious conduct or fraud,[20] or claims related to property or funds that the debtor obtained by false pretenses, embezzlement, or larceny. Any monetary judgment against the debtor for driving while intoxicated cannot be discharged in bankruptcy. When a debtor fails to list a creditor on the bankruptcy schedules (and thus the creditor is not notified of the bankruptcy), that creditor's claims are not dischargeable.

Claims that are not dischargeable in a liquidation bankruptcy include amounts due to the government for taxes, fines, or penalties.[21] Additionally, amounts borrowed by the debtor to pay these taxes will not be discharged. Domestic-support obligations and property settlements arising from a divorce or separation cannot be discharged. Certain student loans and educational debts are not dischargeable (unless payment of the loans imposes an undue hardship on the debtor and the debtor's dependents),[22] nor are amounts due on a retirement account loan. Consumer debts for purchasing luxury items worth more than $550 and cash advances totaling more than $825 generally are not dischargeable.

In the following case, the court considered whether to order the discharge of a debtor's student loan obligations. What does a debtor have to prove to show "undue hardship"?

---

19. Discharges are granted under Chapter 7 only to individuals, not to corporations or partnerships. The latter may use Chapter 11, or they may terminate their existence under state law.

20. Even if a debtor who is sued for fraud settles the lawsuit, the United States Supreme Court has held that the amount due under the settlement agreement may not be discharged in bankruptcy because of the underlying fraud. See *Archer v. Warner,* 538 U.S. 314, 123 S.Ct. 1462, 155 L.Ed.2d 454 (2003).

21. Taxes accruing within three years prior to bankruptcy are nondischargeable, including federal and state income taxes, employment taxes, taxes on gross receipts, property taxes, excise taxes, customs duties, and any other taxes for which the government claims the debtor is liable in some capacity. See 11 U.S.C. Sections 507(a)(8), 523(a)(1).

22. For a case discussing whether a student loan should be discharged because of undue hardship, see *In re Savage,* 311 Bankr. 835 (1st Cir. 2004).

CASE 15.3 In re Mosley

United States Court of Appeals, Eleventh Circuit, 2007. 494 F.3d 1320.

• **Background and Facts** Keldric Mosley incurred student loans while attending Georgia's Alcorn State University between 1989 and 1994. At Alcorn, Mosley joined the U.S. Army Reserve Officers' Training Corps. During training in 1993, Mosley fell from a tank and injured his hip and back. Medical problems from his injuries led him to resign his commission. He left Alcorn to live with his mother in Atlanta from 1994 to 1999. He worked briefly for several employers, but depressed and physically limited by his injury, he was unable to keep any of the jobs. He tried to return to school but could not obtain financial aid because of the debt he had incurred at Alcorn. In 1999, a federal bankruptcy court granted him a discharge under Chapter 7, but it did not include the student loans. In 2000, after a week at the Georgia Regional Hospital, a state-supported mental-health facility, Mosley was prescribed medication through the U.S. Department of Veterans Affairs for depression, back pain, and other problems. By 2004, his monthly income consisted primarily of $210 in disability benefits from the Veterans Administration. Homeless and in debt for $45,000 to Educational Credit Management Corporation, Mosley asked the bankruptcy court to reopen his case. The court granted him a discharge of his student loans on the basis of undue hardship. Educational Credit appealed to the U.S. Court of Appeals for the Eleventh Circuit.

IN THE LANGUAGE OF THE COURT
***JOHN R. GIBSON,* Circuit Judge.**

* * * *

* * * To establish undue hardship [the courts require:]

> (1) that the debtor cannot maintain, based on current income and expenses, a "minimal" standard of living * * * if forced to repay the loans; (2) that additional circumstances exist indicating that this state of affairs is likely to persist for a significant portion of the repayment period of the student loans; and (3) that the debtor has made good faith efforts to repay the loans.

Educational Credit does not contest that Mosley has satisfied the first requirement, an inability to maintain a minimal standard of living, as he lives below the poverty line and has for several years. It contends that the bankruptcy court improperly relaxed Mosley's evidentiary burden [duty to produce enough evidence to prove an assertion] on the second and third requirements * * *. The bankruptcy court concluded that Mosley established undue hardship with his credible testimony that he has tried to obtain work but, for ten years, his "substantial physical and emotional ailments" have prevented him from holding a steady job. * * * Educational Credit argues that corroborating medical evidence independent from the debtor's testimony is required * * * where medical disabilities are the "additional circumstances" * * *.

* * * *

We * * * decline to adopt a rule requiring Mosley to submit independent medical evidence to corroborate his testimony that his depression and back problems were additional circumstances likely to render him unable to repay his student loans. We see no inconsistency between * * * holding that the debtor's detailed testimony was sufficient evidence of undue hardship and the * * * cases cited by Educational Credit where debtors' less detailed testimony was held to be insufficient.

Educational Credit also argues that Mosley's medical prognosis [prediction about how a situation will develop in the future] is a subject requiring specialized medical knowledge * * * and that Mosley was not competent to give his opinion on this matter. Mosley, however, did not purport to give an opinion on his medical prognosis, but rather testified from personal knowledge about how his struggles with depression, back pain, and the side effects of his medication have made it difficult for him to obtain work.

We now turn to Educational Credit's argument that the record does not support a conclusion of undue hardship because Mosley's testimony did not establish * * * that he likely will be unable to repay his student loans in the future and that he has made good faith efforts to repay the loans.

CASE CONTINUES

CASE 15.3 CONTINUED

* * * In showing that "additional circumstances" make it unlikely that he will be able to repay his loans for a significant period of time, Mosley testified that his depression and chronic back pain have frustrated his efforts to work, and thus his ability to repay his loans, as well as to provide himself with shelter, food, and transportation, for several years. * * * Mosley's testimony * * * is * * * unrefuted and is corroborated by his Social Security earnings statements. He testified that his back problems preclude him from heavy lifting, which rules out most of the jobs available [through the Georgia Department of Labor where] he seeks work. Exacerbating [aggravating] the problem, his medications make it difficult for him to function. He did not finish college and has been unable to complete the training necessary to learn a trade. Mosley relies on public assistance programs for health care and food, and * * * there is no reason to believe that Mosley's condition will improve in the future.

The bankruptcy court also correctly concluded that Mosley's testimony established the * * * requirement that he has made good faith efforts to repay his student loans. * * * *Good faith is measured by the debtor's efforts to obtain employment, maximize income, and minimize expenses; his default should result, not from his choices, but from factors beyond his reasonable control.* Mosley has attempted to find work, as demonstrated by the series of jobs he held while living with his mother from 1994 to 1999 and his participation in the [state] labor pool since 2000. Because of his medical conditions, Mosley has been largely unsuccessful, and thus has not had the means even to attempt to make payments. * * * His income has been below the poverty line for years. He lives without a home and car and cannot further minimize his expenses. [Emphasis added.]

• **Decision and Remedy** *The U.S. Court of Appeals for the Eleventh Circuit affirmed the lower court's discharge of the debtor's student loans. The debtor's medical problems, lack of skills, and "dire living conditions" made it unlikely that he would be able to hold a job and repay the loans. Furthermore, the debtor "has made good faith efforts to repay his student loans and would suffer undue hardship if they were excepted from discharge."*

• **The Ethical Dimension** *Should a debtor be required to attempt to negotiate a repayment plan with a creditor to demonstrate good faith? Why or why not?*

• **The Global Dimension** *If this debtor were to relocate to a country with a lower cost of living than the United States, should his change in circumstances be a ground for revoking the discharge? Explain your answer.*

Objections to Discharge In addition to the exceptions to discharge previously discussed, a bankruptcy court may also deny the discharge of the *debtor* (as opposed to the debt). In the latter situation, the assets of the debtor are still distributed to the creditors, but the debtor remains liable for the unpaid portion of all claims. Grounds for the denial of discharge of the debtor include the following:

1. The debtor's concealment or destruction of property with the intent to hinder, delay, or defraud a creditor.
2. The debtor's fraudulent concealment or destruction of financial records.
3. The granting of a discharge to the debtor within eight years of the filing of the petition. (This period was increased from six to eight years by the 2005 act.)
4. The debtor's failure to complete the required consumer education course (unless such a course is unavailable).
5. Proceedings in which the debtor could be found guilty of a felony (basically, a court may not discharge any debt until the completion of felony proceedings against the debtor).

Revocation of Discharge On petition by the trustee or a creditor, the bankruptcy court can, within one year, revoke the discharge decree. The discharge decree will be revoked if it is discovered that the debtor acted fraudulently or dishonestly during the bankruptcy proceedings. The revocation renders the discharge void, allowing creditors not satisfied by the distribution of the debtor's estate to proceed with their claims against the debtor.

Reaffirmation of Debt

An agreement to pay a debt dischargeable in bankruptcy is called a **reaffirmation agreement.** A debtor may wish to pay a debt—for example, a debt owed to a family member, physician, bank, or some other creditor—even though the debt could be discharged in bankruptcy. Also, as noted previously, under the 2005 act a debtor cannot retain secured property while continuing to pay without entering into a reaffirmation agreement.

Reaffirmation Procedures To be enforceable, reaffirmation agreements must be made before the debtor is granted a discharge. The agreement must be signed and filed with the court (along with certain required disclosures, described next). Court approval is required unless the debtor is represented by an attorney during the negotiation of the reaffirmation and submits the proper documents and certifications. Even when the debtor is represented by an attorney, court approval may be required if it appears that the reaffirmation will result in undue hardship on the debtor.[23] When court approval is required, a separate hearing will take place. The court will approve the reaffirmation only if it finds that the agreement will not result in undue hardship to the debtor and that the reaffirmation is consistent with the debtor's best interests.

Reaffirmation Disclosures To discourage creditors from engaging in abusive reaffirmation practices, the 2005 act added more requirements for reaffirmation. The Code now provides specific language for several pages of disclosures that must be given to debtors entering reaffirmation agreements. Among other things, these disclosures explain that the debtor is not required to reaffirm any debt, but that liens on secured property, such as mortgages and cars, will remain in effect even if the debt is not reaffirmed.

The reaffirmation agreement must disclose the amount of the debt reaffirmed, the rate of interest, the date payments begin, and the right to rescind. The disclosures also caution the debtor: "Only agree to reaffirm a debt if it is in your best interest. Be sure you can afford the payments you agree to make." The original disclosure documents must be signed by the debtor, certified by the debtor's attorney, and filed with the court at the same time as the reaffirmation agreement. A reaffirmation agreement that is not accompanied by the original signed disclosures will not be effective.

23. Under the provisions of the 2005 act, if the debtor's monthly income minus the debtor's monthly expenses as shown on her or his completed and signed statement is less than the scheduled payments on the reaffirmed debt, undue hardship will be presumed. The debtor can rebut the presumption by providing a statement that explains and identifies additional sources of funds from which the debtor will make the agreed-on payments.

Reorganizations

The type of bankruptcy proceeding most commonly used by corporate debtors is the Chapter 11 *reorganization*. In a reorganization, the creditors and the debtor formulate a plan under which the debtor pays a portion of the debts and is discharged of the remainder. The debtor is allowed to continue in business. Although this type of bankruptcy is generally a corporate reorganization, any debtors (including individuals but excluding stockbrokers and commodities brokers) who are eligible for Chapter 7 relief are eligible for relief under Chapter 11.[24] In 1994, Congress established a "fast-track" Chapter 11 procedure for small-business debtors whose liabilities do not exceed $2.19 million and who do not own or manage real estate. This allows bankruptcy proceedings without the appointment of committees and can save time and costs.

The same principles that govern the filing of a liquidation (Chapter 7) petition apply to reorganization (Chapter 11) proceedings. The case may be brought either voluntarily or involuntarily. The same guidelines govern the entry of the order for relief. The automatic-stay and adequate protection provisions are applicable in reorganizations as well. The 2005 Bankruptcy Reform Act's exceptions to the automatic stay also apply to Chapter 11 proceedings, as do the new provisions regarding substantial abuse and additional grounds for dismissal (or conversion) of bankruptcy petitions. Additionally, the 2005 act contained specific rules and limitations for *individual* debtors who file a Chapter 11 petition. For example, an individual debtor's postpetition acquisitions and earnings become the property of the bankruptcy estate.

Must Be in the Best Interests of the Creditors

Under Section 305(a) of the Bankruptcy Code, a court, after notice and a hearing, may dismiss or suspend all proceedings in a case at any time if dismissal or suspension would better serve the interests of the creditors. Section 1112 also allows a court, after notice and a hearing, to dismiss a case under reorganization "for cause." Cause includes the absence of a reasonable likelihood of rehabilitation, the inability to effect a plan, and an unreasonable delay by the

24. In addition, railroads are eligible for Chapter 11 relief.

debtor that is prejudicial to (may harm the interests of) creditors.[25]

Workouts

In some instances, creditors may prefer private, negotiated adjustments of creditor-debtor relations, also known as **workouts,** to bankruptcy proceedings. Often, these out-of-court workouts are much more flexible and thus more conducive to a speedy settlement. Speed is critical because delay is one of the most costly elements in any bankruptcy proceeding. Another advantage of workouts is that they avoid the various administrative costs of bankruptcy proceedings.

Debtor in Possession

On entry of the order for relief, the debtor generally continues to operate the business as a **debtor in possession (DIP).** The court, however, may appoint a trustee (often referred to as a *receiver*) to operate the debtor's business if gross mismanagement of the business is shown or if appointing a trustee is in the best interests of the estate.

The DIP's role is similar to that of a trustee in a liquidation. The DIP is entitled to avoid preferential payments made to creditors and fraudulent transfers of assets. The DIP has the power to decide whether to cancel or assume prepetition executory contracts (those that are not yet performed) or unexpired leases. The DIP can also exercise a trustee's strong-arm powers.

Creditors' Committees

As soon as practicable after the entry of the order for relief, a creditors' committee of unsecured creditors is appointed. If the debtor has filed a reorganization plan accepted by the creditors, however, the trustee may decide not to call a meeting of the creditors. The committee may consult with the trustee or the DIP concerning the administration of the case or the formulation of the plan. Additional creditors' committees may be appointed to represent special interest creditors. A court may order the trustee to change the membership of a committee or to increase the number of committee members to include a small-business concern if the court deems it necessary to ensure adequate representation of the creditors.

25. See 11 U.S.C. Section 1112(b). Debtors are not prohibited from filing successive petitions, however. A debtor whose petition is dismissed, for example, can file a new Chapter 11 petition (which may be granted unless it is filed in bad faith).

Orders affecting the estate generally will be entered only with the consent of the committee or after a hearing in which the judge is informed of the position of the committee. As mentioned earlier, businesses with debts of less than $2.19 million that do not own or manage real estate can avoid creditors' committees. In these cases, orders can be entered without a committee's consent.

The Reorganization Plan

A reorganization plan to rehabilitate the debtor is a plan to conserve and administer the debtor's assets in the hope of an eventual return to successful operation and solvency.

Filing the Plan Only the debtor may file a plan within the first 120 days after the date of the order for relief. The 120-day period may be extended but not beyond eighteen months from the date of the order for relief. If the debtor does not meet the 120-day deadline or obtain an extension, and if the debtor fails to procure the required creditor consent (discussed below) within 180 days, any party may propose a plan up to twenty months from the date of the order for relief. (In other words, the 180-day period cannot be extended beyond twenty months past the date of the order for relief.) For a small-business debtor, the time for the debtor's filing is 180 days.

The plan must be fair and equitable and must do the following:

1. Designate classes of claims and interests.
2. Specify the treatment to be afforded the classes. (The plan must provide the same treatment for all claims in a particular class.)
3. Provide an adequate means for execution. (Individual debtors must utilize postpetition assets as necessary to execute the plan.)
4. Provide for payment of tax claims over a five-year period.

Acceptance and Confirmation of the Plan Once the plan has been developed, it is submitted to each class of creditors for acceptance. Each class must accept the plan unless the class is not adversely affected by it. A class has accepted the plan when a majority of the creditors, representing two-thirds of the amount of the total claim, vote to approve it. Confirmation is conditioned on the debtor certifying that all postpetition domestic-support obligations have been paid in full. For small-business debtors, if the plan meets the listed requirements, the court must confirm the plan within forty-five days (unless this period is extended).

Even when all classes of creditors accept the plan, the court may refuse to confirm it if it is not "in the best interests of the creditors."[26] A former spouse or child of the debtor can block the plan if it does not provide for payment of her or his claims in cash. If an unsecured creditor objects to the plan, specific rules apply to the value of property to be distributed under the plan. The plan can also be modified on the request of the debtor, a trustee, or a holder of the unsecured claim. Tax claims must be paid over a five-year period.

Even if only one class of creditors has accepted the plan, the court may still confirm the plan under the Code's so-called **cram-down provision.** In other words, the court may confirm the plan over the objections of a class of creditors. Before the court can exercise this right of cram-down confirmation, it must be demonstrated that the plan is fair and equitable, and does not discriminate unfairly against any creditors.

Discharge The plan is binding on confirmation; however, confirmation of a plan does not discharge an individual debtor. Individual debtors must complete the plan prior to discharge, unless the court orders otherwise. For all other debtors, the court may order discharge at any time after the plan is confirmed. The debtor is given a reorganization discharge from all claims not protected under the plan. This discharge does not apply to any claims that would be denied discharge under liquidation.

Bankruptcy Relief under Chapter 13 and Chapter 12

In addition to bankruptcy relief through liquidation and reorganization, the Code also provides for individuals' repayment plans (Chapter 13) and family-farmer and family-fishermen debt adjustments (Chapter 12).

Individuals' Repayment Plan

Chapter 13 of the Bankruptcy Code provides for "Adjustment of Debts of an Individual with Regular Income." Individuals (not partnerships or corporations) with regular income who owe fixed (liquidated) unsecured debts of less than $336,900 or fixed secured debts of less than $1,010,650 may take advantage of bankruptcy repayment plans. Among those eligible are salaried employees; sole proprietors; and individuals who live on welfare, Social Security, fixed pensions, or investment income. Many small-business debtors have a choice of filing under either Chapter 11 or Chapter 13. Repayment plans offer several advantages, however. One advantage is that they are less expensive and less complicated than reorganization proceedings or, for that matter, even liquidation proceedings.

Filing the Petition A Chapter 13 repayment plan case can be initiated only by the filing of a voluntary petition by the debtor or by the conversion of a Chapter 7 petition (because of a finding of substantial abuse under the means test, for example). Certain liquidation and reorganization cases may be converted to repayment plan cases with the consent of the debtor.[27] A trustee, who will make payments under the plan, must be appointed. On the filing of a repayment plan petition, the automatic stay previously discussed takes effect. Although the stay applies to all or part of the debtor's consumer debt, it does not apply to any business debt incurred by the debtor. The automatic stay also does not apply to domestic-support obligations.

The Bankruptcy Code imposes the requirement of good faith on a debtor at both the time of the filing of the petition and the time of the filing of the plan. The Code does not define good faith—it is determined in each case through a consideration of "the totality of the circumstances." Bad faith can be cause for the dismissal of a Chapter 13 petition, as the following case illustrates.

26. The plan need not provide for full repayment to unsecured creditors. Instead, creditors receive a percentage of each dollar owed to them by the debtor.

27. A Chapter 13 repayment plan may be converted to a Chapter 7 liquidation either at the request of the debtor or, under certain circumstances, "for cause" by a creditor. A Chapter 13 case may be converted to a Chapter 11 case after a hearing.

CASE 15.4 In re Buis

United States Bankruptcy Court, Northern District of Florida, Pensacola Division, 2006. 337 Bankr. 243.

• **Background and Facts** In 2000, Roger and Pauline Buis bought an air show business, including a helicopter, a trailer, and props, from Robert and Annette Hosking. The price was $275,000, which the Buises agreed to pay in installments. The Buises formed Otto Airshows and decorated the helicopter

CASE CONTINUES

CASE 15.1 CONTINUED

as "Otto the Clown." They performed in air shows and took passengers on flights for a fee. In 2003, the Buises began accusing a competitor, Army Aviation Heritage Foundation and Museum, Inc. (AAHF), of safety lapses. AAHF filed a suit in a federal district court against the Buises and their company, alleging defamation. The court issued a summary judgment in AAHF's favor. While the amount of the damages was being determined, the Buises stopped doing business as Otto Airshows. They formed a new firm, Prop and Rotor Aviation, Inc., to which they leased the Otto equipment. Within a month, they filed a bankruptcy petition under Chapter 13. The plan and the schedules did not mention AAHF, the Prop and Rotor lease, a settlement that the Buises received in an unrelated suit, and other items. AAHF filed a motion to dismiss the case, asserting, among other things, that the Buises filed their petition in bad faith.

IN THE LANGUAGE OF THE COURT
***LEWIS M. KILLIAN, JR.*, Bankruptcy Judge.**

* * * *

* * * In considering the totality of circumstances surrounding the debtors' filing of their petition, it is clear to me that *this case was filed in bad faith and therefore should be dismissed.* [Emphasis added.]

First, *the debtors did not accurately state their assets and liabilities on their initial bankruptcy petition.* The debtors failed to list AAHF as a creditor, which is especially hard for the court to comprehend when the debtor admitted that it was AAHF's judgment that pushed them into bankruptcy. The debtors listed income on their schedules from "[r]ent from personal property lease," but did not list any such lease on [the schedules] and did not report any income from leases in their statement of financial affairs or list any agreement with Prop and Rotor anywhere in their schedules * * * . The debtors also did not disclose the $55,000.00 personal injury settlement they received prepetition. In addition to all of these omissions, the debtors also "forgot" about a Kubota lawn tractor worth $10,000 and their generator, worth $400. The debtors did not amend their schedules to reflect any of this until the day of the hearing on this motion. [Emphasis added.]

Next, the timing of the debtors' petition leads to the conclusion of bad faith, in two ways. First, the debtors filed their Chapter 13 petition after they were found liable in the District Court Action and after an unsuccessful mediation with AAHF, but before a final judgment could be entered. * * * It appears to me that *the timing of the bankruptcy filing was an ultimately futile attempt to keep the debtors eligible to file for relief under Chapter 13, because the debts owed to AAHF would be dischargeable in a * * * so-called Chapter 13 "super discharge."* The other reason the timing of the petition is suspect involves the grant of [certain] interests in [some of the Buises' assets to some of their creditors]. While the granting of these * * * interests may not have been fraudulent transfers as a matter of law, they certainly would have been preferences subject to avoidance * * * had they been made within 90 days of the filing of the petition. All of these transfers appear to have been made between 90 and 120 days pre-petition. Thus, the debtors granted these * * * interests, * * * waited 90 days so they would "stick," then filed their petition. The debtor admitted that he began planning to avoid AAHF's judgment through a Chapter 13 bankruptcy shortly after the adverse ruling on summary judgment in the District Court. The timing of the bankruptcy petition further demonstrates both the debtors' attempt to continue in their pre-petition pattern of egregious [flagrant] behavior towards AAHF and their bad faith in filing their petition. [Emphasis added.]

• **Decision and Remedy** *The court dismissed the Buises' petition. The debtors had not included all of their assets and liabilities on their initial petition and had timed its filing to avoid payment on the judgment to AAHF. They had also attempted to transfer interests in some of their assets in preference to certain creditors. The court determined that "the debtors filed their petition in bad faith and it is in the creditors' and estate's best interests that this case be dismissed."*

• **What If the Facts Were Different?** *If AAHF had lost its defamation suit against the Buises, would the result in this case have been the same? Why or why not?*

• **The Global Dimension** *Could the Buises have shipped their assets to Canada or Mexico to prevent them from being included in the bankruptcy estate? Explain.*

The Repayment Plan Only the debtor may file the repayment plan. This plan may provide either for payment of all obligations in full or for payment of a lesser amount.[28] The plan must provide for the following:

1. The turning over to the trustee of such future earnings or income of the debtor as is necessary for execution of the plan.
2. Full payment through deferred cash payments of all claims entitled to priority, such as taxes.[29]
3. Identical treatment of all claims within a particular class. (The Code permits the debtor to list co-debtors, such as guarantors or sureties, as a separate class.)

Time Allowed for Repayment. Prior to the 2005 act, the time for repayment under a plan was usually three years unless the court approved an extension for up to five years. Under the new act, the length of the payment plan (three or five years) is determined by the debtor's family income. If the debtor's family income is greater than the state median family income under the means test (previously discussed), the proposed plan must be for five years.[30] The term may not exceed five years, however.

The Code requires the debtor to make "timely" payments from her or his disposable income, and the trustee must ensure that the debtor commences these payments. The debtor must begin making payments under the proposed plan within thirty days after the plan has been *filed*. Failure of the debtor to make timely payments or to commence payments within the thirty-day period will allow the court to convert the case to a liquidation bankruptcy or to dismiss the petition.

Confirmation of the Plan. After the plan is filed, the court holds a confirmation hearing, at which interested parties (such as creditors) may object to the plan. The hearing must be held at least twenty days, but no more than forty-five days, after the meeting of the creditors. Confirmation of the plan is dependent on the debtor's certification that postpetition domestic-support obligations have been paid in full and that all prepetition tax returns have been filed. The court will confirm a plan with respect to each claim of a secured creditor under any of the following circumstances:

1. If the secured creditors have accepted the plan.
2. If the plan provides that secured creditors retain their liens until there is payment in full or until the debtor receives a discharge.
3. If the debtor surrenders the property securing the claims to the creditors.

In addition, for confirmation, the plan must provide that a creditor with a purchase-money security interest (PMSI) retains its lien until payment of the entire debt for a motor vehicle purchased within 910 days before filing the petition. A PMSI in consumer goods is created when a person buys goods primarily for personal, family, or household purposes, and the seller or lender agrees to extend credit for part or all of the purchase price of the goods. The seller or lender that extends credit to a consumer on a PMSI automatically becomes a secured creditor. For PMSIs on other personal property, the payment plan must cover debts incurred within a one-year period preceding the filing.

Objection to the Plan. Unsecured creditors do not have the power to confirm a repayment plan, but they can object to it. The court can approve a plan over the objection of the trustee or any unsecured creditor only in either of the following situations:

1. When the value of the property (replacement value as of the date of filing) to be distributed under the plan is at least equal to the amount of the claims.
2. When all of the debtor's projected disposable income to be received during the plan period will be applied to making payments. Disposable income is all income received less amounts needed to pay domestic-support obligations and/or amounts needed to meet ordinary expenses to continue the operation of a business. Also excluded from disposable income are charitable contributions up to 15 percent of the debtor's gross income and the reasonable and necessary costs for health insurance for the debtor and his or her dependents.

Modification of the Plan. Prior to completion of payments, the plan may be modified at the request of the debtor, the trustee, or an unsecured creditor. If any

---

28. A plan under Chapter 13 or Chapter 12 (to be discussed shortly) may propose to pay less than 100 percent of prepetition domestic-support obligations that were assigned, but only if disposable income is dedicated to a five-year plan. Disposable income is also redefined to exclude the amounts reasonably necessary to pay current domestic-support obligations.

29. As with a Chapter 11 reorganization plan, full repayment of all claims is not always required.

30. See 11 U.S.C. Section 1322(d) for details on when the court will find that the Chapter 13 plan should extend to a five-year period.

interested party objects to the modification, the court must hold a hearing to determine whether the modified plan will be approved.

Discharge After the debtor has completed all payments, the court grants a discharge of all debts provided for by the repayment plan. Except for allowed claims not provided for by the plan, certain long-term debts provided for by the plan, certain tax claims, payments on retirement accounts, and claims for domestic-support obligations, all other debts are dischargeable. Under prior law, a discharge of debts under a Chapter 13 repayment plan was sometimes referred to as a "superdischarge" because it allowed the discharge of fraudulently incurred debt and claims resulting from malicious or willful injury.

The 2005 Bankruptcy Reform Act, however, deleted most of the "superdischarge" provisions, especially for debts based on fraud. Today, debts for trust fund taxes, taxes for which returns were never filed or filed late (within two years of filing), domestic-support payments, student loans, and injury or property damage from driving under the influence of alcohol or drugs are nondischargeable. The law also excludes fraudulent tax obligations, criminal fines and restitution, fraud by a person acting in a fiduciary capacity, and restitution for willfully and maliciously causing personal injury or death.

Even if the debtor does not complete the plan, a hardship discharge may be granted if failure to complete the plan was due to circumstances beyond the debtor's control and if the value of the property distributed under the plan was greater than what would have been paid in a liquidation. A discharge can be revoked within one year if it was obtained by fraud.

Family Farmers and Fishermen

In 1986, to help relieve economic pressure on small farmers, Congress created Chapter 12 of the Bankruptcy Code. In 2005, Congress extended this protection to family fishermen,[31] modified its provisions somewhat, and made it a permanent chapter in the Bankruptcy Code (previously, the statutes authorizing Chapter 12 had to be periodically renewed by Congress).

For purposes of Chapter 12, a *family farmer* is one whose gross income is at least 50 percent farm dependent and whose debts are at least 50 percent farm related. The total debt for a family farmer must not exceed $3,544,525. A partnership or closely held corporation (see Chapter 18) at least 50 percent owned by the farm family can also qualify as a family farmer.

A *family fisherman* is defined as one whose gross income is at least 50 percent dependent on commercial fishing operations[32] and whose debts are at least 80 percent related to commercial fishing. The total debt for a family fisherman must not exceed $1,642,500. As with family farmers, a partnership or closely held corporation can also qualify.

Filing the Petition The procedure for filing a family-farmer or family-fisherman bankruptcy plan is very similar to the procedure for filing a repayment plan under Chapter 13. The debtor must file a plan not later than ninety days after the order for relief. The filing of the petition acts as an automatic stay against creditors' and co-obligors' actions against the estate.

A farmer or fisherman who has already filed a reorganization or repayment plan may convert it to a Chapter 12 plan. The debtor may also convert a Chapter 12 plan to a liquidation plan.

Content and Confirmation of the Plan The content of a plan under Chapter 12 is basically the same as that of a Chapter 13 repayment plan. The plan can be modified by the debtor but, except for cause, must be confirmed or denied within forty-five days of filing.

Court confirmation of the plan is the same as for a repayment plan. In summary, the plan must provide for payment of secured debts at the value of the collateral. If the secured debt exceeds the value of the collateral, the remaining debt is unsecured. For unsecured debtors, the plan must be confirmed if either (1) the value of the property to be distributed under the plan equals the amount of the claim, or (2) the plan provides that all of the debtor's disposable income to be received in a three-year period (or longer, by court approval) will be applied to making payments. Disposable income is all income received less amounts needed to support the farmer or fisherman and his or her family and to continue the farming or commercial fishing operation. Completion of payments under the plan discharges all debts provided for by the plan. See *Concept Summary 15.2* for a comparison of bankruptcy procedures under Chapters 7, 11, 12, and 13.

31. Although the Code uses the terms *fishermen* and *fisherman*, Chapter 12 provisions apply equally to men and women.

32. Commercial fishing operations include catching, harvesting, or aquaculture raising fish, shrimp, lobsters, urchins, seaweed, shellfish, or other aquatic species or products.

CONCEPT SUMMARY 15.2
Forms of Bankruptcy Relief Compared

Issue	Chapter 7	Chapter 11	Chapters 12 and 13
Purpose	Liquidation.	Reorganization.	Adjustment.
Who Can Petition	Debtor (voluntary) or creditors (involuntary).	Debtor (voluntary) or creditors (involuntary).	Debtor (voluntary) only.
Who Can Be a Debtor	Any "person" (including partnerships, corporations, and municipalities) *except* railroads, insurance companies, banks, savings and loan institutions, investment companies licensed by the Small Business Administration, and credit unions. Farmers and charitable institutions also cannot be involuntarily petitioned. If the court finds the petition to be a substantial abuse of the use of Chapter 7, the debtor may be required to convert to a Chapter 13 repayment plan.	Any debtor eligible for Chapter 7 relief; railroads are also eligible. Individuals have specific rules and limitations.	*Chapter 12*—Any family farmer (one whose gross income is at least 50 percent farm dependent and whose debts are at least 50 percent farm related) or family fisherman (one whose gross income is at least 50 percent dependent on commercial fishing operations and whose debts are at least 80 percent related to commercial fishing) or any partnership or closely held corporation at least 50 percent owned by a family farmer or fisherman, when total debt does not exceed a specified amount ($3,544,525 for farmers and $1,642,500 for fishermen). *Chapter 13*—Any individual (not partnerships or corporations) with regular income who owes fixed unsecured debts of less than $336,900 or fixed secured debts of less than $1,010,650.
Procedure Leading to Discharge	Nonexempt property is sold with proceeds to be distributed (in order) to priority groups. Dischargeable debts are terminated.	Plan is submitted; if it is approved and followed, debts are discharged.	Plan is submitted and must be approved if the value of the property to be distributed equals the amount of the claims or if the debtor turns over disposable income for a three-year or five-year period; if the plan is followed, debts are discharged.
Advantages	On liquidation and distribution, most debts are discharged, and the debtor has an opportunity for a fresh start.	Debtor continues in business. Creditors can either accept the plan, or it can be "crammed down" on them. The plan allows for the reorganization and liquidation of debts over the plan period.	Debtor continues in business or possession of assets. If the plan is approved, most debts are discharged after the plan period.

REVIEWING Creditor-Debtor Relations and Bankruptcy

Three months ago, Janet Hart's husband of twenty years died of cancer. Although he had medical insurance, he left Janet with outstanding medical bills of more than $50,000. Janet has worked at the local library for the past ten years, earning $1,500 per month. Since her husband's death, Janet also receives $1,500 in Social Security benefits and $1,100 in life insurance proceeds every month, for a total monthly income of $4,100. After she pays the mortgage payment of $1,500 and the amounts due on other debts, Janet has barely enough left over to buy groceries for her family (she has two teenage daughters at home). She decides to file for Chapter 7 bankruptcy, hoping for a fresh start. Using the information presented in the chapter, answer the following questions.

1. Under the Bankruptcy Code after the 2005 act, what must Janet do before filing a petition for relief under Chapter 7?
2. How much time does Janet have after filing the bankruptcy petition to submit the required schedules? What happens if Janet does not meet the deadline?
3. Assume that Janet files a petition under Chapter 7. Further assume that the median family income in the state in which Janet lives is $49,300. What steps would a court take to determine whether Janet's petition is presumed to be "substantial abuse" using the means test?
4. Suppose that the court determines that no *presumption* of substantial abuse applies in Janet's case. Nevertheless, the court finds that Janet does have the ability to pay at least a portion of the medical bills out of her disposable income. What would the court likely order in that situation?

TERMS AND CONCEPTS

adequate protection doctrine 375
artisan's lien 364
attachment 364
automatic stay 375
consumer-debtor 371
co-surities 370
cram-down provision 385
creditors' composition agreement 366
default 363
debtor in possession (DIP) 384
discharge 371
garnishment 364
guarantor 368
homestead exemption 370
insider 378
lien 363
liquidation 371
mechanic's lien 363
mortgage 366
mortgagee 367
mortgagor 367
order for relief 375
petition in bankruptcy 372
preference 378
preferred creditor 378
reaffirmation agreement 382
right of contribution 370
right of redemption 367
right of reimbursement 370
right of subrogation 369
surety 367
suretyship 367
trustee 371
U.S. trustee 372
workout 384
writ of attachment 364
writ of execution 364

QUESTIONS AND CASE PROBLEMS

15–1. Burke has been a rancher all her life, raising cattle and crops. Her ranch is valued at $500,000, almost all of which is exempt under state law. Burke has eight creditors and a total indebtedness of $70,000. Two of her largest creditors are Oman ($30,000 owed) and Sneed ($25,000 owed). The other six creditors have claims of less than $5,000 each. A drought has ruined all of Burke's crops and forced her to sell many of her cattle at a loss. She cannot pay off her creditors.

(a) Under the Bankruptcy Code, can Burke, with a $500,000 ranch, voluntarily petition herself into bankruptcy? Explain.
(b) Could either Oman or Sneed force Burke into involuntary bankruptcy? Explain.

15-2. QUESTION WITH SAMPLE ANSWER

Peaslee is not known for his business sense. He started a greenhouse and nursery business two years ago, and because of his lack of experience, he soon was in debt to a number of creditors. On February 1, Peaslee borrowed $5,000 from his father to pay some of these creditors. On May 1, Peaslee paid back the $5,000, depleting his entire working capital. One creditor, the Cool Springs Nursery Supply Corp., extended credit to Peaslee on numerous purchases. Cool Springs pressured Peaslee for payment, and on July 1, Peaslee paid Cool Springs half the amount owed. On September 1, Peaslee voluntarily petitioned himself into bankruptcy. The trustee in bankruptcy claims that both Peaslee's father and Cool Springs must turn over to the debtor's estate the amounts Peaslee paid to them. Discuss fully the trustee's claims.

- **For a sample answer to Question 15–2, go to Appendix I at the end of this text.**

15-3. Natalie is a student at Slippery Stone University. In need of funds to pay for tuition and books, she asks West Bank for a short-term loan. The bank agrees to make a loan if Natalie will have someone who is financially responsible guarantee the loan payments. Sheila, a well-known businessperson and a friend of Natalie's family, calls the bank and agrees to pay the loan if Natalie cannot. Because of Sheila's reputation, the loan is made. Natalie is making the payments, but because of illness she is unable to work for one month. She requests that West Bank extend the loan for three months. West Bank agrees, raising the interest rate for the extended period. Sheila is not notified of the extension (and thus does not consent to it). One month later, Natalie drops out of school. All attempts to collect from Natalie fail. West Bank wants to hold Sheila liable. Discuss the validity of West Bank's claim against Sheila.

15-4. Automatic Stay. On January 22, 2001, Marlene Moffett bought a used 1998 Honda Accord from Hendrick Honda in Woodbridge, Virginia. Moffett agreed to pay $20,024.25, with interest, in sixty monthly installments, and Hendrick retained a security interest in the car. (Hendrick thus had the right to repossess the car in the event of default, subject to Moffett's right of redemption.) Hendrick assigned its rights under the sales agreement to Tidewater Finance Co., which perfected its security interest. The car was Moffett's only means of traveling the forty miles from her home to her workplace. In March and April 2002, Moffett missed two monthly payments. On April 25, Tidewater repossessed the car. On the same day, Moffett filed a Chapter 13 plan in a federal bankruptcy court. Moffett asked that the car be returned to her, in part under the Bankruptcy Code's automatic-stay provision. Tidewater asked the court to terminate the automatic stay so that it could sell the car. How can the interests of both the debtor and the creditor be fully protected in this case? What should the court rule? Explain. [*In re Moffett,* 356 F.3d 518 (4th Cir. 2004)]

15-5. Discharge in Bankruptcy. Between 1980 and 1987, Craig Hanson borrowed funds from Great Lakes Higher Education Corp. to finance his education at the University of Wisconsin. Hanson defaulted on the debt in 1989, and Great Lakes obtained a judgment against him for $31,583.77. Three years later, Hanson filed a bankruptcy petition under Chapter 13. Great Lakes timely filed a proof of claim in the amount of $35,531.08. Hanson's repayment plan proposed to pay $135 monthly to Great Lakes over sixty months, which in total was only 19 percent of the claim, but said nothing about discharging the remaining balance. The plan was confirmed without objection. After Hanson completed the payments under the plan, without any additional proof or argument being offered, the court granted a discharge of his student loans. In 2003, Educational Credit Management Corp. (ECMC), which had taken over Great Lakes' interest in the loans, filed a motion for relief from the discharge. What is the requirement for the discharge of a student loan obligation in bankruptcy? Did Hanson meet this requirement? Should the court grant ECMC's motion? Discuss. [*In re Hanson,* 397 F.3d 482 (7th Cir. 2005)]

15-6. Exceptions to Discharge. Between 1988 and 1992, Lorna Nys took out thirteen student loans, totaling about $30,000, to finance an associate of arts degree in drafting from the College of the Redwoods and a bachelor of arts degree from Humboldt State University (HSU) in California. In 1996, Nys began working at HSU as a drafting technician. As a "Drafter II," the highest-paying drafting position at HSU, Nys's gross income in 2002 was $40,244. She was fifty-one years old, Her net monthly income was $2,299.33, and she had $2,295.05 in monthly expenses, including saving $140 for her retirement, which she planned for age sixty-five. When Educational Credit Management Corp. (ECMC) began to collect payments on Nys's student loans, she filed a Chapter 7 petition in a federal bankruptcy court, seeking a discharge of the loans. ECMC argued that Nys did not show any "additional circumstances" that would impede her ability to repay. What is the standard for the discharge of student loans under Chapter 7? Does Nys meet that standard? Why or why not? [*In re Nys,* 446 F.3d 938 (9th Cir. 2006)]

15-7. CASE PROBLEM WITH SAMPLE ANSWER

James Stout, a professor of economics and business at Cornell College in Iowa City, Iowa, filed a petition in bankruptcy under Chapter 7, seeking to discharge about $95,000 in credit-card debts. At the time, Stout had been divorced for ten years and had custody of his children: Z. S., who attended college, and G. S., who was twelve years old. Stout's ex-wife did not contribute child support. According to Stout, G. S. was an "elite" ice-skater who practiced twenty hours a week and had placed between first and third at more than forty competitive events. He had decided to home school G. S., whose achievements were average for her grade level despite her frequent absences from public school. His petition showed monthly income of $4,227 and expenses of $4,806. The expenses included annual home school costs of $8,400 and annual skating expenses of $6,000. They did not include Z. S.'s college costs, such as airfare for his upcoming studies in Europe, and other items. The trustee allowed monthly expenses of $3,227—with nothing for skating—and asked the court to dismiss the petition. Can the court grant this request? Should it? If so, what might it encourage Stout to do? Explain. [*In re Stout,* 336 Bankr. 138 (N.D. Iowa 2006)]

- **To view a sample answer for Problem 15–7, go to this book's Web site at academic.cengage.com/blaw/cross, select "Chapter 15," and click on "Case Problem with Sample Answer."**

15–8. Attachment. In 2004 and 2005, Kent Avery, on behalf of his law firm—the Law Office of Kent Avery, LLC—contracted with Marlin Broadcasting, LLC, to air commercials on WCCC-FM, 106.9 "The Rock." Avery, who was the sole member of his firm, helped to create the ads, which solicited direct contact with "defense attorney Kent Avery," featured his voice, and repeated his name and experience to make potential clients familiar with him. When WCCC was not paid for the broadcasts, Marlin filed a suit in a Connecticut state court against Avery and his firm, alleging an outstanding balance of $35,250. Pending the court's hearing of the suit, Marlin filed a request for a writ of attachment. Marlin offered in evidence the parties' contracts, the ads' transcripts, and WCCC's invoices. Avery contended that he could not be held personally liable for the cost of the ads. Marlin countered that the ads unjustly enriched Avery by conferring a personal benefit on him to Marlin's detriment. What is the purpose of attachment? What must a creditor prove to obtain a writ of attachment? Did Marlin meet this test? Explain. [*Marlin Broadcasting, LLC v. Law Office of Kent Avery, LLC,* 101 Conn.App. 638, 922 A.2d 1131 (2007)]

15–9. Discharge in Bankruptcy. Rhonda Schroeder married Gennady Shvartsshteyn (Gene) in 1997. Gene worked at Royal Courier and Air Domestic Connect in Illinois, where Melissa Winyard also worked in 1999 and 2000. During this time, Gene and Winyard had an affair. A year after leaving Royal, Winyard filed a petition in a federal bankruptcy court under Chapter 7 and was granted a discharge of her debts. Sometime later, in a letter to Schroeder, who had learned of the affair, Winyard wrote, "I never intentionally wanted any of this to happen. I never wanted to disrupt your marriage." Schroeder obtained a divorce and, in 2005, filed a suit in an Illinois state court against Winyard, alleging "alienation of affection." Schroeder claimed that there had been "mutual love and affection" in her marriage until Winyard engaged in conduct intended to alienate her husband's affection. Schroeder charged that Winyard "caused him to have sexual intercourse with her," resulting in "the destruction of the marital relationship." Winyard filed a motion for summary judgment on the ground that any liability on her part had been discharged in her bankruptcy. Is there an exception to discharge for "willful and malicious conduct"? If so, does Schroeder's claim qualify? Discuss. [*Schroeder v. Winyard,* 375 Ill.App.3d 358, 873 N.E.2d 35, 313 Ill.Dec. 740 (2 Dist. 2007)]

15–10. A QUESTION OF ETHICS

*In January 2003, Gary Ryder and Washington Mutual Bank, F.A., executed a note in which Ryder promised to pay $2,450,000, plus interest at a rate that could vary from month to month. The amount of the first payment was $10,933. The note was to be paid in full by February 1, 2033. A mortgage on Ryder's real property at 345 Round Hill Road in Greenwich, Connecticut, in favor of the bank secured his obligations under the note. The note and mortgage required that he pay the taxes on the property, which he did not do in 2004 and 2005. The bank notified him that he was in default and, when he failed to act, paid $50,095.92 in taxes, penalties, interest, and fees. Other disputes arose between the parties, and Ryder filed a suit in a federal district court against the bank, alleging, in part, breach of contract. He charged, among other things, that some of his timely payments were not processed and were subjected to incorrect late fees, forcing him to make excessive payments and ultimately resulting in "non-payment by Ryder." [*Ryder v. Washington Mutual Bank, F.A., *501 F.Supp.2d 311 (D.Conn. 2007)]*

(a) The bank filed a counterclaim, seeking to foreclose on the mortgage. What should a creditor be required to prove to foreclose on mortgaged property? What would be a debtor's most effective defense? Which party in this case is likely to prevail on the bank's counterclaim? Why?

(b) The parties agreed to a settlement that released the bank from Ryder's claims and required him to pay the note by January 31, 2007. The court dismissed the suit, but when Ryder did not make the payment, the bank asked the court to reopen the case. The bank then asked for a judgment in its favor on Ryder's complaint, arguing that the settlement had "immediately" released the bank from his claims. Does this seem fair? Why or why not?

15–11. VIDEO QUESTION

Go to this text's Web site at **academic.cengage.com/blaw/cross** and select "Chapter 15." Click on "Video Questions" and view the video titled *The River.* Then answer the following questions.

(a) In the video, a crowd (including Mel Gibson) is gathered at a farm auction in which the farming goods of a neighbor (Jim Antonio) are being sold. The people in the crowd, who are upset because they believe that the bank is selling out the farmer, begin chanting "no sale, no sale." In an effort to calm the situation, the farmer tells the crowd that "they've already foreclosed" on his farm. What does he mean?

(b) Assume that the auction is a result of Chapter 7 bankruptcy proceedings. Was the farmer's petition for bankruptcy voluntary or involuntary? Explain.

(c) Suppose that the farmer purchased the homestead three years prior to filing a petition for bankruptcy and that the current market value of the farm is $215,000. What is the maximum amount of equity the farmer could claim as exempt?

(d) Compare the results of a Chapter 12 bankruptcy as opposed to a Chapter 7 bankruptcy for the farmer in the video.

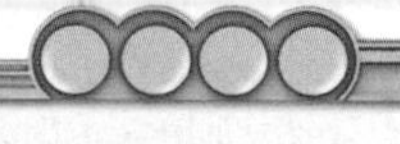

LAW ON THE WEB

For updated links to resources available on the Web, as well as a variety of other materials, visit this text's Web site at

academic.cengage.com/blaw/cross

The Legal Information Institute at Cornell University offers a collection of law materials concerning debtor-creditor relationships, including federal statutes and recent Supreme Court decisions on this topic, at

www.law.cornell.edu/wex/index.php/Debtor_and_creditor

The U.S. Department of Labor's Web site contains a page on garnishment and employees' rights in relation to garnishment proceedings at

www.dol.gov/dol/topic/wages/garnishments.htm

The U.S. Bankruptcy Code is online at

www.law.cornell.edu:80/uscode/11

Another good resource for bankruptcy information is the American Bankruptcy Institute (ABI) at

www.abiworld.org

Legal Research Exercises on the Web

Go to **academic.cengage.com/blaw/cross**, the Web site that accompanies this text. Select "Chapter 15" and click on "Internet Exercises." There you will find the following Internet research exercises that you can perform to learn more about the topics covered in this chapter.

Internet Exercise 15–1: Legal Perspective
Debtor-Creditor Relations

Internet Exercise 15–2: Management Perspective
Bankruptcy Alternatives

UNIT THREE FOCUS ON ETHICS

Ethics and the Commercial Environment

Many aspects of the commercial environment lend themselves to ethical analysis. Businesspersons certainly face ethical questions when they deal with the application of black-letter law to contracts. (*Black-letter law* is an informal term for the principles of law that courts usually accept or that are embodied in statutes.) Courts, for example, generally will not inquire into the adequacy of the consideration given in a contract. In other words, a court will not reevaluate a contract to determine whether what each party gave is equivalent to what that party received.

Ethical questions are also at the core of many principles of the law of sales. Many of the provisions of the Uniform Commercial Code (UCC), such as good faith and commercial reasonableness, though designed to meet the practical needs of business dealings, express ethical standards as well. Product liability also involves ethics. Many of the principles of product liability are based on principles designed to aid individuals injured, without extensive inquiry into issues of fault.

The areas of law covered in the previous unit constitute an important part of the legal environment of business. In each of these areas, new legal (and ethical) challenges have emerged as a result of developments in technology. Today, we are witnessing some of the challenges posed by the use of new communications networks, particularly the Internet. In this *Focus on Ethics* feature, we look at the ethical dimensions of selected topics discussed in the preceding chapters, including some issues that are unique to the cyber age.

Ethics and Freedom of Contract

In Chapter 4, we pointed out the importance of ethical business behavior. But what does acting ethically mean in the area of contracts? If an individual with whom you enter into a contract fails to look after his or her own interests, is that your fault, and should you therefore be doing something about it? If the contract happens to be to your advantage and therefore to the other party's detriment, do you have a responsibility to correct the situation?

The answer to this question is not simple. On the one hand, a common ethical assumption in our society is that individuals should be held responsible for the consequences of their own actions, including their contractual promises. This principle is expressed in the legal concept of freedom of contract.

On the other hand, there are times when courts will hold that the principle *of* freedom of contract should give way to the principle of freedom *from* contract, a principle based on the assumption that people should not be harmed by the actions of others. We look below at some examples of how parties to contracts may be excused from performance under their contracts if that is the only way injustice can be prevented.

Impossibility of Performance The doctrine of impossibility of performance is based to some extent on the ethical question of whether one party should suffer economic loss when it is impossible to perform a contract. The rule that one is "bound by his or her contracts" is not followed when performance becomes impossible. This doctrine, however, is applied only when the parties themselves did not consciously assume the risk of the events that rendered performance impossible. Furthermore, this doctrine rests on the assumption that the party claiming the defense of impossibility has acted ethically.

Unconscionability The doctrine of unconscionability represents a good example of how the law attempts to enforce ethical behavior. Under this doctrine, a contract may be deemed to be so unfair to one party as to be unenforceable—even though that party voluntarily agreed to the contract's terms. Unconscionable action, like unethical action, is incapable of precise definition. Information about the particular facts and specific circumstances surrounding the contract is essential. For example, a contract with a marginally literate consumer might be seen as unfair and unenforceable, whereas the same contract with a major business firm would be upheld by the courts.

Exculpatory Clauses In some situations, courts have also refused to enforce exculpatory clauses on the ground that they are unconscionable or contrary to public policy. An *exculpatory clause* attempts to excuse a party from liability in the event of monetary or physical injury, no matter who is at fault. In some situations, such clauses are upheld. For example, a health club can require its members to sign a clause releasing the club from any liability for injuries the members might incur while using

the club's equipment and facilities. The law permits parties to assume, by express agreement, the risks inherent in certain activities.

Nonetheless, some jurisdictions take a dubious view of exculpatory clauses, particularly when the agreement is between parties with unequal bargaining power. For example, an exculpatory clause that attempts to exempt an employer from *all* liability for negligence toward its employees frequently is held to be against public policy and thus void.[1] The courts reason that disparity in bargaining power and economic necessity force the employee to accept the employer's terms.

Ethics and Sales: Good Faith and Commercial Reasonableness

Good faith and commercial reasonableness are two key concepts that permeate the UCC and help to prevent unethical behavior by businesspersons. These two concepts are read into every contract and impose certain duties on all parties. Section 2–311(1) of the UCC indicates that when parties leave the particulars of performance to be specified by one of the parties, "[a]ny such specification must be made in good faith and within limits set by commercial reasonableness."

Bad Faith Not Required A party can breach the obligation of good faith under the UCC even if the party did not show "bad faith"—that is, even when there is no proof that the party was dishonest. For example, in one case a large manufacturer of recreational boats, Genmar Holdings, Inc., purchased Horizon, a small company that produced a particular type of "deep-V" fishing boat. Genmar bought Horizon to expand into the southern boat market and to prevent Horizon from becoming a potential future competitor. At the time of the sale, Genmar executives promised that Horizon boats would be the "champion" of the facility and vowed to keep Horizon's key employees (including the founder and his family) on as managers. The contract required Genmar to pay Horizon a lump sum in cash as well as paying "earn-out consideration" under a specified formula for five years. The "earn-out" amount depended on the number of Horizon brand boats sold and on the annual gross revenues of the facility.

One year after the sale, Genmar renamed the Horizon brand of boats "Nova" and told employees at the facility to give priority to producing the original Genmar brand of boats over the Nova boats. Because the Genmar boats were more difficult and time consuming to make than the Nova boats, the facility's gross revenues and production decreased, and Genmar was not required to pay the "earn-out" amounts. Eventually, Genmar fired the former Horizon employees and stopped manufacturing the Nova brand of boats entirely. The former employees filed a suit alleging that Genmar had breached the implied covenant of good faith and fair dealing. The defendants argued that they could not have violated good faith because there was no proof that they had engaged in fraud, deceit, or misrepresentation. The court held for the plaintiffs, however, and the decision was affirmed on appeal.[2] It is possible for a party to breach its good faith obligations under the UCC even if the party did not engage in fraud, deceit, or misrepresentation.

Commercial Reasonableness The requirement of commercial reasonableness means that the term subsequently supplied by one party should not come as a surprise to the other. The party filling in the missing term may not take advantage of the opportunity to add a contractual term that will be beneficial to himself or herself (and detrimental to the other party) and then demand contractual performance of the other party that was totally unanticipated. Under the UCC, the party filling in the missing term may not deviate from what is commercially reasonable in the context of the transaction. Courts frequently look to *course of dealing, usage of trade,* and the surrounding circumstances in determining what is commercially reasonable in a given situation.

Oral Contracts and the Statute of Frauds

As you learned in Chapter 9, the Statute of Frauds was originally enacted in England in 1677. The act was intended to prevent harm to innocent parties by requiring written evidence of agreements concerning important transactions.

1. See, for example, *City of Santa Barbara v. Superior Court,* 62 Cal.Rptr.3d 527, 161 P.3d 1095 (2007); and *Health Net of California, Inc. v. Department of Health Services,* 113 Cal.App.4th 224, 6 Cal.Rptr.3d 235 (2003).

2. *O'Tool v. Genmar Holdings, Inc.,* 387 F.3d 1188 (10th Cir. 2004).

(Continued)

UNIT THREE FOCUS ON ETHICS

Detrimental Reliance Under the Statute of Frauds, if a contract is oral when it is required to be in writing, it will not, as a rule, be enforced by the courts. An exception to this rule is made if a party has reasonably relied, to his or her detriment, on the oral contract. Enforcing an oral contract on the basis of a party's reliance arguably undercuts the essence of the Statute of Frauds. The reason that such an exception is made is to prevent the statute—which was created to prevent injustice—from being used to promote injustice. Nevertheless, this use of the doctrine is controversial—as is the Statute of Frauds itself.

Criticisms of the Statute of Frauds Since its inception more than three hundred years ago, the statute has been criticized by some because, although it was created to protect the innocent, it can also be used as a technical defense by a party breaching a genuine, mutually agreed-on oral contract—if the contract falls within the Statute of Frauds. For this reason, some legal scholars believe the act has caused more injustice than it has prevented. Thus, exceptions are sometimes made—such as under the doctrine of promissory estoppel—to prevent unfairness and inequity. Generally, the courts are slow to apply the statute if doing so will result in obvious injustice. In some instances, this has required a good deal of inventiveness on the part of the courts.

Do Gun Makers Have a Duty to Warn?

One of the issues facing today's courts is how tort law principles apply to harms caused by guns. Across the nation, many plaintiffs have filed negligence actions against gun manufacturers claiming that gun makers have a duty to warn users of their products of the dangers associated with gun use. Would it be fair to impose such a requirement on gun manufacturers? Some say no, because such dangers are "open and obvious." (Recall from Chapter 13 that manufacturers and sellers do not have a duty to warn of open and obvious dangers.) Others contend that warnings could prevent numerous gun accidents.

State courts addressing this issue have generally ruled that manufacturers have no duty to warn users of the obvious risks associated with gun use. For example, New York's highest court has held that a gun manufacturer's duty of care does not extend to those who are injured by the illegal use of handguns.[3] Some courts, however, have held that gun makers whose marketing or sales practices cause a large influx of guns into the illegal secondary market could be liable under a public nuisance theory.[4]

Should Civil Liberties Be Sacrificed to Control Crime and Terrorist Activities in the Cyber Age?

In an era when criminal conspirators and terrorists use the Internet to communicate and even to recruit new members, an issue that has come to the forefront is whether it is possible to control many types of crime and terrorist activities without sacrificing some civil liberties. Governments in certain countries, such as Russia, have succeeded in controlling online criminal communications to some extent by monitoring the e-mail and other electronic transmissions of users of specific Internet service providers. In the United States, however, any government attempt to monitor Internet use to detect criminal conspiracies or terrorist activities does not sit well with the American people. The traditional attitude has been that civil liberties must be safeguarded to the greatest extent feasible.

After the terrorist attacks in September 2001, Congress enacted legislation—including the USA Patriot Act mentioned in Chapter 5—that gave law enforcement personnel more authority to conduct electronic surveillance, such as monitoring Web sites and e-mail exchanges. For a time, it seemed that the terrorist attacks might have made Americans more willing to trade off some of their civil liberties for greater national security. Today, though, many complain that this legislation has gone too far in curbing traditional civil liberties guaranteed by the U.S. Constitution. As terrorists find more ways of using the Internet for their purposes, determining the degree to which individuals should sacrifice personal freedoms in exchange for greater protection will likely become even more difficult.

Trademark Protection versus Free Speech Rights

Another legal issue involving questions of fairness pits the rights of trademark owners against the right

3. *Hamilton v. Beretta U.S.A. Corp.*, 96 N.Y.2d 222, 750 N.E.2d 1055, 727 N.Y.S.2d 7 (2001).

4. *City of New York v. Beretta U.S.A. Corp.*, 315 F.Supp.2d 256 (E.D.N.Y. 2004); *Johnson v. Bryco Arms*, 304 F.Supp.2d 383 (E.D.N.Y. 2004); *City of Gary ex rel. King v. Smith & Wesson Corp.*, 801 N.E.2d 1222 (Ind. 2003); *Ileto v. Glock, Inc.*, 349 F.3d 1191 (9th Cir. 2003).

to free speech. The issue—so-called cybergriping—is unique to the cyber age.

Cybergriping Cybergripers are individuals who complain in cyberspace about corporate products, services, or activities. For trademark owners, the issue becomes particularly thorny when cybergriping sites add the word sucks or stinks or some other disparaging term to the domain name of the mark's owners. These sites, sometimes referred to collectively as "sucks" sites, are established solely for the purpose of criticizing the products or services sold by the owners of the marks.

The Question of Trademark Infringement A number of companies have sued the owners of such sites for trademark infringement in the hope that a court or an arbitrating panel will order the site owner to cease using the domain name. Generally, however, the courts have been reluctant to hold that the use of a business's domain name in a "sucks" site infringes on the trademark owner's rights. After all, one of the primary reasons trademarks are protected under U.S. law is to prevent customers from becoming confused over the origins of the goods for sale—and a cybergriping site would certainly not create such confusion. Furthermore, American courts give extensive protection to free speech rights, including the right to express opinions about companies and their products.[5]

Ethics and Bankruptcy

The first goal of bankruptcy law is to provide relief and protection to debtors who have "gotten in over their heads." Society has generally concluded that everyone should be given the chance to start over again. But how far should society go in letting debtors avoid obligations that they voluntarily incurred?

Consider the concept of bankruptcy from the point of view of the creditor. The creditor has extended a transfer of purchasing power from himself or herself to the debtor. That transfer of purchasing power represents a transfer of an asset for an asset. The debtor obtains the asset of money, goods, or services, and the creditor obtains the asset called a secured or unsecured legal obligation to pay. Once the debtor is in bankruptcy, voluntarily or involuntarily, the asset that the creditor owns most often has a diminished value. Indeed, in many circumstances, that asset has no value. Yet the easier it becomes for debtors to hide behind bankruptcy laws, the greater will be the incentive for debtors to use such laws to avoid payment of legally owed sums of money.

Clearly, bankruptcy law is a balancing act between providing a second chance and ensuring that creditors are given "a fair shake." Understandably, ethical issues arise in the process.

The Consequences of Bankruptcy

Under the 2005 Bankruptcy Reform Act, filing for personal bankruptcy (particularly under Chapter 7) has become more difficult. Although it is true that there is less of a stigma attached to bankruptcy today than there once was, bankruptcy is never easy for debtors. Many debtors feel a sense of shame and failure when they petition for bankruptcy. After all, bankruptcy is a matter of public record, and there is no way to avoid a certain amount of publicity. In one case, for example, a couple who filed for Chapter 7 bankruptcy wanted to use their attorney's mailing address in another town on their bankruptcy schedules in an effort to prevent an elderly parent and one of their employers from learning about the bankruptcy. The court, however, held that debtors are not entitled to be protected from publicity surrounding the filing of their cases.[6]

Bankruptcy also has other consequences for debtors, including blemished credit ratings for up to ten years and higher interest charges for new debts, such as those incurred through the purchase of cars or homes. Some private employers may even refuse to hire a job applicant who has filed for bankruptcy. The courts provide little relief for applicants who are denied a job for this reason.[7]

Thus, bankruptcy can have adverse effects for both debtors and creditors. Because of the consequences of bankruptcy, debtors do not always get the fresh start promised by bankruptcy law. At the same time, creditors rarely are able to recover all of the money owed them once a debtor petitions for bankruptcy.

5. Many businesses have concluded that while they cannot control what people say about them, they can make it more difficult for it to be said. Today, businesses commonly register such insulting domain names before the cybergripers themselves can register them.

6. *In the Matter of Laws,* 223 Bankr. 714 (D.Neb. 1998).

7. See, for example, *In re Potter,* 354 Bankr. 301 (D.Ala. 2006); and *In re Stinson,* 285 Bankr. 239 (W.D.Va. 2002).

(Continued)

UNIT THREE ★ FOCUS ON ETHICS ★

DISCUSSION QUESTIONS

1. In determining whether an exculpatory clause should be enforced, why does it matter whether the contract containing the clause involves essential services (such as transportation) or nonessential services (such as skiing or other leisure-time activities)?
2. How can a court objectively measure good faith and commercial reasonableness?
3. Many countries have no Statute of Frauds, and even England, the country that created the original act, has repealed it. Should the United States do likewise? What are some of the costs and benefits to society of the Statute of Frauds?
4. In your opinion, should gun manufacturers have a duty to warn gun users of the dangers of using guns? Would such a warning be effective in preventing gun-related accidents?
5. Many argue that the federal government should not be allowed to monitor the Internet activities and e-mail exchanges of its citizens without obtaining a warrant. Yet others maintain that in some situations, when time is of the essence, such monitoring may be necessary to keep Americans safe from terrorism. Where should the line be drawn between justifiable and unjustifiable governmental interference with American citizens' civil liberties?
6. Is it unethical to avoid paying one's debts by going into bankruptcy? Does a person have a moral responsibility to pay his or her debts?

UNIT FOUR
The Business Environment

CONTENTS

CHAPTER 16

Sole Proprietorships, Franchises, and Partnerships

Anyone who starts a business must first decide which form of business organization will be most appropriate for the new endeavor. In making this decision, the **entrepreneur** (one who initiates and assumes the financial risk of a new enterprise) needs to consider a number of factors, especially (1) ease of creation, (2) the liability of the owners, (3) tax considerations, and (4) the need for capital. In studying this unit on the business environment, keep these factors in mind as you read about the various business organizational forms available to entrepreneurs. You may also find it helpful to refer to Exhibit 18–3 on pages 469–470 in Chapter 18, which compares the major business forms in use today with respect to these and other factors.

Traditionally, entrepreneurs have relied on three major business forms—the sole proprietorship, the partnership, and the corporation. In this chapter, we examine the sole proprietorship and the franchise, which, though not really a separate business organizational form, is widely used today by entrepreneurs. Then we examine the second traditional business form, the partnership.

Section 1 Sole Proprietorships

The simplest form of business organization is a **sole proprietorship.** In this form, the owner is the business; thus, anyone who does business without creating a separate business organization has a sole proprietorship. More than two-thirds of all American businesses are sole proprietorships. They are usually small enterprises—about 99 percent of the sole proprietorships in the United States have revenues of less than $1 million per year. Sole proprietors can own and manage any type of business from an informal, home-office undertaking to a large restaurant or construction firm.

Advantages of the Sole Proprietorship

A major advantage of the sole proprietorship is that the proprietor owns the entire business and receives all of the profits (because she or he assumes all of the risk). In addition, starting a sole proprietorship is often easier and less costly than starting any other kind of business, as few legal formalities are required.[1] No documents need to be filed with the government to start a sole proprietorship (though a state business license may be required to operate certain businesses).

This type of business organization also provides more flexibility than does a partnership or a corporation. The sole proprietor is free to make any decision he or she wishes concerning the business—such as whom to hire, when to take a vacation, and what kind of business to pursue. In addition, the proprietor can sell or transfer all or part of the business to another party at any time and does not need approval from anyone else (as would be required from partners in a partnership or normally from shareholders in a corporation).

A sole proprietor pays only personal income taxes (including Social Security and Medicare taxes) on the business's profits, which are reported as personal

1. Although starting a sole proprietorship involves fewer legal formalities than other business organizational forms, even small sole proprietorships may need to comply with zoning requirements, obtain licenses, and the like.

income on the proprietor's personal income tax return. Sole proprietors are also allowed to establish certain tax-exempt retirement accounts.

Disadvantages of the Sole Proprietorship

The major disadvantage of the sole proprietorship is that, as sole owner, the proprietor alone bears the burden of any losses or liabilities incurred by the business enterprise. In other words, the sole proprietor has unlimited liability, or legal responsibility, for all obligations that arise in doing business. Any lawsuit against the business or its employees can lead to unlimited personal liability for the owner of a sole proprietorship. Creditors can go after the owner's personal assets to satisfy any business debts. This unlimited liability is a major factor to be considered in choosing a business form.

The sole proprietorship also has the disadvantage of lacking continuity on the death of the proprietor. When the owner dies, so does the business—it is automatically dissolved. Another disadvantage is that in raising capital, the proprietor is limited to his or her personal funds and any personal loans that he or she can obtain.

The personal liability of the owner of a sole proprietorship was at issue in the following case. The case involved the federal Cable Communications Act, which prohibits a commercial establishment from broadcasting television programs to its patrons without authorization. The court had to decide whether the owner of a sole proprietorship that installed a satellite television system was personally liable for violating this act by identifying a restaurant as a "residence" for billing purposes.

CASE 16.1 Garden City Boxing Club, Inc. v. Dominguez

United States District Court, Northern District of Illinois, Eastern Division, 2006. __ F.Supp.2d __.

• **Background and Facts** Garden City Boxing Club, Inc. (GCB), which is based in San Jose, California, owned the exclusive right to broadcast via closed-circuit television several prizefights, including the match between Oscar De La Hoya and Fernando Vargas on September 14, 2002. GCB sold the right to receive the broadcasts to bars and other commercial venues. The fee was $20 multiplied by an establishment's maximum fire code occupancy. Antenas Enterprises in Chicago, Illinois, sells and installs satellite television systems under a contract with DISH Network. After installing a system, Antenas sends the buyer's address and other identifying information to DISH. In January 2002, Luis Garcia, an Antenas employee, identified a new customer as Jose Melendez at 220 Hawthorn Commons in Vernon Hills. The address was a restaurant—Mundelein Burrito—but Garcia designated the account as residential. Mundelein's patrons watched the De La Hoya–Vargas match on September 14, as well as three other fights on other dates, for which the restaurant paid only the residential rate to DISH and nothing to GCB. GCB filed a suit in a federal district court against Luis Dominguez, the sole proprietor of Antenas, to collect the fee.

IN THE LANGUAGE OF THE COURT
LEINENWEBER, J. [Judge]

* * * *

Section 605(a) [of the Cable Communications Act] states "[a]n authorized intermediary of a communication violates the Act when it divulges communication through an electronic channel to one other than the addressee." Mundelein Burrito was clearly a commercial establishment. The structure of the building, an exterior identification sign, and its location in a strip mall made this obvious. Mundelein Burrito paid only the residential fee for the four fights it broadcast to its patrons. It was not an authorized addressee of any of the four fights. By improperly listing Mundelein Burrito as a residence, Antenas Enterprises allowed the unauthorized broadcast of the Event, and three additional fights, to Mundelein Burrito. Antenas Enterprises is liable under [Section] 605 of the Act.

* * * *

CASE CONTINUES

CASE 16.1 CONTINUED

The unauthorized broadcast of the four separate events deprived GCB of the full value of its business investment. * * * [Under the Cable Communications Act] an aggrieved party * * * may recover an award of damages "for each violation of [Section 605(a)] involved in the action in a sum of not less than $1,000 or more than $10,000, as the court considers just." If the violation was willful and for purposes of commercial advantage or private financial gain, the court in its discretion may increase the award of damages—by an amount not more than $100,000. The court must award attorneys' fees to the prevailing party.

GCB argues that the Antenas Enterprises failure to properly list Mundelein Burrito resulted in four separate violations. According to the license fee charged for each of the four fights that were illegally broadcast by Mundelein Burrito, the proper amount would have been $20.00 times the maximum fire code occupancy (46) or $3,680.00. Instead, due to the improper identification of the account as residential, Mundelein Burrito paid only $184.40 to broadcast the four events. GCB did not receive any of the $184.40.

* * * [Considering] the willfulness of the defendant's conduct and the deterrent value of the sanction imposed * * * twice the amount of actual damages is reasonable for this case. Therefore, Antenas Enterprises is liable to GCB for the sum of $7,360.00. Pursuant to the Act, GCB is also entitled to reasonable attorneys' fees.

* * * *

GCB argues Luis Dominguez is personally liable for Antenas Enterprises' violation of [Section] 605 of the Act. The term "person" in the Act means an "individual, partnership, association, joint stock company, trust, corporation or governmental entity."

Antenas Enterprises is a sole proprietorship, owned by Dominguez. *A sole proprietor is personally responsible for actions committed by his employees within the scope of their employment.* Accordingly, Dominguez is personally liable for the damages caused by the violation of [Section] 605 of the Act. [Emphasis added.]

- **Decision and Remedy** *The court issued a summary judgment in GCB's favor, holding that the plaintiff was entitled to the amount of Mundelein's fee for which Dominguez was personally liable, plus damages and attorneys' fees.*

- **What If the Facts Were Different?** *If Mundelein had identified itself as a residence when ordering the satellite system, how might the result in this case have been different?*

- **The Global Dimension** *Because the Internet has made it possible for sole proprietorships to do business worldwide without greatly increasing their costs, should they be considered, for some purposes, the equivalent of other business forms? Why or why not?*

Franchises

Instead of setting up a business form for marketing their own products or services, many entrepreneurs opt to purchase a franchise. A **franchise** is an arrangement in which the owner of a trademark, a trade name, or a copyright licenses others to use the trademark, trade name, or copyright in the selling of goods or services. A **franchisee** (a purchaser of a franchise) is generally legally independent of the **franchisor** (the seller of the franchise). At the same time, the franchise is economically dependent on the franchisor's integrated business system. In other words, a franchisee can operate as an independent businessperson but still obtain the advantages of a regional or national organization. Today, franchising companies and their franchisees account for a significant portion of all retail sales in this country. Well-known franchises include McDonald's, 7-Eleven, and Holiday Inn.

Types of Franchises

Many different kinds of businesses now sell franchises, and numerous types of franchises are available. Generally, though, franchises fall into one of three classifications: distributorships, chain-style business operations, and manufacturing or processing-plant arrangements.

Distributorship With a *distributorship,* a manufacturing concern (franchisor) licenses a dealer (franchisee) to sell its product. Often, a distributorship covers an exclusive territory. An example is an automobile dealership or beer distributorship, such as Anheuser-Busch.

Chain-Style Business Operation In a *chain-style business operation,* a franchise operates under a franchisor's trade name and is identified as a member of a select group of dealers that engage in the franchisor's business. The franchisee is generally required to follow standardized or prescribed methods of operation. Often, the franchisor insists that the franchisee maintain certain standards of performance. In addition, the franchisee may be required to obtain materials and supplies exclusively from the franchisor. McDonald's and most other fast-food chains are examples of this type of franchise. Chain-style franchises are also common in service-related businesses, including real estate brokerage firms, such as Century 21, and tax-preparing services, such as H & R Block, Inc.

A Manufacturing or Processing-Plant Arrangement With a *manufacturing* or *processing-plant arrangement,* the franchisor transmits to the franchisee the essential ingredients or formula to make a particular product. The franchisee then markets the product either at wholesale or at retail in accordance with the franchisor's standards. Examples of this type of franchise include Coca-Cola and other soft-drink bottling companies.

Laws Governing Franchising

Because a franchise relationship is primarily a contractual relationship, it is governed by contract law. If the franchise exists primarily for the sale of products manufactured by the franchisor, the law governing sales contracts as expressed in Article 2 of the Uniform Commercial Code applies (see Chapter 11). Additionally, the federal government and most states have enacted laws governing certain aspects of franchising. Generally, these laws are designed to protect prospective franchisees from dishonest franchisors and to prevent franchisors from terminating franchises without good cause.

Federal Regulation of Franchises in Certain Industries The federal government has enacted laws that protect franchisees in certain industries, such as automobile dealerships and service stations. These laws protect the franchisee from unreasonable demands and bad faith terminations of the franchise by the franchisor. If an automobile manufacturer–franchisor terminates a franchise because of a dealer-franchisee's failure to comply with unreasonable demands (for example, failure to attain an unrealistically high sales quota), the manufacturer may be liable for damages.[2] Similarly, federal law prescribes the conditions under which a franchisor of service stations can terminate the franchise.[3] Federal antitrust laws (to be discussed in Chapters 26 and 27) also apply in certain circumstances to prohibit certain types of anticompetitive agreements.

The Franchise Rule In 1978, the Federal Trade Commission (FTC) issued the Franchise Rule, which requires franchisors to disclose material facts that a prospective franchisee needs to make an informed decision concerning the purchase of a franchise.[4] The rule was designed to enable potential franchisees to weigh the risks and benefits of an investment. Basically, the rule requires the franchisor to make numerous written disclosures to prospective franchisees.

For example, a franchisor is required to disclose whether the projected earnings figures are based on actual data or hypothetical examples. If a franchisor makes sales or earnings projections based on actual data for a specific franchise location, the franchisor must disclose the number and percentage of its actual franchises that have achieved this result. All representations made to a prospective franchisee must have a reasonable basis. Franchisors are also required to explain termination, cancellation, and renewal provisions of the franchise contract to potential franchisees before the agreement is signed. Those who violate the Franchise Rule are subject to substantial civil penalties, and the FTC can sue on behalf of injured parties to recover damages.

Online Disclosure Now Allowed In July 2007, amendments to the Franchise Rule went into effect that allow franchisors to provide disclosure documents via the Internet as long as they meet certain requirements. For example, prospective

2. Automobile Dealers' Franchise Act of 1965, also known as the Automobile Dealers' Day in Court Act, 15 U.S.C. Sections 1221 *et seq.*

3. Petroleum Marketing Practices Act (PMPA) of 1979, 15 U.S.C. Sections 2801 *et seq.*

4. 16 C.F.R. Section 436.1.

franchisees must be able to download or save all electronic disclosure documents. The amendments also bring the federal rule into closer alignment with state franchise disclosure laws (discussed next) and require additional disclosures on lawsuits that the franchisor has filed against franchisees and settlement agreements that it has entered into with them.

State Protection for Franchisees State legislation varies but often is aimed at protecting franchisees from unfair practices and bad faith terminations by franchisors. Approximately fifteen states have laws similar to the federal rules requiring franchisors to provide presale disclosures to prospective franchisees.[5] Some states also require a disclosure document (known as a *Uniform Franchise Offering Circular*, or UFOC) to be filed with a state official. To protect franchisees, a state law might require the disclosure of information such as the actual costs of operation, recurring expenses, and profits earned, along with facts substantiating these figures. To protect franchisees against arbitrary or bad faith terminations, the law might also require that certain procedures be followed in terminating a franchising relationship. State deceptive trade practices acts (see Chapter 23) may also prohibit certain types of actions on the part of franchisors.

For example, the Illinois Franchise Disclosure Act prohibits any untrue statement of a material fact in connection with the offer or sale of any franchise. If Miyamoto, a franchisor of bagel stores, understates the start-up costs and exaggerates the anticipated yearly profits from operating a bagel shop to a franchisee, he has violated state law.[6]

The Franchise Contract

The franchise relationship is defined by a contract between the franchisor and the franchisee. The franchise contract specifies the terms and conditions of the franchise and spells out the rights and duties of the franchisor and the franchisee. If either party fails to perform its contractual duties, that party may be subject to a lawsuit for breach of contract. Furthermore, if a franchisee is induced to enter into a franchise contract by the franchisor's fraudulent misrepresentation, the franchisor may be liable for damages. Generally, statutes and the case law governing franchising tend to emphasize the importance of good faith and fair dealing in franchise relationships.

Because each type of franchise relationship has its own characteristics, it is difficult to describe the broad range of details a franchising contract may include. We look next at some of the major issues that typically are addressed in a franchise contract.

Payment for the Franchise The franchisee ordinarily pays an initial fee or lump-sum price for the franchise license (the privilege of being granted a franchise). This fee is separate from the various products that the franchisee purchases from or through the franchisor. In some industries, the franchisor relies heavily on the initial sale of the franchise for realizing a profit. In other industries, the continued dealing between the parties brings profit to both. In most situations, the franchisor receives a stated percentage of the annual sales or annual volume of business done by the franchisee. The franchise agreement may also require the franchisee to pay a percentage of the franchisor's advertising costs and certain administrative expenses.

Business Premises The franchise agreement may specify whether the premises for the business must be leased or purchased outright. Sometimes, a building must be constructed to meet the terms of the agreement. Certainly, the agreement will specify whether the franchisor or the franchisee is responsible for supplying equipment and furnishings for the premises.

Location of the Franchise Typically, the franchisor determines the territory to be served. Some franchise contracts give the franchisee exclusive rights, or "territorial rights," to a certain geographic area. Other franchise contracts, while defining the territory allotted to a particular franchise, either specifically state that the franchise is nonexclusive or are silent on the issue of territorial rights.

Many franchise cases involve disputes over territorial rights, and the implied covenant of good faith and fair dealing often comes into play in this area of franchising. Suppose that the franchise contract either does not give the franchisee exclusive territorial rights or is silent on the issue. If the franchisor allows a competing franchise to be established nearby, the first franchisee may suffer a significant loss in profits. In this situation, a court may hold that the franchisor's actions

5. These states include California, Hawaii, Illinois, Indiana, Maryland, Michigan, Minnesota, New York, North Dakota, Oregon, Rhode Island, South Dakota, Virginia, Washington, and Wisconsin.
6. *Bixby's Food Systems, Inc. v. McKay*, 193 F.Supp.2d 1053 (N.D.Ill. 2002).

breached an implied covenant of good faith and fair dealing.

Business Organization The franchisee's business organization is of great concern to the franchisor. As part of the franchise agreement, the franchisor may require that the business have a particular form and capital structure. The franchise agreement may also provide standards of operation in such aspects of the business as sales quotas, quality, and record keeping. Additionally, a franchisor may retain stringent control over the training of personnel involved in the operation and over administrative aspects of the business.

Quality Control Although the day-to-day operation of the franchise business normally is left up to the franchisee, the franchise agreement may provide for some degree of supervision and control by the franchisor so that it can protect the franchise's name and reputation. When the franchise is a service operation, such as a motel, the contract often states that the franchisor will establish certain standards for the facility and will be permitted to make periodic inspections to ensure that the standards are being maintained.

As a general rule, the validity of a provision permitting the franchisor to establish and enforce certain quality standards is unquestioned. Because the franchisor has a legitimate interest in maintaining the quality of the product or service to protect its name and reputation, it can exercise greater control in this area than would otherwise be tolerated. Increasingly, however, franchisors are finding that if they exercise too much control over the operations of their franchisees, they may incur *vicarious (indirect) liability* under agency theory for the acts of their franchisees' employees (see Chapter 19). The actual exercise of control, or at least the right to control, is the key consideration. If the franchisee controls the day-to-day operations of the business to a significant degree, the franchisor may be able to avoid liability, as the following case illustrates.

EXTENDED CASE 16.2 Kerl v. Dennis Rasmussen, Inc.

Wisconsin Supreme Court, 2004. 2004 WI 86, 273 Wis.2d 106, 682 N.W.2d 328.

DIANE S. SYKES, J. [Justice]

* * * *

* * * [On June 11, 1999] Harvey Pierce ambushed and shot Robin Kerl and her fiancé David Jones in the parking lot of a Madison [Wisconsin] Wal-Mart where Kerl and Jones worked. Kerl was seriously injured in the shooting, and Jones was killed. Pierce, who was Kerl's former boyfriend, then shot and killed himself. At the time of the shooting, Pierce was a work-release inmate at the Dane County jail who was employed at a nearby Arby's [Inc.] restaurant operated by Dennis Rasmussen, Inc. ("DRI"). Pierce had left work without permission at the time of the attempted murder and murder/suicide.

Kerl and Jones' estate sued DRI and Arby's, Inc. [in a Wisconsin state court.] * * * The plaintiffs alleged that Arby's is vicariously [endured for someone else] liable, as DRI's franchisor, for DRI's negligent supervision of Pierce. The * * * court granted summary judgment in favor of Arby's, concluding that there was no basis for vicarious liability. The [state intermediate] court of appeals affirmed. [The plaintiffs appealed to the Wisconsin Supreme Court.]

Vicarious liability under the doctrine of *respondeat superior* depends upon the existence of a master/servant agency relationship. Vicarious liability under *respondeat superior* is a form of liability without fault—the imposition of liability on an innocent party for the tortious conduct of another based upon the existence of a particularized agency relationship. As such, it is an exception to our fault-based liability system, and is imposed only where the principal has control or the right to control the physical conduct of the agent such that a master/servant relationship can be said to exist.

A franchise is a business format typically characterized by the franchisee's operation of an independent business pursuant to a license to use the franchisor's trademark or trade name. A franchise is ordinarily operated in accordance with a detailed franchise or license agreement designed to protect the integrity of the trademark by setting uniform quality, marketing, and operational standards applicable to the franchise.

CASE CONTINUES

CASE 16.2 CONTINUED

The rationale for vicarious liability becomes somewhat attenuated [weak] when applied to the franchise relationship, and vicarious liability premised upon the existence of a master/servant relationship is conceptually difficult to adapt to the franchising context. If the operational standards included in the typical franchise agreement for the protection of the franchisor's trademark were broadly construed as capable of meeting the "control or right to control" test that is generally used to determine *respondeat superior* liability, then franchisors would almost always be exposed to vicarious liability for the torts of their franchisees. We see no justification for such a broad rule of franchisor vicarious liability. If vicarious liability is to be imposed against franchisors, a more precisely focused test is required. [Emphasis added.]

* * * *

Applying these principles here, we conclude that Arby's did not have control or the right to control the day-to-day operation of the specific aspect of DRI's business that is alleged to have caused the plaintiffs' harm, that is, DRI's supervision of its employees. We note first that the license agreement between Arby's and DRI contains a provision that disclaims any agency relationship.

The license agreement contains a plethora [a large number] of general controls on the operation of DRI's restaurant * * *.

These provisions in the license agreement are consistent with the quality and operational standards commonly contained in franchise agreements to achieve product and marketing uniformity and to protect the franchisor's trademark. They are insufficient to establish a master/servant relationship. More particularly, they do not establish that Arby's controlled or had the right to control DRI's hiring and supervision of employees, which is the aspect of DRI's business that is alleged to have caused the plaintiffs' harm.

The agreement's provisions regarding the specific issue of personnel are broad and general.

By the terms of this agreement, DRI has sole control over the hiring and supervision of its employees. Arby's could not step in and take over the management of DRI's employees. Accordingly, we agree with the court of appeals and the [trial] court that there is no genuine issue of material fact as to whether DRI is Arby's servant for purposes of the plaintiffs' *respondeat superior* claim against Arby's: clearly it is not. Arby's cannot be held vicariously liable for DRI's alleged negligent supervision of Pierce.

* * * *

We conclude that the quality, marketing, and operational standards and inspection and termination rights commonly included in franchise agreements do not establish the close supervisory control or right of control over a franchisee necessary to support imposing vicarious liability against the franchisor for all purposes or as a general matter. We hold that *a franchisor may be subject to vicarious liability for the tortious conduct of its franchisee only if the franchisor had control or a right of control over the daily operation of the specific aspect of the franchisee's business that is alleged to have caused the harm.* Because Arby's did not have control or a right of control over DRI's supervision of its employees, there was no master/servant relationship between Arby's and DRI for purposes of the plaintiffs' *respondeat superior* claim against Arby's. Arby's cannot be held vicariously liable for DRI's negligent supervision of Pierce. [Emphasis added.]

The decision of the court of appeals is affirmed.

QUESTIONS

1. Should a franchisor be allowed to control the operation of its franchisee without liability for the franchisee's conduct? Explain your answer.
2. What would constitute the "right to control" under a franchise contract?

Pricing Arrangements Franchises provide the franchisor with an outlet for the firm's goods and services. Depending on the nature of the business, the franchisor may require the franchisee to purchase certain supplies from the franchisor at an established price.[7] A franchisor cannot, however, set the prices at which the franchisee will resell the goods because such price setting may be a violation of state or federal antitrust laws, or both. A franchisor can suggest retail prices but cannot mandate them.

Franchise Termination

The duration of the franchise is a matter to be determined between the parties. Generally, a franchise relationship starts with a short trial period, such as a year, so that the franchisee and the franchisor can determine whether they want to stay in business with one another. Usually, the franchise agreement specifies that termination must be "for cause," such as the death or disability of the franchisee, insolvency of the franchisee, breach of the franchise agreement, or failure to meet specified sales quotas. Most franchise contracts provide that notice of termination must be given. If no set time for termination is specified, then a reasonable time, with notice, is implied. A franchisee must be given reasonable time to wind up the business—that is, to do the accounting and return the copyright or trademark or any other property of the franchisor.

Wrongful Termination Because a franchisor's termination of a franchise often has adverse consequences for the franchisee, much franchise litigation involves claims of wrongful termination. Generally, the termination provisions of contracts are more favorable to the franchisor than to the franchisee. This means that the franchisee, who normally invests a substantial amount of time and financial resources in making the franchise operation successful, may receive little or nothing for the business on termination. The franchisor owns the trademark and hence the business.

It is in this area that statutory and case law become important. The federal and state laws discussed earlier attempt, among other things, to protect franchisees from the arbitrary or unfair termination of their franchises by the franchisors. Generally, both statutory and case law emphasize the importance of good faith and fair dealing in terminating a franchise relationship.

The Importance of Good Faith and Fair Dealing In determining whether a franchisor has acted in good faith when terminating a franchise agreement, the courts generally try to balance the rights of both parties. If a court perceives that a franchisor has arbitrarily or unfairly terminated a franchise, the franchisee will be provided with a remedy for wrongful termination. If a franchisor's decision to terminate a franchise was made in the normal course of the franchisor's business operations, however, and reasonable notice of termination was given to the franchisee, normally a court will not consider the termination wrongful.

Partnerships

Traditionally, one of the most common forms of business organization selected by two or more persons is the *partnership*. A **partnership** arises from an agreement, express or implied, between two or more persons to carry on a business for a profit. Partners are co-owners of a business and have joint control over its operation and the right to share in its profits. In this section, we examine several forms of partnership.

Partnerships are governed both by common law concepts (in particular, those relating to agency) and by statutory law. As in so many other areas of business law, the National Conference of Commissioners on Uniform State Laws has drafted uniform laws for partnerships, and these have been widely adopted by the states.

Agency Concepts and Partnership Law

When two or more persons agree to do business as partners, they enter into a special relationship with one another. To an extent, their relationship is similar to an agency relationship because each partner is deemed to be the agent of the other partners and of the partnership. The agency concepts that you will read about in Chapter 19 thus apply—specifically, the imputation of knowledge of, and responsibility for, acts carried out within the scope of the partnership relationship. In their relationship to one another, partners are also bound by the fiduciary ties that bind an agent and principal under agency law.

Partnership law is distinct from agency law in one significant way, however. A partnership is based on a voluntary contract between two or more competent

7. Although a franchisor can require franchisees to purchase supplies from it, requiring a franchisee to purchase exclusively from the franchisor may violate federal antitrust laws (see Chapters 26 and 27). For two landmark cases in these areas, see *United States v. Arnold, Schwinn & Co.*, 388 U.S. 365, 87 S.Ct. 1956, 18 L.Ed.2d 1249 (1967); and *Fortner Enterprises, Inc. v. U.S. Steel Corp.*, 394 U.S. 495, 89 S.Ct. 1252, 22 L.Ed.2d 495 (1969).

persons who agree to place some or all of their funds or other assets, labor, and skills in a business with the understanding that profits and losses will be shared. In a nonpartnership agency relationship, the agent usually does not have an owernship interest in the business, nor is he or she obligated to bear a portion of ordinary business losses.

The Uniform Partnership Act

The Uniform Partnership Act (UPA) governs the operation of partnerships *in the absence of express agreement* and has done much to reduce controversies in the law relating to partnerships. Except for Louisiana, all of the states, as well as the District of Columbia, have adopted the UPA. A majority of the states have enacted the most recent version of the UPA, which was adopted in 1994 and amended in 1997 to provide limited liability for partners in a limited liability partnership.[8] Excerpts from the latest version of the UPA, including the 1997 amendments, are presented in Appendix E.

When Does a Partnership Exist?

Parties sometimes find themselves in conflict over whether their business enterprise is a legal partnership, especially in the absence of a formal, written partnership agreement. The UPA defines the term *partnership* as "an association of two or more persons to carry on as co-owners a business for profit" [UPA 101(6)]. The *intent* to associate is a key element of a partnership, and one cannot join a partnership unless all other partners consent [UPA 401(i)].

In resolving disputes over whether a partnership exists, courts usually look for the following three essential elements of partnership implicit in the UPA's definition:

1. A sharing of profits or losses.
2. A joint ownership of the business.
3. An equal right to participate in the management of the business.

If the evidence in a particular case is insufficient to establish all three factors, the UPA provides a set of guidelines to be used. For example, the sharing of profits and losses from a business creates a presumption that a partnership exists. No presumption is made, however, if the profits were received as payment of any of the following [UPA 202(c)(3)]:

1. A debt by installments or interest on a loan.
2. Wages of an employee or for the services of an independent contractor.
3. Rent to a landlord.
4. An annuity to a surviving spouse or representative of a deceased partner.
5. A sale of the goodwill of a business or property.

To illustrate: A debtor owes a creditor $5,000 on an unsecured debt. To repay the debt, the debtor agrees to pay (and the creditor, to accept) 10 percent of the debtor's monthly business profits until the loan with interest has been paid. Although the creditor is sharing profits from the business, the debtor and creditor are not presumed to be partners.

Joint Property Ownership and Partnership Status

Joint ownership of property does not in and of itself create a partnership. Therefore, the fact that, say, MacPherson and Bunker own real property as *joint tenants* or as *tenants in common* (forms of joint ownership that will be discussed in Chapter 25) does not by itself establish a partnership. In fact, the sharing of gross returns and even profits from such ownership "does not by itself establish a partnership" [UPA 202(c)(1) and (2)].[9] Thus, if MacPherson and Bunker jointly own a piece of farmland and lease it to a farmer for a share of the profits from the farming operation in lieu of set rental payments, the sharing of the profits ordinarily will not make MacPherson, Bunker, and the farmer partners.

Note, though, that while the sharing of profits from ownership of property does not prove the existence of a partnership, sharing *both profits and losses* usually does. For example, two sisters, Zoe and Cienna, buy a restaurant together, open a joint bank account from which they pay for supplies and expenses, and share the proceeds that the restaurant generates. Zoe manages the restaurant and Cienna handles the bookkeeping. After eight years, Cienna stops keeping the books and does no other work for the restaurant. Zoe, who is now operating the restaurant by herself, no longer wants to share the profits with Cienna. She offers to buy her sister out, but the two cannot agree

8. At the time this book went to press, more than half of the states, as well as the District of Columbia, Puerto Rico, and the U.S. Virgin Islands, had adopted the UPA with the 1997 amendments. We therefore base our discussion of the UPA on the 1997 version and refer to older versions of the UPA in footnotes when necessary.

9. See, for example, *In re Estate of Ivanchak,* 169 Ohio App.3d 140, 862 N.E.2d 151 (2006).

on a fair price. When Cienna files a lawsuit, a question arises as to whether the two sisters were partners in the restaurant. In this situation, a court would find that a partnership existed because the sisters shared management responsibilities, had joint accounts, and shared the profits and the losses of the restaurant equally.

Entity versus Aggregate

A partnership is sometimes called a *company* or a *firm,* terms that suggest that the partnership is an entity separate and apart from its aggregate members. The law of partnership recognizes the independent entity for most purposes but may treat the partnership as a composite of its individual partners for some purposes.

Partnership as an Entity At common law, a partnership was never treated as a separate legal entity. Thus, a common law suit could never be brought by or against the firm in its own name; each individual partner had to sue or be sued. Today, most states provide specifically that a partnership can be treated as an entity for certain purposes. These usually include the capacity to sue or be sued, to collect judgments, and to have all accounting procedures carried out in the name of the partnership. In addition, the UPA clearly states, "A partnership is an entity" and "A partnership may sue and be sued in the name of the partnership" [UPA 201 and 307(a)]. As an entity, a partnership may hold the title to real or personal property in its name rather than in the names of the individual partners. Finally, federal procedural laws frequently permit a partnership to be treated as an entity in such matters as lawsuits in federal courts and bankruptcy proceedings.

Partnership as an Aggregate In one circumstance, the partnership is not regarded as a separate legal entity but is treated as an aggregate of the individual partners. For federal income tax purposes, a partnership is not a taxpaying entity. The income and losses it incurs are "passed through" the partnership framework and attributed to the partners on their individual tax returns. The partnership itself has no tax liability and is responsible only for filing an **information return** with the Internal Revenue Service. In other words, the firm itself pays no taxes. A partner's profit from the partnership (whether distributed or not) is taxed as individual income to the individual partner.

Partnership Formation

As a general rule, agreements to form a partnership can be *oral, written,* or *implied by conduct.* Some partnership agreements, however, must be in writing to be legally enforceable within the Statute of Frauds (see Chapter 9 for details). For example, a partnership agreement that authorizes the partners to deal in transfers of real property must be evidenced by a sufficient writing (or record).

The Partnership Agreement A partnership agreement, called **articles of partnership,** can include virtually any terms that the parties wish, so long as the terms are not illegal or contrary to public policy or statute [UPA 103]. The terms commonly included in a partnership agreement are listed in Exhibit 16–1 on the following page.

Duration of the Partnership The partnership agreement can specify the duration of the partnership by stating that it will continue until a designated date or until the completion of a particular project. This is called a *partnership for a term.* If this type of partnership is dissolved (broken up) without the consent of all of the partners prior to the expiration of the partnership term, the dissolution constitutes a breach of the agreement. The responsible partner can be held liable for any resulting losses.

If no fixed duration is specified, the partnership is a *partnership at will.* Any partner can dissolve this type of partnership at any time without violating the agreement and without incurring liability for losses to other partners that result from the termination.

A Corporation as Partner In a general partnership, the partners are personally liable for the debts incurred by the partnership. If one of the general partners is a corporation, however, what does personal liability mean? Basically, the capacity of corporations to contract is a question of corporate law. At one time, many states had restrictions on corporations becoming partners, although such restrictions have become less common over the years.

The Revised Model Business Corporation Act (see Appendix G) allows corporations generally to make contracts and incur liabilities. The UPA specifically permits a corporation to be a partner. By definition, "a partnership is an association of two or more persons," and the UPA defines *person* as including corporations [UPA 101(10)].

EXHIBIT 16–1 • Terms Commonly Included in a Partnership Agreement

Basic Structure	1. Name of the partnership. 2. Names of the partners. 3. Location of the business and the state law under which the partnership is organized. 4. Purpose of the partnership. 5. Duration of the partnership.
Capital Contributions	1. Amount of capital that each partner is contributing. 2. The agreed-on value of any real or personal property that is contributed instead of cash. 3. How losses and gains on contributed capital will be allocated, and whether contributions will earn interest.
Sharing of Profits and Losses	1. Percentage of the profits and losses of the business that each partner will receive. 2. When distributions of profit will be made and how net profit will be calculated.
Management and Control	1. How management responsibilities will be divided among the partners. 2. Name(s) of the managing partner or partners, and whether other partners have voting rights.
Accounting and Partnership Records	1. Name of the bank in which the partnership will maintain its business and checking accounts. 2. Statement that an accounting of partnership records will be maintained and that any partner or her or his agent can review these records at any time. 3. The dates of the partnership's fiscal year and when the annual audit of the books will take place.
Dissociation and Dissolution	1. Events that will cause the dissociation of a partner or dissolve the partnership, such as the retirement, death, or incapacity of any partner. 2. How partnership property will be valued and apportioned on dissociation and dissolution. 3. Whether an arbitrator will determine the value of partnership property on dissociation and dissolution and whether that determination will be binding.
Arbitration	Whether arbitration is required for any dispute relating to the partnership agreement.

Partnership by Estoppel Sometimes, persons who are not partners nevertheless hold themselves out as partners and make representations that third parties rely on in dealing with them. In such a situation, a court may conclude that a **partnership by estoppel** exists and impose liability—but not partnership *rights*—on the alleged partner or partners. Similarly, a partnership by estoppel may be imposed when a partner represents, expressly or impliedly, that a nonpartner is a member of the firm. Whenever a third person has reasonably and detrimentally relied on the representation that a nonpartner was part of the partnership, partnership by estoppel is deemed to exist. When this occurs, the nonpartner is regarded as an agent whose acts are binding on the partnership [UPA 308].

For example, Moreno owns a small shop. Knowing that Midland Bank will not make a loan on his credit alone, Moreno represents that Lorman, a financially secure businesswoman, is a partner in Moreno's business. Lorman knows of Moreno's misrepresentation but fails to correct it. Midland Bank, relying on the strength of Lorman's reputation and credit, extends a loan to Moreno. Moreno will be liable to the bank for repaying the loan. In many states, Lorman would also be held liable to the bank. Because Lorman has impliedly consented to the misrepresentation, she will normally be estopped (prevented) from denying that she is Moreno's partner. A court will treat Lorman as if she were in fact a partner in Moreno's business insofar as this loan is concerned.

Partnership Operation

The rights and duties of partners are governed largely by the specific terms of their partnership agreement. In the absence of provisions to the contrary in the partnership agreement, the law imposes the rights and duties discussed in the following subsections. The character and nature of the partnership business generally influence the application of these rights and duties.

Rights of Partners The rights of partners in a partnership relate to the following areas: management, interest in the partnership, compensation, inspection of books, accounting, and property.

Management. In a general partnership, "All partners have equal rights in the management and conduct of partnership business" [UPA 401(f)]. Unless the partners agree otherwise, each partner has one vote in management matters *regardless of the proportional size of his or her interest in the firm.* In a large partnership, partners often agree to delegate daily management responsibilities to a management committee made up of one or more of the partners.

The majority rule controls decisions on ordinary matters connected with partnership business, unless otherwise specified in the agreement. Decisions that significantly affect the nature of the partnership or that are not apparently for carrying on the ordinary course of the partnership business, or business of the kind, however, require the *unanimous* consent of the partners [UPA 301(2), 401(i), 401(j)]. Unanimous consent is likely to be required for a decision to undertake any of the following actions:[10]

1. Altering the essential nature of the firm's business as expressed in the partnership agreement or altering the capital structure of the partnership.
2. Admitting new partners or engaging in a completely new business.
3. Assigning partnership property to a trust for the benefit of creditors.
4. Disposing of the partnership's goodwill.
5. Confessing judgment against the partnership or submitting partnership claims to arbitration. (A **confession of judgment** is an act by a debtor permitting a judgment to be entered against him or her by a creditor, for an agreed sum, without the institution of legal proceedings.)
6. Undertaking any act that would make further conduct of partnership business impossible.
7. Amending the terms of the partnership agreement.

10. The previous version of the UPA specifically listed most of these actions as requiring unanimous consent. The current version of the UPA omits the list entirely to allow the courts more flexibility. The Official Comments explain that most of these acts, except for submitting a claim to arbitration, will likely still remain outside the apparent authority of an individual partner.

Interest in the Partnership. Each partner is entitled to the proportion of business profits and losses that is designated in the partnership agreement. If the agreement does not apportion profits (indicate how the profits will be shared), the UPA provides that profits will be shared equally. If the agreement does not apportion losses, losses will be shared in the same ratio as profits [UPA 401(b)].

For example, Rico and Brett form a partnership. The partnership agreement provides for capital contributions of $60,000 from Rico and $40,000 from Brett, but it is silent as to how they will share profits or losses. In this situation, they will share both profits and losses equally. If their partnership agreement had provided that they would share profits in the same ratio as capital contributions, however, 60 percent of the profits would go to Rico, and 40 percent would go to Brett. If the agreement was silent as to losses, losses would be shared in the same ratio as profits (60 percent and 40 percent, respectively).

Compensation. Devoting time, skill, and energy to partnership business is a partner's duty and generally is not a compensable service. Partners can, of course, agree otherwise. For example, the managing partner of a law firm often receives a salary in addition to her or his share of profits for performing special duties, such as managing the office or personnel.

Inspection of Books. Partnership books and records must be kept accessible to all partners. Each partner has the right to receive (and the corresponding duty to produce) full and complete information concerning the conduct of all aspects of partnership business [UPA 403]. Each firm retains books for recording and securing such information. Partners contribute the information, and a bookkeeper typically has the duty to preserve it. The books must be kept at the firm's principal business office (unless the partners agree otherwise). Every partner, whether active or inactive, is entitled to inspect all books and records on demand and can make copies of the materials. The personal representative of a deceased partner's estate has the same right of access to partnership books and records that the decedent would have had [UPA 403].

Accounting of Partnership Assets or Profits. An accounting of partnership assets or profits is required to determine the value of each partner's share in the partnership. An accounting can be performed voluntarily, or it can be compelled by court order. At common law, an accounting was generally not available to partners prior to the dissolution of the partnership. Under UPA 405(b), in contrast, a partner has the right to bring an action for an accounting during the term of the partnership, as well as on the firm's dissolution and winding up.[11] The UPA also provides partners with access to the courts during the term of the partnership to resolve various claims against the partnership and the other partners.

Property Rights. Property acquired *by* a partnership is the property of the partnership and not of the partners individually [UPA 203]. Partnership property includes all property that was originally contributed to the partnership and anything later purchased by the partnership or in the partnership's name (except in rare circumstances) [UPA 204]. A partner may use or possess partnership property only on behalf of the partnership [UPA 401(g)]. A partner is *not* a co-owner of partnership property and has no right to sell, mortgage, or transfer partnership property to another [UPA 501].[12]

In other words, partnership property is owned by the partnership as an entity and not by the individual partners. Thus, a creditor of an individual partner cannot seek to use partnership property to satisfy the partner's debt. Such a creditor can, however, petition a court for a **charging order** to attach the individual partner's *interest* in the partnership (her or his proportionate share of the profits and losses and right to receive distributions) to satisfy the partner's obligation [UPA 502]. (A partner can also assign her or his right to a share of the partnership profits to another to satisfy a debt.)

Duties and Liabilities of Partners

The duties and liabilities of partners that we examine here are basically derived from agency law. Each partner is an agent of every other partner and acts as both a principal and an agent in any business transaction within the scope of the partnership agreement. Each partner is also a general agent of the partnership in carrying out the usual business of the firm "or business of the kind carried on by the partnership" [UPA 301(1)]. Thus, every act of a partner concerning partnership business and "business of the kind" and every contract signed in the partnership's name bind the firm. The UPA affirms general principles of agency law that pertain to the authority of a partner to bind a partnership in contract or tort.

Fiduciary Duties The fiduciary duties that a partner owes to the partnership and the other partners are the duty of care and the duty of loyalty [UPA 404(a)].

Duty of Care. A partner's duty of care is limited to refraining from "grossly negligent or reckless conduct, intentional misconduct, or a knowing violation of law" [UPA 404(c)].[13] A partner is not liable to the partnership for simple negligence or honest errors in judgment in conducting partnership business, but is liable for any grossly negligent or reckless conduct that causes damage to the firm.

Duty of Loyalty. The duty of loyalty requires a partner to account to the partnership for "any property, profit, or benefit" derived by the partner in the conduct of the partnership's business or from the use of its property. A partner must also refrain from dealing with the firm as an adverse party or competing with the partnership in business [UPA 404(b)]. The duty of loyalty can be breached by self-dealing, misusing partnership property, disclosing trade secrets, or usurping a partnership business opportunity.

A classic example is the 1928 case of *Meinhard v. Salmon.*[14] Salmon leased a building on Fifth Avenue in New York City for twenty years. The building had been a hotel, and Salmon wanted to convert it into a commercial building and lease it out to shops and offices. Salmon formed a partnership with Meinhard, who put up half of the capital. Both men received a percentage of the profits and shared the losses equally, but Salmon had the sole power to manage the building. A few months before the lease was set to expire, the property owner approached Salmon about leasing several adjacent properties and constructing a $3 million building on them.

Salmon did not inform Meinhard about this business opportunity and instead signed a new lease in the name of his own business (in which Meinhard was not

11. Under the previous version of the UPA, a partner could bring an action for an accounting only if the partnership agreement provided for an accounting, the partner was wrongfully excluded from the business or its property or books, another partner was in breach of his or her fiduciary duty, or other circumstances rendered it "just and reasonable."

12. Under the previous version of the UPA, partners were *tenants in partnership.* This meant that every partner was a co-owner with all other partners of the partnership property. The current UPA does not recognize this concept.

13. The previous version of the UPA touched only briefly on the duty of loyalty and left the details of the partners' fiduciary duties to be developed under the law of agency.

14. 249 N.Y. 458, 164 N.E. 545 (N.Y.App. 1928).

an owner). The new lease covered the adjacent properties and the original development. In the lawsuit that followed, the court held that Salmon had breached his fiduciary duty by failing to inform Meinhard of a business opportunity and secretly taking advantage of the opportunity himself. The court granted Meinhard a 50 percent interest in the new lease.

Breach and Waiver of Fiduciary Duties. A partner's fiduciary duties may not be waived or eliminated in the partnership agreement, and in fulfilling them, each partner must act consistently with the obligation of good faith and fair dealing [UPA 103(b), 404(d)]. Note that a partner may pursue his or her own interests without automatically violating these duties [UPA 404(e)]. The key is whether the partner has disclosed the interest to the other partners.

For example, a partner who owns a shopping mall may vote against a partnership proposal to open a competing mall, provided that the partner has fully disclosed her interest in the shopping mall to the other partners at the firm. Similarly, suppose that in the case *Meinhard v. Salmon* discussed previously, Salmon had informed Meinhard about the opportunity of leasing and developing the additional properties. If Meinhard was not interested in extending the partnership's lease to cover the nearby properties, then Salmon would have been able to take advantage of the opportunity on his own. A partner cannot make secret profits or put self-interest before his or her duty to the interest of the partnership, however.

Authority of Partners The UPA affirms general principles of agency law that pertain to a partner's authority to bind a partnership in contract. A partner may also subject the partnership to tort liability under agency principles. When a partner is carrying on partnership business or business of the kind with third parties in the usual way, apparent authority exists, and both the partner and the firm share liability.

The partnership will not be liable, however, if the third parties *know* that the partner has no such authority. For example, Patricia, a partner in the partnership of Heise, Green, and Stevens, applies for a loan on behalf of the partnership without authorization from the other partners. The bank manager knows that Patricia has no authority to do so. If the bank manager grants the loan, Patricia will be personally bound, but the firm will not be liable.

A partnership may file a "statement of partnership authority" to limit a partner's capacity to act as the firm's agent or transfer property on its behalf [UPA 105, 303]. Any limit on a partner's authority, however, normally does not affect a third party who does not know about the statement. Statements limiting the partners' authority to transfer real property that are filed with the appropriate state records office (the office that records real property transfers—see Chapter 25) will bind third parties, whether or not they know about the limitation.

The agency concepts relating to apparent authority, actual authority, and ratification that will be discussed in Chapter 19 also apply to partnerships. The extent of *implied authority* is generally broader for partners than for ordinary agents, however.

The Scope of Implied Powers. The character and scope of the partnership business and the customary nature of the particular business operation determine the implied powers of partners. For example, a partnership business that has goods in inventory and makes profits buying and selling those goods is known as a *trading partnership.* In a trading partnership, each partner has a wide range of implied powers, such as to advertise products, hire employees, and extend the firm's credit by issuing or signing checks.

In an ordinary partnership, the partners can exercise all implied powers reasonably necessary and customary to carry on that particular business. Such powers include the authority to make warranties on goods in the sales business and the power to enter into contracts consistent with the firm's regular course of business. Most partners also have the implied authority to make admissions and representations concerning partnership affairs. A partner might also have the implied power to convey (transfer) real property in the firm's name when such conveyances are part of the ordinary course of partnership business.

Authorized versus Unauthorized Actions. If a partner acts within the scope of authority, the partnership is legally bound to honor the partner's commitments to third parties. For example, a partner's authority to sell partnership products carries with it the implied authority to transfer title and to make usual warranties. Hence, in a partnership that operates a retail tire store, any partner negotiating a contract with a customer for the sale of a set of tires can warrant that "each tire will be warranted for normal wear for 40,000 miles."

This same partner, however, does not have the authority to sell office equipment, fixtures, or the partnership's retail facility without the consent of all of the other partners. In addition, because partnerships are formed to generate profits, a partner generally does not have the authority to make charitable contributions without the consent of the other partners. Such actions are not binding on the partnership unless they are ratified by all of the other partners.

Liability of Partners One significant disadvantage associated with a traditional partnership is that the partners are *personally* liable for the debts of the partnership. Moreover, the liability is essentially unlimited because the acts of one partner in the ordinary course of business subject the other partners to personal liability [UPA 305]. The following subsections explain the rules on a partner's liability.

Joint Liability. Each partner in a partnership is jointly liable for the partnership's obligations. **Joint liability** means that a third party must sue all of the partners as a group, but each partner can be held liable for the full amount. Under the prior version of the UPA, which is still in effect in a few states, partners were subject to joint liability on partnership debts and contracts, but not on partnership debts arising from torts.[15] If, for example, a third party sues a partner on a partnership contract, the partner has the right to demand that the other partners be sued with her or him. In fact, if the third party does not sue all of the partners, the assets of the partnership cannot be used to satisfy the judgment. Under the theory of joint liability, the partnership's assets must be exhausted before creditors can reach the partners' individual assets.[16]

Joint and Several Liability. In the majority of the states, under UPA 306(a), partners are both jointly and severally (separately, or individually) liable for all partnership obligations, including contracts, torts, and breaches of trust. **Joint and several liability** means that a third party has the option of suing all of the partners together (jointly) or one or more of the partners separately (severally). This is true even if a partner did not participate in, ratify, or know about whatever it was that gave rise to the cause of action. Normally, though, the partnership's assets must be exhausted before a creditor can enforce a judgment against a partner's separate assets [UPA 307(d)].

A judgment against one partner severally (separately) does not extinguish the others' liability. Those not sued in the first action normally may be sued subsequently, unless the first action was conclusive on the question of liability. Suppose that Renalt brings a malpractice (professional negligence) action against one partner in a firm and then discovers that another partner was involved in the negligence. Normally, he may also file a lawsuit against the second partner (unless the court held that no one at the firm breached the standard of care with regard to Renalt).

If a plaintiff is successful in a suit against a partner or partners, he or she may collect on the judgment only against the assets of those partners named as defendants. A partner who commits a tort is required to indemnify (reimburse) the partnership for any damages it pays. The question in the following case was whether a partnership must indemnify a partner for liability that results from negligent conduct occurring in the ordinary course of the partnership's business.

15. Under the previous version of the UPA, the partners were subject to *joint and several liability,* which is discussed next, on debts arising from torts. States that still follow this rule include Connecticut, West Virginia, and Wyoming.

16. For a case applying joint liability to partnerships, see *Shar's Cars, LLC v. Elder,* 97 P.3d 724 (Utah App. 2004).

CASE 16.3 Moren v. Jax Restaurant

Minnesota Court of Appeals, 2004. 679 N.W.2d 165.
www.lawlibrary.state.mn.us/archive/cap1st.html[a]

• **Background and Facts** "Jax Restaurant" is a partnership that operates Jax Restaurant in Foley, Minnesota. One afternoon in October 2000, Nicole Moren, one of the partners, finished her shift at the restaurant at 4:00 P.M. and picked up her two-year-old son, Remington, from day care. About 5:30 P.M., Moren returned to the restaurant with Remington after Amy Benedetti, the other partner and Moren's sister, asked for help. Moren's husband offered to pick up Remington in twenty minutes. Because Moren

a. In the "Published" section, click on "M–O." On that page, scroll to the name of the case and click on the docket number to access the opinion. The Minnesota State Law Library maintains this Web site.

CASE 16.3 CONTINUED did not want Remington running around the restaurant, she brought him into the kitchen with her, set him on top of the counter, and began rolling out pizza dough using a dough-pressing machine. While she was making pizzas, Remington reached his hand into the dough press. His hand was crushed, causing permanent injuries. Through his father, Remington filed a suit in a Minnesota state court against the partnership, alleging negligence. The partnership filed a complaint against Moren, arguing that it was entitled to indemnity (compensation or reimbursement) from Moren for her negligence. The court issued a summary judgment in favor of Moren on the complaint. The partnership appealed this judgment to a state intermediate appellate court.

IN THE LANGUAGE OF THE COURT
***CRIPPEN,* Judge.**

* * * *

Under Minnesota's Uniform Partnership Act [the most recent version of the UPA], a partnership is an entity distinct from its partners, and as such, a partnership may sue and be sued in the name of the partnership. [Under the UPA] "*[a] partnership is liable for loss or injury caused to a person * * * as a result of a wrongful act or omission, or other actionable conduct, of a partner acting in the ordinary course of business of the partnership or with authority of the partnership.*" Accordingly, a "partnership shall * * * indemnify [reimburse]a partner for liabilities incurred by the partner in the ordinary course of the business of the partnership * * * ." Stated conversely, an "act of a partner which is not apparently for carrying on in the ordinary course the partnership business or business of the kind carried on by the partnership binds the partnership only if the act was authorized by the other partners." Thus, under the plain language of the UPA, *a partner has a right to indemnity from the partnership, but the partnership's claim of indemnity from a partner is not authorized or required.* [Emphasis added.]

The [lower] court correctly concluded that Nicole Moren's conduct was in the ordinary course of business of the partnership and, as a result, indemnity by the partner to the partnership was inappropriate. It is undisputed that one of the cooks scheduled to work that evening did not come in, and that Moren's partner asked her to help in the kitchen. It also is undisputed that Moren was making pizzas for the partnership when her son was injured. Because her conduct at the time of the injury was in the ordinary course of business of the partnership, under the UPA, her conduct bound the partnership and it owes indemnity to her for her negligence.

* * * *

Appellant * * * claims that because Nicole Moren's action of bringing Remington into the kitchen was partly motivated by personal reasons, her conduct was outside the ordinary course of business. Because it has not been previously addressed, there is no Minnesota authority regarding this issue. * * * We conclude that the conduct of Nicole Moren was no less in the ordinary course of business because it also served personal purposes. It is undisputed that Moren was acting for the benefit of the partnership by making pizzas when her son was injured, and even though she was simultaneously acting in her role as a mother, her conduct remained in the ordinary course of the partnership business.

• **Decision and Remedy** *The state intermediate appellate court affirmed the lower court's judgment. "Minnesota law requires a partnership to indemnify its partners for the result of their negligence." The appellate court also reasoned that "the conduct of a partner may be partly motivated by personal reasons and still occur in the ordinary course of business of the partnership." Thus "liability for Nicole Moren's negligence rested with the partnership, even if the partner's conduct partly served her personal interests."*

• **What If the Facts Were Different?** *Suppose that Moren's predominant motive in bringing her son to the restaurant had been to benefit herself by feeding him free pizza. Would the result have been different? Why or why not?*

• **The Legal Environment Dimension** *What seems to have occurred in this case that might have served as an alternative basis for imposing liability on the partnership? (Hint: Who besides Moren had the authority to act on behalf of the partnership?)*

Liability of Incoming Partners. A partner newly admitted to an existing partnership is not personally liable for any partnership obligation incurred before the person became a partner [UPA 306(b)]. In other words, the new partner's liability to existing creditors of the partnership is limited to her or his capital contribution to the firm. Suppose that Smartclub is a partnership with four members. Alex Jaff, a newly admitted partner, contributes $100,000 to the partnership. Smartclub has about $600,000 in debt at the time Jaff joins the firm. Although Jaff's capital contribution of $100,000 can be used to satisfy Smartclub's obligations, Jaff is not personally liable for partnership debts that were incurred before he became a partner. Thus, his personal assets cannot be used to satisfy the partnership's antecedent (prior) debt. If, however, the managing partner at Smartclub borrows funds for the partnership after Jaff becomes a partner, Jaff will be personally liable for those amounts.

Dissociation of a Partner

Dissociation occurs when a partner ceases to be associated in the carrying on of the partnership business. Although a partner always has the *power* to dissociate from the firm, he or she may not have the *right* to dissociate. Dissociation normally entitles the partner to have his or her interest purchased by the partnership, and terminates his or her actual authority to act for the partnership and to participate with the partners in running the business. Otherwise, the partnership can continue to do business without the dissociating partner.[17]

Events Causing Dissociation Under UPA 601, a partner can be dissociated from a partnership in any of the following ways:

1. By the partner's voluntarily giving notice of an "express will to withdraw." (Note that when a partner gives notice of her or his intent to withdraw, the remaining partners must decide whether to continue or give up the partnership business. If they do not agree to continue the partnership, the voluntary dissociation of a partner will dissolve the firm [UPA 801(1)].)
2. By the occurrence of an event agreed to in the partnership agreement.
3. By a unanimous vote of the other partners under certain circumstances, such as when a partner transfers substantially all of her or his interest in the partnership, or when it becomes unlawful to carry on partnership business with that partner.
4. By order of a court or arbitrator if the partner has engaged in wrongful conduct that affects the partnership business, breached the partnership agreement or violated a duty owed to the partnership or the other partners, or engaged in conduct that makes it "not reasonably practicable to carry on the business in partnership with the partner" [UPA 601(5)].
5. By the partner's declaring bankruptcy, assigning his or her interest in the partnership for the benefit of creditors, or becoming physically or mentally incapacitated, or by the partner's death. Note that although the bankruptcy or death of a partner represents that partner's "dissociation" from the partnership, it is not an *automatic* ground for the partnership's dissolution (*dissolution* will be discussed shortly).

Wrongful Dissociation As mentioned, a partner has the power to dissociate from a partnership at any time, but a partner's dissociation can be wrongful in a few circumstances [UPA 602]. When a partner's dissociation is in breach of a partnership agreement, for instance, it is wrongful. For example, a partnership agreement states that it is a breach of the partnership agreement for any partner to assign partnership property to a creditor without the consent of the others. If a partner, Janik, makes such an assignment, she has not only breached the agreement but has also wrongfully dissociated from the partnership. Similarly, if a partner refuses to perform duties required by the partnership agreement—such as accounting for profits earned from the use of partnership property—this breach can be treated as wrongful dissociation.

With regard to a partnership for a definite term or a particular undertaking, dissociation that occurs before the expiration of the term or the completion of the undertaking can be wrongful. In such partnerships, the dissociation normally is considered wrongful if the partner withdraws by express will, is expelled by a court or an arbitrator, or declares bankruptcy [UPA 602].

17. Under the previous version of the UPA, when a partner withdrew from a partnership, the partnership was considered dissolved, its business had to be wound up, and the proceeds had to be distributed to creditors and among partners. The new UPA provisions dramatically changed the law governing partnership breakups and dissolution by no longer requiring that the partnership end if one partner dissociates.

A partner who wrongfully dissociates is liable to the partnership and to the other partners for damages caused by the dissociation. This liability is in addition to any other obligation of the partner to the partnership or to the other partners. Thus, a wrongfully dissociating partner would be liable to the partnership not only for any damage caused by the breach of the partnership agreement, but also for costs incurred to replace the partner's expertise or to obtain new financing.

Effects of Dissociation Dissociation (rightful or wrongful) terminates some of the rights of the dissociated partner, requires that the partnership purchase his or her interest, and alters the liability of the parties to third parties.

Rights and Duties. On a partner's dissociation, his or her right to participate in the management and conduct of the partnership business terminates [UPA 603]. The partner's duty of loyalty also ends. A partner's other fiduciary duties, including the duty of care, continue only with respect to events that occurred before dissociation, unless the partner participates in winding up the partnership's business (to be discussed shortly). For example, Debbie Pearson is a partner who is leaving an accounting firm, Bubb & Pearson. Pearson can immediately compete with the firm for new clients. She must exercise care in completing ongoing client transactions, however, and must account to the firm for any fees received from the old clients based on those transactions.

After a partner's dissociation, his or her interest in the partnership must be purchased according to the rules in UPA 701. The **buyout price** is based on the amount that would have been distributed to the partner if the partnership had been wound up on the date of dissociation. Offset against the price are amounts owed by the partner to the partnership, including damages for wrongful dissociation.

In the following case, the court had to decide how the buyout price of a partner's interest should be determined on his dissociation from his family's ranch business, which had been operated as a partnership for more than twenty years.

CASE 16.4 Warnick v. Warnick

Supreme Court of Wyoming, 2006. 2006 WY 58, 133 P.3d 997.

• **Background and Facts** In 1978, Wilbur and Dee Warnick and their son Randall Warnick bought a ranch in Sheridan County, Wyoming, for $335,000. To operate the ranch, they formed a partnership—Warnick Ranches. The partners' initial capital contributions totaled $60,000, of which Wilbur paid 36 percent, Dee paid 30 percent, and Randall paid 34 percent. Wilbur and Dee moved onto the ranch in 1981. Randall lived and worked on the ranch during the 1981 and 1982 summer haying seasons and again from 1991 to 1998. The partners each contributed funds to the operation and received cash distributions from the partnership. In the summer of 1999, Randall dissociated from the partnership. When the parties could not agree on a buyout price, Randall filed a suit in a Wyoming state court against the other partners and the partnership to recover what he believed to be a fair price. The court awarded Randall $115,783.13—the amount of his cash contributions, plus 34 percent of the partnership assets' increase in value above all partners' cash contributions, with interest from the date of his dissociation. The defendants appealed to the Wyoming Supreme Court, arguing that, in the calculation, $50,000 should be deducted from the appraised value of the ranch, its livestock, and its equipment for the estimated expenses of selling these assets.

IN THE LANGUAGE OF THE COURT
BURKE, **Justice.**

* * * *

The district court was charged with calculating the amount owed to Randall Warnick pursuant to the applicable provisions of [Wyoming Statutes Section 17-21-701 (Wyoming's version of UPA 701)]. That amount, or *the buyout price, is the amount that would have been paid to the dissociating partner following a settlement of partnership accounts upon the*

CASE CONTINUES

CASE 16.4 CONTINUED *winding up of the partnership, if, on the date of dissociation, the assets of the partnership were sold at a price equal to the greater of the liquidation value or the value based on a sale of the business as a going concern without the dissociating partner.* [Emphasis added.]

* * * *

* * * Warnick Ranches claims that the [lower] court erred in the first step of its calculation of the buyout price by overvaluing the ranch assets. The asserted error is the [lower] court's failure to deduct estimated sales expenses of $50,000 from the value of the partnership assets.

Critical to our determination in this case is the recognition that the assets of this partnership were not, in fact, liquidated. Instead, the record reflects that the assets were retained by Warnick Ranches. Randall Warnick's dissociation from the partnership did not require the winding up of the partnership. * * * Accordingly, the deduction urged by Warnick Ranches is for hypothetical costs.

* * * *

* * * Contrary to the interpretation asserted by Warnick Ranches, liquidation value is not the amount of the seller's residual cash following a sale. We find that the meaning of liquidation value in the statute is best understood by comparing it to the other method provided. *When contrasted with "going concern value" it is clear that "liquidation value" simply means the sale of the separate assets rather than the value of the business as a whole.* [Emphasis added.]

Additionally, under either valuation method, * * * [Section] 17-21-701(b) directs that the sale price be determined "on the basis of the amount that would be paid by a willing buyer to a willing seller, neither being under any compulsion to buy or sell, and with knowledge of all relevant facts." * * * This "willing buyer" and "willing seller" language does not present a novel legal concept, as it sets forth precisely what has long been the legal definition or test of "fair market value."

* * * *

Considering the language of [Section 17-21-701(b)] as a whole, we conclude that "liquidation value" does not have the meaning that Warnick Ranches desires, i.e. the amount a seller would "net" upon liquidation. Rather, "liquidation value" represents the sale price of the assets based upon fair market value. It is one thing to say that a business is worth little more than its hard assets. It is quite another * * * to deduct the substantial cost of a liquidation which all parties agree will not take place. Where it is contemplated that a business will continue, it is not appropriate to assume an immediate liquidation with its attendant transactional costs and taxes.

- **Decision and Remedy** *The Wyoming Supreme Court affirmed the judgment of the lower court, holding that "purely hypothetical costs of sale are not a required deduction in valuing partnership assets" to determine the buyout price of a dissociated partner.*

- **The Ethical Dimension** *Was it unethical for Randall to file a suit against his parents to obtain what he regarded as a fair price for his interest? Why or why not?*

- **The Legal Environment Dimension** *How and why might the value of a partnership interest in a going concern differ from the value of the same interest as a result of a liquidation?*

Liability to Third Parties. For two years after a partner dissociates from a continuing partnership, the partnership may be bound by the acts of the dissociated partner based on apparent authority [UPA 702]. In other words, the partnership may be liable to a third party with whom a dissociated partner enters into a transaction if the third party reasonably believed that the dissociated partner was still a partner. Similarly, a dissociated partner may be liable for partnership obligations entered into during a two-year period following dissociation [UPA 703].

To avoid this possible liability, a partnership should notify its creditors, customers, and clients of a partner's dissociation. Also, either the partnership or the dissociated partner can file a statement of dissociation in the appropriate state office to limit the dissociated partner's authority to ninety days after the filing [UPA 704]. Filing this statement helps to minimize the firm's potential liability for the former partner and vice versa.

Partnership Termination

The same events that cause dissociation can result in the end of the partnership if the remaining partners no longer wish to (or are unable to) continue the partnership business. Not every type of dissociation will cause dissolution of the partnership, though. Only certain departures of a partner will trigger dissolution, and generally the partnership can continue if the remaining partners consent [UPA 801].

The termination of a partnership is referred to as **dissolution,** which essentially means the commencement of the winding up process. **Winding up** is the actual process of collecting, liquidating, and distributing the partnership assets.[18] We discuss here the dissolution and winding up of partnership business.

Dissolution Dissolution of a partnership generally can be brought about by the acts of the partners, by operation of law, and by judicial decree [UPA 801]. Any partnership (including one for a fixed term) can be dissolved by the partners' agreement. Similarly, if the partnership agreement states that it will dissolve on a certain event, such as a partner's death or bankruptcy, then the occurrence of that event will dissolve the partnership. A partnership for a fixed term or a particular undertaking is dissolved by operation of law at the expiration of the term or on the completion of the undertaking.

Any event that makes it unlawful for the partnership to continue its business will result in dissolution [UPA 801(4)]. Under the UPA, a court may order dissolution when it becomes obviously impractical for the firm to continue—for example, if the business can only be operated at a loss [UPA 801(5)]. Additionally, a partner's impropriety involving partnership business (for example, fraud perpetrated on the other partners) or improper behavior reflecting unfavorably on the firm may provide grounds for a judicial decree of dissolution. Finally, if dissension between partners becomes so persistent and harmful as to undermine the confidence and cooperation necessary to carry on the firm's business, a court may grant a decree of dissolution.

Winding Up and Distribution of Assets After dissolution, the partnership continues for the limited purpose of the winding up process.[19] The partners cannot create new obligations on behalf of the partnership. They have authority only to complete transactions begun but not finished at the time of dissolution and to wind up the business of the partnership [UPA 803, 804(1)].

Winding up includes collecting and preserving partnership assets, discharging liabilities (paying debts), and accounting to each partner for the value of his or her interest in the partnership. Partners continue to have fiduciary duties to one another and to the firm during this process. UPA 401(h) provides that a partner is entitled to compensation for services in winding up partnership affairs (and reimbursement for expenses incurred in the process) above and apart from his or her share in the partnership profits.

Both creditors of the partnership and creditors of the individual partners can make claims on the partnership's assets. In general, partnership creditors share proportionately with the partners' individual creditors in the partners' assets, which include their interests in the partnership. A partnership's assets are distributed according to the following priorities [UPA 807]:

1. Payment of debts, including those owed to partner and nonpartner creditors.
2. Return of capital contributions and distribution of profits to partners.[20]

If the partnership's liabilities are greater than its assets, the partners bear the losses—in the absence of a contrary agreement—in the same proportion in which they shared the profits (rather than, for example, in proportion to their contributions to the partnership's capital).

Partnership Buy-Sell Agreements Usually, when people enter into partnerships, they are getting along with one another. To prepare for the possibility that the situation might change and they may become unable to work together amicably, the partners should make express arrangements during the formation of

18. Although "winding down" would seem to describe more accurately the process of settling accounts and liquidating the assets of a partnership, English and U.S. statutory and case law have traditionally used "winding up" to denote this final stage of a partnership's existence.

19. Note that at any time after dissolution but before winding up is completed, all of the partners may decide to continue the partnership business and waive the right to have the business wound up [UPA 802].

20. Under the previous version of the UPA, creditors of the partnership had priority over creditors of the individual partners. Also, in distributing partnership assets, third party creditors were paid before partner creditors, and capital contributions were returned before profits.

the partnership to provide for its smooth dissolution. A **buy-sell agreement,** sometimes called simply a *buy-out agreement,* provides for one or more partners to buy out the other or others, should the situation warrant. Agreeing beforehand on who buys what, under what circumstances, and, if possible, at what price may eliminate costly negotiations or litigation later. Alternatively, the agreement may specify that one or more partners will determine the value of the interest being sold and that the other or others will decide whether to buy or sell.

Under UPA 701(a), if a partner's dissociation does not result in a dissolution of the partnership, a buyout of the partner's interest is mandatory. The UPA contains an extensive set of buyout rules that apply when the partners do not have a buyout agreement. Basically, a withdrawing partner receives the same amount through a buyout that he or she would receive if the business were winding up [UPA 701(b)].

REVIEWING Sole Proprietorships, Franchises, and Partnerships

Carlos Del Rey decided to open a Mexican fast-food restaurant and signed a franchise contract with a national chain called La Grande Enchilada. The contract required the franchisee to strictly follow the franchisor's operating manual and stated that failure to do so would be grounds for terminating the franchise contract. The manual set forth detailed operating procedures and safety standards, and provided that a La Grande Enchilada representative would inspect the restaurant monthly to ensure compliance. Nine months after Del Rey began operating his restaurant, a spark from the grill ignited an oily towel in the kitchen. No one was injured, but by the time firefighters were able to put out the fire, the kitchen had sustained extensive damage. The cook told the fire department that the towel was "about two feet from the grill" when it caught fire, which was in compliance with the franchisor's manual that required towels be placed at least one foot from the grills. Nevertheless, the next day La Grande Enchilada notified Del Rey that his franchise would terminate in thirty days for failure to follow the prescribed safety procedures. Using the information presented in the chapter, answer the following questions.

1. What type of franchise was Del Rey's La Grande Enchilada restaurant?
2. If Del Rey operates the restaurant as a sole proprietorship, who bears the loss for the damaged kitchen? Explain.
3. Assume that Del Rey files a lawsuit against La Grande Enchilada, claiming that his franchise was wrongfully terminated. What is the main factor that a court would consider in determining whether the franchise was wrongfully terminated?
4. Would a court be likely to rule that La Grande Enchilada had good cause to terminate Del Rey's franchise in this situation? Why or why not?

TERMS AND CONCEPTS

articles of partnership 409
buyout price 417
buy-sell agreement 420
charging order 412
confession of judgment 411
dissociation 416
dissolution 419
entrepreneur 400
franchise 402
franchisee 402
franchisor 402
information return 409
joint and several liability 414
joint liability 414
partnership 407
partnership by estoppel 410
sole proprietorship 400
winding up 419

QUESTIONS AND CASE PROBLEMS

16–1. Maria, Pablo, and Vicky are recent college graduates who would like to go into business for themselves. They are considering purchasing a franchise. If they enter into a franchising arrangement, they would have the support of a large company that could answer any questions they might have. Also, a firm that has been in business for many years would be experienced in dealing with some of the problems that novice businesspersons might encounter. These and other attributes of franchises can lessen some of the risks of the marketplace. What other aspects of franchising—positive and negative—should Maria, Pablo, and Vicky consider before committing themselves to a particular franchise?

16–2. QUESTION WITH SAMPLE ANSWER

National Foods, Inc., sells franchises to its fast-food restaurants, known as Chicky-D's. Under the franchise agreement, franchisees agree to hire and train employees strictly according to Chicky-D's standards. Chicky-D's regional supervisors are required to approve all job candidates before they are hired and all general policies affecting those employees. Chicky-D's reserves the right to terminate a franchise for violating the franchisor's rules. In practice, however, Chicky-D's regional supervisors routinely approve new employees and individual franchisees' policies. After several incidents of racist comments and conduct by Tim, a recently hired assistant manager at a Chicky-D's, Sharon, a counterperson at the restaurant, resigns. Sharon files a suit in a federal district court against National. National files a motion for summary judgment, arguing that it is not liable for harassment by franchise employees. Will the court grant National's motion? Why or why not?

- **For a sample answer to Question 16–2, go to Appendix I at the end of this text.**

16–3. Daniel is the owner of a chain of shoe stores. He hires Rubya to be the manager of a new store, which is to open in Grand Rapids, Michigan. Daniel, by written contract, agrees to pay Rubya a monthly salary and 20 percent of the profits. Without Daniel's knowledge, Rubya represents himself to Classen as Daniel's partner, showing Classen the agreement to share profits. Classen extends credit to Rubya. Rubya defaults. Discuss whether Classen can hold Daniel liable as a partner.

16–4. Meyer, Knapp, and Cavanna establish a partnership to operate a window-washing service. Meyer contributes $10,000 to the partnership, and Knapp and Cavanna contribute $1,000 each. The partnership agreement is silent as to how profits and losses will be shared. One month after the partnership begins operation, Knapp and Cavanna vote, over Meyer's objection, to purchase another truck for the firm. Meyer believes that because he contributed $10,000, the partnership cannot make any major commitment to purchase over his objection. In addition, Meyer claims that in the absence of any provision in the agreement, profits must be divided in the same ratio as capital contributions. Discuss Meyer's contentions.

16–5. Partnership Status. Charlie Waugh owned and operated an auto parts junkyard in Georgia. Charlie's son, Mack, started working in the business part-time as a child and full-time when he left school at the age of sixteen. Mack oversaw the business's finances, depositing the profits in a bank. Charlie gave Mack a one-half interest in the business, telling him that if "something happened" to Charlie, the entire business would be his. In 1994, Charlie and his wife, Alene, transferred to Mack the land on which the junkyard was located. Two years later, however, Alene and her daughters, Gail and Jewel, falsely convinced Charlie, whose mental competence had deteriorated, that Mack had cheated him. Mack was ordered off the land. Shortly thereafter, Charlie died. Mack filed a suit in a Georgia state court against the rest of the family, asserting, in part, that he and Charlie had been partners and that he was entitled to Charlie's share of the business. Was the relationship between Charlie and Mack a partnership? Is Mack entitled to Charlie's "share"? Explain. [*Waugh v. Waugh,* 265 Ga.App. 799, 595 S.E.2d 647 (2004)]

16–6. Franchise Termination. Walik Elkhatib, a Palestinian Arab, emigrated to the United States in 1971 and became an American citizen. Eight years later, Elkhatib bought a Dunkin' Donuts, Inc., franchise in Bellwood, Illinois. Dunkin' Donuts began offering breakfast sandwiches with bacon, ham, or sausage through its franchises in 1984, but Elkhatib refused to sell these items at his store on the ground that his religion forbade the handling of pork. In 1995, Elkhatib opened a second franchise in Berkeley, Illinois, at which he also refused to sell pork products. The next year, Elkhatib began selling meatless sandwiches at both locations. In 1998, Elkhatib opened a third franchise in Westchester, Illinois. When he proposed to relocate this franchise, Dunkin' Donuts refused to approve the new location and added that it would not renew any of his franchise agreements because he did not carry the full sandwich line. Elkhatib filed a suit in a federal district court against Dunkin' Donuts and others. The defendants filed a motion for summary judgment. Did Dunkin' Donuts act in good faith in its relationship with Elkhatib? Explain. [*Elkhatib v. Dunkin' Donuts, Inc.,* __ F.Supp.2d __ (N.D.Ill. 2004)]

16–7. CASE PROBLEM WITH SAMPLE ANSWER

At least six months before the 1996 Summer Olympic Games in Atlanta, Georgia, Stafford Fontenot, Steve Turner, Mike Montelaro, Joe Sokol, and Doug Brinsmade agreed to sell Cajun food at the Games and began making preparations. Calling themselves

"Prairie Cajun Seafood Catering of Louisiana," on May 19 the group applied for a license with the Fulton County, Georgia, Department of Public Health–Environmental Health Services. Later, Ted Norris received for the sale of a mobile kitchen an $8,000 check drawn on the "Prairie Cajun Seafood Catering of Louisiana" account and two promissory notes, one for $12,000 and the other for $20,000. The notes, which were dated June 12, listed only Fontenot "d/b/a [doing business as] Prairie Cajun Seafood" as the maker. On July 31, Fontenot and his friends signed a partnership agreement, which listed specific percentages of profits and losses. They drove the mobile kitchen to Atlanta, but business was "disastrous." When the notes were not paid, Norris filed a suit in a Louisiana state court against Fontenot, seeking payment. What are the elements of a partnership? Was there a partnership among Fontenot and the others? Who is liable on the notes? Explain. [*Norris v. Fontenot,* 867 So.2d 179 (La.App. 3 Cir. 2004)]

- **To view a sample answer for Problem 16–7, go to this book's Web site at academic.cengage.com/blaw/cross, select "Chapter 16," and click on "Case Problem with Sample Answer."**

16–8. Indications of Partnership. In August 2003, Tammy Duncan began working as a waitress at Bynum's Diner, which was owned by her mother, Hazel Bynum, and her stepfather, Eddie Bynum, in Valdosta, Georgia. Less than a month later, the three signed an agreement under which Eddie was to relinquish his management responsibilities, allowing Tammy to be co-manager. At the end of this six-month period, Eddie would revisit this agreement and could then extend it for another six-month period. The diner's bank account was to remain in Eddie's name. There was no provision with regard to the diner's profit, if any, and the parties did not change the business's tax information. Tammy began doing the bookkeeping, as well as waiting tables and performing other duties. On October 30, she slipped off a ladder and injured her knees. At the end of the six-month term, Tammy quit working at the diner. The Georgia State Board of Workers' Compensation determined that she had been the diner's employee and awarded her benefits under the diner's workers' compensation policy with Cypress Insurance Co. Cypress filed a suit in a Georgia state court against Tammy, arguing that she was not an employee, but a co-owner. What are the essential elements of a partnership? Was Tammy a partner in the business of the diner? Explain. [*Cypress Insurance Co. v. Duncan,* 281 Ga.App. 469, 636 S.E.2d 159 (2006)]

16–9. Sole Proprietorship. James Ferguson operates "Jim's 11-E Auto Sales" in Jonesborough, Tennessee, as a sole proprietorship. In 1999, Consumers Insurance Co. issued a policy to "Jim Ferguson, Jim's 11E Auto Sales" covering "Owned 'Autos' Only." *Auto* was defined to include "a land motor vehicle," which was not further explained in the policy. Coverage extended to damage caused by the owner or driver of an underinsured motor vehicle. In 2000, Ferguson bought and titled in his own name a 1976 Harley-Davidson motorcycle, intending to repair and sell the cycle through his dealership. In October 2001, while riding the motorcycle, Ferguson was struck by an auto driven by John Jenkins. Ferguson filed a suit in a Tennessee state court against Jenkins, who was underinsured with respect to Ferguson's medical bills, and Consumers. The insurer argued, among other things, that because the motorcycle was bought and titled in Ferguson's own name, and he was riding it at the time of the accident, it was his personal vehicle and thus was not covered under the dealership's policy. What is the relationship between a sole proprietor and a sole proprietorship? How might this status affect the court's decision in this case? [*Ferguson v. Jenkins,* 204 S.W.3d 779 (Tenn.App. 2006)]

16–10. A QUESTION OF ETHICS

*In August 2004, Ralph Vilardo contacted Travel Center, Inc., in Cincinnati, Ohio, to buy a trip to Florida in December for his family to celebrate his fiftieth wedding anniversary. Vilardo paid $6,900 to David Sheets, the sole proprietor of Travel Center. Vilardo also paid $195 to Sheets for a separate trip to Florida in February 2005. Sheets assured Vilardo that everything was set, but in fact no arrangements were made. Later, two unauthorized charges for travel services totaling $1,182.35 appeared on Vilardo's credit-card statement. Vilardo filed a suit in an Ohio state court against Sheets and his business, alleging, among other things, fraud and violations of the state consumer protection law. Vilardo served Sheets and Travel Center with copies of the complaint, the summons, a request for admissions, and other documents filed with the court, including a motion for summary judgment. Each of these filings asked for a response within a certain time period. Sheets responded once on his own behalf with a denial of all of Vilardo's claims. Travel Center did not respond. [*Vilardo v. Sheets, *__ Ohio App.3d __, __ N.E.2d __ (12 Dist. 2006)]*

(a) Almost four months after Vilardo filed his complaint, Sheets decided that he was unable to adequately represent himself and retained an attorney who asked the court for more time. Should the court grant this request? Why or why not? Ultimately, what should the court rule in this case?

(b) Sheets admitted that "Travel Center, Inc." was a sole proprietorship. He also argued that liability might be imposed on his business but not on himself. How would you rule with respect to this argument? Why? Would there be anything unethical about allowing Sheets to avoid liability on this basis? Explain.

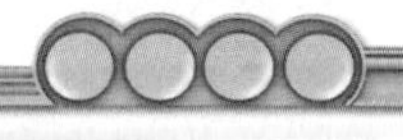

LAW ON THE WEB

For updated links to resources available on the Web, as well as a variety of other materials, visit this text's Web site at

academic.cengage.com/blaw/cross

For some of the advantages and disadvantages of doing business as a partnership, go to the following page, which is part of the U.S. Small Business Administration's Web site. Click on "Forms of Ownership" and then scroll down to "Partnerships."

www.sba.gov/smallbusinessplanner/start/chooseastructure/index.html

For information about FTC regulations on franchising, as well as state laws regulating franchising, go to

www.ftc.gov/bcp/franchise/netfran.htm

A good source of information on the purchase and sale of franchises is Franchising.org, which is online at

www.franchising.org

Legal Research Exercises on the Web

Go to **academic.cengage.com/blaw/cross**, the Web site that accompanies this text. Select "Chapter 16" and click on "Internet Exercises." There you will find the following Internet research exercises that you can perform to learn more about the topics covered in this chapter.

Internet Exercise 16–1: Legal Perspective
Liability of Dissociated Partners

Internet Exercise 16–2: Economic Perspective
Taxation of Partnerships

Internet Exercise 16–3: Management Perspective
Franchises

CHAPTER 17

Limited Liability Companies and Limited Partnerships

In the preceding chapter, we examined sole proprietorships, franchises, and general partnerships. Before we discuss corporations, one of the most prevalent business forms, we pause to examine a relatively new form of business organization called the **limited liability company (LLC).** We also examine business forms designed to limit the liability of partners. The LLC is a hybrid form that combines the limited liability aspects of the corporation and the tax advantages of a partnership. Increasingly, LLCs are becoming an organizational form of choice among businesspersons—a trend encouraged by state statutes permitting their use.

In this chapter, we begin by examining the LLC. We then look at a similar type of entity that is also relatively new—the *limited liability partnership* (LLP). The chapter concludes with a discussion of the *limited partnership* (LP), a special type of partnership in which some of the partners have limited liability, and the *limited liability limited partnership* (LLLP).

Limited Liability Companies

Limited liability companies (LLCs) are governed by state LLC statutes. These laws vary, of course, from state to state. In an attempt to create more uniformity among the states in this respect, in 1995 the National Conference of Commissioners on Uniform State Laws issued the Uniform Limited Liability Company Act (ULLCA). To date, fewer than one-fourth of the states have adopted the ULLCA, and thus the law governing LLCs remains far from uniform.[1] Some provisions are common to most state statutes, however, and we base our discussion of LLCs in this section on these common elements.

Evolution of the LLC

In 1977, Wyoming became the first state to pass legislation authorizing the creation of an LLC. Although LLCs emerged in the United States only in 1977, they have been used for more than a century in other foreign jurisdictions, including several European and South American nations. For example, the South American *limitada* is a form of business organization that operates more or less as a partnership but provides limited liability for the owners.

Taxation of the LLC In the United States, after Wyoming's adoption of an LLC statute, it still was not known how the Internal Revenue Service (IRS) would treat the LLC for tax purposes. In 1988, however, the IRS ruled that Wyoming LLCs would be taxed as partnerships instead of corporations, providing that certain requirements were met. Prior to this ruling, only one additional state—Florida, in 1982—had authorized LLCs. The 1988 ruling encouraged other states to enact LLC statutes, and in less than a decade, all states had done so.

IRS rules that went into effect on January 1, 1997, also encouraged more widespread use of LLCs in the business world. Under these rules, an unincorporated business will automatically be taxed as a partnership

1. Note that the ULLCA was revised in 2006, but no state has yet adopted the revised version of this uniform act.

unless it indicates otherwise on the tax form. The exceptions involve publicly traded companies, companies formed under a state incorporation statute, and certain foreign-owned companies. If a business chooses to be taxed as a corporation, it can indicate this preference by checking a box on the Internal Revenue Service (IRS) form.

Foreign Entities May Be LLC Members Part of the impetus behind creating LLCs in this country is that foreign investors are allowed to become LLC members. Thus, in an era increasingly characterized by global business efforts and investments, the LLC offers U.S. firms and potential investors from other countries flexibility and the opportunity for limited liability and increased tax benefits.

The Nature of the LLC

LLCs share many characteristics with corporations. Like corporations, LLCs are creatures of the state. In other words, they must be formed and operated in compliance with state law. Like the shareholders of a corporation, the owners of an LLC, who are called **members,** enjoy limited liability [ULLCA 303].[2] Also like corporations, LLCs are legal entities apart from their owners. As a legal person, the LLC can sue or be sued, enter into contracts, and hold title to property [ULLCA 201]. The terminology used to describe LLCs formed in other states or nations is also similar to that used in corporate law. For example, an LLC formed in one state but doing business in another state is referred to in the second state as a *foreign LLC.*

2. Members of an LLC can also bring derivative actions, which you will read about in Chapter 18, on behalf of the LLC [ULLCA 101]. As with a corporate shareholder's derivative suit, any damages recovered go to the LLC, not to the members personally. See, for example, *PacLink Communications International, Inc. v. Superior Court,* 90 Cal.App.4th 958, 109 Cal.Rptr.2d 436 (2001).

LLC Formation

As mentioned, LLCs are creatures of statute and thus must follow state statutory requirements. To form an LLC, **articles of organization** must be filed with a central state agency—usually the secretary of state's office [ULLCA 202]. Typically, the articles are required to include such information as the name of the business, its principal address, the name and address of a registered agent, the names of the owners, and information on how the LLC will be managed [ULLCA 203]. The business's name must include the words *Limited Liability Company* or the initials *LLC* [ULLCA 105(a)]. In addition to filing the articles of organization, a few states require that a notice of the intention to form an LLC be published in a local newspaper. Although a majority of the states permit one-member LLCs, some states require at least two members.

Businesspersons sometimes enter into contracts on behalf of a business organization that is not yet formed. For example, as you will read in Chapter 18, persons forming a corporation may enter into contracts during the process of incorporation but before the corporation becomes a legal entity. These contracts are referred to as preincorporation contracts. Once the corporation is formed and adopts the preincorporation contract (by means of a *novation,* discussed in Chapter 9), it can then enforce the contract terms.

In the following case, the question was whether the same principle extends to LLCs. A person in the process of forming an LLC entered into a preorganization contract under which it would be obligated to purchase the Park Plaza Hotel in Hollywood, California. Once the LLC legally existed, the owners of the hotel refused to sell the property to the LLC, claiming that the contract was unenforceable.

EXTENDED CASE 17.1 **02 Development, LLC v. 607 South Park, LLC**

Court of Appeal, Second District, Division 1, California, 2008.
159 Cal.App.4th 609, 71 Cal.Rptr.3d 608.

***ROTHSCHILD,* J. [Judge]**

02 Development, LLC (02 Development), a California limited liability company, appeals from a summary judgment in favor of 607 South Park, LLC (607 South Park), also a California limited liability company, on 02 Development's complaint for breach of a real estate purchase agreement.

BACKGROUND

In March 2004, 607 South Park entered into a written agreement to sell the Park Plaza Hotel to "Creative Environments of Hollywood, Inc., as General Partner of 607 Park View Associates, Ltd., a

CASE CONTINUES

CASE 17.1 CONTINUED

California limited partnership" (Creative Environments) for $8.7 million. In February 2005, Creative Environments and 02 Development executed a contract purporting to assign Creative Environments' rights in the hotel purchase agreement to 02 Development.

02 Development did not exist when the parties executed the assignment agreement. Robert Epstein executed the assignment agreement for 02 Development, and in May 2005 he created 02 Development by executing and filing the appropriate articles of organization [for the LLC] with the California Secretary of State.

02 Development later sued 607 South Park for breach of the hotel purchase agreement. The operative second amended complaint alleged that 607 South Park both refused to perform under the contract and denied that 02 Development held any rights under the purchase and assignment agreements.

607 South Park moved for summary judgment on two grounds: (1) There was no enforceable contract between 607 South Park and 02 Development because 02 Development did not exist when the assignment agreement was executed; and (2) 607 South Park's repudiation of the alleged contract did not cause 02 Development any harm because 02 Development was not ready, willing, and able to fund the purchase of the hotel. In support of the second ground, 607 South Park presented evidence that neither Epstein nor 02 Development had the $8.7 million needed to close the purchase of the hotel or had commitments from anyone else to provide the necessary financing. 607 South Park presented no other evidence concerning 02 Development's ability to fund the purchase of the hotel.

In opposition to the motion, 02 Development argued that a business entity can enforce pre-organization contracts made for its benefit. 02 Development also argued that to prove causation it needed to prove only that it would have been able to fund the purchase of the hotel when required to do so under the contract. Thus, contrary to 607 South Park's argument, 02 Development contended that it did not need to prove that it already had the necessary funds, or already had binding commitments from third parties to provide the funds, when 607 South Park anticipatorily repudiated the contract. All that 02 Development needed to prove was that it would have been able to obtain the necessary funding (or funding commitments) in order to close the transaction on time.

The trial court granted the motion and entered judgment in favor of 607 South Park. 02 Development timely appealed.

* * * *

DISCUSSION

02 Development argues that both grounds for 607 South Park's summary judgment motion fail as a matter of law and that the trial court therefore erred in granting the motion. We agree.

I. Enforceability of Pre-Organization Contracts

It is hornbook law [black letter law] that a corporation can enforce preincorporation contracts made in its behalf, as long as the corporation "has adopted the contract or otherwise succeeded to it." * * * California law does not deviate from that well-established norm. *607 South Park does not argue that limited liability companies should be treated differently from corporations in this respect, and we are aware of no authority that would support such a position.* 607 South Park's first ground for its summary judgment motion—that there is no enforceable contract between 607 South Park and 02 Development because 02 Development did not exist when the assignment agreement was executed—therefore fails as a matter of law. [Emphasis added.]

607 South Park's principal contention to the contrary is that a nonexistent business entity cannot be a party to a contract. The contention is true but irrelevant. *When the assignment agreement was executed, 02 Development did not exist, so it was not then a party to the agreement. But once 02 Development came into existence, it could enforce any pre-organization contract made in its behalf, such as the assignment agreement, if it adopted or ratified it.* [Emphasis added.]

* * * *

II. Causation

In the trial court, 607 South Park contended that in order to prove causation, 02 Development would have to prove either that it had the $8.7 million necessary to fund the transaction or that it had legally binding commitments from third parties to provide the necessary funding. * * * 607 South Park disavows [this contention] on appeal.

CASE 17.1 CONTINUED

Instead, 607 South Park now argues that its motion was based on the proposition that 02 Development "must present admissible evidence that it would have been financially able to close the transaction." But 607 South Park's evidence in support of its motion showed only that 02 Development had neither the $8.7 million to fund the transaction nor legally binding commitments from third parties to provide the funding. *607 South Park presented no evidence that 02 Development would have been unable to arrange for the necessary funding to close the transaction on time if 607 South Park had given it the opportunity instead of repudiating the contract in advance.* Because 607 South Park introduced no evidence to support an argument based on the proposition of law that 607 South Park is now advocating, the burden of production never shifted to 02 Development to present contrary evidence. For all of these reasons, the trial court erred when it granted 607 South Park's motion for summary judgment. [Emphasis added.]

DISPOSITION

The judgment is reversed, and the trial court is directed to enter an order denying 607 South Park's motion for summary judgment.

QUESTIONS

1. Why was it unimportant to the appellate court that 02 Development did not have to prove that it had funding commitments for $8.7 million?
2. What might have been some of the possible reasons that 607 South Park did not agree to sell the property to 02 Development?

Jurisdictional Requirements

One of the significant differences between LLCs and corporations has to do with federal jurisdictional requirements. Under the federal jurisdiction statute, a corporation is deemed to be a citizen of the state where it is incorporated and maintains its principal place of business. The statute does not mention the state citizenship of partnerships, LLCs, and other unincorporated associations, but the courts have tended to regard these entities as citizens of every state in which their members are citizens.

The state citizenship of an LLC may come into play when a party sues the LLC based on diversity of citizenship. Remember from Chapter 2 that when parties to a lawsuit are from different states and the amount in controversy exceeds $75,000, a federal court can exercise diversity jurisdiction. *Total* diversity of citizenship must exist, however. For example, Fong, a citizen of New York, wishes to bring a suit against Skycel, an LLC formed under the laws of Connecticut. One of Skycel's members also lives in New York. Fong will not be able to bring a suit against Skycel in federal court on the basis of diversity jurisdiction because the defendant LLC is also a citizen of New York. The same would be true if Fong was bringing a suit against multiple defendants and one of the defendants lived in New York.

Advantages and Disadvantages of the LLC

The LLC offers many advantages, and relatively few disadvantages, to businesspersons.

Advantages A key advantage of the LLC is that the members are not personally liable for the debts or obligations of the entity: their risk of loss is limited to the amount of their investments. An LLC also offers flexibility in regard to both taxation and management, as will be discussed shortly. Another advantage is that an LLC is an enduring business entity that exists beyond the illness or death of its members. In addition, as mentioned earlier, an LLC can include foreign investors.

An LLC that has *two or more members* can choose to be taxed as either a partnership or a corporation. As will be discussed in Chapter 18, a corporate entity must pay income taxes on its profits, and the shareholders pay personal income taxes on profits distributed as dividends. An LLC that wants to distribute profits to the members may prefer to be taxed as a partnership to avoid the double taxation that occurs with corporate entities. Unless an LLC indicates that it wishes to be taxed as a corporation, the IRS automatically taxes it as a partnership. This means that, as in a partnership, the LLC as an entity pays no taxes but "passes through" its profits to the members, who then personally pay taxes on the profits. If an LLC's members want to reinvest profits in the business, however, rather than distribute the profits to members, they may prefer to be taxed as a corporation. Corporate income tax rates may be lower than personal tax rates.

An LLC that has only *one member* cannot be taxed as a partnership, however. For federal income tax purposes, one-member LLCs are automatically taxed as sole proprietorships unless they indicate that they wish to be taxed as corporations. With respect to state taxes, most states follow the IRS rules, but a few states tax LLCs even though they do not tax partnerships.

Disadvantages The main disadvantage of the LLC is that state LLC statutes are not uniform. Therefore, businesses that operate in more than one state may not receive consistent treatment. Generally, though, most states will apply to a foreign LLC (an LLC formed in another state) the law of the state where the LLC was formed.

The LLC Operating Agreement

As mentioned, an advantage of the LLC form of business is the flexibility it offers in terms of operation and management. The members get to decide who will participate in the management and operation of their business, and how other issues will be resolved. Members normally do this by forming an **operating agreement** [ULLCA 103(a)]. Operating agreements typically contain provisions relating to management, how profits will be divided, the transfer of membership interests, whether the LLC will be dissolved on the death or departure of a member, and other important issues.

In many states, an operating agreement need not be in writing and indeed need not even be formed for an LLC to exist. Generally, though, LLC members should protect their interests by forming a written operating agreement. As with any business arrangement, disputes may arise over any number of issues. If there is no agreement covering the topic under dispute, such as how profits will be divided, the state LLC statute will govern the outcome. For example, most LLC statutes provide that if the members have not specified how profits will be divided, they will be divided equally among the members.

Generally, when an issue is not covered by an operating agreement or by an LLC statute, the principles of partnership law are applied. The following case illustrates what can happen in the absence of a written operating agreement when one of the members of the LLC has a "bad intent."

CASE 17.2 Kuhn v. Tumminelli

Superior Court of New Jersey, Appellate Division, 2004. 366 N.J.Super. 431, 841 A.2d 496.
lawlibrary.rutgers.edu/search.shtml#party[a]

• **Background and Facts** Clifford Kuhn, Jr., and Joseph Tumminelli formed Touch of Class Limousine Service, doing business as Touch of Elegance Limousine Service, under the New Jersey Limited Liability Company Act in 1999. They did not sign a written operating agreement, but orally agreed that Kuhn would provide the financial backing and procure customers, and that Tumminelli would manage the day-to-day operations of the company. Tumminelli embezzled $283,000 from the company after cashing customers' checks at Quick Cash, Inc., a local check-cashing service. Quick Cash deposited the checks in its bank account with First Union National Bank, N.A., which collected on the checks from the drawee banks, Bank of America Corporation and Chase Manhattan Bank, N.A. Kuhn filed a suit in a New Jersey state court against Tumminelli, the banks, and others to recover the embezzled funds. The court ordered Tumminelli to pay Kuhn and to transfer his interest in Touch of Class to Kuhn, but issued a summary judgment in favor of the other defendants. Kuhn appealed to a state intermediate appellate court, arguing, among other things, that Quick Cash and the banks were liable because Tumminelli did not have the authority to cash the company's checks and convert the funds.

a. In the "Which courts do you want to search?" section, click on the small box next to "Appellate Division." In the "Enter Names Here" section, in the "First Name:" box, type "Kuhn"; in the "Second Name:" box, type "Tumminelli"; then click on "Submit Form." In the result, click on the appropriate link to access the opinion. Rutgers University School of Law in Camden, New Jersey, maintains this Web site.

CASE 17.2 CONTINUED

IN THE LANGUAGE OF THE COURT

LEFELT, **J.A.D. [Judge, Appellate Division]**

* * * *

New Jersey enacted the Limited Liability Company Act in 1994. Its purpose was to enable members and managers of LLCs to take advantage of both the limited liability afforded to shareholders and directors of corporations and the pass-through tax advantages available to partnerships.

Under the LLC Act, *when a limited liability company is managed by its members, unless otherwise provided in the operating agreement, each member shall have the authority to bind the limited liability company.* Moreover, except as otherwise provided in an operating agreement, a member or manager may lend money to, borrow money from, act as a surety, guarantor or endorser for, * * * an LLC. [Emphasis added.]

In the absence of a written operating agreement providing to the contrary, Tumminelli as a 50% owner of the LLC had broad authority to bind the LLC * * * and specific authority * * * to endorse and presumably cash checks payable to the LLC. If more limited authority was desired, Kuhn and Tumminelli had to so provide in a written operating agreement.

* * * *

* * * The LLC Act contemplates that its provisions will control unless the members agree otherwise in an operating agreement. *When executing an operating agreement, which must be written if the LLC has more than one member, the members are free to structure the company in a variety of ways and are free to restrict and expand the rights, responsibilities and authority of its managers and members.* [Emphasis added.]

The LLC Act is, therefore, quite flexible and permits the LLC members great discretion to establish the company structure and procedures, with the statute controlling in the absence of a contrary operating agreement. The legislative intent is revealed by the directive that the LLC Act is to be liberally construed to give the maximum effect to the principle of freedom of contract and to the enforceability of operating agreements.

* * * *

Tumminelli was authorized under the LLC Act to endorse the checks. In fact, considering Tumminelli's position at the LLC, his responsibilities, and daily functions along with the statutory grant of authority, it can be inferred that Tumminelli had actual authority to receive the checks, endorse the checks, and cash them at Quick Cash, especially because Kuhn knew that Tumminelli was paying business expenses in cash.

* * * Under Kuhn's argument, even if a person had been authorized to endorse and cash a check, if that person converts the funds to an unauthorized use, a depository bank would be liable, as if the check had been paid on a forged endorsement.

We disagree that an authorized endorsement can become unauthorized by a subsequent unauthorized use of the funds. Rather, we view the circumstances as constituting two acts, the endorsement necessary to obtain the funds and the subsequent use of the funds. These acts are not inseparable. *The misappropriation of the funds is unauthorized, but does not convert an authorized endorsement into a forgery.* [Emphasis added.]

It defies reason to allow an event that occurs after the endorsement to affect the validity of the endorsement. The use to which the agent later puts the check does not affect the agent's authorization to endorse it. The validity of an endorsement does not depend upon the agent's subjective motivation at the time of the endorsement. * * * How can a bank or anyone else protect themselves against someone's bad intent?

If the agent is otherwise authorized * * * the fact that the agent had an improper purpose in making or endorsing the instrument in the authorized form does not prevent a bona fide purchaser in due course, or a subsequent transferee from one, from having the same rights in the instrument and against the principal as if the agent's act were authorized.

• **Decision and Remedy** *The state intermediate appellate court affirmed the lower court's judgment in favor of Quick Cash and the banks. Tumminelli had the authority to accept, indorse, and cash checks on behalf of Touch of Class, under the LLC Act and in the absence of a written*

CASE CONTINUES

CASE 17.2 CONTINUED *operating agreement, which might have specified otherwise. His "bad intent" to convert the funds to his own use did not affect this authority.*

- **What If the Facts Were Different?** *Suppose that Kuhn and Tumminelli had signed a written operating agreement that required both members' indorsements when cashing customers' checks. Assuming that Quick Cash would have known of this requirement, would the result in this case have been different? If so, how?*

- **The Legal Environment Dimension** *What does the outcome in this case suggest to potential members of LLCs who want to avoid the negative consequences of debt and litigation to which Kuhn was subject?*

Management of an LLC

Basically, the members have two options for managing an LLC—the members may decide in their operating agreement to be either a "member-managed" LLC or a "manager-managed" LLC. Most state LLC statutes and the ULLCA provide that unless the articles of organization specify otherwise, an LLC is assumed to be member managed [ULLCA 203(a)(6)].

Participation in Management In a *member-managed* LLC, all of the members participate in management, and decisions are made by majority vote [ULLCA 404(a)]. In a *manager-managed* LLC, the members designate a group of persons to manage the firm. The management group may consist of only members, both members and nonmembers, or only nonmembers. Managers in a manager-managed LLC owe fiduciary duties to the LLC and its members, including the duty of loyalty and the duty of care [ULLCA 409(a), 409(h)], just as corporate directors and officers owe fiduciary duties to the corporation and its shareholders.

Operating Procedures The members of an LLC can include provisions governing decision-making procedures in their operating agreement. For instance, the agreement can include procedures for choosing or removing managers. Although most LLC statutes are silent on this issue, the ULLCA provides that members may choose and remove managers by majority vote [ULLCA 404(b)(3)].

The members are also free to include in the agreement provisions designating when and for what purposes they will hold formal members' meetings. Most state LLC statutes have no provisions regarding members' meetings, which is in contrast to most state laws governing corporations, as you will read in Chapter 18.

Members may also specify in their agreement how voting rights will be apportioned. If they do not, LLC statutes in most states provide that voting rights are apportioned according to each member's capital contributions.[3] Some states provide that, in the absence of an agreement to the contrary, each member has one vote.

Dissociation and Dissolution of an LLC

Recall from Chapter 16 that in the context of partnerships, *dissociation* occurs when a partner ceases to be associated in the carrying on of the partnership business. The same concept applies to LLCs. A member of an LLC has the *power* to dissociate from the LLC at any time, but he or she may not have the *right* to dissociate. Under the ULLCA, the events that trigger a member's dissociation from an LLC are similar to the events causing a partner to be dissociated under the Uniform Partnership Act (UPA). These include voluntary withdrawal, expulsion by other members or by court order, bankruptcy, incompetence, and death. Generally, even if a member dies or otherwise dissociates from an LLC, the other members may continue to carry on the LLC business, unless the operating agreement has contrary provisions.

Effect of Dissociation When a member dissociates from an LLC, he or she loses the right to participate in management and the right to act as an agent for the LLC. His or her duty of loyalty to the LLC also terminates, and the duty of care continues only with respect

3. This is similar to partnership law in the sense that partners in a partnership generally have equal rights in management and equal voting rights unless otherwise specified in a partnership agreement [UPA 401(f)].

to events that occurred before dissociation. Generally, the dissociated member also has a right to have his or her interest in the LLC bought out by the other members of the LLC. The LLC's operating agreement may contain provisions establishing a buyout price, but if it does not, the member's interest is usually purchased at a fair value. In states that have adopted the ULLCA, the LLC must purchase the interest at "fair" value within 120 days after the dissociation.

If the member's dissociation violates the LLC's operating agreement, it is considered legally wrongful, and the dissociated member can be held liable for damages caused by the dissociation. Suppose that Chadwick and Barrel are members in an LLC. Chadwick manages the accounts, and Barrel, who has many connections in the community and is a skilled investor, brings in the business. If Barrel wrongfully dissociates from the LLC, the LLC's business will suffer, and Chadwick can hold Barrel liable for the loss of business resulting from her withdrawal.

Dissolution Regardless of whether a member's dissociation was wrongful or rightful, normally the dissociated member has no right to force the LLC to dissolve. The remaining members can opt to either continue or dissolve the business. Members can also stipulate in their operating agreement that certain events will cause dissolution, or they can agree that they have the power to dissolve the LLC by vote. As with partnerships, a court can order an LLC to be dissolved in certain circumstances, such as when the members have engaged in illegal or oppressive conduct, or when it is no longer feasible to carry on the business.

When an LLC is dissolved, any members who did not wrongfully dissociate may participate in the winding up process. To wind up the business, members must collect, liquidate, and distribute the LLC's assets. Members may preserve the assets for a reasonable time to optimize their return, and they continue to have the authority to perform reasonable acts in conjunction with winding up. In other words, the LLC will be bound by the reasonable acts of its members during the winding up process. Once all of the LLC's assets have been sold, the proceeds are distributed to pay off debts to creditors first (including debts owed to members who are creditors of the LLC). The member's capital contributions are returned next, and any remaining amounts are then distributed to members in equal shares or according to their operating agreement.

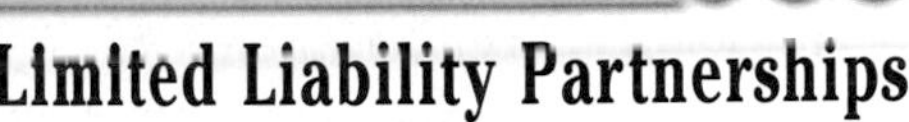

Limited Liability Partnerships

The **limited liability partnership (LLP)** is a hybrid form of business designed mostly for professionals who normally do business as partners in a partnership. The major advantage of the LLP is that it allows a partnership to continue as a pass-through entity for tax purposes but limits the personal liability of the partners.

The first state to enact an LLP statute was Texas, in 1991. Other states quickly followed suit, and by 1997, virtually all of the states had enacted LLP statutes. LLPs must be formed and operated in compliance with state statutes, which may include provisions of the UPA. The appropriate form must be filed with a central state agency, usually the secretary of state's office, and the business's name must include either "Limited Liability Partnership" or "LLP" [UPA 1001, 1002]. In addition, an LLP must file an annual report with the state to remain qualified as an LLP in that state [UPA 1003]. In most states, it is relatively easy to convert a traditional partnership into an LLP because the firm's basic organizational structure remains the same. Additionally, all of the statutory and common law rules governing partnerships still apply (apart from those modified by the LLP statute). Normally, LLP statutes are simply amendments to a state's already existing partnership law.

The LLP is especially attractive for two categories of enterprises: professional services and family businesses. Professional service firms include law firms and accounting firms. *Family limited liability partnerships* are basically business organizations in which the majority of the partners are related to each other.

Liability in an LLP

Traditionally, many professionals, such as attorneys and accountants, have worked together using the partnership business form. As previously discussed, a major disadvantage of the general partnership is the unlimited personal liability of its owner-partners. Each partner in a general partnership is exposed to potential liability for the malpractice of another partner.

The LLP allows professionals to avoid personal liability for the malpractice of other partners. A partner in an LLP is still liable for her or his own wrongful acts, such as negligence, however. Also liable is the partner who supervised the party who committed a wrongful act. This is generally true for all types of partners and partnerships, not just LLPs.

Although LLP statutes vary from state to state, generally each state statute limits the liability of partners in some way. For example, Delaware law protects each innocent partner from the "debts and obligations of the partnership arising from negligence, wrongful acts, or misconduct." In North Carolina, Texas, and Washington, D.C., the statutes protect innocent partners from obligations arising from "errors, omissions, negligence, incompetence, or malfeasance." The UPA more broadly exempts partners from personal liability for any partnership obligation, "whether arising in contract, tort, or otherwise" [UPA 306(c)].

Even though the language of these statutes may seem to apply specifically to attorneys, virtually any group of professionals can use the LLP (depending on the state statute). LLPs are especially popular in the accounting field. All of the "Big Four" firms—the four largest international accountancy and professional services firms—are organized as LLPs, including PricewaterhouseCoopers LLP and Deloitte Development LLP.

Family Limited Liability Partnerships

A **family limited liability partnership (FLLP)** is a limited liability partnership in which the majority of the partners are persons related to each other, essentially as spouses, parents, grandparents, siblings, cousins, nephews, or nieces. A person acting in a fiduciary capacity for persons so related can also be a partner. All of the partners must be natural persons or persons acting in a fiduciary capacity for the benefit of natural persons.

Probably the most significant use of the FLLP form of business organization is in agriculture. Family-owned farms sometimes find this form to their benefit. The FLLP offers the same advantages as other LLPs with certain additional advantages, such as, in Iowa, an exemption from real estate transfer taxes when partnership real estate is transferred among partners.[4]

Limited Partnerships

We now look at a business organizational form that limits the liability of *some* of its owners—the **limited partnership.** Limited partnerships originated in medieval Europe and have been in existence in the United States since the early 1800s. In many ways, limited partnerships are like the general partnerships (discussed in Chapter 16), but they differ from general partnerships in several ways. Because of this, they are sometimes referred to as *special partnerships.*

A limited partnership consists of at least one **general partner** and one or more **limited partners.** A general partner assumes management responsibility for the partnership and has full responsibility for the partnership and for all its debts. A limited partner contributes cash or other property and owns an interest in the firm but does not undertake any management responsibilities and is not personally liable for partnership debts beyond the amount of his or her investment. A limited partner can forfeit limited liability by taking part in the management of the business. A comparison of the characteristics of general partnerships and limited partnerships appears in Exhibit 17–1.[5]

Until 1976, the law governing limited partnerships in all states except Louisiana was the Uniform Limited Partnership Act (ULPA). Since 1976, most states and the District of Columbia have adopted the revised version of the ULPA, known as the Revised Uniform Limited Partnership Act (RULPA). Because the RULPA is the dominant law governing limited partnerships in the United States, we refer to the RULPA in the following discussion. Note, however, that in 2001 the National Conference of Commissioners on Uniform State Laws adopted a new, more flexible version of this law (ULPA 2001), which has been adopted in a minority of states.

Formation of a Limited Partnership

In contrast to the informal, private, and voluntary agreement that usually suffices for a general partnership, the formation of a limited partnership is formal and public. The parties must follow specific statutory requirements and file a certificate with the state. In this regard, a limited partnership resembles a corporation more than it does a general partnership. A limited partnership must have at least one general partner and one limited partner, as mentioned previously. Additionally, the partners must sign a **certificate of limited partnership,** which requires information similar to that found in articles of incorporation

4. Iowa Statutes Section 428A.2.

5. Under the UPA, a general partnership can be converted into a limited partnership and vice versa [UPA 902, 903]. The UPA also provides for the merger of a general partnership with one or more general or limited partnerships [UPA 905].

EXHIBIT 17–1 • A Comparison of General Partnerships and Limited Partnerships

Characteristic	General Partnership (UPA)	Limited Partnership (RULPA)
Creation	By agreement of two or more persons to carry on a business as co-owners for profit.	By agreement of two or more persons to carry on a business as co-owners for profit. Must include one or more general partners and one or more limited partners. Filing of a certificate with the secretary of state is required.
Sharing of Profits and Losses	By agreement; or, in the absence of agreement, profits are shared equally by the partners, and losses are shared in the same ratio as profits.	Profits are shared as required in the certificate agreement, and losses are shared likewise, up to the amount of the limited partners' capital contributions. In the absence of a provision in the certificate agreement, profits and losses are shared on the basis of percentages of capital contributions.
Liability	Unlimited personal liability of all partners.	Unlimited personal liability of all general partners; limited partners liable only to the extent of their capital contributions.
Capital Contribution	No minimum or mandatory amount; set by agreement.	Set by agreement.
Management	By agreement, or in the absence of agreement, all partners have an equal voice.	General partner or partners only. Limited partners have no voice or else are subject to liability as general partners (but *only* if a third party has reason to believe that the limited partner is a general partner). A limited partner may act as an agent or employee of the partnership and vote on amending the certificate or on the sale or dissolution of the partnership.
Duration	Terminated by agreement of the partners, but can continue to do business even when a partner dissociates from the partnership.	Terminated by agreement in the certificate or by retirement, death, or mental incompetence of a general partner in the absence of the right of the other general partners to continue the partnership. Death of a limited partner, unless he or she is the only remaining limited partner, does not terminate the partnership.
Distribution of Assets on Liquidation—Order of Priorities	1. Payment of debts, including those owed to partner and nonpartner creditors. 2. Return of capital contributions and distribution of profit to partners.	1. Outside creditors and partner creditors. 2. Partners and former partners entitled to distributions or partnership assets. 3. Unless otherwise agreed, return of capital contributions and distribution of profit to partners.

(see Chapter 18), such as the name, mailing address, and capital contribution of each general and limited partner. The certificate must be filed with the designated state official—under the RULPA, the secretary of state. The certificate is usually open to public inspection.

Rights and Liabilities of Partners

General partners, unlike limited partners, are personally liable to the partnership's creditors; thus, at least one general partner is necessary in a limited partnership so that someone has personal liability. This policy can be circumvented in states that allow a corporation to be the general partner in a partnership. Because the corporation has limited liability by virtue of corporation statutes, if a corporation is the general partner, no one in the limited partnership has personal liability.

Rights of Limited Partners Subject to the limitations that will be discussed shortly, limited partners have essentially the same rights as general partners, including the right of access to partnership books and the right to other information regarding partnership business. On dissolution of the partnership, limited partners are entitled to a return of their contributions in accordance with the partnership certificate [RULPA 201(a)(10)]. They can also assign their interests subject to the certificate [RULPA 702, 704].

The RULPA provides that a limited partner has the right to sue an outside party on behalf of the firm if the general partners with authority to do so have refused to file suit [RULPA 1001].[6] In addition, investor protection legislation, such as securities laws (discussed in Chapter 28), may give some protection to limited partners.

Liabilities of Limited Partners In contrast to the personal liability of general partners, the liability of a limited partner is limited to the capital that she or he contributes or agrees to contribute to the partnership [RULPA 502].

A limited partnership is formed by good faith compliance with the requirements for signing and filing the certificate, even if it is incomplete or defective. When a limited partner discovers a defect in the formation of the limited partnership, he or she can avoid future liability by filing the appropriate amendment or correction with the state or by renouncing an interest in the profits of the partnership [RULPA 304]. If the limited partner takes neither of these actions on discovery of the defect, however, the firm's creditors can hold the partner personally liable [RULPA 207].

Limited Partners and Management Limited partners enjoy limited liability so long as they do not participate in management [RULPA 303].[7] A limited partner who participates in management will be just as liable as a general partner to any creditor who transacts business with the limited partnership and believes, based on the limited partner's conduct, that the limited partner is a general partner [RULPA 303]. The degree to which a limited partner can participate—by, for example, reviewing partnership operations or providing advice—before being exposed to liability is an unsettled question.[8] A limited partner who knowingly permits his or her name to be used in the name of the limited partnership is liable to creditors who extend credit to the limited partnership without knowledge that the limited partner is not a general partner [RULPA 102, 303(d)].

Although limited partners cannot participate in management, this does not mean that the general partners are totally free of restrictions in running the business. The general partners in a limited partnership have fiduciary obligations to the partnership and to the limited partners.[9]

Dissociation and Dissolution

A general partner has the power to voluntarily dissociate, or withdraw, from a limited partnership unless the partnership agreement specifies otherwise. A limited partner theoretically can withdraw from the partnership by giving six months' notice unless the partnership agreement specifies a term, which most do. Also, some states have passed laws prohibiting the withdrawal of limited partners.

In a limited partnership, a general partner's voluntary dissociation from the firm normally will lead to dissolution *unless* all partners agree to continue the business. Similarly, the bankruptcy, retirement, death, or mental incompetence of a general partner will cause the dissociation of that partner and the dissolution of the limited partnership unless the other members agree to continue the firm [RULPA 801]. Bankruptcy of a limited partner, however, does not dissolve the partnership unless it causes the bankruptcy of the firm. Death or an assignment of the interest of a limited partner does not dissolve a limited partnership [RULPA 702, 704, 705]. A limited partnership can be dissolved by court decree [RULPA 802].

On dissolution, creditors' claims, including those of partners who are creditors, take first priority. After that, partners and former partners receive unpaid distribu-

6. For a case from a jurisdiction that does *not* follow the RULPA in this respect, see *Energy Investors Fund, L.P. v. Metric Constructors, Inc.*, 351 N.C. 331, 525 S.E.2d 441 (2000).

7. Note that the 2001 version of this law that has been adopted in a minority of states provides limited liability to limited partners for entity obligations "even if the limited partner participates in the management and control of the limited partnership" [ULPA 2001, Section 303].

8. The question is unsettled partly because state laws differ on this issue. Factors to be considered under the RULPA are listed in RULPA 303(b), (c).

9. See, for example, *Smith v. Fairfax Realty, Inc.*, 82 P.3d 1064 (Utah Sup.Ct. 2003).

tions of partnership assets and, except as otherwise agreed, amounts representing returns on their contributions and amounts proportionate to their shares of the distributions [RULPA 804].

In the following case, two limited partners wanted the business of the partnership to be sold on its dissolution, while another limited partner and the general partner wanted it to continue.

CASE 17.3 In re Dissolution of Midnight Star Enterprises, L.P.

Supreme Court of South Dakota, 2006. 2006 SD 98, 724 N.W.2d 334.

• **Background and Facts** Midnight Star Enterprises, Limited Partnership, consists of a casino, bar, and restaurant in Deadwood, South Dakota. The owners are Midnight Star Enterprises, Limited (MSEL), the general partner, which owns 22 partnership units; actor Kevin Costner, a limited partner, who owns 71.50 partnership units; and Carla and Francis Caneva, limited partners, who own 3.25 partnership units each. Costner also owns MSEL and thus controls 93.5 partnership units. The Canevas were the business's managers, for which they received salaries and bonuses. When MSEL voiced concerns about the management, communication among the partners broke down. MSEL filed a petition in a South Dakota state court to dissolve the partnership. MSEL hired Paul Thorstenson, an accountant, to determine the firm's fair market value, which he calculated to be $3.1 million. The Canevas solicited a competitor's offer to buy the business for $6.2 million, which the court ruled was the appropriate amount. At the Canevas' request, the court ordered MSEL and Costner to buy the business for that price within ten days or sell it on the open market to the highest bidder. MSEL appealed to the South Dakota Supreme Court.

IN THE LANGUAGE OF THE COURT
***SABERS*, Justice.**

* * * *

MSEL * * * brought a Petition for Dissolution [in a South Dakota state court]. In order to dissolve, the fair market value of Midnight Star had to be assessed. MSEL hired Paul Thorstenson, an accountant, to determine the fair market value. * * * [T]he Canevas solicited an "offer" from Ken Kellar, a Deadwood casino, restaurant, and hotel owner * * * .

* * * Thorstenson determined the fair market value was $3.1 million based on the hypothetical transaction standard of valuation. * * * The * * * court * * * found Kellar's offer of $6.2 million to be the fair market value * * * [and] ordered the majority owners to buy the business for $6.2 million within 10 days or the court would order the business to be sold on the open market. [MSEL appealed to the South Dakota Supreme Court.]

* * * *

[The] Canevas claim the partnership agreement does not allow the general partner to buy out their interest in Midnight Star. Instead, the Canevas argue, the agreement mandates the partnership be sold on the open market upon dissolution. * * * Article 10.4 provides:

> After all of the debts of the Partnership have been paid, the General Partner * * * may distribute in kind any Partnership property provided that a good faith effort is first made to sell * * * such property * * * at its estimated fair value to one or more third parties * * * .

* * * *

* * * This provision clearly states the General Partner "may distribute in kind any partnership property" if the property is first offered to a third party for a fair value. While the General Partner may offer the property on the open market, Article 10.4 does not require it.

This interpretation is reinforced when read together with Article 10.3.1 * * * [which] instructs that "no assets * * * shall be sold or otherwise transferred to [any partner] unless the assets are valued at their then fair market value * * * ." *If Article 10.4 requires a forced sale, then there would be no need to have the fair market value provision of Article 10.3.1.* [Emphasis added.]

* * * Read as a whole, the partnership agreement does not require a mandatory sale upon dissolution. Instead, the general partner can opt to liquidate using either a sale or transfer under Article 10.3.1. * * * Because MSEL decided to pursue dissolution under Article 10.3.1, we decide the correct standard for determining the fair market value of the partnership.

CASE CONTINUES

CASE 17.3 CONTINUED

* * * *

MSEL claims the correct standard * * * is the hypothetical transaction analysis * * *. [The] Canevas argue that * * * the offer from Kellar represented the fair market value * * *.

* * * *

* * * *[There are] sound policy reasons why an offer cannot be the fair market value.* * * * What if a businessman, for personal reasons, offers 10 times the real value of the business? What if the partnership, for personal reasons, such as sentimental value, refuses to sell for that absurdly high offer? *These arbitrary, emotional offers and rejections cannot provide a rational and reasonable basis for determining the fair market value.* [Emphasis added.]

Conversely, the hypothetical transaction standard does provide a rational and reasonable basis for determining the fair market value * * * by removing the irrationalities, strategies, and emotions * * *.

* * * *

Since it was error for the [lower] court to value Midnight Star at $6.2 million, it was also error to force the general partners to buy the business for $6.2 million or sell the business.

* * * *

* * * Instead of ordering the majority partners to purchase the whole partnership for the appraised value, the majority partners should only be required to pay any interests the withdrawing partner is due. * * * The majority partners should only be required to pay the Canevas the value of their 6.5 partnership units * * *.

- **Decision and Remedy** *The South Dakota Supreme Court reversed the judgment of the lower court and remanded the case to allow MSEL and Costner to pay the Canevas the value of their 6.5 partnership units after a revaluation of the partnership. The court concluded that under the partnership agreement, during liquidation, the firm's property could be distributed in kind among the partners if it was first offered for sale to a third party. The court also concluded that the correct value of the business was the accountant's figure, which was based on a fair market value analysis using a hypothetical buyer.*

- **The Legal Environment Dimension** *Why did the court hold that a forced sale of the property of the limited partnership was not appropriate in this case?*

- **The Ethical Dimension** *Under what circumstances might a forced sale of the property of a limited partnership on its dissolution be appropriate?*

Limited Liability Limited Partnerships

A **limited liability limited partnership (LLLP)** is a type of limited partnership. An LLLP differs from a limited partnership in that a general partner in an LLLP has the same liability as a limited partner in a limited partnership. In other words, the liability of all partners is limited to the amount of their investments in the firm.

A few states provide expressly for LLLPs. In states that do not provide for LLLPs but do allow for limited partnerships and limited liability partnerships, a limited partnership should probably still be able to register with the state as an LLLP.

REVIEWING Limited Liability Companies and Limited Partnerships

A bridge on a prominent public roadway in the city of Papagos, Arizona, was deteriorating and in need of repair. The city posted notices seeking proposals for an artistic bridge design and reconstruction. Davidson Masonry, LLC, which was owned and managed by Carl Davidson and his wife,

REVIEWING Limited Liability Companies and Limited Partnerships, Continued

Marilyn Rowe, decided to submit a bid for a decorative concrete project that incorporated artistic metalwork. They contacted Shana Lafayette, a local sculptor who specialized in large-scale metal forms, to help them design the bridge. The city selected their bridge design and awarded them the contract for a commission of $184,000. Davidson Masonry and Lafayette then entered into an agreement to work together on the bridge project. Davidson Masonry agreed to install and pay for concrete and structural work, and Lafayette agreed to install the metalwork at her expense. They agreed that overall profits would be split, with 25 percent going to Lafayette and 75 percent going to Davidson Masonry. Lafayette designed numerous metal sculptures of salmon that were incorporated into colorful decorative concrete forms designed by Rowe, while Davidson performed the structural engineering. Using the information presented in the chapter, answer the following questions.

1. Would Davidson Masonry automatically be taxed as a partnership or a corporation?
2. Is Davidson Masonry member managed or manager managed?
3. Suppose that during construction, Lafayette had entered into an agreement to rent space in a warehouse that was close to the bridge so that she could work on her sculptures near the site where they would eventually be installed. She entered into the contract without the knowledge or consent of Davidson Masonry. In this situation, would a court be likely to hold that Davidson Masonry was bound by the contract that Lafayette entered? Why or why not?
4. Now suppose that Rowe has an argument with her husband and wants to withdraw from being a member of Davidson Masonry. What is the term for such a withdrawal and what effect does it have on the LLC?

TERMS AND CONCEPTS

articles of organization 425
certificate of limited partnership 432
family limited liability partnership (FLLP) 432
general partner 432
limited liability company (LLC) 424
limited liability limited partnership (LLLP) 436
limited liability partnership (LLP) 431
limited partner 432
limited partnership 432
member 425
operating agreement 428

QUESTIONS AND CASE PROBLEMS

17-1. John, Lesa, and Tabir form a limited liability company. John contributes 60 percent of the capital, and Lesa and Tabir each contribute 20 percent. Nothing is decided about how profits will be divided. John assumes that he will be entitled to 60 percent of the profits, in accordance with his contribution. Lesa and Tabir, however, assume that the profits will be divided equally. A dispute over the question arises, and ultimately a court has to decide the issue. What law will the court apply? In most states, what will result? How could this dispute have been avoided in the first place? Discuss fully.

17-2. Asher and Breem form a limited partnership with Asher as the general partner and Breem as the limited partner. Breem puts up $15,000, and Asher contributes some office equipment that he owns. A certificate of limited partnership is properly filed, and business is begun.

One month later, Asher becomes ill. Instead of hiring someone to manage the business, Breem takes over complete management responsibilities. While Breem is in control, he makes a contract with Thaler involving a large sum of money. Asher returns to work. Because of other commitments, Asher and Breem breach the Thaler contract. Thaler contends that Asher and Breem will be personally liable for damages caused by the breach if the damages cannot be satisfied out of the assets of the limited partnership. Discuss this contention.

17-3. QUESTION WITH SAMPLE ANSWER

Dorinda, Luis, and Elizabeth form a limited partnership. Dorinda is a general partner, and Luis and Elizabeth are limited partners. Consider each of the separate events below, and discuss fully which event(s) constitute(s) a dissolution of the limited partnership.

(a) Luis assigns his partnership interest to Ashley.
(b) Elizabeth is petitioned into involuntary bankruptcy.
(c) Dorinda dies.

- **For a sample answer to Question 17-3, go to Appendix I at the end of this text.**

17-4. Joe, a resident of New Jersey, wants to open a restaurant. He asks his friend Kay, an experienced attorney and a New Yorker, for her business and legal advice in exchange for a 20 percent ownership interest in the restaurant. Kay helps Joe negotiate a lease for the restaurant premises and advises Joe to organize the business as a limited liability company (LLC). Joe forms Café Olé, LLC, and with Kay's help, obtains financing. Then, the night before the restaurant opens, Joe tells Kay that he is "cutting her out of the deal." The restaurant proves to be a success. Kay wants to file a suit in a federal district court against Joe and the LLC. Can a federal court exercise jurisdiction over the parties based on diversity of citizenship? Explain.

17-5. Limited Liability Companies. Gloria Duchin, a Rhode Island resident, was the sole shareholder and chief executive officer of Gloria Duchin, Inc. (Duchin, Inc.), which manufactured metallic Christmas ornaments and other novelty items. The firm was incorporated in Rhode Island. Duchin Realty, Inc., also incorporated in Rhode Island, leased real estate to Duchin, Inc. The Duchin entities hired Gottesman Co. to sell Duchin, Inc., and to sign with the buyer a consulting agreement for Gloria Duchin and a lease for Duchin Realty's property. Gottesman negotiated a sale, a consulting agreement, and a lease with Somerset Capital Corp. James Mitchell, a resident of Massachusetts, was the chairman and president of Somerset, and Mary Mitchell, also a resident of Massachusetts, was the senior vice president. The parties agreed that to buy Duchin, Inc., Somerset would create a new limited liability company, JMTR Enterprises, L.L.C., in Rhode Island, with the Mitchells as its members. When the deal fell apart, JMTR filed a suit in a Massachusetts state court against the Duchin entities, alleging, among other things, breach of contract. When the defendants tried to remove the case to a federal district court, JMTR argued that the court did not have jurisdiction because there was no diversity of citizenship between the parties: all of the plaintiffs and defendants were citizens of Rhode Island. Is JMTR correct? Why or why not? [*JMTR Enterprises, L.L.C. v. Duchin*, 42 F.Supp.2d 87 (D.Mass. 1999)]

17-6. Foreign Limited Liability Companies. Walter Matjasich and Cary Hanson organized Capital Care, LLC, in Utah. Capital Care operated, and Matjasich and Hanson managed, Heartland Care Center in Topeka, Kansas. LTC Properties, Inc., held a mortgage on the Heartland facilities. When Heartland failed as a business, its residents were transferred to other facilities. Heartland employees who provided care to the residents for five days during the transfers were not paid wages. The employees filed claims with the Kansas Department of Human Resources for the unpaid wages. Kansas state law provides that a *corporate* officer or manager may be liable for a firm's unpaid wages, but protects limited liability company (LLC) members from personal liability generally and states that an LLC cannot be construed as a corporation. Under Utah state law, however, the members of an LLC can be personally liable for wages due the LLC's employees. Should Matjasich and Hanson be held personally liable for the unpaid wages? Explain. [*Matjasich v. Department of Human Resources*, 271 Kan. 246, 21 P.3d 985 (2001)]

17-7. Limited Liability Companies. Michael Collins entered into a three-year employment contract with E-Magine, LLC. E-Magine was in business for only a brief time, during which it incurred considerable losses. In terminating operations, which ceased before the term of the contract with Collins expired, E-Magine also terminated Collins's services. In exchange for a payment of $24,240, Collins signed a "final payment agreement," which purported to be a settlement of any claims that he might have against E-Magine. Collins filed a suit in a New York state court against E-Magine, its members and managers, and others, alleging, among other things, breach of his employment contract. Collins claimed that signing the "final payment agreement" was the only means for him to obtain what he was owed for past sales commissions and asked the court to impose personal liability on the members and managers of E-Magine for breach of contract. Should the court grant this request? Why or why not? [*Collins v. E-Magine, LLC*, 291 A.D.2d 350, 739 N.Y.S.2d 121 (1 Dept. 2002)]

17-8. CASE PROBLEM WITH SAMPLE ANSWER

Westbury Properties, Inc., and others (collectively, the Westbury group) owned, managed, and developed real property. Jerry Stoker and the Stoker Group, Inc. (the Stokers), also developed real property. The Westbury group entered into agreements with the Stokers concerning a large tract of property in Houston County, Georgia. The parties formed limited liability companies (LLCs), including Bellemeade, LLC (the LLC group), to develop various parcels of the tract for residential purposes. The operating agreements provided that "no Member shall be accountable to the [LLC] or to any other Member with respect to [any other] business or activity even if the business or activity competes with the [LLC's] business." The Westbury group entered into agreements with other parties to develop additional parcels within the tract in competition with the LLC group. The Stokers filed a suit in a Georgia state court against the Westbury group, alleging, among other things, breach of fiduciary duty. What duties do the members of an LLC owe to each other? Under what principle might the terms of an operating agreement alter these duties? In whose favor should the court rule? Discuss. [*Stoker v. Bellemeade, LLC,* 272 Ga.App. 817, 615 S.E.2d 1 (2005)]

- **To view a sample answer for Problem 17–8, go to this book's Web site at academic.cengage.com/blaw/cross, select "Chapter 17," and click on "Case Problem with Sample Answer."**

17–9. Limited Liability Companies. A "Certificate of Formation" (CF) for Grupo Dos Chiles, LLC, was filed with the Delaware secretary of state in February 2000. The CF named Jamie Rivera as the "initial member." The next month, Jamie's mother, Yolanda Martinez, and Alfred Shriver, who had a personal relationship with Martinez at the time, signed an "LLC Agreement" for Grupo, naming themselves "managing partners." Grupo's business was the operation of Dancing Peppers Cantina, a restaurant in Alexandria, Virginia. Identifying themselves as Grupo's owners, Shriver and Martinez borrowed funds from Advanceme, Inc., a restaurant lender. In June 2003, Grupo lost its LLC status in Delaware for failing to pay state taxes, and by the end of July, Martinez and Shriver had ended their relationship. Shriver filed a suit in a Virginia state court against Martinez to wind up Grupo's affairs. Meanwhile, without consulting Shriver, Martinez paid Grupo's back taxes. Shriver filed a suit in a Delaware state court against Martinez, asking the court to dissolve the firm. What effect did the LLC Agreement have on the CF? Did Martinez's unilateral act reestablish Grupo's LLC status? Should the Delaware court grant Shriver's request? Why or why not? [*In re Grupo Dos Chiles, LLC,* __ A.2d __ (Del.Ch. 2006)]

17–10. SPECIAL CASE ANALYSIS

Go to Case 17.1, *02 Development, LLC v. 607 South Park, LLC,* 159 Cal.App.4th 609, 71 Cal.Rptr.3d 608 (2008), on pages 425–426. Read the excerpt and answer the following questions.

(a) **Issue:** What was the main issue in this case?
(b) **Rule of Law:** What rule of law did the court apply?
(c) **Applying the Rule of Law:** Describe how the court applied the rule of law to the facts of this case.
(d) **Conclusion:** What was the court's conclusion in this case?

17–11. A QUESTION OF ETHICS

*Blushing Brides, L.L.C., a publisher of wedding planning magazines in Columbus, Ohio, opened an account with Gray Printing Co. in July 2000. On behalf of Blushing Brides, Louis Zacks, the firm's member-manager, signed a credit agreement that identified the firm as the "purchaser" and required payment within thirty days. Despite the agreement, Blushing Brides typically took up to six months to pay the full amount for its orders. Gray printed and shipped 10,000 copies of a fall/winter 2001 issue for Blushing Brides but had not been paid when the firm ordered 15,000 copies of a spring/summer 2002 issue. Gray refused to print the new order without an assurance of payment. On May 22, Zacks signed a promissory note payable to Gray within thirty days for $14,778, plus interest at 6 percent per year. Gray printed the new order but by October had been paid only $7,500. Gray filed a suit in an Ohio state court against Blushing Brides and Zacks to collect the balance. [*Gray Printing Co. v. Blushing Brides, L.L.C., *__ N.E.2d __ (Ohio App. 10 Dist. 2006)]*

(a) Under what circumstances is a member of an LLC liable for the firm's debts? In this case, is Zacks personally liable under the credit agreement for the unpaid amount on Blushing Brides' account? Did Zacks's promissory note affect the parties' liability on the account? Explain.
(b) Should a member of an LLC assume an ethical responsibility to meet the obligations of the firm? Discuss.
(c) Gray shipped only 10,000 copies of the spring/summer 2002 issue of Blushing Brides' magazine, waiting for the publisher to identify a destination for the other 5,000 copies. The magazine had a retail price of $4.50 per copy. Did Gray have a legal or ethical duty to "mitigate the damages" by attempting to sell or otherwise distribute these copies itself? Why or why not?

For updated links to resources available on the Web, as well as a variety of other materials, visit this text's Web site at

academic.cengage.com/blaw/cross

LLRX.com, a Web site for legal professionals, provides information on LLCs on its Web journal. Go to

www.llrx.com/features/llc.htm

You can find information on filing fees for LLCs at

www.bizcorp.com

Legal Research Exercises on the Web

Go to **academic.cengage.com/blaw/cross**, the Web site that accompanies this text. Select "Chapter 17" and click on "Internet Exercises." There you will find the following Internet research exercises that you can perform to learn more about the topics covered in this chapter.

Internet Exercise 17–1: Legal Perspective
Limited Liability Companies

Internet Exercise 17–2: Management Perspective
Limited Partnerships and Limited Liability Partnerships

CHAPTER 18

Corporations

The corporation is a creature of statute. A **corporation** is an artificial being, existing only in law and neither tangible nor visible. Its existence generally depends on state law, although some corporations, especially public organizations, are created under federal law. Each state has its own body of corporate law, and these laws are not entirely uniform.

The Model Business Corporation Act (MBCA) is a codification of modern corporation law that has been influential in the codification of state corporation statutes. Today, the majority of state statutes are guided by the most recent version of the MBCA, often referred to as the Revised Model Business Corporation Act (RMBCA). Excerpts from the RMBCA are included in Appendix G of this text. Keep in mind, however, that there is considerable variation among the regulations of the states that have used the MBCA or the RMBCA as a basis for their statutes, and several states do not follow either act. Consequently, individual state corporation laws should be relied on to determine corporate law rather than the MBCA or RMBCA.

In this chapter, we examine the corporate form of business enterprise. Under modern law, except as limited by charters, statutes, or constitutions, *a corporation can engage in any act and enter into any contract available to a natural person in order to accomplish the purposes for which it was created.* When a corporation is created, the express and implied powers necessary to achieve its purpose also come into existence.

The Nature and Classification of Corporations

A corporation is a legal entity created and recognized by state law. It can consist of one or more *natural persons* (as opposed to the artificial *legal person* of the corporation) identified under a common name. The corporation substitutes itself for its shareholders in conducting corporate business and in incurring liability, yet its authority to act and the liability for its actions are separate and apart from the individuals who own it.

Corporate Personnel

When an individual purchases a share of stock in a corporation, that person becomes a shareholder and an owner of the corporation. The shareholders elect a *board of directors* who are responsible for the overall management of the corporation. The directors make all policy decisions and hire the *corporate officers* and other employees to run the daily business operations of the corporation.

The body of shareholders can change constantly without affecting the continued existence of the corporation. A shareholder can sue the corporation, and the corporation can sue a shareholder. Additionally, under certain circumstances, a shareholder can sue on behalf of a corporation. The rights and duties of all corporate personnel will be examined later in this chapter.

The Limited Liability of Shareholders

One of the key advantages of the corporate form is the limited liability of its owners (shareholders). Corporate shareholders normally are not personally liable for the obligations of the corporation beyond the extent of their investments. In certain limited situations, however, the "corporate veil" can be pierced and liability for the corporation's obligations extended to shareholders—a concept that will be explained later in this chapter. Additionally, to enable the firm to obtain credit, shareholders in small companies sometimes voluntarily assume personal liability, as guarantors, for corporate obligations.

Corporate Taxation

Corporate profits are taxed by various levels of government. Corporations can do one of two things with corporate profits—retain them or pass them on to shareholders in the form of dividends. The corporation normally receives no tax deduction for dividends distributed to shareholders. Dividends are again taxable (except when they represent distributions of capital) to the shareholder receiving them. This double-taxation feature of the corporation is one of its major disadvantages.[1]

Profits that are not distributed are retained by the corporation. These **retained earnings,** if invested properly, will yield higher corporate profits in the future and thus cause the price of the company's stock to rise. Individual shareholders can then reap the benefits of these retained earnings in the capital gains they receive when they sell their shares.

In recent years, some U.S. corporations have been using holding companies to reduce—or at least defer—their U.S. income taxes. At its simplest, a **holding company** (sometimes referred to as a *parent company*) is a company whose business activity consists of holding shares in another company. Typically, the holding company is established in a low-tax or no-tax offshore jurisdiction. Among the best known are the Cayman Islands, Dubai, Hong Kong, Luxembourg, Monaco, and Panama.

Sometimes, a major U.S. corporation sets up an investment holding company in a low-tax offshore environment. The corporation then transfers its cash, bonds, stocks, and other investments to the holding company. In general, any profits received by the holding company on these investments are taxed at the rate of the offshore jurisdiction in which the company is registered, not the U.S. tax rates applicable to the U.S. corporation or its shareholders. Thus, deposits of cash, for example, may earn interest that is taxed at only a minimal rate. Once the profits are brought "onshore," though, they are taxed at the federal corporate income tax rate, and any payments received by the shareholders are also taxable at the full U.S. rates.

Torts and Criminal Acts

A corporation is liable for the torts committed by its agents or officers within the course and scope of their employment. This principle applies to a corporation exactly as it applies to the ordinary agency relationships, which will be discussed in Chapter 19. It follows the doctrine of *respondeat superior.*

Under modern criminal law (see Chapter 7), a corporation may also be held liable for the criminal acts of its agents and employees, provided the punishment is one that can be applied to the corporation. Although corporations cannot be imprisoned, they can be fined. (Of course, corporate directors and officers can be imprisoned, and in recent years, many have faced criminal penalties for their own actions or for the actions of employees under their supervision.)

The question in the following case was whether a corporation could be convicted for its employee's criminal negligence.

1. Congress enacted a law in 2003 that mitigated this double-taxation feature to some extent by providing a reduced federal tax rate on qualifying dividends. The Jobs Growth Tax Relief Reconciliation Act of 2003, Pub. L. No. 108-27, May 28, 2003, is codified at 26 U.S.C.A. Section 6429.

CASE 18.1 Commonwealth v. Angelo Todesca Corp.

Supreme Judicial Court of Massachusetts, 2006. 446 Mass. 128, 842 N.E.2d 930.
www.findlaw.com/11stategov/ma/maca.html[a]

• **Background and Facts** Brian Gauthier worked as a truck driver for Angelo Todesca Corporation, a trucking and paving company. During 2000, Gauthier drove a ten-wheel tri-axle dump truck, which was designated AT-56. Angelo's safety manual required its trucks to be equipped with back-up alarms, which were to sound automatically whenever the vehicles were in reverse gear. In November,

a. In the "Supreme Court Opinions" section, in the "2006" row, click on "March." When that page opens, scroll to the name of the case and click on its docket number to access the opinion.

CASE 18.1 CONTINUED Gauthier discovered that AT-56's alarm was missing. Angelo ordered a new alarm. Meanwhile, Gauthier continued to drive AT-56. On December 1, Angelo assigned Gauthier to haul asphalt to a work site in Centerville, Massachusetts. At the site, as Gauthier backed up AT-56 to dump its load, he struck a police officer who was directing traffic through the site and facing away from the truck. The officer died of his injuries. The commonwealth of Massachusetts charged Gauthier and Angelo in a Massachusetts state court with, among other wrongful acts, motor vehicle homicide. Angelo was convicted and fined $2,500. On Angelo's appeal, a state intermediate appellate court reversed Angelo's conviction. The state appealed to the Massachusetts Supreme Judicial Court, the state's highest court.

IN THE LANGUAGE OF THE COURT
***SPINA*, J. [Justice]**

* * * *

* * * [On this appeal, the] defendant maintains that a corporation never can be criminally liable for motor vehicle homicide * * * because * * * a "corporation" cannot "operate" a vehicle. *The Commonwealth, however, argues that corporate liability is necessarily vicarious [indirect, or secondary], and that a corporation can be held accountable for criminal acts committed by its agents, including negligent operation of a motor vehicle causing the death of another* * * * . [Emphasis added.]

We agree with the Commonwealth. Because a corporation is not a living person, it can act only through its agents. By the defendant's reasoning, a corporation never could be liable for any crime. A "corporation" can no more serve alcohol to minors, or bribe government officials, or falsify data on loan applications, than operate a vehicle negligently: only human agents, acting for the corporation, are capable of these actions. Nevertheless, * * * *a corporation may be criminally liable for such acts when performed by corporate employees, acting within the scope of their employment and on behalf of the corporation.* [Emphasis added.]

The defendant further contends that it cannot be found vicariously liable for the victim's death because corporate criminal liability requires criminal conduct by the agent, which is lacking in this case. Operating a truck without a back-up alarm, the defendant notes, is not a criminal act: no State or Federal statute requires that a vehicle be equipped with such a device. Although the defendant is correct that criminal conduct of an agent is necessary before criminal liability may be imputed to the corporation, it mischaracterizes the agent's conduct in this case. Gauthier's criminal act, and the conduct imputed to the defendant, was not simply backing up without an alarm, as the defendant contends; rather, the criminal conduct was Gauthier's negligent operation of the defendant's truck, resulting in the victim's death * * * . Clearly, a corporation cannot be criminally liable for acts of employee negligence that are not criminal; however, [a Massachusetts state statute] criminalizes negligence in a very specific context (the operation of a motor vehicle on a public way) and with a specific outcome (resulting in death). Furthermore, nothing in that statute requires that the negligence be based on a statutory violation; the fact that a back-up alarm is not required by statute, then, is irrelevant to the issue whether vehicular homicide committed by an employee can be imputed to the corporation. If a corporate employee violates [this statute] while engaged in corporate business that the employee has been authorized to conduct, we can see no reason why the corporation cannot be vicariously liable for the crime.

- **Decision and Remedy** *The Massachusetts Supreme Judicial Court affirmed Angelo's conviction. The court recognized that a corporation is not a "living person" and "can act only through its agents," which may include its employees. The court reasoned that if an employee commits a crime, "while engaged in corporate business that the employee has been authorized to conduct," a corporation can be held liable for the crime.*

- **What If the Facts Were Different?** *If Gauthier had been an independent contractor rather than Angelo's employee, would the result in this case have been different? Explain.*

- **The Legal Environment Dimension** *Under what circumstances might an employee's supervisor, or even a corporate officer or director, be held liable for the employee's crime?*

Corporate Sentencing Guidelines

Recall from Chapter 7 that the U.S. Sentencing Commission has created standardized sentencing guidelines for federal crimes. The commission subsequently created specific sentencing guidelines for crimes committed by corporate employees (white-collar crimes). The net effect of the guidelines has been a significant increase in the penalties for crimes committed by corporate personnel. Penalties depend on such factors as the seriousness of the offense, the amount involved, and the extent to which top company executives are implicated. Corporate lawbreakers can face fines amounting to hundreds of millions of dollars, though the guidelines allow judges to impose less severe penalties in certain circumstances.

When a company has taken substantial steps to prevent, investigate, and punish wrongdoing, such as by establishing and enforcing crime prevention standards, a court may impose less serious penalties. Many states' corporate laws now require corporations to have adequate systems for detecting and reporting misconduct that can be attributed to corporations. Corporate sentencing guidelines that became effective in 2004 require corporations to train employees on how to comply with relevant laws. Additionally, corporate directors have a fiduciary duty to prevent employee misconduct, which means that if they discover an employee has committed a crime, they have a duty to promptly report it. The Sarbanes-Oxley Act also requires corporate attorneys to report possible corporate misconduct (both civil and criminal) to officials within the corporation. (For a detailed discussion of corporate governance and compliance issues, see Chapter 28.)

Classification of Corporations

Corporations can be classified in several ways. The classification of a corporation normally depends on its location, purpose, and ownership characteristics, as described in the following subsections.

Domestic, Foreign, and Alien Corporations A corporation is referred to as a **domestic corporation** by its home state (the state in which it incorporates). A corporation formed in one state but doing business in another is referred to in the second state as a **foreign corporation.** A corporation formed in another country (say, Mexico) but doing business in the United States is referred to in the United States as an **alien corporation.**

A corporation does not have an automatic right to do business in a state other than its state of incorporation. In some instances, it must obtain a *certificate of authority* in any state in which it plans to do business. Once the certificate has been issued, the corporation generally can exercise in that state all of the powers conferred on it by its home state. If a foreign corporation does business in a state without obtaining a certificate of authority, the state can impose substantial fines and sanctions on the corporation, and sometimes even on its officers, directors, or agents.

Note that most state statutes specify certain activities, such as soliciting orders via the Internet, that are not considered "doing business" within the state. Thus, a foreign corporation normally does not need a certificate of authority to sell goods or services via the Internet or by mail.

Public and Private Corporations A public corporation is one formed by the government to meet some political or governmental purpose. Cities and towns that incorporate are common examples. In addition, many federal government organizations, such as the U.S. Postal Service, the Tennessee Valley Authority, and AMTRAK, are public corporations. Note that a public corporation is not the same as a *publicly held* corporation (often called a *public company*). A publicly held corporation is any corporation whose shares are publicly traded in a securities market, such as the New York Stock Exchange or the over-the-counter market.

In contrast to public corporations (*not* public companies), private corporations are created either wholly or in part for private benefit. Most corporations are private. Although they may serve a public purpose, as a public electric or gas utility does, they are owned by private persons rather than by the government.[2]

Nonprofit Corporations Corporations formed for purposes other than making a profit are called *nonprofit* or *not-for-profit* corporations. Private hospitals, educational institutions, charities, and religious organizations, for example, are frequently organized as nonprofit corporations. The nonprofit corporation is a convenient form of organization that allows various groups to own property and to form contracts without exposing the individual members to personal liability.

---

2. The United States Supreme Court first recognized the property rights of private corporations and clarified the distinction between public and private corporations in the landmark case *Trustees of Dartmouth College v. Woodward,* 17 U.S. (4 Wheaton) 518, 4 L.Ed. 629 (1819).

Close Corporations In terms of numbers, not size, most corporate enterprises in the United States fall into the category of close corporations. A **close corporation** is one whose shares are held by members of a family or by relatively few persons. Close corporations are also referred to as *closely held, family*, or *privately held* corporations. Usually, the members of the small group constituting a close corporation are personally known to each other. Because the number of shareholders is so small, there is no trading market for the shares.

In practice, a close corporation is often operated like a partnership. Some states have enacted special statutory provisions that apply to close corporations. These provisions expressly permit close corporations to depart significantly from certain formalities required by traditional corporation law.[3]

Additionally, a provision added to the RMBCA in 1991 gives a close corporation considerable flexibility in determining its rules of operation [RMBCA 7.32]. If all of a corporation's shareholders agree in writing, the corporation can operate without directors, bylaws, annual or special shareholders' or directors' meetings, stock certificates, or formal records of shareholders' or directors' decisions.[4]

Management of Close Corporations. A close corporation has a single shareholder or a closely knit group of shareholders, who usually hold the positions of directors and officers. Management of a close corporation resembles that of a sole proprietorship or a partnership. As a corporation, however, the firm must meet all specific legal requirements set forth in state statutes.

To prevent a majority shareholder from dominating a close corporation, the corporation may require that more than a simple majority of the directors approve any action taken by the board. Typically, this would apply only to extraordinary actions, such as changing the amount of dividends or dismissing an employee-shareholder, and not to ordinary business decisions.

Transfer of Shares in Close Corporations. By definition, a close corporation has a small number of shareholders. Thus, the transfer of one shareholder's shares to someone else can cause serious management problems. The other shareholders may find themselves required to share control with someone they do not know or like.

Suppose that three brothers, Terry, Damon, and Henry Johnson, are the only shareholders of Johnson's Car Wash, Inc. Terry and Damon do not want Henry to sell his shares to an unknown third person. To avoid this situation, the corporation could restrict the transferability of shares to outside persons. Shareholders could be required to offer their shares to the corporation or the other shareholders before selling them to an outside purchaser. In fact, a few states have statutes that prohibit the transfer of close corporation shares unless certain persons—including shareholders, family members, and the corporation—are first given the opportunity to purchase the shares for the same price.

Control of a close corporation can also be stabilized through the use of a *shareholder agreement.* A shareholder agreement can provide that when one of the original shareholders dies, her or his shares of stock in the corporation will be divided in such a way that the proportionate holdings of the survivors, and thus their proportionate control, will be maintained. Courts are generally reluctant to interfere with private agreements, including shareholder agreements.

S Corporations A close corporation that meets the qualifying requirements specified in Subchapter S of the Internal Revenue Code can operate as an **S corporation.** If a corporation has S corporation status, it can avoid the imposition of income taxes at the corporate level while retaining many of the advantages of a corporation, particularly limited liability.

Qualification Requirements for S Corporations. Among the numerous requirements for S corporation status, the following are the most important:

1. The corporation must be a domestic corporation.
2. The corporation must not be a member of an affiliated group of corporations.
3. The shareholders of the corporation must be individuals, estates, or certain trusts. Nonqualifying trusts and partnerships cannot be shareholders. Corporations can be shareholders under certain circumstances.
4. The corporation must have no more than one hundred shareholders.
5. The corporation must have only one class of stock, although all shareholders do not need to have the same voting rights.

---

3. For example, in some states (such as Maryland), a close corporation need not have a board of directors.

4. Shareholders cannot agree, however, to eliminate certain rights of shareholders, such as the right to inspect corporate books and records or the right to bring *derivative actions* (lawsuits on behalf of the corporation—see page 467).

6. No shareholder of the corporation may be a nonresident alien.

Benefits of S Corporations. At times, it is beneficial for a regular corporation to elect S corporation status. Benefits include the following:

1. When the corporation has losses, the S election allows the shareholders to use the losses to offset other taxable income.
2. When the shareholder's tax bracket is lower than the tax bracket for regular corporations, the S election causes the corporation's entire income to be taxed in the shareholder's bracket (because it is taxed as personal income), whether or not it is distributed. This is particularly attractive when the corporation wants to accumulate earnings for some future business purpose.

In the past, many close corporations opted for S corporation status to obtain these tax benefits. Today, however, the limited liability partnership and the limited liability company (discussed in Chapter 17) offer similar advantages plus additional benefits, including more flexibility in forming and operating the business. Hence, the S corporation has lost some of its appeal.

Professional Corporations Professionals such as physicians, lawyers, dentists, and accountants can incorporate. Professional corporations are typically identified by the letters *P.C.* (professional corporation), *S.C.* (service corporation), or *P.A.* (professional association). In general, the laws governing professional corporations are similar to those governing ordinary business corporations, but there are a few differences with regard to liability that deserve mention.

First, there is generally no limitation on liability for acts of malpractice or obligations incurred because of a breach of duty to a client or patient of the professional corporation. In other words, each shareholder in a professional corporation can be held liable for any malpractice liability incurred by the others within the scope of the corporate business. The reason for this rule is that professionals, in contrast to shareholders in other types of corporations, should not be allowed to avoid liability for their wrongful acts simply by incorporating. Second, in many states, professional persons are liable not only for their own negligent acts, but also for the misconduct of persons under their direct supervision who render professional services on behalf of the corporation. Third, a shareholder in a professional corporation is generally protected from contractual liability and cannot be held liable for the torts—other than malpractice or a breach of duty to clients or patients—that are committed by other professionals at the firm.

Corporate Formation

Up to this point, we have discussed some of the general characteristics of corporations. We now examine the process by which corporations come into existence. Incorporating a business is much simpler today than it was twenty years ago, and many states allow businesses to incorporate online.

One of the most common reasons for creating a corporation is the need for additional capital to finance expansion. Many of the Fortune 500 companies started as sole proprietorships or partnerships and then converted to a corporate entity. A sole proprietor in need of funds can seek partners who will bring capital with them. Although a partnership may be able to secure more funds from potential lenders than the sole proprietor could, the amount is still limited. When a firm wants significant growth, continuing to add partners can result in so many partners that the firm can no longer operate effectively. Therefore, incorporation may be the best choice for an expanding business organization because a corporation can obtain more capital by issuing shares of stock. (Corporate financing is discussed later in this chapter.)

Promotional Activities

In the past, preliminary steps were taken to organize and promote the business prior to incorporating. Contracts were made with investors and others on behalf of the future corporation. Today, however, due to the relative ease of forming a corporation in most states, persons incorporating their business rarely, if ever, engage in preliminary promotional activities. Nevertheless, it is important for businesspersons to understand that they are personally liable for all preincorporation contracts made with investors, accountants, or others on behalf of the future corporation. This personal liability continues until the corporation assumes the preincorporation contracts by *novation* (discussed in Chapter 10).

Incorporation Procedures

Exact procedures for incorporation differ among states, but the basic steps are as follows: (1) select a state of incorporation, (2) secure the corporate name, (3) prepare the articles of incorporation, and (4) file the articles of incorporation with the secretary of state. These steps are discussed in more detail in the following subsections.

Selecting the State of Incorporation The first step in the incorporation process is to select a state in which to incorporate. Because state laws differ, individuals may look for the states that offer the most advantageous tax or incorporation provisions. Another consideration is the fee that a particular state charges to incorporate as well as the annual fees and the fees for specific transactions (such as stock transfers).

Delaware has historically had the least restrictive laws, as well as provisions that favor corporate management. Consequently, many corporations, including a number of the largest, have incorporated there. Delaware's statutes permit firms to incorporate in that state and conduct business and locate their operating headquarters elsewhere. Most other states now permit this as well. Generally, though, closely held corporations, particularly those of a professional nature, incorporate in the state where their principal shareholders live and work. For reasons of convenience and cost, businesses often choose to incorporate in the state in which most of the corporation's business will be conducted.

Securing the Corporate Name The choice of a corporate name is subject to state approval to ensure against duplication or deception. State statutes usually require that the secretary of state run a check on the proposed name in the state of incorporation. In some states, the persons incorporating a firm must do the check themselves at their own expense. Specialized Internet search engines are available for checking corporate names, and many companies will perform this service for a fee. Once cleared, a name can be reserved for a short time, for a fee, pending the completion of the articles of incorporation. All states require the corporation name to include the word *Corporation (Corp.), Incorporated (Inc.), Company (Co.),* or *Limited (Ltd.).*

A new corporation's name cannot be the same as (or deceptively similar to) the name of an existing corporation doing business within the state (see Chapter 14). The name should also be one that can be used as the business's Internet domain name. Suppose that an existing corporation is named Digital Synergy, Inc. A new corporation cannot choose the name Digital Synergy Company because that name is deceptively similar to the first, and the state will be unlikely to allow it. In addition, the new firm would not want to choose the name Digital Synergy Company since it would be unable to acquire an Internet domain name using the name of the business.

If those incorporating a firm contemplate doing business in other states—or over the Internet—they need to check on existing corporate names in those states as well. Otherwise, if the firm does business under a name that is the same as or deceptively similar to an existing company's name, it may be liable for trade name infringement.

Preparing the Articles of Incorporation The primary document needed to incorporate a business is the **articles of incorporation.** The articles include basic information about the corporation and serve as a primary source of authority for its future organization and business functions. The person or persons who execute (sign) the articles are called *incorporators.* Generally, the articles of incorporation *must* include the following information [RMBCA 2.02].

1. The name of the corporation.
2. The number of shares the corporation is authorized to issue.
3. The name and address of the corporation's initial registered agent.
4. The name and address of each incorporator.

In addition, the articles *may* set forth other information, such as the names and addresses of the initial board of directors, the duration and purpose of the corporation, a par value of shares of the corporation, and any other information pertinent to the rights and duties of the corporation's shareholders and directors. Articles of incorporation vary widely depending on the jurisdiction and the size and type of the corporation. Frequently, the articles do not provide much detail about the firm's operations, which are spelled out in the company's **bylaws** (internal rules of management adopted by the corporation at its first organizational meeting).

Shares of the Corporation. The articles must specify the number of shares of stock the corporation is authorized to issue [RMBCA 2.02(a)]. For instance, a company might state that the aggregate number of shares that the corporation has the authority to issue is five thousand. Sometimes, the articles set forth the capital structure of the corporation and other relevant information concerning equity, shares, and credit.

Registered Office and Agent. The corporation must indicate the location and address of its registered office within the state. Usually, the registered office is also the principal office of the corporation. The corporation must also give the name and address of a specific person who has been designated as an *agent* and who can receive legal documents (such as orders to appear in court) on behalf of the corporation.

Incorporators. Each incorporator must be listed by name and address. The incorporators need not have any interest at all in the corporation, and sometimes signing the articles is their only duty. Many states do not have residency or age requirements for incorporators. In some states, only one incorporator is needed, but other states require as many as three. Incorporators frequently participate in the first organizational meeting of the corporation.

Duration and Purpose. A corporation has perpetual existence unless the articles state otherwise. The owners may want to prescribe a maximum duration, however, after which the corporation must formally renew its existence.

The RMBCA does not require a specific statement of purpose to be included in the articles. A corporation can be formed for any lawful purpose. Some incorporators include a general statement of purpose "to engage in any lawful act or activity," while others specify the intended business activities (such as "to engage in the production and sale of agricultural products"). The trend is toward allowing corporate articles to state that the corporation is organized for "any legal business," with no mention of specifics, to avoid the need for future amendments to the corporate articles [RMBCA 2.02(b)(2)(i), 3.01].

Some states prohibit certain licensed professionals, such as physicians or lawyers, from forming a general business corporation and require them instead to incorporate as a professional corporation (discussed previously).[5] Also, in some states, businesses in certain industries—such as banks, insurance companies, or public utilities—cannot be operated in the general corporate form and are governed by special incorporation statutes.

5. See, for example, New Jersey Statutes Annotated Titles 14A:17-1 *et seq.*

Internal Organization. The articles can describe the corporation's internal management structure, although this is usually included in the bylaws adopted after the corporation is formed. The articles of incorporation commence the corporation; the bylaws are formed after commencement by the board of directors. Bylaws cannot conflict with the incorporation statute or the articles of incorporation [RMBCA 2.06].

Under the RMBCA, shareholders may amend or repeal the bylaws. The board of directors may also amend or repeal the bylaws unless the articles of incorporation or provisions of the incorporation statute reserve this power to the shareholders exclusively [RMBCA 10.20]. Typical bylaw provisions describe such matters as voting requirements for shareholders, the election of the board of directors, the methods of replacing directors, and the manner and time of holding shareholders' and board meetings (these corporate activities will be discussed later in this chapter).

Filing the Articles with the State Once the articles of incorporation have been prepared and signed by the incorporators, they are sent to the appropriate state official, usually the secretary of state, along with the required filing fee. In most states, the secretary of state then stamps the articles "Filed" and returns a copy of the articles to the incorporators. Once this occurs, the corporation officially exists. (Note that some states issue a *certificate of incorporation,* or *corporate charter,* which is similar to articles of incorporation, representing the state's authorization for the corporation to conduct business. This procedure was typical under the unrevised MBCA.)

First Organizational Meeting to Adopt Bylaws

After incorporation, the first organizational meeting must be held. Usually, the most important function of this meeting is the adoption of bylaws—the internal rules of management for the corporation. If the articles of incorporation named the initial board of directors, then the directors, by majority vote, call the meeting to adopt the bylaws and complete the company's organization. If the articles did not name the directors (as is typical), then the incorporators hold the meeting to elect the directors, adopt bylaws, and complete the routine business of incorporation (authorizing the issuance of shares and hiring employees, for example). The business transacted depends on the requirements of the state's incorporation statute, the nature of the corporation, the provisions made in the articles, and the desires of the incorporators.

Defects in Formation and Corporate Status

The procedures for incorporation are very specific. If they are not followed precisely, others may be able to challenge the existence of the corporation. Errors in incorporation procedures can become important when, for example, a third party who is attempting to enforce a contract or bring suit for a tort injury learns of them. On the basis of improper incorporation, the plaintiff could seek to make the would-be shareholders personally liable. Additionally, when the corporation seeks to enforce a contract against a defaulting party, that party may be able to avoid liability on the ground of a defect in the incorporation procedure.

To prevent injustice, the courts will sometimes attribute corporate existence to an improperly formed corporation, as discussed below. Occasionally, a corporation may be held to exist by estoppel.

***De Jure* and *De Facto* Corporations** If a corporation has substantially complied with all conditions precedent to incorporation, a corporation is said to have *de jure* (rightful and lawful) existence. In most states and under RMBCA 2.03(b), the secretary of state's filing of the articles of incorporation is conclusive proof that all mandatory statutory provisions have been met [RMBCA 2.03(b)]. Because a *de jure* corporation is one that is properly formed, neither the state nor a third party can attack its existence.[6] If, for example, the articles listed an incorrect address for an incorporator, the corporation was improperly formed, but most courts will uphold its *de jure* status.

Sometimes, there is a defect in complying with statutory mandates—for example, the corporation failed to hold an organizational meeting. Under these circumstances, the corporation may have *de facto* (actual) status, meaning that it will be treated as a legal corporation despite the defect in its formation. A corporation with *de facto* status cannot be challenged by third persons (only by the state). In other words, the shareholders of a *de facto* corporation are still protected by limited liability (provided they are unaware of the defect). The following elements are required for *de facto* status:

1. There must be a state statute under which the corporation can be validly incorporated.
2. The parties must have made a good faith attempt to comply with the statute.
3. The enterprise must already have undertaken to do business as a corporation.

Corporation by Estoppel If a business holds itself out to others as being a corporation but has made no attempt to incorporate, the firm normally will be estopped (prevented) from denying corporate status in a lawsuit by a third party. This usually occurs when a third party contracts with an entity that claims to be a corporation but has not filed articles of incorporation. It can also occur when a third party contracts with a person claiming to be an agent of a corporation that does not in fact exist. When justice requires, the courts treat an alleged corporation as if it were an actual corporation for the purpose of determining the rights and liabilities in particular circumstances. A corporation by estoppel is thus determined by the situation. Recognition of its corporate status does not extend beyond the resolution of the problem at hand.

Corporate Powers

When a corporation is created, the express and implied powers necessary to achieve its purpose also come into existence. The express powers of a corporation are found in its articles of incorporation, in the law of the state of incorporation, and in the state and federal constitutions. Corporate bylaws and the resolutions of the corporation's board of directors also grant or restrict certain powers.

The following order of priority is used if a conflict arises among the various documents involving a corporation:

1. U.S. Constitution.
2. Constitution of the state of incorporation.
3. State statutes.
4. Articles of incorporation.
5. Bylaws.
6. Resolutions of the board of directors.

Certain implied powers arise when a corporation is created. Barring express constitutional, statutory, or charter prohibitions, the corporation has the implied power to perform all acts reasonably appropriate and necessary to accomplish its corporate purposes. For this reason, a corporation has the implied power to borrow funds within certain limits, to lend funds, and to extend credit to those with whom it has a legal or contractual relationship.

6. There is an exception: a few states allow state authorities, in a *quo warranto* proceeding, to bring an action against the corporation for noncompliance with a condition subsequent to incorporation. This might occur if the corporation fails to file annual reports, for example.

To borrow funds, the corporation acts through its board of directors to authorize the loan. Most often, the president or chief executive officer of the corporation will execute the necessary papers on behalf of the corporation. Corporate officers such as these have the implied power to bind the corporation in matters directly connected with the *ordinary* business affairs of the enterprise. A corporate officer does not have the authority to bind the corporation to an action that will greatly affect the corporate purpose or undertaking, such as the sale of substantial corporate assets, however.

Ultra Vires Doctrine

The term ***ultra vires*** means "beyond the power." In corporate law, acts of a corporation that are beyond its express or implied powers are *ultra vires* acts. Most cases dealing with *ultra vires* acts have involved contracts made for unauthorized purposes. For example, Suarez is the chief executive officer of SOS Plumbing, Inc. He enters into a contract with Carlini for the purchase of twenty cases of brandy. It is difficult to see how this contract is reasonably related to the conduct and furtherance of the corporation's stated purpose of providing plumbing installation and services. Hence, a court would probably find the contract to be *ultra vires.*

In some states, when a contract is entirely executory (not yet performed by either party), either party can use a defense of *ultra vires* to prevent enforcement of the contract. Under Section 3.04 of the RMBCA, the shareholders can seek an injunction from a court to prevent the corporation from engaging in *ultra vires* acts. The attorney general in the state of incorporation can also bring an action to obtain an injunction against the *ultra vires* transactions or to institute dissolution proceedings against the corporation on the basis of *ultra vires* acts. The corporation or its shareholders (on behalf of the corporation) can seek damages from the officers and directors who were responsible for the *ultra vires* acts.

SECTION 3 Piercing the Corporate Veil

Occasionally, the owners use a corporate entity to perpetrate a fraud, circumvent the law, or in some other way accomplish an illegitimate objective. In these situations, the court will ignore the corporate structure and **pierce the corporate veil,** exposing the shareholders to personal liability [RMBCA 2.04]. Generally, when the corporate privilege is abused for personal benefit or when the corporate business is treated so carelessly that the corporation and the controlling shareholder are no longer separate entities, the court will require the owner to assume personal liability to creditors for the corporation's debts.

In short, when the facts show that great injustice would result from the use of a corporation to avoid individual responsibility, a court will look behind the corporate structure to the individual shareholder. The following are some of the factors that frequently cause the courts to pierce the corporate veil:

1. A party is tricked or misled into dealing with the corporation rather than the individual.
2. The corporation is set up never to make a profit or always to be insolvent, or it is too "thinly" capitalized—that is, it has insufficient capital at the time it is formed to meet its prospective debts or potential liabilities.
3. Statutory corporate formalities, such as holding required corporation meetings, are not followed.
4. Personal and corporate interests are mixed together, or **commingled,** to the extent that the corporation has no separate identity.

In the following case, when a corporation's creditors sought payment of its debts, the owners took for themselves the small value in the business, filed a bankruptcy petition for the firm, and incorporated under a new name to continue the business. Could the court recover the business assets from the new corporation for distribution to the original firm's creditors?

CASE 18.2 In re Aqua Clear Technologies, Inc.

United States Bankruptcy Court, Southern District of Florida, 2007. 361 Bankr. 567.

• **Background and Facts** Harvey and Barbara Jacobson owned Aqua Clear Technologies, Inc., a small Florida business that installed and serviced home water softening systems. Barbara was Aqua's president, and Sharon, the Jacobsons' daughter, was an officer, but neither participated in the business.

CASE 18.2 CONTINUED Although Harvey controlled the day-to-day operations, he was not an Aqua officer, director, or employee, but an independent contractor in service to it. Aqua had no compensation agreement with the Jacobsons. Instead, whenever Harvey decided that there were sufficient funds, they took funds out of the business for their personal expenses, including the maintenance of their home and payment for their cars, health-insurance premiums, and charges on their credit cards. In December 2004, Aqua filed a bankruptcy petition in a federal bankruptcy court. Three weeks later, Harvey incorporated Discount Water Services, Inc., and continued to service water softening systems for Aqua's customers. Discount appropriated Aqua's equipment and inventory without a formal transfer and advertised Aqua's phone number as Discount's own. Kenneth Welt, Aqua's trustee, initiated a proceeding against Discount, seeking, among other things, to recover Aqua's assets. The trustee contended that Discount was Aqua's "alter ego." (An *alter ego* is the double of something—in this case, the original company.)

IN THE LANGUAGE OF THE COURT
***JOHN K. OLSON*, Bankruptcy Judge.**

* * * *

* * * To disregard the corporate entity form and find that one entity is the alter ego of another, three elements must be established under Florida law:

a. Domination and control of the corporation to such an extent that it has no independent existence;
b. That the corporate form was used fraudulently or for an improper purpose; and
c. That the fraudulent or improper use of the form proximately caused the creditor's injury.

* * * *

The Debtor and Defendant Discount Water were in substantially the same business. They used the same telephone number. They operated from the same business address. They serviced the same geographic area and many of the same customers. Until April 27, 2005, when Barbara Jacobson resigned as President of Discount Water, she was the only President either the Debtor or Discount Water had and a director of both. The Debtor and Discount Water had identical officers and directors. *The Court may presume fraud when a transfer occurs between two corporations controlled by the same officers and directors.* There is no credible evidence before the Court that suggests that Discount Water is anything other than a continuation of the Debtor's business under a new name. [Emphasis added.]

Perhaps the clearest piece of evidence demonstrating the identity of the Debtor and Discount Water is in the following letter sent to Aqua Clear's health insurance carrier:

* * * *

We are changing the name of Aqua Clear Technologies Inc., * * * to DISCOUNT WATER SERVICES INC. Please change your records as soon as possible.

* * * *

Clearly, the author of the letter is declaring that Discount Water Services and the Debtor are one and the same.

* * * The evidence makes clear that the Jacobsons created Discount Water simply to continue the business of the Debtor using the Debtor's assets. The Jacobsons divested the Debtor of such assets as it retained at the time of its bankruptcy filing, motivated in large part by a desire to thwart the collection efforts of * * * judgment creditor[s] * * * . The Jacobsons thus delivered an empty shell of the Debtor to the bankruptcy court in contravention of their duty to their creditors.

*When conducting an analysis concerning a fraud to avoid the liabilities of a predecessor, * * * the bottom line question is whether each entity has run its own race, or whether there has been a relay-style passing of the baton from one to the other.* Here, the assets transferred from the Debtor to Discount Water were in exchange for no bona fide consideration, let alone for reasonably equivalent value. * * * Discount Water took the baton passed by the Debtor and has run with it and in the process has become the Debtor's alter ego. Discount Water is therefore liable to the Debtor's creditors for all of the Debtor's liabilities * * * . [Emphasis added.]

CASE CONTINUES

CASE 18.2 CONTINUED

• **Decision and Remedy** *The court issued a judgment against Discount, and in the trustee's favor, for $108,732.64, which represented the amount of the claims listed in Aqua's bankruptcy schedules. The court also agreed to add the administrative expenses and all other claims allowed against Aqua once those amounts were determined.*

• **The Ethical Dimension** *Was the Jacobsons' disregard for corporate formalities unethical? Why or why not?*

• **The Global Dimension** *If the scope of the Jacobsons' business had been global, should the court have issued a different judgment? Explain.*

The Commingling of Personal and Corporate Assets

The potential for corporate assets to be used for personal benefit is especially great in a close corporation, in which the shares are held by a single person or by only a few individuals, usually family members. In such a situation, the separate status of the corporate entity and the sole shareholder (or family-member shareholders) must be carefully preserved. Certain practices invite trouble for the one-person or family-owned corporation: the commingling of corporate and personal funds; the failure to remit taxes, including payroll and sales taxes; and the shareholders' continuous personal use of corporate property (for example, vehicles).

For example, Donald Park incorporated three sports companies—SSP, SSI, and SSII. His mother was the president of SSP and SSII but did not participate in their operations. Park handled most of the corporations' activities out of his apartment and drew funds from their accounts as needed to pay his personal expenses. None of the three corporations had any employees, issued stock or paid dividends, maintained corporate records, or followed other corporate formalities. Park—misrepresenting himself as the president of SSP and the vice president of SSII—obtained loans on behalf of SSP from Dimmitt & Owens Financial, Inc. When the loans were not paid, Dimmitt filed a suit in a federal district court, seeking, among other things, to impose personal liability on Park. Because Park had commingled corporate funds with his personal funds and failed to follow corporate formalities, the court "pierced the corporate veil" and held him personally responsible for the debt.[7]

Loans to the Corporation

Corporation laws usually do not specifically prohibit a shareholder from lending funds to her or his corporation. When an officer, director, or majority shareholder lends the corporation funds and takes back security in the form of corporate assets, however, the courts will scrutinize the transaction closely. Any such transaction must be made in good faith and for fair value.

SECTION 4 Directors, Officers, and Shareholders

Corporate directors, officers, and shareholders all play different roles within the corporate entity. Sometimes, actions that may benefit the corporation as a whole do not coincide with the separate interests of the individuals making up the corporation. In such situations, it is important to know the rights and duties of all participants in the corporate enterprise, and the ways in which conflicts among corporate participants are resolved.

Role of Directors

The board of directors is the ultimate authority in every corporation. Directors have responsibility for all policymaking decisions necessary to the management of all corporate affairs. Just as shareholders cannot act individually to bind the corporation, the directors must act as a body in carrying out routine corporate business. The board selects and removes the corporate officers, determines the capital structure of the corporation, and declares dividends. Each director has one vote, and customarily the majority rules. The general areas of responsibility of the board of directors are shown in Exhibit 18–1.

Directors are sometimes inappropriately characterized as *agents* because they act on behalf of the corporation. No individual director, however, can act as an agent to bind the corporation; and as a group, directors collectively control the corporation in a way that no agent is able to control a principal. In addition, although

7. *Dimmitt & Owens Financial, Inc. v. Superior Sports Products, Inc.*, 196 F.Supp.2d 731 (N.D.Ill. 2002).

EXHIBIT 18–1 • Directors' Management Responsibilities

Authorize Major Corporate Policy Decisions	Select and Remove Corporate Officers and Other Managerial Employees, and Determine Their Compensation	Make Financial Decisions
Examples: —Oversee major contract negotiations and management-labor negotiations. —Initiate negotiations on sale or lease of corporate assets outside the regular course of business. —Decide whether to pursue new product lines or business opportunities.	*Examples:* —Search for and hire corporate executives and determine the elements of their compensation packages, including stock options. —Supervise managerial employees and make decisions regarding their termination.	*Examples:* —Make decisions regarding the issuance of authorized shares and bonds. —Decide when to declare dividends to be paid to shareholders.

directors occupy positions of trust and control over the corporation, they are not *trustees* because they do not hold title to property for the use and benefit of others.

Few qualifications are required for directors. Only a handful of states impose minimum age and residency requirements. A director may be a shareholder, but that is not necessary (unless the articles of incorporation or bylaws require ownership).

Election of Directors Subject to statutory limitations, the number of directors is set forth in the corporation's articles or bylaws. Historically, the minimum number of directors has been three, but today many states permit fewer. Normally, the incorporators appoint the first board of directors at the time the corporation is created, or the corporation itself names the directors in the articles. The initial board serves until the first annual shareholders' meeting. Subsequent directors are elected by a majority vote of the shareholders.

A director usually serves for a term of one year—from annual meeting to annual meeting. Longer and staggered terms are permissible under most state statutes. A common practice is to elect one-third of the board members each year for a three-year term. In this way, there is greater management continuity.

Removal of Directors. A director can be removed *for cause*—that is, for failing to perform a required duty—either as specified in the articles or bylaws or by shareholder action. Even the board of directors itself may be given power to remove a director for cause, subject to shareholder review. In most states, a director cannot be removed without cause unless the shareholders have reserved the right to do so at the time of election.

Vacancies on the Board of Directors. Vacancies can occur on the board of directors because of death or resignation or when a new position is created through amendment of the articles or bylaws. In these situations, either the shareholders or the board itself can fill the position, depending on state law or on the provisions of the bylaws. Note, however, that even when the bylaws appear to authorize an election, a court can invalidate an election if the directors were attempting to diminish the shareholders' influence in it.

For example, the bylaws of Liquid Audio, a Delaware corporation, authorized a board of five directors. Two directors on the board were elected each year. Another company had offered to buy all of Liquid Audio's stock, but the board of directors rejected this offer. An election was coming up, and the directors feared that the shareholders would elect new directors who would go through with the sale. The directors therefore amended the bylaws to increase the number of directors to seven, thereby diminishing the shareholders' influence in the vote. The shareholders filed an action challenging the election. The Delaware Supreme Court ruled that the directors' action was illegal because they had attempted to diminish the shareholders' right to vote effectively in an election of directors.[8]

8. *MM Companies, Inc. v. Liquid Audio, Inc.*, 813 A.2d 1118 (Del.Sup.Ct. 2003).

Compensation of Directors In the past, corporate directors rarely were compensated, but today they are often paid at least nominal sums and may receive more substantial compensation in large corporations because of the time, work, effort, and especially risk involved. Most states permit the corporate articles or bylaws to authorize compensation for directors. In fact, the Revised Model Business Corporation Act (RMBCA) states that unless the articles or bylaws provide otherwise, the board of directors may set their own compensation [RMBCA 8.11]. Directors also gain through indirect benefits, such as business contacts and prestige, and other rewards, such as stock options.

In many corporations, directors are also chief corporate officers (president or chief executive officer, for example) and receive compensation in their managerial positions. A director who is also an officer of the corporation is referred to as an **inside director,** whereas a director who does not hold a management position is an **outside director.** Typically, a corporation's board of directors includes both inside and outside directors.

Board of Directors' Meetings The board of directors conducts business by holding formal meetings with recorded minutes. The dates of regular meetings are usually established in the articles or bylaws or by board resolution, and no further notice is customarily required. Special meetings can be called, with notice sent to all directors. Today, most states allow directors to participate in board of directors' meetings from remote locations via telephone or Web conferencing, provided that all the directors can simultaneously hear each other during the meeting [RMBCA 8.20].

Unless the articles of incorporation or bylaws specify a greater number, a majority of the board of directors normally constitutes a quorum [RMBCA 8.24]. (A **quorum** is the minimum number of members of a body of officials or other group that must be present for business to be validly transacted.) Some state statutes specifically allow corporations to set a quorum as less than a majority but not less than one-third of the directors.[9]

Once a quorum is present, the directors transact business and vote on issues affecting the corporation. Each director present at the meeting has one vote.[10] Ordinary matters generally require a simple majority vote; certain extraordinary issues may require a greater-than-majority vote. In other words, the affirmative vote of a majority of the directors present at a meeting binds the board of directors with regard to most decisions.

Rights of Directors A corporate director must have certain rights to function properly in that position. The *right to participation* means that directors are entitled to participate in all board of directors' meetings and have a right to be notified of these meetings. As mentioned earlier, the dates of regular board meetings are usually preestablished and no notice of these meetings is required. If special meetings are called, however, notice is required unless waived by the director [RMBCA 8.23].

A director also has a *right of inspection,* which means that each director can access the corporation's books and records, facilities, and premises. Inspection rights are essential for directors to make informed decisions and to exercise the necessary supervision over corporate officers and employees. This right of inspection is virtually absolute and cannot be restricted (by the articles, bylaws, or any act of the board of directors).

When a director becomes involved in litigation by virtue of her or his position or actions, the director may also have a *right to indemnification* (reimbursement) for the legal costs, fees, and damages incurred. Most states allow corporations to indemnify and purchase liability insurance for corporate directors [RMBCA 8.51].

Committees of the Board of Directors

When a board of directors has a large number of members and must deal with a myriad of complex business issues, meetings can become unwieldy. Therefore, the boards of large, publicly held corporations typically create committees, appoint directors to serve on individual committees, and delegate certain tasks to these committees. Committees focus on individual subjects and increase the efficiency of the board. The most common types of committees include the following:

1. *Executive committee.* The board members often elect an executive committee of directors to handle the interim management decisions between board of directors' meetings. The executive committee is limited to making management deci-

9. See, for example, Delaware Code Annotated Title 8, Section 141(b); and New York Business Corporation Law, Section 707.

10. Except in Louisiana, which allows a director to vote by proxy under certain circumstances.

sions about ordinary business matters and conducting preliminary investigations into proposals. It cannot declare dividends, authorize the issuance of shares, amend the bylaws, or initiate any actions that require shareholder approval.

2. *Audit committee.* The audit committee is responsible for the selection, compensation, and oversight of the independent public accountants who audit the corporation's financial records. The Sarbanes-Oxley Act of 2002 requires all publicly held corporations to have an audit committee.
3. *Nominating committee.* This committee chooses the candidates for the board of directors that management wishes to submit to the shareholders in the next election. The committee cannot select directors to fill vacancies on the board, however [RMBCA 8.25].
4. *Compensation committee.* The compensation committee reviews and decides the salaries, bonuses, stock options, and other benefits that are given to the corporation's top executives. The committee may also determine the compensation of directors.
5. *Litigation committee.* This committee decides whether the corporation should pursue requests by shareholders to file a lawsuit against some party that has allegedly harmed the corporation. The committee members investigate the allegations and weigh the costs and benefits of litigation.

In addition to appointing committees, the board of directors can also delegate some of its functions to corporate officers. In doing so, the board is not relieved of its overall responsibility for directing the affairs of the corporation. Instead, corporate officers and managerial personnel are empowered to make decisions relating to ordinary, daily corporate activities within well-defined guidelines.

Corporate Officers and Executives

Officers and other executive employees are hired by the board of directors. At a minimum, most corporations have a president, one or more vice presidents, a secretary, and a treasurer. In most states, an individual can hold more than one office, such as president and secretary, and can be both an officer and a director of the corporation. In addition to carrying out the duties articulated in the bylaws, corporate and managerial officers act as agents of the corporation, and the ordinary rules of agency (discussed in Chapter 19) normally apply to their employment.

Corporate officers and other high-level managers are employees of the company, so their rights are defined by employment contracts. Regardless of the terms of an employment contract, however, the board of directors normally can remove a corporate officer at any time with or without cause—although the officer may then seek damages from the corporation for breach of contract.

The duties of corporate officers are the same as those of directors because both groups are involved in decision making and are in similar positions of control. Hence, officers and directors are viewed as having the same fiduciary duties of care and loyalty in their conduct of corporate affairs, a subject to which we now turn.

Duties and Liabilities of Directors and Officers

Directors and officers are deemed to be fiduciaries of the corporation because their relationship with the corporation and its shareholders is one of trust and confidence. As fiduciaries, directors and officers owe ethical—and legal—duties to the corporation and the shareholders as a whole. These fiduciary duties include the duty of care and the duty of loyalty.

Duty of Care Directors and officers must exercise due care in performing their duties. The standard of *due care* has been variously described in judicial decisions and codified in many state corporation codes. Generally, directors and officers are required to act in good faith, to exercise the care that an ordinarily prudent person would exercise in similar circumstances, and to do what they believe is in the best interests of the corporation [RMBCA 8.30(a), 8.42(a)]. Directors and officers whose failure to exercise due care results in harm to the corporation or its shareholders can be held liable for negligence (unless the business judgment rule applies).

Duty to Make Informed and Reasonable Decisions. Directors and officers are expected to be informed on corporate matters and to conduct a reasonable investigation of the situation before making a decision. This means that they must do what is necessary to keep adequately informed: attend meetings and presentations, ask for information from those who have it, read reports, and review other written materials. In other words, directors and officers must investigate, study, and discuss matters and evaluate alternatives before making a decision. They cannot decide on the spur of the moment without adequate research.

Although directors and officers are expected to act in accordance with their own knowledge and training, they are also normally entitled to rely on information given to them by certain other persons. Most states and Section 8.30(b) of the RMBCA allow a director to make decisions in reliance on information furnished by competent officers or employees, professionals such as attorneys and accountants, and committees of the board of directors (on which the director does not serve). The reliance must be in good faith, of course, to insulate a director from liability if the information later proves to be inaccurate or unreliable.

Duty to Exercise Reasonable Supervision. Directors are also expected to exercise a reasonable amount of supervision when they delegate work to corporate officers and employees. Suppose that Dale, a corporate bank director, fails to attend any board of directors' meetings for five years. In addition, Dale never inspects any of the corporate books or records and generally fails to supervise the efforts of the bank president and the loan committee. Meanwhile, Brennan, the bank president, who is a corporate officer, makes various improper loans and permits large overdrafts. In this situation, Dale (the corporate director) can be held liable to the corporation for losses resulting from the unsupervised actions of the bank president and the loan committee.

Dissenting Directors. Directors are expected to attend board of directors' meetings, and their votes should be entered into the minutes. Sometimes, an individual director disagrees with the majority's vote (which becomes an act of the board of directors). Unless a dissent is entered in the minutes, the director is presumed to have assented. If a decision later leads to the directors being held liable for mismanagement, dissenting directors are rarely held individually liable to the corporation. For this reason, a director who is absent from a given meeting sometimes registers with the secretary of the board a dissent to actions taken at the meeting.

The Business Judgment Rule. Directors and officers are expected to exercise due care and to use their best judgment in guiding corporate management, but they are not insurers of business success. Under the **business judgment rule,** a corporate director or officer will not be liable to the corporation or to its shareholders for honest mistakes of judgment and bad business decisions. Courts give significant deference to the decisions of corporate directors and officers, and consider the reasonableness of a decision at the time it was made, without the benefit of hindsight. Thus, corporate decision makers are not subjected to second-guessing by shareholders or others in the corporation.

The business judgment rule will apply as long as the director or officer (1) took reasonable steps to become informed about the matter, (2) had a rational basis for his or her decision, and (3) did not have a conflict of interest between his or her personal interest and that of the corporation. In fact, unless there is evidence of bad faith, fraud, or a clear breach of fiduciary duties, most courts will apply the rule and protect directors and officers who make bad business decisions from liability for those choices. Consequently, if there is a reasonable basis for a business decision, a court is unlikely to interfere with that decision, even if the corporation suffers as a result.

Duty of Loyalty *Loyalty* can be defined as faithfulness to one's obligations and duties. In the corporate context, the duty of loyalty requires directors and officers to subordinate their personal interests to the welfare of the corporation.

For example, directors may not use corporate funds or confidential corporate information for personal advantage. Similarly, they must refrain from putting their personal interests above those of the corporation. For instance, a director should not oppose a transaction that is in the corporation's best interest simply because pursuing it may cost the director her or his position. Cases dealing with the duty of loyalty typically involve one or more of the following:

1. Competing with the corporation.
2. Usurping (taking personal advantage of) a corporate opportunity.
3. Having an interest that conflicts with the interest of the corporation.
4. Engaging in *insider trading* (using information that is not public to make a profit trading securities, as discussed in Chapter 28).
5. Authorizing a corporate transaction that is detrimental to minority shareholders.
6. Selling control over the corporation.

The following classic case illustrates the conflict that can arise between a corporate official's personal interest and his or her duty of loyalty.

CASE 18.3 Guth v. Loft, Inc.

Supreme Court of Delaware, 1939. 23 Del.Ch. 255, 5 A.2d 503.

• **Background and Facts** Loft, Inc., made and sold candies, syrups, beverages, and food from its offices and plant in Long Island City, New York. Loft operated 115 retail outlets in several states and also sold its products wholesale. Charles Guth was Loft's president. Guth and his family owned Grace Company, which made syrups for soft drinks in a plant in Baltimore, Maryland. Coca-Cola Company supplied Loft with cola syrup. Unhappy with what he felt was Coca-Cola's high price, Guth entered into an agreement with Roy Megargel to acquire the trademark and formula for Pepsi-Cola and form Pepsi-Cola Corporation. Neither Guth nor Megargel could finance the new venture, however, and Grace was insolvent. Without the knowledge of Loft's board, Guth used Loft's capital, credit, facilities, and employees to further the Pepsi enterprise. At Guth's direction, Loft made the concentrate for the syrup, which was sent to Grace to add sugar and water. Loft charged Grace for the concentrate but allowed forty months' credit. Grace charged Pepsi for the syrup but also granted substantial credit. Grace sold the syrup to Pepsi's customers, including Loft, which paid on delivery or within thirty days. Loft also paid for Pepsi's advertising. Finally, losing profits at its stores as a result of switching from Coca-Cola, Loft filed a suit in a Delaware state court against Guth, Grace, and Pepsi, seeking their Pepsi stock and an accounting. The court entered a judgment in the plaintiff's favor. The defendants appealed to the Delaware Supreme Court.

IN THE LANGUAGE OF THE COURT

***LAYTON*, Chief Justice, delivering the opinion of the Court:**

* * * *

Corporate officers and directors are not permitted to use their position of trust and confidence to further their private interests. * * * They stand in a fiduciary relation to the corporation and its stockholders. A public policy, existing through the years, and derived from a profound knowledge of human characteristics and motives, has established *a rule that demands of a corporate officer or director, peremptorily [not open for debate] and inexorably [unavoidably], the most scrupulous observance of his duty, not only affirmatively to protect the interests of the corporation committed to his charge, but also to refrain from doing anything that would work injury to the corporation* * * * . The rule that requires an undivided and unselfish loyalty to the corporation demands that there shall be no conflict between duty and self-interest. [Emphasis added.]

* * * *

* * * *If there is presented to a corporate officer or director a business opportunity which the corporation is financially able to undertake [that] is* * * * *in the line of the corporation's business and is of practical advantage to it* * * * *and, by embracing the opportunity, the self-interest of the officer or director will be brought into conflict with that of his corporation, the law will not permit him to seize the opportunity for himself.* * * * In such circumstances, * * * the corporation may elect to claim all of the benefits of the transaction for itself, and the law will impress a trust in favor of the corporation upon the property, interests and profits so acquired. [Emphasis added.]

* * * *

* * * The appellants contend that no conflict of interest between Guth and Loft resulted from his acquirement and exploitation of the Pepsi-Cola opportunity [and] that the acquisition did not place Guth in competition with Loft * * * . [In this case, however,] Guth was Loft, and Guth was Pepsi. He absolutely controlled Loft. His authority over Pepsi was supreme. As Pepsi, he created and controlled the supply of Pepsi-Cola syrup, and he determined the price and the terms. What he offered, as Pepsi, he had the power, as Loft, to accept. Upon any consideration of human characteristics and motives, he created a conflict between self-interest and duty. He made himself the judge in his own cause. * * * Moreover, a reasonable probability of injury to Loft resulted from the situation forced upon it. Guth was in the same position to impose his terms upon Loft as had been the Coca-Cola Company.

* * * The facts and circumstances demonstrate that Guth's appropriation of the Pepsi-Cola opportunity to himself placed him in a competitive position with Loft with respect to a

CASE CONTINUES

CASE 18.3 CONTINUED

commodity essential to it, thereby rendering his personal interests incompatible with the superior interests of his corporation; and this situation was accomplished, not openly and with his own resources, but secretly and with the money and facilities of the corporation which was committed to his protection.

• **Decision and Remedy** *The Delaware Supreme Court upheld the judgment of the lower court. The state supreme court was "convinced that the opportunity to acquire the Pepsi-Cola trademark and formula, goodwill and business belonged to [Loft], and that Guth, as its President, had no right to appropriate the opportunity to himself."*

• **Impact of This Case on Today's Law** *This early Delaware decision was one of the first to set forth a test for determining when a corporate officer or director has breached the duty of loyalty. The test has two basic parts—whether the opportunity was reasonably related to the corporation's line of business, and whether the corporation was financially able to undertake the opportunity. The court also considered whether the corporation had an interest or expectancy in the opportunity and recognized that when the corporation had "no interest or expectancy, the officer or director is entitled to treat the opportunity as his own."*

• **What If the Facts Were Different?** *Suppose that Loft's board of directors had approved Pepsi-Cola's use of its personnel and equipment. Would the court's decision have been different? Discuss.*

Conflicts of Interest Corporate directors often have many business affiliations, and a director may sit on the board of more than one corporation. Of course, directors are precluded from entering into or supporting businesses that operate in direct competition with corporations on whose boards they serve. Their fiduciary duty requires them to make a full disclosure of any potential conflicts of interest that might arise in any corporate transaction [RMBCA 8.60].

Sometimes, a corporation enters into a contract or engages in a transaction in which an officer or director has a personal interest. The director or officer must make a *full disclosure* of that interest and must abstain from voting on the proposed transaction.

For example, Ballo Corporation needs office space. Stephan Colson, one of its five directors, owns the building adjoining the corporation's headquarters. He negotiates a lease with Ballo for the space, making a full disclosure to Ballo and the other four directors. The lease arrangement is fair and reasonable, and it is unanimously approved by the other members of the corporation's board of directors. Under these circumstances, the contract is valid. The rule is one of reason; otherwise, directors would be prevented from ever having financial dealings with the corporations they serve.

State statutes set different standards for corporate contracts. Generally, though, a contract will not be voidable if (1) it was fair and reasonable to the corporation at the time it was made, (2) there was a full disclosure of the interest of the officers or directors involved in the transaction, and (3) the contract was approved by a majority of the disinterested directors or shareholders [RMBCA 8.62].

Liability of Directors and Officers Directors and officers are exposed to liability on many fronts. They can be liable for negligence in certain circumstances, as previously discussed. Corporate directors and officers may be held liable for the crimes and torts committed by themselves or by corporate employees under their supervision. Additionally, if shareholders perceive that the corporate directors are not acting in the best interests of the corporation, they may sue the directors, in what is called a *shareholder's derivative suit,* on behalf of the corporation. (This type of action will be discussed later in this chapter, in the context of shareholders' rights.) In addition, directors and officers can be held personally liable under a number of statutes, such as statutes enacted to protect consumers or the environment (see Chapters 23 and 24). *Concept Summary 18.1* provides a review of the duties and liabilities of directors and officers.

The Role of Shareholders

The acquisition of a share of stock makes a person an owner of and a shareholder in a corporation.

CONCEPT SUMMARY 18.1
Duties and Liabilities of Directors and Officers

Aspect	Description
DUTIES OF DIRECTORS AND OFFICERS	1. *Duty of care*—Directors and officers are obligated to act in good faith, to use prudent business judgment in the conduct of corporate affairs, and to act in the corporation's best interests. If a director or officer fails to exercise this duty of care, he or she may be answerable to the corporation and to the shareholders for breaching the duty. The *business judgment rule* immunizes a director from liability for a corporate decision as long as it was within the power of the corporation and the authority of the director to make and was an informed, reasonable, and loyal decision.
	2. *Duty of loyalty*—Directors and officers have a fiduciary duty to subordinate their own interests to those of the corporation in matters relating to the corporation.
	3. *Conflicts of interest*—To fulfill their duty of loyalty, directors and officers must make a full disclosure of any potential conflicts between their personal interests and those of the corporation.
LIABILITIES OF DIRECTORS AND OFFICERS	Corporate directors and officers are personally liable for their own torts and crimes (when not protected under the business judgment rule). Additionally, they may be held personally liable for the torts and crimes committed by corporate personnel under their direct supervision (see Chapter 7).

Shareholders own the corporation but have no right to manage it. Basically, the shareholders' ownership control is limited to voting to elect or remove members of the board of directors and deciding whether to approve fundamental changes in the corporation. Shareholders are not agents of the corporation, nor do they have legal title to the corporation's property, such as its buildings and equipment: they simply have an *equitable* (ownership) interest in the firm.

Ordinarily, corporate officers and other employees owe no direct duty to individual shareholders (unless some contract or special relationship exists between them in addition to the corporate relationship). The officers' duty is to act in the best interests of the corporation and its shareholder-owners *as a whole.* In addition, as you will read later in this chapter, controlling shareholders owe a fiduciary duty to minority shareholders.

In this section, we look at the powers of shareholders, which may be established in the articles of incorporation and under the state's general corporation law.

Shareholders' Powers Shareholders must approve fundamental changes affecting the corporation before the changes can be implemented. Hence, shareholder approval normally is required to amend the articles of incorporation or bylaws, to conduct a merger or dissolve the corporation, and to sell all or substantially all of the corporation's assets. Shareholder approval may also be requested (though it is not required) for certain other actions, such as to approve an independent auditor.

Shareholders also have the power to vote to elect or remove members of the board of directors. As described earlier, the first board of directors is either named in the articles of incorporation or chosen by the incorporators to serve until the first shareholders' meeting. From that time on, selection and retention of directors are exclusively shareholder functions.

Directors usually serve their full terms; if the shareholders judge them unsatisfactory, they are simply not reelected. Shareholders have the inherent power, however, to remove a director from office *for cause* (breach of duty or misconduct) by a majority vote.[11] As noted earlier in this chapter, some state statutes (and some articles of incorporation) permit removal of directors

11. A director can often demand court review of removal for cause, however.

without cause by the vote of a majority of the shareholders entitled to vote.[12]

Shareholders' Meetings Shareholders' meetings must occur at least annually. In addition, special meetings can be called to deal with urgent matters. A corporation must notify its shareholders of the date, time, and place of an annual or special shareholders' meeting at least ten days, but not more than sixty days, before the meeting date [RMBCA 7.05].[13] (The date and time of the annual meeting can be specified in the bylaws, however.) Notices of special meetings must include a statement of the purpose of the meeting; business transacted at a special meeting is limited to that purpose.

Proxies. It usually is not practical for owners of only a few shares of stock of publicly traded corporations to attend a shareholders' meeting. Therefore, the law allows stockholders to either vote in person or appoint another person as their agent to vote their shares at the meeting. The signed appointment form or electronic transmission authorizing an agent to vote the shares is called a **proxy** (from the Latin *procurare,* meaning "to manage, take care of"). Management often solicits proxies, but any person can solicit proxies to concentrate voting power. Proxies have been used by groups of shareholders as a device for taking over a corporation. Proxies normally are revocable (that is, they can be withdrawn), unless they are specifically designated as irrevocable. Under RMBCA 7.22(c), proxies last for eleven months, unless the proxy agreement mandates a longer period.

Proxy Materials and Shareholder Proposals. When shareholders want to change a company policy, they can put their ideas up for a shareholder vote. They do this by submitting a shareholder proposal to the board of directors and asking the board to include the proposal in the proxy materials that are sent to all shareholders before meetings. (See this chapter's *Contemporary Legal Debates* feature on pages 462 and 463 for a discussion of a proposal that would increase shareholders' access to the proxy process.)

The Securities and Exchange Commission (SEC), which regulates the purchase and sale of securities (see Chapter 28), has special provisions relating to proxies and shareholder proposals. SEC Rule 14a-8 provides that all shareholders who own stock worth at least $1,000 are eligible to submit proposals for inclusion in corporate proxy materials. The corporation is required to include information on whatever proposals will be considered at the shareholders' meeting along with proxy materials. Only those proposals that relate to significant policy considerations rather than ordinary business operations must be included. Under the SEC's e-proxy rules that went into effect on July 1, 2007,[14] companies now may furnish proxy materials to shareholders by posting them on a Web site (see the discussion of these rules in the *Insight into E-Commerce* feature in Chapter 28).

Proxy Materials Concerning Executive Pay. The issue of executive compensation has become increasingly contentious in recent years. In particular, shareholders have complained about "excessive" executive pay when the returns to shareholders declined during the same period that top executives received tens (or hundreds) of millions of dollars in compensation. Activist shareholders argue that shareholders in general should have a say in what top management earns. At least one bill was submitted to the 110th Congress that would allow investors to vote on the level of executive pay. The proposed law would require corporations to ask the shareholders to vote on whether they approve of executive compensation. Although corporations would be required to include the information in their proxy materials, the bill would give shareholders only an advisory vote on executive pay (shareholder disapproval would not be binding on management).

Shareholder Voting Shareholders exercise ownership control through the power of their votes. Corporate business matters are presented in the form of resolutions, which shareholders vote to approve or disapprove. Each common shareholder is entitled to one vote per share, although the voting techniques discussed below all enhance the power of the shareholder's vote. The articles of incorporation can exclude or limit voting rights, particularly to certain classes of

12. Most states allow *cumulative voting* (which will be discussed shortly) for directors. If cumulative voting is authorized, a director may not be removed if the number of votes against removal would be sufficient to elect a director under cumulative voting. See, for example, California Corporations Code Section 303A. See also Section 8.08(c) of the RMBCA.

13. The shareholder can waive the requirement of notice by signing a waiver form [RMBCA 7.06]. A shareholder who does not receive notice but who learns of the meeting and attends without protesting the lack of notice is said to have waived notice by such conduct.

14. 17 C.F.R. Parts 240, 249, and 274.

shares. For example, owners of preferred shares are usually denied the right to vote [RMBCA 7.21]. If a state statute requires specific voting procedures, the corporation's articles or bylaws must be consistent with the statute.

Quorum Requirements. For shareholders to act during a meeting, a quorum must be present. Generally, this condition is met when shareholders holding more than 50 percent of the outstanding shares are in attendance. In some states, obtaining the unanimous written consent of shareholders is a permissible alternative to holding a shareholders' meeting [RMBCA 7.25].

Once a quorum is present, voting can proceed. A majority vote of the shares represented at the meeting is usually required to pass resolutions. Assume that Novo Pictures, Inc., has 10,000 outstanding shares of voting stock. Its articles of incorporation set the quorum at 50 percent of outstanding shares and provide that a majority vote of the shares present is necessary to pass ordinary matters. Therefore, for this firm, at the shareholders' meeting, a quorum of stockholders representing 5,000 outstanding shares must be present to conduct business, and a vote of at least 2,501 of those shares is needed to pass ordinary resolutions. Thus, if 6,000 shares are represented, a vote of 3,001 will be necessary.

At times, more than a simple majority vote will be required either by statute or by the articles of incorporation. Extraordinary corporate matters, such as a merger, a consolidation, or the dissolution of the corporation, require approval by a higher percentage of the representatives of all corporate shares entitled to vote, not just a majority of those present at that particular meeting [RMBCA 7.27].

Voting Lists. The RMBCA requires a corporation to maintain an alphabetical voting list of shareholders. The corporation prepares the voting list before each shareholders' meeting. Ordinarily, only persons whose names appear on the corporation's stockholder records as owners are entitled to vote.[15] The voting list contains the name and address of each shareholder as shown on the corporate records on a given cutoff date, or *record date.* (Under RMBCA 7.07, the bylaws or board of directors may fix a record date that is as much as seventy days before the meeting.) The voting list also includes the number of voting shares held by each owner. The list is usually kept at the corporate headquarters and must be made available for shareholder inspection [RMBCA 7.20].

Cumulative Voting. Most states permit, and some require, shareholders to elect directors by *cumulative voting,* a voting method designed to allow minority shareholders to be represented on the board of directors.[16] With cumulative voting, each shareholder is entitled to a total number of votes equal to the number of board members to be elected multiplied by the number of voting shares that the shareholder owns. The shareholder can cast all of these votes for one candidate or split them among several nominees for director. All nominees stand for election at the same time. When cumulative voting is not required by statute or under the articles, the entire board can be elected by a majority of shares at a shareholders' meeting.

Suppose that a corporation has 10,000 shares issued and outstanding. The minority shareholders hold 3,000 shares, and the majority shareholders hold the other 7,000 shares. Three members of the board are to be elected. The majority shareholders' nominees are Alomon, Beasley, and Caravel. The minority shareholders' nominee is Dovrik. Can Dovrik be elected to the board by the minority shareholders?

If cumulative voting is allowed, the answer is yes. The minority shareholders have 9,000 votes among them (the number of directors to be elected times the number of shares, or $3 \times 3{,}000 = 9{,}000$ votes). All of these votes can be cast to elect Dovrik. The majority shareholders have 21,000 votes ($3 \times 7{,}000 = 21{,}000$ votes), but these votes must be distributed among three nominees. The principle of cumulative voting is that no matter how the majority shareholders cast their 21,000 votes, they will not be able to elect all three directors if the minority shareholders cast all of their 9,000 votes for Dovrik, as illustrated in Exhibit 18–2 on page 462.

Other Voting Techniques. A group of shareholders can agree in writing prior to a shareholders' meeting, in a *shareholder voting agreement,* to vote their shares together in a specified manner. Such agreements usually are held to be valid and enforceable. A shareholder can also appoint a voting agent and vote by proxy, as mentioned previously.

15. When the legal owner is deceased, bankrupt, mentally incompetent, or in some other way under a legal disability, his or her vote can be cast by a person designated by law to control and manage the owner's property.

16. See, for example, California Corporations Code Section 708. Under RMBCA 7.28, however, no cumulative voting rights exist unless the articles of incorporation so provide.

CONTEMPORARY LEGAL DEBATES

A Shareholder Access Rule

Although shareholders elect the board of directors, shareholders who own a relatively small percentage of the outstanding shares of a corporation are unlikely to be successful even in nominating candidates for director positions. Enter the possibility of a "shareholder access" rule that would make it easier for dissident shareholders to use the proxy process to elect their candidates to the board of directors of a publicly held company. The Securities and Exchange Commission (SEC) made a modest attempt to allow such shareholder access in the early 2000s, but the proposed change was highly controversial and died in 2003.

Recently, however, it has been resurrected. Until late 2006, the SEC interpreted its own rule as specifically allowing a corporation to refuse to include in its proxy materials any shareholder proposal that "relates to an election for membership on the company's board of directors."[a] Now the U.S. Court of Appeals for the Second Circuit has rejected the SEC's interpretation.[b] The court ruled that a corporation could not exclude from its proxy materials a shareholder proposal that, if adopted by the majority of shareholders, would amend the bylaws to require the corporation to publish the names of shareholder-nominated candidates for director positions, in addition to the candidates nominated by the corporation's board of directors.

Investor Activists Are in Favor of Shareholder Access

Whatever action the SEC takes on this interpretation of its rule in the wake of this court decision, shareholder access will remain controversial. Investor activists have always claimed that without a shareholder access rule, directors have little incentive to pay attention to the concerns of their shareholders. Furthermore, the current system not only discourages shareholders from trying to take an active role in guiding the corporation but also leads to litigation. Because shareholders have no way to engage in dialogue with the corporation to alter what they regard as questionable behavior, they have no choice but to resort to lawsuits against the company. The media have also generally applauded shareholder access as a way to level the playing field between small shareholders and giant corporations.

a. Rule 14a-8(i)8; 17 C.F.R. Section 240.14a-8.

b. *American Federation of State, County, & Municipal Employees v. American International Group, Inc.*, 462 F.3d 121 (2d Cir. 2006). Note that the SEC disagreed with the court in this case and has since proposed a change to clarify its rules. 72 *Federal Register* 43488-01 (August 3, 2007).

Another technique is for shareholders to enter into a *voting trust.* A **voting trust** is an agreement (a trust contract) under which a shareholder transfers the shares to a trustee, usually for a specified period of time. The trustee is then responsible for voting the shares on behalf of the beneficiary-shareholder. The agreement can specify how the trustee is to vote, or it can allow the trustee to use his or her discretion. The trustee takes physical possession of the stock certificate and in return gives the shareholder a *voting trust certificate.* The shareholder retains other rights of ownership (for example, the right to receive dividend payments) except the power to vote the shares [RMBCA 7.30].

In the following case, corporate management was concerned about losing a proxy contest. The corpora-

EXHIBIT 18–2 • Results of Cumulative Voting

Ballot	Majority Shareholder Votes			Minority Shareholder Votes	Directors Elected
	Alomon	*Beasley*	*Caravel*	*Dovrik*	
1	10,000	10,000	1,000	9,000	Alomon, Beasley, Dovrik
2	9,001	9,000	2,999	9,000	Alomon, Beasley, Dovrik
3	6,000	7,000	8,000	9,000	Beasley, Caravel, Dovrik

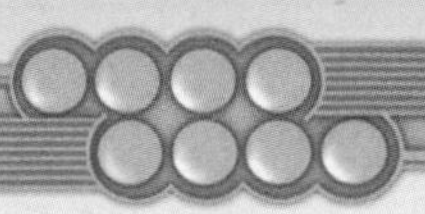

Shareholder Access May Mean Lower Returns for Shareholders

Others are not so sure that shareholder access will benefit shareholders. Opponents of shareholder access, such as law professor Lynn A. Stout of the UCLA-Sloan Research Program on Business Organizations, argue that such a rule is unnecessary because shareholders today have more influence and power over top management and directors than ever before. Shareholders can join in class-action lawsuits against corporations, and they gained additional protections under the Sarbanes-Oxley Act of 2002. Moreover, small investors can purchase their shares through mutual funds, which wield much more power than individual shareholders.

Furthermore, says Professor Stout, shareholder access would dramatically accelerate "an already dangerous trend: 'the flight of corporations away from public investors into the arms of private equity.'" An increasing number of public corporations are going private because they have been purchased by private equity firms. A shareholder access rule could enhance this process because the rule would impose additional costs on publicly held companies. As the costs of having public shareholders increase, more top managers may decide that the corporation should eliminate the shareholders. In other words, more publicly held companies will let private equity firms know that they are for sale. When a company is taken private, its public shareholders receive a small premium over the market value of their shares, but once the company goes private, of course, they are no longer shareholders and are unable to benefit from the company's growth under new management (if that growth materializes). Consequently, in the long run public shareholders may earn lower returns if a shareholder access rule is adopted.

WHERE DO YOU STAND?

Several dozen managers and directors of foreign-based pension plans and insurance companies—which invest in U.S. securities—wrote a joint letter to the head of the SEC. In that letter, they stated that "experience in the United Kingdom, Australia, and the Netherlands has shown that boards whose members may be removed by shareholders are much more sensitive to shareholder opinion and are much more likely to engage in a meaningful dialogue with the institutions that holds their shares." How important is such a dialogue? What might be some of the topics of such a dialogue?

tion's chief executive officer (CEO) then entered into an agreement with a shareholder who would support management's candidates in return for a seat on the board of directors. A shareholder who opposed the deal filed a lawsuit claiming that this agreement was illegal and a breach of the officer's fiduciary duty.

EXTENDED CASE 18.4 Portnoy v. Cryo-Cell International, Inc.

Court of Chancery of Delaware, 2008. 940 A.2d 43.

***STRINE,* V.C. [Vice Chancellor]**

This case involves a challenge to the results of a contested corporate election. Cryo-Cell International, Inc. ("Cryo-Cell" or the "Company") is a small public company that has struggled to succeed. By early 2007, several of its large stockholders were considering mounting a proxy contest to replace the board.

One of those stockholders, Andrew Filipowski, used management's fear of replacement to strike a deal for himself to be included in the management slate for the 2007 annual meeting. Another stockholder, plaintiff David Portnoy, filed a dissident slate (the "Portnoy Slate").

* * * [The company's CEO] Walton ginned up a plan with Filipowski to win the proxy contest. That plan involved Walton acting as a "matchmaker" by finding stockholders willing to sell their shares to Filipowski. In exchange for this alliance, Walton promised Filipowski that if their

CASE CONTINUES

CASE 18.4 CONTINUED

"Management Slate" prevailed, Cryo-Cell's board would, using their power as corporate directors, expand the board to add another seat that Filipowski's designee would fill. * * * This plan was not disclosed to the Cryo-Cell stockholders, who did not realize that if they voted for management, they would in fact be electing a seven, not six member board, with two, not one, Filipowski representatives.

* * * *

The post-meeting vote count resulted in the Management Slate squeaking out a victory by an extremely small margin. Immediately after that, Walton began preparing to add Filipowski's designee to the Cryo-Cell board. Only after this challenge was brought to the election by Portnoy did that process slow down, and only for the obvious reason that the litigation was brought.

* * * *

After it became clear that the Management Slate had prevailed, Walton and the board immediately began to follow through on their agreement to give the Filipowski Group an additional board seat.

* * * *

Portnoy has brought this claim under [Delaware corporation law] challenging the seating of the Management Slate. He claims that the election results should be overturned because the Management Slate would not have been elected had the following alleged breaches of duty not occurred:

1) A supposedly improper agreement by the Cryo-Cell board to include Filipowski on the Management Slate, not because they believed that was in the best interests of Cryo-Cell and its stockholders, but merely as consideration for Filipowski's agreement to vote for the incumbent board members in the proxy fight;

2) A supposedly improper promise by Walton that the incumbent board members would, if reelected, add another Filipowski designee * * * to the board if Filipowski continued to buy up more shares and if that conduct resulted in the Management Slate winning the election;

* * * *

Portnoy claims that all aspects of the incumbents' dealings with Filipowski are tainted by fiduciary misconduct. As he sees it, the incumbents had already marked out the key characteristics they were looking for in additional board members—healthcare industry and stem cell industry experience—and that Filipowski did not have those. Walton, and a board that Portnoy rightly portrays as having every appearance of largely following her lead without much question, simply made a bargain to add Filipowski to the Management Slate, not because they thought his service would help Cryo-Cell but because it would ensure that the large bloc of votes Filipowski controlled would vote for their re-election. That is, this was an entrenchment-motivated decision. Portnoy contends that the deal struck between Walton and the other incumbents, on the one hand, and Filipowski, on the other, to add Filipowski to the Management Slate in exchange for his support in the proxy fight constituted an illegal vote-buying arrangement.

On this [latter] claim, * * * I find in favor of the defendants. My conclusion rests on several grounds. Initially, I note that an arrangement of this kind fits comfortably, as a linguistic matter, within the traditional definition of so-called "vote buying" used in our jurisprudence. * * * I have no doubt that the voting agreement between the Filipowski Group and the incumbents was only assented to by Filipowski after he was offered a candidacy on the Management Slate.

* * * *

The notion that judges should chew over the complicated calculus made by incumbent boards considering whether to add to the management slate candidates proposed by a large blockholder whose velvety suggestions were cloaking an unmistakably clenched fist seems to run against many of the sound reasons for the business judgment rule. There is, thankfully, a practical and civic dynamic in much of our nation's human relations, including in commerce, by which clashes of viewpoint are addressed peaceably through give and take. *When stockholders can decide for themselves whether to seat a candidate who obtained a place on a management slate by way of such bargaining, it seems unwise to formulate a standard that involves the potential for excessive and imprecise judicial involvement.* [Emphasis added.]

* * * *

In my view, a mere offer of a position on a management slate should not be considered a vote-buying arrangement subject to a test of entire fairness, and for that reason, I see no reason to con-

CASE 18.4 CONTINUED

demn the addition of Filipowski to the Management Slate. As an alternative matter, the defendants have convinced me that there was nothing unfair about joining forces with Filipowski in this manner. In this regard, I note that there is not a hint that Filipowski sought to receive financial payments from Cryo-Cell in the form of contracts or consulting fees or other such arrangements. What he sought was influence on the board of a company in which he owned a large number of shares, an ownership interest that gave him an incentive to increase the company's value. Stockholders knew he sought a seat and he had to obtain their votes to get on the board.

For all these reasons, I conclude that Portnoy's attack on this aspect of the incumbents' dealings with Filipowski fails.

* * * *

I reach a different conclusion, however, about the later arrangement that was reached with Filipowski shortly before the annual meeting. * * * Walton * * * promised Filipowski that if the Management Slate won, the incumbent board majority would use its powers under the Company's bylaws to expand the Cryo-Cell board from six members to seven and to fill the new seat with Filipowski's designee.

* * * *

I believe that this arrangement differed in materially important respects from the prior agreement to place Filipowski on the Management Slate. For starters, Walton did not merely promise someone a shot at getting elected by the stockholders by running in the advantaged posture of being a member of a management slate. She promised that she and her incumbent colleagues would use their powers as directors of Cryo-Cell to increase the size of the board and seat [Filipowski's designee]. This was therefore a promise that would not be, for the duration of the term, subject to prior approval by the electorate.

* * * *

* * * There is a very clear and important, but narrow, reason why this later arrangement with Filipowski was improper and inequitably tainted the election process: it was a very material event that was not disclosed to the Cryo-Cell stockholders.

* * * *

* * * I find that Portnoy has proven that serious breaches of fiduciary duty tainted the election.

* * * *

* * * I think the remedy that best vindicates the interests of Cryo-Cell stockholders as a class is to order a prompt special meeting at which a new election will be held and presided over by a special master.

QUESTIONS

1. **What was the main reason that it was acceptable to add Filipowski to the management slate of proposed directors but not so to agree to increase the board by one director with that director being Filipowski's designee?**
2. **For what reason was the business judgment rule introduced in this opinion?**

Rights of Shareholders

Shareholders possess numerous rights. A significant right—the right to vote their shares—has already been discussed. We now look at some additional rights of shareholders in the following subsections.

Stock Certificates A **stock certificate** is a certificate issued by a corporation that evidences ownership of a specified number of shares in the corporation. In jurisdictions that require the issuance of stock certificates, shareholders have the right to demand that the corporation issue certificates and record their names and addresses in the corporate stock record books. In most states and under RMBCA 6.26, the board of directors may provide that shares of stock will be uncertificated (that is, no actual, physical stock certificates will be issued). When shares are uncertificated, the corporation may be required to send each shareholder a letter or some other notice containing the same information that is required to be included on the face of stock certificates.

Stock is intangible personal property, and the ownership right exists independently of the certificate itself. If a stock certificate is lost or destroyed, ownership is not destroyed with it. A new certificate can be issued to replace the one that was lost or destroyed.[17] Notice of shareholders' meetings, dividends, and operational and financial reports are all distributed according to the recorded ownership listed in the corporation's books, not on the basis of possession of the certificate.

Preemptive Rights Sometimes, the articles of incorporation grant preemptive rights to shareholders [RMBCA 6.30]. With **preemptive rights,** a shareholder receives a preference over all other purchasers to subscribe to or purchase a prorated share of a new issue of stock. In other words, a shareholder who is given preemptive rights can purchase the same percentage of the new shares being issued as she or he already holds in the company. This right does not apply to **treasury shares**—shares that are authorized but have not been issued.

Preemptive rights allow each shareholder to maintain her or his proportionate control, voting power, or financial interest in the corporation. Generally, preemptive rights apply only to additional, newly issued stock sold for cash, and the preemptive rights must be exercised within a specified time period, which is usually thirty days.

For example, Tron Corporation authorizes and issues 1,000 shares of stock, and Omar Loren purchases 100 shares, making him the owner of 10 percent of the company's stock. Subsequently, Tron, by vote of its shareholders, authorizes the issuance of another 1,000 shares (by amending the articles of incorporation). This increases its capital stock to a total of 2,000 shares. If preemptive rights have been provided, Loren can purchase one additional share of the new stock being issued for each share he already owns—or 100 additional shares. Thus, he can own 200 of the 2,000 shares outstanding, and his relative position as a shareholder will be maintained. If preemptive rights are not reserved, his proportionate control and voting power will be diluted from that of a 10 percent shareholder to that of a 5 percent shareholder because the additional 1,000 shares were issued.

Preemptive rights are most important in close corporations because each shareholder owns a relatively small number of shares but controls a substantial interest in the corporation. Without preemptive rights, it would be possible for a shareholder to lose his or her proportionate control over the firm.

Stock Warrants **Stock warrants** are rights to buy stock at a stated price by a specified date that are given by the company. Usually, when preemptive rights exist and a corporation is issuing additional shares, it gives its shareholders stock warrants. Warrants are often publicly traded on securities exchanges.

Dividends As mentioned, a **dividend** is a distribution of corporate profits or income *ordered by the directors* and paid to the shareholders in proportion to their respective shares in the corporation. Dividends can be paid in cash, property, stock of the corporation that is paying the dividends, or stock of other corporations.[18]

Sources of Funds for Dividends. State laws vary, but every state determines the general circumstances and legal requirements under which dividends are paid. State laws also control the sources of revenue to be used; only certain funds are legally available for paying dividends. Once declared, a cash dividend becomes a corporate debt enforceable at law like any other debt. Depending on state law, dividends may be paid from the following sources:

1. *Retained earnings.* All states allow dividends to be paid from the undistributed net profits earned by the corporation, including capital gains from the sale of fixed assets. As mentioned previously, the undistributed net profits are called *retained earnings.*
2. *Net profits.* A few states allow dividends to be issued from current net profits without regard to deficits in prior years.
3. *Surplus.* A number of states allow dividends to be paid out of any kind of surplus.

Directors' Failure to Declare a Dividend. When directors fail to declare a dividend, shareholders can ask a court to compel the directors to meet and declare a dividend. To succeed, the shareholders must show that the directors have acted so unreasonably in

17. For a lost or destroyed certificate to be reissued, a shareholder normally must furnish an *indemnity bond,* which is a written promise to reimburse the holder for any actual or claimed loss caused by the issuer's or some other person's conduct. The bond protects the corporation against potential loss should the original certificate reappear at some future time in the hands of a bona fide purchaser. See Sections 8–302 and 8–405(2) of the Uniform Commercial Code.

18. On one occasion, a distillery declared and paid a "dividend" in bonded whiskey.

withholding the dividend that their conduct is an abuse of their discretion.

Often, a corporation accumulates large cash reserves for a legitimate corporate purpose, such as expansion or research. The mere fact that the firm has sufficient earnings or surplus available to pay a dividend is not enough to compel the directors to distribute funds that, in the board's opinion, should not be distributed.[19] The courts are hesitant to interfere with corporate operations and will not compel directors to declare dividends unless abuse of discretion is clearly shown.

Inspection Rights Shareholders in a corporation enjoy both common law and statutory inspection rights. The RMBCA provides that every shareholder is entitled to examine specified corporate records [RMBCA 16.02]. This includes inspecting voting lists, as discussed earlier [RMBCA 7.20]. A shareholder who is denied the right of inspection can seek a court order to compel the inspection. The shareholder's right of inspection is limited, however, to the inspection and copying of corporate books and records for a *proper purpose,* provided the request is made in advance. The shareholder may inspect in person, or an attorney, accountant, or other authorized assistant may do so as the shareholder's agent.

The power of inspection is fraught with potential abuses, and the corporation is allowed to protect itself from them. For example, a shareholder can properly be denied access to corporate records to prevent harassment or to protect trade secrets or other confidential corporate information.[20] Some states require that a shareholder must have held her or his shares for a minimum period of time immediately preceding the demand to inspect or must hold a minimum number of outstanding shares.

Transfer of Shares Corporate stock represents an ownership right in intangible personal property. The law generally recognizes the right of an owner to transfer property to another person unless there are valid restrictions on its transferability. Although stock certificates are negotiable and freely transferable by indorsement and delivery, transfer of stock in closely held corporations (see page 445) is usually restricted. These restrictions must be reasonable and may be found in the bylaws or stated in a shareholder agreement. The existence of any restrictions on transferability must always be indicated on the face of the stock certificate.

When shares are transferred, a new entry is made in the corporate stock book to indicate the new owner. Until the corporation is notified and the entry is complete, all rights—including voting rights, notice of shareholders' meetings, and the right to dividend distributions—remain with the current record owner.

Rights on Dissolution When a corporation is dissolved and its outstanding debts and the claims of its creditors have been satisfied, the remaining assets are distributed on a pro rata basis among the shareholders. The articles of incorporation may provide that certain classes of preferred stock will be given priority. If no class of stock has been given preferences in the distribution of assets, all of the stockholders share the remaining assets. In some circumstances, such as when the board of directors is mishandling corporate assets or is allowing a deadlock to irreparably injure the corporation, shareholders can petition a court to have the corporation dissolved [RMBCA 1430].

The Shareholder's Derivative Suit When the corporation is harmed by the actions of a third party, the directors can bring a lawsuit in the name of the corporation against that party. If the corporate directors fail to bring a lawsuit, shareholders can do so "derivatively" in what is known as a **shareholder's derivative suit.** A shareholder cannot bring a derivative suit until ninety days after making a written demand on the corporation (the board of directors) to take suitable action [RMBCA 7.40]. Only if the directors refuse to take appropriate action can the derivative suit go forward.

The right of shareholders to bring a derivative action is especially important when the wrong suffered by the corporation results from the actions of the corporate directors. This is because the directors and officers would probably be unwilling to take any action against themselves. Nevertheless, a court will dismiss a derivative suit if the majority of directors or an independent panel determines in good faith that the lawsuit is not in the best interests of the corporation [RMBCA 7.44].

When shareholders bring a derivative suit, they are not pursuing rights or benefits for themselves personally but are acting as guardians of the corporate entity. Therefore, if the suit is successful, any damages recovered normally go into the corporation's treasury, not to the shareholders personally. (The shareholders may be

19. A striking exception to this rule was made in *Dodge v. Ford Motor Co.,* 204 Mich. 459, 170 N.W. 668 (1919), when Henry Ford, the president and major stockholder of Ford Motor Company, refused to declare a dividend notwithstanding the firm's large capital surplus. The court, holding that Ford had abused his discretion, ordered the company to declare a dividend.

20. See, for example, *Disney v. Walt Disney Co.,* 857 A.2d 444 (Del.Ch. 2004).

entitled to reimbursement for reasonable expenses of the lawsuit, including attorneys' fees.)

Liability of Shareholders

One of the hallmarks of the corporate organization is that shareholders are not personally liable for the debts of the corporation. If the corporation fails, the shareholders can lose their investments, but that is generally the limit of their liability. As discussed on page 450, however, in certain instances of fraud, undercapitalization, or careless observance of corporate formalities, a court will *pierce the corporate veil* (disregard the corporate entity) and hold the shareholders individually liable. But these situations are the exception, not the rule.

A shareholder can also be personally liable in certain other rare instances. One relates to *watered stock*. Also, in some instances, a majority shareholder who engages in oppressive conduct or attempts to exclude minority shareholders from receiving certain benefits can be held personally liable.

Watered Stock When a corporation issues shares for less than their fair market value, the shares are referred to as **watered stock.**[21] Usually, the shareholder who receives watered stock must pay the difference to the corporation (the shareholder is personally liable). In some states, the shareholder who receives watered stock may be liable to creditors of the corporation for unpaid corporate debts.

For example, during the formation of a corporation, Gomez, one of the incorporators, transfers his property, Sunset Beach, to the corporation for 10,000 shares of stock at a par value of $100 per share for a total price of $1 million. After the property is transferred and the shares are issued, Sunset Beach is carried on the corporate books at a value of $1 million. On appraisal, it is discovered that the market value of the property at the time of transfer was only $500,000. The shares issued to Gomez are therefore watered stock, and he is liable to the corporation for the difference between the value of the shares and the value of the property.

Duties of Majority Shareholders In some instances, a majority shareholder is regarded as having a fiduciary duty to the corporation and to the minority shareholders. This occurs when a single shareholder (or a few shareholders acting in concert) owns a sufficient number of shares to exercise *de facto* (actual) control over the corporation. In these situations, the majority shareholders owe a fiduciary duty to the minority shareholders. A breach of fiduciary duties by those who control a closely held corporation normally constitutes what is known as *oppressive conduct.*

A common example of a breach of fiduciary duty occurs when the majority shareholders "freeze out" the minority shareholders and exclude them from certain benefits of participating in the firm. For example, Brodie, Jordan, and Barbuto formed a close corporation to operate a machine shop. Each owned one-third of the shares in the company, and all three were directors. Brodie served as the corporate president for twelve years but thereafter met with the other shareholders only a few times a year. After disagreements arose, Brodie asked the company to purchase his shares, but his requests were refused. A few years later, Brodie died and his wife inherited his shares in the company. Jordan and Barbuto refused to perform a valuation of the company, denied her access to the corporate information she requested, did not declare any dividends, and refused to elect her as a director. In this situation, a court found that the majority shareholders had violated their fiduciary duty to Brodie's wife.[22]

Major Business Forms Compared

As mentioned in Chapter 16, when deciding which form of business organization to choose, businesspersons normally consider several factors, including ease of creation, the liability of the owners, tax considerations, and the need for capital. Each major form of business organization offers distinct advantages and disadvantages with respect to these and other factors. Exhibit 18–3 on pages 469–470 summarizes the essential advantages and disadvantages of each of the forms of business organization discussed in Chapters 16 through 18.

21. The phrase *watered stock* was originally used to describe cattle that were kept thirsty during a long drive and then were allowed to drink large quantities of water just prior to their sale. The increased weight of the "watered stock" allowed the seller to reap a higher profit.

22. *Brodie v. Jordan,* 447 Mass. 866, N.E.2d 1076 (2006).

EXHIBIT 18–3 • Major Forms of Business Compared

Characteristic	Sole Proprietorship	Partnership	Corporation
Method of Creation	Created at will by owner.	Created by agreement of the parties.	Authorized by the state under the state's corporation law.
Legal Position	Not a separate entity; owner is the business.	A traditional partnership is a separate legal entity in most states.	Always a legal entity separate and distinct from its owners—a legal fiction for the purposes of owning property and being a party to litigation.
Liability	Unlimited liability.	Unlimited liability.	Limited liability of shareholders—shareholders are not liable for the debts of the corporation.
Duration	Determined by owner; automatically dissolved on owner's death.	Terminated by agreement of the partners, but can continue to do business even when a partner dissociates from the partnership.	Can have perpetual existence.
Transferability of Interest	Interest can be transferred, but individual's proprietorship then ends.	Although partnership interest can be assigned, assignee does not have full rights of a partner.	Shares of stock can be transferred.
Management	Completely at owner's discretion.	Each partner has a direct and equal voice in management unless expressly agreed otherwise in the partnership agreement.	Shareholders elect directors, who set policy and appoint officers.
Taxation	Owner pays personal taxes on business income.	Each partner pays income taxes in proportion to her or his share of the net profits, whether or not they are distributed.	Double taxation—corporation pays income tax on net profits, with no deduction for dividends, and shareholders pay income tax on disbursed dividends they receive.
Organizational Fees, Annual License Fees, and Annual Reports	None or minimal.	None or minimal.	All required.
Transaction of Business in Other States	Generally no limitation.	Generally no limitation.[a]	Normally must file a foreign qualification form to do business in another state.

a. A few states have enacted statutes requiring that foreign partnerships qualify to do business there.

EXHIBIT CONTINUES

EXHIBIT 18–3 • Major Forms of Business Compared, Continued

Characteristic	Limited Partnership	Limited Liability Company	Limited Liability Partnership
Method of Creation	Created by agreement to carry on a business for a profit. At least one party must be a general partner and the other(s) limited partner(s). Certificate of limited partnership is filed. Charter must be issued by the state.	Created by an agreement of the member-owners of the company. Articles of organization are filed. Charter must be issued by the state.	Created by agreement of the partners. A statement of qualification for the limited liability partnership is filed.
Legal Position	Treated as a legal entity.	Treated as a legal entity.	Generally, treated same as a traditional partnership.
Liability	Unlimited liability of all general partners; limited partners are liable only to the extent of capital contributions.	Member-owners' liability is limited to the amount of capital contributions or investments.	Varies, but under the Uniform Partnership Act, liability of a partner for acts committed by other partners is limited.
Duration	By agreement in certificate, or by termination of the last general partner (retirement, death, and the like) or last limited partner.	Unless a single-member LLC, can have perpetual existence (same as a corporation).	Remains in existence until cancellation or revocation.
Transferability of Interest	Interest can be assigned (same as traditional partnership), but if assignee becomes a member with consent of other partners, certificate must be amended.	Member interests are freely transferable.	Interest can be assigned same as in a traditional partnership.
Management	General partners have equal voice or by agreement. Limited partners may not retain limited liability if they actively participate in management.	Member-owners can fully participate in management, or management is selected by member-owners who manage on behalf of the members.	Same as a traditional partnership.
Taxation	Generally taxed as a partnership.	LLC is not taxed, and members are taxed personally on profits "passed through" the LLC.	Same as a traditional partnership.
Organizational Fees, Annual License Fees, and Annual Reports	Organizational fee required; usually not others.	Organizational fee required; others vary with states.	Fees are set by each state for filing statements of qualification, foreign qualification, and annual reports.
Transaction of Business in Other States	Generally no limitations.	Generally no limitation, but may vary depending on state.	Must file a statement of foreign qualification before doing business in another state.

REVIEWING Corporations

David Brock is on the board of directors of Firm Body Fitness, Inc., which owns a string of fitness clubs in New Mexico. Brock owns 15 percent of the Firm Body stock and is also employed as a tanning technician at one of the fitness clubs. After the January financial report showed that Firm Body's tanning division was operating at a substantial net loss, the board of directors, led by Marty Levinson, discussed the possibility of terminating the tanning operations. Brock successfully convinced a majority of the board that the tanning division was necessary to market the clubs' overall fitness package. By April, the tanning division's financial losses had risen. The board hired a business analyst, who conducted surveys and determined that the tanning operations did not significantly increase membership. A shareholder, Diego Peñada, discovered that Brock owned stock in Sunglow, Inc., the company from which Firm Body purchased its tanning equipment. Peñada notified Levinson, who privately reprimanded Brock. Shortly thereafter Brock and Mandy Vail, who owned 37 percent of the Firm Body stock and also held shares of Sunglow, voted to replace Levinson on the board of directors. Using the information presented in the chapter, answer the following questions.

1. What duties did Brock, as a director, owe to Firm Body?
2. Does the fact that Brock owned shares in Sunglow establish a conflict of interest? Why or why not?
3. Suppose that Firm Body brought an action against Brock claiming that he had breached the duty of loyalty by not disclosing his interest in Sunglow to the other directors. What theory might Brock use in his defense?
4. Now suppose that Firm Body did not bring an action against Brock. What type of lawsuit might Peñada be able to bring based on these facts?

TERMS AND CONCEPTS

alien corporation 444
articles of incorporation 447
business judgment rule 456
bylaws 447
close corporation 445
commingle 450
corporation 441
dividend 466
domestic corporation 444
foreign corporation 444
holding company 442
inside director 454
outside director 454
pierce the corporate veil 450
preemptive rights 466
proxy 460
quorum 454
retained earnings 442
S corporation 445
shareholder's derivative suit 467
stock certificate 465
stock warrant 466
treasury share 466
***ultra vires* 450**
voting trust 462
watered stock 468

QUESTIONS AND CASE PROBLEMS

18–1. Jonathan, Gary, and Ricardo are active members of a partnership called Swim City. The partnership manufactures, sells, and installs outdoor swimming pools in the states of Arkansas and Texas. The partners want to continue to be active in management and to expand the business into other states as well. They are also concerned about rather large recent judgments entered against swimming pool companies throughout the United States. Based on these facts only, discuss whether the partnership should incorporate.

18-2. QUESTION WITH SAMPLE ANSWER

AstroStar, Inc., has a board of directors consisting of three members (Eckhart, Dolan, and Macero) and has approximately five hundred shareholders. At a regular board meeting, the board selects Galiard as president of the corporation by a two-to-one vote, with Eckhart dissenting. The minutes of the meeting do not register Eckhart's dissenting vote. Later, an audit discovers that Galiard is a former convict and has embezzled $500,000 from the corporation that is not covered by insurance. Can the corporation hold directors Eckhart, Dolan, and Macero personally liable? Discuss.

- **For a sample answer to Question 18–2, go to Appendix I at the end of this text.**

18-3. Oxy Corp. is negotiating with the Wick Construction Co. for the renovation of the Oxy corporate headquarters. Wick, the owner of the Wick Construction Co., is also one of the five members of the board of directors of Oxy. The contract terms are standard for this type of contract. Wick has previously informed two of the other directors of his interest in the construction company. Oxy's board approves the contract by a three-to-two vote, with Wick voting with the majority. Discuss whether this contract is binding on the corporation.

18-4. Superal Corp. authorized 100,000 shares and issued all of them during its first six months in operation. Avril purchased 10,000 of the shares (10 percent). Later, Superal reacquired 10,000 of the shares it originally issued. With shareholder approval, Superal has now amended its articles so as to authorize and issue another 100,000 shares. It has also, by a resolution of the board of directors, made plans to reissue the 10,000 shares of treasury stock (the shares reacquired by the corporation). The corporate articles do not include a provision dealing with shareholders' preemptive rights. Because of her ownership of 10 percent of Superal, Avril claims that she has the preemptive right to purchase 10,000 shares of the new issue and 1,000 shares of the stock being reissued. Discuss her claims.

18-5. Fiduciary Duties and Liabilities. In 1978, David Brandt and Dean Somerville incorporated Posilock Puller, Inc. (PPI), to make and market bearing pullers. Each received half of the stock. Initially operating out of McHenry, North Dakota, PPI moved to Cooperstown, North Dakota, in 1984 into a building owned by Somerville. After the move, Brandt's participation in PPI diminished, and Somerville's increased. In 1998, Somerville formed PL MFG as his own business to make components for the bearing pullers and sell the parts to PPI. The start-up costs included a $450,000 loan from Sheyenne Valley Electric Cooperative. PPI executed the loan documents and indorsed the check. The proceeds were deposited into an account for PL MFG, which did not sign a promissory note payable to PPI until 2000. When Brandt learned of PL MFG and the loan, he filed a suit in a North Dakota state court against Somerville, alleging, in part, a breach of fiduciary duty. What fiduciary duty does a director owe to his or her corporation? What does this duty require? Should the court hold Somerville liable? Why or why not? [*Brandt v. Somerville*, 2005 ND 35, 692 N.W.2d 144 (2005)]

18-6. CASE PROBLEM WITH SAMPLE ANSWER

Thomas Persson and Jon Nokes founded Smart Inventions, Inc., in 1991 to market household consumer products. The success of their first product, the Smart Mop, continued with later products, which were sold through infomercials and other means. Persson and Nokes were the firm's officers and equal shareholders, with Persson responsible for product development and Nokes in charge of day-to-day operations. By 1998, they had become dissatisfied with each other's efforts. Nokes represented the firm as financially "dying," "in a grim state, . . . worse than ever," and offered to buy all of Persson's shares for $1.6 million. Persson accepted. On the day that they signed the agreement to transfer the shares, Smart Inventions began marketing a new product—the Tap Light—which was an instant success, generating millions of dollars in revenues. In negotiating with Persson, Nokes had intentionally kept the Tap Light a secret. Persson filed a suit in a California state court against Smart Inventions and others, asserting fraud and other claims. Under what principle might Smart Inventions be liable for Nokes's fraud? Is Smart Inventions liable in this case? Explain. [*Persson v. Smart Inventions, Inc.*, 125 Cal.App.4th 1141, 23 Cal.Rptr.3d 335 (2 Dist. 2005)]

- **To view a sample answer for Problem 18–6, go to this book's Web site at academic.cengage.com/blaw/cross, select "Chapter 18," and click on "Case Problem with Sample Answer."**

18-7. Duties of Majority Shareholders. Steve and Marie Venturini were involved in the operation of Steve's Sizzling Steakhouse in Carlstadt, New Jersey, from the day their parents opened it in the 1930s. By the 1980s, Steve, Marie, and her husband Joe were running it. The business was a corporation with Steve and Marie each owning half of the stock. Steve died in 2001, leaving his stock in equal shares to his sons Steve and Gregg. Son Steve had never worked there. Gregg did occasional maintenance work until his father's death. Despite their lack of participation, the sons were paid more than $750 per week each. In 2002, Marie's son Blaise, who had obtained a college degree in restaurant management while working part-time at the steakhouse, took over its management. When his cousins became threatening, he denied them access to the business and its books. Marie refused Gregg and Steve's offer of about $1.4 million for her stock in the restaurant, and they refused her offer of about $800,000 for theirs. They filed a suit in a New

Jersey state court against her, claiming, among other things, a breach of fiduciary duty. Should the court order the aunt to buy out the nephews or the nephews to buy out the aunt, or neither? Why? [*Venturini v. Steve's Steakhouse, Inc.*, __ N.J.Super. __, __ A.2d __ (Ch.Div. 2006)]

18–8. Fiduciary Duties and Liabilities. Harry Hoaas and Larry Griffiths were shareholders in Grand Casino, Inc., which owned and operated a casino in Watertown, South Dakota. Griffiths owned 51 percent of the stock and Hoaas 49 percent. Hoaas managed the casino, which Griffiths typically visited once a week. At the end of 1997, an accounting showed that the cash on hand was less than the amount posted in the casino's books. Later, more shortfalls were discovered. In October 1999, Griffiths did a complete audit. Hoaas was unable to account for $135,500 in missing cash. Griffiths then kept all of the casino's most recent profits, including Hoaas's $9,447.20 share, and, without telling Hoaas, sold the casino for $100,000 and kept all of the proceeds. Hoaas filed a suit in a South Dakota state court against Griffiths, asserting, among other things, a breach of fiduciary duty. Griffiths countered with evidence of Hoaas's misappropriation of corporate cash. What duties did these parties owe each other? Did either Griffiths or Hoaas, or both of them, breach those duties? How should their dispute be resolved? How should their finances be reconciled? Explain. [*Hoaas v. Griffiths*, 2006 SD 27, 714 N.W.2d 61 (2006)]

18–9. Improper Incorporation. Denise Rubenstein and Christopher Mayor agreed to form Bayshore Sunrise Corp. (BSC) in New York to rent certain premises and operate a laundromat. BSC entered into a twenty-year commercial lease with Bay Shore Property Trust on April 15, 1999. Mayor signed the lease as the president of BSC. The next day—April 16—BSC's certificate of incorporation was filed with New York's secretary of state. Three years later, BSC defaulted on the lease, which resulted in its termination. Rubenstein and BSC filed a suit in a New York state court against Mayor, his brother-in-law Thomas Castellano, and Planet Laundry, Inc., claiming wrongful interference with a contractual relationship. The plaintiffs alleged that Mayor and Castellano conspired to squeeze Rubenstein out of BSC and arranged the default on the lease so that Mayor and Castellano could form and operate their own business, Planet Laundry, at the same address. The defendants argued that they could not be liable on the plaintiffs' claim because there had never been an enforceable lease—BSC lacked the capacity to enter into contracts on April 15. What theory might Rubenstein and BSC assert to refute this argument? Discuss. [*Rubenstein v. Mayor*, 41 A.D.3d 826, 839 N.Y.S.2d 170 (2 Dept. 2007)]

18–10. A QUESTION OF ETHICS

*New Orleans Paddlewheels, Inc. (NOP), is a Louisiana corporation formed in 1982 when James Smith, Sr., and Warren Reuther were its only shareholders, with each holding 50 percent of the stock. NOP is part of a sprawling enterprise of tourism and hospitality companies in New Orleans. The positions on the board of each company were split equally between the Smith and Reuther families. At Smith's request, his son James Smith, Jr. (JES), became involved in the businesses. In 1999, NOP's board elected JES as president, to be in charge of day-to-day operations, and Reuther as chief executive officer (CEO), to be in charge of marketing and development. Over the next few years, animosity developed between Reuther and JES. In October 2001, JES terminated Reuther as CEO and denied him access to the offices and books of NOP and the other companies, literally changing the locks on the doors. At the next meetings of the boards of NOP and the overall enterprise, deadlock ensued, with the directors voting along family lines on every issue. Complaining that the meetings were a "waste of time," JES began to run the entire enterprise by taking advantage of an unequal balance of power on the companies' executive committees. In NOP's subsequent bankruptcy proceeding, Reuther filed a motion for the appointment of a trustee to formulate a plan for the firm's reorganization, alleging, among other things, misconduct by NOP's management. [*In re New Orleans Paddlewheels, Inc., *350 Bankr. 667 (E.D.La. 2006)]*

(a) Was Reuther legally entitled to have access to the books and records of NOP and the other companies? JES maintained, among other things, that NOP's books were "a mess." Was JES's denial of that access unethical? Explain.

(b) How would you describe JES's attempt to gain control of NOP and the other companies? Were his actions deceptive and self-serving in the pursuit of personal gain or legitimate and reasonable in the pursuit of a business goal? Discuss.

18–11. VIDEO QUESTION

Go to this text's Web site at **academic.cengage.com/blaw/cross** and select "Chapter 18." Click on "Video Questions" and view the video titled *Corporation or LLC: Which Is Better?* Then answer the following questions.

(a) Compare the liability that Anna and Caleb would be exposed to as shareholders/owners of a corporation versus as members of a limited liability company (LLC).

(b) How does the taxation of corporations and LLCs differ?

(c) Given that Anna and Caleb conduct their business (Wizard Internet) over the Internet, can you think of any drawbacks to forming an LLC?

(d) If you were in the position of Anna and Caleb, would you choose to create a corporation or an LLC? Why?

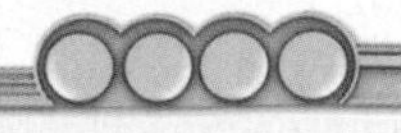

LAW ON THE WEB

For updated links to resources available on the Web, as well as a variety of other materials, visit this text's Web site at

academic.cengage.com/blaw/cross

Cornell University's Legal Information Institute has links to state corporation statutes at

www.law.cornell.edu/topics/state_statutes.html

The Center for Corporate Law at the University of Cincinnati College of Law is a good source of information on corporate law. Go to

www.law.uc.edu/CCL

One of the best sources on the Web for information on corporations, including their directors, is the EDGAR database of the Securities and Exchange Commission (SEC) at

www.sec.gov/edgar.shtml

Legal Research Exercises on the Web

Go to **academic.cengage.com/blaw/cross**, the Web site that accompanies this text. Select "Chapter 18" and click on "Internet Exercises." There you will find the following Internet research exercises that you can perform to learn more about the topics covered in this chapter.

Internet Exercise 18–1: Legal Perspective
Liability of Officers and Directors

Internet Exercise 18–2: Management Perspective
Online Incorporation

UNIT FOUR FOCUS ON ETHICS

Ethics and the Business Environment

In Chapter 4, we examined the importance of ethical standards in the business context. We also offered suggestions on how business decision makers can create an ethical workplace. Here, we look at selected areas in which the relationships within specific business organizational forms may raise ethical issues.

Fiduciary Duties of All Partners and Corporate Directors

The law of agency, which will be outlined in Chapter 19, permeates virtually all relationships within any partnership or corporation. An important duty that arises in the law of agency, and applies to all partners and corporate directors, officers, and management personnel, is the duty of loyalty. As caretakers of the shareholders' wealth, corporate directors and officers also have a fiduciary duty to exercise care when making decisions affecting the corporate enterprise.

The Duty of Loyalty Every individual has his or her own personal interests, which may at times conflict with the interests of the partnership or corporation with which he or she is affiliated. In particular, a partner or a corporate director may face a conflict between personal interests and the interests of the business entity. Corporate officers and directors may find themselves in a position to acquire assets that would also benefit the corporation if acquired in the corporation's name. If an officer does purchase the asset without offering the opportunity to the corporation, however, she or he may be liable for usurping a corporate opportunity.[1]

Most courts also hold that a corporate officer or director has a fiduciary duty to disclose improper conduct to the corporation. The Supreme Court of Arkansas weighed in on this issue in 2007. Thomas Coughlin was a top executive in theft prevention at Wal-Mart who held several other high-level positions prior to becoming a member of the corporation's board of directors. He retired in 2005 and entered into a retirement agreement and release of claims with Wal-Mart under which he was to receive millions of dollars in benefits over the years.

Then Wal-Mart discovered that Coughlin, prior to retiring, had been abusing his position of authority and conspiring with subordinates to misappropriate hundreds of thousands of dollars in property and cash through various fraudulent schemes. Wal-Mart filed a lawsuit alleging that Coughlin had breached his fiduciary duty of loyalty by failing to disclose his misconduct before entering a self-dealing contract. Ultimately, the state's highest court agreed and held that the director's fiduciary duty obligated him to divulge material facts of *past* fraud to the corporation before entering the contract. The court stated, "[W]e are persuaded, in addition, that the majority view is correct, which is that the failure of a fiduciary to disclose material facts of his fraudulent conduct to his corporation prior to entering into a self-dealing contract with that corporation will void that contract."[2]

The Duty of Care In addition to the duty of loyalty, every corporate director or officer owes a duty of care. *Due care* means that officers and directors must keep themselves informed and make businesslike judgments. Officers have a duty to disclose material information that shareholders need for competent decision making. Some courts have even suggested that corporate directors have a duty to detect and "ferret out" wrongdoing within the corporation.[3] In fact, a number of courts applying Delaware law have recognized that directors may be held liable for failing to exercise proper oversight.[4] Corporate law also creates other structures to protect shareholder interests, such as the right to inspect books and records.

Although traditionally the duty of care did not require directors to monitor the behavior of corporate employees to detect and prevent wrongdoing, the tide may be changing. Since the corporate sentencing guidelines were first issued in 1991, courts have the power to impose substantial penalties on corporations and corporate directors for criminal wrongdoing. The guidelines allow these penalties to be mitigated,

1. For a landmark case on this issue, see *Guth v. Loft, Inc.,* 5 A.2d 503 (Del. 1939), presented as Case 18.3 in Chapter 18.

2. *Wal-Mart Stores, Inc. v. Coughlin,* 369 Ark. 365, ___ S.W.3d ___ (2007).

3. *In re Caremark International, Inc. Derivative Litigation,* 698 A.2d 959 (Del.Ch. 1996); also see *Forsyhe v. ESC Fund Management Co. (U.S.), Inc.,* 2007 WL 2982247 (Del.Ch. 2007).

4. See, for example, *McCall v. Scott,* 239 F.3d 808 (6th Cir. 2001); *Guttman v. Huang,* 823 A.2d 492 (Del.Ch. 2003); *Landy v. D'Alessandro,* 316 F.Supp.2d 49 (D.Mass. 2004); and *Miller v. U.S. Foodservice, Inc.,* 361 F.Supp.2d 470 (D.Md. 2005).

(Continued)

UNIT FOUR · FOCUS ON ETHICS

though, if a company can show that it has an effective compliance program in place to detect and prevent wrongdoing by corporate personnel. The Sarbanes-Oxley Act of 2002 required the sentencing commission to revise these guidelines, and now the penalties for white-collar crimes, such as federal mail and wire fraud, have increased dramatically.

Fiduciary Duties to Creditors It is a long-standing principle that corporate directors ordinarily owe fiduciary duties only to a corporation's shareholders. Directors who favor the interests of other corporate "stakeholders," such as creditors, over those of the shareholders have been held liable for breaching these duties. The picture changes, however, when a corporation approaches insolvency. At this point, the shareholders' equity interests in the corporation may be worthless, while the interests of creditors become paramount. In this situation, do the fiduciary duties of loyalty and care extend to the corporation's creditors as well as to the shareholders? The answer to this question, according to some courts, is yes. In a leading case on this issue, a Delaware court noted that "[t]he possibility of insolvency can do curious things to incentives, exposing creditors to risks of opportunistic behavior and creating complexities for directors." The court held that when a corporation is on the brink of insolvency, the directors assume a fiduciary duty to other stakeholders that sustain the corporate entity, including creditors.[5]

Franchise Relationships

Franchise relationships present several significant ethical issues. One issue has to do with the franchisor's quality control over the franchisee's activities. On the one hand, if the franchisor ignores the problem of quality control, the reputation of the franchisor's business may suffer. On the other hand, if a franchisor's control over the operations of the franchisee is too extensive, the franchisor may be liable for the torts of the franchisee's employees under agency theory (see Chapter 19). Even when an independent business entity purchases a franchise and the franchise agreement specifies that no agency relationship exists, the courts may find otherwise.

Another issue today is how to adapt certain protections for franchisees to the online world. This issue has become increasingly important as more and more prospective franchisees are going online to find information about particular franchises. Recall from Chapter 16 that the Franchise Rule of the Federal Trade Commission (FTC) imposes certain disclosure requirements on franchisors and that states also have rules. Does a franchisor advertising on the Internet have to comply with fifty different state franchise regulations? Generally, how can the interests of franchisees be protected in the cyber environment?

In view of these problems, the FTC has proposed a rule that would require online franchisors to state very clearly that franchisees would not be entitled to exclusive territorial rights. Notwithstanding these changes, however, one problem would remain: given the speed with which online franchises can be created, it may be difficult—if not impossible—for the FTC to effectively regulate these relationships.

DISCUSSION QUESTIONS

1. Do you agree that when a corporation is approaching insolvency, the directors' fiduciary obligations should extend to the corporation's creditors as well as to the shareholders? In this situation, should the fiduciary duties owed to creditors take priority over the duties to shareholders? Why or why not?
2. As explained, if a franchisor exercises "too much control" over a franchisee's business operations, a court may deem the franchisor to be liable as an employer for the torts committed by the franchisee's employees. How can holding franchisors liable in such circumstances be squared with the doctrine of freedom of contract (see Chapter 9)?

5. *Credit Lyonnais Bank Nederland N.V. v. Pathe Communications Corp.*, 1991 WL 277613 (Del.Ch. 1991). See also *Production Resources Group, LLC v. NCT Group, Inc.*, 863 A.2d 772 (Del.Ch. 2004); and *In re Amcast Industrial Corp.*, 365 Bankr. 91 (S.D. Ohio 2007).

UNIT FIVE

The Employment Environment

CONTENTS

CHAPTER 19

Agency

One of the most common, important, and pervasive legal relationships is that of **agency.** In an agency relationship involving two parties, one of the parties, called the *agent,* agrees to represent or act for the other, called the *principal.* The principal has the right to control the agent's conduct in matters entrusted to the agent. By using agents, a principal can conduct multiple business operations simultaneously in various locations. Thus, for example, contracts that bind the principal can be made at different places with different persons at the same time.

A familiar example of an agent is a corporate officer who serves in a representative capacity for the owners of the corporation. In this capacity, the officer has the authority to bind the principal (the corporation) to a contract. Indeed, agency law is essential to the existence and operation of a corporate entity because only through its agents can a corporation function and enter into contracts.

Most employees are also considered to be agents of their employers. Thus, some of the concepts that you will learn about in Chapters 20 and 21, on employment law, are based on agency law. Generally, agency relationships permeate the business world. For that reason, an understanding of the law of agency is crucial to understanding business law.

Agency Relationships

Section 1(1) of the *Restatement (Second) of Agency*[1] defines *agency* as "the fiduciary relation [that] results from the manifestation of consent by one person to another that the other shall act in his [or her] behalf and subject to his [or her] control, and consent by the other so to act." The term **fiduciary** is at the heart of agency law. The term can be used both as a noun and as an adjective. When used as a noun, it refers to a person having a duty created by his or her undertaking to act primarily for another's benefit in matters connected with the undertaking. When used as an adjective, as in the phrase "fiduciary relationship," it means that the relationship involves trust and confidence.

Agency relationships commonly exist between employers and employees. Agency relationships may sometimes also exist between employers and independent contractors who are hired to perform special tasks or services.

Employer-Employee Relationships

Normally, all employees who deal with third parties are deemed to be agents. A salesperson in a department store, for instance, is an agent of the store's owner (the principal) and acts on the owner's behalf. Employment laws (state and federal) apply only to the employer-employee relationship. Statutes governing Social Security, withholding taxes, workers' compensation, unemployment compensation, workplace safety, employment discrimination, and other aspects of

1. The *Restatement (Second) of Agency* is an authoritative summary of the law of agency and is often referred to by judges in their decisions and opinions.

employment (see Chapters 20 and 21) are applicable only when an employer-employee relationship exists. *These laws do not apply to an independent contractor.*

Because employees who deal with third parties are normally deemed to be agents of their employers, agency law and employment law overlap considerably. Agency relationships, though, as will become apparent, can exist outside an employer-employee relationship, and thus agency law has a broader reach than employment law does.

Employer–Independent Contractor Relationships

Independent contractors are not employees because, by definition, those who hire them have no control over the details of their work performance. Section 2 of the *Restatement (Second) of Agency* defines an **independent contractor** as follows:

> [An independent contractor is] a person who contracts with another to do something for him [or her] but who is not controlled by the other nor subject to the other's right to control with respect to his [or her] physical conduct in the performance of the undertaking. He [or she] may or may not be an agent.

Building contractors and subcontractors are independent contractors; a property owner who hires a contractor and subcontractors to complete a project does not control the details of the way they perform their work. Truck drivers who own their vehicles and hire out on a per-job basis are independent contractors, but truck drivers who drive company trucks on a regular basis usually are employees.

The relationship between a principal and an independent contractor may or may not involve an agency relationship. To illustrate: An owner of real estate who hires a real estate broker to negotiate the sale of her property not only has contracted with an independent contractor (the real estate broker) but also has established an agency relationship for the specific purpose of selling the property. Another example is an insurance agent, who is both an independent contractor and an agent of the insurance company for which he or she sells policies. (Note that an insurance *broker,* in contrast, normally is an agent of the person obtaining insurance and not of the insurance company.)

Determining Employee Status

The courts are frequently asked to determine whether a particular worker is an employee or an independent contractor. How a court decides this issue can have a significant effect on the rights and liabilities of the parties. For example, employers are required to pay certain taxes, such as Social Security and unemployment taxes, for employees but not for independent contractors.

Criteria Used by the Courts In deciding whether a worker is categorized as an employee or an independent contractor, courts often consider the following questions:

1. How much control does the employer exercise over the details of the work? (If the employer exercises considerable control over the details of the work and the day-to-day activities of the worker, this indicates employee status. This is perhaps the most important factor weighed by the courts in determining employee status.)
2. Is the worker engaged in an occupation or business distinct from that of the employer? (If so, this points to independent-contractor, not employee, status.)
3. Is the work usually done under the employer's direction or by a specialist without supervision? (If the work is usually done under the employer's direction, this indicates employee status.)
4. Does the employer supply the tools at the place of work? (If so, this indicates employee status.)
5. For how long is the person employed? (If the person is employed for a long period of time, this indicates employee status.)
6. What is the method of payment—by time period or at the completion of the job? (Payment by time period, such as once every two weeks or once a month, indicates employee status.)
7. What degree of skill is required of the worker? (If a great degree of skill is required, this may indicate that the person is an independent contractor hired for a specialized job and not an employee.)

Sometimes, workers may benefit from having employee status—for tax purposes and to be protected under certain employment laws, for example. As mentioned earlier, federal statutes governing employment discrimination apply only when an employer-employee relationship exists. The question in the following case was whether, for the purpose of applying one of these statutes, a television show's co-host was an employee or an independent contractor.

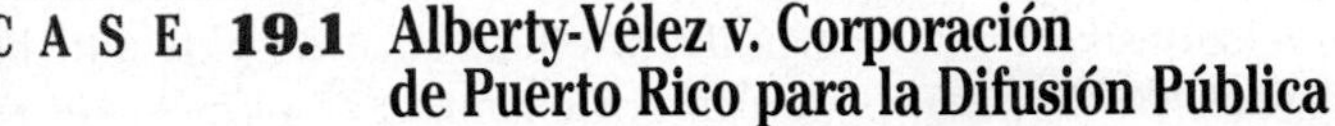

CASE 19.1 Alberty-Vélez v. Corporación de Puerto Rico para la Difusión Pública

United States Court of Appeals, First Circuit, 2004. 361 F.3d 1.
www.ca1.uscourts.gov[a]

• **Background and Facts** In July 1993, Victoria Lis Alberty-Vélez (Alberty) began to co-host a new television show, *Desde Mi Pueblo,* on WIPR, a television station in Puerto Rico. The show profiled Puerto Rican cities and towns. Instead of signing a single contract, Alberty signed a new contract for each episode. Each contract obligated her to work a certain number of days. She was not obliged to do other work for WIPR, and WIPR was not obliged to contract with her for other work. During the filming, Alberty was responsible for providing her own clothing, shoes, accessories, hairstylist, and other services and materials. She was paid a lump sum, ranging from $400 to $550, for each episode. WIPR did not withhold income or Social Security taxes and did not provide health insurance, life insurance, a retirement plan, paid sick leave, maternity leave, or vacation pay. Alberty became pregnant, and after November 1994, WIPR stopped contracting with her. She filed a suit in a federal district court against WIPR's owner, Corporación de Puerto Rico para la Difusión Pública, alleging, among other things, discrimination on the basis of her pregnancy in violation of a federal statute. The court issued a judgment in the defendant's favor. Alberty appealed to the U.S. Court of Appeals for the First Circuit.

IN THE LANGUAGE OF THE COURT
***HOWARD,* Circuit Judge.**

* * * *

* * * We * * * will apply the common law test to determine whether Alberty was WIPR's employee or an independent contractor.

Under the common law test, a court must consider * * * *the hiring party's right to control the manner and means by which the product is accomplished.* Among other factors relevant to this inquiry are the skills required; the source of the instrumentalities [means] and tools; the location of the work; the duration of the relationship between the parties; whether the hiring party has the right to assign additional projects to the hired party; the extent of the hired party's discretion over when and how long to work; the method of payment; * * * whether the work is part of the regular business of the hiring party; whether the hiring party is in business; the provision of employee benefits; and the tax treatment of the hired party. [Emphasis added.]

* * * *

Several factors favor classifying Alberty as an independent contractor. First, a television actress is a skilled position requiring talent and training not available on-the-job. In this regard, Alberty possesses a master's degree in public communications and journalism; is trained in dance, singing, and modeling; taught within the drama department at the University of Puerto Rico; and acted in several theater and television productions prior to her affiliation with "Desde Mi Pueblo."

Second, Alberty provided the tools and instrumentalities necessary for her to perform. Specifically, she provided, or obtained sponsors to provide, the costumes, jewelry, and other image-related supplies and services necessary for her appearance.

Third, WIPR could not assign Alberty work in addition to filming "Desde Mi Pueblo."

Fourth, the method of payment favors independent-contractor status. Alberty received a lump sum fee for each episode. Her compensation was based on completing the filming, not the time consumed. If she did not film an episode she did not get paid.

Fifth, WIPR did not provide Alberty with benefits.

Sixth, Alberty's tax treatment suggests independent-contractor status.

Despite these factors favoring independent-contractor status, Alberty argues that she was WIPR's employee because WIPR controlled the manner of her work by directing her during filming, dictated the location of her work by selecting the filming sites, and determined the hours of her work * * * . *While "control" over the manner, location, and hours of work is often critical to*

a. In the right-hand column, click on "Opinions." When that page opens, under "General Search," type "02-2187" in the "Opinion Number begins with" box and click on "Submit Query." In the result, click on the appropriate link to access the opinion. The U.S. Court of Appeals for the First Circuit maintains this Web site.

CASE 19.1 CONTINUED *the independent contractor/employee analysis, it must be considered in light of the work performed and the industry at issue.* Considering the tasks that an actor performs, we do not believe that the sort of control identified by Alberty necessarily indicates employee status. [Emphasis added.]

* * * *

* * * Alberty's work on "Desde Mi Pueblo" required her to film at the featured sites at the required times and to follow the instructions of the director. WIPR could only achieve its goal of producing its program by having Alberty follow these directions. Just as an orchestra musician is subject to the control of the conductor during concerts and rehearsals, an actor is subject to the control of the director during filming.

* * * *

While no one factor is dispositive [determines the outcome], it is clear, based on the parties' entire relationship, that a reasonable fact finder could only conclude that Alberty was an independent contractor. * * * Accordingly, we conclude that Alberty was an independent contractor as a matter of law and therefore cannot maintain [this] action against WIPR.

● **Decision and Remedy** *The U.S. Court of Appeals for the First Circuit affirmed the lower court's judgment in WIPR's favor. The court stated, "The parties structured their relationship through the use of set length contracts that permitted Alberty the freedom to pursue other opportunities and assured WIPR that it would not have to pay Alberty for the weeks that it was not filming. Further, the lack of benefits, the method of payment, and the parties' own description of their relationship in tax documents all indicate independent-contractor status."*

● **What If the Facts Were Different?** *Suppose that Alberty had been a full-time, hourly worker and that such status was common among television hosts, but WIPR had manipulated the benefits and tax withholdings to favor independent-contractor status. How might the result have been different?*

● **The Global Dimension** *Would Alberty have been defined as an employee if she had been a foreign correspondent who reported on stories from international locations and WIPR had paid her travel and related expenses? Explain.*

Criteria Used by the IRS Businesspersons should be aware that the Internal Revenue Service (IRS) has established its own criteria for determining whether a worker is an independent contractor or an employee. Although the IRS once considered twenty factors in determining a worker's status, guidelines in effect since 1997 encourage IRS examiners to look closely at just one of those factors—the degree of control the business exercises over the worker.

The IRS tends to scrutinize closely a firm's classification of a worker as an independent contractor rather than an employee because employers can avoid certain tax liabilities by hiring independent contractors instead of employees. Even when a firm has classified a worker as an independent contractor, if the IRS decides that the worker is actually an employee, the employer will be responsible for paying any applicable Social Security, withholding, and unemployment taxes. For example, in one widely publicized case, Microsoft Corporation was ordered to pay back payroll taxes for hundreds of temporary workers who had contractually agreed to work for Microsoft as independent contractors.[2]

Employee Status and "Works for Hire" Under the Copyright Act of 1976, any copyrighted work created by an employee within the scope of her or his employment at the request of the employer is a "work for hire," and the employer owns the copyright to the work. In contrast, when an employer hires an independent contractor—a freelance artist, writer, or computer programmer, for example—the independent contractor normally owns the copyright. In this situation, the employer can own the copyright only if the parties agree in writing that the work is a "work for hire" and the work falls into one of nine specific categories, including audiovisual and other works.

2. *Vizcaino v. U.S. District Court for the Western District of Washington*, 173 F.3d 713 (9th Cir. 1999).

In one case, for example, Graham marketed CD-ROM discs containing compilations of software programs that are available free to the public. Graham hired James to create a file-retrieval program that allowed users to access the software on the CDs. James built into the final version of the program a notice stating that he was the author of the program and owned the copyright. Graham removed the notice. When James sold the program to another CD-ROM publisher, Graham filed a suit claiming that James's file-retrieval program was a "work for hire" and that Graham owned the copyright to the program. The court, however, decided that James—a skilled computer programmer who controlled the manner and method of his work—was an independent contractor and not an employee for hire. Thus, James owned the copyright to the file-retrieval program.[3]

Formation of the Agency Relationship

Agency relationships normally are *consensual;* in other words, they come about by voluntary consent and agreement between the parties. Generally, the agreement need not be in writing,[4] and consideration is not required.

A person must have contractual capacity to be a principal.[5] Those who cannot legally enter into contracts directly should not be allowed to do so indirectly through an agent. Any person can be an agent, however, regardless of whether he or she has the capacity to contract. Because an agent derives the authority to enter into contracts from the principal and because a contract made by an agent is legally viewed as a contract of the principal, it is immaterial whether the agent personally has the legal capacity to make that contract. Thus, even a minor or a person who is legally incompetent can be appointed as an agent.

3. *Graham v. James,* 144 F.3d 229 (2d Cir. 1998).

4. There are two main exceptions to the statement that agency agreements need not be in writing. An agency agreement must be in writing (1) whenever agency authority empowers the agent to enter into a contract that the Statute of Frauds requires to be in writing (this is called the *equal dignity rule,* to be discussed on page 490) and (2) whenever an agent is given power of attorney.

5. Note that some states allow a minor to be a principal. When a minor is permitted to be a principal, however, any resulting contracts will be voidable by the minor principal but *not* by the adult third party.

An agency relationship can be created for any legal purpose. An agency relationship created for a purpose that is illegal or contrary to public policy is unenforceable. If LaSalle (as principal) contracts with Burke (as agent) to sell illegal narcotics, the agency relationship is unenforceable because selling illegal narcotics is a felony and is contrary to public policy. It is also illegal for physicians and other licensed professionals to employ unlicensed agents to perform professional actions.

Generally, an agency relationship can arise in four ways: by agreement of the parties, by ratification, by estoppel, and by operation of law. We look here at each of these possibilities.

Agency by Agreement

Most agency relationships are based on an express or implied agreement that the agent will act for the principal and that the principal agrees to have the agent so act. An agency agreement can take the form of an express written contract. For example, Henchen enters into a written agreement with Vogel, a real estate agent, to sell Henchen's house. An agency relationship exists between Henchen and Vogel for the sale of the house and is detailed in a document that both parties sign.

Many express agency relationships are created by oral agreement and are not based on a written contract. Suppose that Henchen asks Grace, a gardener, to contract with others for the care of his lawn on a regular basis. If Grace agrees, an agency relationship exists between Henchen and Grace for the lawn care.

An agency agreement can also be implied by conduct. For example, a hotel expressly allows only Hans Cooper to park cars, but Hans has no employment contract there. The hotel's manager tells Hans when to work, as well as where and how to park the cars. The hotel's conduct manifests a willingness to have Hans park its customers' cars, and Hans can infer from the hotel's conduct that he has authority to act as a parking valet. Thus, there is an implied agreement that Hans is an agent for the hotel and provides valet parking services for hotel guests.

Agency by Ratification

On occasion, a person who is in fact not an agent may make a contract on behalf of another (a principal). If the principal approves or affirms that contract by word or by action, an agency relationship is created by ratification. Ratification involves a question of intent, and intent can be expressed by either words or conduct.

The basic requirements for ratification will be discussed later in this chapter.

Agency by Estoppel

When a principal causes a third person to believe that another person is the principal's agent, and the third person acts to his or her detriment in reasonable reliance on that belief, the principal is "estopped to deny" (prevented from denying) the agency relationship. In such a situation, the principal's actions have created the *appearance* of an agency that does not in fact exist. The third person must prove that he or she *reasonably* believed that an agency relationship existed, however.[6]

Suppose that Jayden accompanies Grant, a seed sales representative, to call on a customer, Palko, who owns a seed store. Jayden has performed independent sales work but has never signed an employment agreement with Grant. Grant boasts to Palko that he wishes he had three more assistants "just like Jayden." By making this representation, Grant creates the impression that Jayden is his agent and has authority to solicit orders. Palko has reason to believe from Grant's statements that Jayden is an agent for Grant. Palko then places seed orders with Jayden. If Grant does not correct the impression that Jayden is an agent, Grant will be bound to fill the orders just as if Jayden were really his agent. Grant's representation to Palko has created the impression that Jayden is Grant's agent and has authority to solicit orders.

Note that the acts or declarations of a purported *agent* in and of themselves do not create an agency by estoppel. Rather, it is the deeds or statements *of the principal* that create an agency by estoppel. If Jayden walked into Palko's store and claimed to be Grant's agent, when in fact he was not, and Grant had no knowledge of Jayden's representations, Grant would not be bound to any deal struck by Jayden and Palko.

Under what other circumstances might a third party reasonably believe that a person is an agent of and has the authority to act for a principal when the person does not actually have this authority? The following case provides an illustration.

6. These concepts also apply when a person who is in fact an agent undertakes an action that is beyond the scope of her or his authority, as will be discussed later in this chapter.

CASE 19.2 Motorsport Marketing, Inc. v. Wiedmaier, Inc.

Missouri Court of Appeals, Western District, 2006. 195 S.W.3d 492.
www.courts.mo.gov[a]

• **Background and Facts** Wiedmaier, Inc., owns and operates Wiedmaier Truck Stop in St. Joseph, Missouri. The owners are Marsha Wiedmaier and her husband, Jerry. Their son Michael does not own an interest in the firm, but in 2002 and 2003, he worked for it as a fuel truck operator. Motorsport Marketing, Inc., sells racing collectibles and memorabilia to retail outlets. In April 2003, Michael faxed a credit application to Motorsport's sales manager, Lesa James. Michael's mother, Marsha, signed the form as "Secretary-Owner" of Wiedmaier; after she signed, Michael added himself to the list of owners. A credit line was approved. Michael formed Extreme Diecast, LLC, and told Motorsport that it was part of Wiedmaier. He then began ordering Motorsport merchandise. By early 2004, however, Michael had stopped making payments on the account, quit his job, and moved to Columbus, Ohio. Patrick Rainey, the president of Motorsport, contacted Marsha about the account, but she refused to pay. Motorsport filed a suit in a Missouri state court against Wiedmaier and others to collect the unpaid amount. The court entered a judgment in favor of Motorsport, assessing liability against the defendants for the outstanding balance of $93,388.58, plus $13,406.38 in interest and $25,165.93 in attorneys' fees. The defendants appealed to a state intermediate appellate court.

IN THE LANGUAGE OF THE COURT
***VICTOR C. HOWARD*, Presiding Judge.**

* * * *
* * *

a. In the "Quick Links" box, click on "Opinion & Minutes." When that page opens, click on the "Missouri Court of Appeals, Western District opinions" link. At the bottom of the next page, click on the "Search Opinions" link. In that page's "Search for" box, type "Wiedmaier" and click on "Search." In the result, click on the name of the case to access the opinion. The Missouri state courts maintain this Web site.

CASE CONTINUES

CASE 19.2 CONTINUED To establish the apparent authority of a purported agent, Motorsport must show that

> *(1) the principal manifested his consent to the exercise of such authority or knowingly permitted the agent to assume the exercise of such authority; (2) the person relying on this exercise of authority knew of the facts and, acting in good faith, had reason to believe, and actually believed, the agent possessed such authority; and (3) the person relying on the appearance of authority changed his position and will be injured or suffer loss if the transaction executed by the agent does not bind the principal.* * * * [Emphasis added.]

We find that Motorsport has shown that each of the criteria for establishing Michael's apparent agency has been satisfied. First, * * * [t]he credit application constituted a direct communication from Wiedmaier, Inc. (through Marsha) to Motorsport causing Motorsport to reasonably believe that Michael had authority to act for Wiedmaier, Inc.

Second, Motorsport, relying on Michael's exercise of authority and acting in good faith, had reason to believe, and actually believed, that Michael possessed such authority. Motorsport received a credit application from Wiedmaier, Inc. signed by owner Marsha Wiedmaier, listing Michael as an owner. Motorsport had no reason to believe that Michael was not an owner of Wiedmaier or was otherwise unauthorized to act on Wiedmaier, Inc.'s behalf.

Wiedmaier, Inc. argues that even if Motorsport's reliance on Michael's apparent authority was reasonably prudent on April 10, 2003, when Michael submitted the credit application, such reliance could not have been and was not reasonably prudent from and after June 23, 2003. At that time, Michael personally made the first payment on the account with a check drawn on the account of Extreme Diecast. * * * At the very least, Wiedmaier, Inc. argues, Motorsport had "red flags waving all around it suggesting that Michael was something other than the agent of Wiedmaier, Inc."

We find that this argument is without merit. * * * It is a common practice for a truck stop to have a separate division with a separate name to handle its diecast and other related merchandise, and * * * Michael represented that this is exactly what Extreme Diecast was. * * * This evidence explains what Wiedmaier, Inc. characterizes as "red flags" concerning Michael's authority to act on behalf of Wiedmaier, Inc., and negates any alleged duty on Motorsport's part to investigate Michael's authority.

Third, Motorsport changed its position and will be injured or suffer loss if the transaction executed by Michael does not bind Wiedmaier, Inc. Motorsport extended credit to Wiedmaier, Inc. based on its interaction with Michael and based on its belief that it was dealing with Wiedmaier, Inc. Marsha Wiedmaier has refused to pay the account balance. If the transaction executed by Michael does not bind Wiedmaier, Inc., Motorsport will suffer the loss of the balance due on the account.

- **Decision and Remedy** *The state intermediate appellate court affirmed the judgment of the lower court, echoing the conclusion that "Michael acted as an apparent agent of Wiedmaier, Inc., in its dealings with Motorsport." In other words, Motorsport reasonably believed that Michael acted as Wiedmaier's agent in ordering merchandise.*

- **What If the Facts Were Different?** *Suppose that Motorsport's sales manager had telephoned Marsha Wiedmaier. Further suppose that Marsha had vouched for Michael's creditworthiness but informed Motorsport that she and her husband owned Wiedmaier and that Michael worked for them. How might the outcome of this case have been different in that situation?*

- **The E-Commerce Dimension** *Should the court have applied the law differently in this case if Michael had done business with Motorsport entirely online? Explain.*

Agency by Operation of Law

The courts may find an agency relationship in the absence of a formal agreement in other situations as well. This may occur in family relationships. For example, suppose that one spouse purchases certain basic necessaries (such as food or clothing) and charges them to the other spouse's charge account. The courts will often rule that the latter is liable for payment for the necessaries, either because of a social policy of promoting the general welfare of the spouse or because of a legal duty to supply necessaries to family members.

Agency by operation of law may also occur in emergency situations, when the agent's failure to act outside the scope of her or his authority would cause the principal substantial loss. If the agent is unable to contact the principal, the courts will often grant this emergency power. For example, a railroad engineer may contract on behalf of his or her employer for medical care for an injured motorist hit by the train. *Concept Summary 19.1* reviews the various ways that agencies are formed.

Duties of Agents and Principals

Once the principal-agent relationship has been created, both parties have duties that govern their conduct. As discussed previously, the principal-agent relationship is *fiduciary*—one of trust. In a fiduciary relationship, each party owes the other the duty to act with the utmost good faith. In this section, we examine the various duties of agents and principals.

Agent's Duties to the Principal

Generally, the agent owes the principal five duties—performance, notification, loyalty, obedience, and accounting.

Performance An implied condition in every agency contract is the agent's agreement to use reasonable diligence and skill in performing the work. When an agent fails to perform his or her duties, liability for breach of contract may result. The degree of skill or care required of an agent is usually that expected of a reasonable person under similar circumstances. Generally, this is interpreted to mean ordinary care. If an agent has represented herself or himself as possessing special skills, however, the agent is expected to exercise the degree of skill or skills claimed. Failure to do so constitutes a breach of the agent's duty.

Not all agency relationships are based on contract. In some situations, an agent acts gratuitously—that is, without payment. A gratuitous agent cannot be liable for breach of contract, as there is no contract; he or she is subject only to tort liability. Once a gratuitous agent has begun to act in an agency capacity, he or she has the duty to continue to perform in that capacity in an acceptable manner and is subject to the same standards of care and duty to perform as other agents.

For example, Bower's friend Alcott is a real estate broker. Alcott offers to sell Bower's farm at no charge. If Alcott never attempts to sell the farm, Bower has no legal cause of action to force her to do so. If Alcott does find a buyer, however, but negligently fails to follow through with the sales contract, causing the buyer to seek other property, then Bower can sue Alcott for negligence.

Notification An agent is required to notify the principal of all matters that come to her or his attention

CONCEPT SUMMARY 19.1
Formation of the Agency Relationship

Method of Formation	Description
BY AGREEMENT	The agency relationship is formed through express consent (oral or written) or implied by conduct.
BY RATIFICATION	The principal either by act or by agreement ratifies the conduct of a person who is not in fact an agent.
BY ESTOPPEL	The principal causes a third person to believe that another person is the principal's agent, and the third person acts to his or her detriment in reasonable reliance on that belief.
BY OPERATION OF LAW	The agency relationship is based on a social duty (such as the need to support family members) or formed in emergency situations when the agent is unable to contact the principal and failure to act outside the scope of the agent's authority would cause the principal substantial loss.

concerning the subject matter of the agency. This is the *duty of notification,* or the duty to inform. For example, suppose that Lang, an artist, is about to negotiate a contract to sell a series of paintings to Barber's Art Gallery for $25,000. Lang's agent learns that Barber is insolvent and will be unable to pay for the paintings. Lang's agent has a duty to inform Lang of Barber's insolvency because it is relevant to the subject matter of the agency—the sale of Lang's paintings. Generally, the law assumes that the principal is aware of any information acquired by the agent that is relevant to the agency—regardless of whether the agent actually passes on this information to the principal. It is a basic tenet of agency law that notice to the agent is notice to the principal.

Loyalty Loyalty is one of the most fundamental duties in a fiduciary relationship. Basically stated, the agent has the duty to act *solely for the benefit of his or her principal* and not in the interest of the agent or a third party. For example, an agent cannot represent two principals in the same transaction unless both know of the dual capacity and consent to it. The duty of loyalty also means that any information or knowledge acquired through the agency relationship is confidential. It is a breach of loyalty to disclose such information either during the agency relationship or after its termination. Typical examples of confidential information are trade secrets and customer lists compiled by the principal (see Chapter 14).

In short, the agent's loyalty must be undivided. The agent's actions must be strictly for the benefit of the principal and must not result in any secret profit for the agent. For example, Don Cousins contracts with Leo Hodgins, a real estate agent, to negotiate the purchase of an office building as an investment. While working for Cousins, Hodgins discovers that the property owner will sell the building only as a package deal with another parcel. If Hodgins then forms a limited partnership with his brother to buy the two properties and resell the building to Cousins, has he breached his fiduciary duties? The answer is yes, because as a real estate agent, Hodgins had a duty to communicate all offers to his principal and not to secretly purchase the property and then resell it to his principal. Hodgins is required to act in Cousins's best interests and can become the purchaser in this situation only with Cousins's knowledge and approval.[7]

Obedience When an agent is acting on behalf of the principal, the agent has a duty to follow all lawful and clearly stated instructions given by the principal. Any deviation from such instructions is a violation of this duty. During emergency situations, however, when the principal cannot be consulted, the agent may deviate from the instructions without violating this duty. Whenever instructions are not clearly stated, the agent can fulfill the duty of obedience by acting in good faith and in a manner reasonable under the circumstances.

Accounting Unless an agent and a principal agree otherwise, the agent has a duty to keep and make available to the principal an account of all property and funds received and paid out on behalf of the principal. The agent has a duty to maintain separate accounts for the principal's funds and the agent's personal funds, and the agent must not intermingle the funds in these accounts. Whenever a licensed professional (such as an attorney) violates this duty to account, he or she may be subject to disciplinary proceedings carried out by the appropriate regulatory institution (such as the state bar association) in addition to being liable to the principal (the professional's client) for failure to account.

A bank acts as an agent for its customer when collecting an item presented for payment. Suppose that the item is an international check to be paid in currency subject to a variable rate of exchange. Does the bank have a duty to account for the difference between the amount paid to the customer and the amount collected on the check? That was a question in the following case.

7. *Cousins v. Realty Ventures, Inc.*, 844 So.2d 860 (La.App. 5 Cir. 2003).

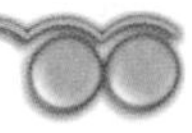

EXTENDED CASE 19.3 Gossels v. Fleet National Bank

Appeals Court of Massachusetts, Suffolk, 2007. 69 Mass.App.Ct. 797, 876 N.E.2d 872.

GELINAS, J. [Justice]

* * * *

* * * [Peter] Gossels received a check from the German government for 85,071.19 euros, drawn on Dresdner Bank of Germany. [The check was a payment in reparation for the seizure by the Third Reich of property belonging to Gossels's family.] On October 15, 1999, he took the

CASE 19.3 CONTINUED

check to a branch of Fleet [National Bank] in Boston and presented it to the international teller.

* * * [The] teller failed to inform Gossels * * * that Fleet paid international checks at a "retail exchange rate" several percentage points lower than the interbank "spot rate" for foreign currency.

As Gossels started to indorse the check, the international teller also incorrectly instructed Gossels not to indorse the check * * * .

* * * *

Fleet, as collecting bank, sent the check to * * * Fleet's foreign correspondent bank in Germany, Deutsche Bank [which sent it to Dresdner Bank. After a delay to obtain Gossels's indorsement] Dresdner Bank debited the funds from the appropriate account and sent 85,071.19 euros to Deutsche Bank, which * * * credited 84,971.19 euros to Fleet's account at Deutsche Bank (100 euros having been deducted as a collection fee).

On December 15, 1999, Gossels received notice from Fleet that it had credited his account with check proceeds in the amount of $81,754.77, which was based on the December 15, 1999, retail exchange rate offered by Fleet for 84,971.19 euros. The same number of euros would have been worth $88,616.45 based on the October 15, 1999, retail exchange rate offered by Fleet, or $92,023.80 based on the October 15, 1999, spot rate offered by Dresdner Bank.

[When Gossels learned of the different rates, he filed a suit in a Massachusetts state court against Fleet. The court entered a judgment for Gossels on a ground of negligent misrepresentation. Both parties appealed to a state intermediate appellate court.]

* * * *

Under [Section 4–201(a) of the Uniform Commercial Code] Fleet became Gossels's agent when he passed the check to Fleet, and Fleet accepted the check, for collection.

* * * *

As Gossels's agent and fiduciary, Fleet was obliged to disclose fully all facts material to the transaction. *The principal has a right to be informed of all material facts known to the agent in reference to the transaction in which he is acting for his principal, and good faith requires a disclosure of such facts by the agent. Whenever facts known to the agent but not to the principal may affect the desires and conduct of the principal, the agent must communicate that information to the principal * * * particularly if the agent is engaging in any arrangement * * * adverse to the principal's interest.* [Emphasis added.]

* * * *

* * * Fleet was required, as a fiduciary, to advise Gossels that it would pay his international check at a retail exchange rate that was several percentage points lower than the spot rate it received for foreign currency. * * * Nowhere in the transaction did Fleet reveal that it would pay Gossels, its principal, a retail rate of exchange substantially less than the spot rate it obtained for the item, which former rate was set out daily on a "secret" rate sheet that bank employees were advised not to disclose to the public, and that it would profit by effectively keeping the difference.

* * * *

* * * By failing to disclose the rate, and by withholding the amount without giving Gossels an adequate explanation, Fleet further committed a breach of its fiduciary duty to give a complete accounting of the disposition of the funds * * * . *An agent or fiduciary is under a duty to keep and render accounts and, when called upon for an accounting, has the burden of proving that he properly disposed of funds which he is shown to have received for his principal * * * .* [Emphasis added.]

* * * If there is no prior agreement with regard to the profit, the agent must not only render an account of it, but must pay the funds over to the principal. Fleet was bound to account for the amounts it kept in the rate arbitrage [the profits it earned on the transaction], and to pay it over to Gossels.

* * * *

* * * The [trial] judge's finding * * * that Fleet is liable to Gossels for negligent misrepresentation has not been shown to be erroneous. Fleet is also liable to Gossels * * * for breach of fiduciary duty. * * * The judgment is vacated and we remand the case to the trial court for entry of a single judgment in favor of Gossels on the aforementioned claims * * * .

CASE CONTINUES

CASE 19.3 CONTINUED

QUESTIONS

1. Was the specific exchange rate that the bank used important to the disposition of this case? Explain.
2. Should the court have considered whether the bank had a corrupt intent to deprive its customer of funds? Why or why not?

Principal's Duties to the Agent

The principal also has certain duties to the agent. These duties relate to compensation, reimbursement and indemnification, cooperation, and safe working conditions.

Compensation In general, when a principal requests certain services from an agent, the agent reasonably expects payment. The principal therefore has a duty to pay the agent for services rendered. For example, when an accountant or an attorney is asked to act as an agent, an agreement to compensate the agent for this service is implied. The principal also has a duty to pay that compensation in a timely manner. Except in a gratuitous agency relationship, in which the agent does not act in exchange for payment, the principal must pay the agreed-on value for the agent's services. If no amount has been expressly agreed on, then the principal owes the agent the customary compensation for such services.

Reimbursement and Indemnification Whenever an agent disburses funds to fulfill the request of the principal or to pay for necessary expenses in the course of a reasonable performance of her or his agency duties, the principal has the duty to reimburse the agent for these payments.[8] Agents cannot recover for expenses incurred by their own misconduct or negligence, though.

Subject to the terms of the agency agreement, the principal has the duty to *indemnify* (compensate) an agent for liabilities incurred because of authorized and lawful acts and transactions. For example, if the agent, on the principal's behalf, forms a contract with a third party, and the principal fails to perform the contract, the third party may sue the agent for damages. In this situation, the principal is obligated to compensate the agent for any costs incurred by the agent as a result of the principal's failure to perform the contract.

Additionally, the principal must indemnify the agent for the value of benefits that the agent confers on the principal. The amount of indemnification is usually specified in the agency contract. If it is not, the courts will look to the nature of the business and the type of benefits to determine the amount. Note that this rule applies to acts by gratuitous agents as well.

Cooperation A principal has a duty to cooperate with the agent and to assist the agent in performing his or her duties. The principal must do nothing to prevent that performance. For example, when a principal grants an agent an exclusive territory, creating an *exclusive agency*, the principal cannot compete with the agent or appoint or allow another agent to so compete in violation of the exclusive agency. If the principal does so, she or he will be exposed to liability for the agent's lost sales or profits.

Safe Working Conditions The common law requires the principal to provide safe working premises, equipment, and conditions for all agents and employees. The principal has a duty to inspect working areas and to warn agents and employees about any unsafe situations. When the agent is an employee, the employer's liability is frequently covered by state workers' compensation insurance, and federal and state statutes often require the employer to meet certain safety standards (see Chapter 20).

Rights and Remedies of Agents and Principals

It is said that every wrong has its remedy. In business situations, disputes between agents and principals may arise out of either contract or tort law and carry corresponding remedies. These remedies include monetary damages, termination of the agency relationship, an injunction, and required accountings.

8. This principle applies to acts by gratuitous agents as well. If a finder of a dog that becomes sick takes the dog to a veterinarian and pays the required fees for the veterinarian's services, the agent is entitled to be reimbursed by the owner of the dog for those fees.

Agent's Rights and Remedies against the Principal

For every duty of the principal, the agent has a corresponding right. Therefore, the agent has the right to be compensated, reimbursed, and indemnified and to work in a safe environment. An agent also has the right to perform agency duties without interference by the principal.

Tort and Contract Remedies Remedies of the agent for breach of duty by the principal follow normal contract and tort remedies. For example, Aaron Hart, a builder who has just constructed a new house, contracts with a real estate agent, Fran Boller, to sell the house. The contract calls for the agent to have an exclusive, ninety-day listing and to receive 6 percent of the selling price when the home is sold. Boller holds several open houses and shows the home to a number of potential buyers. One month before the ninety-day listing terminates, Hart agrees to sell the house to another buyer—not one to whom Boller has shown the house—after the ninety-day listing expires. Hart and the buyer agree that Hart will reduce the price of the house by 3 percent because he will sell it directly and thus will not have to pay Boller's commission. In this situation, if Boller learns of Hart's actions, she can terminate the agency relationship and sue Hart for damages—including the 6 percent commission she should have earned on the sale of the house.

Demand for an Accounting An agent can also withhold further performance and demand that the principal give an accounting. For example, a sales agent may demand an accounting if the agent and principal disagree on the amount of commissions the agent should have received for sales made during a specific period of time.

No Right to Specific Performance When the principal-agent relationship is not contractual, the agent has no right to specific performance. An agent can recover for past services and future damages but cannot force the principal to allow him or her to continue acting as an agent.

Principal's Rights and Remedies against the Agent

In general, a principal has contract remedies for an agent's breach of fiduciary duties. The principal also has tort remedies if the agent commits misrepresentation, negligence, deceit, libel, slander, or trespass. In addition, any breach of a fiduciary duty by an agent may justify the principal's termination of the agency. The main actions available to the principal are constructive trust, avoidance, and indemnification.

Constructive Trust Anything that an agent obtains by virtue of the employment or agency relationship belongs to the principal. An agent commits a breach of fiduciary duty if he or she secretly retains benefits or profits that, by right, belong to the principal. For example, Andrews, a purchasing agent for Metcalf, receives cash rebates from a customer. If Andrews keeps the rebates for himself, he violates his fiduciary duty to his principal, Metcalf. On finding out about the cash rebates, Metcalf can sue Andrews and recover them.

Avoidance When an agent breaches the agency agreement or agency duties under a contract, the principal has a right to avoid any contract entered into with the agent. This right of avoidance is at the election of the principal.

Indemnification In certain situations, when a principal is sued by a third party for an agent's negligent conduct, the principal can sue the agent for an equal amount of damages. This is called *indemnification*. The same holds true if the agent violates the principal's instructions. For example, Parke (the principal) owns a used-car lot where Moore (the agent) works as a salesperson. Parke tells Moore to make no warranties for the used cars. Moore is eager to make a sale to Walters, a customer, and adds a 50,000-mile warranty for the car's engine. Parke may still be liable to Walters for engine failure, but if Walters sues Parke, Parke normally can then sue Moore for indemnification for violating his instructions.

Sometimes, it is difficult to distinguish between instructions of the principal that limit an agent's authority and those that are merely advice. For example, Gutierrez (the principal) owns an office supply company; Logan (the agent) is the manager. Gutierrez tells Logan, "Don't purchase any more inventory this month." Gutierrez goes on vacation. A large order comes in from a local business, and the inventory on hand is insufficient to meet it. What is Logan to do? In this situation, Logan probably has the inherent authority to purchase more inventory despite Gutierrez's command. It is unlikely that Logan would be required to indemnify Gutierrez in the event that the local business subsequently canceled the order.

Scope of Agent's Authority

The liability of a principal to third parties with whom an agent contracts depends on whether the agent had the authority to enter into legally binding contracts on the principal's behalf. An agent's authority can be either *actual* (express or implied) or *apparent*. If an agent contracts outside the scope of his or her authority, the principal may still become liable by ratifying the contract.

Express Authority

Express authority is authority declared in clear, direct, and definite terms. Express authority can be given orally or in writing. In most states, the **equal dignity rule** requires that if the contract being executed is or must be in writing, then the agent's authority must also be in writing. Failure to comply with the equal dignity rule can make a contract voidable *at the option of the principal*. The law regards the contract at that point as a mere offer. If the principal decides to accept the offer, the acceptance must be ratified, or affirmed, in writing.

Assume that Pattberg (the principal) orally asks Austin (the agent) to sell a ranch that Pattberg owns. Austin finds a buyer and signs a sales contract (a contract for an interest in realty must be in writing) on behalf of Pattberg to sell the ranch. The buyer cannot enforce the contract unless Pattberg subsequently ratifies Austin's agency status in writing. Once the contract is ratified, either party can enforce rights under the contract.

Modern business practice allows an exception to the equal dignity rule. An executive officer of a corporation, when acting for the corporation in an ordinary business situation, is not required to obtain written authority from the corporation. In addition, the equal dignity rule does not apply when the agent acts in the presence of the principal or when the agent's act of signing is merely perfunctory. Thus, if Healy (the principal) negotiates a contract but is called out of town the day it is to be signed and orally authorizes Scougall to sign, the oral authorization is sufficient.

Power of Attorney Giving an agent a **power of attorney** confers express authority.[9] The power of attorney is a written document and is usually notarized. (A document is notarized when a **notary public**—a public official authorized to attest to the authenticity of signatures—signs and dates the document and imprints it with her or his seal of authority.) Most states have statutory provisions for creating a power of attorney. A power of attorney can be special (permitting the agent to perform specified acts only), or it can be general (permitting the agent to transact all business for the principal). Because of the extensive authority granted to an agent by a general power of attorney (see Exhibit 19–1), it should be used with great caution and usually only in exceptional circumstances. Ordinarily, a power of attorney terminates on the incapacity or death of the person giving the power.[10]

Implied Authority

An agent has the **implied authority** to do what is reasonably necessary to carry out express authority and accomplish the objectives of the agency. Authority can also be implied by custom or inferred from the position the agent occupies. For example, Carlson is employed by Packard Grocery to manage one of its stores. Packard has not expressly stated that Carlson has authority to contract with third persons. Nevertheless, authority to manage a business implies authority to do what is reasonably required (as is customary or can be inferred from a manager's position) to operate the business. This includes making contracts for hiring personnel, for buying merchandise and equipment, and even for advertising the products sold in the store.

In general, implied authority is authority customarily associated with the position occupied by the agent or authority that can be inferred from the express authority given to the agent to perform fully his or her duties. For example, an agent who has authority to solicit orders for goods sold by the principal generally would not have the authority to collect payments for the goods unless the agent possesses the goods. The test is whether it was reasonable for the agent to believe that she or he had the authority to enter into the contract in question.

Also note that an agent's implied authority cannot contradict his or her express authority. Thus, if a princi-

9. An agent who holds a power of attorney is called an *attorney-in-fact* for the principal. The holder does not have to be an attorney-at-law (and often is not).

10. A *durable* power of attorney, however, continues to be effective despite the principal's incapacity. An elderly person, for example, might grant a durable power of attorney to provide for the handling of property and investments or specific health-care needs should he or she become incompetent.

EXHIBIT 19–1 • A Sample General Power of Attorney

GENERAL POWER OF ATTORNEY

Know All Men by These Presents:

That I, __________, hereinafter referred to as PRINCIPAL, in the County of __________ State of __________, do(es) appoint __________ as my true and lawful attorney.

In principal's name, and for principal's use and benefit, said attorney is authorized hereby;

(1) To demand, sue for, collect, and receive all money, debts, accounts, legacies, bequests, interest, dividends, annuities, and demands as are now or shall hereafter become due, payable, or belonging to principal, and take all lawful means, for the recovery thereof and to compromise the same and give discharges for the same;
(2) To buy and sell land, make contracts of every kind relative to land, any interest therein or the possession thereof, and to take possession and exercise control over the use thereof;
(3) To buy, sell, mortgage, hypothecate, assign, transfer, and in any manner deal with goods, wares and merchandise, choses in action, certificates or shares of capital stock, and other property in possession or in action, and to make, do, and transact all and every kind of business of whatever nature;
(4) To execute, acknowledge, and deliver contracts of sale, escrow instructions, deeds, leases including leases for minerals and hydrocarbon substances and assignments of leases, covenants, agreements and assignments of agreements, mortgages and assignments of mortgages, conveyances in trust, to secure indebtedness or other obligations, and assign the beneficial interest thereunder, subordinations of liens or encumbrances, bills of lading, receipts, evidences of debt, releases, bonds, notes, bills, requests to reconvey deeds of trust, partial or full judgments, satisfactions of mortgages, and other debts, and other written instruments of whatever kind and nature, all upon such terms and conditions as said attorney shall approve.

GIVING AND GRANTING to said attorney full power and authority to do all and every act and thing whatsoever requisite and necessary to be done relative to any of the foregoing as fully to all intents and purposes as principal might or could do if personally present.

All that said attorney shall lawfully do or cause to be done under the authority of this power of attorney is expressly approved.

Dated: __________ /s/__________

State of __________ }
County of __________ } SS.

On __________, before me, the undersigned, a Notary Public in and for said State, personally appeared __________
____
known to me to be the person __________ whose name __________ subscribed to the within instrument and acknowledged that __________ executed the same.

Witness my hand and official seal. (Seal) __________
Notary Public in and for said State.

pal has limited an agent's authority—by forbidding a manager to enter contracts to hire additional workers, for example—then the fact that managers customarily would have such authority is irrelevant.

Apparent Authority and Estoppel

Actual authority (express or implied) arises from what the principal makes clear *to the agent.* Apparent authority, in contrast, arises from what the principal causes a third party to believe. An agent has **apparent authority** when the principal, by either word or action, causes a *third party* reasonably to believe that the agent has authority to act, even though the agent has no express or implied authority. If the third party changes his or her position in reliance on the principal's representations, the principal may be *estopped* (prevented) from denying that the agent had authority.

Apparent authority usually comes into existence through a principal's pattern of conduct over time. For example, Bain is a traveling salesperson with the authority to solicit orders for a principal's goods. Because she does not carry any goods with her, she normally would not have the implied authority to collect payments from customers on behalf of the principal. Suppose that she does accept payments from Corgley Enterprises, however, and submits them to the principal's accounting department for processing. If the principal does nothing to stop Bain from continuing this practice, a pattern develops over time, and the principal confers apparent authority on Bain to accept payments from Corgley.

At issue in the following case was a question of apparent authority or, as the court referred to it, "ostensible agency."

CASE 19.4 Ermoian v. Desert Hospital

Court of Appeal of California, Fourth District, Division 2, 2007.
152 Cal.App.4th 475, 61 Cal.Rptr.3d 754.

• **Background and Facts** In 1990, Desert Hospital in California established a comprehensive perinatal services program (CPSP) to provide obstetrical care to women who were uninsured (*perinatal* is often defined as relating to the period from about the twenty-eighth week of pregnancy to around one month after birth). The CPSP was set up in an office suite across from the hospital and named "Desert Hospital Outpatient Maternity Services Clinic." The hospital contracted with a corporation controlled by Dr. Morton Gubin, which employed Dr. Masami Ogata, to provide obstetrical services. In January 1994, Jackie Shahan went to the hospital's emergency room because of cramping and other symptoms. The emergency room physician told Shahan that she was pregnant and referred her to the clinic. Shahan visited the clinic throughout her pregnancy. On May 15, Shahan's baby, named Amanda, was born with brain abnormalities that left her severely mentally retarded and unable to care for herself. Her conditions could not have been prevented, treated, or cured *in utero.* Amanda filed a suit in a California state court against the hospital and others, alleging "wrongful life." She claimed that the defendants negligently failed to inform her mother of her abnormalities before her birth, depriving her mother of the opportunity to make an informed choice to terminate the pregnancy. The court ruled in the defendants' favor, holding, among other things, that the hospital was not liable because Drs. Gubin and Ogata were not its employees. Amanda appealed to a state intermediate appellate court, contending in part that the physicians were the hospital's "ostensible agents."

IN THE LANGUAGE OF THE COURT

KING, J. [Judge]

* * * *

Agency may be either actual or ostensible [apparent]. Actual agency exists when the agent is really employed by the principal. Here, there was evidence that the physicians were not employees of the Hospital, but were physicians with a private practice who contracted with the Hospital to perform obstetric services at the clinic. The written contract between the Hospital and Dr. Gubin's corporation (which employed Dr. Ogata) describes Dr. Gubin and his corporation as "independent contractors with, and not as employees of, [the] Hospital." [Maria Sterling, a registered nurse at the clinic and Shahan's CPSP case coordinator] testified that Drs. Gubin and Ogata, not the Hospital, provided the obstetric services to the clinic's patients. Donna McCloudy, a director of nursing [who set up the CPSP] at the Hospital, testified that while the Hospital provided some aspects of the CPSP services, "independent physicians * * * provided the obstetrical care * * * ." Based upon such evidence, the [trial] court reasonably concluded that the physicians were not the employees or actual agents of the Hospital for purposes of vicarious [indirect] liability.

Ostensible [apparent] agency on the other hand, may be implied from the facts of a particular case, and if a principal by his acts has led others to believe that he has conferred authority upon an agent, he cannot be heard to assert, as against third parties who have relied thereon in good faith, that he did not intend to confer such power * * * . The doctrine establishing the principles of liability for the acts of an ostensible agent rests on the doctrine of estoppel. *The essential elements are representations by the principal, justifiable reliance thereon by a third party, and change of position or injury resulting from such reliance.* Before recovery can be had against the principal for the acts of an ostensible agent, the person dealing with an agent must do so with belief in the

CASE 19.4 CONTINUED

agent's authority and this belief must be a reasonable one. Such belief must be generated by some act or neglect by the principal sought to be charged and the person relying on the agent's apparent authority must not be guilty of neglect. [Emphasis added.]

* * * *

Here, the Hospital held out the clinic and the personnel in the clinic as part of the Hospital. Furthermore, it was objectively reasonable for Shahan to believe that Drs. Gubin and Ogata were employees of the Hospital. The clinic was located across the street from the Hospital. It used the same name as the Hospital and labeled itself as an outpatient clinic. Numerous professionals at the clinic were employees of the Hospital. [Carol Cribbs, a comprehensive perinatal health worker at the clinic] and Sterling indicated to Shahan that they were employees of the Hospital and that the program was run by the Hospital. Sterling personally set up all of Shahan's appointments at the main Hospital rather than giving Shahan a referral for the various tests. Shahan was referred by individuals in the emergency room specifically to Dr. Gubin. When she called for an appointment she was told by the receptionist that she was calling the Hospital outpatient clinic which was the clinic of Dr. Gubin. On days when Shahan would see either Dr. Gubin or Dr. Ogata at the clinic, she would also see either Cribbs or Sterling, whom she knew were employed by the Hospital.

* * * At her first appointment she signed a document titled "patient rights and responsibilities," which would unambiguously lead a patient to the conclusion that the clinic "was a one-stop shop for the patient," and that all individuals at the clinic were connected with the Hospital. All of Shahan's contacts with the physicians were at the Hospital-run clinic. Most, if not all, of the physician contacts occurred in conjunction with the provision of other services by either Sterling or Cribbs. The entire appearance created by the Hospital, and those associated with it, was that the Hospital was the provider of the obstetrical care to Shahan.

• **Decision and Remedy** *The state intermediate appellate court decided that, contrary to the lower court's finding, Drs. Gubin and Ogata were "ostensible agents of the Hospital." The appellate court affirmed the lower court's ruling, however, on Amanda's "wrongful life" claim, concluding that the physicians were not negligent in failing to advise Shahan to have an elective abortion.*

• **The Ethical Dimension** *Does a principal have an ethical responsibility to inform an unaware third party that an apparent (ostensible) agent does not in fact have authority to act on the principal's behalf?*

• **The E-Commerce Dimension** *Could Amanda have established Drs. Gubin and Ogata's apparent authority if Desert Hospital had maintained a Web site that advertised the services of the CPSP clinic and stated clearly that the physicians were not its employees? Explain.*

Emergency Powers

When an unforeseen emergency demands action by the agent to protect or preserve the property and rights of the principal, but the agent is unable to communicate with the principal, the agent has emergency power. For example, Fulsom is an engineer for Pacific Drilling Company. While Fulsom is acting within the scope of his employment, he is severely injured in an accident at an oil rig many miles from home. Dudley, the rig supervisor, directs Thompson, a physician, to give medical aid to Fulsom and to charge Pacific for the medical services. Dudley, an agent, has no express or implied authority to bind the principal, Pacific Drilling, for Thompson's medical services. Because of the emergency situation, however, the law recognizes Dudley as having authority to act appropriately under the circumstances.

Ratification

Ratification occurs when the principal affirms, or accepts responsibility for, an agent's *unauthorized* act. When ratification occurs, the principal is bound to the agent's act, and the act is treated as if it had been authorized by the principal *from the outset*. Ratification can be either express or implied.

If the principal does not ratify the contract, the principal is not bound, and the third party's agreement with the agent is viewed as merely an unaccepted offer. Because the third party's agreement is an unaccepted offer, the third party can revoke it at any time, without liability, before the principal ratifies the contract. The agent, however, may be liable to the third party for misrepresenting her or his authority.

The requirements for ratification can be summarized as follows:

1. The agent must have acted on behalf of an identified principal who subsequently ratifies the action.
2. The principal must know all of the material facts involved in the transaction. If a principal ratifies a contract without knowing all of the facts, the principal can rescind (cancel) the contract.[11]
3. The principal must affirm the agent's act in its entirety.
4. The principal must have the legal capacity to authorize the transaction at the time the agent engages in the act and at the time the principal ratifies. The third party must also have the legal capacity to engage in the transaction.
5. The principal's affirmation (ratification) must occur before the third party withdraws from the transaction.
6. The principal must observe the same formalities when approving the act done by the agent as would have been required to authorize it initially.

11. If the third party has changed position in reliance on the apparent contract, however, the principal can rescind but must reimburse the third party for any costs.

Concept Summary 19.2 summarizes the rules concerning an agent's authority to bind the principal and a third party.

Liability for Contracts

Liability for contracts formed by an agent depends on how the principal is classified and on whether the actions of the agent were authorized or unauthorized. Principals are classified as disclosed, partially disclosed, or undisclosed.

A **disclosed principal** is a principal whose identity is known by the third party at the time the contract is made by the agent. A **partially disclosed principal** is a principal whose identity is not known by the third party, but the third party knows that the agent is or may be acting for a principal at the time the contract is made. An **undisclosed principal** is a principal whose identity is totally unknown by the third party, and the third party has no knowledge that the agent is acting in an agency capacity at the time the contract is made.

CONCEPT SUMMARY 19.2
Authority of an Agent to Bind the Principal and a Third Party

Authority of Agent	Definition	Effect on Principal and Third Party
EXPRESS AUTHORITY	Authority expressly given by the principal to the agent.	Principal and third party are bound in contract.
IMPLIED AUTHORITY	Authority implied (1) by custom, (2) from the position in which the principal has placed the agent, or (3) because such authority is necessary if the agent is to carry out expressly authorized duties and responsibilities.	Principal and third party are bound in contract.
APPARENT AUTHORITY	Authority created when the conduct of the principal leads a third party to believe that the principal's agent has authority.	Principal and third party are bound in contract.
UNAUTHORIZED ACTS	Acts committed by an agent that are outside the scope of his or her express, implied, or apparent authority.	Principal and third party are not bound in contract—*unless* the principal ratifies prior to the third party's withdrawal.

Authorized Acts

If an agent acts within the scope of her or his authority, normally the principal is obligated to perform the contract regardless of whether the principal was disclosed, partially disclosed, or undisclosed. Whether the agent may also be held liable under the contract, however, depends on the disclosed, partially disclosed, or undisclosed status of the principal.

Disclosed or Partially Disclosed Principal A disclosed or partially disclosed principal is liable to a third party for a contract made by the agent. If the principal is disclosed, an agent has no contractual liability for the nonperformance of the principal or the third party. If the principal is partially disclosed, in most states the agent is also treated as a party to the contract, and the third party can hold the agent liable for contractual nonperformance.[12]

Undisclosed Principal When neither the fact of an agency relationship nor the identity of the principal is disclosed, the undisclosed principal is bound to perform just as if the principal had been fully disclosed at the time the contract was made.

When a principal's identity is undisclosed and the agent is forced to pay the third party, the agent is entitled to be *indemnified* (compensated) by the principal. The principal had a duty to perform, even though his or her identity was undisclosed, and failure to do so will make the principal ultimately liable. Once the undisclosed principal's identity is revealed, the third party generally can elect to hold either the principal or the agent liable on the contract.

Conversely, the undisclosed principal can require the third party to fulfill the contract, *unless* (1) the undisclosed principal was expressly excluded as a party in the written contract; (2) the contract is a negotiable instrument signed by the agent with no indication of signing in a representative capacity;[13] or (3) the performance of the agent is personal to the contract, allowing the third party to refuse the principal's performance.

Unauthorized Acts

If an agent has no authority but nevertheless contracts with a third party, the principal cannot be held liable on the contract. It does not matter whether the principal was disclosed, partially disclosed, or undisclosed. The agent is liable, however. For example, Scammon signs a contract for the purchase of a truck, purportedly acting as an agent under authority granted by Johnson. In fact, Johnson has not given Scammon any such authority. Johnson refuses to pay for the truck, claiming that Scammon had no authority to purchase it. The seller of the truck is entitled to hold Scammon liable for payment.

If the principal is disclosed or partially disclosed, the agent is liable as long as the third party relied on the agency status. The agent's liability here is based on the theory of breach of the *implied warranty of authority*, not on breach of the contract itself.[14] The agent's implied warranty of authority can be breached intentionally or by a good faith mistake.[15] For example, Kilmer (the principal) is a reclusive artist who hires Higgs (the agent) to solicit offers for particular paintings from various galleries, but does not authorize him to enter into sales agreements. Olaf, a gallery owner, desires to buy two of Kilmer's paintings right away for an upcoming show. Higgs tells Olaf that he will draw up a sales contract. By doing so, Higgs impliedly warrants that he has the authority to enter into sales contracts on behalf of Kilmer. If it later turns out that Kilmer does not wish to ratify the sales contract signed by Higgs, Olaf cannot hold Kilmer liable, but he can hold Higgs liable for breaching the implied warranty of authority.

Note that if the third party knows at the time the contract is made that the agent does not have authority, then the agent is not liable. Similarly, if the agent expresses to the third party *uncertainty* as to the extent of her or his authority, the agent is not personally liable.

Actions by E-Agents

Although standard agency principles once applied only to *human* agents, today these same agency principles are being applied to e-agents. An electronic agent, or **e-agent,** is a semiautonomous computer program that is capable of executing specific tasks. E-agents used in e-commerce include software that can search through many databases and retrieve only relevant information for the user.

12. *Restatement (Second) of Agency,* Section 321.
13. Under the Uniform Commercial Code (UCC), only the agent is liable if the instrument neither names the principal nor shows that the agent signed in a representative capacity [UCC 3–402(b)(2)].
14. The agent is not liable on the contract because the agent was never intended personally to be a party to the contract.
15. If the agent intentionally misrepresents his or her authority, then the agent can also be liable in tort for fraud.

The Uniform Electronic Transactions Act (UETA), which has been adopted at least in part by the majority of the states (see Chapter 11), includes several provisions relating to the principal's liability for the actions of e-agents. Section 15 of the UETA states that e-agents may enter into binding agreements on behalf of their principals. Presumably, then—at least in those states that have adopted the act—the principal will be bound by the terms in a contract entered into by an e-agent. Thus, if you place an order over the Internet, the company (principal) whose system took the order via an e-agent cannot claim that it did not receive your order.

The UETA also stipulates that if an e-agent does not provide an opportunity to prevent errors at the time of the transaction, the other party to the transaction can avoid the transaction. Therefore, if an e-agent fails to provide an on-screen confirmation of a purchase or sale, the other party can avoid the effect of any errors. For example, Finig wants to purchase three each of three different items (a total of nine items). The e-agent mistakenly records an order for thirty-three of a single item and does not provide an on-screen verification of the order. If thirty-three items are then sent to Finig, he can avoid the contract to purchase them.

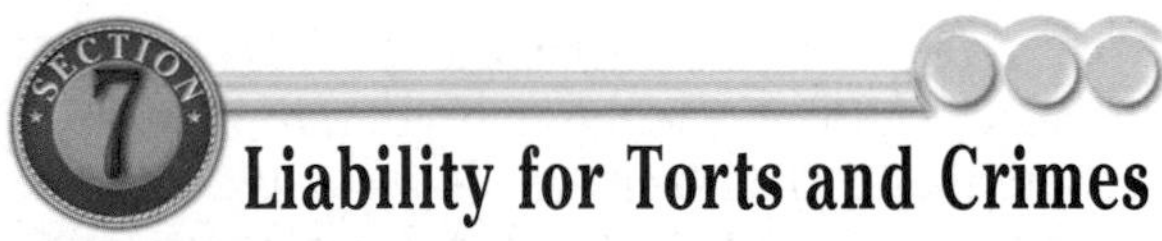

Liability for Torts and Crimes

Obviously, any person, including an agent, is liable for his or her own torts and crimes. Whether a principal can also be held liable for an agent's torts and crimes depends on several factors, which we examine here. In some situations, a principal may be held liable not only for the torts of an agent but also for the torts committed by an independent contractor.

Principal's Tortious Conduct

A principal conducting an activity through an agent may be liable for harm resulting from the principal's own negligence or recklessness. Thus, a principal may be liable for giving improper instructions, authorizing the use of improper materials or tools, or establishing improper rules that result in the agent's committing a tort. For instance, if Jack knows that Lucy cannot drive but nevertheless tells her to use the company truck to deliver some equipment to a customer, he will be liable for his own negligence to anyone injured by her negligent driving.

Principal's Authorization of Agent's Tortious Conduct

Similarly, a principal who authorizes an agent to commit a tort may be liable to persons or property injured thereby, because the act is considered to be the principal's. For example, Selkow directs his agent, Warren, to cut the corn on specific acreage, which neither of them has the right to do. The harvest is therefore a trespass (a tort), and Selkow is liable to the owner of the corn.

Note that an agent acting at the principal's direction can be liable as a *tortfeasor* (one who commits a wrong, or tort), along with the principal, for committing the tortious act even if the agent was unaware that the act was wrong. Assume in the above example that Warren, the agent, did not know that Selkow lacked the right to harvest the corn. Warren can still be held liable to the owner of the field for damages, along with Selkow, the principal.

Liability for Agent's Misrepresentation

A principal is exposed to tort liability whenever a third person sustains a loss due to the agent's misrepresentation. The principal's liability depends on whether the agent was actually or apparently authorized to make representations and whether the representations were made within the scope of the agency. The principal is always directly responsible for an agent's misrepresentation made within the scope of the agent's authority.

Assume that Bassett is a demonstrator for Moore's products. Moore sends Bassett to a home show to demonstrate the products and to answer questions from consumers. Moore has given Bassett authority to make statements about the products. If Bassett makes only true representations, all is fine; but if he makes false claims, Moore will be liable for any injuries or damages sustained by third parties in reliance on Bassett's false representations.

Apparent Implied Authority When a principal has placed an agent in a position of apparent authority—making it possible for the agent to defraud a third party—the principal may also be liable for the agent's fraudulent acts. For example, Frendak is a loan officer at First Security Bank. In the ordinary course of the job, Frendak approves and services loans and has access to the credit records of all customers. Frendak falsely represents to a borrower, McMillan, that the bank feels insecure about McMillan's loan and intends to call it in unless McMillan provides additional collateral, such as stocks and bonds. McMillan gives Frendak numerous stock certificates, which Frendak keeps in her own possession and later uses to make personal investments. The bank is liable to McMillan for losses sustained on the stocks even though the bank was unaware of the fraudulent scheme.

If, in contrast, Frendak had been a recently hired junior bank teller rather than a loan officer when she told McMillan that the bank required additional security for the loan, McMillan would not have been justified in relying on her representation. In that situation, the bank normally would not be liable to McMillan for the losses sustained.

Innocent Misrepresentation Tort liability based on fraud requires proof that a material misstatement was made knowingly and with the intent to deceive. An agent's innocent mistakes occurring in a contract transaction or involving a warranty contained in the contract can provide grounds for the third party's rescission of the contract and the award of damages. Moreover, justice dictates that when a principal knows that an agent is not accurately advised of facts but does not correct either the agent's or the third party's impressions, the principal is directly responsible to the third party for resulting damages. The point is that the principal is always directly responsible for an agent's misrepresentation made within the scope of authority.

Liability for Agent's Negligence

Under the doctrine of ***respondeat superior,***[16] the principal-employer is liable for any harm caused to a third party by an agent-employee within the scope of employment. This doctrine imposes **vicarious liability**, or indirect liability, on the employer—that is, liability without regard to the personal fault of the employer for torts committed by an employee in the course or scope of employment.[17] Third parties injured through the negligence of an employee can sue either that employee or the employer, if the employee's negligent conduct occurred while the employee was acting within the scope of employment.

Rationale Underlying the Doctrine of *Respondeat Superior* At early common law, a servant (employee) was viewed as the master's (employer's) property. The master was deemed to have absolute control over the servant's acts and was held strictly liable for them no matter how carefully the master supervised the servant. The rationale for the doctrine of *respondeat superior* is based on the social duty that requires every person to manage his or her affairs, whether accomplished by the person or through agents, so as not to injure another. Liability is imposed on employers because they are deemed to be in a better financial position to bear the loss. The superior financial position carries with it the duty to be responsible for damages.

Generally, public policy requires that an injured person be afforded effective relief, and a business enterprise is usually better able to provide that relief than is an individual employee. Employers normally carry liability insurance to cover any damages awarded as a result of such lawsuits. They are also able to spread the cost of risk over the entire business enterprise.

The doctrine of *respondeat superior,* which the courts have applied for nearly two centuries, continues to have practical implications in all situations involving principal-agent (employer-employee) relationships. Today, the small-town grocer with one clerk and the multinational corporation with thousands of employees are equally subject to the doctrinal demand of "let the master respond." (Keep this principle in mind as you read through Chapters 20 and 21.)

Determining the Scope of Employment The key to determining whether a principal may be liable for the torts of an agent under the doctrine of *respondeat superior* is whether the torts are committed within the scope of the agency or employment. The *Restatement (Second) of Agency,* Section 229, outlines the following general factors that courts will consider in determining whether a particular act occurred within the course and scope of employment:

1. Whether the employee's act was authorized by the employer.
2. The time, place, and purpose of the act.
3. Whether the act was one commonly performed by employees on behalf of their employers.
4. The extent to which the employer's interest was advanced by the act.
5. The extent to which the private interests of the employee were involved.

16. Pronounced ree-*spahn*-dee-uht soo-*peer*-ee-your. The doctrine of *respondeat superior* applies not only to employer-employee relationships but also to other principal-agent relationships in which the principal has the right of control over the agent.

17. The theory of *respondeat superior* is similar in this respect to the theory of strict liability covered in Chapter 13.

6. Whether the employer furnished the means or instrumentality (for example, a truck or a machine) by which an injury was inflicted.
7. Whether the employer had reason to know that the employee would perform the act in question and whether the employee had done it before.
8. Whether the act involved the commission of a serious crime.

The Distinction between a "Detour" and a "Frolic" A useful insight into the concept of "scope of employment" may be gained from Judge Baron Parke's classic distinction between a "detour" and a "frolic" in the case of *Joel v. Morison* (1834).[18] In this case, the English court held that if a servant merely took a detour from his master's business, the master will be responsible. If, however, the servant was on a "frolic of his own" and not in any way "on his master's business," the master will not be liable.

Consider an example. Mandel, a traveling salesperson, while driving his employer's vehicle to call on a customer, decides to stop at the post office—which is one block off his route—to mail a personal letter. As Mandel approaches the post office, he negligently runs into a parked vehicle owned by Chan. In this situation, because Mandel's detour from the employer's business is not substantial, he is still acting within the scope of employment, and the employer is liable. The result would be different, though, if Mandel had decided to pick up a few friends for cocktails in another city and in the process had negligently run his vehicle into Chan's. In that circumstance, the departure from the employer's business would be substantial, and the employer normally would not be liable to Chan for damages. Mandel would be considered to have been on a "frolic" of his own.

Employee Travel Time An employee going to and from work or to and from meals is usually considered to be outside the scope of employment. In contrast, all travel time of traveling salespersons or others whose jobs require them to travel is normally considered to be within the scope of employment for the duration of the business trip, including the return trip home, unless there is a significant departure from the employer's business.

Notice of Dangerous Conditions The employer is charged with knowledge of any dangerous conditions discovered by an employee and pertinent to the employment situation. Suppose that Brad, a maintenance employee in an apartment building, notices a lead pipe protruding from the ground in the building's courtyard. Brad neglects either to fix the pipe or to inform his employer of the danger. John falls on the pipe and is injured. The employer is charged with knowledge of the dangerous condition regardless of whether Brad actually informed the employer. That knowledge is imputed to the employer by virtue of the employment relationship.

Borrowed Servants Employers sometimes lend the services of their employees to other employers. Suppose that an employer leases ground-moving equipment to another employer and sends along an employee to operate the machinery. Who is liable for injuries caused by the employee's negligent actions on the job site? Liability turns on *which employer had the primary right to control* the employee at the time the injuries occurred. Generally, the employer who rents out the equipment is presumed to retain control over her or his employee. If the rental is for a relatively long period of time, however, control may be deemed to pass to the employer who is renting the equipment and presumably controlling and directing the employee.

Liability for Agent's Intentional Torts

Most intentional torts that employees commit have no relation to their employment; thus, their employers will not be held liable. Nevertheless, under the doctrine of *respondeat superior*, the employer can be liable for intentional torts of the employee that are committed within the course and scope of employment, just as the employer is liable for negligence. For example, an employer is liable when an employee (such as a "bouncer" at a nightclub or a security guard at a department store) commits the tort of assault and battery or false imprisonment while acting within the scope of employment.

In addition, an employer who knows or should know that an employee has a propensity for committing tortious acts is liable for the employee's acts even if they would not ordinarily be considered within the scope of employment. For example, if an employer hires a bouncer knowing that he has a history of arrests for criminal assault and battery, the employer may be liable if the employee viciously attacks a patron in the parking lot after hours.

An employer is also liable for permitting an employee to engage in reckless actions that can injure

18. 6 Car. & P. 501, 172 Eng. Rep. 1338 (1834).

others. For example, an employer observes an employee smoking while filling containerized trucks with highly flammable liquids. Failure to stop the employee will cause the employer to be liable for any injuries that result if a truck explodes. Needless to say, most employers purchase liability insurance to cover their potential liability for employee conduct in many situations.

Liability for Independent Contractor's Torts

Generally, an employer is not liable for physical harm caused to a third person by the negligent act of an independent contractor in the performance of the contract. This is because the employer does not have *the right to control* the details of an independent contractor's performance. Exceptions to this rule are made in certain situations, though, such as when the contract involves unusually hazardous activities—for example, blasting operations, the transportation of highly volatile chemicals, or the use of poisonous gases. In these situations, an employer cannot be shielded from liability merely by using an independent contractor. Strict liability is imposed on the employer-principal as a matter of law. Also, in some states, strict liability may be imposed by statute.

Liability for Agent's Crimes

An agent is liable for his or her own crimes. A principal or employer is not liable for an agent's or employee's crime simply because the agent or employee committed the crime while otherwise acting within the scope of authority or employment. An exception to this rule is made when the principal or employer participated in the crime by conspiracy or other action. In some jurisdictions, under specific statutes, a principal may be liable for an agent's violating, in the course and scope of employment, such regulations as those governing sanitation, prices, weights, and the sale of liquor.

Section 8 Termination of an Agency

Agency law is similar to contract law in that both an agency and a contract may be terminated by an act of the parties or by operation of law. Once the relationship between the principal and the agent has ended, the agent no longer has the right (*actual* authority) to bind the principal. For an agent's *apparent* authority to be terminated, though, third persons may also need to be notified that the agency has been terminated.

Termination by Act of the Parties

An agency relationship may be terminated by act of the parties in a number of ways, including those discussed here.

Lapse of Time An agency agreement may specify the time period during which the agency relationship will exist. If so, the agency ends when that time expires. For example, Akers signs an agreement of agency with Janz "beginning January 1, 2009, and ending December 31, 2010." The agency is automatically terminated on December 31, 2010. If no definite time is stated, then the agency continues for a reasonable time and can be terminated at will by either party. What constitutes a reasonable time depends on the circumstances and the nature of the agency relationship.

Purpose Achieved An agent can be employed to accomplish a particular objective, such as the purchase of stock for a cattle rancher. In that situation, the agency automatically ends after the cattle have been purchased. If more than one agent is employed to accomplish the same purpose, such as the sale of real estate, the first agent to complete the sale automatically terminates the agency relationship for all the others.

Occurrence of a Specific Event An agency can be created to terminate on the happening of a certain event. For example, if Posner appoints Rubik to handle her business affairs while she is away, the agency automatically terminates when Posner returns.

Mutual Agreement Recall from basic contract law that parties can rescind (cancel) a contract by mutually agreeing to terminate the contractual relationship at any time. The same holds true in agency law regardless of whether the agency contract is in writing or whether it is for a specific duration.

At the Option of One Party As a *general* rule, either party can terminate the agency relationship—because agency is a consensual relationship, and thus neither party can be compelled to continue in the relationship. The agent's act is said to be a *renunciation* of authority. The principal's act is a *revocation* of authority. Although both parties may have the *power* to terminate the agency, they may not possess the *right* to terminate and may therefore be liable for breach of contract.

Wrongful Termination. Wrongful termination can subject the canceling party to a lawsuit for breach of contract. For example, Rawlins has a one-year employment contract with Munro to act as agent in return for $65,000. Munro has the *power* to discharge Rawlins before the contract period expires. If Munro discharges Rawlins, though, he can be sued for breaching the contract and will be liable to Rawlins for damages because he had no *right* to terminate the agency.

Even in an agency at will—that is, an agency that either party may terminate at any time—the principal who wishes to terminate must give the agent *reasonable* notice. The notice must be at least sufficient to allow the agent to recoup his or her expenses and, in some situations, to make a normal profit.

Agency Coupled with an Interest. A special rule applies in an *agency coupled with an interest.* This type of agency is not an agency in the usual sense because it is created for the agent's benefit instead of for the principal's benefit. Suppose that Julie borrows $5,000 from Rob, giving Rob some of her jewelry and signing a letter authorizing him to sell the jewelry as her agent if she fails to repay the loan. After Julie receives the $5,000 from Rob, she attempts to revoke his authority to sell the jewelry as her agent. Julie will not succeed in this attempt because a principal cannot revoke an agency created for the agent's benefit.

An agency coupled with an interest should not be confused with a situation in which the agent merely derives proceeds or profits from the sale of the subject matter. For example, an agent who merely receives a commission from the sale of real property does not have a beneficial interest in the property itself.

Notice of Termination When an agency has been terminated by act of the parties, it is the principal's duty to inform any third parties who know of the existence of the agency that it has been terminated (notice of the termination may be given by others, however).

Although an agent's actual authority ends when the agency is terminated, an agent's *apparent authority* continues until the third party receives notice (from any source) that such authority has been terminated. If the principal knows that a third party has dealt with the agent, the principal is expected to notify that person *directly*. For third parties who have heard about the agency but have not yet dealt with the agent, *constructive notice* is sufficient.[19]

No particular form is required for notice of termination of the principal-agent relationship to be effective. The principal can personally notify the agent, or the agent can learn of the termination through some other means. For example, Manning bids on a shipment of steel, and Stone is hired as an agent to arrange transportation of the shipment. When Stone learns that Manning has lost the bid, Stone's authority to make the transportation arrangement terminates. If the agent's authority is written, however, normally it must be revoked in writing (unless the written document contained an expiration date).

Termination by Operation of Law

Certain events will terminate agency authority automatically because their occurrence makes it impossible for the agent to perform or improbable that the principal would continue to want performance. We look at these events here. Note that when an agency terminates by operation of law, there is no duty to notify third persons—unless the agent's authority is coupled with an interest.

Death or Insanity The general rule is that the death or insanity of either the principal or the agent automatically and immediately terminates an ordinary agency relationship.[20] Knowledge of the death or insanity is not required. For example, Grey sends Bosley to Japan to purchase a rare book. Before Bosley makes the purchase, Grey dies. Bosley's agent status is terminated at the moment of Grey's death, even though Bosley does not know that Grey has died. (Some states, however, have changed the common law by statute to make knowledge of the principal's death a requirement for agency termination.)

An agent's transactions that occur after the death of the principal are not binding on the principal's estate. Assume that Bosley is hired by Grey to collect a debt from Cochran (a third party). Grey dies, but Bosley, not knowing of Grey's death, still collects the debt from Cochran. Cochran's payment to Bosley is no longer legally sufficient to discharge the debt to Grey because Bosley no longer has Grey's authority to collect the funds. If Bosley absconds with the funds, Cochran must pay the debt again to Grey's estate.

19. With *constructive notice* of a fact, knowledge of the fact is imputed by law to a person if he or she could have discovered the fact by proper diligence. Constructive notice is often accomplished by publication in a newspaper.

20. There is an exception to this rule in banking. Under UCC 4–405, when the bank has knowledge of the customer's death, it has authority for ten days after the death to pay checks (but not notes or drafts) drawn by the customer unless it receives a stop-payment order from someone who has an interest in the account, such as an heir.

Impossibility When the specific subject matter of an agency is destroyed or lost, the agency terminates. For example, Gonzalez employs Raich to sell Gonzalez's house. Prior to any sale, the house is destroyed by fire. Raich's agency and authority to sell the house terminate. Similarly, when it is impossible for the agent to perform the agency lawfully because of a change in the law, the agency terminates.

Changed Circumstances When an event occurs that has such an unusual effect on the subject matter of the agency that the agent can reasonably infer that the principal will not want the agency to continue, the agency terminates. Suppose that Baird hires Joslen to sell a tract of land for $40,000. Subsequently, Joslen learns that there is oil under the land and that the land is therefore worth $1 million. The agency and Joslen's authority to sell the land for $40,000 are terminated.

Bankruptcy If either the principal or the agent petitions for bankruptcy, the agency is *usually* terminated. In certain circumstances, such as when the agent's financial status is irrelevant to the purpose of the agency, the agency relationship may continue. *Insolvency* (defined as the inability to pay debts when they come due or when liabilities exceed assets), as distinguished from bankruptcy, does not necessarily terminate the relationship.

War When the principal's country and the agent's country are at war with each other, the agency is terminated. In this situation, the agency is automatically suspended or terminated because there is no way to enforce the legal rights and obligations of the parties. See *Concept Summary 19.3* for a synopsis of the rules governing the termination of an agency.

CONCEPT SUMMARY 19.3 Termination of an Agency

Method of Termination	Rules	Termination of Agent's Authority
ACT OF THE PARTIES		
1. Lapse of time.	Automatic at end of the stated time.	
2. Purpose achieved.	Automatic on the completion of the purpose.	
3. Occurrence of a specific event.	Normally automatic on the happening of the event.	**Notice to Third Parties Required—**
4. Mutual agreement.	Mutual consent required.	1. Direct to those who have dealt with agency.
5. At the option of one party (revocation, if by principal; renunciation, if by agent).	Either party normally has a right to terminate the agency but may lack the power to do so, which can lead to liability for breach of contract.	2. Constructive to all others.
OPERATION OF LAW		
1. Death or insanity.	Automatic on the death or insanity of either the principal or the agent (except when the agency is coupled with an interest).	
2. Impossibility—destruction of the specific subject matter.	Applies any time the agency cannot be performed because of an event beyond the parties' control.	**No Notice Required—** Automatic on the happening of the event.
3. Changed circumstances.	Events so unusual that it would be inequitable to allow the agency to continue to exist.	
4. Bankruptcy.	A bankruptcy decree (not mere insolvency) usually terminates the agency.	
5. War between principal's country and agent's country.	Automatically suspends or terminates the agency—no way to enforce legal rights.	

REVIEWING Agency

Lynne Meyer, on her way to a business meeting and in a hurry, stopped at a Buy-Mart store for a new pair of nylons to wear to the meeting. There was a long line at one of the checkout counters, but a cashier, Valerie Watts, opened another counter and began loading the cash drawer. Meyer told Watts that she was in a hurry and asked Watts to work faster. Instead, Watts only slowed her pace. At this point, Meyer hit Watts. It is not clear from the record whether Meyer hit Watts intentionally or, in an attempt to retrieve the nylons, hit her inadvertently. In response, Watts grabbed Meyer by the hair and hit her repeatedly in the back of the head, while Meyer screamed for help. Management personnel separated the two women and questioned them about the incident. Watts was immediately fired for violating the store's no-fighting policy. Meyer subsequently sued Buy-Mart, alleging that the store was liable for the tort (assault and battery) committed by its employee. Using the information presented in the chapter, answer the following questions.

1. Under what doctrine discussed in this chapter might Buy-Mart be held liable for the tort committed by Watts?
2. What is the key factor in determining whether Buy-Mart is liable under this doctrine?
3. How is Buy-Mart's potential liability affected depending on whether Watts's behavior constituted an intentional tort or a tort of negligence?
4. Suppose that when Watts applied for the job at Buy-Mart, she disclosed in her application that she had previously been convicted of felony assault and battery. Nevertheless, Buy-Mart hired Watts as a cashier. How might this fact affect Buy-Mart's liability for Watts's actions?

TERMS AND CONCEPTS

agency 478
apparent authority 491
disclosed principal 494
e-agent 495
equal dignity rule 490
express authority 490
fiduciary 478
implied authority 490
independent contractor 479
notary public 490
partially disclosed principal 494
power of attorney 490
ratification 493
***respondeat superior* 497**
undisclosed principal 494
vicarious liability 497

QUESTIONS AND CASE PROBLEMS

19–1. Paul Gett is a well-known, wealthy financial expert. Adam Wade, Gett's friend, tells Timothy Brown that he is Gett's agent for the purchase of rare coins and shows Brown a local newspaper clipping mentioning Gett's interest in coin collecting. Brown, knowing of Wade's friendship with Gett, contracts with Wade to sell a rare coin valued at $25,000 to Gett. Wade takes the coin and disappears with it. On the payment due date, Brown seeks to collect from Gett. Gett denies liability and claims that Wade was never his agent. Discuss fully whether an agency was in existence at the time the contract for the rare coin was made.

19–2. QUESTION WITH SAMPLE ANSWER

Peter hires Alice as an agent to sell a piece of property he owns. The price is to be at least $30,000. Alice discovers that the fair market value of Peter's property is actually at least $45,000 and could be higher because a shopping mall is going to be built nearby. Alice forms a real estate partnership with her cousin Carl, and she prepares for Peter's signature a contract for the sale of the property to Carl for $32,000. Peter signs the contract. Just before closing and passage of title, Peter learns about the shopping mall and the increased fair market value of his property. Peter refuses to deed the property to Carl. Carl claims that Alice, as agent, solicited a price above that agreed on when the agency was created and that the contract is therefore binding and enforceable. Discuss fully whether Peter is bound to this contract.

- **For a sample answer to Question 19–2, go to Appendix I at the end of this text.**

19–3. Lei Chu-Ming is a purchasing agent-employee for the A & B Coal Supply partnership. Chu-Ming has authority to purchase the coal needed by A & B to satisfy the needs of its customers. While Chu-Ming is leaving a coal mine from which she has just purchased a large quantity of coal, her car breaks down. She walks into a small roadside grocery store for help. While there, she runs into Darin Wilson, who owns 360 acres back in the mountains with all mineral rights. Wilson, in need of cash, offers to sell Chu-Ming the property for $1,500 per acre. On inspection of the property, Chu-Ming forms the opinion that the subsurface contains valuable coal deposits. Chu-Ming contracts to purchase the property for A & B Coal Supply, signing the contract "A & B Coal Supply, Lei Chu-Ming, agent." The closing date is August 1. Chu-Ming takes the contract to the partnership. The managing partner is furious, as A & B is not in the property business. Later, just before closing, both Wilson and the partnership learn that the value of the land is at least $15,000 per acre. Discuss the rights of A & B and Wilson concerning the land contract.

19–4. Ankir is hired by Jamison as a traveling salesperson. Ankir not only solicits orders but also delivers the goods and collects payments from his customers. Ankir deposits all payments in his private checking account and at the end of each month draws sufficient cash from his bank to cover the payments made. Jamison is totally unaware of this procedure. Because of a slowdown in the economy, Jamison tells all his salespeople to offer 20 percent discounts on orders. Ankir solicits orders, but he offers only 15 percent discounts, pocketing the extra 5 percent paid by customers. Ankir has not lost any orders by this practice, and he is rated as one of Jamison's top salespersons. Jamison learns of Ankir's actions. Discuss fully Jamison's rights in this matter.

19–5. Principal's Duties to Agent. Josef Boehm was an officer and the majority shareholder of Alaska Industrial Hardware, Inc. (AIH), in Anchorage, Alaska. In August 2001, Lincolnshire Management, Inc., in New York, created AIH Acquisition Corp. to buy AIH. The three firms signed a "commitment letter" to negotiate "a definitive stock purchase agreement" (SPA). In September, Harold Snow and Ronald Braley began to work, on Boehm's behalf, with Vincent Coyle, an agent for AIH Acquisition, to produce an SPA. They exchanged many drafts and dozens of e-mails. Finally, in February 2002, Braley told Coyle that Boehm would sign the SPA "early next week." That did not occur, however, and at the end of March, after more negotiations and drafts, Boehm demanded more money. AIH Acquisition agreed and, following more work by the agents, another SPA was drafted. In April, the parties met in Anchorage. Boehm still refused to sign. AIH Acquisition and others filed a suit in a federal district court against AIH. Did Boehm violate any of the duties that principals owe to their agents? If so, which duty, and how was it violated? Explain. [*AIH Acquisition Corp., LLC v. Alaska Industrial Hardware, Inc.*, __ F.Supp.2d __ (S.D.N.Y. 2004)]

19–6. CASE PROBLEM WITH SAMPLE ANSWER

In July 2001, John Warren viewed a condominium in Woodland Hills, California, as a potential buyer. Hildegard Merrill was the agent for the seller. Because Warren's credit rating was poor, Merrill told him he needed a co-borrower to obtain a mortgage at a reasonable rate. Merrill said that her daughter Charmaine would "go on title" until the loan and sale were complete if Warren would pay her $10,000. Merrill also offered to defer her commission on the sale as a loan to Warren so that he could make a 20 percent down payment on the property. He agreed to both plans. Merrill applied for and secured the mortgage in Charmaine's name alone by misrepresenting her daughter's address, business, and income. To close the sale, Merrill had Warren remove his name from the title to the property. In October, Warren moved into the condominium, repaid Merrill the amount of her deferred commission, and began paying the mortgage. Within a few months, Merrill had Warren evicted. Warren filed a suit in a California state court against Merrill and Charmaine. Who among these parties was in an agency relationship? What is the basic duty that an agent owes a principal? Was the duty breached here? Explain. [*Warren v. Merrill*, 143 Cal.App.4th 96, 49 Cal.Rptr.3d 122 (2 Dist. 2006)]

- **To view a sample answer for Problem 19–6, go to this book's Web site at academic.cengage.com/blaw/cross, select "Chapter 19," and click on "Case Problem with Sample Answer."**

19–7. Apparent Authority. Lee Dennegar and Mark Knutson lived in Dennegar's house in Raritan, New Jersey. Dennegar paid the mortgage and other household expenses. With Dennegar's consent, Knutson managed their household's financial affairs and the "general office functions concerned with maintaining the house." Dennegar allowed Knutson to handle the mail and "to do with it as he chose." Knutson wrote checks for Dennegar to sign, although Knutson signed Dennegar's name to many of the checks with Dennegar's consent. AT&T Universal issued a credit card in Dennegar's name in February 2001. Monthly statements were mailed to Dennegar's house, and payments were sometimes made on those statements. Knutson died in June 2003. The unpaid charges on the card of $14,752.93 were assigned to New Century Financial Services, Inc. New Century filed a suit in a New Jersey state court against Dennegar to collect the unpaid amount. Dennegar claimed that he never applied for or used the card and knew nothing about it. Under what theory could Dennegar be liable for the charges? Explain. [*New Century Financial Services, Inc. v. Dennegar,* 394 N.J.Super. 595, 928 A.2d 48 (A.D. 2007)]

19–8. Agent's Duties to Principal. Su Ru Chen owned the Lucky Duck Fortune Cookie Factory in Everett, Massachusetts, which made Chinese-style fortune cookies for restaurants. In November 2001, Chen listed the business for sale with Bob Sun, a real estate broker, for $35,000. Sun's daughter Frances and her fiancé, Chiu Chung Chan, decided that Chan would buy the business. Acting as a broker on Chen's (the seller's) behalf, Frances asked about the Lucky Duck's finances. Chen said that each month the business sold at least 1,000 boxes of cookies at a $2,000 profit. Frances negotiated a price of $23,000, which Chan (her fiancé) paid. When Chan began to operate the Lucky Duck, it became clear that the demand for the cookies was actually about 500 boxes per month—a rate at which the business would suffer losses. Less than two months later, the factory closed. Chan filed a suit in a Massachusetts state court against Chen, alleging fraud, among other things. Chan's proof included Frances's testimony as to what Chen had said to her. Chen objected to the admission of this testimony. What is the basis for this objection? Should the court admit the testimony? Why or why not? [*Chan v. Chen,* 70 Mass.App.Ct. 79, 872 N.E.2d 1153 (2007)]

19–9. A QUESTION OF ETHICS

*Emergency One, Inc. (EO), makes fire and rescue vehicles. Western Fire Truck, Inc., contracted with EO to be its exclusive dealer in Colorado and Wyoming through December 2003. James Costello, a Western salesperson, was authorized to order EO vehicles for his customers. Without informing Western, Costello e-mailed EO about Western's difficulties in obtaining cash to fund its operations. He asked about the viability of Western's contract and his possible employment with EO. On EO's request, and in disregard of Western's instructions, Costello sent some payments for EO vehicles directly to EO. In addition, Costello, with EO's help, sent a competing bid to a potential Western customer. EO's representative e-mailed Costello, "You have my permission to kick [Western's] ass." In April 2002, EO terminated its contract with Western, which, after reviewing Costello's e-mail, fired Costello. Western filed a suit in a Colorado state court against Costello and EO, alleging, among other things, that Costello breached his duty as an agent and that EO aided and abetted the breach. [*Western Fire Truck, Inc. v. Emergency One, Inc., *134 P.3d 570 (Colo.App. 2006)]*

(a) Was there an agency relationship between Western and Costello? In determining whether an agency relationship exists, is the *right* to control or the *fact* of control more important? Explain.
(b) Did Costello owe Western a duty? If so, what was the duty? Did Costello breach it? How?
(c) A Colorado state statute allows a court to award punitive damages in "circumstances of fraud, malice, or willful and wanton conduct." Did any of these circumstances exist in this case? Should punitive damages be assessed against either defendant? Why or why not?

19–10. VIDEO QUESTION

Go to this text's Web site at **academic.cengage.com/blaw/cross** and select "Chapter 19." Click on "Video Questions" and view the video titled *Fast Times at Ridgemont High.* Then answer the following questions.

(a) Recall from the video that Brad (Judge Reinhold) is told to deliver an order of Captain Hook Fish and Chips to IBM. Is Brad an employee or an independent contractor? Why?
(b) Assume that Brad is an employee and agent of Captain Hook Fish and Chips. What duties does he owe Captain Hook? What duties does Captain Hook, as principal, owe Brad?
(c) In the video, Brad throws part of his uniform and several bags of the food that he is supposed to deliver out of his car window while driving. Assuming Brad is an agent-employee of Captain Hook Fish and Chips, did these actions violate any of his duties as an agent? Explain.

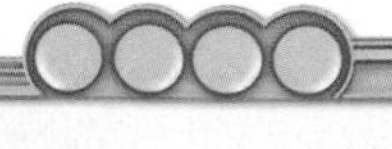

LAW ON THE WEB

For updated links to resources available on the Web, as well as a variety of other materials, visit this text's Web site at

academic.cengage.com/blaw/cross

The Legal Information Institute (LII) at Cornell University is an excellent source for information on agency law, including court cases involving agency concepts. You can access the LII's Web page on this topic at

www.law.cornell.edu/wex/index.php/Agency

There are now numerous "shopping bots" (e-agents) that will search the Web to obtain the best prices for specified products. You can obtain the latest reviews on the merits of various shopping bots by going to

www.botspot.com

Legal Research Exercises on the Web

Go to **academic.cengage.com/blaw/cross**, the Web site that accompanies this text. Select "Chapter 19" and click on "Internet Exercises." There you will find the following Internet research exercises that you can perform to learn more about the topics covered in this chapter.

Internet Exercise 19–1: Legal Perspective
Employees or Independent Contractors?

Internet Exercise 19–2: Management Perspective
Problems with Using Independent Contractors

Internet Exercise 19–3: Management Perspective
Liability in Agency Relationships

CHAPTER 20

Employment Relationships

Traditionally, employment relationships in the United States were governed primarily by the common law. Today, in contrast, the workplace is regulated extensively by federal and state statutes. Recall from Chapter 1 that common law doctrines apply only to areas *not* covered by statutory law. Common law doctrines have thus been displaced to a significant extent by statutory law. In this chapter, we look at the most significant laws regulating employment relationships. We examine other important laws regulating the workplace, including those covering employment discrimination, immigration, and labor unions, in Chapters 21 and 22.

Keep in mind, however, that certain aspects of employment relationships are still governed by common law rules, including the rules under contract, tort, and agency law discussed in previous chapters of this text. Given that many employees (those who deal with third parties) normally are deemed to be agents of their employer, agency concepts are especially relevant in the employment context, as is the distinction between employees and independent contractors. Generally, the laws discussed in this chapter and in Chapter 21 apply only to the employer-employee relationship and not to independent contractors. Here, we begin our discussion by examining one other common law doctrine that has not been entirely displaced by statutory law—that of employment at will.

Employment at Will

Traditionally, employment relationships have generally been governed by the common law doctrine of **employment at will.** Under this doctrine, either the employer or the employee may terminate an employment contract at any time and for any reason, unless the contract specifically provides to the contrary. This doctrine is still in widespread use, and only one state (Montana) does not apply it. Nonetheless, as has occurred in many other areas of employment law, federal and state statutes have partially displaced the common law and now prevent this doctrine from being applied in a number of circumstances. Today, an employer may not fire an employee if to do so would violate a federal or state statute, such as one prohibiting termination of employment for discriminatory reasons (see Chapter 21).

Exceptions to the Employment-at-Will Doctrine

Under the employment-at-will doctrine, as mentioned, an employer may hire and fire employees at will (regardless of the employees' performance) without liability, unless the decision violates the terms of an employment contract or statutory law. Because of the harsh effects of the employment-at-will doctrine for employees, courts have carved out various exceptions to this doctrine. These exceptions are based on contract theory, tort theory, and public policy.

Exceptions Based on Contract Theory Some courts have held that an *implied* employment contract exists between the employer and the employee. If the employee is fired outside the terms of the implied contract, he or she may succeed in an action for breach of contract even though no written employment contract exists.

For example, an employer's manual or personnel bulletin may state that, as a matter of policy, workers will be dismissed only for good cause. If the employee is aware of this policy and continues to work for the employer, a court may find that there is an implied contract based on the terms stated in the manual or bulletin. Generally, the key consideration in determining whether an employment manual creates an implied contractual obligation is the employee's reasonable expectations.

Oral promises that an employer makes to employees regarding discharge policy may also be considered part of an implied contract. If the employer fires a worker in a manner contrary to what was promised, a court may hold that the employer has violated the implied contract and is liable for damages. Most state courts will consider this claim and judge it by traditional contract standards. In some cases, courts have held that an implied employment contract existed even though the employees agreed in writing to be employees at will.[1] In a few states, courts have gone further and held that all employment contracts contain an implied covenant of good faith. In those states, if an employer fires an employee for an arbitrary or unjustified reason, the employee can claim that the covenant of good faith was breached and the contract violated.

Exceptions Based on Tort Theory In some situations, the discharge of an employee may give rise to an action for wrongful discharge under tort theories. Abusive discharge procedures may result in intentional infliction of emotional distress or defamation. In addition, some courts have permitted workers to sue their employers under the tort theory of fraud. Under this theory, an employer may be held liable for making false promises to a prospective employee if the person detrimentally relies on the employer's representations by taking the job.

Suppose that an employer induces a prospective employee to leave a lucrative position and move to another state by offering "a long-term job with a thriving business." In fact, the employer is having significant financial problems. Furthermore, the employer is planning a merger that will result in the elimination of the position offered to the prospective employee. If the person takes the job in reliance on the employer's representations and is laid off shortly thereafter, he or she may be able to bring an action against the employer for fraud.[2]

Exceptions Based on Public Policy Another common law exception to the employment-at-will doctrine is made on the basis of public policy. Courts may apply this exception when an employer fires a worker for reasons that violate a fundamental public policy of the jurisdiction.

Generally, the courts require that the public policy involved be expressed clearly in the statutory law governing the jurisdiction. The public policy against employment discrimination, for instance, is expressed clearly in federal and state statutes. Thus, if a worker is fired for discriminatory reasons but has no cause of action under statutory law (because, for example, the workplace has too few employees to be covered by the statute, discussed in Chapter 21) that worker may succeed in a suit against the employer for wrongful discharge in violation of public policy.[3] Firing an employee for filing a workers' compensation claim (discussed later in this chapter) is another example of the strong public policy that must exist for a court to find an exception to the employment-at-will doctrine.[4]

Occasionally, a discharge can violate public policy if it is done in retaliation for an employee's refusing to engage in criminal conduct or reporting an employer's unlawful conduct to authorities (commonly referred to as *whistleblowing*). Does the public policy exception apply to a nursing home employee who is fired for reporting the abuse of a patient as required by a state statute? That was the question in the following case.

---

1. See, for example, *Kuest v. Regent Assisted Living, Inc.*, 111 Wash.App. 36, 43 P.3d 23 (2002).

2. See, for example, *Lazar v. Superior Court of Los Angeles Co.*, 12 Cal.4th 631, 909 P.2d 981, 49 Cal.Rptr.2d 377 (1996); and *Helmer v. Bingham Toyota Isuzu*, 129 Cal.App. 4th 1121, 29 Cal.Rptr.3d 136 (2005).

3. See, for example, *Wholey v. Sears Roebuck*, 370 Md. 38, 803 A.2d 482 (2002).

4. Note that some states, such as Ohio, have limited an employee's ability to sue for wrongful discharge based on the public policy exception. See, for example, *Bickers v. W.&S. Life Insurance Co.*, 116 Ohio St.3d 351, 879 N.E.2d 201 (2007).

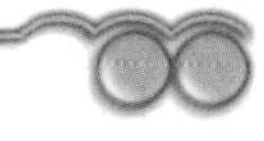

CASE 20.1 Wendeln v. The Beatrice Manor, Inc.

Supreme Court of Nebraska, 2006. 271 Neb. 373, 712 N.W.2d 226.

• **Background and Facts** Rebecca Wendeln, a twenty-one-year-old certified nursing assistant, worked as a staffing coordinator at The Beatrice Manor, Inc., in Beatrice, Nebraska. One of the patients at Beatrice Manor was wheelchair-bound. Moving the patient required two persons and a gait belt (an ambulatory aid used to transfer or mobilize patients). In December 2001, two medical aides told Wendeln that the patient had been improperly moved and had been injured. Wendeln reported the incident to the Nebraska Department of Health and Human Services, as required under the state Adult Protective Services Act (APSA). A few days later, Wendeln's supervisor angrily confronted her about the report. Intimidated, Wendeln asked for a day off, which was granted. On her return, she was fired. She filed a suit in a Nebraska state court against Beatrice Manor, alleging, among other things, that her discharge was a violation of the state's public policy. A jury returned a verdict in her favor, awarding damages of $79,000. Beatrice Manor appealed to the Nebraska Supreme Court.

IN THE LANGUAGE OF THE COURT
McCORMACK, J. [Justice]

* * * *

* * * Beatrice Manor asserts that * * * "[t]here is no clear legislative enactment declaring an important public policy with such clarity as to provide a basis for [Wendeln's] civil action for wrongful discharge."

The clear rule in Nebraska is that unless constitutionally, statutorily, or contractually prohibited, an employer, without incurring liability, may terminate an at-will employee at any time with or without reason. We recognize, however, a public policy exception to the at-will employment doctrine. *Under the public policy exception, we will allow an employee to claim damages for wrongful discharge when the motivation for the firing contravenes public policy.* * * * However, * * * it [is] important that abusive discharge claims of employees at-will be limited to manageable and clear standards. Thus, the right of an employer to terminate employees at will should be restricted only by exceptions created by statute or to those instances where a very clear mandate of public policy has been violated. [Emphasis added.]

* * * An employee could state a cause of action for retaliatory discharge based upon the allegation that the employee was terminated from her employment because she filed a workers' compensation claim. * * * Nebraska law neither specifically prohibit[s] an employer from discharging an employee for filing a workers' compensation claim, nor specifically [makes] it a crime for an employer to do so. Nevertheless, * * * the general purpose and unique nature of the Nebraska Workers' Compensation Act itself provides a mandate for public policy. * * * The Nebraska Workers' Compensation Act was meant to create * * * rights for employees and * * * such [a] beneficent purpose would be undermined by failing to adopt a rule which allows a retaliatory discharge claim for employees discharged for filing a workers' compensation claim. This is because were we not to recognize such a public policy exception to the employment-at-will doctrine, the * * * rights granted by the Nebraska Workers' Compensation Act could simply be circumvented by the employer's threatening to discharge the employee if he or she exercised those rights.

* * * *

* * * [In Nebraska] the law imposes an affirmative obligation upon an employee to prevent abuse or neglect of nursing home residents, and the employee fulfills that obligation by reporting the abuse [and may be subject to criminal sanctions for failing to do so. *An] employer's termination of employment for fulfillment of the legal obligation exposes the employer to a wrongful termination action under the fundamental and well-defined public policy of protecting nursing home residents from abuse and neglect.* * * * By applying the public policy exception * * *, employees [are] relieved of the onerous burden of choosing between equally destructive alternatives: report and be terminated, or fail to report and be prosecuted. [Emphasis added.]

* * * The purpose of the APSA would be circumvented if employees mandated by the APSA to report suspected patient abuse could be threatened with discharge for making such a report.

CASE 20.1 CONTINUED The [Nebraska] Legislature articulates public policy when it declares certain conduct to be in violation of the criminal law. The APSA makes a clear public policy statement by utilizing the threat of criminal sanction to ensure the implementation of the reporting provisions set forth to protect the vulnerable adults with which the APSA is concerned. Thus, we determine that a public policy exception to the employment-at-will doctrine applies to allow a cause of action for retaliatory discharge when an employee is fired for making a report of abuse as mandated by the APSA.

• **Decision and Remedy** *The state supreme court affirmed the trial court's judgment. The appellate court emphasized that under the employment-at-will doctrine an employer may fire an at-will employee at any time with or without cause. The court recognized an exception to this principle, however, "for wrongful discharge when the motivation for the firing contravenes public policy." Under this exception, an employee has a cause of action for retaliatory discharge when she is fired for reporting abuse of a nursing home patient, as state law requires.*

• **The Ethical Dimension** *Is it fair to sanction an employer for discharging an employee who reports on the employer's unsafe or illegal actions to government authorities or others? Discuss.*

• **The Global Dimension** *In many countries, discharging an employee is more difficult and costly for the employer than it is in the United States. Why?*

Wrongful Discharge

Whenever an employer discharges an employee in violation of an employment contract or a statutory law protecting employees, the employee may bring an action for **wrongful discharge.** Even if an employer's actions do not violate any express employment contract or statute, the employer may still be subject to liability under a common law doctrine, such as a tort theory or agency. For example, an employer discharges a female employee and publicly discloses private facts about her sex life to her co-workers. In that situation, the employee could bring a wrongful discharge claim against the employer based on the tort of invasion of privacy (see Chapter 12).

SECTION 2 Wage and Hour Laws

In the 1930s, Congress enacted several laws regulating the wages and working hours of employees. In 1931, Congress passed the Davis-Bacon Act,[5] which requires the payment of "prevailing wages" to employees of contractors and subcontractors working on government construction projects. In 1936, the Walsh-Healey Act[6] was passed. This act requires that a minimum wage, as well as overtime pay at 1.5 times regular pay rates, be paid to employees of manufacturers or suppliers entering into contracts with agencies of the federal government.

In 1938, with the passage of the Fair Labor Standards Act[7] (FLSA), Congress extended wage-hour requirements to cover all employers engaged in interstate commerce or in the production of goods for interstate commerce. Here we examine the FLSA's provisions in regard to child labor, maximum hours, and minimum wages, and overtime exceptions.

Child Labor

The FLSA prohibits oppressive child labor. Children under fourteen years of age are allowed to do certain types of work, such as deliver newspapers, work for their parents, and be employed in the entertainment and (with some exceptions) agricultural areas. Children who are fourteen or fifteen years of age are allowed to work, but not in hazardous occupations. There are also numerous restrictions on how many hours per day and per week they can work. For example, minors under the age of sixteen cannot work during school hours, for more than three hours on a school day (or eight hours on a nonschool day), for more than eighteen hours during a school week (or forty hours during a nonschool week), or before 7 A.M. or after 7 P.M. (9 P.M. during the summer). Most states require persons under sixteen years of age to obtain work permits.

5. 40 U.S.C. Sections 276a–276a-5.
6. 41 U.S.C. Sections 35–45.
7. 29 U.S.C. Sections 201–260.

Working times and hours are not restricted for persons between the ages of sixteen and eighteen, but they cannot be employed in hazardous jobs or in jobs detrimental to their health and well-being. None of these restrictions apply to those over the age of eighteen.

Hours and Wages

The FLSA provides that a **minimum wage** of a specified amount ($7.25 per hour as of 2009) must be paid to employees in covered industries. Congress periodically revises this minimum wage.[8] Under the FLSA, the term *wages* includes the reasonable costs of the employer in furnishing employees with board, lodging, and other facilities if they are customarily furnished by that employer.

Under the FLSA, any employee who works more than forty hours per week must be paid no less than 1.5 times her or his regular pay for all hours over forty. Note that the FLSA overtime provisions apply only after an employee has worked more than forty hours per *week*. Thus, employees who work for ten hours a day, four days per week, are not entitled to overtime pay because they do not work more than forty hours per week.

Overtime Exemptions

Certain employees—usually executive, administrative, and professional employees; outside salespersons; and computer programmers—are exempt from the overtime provisions of the FLSA. Employers are not required to pay overtime wages to exempt employees. In order for an exemption to apply, an employee's specific job duties and salary must meet all the requirements of the U.S. Department of Labor (DOL) regulations. In the past, because the salary limits were low and the duties tests were complex and confusing, some employers were able to avoid paying overtime wages to their employees. This prompted the DOL to substantially revise the overtime regulations in 2004 for the first time in more than fifty years. The revisions effectively expanded the number of workers eligible for overtime by nearly tripling the salary threshold.[9]

Employers can continue to pay overtime to ineligible employees if they want to do so, but they cannot waive or reduce the overtime requirements of the FLSA. The exemptions to the overtime-pay requirement do not apply to manual laborers or other workers who perform tasks involving repetitive operations with their hands (such as nonmanagement production-line employees, for example). The exemptions also do not apply to police, firefighters, licensed nurses, and other public-safety workers. White-collar workers who earn more than $100,000 per year, computer programmers, dental hygienists, and insurance adjusters are typically exempt—though they must also meet certain other criteria. An employer cannot deny overtime wages to an employee based solely on the employee's job title.[10] (Does the FLSA require employers to pay overtime wages to workers who telecommute? See this chapter's *Emerging Trends* feature on pages 514–515 for a discussion of this issue.)

Under the overtime-pay regulations, an employee qualifies for the executive exemption if, among other requirements, his or her "primary duty" is management. This requirement was the focus of the dispute in the following case.

8. Note that many state and local governments also have minimum-wage laws; these laws may provide for higher minimum-wage rates than that required by the federal government.

9. 29 C.F.R. Section 541.

10. See, for example, *In re Wal-Mart Stores, Inc.*, 395 F.3d 1177 (10th Cir. 2005); and *Martin v. Indiana Michigan Power Co.*, 381 F.3d 574 (6th Cir. 2004).

CASE 20.2 Mims v. Starbucks Corp.

United States District Court, Southern District of Texas, 2007. __ F.Supp.2d __.

• **Company Profile** Starbucks Corporation (**www.starbucks.com**) is the largest and best-known purveyor of specialty coffees and coffee products in North America. Named after the first mate in Herman Melville's *Moby Dick,* Starbucks does business in more than 10,000 retail locations in the United States and forty-one foreign countries and territories. Starbucks also supplies premium, fresh-roasted coffee to bookstores, grocery stores, restaurants, airlines, sports and entertainment venues, movie theaters, hotels, and cruise ship lines throughout the world. Starbucks' success is predicated on the consistently high quality of its coffees and the other products and services it provides. Starbucks has a reputation for excellence and is recognized for its knowledgeable staff and service.

CASE 20.2 CONTINUED

• **Background and Facts** In Starbucks Corporation's stores, baristas wait on customers, make drinks for customers, serve customers, operate the cash register, clean the store, and maintain its equipment. In each store, a manager supervises and motivates six to thirty employees, including baristas, shift supervisors, and assistant managers. The manager oversees customer service and processes employee records, payrolls, and inventory counts. He or she also develops strategies to increase revenues, control costs, and comply with corporate policies. Kevin Keevican was hired as a barista in March 2000. Keevican was subsequently promoted to shift supervisor, assistant manager, and, in November 2001, manager. During his tenure, Keevican doubled pastry sales at one store, nearly tripled revenues at another, and won sales awards at both. As a manager, Keevican worked seventy hours a week for $650 to $800, a 10 to 20 percent bonus, and fringe benefits that were not available to baristas, such as paid sick leave. Keevican resigned in 2004. He and other former managers, including Kathleen Mims, filed a suit in a federal district court against Starbucks, seeking unpaid overtime and other amounts. The plaintiffs admitted that they performed many managerial tasks, but argued that they spent 70 to 80 percent of their time on barista chores. Starbucks filed a motion for summary judgment.

IN THE LANGUAGE OF THE COURT
***EWING WERLEIN, JR.*, United States District Judge.**

* * * *

* * * An employee's primary duty is usually what the employee does that is of principal value to the employer, not the collateral tasks that she may also perform, even if they consume more than half her time.

* * * *

Where an employee spends less than 50 percent of his time on management, as both Plaintiffs claim they did, management may still be the employee's primary duty if certain pertinent factors support such a conclusion. *The four factors ordinarily considered are: (1) the relative importance of managerial duties compared to other duties; (2) the frequency with which the employee makes discretionary decisions; (3) the employee's relative freedom from supervision; and (4) the relationship between the employee's salary and the wages paid to employees who perform relevant nonexempt work.* * * * [Emphasis added.]

* * * *

The uncontroverted [not put into question] * * * record establishes that Plaintiffs' significant managerial functions—such as ordering and controlling inventory; deciding whom to interview and hire for barista positions; training and scheduling employees; special marketing promotions; and monitoring labor costs—were critical to the successes of their respective stores. If Plaintiffs while each managing a store with annual sales exceeding $1 million were able to spend 70 or 80 percent of their time pouring coffee and performing other barista chores that six to 30 subordinates also performed, those activities of the manager quite obviously were of minor importance to Defendant when compared to the significant management responsibilities performed during the other 20 to 30 percent of their time, management responsibilities that directly influenced the ultimate commercial and financial success or failure of the store.

* * * *

It is uncontroverted that Plaintiffs, as the highest-ranking employees in their stores, made decisions on matters such as deciding whom to interview and hire as a barista, whom to assign to train new hires, when to discipline employees, whom to deploy in certain positions, what promotions to run, and the amount of product to order for efficient inventory control. Plaintiffs argue, however, that they infrequently exercised discretion because they worked under the "ultimate managing authority" of their district managers, who had authority to hire more senior employees, approve changes to Plaintiffs' work schedules, set rates of pay for newly-hired employees if the pay exceeded Starbucks's guidelines, and establish guidelines for Plaintiffs when completing performance reviews. *However, the manager of a local store in a modern multi-store organization has management as his or her primary duty even though the discretion usually associated with management may be limited by the company's desire for standardization and uniformity.* * * * [Emphasis added.]

CASE CONTINUES

CASE 20.2 CONTINUED

Plaintiffs also contend that they were not relatively free from supervision because their district managers spent "substantial amounts of time" in Plaintiffs' stores. * * * On the other hand, it is uncontroverted that each Plaintiff as store manager was the single highest-ranking employee in his particular store and was responsible on site for that store's day-to-day overall operations. Indeed, department and assistant managers have been held exempt under the executive exemption even when their superiors worked in close proximity to them at the same location. Viewing the evidence in the light most favorable to Plaintiffs, Plaintiffs still were vested with enough discretionary power and freedom from supervision to qualify for the executive exemption.

* * * *

The final factor is the relationship between Plaintiffs' salary and the wages paid to non-exempt employees. Plaintiffs argue, with no supporting evidence, that their compensation "approximated that received by some assistant store managers." It is undisputed, however, that Plaintiffs received nearly twice the total annual compensation received by their highest-paid shift supervisors, and Plaintiffs received bonuses and benefits not available to other employees (including assistant managers). This marked disparity in pay and benefits between Plaintiffs and the non-exempt employees is a hallmark of exempt status.

- **Decision and Remedy** *The court issued a summary judgment in Starbucks' favor and dismissed the claims of the plaintiffs, who were exempt from the FLSA's overtime provisions as executive employees. The court concluded that during their employment the plaintiffs' "primary duty" was management.*

- **What If the Facts Were Different?** *Suppose that Keevican's job title had been "glorified barista" instead of "manager." Would the result have been different? Explain.*

- **The Legal Environment Dimension** *What might the court have concluded if the store could have operated successfully without the plaintiffs' performing their "managerial" functions?*

Worker Health and Safety

Under the common law, employees injured on the job had to rely on tort law, contract law, or agency law principles (discussed in Chapter 19) to seek recovery from their employers. Today, numerous state and federal statutes protect employees from the risk of accidental injury, death, or disease resulting from their employment. This section discusses the primary federal statute governing health and safety in the workplace, along with state workers' compensation acts.

The Occupational Safety and Health Act

At the federal level, the primary legislation protecting employees' health and safety is the Occupational Safety and Health Act of 1970.[11] Congress passed this act in an attempt to ensure safe and healthful working conditions for practically every employee in the country. The act not only imposes a general duty on employers to keep workplaces safe but also requires them to meet specific standards.

Enforcement Agencies Three federal agencies develop and enforce the standards set by the Occupational Safety and Health Act. The Occupational Safety and Health Administration (OSHA), which is part of the U.S. Department of Labor, has the authority to promulgate standards, make inspections, and enforce the act. OSHA has issued safety standards governing many workplace details, such as the structural stability of ladders and the requirements for railings. OSHA also establishes standards that protect employees against exposure to substances that may be harmful to their health.

The National Institute for Occupational Safety and Health is part of the U.S. Department of Health and Human Services. It conducts research on safety and health problems and recommends standards for OSHA to adopt. Finally, the Occupational Safety and Health Review Commission is an independent agency set up to handle appeals from actions taken by OSHA administrators.

11. 29 U.S.C. Sections 553, 651–678.

Procedures and Violations OSHA compliance officers may enter and inspect the facilities of any establishment covered by the Occupational Safety and Health Act.[12] Employees may also file complaints of violations. Under the act, an employer cannot discharge an employee who files a complaint or who, in good faith, refuses to work in a high-risk area if bodily harm or death might result.

Employers with eleven or more employees are required to keep occupational injury and illness records for each employee. Each record must be made available for inspection when requested by an OSHA inspector. Whenever a work-related injury or disease occurs, employers must make reports directly to OSHA. Whenever an employee is killed in a work-related accident or when five or more employees are hospitalized in one accident, the employer must notify the Department of Labor within forty-eight hours. If the company fails to do so, it will be fined. Following the accident, a complete inspection of the premises is mandatory.

Criminal penalties for willful violation of the Occupational Safety and Health Act are limited. Employers may be prosecuted under state laws, however. In other words, the act does not preempt state and local criminal laws.[13]

State Workers' Compensation Laws

State **workers' compensation laws** establish an administrative procedure for compensating workers injured on the job. Instead of suing, an injured worker files a claim with the administrative agency or board that administers the local workers' compensation claims.

Employees Who Are Covered by Workers' Compensation Most workers' compensation statutes are similar. No state covers all employees. Typically, domestic workers, agricultural workers, temporary employees, and employees of common carriers (companies that provide transportation services to the public) are excluded, but minors are covered. Usually, the statutes allow employers to purchase insurance from a private insurer or a state fund to pay workers' compensation benefits in the event of a claim. Most states also allow employers to be *self-insured*—that is, employers that show an ability to pay claims do not need to buy insurance.

Requirements for Receiving Workers' Compensation In general, the right to recover benefits is predicated wholly on the existence of an employment relationship and the fact that the worker's injury was *accidental* and *occurred on the job or in the course of employment,* regardless of fault. Intentionally inflicted self-injury, for example, would not be considered accidental and hence would not be covered. If an injury occurs while an employee is commuting to or from work, it usually will not be considered to have occurred on the job or in the course of employment and hence will not be covered.

An employee must notify his or her employer of an injury promptly (usually within thirty days of the injury's occurrence). Generally, an employee must also file a workers' compensation claim with the appropriate state agency or board within a certain period (sixty days to two years) from the time the injury is first noticed, rather than from the time of the accident.

Workers' Compensation versus Litigation An employee who accepts workers' compensation benefits is prohibited from suing for injuries caused by the employer's negligence. By barring lawsuits for negligence, workers' compensation laws also prevent employers from raising common law defenses to negligence, such as contributory negligence or assumption of risk, to avoid liability. A worker may sue an employer who *intentionally* injures the worker, however.

Income Security, Pension, and Health Plans

Federal and state governments participate in insurance programs designed to protect employees and their families from the financial impact of retirement,

12. In 1978, the United States Supreme Court held that warrantless inspections violated the warrant clause of the Fourth Amendment to the U.S. Constitution. See *Marshall v. Barlow's, Inc.*, 436 U.S. 307, 98 S.Ct. 1816, 56 L.Ed.2d 305 (1978). Although this case has not been overruled, the Supreme Court subsequently indicated that statutory inspection programs can provide a constitutionally adequate substitute for a warrant. See *Donovan v. Dewey*, 452 U.S. 594, 101 S.Ct. 2534, 69 L.Ed.2d 262 (1981).

13. *Pedraza v. Shell Oil Co.*, 942 F.2d 48 (1st Cir. 1991); *cert.* denied, 502 U.S. 1082, 112 S.Ct. 993, 117 L.Ed.2d 154 (1992). See also *In re Welding Fume Products Liability Litigation*, 364 F. Supp.2d 669 (N.D. Ohio 2005).

EMERGING TRENDS IN THE LEGAL ENVIRONMENT OF BUSINESS

Paying Overtime in the Virtual Workforce

According to WorldatWork, a research organization for human resources professionals, nearly 46 million U.S. workers perform at least part of their job at home, and close to 13 million of them are full-time *telecommuters,* meaning that they work at home or off-site by means of an electronic linkup to the central workplace. Just because employees work at a remote location does not mean that they are automatically exempt from overtime-pay requirements (or minimum-wage laws). Federal (and sometimes state and local) wage and hour laws often apply to the virtual workforce, as many businesses are finding out the unfortunate way—through litigation.

Telecommuters and Overtime-Pay Requirements

As described in the text, the U.S. Department of Labor revised its regulations in 2004 to clarify how overtime exemptions apply to employees in various occupations. The new regulations established a primary duty test to be used in classifying workers.[a] In general, workers whose primary duty involves the exercise of discretion and independent judgment are more likely to be exempt from the overtime-pay requirements. So are those whose positions require advanced knowledge or specialized instructions, such as computer systems analysts and software engineers.

Although the regulations appear detailed, they do not specifically address how these exemptions apply to telecommuters. Since the new rules went into effect in 2004, telecommuters have filed a barrage of lawsuits claiming that their employers violated the Fair Labor Standards Act by failing to pay them for overtime work and to compensate them for work-related tasks.

An Increasing Number of Cases and Settlements

To date, more cases have been filed in California than in any other state—mostly by telecommuting information technology workers, pharmaceutical sales representatives, and insurance company employees. Suits are also pending in Colorado, the District of Columbia, Illinois, Missouri, New Jersey, New York, and Ohio.

Some defendants with large numbers of employees have decided to settle before the case goes to trial. Computer Sciences Corporation in El Segundo, California, for example, paid $24 million to settle a case brought by telecommuters and call-center

a. See 29 C.F.R. Sections 541.203 and 541.400.

disability, death, hospitalization, and unemployment. The key federal law on this subject is the Social Security Act of 1935.[14]

Social Security

The Social Security Act of 1935 provides for old-age (retirement), survivors', and disability insurance. The act is therefore often referred to as OASDI. Both employers and employees must "contribute" under the Federal Insurance Contributions Act (FICA)[15] to help pay for benefits that will partially make up for the employees' loss of income on retirement.

The basis for the employee's and the employer's contribution is the employee's annual wage base—the maximum amount of the employee's wages that is subject to the tax. The employer withholds the employee's FICA contribution from the employee's wages and then matches this contribution. The annual wage base increases each year to take into account the rising cost of living. In 2008, employers were required to withhold 6.2 percent of each employee's wages, up to a maximum wage base of $102,000, and to match this contribution.

Retired workers are eligible to receive monthly payments from the Social Security Administration, which administers the Social Security Act. Social Security benefits are fixed by statute but increase automatically with increases in the cost of living.

Medicare

Medicare, a federal government health-insurance program, is administered by the Social Security Administration for people sixty-five years of age and older and for some under age sixty-five who have a disability. It originally had two parts, one pertaining to hospital costs and the other to nonhospital medical costs, such as visits to physicians' offices. People who have Medicare hospital insurance can obtain additional federal medical insurance if they pay small monthly premiums, which increase as the cost of medical care rises.

As with Social Security contributions, both the employer and the employee "contribute" to Medicare, but unlike Social Security, there is no cap on the

14. 42 U.S.C. Sections 301–1397e.
15. 26 U.S.C. Sections 3101–3125.

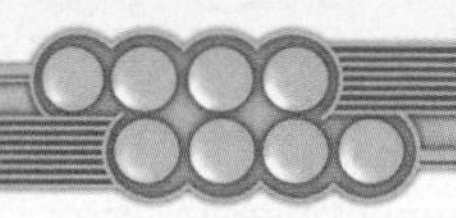

employees,[b] and International Business Machines Corporation (IBM) settled a similar suit for $65 million.[c] Other defendants have refused to settle. Farmers Insurance Exchange went to trial but lost and faced a significant jury verdict. On appeal to the U.S. Court of Appeals for the Ninth Circuit, however, the company prevailed.[d] In contrast, Advanced Business Integrators, Inc., had to pay nearly $50,000 in overtime compensation to a computer consultant who had spent the majority of his work time at customers' sites training their employees in the use of his employer's software.[e]

b. *Computer Sciences Corp.*, No. 03-08201 (C.D.Cal., settled in 2005).

c. *International Business Machines Corp.*, No. 06-00430 (N.D.Cal., settled in 2006).

d. *In re Farmers Insurance Exchange, Claims Representatives' Overtime Pay Litigation*, 481 F.3d 1119 (9th Cir. 2007).

e. *Eicher v. Advanced Business Integrators, Inc.*, 151 Cal.App.4th 1363, 61 Cal.Rptr.3d 114 (2007).

IMPLICATIONS FOR THE BUSINESSPERSON

1. The litigation discussed here illustrates the importance of properly tracking hours worked for compensation purposes. Even though recording the hours worked by telecommuters may be difficult, allowing employees to work from home without an accounting of how many hours they actually work may lead to class-action claims for overtime pay.
2. Businesspersons may consider whether a particular job is appropriate for telecommuting and then allow only exempt employees to telecommute.

FOR CRITICAL ANALYSIS

1. Why might telecommuting employees sometimes accept being wrongly classified as "executives" or "professionals" under the overtime-pay requirements and thus be exempt from overtime pay?
2. If more class-action lawsuits claiming overtime pay for telecommuters are successful, what do you think will be the effect on telecommuting? Why?

RELEVANT WEB SITES

To locate information on the Web concerning the issues discussed in this feature, go to this text's Web site at **academic.cengage.com/blaw/cross**, select "Chapter 20," and click on "Emerging Trends."

amount of wages subject to the Medicare tax. In 2008, both the employer and the employee were required to pay 1.45 percent of *all* wages and salaries to finance Medicare. Thus, for Social Security and Medicare together, in 2008 the employer and employee each paid 7.65 percent of the first $102,000 of income (6.2 percent for Social Security + 1.45 percent for Medicare), for a combined total of 15.3 percent. In addition, all wages and salaries above $102,000 were taxed at a combined (employer and employee) rate of 2.9 percent for Medicare. Self-employed persons pay both the employer and the employee portions of the Social Security and Medicare taxes (15.3 percent of income up to $102,000 and 2.9 percent of income above that amount in 2008).

Private Pension Plans

The Employee Retirement Income Security Act (ERISA) of 1974[16] is the major federal act regulating employee retirement plans set up by employers to supplement Social Security benefits. This statute empowers the Labor Management Services Administration of the U.S. Department of Labor to enforce its provisions governing employers who have private pension funds for their employees. ERISA does not require an employer to establish a pension plan. When a plan exists, however, ERISA provides standards for its management.

A key provision of ERISA concerns vesting. **Vesting** gives an employee a legal right to receive pension benefits at some future date when she or he stops working. Before ERISA was enacted, some employees who had worked for companies for as long as thirty years received no pension benefits when their employment terminated because those benefits had not vested. ERISA establishes complex vesting rules. Generally, however, all of an employee's contributions to a pension plan vest immediately, and the employee's rights to the employer's contributions vest after five years of employment.

In an attempt to prevent mismanagement of pension funds, ERISA has established rules on how they must be invested. Managers must choose investments

16. 29 U.S.C. Sections 1001 *et seq.*

cautiously and must diversify the plan's investments to minimize the risk of large losses. ERISA also includes detailed record-keeping and reporting requirements.

Unemployment Compensation

To ease the financial impact of unemployment, the United States has a system of unemployment insurance. The Federal Unemployment Tax Act (FUTA) of 1935[17] created a state-administered system that provides unemployment compensation to eligible individuals. Under this system, employers pay into a fund, and the proceeds are paid out to qualified unemployed workers. FUTA and state laws require employers that fall under the provisions of the act to pay unemployment taxes at regular intervals.

FUTA generally determines covered employment and imposes certain requirements on state unemployment programs, but the states determine individual eligibility requirements and benefit amounts. To be eligible for unemployment compensation, a worker must be willing and able to work and be actively seeking employment. Workers who have been fired for misconduct or who have left their jobs without good cause normally are not eligible for benefits.

COBRA

Federal legislation also addresses the issue of health insurance for workers who have lost their jobs and are no longer eligible for group health-insurance plans. Employers who have twenty or more employees and provide a group health plan must comply with the requirements of the Consolidated Omnibus Budget Reconciliation Act (COBRA) of 1985.[18] COBRA basically gives employees a right to continue the group health benefits provided by their employers for a limited time after the voluntary or involuntary loss of employment. The act also applies to workers who are no longer eligible for coverage under the employer's health plan because their hours have been decreased. Spouses, former spouses, and dependent children who were covered under the plan also have the right to continue health coverage.

Procedures under COBRA An employer must notify an employee of COBRA's provisions if the worker faces termination or a reduction of hours that would affect her or his eligibility for coverage under the plan. The worker has sixty days (beginning with the date that the group coverage would stop) to decide whether to continue with the employer's group insurance plan. If the worker chooses to discontinue the coverage, then the employer has no further obligation. If the worker chooses to continue coverage, the employer is obligated to keep the policy active for up to eighteen months but is not required to pay for the coverage.[19]

Usually, the worker (or beneficiary) must pay the premiums for continued coverage, plus an additional 2 percent administrative fee. The coverage provided must be the same as that enjoyed by the worker prior to the termination or reduction of employment. If family members were originally included, for example, COBRA prohibits their exclusion.

Employer's Obligations under COBRA The employer is relieved of the responsibility to provide COBRA coverage if the worker fails to pay the premium, becomes eligible for Medicare, or is covered under another health plan (such as a spouse's or new employer's). The employer is also relieved of the obligation if the employer completely cancels its group benefit plan for all employees. An employer that fails to comply with COBRA risks substantial penalties, such as a tax of up to 10 percent of the annual cost of the group plan or $500,000, whichever is less.

Employer-Sponsored Group Health Plans

The Health Insurance Portability and Accountability Act (HIPAA),[20] which was discussed in Chapter 5 in the context of its privacy protections, contains provisions that affect employer-sponsored group health plans. HIPAA does not require employers to provide health insurance, but it does establish requirements for those that do. One provision of HIPAA limits an employer's ability to exclude persons from coverage for "preexisting conditions" to conditions for which medical treatment was received within the previous six months (excluding pregnancy). Another provision requires that an employee be given credit for previous health coverage (including COBRA coverage) to decrease any waiting period before coverage becomes effective.

17. 26 U.S.C. Sections 3301–3310.
18. 29 U.S.C. Sections 1161–1169.
19. Certain events, such as a disability, can extend the period of COBRA coverage. Also, COBRA does not prohibit health plans from offering continuation health coverage that goes beyond COBRA periods.
20. 29 U.S.C.A. Sections 1181 *et seq.*

In addition, employers that are plan sponsors have significant responsibilities regarding the manner in which they collect, use, and disclose the health information of employees and their families. Employers must comply with numerous administrative, technical, and procedural safeguards (such as training employees, designating privacy officials, and distributing privacy notices) to ensure that employees' health information is not disclosed to unauthorized parties. Failure to comply with HIPAA regulations can result in civil penalties of up to $100 per person per violation (with a cap of $25,000 per year). The employer is also subject to criminal prosecution for certain types of HIPAA violations and can face up to $250,000 in criminal fines and imprisonment for up to ten years if convicted.

Section 5 Family and Medical Leave

In 1993, Congress passed the Family and Medical Leave Act (FMLA)[21] to protect employees who need time off work for family or medical reasons. A majority of the states also have legislation allowing for a leave from employment for family or medical reasons, and many employers maintain private family-leave plans for their workers.

Coverage and Application of the FMLA

The FMLA requires employers who have fifty or more employees to provide an employee with up to twelve weeks of unpaid family or medical leave during any twelve-month period. Generally, an employee may take family leave to care for a newborn baby, an adopted child, or a foster child, and medical leave when the employee or the employee's spouse, child, or parent has a "serious health condition" requiring care.[22] Employees suffering from certain chronic health conditions, such as asthma, diabetes, and pregnancy, may take FMLA leave for their own incapacities that require absences of fewer than three days.

The employer must continue the worker's health-care coverage and guarantee employment in the same position or a comparable position when the employee returns to work. An important exception to the FMLA, however, allows the employer to avoid reinstating a *key employee*—defined as an employee whose pay falls within the top 10 percent of the firm's workforce. (The employer must continue to maintain health benefits for the key employee during the leave, however.) Also, the act does not apply to part-time or newly hired employees (those who have worked for less than one year).

The FMLA expressly covers private and public (government) employees. Nevertheless, some states argued that public employees could not sue their state employers in federal courts to enforce their FMLA rights unless the states consented to be sued.[23] This argument came before the United States Supreme Court in the following case.

21. 29 U.S.C. Sections 2601, 2611–2619, 2651–2654.

22. The foster care must be state sanctioned before such an arrangement falls within the coverage of the FMLA.

23. Under the Eleventh Amendment to the U.S. Constitution, a state is immune from suit in a federal court unless the state agrees to be sued.

EXTENDED CASE 20.3 Nevada Department of Human Resources v. Hibbs

Supreme Court of the United States, 2003. 538 U.S. 721, 123 S.Ct. 1972, 155 L.Ed.2d 953.

Chief Justice *REHNQUIST* Delivered the Opinion of the Court.

* * * *

Petitioners include the Nevada Department of Human Resources (Department) * * *. Respondent William Hibbs (hereinafter respondent) worked for the Department's Welfare Division. In April and May 1997, he sought leave under the FMLA to care for his ailing wife, who was recovering from a car accident and neck surgery. The Department granted his request for the full 12 weeks of FMLA leave and authorized him to use the leave intermittently as needed between May and December 1997. Respondent did so until August 5, 1997, after which he did not return to work. In October 1997, the Department informed respondent that he had exhausted his FMLA leave, that no further leave would be granted, and that he must report to work by November 12, 1997. Respondent failed to do so and was terminated.

CASE CONTINUES

CASE 20.3 CONTINUED

Respondent sued petitioners in [a] United States District Court * * * . The District Court awarded petitioners summary judgment on the grounds that the FMLA claim was barred by the [U.S. Constitution's] Eleventh Amendment * * * . Respondent appealed * * * . The Ninth Circuit reversed.

We granted *certiorari* * * * .

* * * *

The history of the many state laws limiting women's employment opportunities is chronicled in—and, until relatively recently, was sanctioned by—this Court's own opinions. For example, in [previous cases] the Court upheld state laws prohibiting women from practicing law and tending bar * * * . State laws frequently subjected women to distinctive restrictions, terms, conditions, and benefits for those jobs they could take. In [one case] for example, this Court approved a state law limiting the hours that women could work for wages, and observed that 19 States had such laws at the time. Such laws were based on the related beliefs that (1) woman is, and should remain, the center of home and family life, and (2) a proper discharge of a woman's maternal functions—having in view not merely her own health, but the well-being of the race—justifies legislation to protect her from the greed as well as the passion of man. Until [1971] it remained the prevailing doctrine that government, both federal and state, could withhold from women opportunities accorded men so long as any basis in reason—such as the above beliefs—could be conceived for the discrimination.

Congress responded to this history of discrimination by abrogating [revoking] States' sovereign immunity in Title VII of the Civil Rights Act of 1964 * * * .[a] But state gender discrimination did not cease. * * * According to evidence that was before Congress when it enacted the FMLA, States continue[d] to rely on invalid gender stereotypes in the employment context, specifically in the administration of leave benefits.

* * * *

Congress * * * heard testimony that parental leave for fathers * * * is rare. Even * * * where child-care leave policies do exist, men, both in the public and private sectors, receive notoriously discriminatory treatment in their requests for such leave. Many States offered women extended "maternity" leave that far exceeded the typical 4- to 8-week period of physical disability due to pregnancy and childbirth, but very few States granted men a parallel benefit: Fifteen States provided women up to one year of extended maternity leave, while only four provided men with the same. This and other differential leave policies were not attributable to any differential physical needs of men and women, but rather to the pervasive sex-role stereotype that caring for family members is women's work.

* * * *

* * * Because employers continued to regard the family as the woman's domain, they often denied men similar accommodations or discouraged them from taking leave. These mutually reinforcing stereotypes created a self-fulfilling cycle of discrimination that forced women to continue to assume the role of primary family caregiver, and fostered employers' stereotypical views about women's * * * value as employees.

* * * *

By creating an across-the-board, routine employment benefit for all eligible employees, Congress sought to ensure that family-care leave would no longer be stigmatized as an inordinate drain on the workplace caused by female employees, and that employers could not evade leave obligations simply by hiring men. *By setting a minimum standard of family leave for all eligible employees, irrespective of gender, the FMLA attacks the formerly state-sanctioned stereotype that only women are responsible for family caregiving, thereby reducing employers' incentives to engage in discrimination by basing hiring and promotion decisions on stereotypes.* [Emphasis added.]

* * * *

* * * The FMLA is narrowly targeted at the fault line between work and family—precisely where sex-based overgeneralization has been and remains strongest—and affects only one aspect of the employment relationship.

* * * *

a. This statute will be discussed in detail in Chapter 21.

CASE 20.3 CONTINUED

For the above reasons, we conclude that [the FMLA] is congruent [harmonious] and proportional to its remedial object, and can be understood as responsive to, or designed to prevent, unconstitutional behavior. The judgment of the Court of Appeals [holding that the Eleventh Amendment did not bar the plaintiff's suit] is therefore *Affirmed*.

QUESTIONS

1. What did the Court hold with respect to the primary issue in this case?
2. How might a law foster discrimination even when the law is not obviously discriminatory?

Remedies for Violations of the FMLA

Remedies for violations of the FMLA can include (1) damages for lost benefits, denied compensation, and actual monetary losses (such as the cost of providing for care of the family member) up to an amount equivalent to the employee's wages for twelve weeks; (2) job reinstatement; and (3) promotion, if a promotion had been denied. A successful plaintiff is entitled to court costs, attorneys' fees, and—in cases involving bad faith on the part of the employer—two times the amount of damages awarded by a judge or jury. Supervisors may also be subject to personal liability, as employers, for violations of the act when the supervisor exercises sufficient control over the employee's leave.[24]

Employers generally are required to notify employees when an absence will be counted against leave authorized under the act. If an employer fails to provide such notice, and the employee consequently suffers an injury because he or she did not receive notice, the employer may be sanctioned.[25]

Interaction with Other Laws

The FMLA does not affect any other federal or state law that prohibits discrimination. Nor does it supersede any state or local law that provides more generous family- or medical-leave protection. For example, if a California state law allows employees who are disabled by pregnancy to take up to four months of unpaid leave, an employer in California would have to comply with that law (in addition to the provisions of the FMLA). Also, an employer who is obligated to provide more extensive leave under a collective bargaining agreement must do so, regardless of the FMLA.

Employee Privacy Rights

In the last thirty years, concerns about the privacy rights of employees have arisen in response to the sometimes invasive tactics used by employers to monitor and screen workers. Perhaps the greatest privacy concern in today's employment arena has to do with electronic monitoring of employees' activities. Clearly, employers need to protect themselves from liability for their employees' online activities. They also have a legitimate interest in monitoring the productivity of their workers. At the same time, employees expect to have a certain zone of privacy in the workplace. Indeed, many lawsuits have alleged that employers' intrusive monitoring practices violate employees' privacy rights.

Electronic Monitoring in the Workplace

According to the American Management Association, more than two-thirds of employers engage in some form of electronic monitoring of their employees. Types of monitoring include monitoring workers' Web site connections, reviewing employees' e-mail and computer files, video recording of employee job performance, and recording and reviewing telephone conversations and voice mail.

Various specially designed software products have made it easier for an employer to track employees' Internet use. Software allows an employer to track almost every move an employee makes on the Internet, including the specific Web sites visited and

24. See, for example, *Rupnow v. TRC, Inc.*, 999 F.Supp. 1047 (N.D. Ohio 1998); and *Mueller v. J. P. Morgan Chase & Co.*, 2007 WL 915160 (N.D. Ohio 2007).

25. *Ragsdale v. Wolverine World Wide, Inc.*, 535 U.S. 81, 122 S.Ct. 1155, 152 L.Ed.2d 167 (2002); and *Mondaine v. American Drug Stores, Inc.*, 408 F. Supp.2d 1169 (D.Kan. 2006).

the time spent surfing the Web. Filtering software, which was discussed in Chapter 5, can be used to prevent access to certain Web sites, such as sites containing sexually explicit images. Other filtering software may be used to screen incoming e-mail for viruses and to block junk e-mail (spam).

Although the use of filtering software by public employers (government agencies) has led to charges that blocking access to Web sites violates employees' rights to free speech, this issue does not arise in private businesses. This is because the First Amendment's protection of free speech applies only to *government* restraints on speech, not restraints imposed in the private sector.

Employee Privacy Protection under Constitutional and Tort Law Recall from Chapter 5 that the United States Supreme Court has inferred a personal right to privacy from the constitutional guarantees provided by the First, Third, Fourth, Fifth, and Ninth Amendments to the Constitution. Tort law (see Chapter 12), state constitutions, and a number of state and federal statutes also provide for privacy rights.

When determining whether an employer should be held liable for violating an employee's privacy rights, the courts generally weigh the employer's interests against the employee's reasonable expectation of privacy. Normally, if employees are informed that their communications are being monitored, they cannot reasonably expect those communications to be private. If employees are not informed that certain communications are being monitored, however, the employer may be held liable for invading their privacy. For this reason, today most employers that engage in electronic monitoring notify their employees about the monitoring.

For the most part, courts have held that an employer's monitoring of electronic communications in the workplace does not violate employees' privacy rights. Even if employees are not informed that their e-mail will be monitored, courts have generally concluded that employees have no expectation of privacy if the employer provided the e-mail system.[26] Courts have even found that employers have a right to monitor the e-mail of an independent contractor (such as an insurance agent) when the employer provided the e-mail service and was authorized to access stored messages.[27]

26. For a leading case on this issue, see *Smyth v. Pillsbury Co.*, 914 F. Supp. 97 (E.D.Pa. 1996).

27. See *Fraser v. Nationwide Mutual Insurance Co.*, 352 F.3d 107 (3d Cir. 2004).

The Electronic Communications Privacy Act The major statute with which employers must comply is the Electronic Communications Privacy Act (ECPA) of 1986.[28] This act amended existing federal wiretapping law to cover electronic forms of communications, such as communications via cellular telephones or e-mail. The ECPA prohibits the intentional interception of any wire or electronic communication or the intentional disclosure or use of the information obtained by the interception. Excluded from coverage, however, are any electronic communications through devices that are "furnished to the subscriber or user by a provider of wire or electronic communication service" and that are being used by the subscriber or user, or by the provider of the service, "in the ordinary course of its business."

This "business-extension exception" to the ECPA permits an employer to monitor employees' electronic communications in the ordinary course of business. It does not, however, permit an employer to monitor employees' personal communications. Under another exception to the ECPA, however, an employer may avoid liability under the act if the employees consent to having their electronic communications intercepted by the employer. Thus, an employer may be able to avoid liability under the ECPA by simply requiring employees to sign forms indicating that they consent to such monitoring.

Other Types of Monitoring

In addition to monitoring their employees' online activities, employers also engage in other types of employee screening and monitoring practices. The practices discussed below have often been challenged as violations of employee privacy rights.

Lie-Detector Tests At one time, many employers required employees or job applicants to take polygraph examinations (lie-detector tests). To protect the privacy interests of employees and job applicants, in 1988 Congress passed the Employee Polygraph Protection Act.[29] The act prohibits employers from (1) requiring or causing employees or job applicants to take lie-detector tests or suggesting or requesting that they do so; (2) using, accepting, referring to, or asking about the results of lie-detector tests taken by employees or applicants; and (3) taking or threatening negative employment-related action against employees or

28. 18 U.S.C. Sections 2510–2521.

29. 29 U.S.C. Sections 2001 *et seq.*

applicants based on results of lie-detector tests or on their refusal to take the tests.

Employers excepted from these prohibitions include federal, state, and local government employers; certain security service firms; and companies manufacturing and distributing controlled substances. Other employers may use polygraph tests when investigating losses attributable to theft, including embezzlement and the theft of trade secrets.

Drug Testing In the interests of public safety and to reduce unnecessary costs, many employers, including the government, require their employees to submit to drug testing.

Public Employers. Government (public) employers, of course, are constrained in drug testing by the Fourth Amendment to the U.S. Constitution, which prohibits unreasonable searches and seizures (see Chapter 5). Drug testing of public employees is allowed by statute for transportation workers and is normally upheld by the courts when drug use in a particular job may threaten public safety.[30] The Federal Aviation Administration also requires drug and alcohol testing of all employees and contractors (including employees of foreign air carriers) who perform safety-related functions.[31] When there is a reasonable basis for suspecting public employees of drug use, courts often find that drug testing does not violate the Fourth Amendment.

Private Employers. The Fourth Amendment does not apply to drug testing conducted by private employers.[32] Hence, the privacy rights and drug testing of private-sector employees are governed by state law, which varies from state to state. When testing is not allowed by state statute, employees sometimes file suit against their employers for the tort of invasion of privacy, although such claims have not met with much success.

Many states have statutes that allow drug testing by private employers but put restrictions on when and how the testing may be performed. A collective bargaining agreement may also provide protection against drug testing (or authorize drug testing under certain conditions). The permissibility of a private employee's drug test often hinges on whether the employer's testing was reasonable. Random drug tests and even "zero-tolerance" policies (that deny a "second chance" to employees who test positive for drugs) have been held to be reasonable.[33]

AIDS and HIV Testing A number of employers test their workers for acquired immune deficiency syndrome (AIDS) or the presence of human immunodeficiency virus (HIV), the virus that causes AIDS. Some state laws restrict such testing, and federal statutes—particularly the Americans with Disabilities Act of 1990[34] (see Chapter 21)—offer some protection to employees or job applicants who have AIDS or have tested positive for HIV. Employees may not be discharged and job applicants may not be discriminated against based on the results of AIDS tests. Employers are also required to safeguard a person's protected medical information and cannot disclose an employee's test results to unauthorized parties under HIPAA, which was discussed earlier in this chapter.

30. Omnibus Transportation Employee Testing Act of 1991, Pub. L. No. 102-143, Title V, 105 Stat. 917 (1991).

31. Antidrug and Alcohol Misuse Prevention Program for Personnel Engaged in Specified Aviation Activities, 71 *Federal Register* 1666 (January 10, 2006), enacted pursuant to 49 U.S.C. Section 45102(a)(1).

32. See *Chandler v. Miller,* 520 U.S. 305, 117 S.Ct. 1295, 137 L.Ed.2d 513 (1997).

33. See *CITGO Asphalt Refining Co. v. Paper, Allied-Industrial, Chemical, and Energy Workers International Union Local No. 2-991,* 385 F.3d 809 (3d Cir. 2004).

34. 42 U.S.C. Sections 12102–12118.

REVIEWING Employment Relationships

Rick Saldona began working as a traveling salesperson for Aimer Winery in 1979. Sales constituted 90 percent of Saldona's work time. Saldona worked an average of fifty hours per week but received no overtime pay. In June 2009, Saldona's new supervisor, Caesar Braxton, claimed

REVIEWING CONTINUES

REVIEWING Employment Relationships, Continued

that Saldona had been inflating his reported sales calls and required Saldona to submit to a polygraph test. Saldona reported Braxton to the U.S. Department of Labor, which prohibited Aimer from requiring Saldona to take a polygraph test for this purpose. In August 2009, Saldona's wife, Venita, fell from a ladder and sustained a head injury while employed as a full-time agricultural harvester. Saldona delivered to Aimer's Human Resources Department a letter from his wife's physician indicating that she would need daily care for several months, and Saldona took leave until December 2009. Aimer had sixty-three employees at that time. When Saldona returned to Aimer, he was informed that his position had been eliminated because his sales territory had been combined with an adjacent territory. Using the information presented in the chapter, answer the following questions.

1. Would Saldona have been legally entitled to receive overtime pay at a higher rate? Why or why not?
2. What is the maximum length of time Saldona would have been allowed to take leave to care for his injured spouse?
3. Would Aimer likely be able to avoid reinstating Saldona under the *key employee* exception? Why or why not?
4. Under what circumstances would Aimer have been allowed to require an employee to take a polygraph test?

TERMS AND CONCEPTS

employment at will 506
minimum wage 510
vesting 515
workers' compensation law 513
wrongful discharge 509

QUESTIONS AND CASE PROBLEMS

20–1. Calzoni Boating Co. is an interstate business engaged in manufacturing and selling boats. The company has five hundred nonunion employees. Representatives of these employees are requesting a four-day, ten-hours-per-day workweek, and Calzoni is concerned that this would require paying time and a half after eight hours per day. Which federal act is Calzoni thinking of that might require this? Will the act in fact require paying time and a half for all hours worked over eight hours per day if the employees' proposal is accepted? Explain.

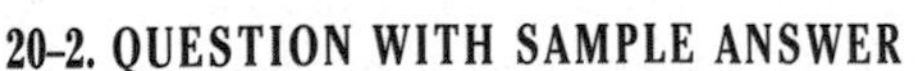

20–2. QUESTION WITH SAMPLE ANSWER

Denton and Carlo were employed at an appliance plant. Their job required them to perform occasional maintenance work while standing on a wire mesh twenty feet above the plant floor. Other employees had fallen through the mesh, and one of them had been killed by the fall. When Denton and Carlo were asked by their supervisor to perform tasks that would likely require them to walk on the mesh, they refused because of their fear of bodily harm or death. Because of their refusal to do the requested work, the two employees were fired from their jobs. Was their discharge wrongful? If so, under what federal employment law? To what federal agency or department should they turn for assistance?

- **For a sample answer to Question 20–2, go to Appendix I at the end of this text.**

20–3. Performance Monitoring. Patience Oyoyo worked as a claims analyst in the claims management department of Baylor Healthcare Network, Inc. When questions arose about Oyoyo's performance on several occasions, department manager Debbie Outlaw met with Oyoyo to discuss, among other things, Oyoyo's personal use of a business phone. Outlaw reminded Oyoyo that company policy prohibited excessive personal calls and that these would result in the termination of her employment. Outlaw began to monitor Oyoyo's phone usage, noting lengthy outgoing calls on several occasions, including some long-distance calls. Eventually, Outlaw terminated Oyoyo's employment, and Oyoyo filed a suit in a federal district court against Baylor. Oyoyo asserted in part that in monitoring her phone calls, the employer had invaded her privacy. Baylor asked the court to dismiss this claim. In whose favor should the court rule, and why? [*Oyoyo v. Baylor Healthcare Network, Inc.*, __ F.Supp.2d __ (N.D.Tex. 2000)]

20–4. Hours and Wages. Tradesmen International, Inc., leases skilled tradespersons (field employees) to construction contractors. To receive a job offer through Tradesmen, applicants must either complete an Occupational Safety and Health Administration (OSHA) ten-hour general construction safety course or commit to registering for the course within sixty days and completing it within a reasonable time. The class instruction has no effect on the trade skills of any field employee. The classes are held outside of regular working hours. Employees perform no work in the class and are not compensated for the time spent in the class. Elaine Chao, the U.S. secretary of labor, filed a suit in a federal district court against Tradesmen for failing to pay overtime compensation to those who attend the class. Does Tradesmen's practice—requiring the class as a prerequisite to employment but not paying applicants to attend it—violate the Fair Labor Standards Act? Explain. [*Chao v. Tradesmen International, Inc.*, 310 F.3d 904 (6th Cir. 2002)]

20–5. Workers' Compensation Laws. The Touch of Class Lounge is in a suburban shopping plaza, or strip mall, in Omaha, Nebraska. Patricia Bauer, the Lounge's owner, does not own the parking lot, which is provided for the common use of all of the businesses in the plaza. Stephanie Zoucha was a bartender at the Lounge. Her duties ended when she locked the door after closing. On June 4, 2001, at 1:15 A.M., Zoucha closed the bar and locked the door from the inside. An hour later, she walked to her car in the parking lot, where she was struck with "[l]ike a tire iron on the back of my head." Zoucha sustained a skull fracture and other injuries, including significant cognitive damage (impairment of speech and thought formation). Her purse, containing her tip money, was stolen. She identified her attacker as William Nunez, who had been in the Lounge earlier that night. Zoucha filed a petition in a Nebraska state court to obtain workers' compensation. What are the requirements for receiving workers' compensation? Should Zoucha's request be granted or denied? Why? [*Zoucha v. Touch of Class Lounge*, 269 Neb. 89, 690 N.W.2d 610 (2005)]

20–6. CASE PROBLEM WITH SAMPLE ANSWER

Jennifer Willis worked for Coca Cola Enterprises, Inc. (CCE), in Louisiana as a senior account manager. On a Monday in May 2003, Willis called her supervisor to tell him that she was sick and would not be able to work that day. She also said that she was pregnant, but she did not say she was sick *because* of the pregnancy. On Tuesday, she called to ask where to report to work and was told that she could not return without a doctor's release. She said that she had a doctor's appointment on "Wednesday," which her supervisor understood to be the next day. Willis meant the *following* Wednesday. More than a week later, during which time Willis did not contact CCE, she was told that she had violated CCE's "No Call/No Show" policy. Under this policy, "an employee absent from work for three consecutive days without notifying the supervisor during that period will be considered to have voluntarily resigned." She was fired. Willis filed a suit in a federal district court against CCE under the Family and Medical Leave Act (FMLA). To be eligible for FMLA leave, an employee must inform an employer of the reason for the leave. Did Willis meet this requirement? Did CCE's response to Willis's absence violate the FMLA? Explain. [*Willis v. Coca Cola Enterprises, Inc.*, 445 F.3d 413 (5th Cir. 2006)]

- **To view a sample answer for Problem 20–6, go to this book's Web site at academic.cengage.com/blaw/cross, select "Chapter 20," and click on "Case Problem with Sample Answer."**

20–7. Unemployment Insurance. Mary Garas, a chemist, sought work in Missouri through Kelly Services, Inc. Kelly is a staffing agency that places individuals in jobs of varying duration with other companies. Through Kelly, Garas worked at Merial Co. from April 2005 to February 2006. After the assignment ended, Garas asked Kelly for more work. Meanwhile, she filed a claim for unemployment benefits with the Missouri Division of Employment Security (DES). In March, Kelly recruiter Rebecca Cockrum told Garas about a temporary assignment with Celsis Laboratory. Garas said that she would prefer a "more stable position," but later asked Cockrum to submit her résumé to Celsis. Before the employer responded, Kelly told the DES that Garas had refused suitable work. Under a Missouri state statute, a claim for unemployment benefits must be denied if "the claimant failed without good cause . . . to accept suitable work when offered the claimant . . . by an employer by whom the individual was formerly employed." The DES denied Garas's claim for benefits. She filed an appeal with a state court. Was the DES's denial right or wrong? Why? [*Garas v. Kelly Services, Inc.*, 211 S.W.3d 149 (Mo.App.E.D. 2007)]

20–8. A QUESTION OF ETHICS

Beverly Tull had worked for Atchison Leather Products, Inc., in Kansas for ten years when, in 1999, she began to complain of hand, wrist, and shoulder pain. Atchison recommended that she contact a certain physician, who in April 2000 diagnosed the condition as carpal tunnel syndrome "severe enough" for surgery. In August, Tull filed a claim with the state workers' compensation board. Because Atchison changed workers' *compensation insurance companies every year, a dispute arose as to which company should pay Tull's claim. Fearing liability, no insurer would authorize treatment, and Tull was forced to delay surgery until December. The board granted her temporary total disability benefits for the subsequent six weeks that she missed work. On April 23, 2002, Berger Co. bought Atchison. The new employer adjusted Tull's work so that it was less demanding and stressful, but she continued to suffer pain. In July, a physician diagnosed her condition as permanent. The board granted her permanent partial disability benefits. By May 2005, the bickering over the financial responsibility for Tull's claim involved five insurers—four of which had each covered Atchison for a single year and one of which covered Berger. [*Tull v. Atchison Leather Products, Inc., *37 Kan.App.2d 87, 150 P.3d 316 (2007)]*

(a) When an injured employee files a claim for workers' compensation, a proceeding is held to assess the injury and determine the amount of compensation. Should a dispute between insurers over the payment of the claim be resolved in the same proceeding? Why or why not?
(b) The board designated April 23, 2002, as the date of Tull's injury. What is the reason for determining the date of a worker's injury? Should the board in this case have selected this date or a different date? Why?
(c) How should the board assess liability for the payment of Tull's medical expenses and disability benefits? Would it be appropriate to impose joint and several liability on the insurers (holding each of them responsible for the full amount of damages), or should the individual liability of each of them be determined? Explain.

20-9. VIDEO QUESTION

Go to this text's Web site at **academic.cengage.com/blaw/cross** and select "Chapter 20." Click on "Video Questions" and view the video titled *Employment at Will.* Then answer the following questions.

(a) In the video, Laura asserts that she can fire Ray "for any reason; for no reason." Is this true? Explain your answer.
(b) What exceptions to the employment-at-will doctrine are discussed in the chapter? Does Ray's situation fit into any of these exceptions?
(c) Assume that you are the employer in this scenario. What arguments can you make that Ray should not be able to sue for wrongful discharge in this situation?

LAW ON THE WEB

For updated links to resources available on the Web, as well as a variety of other materials, visit this text's Web site at

academic.cengage.com/blaw/cross

The U.S. Department of Labor offers an FLSA Overtime Calculator and a variety of other information to assist both employers and workers at

www.dol.gov/elaws

The American Civil Liberties Union (ACLU) has a page on its Web site devoted to employee privacy rights with respect to electronic monitoring. Go to

www.aclu.org/privacy/workplace/index.html

An excellent Web site for information on employee benefits—including the full text of relevant statutes, such as the FMLA and COBRA, as well as case law and current articles—is BenefitsLink. Go to

www.benefitslink.com/index.html

Legal Research Exercises on the Web

Go to **academic.cengage.com/blaw/cross**, the Web site that accompanies this text. Select "Chapter 20" and click on "Internet Exercises." There you will find the following Internet research exercises that you can perform to learn more about the topics covered in this chapter.

Internet Exercise 20–1: Legal Perspective
Workers' Compensation

Internet Exercise 20–2: Management Perspective
Workplace Monitoring and Surveillance

CHAPTER 21 Employment Discrimination

Out of the 1960s civil rights movement to end racial and other forms of discrimination grew a body of law protecting employees against discrimination in the workplace. This protective legislation further eroded the employment-at-will doctrine, which was discussed in Chapter 20. In the past several decades, judicial decisions, administrative agency actions, and legislation have restricted the ability of employers, as well as unions, to discriminate against workers on the basis of race, color, religion, national origin, gender, age, or disability. A class of persons defined by one or more of these criteria is known as a **protected class.**

Several federal statutes prohibit **employment discrimination** against members of protected classes. The most important statute is Title VII of the Civil Rights Act of 1964.[1] Title VII prohibits employment discrimination on the basis of race, color, religion, national origin, and gender. The Age Discrimination in Employment Act of 1967[2] and the Americans with Disabilities Act of 1990[3] prohibit discrimination on the basis of age and disability, respectively. The protections afforded under these laws extend to U.S. citizens who are working abroad for U.S. firms or for companies that are controlled by U.S. firms—*unless* to do so would violate the laws of the countries in which their workplaces are located. This "foreign laws exception" prevents employers from being subjected to conflicting laws.

This chapter focuses on the kinds of discrimination prohibited by these federal statutes. Note, however, that discrimination against employees on the basis of any of the above-mentioned criteria may also violate state human rights statutes or other state laws prohibiting discrimination.

1. 42 U.S.C. Sections 2000e–2000e-17.
2. 29 U.S.C. Sections 621–634.
3. 42 U.S.C. Sections 12102–12118.

SECTION 1 Title VII of the Civil Rights Act of 1964

Title VII of the Civil Rights Act of 1964 and its amendments prohibit job discrimination against employees, applicants, and union members on the basis of race, color, national origin, religion, and gender at any stage of employment. It prohibits discrimination in decisions concerning hiring, firing, promotion, demotion, discipline, compensation, opportunities for additional job training, and any other term and condition of employment.

Title VII expressly applies to employers affecting interstate commerce with fifteen or more employees, labor unions with fifteen or more members, labor unions that operate hiring halls (to which members go regularly to be rationed jobs as they become available), employment agencies, and state and local governing units or agencies. A special section of the act prohibits discrimination in most federal government employment. When Title VII applies to the employer, any employee—including an undocumented (alien) worker—can bring an action for employment discrimination. Moreover, an employer with fewer than fifteen employees is not automatically shielded from a lawsuit filed under Title VII.[4]

The Equal Employment Opportunity Commission

The Equal Employment Opportunity Commission (EEOC) monitors compliance with Title VII. A victim of alleged discrimination, before bringing a suit against the employer, must first file a claim with the EEOC. The EEOC may investigate the dispute and attempt to obtain the parties' voluntary consent to an out-of-court settlement. If voluntary agreement cannot be reached, the EEOC may then file a suit against the employer on the employee's behalf. If the EEOC decides not to investigate the claim, the victim may bring his or her own lawsuit against the employer.

The EEOC does not investigate every claim of employment discrimination. Generally, it takes only "priority cases," such as cases that affect many workers, cases involving retaliatory discharge (firing an employee in retaliation for submitting a claim with the EEOC), and cases involving types of discrimination that are of particular concern to the EEOC. In recent years, the EEOC has been receiving and investigating an increasing number of claims of religious discrimination in the workplace.[5]

Intentional and Unintentional Discrimination

Title VII of the Civil Rights Act of 1964 prohibits both intentional and unintentional discrimination.

Intentional Discrimination Intentional discrimination by an employer against an employee is known as **disparate-treatment discrimination.** Because intent may sometimes be difficult to prove, courts have established certain procedures for resolving disparate-treatment cases. Suppose that a woman applies for employment with a construction firm and is rejected. If she sues on the basis of disparate-treatment discrimination in hiring, she must show that (1) she is a member of a protected class, (2) she applied and was qualified for the job in question, (3) she was rejected by the employer, and (4) the employer continued to seek applicants for the position or filled the position with a person not in a protected class.

If the woman can meet these relatively easy requirements, she makes out a ***prima facie* case** of illegal discrimination. Making out a *prima facie* case of discrimination means that the plaintiff has met her initial burden of proof and will win in the absence of a legally acceptable employer defense. (Defenses to claims of employment discrimination will be discussed later in this chapter.) The burden then shifts to the employer-defendant, who must articulate a legal reason for not hiring the plaintiff. For example, the employer might say that the plaintiff was not hired because she lacked sufficient experience or training. To prevail, the plaintiff must then show that the employer's reason is a *pretext* (not the true reason) and that discriminatory intent actually motivated the employer's decision.

Unintentional Discrimination Employers often use interviews and testing procedures to choose from among a large number of applicants for job openings. Minimum educational requirements are also common. Employer practices, such as those involving educational requirements, may have an unintended discriminatory impact on a protected class. **Disparate-impact discrimination** occurs when a protected group of people is adversely affected by an employer's practices, procedures, or tests, even though they do not appear to be discriminatory. In a disparate-impact discrimination case, the complaining party must first show statistically that the employer's practices, procedures, or tests are discriminatory in effect. The plaintiff must show a causal link between the practice and the discriminatory effect. Once the plaintiff has made out a *prima facie* case, the burden of proof shifts to the employer to show that the practices or procedures in question were justified. There are two ways of proving that disparate-impact discrimination exists, as discussed next.

Pool of Applicants. A plaintiff can prove a disparate impact by comparing the employer's workforce to the pool of qualified individuals available in the local labor market. The plaintiff must show that as a result of educational or other job requirements or hiring procedures, the percentage of nonwhites, women, or members of other protected classes in the employer's workforce does not reflect the percentage of that group in the pool of qualified applicants. If a person

4. The United States Supreme Court has held that courts still have jurisdiction to hear Title VII claims by employees against their employers even if the employer has fewer than fifteen employees. *Arbaugh v. Y&H Corp.*, 546 U.S. 500, 126 S.Ct. 1235, 163 L.Ed.2d 1097 (2006).

5. Dick Dahl, "EEOC Reports 10 Percent Increase in Charges," *Lawyers USA*, February 26, 2007.

challenging an employment practice can show a connection between the practice and the disparity, she or he makes out a *prima facie* case and need not provide evidence of discriminatory intent.

Rate of Hiring. Disparate-impact discrimination can also occur when an educational or other job requirement or hiring procedure excludes members of a protected class from an employer's workforce at a substantially higher rate than nonmembers, regardless of the racial balance in the employer's workforce. This "rates analysis" compares the selection rate for whites with that for nonwhites (or other members of a protected class). The plaintiff does not have to prove that the workforce does not reflect the percentage of qualified nonwhite persons available in the local labor market.

The EEOC has devised a test, called the "four-fifths rule" or the "80 percent rule," to determine whether an employment examination is discriminatory on its face. Under this rule, a selection rate for protected classes that is less than four-fifths, or 80 percent, of the rate for the group with the highest rate will generally be regarded as evidence of disparate impact. To illustrate: One hundred majority-group applicants take an employment test, and fifty pass the test and are hired. One hundred minority-group applicants take the test, and twenty pass the test and are hired. Because twenty is less than four-fifths (80 percent) of fifty, the test would be considered discriminatory under the EEOC guidelines.

Discrimination Based on Race, Color, and National Origin

Title VII prohibits employers from discriminating against employees or job applicants on the basis of race, color, or national origin. If an employer's standards or policies for selecting or promoting employees have a discriminatory effect on employees or job applicants in these protected classes, then a presumption of illegal discrimination arises. To avoid liability, the employer must then show that its standards or policies have a substantial, demonstrable relationship to realistic qualifications for the job in question.

For example, suppose that a city fires Cheng Mai, a Chinese American, who has worked in the city's planning department for two years. Mai claims that he was fired because of his national origin and presents evidence that the city's "residents only" policy has a discriminatory effect on Chinese Americans. The policy requires all city employees to become residents of the city within a reasonable time after being hired. Cheng Mai has not moved to the city but instead has continued to live with his wife and children in a nearby town that has a small population of Chinese Americans. Although residency requirements sometimes violate antidiscrimination laws, if the city can show that its residency requirement has a substantial, demonstrable relationship to realistic qualifications for the job in question, then normally it will not be illegal.

Reverse Discrimination Note that discrimination based on race can also take the form of *reverse discrimination,* or discrimination against "majority" individuals, such as white males. For example, in one Pennsylvania case, an African American woman fired four white men from their management positions at a school district. The men filed a lawsuit for racial discrimination alleging that the woman was trying to eliminate white males from the department. The woman claimed that the terminations were part of a reorganization plan to cut costs in the department. The jury sided with the men and awarded them nearly $3 million in damages. The verdict was upheld on appeal (though the damages award was reduced slightly).[6]

Potential "Section 1981" Claims Victims of racial or ethnic discrimination may also have a cause of action under 42 U.S.C. Section 1981. This section, which was enacted as part of the Civil Rights Act of 1866 to protect the rights of freed slaves, prohibits discrimination on the basis of race or ethnicity in the formation or enforcement of contracts. Because employment is often a contractual relationship, Section 1981 can provide an alternative (and potentially advantageous) basis for a plaintiff's action.[7] Unlike Title VII, Section 1981 does not place a cap on damages (see the discussion of Title VII remedies later in this chapter). Thus, if an employee can prove that he or she was discriminated against in the formation or enforcement of a contract, the employee may be able to obtain a larger damages award under Section 1981 than would be available under Title VII.

Discrimination Based on Religion

Title VII of the Civil Rights Act of 1964 also prohibits government employers, private employers, and unions

6. *Johnston v. School District of Philadelphia,* 2006 WL 999966 (E.D.Pa. 2006).

7. See, for example, *E.E.O.C. v. Sephora USA, LLC,* 419 F.Supp.2d 408 (S.D.N.Y. 2005).

from discriminating against persons because of their religion. An employer must "reasonably accommodate" the religious practices of its employees, unless to do so would cause undue hardship to the employer's business. For example, if an employee's religion prohibits him from working on a certain day of the week or at a certain type of job, the employer must make a reasonable attempt to accommodate these religious requirements. Employers must reasonably accommodate an employee's religious belief even if the belief is not based on the doctrines of a traditionally recognized religion, such as Christianity or Judaism, or a denomination, such as Baptist. The only requirement is that the belief be sincerely held by the employee.[8]

Discrimination Based on Gender

Under Title VII, as well as under other federal acts (including those discussed here), employers are forbidden from discriminating against employees on the basis of gender. Employers are prohibited from classifying jobs as male or female and from advertising in help-wanted columns that are designated male or female unless the employer can prove that the gender of the applicant is essential to the job. Furthermore, employers cannot have separate male and female seniority lists. Generally, to succeed in a suit for gender discrimination, a plaintiff must demonstrate that gender was a determining factor in the employer's decision to hire, fire, or promote him or her. Typically, this involves looking at all of the surrounding circumstances.

The Equal Pay Act of 1963[9] prohibits employers from engaging in gender-based wage discrimination. For the act's equal pay requirements to apply, the male and female employees must work at the same establishment doing similar work. The work need not be identical, provided there is substantial equality of skill, effort, responsibility, and working conditions. To determine whether the Equal Pay Act has been violated, a court will look to the primary duties of the two jobs. It is the job content rather than the job description that controls.[10] If a court finds that the wage differential is due to any factor other than gender, such as a seniority or merit system, then it does not violate the Equal Pay Act.

The Pregnancy Discrimination Act of 1978,[11] which amended Title VII, expanded the definition of gender discrimination to include discrimination based on pregnancy. Women affected by pregnancy, childbirth, or related medical conditions must be treated—for all employment-related purposes, including the provision of benefits under employee benefit programs—the same as other persons not so affected but similar in ability to work.

Constructive Discharge

The majority of Title VII complaints involve unlawful discrimination in decisions to hire or fire employees. In some situations, however, employees who leave their jobs voluntarily can claim that they were "constructively discharged" by the employer. **Constructive discharge** occurs when the employer causes the employee's working conditions to be so intolerable that a reasonable person in the employee's position would feel compelled to quit.

Proving Constructive Discharge The plaintiff must present objective proof of intolerable working conditions, which the employer knew or had reason to know about yet failed to correct within a reasonable time period. Courts generally also require the employee to show causation—that the employer's unlawful discrimination caused the working conditions to be intolerable. Put a different way, the employee's resignation must be a foreseeable result of the employer's discriminatory action.

For example, Khalil's employer humiliates him by informing him in front of his co-workers that he is being demoted to an inferior position. Khalil's co-workers then continually insult, harass, and make derogatory remarks to him about his national origin (he is from Iraq). The employer is aware of this discriminatory treatment but does nothing to remedy the situation, despite repeated complaints from Khalil. After several months, Khalil quits his job and files a Title VII claim. In this situation, Khalil would likely have sufficient evidence to maintain an action for constructive discharge in violation of Title VII. Although courts weigh the facts on a case-by-case basis, employee demotion is one of the most frequently cited reasons for a finding of constructive discharge, particularly when the employee was subjected to humiliation.

Applies to All Title VII Discrimination Note that constructive discharge is a theory that plain-

8. *Frazee v. Illinois Department of Employment Security*, 489 U.S. 829, 109 S.Ct. 1514, 103 L.Ed.2d 914 (1989); and *Watts v. Florida International University*, 495 F.3d 1289 (11th Cir. 2007).

9. 29 U.S.C. Section 206(d).

10. For an illustration of the factors courts consider in wage-discrimination claims under the Equal Pay Act, see *Beck-Wilson v. Principi*, 441 F.3d 353 (6th Cir. 2006).

11. 42 U.S.C. Section 2000e(k).

tiffs can use to establish any type of discrimination claims under Title VII, including race, color, national origin, religion, gender, pregnancy, and sexual harassment. Constructive discharge has also been successfully used in situations that involve discrimination based on age or disability (both of which will be discussed later in this chapter). Constructive discharge is most commonly asserted in cases involving sexual harassment, however.

Sexual Harassment

Title VII also protects employees against **sexual harassment** in the workplace. Sexual harassment can take two forms: *quid pro quo* harassment and hostile-environment harassment. *Quid pro quo* is a Latin phrase that is often translated as "something in exchange for something else." *Quid pro quo* harassment occurs when sexual favors are demanded in return for job opportunities, promotions, salary increases, or other benefits. Hostile-environment claims, in contrast, arise when a person is subjected to unwelcome sexual advances, requests for sexual favors, and other verbal or physical conduct or communication of a sexual nature. The United States Supreme Court has stated that hostile-environment harassment occurs when "the workplace is permeated with discriminatory intimidation, ridicule, and insult, that is sufficiently severe or pervasive to alter the conditions of the victim's employment and create an abusive working environment."[12]

The courts determine whether the sexually offensive conduct was sufficiently severe or pervasive as to create a hostile environment on a case-by-case basis. Typically, a single incident of sexually offensive conduct is not enough to permeate the work environment (although there have been exceptions when the conduct was particularly severe). For example, if a male supervisor makes suggestive gestures and tells a female employee on one occasion that he would like to have sexual relations with her, that may not be enough to make the work environment hostile.[13] If a supervisor repeatedly makes sexually offensive comments, however, or asks for specific details about the sexual conduct of a co-worker on several occasions, this may be enough to create a hostile environment.[14]

Harassment by Supervisors For an employer to be held liable for a supervisor's sexual harassment, the supervisor must have taken a *tangible employment action* against the employee. A **tangible employment action** is a significant change in employment status, such as firing or failing to promote an employee, reassigning the employee to a position with significantly different responsibilities, or effecting a significant change in employment benefits.

Only a supervisor, or another person acting with the authority of the employer, can cause this sort of injury. A co-worker can sexually harass another employee, and anyone who has regular contact with an employee can inflict psychological injuries by offensive conduct. A co-worker cannot dock another's pay, demote her or him, or set conditions for continued employment, however.

Supreme Court Guidelines. In 1998, in two separate cases, the United States Supreme Court issued some significant guidelines relating to the liability of employers for their supervisors' harassment of employees in the workplace. In *Faragher v. City of Boca Raton*,[15] the Court held that an employer (a city) could be held liable for a supervisor's harassment of employees even though the employer was unaware of the behavior. The Court reached this conclusion primarily because, although the city had a written policy against sexual harassment, the policy had not been distributed to city employees. Additionally, the city had not established any procedures that could be followed by employees who felt that they were victims of sexual harassment. In *Burlington Industries, Inc. v. Ellerth*,[16] the Court ruled that a company could be held liable for the harassment of an employee by one of its vice presidents even though the employee suffered no adverse job consequences.

In these two cases, the Court set forth some commonsense guidelines on liability for harassment in the workplace that are helpful to employers and employees alike. On the one hand, employees benefit by the ruling that employers may be held liable for their supervisors' harassment even though the employers were unaware of the actions and even though the employees suffered no adverse job consequences. On the other hand, the Court made it clear in both decisions that employers have an affirmative defense against liability for their supervisors'

12. *Harris v. Forklift Systems*, 510 U.S. 17, 114 S.Ct. 367, 126 L.Ed.2d 295 (1993). See also *Baker v. Via Christi Regional Medical Center*, 491 F.Supp.2d 1040 (D.Kan. 2007).

13. *Pomales v. Celulares Telefonica, Inc.*, 447 F.3d 79 (1st Cir. 2006); and *Fontanez-Nunez v. Janssen Ortho, LLC*, 447 F.3d 50 (1st Cir. 2006).

14. See, for example, *Fye v. Oklahoma Corp. Commission*, 2006 WL 895237 (10th Cir. 2006).

15. 524 U.S. 775, 118 S.Ct. 2275, 141 L.Ed.2d 662 (1998).

16. 524 U.S. 742, 118 S.Ct. 2257, 141 L.Ed.2d 633 (1998).

harassment of employees if the employers can show the following:

1. That they have taken "reasonable care to prevent and correct promptly any sexually harassing behavior" (by establishing effective harassment policies and complaint procedures, for example).
2. That the employees suing for harassment failed to follow these policies and procedures.

In 2004, the Supreme Court further clarified the tangible employment action requirement as it applies in constructive discharge cases. The Court held that "[t]o establish constructive discharge, a plaintiff alleging sexual harassment must show that the work environment became so intolerable that resignation was a fitting response. An employer may then assert the *Ellerth/Faragher* affirmative defense unless the plaintiff quit in reasonable response to a tangible employment action."[17]

17. *Pennsylvania State Police v. Suders*, 542 U.S. 129, 124 S.Ct. 2342, 159 L.Ed.2d 204 (2004).

Retaliation by Employer. Charges of sexual harassment by supervisors—and other claims under Title VII as well—have sometimes resulted in attempts by the employer to retaliate against the employee bringing the claim by demoting him or her or by making some other change in his or her employment status. Title VII includes an antiretaliation provision that makes it unlawful for an employer to "discriminate against" an employee or applicant who has "opposed" a practice that Title VII prohibits. In a *retaliation claim*, the individual asserts that she or he has suffered a harm as a result of making a charge, testifying, or participating in a Title VII investigation or proceeding.

The courts disagreed, however, on what the plaintiff had to show to prove retaliation. Some courts required a plaintiff to show that the challenged action resulted in an adverse effect on the terms or conditions of *employment*. Other courts required a plaintiff to show only that the challenged action would have been material to a reasonable employee. In the following case, the United States Supreme Court considered whether Title VII's ban on retaliation covers acts that are not job related.

EXTENDED CASE 21.1 Burlington Northern and Santa Fe Railway Co. v. White

Supreme Court of the United States, 2006. 548 U.S. 53, 126 S.Ct. 2405, 165 L.Ed.2d 345.

Justice *BREYER* delivered the opinion of the Court.

* * * *

* * * Sheila White [was] the only woman working in the Maintenance of Way department at [Burlington Northern & Santa Fe Railway Company's] Tennessee Yard.

In September 1997, White complained to Burlington officials that her * * * supervisor, Bill Joiner, had repeatedly told her that women should not be working in the Maintenance of Way department. [Joiner was disciplined. White was reassigned from forklift duty to "track laborer" tasks.]

* * * *

On October 10, White filed a complaint with the Equal Employment Opportunity Commission (EEOC * * *).

[In December, White's supervisor, Percy Sharkey, complained to Burlington officials that White had been insubordinate. She was suspended without pay but reinstated after an investigation and awarded back pay for the period of the suspension. White filed a second charge with the EEOC.]

* * * *

* * * [Later] White filed this Title VII action against Burlington in federal [district] court. * * * [S]he claimed that Burlington's actions—(1) changing her job responsibilities, and (2) suspending her * * * without pay—amounted to unlawful retaliation in violation of Title VII. A jury found in White's favor * * * [and] awarded her $43,500 in * * * damages * * * .

* * * [On appeal, the U.S. Court of Appeals for the Sixth Circuit held that Title VII's antiretaliation ban is limited to acts that adversely affect the terms, conditions, or benefits of employment, and] affirmed the District Court's judgment in White's favor on both retaliation claims. [Burlington appealed to the United States Supreme Court.]

* * * *

* * * The language of the [antidiscrimination] provision differs from that of the antiretaliation provision in important ways.

CASE 21.1 CONTINUED

The * * * words in the [antidiscrimination] provision—"hire," "discharge," "compensation, terms, conditions, or privileges of employment," "employment opportunities," and "status as an employee"—explicitly limit the scope of that provision to actions that affect employment or alter the conditions of the workplace. No such limiting words appear in the anti-retaliation provision.

* * * The two provisions differ not only in language but in purpose as well. The anti-discrimination provision seeks a workplace where individuals are not discriminated against because of their racial, ethnic, religious, or gender-based status. *The anti-retaliation provision seeks to secure that primary objective by preventing an employer from interfering (through retaliation) with an employee's efforts to secure or advance enforcement of the Act's basic guarantees.* The [antidiscrimination] provision seeks to prevent injury to individuals based on who they are, i.e., their status. *The anti-retaliation provision seeks to prevent harm to individuals based on what they do, i.e., their conduct.* [Emphasis added.]

To secure the first objective, Congress did not need to prohibit anything other than employment-related discrimination.

But one cannot secure the second objective by focusing only upon employer actions and harm that concern employment and the workplace. * * * *An employer can effectively retaliate against an employee by taking actions not directly related to his employment or by causing him harm outside the workplace.* [Emphasis added.]

* * * *

* * * We conclude that * * * the anti-retaliation provision extends beyond workplace-related or employment-related retaliatory acts * * * .

* * * *

* * * A plaintiff must show that a reasonable employee would have found the challenged action materially adverse, which in this context means it well might have dissuaded a reasonable worker from making or supporting a charge of discrimination.

* * * *

* * * [In this case] the track labor duties were by all accounts more arduous and dirtier; * * * the forklift operator position required more qualifications, which is an indication of prestige; and * * * the forklift operator position was objectively considered a better job and the male employees resented White for occupying it. Based on this record, a jury could reasonably conclude that the reassignment of responsibilities would have been materially adverse to a reasonable employee.

* * * *

For these reasons, the judgment of the Court of Appeals is affirmed.

QUESTIONS

1. Why did the Court evaluate the language of Title VII's "antidiscrimination" and "antiretaliation" provisions in this case?
2. What was the Court's interpretation of those provisions?

Harassment by Co-Workers and Nonemployees Often, employees alleging harassment complain that the actions of co-workers, not supervisors, are responsible for creating a hostile working environment. In such cases, the employee still has a cause of action against the employer. Generally, though, the employer will be held liable only if it knew or should have known about the harassment and failed to take immediate remedial action.

Employers may also be liable for harassment by *nonemployees* under certain conditions. Suppose that a restaurant owner or manager knows that a particular customer repeatedly harasses a waitress and permits the harassment to continue. In this situation, the restaurant owner may be liable under Title VII even though the customer is not an employee of the restaurant. The issue turns on the control that the employer exerts over a nonemployee. In one case, the owner of a Pizza Hut franchise was held liable for the harassment of a waitress by two male customers because no steps were taken to prevent the harassment.[18]

18. *Lockard v. Pizza Hut, Inc.*, 162 F.3d 1062 (10th Cir. 1998).

In another case, a female sales representative at Merck & Company, Inc., was temporarily assigned to work in Mexico at Merck-Mexico (a subsidiary of Merck & Company). She claimed that she was being sexually harassed and informed the supervisor in Mexico, who allegedly warned her not to report the harassment to Merck's U.S. headquarters. When she filed a lawsuit, Merck argued that it should not be liable because the alleged harassers were employed by Merck-Mexico and not by the U.S.-based Merck & Company. Although the trial court granted a summary judgment in Merck's favor, an appellate court reversed that decision. The appellate court held that there was a sufficient issue of fact as to whether Merck and its corporate affiliate in Mexico could be considered a single employer for purposes of a Title VII claim. In other words, the court ruled that there was enough evidence of Merck's control over the alleged harassers for the employee to take her case to a jury trial.[19]

Same-Gender Harassment The courts have also had to address the issue of whether men who are harassed by other men, or women who are harassed by other women, are also protected by laws that prohibit gender-based discrimination in the workplace. For example, what if the male president of a firm demands sexual favors from a male employee? Does this action qualify as sexual harassment? For some time, the courts were widely split on this question. In 1998, in *Oncale v. Sundowner Offshore Services, Inc.*,[20] the Supreme Court resolved the issue by holding that Title VII protection extends to situations in which individuals are harassed by members of the same gender.

Nonetheless, it can be difficult to prove that the harassment in same-gender harassment cases is "based on sex." Suppose that a gay man is harassed by another man at the workplace. The harasser is not a homosexual and does not treat all men with hostility—just this one man. Does the victim in this situation have a cause of action under Title VII? A court may find that the harasser's conduct does not qualify as sexual harassment under Title VII because it was based on the employee's sexual orientation, not on his "sex."[21]

Note that although Title VII does not prohibit discrimination or harassment based on a person's sexual orientation, a growing number of companies are voluntarily establishing nondiscrimination policies that include sexual orientation. According to some reports, at the end of 2006, approximately 80 percent of the companies in the Fortune 500 had banned workplace discrimination on the basis of sexual orientation.[22] In addition, an increasing number of states have passed legislation that explicitly prohibits sexual orientation discrimination in the workplace.[23]

Online Harassment

Employees' online activities can create a hostile working environment in many ways. Racial jokes, ethnic slurs, or other comments contained in e-mail may become the basis for a claim of hostile-environment harassment or other forms of discrimination. A worker who regularly sees sexually explicit images on a co-worker's computer screen may find the images offensive and claim that they create a hostile working environment. For a discussion of some new areas in which an employer may potentially be liable for an employee's online conduct, see this chapter's *Emerging Trends* feature on pages 536 and 537.

Nevertheless, employers may be able to avoid liability for online harassment by taking prompt remedial action. For example, in one case Angela Daniels, an employee under contract to WorldCom Corporation, received racially harassing e-mailed jokes from another employee. After receiving the jokes, Daniels complained to WorldCom managers. Shortly afterward, the company issued a warning to the offending employee about the proper use of the e-mail system and held two meetings to discuss company policy on the use of the system. In Daniels's discrimination suit against WorldCom, a federal district court concluded that the employer was not liable for its employee's racially harassing e-mails because the employer took prompt remedial action.[24]

Remedies under Title VII

Employer liability under Title VII may be extensive. If the plaintiff successfully proves that unlawful discrimi-

19. *Torres-Negron v. Merck & Company, Inc.*, 488 F.3d 34 (1st Cir. 2007).
20. 523 U.S. 75, 118 S.Ct. 998, 140 L.Ed.2d 207 (1998).
21. See, for example, *McCown v. St. John's Health System*, 349 F.3d 540 (8th Cir. 2003); and *Rene v. MGM Grand Hotel, Inc.*, 305 F.3d 1061 (9th Cir. 2002).
22. Marc Gunther, "Corporate America backs gay rights: Gay rights are good business, no matter the politics," April 26, 2006, as reported on *Plugged In*, a daily column by writers of *Fortune* magazine.
23. See, for example, 775 Illinois Compiled Statutes 5/1–103.
24. *Daniels v. WorldCom Corp.*, 1998 WL 91261 (N.D.Tex. 1998). See also *Musgrove v. Mobil Oil Corp.*, 2003 WL 21653125 (N.D.Tex. 2003).

nation occurred, he or she may be awarded reinstatement, back pay, retroactive promotions, and damages. Compensatory damages are available only in cases of intentional discrimination. Punitive damages may be recovered against a private employer only if the employer acted with malice or reckless indifference to an individual's rights. The statute limits the total amount of compensatory and punitive damages that the plaintiff can recover from specific employers (ranging from $50,000 against employers with one hundred or fewer employees to $300,000 against employers with more than five hundred employees).

Section 2 Discrimination Based on Age

Age discrimination is potentially the most widespread form of discrimination, because anyone—regardless of race, color, national origin, or gender—could be a victim at some point in life. The Age Discrimination in Employment Act (ADEA) of 1967, as amended, prohibits employment discrimination on the basis of age against individuals forty years of age or older. The act also prohibits mandatory retirement for nonmanagerial workers. The United States Supreme Court has made it clear that the text and the legislative history of the ADEA show that it was meant to protect relatively old workers from discrimination that gives an unfair advantage to the relatively young. Therefore, the ADEA does not necessarily prohibit an employer from eliminating a health-insurance benefits program for workers under age fifty but retaining the program for workers over fifty.[25]

For the act to apply, an employer must have twenty or more employees, and the employer's business activities must affect interstate commerce. The EEOC administers the ADEA, but the act also permits private causes of action against employers for age discrimination.

Procedures under the ADEA

The burden-shifting procedure under the ADEA is similar to that under Title VII. If a plaintiff can establish that he or she (1) was a member of the protected age group, (2) was qualified for the position from which he or she was discharged, and (3) was discharged under circumstances that give rise to an inference of discrimination, the plaintiff has established a *prima facie* case of unlawful age discrimination. The burden then shifts to the employer, who must articulate a legitimate reason for the discrimination. If the plaintiff can prove that the employer's reason is only a pretext and that the plaintiff's age was a determining factor in the employer's decision, the employer will be held liable under the ADEA.

If an employer offers several nondiscriminatory reasons, based on a variety of events, for an act of alleged discrimination, does the employee need to rebut every reason by proving that the events did not occur? That was the question in the following case.

25. *General Dynamics Land Systems, Inc. v. Cline*, 540 U.S. 581, 124 S.Ct. 1236, 157 L.Ed.2d 1094 (2004).

CASE 21.2 Cash Distributing Co. v. Neely

Mississippi Supreme Court, 2007. 947 So.2d 286.
www.mssc.state.ms.us[a]

Background and Facts Cash Distributing Company is a distributorship for Anheuser-Busch Corporation products, including Budweiser and Michelob beers. The company has offices in Columbus, Starkville, and Tupelo, Mississippi. In 1973, James Neely began to work for Cash. At the time, the company often relaxed or ignored Anheuser-Busch rules. By the late 1990s, Neely had become the manager of the Columbus office. In 1997, Anheuser-Busch began to insist on Cash's compliance with certain standards. Danny Cash, Cash's chief executive officer, announced that he intended to strictly enforce the new rules. Part of the newly required documentation was a tracking form to detect out-of-date beer. Danny also required Neely to, among other things, submit daily call sheets to disclose where he had been and what he had done and to submit regular written employee evaluations. Neely generally refused to

a. In the center of the page, click on the "Search this site" link. On the next page, click on "Plain English." When that page opens, in the "Enter the ISYS Plain English query:" box, type "2004-CT-01124-SCT" and click on "Search." In the result, click on the item that includes that number to access the opinion. The Mississippi Supreme Court maintains this Web site.

CASE CONTINUES

CASE 21.2 CONTINUED

provide the new documents. In March 2000, Danny terminated Neely's employment, replacing him with Tony Carley, who was then thirty-eight years old. Neely filed a suit in a Mississippi state court against Cash, alleging, among other things, a violation of the ADEA. Neely was awarded $120,000 in back pay. Both parties appealed to a state intermediate appellate court, which reversed the lower court's failure to grant additional remedies to Neely. Cash appealed to the Mississippi Supreme Court.

IN THE LANGUAGE OF THE COURT
***DICKINSON,* Justice, for the Court.**

* * * *

Where a plaintiff establishes a *prima facie* case, discrimination is presumed unless the employer provides a nondiscriminatory explanation for the adverse employment action. * * *

* * * *

* * * *[An] ADEA plaintiff [does not need] to rebut with specific evidence each and every nondiscriminatory reason offered by an employer for [a] termination.* * * * The plaintiff must * * * have an opportunity to prove * * * that the legitimate reasons offered by the defendant were not its true reasons, but were a pretext for discrimination. Requiring courts to provide this opportunity is, we think, quite different from saying that the plaintiff must present specific rebuttal evidence as to each nondiscriminatory reason for the dismissal. [Emphasis added.]

* * * *

Cash argues that Neely failed to rebut every nondiscriminatory reason offered for his termination. We take Cash's argument to mean that Neely had to offer proof that each of the events Cash claims led to his dismissal did not actually happen. For instance, under Cash's view of the rebuttal requirement, once Cash asserts it terminated Neely because he refused to fill out certain forms, Neely must come forward with some proof that he actually did fill out the forms. * * * [But a jury's] disbelief of the reasons put forward by the defendant does not require the [jury] to disbelieve a particular event occurred, but rather requires the [jury] to find that—even if it did occur—it was not the motivating reason for the dismissal. The jury in this case could very well have found that all of Danny's testimony about Neely's insubordination, while true, was not the real reason for Neely's dismissal.

Stated another way, * * * Neely [is required to] rebut Cash's nondiscriminatory reasons for the dismissal [only] by persuading the jury that, true or not, the reasons offered by Cash were not the motivating reasons for his termination. Thus, Neely was free to admit that some or all of the wrongful acts attributed to him by Cash were true but were not the real reason for his dismissal.

It is not enough, of course, for Neely simply to make the claim. He must produce some proof which persuades the jury that the true reason for his termination was impermissible age discrimination.

* * * *

Cash does not contest that Neely established a *prima facie* case of discrimination under the ADEA. Instead, Cash claims it discharged Neely for the nondiscriminatory reasons of insubordination and his failure to discover and report out-of-date product on a particular occasion while riding with a salesman. Neely might have claimed that this event never happened at all, which would have served as evidence to rebut Cash's proffered [offered] reason for termination.

Instead, Neely did not deny that most of the events claimed by Cash occurred. However, Neely offered substantial evidence that these events were not the reason for his termination. For instance, Neely offered evidence that despite Cash's claims of insubordination and poor performance, his operation in Columbus received perfect scores following several evaluations by the Brewery. Neely also offered evidence that out-of-date product was fairly common and that the extremely meticulous audit of his territory was unprecedented, amounting to (according to another witness) a "witch hunt."

Additionally, Neely offered evidence showing that Danny possessed discriminatory *animus* toward him.

The jury in this case obviously credited Neely's account of his dismissal and the evidence supporting it over explanations supplied by Cash. This Court has no basis to disturb that decision on appeal. The jury was free to find that even if, as Cash claimed, Neely had been insubordinate, that

CASE 21.2 CONTINUED justification was pretextual [untrue] based on evidence of unequal treatment [and] age-related statements made by Cash's CEO * * * .

• **Decision and Remedy** *The Mississippi Supreme Court affirmed the lower court's judgment. An employee can prevail in an ADEA suit without rebutting every nondiscriminatory reason that an employer offers for an act of discrimination. Neely did not have to prove that the events Cash claimed led to his dismissal did not actually happen.*

• **What If the Facts Were Different?** *If Neely had admitted that he had committed all of the "wrongful" acts attributed to him by Cash, would the outcome of this case have been different? Why or why not?*

• **The Legal Environment Dimension** *Why is discrimination presumed under the ADEA when a plaintiff establishes a* prima facie *case, unless the employer provides a nondiscriminatory explanation for the adverse employment action?*

Replacing Older Workers with Younger Workers

Numerous age discrimination cases have been brought against employers who, to cut costs, replaced older, higher-salaried employees with younger, lower-salaried workers. Whether a firing is discriminatory or simply part of a rational business decision to prune the company's ranks is not always clear. Companies typically defend a decision to discharge a worker by asserting that the worker could no longer perform her or his duties or that the worker's skills were no longer needed.

The employee must prove that the discharge was motivated, at least in part, by age bias. Proof that qualified older employees are generally discharged before employees who are younger or that co-workers continually made unflattering age-related comments about the discharged worker may be enough. The plaintiff does not need to prove that she or he was replaced by a person "outside the protected class" (under the age of forty years), so long as the replacement is younger (or substantially younger) than the plaintiff. Nevertheless, the bigger the age gap, the more likely the individual is to succeed in showing age discrimination.

State Employees Not Covered by the ADEA

Generally, the states are immune under the Eleventh Amendment from lawsuits brought by private individuals in federal court—unless a state consents to the suit. For example, in separate cases, professors and librarians contended that their employers—two Florida state universities—denied them salary increases and other benefits because they were getting old and their successors could be hired at lower cost. The universities claimed that as agencies of a sovereign state, they could not be sued without the state's consent. The cases ultimately reached the United States Supreme Court, which held that the Eleventh Amendment bars private parties from suing state employers for violations of the ADEA.[26]

State immunity under the Eleventh Amendment is not absolute, however, as the Supreme Court explained in 2004. In some situations, such as when fundamental rights are at stake, Congress has the power to abrogate (abolish) state immunity to private suits through legislation that unequivocally shows Congress's intent to subject states to private suits.[27] Generally, though, the Court has found that state employers are immune from private suits brought by employees under the ADEA (for age discrimination), the Americans with Disabilities Act (for disability-based discrimination),[28] and the Fair Labor Standards Act (the wage and hour laws that were discussed in Chapter 20).[29] As explained in Chapter 20, state employers are not immune from the requirements of the Family and Medical Leave Act (FMLA).[30]

26. *Kimel v. Florida Board of Regents,* 528 U.S. 62, 120 S.Ct. 631, 145 L.Ed.2d 522 (2000).

27. *Tennessee v. Lane,* 541 U.S. 509, 124 S.Ct. 1978, 158 L.Ed.2d 820 (2004).

28. *Board of Trustees of the University of Alabama v. Garrett,* 531 U.S. 356, 121 S.Ct. 955, 148 L.Ed.2d 866 (2001).

29. *Alden v. Maine,* 527 U.S. 706, 119 S.Ct. 2240, 144 L.Ed.2d 636 (1999).

30. *Nevada Department of Human Resources v. Hibbs,* 538 U.S. 721, 123 S.Ct. 1972, 155 L.Ed.2d 953 (2003). This case was presented in Chapter 20 as Extended Case 20.3.

EMERGING TRENDS IN THE LEGAL ENVIRONMENT OF BUSINESS
New Issues in Online Privacy and Employment Discrimination

As computers come to be used for more aspects of both personal and professional life, the line between personal use and work-related use is becoming blurred. As this chapter has explained, employers are legally required to prevent discrimination in the workplace, including a hostile environment created by workers' online activities. That employers have a right—or even obligation—to monitor their employees' computer use to this end is generally established. Indeed, as discussed in Chapter 20, courts generally have held that employees have no expectation of privacy in their workplace computers when a private employer supplies the equipment. The limits of this privacy exception are still being tested, however, as a number of issues related to computers, privacy, and employment discrimination remain unresolved. A new issue that is just emerging is whether employers can obtain information about job applicants by conducting online searches when asking for the same information on a job application or in an interview might be illegal.

Searches of Workplace Computers

An employee who uses his or her workplace computer to view sexually explicit photographs may create a hostile environment if the photographs can be seen by other employees. Furthermore, if the photographs involve children, the employee's activities may be illegal. Courts generally have held that employers can search a workplace computer for evidence of employee misconduct[a] and that they can also consent to a search by government officials. If the computer is in a locked office, however, does the employee have a greater expectation of privacy? In *United States v. Ziegler*[b] in 2007, the court had to answer this question.

The Internet service provider for Frontline Processing Corporation informed the Federal Bureau of Investigation (FBI) that one of Frontline's computers had been used to access child-pornography Web sites in violation of federal criminal law. The FBI investigated and determined that Jeffrey Ziegler, Frontline's director of operations, had used the computer in his office to search for and view online photos of "very young girls in various states of undress." Frontline agreed to cooperate with the FBI, and at some point, corporate employees entered Ziegler's locked office and made a backup copy of the hard drive on his computer without his consent.

Ziegler appealed his subsequent conviction for possessing child pornography on the ground that the search of his computer violated his Fourth Amendment rights against unreasonable search and seizure. The U.S. Court of Appeals for the Ninth Circuit first held that Ziegler had no reasonable expectation of privacy, but on rehearing, the court changed its ruling and held that Ziegler did have a reasonable expectation of privacy in the contents of the computer in his locked office. Because the employer (Frontline) owned the computer, however, the court held that Frontline's consent validated the search. According to the court, a "computer is the type of workplace property that remains within control of the employer 'even if the employee has placed personal items in it.' "

Unresolved Issues

Certainly, the trend is clearly toward limiting employees' expectations of privacy in employer-owned computers in the workplace, but several questions still remain open.

What expectations of privacy does an employee have in a laptop computer that is provided by the company but is used by the

a. See, for example, *Twymon v. Wells Fargo & Co.*, 462 F.3d 925 (8th Cir. 2006); and *Griffis v. Pinal County*, 213 Ariz. 300, 141 P.3d 780 (2006).

b. 474 F.3d 1184 (9th Cir. 2007). See also *Doe v. XYC Corp.*, 382 N.J.Super. 122, 887 A.2d 1156 (2005).

Discrimination Based on Disability

The Americans with Disabilities Act (ADA) of 1990 is designed to eliminate discriminatory employment practices that prevent otherwise qualified workers with disabilities from fully participating in the national labor force. Prior to 1990, the major federal law providing protection to those with disabilities was the Rehabilitation Act of 1973. That act protected only federal government employees and those employed under federally funded programs. The ADA extends federal protection against disability-based discrimination to all workplaces with fifteen or more workers (with the exception of state government employers, who are generally immune under the Eleventh Amendment, as just discussed). Basically, the ADA requires that employers "reasonably accommodate" the needs of persons with disabilities unless to do so would cause the employer to suffer an "undue hardship."

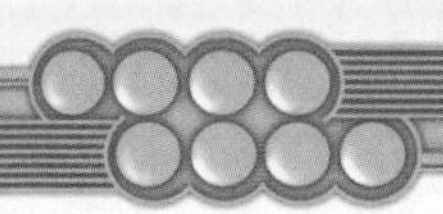

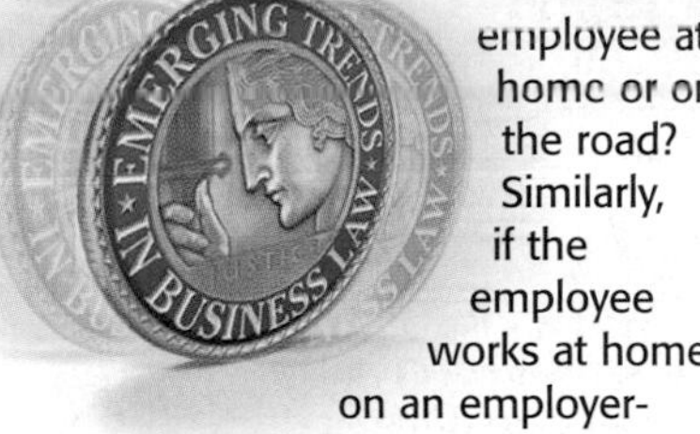

employee at home or on the road? Similarly, if the employee works at home on an employer-owned computer, to what degree can the employer justify monitoring the employee's online activities? Although computers in remote locations could be used to send harassing e-mail, other employees are unlikely to view offensive material on such computers, so that justification for monitoring Internet use seems less valid.

Other issues have to do with whether employers must tell employees that their computer use will be monitored and the degree to which employers should monitor employees' online activities that are mostly personal. To date, only two states (Connecticut and Delaware) have passed laws specifically requiring private employers to inform employees that their workplace Internet activities will be monitored. Personal blogs raise an even more complex issue: Does an employer have the right to monitor its employees' personal blogs? If an employee's personal blog contains racially or sexually offensive comments about co-workers, what should the employer do? Thus far, in most of the cases involving employees dismissed for computer misuse, the employer had a written Internet policy and presented evidence that the employee knew about and disregarded the policy. According to recent surveys, however, most organizations do not have policies on employees' blogs.

Facebook, MySpace, and Job Applications

Even more problematic is another issue that is just emerging. Today, many college students and recent graduates belong to social networking sites such as Facebook.com and MySpace.com, at which they can post photographs, comments, blogs, or even videos about themselves. Some of this material is sexually suggestive, to say the least. A number of employers have begun to use search engines to search for information on job applicants. A search may turn up photos that the applicant intended to be viewed only by close friends. Such searches may reveal information about the applicant's marital status, sexual orientation, or political or religious views that the employer could not ask for on a job application or discuss in a job interview. Nevertheless, this information is now readily available to employers.

Some colleges and employment counselors are beginning to advise job seekers to make sure that they remove any information they do not want a prospective employer to see, but the issue of whether employers have a right to search for this information is likely to persist.

IMPLICATIONS FOR THE BUSINESSPERSON

1. Employers should explicitly inform all employees that their company-provided computers, even if used at home, can be monitored by the employer.

2. It is not illegal for employers to conduct an online search for information about job applicants, including their blogs and their postings at social networks such as Facebook and MySpace.

FOR CRITICAL ANALYSIS

1. Suppose that an employee writes a message to like-minded persons concerning religious beliefs or political views. Can the employee be fired in that situation? Who decides what is acceptable Internet activity when there is no written policy?

2. How might an employee avoid the possibility that his or her employer will discover objectionable items on the employee's computer?

RELEVANT WEB SITES

To locate information on the Web concerning the issues discussed in this feature, go to this text's Web site at **academic.cengage.com/blaw/cross**, select "Chapter 21" and click on "Emerging Trends."

Procedures under the ADA

To prevail on a claim under the ADA, a plaintiff must show that he or she (1) has a disability, (2) is otherwise qualified for the employment in question, and (3) was excluded from the employment solely because of the disability. As in Title VII cases, a claim alleging violation of the ADA may be commenced only after the plaintiff has pursued the claim through the EEOC, which administers the provisions of the act relating to disability-based discrimination in the employment context. The EEOC may decide to investigate and perhaps even sue the employer on behalf of the employee. The EEOC can bring a suit on behalf of the employee under the ADA even if the employee signed an arbitration agreement with the employer.[31]

If the EEOC decides not to sue, then the employee may do so. Plaintiffs in lawsuits brought under the ADA may seek many of the same remedies that are available under Title VII. These include reinstatement, back pay, a limited amount of compensatory and punitive

31. This was the Supreme Court's ruling in *EEOC v. Waffle House, Inc.*, 534 U.S. 279, 122 S.Ct. 754, 151 L.Ed.2d 755 (2002).

damages (for intentional discrimination), and certain other forms of relief. Repeat violators may be ordered to pay fines of up to $100,000.

What Is a Disability?

The ADA broadly defines *persons with disabilities* as persons with physical or mental impairments that "substantially limit" their everyday activities. More specifically, the ADA defines a *disability* as "(1) a physical or mental impairment that substantially limits one or more of the major life activities of such individuals; (2) a record of such impairment; or (3) being regarded as having such an impairment."

Health conditions that have been considered disabilities under federal law include blindness, alcoholism, heart disease, cancer, muscular dystrophy, cerebral palsy, paraplegia, diabetes, acquired immune deficiency syndrome (AIDS), testing positive for the human immunodeficiency virus (HIV, the virus that causes AIDS), and morbid obesity (which exists when an individual's weight is two times that of a normal person). The ADA excludes from coverage certain conditions, such as kleptomania (the obsessive desire to steal).

Although the ADA's definition of disability is broad, starting in 1999, the United States Supreme Court has issued a series of decisions narrowing the definition of what constitutes a disability under the act.

Correctable Conditions In 1999, the Supreme Court reviewed a case raising the issue of whether severe myopia, or nearsightedness, which can be corrected with lenses, qualifies as a disability under the ADA. The Supreme Court ruled that it does not.[32] The determination of whether a person is substantially limited in a major life activity is based on how the person functions when taking medication or using corrective devices, not on how the person functions without these measures.

In a similar case in 2002, a federal appellate court held that a pharmacist suffering from diabetes, which could be corrected by insulin, did not have a cause of action against his employer under the ADA.[33] In other cases decided in the early 2000s, the courts have held that plaintiffs with bipolar disorder, epilepsy, and other such conditions do *not* fall under the ADA's protections if the conditions can be corrected.

32. *Sutton v. United Airlines, Inc.*, 527 U.S. 471, 119 S.Ct. 2139, 144 L.Ed.2d 450 (1999).

33. *Orr v. Walmart Stores, Inc.*, 297 F.3d 720 (8th Cir. 2002).

Repetitive-Stress Injuries For some time, the courts were divided on the issue of whether carpal tunnel syndrome (or any other repetitive-stress injury) constitutes a disability under the ADA. Carpal tunnel syndrome is a condition of pain and weakness in the hand caused by repetitive compression of a nerve in the wrist. In 2002, in a case involving this issue, the Supreme Court unanimously held that it does not. The Court stated that although the employee could not perform the manual tasks associated with her job, the condition did not constitute a disability under the ADA because it did not "substantially limit" the major life activity of performing manual tasks.[34]

Reasonable Accommodation

If a job applicant or an employee with a disability can perform essential job functions with reasonable accommodation, the employer must make the accommodation. Required modifications may include installing ramps for a wheelchair, establishing flexible working hours, creating or modifying job assignments, and designing or improving training materials and procedures.

Generally, employers should give primary consideration to employees' preferences in deciding what accommodations should be made. If an applicant or employee fails to let the employer know how his or her disability can be accommodated, the employer may avoid liability for failing to hire or retain the individual on the ground that the individual has failed to meet the "otherwise qualified" requirement.

Undue Hardship Employers who do not accommodate the needs of persons with disabilities must demonstrate that the accommodations would cause *undue hardship*. Generally, the law offers no uniform standards for identifying what is an undue hardship other than the imposition of a "significant difficulty or expense" on the employer.

Usually, the courts decide whether an accommodation constitutes an undue hardship on a case-by-case basis. For example, suppose that Bryan Lockhart works for a cell phone company that provides parking to its employees. Lockhart, who uses a wheelchair, informs the company supervisors that the parking spaces are so narrow that he is unable to extend the ramp on his van that allows him to get in and out of the vehicle. Lockhart therefore requests that the company reason-

34. *Toyota Motor Manufacturing, Kentucky, Inc. v. Williams*, 534 U.S. 184, 122 S.Ct. 681, 151 L.Ed.2d 615 (2002).

ably accommodate his needs by paying a monthly fee for him to use a larger parking space in an adjacent lot. In this situation, a court would likely find that it would not be an undue hardship for the employer to pay for additional parking for Lockhart.

Job Applications and Preemployment Physical Exams Employers must modify their job-application and selection process so that those with disabilities can compete for jobs with those who do not have disabilities. A job announcement that has only a phone number, for example, would discriminate against potential job applicants with hearing impairments. Thus, the job announcement must also provide another way for applicants to contact the prospective employer. Employers are also restricted in the kinds of questions they may ask on job-application forms and during preemployment interviews.

Additionally, employers cannot require persons with disabilities to submit to preemployment physicals unless such exams are required of all other applicants. An employer can condition an offer of employment on the applicant's successfully passing a medical examination, but can disqualify the applicant only if the medical problems discovered would render the applicant unable to perform the job. For example, when filling the position of delivery truck driver, a company cannot screen out all applicants who are unable to meet the U.S. Department of Transportation's hearing standard. The company would first have to prove that drivers who are deaf are not qualified to perform the essential job function of driving safely and pose a higher risk of accidents than drivers who are not deaf.[35]

Substance Abusers Drug addiction is considered a disability under the ADA because it is a substantially limiting impairment. Note that the ADA only protects persons with *former* drug addictions—those who have completed a supervised drug-rehabilitation program or who are currently participating in a supervised rehabilitation program. Those who are currently using illegal drugs are not protected by the act, nor are persons who have used drugs casually in the past. They are not considered addicts and therefore do not have a disability (addiction).

People suffering from alcoholism are protected by the ADA. Employers cannot legally discriminate against employees simply because they suffer from alcoholism and must treat them the same way other employees are treated. For example, an employee with alcoholism who comes to work late because she or he was drinking excessively the night before cannot be disciplined any differently than an employee who comes to work late for another reason. Of course, employers have the right to prohibit the use of alcohol in the workplace and can require that employees not be under the influence of alcohol while working. Employers can also fire or refuse to hire a person with alcoholism if he or she poses a substantial risk of harm either to himself or herself or to others and the risk cannot be reduced by reasonable accommodation.

Health-Insurance Plans Workers with disabilities must be given equal access to any health insurance provided to other employees. Nevertheless, employers can exclude from coverage preexisting health conditions and certain types of diagnostic or surgical procedures. An employer can also put a limit, or cap, on health-care payments under its particular group health policy as long as the cap is applied equally to all insured employees and does not discriminate on the basis of disability. Whenever a group health-care plan makes a disability-based distinction in its benefits, the plan violates the ADA (unless the employer can justify its actions under the business necessity defense, as will be discussed later in this chapter).

Association Discrimination

The ADA contains an "association provision" that protects qualified individuals from employment discrimination based on a known disability of a person with whom the qualified individual is known to have a relationship or an association.[36] The purpose of this provision is to prevent employers from taking adverse employment actions based on stereotypes or assumptions about individuals who associate with people who have disabilities. An employer cannot, for instance, refuse to hire the parent of a child with a disability based on the assumption that the person will miss work too often or be unreliable.

To establish a *prima facie* case of association discrimination under the ADA, the plaintiff must show that she or he (1) was qualified for the job, (2) was subjected to adverse employment action, and (3) was known by her or his employer to have a relative or an associate with a disability. In addition, the plaintiff must

35. *Bates v. United Parcel Service, Inc.*, 465 F.3d 1069 (9th Cir. 2006).

36. 42 U.S.C. Section 12112(b)(4).

show that the adverse employment action occurred under circumstances raising a reasonable inference that the disability of the relative or associate was a determining factor in the employer's decision.

In the following case, a man claimed that his employer unlawfully discriminated against him based on his wife's disability. Although the case involved a state law that offers slightly more protection than the ADA, the opinion shows how courts analyze association discrimination claims.

CASE 21.3 Francin v. Mosby, Inc.

Missouri Court of Appeals, Eastern District, Division Three, 2008. ___ S.W.3d ___.
www.courts.mo.gov[a]

• **Background and Facts** Randall Francin began working at Mosby, Inc., (doing business as Elsevier) in 1991. He worked as a production assistant until March 2002, when his position was eliminated within the company due to organizational restructuring. Francin was rehired a few months later as an associate database publishing editor. In his new position, Francin updated drug information and proofread information contained in drug inserts. In 2003, Francin's wife was diagnosed with amyotrophic lateral sclerosis (ALS). He discussed his potential rights for leave under the Family Medical Leave Act (discussed in Chapter 20) with a representative from the human resources department at Elsevier. Francin received a "merit award increase" in salary in January 2004. Later in 2004, Francin's supervisor resigned. During an interview with a new boss, Francin informed him of his wife's illness. On September 21, 2004, Francin was fired. Francin filed a suit under the Missouri Human Rights Act (MHRA), alleging that Elsevier discriminated against him because of his association with a person with a disability. Elsevier filed a motion for summary judgment, which was granted by the trial court. On appeal, Francin claimed that the trial court erred in granting summary judgment because there was a genuine issue of material fact concerning whether his wife's disability was a contributing factor in the decision to terminate his employment.

IN THE LANGUAGE OF THE COURT
AHRENS, Judge.

* * * *

* * * Summary judgment is appropriate only where the record shows there are no genuine disputes of material fact and the moving party is entitled to judgment as a matter of law. * * * *If there is a dispute over facts that might affect the outcome of the action, summary judgment is not proper because the determination of such facts is for the fact finder at trial.* [Emphasis added.]

As a threshold matter, in its brief Elsevier asserts Francin's claim of discrimination is not a cognizable [recognizable] claim because he only asserted his termination was due to a stated intention to be absent, rather than a real absence. Elsevier's claim is based largely on cases interpreting the federal Americans with Disabilities Act ("ADA") in Federal courts. Elsevier argues that the MHRA is "patterned under and consistent with" the protections afforded by the ADA.

Here, Section 213.070(4) of the Missouri Human Rights Act provides that it is unlawful to "discriminate in any manner against any other person because of such person's association with any person protected by this chapter." [This section] does not qualify this discrimination with any requirement that an employee actually take leave under the Family and Medical Leave Act, as Elsevier attempts to argue. Instead, the statute merely provides a cause of action where an employee is discriminated against for his association with a person protected by the MHRA. Francin claims Elsevier discriminated against him by terminating him because of his association with his wife, who suffered from ALS. Francin presented a cognizable claim for discrimination under [this section], and Elsevier's argument is without merit.

a. Click on "Opinions & Minutes" under the "Quick Links" menu. Select the link for opinions from the Missouri Court of Appeals, Eastern District, and scroll down to the listings under the date 1/8/08. Find the plaintiff's name "Randall Francin" and click on it to access the opinion (the line ends with the case number ED89814). This is the official Web site of the Missouri courts.

CASE 21.3 CONTINUED

Turning to the merits of Francin's appeal, Francin argues there was a genuine issue of material fact concerning whether his wife's disability was a contributing factor to Maheswaran's [Francin's new boss's] decision to terminate him. According to Francin, this genuine issue of material fact is based upon the evidence of Francin's satisfactory performance coupled with the close timing of the decision to his notification to Maheswaran of his wife's condition.

* * * *

The contradictory evidence regarding Francin's job performance and the memos from [his boss's] meetings with Francin noting [his wife's] illness and [its] effect on Francin, coupled with the close timing of Francin's termination is sufficient to create a genuine issue of material fact concerning whether Francin's wife's illness was a contributing factor to Elsevier's decision to terminate him. Therefore, Elsevier was not entitled to judgment as a matter of law, and the trial court erred in granting summary judgment in favor of Elsevier.

- **Decision and Remedy** *The Missouri Court of Appeals, Eastern District, reversed the trial court's decision and remanded the case for further proceedings.*

- **What If the Facts Were Different?** *Assume that Francin had only discussed his wife's illness with a human resources officer in the company and never mentioned it to his new boss. Would the outcome of the appeal have been different? Explain.*

- **The Ethical Dimension** *Did Elsevier have any ethical duty to keep Francin employed, even if he did indicate he might take time off under the Family Medical Leave Act?*

Defenses to Employment Discrimination

The first line of defense for an employer charged with employment discrimination is, of course, to assert that the plaintiff has failed to meet his or her initial burden of proof—proving that discrimination did in fact occur. As noted, plaintiffs bringing cases under the ADA may find it difficult to meet this initial burden because they must prove that their alleged disabilities are disabilities covered by the ADA. Furthermore, plaintiffs in ADA cases must prove that they were otherwise qualified for the job.

Once a plaintiff succeeds in proving that discrimination occurred, then the burden shifts to the employer to justify the discriminatory practice. Often, employers attempt to justify the discrimination by claiming that it was the result of a business necessity, a bona fide occupational qualification, or a seniority system. Alternatively, they may assert that employee misconduct should limit their liability. In some situations, as noted earlier, an effective antiharassment policy and prompt remedial action when harassment occurs may shield employers from liability for sexual harassment under Title VII.

Business Necessity

An employer may defend against a claim of *disparate-impact* (unintentional) discrimination by asserting that a practice that has a discriminatory effect is a **business necessity.** If requiring a high school diploma, for example, is shown to have a discriminatory effect, an employer might argue that a high school education is required for workers to perform the job at a required level of competence. If the employer can demonstrate to the court's satisfaction that a definite connection exists between a high school education and job performance, then the employer normally will succeed in this business necessity defense.

Bona Fide Occupational Qualification

Another defense applies when discrimination against a protected class is essential to a job—that is, when a particular trait is a **bona fide occupational qualification (BFOQ).** Race, color, and national origin, however, can never be justified as a BFOQ.

Generally, courts have restricted the BFOQ defense to instances in which the employee's gender or religion is essential to the job. For example, a women's clothing boutique might legitimately hire only female salespersons if part of a salesperson's job involves assisting clients in the boutique's dressing rooms.

Similarly, a state prison might legitimately respond to prior complaints of sexual abuse of female prisoners by hiring only female staff to work in the prison units housing women.[37]

Seniority Systems

An employer with a history of discrimination may have no members of protected classes in upper-level positions. Even if the employer now seeks to be unbiased, it may face a lawsuit seeking a court order that members of protected classes be promoted ahead of schedule to compensate for past discrimination. If no present intent to discriminate is shown, however, and if promotions or other job benefits are distributed according to a fair **seniority system** (in which workers with more years of service are promoted first or laid off last), the employer normally has a good defense against the suit.

According to the United States Supreme Court, this defense may also apply to claims of discrimination under the ADA. If an employee with a disability requests an accommodation (such as an assignment to a particular position) that conflicts with an employer's seniority system, the accommodation will generally not be considered "reasonable" under the act.[38]

After-Acquired Evidence of Employee Misconduct

In some situations, employers have attempted to avoid liability for employment discrimination on the basis of "after-acquired evidence" of an employee's misconduct. For example, suppose that an employer fires a worker, who then sues the employer for employment discrimination. During pretrial investigation, the employer learns that the employee made material misrepresentations on his employment application—misrepresentations that, had the employer known about them, would have served as a ground to fire the individual. Can this after-acquired evidence be used as a defense?

According to the United States Supreme Court, after-acquired evidence of wrongdoing cannot be used to shield an employer entirely from liability for employment discrimination. It may, however, be used to limit the amount of damages for which the employer is liable.[39]

Affirmative Action

The laws discussed in this chapter were designed to reduce or eliminate discriminatory practices with respect to hiring, retaining, and promoting employees. **Affirmative action** programs go a step further and attempt to "make up" for past patterns of discrimination by giving members of protected classes preferential treatment in hiring or promotion. During the 1960s, all federal and state government agencies, private companies that contracted to do business with the federal government, and institutions that received federal funding were required to implement affirmative action policies.

Title VII of the Civil Rights Act of 1964 neither requires nor prohibits affirmative action. Thus, most private companies and organizations have not been required to implement affirmative action policies, though many have done so voluntarily.

Affirmative action programs have aroused much controversy during the last forty years, particularly when they result in *reverse discrimination*, which as mentioned previously, is discrimination against members of a majority group, such as white males. At issue is whether affirmative action programs, because of their inherently discriminatory nature, violate employee rights or the equal protection clause of the Fourteenth Amendment to the U.S. Constitution.

The *Bakke* Case

An early case addressing this issue outside the employment context, *Regents of the University of California v. Bakke*,[40] involved an affirmative action program implemented by the University of California at Davis. Allan Bakke, who had been turned down for medical school at the Davis campus, sued the university for reverse discrimination after he discovered that his academic record was better than the records of some of the minority applicants who had been admitted to the program.

37. *Everson v. Michigan Department of Corrections*, 391 F.3d 737 (6th Cir. 2004).
38. *U.S. Airways, Inc. v. Barnett*, 535 U.S. 391, 122 S.Ct. 1516, 152 L.Ed.2d 589 (2002).
39. *McKennon v. Nashville Banner Publishing Co.*, 513 U.S. 352, 115 S.Ct. 879, 130 L.Ed.2d 852 (1995). See also *EEOC v. Dial Corp.*, 469 F.3d 735 (8th Cir. 2006).
40. 438 U.S. 265, 98 S.Ct. 2733, 57 L.Ed.2d 750 (1978).

The United States Supreme Court held that affirmative action programs were subject to intermediate scrutiny. Recall from the discussion of the equal protection clause in Chapter 5 that any law or action evaluated under a standard of intermediate scrutiny, to be constitutionally valid, must be substantially related to important government objectives. Applying this standard, the Court held that the university could give favorable weight to minority applicants as part of a plan to increase minority enrollment so as to achieve a more culturally diverse student body. The Court stated, however, that the use of a quota system, in which a certain number of places are explicitly reserved for minority applicants, violated the equal protection clause of the Fourteenth Amendment.

The *Adarand* Case

Although the *Bakke* case and later court decisions alleviated the harshness of the quota system, today's courts are going even further in questioning the constitutional validity of affirmative action programs. In 1995, in its landmark decision in *Adarand Constructors, Inc. v. Peña,*[41] the United States Supreme Court held that any federal, state, or local affirmative action program that uses racial or ethnic classifications as the basis for making decisions is subject to strict scrutiny by the courts.

In effect, the Court's ruling in *Adarand* means that an affirmative action program is constitutional only if it attempts to remedy past discrimination and does not make use of quotas or preferences. Furthermore, once such a program has succeeded in the goal of remedying past discrimination, it must be changed or dropped. Since then, other federal courts have followed the Supreme Court's lead by declaring affirmative action programs invalid unless they attempt to remedy past or current discrimination.

The *Hopwood* Case

In 1996, in *Hopwood v. State of Texas,*[42] the U.S. Court of Appeals for the Fifth Circuit held that an affirmative action program at the University of Texas School of Law in Austin violated the equal protection clause. In that case, two white law school applicants sued the university when they were denied admission. The court decided that the affirmative action policy unlawfully discriminated in favor of minority applicants. In its decision, the court directly challenged the *Bakke* decision by stating that the use of race even as a means of achieving diversity on college campuses "undercuts the Fourteenth Amendment." The United States Supreme Court declined to hear the case, thus letting the lower court's decision stand. Federal appellate court decisions since then have been divided on whether such programs are constitutional.[43]

Subsequent Court Decisions

In 2003, the United States Supreme Court reviewed two cases involving issues similar to that in the *Hopwood* case. Both cases involved admissions programs at the University of Michigan. In *Gratz v. Bollinger,*[44] two white applicants who were denied undergraduate admission to the university alleged reverse discrimination. The school's admission policy gave each applicant a score based on a number of factors, including grade point average, standardized test scores, and personal achievements. The system *automatically* awarded every "underrepresented" minority (African American, Hispanic, and Native American) applicant twenty points—one-fifth of the points needed to guarantee admission. The Court held that this policy violated the equal protection clause.

In contrast, in *Grutter v. Bollinger,*[45] the Court held that the University of Michigan Law School's admission policy was constitutional. In that case, the Court concluded that "[u]niversities can, however, consider race or ethnicity more flexibly as a 'plus' factor in the context of individualized consideration of each and every applicant." The significant difference between the two admissions policies, in the Court's view, was that the law school's approach did not apply a mechanical formula giving "diversity bonuses" based on race or ethnicity.

In 2007, the United States Supreme Court ruled on two more cases involving racial classifications used in assigning students to schools in Seattle, Washington, and Jefferson County, Kentucky. Both school districts had adopted student assignment plans that relied on race to determine which schools certain children attended. The Seattle school district plan classified children as white or nonwhite and used the racial classifications as a "tiebreaker" to determine the particular

41. 515 U.S. 200, 115 S.Ct. 2097, 132 L.Ed.2d 158 (1995).
42. 84 F.3d 720 (5th Cir. 1996).

43. See, for example, *Johnson v. Board of Regents of the University of Georgia,* 263 F.3d 1234 (11th Cir. 2001); and *Smith v. University of Washington School of Law,* 233 F.3d 1188 (9th Cir. 2000).
44. 539 U.S. 244, 123 S.Ct. 2411, 156 L.Ed.2d 257 (2003).
45. 539 U.S. 306, 123 S.Ct. 2325, 156 L.Ed.2d 304 (2003).

high school students attended. The school district in Jefferson County classified students as black or other to assign children to elementary schools. A group of parents from the relevant public schools filed lawsuits claiming that the school districts' racial preferences violated the equal protection clause. The Supreme Court applied strict scrutiny and held that the school districts failed to show that use of racial classifications in their student assignment plans was necessary to achieve their stated goal of racial diversity.[46]

State Laws Prohibiting Discrimination

Although the focus of this chapter is on federal legislation, most states also have statutes that prohibit employment discrimination. Generally, the same kinds of discrimination are prohibited under federal and state legislation. In addition, state statutes often provide protection for certain individuals who are not protected under federal laws. For example, a New Jersey appellate court held that anyone over the age of eighteen was entitled to sue for age discrimination under the state law, which specified no threshold age limit.[47]

Furthermore, state laws prohibiting discrimination may apply to firms with fewer employees than the threshold number required under federal statutes, thus offering protection to more workers. Even when companies are too small to be covered by state statutes, state courts may uphold employees' rights against discrimination in the workplace for public-policy reasons.[48] State laws may also provide for additional damages, such as damages for emotional distress, that are not provided for under federal statutes.[49] Finally, some states, such as California and Washington, have passed laws that end affirmative action programs in those states or modify admission policies at state-sponsored universities.

46. The court consolidated the two cases and issued only one opinion to address the issues presented by both cases. *Parents Involved in Community Schools v. Seattle School Dist. No. 1*, ___ U.S.___, 127 S.Ct. 2738, 168 L.Ed.2d 508 (2007).

47. *Bergen Commercial Bank v. Sisler*, 307 N.J.Super. 333, 704 A.2d 1017 (1998).

48. See, for example, *Roberts v. Dudley, D.V.M.*, 92 Wash.App. 652, 966 P.2d 377 (1998); and *Insignia Residential Corp. v. Ashton*, 359 Md. 560, 755 A.2d 1080 (2000).

49. For a reverse discrimination case in which a former police officer was awarded nearly $80,000 in emotional distress damages based on a violation of New Jersey's Law Against Discrimination, see *Klawitter v. City of Trenton*, 395 N.J.Super. 302, 928 A.2d 900 (2007).

REVIEWING Employment Discrimination

Amaani Lyle, an African American woman, was hired by Warner Brothers Television Productions to be a scriptwriters' assistant for the writers of *Friends*, a popular, adult-oriented television series. One of her essential job duties was to type detailed notes for the scriptwriters during brainstorming sessions in which they discussed jokes, dialogue, and story lines. The writers then combed through Lyle's notes after the meetings for script material. During these meetings, the three male scriptwriters told lewd and vulgar jokes and made sexually explicit comments and gestures. They often talked about their personal sexual experiences and fantasies, and some of these conversations were then used in episodes of *Friends*.

Lyle never complained that she found the writers' conduct during the meetings offensive. After four months, Lyle was fired because she could not type fast enough to keep up with the writers' conversations during the meetings. She filed a suit against Warner Brothers, alleging sexual harassment and claiming that her termination was based on racial discrimination. Using the information presented in the chapter, answer the following questions.

1. Would Lyle's claim of racial discrimination be for intentional (disparate-treatment) or unintentional (disparate-impact) discrimination? Explain.
2. Can Lyle establish a *prima facie* case of racial discrimination? Why or why not?

REVIEWING Employment Discrimination, Continued

3. When Lyle was hired, she was told that typing speed was extremely important to the position. At the time, she maintained that she could type eighty words per minute, so she was not given a typing test. It later turned out that Lyle could type only fifty words per minute. What impact might typing speed have on Lyle's lawsuit?
4. Lyle's sexual-harassment claim is based on the hostile work environment created by the writers' sexually offensive conduct at meetings that she was required to attend. The writers, however, argue that their behavior was essential to the "creative process" of writing for *Friends,* a show that routinely contained sexual innuendos and adult humor. Which defense discussed in the chapter might Warner Brothers assert using this argument?

TERMS AND CONCEPTS

affirmative action 542
bona fide occupational qualification (BFOQ) 541
business necessity 541
constructive discharge 528
disparate-impact discrimination 526
disparate-treatment discrimination 526
employment discrimination 525
***prima facie* case 526**
protected class 525
seniority system 542
sexual harassment 529
tangible employment action 529

QUESTIONS AND CASE PROBLEMS

21-1. Discuss fully whether either of the following actions would constitute a violation of Title VII of the 1964 Civil Rights Act, as amended:

(a) Tennington, Inc., is a consulting firm and has ten employees. These employees travel on consulting jobs in seven states. Tennington has an employment record of hiring only white males.

(b) Novo Films is making a movie about Africa and needs to employ approximately one hundred extras for this picture. Novo advertises in all major newspapers in Southern California for the hiring of these extras. The ad states that only African Americans need apply.

21-2. QUESTION WITH SAMPLE ANSWER

Chinawa, a major processor of cheese sold throughout the United States, employs one hundred workers at its principal processing plant. The plant is located in Heartland Corners, which has a population that is 50 percent white and 25 percent African American, with the balance Hispanic American, Asian American, and others. Chinawa requires a high school diploma as a condition of employment for its cleaning crew. Three-fourths of the white population complete high school, compared with only one-fourth of those in the minority groups. Chinawa has an all-white cleaning crew. Has Chinawa violated Title VII of the Civil Rights Act of 1964? Explain.

- **For a sample answer to Question 21-2, go to Appendix I at the end of this text.**

21-3. Discrimination Based on Disability. PGA Tour, Inc., sponsors professional golf tournaments. A player may enter in several ways, but the most common method is to compete successfully in a three-stage qualifying tournament known as the "Q-School." Anyone may enter the Q-School by submitting two letters of recommendation and paying $3,000 to cover greens fees and the cost of a golf cart, which is permitted during the first two stages, but is prohibited during the third stage. The rules governing the events include the "Rules of Golf," which apply at all levels of amateur and professional golf and do not prohibit the use of golf carts, and the "hard card," which applies specifically to the PGA tour and requires the players to walk the course during most of a tournament. Casey Martin is a talented golfer with a degenerative circulatory disorder that prevents him from walking golf courses. Martin entered the Q-School and asked for permission to use a cart during the third stage. PGA refused. Martin filed a suit in a federal district court against PGA, alleging a violation of the Americans with Disabilities Act. Is a golf cart in these circumstances a "reasonable accommodation" under the ADA? Why or why not? [*PGA Tour, Inc. v. Martin,* 531 U.S. 1049, 121 S.Ct. 652, 148 L.Ed.2d 556 (2001)]

21–4. Discrimination Based on Age. The United Auto Workers (UAW) is the union that represents the employees of General Dynamics Land Systems, Inc. In 1997, a collective bargaining agreement between UAW and General Dynamics eliminated the company's obligation to provide health insurance to employees who retired after the date of the agreement, except for current workers at least fifty years of age. Dennis Cline and 194 other employees over the age of forty but under age fifty objected to this term. They complained to the Equal Employment Opportunity Commission, claiming that the agreement violated the Age Discrimination in Employment Act (ADEA) of 1967. The ADEA forbids discriminatory preference for the "young" over the "old." Does the ADEA also prohibit favoring the old over the young? How should the court rule? Explain. [*General Dynamics Land Systems, Inc. v. Cline,* 540 U.S. 581, 124 S.Ct. 1236, 157 L.Ed.2d 1094 (2004)]

21–5. CASE PROBLEM WITH SAMPLE ANSWER

Kimberly Cloutier began working at the Costco store in West Springfield, Massachusetts, in July 1997. Cloutier had multiple earrings and four tattoos, but no facial piercings. In June 1998, Costco promoted Cloutier to cashier. Over the next two years, she engaged in various forms of body modification, including facial piercing and cutting. In March 2001, Costco revised its dress code to prohibit all facial jewelry except earrings. Cloutier was told that she would have to remove her facial jewelry. She asked for a complete exemption from the code, asserting that she was a member of the Church of Body Modification and that eyebrow piercing was part of her religion. She was told to remove the jewelry, cover it, or go home. She went home and was later discharged for her absence. Cloutier filed a suit in a federal district court against Costco, alleging religious discrimination in violation of Title VII. Does an employer have an obligation to accommodate its employees' religious practices? If so, to what extent? How should the court rule in this case? Discuss. [*Cloutier v. Costco Wholesale Corp.,* 390 F.3d 126 (1st Cir. 2004)]

- **To view a sample answer for Problem 21–5, go to this book's Web site at academic.cengage.com/blaw/cross, select "Chapter 21," and click on "Case Problem with Sample Answer."**

21–6. Discrimination Based on Gender. For twenty years, Darlene Jespersen worked as a bartender at Harrah's Casino in Reno, Nevada. In 2000, Harrah's implemented a "Personal Best" program that included new grooming standards. Among other requirements, women were told to wear makeup "applied neatly in complimentary colors." Jespersen, who never wore makeup off the job, felt so uncomfortable wearing it on the job that it interfered with her ability to perform. Unwilling to wear makeup and not qualifying for another position at Harrah's with similar compensation, Jespersen quit the casino. She filed a suit in a federal district court against Harrah's Operating Co., the casino's owner, alleging that the makeup policy discriminated against women in violation of Title VII of the Civil Rights Act of 1964. Harrah's argued that any burdens under the new program fell equally on both genders, citing the "Personal Best" short-hair standard that applied only to men. Jespersen responded by describing her personal reaction to the makeup policy and emphasizing her exemplary record during her tenure at Harrah's. In whose favor should the court rule? Why? [*Jespersen v. Harrah's Operating Co.,* 444 F.3d 1104 (9th Cir. 2006)]

21–7. Discrimination Based on Disability. Cerebral palsy limits Steven Bradley's use of his legs. He uses forearm crutches for short-distance walks and a wheelchair for longer distances. Standing for more than ten or fifteen minutes is difficult. With support, however, Bradley can climb stairs and get on and off a stool. His condition also restricts the use of his fourth finger to, for example, type, but it does not limit his ability to write—he completed two years of college. His grip strength is normal, and he can lift heavy objects. In 2001, Bradley applied for a "greeter" or "cashier" position at a Wal-Mart Stores, Inc., Supercenter in Richmond, Missouri. The job description stated, "No experience or qualification is required." Bradley indicated that he was available for full- or part-time work from 4:00 P.M. to 10:00 P.M. any evening. His employment history showed that he currently worked as a proofreader and that he had previously worked as an administrator. His application was rejected, according to Janet Daugherty, the personnel manager, based on his "work history" and the "direct threat" that he posed to the safety of himself and others. Bradley claimed, however, that the store refused to hire him due to his disability. What steps must Bradley follow to pursue his claim? What does he need to show to prevail? Is he likely to meet these requirements? Discuss. [*EEOC v. Wal-Mart Stores, Inc.,* 477 F.3d 561 (8th Cir. 2007)]

21–8. A QUESTION OF ETHICS

Titan Distribution, Inc., employed Quintak, Inc., to run its tire mounting and distribution operation *in Des Moines, Iowa. Robert Chalfant worked for Quintak as a second shift supervisor at Titan. He suffered a heart attack in 1992 and underwent heart bypass surgery in 1997. He also had arthritis. In July 2002, Titan decided to terminate Quintak. Chalfant applied to work at Titan. On his application, he described himself as disabled. After a physical exam, Titan's physician concluded that Chalfant could work in his current capacity, and he was notified that he would be hired. Despite the notice, Nadis Barucic, a Titan employee, wrote "not pass px" at the top of his application, and he was not hired. He took a job with AMPCO Systems, a parking ramp management company. This work involved walking up to five miles a day and lifting more weight than he had at Titan. In September, Titan eliminated its second shift. Chalfant filed a suit in a federal district court against Titan, in part, under the Americans with Disabilities Act (ADA). Titan argued that it had not hired Chalfant because he did not pass the physical, but no one—including Barucic—could explain why she had written "not pass px" on his application. Later, Titan claimed that Chalfant was not hired because the entire second shift was going to be eliminated. [*Chalfant v. Titan Distribution, Inc., *475 F.3d 982 (8th Cir. 2007)]*

(a) What must Chalfant establish to make his case under the ADA? Can he meet these requirements? Explain.
(b) In employment-discrimination cases, punitive damages can be appropriate when an employer acts with malice or reckless indifference in regard to an employee's protected rights. Would an award of punitive damages to Chalfant be appropriate in this case? Discuss.

21-9. SPECIAL CASE ANALYSIS

Go to Case 21.1, *Burlington Northern and Santa Fe Railway Co. v. White,* 548 U.S. 53, 126 S.Ct. 2405, 165 L.Ed.2d 345 (2006), on pages 530 and 531. Read the excerpt and answer the following questions.

(a) **Issue:** What was the main issue in this case?
(b) **Rule of Law:** What rule of law did the Court apply?
(c) **Applying the Rule of Law:** Describe how the Court applied the rule of law to the facts of this case.
(d) **Conclusion:** What was the Court's conclusion in this case?

21-10. VIDEO QUESTION

Go to this text's Web site at **academic.cengage.com/blaw/cross** and select "Chapter 21." Click on "Video Questions" and view the video titled *Parenthood.* Then answer the following questions.

(a) In the video, Gil (Steve Martin) threatens to leave his job when he discovers that his boss is promoting another person to partner instead of him. His boss (Dennis Dugan) laughs and tells him that the threat is not realistic because if Gil leaves, he will be competing for positions with workers who are younger than he is and willing to accept lower salaries. If Gil takes his employer's advice and stays in his current position, can he sue his boss for age discrimination based on the boss's statements? Why or why not?
(b) Suppose that Gil leaves his current position and applies for a job at another firm. The prospective employer refuses to hire him based on his age. What would Gil have to prove to establish a *prima facie* case of age discrimination? Explain your answer.
(c) What defenses might Gil's current employer raise if Gil sues for age discrimination?

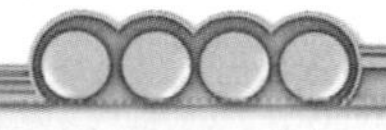

LAW ON THE WEB

For updated links to resources available on the Web, as well as a variety of other materials, visit this text's Web site at

academic.cengage.com/blaw/cross

The Employment Law Information Network provides access to many articles on age discrimination and other employment issues at

www.elinfonet.com/fedindex/2

The New York State Governor's Office of Employee Relations maintains an interactive site on sexual harassment and how to prevent sexual harassment in the workplace. Go to

www.goer.state.ny.us/Train/onlinelearning/SH/intro.html

An abundance of helpful information on disability-based discrimination, including the text of the Americans with Disabilities Act of 1990, can be found at the following Web site:

www.jan.wvu.edu/links/adalinks.htm

An excellent source for information on various forms of employment discrimination is the Equal Employment Opportunity Commission's Web site at

www.eeoc.gov

Legal Research Exercises on the Web

Go to **academic.cengage.com/blaw/cross**, the Web site that accompanies this text. Select "Chapter 21" and click on "Internet Exercises." There you will find the following Internet research exercises that you can perform to learn more about the topics covered in this chapter.

Internet Exercise 21–1: Legal Perspective
Americans with Disabilities

Internet Exercise 21–2: Management Perspective
Equal Employment Opportunity

Internet Exercise 21–3: Social Perspective
Religious and National-Origin Discrimination

CHAPTER 22 Immigration and Labor Law

During the nineteenth century, two separate forces began to affect the employment environment in the United States—a rise in immigration and the Industrial Revolution. Both led to significant changes in the legal environment of the workplace, which we will examine in this chapter. Legislation was enacted to prohibit employers from hiring illegal immigrants. Immigration law has evolved over the years into a myriad of complex rules that employers need to follow when hiring foreign-born workers. The laws on immigration are also in a state of transition, as politicians and others debate what reforms are needed to best serve the interests of both employers and workers.

During the Industrial Revolution, fewer Americans were self-employed than ever before, and employers generally set the terms of employment. Moreover, with increasing industrialization, the size of workplaces and the number of on-the-job hazards increased. Workers came to believe that to counter the power and freedom of their employers and to protect themselves, they needed to organize into unions. Employers discouraged—sometimes forcibly—collective activities such as unions. In support of unionization, Congress enacted such legislations as the Railway Labor Act of 1926.[1] These laws were often restricted to particular industries. Beginning in 1932, Congress enacted a number of statutes that increased employees' rights generally. At the heart of these rights is the right to join unions and engage in *collective bargaining* with management to negotiate working conditions, salaries, and benefits for a group of workers.

This chapter begins with a discussion of immigration law from its beginnings to its current state, and its importance to today's business owners and employers. We then describe the development of labor law and the legal recognition of the right to form unions. Next, the chapter examines the process of unionizing a company, the collective bargaining required of a unionized employer, and the strikes and lockouts that may result if bargaining fails. We also look at the labor practices that are considered unfair under federal law, and briefly discuss the rights of nonunion employees.

1. 45 U.S.C. Sections 151–188.

SECTION 1 The Law Governing Immigration

The United States is known as a nation of immigrants. Until 1875, there was no legislation restricting immigration, and the United States Supreme Court had declared state laws regulating immigration to be unconstitutional. The late nineteenth century saw the first federal immigration restrictions, beginning with a law excluding convicts and prostitutes. This coincided with a huge surge in immigration from new sources (including China, Ireland, and Southern and Eastern Europe). In 1890, more than 40 percent of New York City's population was foreign born. Immigration peaked at the beginning of the twentieth century. After that time, immigration waned, but recent years have seen a marked increase in illegal immigration from Latino countries, especially Mexico.

The rapid growth in immigration saw an increase in exclusionary laws. In 1924, Congress created a permanent national origin quota system that based legal immigration on the proportion of persons from a foreign country enumerated in the 1890 census. This was modified in the 1952 McCarran-Walter Act,[2] which continued the quota system, set standards for deportation, and first created preferences for aliens with special skills. The national origin and racial quotas were eliminated in 1965. The next major statute was the Immigration Reform and Control Act of 1986 (IRCA),[3] which provided amnesty to certain groups of illegal aliens then living in the United States and also established a system of sanctions against employers for hiring illegal immigrants lacking work authorization.

Both legal and illegal immigration have been surging in recent decades, as illustrated in Exhibit 22–1. The expansion of immigration has made an understanding of related legal requirements for business steadily more important. Employers must take steps to avoid hiring illegal immigrants or face serious penalties.

Law and Illegal Immigration

Today, there are an estimated 11 to 12 million illegal immigrants living in the United States. The overwhelming majority of these immigrants hold jobs, and they are the subject of considerable political controversy.

2. 8 U.S.C. Sections 1101 *et seq.*

3. This act amended various provisions of the McCarran-Walter Act, including 8 U.S.C. Sections 1160, 1187, 1188, 1255a, 1324a, 1324b, 1364, and 1365.

EXHIBIT 22–1 • Foreign-Born Population and Illegal Aliens, 1960–2010 (in Millions)

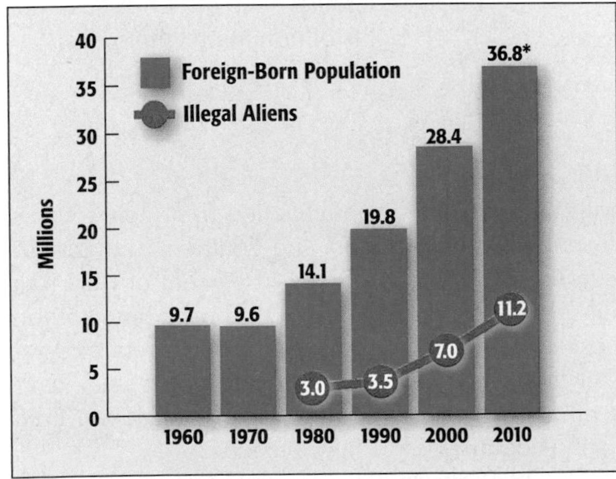

*Authors' estimates.
Source: U.S. Census Bureau, Center for Immigration Studies.

Many contend that the immigrants take jobs from American citizens or hold down wages for such jobs. The 1986 immigration reform just mentioned (IRCA) was intended to prevent this and made it illegal to hire, recruit, or refer for a fee someone not authorized to work in the country. The federal government—through Immigration and Customs Enforcement officers—conducts random compliance audits, and the federal government has further engaged in enforcement actions against employers who hire illegal immigrants. This section sets out the compliance requirements for companies.

I-9 Employment Verification

To comply with current law (based on the 1986 act), employers must perform **I-9 verifications** for new hires and this includes even those hired as "contractors" or "day workers" if they work under the employer's direct supervision. Form I-9, Employment Eligibility Verification, available from the U.S. Citizenship and Immigration Services,[4] must be completed within three days of the worker's commencement of employment. The three-day period is to allow the employer to verify the documents and the form's accuracy. The I-9 form requires employers to review and verify documents establishing the prospective worker's identity and eligibility for employment in the United States. Acceptable documents include a U.S. passport establishing a person's citizenship or others, such as a Permanent Resident Card or Alien Registration Receipt Card, that authorize a foreign citizen to work in the country.

The employer must attest, under penalty of perjury, that an employee produced documents establishing his or her identity and legal employability. The employee must state that he or she is a U.S. citizen or otherwise authorized to work in the United States. The employer is the party legally responsible for any problems with the I-9 verification process. Companies need to establish compliance procedures and keep completed I-9 forms on file for at least three years for potential future government inspection.

The 1986 act only prohibits "knowing" violations, but these include cases in which an employer "should have known" that the worker was unauthorized. Good

4. The U.S. Citizenship and Immigration Services is a federal agency that is part of the U.S. Department of Homeland Security.

faith is a defense under the statute, and employers are legally entitled to rely on documentation of authorization to work that reasonably appears on its face to be genuine, even if it is later established to be counterfeit. Good faith is not a defense, however, to the failure to possess the proper paperwork. Moreover, if an employer subsequently learns that an employee is not authorized to work in this country, it must promptly discharge that employee or be in violation of the law.

Enforcement

The U.S. Immigration and Customs Enforcement (ICE) was established in 2003 as the largest investigative arm of the U.S. Department of Homeland Security. ICE has a General Inspection Program that conducts random compliance audits. Other audits may occur after the agency receives a written complaint alleging an employer's violations. Government inspections involve a review of an employer's file of I-9 forms. The government need not obtain a subpoena or a warrant to conduct such an inspection.

EXHIBIT 22–2 • Worksite Enforcement Arrests by the U.S. Immigration and Customs Enforcement

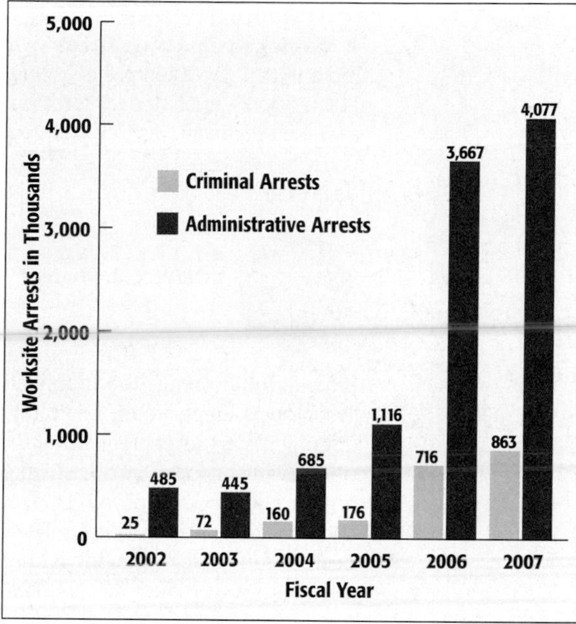

Source: U.S. Immigration and Customs Enforcement, 2008.

Administrative Actions After investigation and discovery of a possible violation, ICE will bring an administrative action and issue a Notice of Intent to Fine, which sets out the charges against the employer. The employer has a right to a hearing on the enforcement action, if it files a request within thirty days. This hearing is conducted before an *administrative law judge* (see Chapter 6), and the employer has a right to counsel and to *discovery* (see Chapter 2). The typical defense in such actions is good faith or substantial compliance with the documentation provisions.

In past years, the threat of enforcement was regarded as minimal, but the federal government has substantially increased its enforcement activities. This is demonstrated by ICE data presented in Exhibit 22–2. In 2007, ICE raided and identified hundreds of illegal workers at plants owned by companies including Koch Foods, Fresh Del Monte Produce, Tarrasco Steel, and Jones Industrial Network.

Criminal Actions ICE has increasingly sought criminal punishment for acts such as harboring an alien or illegally inducing illegal immigration. In January 2008, an employee of George's Processing, Inc., was convicted by a Missouri federal jury after an ICE raid resulted in the arrest of 136 illegal aliens at the plant. The convicted management employee was in the human resources department of the company and was involved in the hiring process. Evidence suggested that she helped applicants complete their I-9 forms, with knowledge that they had fraudulently obtained identity documents. The potential penalty for this crime is ten years in prison without parole.

A company may present a defense demonstrating that the employee alleged to be in violation was truly an independent contractor rather than an employee and therefore not subject to the I-9 requirements. Even for independent contractors, though, a party's actual knowledge that a worker was unauthorized is illegal. Ultimately, the administrative law judge reviewing the case makes a ruling and assesses penalties if he or she finds a violation. This hearing may be appealed administratively or to a federal court.

Individuals who believe they have suffered as a result of illegal hiring have no direct cause of action to sue an employer under current law. They may sue under the Racketeer Influenced and Corrupt Organizations Act (RICO), though, using the violations as a predicate illegal act.[5] The following case illustrates such an action.

5. RICO was discussed in Chapter 7.

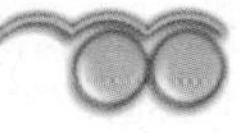

CASE 22.1 Trollinger v. Tyson Foods, Inc.

United States District Court, Eastern District of Tennessee, 2007. ___ F.Supp.2d ___.

• **Background and Facts** Tyson Foods, Inc., is one of the nation's largest poultry processors, with more than 100,000 employees. One of its plants was located in Shelbyville, Tennessee. In December 2001, Tyson was indicted for conspiring to smuggle illegal aliens into the country and employ them. Soon after the indictment was filed, four former workers at the Shelbyville facility filed this action against Tyson under the Racketeer Influenced and Corrupt Organizations Act (RICO), alleging that Tyson engaged in an illegal scheme to depress wages by hiring illegal immigrants. Tyson moved to dismiss the complaint.

IN THE LANGUAGE OF THE COURT
COLLIER, J. [Judge]

* * * *

* * * The Complaint alleges Defendants engaged in a long-term pattern and practice of violating [the Immigration Reform and Control Act]. * * * The Complaint states Tyson signs Employment Eligibility Verification Forms (I-9 forms) in mass quantities before any documents are inspected, more than three days after new hires have been employed, and based on a review of copies of documents rather than reviewing the original documents. The Complaint further alleges Tyson prohibits its employees from taking into account obvious facts which indicate that documents do not relate to the people tendering them; rehires persons whom it previously hired under different names, usually after a short absence; hires workers who appear decades younger than the pictures on their stolen identity documents; uses temporary employment placement services to hire illegal immigrants and then "loan" them to Tyson for a fee; and gives employees leave to "get good documents" after Tyson learns the initial documents submitted by the illegal alien actually belong to someone else.

* * * *

In the context of the present illegal immigration problem in the United States, it is widely, if not universally, known that illegal immigration from Mexico is done in substantial part through smuggling. It is also of note that Tyson's processing plants are all located in areas where the predominant illegal alien population is from Mexico. *This knowledge along with the above allegations satisfies the requirement that the Complaint alleges Defendants had a subjective belief that large numbers of its illegal alien employees had been brought into the United States illegally.* [Emphasis added.]

• **Decision and Remedy** *The court denied Tyson's motion to dismiss the complaint.*

• **What If the Facts Were Different?** *Assume that Tyson's human resource managers were acting on their own, in clear violation of that company's written employment policy. Would the judge have ruled differently? Why or why not?*

• **The Global Dimension** *Many businesses in U.S. communities near the border with Mexico rely on the purchasing power of immigrants, both legal and illegal. What incentives, if any, do these businesses have in helping enforce U.S. immigration laws?*

Penalties

In general, the federal government (through ICE) enforces the current immigration laws. An employer who violates the law by hiring an unauthorized alien is subject to substantial penalties. A first offense can result in a civil fine of up to $2,200 for each unauthorized employee. Fines rise to $5,000 per employee for a second offense and up to $11,000 for subsequent offenses by the same employer. Criminal penalties apply to employers who have engaged in a "pattern or practice of violations," and these penalties include additional fines and imprisonment. A company may also be barred from future government contracts for violations.

ICE regulations provide a list of circumstances that may warrant the mitigation or aggravation of penalties. Considerations include whether the company is a small business and the relative cooperation of the employer in the investigation. In determining the amount of the penalty, ICE also considers the seriousness of the violation (such as intentional falsification of documents) and the employer's past compliance.

Anti-Discrimination Provisions

The passage of the Immigration Reform and Control Act (ICRA) led to concerns about discrimination based on national origin. Some employers reportedly refused to hire Latinos out of concern for violating the statute. Amendments to the act established prohibitions on unfair immigration-related employment practices. The ICRA now provides that it is an unfair immigration-related practice for an employer to discriminate against any individual (other than an unauthorized alien) with respect to hiring or discharging the individual from employment.[6] Companies must exercise reasonable care to evaluate the required I-9 documents in a fair and consistent manner. They may not require greater proof from some prospective employees or reject apparently sufficient documentation of work authorization or citizenship.

A prospective employee who believes that he or she has been subject to discrimination may file a charge with the Office of Special Counsel for Immigration Related Unfair Employment Practices (OSC). The OSC investigates the charge and may file a complaint with an administrative law judge if it finds the complaint has merit. If the OSC fails to file such a complaint within 120 days, the private party may bring a private action for discrimination. The standards and procedures for evaluating the action parallel those of Title VII of the Civil Rights Act, which was discussed in Chapter 21.

Law and Legal Immigration

The immigration laws of this country are very elaborate, and individuals can seek authorization to enter the country under numerous different authorities. These include provisions for refugees who can demonstrate certain persecution from their home country's government. This section focuses on the rules for those who immigrate in order to work in the United States. U.S. businesses can benefit from hiring immigrants who have abilities surpassing those of available domestic workers. Our immigration laws have long made provisions for businesses to hire especially qualified foreign workers. The Immigration Act of 1990 placed caps on the number of visas (entry permits) that can be issued to immigrants each year.

Most temporary visas are set aside for workers who can be characterized as "persons of extraordinary ability," members of the professions holding advanced degrees, or other skilled workers and professionals. To hire these individuals, employers must submit a petition with the Citizenship and Immigration Services, which determines whether the job candidate meets the legal standards. Each visa is for a specific job, and there are legal limits on the employee's ability to switch jobs once in the United States.

Self-Authorized Immigrant Job Candidates

A company seeking to hire a noncitizen worker may do so, if the worker is self-authorized. This means that the worker is either (a) a lawful permanent resident or (b) has a valid temporary Employment Authorization Document (EAD). Lawful permanent residents can prove their status to an employer by presenting an **I-551 Alien Registration Receipt,** known as a "green card," or a properly stamped foreign passport.

When an Immigrant Is Not Self-Authorized

Many workers are not already self-authorized, though, and employers may obtain a labor certification, or green card, for those immigrants whom they wish to hire. Fifty thousand new green card immigrants are authorized each year. To take advantage of this authority, the job must be for a permanent, full-time position.

To gain such authorization for hiring a foreign worker, the employer must show that no American worker is qualified, willing, and able to take the job. This requires publication of the bona fide job opening in suitable newspapers or professional journals within six months of the hiring action. The government has detailed regulations governing the nature of this publication.[7] Any U.S. applicants must be interviewed and

6. 8 U.S.C. Section 1324b.

7. The most relevant regulations can be found at 20 C.F.R. 655 (for temporary employment) and 20 C.F.R. 656 (for permanent employment).

hired for the position if they meet its stated qualifications. The qualifications are also evaluated for their business necessity. A group of administrative law judges rejected one company's notice for hiring kitchen supervisors, because the company required that the applicants speak Spanish.[8]

The employer must also determine from a state agency what the "prevailing wage" for the position is in the location and must offer the immigrating worker at least 100 percent of that prevailing wage. The prevailing wage rate is defined as the average wage paid to similarly employed workers in the requested occupation in the area of intended employment. Fringe benefits are also considered in this calculation.

A separate authorization system provides for the temporary entry and hiring of nonimmigrant visa workers. These are individuals who enter the country for a period of time and who are restricted to an activity consistent with their visas. Applicants must express an intention to depart the country at the expiration of their requested stay, though they may apply for an extension of the stay.

The H-1B Visa Program The most common and controversial visa program today involves the H-1B visa system. These individuals may stay and work in the country for three to six years and work only for the sponsoring employer. The recipients of these visas include many high-tech workers. Sixty-five thousand slots for new immigrants were set aside for H-1B visas; the number was temporarily increased to 195,000, but that law expired and the cap returned to 65,000 in 2004. The available slots go quickly, and many businesses, such as Microsoft, have lobbied Congress to expand the number of H1-B visas offered to immigrants. In recent years, the total allotment of H1-B visas has been filled within the first few weeks of the year, leaving no slots available for the remaining eleven months.

The criteria for such a visa include the potential employee's "specialty occupation," which is defined as having highly specialized knowledge and the attainment of a bachelor's or higher degree or its equivalent. Qualifying jobs may include computer programmers, electronics specialists, complex business managers, engineers, professionals, and other jobs. In one 2006 ruling, ICE found that the position of "accountant" did not qualify as a specialty occupation because the American Council for Accountancy and Taxation did not require a degree for an individual to be credentialed as such.

Labor Certification Before an employer can submit an H-1B application, it must obtain a Labor Certification application filed on a form known as ETA 9035. The employer must agree to provide a wage level at least equal to those offered to other individuals with similar experience and qualifications and attest that the hiring will not adversely affect other workers similarly employed. The employer must inform U.S. workers of the intent to hire a foreign worker by posting the form. The U.S. Department of Labor reviews the applications and may reject them for incompleteness or inaccuracies.

In 2002, a former employee of Sun Microsystems complained to the Justice Department that the company was discriminating against American workers in favor of H-1B visa holders. Sun had laid off nearly 4,000 domestic workers while applying for thousands of temporary visa employees. The court ultimately found that Sun had violated only minor technical requirements and ordered it only to change its posting practices for applicants for open positions.

H-2, O, L, and E Visas Other specialty temporary nonimmigrant visas are available for other categories of employees. H-2 visas provide for workers performing agricultural labor of a seasonal nature. O visas provide entry for persons who have "extraordinary ability in the sciences, arts, education, business or athletics which has been demonstrated by sustained national or international acclaim." L visas allow companies to bring some of their foreign managers or executives to work inside the country. E visas permit the entry of certain foreign investors or entrepreneurs.

Immigration Reform on the Horizon

For many years, the president, members of Congress, business owners, and citizens have debated proposals for immigration reform. Some of the proposals would have allowed illegal immigrants to remain legally in this country and would have allowed many of them to eventually become citizens. At the other extreme, anti-immigration proposals would have required all illegal immigrants to leave this country and go through the full procedures for obtaining a legal way to return in order to work. At the writing of this edition, too many factors were at play to predict what immigration reform would look like in the years to come.

8. *In the matter of Malnati Organization, Inc.*, 2007-INA-00035 (Bd. Alien Lab. Cert. App. 2007).

One thing is certain: problems with immigration will remain. The average wage differential between Mexico and the United States is more than 400 percent. This wage differential is larger than between any other two countries in the world that share a contiguous border. Thus, the incentives facing those south of the border will remain the same until economic growth in Mexico (and other Latin American countries) boosts average wage rates to be closer to those in the United States.

Federal Labor Laws

Federal labor laws governing union-employer relations have developed considerably since the first law was enacted in 1932. Initially, the laws were concerned with protecting the rights and interests of workers. Subsequent legislation placed some restraints on unions and granted rights to employers. We look here at four major federal statutes regulating union-employer relations.

Norris-LaGuardia Act

Congress protected peaceful strikes, picketing, and boycotts in 1932 in the Norris-LaGuardia Act.[9] The statute restricted the power of federal courts to issue injunctions against unions engaged in peaceful strikes. In effect, this act declared a national policy permitting employees to organize.

National Labor Relations Act

One of the foremost statutes regulating labor is the National Labor Relations Act (NLRA) of 1935.[10] The purpose of the NLRA was to secure for employees the rights to organize; to bargain collectively through representatives of their own choosing; and to engage in concerted activities for organizing, collective bargaining, and other purposes. The NLRA specifically defined a number of employer practices as unfair to labor:

1. Interference with the efforts of employees to form, join, or assist labor organizations or to engage in concerted activities for their mutual aid or protection.
2. An employer's domination of a labor organization or contribution of financial or other support to it.
3. Discrimination in the hiring of or the awarding of tenure to employees for reason of union affiliation.
4. Discrimination against employees for filing charges under the act or giving testimony under the act.
5. Refusal to bargain collectively with the duly designated representative of the employees.

To ensure that employees' rights would be protected, the NLRA established the National Labor Relations Board (NLRB). The NLRB has the authority to investigate employees' charges of unfair labor practices and to file complaints against employers in response to these charges. When violations are found, the NLRB may also issue **cease-and-desist orders**—orders compelling employers to stop engaging in the unfair practices. Cease-and-desist orders can be enforced by a federal appellate court if necessary. Disputes over alleged unfair labor practices are first decided by the NLRB and may then be appealed to a federal court.

To be protected under the NLRA, an individual must be an employee or a job applicant (otherwise, the NLRA's ban on discrimination in regard to hiring would mean little). Additionally, the United States Supreme Court has held that individuals who are hired by a union to organize a company (union organizers) are to be considered employees of the company for NLRA purposes.[11]

Labor-Management Relations Act

The Labor-Management Relations Act (LMRA) of 1947[12] was passed to proscribe certain unfair union practices, such as the *closed shop*. A **closed shop** is a firm that requires union membership by its workers as a condition of employment. Although the act made the closed shop illegal, it preserved the legality of the union shop. A **union shop** is a firm that does not require union membership as a prerequisite for employment but can, and usually does, require that workers join the union after a specified amount of time on the job.

The LMRA also prohibited unions from refusing to bargain with employers, engaging in certain types of picketing, and *featherbedding* (causing employers to hire more employees than necessary). In addition, the act allowed individual states to pass their own **right-to-work laws**—laws making it illegal for

9. 29 U.S.C. Sections 101–110, 113–115.
10. 20 U.S.C. Sections 151–169.
11. *NLRB v. Town & Country Electric, Inc.*, 516 U.S. 85, 116 S.Ct. 450, 133 L.Ed.2d 371 (1995).
12. 29 U.S.C. Sections 141 *et seq.*

union membership to be required for *continued* employment in any establishment. Thus, union shops are technically illegal in the twenty-two states that have right-to-work laws.

Labor-Management Reporting and Disclosure Act

The Labor-Management Reporting and Disclosure Act (LMRDA) of 1959[13] established an employee bill of rights and reporting requirements for union activities. The act strictly regulates unions' internal business procedures, including elections. For example, the LMRDA requires unions to hold regularly scheduled elections of officers using secret ballots. Former convicts are prohibited from holding union office. Moreover, union officials are accountable for union property and funds. Members have the right to attend and to participate in union meetings, to nominate officers, and to vote in most union proceedings.

The act also outlawed *hot-cargo agreements* and *secondary boycotts,* as will be discussed later in this chapter.

Coverage and Procedures

Coverage of the federal labor laws is broad and extends to all employers whose business activity either involves or affects interstate commerce. Some workers are specifically excluded from these laws. Railroads and airlines are not covered by the NLRA but are covered by a separate act, the Railway Labor Act, which closely parallels the NLRA. Other types of workers, such as agricultural workers and domestic servants, are excluded from the NLRA and have no coverage under separate legislation.

When a union or employee believes that the employer has violated federal labor law (or vice versa), the union or employee files a charge with a regional office of the NLRB. The form for an employee to use to file an unfair labor practice charge against an employer is shown in Exhibit 22–3. The charge is investigated, and if it is found worthy, the regional director files a complaint. An administrative law judge (ALJ) initially hears the complaint and rules on it (see Chapter 6). The board reviews the ALJ's findings and decision. If the NLRB finds a violation, it may issue remedial orders (including requiring rehiring of discharged workers). The NLRB decision may be appealed to a U.S. court of appeals.

13. 29 U.S.C. Sections 401 *et seq.*

SECTION 3 The Decision to Form or Select a Union

The key starting point for labor relations law is the decision by a company's employees to form a union, which is usually referred to in the law as their bargaining representative. Many workplaces have no union, and workers bargain individually with the employer. If the workers decide that they want the added power of collective union representation, they must follow certain steps to have a union certified. Usually, the employer will resist these efforts to unionize.

Preliminary Organizing

Suppose that a national union, such as the Communication Workers of America (CWA), wants to organize workers who produce semiconductor chips. The union would visit a manufacturing plant of a company—SemiCo in this example. If some SemiCo workers are interested in joining the union, they must begin organizing. An essential part of the process is to decide exactly which workers will be covered in the planned union. Will all manufacturing workers be covered or just those engaged in a single stage in the manufacturing process?

The first step in forming a union is to get the relevant workers to sign **authorization cards.** These cards usually state that the worker desires to have a certain union, such as the CWA, represent the workforce. If a majority of the workers sign authorization cards, the organizers can present the cards to the employer and ask for formal recognition of the union. The employer is not required to recognize the union at this point, but it may do so voluntarily on a showing of majority support. (Under legislation that was proposed in 2007, the employer would have been required to recognize the union as soon as a majority of the workers had signed authorization cards—without holding an election, as described next.)[14]

If the employer refuses to voluntarily recognize the union after a majority of the workers sign authorization cards—or if fewer than 50 percent of the workers sign authorization cards—the union organizers can

14. The U.S. House of Representatives passed the Employee Free Choice Act, also known as the Card Check Bill (H.R. 800), in March 2007, but the bill (S 1041) was defeated in the U.S. Senate in June 2007. Because this pro-labor measure enjoyed wide support, similar legislation is likely to be proposed in the future.

EXHIBIT 22-3 • Unfair Labor Practice Complaint Form

FORM EXEMPT UNDER 44 U.S.C 3512

FORM NLRB-501
(9-07)

UNITED STATES OF AMERICA
NATIONAL LABOR RELATIONS BOARD
CHARGE AGAINST EMPLOYER

DO NOT WRITE IN THIS SPACE	
Case	Date Filed / /

INSTRUCTIONS:
File an original together with four copies and a copy for each additional charged party named in item 1 with NLRB Regional Director for the region in which the alleged unfair labor practice occurred or is occurring.

1. EMPLOYER AGAINST WHOM CHARGE IS BROUGHT

a. Name of Employer		b. Number of workers employed
c. Address *(Street, city, state, and ZIP code)*	d. Employer Representative	e. Telephone No. ( ) - Fax No. ( ) -
f. Type of Establishment *(factory, mine, wholesaler, etc.)*	g. Identify principal product or service	

h. The above-named employer has engaged in and is engaging in unfair labor practices within the meaning of section 8(a), subsections (1) and *(list subsections)* ______________________ of the National Labor Relations Act, and these unfair labor practices are practices affecting commerce within the meaning of the Act, or these unfair labor practices are unfair practices affecting commerce within the meaning of the Act and the Postal Reorganization Act.

2. Basis of the Charge *(set forth a clear and concise statement of the facts constituting the alleged unfair labor practices)*

3. Full name of party filing charge *(if labor organization, give full name, including local name and number)*

4a. Address *(Street and number, city, state, and ZIP code)*	4b. Telephone No. ( ) - Fax No. ( ) -

5. Full name of national or international labor organization of which it is an affiliate or constituent unit *(to be filled in when charge is filed by a labor organization)*

6. DECLARATION
I declare that I have read the above charge and that the statements are true to the best of my knowledge and belief.

By ______________________
(signature of representative or person making charge)

____
(Print/type name and title or office, if any)

(fax) ( ) - ______________

Address ______________________ ( ) - ______________ / /
(Telephone No.) *(date)*

WILLFUL FALSE STATEMENTS ON THIS CHARGE CAN BE PUNISHED BY FINE AND IMPRISONMENT (U.S. CODE, TITLE 18, SECTION 1001)

PRIVACY ACT STATEMENT

Solicitation of the information on this form is authorized by the National Labor Relations Act (NLRA), 29 U.S.C. § 151 *et seq.* The principal use of the information is to assist the National Labor Relations Board (NLRB) in processing unfair labor practice and related proceedings or litigation. The routine uses for the imformation are fully set forth in the Federal Register, 71 Fed. Reg. 74942-43 (Dec. 13, 2006). The NLRB will further explain these uses upon request. Disclosure of this information to the NLRB is voluntary; however, failure to supply the information will cause the NLRB to decline to invoke its processes.

petition the NLRB for an election. For an election to be held, the NLRB requires that unionizers demonstrate that at least 30 percent of the workers to be represented support a union or an election on unionization. The NLRB supervises the election and ensures that the voting is secret and that the voters are eligible. If the proposed union receives majority support (more than 50 percent of the votes) in a fair election, the NLRB certifies the union as the bargaining representative for the employees.

Appropriate Bargaining Unit

The NLRB considers the employees' petition as a basis for calling an election. In addition to a sufficient showing of interest in unionization, the proposed union must represent an **appropriate bargaining unit.**

Not every group of workers can form together into a single union. One key requirement of an appropriate bargaining unit is a *mutuality of interest* among all the workers to be represented. Groups of workers with significantly conflicting interests may not be represented in a single union.

Job Similarity One factor in determining the mutuality of interest is the *similarity of the jobs* of all the workers to be unionized. The NLRB considers factors such as similar levels of skill and qualifications, similar levels of wages and benefits, and similar working conditions. If represented workers have vastly different working conditions, they are unlikely to have the mutuality of interest necessary to bargain as a single unit with their employer.

One issue of job similarity has involved companies that employ both general industrial workers and craft workers (those with specialized skills, such as electricians). On many occasions, the NLRB has found that industrial and craft workers should be represented by different unions, although this is not an absolute rule.

Work-Site Proximity A second factor in determining the appropriate bargaining unit is *geographical.* If workers at only a single manufacturing plant are to be unionized, the geographical factor is not a problem. Even if the workers desire to join a national union, such as the CWA, they can join together in a single "local" division of that union. Geographical disparity may become a problem if a union is attempting to join workers at many different manufacturing sites together into a single union.

Nonmanagement Employees A third factor to be considered is the rule against unionization of *management* employees. The labor laws differentiate between labor and management and preclude members of management from being part of a union. There is no clear-cut definition of *management,* but supervisors are considered management and may not be included in worker unions. A supervisor is an individual who has the discretionary authority, as a representative of the employer, to make decisions such as hiring, suspending, promoting, firing, or disciplining other workers. Professional employees, including legal and medical personnel, may be considered labor rather than management.

Moving toward Certification

A union, then, becomes certified through a procedure that begins with petitioning the NLRB. The proposed union must present authorization cards or other evidence showing an employee interest level of at least 30 percent. The organization must also show that the proposed union represents an appropriate bargaining unit. If the workers are under the NLRA's jurisdiction and if no other union has been certified within the past twelve months for these workers, the NLRB will schedule an election.

Union Election

Labor law provides for an election to determine whether employees choose to be represented by a union and, if so, which union. The NLRB supervises this election, ensuring secret voting and voter eligibility. The election is usually held about a month after the NLRB orders the vote (although it may be much longer, if management disputes the composition of an appropriate bargaining unit). If the election is a fair one, and if the proposed union receives majority support, the board certifies the union as the bargaining representative. Otherwise, the board will not certify the union.

Sometimes, a plant with an existing union may attempt to *decertify* (de-unionize) the union. Although this action may be encouraged by management, it must be conducted by the employees. This action also requires a petition to the NLRB, with a showing of 30 percent employee support and no certification within the past year. The NLRB may grant this petition and call for a decertification election.

Union Election Campaigns

Union organizers may campaign among workers to solicit votes for unionization. Considerable litigation has arisen over the rights of workers and outside union supporters to conduct such campaigns.

The Employer's Right to Limit Campaign Activities The employer retains great control over any activities, including unionization campaigns, that take place on company property and company time. Employers may lawfully use this authority to limit the campaign activities of union supporters. For example, management may prohibit all solicitations and distribution of pamphlets on company property as long as it has a legitimate business reason for doing so (such as to ensure safety or to prevent interference with business). The employer may also reasonably limit the places where solicitation occurs (for example, limit it to the lunchroom), limit the times during which solicitation can take place, and prohibit all outsiders from access to the workplace. All these actions are lawful.

For example, a union is seeking to organize clerks at a department store owned by Amanti Enterprises. Amanti can prohibit all union solicitation in areas of the store open to the public because the unionizing activities could interfere with the store's business. It can also restrict union-related activities to coffee breaks and lunch hours. Amanti cannot, however, allow solicitation for charitable causes during work hours or in the public part of the store if it prohibits union-related solicitation.

Restrictions on Management There are some legal restrictions on management regulation of union solicitation. The key restriction is the *nondiscrimination* rule. An employer may prohibit all solicitation during work time or in certain places but may not selectively prohibit union solicitation during work time. If the employer permits political candidates to campaign on the employer's premises, for example, it also must permit union solicitation.

Workers' Rights and Obligations Workers have a right to some reasonable opportunity to campaign. For example, the United States Supreme Court held that employees have a right to distribute a pro-union newsletter in nonworking areas on the employer's property during nonworking time. In this case, management had the burden to show some material harm from this action and could not do so.[15] Like an employer, a union and its supporters may not engage in unfair labor practices during a union election campaign.[16]

Management Election Campaign

Management may also campaign among its workers against the union (or for decertification of an existing union). Campaign tactics, however, are carefully monitored and regulated by the NLRB. Otherwise, the economic power of management might allow coercion of the workers.

Management still has many advantages in the campaign. For example, management is allowed to call all workers together during work time and make a speech against unionization. Management need not give the union supporters an equal opportunity for rebuttal. The NLRB does restrict what management may say in such a speech, however.

No Threats In campaigning against the union, the employer may not make threats of reprisals if employees vote to unionize. A supervisor may not state, "If the union wins, you'll all be fired." This would be a threat. Employers must be very careful on this issue. Suppose an employer says, "Our competitor's plant in town became unionized, and half the workers lost their jobs." The NLRB might consider this to be a veiled threat and therefore unfair.

"Laboratory Conditions" Obviously, union election campaigns are not like national political campaigns, when a political party can make almost any claim. The NLRB tries to maintain "laboratory conditions" for a fair election that is unaffected by pressure. In establishing such conditions, the board considers the totality of circumstances in the campaign. The NLRB is especially strict about promises (or threats) made by the employer at the last minute, immediately before the election, because the union lacks an opportunity to respond effectively to these last-minute statements.

There is even a specific rule that prohibits an employer from making any election speech on company time, to massed assemblies of workers, within

15. *Eastex, Inc. v. NLRB,* 437 U.S. 556, 98 S.Ct. 2505, 57 L.Ed.2d 428 (1978).

16. See, for example, *Associated Rubber Co. v. NLRB,* 296 F.3d 1055 (11th Cir. 2002).

twenty-four hours of the time for voting. Such last-minute speeches are permitted only if employees attend voluntarily and on their own time.

The employer is also prohibited from taking actions that might intimidate its workers. Employers may not undertake certain types of surveillance of workers or even create the impression of observing workers to identify union sympathizers. Management also is limited in its ability to question individual workers about their positions on unionization.

In the following case, the question was whether management officials' brief interruptions of unionizing activities constituted illegal surveillance.

EXTENDED CASE 22.2 Local Joint Executive Board of Las Vegas; Culinary Workers Union Local #226; and Bartenders Union Local 165, AFL-CIO v. NLRB

United States Court of Appeals, Ninth Circuit, 2008. 515 F.3d 942.

***CALLAHAN,* Circuit Judge:**

Local Joint Executive Board of Las Vegas, the Culinary Workers Unions Local 226, and the Bartenders Unions, Local 165, AFL-CIO [American Federation of Labor and Congress of Industrial Organizations] ("the Unions"), petition this court for review of a decision by the National Labor Relations Board ("the Board") reversing the Administrative Law Judge's ("ALJ") conclusion that agents of Aladdin Gaming, LLC ("the Company"), engaged in illegal surveillance in violation of Section 8(a)(1) of the National Labor Relations Act ("NLRA" or "the Act"). We deny the Unions' petition for review.

The Company operates a hotel and casino in Las Vegas, Nevada. On May 30, 2003, the Unions began an open campaign to organize the housekeeping, food, and beverage departments. * * * The issue in this appeal is whether two incidents where human resources managers [Ms. Sapien and Ms. Briand] interrupted employees who were discussing union cards in an open dining room constitute unlawful surveillance under Section 8(a)(1) [of the National Labor Relations Act (NLRA)].

* * * *

Section 8(a)(1) of the NLRA states that "[i]t shall be an unfair labor practice for an employer (1) to interfere with, restrain, or coerce employees in the exercise of the rights guaranteed in section 157 of this title." The Board has interpreted Section 8(a)(1) to make observation of union activity unlawful, "if the observation goes beyond casual and becomes unduly intrusive." * * * "The test for determining whether an employer engages in unlawful surveillance or whether it creates the impression of surveillance is an objective one and involves the determination of whether the employer's conduct, under the circumstances, was such as would tend to interfere with, restrain or coerce employees in the exercise of the rights guaranteed under Section 7 of the [National Labor Relations] Act."

The NLRB refined the objective test for surveillance by announcing that, "[i]ndicia of coerciveness include the duration of the observation, the employer's distance from its employees while observing them, and whether the employer engaged in other coercive behavior during its observation." We determine that this three-factor test is "rational and consistent" with the NLRA, and accordingly, we defer to the Board's interpretation of when surveillance becomes coercive and the application of the test to these facts. By announcing factors to consider when deciding when otherwise lawful observation becomes coercive, the Board exercised its "primary power of interpretation and application of the Act" granted by Congress.

In addition, the NLRB found that the views expressed by [human resources managers] Ms. Sapien and Ms. Briand were protected under Section 8(c) of the NLRA. "Section 8(c) of the Act specifically prohibits [the Board] from finding that an uncoercive speech, whenever delivered by the employer, constitutes an unfair labor practice." The Supreme Court has stated that "an employer's free speech right to communicate his views to his employees is firmly established and cannot be infringed by a union or the Board." "Thus, *an employer is free to communicate to his employees any of his general views about unionism or any of his specific views about a particular union, so long as the communications do not contain 'a threat of reprisal or force or promise of benefit.*'" Of course, "any assessment of the precise scope of employer expression . . . must be made

CASE 22.2 CONTINUED

in the context of its labor relations setting. Thus, an employer's rights cannot outweigh the equal rights of the employees to associate freely, as those rights are embodied in Section 7 and protected by [the NLRA]." [Emphasis added.]

There is no evidence that either Ms. Sapien or Ms. Briand used threats, force, or promises of benefits that would strip their speech of the protections of Section 8(c). Ms. Sapien attempted to give the buffet servers additional facts to consider before signing the union cards. Ms. Briand told Ms. Felix [an employee] that Ms. Bueno [another employee] should not sign a union card without fully understanding the consequences and provided her opinion that the union may not be able to deliver on its promises. Ms. Felix voluntarily translated Ms. Briand's comments for Ms. Bueno. After Ms. Felix explained the translation, Ms. Briand left.

The unions do not contend that the observations of organizing activity by Ms. Sapien or Ms. Briand were unlawful by themselves. The unions argue that the interruption of protected union activity, even to express opinions protected by Section 8(c), makes the otherwise lawful observation unlawful.

We defer to the Board's conclusion that Ms. Sapien's and Ms. Briand's brief, spontaneous interruptions were not coercive because it is "rational and consistent" with the Act. Applying its new three-factor test, the Board reasonably determined that where the duration of the observation was short and the employer's behavior was not out of the ordinary, verbally interrupting organizing activity does not necessarily violate [the NLRA]. The Board's creation of a three-factor test for unlawful surveillance is "reasonably defensible." * * * Therefore, the petition for review is DENIED.

QUESTIONS

1. Why did the administrative law judge originally rule that the two brief verbal interventions by the company's human resources managers were in violation of the National Labor Relations Act?
2. Do you think the result in this case would have been different if there had been two dozen similar incidents? If so, how?

NLRB Options If the employer issues threats or engages in other unfair labor practices and then wins the election, the NLRB may invalidate the results. The NLRB may certify the union, even though it lost the election, and direct the employer to recognize the union as the employees' exclusive bargaining representative. Or the NLRB may ask a court to order a new election.

Section 5 Collective Bargaining

If a fair election is held and the union wins, the NLRB will certify the union as the *exclusive bargaining representative* of the workers. Unions may provide a variety of services to their members, but the central legal right of a union is to serve as the sole representative of the group of workers in bargaining with the employer over the workers' rights.

The concept of bargaining is at the heart of the federal labor laws. When a union is officially recognized, it may make a demand to bargain with the employer. The union then sits at the table opposite the representatives of management to negotiate contracts for its workers. The terms of employment that result from the negotiations apply to all workers in the bargaining unit, even those who do not choose to belong to the union. This process is known as **collective bargaining.** Such bargaining is like most other business negotiations, and each side uses its economic power to pressure or persuade the other side to grant concessions.

Bargaining does not mean that either side must give in on demands or even that the sides must always compromise. It does mean that a demand must be taken seriously and considered as part of a package to be negotiated. Most important, both sides must bargain in "good faith."

Subjects of Bargaining

A common issue in collective bargaining concerns the subjects over which the parties can bargain. The law makes certain subjects mandatory for collective bargaining. These topics cannot be "taken off the table" unilaterally but must be discussed and bargained over.

Terms and Conditions of Employment The NLRA provides that employers may bargain with workers over wages, hours of work, and other terms and conditions of employment. These are broad terms that cover many employment issues. Suppose that a union wants a contract provision granting all workers four weeks of paid vacation. The company need not give in to this demand but must at least consider it and bargain over it.

Many other employment issues are also considered appropriate subjects for collective bargaining. These include safety rules, insurance coverage, pension and other employee benefit plans, procedures for employee discipline, procedures for employee grievances against the company, and even the price of food sold in the company cafeteria.

A few subjects are illegal in collective bargaining. Management need not bargain over a provision that would be illegal if included in a contract. Thus, if a union presents a demand for **featherbedding** (the hiring of unnecessary excess workers) or for an unlawful closed shop, management need not respond to these demands.

Closing or Relocating a Plant Management need not bargain with a union over the decision to close a particular facility. Similarly, management need not bargain over a decision to relocate a plant if the move involves a basic change in the nature of the employer's operation. Management may choose to bargain over such decisions, however, to obtain concessions on other bargaining subjects.

Management must bargain over the economic consequences of such decisions. Thus, issues such as **severance pay** (compensation for the termination of employment) in the event of a plant shutdown are appropriate for collective bargaining. Also, if a relocation does *not* involve a basic change in the nature of an operation, management must bargain over the decision unless it can show (1) that the work performed at the new location varies significantly from the work performed at the former plant; (2) that the work performed at the former plant is to be discontinued entirely and not moved to the new location; (3) that the move involves a change in the scope and direction of the enterprise; (4) that labor costs were not a factor in the decision; or (5) that even if labor costs were a factor, the union could not have offered concessions that would have changed the decision to relocate.

Privacy Issues Employee privacy rights were discussed in Chapter 20. Are these rights, and their potential or real violations, appropriate subjects for collective bargaining? The NLRB has determined that physical examinations, requirements for drug or alcohol testing, and polygraph (lie-detector) testing are mandatory subjects of bargaining. The question in the following case was whether the use of hidden surveillance cameras in the workplace could also be bargained over.

CASE 22.3 National Steel Corp. v. NLRB

United States Court of Appeals, Seventh Circuit, 2003. 324 F.3d 928.
laws.lp.findlaw.com/7th/952521.html[a]

• **Background and Facts** National Steel Corporation operates a plant in Granite City, Illinois, where it employs approximately three thousand employees, who are represented by ten different unions and covered by seven different collective bargaining agreements. National Steel uses more than one hundred video cameras in plain view to monitor areas of the plant and periodically employs hidden cameras to investigate suspected misconduct. In February 1999, National Steel installed a hidden camera to discover who was using a manager's office when the manager was not at work. The camera revealed a union member using the office to make long-distance phone calls. When National Steel discharged the employee, the union asked the company about other hidden cameras and indicated that it wanted to bargain over their use. National Steel refused to supply the information. The union filed a charge with the NLRB, which ordered National Steel to provide the information and bargain over the use of the cameras. National Steel appealed to the U.S. Court of Appeals for the Seventh Circuit.

IN THE LANGUAGE OF THE COURT
WILLIAMS, **Circuit Judge.**

* * * *

The [National Labor Relations] Board determined * * * that the use of hidden surveillance cameras is a mandatory subject of collective bargaining because it found the instal-

a. This is a page within the Web site maintained by Findlaw.

CASE 22.3 CONTINUED

lation and use of such cameras "analogous to physical examinations, drug/alcohol testing requirements, and polygraph testing, all of which the Board has found to be mandatory subjects of bargaining." It found that hidden cameras are focused primarily on the "working environment" that employees experience on a daily basis and are used to expose misconduct or violations of the law by employees or others. The Board held that such changes in an employer's methods have "serious implications for its employees' job security." The Board found that the use of such devices "is not entrepreneurial in character [and] is not fundamental to the basic direction of the enterprise." We find the Board's legal conclusion * * * objectively reasonable and wholly supported.

* * * According to National Steel, requiring it to bargain over hidden surveillance cameras, especially as to their locations precludes an employer from meaningfully using such devices because bargaining itself will compromise the secrecy that is required for them to be effective.

* * * The Board acknowledged an employer's need for secrecy if hidden surveillance cameras are to serve a purpose. The Board's order to National Steel preserves those managerial interests while also honoring the union's collective bargaining rights. It only requires National Steel to negotiate with the unions over the company's installation and use of hidden surveillance cameras and * * * does not dictate how the legitimate interests of the parties are to be accommodated in the process. The Board's order does not mandate an outcome of negotiations, nor does it make any suggestion that National Steel must yield any prerogatives, other than yielding the right to proceed exclusive of consultation with the union. * * * *Here, the Board's order is consistent with the [National Labor Relations] Act's requirement that parties resolve their differences through good faith bargaining;* it simply directs National Steel to initiate an accommodation process, and to provide assertedly confidential information in accord with whatever accommodation the parties agree upon (such as a confidentiality agreement * * *). The Board's order does not eliminate National Steel's management right to use hidden cameras and it seeks to preserve the level of confidentiality necessary to allow for the continued effective use of such devices. [Emphasis added.]

• **Decision and Remedy** *The U.S. Court of Appeals for the Seventh Circuit upheld the NLRB's order to National Steel to bargain over the use of hidden surveillance cameras in the workplace. The court emphasized that this order did not prohibit their use, but only made that use a subject of collective bargaining.*

• **The Ethical Dimension** *Can an employer's interests ever justify the use of hidden video cameras in the workplace? Explain your answer.*

• **The Global Dimension** *Suppose that a company used hidden video cameras only in the areas of a plant that employed foreign-born workers (immigrants). Would this violate the antidiscrimination provisions of the Immigration Reform and Control Act (IRCA) discussed earlier in this chapter? Why or why not?*

Good Faith Bargaining

Parties engaged in collective bargaining often claim that the other side is not bargaining in good faith, as required by labor law. Although good faith is a matter of subjective intent, a party's actions are used to evaluate the finding of good or bad faith in bargaining.

Obviously, the employer must be willing to meet with union representatives. Excessive delaying tactics may be proof of bad faith, as is insistence on obviously unreasonable contract terms. Suppose that a company makes a single overall contract offer on a take-it-or-leave-it basis and refuses to consider modifications of individual terms. This also is considered bad faith in bargaining.

While bargaining is going on, management may not make unilateral changes in important working conditions, such as wages or hours of employment. These changes must be bargained over. Once bargaining reaches an impasse, management may make such unilateral changes. The law also includes an exception permitting unilateral changes in cases of business necessity.

A series of decisions have found other actions to constitute bad faith in bargaining, including the following:

1. Engaging in a campaign among workers to undermine the union.
2. Constantly shifting positions on disputed contract terms.

3. Sending bargainers who lack authority to commit the company to a contract.

If an employer (or a union) refuses to bargain in good faith without justification, it has committed an unfair labor practice, and the other party may petition the NLRB for an order requiring good faith bargaining. Except in extreme situations, the NLRB does not have authority to require a party to accede to any specific contract terms. The NLRB may require a party to reimburse the other side for its litigation expenses.

Strikes and Lockouts

The law does not require parties to reach a contract agreement in collective bargaining. Even when parties have bargained in good faith, they may be unable to reach a final agreement. When extensive collective bargaining has been conducted and the parties still cannot agree, an impasse has been reached.

When bargaining has reached an impasse, the union may call a strike against the employer to pressure it into making concessions. A **strike** occurs when the unionized workers leave their jobs and refuse to work. The workers also typically picket the plant, standing outside the facility with signs that complain of management's unfairness. A strike is an extreme action. Striking workers lose their right to be paid, and management loses production and may lose customers, if it cannot fill their orders. Labor law regulates the circumstances and conduct of strikes.

A union may strike when the employer has engaged in unfair labor practices, but most strikes are "economic strikes," which are initiated because the union wants a better contract. For example, in 2007, the United Auto Workers engaged in an economic strike when General Motors (GM) proposed that its workers accept wage cuts and pay much higher monthly premiums for health care. Approximately 73,000 GM employees walked off the job, shutting down several plants in the United States and Canada. Although the strike was settled quickly, it nevertheless resulted in lost production and profits for the company, its suppliers, and its contractors, as well as lost wages for the strikers.

The Right to Strike

The right to strike is guaranteed by the NLRA, within limits, and strike activities, such as picketing, are protected by the free speech guarantee of the First Amendment to the U.S. Constitution. Nonworkers have a right to participate in picketing an employer. The NLRA also gives workers the right to refuse to cross a picket line of fellow workers who are engaged in a lawful strike. Employers are permitted to hire replacement workers to substitute for the striking workers.

Illegal Strikes

An otherwise lawful strike may become illegal because of the conduct of the strikers. Violent strikes (including the threat of violence) are illegal. The use of violence against management employees or substitute workers is illegal. Certain forms of "massed picketing" are also illegal. If the strikers form a barrier and deny management or other nonunion workers access to the plant, the strike is illegal. Similarly, "sit-down" strikes, in which employees simply stay in the plant without working, are illegal.

Secondary Boycotts A strike directed against someone other than the strikers' employer, such as the companies that sell materials to the employer, is a **secondary boycott.** Suppose that the unionized workers of SemiCo (our hypothetical semiconductor company) go out on strike. To increase their economic leverage, the workers picket the leading suppliers and customers of SemiCo in an attempt to hurt the company's business. SemiCo is considered the primary employer, and its suppliers and customers are considered secondary employers. Picketing of the suppliers or customers is a secondary boycott, which was made illegal by the Taft-Hartley Act.

Common Situs Picketing. A controversy may arise in a strike when both the primary employer and a secondary employer occupy the same job site. In this situation, it may be difficult to distinguish between lawful picketing of the primary employer and an unlawful strike against a secondary employer. The law permits a union to picket a site occupied by both primary and secondary employers, an act called **common situs picketing.** If evidence indicates that the strike is directed against the secondary employer, however, it may become illegal. For example, if a union sends a threatening letter to the secondary employer about the strike, that fact may show that the picketing includes an illegal secondary boycott.

Hot-Cargo Agreements. When employers voluntarily agree with unions not to handle, use, or deal in nonunion-produced goods of other employers, it is known as a **hot-cargo agreement.** This particular type of secondary boycott was *not* made illegal by the Taft-Hartley Act, because that act only prevented unions from inducing *employees* to strike or otherwise act to force employers not to handle these goods. The Landrum-Griffin Act addressed this problem:

> It shall be [an] unfair labor practice for any labor organization and any employer to enter into any contract or any agreement . . . whereby such employer . . . agrees to refrain from handling, using, selling, transporting or otherwise dealing in any of the products of any other employer, or to cease doing business with any other person.

Hot-cargo agreements are therefore illegal. Parties injured by an illegal hot-cargo agreement or other secondary boycott may sue the union for damages.

A union may legally urge consumer boycotts of the primary employer, even at the site of a secondary employer. Suppose that a union is on strike against SemiCo, which manufactures semiconductors that are bought by Intellect, Inc., a distributor of electronic components. Intellect sells SemiCo's semiconductors to computer manufacturers. The striking workers can urge the manufacturers not to buy SemiCo's products. The workers cannot urge a total boycott of Intellect, as that would constitute a secondary boycott.

Wildcat Strikes A **wildcat strike** occurs when a minority group of workers, perhaps dissatisfied with a union's representation, calls its own strike. The union is the exclusive bargaining representative of a group of workers, and only the union can call a strike. A wildcat strike, unauthorized by the certified union, is illegal.

Strikes That Threaten National Health or Safety The law also places some restrictions on strikes that threaten national health or safety. The law, however, does not prohibit such strikes, nor does it require the settlement of labor disputes that threaten the national welfare. The Taft-Hartley Act simply provides time to encourage the settlement of these disputes, called the "cooling-off period."

One of the most controversial aspects of the Taft-Hartley Act was the establishment of this **eighty-day cooling-off period**—a provision allowing federal courts to issue injunctions against strikes that would create a national emergency. The president of the United States can obtain a court injunction that will last for eighty days, and presidents have occasionally used this provision. During these eighty days, the president and other government officials can work with the employer and the union to produce a settlement and avoid a strike that may cause a national emergency.

Strikes That Contravene No-Strike Clauses A strike may also be illegal if it contravenes a *no-strike clause.* The previous collective bargaining agreement between a union and an employer may have contained a clause in which the union agreed not to strike (a **no-strike clause**). The law permits the employer to enforce this no-strike clause and obtain an injunction against the strike in some circumstances.

Replacement Workers

Suppose that SemiCo's workers go out on strike. SemiCo is not required to shut down its operations but may find substitute workers to replace the strikers, if possible. These substitute workers are often called "scabs" by union supporters. An employer may even give the replacement workers permanent positions with the company.

Even the National Football League (NFL), when struck by the players in 1987, found replacements to play for the NFL teams. Although some scoffed at the ability of the replacement players, the tactic was largely successful for management, as the strike was called off after only three weeks. An employer can even use an employment agency to recruit replacement workers.[17]

The Rights of Strikers after a Strike Ends

An important issue concerns the rights of strikers after a strike ends. In a typical economic strike, the employer has a right to hire permanent replacements during the strike and need not terminate the replacement workers when the economic strikers seek to return to work. In other words, striking workers are not guaranteed the right to return to their jobs after the strike if satisfactory replacement workers have been found.

If the employer has not hired replacement workers to fill the strikers' positions, however, then the employer must rehire the economic strikers to fill any vacancies. Employers may not discriminate against former economic strikers, and those who are rehired retain their seniority rights. Different rules apply when a union strikes because the employer has engaged in unfair

17. *Professional Staff Nurses Association v. Dimensions Health Corp.,* 110 Md.App. 270, 677 A.2d 87 (1996).

labor practices. In this situation, the employer may still hire replacements but must give the strikers back their jobs once the strike is over.

Lockouts

Lockouts are the employer's counterpart to the worker's right to strike. A **lockout** occurs when the employer shuts down to prevent employees from working. Lockouts are usually used when the employer believes that a strike is imminent.

Lockouts may be a legal employer response. In the leading Supreme Court case on this issue, a union and an employer had reached a stalemate in collective bargaining. The employer feared that the union would delay a strike until the busy season and thereby cause the employer to suffer more greatly from the strike. The employer called a lockout before the busy season to deny the union this leverage, and the Supreme Court held that this action was legal.[18]

Some lockouts are illegal, however. An employer may not use its lockout weapon as a tool to break the union and pressure employees into decertification. Consequently, an employer must show some economic justification for instituting a lockout.

Unfair Labor Practices

The preceding sections have discussed unfair labor practices involved in the significant acts of union elections, collective bargaining, and strikes. Many unfair labor practices may occur within the normal working relationship as well. The most important of these practices are discussed in the following sections. Exhibit 22–4 lists the basic unfair labor practices.

Employer's Refusal to Recognize the Union and to Negotiate

As noted above, once a union has been certified as the exclusive representative of a bargaining unit, an employer must recognize and bargain in good faith with the union over issues affecting all employees who are within the bargaining unit. Failure to do so is an unfair labor practice. Because the National Labor Relations Act embraces a policy of majority rule, certification of the union as the bargaining unit's representative binds *all* of the employees in that bargaining unit. Thus, the union must fairly represent all the members of the bargaining unit.

Certification does not mean that a union will continue indefinitely as the exclusive representative of the bargaining unit. If the union loses the majority support of those it represents, an employer is not obligated to continue recognition of, or negotiation with, the union. As a practical matter, a newly elected representative needs time to establish itself among the workers and to begin to formulate and implement its programs. Therefore, as a matter of labor policy, a union is immune from attack by employers and from repudiation by the employees for a period of one year after certification. During this period, it is *presumed* that the union enjoys majority support among the employees; the employer cannot refuse to deal with the union as the employees' exclusive representative, even if the employees prefer not to be represented by that union.

18. *American Ship Building Co. v. NLRB,* 380 U.S. 300, 85 S.Ct. 955, 13 L.Ed.2d 855 (1965).

EXHIBIT 22–4 • Basic Unfair Labor Practices

Employers *It is unfair to . . .*	**Unions** *It is unfair to . . .*
1. Refuse to recognize a union and refuse to bargain in good faith. **2.** Interfere with, restrain, or coerce employees in their efforts to form a union and bargain collectively. **3.** Dominate a union. **4.** Discriminate against union workers. **5.** Punish employees for engaging in concerted activity.	**1.** Refuse to bargain in good faith. **2.** Picket to coerce unionization without the support of a majority of the employees. **3.** Demand the hiring of unnecessary excess workers. **4.** Discriminate against nonunion workers. **5.** Agree to participate in a secondary boycott. **6.** Engage in an illegal strike. **7.** Charge excessive membership fees.

Beyond the one-year period, the presumption of majority support continues, but it is *rebuttable*. An employer may rebut (attempt to refute) the presumption with objective evidence that a majority of employees do not wish to be represented by the union. If the evidence is sufficient to support a *good faith belief* that the union no longer enjoys majority support among the employees, the employer may refuse to continue to recognize and negotiate with the union.[19]

Employer's Interference in Union Activities

The NLRA declares it to be an unfair labor practice for an employer to interfere with, restrain, or coerce employees in the exercise of their rights to form a union and bargain collectively. Unlawful employer interference may take a variety of forms.

Courts have found it an unfair labor practice for an employer to make threats that may interfere with an employee's decision to join a union. Even asking employees about their views on the union may be considered coercive. Employees responding to such questioning must be able to remain anonymous and must receive assurances against employer reprisals. Employers also may not prohibit certain forms of union activity in the workplace. If an employee has a grievance with the company, the employer cannot prevent the union's participation in support of the employee, for example.

If an employer has unlawfully interfered with the operation of a union, the NLRB or a reviewing court may issue a cease-and-desist order halting the practice. The company typically is required to post the order on a bulletin board and renounce its past unlawful conduct.

Employer's Domination of a Union

In the early days of unionization, employers fought back by forming employer-sponsored unions to represent employees. These "company unions" were seldom more than the puppets of management. The NLRA outlawed company unions and any other form of employer domination of workers' unions.

Under the law against employer domination, an employer can have no say in which employees belong to the union or which employees serve as union officers. Nor may supervisors or other management personnel participate in union meetings.

Company actions that support a union may be considered improper potential domination. For this reason, a company cannot give union workers pay for time spent on union activities, because this is considered undue support for the union. The company may not provide financial aid to a union and may not solicit workers to join a union.

Employer's Discrimination against Union Employees

The NLRA prohibits employers from discriminating against workers because they are union officers or are otherwise associated with a union. When workers must be laid off, the company cannot consider union participation as a criterion for deciding whom to fire.

The provisions prohibiting discrimination also apply to hiring decisions. Suppose that certain employees of SemiCo are represented by a union, but the company is attempting to weaken the union's strength. The company is prohibited from requiring potential new hires to guarantee that they will not join the union.

Discriminatory punishment of union members or officers can be difficult to prove. The company will claim to have good reasons for its action. The NLRB has specified a series of factors to be considered in determining whether an action had an unlawful, discriminatory motivation. These include giving inconsistent reasons for the action, applying rules inconsistently and more strictly against union members, failing to give an expected warning prior to discharge or other discipline, and acting contrary to worker seniority.

The decision to close a facility cannot be made with a discriminatory motive. If a company has several facilities and only one is unionized, the company cannot shut down the union plant simply because of the union. The company could shut down the union plant if it were demonstrably less efficient than the other facilities, however.

Union's Unfair Labor Practices

Certain union activities are declared to be unfair labor practices by the Taft-Hartley Act. Secondary boycotts, discussed above, are one such union unfair labor practice.

Coercion Another significant union unfair labor practice is coercion or restraint on an employee's

19. An employer cannot agree to a collective bargaining agreement and later refuse to abide by it, however, on the ground of a good faith belief that the union did not have majority support when the agreement was negotiated. See *Auciello Iron Works, Inc. v. NLRB*, 517 U.S. 781, 116 S.Ct. 1754, 135 L.Ed.2d 64 (1996).

decision to participate in or refrain from participating in union activities. Obviously, it is unlawful for a union to threaten an employee or a family with violence for failure to join the union. The law's prohibition includes economic coercion as well. Suppose that a union official declares, "We have a lot of power here; you had better join the union, or you may lose your job." This threat is an unfair labor practice.

The NLRA provides unions with the authority to regulate their own internal affairs, which includes disciplining union members. This discipline cannot be used in an improperly coercive fashion, however. For example, Stan Kowalski is a union member who feels that the union is no longer providing proper representation for employees at his workplace. He starts a campaign to decertify the union. The union may expel Kowalski from membership, but it may not fine or otherwise discipline the worker.

Discrimination Another significant union unfair labor practice is discrimination. A union may not discriminate against workers because they refuse to join. This provision also prohibits a union from using its influence to cause an employer to discriminate against workers who refuse to join the union. A union cannot force an employer to deny promotions to workers who fail to join the union.

Other Unfair Practices Other union unfair labor practices include featherbedding (discussed earlier in this chapter), participation in picketing to coerce unionization without majority employee support, and refusal to engage in good faith bargaining with employer representatives.

Unions are allowed to bargain for certain "union security clauses" in contracts. Although closed shops are illegal, a union can bargain for a provision that requires workers to contribute to the union within thirty days after they are hired. This is typically called an *agency shop,* or *union shop, clause.*

The union shop clause can compel workers to begin paying dues to the certified union but cannot require the worker to "join" the union. Dues payment can be required to prevent workers from taking the benefits of union bargaining without contributing to the union's efforts. The clause cannot require workers to contribute their efforts to the union, however, or to go out on strike.

Even a requirement of dues payment has its limits. Excessive initiation fees or dues may be illegal. Unions often use their revenues to contribute to causes or to lobby politicians. A nonunion employee subject to a union shop clause who must pay dues cannot be required to contribute to this sort of union expenditure.

Rights of Nonunion Employees

Most labor law involves the formation of unions and associated rights. Even nonunion employees have some similar rights, however. Most workers do not belong to unions, so this issue is significant. The NLRA protects concerted employee action, for example, and does not limit its protection to certified unions.

Concerted Activity

Data from the NLRB indicate that growing numbers of nonunion employees are challenging employer barriers to their **concerted action.** Protected concerted action is that taken by employees for their mutual benefit regarding wages, hours, or terms and conditions of employment.

Even an action by a *single* employee may be protected concerted activity, if that action is taken for the benefit of other employees and if the employee has at least discussed the action with other approving workers. If only a single worker engages in a protest or walkout, the employer will not be liable for an unfair labor practice if it fires the worker unless the employer is aware that this protest or walkout is concerted activity taken with the assent of other workers.

In the following case, an employer discharged an employee for "complaining." The employee claimed that this "complaining" constituted concerted activity on behalf of herself and other employees.

CASE **22.4** **NLRB v. Hotel Employees and Restaurant Employees International Union Local 26, AFL-CIO**

United States Court of Appeals, First Circuit, 2006. 446 F.3d 200.
www.ca1.uscourts.gov[a]

a. In the right-hand column, click on "Opinions." When that page opens, in the "Opinion Number begins with" box, type "05-1924" and click on "Submit Search." From the result, in the "Click for Opinion" column, click on the link to read the case. The U.S. Court of Appeals for the First Circuit maintains this Web site.

CASE 22.4 CONTINUED

• Background and Facts The Hotel Employees and Restaurant Employees International Union, Local 26, AFL-CIO (the Union), represents 5,800 hotel workers in Boston, Massachusetts. In 1997, the Union hired Janice Loux as its president. In September 1998, Loux hired Emma Johnson as a researcher. In June 1999, the Logan Airport Ramada Inn near Boston announced that it would be closing and all employees would be discharged. Hilton Hotels Corporation would reopen the hotel, but the discharged employees would not be given a right of reemployment. Loux scheduled a leafleting campaign against Hilton. Each Union employee was to leaflet in a two-hour shift at times varying from day to day, in addition to other job duties. During the campaign, Johnson repeatedly asked Loux to allow employees to switch shifts. Loux refused. On August 6, the Union reached an agreement with Hilton and the leafleting stopped. Less than two weeks later, Loux fired Johnson for "complaining about the Hilton campaign." Johnson filed an unfair labor practice charge with the National Labor Relations Board (NLRB) against the Union. The NLRB concluded that the Union discharged Johnson "because of her protected concerted activity." The Union petitioned the U.S. Court of Appeals for the First Circuit for review.

IN THE LANGUAGE OF THE COURT
***BOWMAN,* Senior Circuit Judge.**

* * * *

* * * The Union argues that Johnson did not engage in concerted activity, but rather engaged in self-motivated complaining about her schedule.

To qualify as concerted activity, conduct need not take place in a union setting and it is not necessary that a collective bargaining agreement be in effect. It is sufficient that the complaining employee intends or contemplates, as an end result, group activity which will also benefit some other employees. We recognize that even a conversation can constitute concerted activity, but to qualify as such, it must appear at the very least that it was engaged in with the object of initiating or inducing or preparing for group action or that it had some relation to group action in the interest of the employees. [Emphasis added.]

We conclude * * * that Johnson engaged in concerted activity. * * * Johnson polled co-employees about their desire to switch shifts and/or work only one day per weekend, she informed co-employees that she would present her ideas to Loux at a staff meeting, and she later presented her ideas that would benefit all employees to Loux. Johnson also gave Loux alternative weekend schedules that either would have granted employees one weekend day off per week or at least ensured that the employees did not work in the middle of both weekend days. Some employees supported Johnson's ideas. * * * *Johnson's conduct related to group action that would have benefited the Union's employees such that it constituted concerted activity.* [Emphasis added.]

* * * *

[Next] we ask whether * * * Loux discharged Johnson because she engaged in protected concerted activity. * * * After Loux announced that the leafletting campaign could last up to four months, that employees could not take any vacations until it was concluded, and that employees would work seven days per week during the campaign, Johnson began to discuss schedule changes openly with co-employees. Johnson then advocated to Loux on behalf of the employees for the ability to switch shifts or be allowed to work four-hour shifts on one weekend day so that they could enjoy one day off per week.

* * * Loux knew about this activity [and] * * * Loux's motivation for discharging Johnson was rooted in Johnson's protesting the leafletting schedule. For instance, * * * Johnson's [job performance was rated in May 1999] as very good * * * . Soon after, in July 1999, Loux initiated the leafletting campaign against the Hilton and Johnson began voicing complaints about the leafletting schedule. That is when Loux became extremely critical of Johnson's performance and attitude. * * * Johnson was discharged because she complained about the Hilton campaign. * * * Thus, we conclude * * * that *a motivating factor in the Union's discharge of Johnson was her protected concerted activity.* [Emphasis added.]

* * * *

The Union admits that Johnson's poor attitude during the leafletting activities was a reason for her discharge. * * * This criticism is inextricably related to the fact that Johnson made herself

CASE CONTINUES

CASE 22.4 CONTINUED

a pest in Loux's eyes by continually complaining about the * * * leafletting schedule. * * * Johnson may have been an irritant to Loux because she was challenging the schedule; but that irritating activity by Johnson is protected by * * * the NLRA.

• **Decision and Remedy** *The U.S. Court of Appeals for the First Circuit denied the Union's petition for review. The court affirmed the NLRB's conclusion that the Union was liable for discharging Johnson. "A consistent theme runs through the * * * testimony and supports the * * * finding that Johnson's protected concerted activity motivated Loux to discharge her."*

• **The Legal Environment Dimension** *Would Emma Johnson have been able to file a wrongful discharge claim (discussed in Chapter 21) against Hilton Hotels based on these facts? Discuss.*

• **The Ethical Dimension** *Should an employee's complaints be considered protected "concerted" activity? Is the holding of this case fair to the employer? Why or why not?*

Safety

A common circumstance for nonunion activity is concern over workplace safety. The Labor-Management Relations Act authorizes an employee to walk off the job if he or she has a good faith belief that the working conditions are abnormally dangerous. The employer cannot lawfully discharge the employee under these conditions.

Suppose that Knight Company operates a plant building mobile homes. A large ventilation fan at the plant blows dust and abrasive materials into the faces of workers. The workers have complained, but Knight Company has done nothing. The workers finally refuse to work until the fan is modified, and Knight fires them. The NLRB will find that the walkout is a protected activity and can command Knight to rehire the workers with back pay.

To be protected under federal labor law, a safety walkout must be *concerted* activity. If a single worker walks out over a safety complaint, other workers must be affected by the safety issue for the walkout to be protected under the LMRA.

Employee Committees

Personnel specialists note that worker problems are often attributable to a lack of communication between labor and management. In a nonunion workforce, a company may wish to create some institution to communicate with workers and act together with them to improve workplace conditions. This institution, generally called an **employee committee,** is composed of representatives from both management and labor. The committee meets periodically and has some authority to create rules. The committee gives employees a forum to voice their dissatisfaction with certain conditions and gives management a conduit to inform workers fully of policy decisions.

The creation of an employee committee may be entirely motivated by good intentions on the company's part and may serve the interests of workers as well as management. Nevertheless, employee committees are fraught with potential problems under federal labor laws, and management must be aware of these difficulties. The central problem with employee committees is that they may become the functional equivalent of unions dominated by management, in violation of the NLRA. Thus, these committees cannot perform union functions. For example, the employee representatives on an employee committee should not present a package of proposals on wages and terms of employment, because this is the role of a union negotiating committee.

REVIEWING Immigration and Labor Law

In April 2008, several employees of Javatech, Inc., a computer hardware developer with 250 employees, formed the Javatech Employees Union (JEU). In June, the National Labor Relations Board (NLRB) conducted an election that showed that a majority of Javatech employees

REVIEWING Immigration and Labor Law, Continued

supported the union. JEU began bargaining with management over wages and benefits. In January 2009, Javatech management offered JEU a 1 percent annual wage increase to all employees with no other changes in employment benefits. JEU countered by requesting a 3 percent wage increase and an employee health-insurance package. Javatech management responded that the 1 percent wage increase was the company's only offer. JEU petitioned the NLRB for an order requesting good faith bargaining. After meeting with an NLRB representative, Javatech management still refused to consider modifying its position. JEU leaders then became embroiled in a dispute about whether JEU should accept this offer or go on strike. New union leaders were elected in July 2009, and the employer refused to meet with the new JEU representatives, claiming that the union no longer had majority support from employees. In August 2009, a group of seven Javatech engineers began feeling ill while working with a new adhesive used in creating motherboards. The seven engineers discussed going on strike without union support. Before reaching agreement, one of the engineers, Rosa Molina, became dizzy while working with the adhesive and walked out of the workplace. Using the information presented in the chapter, answer the following questions.

1. How many of Javatech's 250 employees must have signed authorization cards to allow JEU to petition the NLRB for an election?
2. What must Javatech change in its collective bargaining negotiations to demonstrate that it is bargaining in good faith with JEU, as required by labor law?
3. Could the seven engineers legally call a strike? What would this be called?
4. Would Molina's safety walkout be protected under the Labor-Management Relations Act?

TERMS AND CONCEPTS

appropriate bargaining unit 558
authorization card 556
cease-and-desist order 555
closed shop 555
collective bargaining 561
common situs picketing 564
concerted action 568
eighty-day cooling-off period 565
employee committee 570
featherbedding 562
hot-cargo agreement 565
I-9 verification 550
I-551 Alien Registration Receipt 553

lockout 566
no-strike clause 565
right-to-work law 555
secondary boycott 564
severance pay 562
strike 564
union shop 555
wildcat strike 565

QUESTIONS AND CASE PROBLEMS

22-1. A group of employees at the Briarwood Furniture Co.'s manufacturing plant were interested in joining a union. A representative of the American Federation of Labor and Congress of Industrial Organizations (AFL-CIO) told the group that her union was prepared to represent the workers and suggested that the group begin organizing by obtaining authorization cards from their fellow employees. After obtaining 252 authorization cards from among Briarwood's 500 nonmanagement employees, the organizers requested that the company recognize the AFL-CIO as the official representative of the employees. The company refused. Has the company violated federal labor laws? What should the organizers do?

22–2. The Briarwood Furniture Co., discussed in the preceding problem, employs 400 unskilled workers and 100 skilled workers in its plant. The unskilled workers operate the industrial machinery used in processing Briarwood's line of standardized plastic office furniture. The skilled workers, who work in an entirely separate part of the plant, are experienced artisans who craft Briarwood's line of expensive wood furniture products. Do you see any problems with a single union's representing all the workers at the Briarwood plant? Explain. Would your answers to Problem 22–1 change if you knew that 51 of the authorization cards had been signed by the skilled workers, with the remainder signed by the unskilled workers?

22–3. QUESTION WITH SAMPLE ANSWER

Suppose that Consolidated Stores is undergoing a unionization campaign. Prior to the election, management says that the union is unnecessary to protect workers. Management also provides bonuses and wage increases to the workers during this period. The employees reject the union. Union organizers protest that the wage increases during the election campaign unfairly prejudiced the vote. Should these wage increases be regarded as an unfair labor practice? Discuss.

- **For a sample answer to Question 22–3, go to Appendix I at the end of this text.**

22–4. SimpCo was engaged in ongoing negotiations over a new labor contract with the union representing the company's employees. As the deadline for expiration of the old labor contract drew near, several employees who were involved in union activities were disciplined for being late to work. The union claimed that other employees had not been dealt with as harshly and that the company was discriminating on the basis of union activity. When the negotiations failed to prove fruitful and the old contract expired, the union called a strike. The company claimed that the action was an economic strike to press the union's demands for higher wages. The union contended that the action was an unfair labor practice strike because of the alleged discrimination. What importance does the distinction have for the striking workers and the company?

22–5. Secondary Boycotts. For many years, grapefruit was shipped to Japan from Fort Pierce and Port Canaveral, Florida. In 1990, Coastal Stevedoring Co. in Fort Pierce and Port Canaveral Stevedoring, Ltd., in Port Canaveral—nonunion firms—were engaged in a labor dispute with the International Longshoremen's Association (ILA). The ILA asked the National Council of Dockworkers' Unions of Japan to prevent Japanese shippers from using nonunion stevedores in Florida, and the council warned Japanese firms that their workers would not unload fruit loaded in the United States by nonunion labor. The threat caused all citrus shipments from Florida to Japan to go through Tampa, where they were loaded by stevedores represented by the ILA. Coastal, Canaveral, and others complained to the National Labor Relations Board (NLRB), alleging that the ILA's request of the Japanese unions was an illegal secondary boycott. How should the NLRB rule? [*International Longshoremen's Association, AFL-CIO*, 313 N.L.R.B. No. 53 (1993)]

22–6. Union Recognition. The International Association of Machinists and Aerospace Workers was certified as the exclusive representative of a unit of employees of F & A Food Sales, Inc. The employees were associated with F & A's trucking operations. The parties negotiated a collective bargaining agreement (CBA) that recognized the union as the employees' representative and reserved F & A's right to subcontract work as the company deemed necessary. Five months after negotiating the CBA, F & A subcontracted the services performed by the unit to Ryder Dedicated Logistics, Inc. Ryder operated from the same facility, used the same trucks, and employed substantially the same employees as had F & A. The union did not represent the workers while Ryder employed them. Seventeen months later, Ryder terminated the subcontract, and F & A resumed its own trucking operations with the same facility, the same trucks, and many of the same employees. The union asserted its right to represent the employees under the CBA. F & A refused to recognize the union. The union filed a charge of unfair labor practice with the NLRB. Is the CBA still in effect? Is the union still the representative of this unit of employees? Explain. [*National Labor Relations Board v. F & A Food Sales, Inc.*, 202 F.3d 1258 (10th Cir. 2000)]

22–7. CASE PROBLEM WITH SAMPLE ANSWER

The New York Department of Education's e-mail policy prohibits the use of the e-mail system for unofficial purposes, except that officials of the New York Public Employees Federation (PEF), the union representing state employees, can use the system for some limited communications, including the scheduling of union meetings and activities. In 1998, Michael Darcy, an elected PEF official, began sending mass, union-related e-mails to employees, including a summary of a union delegates' convention, a union newsletter, a criticism of proposed state legislation, and a criticism of the state governor and the Governor's Office of Employee Relations. Richard Cate, the Department's chief operating officer, met with Darcy and reiterated the Department's e-mail policy. When Darcy refused to stop his use of the e-mail system, Cate terminated his access to it. Darcy filed a complaint with the New York Public Employment Relations Board, alleging an unfair labor practice. Do the circumstances support Cate's action? Why or why not? [*Benson v. Cuevas*, 293 A.D.2d 927, 741 N.Y.S.2d 310 (3 Dept. 2002)]

- **To view a sample answer for Problem 22–7, go to this book's Web site at academic.cengage.com/blaw/cross, select "Chapter 22," and click on "Case Problem with Sample Answer."**

22-8. Collective Bargaining. Verizon New York, Inc. (VNY), provides telecommunications services. VNY and the Communications Workers of America (CWA) are parties to collective bargaining agreements covering installation and maintenance employees. At one time, VNY supported annual blood drives. VNY, CWA, and charitable organizations jointly set dates, arranged appointments, and adjusted work schedules for the drives. For each drive, about a thousand employees, including managers, spent up to four hours traveling to a donor site, giving blood, recovering, and returning to their jobs. Employees received full pay for the time. In 2001, VNY told CWA that it would no longer allow employees to participate "on Company time," claiming that it experienced problems meeting customer requests for service during the drives. CWA filed a complaint with the National Labor Relations Board (NLRB), asking that VNY be ordered to bargain over the decision. Did VNY commit an unfair labor practice? Should the NLRB grant CWA's request? Why or why not? [*Verizon New York, Inc. v. National Labor Relations Board*, 360 F.3d 206 (D.C. Cir. 2004)]

22-9. Collective Bargaining. Ceridian Corp. provides employment services to other companies. One of its divisions offers counseling to its customers' employees through a call-in center in Eagan, Minnesota. Under Ceridian's "Personal Days Off" (PDO) policy, employees can use a certain amount of paid time off each year for whatever purpose they wish, but unpaid leave is not available. Employees who take time off in excess of their PDO are subject to discipline, including discharge. In June 2003, the National Labor Relations Board (NLRB) certified Service Employees International Union 113 as the exclusive collective bargaining representative for 130 employees at the call-in center. The union assembled a six-employee team to negotiate a collective bargaining agreement. Ceridian refused to meet with the team during nonworking hours or to grant the members unpaid leave to attend bargaining sessions during working hours, but required them to use their PDO instead. The union filed an unfair-labor-practice charge with the NLRB against Ceridian, alleging that the employer impermissibly interfered with its employees' choice of bargaining representatives. Did Ceridian commit an unfair labor practice? Explain. [*Ceridian Corp. v. National Labor Relations Board*, 435 F.3d 352 (D.C. Cir. 2006)]

22-10. A QUESTION OF ETHICS

*Salvatore Monte was president of Kenrich Petrochemicals, Inc. Helen Chizmar had been Kenrich's office manager since 1963. Among the staff that Chizmar supervised were her sister, daughter, and daughter-in-law. In 1987, Chizmar's relatives and four other staff members designated the Oil, Chemical, and Atomic Workers International Union as their bargaining representative. Chizmar was not involved, but when Monte was notified that his office was unionizing, he told Chizmar that someone else could do her job for "$20,000 less" and fired her. He told another employee that one of his reasons for firing Chizmar was that he "was not going to put up with any union bullsh—." During negotiations with the union, Monte said that he planned to "get rid of the whole family." Chizmar's family complained to the National Labor Relations Board (NLRB) that the firing was an unfair labor practice. The NLRB agreed and ordered that Chizmar be reinstated with back pay. Kenrich appealed. In view of these facts, consider the following questions. [*Kenrich Petrochemicals, Inc. v. NLRB, *907 F.2d 400 (3d Cir. 1990)]*

(a) The National Labor Relations Act does not protect supervisors who engage in union activities. Should the appellate court affirm the NLRB's order nonetheless?
(b) If the appellate court does not affirm the NLRB's order, what message will be sent to the supervisors and employees of Kenrich?
(c) Is there anything Kenrich could (legally) do to avoid the unionization of its employees? Would it be ethical to counter the wishes of the employees to unionize?

LAW ON THE WEB

For updated links to resources available on the Web, as well as a variety of other materials, visit this text's Web site at

academic.cengage.com/blaw/cross

The American Federation of Labor–Congress of Industrial Organizations (AFL-CIO) provides links to labor-related resources at

www.aflcio.org

The National Labor Relations Board is online at
www.nlrb.gov

Legal Research Exercises on the Web

Go to **academic.cengage.com/blaw/cross**, the Web site that accompanies this text. Select "Chapter 22" and click on "Internet Exercises." There you will find the following Internet research exercises that you can perform to learn more about the topics covered in this chapter.

Internet Exercise 22–1: Legal Perspective
The National Labor Relations Board

Internet Exercise 22–2: Management Perspective
Mail Policies and Union Activity

Internet Exercise 22–3: Historical Perspective
Labor Unions and Labor Law

UNIT FIVE · FOCUS ON ETHICS

Ethics and the Employment Environment

Ethical principles—and challenging ethical issues—pervade the employment environment. In part, this is because employment relationships often involve intricate duties of agency. As you read in Chapter 19, when one person agrees to act on behalf of another, as an agent does in an agency relationship, that person assumes certain ethical responsibilities. Similarly, the principal also assumes certain ethical duties. In essence, agency law gives legal force to the ethical duties arising in an agency relationship. Although agency law also focuses on the rights of agents and principals, those rights are framed by the concept of duty—that is, an agent's duty becomes a right for the principal and vice versa.

Employees who deal with third parties are also deemed to be agents and thus share the ethical (and legal) duties imposed under agency law. In the employment context, however, it is not always possible for an employee to negotiate favorable employment terms. Often, an employee who is offered a job either accepts the job on the employer's terms or looks elsewhere for a position. Although numerous federal and state statutes protect employees, in some situations employees still have little recourse against their employers. At the same time, employers complain that statutes regulating employment relationships impose so many requirements that they find it hard to exercise a reasonable amount of control over their workplaces.

In the following pages, we focus on the ethical dimensions of selected issues in agency and employment law.

The Agent's Duty to the Principal

The very nature of the principal-agent relationship is one of trust, which we call a fiduciary relationship. Because of the nature of this relationship, an agent is considered to owe certain duties to the principal. These duties include being loyal and obedient, informing the principal of important facts concerning the agency, accounting to the principal for property or money received, and performing with reasonable diligence and skill.

Thus, ethical conduct would prevent an agent from representing two principals in the same transaction, making a secret profit from the agency relationship, or failing to disclose the interest of the agent in property the principal was purchasing. The expected ethical conduct of the agent has evolved into rules that, if breached, cause the agent to be held legally liable.

Does an Agent Also Have a Duty to Society? A question that sometimes arises is whether an agent's obligation extends beyond the duty to the principal and includes a duty to society as well. Consider, for example, the situation faced by an employee who knows that her employer is engaging in an unethical—or even illegal—practice, such as marketing an unsafe product. Does the employee's duty to the principal include keeping silent about this practice, which may harm users of the product? Does the employee have a duty to protect consumers by disclosing this information to the public, even if she loses her job as a result? Some scholars have argued that many of the greatest evils in the past thirty years have been accomplished in the name of duty to the principal.

Does an Agent's Breach of Loyalty Terminate the Agent's Authority? Suppose that an employee-agent who is authorized to access company trade secrets contained in computer files takes those secrets to a competitor for whom the employee is about to begin working. Clearly, in this situation the agent has violated the ethical—and legal—duty of loyalty to the principal. Does this breach of loyalty mean that the employee's act of accessing the trade secrets was unauthorized? The question has significant implications because if the act was unauthorized, the employee will be subject to state and federal laws prohibiting unauthorized access to computer information and data. If the act was authorized, the employee will not be subject to such laws. Although one court has held that the moment the employee accessed trade secrets for the purpose of divulging them to a competitor, the employee's authority as an agent terminated,[1] most courts have held that an agent's authority continues.

In one case, for example, three employees of Lockheed Martin Corporation copied confidential information and trade secrets from Lockheed's computer network onto compact discs and

1. *Shurgard Storage Centers, Inc. v. Safeguard Self Storage, Inc.*, 119 F.Supp.2d 1121 (W.D.Wash. 2000).

(Continued)

UNIT FIVE FOCUS ON ETHICS

BlackBerries (personal digital assistants). Lockheed had authorized the employee-agents to access these files but was understandably upset when the three resigned and went to work for a competitor taking the trade secrets with them. Lockheed sued the former agents under the Computer Fraud and Abuse Act (discussed in Chapter 12), arguing that they accessed the data without authorization. The federal district court, however, held that the individuals did have authorization to access the computer network and did not lose this authorization when they breached the duty of loyalty. Therefore, the court dismissed the case.[2]

The Principal's Duty to the Agent

Just as agents owe certain duties to their principals, so do principals owe duties to their agents, such as compensation and reimbursement for job-related expenses. Principals also owe their agents a duty of cooperation. One might expect principals to cooperate with their agents out of self-interest, but this does not always happen. Suppose that a principal hires an agent on commission to sell a building, and the agent puts considerable time and expense into finding a buyer. If the principal changes his mind and decides to retain the building, he may try to prevent the agent from completing the sale. Is such action ethical? Does it violate the principal's duty of cooperation? What alternatives would the principal have?

Although a principal is legally obligated to fulfill certain duties to the agent, these duties do not include any specific duty of loyalty. Some argue that employers' failure to be loyal to their employees has resulted in a reduction in employee loyalty to employers. After all, they maintain, why should an employee be loyal to an employer's interests over the years when the employee knows that the employer has no corresponding legal duty to be loyal to the employee's interests? Employers who do show a sense of loyalty toward their employees—for example, by not laying off longtime, faithful employees when business is slow or when those employees could be replaced by younger workers at lower cost—base that loyalty primarily on ethical, not legal, considerations.

Apparent Authority and Agency by Estoppel

Agency law is designed to enforce the ethical or fiduciary duties that arise once an agency relationship is established. To perhaps an even greater extent, agency law is designed to protect third parties—people outside the agency relationship. The doctrines of apparent authority and agency by estoppel stem primarily from ethical considerations that arise when third parties suffer a loss from an apparent agency relationship.

Sometimes, a third party may be led by the actions of the principal to believe that an individual is acting in the capacity of an agent, when in fact the individual is not an agent at all. For instance, a patient treated by a physician in a hospital's emergency room may assume that the physician is an agent of the hospital, even though the physician is an independent contractor and has no agency relationship with the hospital. If the patient suffers harm because of the physician's negligence and sues the hospital, some courts may hold the hospital liable under a theory of apparent agency.

For example, in one case a man and his wife were shopping at a mall when the man experienced signs and symptoms of a stroke. His wife called an ambulance and asked the driver to take her husband to a hospital that could render emergency services for a stroke. He was taken to Kenner Regional Medical Center in Louisiana and seen by Dr. Roland LeBlanc. After many hours of waiting at Kenner Regional, the man's family had him transferred to another hospital for treatment of a stroke. Later, the family filed a lawsuit against Kenner Regional based on Dr. LeBlanc's negligent failure to render emergency services for the stroke in a timely manner. Because Dr. LeBlanc was not an employee but only an independent contractor at the hospital, the trial court granted a summary judgment dismissing Kenner Regional from the lawsuit. The appellate court reversed, however, reasoning that the man was entitled to assume that the treating physician at the emergency room was an employee of the hospital.[3] It would be unethical to allow the hospital to avoid liability for the negligent conduct of the physicians it has working in its emergency room simply because of the physicians' status as independent contractors.

2. *Lockheed Martin Corp. v. Speed,* 2006 WL 2683058 (M.D.Fla. 2006). See also *Cenveo Corp. v. CelumSolutions Software GMBH & Co. KG,* 504 F.Supp.2d 574 (D.Minn. 2007).

3. *Arroyo v. East Jefferson General Hospital,* 956 So.2d 661 (La.App. 2007); see also the case presented in Chapter 19 as Case 19.4 *Ermoian v. Desert Hospital,* 152 Cal.App.4th 475, 61 Cal.Rptr.3d 754 (2007).

Focus on Ethics

Respondeat Superior

Agency law is designed to enforce the ethical or fiduciary duties that arise once an agency relationship is established. To perhaps an even greater extent, agency law is designed to protect third parties—people outside the agency relationship.

One legal concept that addresses the effect of agency relationships on third parties is the doctrine of *respondeat superior.* The doctrine raises a significant ethical question: Why should innocent employers be required to assume responsibility for the tortious, or wrongful, actions of their agent-employees? The answer has to do with the courts' perception that when one of two innocent parties must suffer a loss, the party in the best position to prevent that loss should bear the burden. In an employment relationship, for example, the employer has more control over the employee's behavior than a third party to the relationship does.

Another reason for retaining the doctrine of *respondeat superior* in our laws is based on the employer's assumed ability to pay any damages that are incurred by a third party. Our collection of shared beliefs suggests that an injured party should be afforded the most effective relief possible. Thus, even though an employer may be absolutely innocent, the employer has "deeper pockets" than the employee and will be more likely to have the funds necessary to make the injured party whole.

Employee versus Independent Contractor

An aspect of agency law that has troubled employers and employees alike on numerous occasions has to do with a worker's declared status as an independent contractor. Not surprisingly, many employers prefer to designate certain workers as independent contractors rather than as employees. Yet, increasingly, the courts are holding that certain workers who are designated as independent contractors are, in fact, employees if the employer exercises a significant degree of control over their performance. It does not matter whether the parties had specified, in written contracts, that the workers were independent contractors.

For example, in one case a group of drivers for a delivery service agreed to work as independent contractors and to use their own cars to make deliveries. Each driver signed a contract explicitly agreeing to work as an independent contractor. Nonetheless, a court held that the workers qualified as employees because they were dependent for their business on the employer. The delivery service "procured the customers, set the delivery prices, made the delivery assignments, billed the customers, set the commission rate, and paid the drivers."[4]

Why should a court interfere if a worker agrees to be classified as an independent contractor? The answer is, at least in part, that issues of fairness may be involved. The common law of agency, as developed and applied by the courts, implicitly recognizes these issues. After all, if a worker is an independent contractor, the worker must pay all Social Security taxes, instead of sharing them with his or her employer. Additionally, the worker will not be entitled to employer-provided benefits—such as group health insurance, pension plans, and stock options—that are available to employees. Furthermore, the worker will not receive the legal protections afforded to employees under such laws as those prohibiting employment discrimination (see Chapter 21).

For some types of work, especially work that requires great expertise, the worker may have sufficient bargaining power to negotiate favorable contract terms with the employer. Often, however, workers lack such power. If an employer states that a worker is being hired as an independent contractor, what can the worker do? Generally, in this situation the worker has only two options—accept the arrangement or forfeit the job.

At-Will Employment

Because of the extensive array of statutory protections for workers, it is easy to lose sight of the fact that the majority of workers in the United States have the legal status of "employees at will" (see Chapter 20). An employer may fire at-will employees for any reason or no reason if they do not have employment contracts—unless, of course, the employees fall under the protection of a state or federal statute.

Statutes Do Not Protect All Employees A problem faced by many at-will employees is that federal and state statutes regulating the workplace do not apply to all employers. As already mentioned, the Family and Medical Leave Act applies only to employers that have fifty or more workers. Additionally, the

4. *AFM Messenger Service, Inc. v. The Department of Employment Security,* 198 Ill.2d 380, 763 N.E.2d 272, 261 Ill.Dec. 302 (2001).

(Continued)

UNIT FIVE FOCUS ON ETHICS

major federal law prohibiting employment discrimination applies only to firms that have twenty-five or more employees and are engaged in interstate commerce. Similarly, state laws apply only to firms with a threshold number of employees, such as eight or ten employees. Even if an employer is subject to such statutes, these laws do not apply to many types of employment disputes, such as whether an employment contract was formed.

Exceptions to the At-Will Doctrine Sometimes, the only hope for plaintiffs in many employment disputes is that a court will make an exception to the at-will doctrine—on the basis of public policy, for example. The public-policy exception, though, remains just that—an exception. Often, courts are reluctant to make such an exception unless it can be justified by a clearly expressed public policy.

DISCUSSION QUESTIONS

1. How much obedience and loyalty does an agent-employee owe a principal-employer? What if the employer engages in an activity—or requests that the employee engage in an activity—that violates the employee's ethical standards but does not necessarily violate any public policy or law? In such a situation, does an employee's duty to abide by her or his own ethical standards override the employee's duty of loyalty to the employer?
2. When an agent acts in violation of his or her ethical or legal duty to the principal, should that action terminate the agent's authority to act on behalf of the principal? Why or why not?
3. If an agent injures a third party during the course of employment, under the doctrine of *respondeat superior,* the employer may be held liable for the agent's actions even though the employer did not authorize the action and was not even aware of it. Do you think that it is fair to hold employers liable in such situations? Do you think that it would be more equitable to hold that the employee alone should bear the responsibility for his or her tortious (legally wrongful) actions to third parties, even when the actions are committed within the scope of employment?

UNIT SIX
The Regulatory Environment

CONTENTS

CHAPTER 23

Consumer Protection

All statutes, agency rules, and common law judicial decisions that serve to protect the interests of consumers are classified as **consumer law.** Traditionally, in disputes involving consumers, it was assumed that the freedom to contract carried with it the obligation to live by the deal made. Over time, this attitude has changed considerably. Today, myriad federal and state laws protect consumers from unfair trade practices, unsafe products, discriminatory or unreasonable credit requirements, and other problems related to consumer transactions. Nearly every agency and department of the federal government has an office of consumer affairs, and most states have one or more such offices to help consumers. Also, typically the attorney general's office assists consumers at the state level.

In this chapter, we examine some of the major laws and regulations protecting consumers. Because of the wide variation among state consumer protection laws, our primary focus in this chapter is on federal legislation. Realize, though, that state laws often provide more sweeping and significant protections for the consumer than do federal laws. Exhibit 23–1 indicates many of the areas of consumer law that are regulated by federal statutes.

Deceptive Advertising

One of the earliest federal consumer protection laws—and still one of the most important—was the Federal Trade Commission Act of 1914 (mentioned in Chapter 6).[1] The act created the Federal Trade Commission (FTC) to carry out the broadly stated goal of preventing unfair and deceptive trade practices, including deceptive advertising.[2]

1. 15 U.S.C. Sections 41–58.
2. 15 U.S.C. Section 45.

EXHIBIT 23–1 • Selected Areas of Consumer Law Regulated by Statutes

CONSUMER LAW	
Advertising	*Example*—The Federal Trade Commission Act of 1914
Labeling and Packaging	*Example*—The Fair Packaging and Labeling Act of 1966
Sales	*Example*—The FTC Mail-Order Rule of 1975
Food and Drugs	*Example*—The Federal Food, Drug and Cosmetic Act of 1938
Product Safety	*Example*—The Consumer Product Safety Act of 1972
Credit Protection	*Example*—The Consumer Credit Protection Act of 1968

Generally, **deceptive advertising** occurs if a reasonable consumer would be misled by the advertising claim. Vague generalities and obvious exaggerations are permissible. These claims are known as *puffery*. When a claim takes on the appearance of literal authenticity, however, it may create problems. Advertising that *appears* to be based on factual evidence but in fact is not reasonably supported by some evidence will be deemed deceptive.

Some advertisements contain "half-truths," meaning that the presented information is true but incomplete and therefore leads consumers to a false conclusion. For example, the makers of Campbell's soups advertised that "most" Campbell's soups were low in fat and cholesterol and thus were helpful in fighting heart disease. What the ad did not say was that Campbell's soups are high in sodium, and high-sodium diets may increase the risk of heart disease. The FTC ruled that Campbell's claims were thus deceptive. Advertising that contains an endorsement by a celebrity may be deemed deceptive if the celebrity does not actually use the product.

In the following case brought by the FTC, *WIRED* magazine had already put the product in question on its list of top ten "Snake-Oil Gadgets."

CASE 23.1 Federal Trade Commission v. QT, Inc.

United States Court of Appeals, Seventh Circuit, 2008. 512 F.3d 858.
www.ca7.uscourts.gov[a]

Background and Facts QT, Inc., and assorted related companies, heavily promoted the Q-Ray Ionized Bracelet on television infomercials as well as on its Web site. In its promotions, the company made many claims about the pain-relief powers of these bracelets. The bracelet offered immediate, significant, or complete pain relief and could cure chronic pain. At trial in the U.S. District Court for the Northern District of Illinois, the presiding judge labeled all such claims as fraudulent, forbid further promotional claims, and ordered the company to pay $16 million, plus interest, into a fund to be distributed to all customers. QT, Inc., appealed.

IN THE LANGUAGE OF THE COURT
***EASTERBROOK*, Chief Judge.**

* * * According to the district court's findings, almost everything that defendants have said about the bracelet is false. Here are some highlights:

- Defendants promoted the bracelet as a miraculous cure for chronic pain, but it has no therapeutic effect.
- Defendants told consumers that claims of "immediate, significant or complete pain relief" had been "test-proven"; they hadn't.

* * * *

- Defendants represented that the therapeutic effect wears off in a year or two, despite knowing that the bracelet's properties do not change. This assertion is designed to lead customers to buy new bracelets. Likewise the false statement that the bracelet has a "memory cycle specific to each individual wearer" so that only the bracelet's original wearer can experience pain relief is designed to increase sales by eliminating the second-hand market and "explaining" the otherwise-embarrassing fact that the buyer's friends and neighbors can't perceive any effect.

The magistrate judge [the judge presiding over the trial] did not commit a clear error, or abuse his discretion, in concluding that the defendants set out to bilk unsophisticated persons who found themselves in pain from arthritis and other chronic conditions.

Defendants maintain that the magistrate judge subjected their statements to an excessively rigorous standard of proof.

a. In the box for the case number, type "07" and "1662" and then click on "List Case." Follow the links to access the opinion. The U.S. Court of Appeals for the Seventh Circuit maintains this Web site.

CASE CONTINUES

CASE 23.1 CONTINUED

* * * *The Federal Trade Commission Act forbids false and misleading statements, and a statement that is plausible but has not been tested in the most reliable way cannot be condemned out of hand.* [Emphasis added.]

* * * For the Q-Ray Ionized Bracelet, * * * all statements about how the product works—Q-Rays, ionization, enhancing the flow of bio-energy, and the like—are blather. Defendants might as well have said: "Beneficent creatures from the 17th Dimension use this bracelet as a beacon to locate people who need pain relief, and whisk them off to their homeworld every night to provide help in ways unknown to our science."

* * * *Proof is what separates an effect new to science from a swindle.* Defendants themselves told customers that the bracelet's efficacy had been "test-proven"; * * * but defendants have no proof of the Q-Ray Ionized Bracelet's efficacy. The "tests" on which they relied were bunk. * * * What remain are testimonials, which are not a form of proof * * *. That's why the "testimonial" of someone who keeps elephants off the streets of a large city by snapping his fingers is the basis of a joke rather than proof of cause and effect. [Emphasis added.]

* * * *

Physicians know how to treat pain. Why pay $200 for a Q-Ray Ionized Bracelet when you can get relief from an aspirin tablet that costs 1¢?

- **Decision and Remedy** *The U.S. Court of Appeals for the Seventh Circuit affirmed the district court's decision. QT, Inc., was required to stop its deceptive advertising and to pay the $16 million, plus interest, so that its customers could be reimbursed.*

- **What If the Facts Were Different?** *Assume that the defendant had actually done scientific studies, but they were inconclusive. How might the judge have ruled in that situation?*

- **The Ethical Dimension** *Most people have seen infomercials. Do the fraudulent promotional claims of QT, Inc., in such infomercials mean that all products "pitched" on television are suspect? Why or why not?*

Bait-and-Switch Advertising

The FTC has issued rules that govern specific advertising techniques. One of the most important rules is contained in the FTC's "Guides Against Bait Advertising,"[3] issued in 1968. The rule seeks to prevent **bait-and-switch advertising**—that is, advertising a very low price for a particular item that will likely be unavailable to the consumer, who will then be encouraged to purchase a more expensive item. The low price is the "bait" to lure the consumer into the store. The salesperson is instructed to "switch" the consumer to a different, more expensive item. Under the FTC guidelines, bait-and-switch advertising occurs if the seller refuses to show the advertised item, fails to have a reasonable quantity of the item in stock, fails to promise to deliver the advertised item within a reasonable time, or discourages employees from selling the item.

Online Deceptive Advertising

Deceptive advertising may occur in the online environment as well. The FTC has been quite active in monitoring online advertising and has identified hundreds of Web sites that have made false or deceptive advertising claims for products ranging from medical treatments for various diseases to exercise equipment and weight-loss aids.

The FTC has issued guidelines to help online businesses comply with existing laws prohibiting deceptive advertising.[4] These guidelines include three basic requirements. First, all ads—both online and offline—must be truthful and not misleading. Second, any claims made in an ad must be substantiated; that is, advertisers must have evidence to back up their claims. Third, ads cannot be "unfair," which the FTC defines as "caus[ing] or . . . likely to cause substantial consumer injury that consumers could not reasonably avoid and that is not outweighed by the benefit to consumers or competition."

The guidelines also call for "clear and conspicuous" disclosure of any qualifying or limiting information. The FTC suggests that advertisers should assume that consumers will not read an entire Web page. Therefore, to satisfy the "clear and conspicuous" requirement, online advertisers should place the dis-

3. 16 C.F.R. Part 238.

4. *Advertising and Marketing on the Internet: Rules of the Road,* September 2000.

closure as close as possible to the claim being qualified or include the disclosure within the claim itself. If such placement is not feasible, the next-best location is on a section of the page to which a consumer can easily scroll. Generally, hyperlinks to a disclosure are recommended only for lengthy disclosures or for disclosures that must be repeated in a variety of locations on the Web page.

FTC Actions against Deceptive Advertising

The FTC receives complaints from many sources, including competitors of alleged violators, consumers, consumer organizations, trade associations, Better Business Bureaus, government organizations, and state and local officials. When the agency receives numerous and widespread complaints about a particular problem, it will investigate. If the FTC concludes that a given advertisement is unfair or deceptive, it drafts a formal complaint, which is sent to the alleged offender. The company may agree to settle the complaint without further proceedings; if not, the FTC can conduct a hearing in which the company can present its defense (see Chapter 6).

If the FTC succeeds in proving that an advertisement is unfair or deceptive, it usually issues a **cease-and-desist order** requiring the company to stop the challenged advertising. It might also impose a sanction known as **counteradvertising** by requiring the company to advertise anew—in print, on the Internet, on radio, and on television—to inform the public about the earlier misinformation. The FTC may institute **multiple product orders,** which require a firm to cease and desist from false advertising in regard to all of its products, not just the product that was the subject of the action.

In some instances, the FTC may seek other remedies. In the following case, for example, after receiving more than five hundred consumer complaints, the FTC sought restitution of the amounts that the consumers had paid.

EXTENDED CASE 23.2 Federal Trade Commission v. Verity International, Ltd.

United States Court of Appeals, Second Circuit, 2006. 443 F.3d 48.

***JOHN M. WALKER, JR.*, Chief Judge.**

The incessant demand for pornography, some have said, is an engine of technological development. The telephonic system at dispute in this appeal is an example of that phenomenon—it was designed and implemented to ensure that consumers paid charges for accessing pornography and other adult entertainment. The system identified the user of an online adult-entertainment service by the telephone line used to access that service and then billed the telephone-line subscriber for the cost of that service as if it was a charge for an international phone call to Madagascar. This system had the benefit that the user's credit card never had to be processed, but it had a problem as well: It was possible for someone to access an adult-entertainment service over a telephone line without authorization from the telephone-line subscriber who understood herself contractually bound to pay all telephone charges, including those that disguised fees for the adult entertainment.

The Federal Trade Commission ("FTC") took a dim view of this billing system and brought suit [in a federal district court] to shut it down as a deceptive and unfair trade practice within the meaning of [Section] 5(a)(1) of the Federal Trade Commission Act ("FTC Act"). The FTC sued Verity International, Ltd. ("Verity") and Automatic Communications, Ltd. ("ACL"), corporations that operated this billing system, as well as Robert Green and Marilyn Shein, who controlled these corporations.

* * * *

* * * [The] court entered * * * [a judgment] against the defendants-appellants for a total of $17.9 million. * * * The defendants-appellants timely appealed * * * [to the U.S. Court of Appeals for the Second Circuit].

* * * *

* * * *To prove a deceptive act or practice under [Section] 5(a)(1) [of the FTC Act], the FTC must show three elements: (1) a representation, omission, or practice, that (2) is likely to mislead consumers acting reasonably under the circumstances, and [that] (3) * * * is material.* [Emphasis added.]

CASE CONTINUES

CASE 23.2 CONTINUED

The FTC contends that the first element is satisfied by proof that the defendants-appellants caused telephone-line subscribers to receive explicit and implicit representations that they could not successfully avoid paying charges for adult entertainment that had been accessed over their phone lines—what we call a "representation of uncontestability [cannot be disputed]." * * * The defendants-appellants caused charges for adult entertainment to appear on * * * phone bills as telephone calls, thereby capitalizing on the common and well-founded perception held by consumers that they must pay their telephone bills, irrespective of whether they made or authorized the calls. * * * [This] conveyed a representation of uncontestability.

* * * [As for the second element, the] FTC contends that the representation of uncontestability was false and therefore likely to mislead consumers who did not use or authorize others to use the adult entertainment in question; the defendants-appellants contend that the representation was rendered true by * * * agency principles.

*Under common law agency principles, a person is liable to pay for services that she does not herself contract for if another person has * * * authority to consent on her behalf to pay for the services.* [Emphasis added.]

* * * [But a] computer * * * is not primarily understood as a payment mechanism, and in the ordinary habits of human behavior, one does not reasonably infer that because a person is authorized to use a computer, the subscriber to the telephone line connected to that computer has authorized the computer user to purchase online content * * * .

* * * The FTC proved the second element of its * * * claim.

Finally [with respect to the third element] * * * telephone-line subscribers found the representation material to their decision whether to pay the billed charges because of the worry of telephone-line disconnection, the perception of the futility of challenging the charges, the desire to avoid credit-score injury, or some combination of these factors.

* * * *

The district court measured the appropriate amount of [the judgment] as "the full amount lost by consumers." This was error. The appropriate measure * * * is the benefit unjustly received by the defendants.

* * * *

* * * [Phone service providers] received some fraction of the money * * * before any payments were made to the defendants-appellants.

* * * *

* * * [Also] some fraction of consumers * * * actually used or authorized others to use the services at issue * * * .

* * * *

We affirm all components of the district court's * * * order of relief except for the monetary judgment * * * . The case is remanded to the district court for further proceedings consistent with this opinion.

QUESTIONS

1. How might the defendants have avoided the charges against them in this case?
2. As an administrative agency, what powers might the FTC use to determine more precisely the number of consumers who paid their phone bills but did not use, or authorize others to use, the defendants' services?

Telemarketing and Electronic Advertising

The Telephone Consumer Protection Act (TCPA)[5] prohibits telephone solicitation using an automatic telephone dialing system or a prerecorded voice. Most states also have statutes regulating telephone solicitation. The TCPA also makes it illegal to transmit ads via fax without first obtaining the recipient's permission. (Similar issues have arisen with respect to junk e-mail, called *spam*—see Chapters 7 and 12.)

The Federal Communications Commission (FCC) enforces the TCPA. The FCC imposes substantial fines

5. 47 U.S.C. Sections 227 *et seq.*

($11,000 each day) on companies that violate the junk fax provisions of the act and has even fined one company as much as $5.4 million.[6] The TCPA also provides for a private right of action under which consumers can recover actual losses resulting from a violation of the act or receive $500 in damages for each violation, whichever is greater. If a court finds that a defendant willfully or knowingly violated the act, the court has the discretion to treble (triple) the amount of damages awarded.

The Telemarketing and Consumer Fraud and Abuse Prevention Act of 1994[7] directed the FTC to establish rules governing telemarketing and to bring actions against fraudulent telemarketers. The FTC's Telemarketing Sales Rule of 1995[8] requires a telemarketer to identify the seller's name, describe the product being sold, and disclose all material facts related to the sale (such as the total cost of the goods being sold). The rule makes it illegal for telemarketers to misrepresent information or facts about their goods or services. A telemarketer must also remove a consumer's name from its list of potential contacts if the customer so requests. An amendment to the Telemarketing Sales Rule established the national Do Not Call Registry, which became effective in October 2003. Telemarketers must refrain from calling those consumers who have placed their names on the list.

SECTION 2 Labeling and Packaging Laws

A number of federal and state laws deal specifically with the information given on labels and packages. In general, labels must be accurate, and they must use words that are easily understood by the ordinary consumer. For example, a box of cereal cannot be labeled "giant" if that would exaggerate the amount of cereal contained in the box.

In some instances, labels must specify the raw materials used in the product, such as the percentage of cotton, nylon, or other fiber used in a garment. In other instances, the product must carry a warning. Cigarette packages and advertising, for example, must include one of several warnings about the health hazards associated with smoking.[9]

Federal Statutes

There are numerous federal laws regulating the labeling and packaging of products. These include the Wool Products Labeling Act of 1939,[10] the Fur Products Labeling Act of 1951,[11] the Flammable Fabrics Act of 1953,[12] and the Fair Packaging and Labeling Act of 1966.[13] The Comprehensive Smokeless Tobacco Health Education Act of 1986,[14] for example, requires that producers, packagers, and importers of smokeless tobacco label their product with one of several warnings about the use of smokeless tobacco.

Food Labeling

Because the quality and safety of food are so important to consumers, several statutes deal specifically with food labeling. The Fair Packaging and Labeling Act requires that food product labels identify (1) the product; (2) the net quantity of the contents and, if the number of servings is stated, the size of the serving; (3) the manufacturer; and (4) the packager or distributor. The act includes additional requirements concerning descriptions on packages, savings claims, components of nonfood products, and standards for the partial filling of packages.

Food products must bear labels detailing the nutritional content, including how much fat the food contains and what kind of fat it is. The Nutrition Labeling and Education Act of 1990[15] requires standard nutrition facts (including fat content) on food labels; regulates the use of such terms as *fresh* and *low fat;* and authorizes certain health claims, subject to the federal Food and Drug Administration's approval. The FTC enforces these rules.

Sales

A number of statutes protect consumers by requiring the disclosure of certain terms in sales transactions and providing rules governing unsolicited merchandise and various forms of sales, such as door-to-door sales, mail-order sales, and referral sales. The FTC has regulatory authority in this area, as do other federal

6. See *Missouri ex rel. Nixon v. American Blast Fax, Inc.,* 323 F.3d 649 (8th Cir. 2003); *cert.* denied, 540 U.S. 1104, 124 S.Ct. 1043, 157 L.Ed.2d 888 (2004).
7. 15 U.S.C. Sections 6101–6108.
8. 16 C.F.R. Sections 310.1–310.8.
9. 15 U.S.C. Sections 1331–1341.
10. 15 U.S.C. Section 68.
11. 15 U.S.C. Section 69.
12. 15 U.S.C. Section 1191.
13. 15 U.S.C. Sections 1451 *et seq.*
14. 15 U.S.C. Sections 4401–4408.
15. 21 U.S.C. Section 343.1.

agencies. The Federal Reserve Board of Governors, for example, has issued **Regulation Z,**[16] which governs credit provisions associated with sales contracts, as discussed later in this chapter.

Many states have also enacted laws governing consumer sales transactions. Moreover, states have protected consumers to a certain extent through adopting the Uniform Commercial Code (discussed in Chapter 11) and, in a few states, the Uniform Consumer Credit Code.

Door-to-Door Sales

Door-to-door sales are singled out for special treatment in the laws of most states, largely because of the potential for high-pressure sales tactics. Repeat purchases are not as likely as they are in stores, so the seller has less incentive to cultivate the goodwill of the purchaser. Furthermore, the seller is unlikely to present alternative products and their prices. Thus, a number of states have passed "cooling-off" laws that permit the buyers of goods sold door to door to cancel their contracts within a specified period of time, usually two to three business days after the sale.

An FTC regulation also requires sellers to give consumers three days to cancel any door-to-door sale, and this rule applies in addition to any state law. The FTC rule further requires that consumers be notified in Spanish of this right if the oral negotiations for the sale were in that language.

Telephone and Mail-Order Sales

The FTC Mail or Telephone Order Merchandise Rule of 1993, which amended the FTC Mail-Order Rule of 1975,[17] provides specific protections for consumers who purchase goods over the phone or through the mail. The 1993 rule extended the 1975 rule to include sales orders transmitted using computers, fax machines, or other means involving a telephone line. Among other things, the rule requires merchants to ship orders within the time promised in their catalogues or advertisements and to notify consumers when orders cannot be shipped on time. Merchants must also issue a refund within a specified period of time when a consumer cancels an order.

In addition, under the Postal Reorganization Act of 1970,[18] a consumer who receives *unsolicited* merchandise sent by U.S. mail can keep it, throw it away, or dispose of it in any manner that she or he sees fit. The recipient will not be obligated to the sender. Suppose that Serena receives a copy of the "Cookbook of the Month" from a company via U.S. mail, even though she did not order the cookbook. She gives it to her friend, Vaya, who loves to cook. The following month, Serena receives a bill for $49.99 from the company that sent the cookbook. Under the 1970 act, because the cookbook was sent to her unsolicited through the U.S. mail, Serena is not obligated to pay the bill.

Online Sales

Protecting consumers from fraudulent and deceptive sales practices conducted via the Internet has proved to be a challenging task. Nonetheless, the FTC and other federal agencies have brought a number of enforcement actions against those who perpetrate online fraud. Additionally, the federal statute prohibiting wire fraud that was discussed in Chapter 7 applies to online transactions.

Some states have amended their consumer protection statutes to cover Internet transactions as well. For example, the California legislature revised its Business and Professions Code to include transactions conducted over the Internet or by "any other electronic means of communication." Previously, that code covered only telephone, mail-order catalogue, radio, and television sales. Now any entity selling over the Internet in California must explicitly create an on-screen notice indicating its refund and return policies, where its business is physically located, its legal name, and a number of other details. Various states are also setting up information sites to help consumers protect themselves.

Credit Protection

Because of the extensive use of credit by American consumers, credit protection has become an especially important area of consumer protection legislation. A key statute regulating the credit and credit-card industries is Title I of the Consumer Credit Protection Act (CCPA),[19] which is commonly referred to as the Truth-in-Lending Act (TILA).

The Truth-in-Lending Act

The TILA is basically a *disclosure law.* It is administered by the Federal Reserve Board and requires sellers and

16. 12 C.F.R. Sections 226.1–226.30.
17. 16 C.F.R. Sections 435.1–435.2.
18. 39 U.S.C. Section 3009.
19. 15 U.S.C. Sections 1601–1693r.

lenders to disclose credit terms or loan terms so that individuals can shop around for the best financing arrangements. TILA requirements apply only to persons who, in the ordinary course of business, lend funds, sell on credit, or arrange for the extension of credit. Thus, sales or loans made between two consumers do not come under the protection of the act. Additionally, this law protects only debtors who are natural persons (as opposed to the artificial "person" of a corporation); it does not extend to other legal entities.

The disclosure requirements are contained in Regulation Z, which was promulgated (publicized) by the Federal Reserve Board. If the contracting parties are subject to the TILA, the requirements of Regulation Z apply to any transaction involving an installment sales contract that calls for payment to be made in more than four installments. Transactions subject to Regulation Z typically include installment loans, retail and installment sales, car loans, home-improvement loans, and certain real estate loans if the amount of financing is less than $25,000.

Under the provisions of the TILA, all of the terms of a credit instrument must be clearly and conspicuously disclosed. The TILA provides for contract rescission (cancellation) if a creditor fails to follow *exactly* the procedures required by the act.[20] TILA requirements are strictly enforced.

Equal Credit Opportunity In 1974, Congress enacted the Equal Credit Opportunity Act (ECOA)[21] as an amendment to the TILA. The ECOA prohibits the denial of credit solely on the basis of race, religion, national origin, color, gender, marital status, or age. The act also prohibits credit discrimination on the basis of whether an individual receives certain forms of income, such as public-assistance benefits.

Under the ECOA, a creditor may not require the signature of an applicant's spouse, other than as a joint applicant, on a credit instrument if the applicant qualifies under the creditor's standards of creditworthiness for the amount and terms of the credit request. For example, Tonja, an African American, applied for financing with a used-car dealer. The dealer looked at Tonja's credit report and, without submitting the application to the lender, decided that she would not qualify. Instead of informing Tonja that she did not qualify, the dealer told her that she needed a cosigner on the loan to purchase the car. According to a federal appellate court, the dealer qualified as a creditor in this situation because the dealer unilaterally denied the credit and thus could be held liable under the ECOA.[22]

Credit-Card Rules The TILA also contains provisions regarding credit cards. One provision limits the liability of a cardholder to $50 per card for unauthorized charges made before the creditor is notified that the card has been lost. Another provision prohibits a credit-card company from billing a consumer for any unauthorized charges if the credit card was improperly issued by the company. Suppose that a consumer receives an unsolicited credit card in the mail and the card is later stolen and used by the thief to make purchases. In this situation, the consumer to whom the card was sent will not be liable for the unauthorized charges.

Other provisions of the act set out specific procedures for both the credit-card company and its cardholder to use in settling disputes related to credit-card purchases. These procedures would be used if, for example, a cardholder thinks that an error has occurred in billing or wishes to withhold payment for a faulty product purchased by credit card.

Consumer Leases The Consumer Leasing Act (CLA) of 1988[23] amended the TILA to provide protection for consumers who lease automobiles and other goods. The CLA applies to those who lease or arrange to lease consumer goods in the ordinary course of their business. The act applies only if the goods are priced at $25,000 or less and if the lease term exceeds four months. The CLA and its implementing regulation, Regulation M,[24] require lessors to disclose in writing (or by electronic record) all of the material terms of the lease.

The Fair Credit Reporting Act

In 1970, to protect consumers against inaccurate credit reporting, Congress enacted the Fair Credit Reporting Act (FCRA).[25] The act provides that consumer credit reporting agencies may issue credit reports to users only for specified purposes, including the extension of credit, the issuance of insurance policies, and compliance with a court order, and in

20. Note, however, that amendments to the TILA enacted in 1995 prevent borrowers from rescinding loans because of minor clerical errors in closing documents [15 U.S.C. Sections 1605, 1631, 1635, 1640, and 1641].

21. 15 U.S.C. Sections 1691–1691f.

22. *Treadway v. Gateway Chevrolet Oldsmobile, Inc.*, 362 F.3d 971 (7th Cir. 2004).

23. 15 U.S.C. Sections 1667–1667e.

24. 12 C.F.R. Part 213.

25. 15 U.S.C. Sections 1681–1681t.

response to a consumer's request for a copy of his or her own credit report. The act further provides that whenever a consumer is denied credit or insurance on the basis of her or his credit report, or is charged more than others ordinarily would be for credit or insurance, the consumer must be notified of that fact and of the name and address of the credit reporting agency that issued the credit report.

Under the FCRA, consumers may request the source of any information being given out by a credit agency, as well as the identity of anyone who has received an agency's report. Consumers are also permitted to access the information about them contained in a credit reporting agency's files. If a consumer discovers that an agency's files contain inaccurate information about his or her credit standing, the agency, on the consumer's written request, must investigate the matter and delete any unverifiable or erroneous information within a reasonable period of time. As part of its investigation, the agency should systematically examine its records and contact the creditor whose information the consumer disputes.[26] An agency that fails to comply with the act is liable for actual damages, plus additional damages not to exceed $1,000 and attorneys' fees.[27] The FCRA allows an award of punitive damages for a "willful" violation.[28]

Fair and Accurate Credit Transactions Act

In an effort to combat identity theft (discussed in Chapter 7), Congress passed the Fair and Accurate Credit Transactions Act (FACT Act) of 2003.[29] The act established a national fraud alert system so that consumers who suspect that they have been or may be victimized by identity theft can place an alert on their credit files. The act also requires the major credit reporting agencies to provide consumers with free copies of their own credit reports every twelve months. Another provision requires account numbers on credit-card receipts to be shortened (truncated) so that merchants, employees, or others who may have access to the receipts do not have the consumers' names and full credit-card numbers. The act further mandates that financial institutions work with the Federal Trade Commission to identify "red flag" indicators of identity theft and to develop rules for disposing of sensitive credit information.

The FACT Act gives consumers who have been victimized by identity theft some assistance in rebuilding their credit reputations. For example, credit reporting agencies must stop reporting allegedly fraudulent account information once the consumer establishes that identify theft has occurred. Business owners and creditors are required to provide consumers with copies of any records that can help the consumer prove that the particular account or transaction is fraudulent (records showing that an account was created by a fraudulent signature, for example). In addition, the act allows consumers to report the accounts affected by identity theft directly to creditors in order to help prevent the spread of erroneous credit information.

The Fair Debt Collection Practices Act

In 1977, Congress enacted the Fair Debt Collection Practices Act (FDCPA)[30] in an attempt to curb what were perceived to be abuses by collection agencies. The act applies only to specialized debt-collection agencies that regularly attempt to collect debts on behalf of someone else, usually for a percentage of the amount owed. Creditors attempting to collect debts are not covered by the act unless, by misrepresenting themselves, they cause debtors to believe they are collection agencies.

Requirements under the Act The act explicitly prohibits a collection agency from using any of the following tactics:

1. Contacting the debtor at the debtor's place of employment if the debtor's employer objects.
2. Contacting the debtor during inconvenient or unusual times (for example, calling the debtor at three o'clock in the morning) or at any time if the debtor is being represented by an attorney.
3. Contacting third parties other than the debtor's parents, spouse, or financial adviser about payment of a debt unless a court authorizes such action.

26. See, for example, *Johnson v. MBNA America Bank, N.A.*, 357 F.3d 426 (4th Cir. 2004).

27. 15 U.S.C. Section 1681n.

28. Under the FCRA, if an insurance company *raises* a customer's rates because of a credit score, the insurance company is required to notify the individual. In 2007, the United States Supreme Court held that even the failure to notify *new* customers that they are paying higher insurance rates as a result of their credit scores is an adverse action that can be considered a *willful* violation of the FCRA. *Safeco Insurance Co. of America v. Burr*, ___ U.S. ___, 127 S.Ct. 2201, 167 L.Ed.2d 1045 (2007).

29. Pub. L. No. 108-159, 117 Stat. 1952 (December 4, 2003).

30. 15 U.S.C. Section 1692.

4. Using harassment or intimidation (for example, using abusive language or threatening violence) or employing false or misleading information (for example, posing as a police officer).
5. Communicating with the debtor at any time after receiving notice that the debtor is refusing to pay the debt, except to advise the debtor of further action to be taken by the collection agency.

The FDCPA also requires a collection agency to include a **validation notice** whenever it initially contacts a debtor for payment of a debt or within five days of that initial contact. The notice must state that the debtor has thirty days in which to dispute the debt and to request a written verification of the debt from the collection agency. The debtor's request for debt validation must be in writing.

The following case involved contacting a third party other than the debtor's parents, spouse, or financial adviser about the payment of a debt. A consumer alleged that a debt collection company violated Colorado's fair debt collection statute when it hired a third party—an automated mailing service—to send her the required validation notice. Although the case was brought under Colorado's fair debt collection statute, the state statute parallels the relevant portions of the FDCPA and both prohibit communications between a debt collector and third parties.

CASE 23.3 Flood v. Mercantile Adjustment Bureau, LLC

Supreme Court of Colorado, 2008. 176 P.3d 769.
www.courts.state.co.us/supct/supctopinion.htm[a]

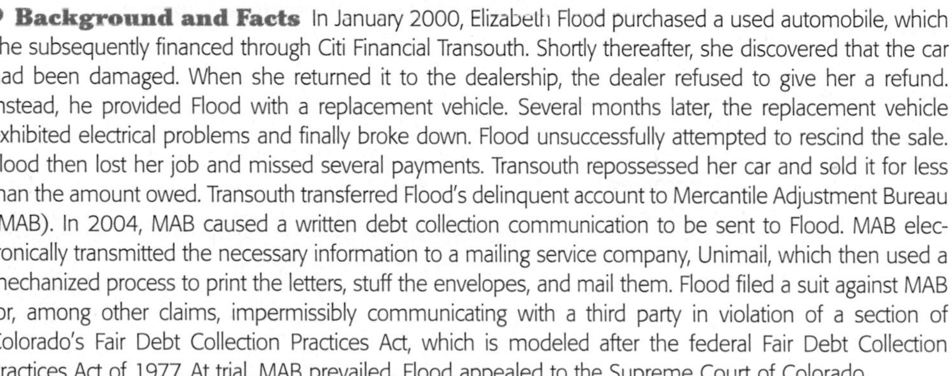

• **Background and Facts** In January 2000, Elizabeth Flood purchased a used automobile, which she subsequently financed through Citi Financial Transouth. Shortly thereafter, she discovered that the car had been damaged. When she returned it to the dealership, the dealer refused to give her a refund. Instead, he provided Flood with a replacement vehicle. Several months later, the replacement vehicle exhibited electrical problems and finally broke down. Flood unsuccessfully attempted to rescind the sale. Flood then lost her job and missed several payments. Transouth repossessed her car and sold it for less than the amount owed. Transouth transferred Flood's delinquent account to Mercantile Adjustment Bureau (MAB). In 2004, MAB caused a written debt collection communication to be sent to Flood. MAB electronically transmitted the necessary information to a mailing service company, Unimail, which then used a mechanized process to print the letters, stuff the envelopes, and mail them. Flood filed a suit against MAB for, among other claims, impermissibly communicating with a third party in violation of a section of Colorado's Fair Debt Collection Practices Act, which is modeled after the federal Fair Debt Collection Practices Act of 1977. At trial, MAB prevailed. Flood appealed to the Supreme Court of Colorado.

IN THE LANGUAGE OF THE COURT
HOBBES, **Justice**

* * * *

[Two previous courts] ruled that the debt collection communication that Mercantile Adjustment Bureau, LLC ("MAB") sent to Elizabeth Flood complied with the notice provisions of section 12-14-109 [of Colorado's Fair Debts Collection Practices Act], and that MAB did not violate section 12-14-105(2) [of that act] when it utilized an automated mailing service to print and mail the communication.

* * * *

* * * Flood * * * alleged that MAB impermissibly communicated with a third party, in violation of section 12-14-105(2), by outsourcing the printing and mailing of its collection communications to Unimail [a mailing service company].

* * * *

In the case before us, the relevant provisions of the Colorado statute parallel the federal statute. Because the Colorado statute is patterned on the federal statute, we look to federal case law for persuasive guidance bearing on the construction of our state's law.

---

a. Click on "Supreme Court Case Announcements by Date," then click on "2008," and then on "01/22/08."

CASE CONTINUES

CASE 23.3 CONTINUED

* * * *

Flood * * * argues that MAB violated the [Colorado statute] by using an automated mailing service to prepare and mail its debt collection communications. With certain exceptions, [the statute] prohibits communications between a debt collector and third parties. Our analysis * * * leads us to conclude that the [Colorado legislature] did not intend for section 12-14-105(2) [of the Colorado act] to prohibit a debt collector from using an automated mailing service. The federal statute contains a nearly identical provision. *The purpose of [this federal provision] is to "protect a consumer's reputation and privacy, as well as to prevent loss of jobs resulting from a debt collector's communication with a consumer's employer concerning the collection of a debt."* [Emphasis added.]

The record here shows that MAB utilized an entirely automated printing and mailing service. The county court found that MAB electronically transmitted the information included in its collection communications to Unimail. Unimail then printed the collection communications, which were mechanically stuffed into envelopes. The county court concluded that the use of such a highly automated procedure did not violate section 12-14-105(2) because it did not threaten the consumer with the risk of being coerced or embarrassed into paying a debt because the debt collector contacted an employer, family member, friend, or other third party.

We agree with the holding of the county court. The use of an automated mailing service, such as Unimail, by a debt collector is a *de minimus* [trivial] communication with a third party that cannot reasonably be perceived as a threat to the consumer's privacy or reputation.

Accordingly, we hold that MAB's use of Unimail to automatically print and mail its debt collection communications did not violate section 12-14-105(2). Thus, we affirm that part of the district court's judgment upholding the county court's judgment on this issue.

- **Decision and Remedy** *The Supreme Court of Colorado held that Mercantile Adjustment Bureau did not violate Colorado's statute prohibiting communications with a third party about an outstanding debt. The state supreme court affirmed the lower court's opinion on this issue, but reversed the decision on other grounds (the letter sent contained contradictory language and failed to effectively convey the required notices regarding the debtor's rights).*

- **What If the Facts Were Different?** *Assume that Unimail had spotcheckers who randomly pulled printed communications to debtors prior to mailing. These checkers read the letters to make sure that they were accurate. Would the court have still ruled in favor of Mercantile Adjustment Bureau? Why or why not?*

- **The Legal Environment Dimension** *Why might this ruling actually benefit debtors in the long run?*

Enforcement of the Act The enforcement of the FDCPA is primarily the responsibility of the Federal Trade Commission. The act provides that a debt collector who fails to comply with the act is liable for actual damages, plus additional damages not to exceed $1,000[31] and attorneys' fees.

Cases brought under the FDCPA sometimes raise questions as to who qualifies as a debt collector or debt-collection agency subject to the act. For example, in the past courts were issuing conflicting opinions on whether attorneys who attempted to collect debts owed to their clients were subject to the FDCPA's provisions. In 1995, however, the United States Supreme Court resolved this issue when it held that an attorney who regularly tries to obtain payment of consumer debts through legal proceedings meets the FDCPA's definition of "debt collector."[32]

Garnishment of Wages

Despite the increasing number of protections afforded debtors, creditors are not without means of securing

31. According to the U.S. Court of Appeals for the Sixth Circuit, the $1,000 limit on damages applies to each lawsuit, not to each violation. See *Wright v. Finance Service of Norwalk, Inc.*, 22 F.3d 647 (6th Cir. 1994).

32. *Heintz v. Jenkins*, 514 U.S. 291, 115 S.Ct. 1489, 131 L.Ed.2d 395 (1995).

payment on debts. One of these is the right to garnish a debtor's wages after the debt has gone unpaid for a prolonged period. Recall from Chapter 15 that in a *garnishment* process, a creditor directly attaches, or seizes, a portion of the debtor's assets (such as wages) that are in the possession of a third party (such as an employer).

State law governs the garnishment process, but the law varies among the states as to how easily garnishment can be obtained. Indeed, a few states, such as Texas, prohibit garnishment of wages except for child support and court-approved spousal maintenance. Constitutional due process and federal legislation under the TILA also provide certain protections against abuse.[33] In general, the debtor is entitled to notice and an opportunity to be heard. Moreover, wages cannot be garnished beyond 25 percent of the debtor's after-tax earnings, and the garnishment must leave the debtor with at least a specified minimum income.

SECTION 5 Consumer Health and Safety

The laws discussed earlier regarding the labeling and packaging of products go a long way toward promoting consumer health and safety. There is a significant distinction, however, between regulating the information dispensed about a product and regulating the actual content of the product. The classic example is tobacco products. Producers of tobacco products are required to warn consumers about the hazards associated with the use of their products, but the sale of tobacco products has not been subjected to significant restrictions or banned outright despite the obvious dangers to health.[34] We now examine various laws that regulate the actual products made available to consumers.

The Federal Food, Drug and Cosmetic Act

The first federal legislation regulating food and drugs was enacted in 1906 as the Pure Food and Drugs Act. That law, as amended in 1938, exists today as the Federal Food, Drug and Cosmetic Act (FDCA).[35] The act protects consumers against adulterated and misbranded foods and drugs. As to foods, in its present form, the act establishes food standards, specifies safe levels of potentially hazardous food additives, and sets classifications of foods and food advertising. Most of these statutory requirements are monitored and enforced by the Food and Drug Administration (FDA).

The FDCA also charges the FDA with the responsibility of ensuring that drugs are safe before they are marketed to the public. Under an extensive set of procedures established by the FDA, drugs must be shown to be effective as well as safe, and the use of some food additives suspected of being carcinogenic is prohibited. A 1976 amendment to the FDCA[36] authorizes the FDA to regulate medical devices, such as pacemakers and other health devices and equipment, and to withdraw from the market any such device that is mislabeled.

The question in the following case was whether the U.S. Constitution provides terminally ill patients with a right of access to experimental drugs that have passed limited safety trials but have not been proved safe and effective.

33. 15 U.S.C. Sections 1671–1677.

34. We are ignoring recent civil litigation concerning the liability of tobacco product manufacturers for injuries that arise from the use of tobacco. See, for example, *Philip Morris USA v. Williams*, __U.S.__, 127 S.Ct. 1057, 166 L.Ed.2d 940 (2007).

35. 21 U.S.C. Sections 301–393.

36. 21 U.S.C. Sections 352(o), 360(j), 360(k), and 360c–360k.

CASE 23.4 Abigail Alliance for Better Access to Developmental Drugs v. von Eschenbach

United States Court of Appeals, District of Columbia Circuit, 2007. 495 F.3d 695.

• **Background and Facts** The Food and Drug Administration (FDA) and Congress have created programs to provide terminally ill patients with access to promising experimental drugs before the completion of the clinical-testing process—which can be lengthy. The Abigail Alliance for Better Access to Developmental Drugs (Alliance), an organization of terminally ill patients and their supporters, asked the FDA to expand this access. The FDA responded that, among other things, "a reasonably precise estimate of response rate" and "enough experience to detect serious adverse effects" are "critical" in determining

CASE CONTINUES

CASE 23.4 CONTINUED when experimental drugs should be made available. Accordingly, "it does not serve patients well to make drugs too widely available before there is a reasonable assessment of such risks to guide patient decisions, and experience in managing them." Accepting Alliance's proposal "would upset the appropriate balance * * * by giving almost total weight to the goal of early availability and giving little recognition to the importance of marketing drugs with reasonable knowledge for patients and physicians of their likely clinical benefit and their toxicity." Alliance filed a suit in a federal district court against FDA commissioner Andrew von Eschenbach and others, arguing that the Constitution provides terminally ill patients with a fundamental right of access to experimental drugs. The court ruled in the defendants' favor. Alliance appealed to the U.S. Court of Appeals for the District of Columbia Circuit.

IN THE LANGUAGE OF THE COURT
***GRIFFITH,* Circuit Judge:**

* * * *

* * * [The due process clause of the Fifth Amendment to the Constitution] provides heightened protection against government interference with certain fundamental rights [by subjecting that interference to strict scrutiny] * * * .

* * * *

* * * *The Due Process Clause specially protects those fundamental rights * * * which are, objectively, deeply rooted in this Nation's history and tradition * * ** . [Emphasis added.]

* * * *

Drug regulation in the United States began with the Colonies and the States * * * . In the early history of our Nation, we observe not a tradition of protecting a right of access to drugs, but rather governments responding to the risks of new compounds as they become aware of and able to address those risks.

* * * *

The current regime of federal drug regulation began to take shape with the Food, Drug, and Cosmetic Act [FDCA] of 1938. The Act required that drug manufacturers provide proof that their products were safe before they could be marketed.

* * * Congress amended the FDCA in 1962 to explicitly require that the FDA only approve drugs deemed effective for public use. Thus, the Alliance argues that, prior to 1962, patients were free to make their own decisions whether a drug might be effective. * * * Alliance's argument ignores our Nation's history of drug safety regulation * * * . Nor can the Alliance override current FDA regulations simply by insisting that drugs which have completed [some] testing are safe enough for terminally ill patients. Current law bars public access to drugs undergoing clinical testing on safety grounds. *The fact that a drug * * * is safe for limited clinical testing in a controlled and closely monitored environment after detailed scrutiny of each trial participant does not mean that a drug is safe for use beyond supervised trials.* [Emphasis added.]

* * * *

* * * We conclude that the Alliance has not provided evidence of a right to procure and use experimental drugs that is deeply rooted in our Nation's history and traditions.

* * * *

Because the Alliance's claimed right is not fundamental, the Alliance's claim of a right of access to experimental drugs is subject only to rational basis scrutiny. *The rational basis test requires that the Alliance prove that the government's restrictions bear no rational relationship to a legitimate state interest.* [Emphasis added.]

* * * *

Applying the rational basis standard to the Alliance's complaint, we cannot say that the government's interest does not bear a rational relation to a legitimate state interest. * * * For the terminally ill, as for anyone else, a drug is unsafe if its potential for inflicting death or physical injury is not offset by the possibility of therapeutic benefit.

* * * Thus, we must conclude that * * * the Government has a rational basis for ensuring that there is a scientifically and medically acceptable level of knowledge about the risks and benefits of such a drug.

● **Decision and Remedy** *The U.S. Court of Appeals for the District of Columbia Circuit affirmed the lower court's decision, holding that terminally ill patients do not have a fundamental con-*

CASE 23.4 CONTINUED

stitutional right of access to experimental drugs. Furthermore, "the FDA's policy of limiting access to investigational drugs is rationally related to the legitimate state interest of protecting patients, including the terminally ill, from potentially unsafe drugs with unknown therapeutic effects."

- **The Global Dimension** *Should the court have ruled that as long as a drug has been approved for use in any country, terminally ill patients in the United States should be given access to it? Explain.*

- **The Legal Environment Dimension** *In light of the analysis in this case, what option is left to those who believe that terminally ill patients—not the government—should make the decision about whether to accept the risk associated with experimental drugs?*

The Consumer Product Safety Act

Consumer product-safety legislation began in 1953 with the passage of the Flammable Fabrics Act, which prohibits the sale of highly flammable clothing or materials. Over the next two decades, Congress enacted legislation regarding the design or composition of specific classes of products. Then, in 1972, Congress enacted the Consumer Product Safety Act,[37] creating the first comprehensive scheme of regulation over matters of consumer safety. The act also established the Consumer Product Safety Commission (CPSC), which has far-reaching authority over consumer safety.

The CPSC's Authority The CPSC conducts research on the safety of individual consumer products and maintains a clearinghouse on the risks associated with various products. The Consumer Product Safety Act authorizes the CPSC to set standards for consumer products and to ban the manufacture and sale of any product that it deems to be potentially hazardous to consumers. The CPSC also has authority to remove from the market any products it believes to be imminently hazardous and to require manufacturers to report on any products already sold or intended for sale if the products have proved to be dangerous. The CPSC also has authority to administer other product-safety legislation, such as the Child Protection and Toy Safety Act of 1969[38] and the Federal Hazardous Substances Act of 1960.[39]

The CPSC's authority is sufficiently broad to allow it to ban any product that it believes poses an "unreasonable risk" to consumers. This includes the authority to ban the importation of hazardous products into the United States. Some of the products that the CPSC has banned include various types of fireworks, cribs, and toys, as well as many products containing asbestos or vinyl chloride.

Notification Requirements The Consumer Product Safety Act requires the distributors of consumer products to notify the CPSC immediately if they receive information that a product "contains a defect which . . . creates a substantial risk to the public" or "an unreasonable risk of serious injury or death."

For example, Aroma Housewares Company had been distributing a particular model of juicer for just over a year when it began receiving letters from customers. They complained that during operation the juicer had suddenly exploded, sending pieces of glass and razor-sharp metal across the room. The company received twenty-three letters from angry consumers about the exploding juicer but waited more than six months before notifying the CPSC that the product posed a significant risk to the public. In a suit filed by the federal government, the court held that when a company first receives information regarding a threat, the company is required to report the problem within twenty-four hours to the CPSC. The court also found that even if the company had to investigate the allegations, it should not have taken more than ten days to verify the information and report the problem. The court therefore held that the company had violated the law and ordered it to pay damages.[40]

37. 15 U.S.C. Sections 2051–2083.

38. This act consists of amendments to 15 U.S.C. Sections 1261, 1262, and 1274.

39. 15 U.S.C. Sections 1261–1277.

40. *United States v. Miram Enterprises, Inc.*, 185 F.Supp.2d 1148 (S.D.Ca. 2002).

REVIEWING Consumer Protection

Leota Sage saw a local motorcycle dealer's newspaper advertisement for a MetroRider EZ electric scooter for $1,699. When she went to the dealership, however, she learned that the EZ model had been sold out. The salesperson told Sage that he still had the higher-end MetroRider FX model in stock for $2,199 and would offer her one for $1,999. Sage was disappointed but decided to purchase the FX model. When Sage said that she wished to purchase the scooter on credit, she was directed to the dealer's credit department. As she filled out the credit forms, the clerk told Sage, who is an African American, that she would need a cosigner to obtain a loan. Sage could not understand why she would need a cosigner and asked to speak to the store manager. The manager apologized, told her that the clerk was mistaken, and said that he would "speak to" the clerk about that. The manager completed Sage's credit application, and Sage then rode the scooter home. Seven months later, Sage received a letter from the manufacturer informing her that a flaw had been discovered in the scooter's braking system and that the model had been recalled. Using the information presented in the chapter, answer the following questions.

1. Had the dealer engaged in deceptive advertising? Why or why not?
2. Suppose that Sage had ordered the scooter through the dealer's Web site but the dealer had been unable to deliver it by the date promised. What would the FTC have required the merchant to do in that situation?
3. Assuming that the clerk had required a cosigner based on Sage's race or gender, what act prohibits such credit discrimination?
4. What organization has the authority to ban the sale of scooters based on safety concerns?

TERMS AND CONCEPTS

bait-and-switch advertising 582
cease-and-desist order 583
consumer law 580
counteradvertising 583
deceptive advertising 581
multiple product order 583
Regulation Z 586
validation notice 589

QUESTIONS AND CASE PROBLEMS

23–1. Andrew, a resident of California, received an advertising circular in the U.S. mail announcing a new line of regional cookbooks distributed by the Every-Kind Cookbook Co. Andrew didn't want any books and threw the circular away. Two days later, Andrew received in the mail an introductory cookbook entitled *Lower Mongolian Regional Cookbook,* as announced in the circular, on a "trial basis" from Every-Kind. Andrew was not interested but did not go to the trouble to return the cookbook. Every-Kind demanded payment of $20.95 for the *Lower Mongolian Regional Cookbook.* Discuss whether Andrew can be required to pay for the book.

23–2. Maria Ochoa receives two new credit cards on May 1. She had solicited one of them from Midtown Department Store, and the other arrived unsolicited from High-Flying Airlines. During the month of May, Ochoa makes numerous credit-card purchases from Midtown Department Store, but she does not use the High-Flying Airlines card. On May 31, a burglar breaks into Ochoa's home and steals both credit cards, along with other items. Ochoa notifies the Midtown Department Store of the theft on June 2, but she fails to notify High-Flying Airlines. Using the Midtown credit card, the burglar makes a $500 purchase on June 1 and a $200 purchase on June 3. The burglar then charges a vacation flight on the High-Flying Airlines card for $1,000 on June 5. Ochoa receives the bills for these charges and refuses to pay them. Discuss Ochoa's liability in these situations.

23-3. QUESTION WITH SAMPLE ANSWER

On June 28, a salesperson for Renowned Books called on the Gonchars at their home. After a very persuasive sales pitch by the agent, the Gonchars agreed in writing to purchase a twenty-volume set of historical encyclopedias from Renowned Books for a total of $299. A down payment of $35 was required, with the remainder of the cost to be paid in monthly payments over a one-year period. Two days later, the Gonchars, having second thoughts, contacted the book company and stated that they had decided to rescind the contract. Renowned Books said this would be impossible. Has Renowned Books violated any consumer law by not allowing the Gonchars to rescind their contract? Explain.

- **For a sample answer to Question 23–3, go to Appendix I at the end of this text.**

23-4. Fair Debt Collection. CrossCheck, Inc., provides check-authorization services to retail merchants. When a customer presents a check, the merchant contacts CrossCheck, which estimates the probability that the check will clear the bank. If the check is within an acceptable statistical range, CrossCheck notifies the merchant. If the check is dishonored, the merchant sends it to CrossCheck, which pays it. CrossCheck then attempts to redeposit the check. If this fails, CrossCheck takes further steps to collect the amount. CrossCheck attempts to collect on more than two thousand checks per year and spends $2 million on these efforts, which involve about 7 percent of its employees and 6 percent of its total expenses. William Winterstein took his truck to C&P Auto Service Center, Inc., for a tune-up and paid for the service with a check. C&P contacted CrossCheck and, on its recommendation, accepted the check. When the check was dishonored, C&P mailed it to CrossCheck, which reimbursed C&P and sent a letter to Winterstein requesting payment. Winterstein filed a suit in a federal district court against CrossCheck, asserting that the letter violated the Fair Debt Collection Practices Act. CrossCheck filed a motion for summary judgment. On what ground might the court grant the motion? Explain. [*Winterstein v. CrossCheck, Inc.*, 149 F.Supp.2d 466 (N.D.Ill. 2001)]

23-5. Fair Credit Reporting Act. Source One Associates, Inc., is based in Poughquag, New York. Peter Easton, Source One's president, is responsible for its daily operations. Between 1995 and 1997, Source One received requests from persons in Massachusetts seeking financial information about individuals and businesses. To obtain this information, Easton first obtained the targeted individuals' credit reports through Equifax Consumer Information Services by claiming that the reports would be used only in connection with credit transactions involving the consumers. From the reports, Easton identified financial institutions at which the targeted individuals held accounts. He then called the institutions to learn the account balances by impersonating either officers of the institutions or the account holders. The information was then provided to Source One's customers for a fee. Easton did not know why the customers wanted the information. The state ("commonwealth") of Massachusetts filed a suit in a Massachusetts state court against Source One and Easton, alleging, among other things, violations of the Fair Credit Reporting Act (FCRA). Did the defendants violate the FCRA? Explain. [*Commonwealth v. Source One Associates, Inc.*, 436 Mass. 118, 763 N.E.2d 42 (2002)]

23-6. Deceptive Advertising. "Set Up & Ready to Make Money in Minutes Guaranteed!" the ads claimed. "The Internet Treasure Chest (ITC) will give you everything you need to start your own exciting Internet business including your own worldwide Web site all for the unbelievable price of only $59.95." The ITC "contains virtually everything you need to quickly and easily get your very own worldwide Internet business up, running, stocked with products, able to accept credit cards and ready to take orders almost immediately." What ITC's marketers—Damien Zamora and end70 Corp.—did not disclose were the significant additional costs required to operate the business: domain name registration fees, monthly Internet access and hosting charges, monthly fees to access the ITC product warehouse, and other "upgrades." The Federal Trade Commission filed a suit in a federal district court against end70 and Zamora, seeking an injunction and other relief. Are the defendants' claims "deceptive advertising"? If so, what might the court order the defendants to do to correct any misrepresentations? [*Federal Trade Commission v. end70 Corp.*, __ F.Supp.2d __ (N.D.Tex. 2003)]

23-7. CASE PROBLEM WITH SAMPLE ANSWER

One of the products that McDonald's Corp. sells is the Happy Meal®, which consists of a McDonald's food entree, a small order of french fries, a small drink, and a toy. In the early 1990s, McDonald's began to aim its Happy Meal marketing at children aged one to three. In 1995, McDonald's began making nutritional information for its food products available in documents known as "McDonald's Nutrition Facts." Each document lists each food item that the restaurant serves and provides a nutritional breakdown, but the Happy Meal is not included. Marc Cohen filed a suit in an Illinois state court against McDonald's, alleging, among other things, that the defendant had violated a state law prohibiting consumer fraud and deceptive business practices by failing to adhere to the National Labeling and Education Act (NLEA) of 1990. The NLEA sets out different requirements for products specifically intended for children under the age of four—generally, the products cannot declare the percent of daily value of nutritional components. Would this requirement be readily understood by a consumer who is not familiar with nutritional standards? Why or why not? Should a state court impose such regulations? Explain. [*Cohen v. McDonald's Corp.*, 347 Ill.App.3d 627, 808 N.E.2d 1, 283 Ill.Dec. 451 (1 Dist. 2004)]

- **To view a sample answer for Problem 23–7, go to this book's Web site at academic.cengage.com/blaw/cross, select "Chapter 23," and click on "Case Problem with Sample Answer."**

23–8. Debt Collection. 55th Management Corp. in New York City owns residential property that it leases to various tenants. In June 2000, claiming that one of the tenants, Leslie Goldman, owed more than $13,000 in back rent, 55th retained Jeffrey Cohen, an attorney, to initiate nonpayment proceedings. Cohen filed a petition in a New York state court against Goldman, seeking recovery of the unpaid rent and at least $3,000 in attorneys' fees. After receiving notice of the petition, Goldman filed a suit in a federal district court against Cohen. Goldman contended that the notice of the petition constituted an initial contact that, under the Fair Debt Collection Practices Act (FDCPA), required a validation notice. Because Cohen did not give Goldman a validation notice at the time, or within five days, of the notice of the petition, Goldman argued that Cohen was in violation of the FDCPA. Should the filing of a suit in a state court be considered "communication," requiring a debt collector to provide a validation notice under the FDCPA? Why or why not? [*Goldman v. Cohen,* 445 F.3d 152 (2d Cir. 2006)]

23–9. A QUESTION OF ETHICS

*After graduating from law school—and serving time in prison for attempting to collect debts by posing as an FBI agent—Barry Sussman theorized that if a debt-collection business collected only debts that it owned as a result of buying checks written on accounts with insufficient funds (NSF checks), it would not be subject to the Federal Debt Collection Practices Act (FDCPA). Sussman formed Check Investors, Inc., to act on his theory. Check Investors bought more than 2.2 million NSF checks, with an estimated face value of about $348 million, for pennies on the dollar. Check Investors added a fee of $125 or $130 to the face amount of each check (which exceeds the legal limit in most states) and aggressively pursued its drawer to collect. The firm's employees were told to accuse drawers of being criminals and to threaten them with arrest and prosecution. The threats were false. Check Investors never took steps to initiate a prosecution. The employees contacted the drawers' family members and used "saturation phoning"—phoning a drawer numerous times in a short period. They used abusive language, referring to drawers as "deadbeats," "retards," "thieves," and "idiots." Between January 2000 and January 2003, Check Investors netted more than $10.2 million from its efforts. [*Federal Trade Commission v. Check Investors, Inc., *502 F.3d 159 (3d Cir. 2007)]*

(a) The Federal Trade Commission filed a suit in a federal district court against Check Investors and others, alleging, in part, violations of the FDCPA. Was Check Investors a "debt collector," collecting "debts," within the meaning of the FDCPA? If so, did its methods violate the FDCPA? Were its practices unethical? What might Check Investors argue in its defense? Discuss.

(b) Are "deadbeats" the primary beneficiaries of laws such as the FDCPA? If not, how would you characterize debtors who default on their obligations?

23–10. VIDEO QUESTION

Go to this text's Web site at **academic.cengage.com/blaw/cross** and select "Chapter 23." Click on "Video Questions" and view the video titled *Advertising Communication Law: Bait and Switch.* Then answer the following questions.

(a) Is the auto dealership's advertisement for the truck in the video deceptive? Why or why not?

(b) Is the advertisement for the truck an offer to which the dealership is bound? Does it matter if Betty detrimentally relied on the advertisement?

(c) Is Tony committed to buying Betty's trade-in truck for $3,000 because that is what he told her over the phone?

LAW ON THE WEB

For updated links to resources available on the Web, as well as a variety of other materials, visit this text's Web site at

academic.cengage.com/blaw/cross

For a government-sponsored Web site containing reports on consumer issues, go to

www.consumer.gov

The Federal Trade Commission (FTC) offers extensive information on consumer protection laws, consumer problems, enforcement issues, and other topics relevant to consumer law at its Web site. Go to

www.ftc.gov

and click on "Consumer Protection."

To learn more about the FTC's "cooling-off" rule, you can access it directly by going to the following URL:

www.ftc.gov/bcp/edu/pubs/consumer/products/pro03.shtm

Legal Research Exercises on the Web

Go to **academic.cengage.com/blaw/cross**, the Web site that accompanies this text. Select "Chapter 23" and click on "Internet Exercises." There you will find the following Internet research exercises that you can perform to learn more about the topics covered in this chapter.

Internet Exercise 23–1: Legal Perspective
The Food and Drug Administration

Internet Exercise 23–2: Management Perspective
Internet Advertising and Marketing

CHAPTER 24

Environmental Law

Concerns over the degradation of the environment have increased over time in response to the environmental effects of population growth, urbanization, and industrialization. Environmental protection is not without a price, however. For many businesses, the costs of complying with environmental regulations are high, and for some they may seem too high. A constant tension exists between the desire to increase profits and productivity and the need to protect the environment. In this chapter, we discuss **environmental law,** which consists of all laws and regulations designed to protect and preserve our environmental resources.

Common Law Actions

Common law remedies against environmental pollution originated centuries ago in England. Those responsible for operations that created dirt, smoke, noxious odors, noise, or toxic substances were sometimes held liable under common law theories of nuisance or negligence. Today, injured individuals continue to rely on the common law to obtain damages and injunctions against business polluters.

Nuisance

Under the common law doctrine of **nuisance,** persons may be held liable if they use their property in a manner that unreasonably interferes with others' rights to use or enjoy their own property. Courts typically balance the equities between the harm caused by the pollution and the costs of stopping it. Courts have often denied injunctive relief on the ground that the hardships that would be imposed on the polluter and on the community are greater than the hardships suffered by the plaintiff. For example, a factory that causes neighboring landowners to suffer from smoke, soot, and vibrations may be left in operation if it is the core of the local economy. The injured parties may be awarded only monetary damages, which may include compensation for the decline in the value of their property caused by the factory's operation.

A property owner may be given relief from pollution if he or she can identify a distinct harm separate from that affecting the general public. This harm is referred to as a "private" nuisance. Under the common law, individuals were denied *standing* (access to the courts—see Chapter 2) unless they suffered a harm distinct from the harm suffered by the public at large. Some states still require this. For example, in one case a group of individuals who made their living by commercial fishing in a major river in New York filed a suit seeking damages and an injunction against a company that was polluting the river. The New York court found that the plaintiffs had standing because they were particularly harmed by the pollution in the river.[1] A public authority (such as a state's attorney general), however, can sue to abate a "public" nuisance.

Negligence and Strict Liability

An injured party may sue a business polluter in tort under the negligence and strict liability theories discussed in Chapters 12 and 13. The basis for a negligence action is a business's alleged failure to use reasonable care toward a party whose injury was foreseeable and was caused by the lack of reasonable

1. *Lee v. General Electric Co.*, 538 N.Y.S.2d 844, 145 A.D.2d 291 (1989).

care. For example, employees might sue an employer whose failure to use proper pollution controls contaminated the air, causing the employees to suffer respiratory illnesses. A developing area of tort law involves **toxic torts**—actions against toxic polluters.

Businesses that engage in ultrahazardous activities—such as the transportation of radioactive materials—are strictly liable for any injuries the activities cause. In a strict liability action, the injured party need not prove that the business failed to exercise reasonable care.

Federal, State, and Local Regulation

All levels of government in the United States regulate some aspect of the environment. In this section, we look at the various ways in which the federal, state, and local governments control business activities and land use in the interests of environmental preservation and protection.

Federal Regulation

Congress has passed a number of statutes to control the impact of human activities on the environment. Exhibit 24–1 on the next page lists and summarizes the major federal environmental statutes, most of which are discussed in this chapter. Some of these statutes were passed in an attempt to improve air and water quality. Others specifically regulate toxic chemicals, including pesticides, herbicides, and hazardous wastes.

Environmental Regulatory Agencies The primary federal agency regulating environmental law is the Environmental Protection Agency (EPA), which was created in 1970 to coordinate federal environmental responsibilities. Other federal agencies with authority for regulating specific environmental matters include the Department of the Interior, the Department of Defense, the Department of Labor, the Food and Drug Administration, and the Nuclear Regulatory Commission. These regulatory agencies—and all other agencies of the federal government—must take environmental factors into consideration when making significant decisions.

Most federal environmental laws provide that private parties can sue to enforce environmental regulations if government agencies fail to do so—or can sue to protest agency enforcement actions if they believe that these actions go too far. Typically, a threshold hurdle in such suits is meeting the requirements for standing to sue (see Chapter 2).

State and local regulatory agencies also play a significant role in carrying out federal environmental legislation. Typically, the federal government relies on state and local governments to implement federal environmental statutes and regulations such as those regulating air quality.

Environmental Impact Statements The National Environmental Policy Act (NEPA) of 1969[2] requires that an **environmental impact statement (EIS)** be prepared for every major federal action that significantly affects the quality of the environment. An EIS must analyze (1) the impact on the environment that the action will have, (2) any adverse effects on the environment and alternative actions that might be taken, and (3) irreversible effects the action might generate.

An action qualifies as "major" if it involves a substantial commitment of resources (monetary or otherwise). An action is "federal" if a federal agency has the power to control it. Construction by a private developer of a ski resort on federal land, for example, may require an EIS. Building or operating a nuclear plant, which requires a federal permit, or constructing a dam as part of a federal project requires an EIS. If an agency decides that an EIS is unnecessary, it must issue a statement supporting this conclusion. EISs have become instruments for private individuals, consumer interest groups, businesses, and others to challenge federal agency actions on the basis that the actions improperly threaten the environment.

State and Local Regulation

Many states regulate the degree to which the environment may be polluted. Thus, for example, even when state zoning laws permit a business's proposed development, the proposal may have to be altered to lessen the development's impact on the environment. State laws may restrict a business's discharge of chemicals into the air or water or regulate its disposal of toxic wastes. States may also regulate the disposal or recycling of other wastes, including glass, metal, and plastic containers and paper. Additionally, states may restrict the emissions from motor vehicles.

City, county, and other local governments oversee certain aspects of the environment. For instance, local

2. 42 U.S.C. Sections 4321–4370d.

EXHIBIT 24–1 • Major Federal Environmental Statutes

Popular Name	Purpose	Statute Reference
Rivers and Harbors Appropriations Act (1899)	To prohibit ships and manufacturers from discharging and depositing refuse in navigable waterways.	33 U.S.C. Sections 401–418.
Federal Insecticide, Fungicide, and Rodenticide Act (1947)	To control the use of pesticides and herbicides.	7 U.S.C. Sections 136–136y.
Federal Water Pollution Control Act (1948)	To eliminate the discharge of pollutants from major sources into navigable waters.	33 U.S.C. Sections 1251–1387.
Clean Air Act (1963, 1970)	To control air pollution from mobile and stationary sources.	42 U.S.C. Sections 7401–7671q.
National Environmental Policy Act (1969)	To limit environmental harm from federal government activities.	42 U.S.C. Sections 4321–4370d.
Endangered Species Act (1973)	To protect species that are threatened with extinction.	16 U.S.C. Sections 1531–1544.
Safe Drinking Water Act (1974)	To regulate pollutants in public drinking water systems.	42 U.S.C. Sections 300f to 300j-25.
Resource Conservation and Recovery Act (1976)	To establish standards for hazardous waste disposal.	42 U.S.C. Sections 6901–6986.
Toxic Substances Control Act (1976)	To regulate toxic chemicals and chemical compounds.	15 U.S.C. Sections 2601–2692.
Comprehensive Environmental Response, Compensation, and Liability Act (1980)	To regulate the clean-up of hazardous waste–disposal sites.	42 U.S.C. Sections 9601–9675.
Oil Pollution Act (1990)	To establish liability for the clean-up of navigable waters after oil-spill disasters.	33 U.S.C. Sections 2701–2761.
Small Business Liability Relief and Brownfields Revitalization Act (2002)	To allow developers who comply with state voluntary clean-up programs to avoid federal liability for the properties that they decontaminate and develop.	42 U.S.C. Section 9628.

zoning laws control some land use. These laws may be designed to inhibit or direct the growth of cities and suburbs or to protect the natural environment. In the interest of safeguarding the environment, such laws may prohibit certain land uses.

Other aspects of the environment may also be subject to local regulation. Methods of waste and garbage removal and disposal, for example, can have a substantial impact on a community. The appearance of buildings and other structures, including advertising signs and billboards, may affect traffic safety, property values, or local aesthetics. Noise generated by a business or its customers may be annoying, disruptive, or damaging to its neighbors. The location and condition of parks, streets, and other public uses of land subject to local control affect the environment and can also affect business.

Air Pollution

Federal involvement with air pollution goes back to the 1950s and 60s, when Congress authorized funds for air-pollution research and passed the Clean Air Act.[3]

3. 42 U.S.C. Sections 7401–7671q.

The act focused on multistate air pollution and provided assistance to the states. Amendments to the Clean Air Act, particularly those made in 1970, 1977, and 1990, strengthened the government's authority to regulate air quality. These laws provide the basis for issuing regulations to control pollution coming primarily from mobile sources (such as automobiles) and stationary sources (such as electric utilities and industrial plants).

Mobile Sources

Automobiles and other vehicles are referred to as mobile sources of pollution. The EPA has issued regulations specifying standards for mobile sources of pollution, as well as for service stations. The agency periodically updates these standards in light of new developments and data.

Motor Vehicles Regulations governing air pollution from automobiles and other mobile sources specify pollution standards and time schedules for meeting these standards. For example, the 1990 amendments to the Clean Air Act required automobile manufacturers to cut new automobiles' exhaust emissions of nitrogen oxide by 60 percent and emissions of other pollutants by 35 percent by 1998. Regulations that became effective beginning with 2004 model cars called for nitrogen oxide tailpipe emissions to be cut by nearly 10 percent by 2007. For the first time, sport-utility vehicles (SUVs) and light trucks were required to meet the same emission standards as automobiles. The amendments also required service stations to sell gasoline with a higher oxygen content in certain cities, and to sell even cleaner-burning gasoline in the most polluted urban areas.

When individuals or groups oppose regulations, they often file lawsuits in an attempt to *prevent* an agency from taking some regulatory action. As mentioned earlier, however, private parties also sometimes file lawsuits in an effort to *compel* an agency to take action in an area in which it has failed to act. A group of private organizations and several states recently took such an action when they sued to require the EPA to adopt rules to regulate carbon dioxide emissions from automobiles under the Clean Air Act. For a discussion of the United States Supreme Court's decision in this case, see this chapter's *Contemporary Legal Debates* feature on the following two pages.

Updating Pollution-Control Standards As mentioned, the EPA attempts to update pollution-control standards when new scientific information becomes available. For example, studies conducted in the 1990s concluded that very small particles (2.5 microns, or millionths of a meter) of soot affect our health as significantly as larger particles. Based on this evidence, in 1997 the EPA issued new particulate standards for motor vehicle exhaust systems and other sources of pollution. The EPA also set a more rigorous standard for ozone (the basic ingredient of smog), which is formed when sunlight combines with pollutants from cars and other sources.

The EPA's particulate standards and ozone standard were challenged in court by a number of business groups that claimed that the EPA had exceeded its authority under the Clean Air Act by issuing the stricter rules. Additionally, the groups claimed that the EPA had to take economic costs into account when developing new regulations. In 2000, however, the United States Supreme Court upheld the EPA's authority under the Clean Air Act to issue the standards. The Court also held that the EPA did not have to take economic costs into account when creating new rules.[4]

In 2006, the EPA again reevaluated its particulate standards and found that more than two hundred counties were not meeting the standards set in 1997. The EPA issued new regulations for daily (twenty-four hour) exposure to particles of soot but did not change the annual particulate standards.[5]

Stationary Sources

The Clean Air Act also authorizes the EPA to establish air-quality standards for stationary sources (such as manufacturing plants) but recognizes that the primary responsibility for implementing these standards rests with state and local governments. The standards are aimed at controlling hazardous air pollutants—that is, those likely to cause death or serious irreversible or incapacitating illness such as cancer or neurological and reproductive damage.

Listing of Regulated Hazardous Air Pollutants When Congress amended the Clean Air Act in 1970, it required the EPA to list all regulated hazardous air pollutants (HAPs) on a prioritized schedule. The EPA listed only eight substances for the next eighteen years. In 1990, Congress again amended the act and required the EPA to list more substances as

4. *Whitman v. American Trucking Associations,* 531 U.S. 457, 121 S.Ct. 903, 149 L.Ed.2d 1 (2001).
5. 40 C.F.R. Part 50.

CONTEMPORARY LEGAL DEBATES

Should the EPA Take the Threat of Global Warming into Account?

For some time, environmental groups have argued that Congress should take action to curb emissions of so-called greenhouse gases, including carbon dioxide, which build up in the atmosphere and supposedly create a "greenhouse effect," leading to global warming. They wanted Congress to mandate that the Environmental Protection Agency (EPA) consider global warming effects when instituting regulations, particularly with respect to carbon dioxide emissions from automobiles.

If Congress Won't Act, Go to Court to Force the EPA to Act

In 1999, frustrated by Congress's apparent lack of concern about global warming, environmental groups went directly to the EPA and petitioned the agency to use its authority under the Clean Air Act to regulate greenhouse gases, including carbon dioxide emissions from motor vehicles. In 2003, however, the EPA denied their petition, stating, among other things, that the Clean Air Act did not authorize it to address global climate change or to regulate carbon dioxide emissions. As a result of the EPA's refusal to take action, the environmental groups and several states brought a lawsuit to force the EPA to act. At issue in the case was not only whether the EPA has the authority to regulate carbon dioxide under the Clean Air Act but also whether the plaintiffs had *standing* to bring their case at all.

The Supreme Court Agrees

In 2007, in *Massachusetts v. Environmental Protection Agency*,[a] the United States Supreme Court issued what may turn out to be a landmark decision supporting the plaintiffs. As to whether the plaintiffs had standing to sue, recall from the discussion earlier in this chapter that ordinarily a plaintiff must have suffered a particularized harm that is distinct from that experienced by the public at large. In this case, Massachusetts asserted that it had standing because its coastline, including lands owned by the state, faced an imminent threat from rising sea levels caused by global warming. The Court agreed, declaring that "the harm associated with climate changes is serious and well recognized," including "severe and irreversible changes to natural ecosystems" and "a precipitate rise in sea levels." The EPA had argued that because global warming has widespread effects, an individual plaintiff could not show the particularized harm that standing requires, but the Court said that the fact that these effects are widely shared does not minimize their

a. ___ U.S. ___, 127 S.Ct. 1438, 167 L.Ed.2d 248 (2007).

HAPs. In all, 189 substances, including asbestos, benzene, beryllium, cadmium, and vinyl chloride, have been classified as hazardous. They are emitted from stationary sources by a variety of business activities, including smelting (melting ore to produce metal), dry cleaning, house painting, and commercial baking.

Mercury is one of the listed hazardous substances. The EPA attempted nonetheless to remove mercury from its list of designated HAPs emitted from electric utility steam-generating units. In the following case, New Jersey and others challenged this delisting.

CASE 24.1 State of New Jersey v. Environmental Protection Agency

United States Court of Appeals for the District of Columbia Circuit, 2008. ___ F.3d ___.
www.cadc.uscourts.gov/bin/opinions/allopinions.asp[a]

• **Background and Facts** The Environmental Protection Agency (EPA) published a rule—the Delisting Rule—that had the effect of removing from its regulation the emissions of mercury from steam-generating electricity plants that used coal or oil as their energy sources. This Delisting Rule ran counter to the EPA's own conclusions at the end of 2000 that it was "appropriate and necessary" to regulate mercury emissions. At that time, it placed mercury on its list of hazardous air pollutants (HAPs) to be moni-

a. This is the opinions page of the Court of Appeals for the District of Columbia. Select "February" and "2008" from the drop-down menus for "Month" and "Year" and click on "Go!" Scroll down to the listing for case number "05-1097" and click on the link to access the opinion.

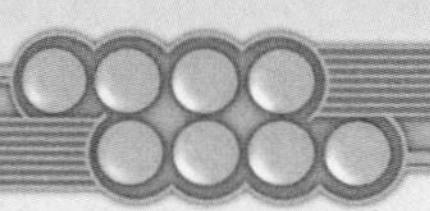

impact on Massachusetts. Hence, Massachusetts had standing to bring a lawsuit to force the EPA to take action to protect the state and its residents.

The Court also found that the Clean Air Act gives the EPA the authority to regulate carbon dioxide. The agency had contended that the statutory language did not include carbon dioxide, but the Court pointed out that the statute defines an air pollutant as "any physical, chemical, . . . substance which is emitted into or otherwise enters the ambient air"—a definition that would include all airborne compounds. Thus, the statute's mandate that the EPA should regulate "any air pollutant" from cars that might "endanger public health or welfare" provides authority to regulate carbon dioxide.

But Others Are Critical

Although environmental groups hailed the decision, others were highly critical. Many observers questioned the Court's ruling on standing. They pointed out that Massachusetts had presented no exhibits to support witnesses' statements that Massachusetts would actually lose coastal land as a result of rising sea levels. Hence, there was no imminent harm—and thus no case or controversy, as required by Article III of the U.S. Constitution. To date, at least two federal courts have declined to extend the ruling to other subjects.[b]

The Court's interpretation of the Clean Air Act has also been controversial. Critics have pointed out that when Congress last amended the Clean Air Act in 1990, there were already major studies on global warming. Nevertheless, Congress did not include amendments that would have forced the EPA to set carbon dioxide emission standards. If Congress chose not to force the EPA to act, why should the Court do so? In his dissent, Justice Antonin Scalia also criticized the majority's broad definition of "pollutant." He pointed out that the dictionary defines "pollute" as "to make or render impure or unclean," a definition that hardly applies to carbon dioxide, which, after all, is the principal product of human respiration.

WHERE DO YOU STAND?

Some argue that the requirement that plaintiffs have standing is one of the self-restraints on the power of the federal courts. Do you think that the Supreme Court's decision in the *Massachusetts* case diluted the standards for standing? Why or why not? Will the Supreme Court's new approach to standing increase or decrease the role of the courts in U.S. public life? Why?

b. See *United States v. Genendo Pharmaceutical, N.V.,* 485 F.3d 958 (7th Cir. 2007); and *American Civil Liberties Union v. National Security Agency,* 493 F.3d 644 (6th Cir. 2007).

CASE 24.1 CONTINUED tored at electricity-generating sites. New Jersey and fourteen additional states, plus various state agencies, challenged the EPA's action.

IN THE LANGUAGE OF THE COURT
***ROGERS,* Circuit Judge.**

* * * *

First, Congress required EPA to regulate more than one hundred specific HAPs [hazardous air pollutants], including mercury and nickel compounds. Further, EPA was required to list and to regulate, on a prioritized schedule, "all categories and subcategories of major sources and areas sources" that emit one or more HAPs. *In seeking to ensure that regulation of HAPs reflects the "maximum reduction in emissions which can be achieved by application of [the] best available control technology," Congress imposed specific, strict pollution control requirements on both new and existing sources of HAPs.* [Emphasis added.]

Second, Congress restricted the opportunities for EPA and others to intervene in the regulation of HAP sources. For HAPs that result in health effects other than cancer, as is true of mercury, Congress directed that the Administrator "may delete any source category" from the section 112(c)(1) list only after determining that "emissions from no source in the category or subcategory concerned . . . exceed a level which is adequate to protect public health with an ample margin of safety and no adverse environmental effect will result from emissions from any source."

CASE CONTINUES

CASE 24.1 CONTINUED

* * * *

EPA maintains that it possesses authority to remove EGUs [electrical generating units] from * * * [the] list under the "fundamental principle of administrative law that an agency has inherent authority to reverse an earlier administrative determination or ruling where an agency has a principled basis for doing so."

EPA states in its brief that it has previously removed sources listed * * * without satisfying the requirements of [the statute]. But previous statutory violations cannot excuse the one now before the court. "We do not see how merely applying an unreasonable statutory interpretation for several years can transform it into a reasonable interpretation."

• **Decision and Remedy** *The U.S. Court of Appeals for the District of Columbia Circuit ruled in favor of New Jersey and the other plaintiffs. The EPA was required to rescind its delisting of mercury.*

• **What If the Facts Were Different?** *Assume that the EPA had carried out scientific tests that showed mercury was relatively harmless as a by-product of electricity generation. How might this have affected the court's ruling?*

• **The Global Dimension** *Because air pollution knows no borders, how did this ruling affect our neighboring countries?*

Air Pollution Control Standards The EPA sets primary and secondary levels of ambient standards—that is, the maximum levels of certain pollutants—and the states formulate plans to achieve those standards. Different standards apply depending on whether the sources of pollution are located in clean areas or polluted areas and whether they are already existing sources or major new sources. Major new sources include existing sources modified by a change in a method of operation that increases emissions. Performance standards for major sources require the use of the *maximum achievable control technology*, or MACT, to reduce emissions. The EPA issues guidelines as to what equipment meets this standard.[6]

The pollution-control schemes established under the Clean Air Act are known as New Source Performance Standards (NSPS) and Prevention of Significant Deterioration (PSD). The NSPS and PSD provisions' definitions of the term *modification* were at the center of the dispute in the following case.

6. The EPA has also issued rules to regulate hazardous air pollutants emitted by landfills. 40 C.F.R. Sections 60.750–759.

EXTENDED CASE 24.2 **Environmental Defense v. Duke Energy Corp.**

Supreme Court of the United States, 2007. __ U.S. __, 127 S.Ct. 1423, 167 L.Ed.2d 295.
www.law.cornell.edu/supct/index.html[a]

Justice *SOUTER* delivered the opinion of the Court.

* * * *

* * * Section 111(a) of the [Clean Air Amendments of] 1970 * * * defined [modification] within the NSPS [New Source Performance Standards] scheme as "any physical change in, or change in the method of operation of, a stationary source which increases the amount of any air pollutant emitted by such source or which results in the emission of any air pollutant not previously emitted."

EPA's 1975 regulations implementing NSPS * * * [identified] "a modification within the meaning of [S]ection 111" * * * as a change that "increase[s] * * * the emission rate," which "shall be expressed as [kilograms per hour] of any pollutant discharged into the atmosphere."

a. In the "Archive of Decisions" section, in the "By party" subsection, click on "1990-present." In the result, in the "2006-2007" row, click on "1st party." On the next page, scroll to the name of the case and click on it. On that page, click on the appropriate link to access the opinion. Cornell University Law School maintains this Web site.

CASE 24.2 CONTINUED

* * * The Clean Air Act Amendments of 1977 included the PSD [Prevention of Significant Deterioration] provisions, which * * * required a PSD permit before a "major emitting facility" could be "constructed" * * * . "The term 'construction' * * * includes the modification (as defined in [S]ection 111(a)) * * * ."

* * * *

* * * EPA's 1980 PSD regulations require a permit for a modification (with the same statutory definition) only when it is a major one and only when it would increase the actual annual emission of a pollutant above the actual average for the two prior years.

* * * *

* * * Duke Energy Corporation runs 30 coal-fired electric generating units at eight plants in North and South Carolina. The units were placed in service between 1940 and 1975, and each includes a boiler containing thousands of steel tubes arranged in sets. Between 1988 and 2000, Duke replaced or redesigned 29 tube assemblies in order to extend the life of the units and allow them to run longer each day.

The United States filed this action [in a federal district court] in 2000, claiming, among other things, that Duke violated the PSD provisions by doing this work without permits. Environmental Defense [and other private organizations] filed a complaint charging similar violations.

* * * [T]he District Court [ruled that] a PSD "major modification" can occur "only if the project increases the hourly rate of emissions" [and issued a judgment in Duke's favor] * * * .

* * * *

[On the plaintiffs' appeal, the U.S.] Court of Appeals for the Fourth Circuit affirmed * * * . "Identical statutory definitions of the term 'modification'" in the NSPS and PSD provisions * * * "[have] affirmatively mandated that this term be interpreted identically" in the regulations * * * . [The plaintiffs appealed to the United States Supreme Court.]

* * * *

In applying the 1980 PSD regulations to Duke's conduct, the Court of Appeals thought that, by defining the term "modification" identically in its NSPS and PSD provisions, the Act required EPA to conform its PSD interpretation of that definition to any such interpretation it reasonably adhered to under NSPS. *But principles of statutory construction are not so rigid.* * * * *Most words have different shades of meaning and consequently may be variously construed, not only when they occur in different statutes, but when used more than once in the same statute or even in the same section.* Thus, the natural presumption that identical words used in different parts of the same act are intended to have the same meaning * * * readily yields whenever there is such variation in the connection in which the words are used as reasonably to warrant the conclusion that they were employed in different parts of the act with different intent. *A given term in the same statute may take on distinct characters from association with distinct statutory objects calling for different implementation strategies.* [Emphasis added.]

* * * *

The Court of Appeals's reasoning that the PSD regulations must conform to their NSPS counterparts led the court to read those PSD regulations in a way that seems to us too far a stretch * * * .

* * * The regulatory language simply cannot be squared with a regime under which "hourly rate of emissions" is dispositive [a controlling factor].

* * * *

The judgment of the Court of Appeals is vacated, and the case is remanded for further proceedings consistent with this opinion.

QUESTIONS

1. What would support an argument that the Court should have given the term *modification* a definition that would be common to both regulations?
2. Did the U.S. Court of Appeals for the Fourth Circuit's attempt to equate the NSPS and PSD regulations implicitly—without analysis or discussion—invalidate those regulations? Explain.

Violations of the Clean Air Act

For violations of emission limits under the Clean Air Act, the EPA can assess civil penalties of up to $25,000 per day. Additional fines of up to $5,000 per day can be assessed for other violations, such as failing to maintain the required records. To penalize those who find it more cost-effective to violate the act than to comply with it, the EPA is authorized to impose a penalty equal to the violator's economic benefits from noncompliance. Persons who provide information about violators may be paid up to $10,000. Private citizens can also sue violators.

Those who knowingly violate the act may be subject to criminal penalties, including fines of up to $1 million and imprisonment for up to two years (for false statements or failure to report violations). Corporate officers are among those who may be subject to these penalties.

Water Pollution

Water pollution stems mostly from industrial, municipal, and agricultural sources. Pollutants entering streams, lakes, and oceans include organic wastes, heated water, sediments from soil runoff, nutrients (including fertilizers and human and animal wastes), and toxic chemicals and other hazardous substances. We look here at laws and regulations governing water pollution.

Navigable Waters

Federal regulations governing water pollution can be traced back to the Rivers and Harbors Appropriations Act of 1899.[7] These regulations prohibited ships and manufacturers from discharging or depositing refuse in navigable waterways. Once limited to waters actually used for navigation, the term *navigable waters* is today interpreted to include intrastate lakes and streams used by interstate travelers and industries, as well as coastal and freshwater wetlands (*wetlands* will be defined shortly).

The Clean Water Act In 1948, Congress passed the Federal Water Pollution Control Act (FWPCA),[8] but its regulatory system and enforcement powers proved to be inadequate. In 1972, amendments to the FWPCA—known as the Clean Water Act—established the following goals: (1) make waters safe for swimming, (2) protect fish and wildlife, and (3) eliminate the discharge of pollutants into the water. The act requires municipal and industrial polluters to apply for permits before discharging wastes into navigable waters. The Clean Water Act also set specific schedules, which were extended by amendment in 1977 and by the Water Quality Act of 1987.[9] Under these schedules, the EPA establishes limits for discharges of various types of pollutants based on the technology available for controlling them.

Before a company can obtain a federal license to "discharge" into navigable waters, the affected state must certify that water-protection laws will not be violated. Can a river routed through a hydropower dam "discharge" into itself for purposes of the Clean Water Act, thus requiring the dam's owner to obtain state approval? That was the question in the following case.

7. 33 U.S.C. Sections 401–418.
8. 33 U.S.C. Sections 1251–1387.
9. This act amended 33 U.S.C. Section 1251.

CASE 24.3 S. D. Warren Co. v. Maine Board of Environmental Protection

Supreme Court of the United States, 2006. 547 U.S. 370, 126 S.Ct. 1843, 164 L.Ed.2d 625.
www.findlaw.com/casecode/supreme.html[a]

• **Background and Facts** S. D. Warren Company generates electricity for a paper mill by operating hydropower dams in the Presumpscot River, which runs for twenty-five miles through southern Maine. Each dam creates a pond, from which water funnels into a canal, through turbines, and back to the riverbed. Operating the dams requires a license from the Federal Energy Regulatory Commission (FERC). Under the Clean Water Act, a license for an activity that causes a "discharge" into navigable waters requires the state in which the discharge occurs to certify that the discharge will not violate water-quality standards. To renew the licenses for the dams in 1999, Warren applied for certification from the Maine Department of

a. In the "Browsing" section, click on "2006 Decisions." When that page opens, scroll to the name of the case and click on it to read the opinion.

CASE 24.3 CONTINUED *Environmental Protection. The agency told Warren to maintain a minimum stream flow in the river and to allow passage for migratory fish and eels. Warren appealed to the state Board of Environmental Protection, which upheld the requirements. FERC licensed the dams subject to the conditions. Warren filed a suit in a Maine state court against the state agency, arguing that the dams do not result in discharges. The court ruled in the agency's favor. Warren appealed to the Supreme Judicial Court of Maine, the state's highest court, which affirmed the lower court's ruling. Warren appealed to the United States Supreme Court.*

IN THE LANGUAGE OF THE COURT
Justice *SOUTER* delivered the opinion of the Court.

* * * *

The dispute turns on the meaning of the word "discharge," the key to the state certification requirement under [the Clean Water Act]. * * * *[S]ince it is neither defined in the statute nor a term of art, we are left to construe it in accordance with its ordinary or natural meaning.* [Emphasis added.]

When it applies to water, "discharge" commonly means a "flowing or issuing out," [according to] Webster's New International Dictionary * * * *, and this ordinary sense has consistently been the meaning intended when this Court has used the term in prior water cases.* [Emphasis added.]

* * * *

* * * This Court has not been alone, for the Environmental Protection Agency (EPA) and FERC have each regularly read "discharge" as having its plain meaning and thus covering releases from hydroelectric dams. Warren is, of course, entirely correct in cautioning us that because neither the EPA nor FERC [Federal Energy Regulatory Commission] has formally settled the definition, or even set out agency reasoning, these expressions of agency understanding do not command deference from this Court. But even so, the administrative usage of "discharge" in this way confirms our understanding of the everyday sense of the term.

* * * *

Congress passed the Clean Water Act to "restore and maintain the chemical, physical, and biological integrity of the Nation's waters," the "national goal" being to achieve "water quality which provides for the protection and propagation of fish, shellfish, and wildlife and provides for recreation in and on the water." To do this, the Act does not stop at controlling the "addition of pollutants," but deals with "pollution" generally, which Congress defined to mean "the man-made or man-induced alteration of the chemical, physical, biological, and radiological integrity of water."

The alteration of water quality as thus defined is a risk inherent in limiting river flow and releasing water through turbines. Warren itself admits that its dams "can cause changes in the movement, flow, and circulation of a river * * * caus[ing] a river to absorb less oxygen and to be less passable by boaters and fish." And several [other parties who submitted briefs in this case] alert us to the chemical modification caused by the dams, with "immediate impact on aquatic organisms, which of course rely on dissolved oxygen in water to breathe." Then there are the findings of the Maine Department of Environmental Protection that led to this appeal:

> The record in this case demonstrates that Warren's dams have caused long stretches of the natural river bed to be essentially dry and thus unavailable as habitat for indigenous populations of fish and other aquatic organisms; that the dams have blocked the passage of eels and sea-run fish to their natural spawning and nursery waters; that the dams have eliminated the opportunity for fishing in long stretches of river, and that the dams have prevented recreational access to and use of the river.

Changes in the river like these fall within a State's legitimate legislative business, and the Clean Water Act provides for a system that respects the States' concerns. [Emphasis added.]

State certifications under [the Clean Water Act] are essential in the scheme to preserve state authority to address the broad range of pollution * * * .

Reading [the Clean Water Act] to give "discharge" its common and ordinary meaning preserves the state authority apparently intended.

• **Decision and Remedy** *The United States Supreme Court affirmed the decision of the Maine Supreme Judicial Court. Under the Clean Water Act, an activity that may result in a "discharge"*

CASE CONTINUES

CASE 24.3 CONTINUED *into navigable waters under a federal license requires state approval. Water flowing through a hydropower dam operated under a federal license constitutes such a "discharge."*

- **What If the Facts Were Different?** *Would the result in this case have been different if the quality of the water flowing through the turbines of Warren's dams improved before returning to the river? Why or why not?*

- **The Global Dimension** *Should the Court have ruled differently if the discharge had been into international or foreign waters rather than into the waters of the United States? Explain.*

Standards for Equipment Regulations, for the most part, specify that the *best available control technology,* or BACT, be installed. The EPA issues guidelines as to what equipment meets this standard; essentially, the guidelines require the most effective pollution-control equipment available. New sources must install BACT equipment before beginning operations. Existing sources are subject to timetables for the installation of BACT equipment and must immediately install equipment that utilizes the *best practical control technology,* or BPCT. The EPA also issues guidelines as to what equipment meets this standard.

Wetlands The Clean Water Act prohibits the filling or dredging of wetlands unless a permit is obtained from the Army Corps of Engineers. The EPA defines **wetlands** as "those areas that are inundated or saturated by surface or ground water at a frequency and duration sufficient to support, and that under normal circumstances do support, a prevalence of vegetation typically adapted for life in saturated soil conditions." The EPA's broad interpretation of what constitutes a wetland for purposes of regulation by the federal government has generated substantial controversy.

The Migratory Bird Rule. One of the most controversial regulations was the "migratory bird rule" issued by the Army Corps of Engineers. Under this rule, any bodies of water that could affect interstate commerce, including seasonal ponds or waters "used or suitable for use by migratory birds" that fly over state borders, were "navigable waters" subject to federal regulation under the Clean Water Act as wetlands. The rule was challenged in a case brought by a group of communities that wanted to build a landfill in a tract of land northwest of Chicago. The Army Corps of Engineers refused to grant a permit for the landfill on the ground that the shallow ponds on the property formed a habitat for migratory birds.

Ultimately, the United States Supreme Court held that the Army Corps of Engineers had exceeded its authority under the Clean Water Act. The Court stated that it was not prepared to hold that isolated and seasonable ponds, puddles, and "prairie potholes" become "navigable waters of the United States" simply because they serve as a habitat for migratory birds.[10]

Seasonal Bodies of Water. The United States Supreme Court revisited the issue of wetlands in 2006, again scaling back the reach of the Clean Water Act. Two disputes had arisen as to whether certain properties in Michigan could be developed by the owners or were protected as wetlands, and the Court consolidated the cases on appeal. One involved property deemed to be wetlands because it was near an unnamed ditch that flowed into the Sutherland-Oemig Drain, which ultimately connected to Lake St. Clair. The other involved acres of marshy land, some of which was adjacent to a creek that flowed into a river, which flowed into yet another river, eventually reaching Saginaw Bay. Although the lower courts had concluded that both properties were wetlands under the Clean Water Act, the Supreme Court reversed these decisions. The Court held that the act covers "only those wetlands with a continuous surface connection to bodies that are waters of the United States in their own right." The Court further held that navigable waters under the act include only relatively permanent, standing or flowing bodies of water—not intermittent or temporary flows of water.[11]

10. *Solid Waste Agency of Northern Cook County v. U.S. Army Corps of Engineers,* 531 U.S. 159, 121 S.Ct. 675, 148 L.Ed.2d 576 (2001).

11. *Rapanos v. United States,* 547 U.S. 715, 126 S.Ct. 2208, 165 L.Ed.2d 159 (2006).

Violations of the Clean Water Act Under the Clean Water Act, violators are subject to a variety of civil and criminal penalties. Depending on the violation, civil penalties range from $10,000 to $25,000 per day, but not more than $25,000 per violation. Criminal penalties, which apply only if an act was intentional, range from a fine of $2,500 per day and imprisonment for up to one year to a fine of $1 million and fifteen years' imprisonment. Injunctive relief and damages can also be imposed. The polluting party can be required to clean up the pollution or pay for the cost of the clean-up.

Drinking Water

Another statute governing water pollution is the Safe Drinking Water Act.[12] Passed in 1974, this act requires the EPA to set maximum levels for pollutants in public water systems. Operators of public water supply systems must come as close as possible to meeting the EPA's standards by using the best available technology that is economically and technologically feasible. The EPA is particularly concerned about contamination from underground sources. Pesticides and wastes leaked from landfills or disposed of in underground injection wells are among the more than two hundred pollutants known to exist in groundwater used for drinking in at least thirty-four states. Many of these substances are associated with cancer and may cause damage to the central nervous system, liver, and kidneys.

The act was amended in 1996 to give the EPA greater flexibility in setting regulatory standards governing drinking water. These amendments also imposed requirements on suppliers of drinking water. Each supplier must send to every household it supplies with water an annual statement describing the source of its water, the level of any contaminants contained in the water, and any possible health concerns associated with the contaminants.

Ocean Dumping

The Marine Protection, Research, and Sanctuaries Act of 1972[13] (known popularly as the Ocean Dumping Act) regulates the transportation and dumping of material (pollutants) into ocean waters. It prohibits entirely the ocean dumping of radiological, chemical, and biological warfare agents and high-level radioactive waste.

The act also established a permit program for transporting and dumping other materials, and designated certain areas as marine sanctuaries. Each violation of any provision or permit requirement in the Ocean Dumping Act may result in a civil penalty of up to $50,000. A knowing violation is a criminal offense that may result in a $50,000 fine, imprisonment for not more than a year, or both. A court may also grant an injunction to prevent an imminent or continuing violation.

Oil Pollution

In response to the worst oil spill in North American history—more than 10 million gallons of oil that leaked into Alaska's Prince William Sound from the *Exxon Valdez* supertanker—Congress passed the Oil Pollution Act of 1990.[14] Under this act, any onshore or offshore oil facility, oil shipper, vessel owner, or vessel operator that discharges oil into navigable waters or onto an adjoining shore may be liable for clean-up costs, as well as damages. The act created an oil clean-up and economic compensation fund, and required oil tankers using U.S. ports to be double hulled by the year 2011 (to limit the severity of accidental spills).

Under the act, damage to natural resources, private property, and the local economy, including the increased cost of providing public services, is compensable. The penalties range from $2 million to $350 million, depending on the size of the vessel and on whether the oil spill came from a vessel or an offshore facility. The party held responsible for the clean-up costs can bring a civil suit for contribution from other potentially liable parties.

Toxic Chemicals

Originally, most environmental clean-up efforts were directed toward reducing smog and making water safe for fishing and swimming. Today, control of toxic chemicals used in agriculture and in industry has become increasingly important.

Pesticides and Herbicides

The Federal Insecticide, Fungicide, and Rodenticide Act (FIFRA) of 1947[15] regulates pesticides and herbicides. Under FIFRA, pesticides and herbicides must be

12. 42 U.S.C. Sections 300f to 300j-25.
13. 16 U.S.C. Sections 1401–1445.
14. 33 U.S.C. Sections 2701–2761.
15. 7 U.S.C. Sections 136–136y.

(1) registered before they can be sold, (2) certified and used only for approved applications, and (3) used in limited quantities when applied to food crops. The EPA can cancel or suspend registration of substances that are identified as harmful and may also inspect factories where the chemicals are made. Under 1996 amendments to FIFRA, there must be no more than a one-in-a-million risk to people of developing cancer from any kind of exposure to the substance, including eating food that contains pesticide residues.[16]

It is a violation of FIFRA to sell a pesticide or herbicide that is either unregistered or has had its registration canceled or suspended. It is also a violation to sell a pesticide or herbicide with a false or misleading label or to destroy or deface any labeling required under the act. For example, it is an offense to sell a substance that has a chemical strength different from the concentration declared on the label. Penalties for commercial dealers include imprisonment for up to one year and a fine up to $25,000 (producers can be fined up to $50,000). Farmers and other private users of pesticides or herbicides who violate the act are subject to a $1,000 fine and incarceration for up to thirty days.

Can a state regulate the sale and use of federally registered pesticides? Tort suits against pesticide manufacturers were common long before the enactment of FIFRA in 1947 and continued to be a feature of the legal landscape at the time FIFRA was amended. Until it heard the following case, however, the United States Supreme Court had never considered whether the statute preempts claims arising under state law.

16. 21 U.S.C. Section 346a.

CASE 24.4 Bates v. Dow Agrosciences, LLC

Supreme Court of the United States, 2005. 544 U.S. 431, 125 S.Ct. 1788, 161 L.Ed.2d 687.
www.findlaw.com/casecode/supreme.html[a]

Background and Facts The Environmental Protection Agency (EPA) conditionally registered Strongarm, a new weed-killing pesticide, on March 8, 2000.[b] Dow Agrosciences, LLC, immediately sold Strongarm to Texas peanut farmers, who normally plant their crops around May 1. The label stated, "Use of Strongarm is recommended in all areas where peanuts are grown." When the farmers applied Strongarm to their fields, the pesticide damaged their crops while failing to control the growth of weeds. After unsuccessfully attempting to negotiate with Dow, the farmers announced their intent to sue Strongarm's maker for violations of Texas state law. Dow filed a suit in a federal district court against the peanut farmers, asserting that FIFRA preempted their claims. The court issued a summary judgment in Dow's favor. The farmers appealed to the U.S. Court of Appeals for the Fifth Circuit, which affirmed the lower court's judgment. The farmers appealed to the United States Supreme Court.

IN THE LANGUAGE OF THE COURT
Justice *STEVENS* delivered the opinion of the Court.

* * * *

Under FIFRA * * *, [a] pesticide is misbranded if its label contains a statement that is false or misleading in any particular, including a false or misleading statement concerning the efficacy of the pesticide. *A pesticide is also misbranded if its label does not contain adequate instructions for use, or if its label omits necessary warnings or cautionary statements.* [Emphasis added.]

* * * *

* * * [Section] 136v provides:

> (a) * * * A State may regulate the sale or use of any federally registered pesticide or device in the State, but only if and to the extent [that] the regulation does not permit any sale or use prohibited by [FIFRA].
> (b) * * * Such State shall not impose or continue in effect any requirements for labeling or packaging in addition to or different from those required under [FIFRA].

* * * *

* * * *Nothing in the text of FIFRA would prevent a State from making the violation of a federal labeling or packaging requirement a state offense,* thereby imposing its own sanctions on pes-

a. In the "Browsing" section, click on "2005 Decisions." In the result, click on the name of the case to access the opinion.
b. Strongarm might more commonly be called an herbicide, but FIFRA classifies it as a pesticide.

CASE 24.4 CONTINUED

ticide manufacturers who violate federal law. The imposition of state sanctions for violating state rules that merely duplicate federal requirements is equally consistent with the text of [Section] 136v. [Emphasis added.]

* * * *

* * * For a particular state rule to be preempted, it must satisfy two conditions. First, it must be a requirement "for labeling or packaging"; rules governing the design of a product, for example, are not preempted. Second, it must impose a labeling or packaging requirement that is "in addition to or different from those required under [FIFRA]." A state regulation requiring the word "poison" to appear in red letters, for instance, would not be preempted if an EPA regulation imposed the same requirement.

* * * Rules that require manufacturers to design reasonably safe products, to use due care in conducting appropriate testing of their products, to market products free of manufacturing defects, and to honor their express warranties or other contractual commitments plainly do not qualify as requirements for "labeling or packaging." None of these common-law rules requires that manufacturers label or package their products in any particular way. Thus, petitioners' claims for defective design, defective manufacture, negligent testing, and breach of express warranty are not preempted.

* * * *

Dow * * * argues that [this] "parallel requirements" reading of [Section] 136v(b) would "give juries in 50 States the authority to give content to FIFRA's misbranding prohibition, establishing a crazy-quilt of anti-misbranding requirements * * * ." Conspicuously absent from the submissions by Dow * * * is any plausible alternative interpretation of "in addition to or different from" that would give that phrase meaning. Instead, they appear to favor reading those words out of the statute * * * . This amputated version of [Section] 136v(b) would no doubt have clearly and succinctly commanded the pre-emption of *all* state requirements concerning labeling. *That Congress added the remainder of the provision is evidence of its intent to draw a distinction between state labeling requirements that are preempted and those that are not.* [Emphasis added.]

* * * *

In sum, under our interpretation, [Section] 136v(b) * * * preempts competing state labeling standards—imagine 50 different labeling regimes prescribing the color, font size, and wording of warnings—that would create significant inefficiencies for manufacturers. The provision also preempts any statutory or common-law rule that would impose a labeling requirement that diverges from those set out in FIFRA * * * . *It does not, however, preempt any state rules that are fully consistent with federal requirements.* [Emphasis added.]

- **Decision and Remedy** *The United States Supreme Court vacated the lower court's judgment. A state can regulate the sale and use of federally registered pesticides to the extent that it does not permit anything that FIFRA prohibits, but a state cannot impose any requirements for labeling or packaging in addition to or different from those that FIFRA requires. The Court remanded the case, however, for further proceedings subject to this standard, concerning certain state law claims "on which we have not received sufficient briefing."*

- **What If the Facts Were Different?** *Suppose that FIFRA required Strongarm's label to include the word* CAUTION, *and the Texas peanut farmers filed their claims under a state regulation that required the label to use the word* DANGER. *Would the result have been different?*

- **The Legal Environment Dimension** *According to the Court's interpretation, what is required for a state regulation or rule to be preempted under FIFRA? Why is this significant?*

Toxic Substances

The first comprehensive law covering toxic substances was the Toxic Substances Control Act of 1976.[17] The act was passed to regulate chemicals and chemical compounds that are known to be toxic—such as asbestos and polychlorinated biphenyls, popularly known as PCBs—and to institute investigation of any possible harmful effects from new chemical compounds. The regulations authorize the EPA to require that manufacturers, processors, and other entities planning to use

17. 15 U.S.C. Sections 2601–2692.

chemicals first determine their effects on human health and the environment. The EPA can regulate substances that may pose an imminent hazard or an unreasonable risk of injury to health or the environment. The EPA may require special labeling, limit the use of a substance, set production quotas, or prohibit the use of a substance altogether.

SECTION 6 Hazardous Wastes

Some industrial, agricultural, and household wastes pose more serious threats than others. If not properly disposed of, these toxic chemicals may present a substantial danger to human health and the environment. If released into the environment, they may contaminate public drinking water resources.

Resource Conservation and Recovery Act

In 1976, Congress passed the Resource Conservation and Recovery Act (RCRA)[18] in reaction to a growing concern about the effects of hazardous waste materials on the environment. The RCRA required the EPA to establish regulations to determine which forms of solid waste should be considered hazardous and to establish regulations to monitor and control hazardous waste disposal. The act also requires all producers of hazardous waste materials to label and package properly any hazardous waste to be transported. The RCRA was amended in 1984 and 1986 to decrease the use of land containment in the disposal of hazardous waste and to require smaller generators of hazardous waste to comply with the act.

Under the RCRA, a company may be assessed a civil penalty of up to $25,000 for each violation.[19] The penalty is based on the seriousness of the violation, the probability of harm, and the extent to which the violation deviates from RCRA requirements. Criminal penalties include fines up to $50,000 for each day of violation, imprisonment for up to two years (in most instances), or both. Criminal fines and the time of imprisonment can be doubled for certain repeat offenders.

Superfund

In 1980, Congress passed the Comprehensive Environmental Response, Compensation, and Liability Act (CERCLA),[20] commonly known as Superfund. The basic purpose of Superfund is to regulate the cleanup of disposal sites in which hazardous waste is leaking into the environment. A special federal fund was created for that purpose.

Superfund provides that when a release or a threatened release of hazardous chemicals from a site occurs, the EPA can clean up the site and recover the cost of the clean-up from the following persons: (1) the person who generated the wastes disposed of at the site, (2) the person who transported the wastes to the site, (3) the person who owned or operated the site at the time of the disposal, or (4) the current owner or operator. A person falling within one of these categories is referred to as a **potentially responsible party (PRP).**

Liability under Superfund is usually joint and several—that is, a PRP who generated *only a fraction of the hazardous waste* disposed of at the site may nevertheless be liable for *all* of the clean-up costs. CERCLA authorizes a party who has incurred clean-up costs to bring a "contribution action" against any other person who is liable or potentially liable for a percentage of the costs.

18. 42 U.S.C. Sections 6901–6986.
19. 42 U.S.C. Section 6928(a).
20. 42 U.S.C. Sections 9601–9675.

REVIEWING Environmental Law

In the late 1980s, residents of Lake Caliopa, Minnesota, began noticing an unusually high number of lung ailments among their population. A group of concerned local citizens pooled their resources and commissioned a study of the frequency of these health conditions per capita as compared to national averages. The study concluded that residents of Lake Caliopa experienced four to seven times the frequency of asthma, bronchitis, and emphysema as the population nationwide.

REVIEWING Environmental Law, Continued

During the study period, citizens began expressing concerns about the large volumes of smog emitted by the Cotton Design apparel manufacturing plant on the outskirts of town. The plant had opened its production facility two miles east of town beside the Tawakoni River in 1997 and employed seventy full-time workers by 2008.

Just downstream on the Tawakoni River, the city of Lake Caliopa operated a public water works facility, which supplied all city residents with water. In August 2008, the Minnesota Pollution Control Agency required Cotton Design to install new equipment to control air and water pollution. In May 2009, thirty citizens brought a class-action lawsuit in a Minnesota state court against Cotton Design for various respiratory ailments allegedly caused or compounded by smog from Cotton Design's factory. Using the information presented in the chapter, answer the following questions.

1. Under the common law, what would each plaintiff be required to identify in order to be given relief by the court?
2. Are air-quality regulations typically overseen by federal, state, or local governments?
3. What standard for limiting emissions into the air does Cotton Design's pollution-control equipment have to meet?
4. What information must the city send to every household that the city supplies with water?

TERMS AND CONCEPTS

environmental impact statement (EIS) 599
environmental law 598
nuisance 598
potentially responsible party (PRP) 612
toxic tort 599
wetlands 608

QUESTIONS AND CASE PROBLEMS

24–1. Some scientific knowledge indicates that there is no safe level of exposure to a cancer-causing agent. In theory, even one molecule of such a substance has the potential for causing cancer. Section 112 of the Clean Air Act requires that all cancer-causing substances be regulated to ensure a margin of safety. Some environmental groups have argued that all emissions of such substances must be eliminated to attain such a margin of safety. Total elimination would likely shut down many major U.S. industries. Should the Environmental Protection Agency totally forbid all emissions of cancer-causing chemicals? Discuss.

24–2. QUESTION WITH SAMPLE ANSWER

Fruitade, Inc., is a processor of a soft drink called Freshen Up. Fruitade uses returnable bottles, which it cleans with a special acid to allow for further beverage processing. The acid is diluted with water and then allowed to pass into a navigable stream. Fruitade crushes its broken bottles and throws the crushed glass into the stream. Discuss fully any environmental laws that Fruitade has violated.

- **For a sample answer to Question 24–2, go to Appendix I at the end of this text.**

24–3. Moonbay is a home-building corporation that primarily develops retirement communities. Farmtex owns a number of feedlots in Sunny Valley. Moonbay purchased 20,000 acres of farmland in the same area and began building and selling homes on this acreage. In the meantime, Farmtex continued to expand its feedlot business, and eventually only 500 feet separated the two operations. Because of the odor and flies from the feedlots, Moonbay found it difficult to sell the homes in its development. Moonbay wants to enjoin (prevent) Farmtex from operating its feedlot in the vicinity of the retirement home development. Under what common law theory would Moonbay file this action? Has Farmtex violated any federal environmental laws? Discuss.

24–4. Clean Water Act. Attique Ahmad owned the Spin-N-Market, a convenience store and gas station. The gas pumps were fed by underground tanks, one of which had a leak at its top that allowed water to enter. Ahmad emptied the tank by pumping its contents into a storm drain and a sewer system. Through the storm drain, gasoline flowed into a creek, forcing the city to clean the water. Through the sewer system, gasoline flowed into a sewage treatment plant, forcing the city to evacuate the plant and two nearby schools. Ahmad was charged with discharging a pollutant without a permit, which is a criminal violation of the Clean Water Act. The act provides that a person who "knowingly violates" the act commits a felony. Ahmad claimed that he had believed he was discharging only water. Did Ahmad commit a felony? Why or why not? Discuss fully. [*United States v. Ahmad,* 101 F.3d 386 (5th Cir. 1996)]

24–5. Environmental Impact Statement. Greers Ferry Lake is in Arkansas, and its shoreline is under the management of the U.S. Army Corps of Engineers, which is part of the U.S. Department of Defense (DOD). The Corps's 2000 Shoreline Management Plan (SMP) rezoned numerous areas along the lake, authorized the Corps to issue permits for the construction of new boat docks in the rezoned areas, increased by 300 percent the area around habitable structures that could be cleared of vegetation, and instituted a Wildlife Enhancement Permit to allow limited modifications of the shoreline. In relation to the SMP's adoption, the Corps issued a Finding of No Significant Impact, which declared that no environmental impact statement (EIS) was necessary. The Corps issued thirty-two boat dock construction permits under the SMP before Save Greers Ferry Lake, Inc., filed a suit in a federal district court against the DOD, asking the court to, among other things, stop the Corps from acting under the SMP and order it to prepare an EIS. What are the requirements for an EIS? Is an EIS needed in this case? Explain. [*Save Greers Ferry Lake, Inc. v. Department of Defense,* 255 F.3d 498 (8th Cir. 2001)]

24–6. CERCLA. Beginning in 1926, Marietta Dyestuffs Co. operated an industrial facility in Marietta, Ohio, to make dyes and other chemicals. In 1944, Dyestuffs became part of American Home Products Corp. (AHP), which sold the Marietta facility to American Cyanamid Co. in 1946. In 1950, AHP sold the rest of the Dyestuffs assets and all of its stock to Goodrich Co., which immediately liquidated the acquired corporation. Goodrich continued to operate the dissolved corporation's business, however. Cyanamid continued to make chemicals at the Marietta facility, and in 1993, it created Cytec Industries, Inc., which expressly assumed all environmental liabilities associated with Cyanamid's ownership and operation of the facility. Cytec spent nearly $25 million on clean-up costs and filed a suit in a federal district court against Goodrich to recover, under CERCLA, a portion of the costs attributable to the clean-up of hazardous wastes that may have been discarded at the site between 1926 and 1946. Cytec filed a motion for summary judgment in its favor. Should the court grant Cytec's motion? Explain. [*Cytec Industries, Inc. v. B. F. Goodrich Co.,* 196 F.Supp.2d 644 (S.D. Ohio 2002)]

24–7. CASE PROBLEM WITH SAMPLE ANSWER

William Gurley was the president and majority stockholder in Gurley Refining Co. (GRC). GRC bought used oil, treated it, and sold it. The refining process created a by-product residue of oily waste. GRC disposed of this waste by dumping it at, among other locations, a landfill in West Memphis, Arkansas. In February 1992, after detecting hazardous chemicals at the site, the Environmental Protection Agency (EPA) asked Gurley about his assets, the generators of the material disposed of at the landfill, site operations, and the structure of GRC. Gurley refused to respond, except to suggest that the EPA ask GRC. In October, the EPA placed the site on its clean-up list and again asked Gurley for information. When he still refused to respond, the EPA filed a suit in a federal district court against him, asking the court to impose a civil penalty. In February 1999, Gurley finally answered the EPA's questions. Under CERCLA, a court may impose a civil penalty "not to exceed $25,000 for each day of noncompliance against any person who unreasonably fails to comply" with an information request. Should the court assess a penalty in this case? Why or why not? [*United States v. Gurley,* 384 F.3d 316 (6th Cir. 2004)]

- **To view a sample answer for Problem 24–7, go to this book's Web site at academic.cengage.com/blaw/cross, select "Chapter 24," and click on "Case Problem with Sample Answer."**

24–8. Clean Water Act. The Anacostia River, which flows through Washington, D.C., is one of the ten most polluted rivers in the country. For bodies of water such as the Anacostia, the Clean Water Act requires states (which, under the act, include the District of Columbia) to set a "total maximum daily load" (TMDL) for pollutants. A TMDL is to be set "at a level necessary to implement the applicable water-quality standards with seasonal variations." The Anacostia contains biochemical pollutants that consume oxygen, putting the river's aquatic life at risk for suffocation. In addition, the river is murky, stunting the growth of plants that rely on sunlight and impairing recreational use. The Environmental Protection Agency (EPA) approved one TMDL limiting the *annual* discharge of oxygen-depleting pollutants and a second limiting the *seasonal* discharge of pollutants contributing to turbidity. Neither TMDL limited daily discharges. Friends of the Earth, Inc. (FoE), asked a federal district court to review the TMDLs. What is FoE's best argument in this dispute? What is the EPA's likely response? What should the court rule, and why? [*Friends of the Earth, Inc. v. Environmental Protection Agency,* 446 F.3d 140 (D.C.Cir. 2006)]

24–9. Environmental Impact Statement. The fourth largest crop in the United States is alfalfa, of which 5 percent is exported to Japan. RoundUp Ready alfalfa is genetically engineered to resist glyphosate, the active ingredient in the herbicide RoundUp. The U.S. Department of Agriculture (USDA) regulates genetically engineered agricultural products through the Animal and Plant Health Inspection Service (APHIS). APHIS concluded that RoundUp Ready alfalfa does not have any harmful health effects on humans or livestock and deregulated it. Geertson Seed Farms and others filed a suit in a federal district court against Mike Johanns (the secretary of the USDA) and others, asserting that APHIS's decision required the preparation of an environmental impact statement (EIS). The plaintiffs argued, among other things, that the introduction of RoundUp Ready alfalfa might significantly decrease the availability of, or even eliminate, all nongenetically engineered varieties. The plaintiffs were concerned that the RoundUp Ready alfalfa might contaminate standard alfalfa because alfalfa is pollinated by bees, which can travel as far as two miles from a pollen source. If contamination occurred, farmers would not be able to market "contaminated" varieties as "organic," which would impact the sales of "organic" livestock and exports to Japan, which does not allow the import of glyphosate-tolerant alfalfa. Should an EIS be prepared in this case? Why or why not? [*Geertson Seed Farms v. Johanns,* __ F.Supp.2d __ (N.D.Cal. 2007)]

24–10. A QUESTION OF ETHICS

*In the Clean Air Act, Congress allowed California, which has particular problems with clean air, to adopt its own standard for emissions from cars and trucks, subject to the approval of the Environmental Protection Agency (EPA) according to certain criteria. Congress also allowed other states to adopt California's standard after the EPA's approval. In 2004, in an effort to address global warming, the California Air Resources Board amended the state's standard to attain "the maximum feasible and cost-effective reduction of GHG [greenhouse gas] emissions from motor vehicles." The regulation, which applies to new passenger vehicles and light-duty trucks for 2009 and later, imposes decreasing limits on emissions of carbon dioxide through 2016. While EPA approval was pending, Vermont and other states adopted similar standards. Green Mountain Chrysler Plymouth Dodge Jeep and other auto dealers, automakers, and associations of automakers filed a suit in a federal district court against George Crombie (secretary of the Vermont Agency of Natural Resources) and others, seeking relief from the state regulations. [*Green Mountain Chrysler Plymouth Dodge Jeep v. Crombie, *508 F.Supp.2d 295 (D.Vt. 2007)]*

(a) Under the Environmental Policy and Conservation Act (EPCA) of 1975, the National Highway Traffic Safety Administration sets fuel economy standards for new cars. The plaintiffs argued, among other things, that the EPCA, which prohibits states from adopting separate fuel economy standards, preempts Vermont's GHG regulation. Do the GHG rules equate to the fuel economy standards? Discuss.

(b) Do Vermont's rules tread on the efforts of the federal government to address global warming internationally? Who should regulate GHG emissions? The federal government? The state governments? Both? Neither? Why?

(c) The plaintiffs claimed that they would go bankrupt if they were forced to adhere to the state's GHG standards. Should they be granted relief on this basis? Does history support their claim? Explain.

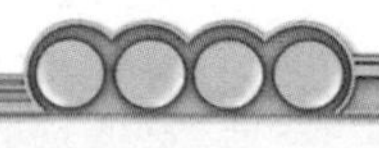

LAW ON THE WEB

For updated links to resources available on the Web, as well as a variety of other materials, visit this text's Web site at

academic.cengage.com/blaw/cross

For information on the standards, guidelines, and regulations of the Environmental Protection Agency (EPA), go to the EPA's Web site at

www.epa.gov

To learn about the Resource Conservation and Recovery Act's "buy-recycled" requirements and other steps that the federal government has taken toward "greening the environment," go to

www.epa.gov/cpg

The Law Library of the Indiana University School of Law provides numerous links to online environmental law sources. Go to

www.law.indiana.edu/library/services/onl_env.shtml

Legal Research Exercises on the Web

Go to **academic.cengage.com/blaw/cross**, the Web site that accompanies this text. Select "Chapter 24" and click on "Internet Exercises." There you will find the following Internet research exercises that you can perform to learn more about the topics covered in this chapter.

Internet Exercise 24–1: Legal Perspective
Nuisance Law

Internet Exercise 24–2: Management Perspective
Complying with Environmental Regulation

Internet Exercise 24–3: Ethical Perspective
Environmental Justice

CHAPTER 25

Land-Use Control and Real Property

Property ownership confers certain rights. An owner generally has the right to possess the property; the right either to use the property or to derive profits from another's use of the property; and the right to *alienate*[1] the property—that is, to sell, bequeath (pass on through a will), or give to others the same rights of ownership. Not all forms of ownership provide such a complete bundle of rights, but one or more of these attributes are normally included when we say that property is "owned."

1. *Alienate* derives from the Latin word *alienus* (alien), which is from the Latin *alus* (other). In legal terms, alienate means to transfer the title to property.

Even for one who possesses the entire bundle of rights we have delineated, however, ownership is not absolute. The law places restrictions on how property may be used. It also imposes duties on the owners regarding how the land is to be maintained. In addition, individual owners may agree with others to restrict or limit the use of their property. Thus, property owners cannot always do with their property whatever they wish. Nuisance and environmental laws, for example, restrict how people carry out certain types of activities on their own land. Briefly stated, the rights of every property owner are subject to certain conditions and limitations.

In this chapter, we first look at the nature of ownership rights in real property. We then examine the legal requirements involved in the transfer of real property, including the kinds of rights that are transferred by various types of deeds; the procedures used in the sale of real estate; and a way in which real property can, under certain conditions, be transferred merely by possession. We also discuss the right of government to take, for compensation, private land for public use, as well as other types of restrictions on the ownership and use of property.

The Nature of Real Property

Real property (sometimes called *realty* or *real estate*) consists of land and the buildings, plants, and trees that it contains. Everything else is **personal property.** Personal property is movable; real property is immovable. Real property usually means land and structures, but it also includes airspace and subsurface rights, plant life and vegetation, and *fixtures* (as will be discussed shortly).

Land and Structures

Land includes the soil on the surface of the earth and the natural products or artificial structures that are attached to it. Land further includes all the waters contained on or under its surface and much, but not necessarily all, of the airspace above it. The exterior boundaries of land extend down to the center of the earth and up to the farthest reaches of the atmosphere (subject to certain qualifications).

Airspace and Subsurface Rights

The owner of real property has relatively exclusive rights to both the airspace above the land and the soil and minerals underneath it. Any limitations on either airspace rights or subsurface rights, called *encumbrances,* normally must be indicated on the document that transfers title at the time of purchase. The ways in which ownership rights in real property can be limited will be examined in detail later in this chapter.

Airspace Rights Early cases involving airspace rights dealt with such matters as whether a telephone wire could be run across a person's property when the wire did not touch any of the property[2] and whether a bullet shot over a person's land constituted trespass.[3] Today, disputes concerning airspace rights may involve the right of commercial and private planes to fly over property and the right of individuals and governments to seed clouds and produce artificial rain. Flights over private land normally do not violate property rights unless the flights are so low and so frequent that they directly interfere with the owner's enjoyment and use of the land.

Subsurface Rights In many states, land ownership can be separated from ownership of its subsurface. In other words, the owner of the surface may sell subsurface rights to another person. Subsurface rights can be extremely valuable, as these rights include the ownership of minerals, oil, or natural gas. But a subsurface owner's rights would be of little value if he or she could not use the surface to exercise those rights. Hence, a subsurface owner will have a right (called a *profit*, discussed later in this chapter) to go onto the surface of the land to, for example, find and remove minerals.

When the ownership is separated into surface and subsurface rights, each owner can pass title to what she or he owns without the consent of the other owner. Of course, conflicts may arise between surface and subsurface owners when attempts are made to excavate below the surface. One party's interest may become subservient (secondary) to the other party's interest either by statute or case law. At common law and generally today, if the owners of the subsurface rights excavate, they are absolutely liable if their excavation causes the surface to collapse. Depending on the circumstances, the excavators may also be liable for any damage to structures on the land. Many states have statutes that extend excavators' liability to include damage to structures on the property. Typically, these statutes provide exact guidelines as to the requirements for excavations of various depths.

2. *Butler v. Frontier Telephone Co.*, 186 N.Y. 486, 79 N.E. 716 (1906). Stringing a wire across someone's property violates the airspace rights of that person. Leaning walls and projecting eave spouts and roofs also violate the airspace rights of the property owner.

3. *Herrin v. Sutherland*, 74 Mont. 587, 241 P. 328 (1925). Shooting over a person's land normally constitutes trespass.

Plant Life and Vegetation

Plant life, both natural and cultivated, is also considered to be real property. In many instances, the natural vegetation, such as trees, adds greatly to the value of realty. When a parcel of land is sold and the land has growing crops on it, the sale includes the crops, unless otherwise specified in the sales contract. When crops are sold by themselves, however, they are considered to be personal property or goods rather than real property. Consequently, the sale of crops is a sale of goods and thus is governed by the Uniform Commercial Code (see Chapter 11) rather than by real property law.

Fixtures

Certain personal property can become so closely associated with the real property to which it is attached that the law views it as real property. Such property is known as a **fixture—**a thing affixed to realty. A thing is affixed to realty when it is attached to the realty by roots; embedded in it; or permanently attached by means of cement, plaster, bolts, nails, or screws. The fixture can be physically attached to real property or attached to another fixture; it can even be an item, such as a statue, that is not physically attached to the land, as long as the owner *intends* the property to be a fixture.

Fixtures are included in the sale of land if the sales contract does not provide otherwise. The sale of a house includes the land and the house and garage on it, as well as the cabinets, plumbing, and windows. Because these are permanently affixed to the property, they are considered to be a part of it. Unless otherwise agreed, however, the curtains and throw rugs are not included. Items such as drapes and window-unit air conditioners are difficult to classify. Thus, a contract for the sale of a house or commercial property should indicate which items of this sort are included in the sale.

The issue of whether an item is a fixture (and thus real estate) or not a fixture (and thus personal property) often arises with respect to land sales, real property taxation, insurance coverage, and divorces. Generally, when the courts need to determine whether a certain item is a fixture, they examine the intention of the party who placed the object on the real property. If the facts indicate that the person intended the item to be a fixture, then it normally will be considered a fixture.

Ownership and Other Interests in Real Property

Ownership of property is an abstract concept that cannot exist independently of the legal system. No one can actually possess, or *hold*, a piece of land, the air above, the earth below, and all the water contained on it. One can only possess *rights* in real property. Numerous rights are involved in real property ownership, which is why property ownership is often viewed as a bundle of rights. These rights include the right to possess the property and the right to dispose of the property—by sale, gift, rental, and lease, for example. Traditionally, ownership interests in real property were referred to as *estates in land*, which include fee simple estates, life estates, and leasehold estates. We examine these estates in land, forms of concurrent ownership, and certain other interests in real property that is owned by others in the following subsections.

Ownership in Fee Simple

A person who holds the entire bundle of rights is said to be the owner in **fee simple absolute.** In a fee simple absolute, the owner has the greatest aggregation of rights, privileges, and power possible. The owner can give the property away or dispose of the property by *deed* (the instrument used to transfer property, as discussed later in this chapter) or by a will. When there is no will, the fee simple passes to the owner's legal heirs on her or his death. A fee simple absolute is potentially infinite in duration and is assigned forever to a person and her or his heirs without limitation or condition.[4] The owner has the right of *exclusive* possession and use of the property.

The rights that accompany a fee simple absolute include the right to use the land for whatever purpose the owner sees fit. Of course, other laws, including applicable zoning, noise, and environmental laws, may limit the owner's ability to use the property in certain ways.

In the following case, the court had to decide whether the noise—rock and roll music, conversation, and clacking pool balls—coming from a local bar (called a "saloon" during the days of cowboys in the United States) unreasonably interfered with a neighboring property owner's rights.

4. Note that in *fee simple defeasible*, ownership in fee simple will automatically terminate if a stated event occurs, such as when property is conveyed (transferred) to a school board only as long as it is used for school purposes. In addition, the fee simple may be subject to a *condition subsequent*, meaning that if a stated event occurs, the prior owner of the property can bring an action to regain possession of the property.

CASE 25.1 Biglane v. Under the Hill Corp.

Mississippi Supreme Court, 2007. 949 So.2d 9.
www.mssc.state.ms.us[a]

Background and Facts In 1967, Nancy and James Biglane bought and refurbished a building at 27 Silver Street in Natchez, Mississippi, and opened the lower portion as a gift shop. In 1973, Andre Farish and Paul O'Malley bought the building next door, at 25 Silver Street, and opened the Natchez Under the Hill Saloon. Later, the Biglanes converted the upper floors of their building into an apartment and moved in. Despite installing insulated walls and windows, locating the bedroom on the side of the building away from the Saloon, and placing the air-conditioning unit on the side nearest the Saloon, the Biglanes had a problem: the noise of the Saloon kept them wide awake at night. During the summer, the Saloon, which had no air-conditioning, opened its windows and doors, and live music echoed up and down the street. The Biglanes asked the Saloon to turn the music down, and it was: thicker windows were installed, the loudest band was replaced, and the other bands were asked to keep their output below a certain level of decibels. Still dissatisfied, the Biglanes filed a suit in a Mississippi state court against the Saloon. The court enjoined the defendant from opening doors or windows when music was playing and ordered it to prevent its patrons from loitering in the street. Both parties appealed to the Mississippi Supreme Court.

a. In the center of the page, click on the "Search this site" link. On the next page, click on "Plain English." When that page opens, in the "Enter the ISYS Plain English query:" box, type "2005-CA-01751-SCT" and click on "Search." In the result, click on the first item in the list that includes that number to access the opinion. The Mississippi Supreme Court maintains this Web site.

CASE CONTINUES

CASE 25.1 CONTINUED

IN THE LANGUAGE OF THE COURT
DIAZ, **Justice, for the Court.**

* * * *

An entity is subject to liability * * * *when its conduct is a legal cause of an invasion of another's interest in the private use and enjoyment of land and that invasion is* * * * *intentional and unreasonable* * * * . [Emphasis added.]

* * * [The trial court] found ample evidence that the Biglanes frequently could not use or enjoy their property—significantly, that Mrs. Biglane often slept away from the apartment on weekends to avoid the noise and that she could not have her grandchildren over on the weekends because of the noise. The audiologist [one who diagnoses hearing problems] who testified for the Biglanes concluded that the noise levels were excessive and unreasonable * * * .

* * * *

* * * The trial court weighed the fact that the Biglanes knew or should have known that there was going to be some sort of noise associated with living within five feet of a * * * saloon which provides live music on the weekends.

* * * *

* * * *A reasonable use of one's property cannot be construed to include those uses which produce obnoxious noises, which in turn result in a material injury to owners of property in the vicinity, causing them to suffer substantial annoyance, inconvenience, and discomfort.* [Emphasis added.]

Accordingly, even a lawful business—which the Under the Hill Saloon certainly is—may * * * [not interfere] with its neighbors' enjoyment of their property. We recognize that each * * * case must be decided upon its own peculiar facts, taking into consideration the location and the surrounding circumstances. Ultimately, it is not necessary that other property owners should be driven from their dwellings, because it is enough that the enjoyment of life and property is rendered materially uncomfortable and annoying.

* * * *

In the case at hand, the trial court exercised its power to permit continued operation of the Saloon while setting conditions to its future operation. Namely, it found that the Saloon could not operate its business with its doors and windows opened during any time that amplified music is being played inside the saloon. The * * * court found that such a limitation is reasonable in that it should help contain the noise within the saloon, and should discourage the bar patrons from congregating or loitering in the streets outside of the saloon.

From a review of the record it is clear that the * * * court balanced the interests between the Biglanes and the Saloon in a quest for an equitable remedy that allowed the couple to enjoy their private apartment while protecting a popular business and tourist attraction from overregulation.

• **Decision and Remedy** *The Mississippi Supreme Court affirmed the lower court's injunction. The Saloon unreasonably interfered with the Biglanes' rights. "One landowner may not use his land so as to unreasonably annoy, inconvenience, or harm others."*

• **The Ethical Dimension** *At one point in their dispute, the Biglanes blocked off two parking lots that served the Saloon. Was this an unreasonable interference with the Saloon's rights? Explain.*

• **The Legal Environment Dimension** *Could repulsive odors emanating from a neighbor's property constitute unreasonable interference with a property owner's rights? Why or why not?*

Life Estates

A **life estate** is an estate that lasts for the life of some specified individual. A **conveyance,** or transfer of real property, "to A for his life" creates a life estate.[5] In a life estate, the life tenant's ownership rights cease to exist on the life tenant's death. The life tenant has the right to use the land, provided no **waste** (injury to the land) is committed. In other words, the life tenant cannot use the land in a manner that would adversely affect its value. The life tenant can use the land to harvest crops or, if mines and oil wells are already on the land, can

5. A less common type of life estate is created by the conveyance "to A for the life of B." This is known as an estate *pur autre vie*—that is, an estate for the duration of the life of another.

extract minerals and oil from it, but the life tenant cannot exploit the land by creating new wells or mines.

With few exceptions, the owner of a life estate has an exclusive right to possession during his or her lifetime. In addition, the life tenant has the right to mortgage the life estate and create other interests in the land, but none can extend beyond the life of the tenant.

Along with these rights, the life tenant also has some duties—to keep the property in repair and to pay property taxes. In sum, the owner of the life estate has the same rights as a fee simple owner except that she or he must maintain the value of the property during her or his tenancy, less the decrease in value resulting from the normal use of the property allowed by the life tenancy.

Concurrent Ownership

Persons who share ownership rights simultaneously in particular property (including real property and personal property) are said to be concurrent owners. There are two principal types of **concurrent ownership:** *tenancy in common* and *joint tenancy.* Concurrent ownership rights can also be held in a tenancy by the entirety or as community property, although these types of concurrent ownership are less common.

Tenancy in Common The term **tenancy in common** refers to a form of co-ownership in which each of two or more persons owns an undivided interest in the property. The interest is undivided because each tenant has rights in the whole property. On the death of a tenant in common, that tenant's interest in the property passes to her or his heirs.

For example, four friends purchase a condominium unit in Hawaii together as tenants in common. This means that each of them has an ownership interest (one-fourth) in the whole. If one of the four owners, Trey, dies a year after the purchase, his ownership interest passes to his heirs (his wife and children, for example) rather than to the other tenants in common.

Unless the co-tenants have agreed otherwise, a tenant in common can transfer her or his interest in the property to another without the consent of the remaining co-owners. Generally, it is presumed that a co-tenancy is a tenancy in common unless there is a clear intention to establish a joint tenancy (discussed next).

Joint Tenancy In a **joint tenancy,** each of two or more persons owns an undivided interest in the property, but a deceased joint tenant's interest passes to the surviving joint tenant or tenants. The right of a surviving joint tenant to inherit a deceased joint tenant's ownership interest—referred to as a *right of survivorship*—distinguishes a joint tenancy from a tenancy in common. Suppose that Jerrold and Eva are married and purchase a house as joint tenants. The title to the house clearly expresses the intent to create a joint tenancy because it says "to Jerrold and Eva as joint tenants with right of survivorship." Jerrold has three children from a prior marriage. If Jerrold dies, his interest in the house automatically passes to Eva rather than to his children from the prior marriage.

Although a joint tenant can transfer her or his rights by sale or gift to another without the consent of the other joint tenants, doing so terminates the joint tenancy. In such a situation, the person who purchases the property or receives it as a gift becomes a tenant in common, not a joint tenant. For example, three brothers, Brody, Saul, and Jacob, own a parcel as joint tenants. Brody is experiencing financial difficulties and sells his interest in the property to Beth. The sale terminates the joint tenancy, and now Beth, Saul, and Jacob hold the property as tenants in common.

A joint tenant's interest can also be levied against (seized by court order) to satisfy the tenant's judgment creditors. If this occurs, the joint tenancy terminates, and the remaining owners hold the property as tenants in common. (Judgment creditors can also seize the interests of tenants in a tenancy in common.)

Tenancy by the Entirety A **tenancy by the entirety** is a less common form of ownership that typically is created by a conveyance (transfer) of real property to a husband and wife. It differs from a joint tenancy in that neither spouse may separately transfer his or her interest during his or her lifetime unless the other spouse consents. In some states in which statutes give the wife the right to convey her property, this form of concurrent ownership has effectively been abolished. A divorce, either spouse's death, or mutual agreement will terminate a tenancy by the entirety.

Community Property Only a limited number of states[6] allow property to be owned by a married couple as **community property.** If property is held as community property, each spouse technically owns an undivided one-half interest in the property. This type of

6. These states include Alaska, Arizona, California, Idaho, Louisiana, Nevada, New Mexico, Texas, Washington, and Wisconsin. Puerto Rico allows property to be owned as community property as well.

ownership applies to most property acquired by the husband or the wife during the course of the marriage. It generally does not apply to property acquired prior to the marriage or to property acquired by gift or inheritance during the marriage. After a divorce, community property is divided equally in some states and according to the discretion of the court in other states.

Leasehold Estates

A **leasehold estate** is created when a real property owner or lessor (landlord) agrees to convey the right to possess and use the property to a lessee (tenant) for a certain period of time. In every leasehold estate, the tenant has a *qualified* right to exclusive, though *temporary*, possession (qualified by the landlord's right to enter onto the premises to ensure that the tenant is not causing damage to the property). The tenant can use the land—for example, by harvesting crops—but cannot injure it by such activities as cutting down timber for sale or extracting oil.

Here, we look at the types of leasehold estates, or tenancies, that can be created when real property is leased.

Fixed-Term Tenancy or Tenancy for Years A **fixed-term tenancy,** also called a *tenancy for years,* is created by an express contract by which property is leased for a specified period of time, such as a month, a year, or a period of years. Signing a one-year lease to occupy an apartment, for instance, creates a tenancy for years. Note that the term need not be specified by date and can be conditioned on the occurrence of an event, such as leasing a cabin for the summer or an apartment during Mardi Gras. At the end of the period specified in the lease, the lease ends (without notice), and possession of the property returns to the lessor. If the tenant dies during the period of the lease, the lease interest passes to the tenant's heirs as personal property. Often, leases include renewal or extension provisions.

Periodic Tenancy A **periodic tenancy** is created by a lease that does not specify how long it is to last but does specify that rent is to be paid at certain intervals. This type of tenancy is automatically renewed for another rental period unless properly terminated. For example, Jewel, LLC, enters into a lease with Capital Properties. The lease states, "Rent is due on the tenth day of every month." This provision creates a periodic tenancy from month to month. This type of tenancy can also extend from week to week or from year to year. A periodic tenancy sometimes arises when a landlord allows a tenant under a tenancy for years to *hold over* (retain possession after the lease term ends) and continue paying monthly or weekly rent.

Under the common law, to terminate a periodic tenancy, the landlord or tenant must give at least one period's notice to the other party. If the tenancy is month to month, for example, one month's notice must be given. State statutes often require a different period for notice of termination in a periodic tenancy, however.

Tenancy at Will In a **tenancy at will,** either the landlord or the tenant can terminate the tenancy without notice. This type of tenancy can arise if a landlord rents property to a tenant "for as long as both agree" or allows a person to live on the premises without paying rent. Tenancy at will is rare today because most state statutes require a landlord to provide some period of notice to terminate a tenancy (as previously noted). States may also require a landowner to have sufficient cause (reason) to end a residential tenancy. Certain events, such as the death of either party or the voluntary commission of waste by the tenant, automatically terminate a tenancy at will.

Tenancy at Sufferance The mere possession of land without right is called a **tenancy at sufferance.** A tenancy at sufferance is not a true tenancy because it is created when a tenant *wrongfully* retains possession of property. Whenever a tenancy for years or a periodic tenancy ends and the tenant continues to retain possession of the premises without the owner's permission, a tenancy at sufferance is created.

Nonpossessory Interests

In contrast to the types of property interests just described, some interests in land do not include any rights to possess the property. These interests, known as **nonpossessory interests,** include *easements, profits,* and *licenses.* Nonpossessory interests are basically interests in real property owned by others. (See *Concept Summary 25.1* for a review of the interests that can exist in real property.)

An **easement** is the right of a person to make limited use of another person's real property without taking anything from the property. An easement, for

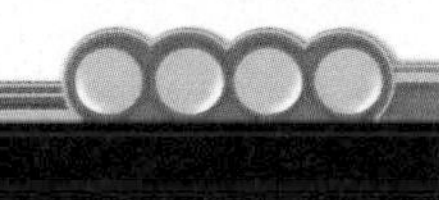

CONCEPT SUMMARY 25.1
Interests in Real Property

Type of Interest	Description
OWNERSHIP INTERESTS	1. *Fee simple absolute*—The most complete form of ownership. 2. *Life estate*—An estate that lasts for the life of a specified individual. 3. *Concurrent interests*—When two or more persons hold title to property together, concurrent ownership exists. a. A tenancy in common exists when two or more persons own an undivided interest in property; on a tenant's death, that tenant's property interest passes to his or her heirs. b. A joint tenancy exists when two or more persons own an undivided interest in property, with a right of survivorship; on the death of a joint tenant, that tenant's property interest transfers to the remaining tenant(s), not to the heirs of the deceased. c. A tenancy by the entirety is a form of co-ownership between a husband and wife that is similar to a joint tenancy, except that a spouse cannot transfer separately her or his interest during her or his lifetime. d. Community property is a form of co-ownership between a husband and wife in which each spouse technically owns an undivided one-half interest in property acquired during the marriage. This type of ownership occurs in only a few states.
LEASEHOLD INTERESTS	A leasehold interest, or estate, is an interest in real property that is held for only a limited period of time, as specified in the lease agreement. Types of tenancies relating to leased property include the following: 1. *Fixed-term tenancy (tenancy for years)*—Tenancy for a period of time stated by express contract. 2. *Periodic tenancy*—Tenancy for a period determined by the frequency of rent payments; automatically renewed unless proper notice is given. 3. *Tenancy at will*—Tenancy for as long as both parties agree; no notice of termination is required. 4. *Tenancy at sufferance*—Possession of land without legal right.
NONPOSSESSORY INTERESTS	Interests that involve the right to use real property but not to possess it. Easements, profits, and licenses are nonpossessory interests.

example, can be the right to walk across another's property. In contrast, a **profit** is the right to go onto land owned by another and take away some part of the land itself or some product of the land. For example, Akmed, the owner of Sandy View, gives Ann the right to go there and remove all the sand and gravel that she needs for her cement business. Ann has a profit.

Easements and profits can be classified as either *appurtenant* or *in gross*. Because easements and profits are similar and the same rules apply to both, we discuss them together.

Easement or Profit Appurtenant An easement or profit *appurtenant* arises when the owner of one piece of land has a right to go onto (or remove things from) an adjacent piece of land owned by another. The land that is benefited by the easement is called the *dominant estate*, and the land that is burdened is called the *servient estate*. Because easements appurtenant are intended to *benefit the land*, they run with (are conveyed with) the land when it is transferred.[7] Suppose that Owen has a right to drive his car

7. See, for example, *Webster v. Ragona*, 7 A.D.3d 850, 776 N.Y.S.2d 347 (2004).

across Green's land, which is adjacent to Owen's property. This right-of-way over Green's property is an easement appurtenant to Owen's land and can be used only by Owen. If Owen sells his land, the easement runs with the land to benefit the new owner.

Easement or Profit in Gross An easement or profit *in gross* exists when someone who does not own an adjacent tract of land has a right to use or take things from another's land. These easements are intended to *benefit a particular person or business,* not a particular piece of land, and cannot be transferred. For example, Avery owns a parcel of land with a marble quarry. Avery conveys to Classic Stone Corporation the right to come onto her land and remove up to five hundred pounds of marble per day. Classic Stone owns a profit in gross and cannot transfer this right to another. Similarly, when a utility company is granted an easement to run its power lines across another's property, it obtains an easement in gross.

Creation of an Easement or Profit Most easements and profits are created by an express grant in a contract, deed, or will. This allows the parties to include terms defining the extent and length of time of use. In some situations, an easement or profit can also be created without an express agreement.

An easement or profit may arise by *implication* when the circumstances surrounding the division of a parcel of property imply its creation. For example, Barrow divides a parcel of land that has only one well for drinking water. If Barrow conveys the half without a well to Dean, a profit by implication arises because Dean needs drinking water.

An easement may also be created by *necessity.* An easement by necessity does not require division of property for its existence. A person who rents an apartment, for example, has an easement by necessity in the private road leading up to the dwelling.

An easement arises by *prescription* when one person exercises an easement, such as a right-of-way, on another person's land without the landowner's consent, and the use is apparent and continues for a period of time equal to the applicable statute of limitations. (In much the same way, title to property may be obtained by *adverse possession,* which will be discussed later in this chapter.)

Termination of an Easement or Profit An easement or profit can be terminated or extinguished in several ways. The simplest way is to deed it back to the owner of the land that is burdened by it. Another way is to abandon it and create evidence of intent to relinquish the right to use it. Mere nonuse will not extinguish an easement or profit *unless the nonuse is accompanied by an overt act showing the intent to abandon.* Also, if the owner of an easement or profit becomes the owner of the property burdened by it, then it is merged into the property.

Licenses In the context of real property, a **license** is the revocable right of a person to come onto another person's land. It is a personal privilege that arises from the consent of the owner of the land and can be revoked by the owner. A ticket to attend a movie at a theater is an example of a license. Assume that a Broadway theater owner issues a ticket to see a play to Alena. If Alena is refused entry because she is improperly dressed, she has no right to force her way into the theater. The ticket is only a revocable license, not a conveyance of an interest in property.

In essence, a license grants a person the authority to enter the land of another and perform a specified act or series of acts without obtaining any permanent interest in the land. What happens when a person with a license exceeds the authority granted and undertakes an action that is not permitted? That was the central issue in the following case.

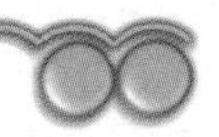

CASE 25.2 Roman Catholic Church of Our Lady of Sorrows v. Prince Realty Management, LLC

New York Supreme Court, Appellate Division, Second Department, 2008.
47 A.D.3d 909, 850 N.Y.S.2d 569.

• **Background and Facts** The Roman Catholic Church of Our Lady of Sorrows (the Church) and Prince Realty Management, LLC (Prince), own adjoining property in Queens County, New York. On August 19, 2005, the parties entered into an agreement by which the Church granted Prince a three-month license to use a three-foot strip of its property immediately adjacent to Prince's property. The license specifically authorized Prince to remove an existing chainlink fence on the licensed strip and to "put up plywood panels surrounding the construction site, including the [licensed strip]." The license also required that Prince

CASE 25.2 CONTINUED

restore the boundary line between the properties with a new brick fence. The purpose of the license was to allow Prince to erect a temporary plywood fence in order to protect Prince's property during the construction of a new building. During the term of the license, Prince installed structures consisting of steel piles and beams on the licensed property. The Church objected to the installation of these structures, and repeatedly demanded that they be removed. The Church commenced an action to recover damages for breach of the license and for trespass. The trial court concluded that the Church had made a *prima facie* case showing that structures were placed upon its property by the defendant in violation of the license, and that Prince had failed to dispute the plaintiff's claim that it had violated the agreement. Prince appealed.

IN THE LANGUAGE OF THE COURT
***SKELOS*, J.P. [Justice Presiding]**

* * * *

The [trial court] properly granted the plaintiff summary judgment on its causes of action alleging breach of the license and trespass. *"A license, within the context of real property law, grants the licensee a revocable non-assignable privilege to do one or more acts upon the land of the licensor, without granting possession of any interest therein. A license is the authority to do a particular act or series of acts upon another's land, which would amount to a trespass without such permission."* Here, the evidentiary [related to the evidence] proof submitted by the plaintiff * * * established that the license granted the defendant a privilege to use a three-foot strip of its land for specified purposes, primarily consisting of the temporary erection of wooden fencing to protect the defendant's property during construction of a building, the removal of an existing chain link fence, and the installation of a new brick fence upon completion of the license. The plaintiff also submitted uncontroverted evidence that the defendant installed structures consisting of steel piles and beams on the licensed strip of property. Contrary to the defendant's contention, the license did not permit it to install structures of this nature on the plaintiff's property. Moreover, in opposition to the establishment of a *prima facie* case for summary judgment, the defendant offered no proof that the installation of these structures was reasonably related to its licensed use of the property. [Emphasis added.]

In addition, since the plaintiff established as a matter of law that the defendant violated the license by installing unauthorized structures on its property, the plaintiff also established as a matter of law that the defendant's installation of these structures constituted a trespass regardless of whether they were subsequently removed.

- **Decision and Remedy** *The New York appellate court held that a license did not permit the adjoining property owner (Prince) to install structures consisting of steel piles and beams on the licensed strip of property.*

- **The Ethical Dimension** *While the Church pastor requested that the steel piles and beams be removed, the defendant resisted, but eventually did remove them. Was it still appropriate for the Church to file this lawsuit? Explain your answer.*

- **The Legal Environment Dimension** *The Church sued for damages. What would be an appropriate calculation of those damages?*

Transfer of Ownership

Ownership of real property can pass from one person to another in a number of ways. Commonly, ownership interests in land are transferred by sale, and the terms of the transfer are specified in a real estate sales contract. Often, real estate brokers or agents who are licensed by the state assist the buyers and sellers during the sales transaction. Real property ownership can also be transferred by gift, by will or inheritance, by possession, or by eminent domain. In the subsections that follow, we focus primarily on voluntary sales of real property. We then consider adverse possession, which is an involuntary method of transferring title to real property. *Eminent domain* will be discussed later in this chapter.

Listing Agreements

In a typical real estate transaction, the seller employs a real estate agent to find a buyer for the property by entering into a listing agreement with the agent. The listing agreement specifies the duration of the listing with that real estate agent, the terms under which the seller will sell the property, and the amount of commission the seller will pay. There are different types of listing agreements. If the contract gives the agent an exclusive right to sell the property, then only that real estate agent is authorized to sell the property for a specified period of time. For example, a seller might give the agent thirty days of exclusive agency. If a buyer is found within the thirty-day period, the agent will be paid the full amount of the commission even if the agent was not responsible for finding that buyer. After the thirty-day period ends, if another real estate agent procures a buyer, the listing agent may have to split the commission. In an open listing, the seller agrees to pay a commission to the real estate agent who brings in a buyer. An open listing is nonexclusive, and thus agents with other real estate firms may attempt to find a buyer and share in the commission with the listing agent.

Although many sales of real estate involve listing agreements, it is not necessary for a property owner to list the property with a real estate agent. Many owners offer their properties for sale directly without an agent. The ability to advertise real properties for sale via the Internet has made it easier for an owner to find a buyer without using an agent. Because an agent is not essential, listing agreements are not shown in Exhibit 25–1, which summarizes the steps involved in any sale of real property.

Real Estate Sales Contracts

The sale of real estate is in some ways similar to the sale of goods because it involves a transfer of ownership, often with specific warranties. In a sale of real

EXHIBIT 25–1 • Steps Involved in the Sale of Real Estate

BUYER'S PURCHASE OFFER
Buyer offers to purchase Seller's property. The offer may be conditioned on Buyer's ability to obtain financing, on satisfactory inspections of the premises, on title examination, and the like. Included with the offer is earnest money, which will be placed in an escrow account.

SELLER'S RESPONSE
If Seller accepts Buyer's offer, then a contract is formed. Seller could also reject the offer or make a counteroffer that modifies Buyer's terms. Buyer may accept or reject Seller's counteroffer or make a counteroffer that modifies Seller's terms.

PURCHASE AND SALE AGREEMENT
Once an offer or a counteroffer is accepted, a purchase and sale agreement is formed.

TITLE EXAMINATION AND INSURANCE
The examiner investigates and verifies Seller's rights in the property and discloses any claims or interests held by others. Buyer (and/or Seller) may purchase title insurance to protect against a defect in title.

FINANCING
Buyer may seek a mortgage loan to finance the purchase. Buyer agrees to grant lender an interest in the property as security for Buyer's indebtedness.

INSPECTION
Buyer has the property inspected for any physical problems, such as major structural or mechanical defects and insect infestation.

ESCROW
Buyer's purchase funds (including earnest money) are held in an escrow account by an escrow agent (such as a title company or a bank). This agent holds the deed transferring title received from Seller and any funds received from Buyer until all conditions of the sale have been met.

CLOSING
The escrow agent transfers the deed to Buyer and the proceeds of the sale to Seller. The proceeds are the purchase price less any amount already paid by Buyer and any closing costs to be paid by Seller. Included in the closing costs are fees charged for services performed by the lender, escrow agent, and title examiner. The purchase and sale of the property is complete.

estate, however, certain formalities are observed that are not required in a sale of goods. The sale of real estate is a complicated transaction. Usually, after substantial negotiation between the parties (offers, counteroffers, responses), the parties enter into a detailed contract setting forth their agreement. A contract for a sale of land includes such terms as the purchase price, the type of deed the buyer will receive, the condition of the premises, and any items that will be included.

Contingencies Unless the buyer pays cash for the property, the buyer must obtain financing through a mortgage loan. (As discussed in Chapter 15, a *mortgage* is a loan made by an individual or institution, such as a banking institution or trust company, for which the property is given as security.) Real estate sales contracts are often made contingent on the buyer obtaining financing at or below a specified rate of interest. The contract may also be contingent on the buyer selling other real property, the seller obtaining a survey and title insurance, and the property passing one or more inspections. Normally, the buyer is responsible for having the premises inspected for physical or mechanical defects and for insect infestation.

Closing Date and Escrow The contract usually fixes a date for performance, or **closing,** that is frequently four to twelve weeks after the contract is signed. On this day, the seller conveys the property to the buyer by delivering the deed to the buyer in exchange for payment of the purchase price. Deposits toward the purchase price normally are held in a special account, called an **escrow account,** until all of the conditions of sale have been met. Once the closing takes place, the funds remaining in the escrow account (after payments have been made to the escrow agency, title insurance company, and any lien holders) are transferred to the seller. The *escrow agent,* which may be a title company, bank, or special escrow company, acts as a neutral party in the sales transaction and facilitates the sale by allowing the buyer and seller to close the transaction without having to exchange documents and funds.

Implied Warranties in the Sale of New Homes The common law rule of *caveat emptor* ("let the buyer beware") held that the seller of a home made no warranty as to its soundness or fitness (unless the contract or deed stated otherwise). Today, however, most states imply a warranty—the **implied warranty of habitability**—in the sale of new homes. The seller of a new house warrants that it will be fit for human habitation even if the deed or contract of sale does not include such a warranty.

Essentially, the seller is warranting that the house is in reasonable working order and is of reasonably sound construction. To recover damages for breach of the implied warranty of habitability, the purchaser of the house is required to prove only that it is somehow defective and that the defect caused the damage. Thus, under this theory, the seller of a new home is in effect a guarantor of its fitness. In some states, the warranty protects not only the first purchaser but any subsequent purchaser as well.

Seller's Duty to Disclose Hidden Defects In most jurisdictions, courts impose on sellers a duty to disclose any known defect that materially affects the value of the property and that the buyer could not reasonably discover. Failure to disclose such a material defect gives the buyer a right to rescind the contract and to sue for damages based on fraud or misrepresentation.

A dispute may arise over whether the seller knew of the defect before the sale, and there is normally a limit to the time within which the buyer can bring a suit against the seller based on the defect. For example, in Louisiana, where the following case was decided, the prescribed limit for a suit against a seller who knew, or can be presumed to have known, of the defect is one year from the day that the buyer discovered it. If the seller did not know of the defect, the limit is one year from the date of the sale.

CASE 25.3 Whitehead v. Humphrey

Court of Appeal of Louisiana, Second Circuit, 2007. 954 So.2d 859.

• **Background and Facts** Matthew Humphrey paid $44,000 for a home in Webster Parish, Louisiana, in the fall of 2003 and partially renovated it. Among other things, he replaced rotten wood underneath a bedroom window, leveled the porch, painted the interior, replaced sheetrock, tore out a wall, replaced a window, dug up eighty feet of field line for the septic system, and pumped out the septic

CASE CONTINUES

CASE 25.3 CONTINUED tank. In February 2004, Terry and Tabitha Whitehead bought the house for $67,000. A few months after they moved in, problems began to develop with the air-conditioning unit, the fireplace, and the plumbing in the bathrooms. In May 2005, they discovered rotten wood behind the tile in the bathroom and around the front porch. In October, the Whiteheads filed a suit in a Louisiana state court against Humphrey, seeking to rescind the sale. The court awarded the plaintiffs the cost of repairing the fireplace ($1,675) and replacing some of the bad wood ($7,695). The Whiteheads appealed to a state intermediate appellate court.

IN THE LANGUAGE OF THE COURT
CARAWAY, **J. [Judge]**

* * * *

Terry Whitehead testified that when they were looking at the house to buy, the yard was a mess because all of the field lines for the sewer system had been dug up. However, he did not realize at that time that the septic tank was located under the driveway. As part of her pre-inspection of the house, Tabitha Whitehead testified that she flushed both of the toilets and they both worked.

The Whiteheads' initial problem concerned the master bathroom and began three or four months after they moved into the house. When the water backed up in the main bathroom in the spring of 2004, Tabitha called Roto-Rooter to correct the flow. It was then that she learned the septic tank was located under the driveway. This meant that the traffic across the driveway could cause problems with the tank and lines.

In May 2005 * * * [t]he Whiteheads * * * began using the rear bathroom and experienced the same backing-up problem. At that time, the Whiteheads consulted Cook's Plumbing which provided the Whiteheads with an estimate totaling $12,000 which included relocation of the septic system and correction of other problems.

This evidence reveals that prior to the sale, the vendor and vendee were alerted to an issue regarding the sewer system. Corrective actions were taken, and no problems concerning the flushing of the toilets and flowage through the underground system prevented the Whiteheads from completing their purchase. *From this evidence, the ruling of the trial court * * * can be upheld from the view that neither side understood that a latent defect remained unresolved.* [Emphasis added.]

* * * *

Accordingly, we find no manifest error in the trial court's factual determination that the Whiteheads discovered that the sewer system remained a problem with their residence in the spring of 2004, and therefore their failure to have filed suit within one year of that discovery caused [the limitations period] to run against that claim.

On the other hand, the trial court expressly found that Humphrey had knowledge of the rotten boards or sills underneath the house which were improperly repaired by Humphrey prior to the sale. * * * The evidence showed that the Whiteheads first discovered this problem in May 2005, five months prior to [their law]suit.

* * * *

The trial court's judgment refused to rescind the sale and awarded a reduction in price based upon the cost of repairs of the defects in the fireplace and the wooden sills. From our review of the nature of these two defects, we find that the court properly used its discretion in rejecting rescission, and appellants' assignment of error seeking rescission and return of the sale price is without merit.

• **Decision and Remedy** *The state intermediate appellate court affirmed the lower court's conclusions regarding the defects in the Whiteheads' home. Rescission was not warranted for the sewer problems because the Whiteheads waited too long after their discovery to file a claim against Humphrey. The other defects "could be repaired with relative ease" and the "costs of those repairs were a small fraction of the sale price."*

• **The Ethical Dimension** *Should the court have rescinded the sale despite the running of the limitations period on the Whiteheads' sewer claim? Why or why not?*

CASE 25.3 CONTINUED • **The Legal Environment Dimension** *In Louisiana, a seller who knows of a defect and does not inform a buyer can be liable for the buyer's attorneys' fees in a suit based on that defect. Did Humphrey qualify as such a "bad faith" seller in this case? Explain.*

Deeds

Possession and title to land are passed from person to person by means of a **deed**—the instrument of conveyance of real property. A deed is a writing signed by an owner of real property by which title to it is transferred to another.[8] Deeds must meet certain requirements, but unlike a contract, a deed does not have to be supported by legally sufficient consideration. Gifts of real property are common, and they require deeds even though there is no consideration for the gift. To be valid, a deed must include the following:

1. The names of the *grantor* (the giver or seller) and the *grantee* (the donee or buyer).
2. Words evidencing the intent to convey (for example, "I hereby bargain, sell, grant, or give"). No specific words are necessary, and if the deed does *not* specify the estate being transferred, it presumptively transfers it in fee simple absolute.
3. A legally sufficient description of the land. (The description must include enough detail to distinguish the property being conveyed from every other parcel of land. The property can be identified by reference to an official survey or recorded plat map, or each boundary can be described by *metes and bounds*. **Metes and bounds** is a system of measuring boundary lines by the distance between two points, often using physical features of the local geography. For example, "beginning at the southwesterly intersection of Court and Main Streets, then West 40 feet to the fence, then South 100 feet, then Northeast approximately 120 feet back to the beginning.")
4. The grantor's (and usually his or her spouse's) signature.
5. Delivery of the deed.

Warranty Deeds Different types of deeds provide different degrees of protection against defects of title. A **warranty deed** makes the greatest number of warranties and thus provides the most extensive protection against defects of title. In most states, special language is required to create a warranty deed.

Warranty deeds include a number of *covenants,* or promises, that the grantor makes to the grantee. These covenants include a covenant that the grantor has the title to, and the power to convey, the property; a covenant of quiet enjoyment (a warranty that the buyer will not be disturbed in her or his possession of the land); and a covenant that transfer of the property is made without knowledge of adverse claims of third parties.

Generally, the warranty deed makes the grantor liable for all defects of title by the grantor and previous titleholders. For example, Julio sells a two-acre lot and office building by warranty deed. Subsequently, a third person appears, shows that she has better title than Julio had, and forces the buyer off the property. Here, the covenant of quiet enjoyment has been breached, and the buyer can sue Julio to recover the purchase price of the land, plus any other damages incurred as a result.

Special Warranty Deed In contrast to the warranty deed, the **special warranty deed,** which is frequently referred to as a *limited warranty deed,* warrants only that the grantor or seller held good title during his or her ownership of the property. In other words, the grantor is not warranting that there were no defects of title when the property was held by previous owners.

If the special warranty deed discloses all liens or other encumbrances, the seller will not be liable to the buyer if a third person subsequently interferes with the buyer's ownership. If the third person's claim arises out of, or is related to, some act of the seller, however, the seller will be liable to the buyer for damages.

Quitclaim Deed A **quitclaim deed** offers the least amount of protection against defects in the title. Basically, a quitclaim deed conveys to the grantee whatever interest the grantor had; so, if the grantor had no interest, then the grantee receives no interest. Naturally, if the grantor had a defective title or no title at all, a conveyance by warranty deed or special warranty deed

8. Note that in some states when a person purchases real property, the bank or lender receives a *trust deed* on the property until the homeowner pays off the mortgage. Despite its name, a trust deed is not used to transfer property. Instead, it is similar to a mortgage in that the lender holds the property as security for a loan.

would not cure the defects. Such deeds, however, will give the buyer a cause of action to sue the seller.

A quitclaim deed can and often does serve as a release of the grantor's interest in a particular parcel of property. For instance, Sandor owns a strip of waterfront property on which he wants to build condominiums. Lanz has an easement on a portion of the property, which might interfere with Sandor's plans for the development. Sandor can negotiate with Lanz to deed the easement back to Sandor. Lanz's signing of a quitclaim deed would constitute such a transfer.

Grant Deed With a **grant deed,** the grantor simply states, "I grant the property to you" or "I convey, or bargain and sell, the property to you." By state statute, grant deeds carry with them an implied warranty that the grantor owns the property and has not previously transferred it to someone else or encumbered it, except as set out in the deed.

Sheriff's Deed A **sheriff's deed** is a document giving ownership rights to a buyer of property at a sheriff's sale, which is a sale held by a sheriff when the owner of the property has failed to pay a court judgment against her or him. Typically, the property was subject to a mortgage or tax payments, and the owner defaulted on the payments. After a statutory period of time during which the defaulting owner can redeem the property, the deed is delivered to the purchaser.

Recording Statutes

Once the seller delivers the deed to the buyer (at closing), legal title to the property is conveyed. Nevertheless, the buyer should promptly record the deed with the state records office to establish superior ownership rights against any third parties who might make a claim to the property. Every state has a **recording statute,** which allows deeds to be recorded in the public record. Recording a deed involves a fee, which the buyer typically pays because he or she is the one who will be protected by recording the deed.

Recording a deed gives notice to the public that a certain person is now the owner of a particular parcel of real estate. Putting everyone on notice as to the true owner is intended to prevent the previous owners from fraudulently conveying the land to other purchasers. Deeds are generally recorded in the county in which the property is located. Many state statutes require that the grantor sign the deed in the presence of two witnesses before it can be recorded.

Marketable Title The question of title to a particular parcel of property is especially important to the buyer. A grantor (seller) is obligated to transfer **marketable title,** or good title, to the grantee (buyer). Marketable title means that the grantor's ownership is free from encumbrances (except those disclosed by the grantor) and free of defects. If the buyer signs a real estate sales contract and then discovers that the seller does not have a marketable title, the buyer can withdraw from the contract. For example, Chan enters an agreement to buy Fortuna Ranch from Hal. Chan then discovers that Hal has previously given Pearl an unexpired option to purchase the ranch. In this situation, the title is not marketable because Pearl could exercise the option and Hal would be compelled to sell the ranch to her. Therefore, Chan can withdraw from the contract to buy the property.

Title Search Because each document affecting ownership of property is recorded, recording provides a chronological public record of all transactions concerning the property. Systematically examining this record for transactions creating interests or rights in a specific parcel of real property is called a **title search.** A prospective buyer or lender generally performs a title search to determine whether the seller truly owns the interest that he or she is attempting to convey and whether anyone else has an interest in the property. A title search should—but does not always—reveal encumbrances on the property, such as the existence of an easement or lien.

Methods of Ensuring Good Title To ensure that the title is marketable, a grantee has several options depending on the state. The grantee may hire an attorney to examine an *abstract of title* (history of what the public records show regarding the title to the property) and provide an opinion as to whether the title is marketable. If the title is defective, the attorney's opinion will specify the nature of the defects. The attorney is liable to the grantee for any loss caused by her or his negligence.

An alternative method available in a few states is the *Torrens system* of title registration. Under this system, the title is registered in a judicial proceeding; all parties claiming an interest in the property are notified of the proceeding and are given an opportunity to assert their claims. After the hearing, the court issues a certificate of title, which is similar to an automobile title, to the person found to be the owner. All encumbrances (such as liens for unpaid taxes, mechanic's liens, or restrictive covenants, discussed next) are noted on the certificate, and when the property is sold, the certificate is transferred to the grantee along with the deed.

The most common method of assuring title is through **title insurance,** which insures the grantee against loss from defects in title to real property. When financing the purchase of real property, many lenders require title insurance to protect their interests in the collateral for the loan. Title insurance is becoming less significant, though, because title information and records are now available electronically and thus are easy to access.

Restrictive Covenants

Deeds may include voluntary agreements between individuals that limit the use of the property. For example, easements, profits, and licenses, which were discussed earlier, may place limitations on a property owner's rights. Also, deeds sometimes include a **restrictive covenant,** which is a private restriction on the use of land. If the restriction is binding on the party who purchases the property originally as well as on subsequent purchasers—in other words, if its benefit or obligation passes with the land's ownership—it is said to "run with the land."

Covenants Running with the Land A restrictive covenant that runs with the land goes with the land and cannot be separated from it. Consider an example. Owen is the owner of Grasslands, a twenty-acre estate whose northern half contains a small reservoir. Owen wishes to convey the northern half to Arid City, but before he does, he digs an irrigation ditch connecting the reservoir with the lower ten acres, which he uses as farmland. When Owen conveys the northern ten acres to Arid City, he enters into an agreement with the city. The agreement, which is contained in the deed, states, "Arid City, its heirs and assigns, promises not to remove more than five thousand gallons of water per day from the Grasslands reservoir." Owen has created a restrictive covenant running with the land under which Arid City and all future owners of the northern ten acres of Grasslands are limited as to the amount of water they can draw from its reservoir.

Four requirements must be met for a covenant running with the land to be enforceable. If they are not met, the covenant will apply to the two original parties to a contract only and will not run with the land to future owners. The requirements are as follows:

1. The covenant running with the land must be created in a written agreement (usually it is in the deed).
2. The parties must intend that the covenant run with the land. In other words, the instrument that contains the covenant must state not only that the promisor is bound by the terms of the covenant but also that all the promisor's "successors, heirs, or assigns" will be bound.
3. The covenant must touch and concern the land—that is, the limitations on the activities of the owner of the burdened land must have some connection with the land. For example, a purchaser of land cannot be bound by a covenant requiring him or her to drive only Ford pickups, because such a restriction has no relation to the land purchased.
4. The successors to the original parties to the covenant must have notice of the covenant.

To satisfy the last requirement, the notice may be actual or constructive. For example, in the course of developing a fifty-lot suburban subdivision, Levitt records a declaration of restrictions that effectively limits construction on each lot to one single-family house. In each lot's deed is a reference to the declaration with a provision that the purchaser and his or her successors are bound to those restrictions. Thus, each purchaser assumes ownership with notice of the restrictions. If an owner attempts to build a duplex (or any structure that does not comply with the restrictions) on a lot, the other owners may obtain a court order enjoining the construction.

In fact, Levitt might simply have included the restrictions on the subdivision's map, filed the map in the appropriate public office, and included a reference to the map in each deed. In this way, each owner would have been held to have constructive notice of the restrictions.

Illegal Restrictive Covenants Restrictive covenants have sometimes been used to perpetuate neighborhood segregation, and in these cases they have been invalidated by the courts. In the United States Supreme Court case of *Shelley v. Kraemer,*[9] restrictive covenants proscribing resale to minority groups were declared unconstitutional and could no longer be enforced in courts of law. In addition, the Civil Rights Act of 1968 (also known as the Fair Housing Act) prohibits all discrimination based on

9. 334 U.S. 1, 68 S.Ct. 836, 92 L.Ed. 1161 (1948).

race, color, religion, gender, familial status, or national origin in the sale and leasing of housing.

Adverse Possession

A person who wrongfully possesses (by occupying or using) the real property of another may eventually acquire title to it through **adverse possession.** Adverse possession is a means of obtaining title to land without delivery of a deed and without the consent of—or payment to—the true owner. Thus, adverse possession is a method of involuntarily transferring title to the property from the true owner to the adverse possessor.

Essentially, when one person possesses the real property of another for a certain statutory period of time (three to thirty years, with ten years being most common), that person acquires title to the land. For property to be held adversely, four elements must be satisfied:

1. Possession must be *actual and exclusive*—that is, the possessor must physically occupy the property. This requirement is clearly met if the possessor lives on the property, but it may also be met if the possessor builds fences, erects structures, plants crops, or even grazes animals on the land.
2. The possession must be *open, visible, and notorious,* not secret or clandestine. The possessor must occupy the land for all the world to see. This requirement of obviousness ensures that the true owner is on notice that someone is possessing the owner's property wrongfully.
3. Possession must be *continuous and peaceable for the required period of time.* This requirement means that the possessor must not be interrupted in the occupancy by the true owner or by the courts. *Continuous* does not mean constant—it simply means that the possessor has continuously occupied the property in some fashion for the statutory time and has not used force to possess the land.
4. Possession must be *hostile and adverse.* In other words, the possessor cannot be living on the property with the owner's permission and must claim the property as against the whole world.

There are a number of public-policy reasons for the adverse possession doctrine. These include society's interest in resolving boundary disputes, in quieting (determining) title when title to property is in question, and in ensuring that real property remains in the stream of commerce. More fundamentally, policies behind the doctrine include punishing owners who do not take action when they see adverse possession and rewarding possessors for putting land to productive use.

Public Control of Land Use

Land-use control is the control over the ownership and uses of real property by authorized public agencies. Land use is subject to regulation by the state within whose political boundaries the land is located. Most states authorize control over land use through various planning boards and zoning authorities at a city or county level. The federal government does not engage in land-use control under normal circumstances, except with respect to federally owned land.[10] The federal government does influence state and local regulation, however, through the allocation of federal funds. Stipulations on land use may be a condition to the states' receiving such funds.

Sources of Public Control

The states' power to control the use of land through legislation is derived from their *police power* and the doctrine of *eminent domain.* Under their police power, state governments enact legislation that promotes the health, safety, and welfare of their citizens. This legislation includes land-use controls. The power of **eminent domain** is the government's authority to take private property for public use or purpose without the owner's consent. Typically, this is accomplished through a judicial proceeding to obtain title to the land.

Police Power

As an exercise of its police power,[11] a state can regulate the use of land within its jurisdiction. A few states control land use at the state level. Hawaii, for instance, employs a statewide land-use classification scheme. Some states have a land-permit process that operates in conjunction with local control. Florida, for example, uses such a scheme in certain areas of "critical environmental concern" to permit or prohibit develop-

10. Federal (and state) laws concerning environmental matters—such as air and water quality, the protection of endangered species, and the preservation of natural wetlands—are also a source of land-use control.

11. As pointed out in Chapter 5, the police power of a state encompasses the right to regulate private activities to protect or promote the public order, health, safety, morals, and general welfare.

ment on the basis of available roads, sewers, and so on. Vermont also utilizes a statewide land-permit scheme.

Usually, however, a state authorizes its city or county governments to regulate the use of land within their local jurisdictions. A state confers this power through *enabling legislation.* Enabling legislation normally requires local governments to devise *general plans* before imposing other land-use controls. Enabling acts also typically authorize local bodies to enact *zoning laws* to regulate the use of land and the types of, and specifications for, structures. Local planning boards may regulate the development of subdivisions, in which private developers subdivide large tracts of land and construct commercial or residential units for resale to others. Local governments may also enact growth-management ordinances to control development in their jurisdictions.

Government Plans Most states require that land-use laws follow a local government's general plan. A **general plan** is a comprehensive, long-term scheme dealing with the physical development, and in some cases redevelopment, of a city or community. It addresses such concerns as types of housing, protection of natural resources, provision of public facilities and transportation, and other issues related to land use. A plan indicates the direction of growth in a community and the contributions that private developers must make toward providing such public facilities as roads. If a proposed use is not authorized by the general plan, the plan may be amended to permit the use. (A plan may also be amended to preclude a proposed use.)

Even when a proposed use complies with a general plan, it may not be allowed. Most jurisdictions have requirements in addition to those in the general plan. These requirements are included in specific plans—also called special, area, or community plans. Specific plans typically pertain to only a portion of a jurisdiction's area. For example, a specific plan may concern a downtown area subject to redevelopment efforts, an area with special environmental concerns, or an area with increased public transportation needs arising from population growth.

Zoning Laws In addition to complying with a general plan and any specific plans, a particular land use must comply with zoning laws. The term **zoning** refers to the dividing of an area into districts to which specific land-use regulations apply. A typical zoning law consists of a zoning map and a zoning ordinance. The zoning map indicates the characteristics of each parcel of land within an area and divides that area into districts. The zoning ordinance specifies the restrictions on land use within those districts.

Zoning ordinances generally include two types of restrictions. One type pertains to the kind of land use—such as commercial versus residential—to which property within a particular district may be put. The second type dictates the engineering features and architectural design of structures built within that district.

Use Restrictions. Districts are typically zoned for residential, commercial, industrial, or agricultural use. Each district may be further subdivided for degree or intensity of use. For example, a residential district may be subdivided to permit a certain number of apartment buildings and a certain number of units in each building. Commercial and industrial districts are often zoned to permit *heavy* or *light* activity. Heavy activity might include the operation of large factories. Light activity might include the operation of professional office buildings or small retail shops. Zoning that specifies the use to which property may be put is referred to as **use zoning.**

Structural Restrictions. Restrictions known as bulk regulations cover such details as minimum floor-space requirements and minimum lot-size restrictions. For example, a particular district's minimum floor-space requirements might specify that a one-story building contain a minimum of 1,240 square feet of floor space, and minimum lot-size restrictions might specify that each single-family dwelling be built on a lot that is at least one acre in size. Referred to collectively as **bulk zoning,** these regulations also dictate *setback* (the distance between a building and a street, sidewalk, or other boundary) and the height of buildings, with different requirements for buildings in different areas.

Restrictions related to structure may also be concerned with such matters as architectural control, the overall appearance of a community, and the preservation of historic buildings. An ordinance may require that all proposed construction be approved by a design review board composed of local architects. A community may restrict the size and placement of outdoor advertising, such as billboards and business signs. A property owner may be prohibited from tearing down or remodeling a historic landmark or building. In challenges against these types of restrictions, the courts have generally upheld the regulations.

Variances. A **zoning variance** allows property to be used or structures to be built in some way that varies from the restrictions of a zoning ordinance. A variance may exempt property from a use restriction to allow, for example, a bakery shop in a residential area. Or, a variance may exempt a building from a height restriction so that, for example, a two-story house can be built in a district in which houses are otherwise limited to one floor. Some jurisdictions do not permit variances from use restrictions.

Variances are normally granted by local adjustment boards. In general, a property owner must meet three criteria to obtain a variance:

1. The owner must find it impossible to realize a reasonable return on the land as currently zoned.
2. The adverse effect of the zoning ordinance must be particular to the party seeking the variance and not have a similar effect on other owners in the same zone.
3. Granting the variance must not substantially alter the essential character of the zoned area.

Courts tend to be rather lenient about the first two requirements. By far the most important criterion in granting a variance is whether it will substantially alter the character of the neighborhood.

In contrast to a "use" provision, an "area" restriction regulates the area, height, density, setback, or sideline attributes of a building or other development on a piece of property. For example, an area provision may dictate the distance between buildings.

Subdivision Regulations When subdividing a parcel of land into smaller plots, a private developer must comply not only with local zoning ordinances but also with local subdivision regulations. Subdivision regulations are different from zoning ordinances, although they may be administered by the same local agencies that oversee the zoning process. In the design of a subdivision, the local authorities may demand, for example, the allocation of space for a public park or school or may require a developer to construct streets to accommodate a specific level of traffic.

Growth-Management Ordinances To prevent population growth from racing ahead of the community's ability to provide necessary public services, local authorities may enact a growth-management ordinance to limit, for example, the number of residential building permits. A property owner may thus be precluded from constructing a residential building on his or her property even if the area is zoned for the use and the proposed structure complies with all other requirements. A growth-management ordinance may prohibit the issuance of residential building permits for a specific period of time, until the occurrence of a specific event (such as a decline in the total number of residents in the community), or on the basis of the availability of necessary public services (such as the capacity for drainage in the area or the proximity of hospitals and police stations).

Limitations on the Exercise of Police Power The government's exercise of its police power to regulate the use of land is limited in at least three ways. Two of these limitations arise under the Fourteenth Amendment to the Constitution. The third limitation arises under the Fifth Amendment and requires that, under certain circumstances, the government must compensate an owner who is deprived of the use of his or her property.

Due Process and Equal Protection. A government cannot regulate the use of land in a way that violates either the due process clause or the equal protection clause of the Fourteenth Amendment. A government may be deemed to violate the due process clause if it acts arbitrarily or unreasonably.[12] Thus, there must be a *rational basis* for classifications that are imposed on property. Any classification that is reasonably related to the health or general welfare of the public is deemed to have a rational basis.

Under the equal protection clause, land-use controls cannot be discriminatory. A zoning ordinance is discriminatory if it affects one parcel of land in a way in which it does not affect surrounding parcels and if there is no rational basis for the difference. For example, classifying a single parcel in a way that does not accord with a general plan is discriminatory. Similarly, a zoning ordinance cannot be racially discriminatory. For example, a community may not zone itself to exclude all low-income housing if the intention is to exclude minorities.

Just Compensation. Under the Fifth Amendment, private property may not be taken for a public purpose without the payment of just compensation.[13] If gov-

12. See, for example, *United Artists Theatre Circuit, Inc. v. Township of Warrington, Pennsylvania,* 316 F.3d 392 (3d Cir. 2003).

13. Although the Fifth Amendment pertains to actions taken by the federal government, the Fourteenth Amendment has been interpreted as extending this limitation to state actions.

ernment restrictions on a landowner's property rights are overly burdensome, the regulation may be deemed a **taking.** A taking occurs when a regulation denies an owner the ability to use his or her property for any reasonable income-producing or private purpose for which it is suited. This requires the government to pay the owner.

Suppose that Perez purchases a large tract of land with the intent to subdivide and develop it into residential properties. At the time of the purchase, there are no zoning laws restricting use of the land. After Perez has taken significant steps to develop the property, the county attempts to zone the tract "public parkland only." If this prohibits Perez from developing any of the land, it will be deemed a taking. If the county does not fairly compensate Perez, the regulation will be held unconstitutional and void.

The distinction between an ordinance that merely restricts land use and an outright taking is crucial. A restriction is simply an exercise of the state's police power; even though it limits a property owner's land use, the owner generally need not be compensated for the limitation. An ordinance that completely deprives an owner of use or benefit of property, or an outright governmental taking of property, however, must be compensated.

Eminent Domain

As noted earlier, no ownership rights in real property can ever truly be absolute. Even ownership in real property in fee simple absolute is limited by a superior ownership. Just as the king was the ultimate landowner in medieval England, today the government has an ultimate ownership right in all land in the United States. This right, known as *eminent domain,* is sometimes referred to as the *condemnation power* of government to take land for public use. It gives the government the right to acquire possession of real property in the manner directed by the U.S. Constitution and the laws of the state whenever the public interest requires it. Property may be taken only for public use, not for private benefit.

For example, when a new public highway is to be built, the government decides where to build it and how much land to condemn. After the government determines that a particular parcel of land is necessary for public use, it will first offer to buy the property. If the owner refuses the offer, the government brings a judicial **(condemnation)** proceeding to obtain title to the land. Then, in another proceeding, the court determines the *fair value* of the land, which is usually approximately equal to its market value.

When the government takes land owned by a private party for public use, the government must compensate the private party. Under the so-called *takings clause* of the Fifth Amendment to the U.S. Constitution, the government may not take private property for public use without "just compensation." State constitutions contain similar provisions.

Can the power of eminent domain be used to further economic development? That was the question in the following case.

EXTENDED CASE 25.4

Kelo v. City of New London, Connecticut

Supreme Court of the United States, 2005. 545 U.S. 469, 125 S.Ct. 2655, 162 L.Ed.2d 439.
www.findlaw.com/casecode/supreme.html[a]

Justice *STEVENS* delivered the opinion of the Court.

* * * *

The city of New London (hereinafter City) sits at the junction of the Thames River and the Long Island Sound in southeastern Connecticut. Decades of economic decline led a state agency in 1990 to designate the City a "distressed municipality." In 1996, the Federal Government closed the Naval Undersea Warfare Center, which had been located in the Fort Trumbull area of the City and had employed over 1,500 people. In 1998, the City's unemployment rate was nearly double that of the State, and its population of just under 24,000 residents was at its lowest since 1920.

These conditions prompted state and local officials to target New London * * * for economic revitalization. * * * In February [1998] the pharmaceutical company Pfizer Inc. announced that it would build a $300 million research facility on a site immediately adjacent to Fort Trumbull; local planners hoped that Pfizer would draw new business to the area * * * .

* * * *

a. In the "Browsing" section, click on "2005 Decisions." In the result, click on "Kelo v. New London" to access the opinion.

CASE CONTINUES

CASE 25.4 CONTINUED

The city council approved [a] plan in January 2000 [to redevelop the area that once housed the federal facility]. The [City] successfully negotiated the purchase of most of the real estate in the 90-acre area, but its negotiations with [some of the property owners] failed. As a consequence, in November 2000, the [City] initiated * * * condemnation proceedings * * *.

* * * *

* * * Susette Kelo has lived in the Fort Trumbull area since 1997. * * * She prizes [her house] for its water view.

In December 2000 [Kelo and others] brought this action in [a Connecticut state court against the City and others]. They claimed, among other things, that the taking of their properties would violate the "public use" restriction in the [U.S. Constitution's] Fifth Amendment. * * * [The court issued a ruling partly in favor of both sides].

* * * Both sides took appeals to the Supreme Court of Connecticut [which] held * * * that all of the City's proposed takings were valid.

* * * *

We granted *certiorari* to determine whether a city's decision to take property for the purpose of economic development satisfies the "public use" requirement of the Fifth Amendment.

* * * *

* * * This Court long ago rejected any literal requirement that condemned property be put into use for the general public. * * * Not only was the "use by the public" test difficult to administer (*e.g.*, what proportion of the public need have access to the property? at what price?), but it proved to be impractical given the diverse and always evolving needs of society. Accordingly, * * * *this Court* * * * *embraced the broader and more natural interpretation of public use as "public purpose."* * * * [Emphasis added.]

The disposition of this case therefore turns on the question whether the City's development plan serves a "public purpose."

* * * *

Viewed as a whole, our jurisprudence has recognized that the needs of society have varied between different parts of the Nation, just as they have evolved over time in response to changed circumstances. * * * *For more than a century, our public use jurisprudence has wisely eschewed [avoided] rigid formulas and intrusive scrutiny in favor of affording legislatures broad latitude in determining what public needs justify the use of the takings power.* [Emphasis added.]

* * * *

Those who govern the City were not confronted with the need to remove blight in the Fort Trumbull area, but their determination that the area was sufficiently distressed to justify a program of economic rejuvenation is entitled to our deference. The City has carefully formulated an economic development plan that it believes will provide appreciable benefits to the community, including—but by no means limited to—new jobs and increased tax revenue. As with other exercises in urban planning and development, the City is endeavoring to coordinate a variety of commercial, residential, and recreational uses of land, with the hope that they will form a whole greater than the sum of its parts. To effectuate this plan, the City has invoked a state statute that specifically authorizes the use of eminent domain to promote economic development. Given the comprehensive character of the plan, the thorough deliberation that preceded its adoption, and the limited scope of our review, it is appropriate for us * * * to resolve the challenges of the individual owners, not on a piecemeal basis, but rather in light of the entire plan. *Because that plan unquestionably serves a public purpose, the takings challenged here satisfy the public use requirement of the Fifth Amendment.* [Emphasis added.]

* * * *

The judgment of the Supreme Court of Connecticut is affirmed.

QUESTIONS

1. Why did the United States Supreme Court grant *certiorari* in this case, and what did the Court hold with respect to the principal issue?
2. Considering the impact of the majority's ruling, what are some arguments against this decision?

Legislation Prohibiting Takings for Economic Development

The increasingly widespread use of eminent domain for economic development has generated substantial controversy. Although the United States Supreme Court approved this type of taking in the *Kelo* case that was just discussed, the Court also recognized that individual states have the right to pass laws that prohibit takings for economic development. Thirty-five states have done exactly that, limiting the government's ability to take private property and give it to private developers. At least eight states have amended their state constitutions, and a number of other states have passed ballot measures.

REVIEWING Land-Use Control and Real Property

Vern Shoepke purchased a two-story home from Walter and Eliza Bruster in the town of Roche, Maine. The warranty deed did not specify what covenants would be included in the conveyance. The property was adjacent to a public park that included a popular Frisbee golf course. (Frisbee golf is a sport similar to golf but using Frisbees.) Wayakichi Creek ran along the north end of the park and along Shoepke's property. The deed allowed Roche citizens the right to walk across a five-foot-wide section of the lot beside Wayakichi Creek as part of a two-mile public trail system. Teenagers regularly threw Frisbee golf discs from the walking path behind Shoepke's property over his yard to the adjacent park. Shoepke habitually shouted and cursed at the teenagers, demanding that they not throw objects over his yard. Six months later, the town of Roche passed an ordinance to appropriate all necessary land along the Wayakichi trail to widen the path to ten feet. Using the information presented in the chapter, answer the following questions.

1. What is the term for the right of Roche citizens to walk across Shoepke's land on the trail?
2. In the warranty deed that was used in the property transfer from the Brusters to Shoepke, what covenants would be inferred by most courts?
3. Suppose that Shoepke wants to file a trespass lawsuit against some teenagers who continually throw Frisbees over his land. Shoepke discovers, however, that when the city put in the Frisbee golf course, the neighborhood homeowners signed an agreement that limited their right to complain about errant Frisbees. What is this type of promise or agreement called in real property law?
4. What is the term for Roche's power to appropriate Shoepke's property for public use? Is this a restriction or taking?

TERMS AND CONCEPTS

adverse possession 632
bulk zoning 633
closing 627
community property 621
concurrent ownership 621
condemnation 635
conveyance 620
deed 629
easement 622
eminent domain 632
escrow account 627
fee simple absolute 619
fixed-term tenancy 622
fixture 618
general plan 633
grant deed 630
implied warranty of habitability 627
joint tenancy 621
land-use control 632
leasehold estate 622
license 624
life estate 620
marketable title 630

metes and bounds 629
nonpossessory interest 622
periodic tenancy 622
personal property 617
profit 623
quitclaim deed 629
real property 617
recording statute 630
restrictive covenant 631
sheriff's deed 630
special warranty deed 629
taking 635
tenancy at sufferance 622
tenancy at will 622
tenancy by the entirety 621
tenancy in common 621
title insurance 631
title search 630
use zoning 633
warranty deed 629
waste 620
zoning 633
zoning variance 634

QUESTIONS AND CASE PROBLEMS

25-1. Glenn is the owner of a lakeside house and lot. He deeds the house and lot "to my wife, Livia, for life, then to my daughter, Sarina." What is Livia's interest called? Is there any limitation on her rights to use the property as she wishes? Discuss.

25-2. Madison owned a tract of land, but he was not sure that he had full title to the property. When Rafael expressed an interest in buying the land, Madison sold it to Rafael and executed a quitclaim deed. Rafael properly recorded the deed immediately. Several months later, Madison learned that he had had full title to the tract of land. He then sold the land to Linda by warranty deed. Linda knew of the earlier purchase by Rafael but took the deed anyway and later sued to have Rafael evicted from the land. Linda claimed that because she had a warranty deed, her title to the land was better than that conferred by Rafael's quitclaim deed. Will Linda succeed in claiming title to the land? Explain.

25-3. QUESTION WITH SAMPLE ANSWER

The county intends to rezone an area from industrial use to residential use. Land within the affected area is largely undeveloped, but nonetheless it is expected that the proposed action will reduce the market value of the affected land by as much as 50 percent. Will the landowners be successful in suing to have the action declared a taking of their property, entitling them to just compensation?

- **For a sample answer to Question 25-3, go to Appendix I at the end of this text.**

25-4. Suppose that as a condition of a developer's receiving approval for constructing a new residential community, the local authorities insist that the developer dedicate, or set aside, land for a new hospital. The hospital would serve not only the proposed residential community but also the rest of the city. If the developer challenges the condition in court, under what standard might the court invalidate the condition?

25-5. To prevent population growth from racing ahead of the local government's ability to provide adequate police and fire protection, as well as road development for the increase in traffic, the local planning board imposes an ordinance limiting the issuance of residential building permits to one thousand per year for the next three years. A property developer who owns several tracts zoned for residential housing and whose development plans comply with all other existing ordinances challenges the ban in court. Will she succeed? Discuss all the relevant issues. What difference would it make if the developer had already expended considerable resources and taken the last step toward approval of the development project?

25-6. Adverse Possession. In 1972, Ted Pafundi bought a quarry in West Pawlet, Vermont, from his neighbor, Marguerite Scott. The deed vaguely described the eastern boundary of the quarry as "the westerly boundary of the lands of" the neighboring property owners. Pafundi quarried green slate from the west wall until his death in 1979, when his son Gary began to work the east wall until *his* death in 1989. Gary's daughter Connie then took over operations. All of the Pafundis used the floor of the quarry as their base of operations. In 1992, N.A.S. Holdings, Inc., bought the neighboring property. A survey revealed that virtually the entire quarry was within the boundaries of N.A.S.'s property and that twenty years earlier, Ted had actually bought only a small strip of land on the west side. When N.A.S. attempted to begin quarrying, Connie blocked the access. N.A.S. filed a suit in a Vermont state court against Connie, seeking to establish title. Connie argued that she had title to the quarry through adverse possession under a state statute with a possessory period of fifteen years. What are the elements to acquire title by adverse possession? Are they satisfied in this case? In whose favor should the court rule, and why? [*N.A.S. Holdings, Inc. v. Pafundi,* 169 Vt. 437, 736 A.2d 780 (1999)]

25-7. Easements. The Wallens family owned a cabin on Lummi Island in the state of Washington. A driveway ran from the cabin across their property to South Nugent Road. In 1952, Floyd Massey bought the adjacent lot and built a cabin. To gain access to his property, he used a bulldozer to extend the driveway without the Wallenses' permission but also without their objection. In 1975, the Wallenses sold their property to Wright Fish Co. Massey continued to use and maintain the driveway without permission or objection. In 1984, Massey sold his property to Robert Drake. Drake and his employees continued to use and maintain the driveway without permission or objection, although Drake knew it was located largely on Wright's property. In 1997, Wright sold its lot to Robert Smersh. The next year, Smersh told Drake to stop using the driveway. Drake filed a suit in a Washington state court against Smersh, claiming an easement by prescription (which is created by meeting the same requirements as adverse possession). Does Drake's use of the driveway meet all of the requirements? What should the court rule? Explain. [*Drake v. Smersh*, 122 Wash.App. 147, 89 P.3d 726 (Div. 1 2004)]

25-8. CASE PROBLEM WITH SAMPLE ANSWER

The Hope Partnership for Education, a religious organization, proposed to build a private independent middle school in a blighted neighborhood in Philadelphia, Pennsylvania. In 2002, the Hope Partnership asked the Redevelopment Authority of the City of Philadelphia to acquire specific land for the project and sell it to the Hope Partnership for a nominal price. The land included a house at 1839 North Eighth Street owned by Mary Smith, whose daughter Veronica lived there with her family. The Authority offered Smith $12,000 for the house and initiated a taking of the property. Smith filed a suit in a Pennsylvania state court against the Authority, admitting that the house was a "substandard structure in a blighted area," but arguing that the taking was unconstitutional because its beneficiary was private. The Authority asserted that only the public purpose of the taking should be considered, not the status of the property's developer. On what basis can a government entity use the power of eminent domain to take property? What are the limits to this power? How should the court rule? Why? [*Redevelopment Authority of City of Philadelphia v. New Eastwick Corp.*, 588 Pa. 789, 906 A.2d 1197 (2006)]

- **To view a sample answer for Problem 25–8, go to this book's Web site at academic.cengage.com/blaw/cross, select "Chapter 25," and click on "Case Problem with Sample Answer."**

25-9. Ownership in Fee Simple. Thomas and Teresa Cline built a house on a 76-acre parcel of real estate next to Roy Berg's home and property in Augusta County, Virginia. The homes were about 1,800 feet apart but in view of each other. After several disagreements between the parties, Berg equipped an 11-foot tripod with motion sensors and floodlights that intermittently illuminated the Clines' home. Berg also installed surveillance cameras that tracked some of the movement on the Clines' property. The cameras transmitted on an open frequency, which could be received by any television within range. The Clines asked Berg to turn off, or at least redirect, the lights. When he refused, they erected a fence for 200 feet along the parties' common property line. The 32-foot-high fence consisted of 20 utility poles spaced 10 feet apart with plastic wrap stretched between the poles. This effectively blocked the lights and cameras. Berg filed a suit against the Clines in a Virginia state court, complaining that the fence interfered unreasonably with his use and enjoyment of his property. He asked the court to order the Clines to take the fence down. What are the limits on an owner's use of property? How should the court rule in this case? Why? [*Cline v. Berg*, 273 Va. 142, 639 S.E.2d 231 (2007)]

25-10. A QUESTION OF ETHICS

*In 1999, Stephen and Linda Kailin bought the Monona Center, a mall in Madison, Wisconsin, from Perry Armstrong for $760,000. The contract provided, "Seller represents to Buyer that as of the date of acceptance Seller had no notice or knowledge of conditions affecting the Property or transaction" other than certain items disclosed at the time of the offer. Armstrong told the Kailins of the Center's eight tenants, their lease expiration dates, and the monthly and annual rent due under each lease. One of the lessees, Ring's All-American Karate, occupied about a third of the Center's space under a five-year lease. Because of Ring's financial difficulties, Armstrong had agreed to reduce its rent for nine months in 1997. By the time of the sale to the Kailins, Ring owed $13,910 in unpaid rent, but Armstrong did not tell the Kailins, who did not ask. Ring continued to fail to pay rent and finally vacated the Center. The Kailins filed a suit in a Wisconsin state court against Armstrong and others, alleging, among other things, misrepresentation. [*Kailin v. Armstrong, *2002 WI App 70, 252 Wis.2d 676, 643 N.W.2d 132 (2002)]*

(a) Did Armstrong have a duty to disclose Ring's delinquency and default to the Kailins? Does the failure of a tenant to pay rent constitute a defect that affects the value of the property? Why or why not?

(b) Could the Kalins reasonably have discovered Ring's delinquency in rent payments? Explain.

25-11. SPECIAL CASE ANALYSIS

Go to Case 25.4, *Kelo v. City of New London, Connecticut,* 545 U.S. 469, 125 S.Ct. 2655, 162 L.Ed.2d 439 (2005), on pages 635–636. Read the excerpt and answer the following questions.

(a) **Issue:** What was the main issue in this case?

(b) **Rule of Law:** What rule of law did the Court apply?

(c) **Applying the Rule of Law:** Describe how the Court applied the rule of law to the facts of this case.

(d) **Conclusion:** What was the Court's conclusion in this case?

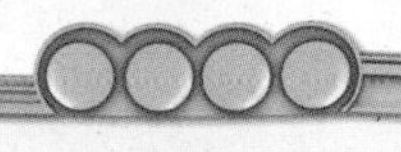

LAW ON THE WEB

For updated links to resources available on the Web, as well as a variety of other materials, visit this text's Web site at

academic.cengage.com/blaw/cross

For links to numerous sources relating to real property, go to

www.findlaw.com/01topics/index.html

and click on "Property Law & Real Estate."

For information on condemnation procedures and rules under one state's (California's) law, go to

www.eminentdomainlaw.net/propertyguide.html

Legal Research Exercises on the Web

Go to **academic.cengage.com/blaw/cross**, the Web site that accompanies this text. Select "Chapter 25" and click on "Internet Exercises." There you will find the following Internet research exercises that you can perform to learn more about the topics covered in this chapter.

Internet Exercise 25–1: Legal Perspective
Eminent Domain

Internet Exercise 25–2: Management Perspective
How to Challenge a Condemnation of Property

APPENDIX A

How to Brief Cases and Analyze Case Problems

HOW TO BRIEF CASES

To fully understand the law with respect to business, you need to be able to read and understand court decisions. To make this task easier, you can use a method of case analysis that is called *briefing*. There is a fairly standard procedure that you can follow when you "brief" any court case. You must first read the case opinion carefully. When you feel you understand the case, you can prepare a brief of it.

Although the format of the brief may vary, typically it will present the essentials of the case under headings such as those listed below.

1. Citation. Give the full citation for the case, including the name of the case, the date it was decided, and the court that decided it.
2. Facts. Briefly indicate (a) the reasons for the lawsuit; (b) the identity and arguments of the plaintiff(s) and defendant(s), respectively; and (c) the lower court's decision—if appropriate.
3. Issue. Concisely phrase, in the form of a question, the essential issue before the court. (If more than one issue is involved, you may have two—or even more—questions here.)
4. Decision. Indicate here—with a "yes" or "no," if possible—the court's answer to the question (or questions) in the *Issue* section above.
5. Reason. Summarize as briefly as possible the reasons given by the court for its decision (or decisions) and the case or statutory law relied on by the court in arriving at its decision.

AN EXAMPLE OF A BRIEFED SAMPLE COURT CASE

As an example of the format used in briefing cases, we present here a briefed version of the sample court case that was presented in Exhibit 1–6 on page 24.

BERGER V. CITY OF SEATTLE
United States Court of Appeals,
Ninth Circuit, 2008.
512 F.3d 582.

FACTS The Seattle Center is an entertainment "zone" in downtown Seattle, Washington, that attracts nearly ten million tourists each year. The center encompasses theaters, arenas, museums, exhibition halls, conference rooms, outdoor stadiums, and restaurants, and features street performers. Under the authority of the city, the center's director issued rules in 2002 to address safety concerns and other matters. Among other things, street performers were required to obtain permits and wear badges. After members of the public filed numerous complaints of threatening behavior by street performer and balloon artist Michael Berger, Seattle Center staff cited Berger for several rules violations. He filed a suit in a federal district court against the city and others, alleging, in part, that the rules violated his free speech rights under the First Amendment to the U.S. Constitution. The court issued a judgment in the plaintiff's favor. The city appealed to the U.S. Court of Appeals for the Ninth Circuit.

ISSUE Did the rules issued by the Seattle Center under the city's authority meet the requirements for valid restrictions on speech under the First Amendment?

DECISION Yes. The U.S. Court of Appeals for the Ninth Circuit reversed the decision of the lower court and remanded the case for further proceedings. "Such content neutral and narrowly tailored rules * * * must be upheld."

REASON The court concluded first that the rules requiring permits and badges were "content neutral." Time, place, and manner restrictions do not violate the First Amendment if they burden all expression equally and do not allow officials to treat different messages differently. In

this case, the rules met this test and thus did not discriminate based on content. The court also concluded that the rules were "narrowly tailored" to "promote a substantial government interest that would be achieved less effectively" otherwise. With the rules, the city was trying to "reduce territorial disputes among performers, deter patron harassment, and facilitate the identification and apprehension of offending performers." This was pursuant to the valid governmental objective of protecting the safety and convenience of the other performers and the public generally. The public's complaints about Berger and others showed that unregulated street performances posed a threat to these interests. The court was "satisfied that the city's permit scheme was designed to further valid governmental objectives."

REVIEW OF SAMPLE COURT CASE

Here, we provide a review of the briefed version to indicate the kind of information that is contained in each section.

CITATION The name of the case is *Berger v. City of Seattle.* Berger is the plaintiff; the City of Seattle is the defendant. The U.S. Court of Appeals for the Ninth Circuit decided this case in 2008. The citation states that this case can be found in volume 512 of the *Federal Reporter, Third Series,* on page 582.

FACTS The *Facts* section identifies the plaintiff and the defendant, describes the events leading up to this suit, the allegations made by the plaintiff in the initial suit, and (because this case is an appellate court decision) the lower court's ruling and the party appealing. The party appealing's argument on appeal is also sometimes included here.

ISSUE The *Issue* section presents the central issue (or issues) decided by the court. In this case, the U.S. Court of Appeals for the Ninth Circuit considered whether certain rules imposed on street performers by local government authorities satisfied the requirements for valid restrictions on speech under the First Amendment to the U.S. Constitution.

DECISION The *Decision* section includes the court's decision on the issues before it. The decision reflects the opinion of the judge or justice hearing the case. Decisions by appellate courts are frequently phrased in reference to the lower court's decision. In other words, the appellate court may "affirm" the lower court's ruling or "reverse" it. Here, the court determined that Seattle's rules were "content neutral" and "narrowly tailored" to "promote a substantial government interest that would otherwise be achieved less effectively." The court found in favor of the city and reversed the lower court's ruling in the plaintiff's (Berger's) favor.

REASON The *Reason* section includes references to the relevant laws and legal principles that the court applied in coming to its conclusion in the case. The relevant law in the *Berger* case included the requirements under the First Amendment for evaluating the purpose and effect of government regulation with respect to expression. This section also explains the court's application of the law to the facts in this case.

ANALYZING CASE PROBLEMS

In addition to learning how to brief cases, students of business law and the legal environment also find it helpful to know how to analyze case problems. Part of the study of business law and the legal environment usually involves analyzing case problems, such as those included in this text at the end of each chapter.

For each case problem in this book, we provide the relevant background and facts of the lawsuit and the issue before the court. When you are assigned one of these problems, your job will be to determine how the court should decide the issue, and why. In other words, you will need to engage in legal analysis and reasoning. Here, we offer some suggestions on how to make this task less daunting. We begin by presenting a sample problem:

> While Janet Lawson, a famous pianist, was shopping in Quality Market, she slipped and fell on a wet floor in one of the aisles. The floor had recently been mopped by one of the store's employees, but there were no signs warning customers that the floor in that area was wet. As a result of the fall, Lawson injured her right arm and was unable to perform piano concerts for the next six months. Had she been able to perform the scheduled concerts, she would have earned approximately $60,000 over that period of time. Lawson sued Quality Market for this amount, plus another $10,000 in medical expenses. She claimed that the store's failure to warn customers of the wet floor constituted negligence and therefore the market was liable for her injuries. Will the court agree with Lawson? Discuss.

UNDERSTAND THE FACTS

This may sound obvious, but before you can analyze or apply the relevant law to a specific set of facts, you must clearly understand those facts. In other words, you should read through the case problem carefully—more than once, if necessary—to make sure you understand the identity of the plaintiff(s) and defendant(s) in the case and the progression of events that led to the lawsuit.

In the sample case problem just given, the identity of the parties is fairly obvious. Janet Lawson is the one bringing the suit; therefore, she is the plaintiff. Quality Market, against whom she is bringing the suit, is the defendant. Some of the case problems you may work on have multiple plaintiffs or defendants. Often, it is helpful to use abbreviations for the parties. To indicate a reference to a plaintiff, for example, the *pi* symbol—π—is often used,

and a defendant is denoted by a *delta*—Δ—a triangle.

The events leading to the lawsuit are also fairly straightforward. Lawson slipped and fell on a wet floor, and she contends that Quality Market should be liable for her injuries because it was negligent in not posting a sign warning customers of the wet floor.

When you are working on case problems, realize that the facts should be accepted as they are given. For example, in our sample problem, it should be accepted that the floor was wet and that there was no sign. In other words, avoid making conjectures, such as "Maybe the floor wasn't too wet," or "Maybe an employee was getting a sign to put up," or "Maybe someone stole the sign." Questioning the facts as they are presented only adds confusion to your analysis.

LEGAL ANALYSIS AND REASONING

Once you understand the facts given in the case problem, you can begin to analyze the case. Recall from Chapter 1 that the IRAC method is a helpful tool to use in the legal analysis and reasoning process. IRAC is an acronym for **I**ssue, **R**ule, **A**pplication, **C**onclusion. Applying this method to our sample problem would involve the following steps:

1. First, you need to decide what legal **issue** is involved in the case. In our sample case, the basic issue is whether Quality Market's failure to warn customers of the wet floor constituted negligence. As discussed in Chapter 12, negligence is a *tort*—a civil wrong. In a tort lawsuit, the plaintiff seeks to be compensated for another's wrongful act. A defendant will be deemed negligent if he or she breached a duty of care owed to the plaintiff and the breach of that duty caused the plaintiff to suffer harm.
2. Once you have identified the issue, the next step is to determine what **rule of law** applies to the issue. To make this determination, you will want to review carefully the text of the chapter in which the relevant rule of law for the problem appears. Our sample case problem involves the tort of negligence, which is covered in Chapter 12. The applicable rule of law is the tort law principle that business owners owe a duty to exercise reasonable care to protect their customers ("business invitees"). Reasonable care, in this context, includes either removing—or warning customers of—*foreseeable* risks about which the owner *knew* or *should have known.* Business owners need not warn customers of "open and obvious" risks, however. If a business owner breaches this duty of care (fails to exercise the appropriate degree of care toward customers), and the breach of duty causes a customer to be injured, the business owner will be liable to the customer for the customer's injuries.
3. The next—and usually the most difficult—step in analyzing case problems is the **application** of the relevant rule of law to the specific facts of the case you are studying. In our sample problem, applying the tort law principle just discussed presents few difficulties. An employee of the store had mopped the floor in the aisle where Lawson slipped and fell, but no sign was present indicating that the floor was wet. That a customer might fall on a wet floor is clearly a foreseeable risk. Therefore, the failure to warn customers about the wet floor was a breach of the duty of care owed by the business owner to the store's customers.
4. Once you have completed Step 3 in the IRAC method, you should be ready to draw your **conclusion.** In our sample problem, Quality Market is liable to Lawson for her injuries, because the market's breach of its duty of care caused Lawson's injuries.

The fact patterns in the case problems presented in this text are not always as simple as those presented in our sample problem. Often, for example, a case has more than one plaintiff or defendant. A case may also involve more than one issue and have more than one applicable rule of law. Furthermore, in some case problems the facts may indicate that the general rule of law should not apply. For example, suppose that a store employee advised Lawson not to walk on the floor in the aisle because it was wet, but Lawson decided to walk on it anyway. This fact could alter the outcome of the case because the store could then raise the defense of *assumption of risk* (see Chapter 12). Nonetheless, a careful review of the chapter should always provide you with the knowledge you need to analyze the problem thoroughly and arrive at accurate conclusions.

APPENDIX B

The Constitution of the United States

Preamble

We the People of the United States, in Order to form a more perfect Union, establish Justice, insure domestic Tranquility, provide for the common defence, promote the general Welfare, and secure the Blessings of Liberty to ourselves and our Posterity, do ordain and establish this Constitution for the United States of America.

Article I

Section 1. All legislative Powers herein granted shall be vested in a Congress of the United States, which shall consist of a Senate and House of Representatives.

Section 2. The House of Representatives shall be composed of Members chosen every second Year by the People of the several States, and the Electors in each State shall have the Qualifications requisite for Electors of the most numerous Branch of the State Legislature.

No Person shall be a Representative who shall not have attained to the Age of twenty five Years, and been seven Years a Citizen of the United States, and who shall not, when elected, be an Inhabitant of that State in which he shall be chosen.

Representatives and direct Taxes shall be apportioned among the several States which may be included within this Union, according to their respective Numbers, which shall be determined by adding to the whole Number of free Persons, including those bound to Service for a Term of Years, and excluding Indians not taxed, three fifths of all other Persons. The actual Enumeration shall be made within three Years after the first Meeting of the Congress of the United States, and within every subsequent Term of ten Years, in such Manner as they shall by Law direct. The Number of Representatives shall not exceed one for every thirty Thousand, but each State shall have at Least one Representative; and until such enumeration shall be made, the State of New Hampshire shall be entitled to chuse three, Massachusetts eight, Rhode Island and Providence Plantations one, Connecticut five, New York six, New Jersey four, Pennsylvania eight, Delaware one, Maryland six, Virginia ten, North Carolina five, South Carolina five, and Georgia three.

When vacancies happen in the Representation from any State, the Executive Authority thereof shall issue Writs of Election to fill such Vacancies.

The House of Representatives shall chuse their Speaker and other Officers; and shall have the sole Power of Impeachment.

Section 3. The Senate of the United States shall be composed of two Senators from each State, chosen by the Legislature thereof, for six Years; and each Senator shall have one Vote.

Immediately after they shall be assembled in Consequence of the first Election, they shall be divided as equally as may be into three Classes. The Seats of the Senators of the first Class shall be vacated at the Expiration of the second Year, of the second Class at the Expiration of the fourth Year, and of the third Class at the Expiration of the sixth Year, so that one third may be chosen every second Year; and if Vacancies happen by Resignation, or otherwise, during the Recess of the Legislature of any State, the Executive thereof may make temporary Appointments until the next Meeting of the Legislature, which shall then fill such Vacancies.

No Person shall be a Senator who shall not have attained to the Age of thirty Years, and been nine Years a Citizen of the United States, and who shall not, when elected, be an Inhabitant of that State for which he shall be chosen.

The Vice President of the United States shall be President of the Senate, but shall have no Vote, unless they be equally divided.

The Senate shall chuse their other Officers, and also a President pro tempore, in the Absence of the Vice President, or when he shall exercise the Office of President of the United States.

The Senate shall have the sole Power to try all Impeachments. When sitting for that Purpose, they shall be on Oath or Affirmation. When the President of the United States is tried, the Chief Justice shall preside: And no Person shall be convicted without the Concurrence of two thirds of the Members present.

Judgment in Cases of Impeachment shall not extend further than to removal from Office, and disqualification to hold and enjoy any Office of honor, Trust, or Profit under the United States: but the Party convicted shall nevertheless be liable and subject to Indictment, Trial, Judgment, and Punishment, according to Law.

Section 4. The Times, Places and Manner of holding Elections for Senators and Representatives, shall be prescribed in each State by the Legislature thereof; but the Congress may at any time by Law make or alter such Regulations, except as to the Places of chusing Senators.

The Congress shall assemble at least once in every Year, and such Meeting shall be on the first Monday in December, unless they shall by Law appoint a different Day.

Section 5. Each House shall be the Judge of the Elections, Returns, and Qualifications of its own Members, and a Majority of each shall constitute a Quorum to do Business; but a smaller Number may adjourn from day to day, and may be authorized to compel the Attendance of absent Members, in such Manner, and under such Penalties as each House may provide.

Each House may determine the Rules of its Proceedings, punish its Members for disorderly Behavior, and, with the Concurrence of two thirds, expel a Member.

Each House shall keep a Journal of its Proceedings, and from time to time publish the same, excepting such Parts as may in their Judgment require Secrecy; and the Yeas and Nays of the Members of either House on any question shall, at the Desire of one fifth of those Present, be entered on the Journal.

Neither House, during the Session of Congress, shall, without the Consent of the other, adjourn for more than three days, nor to any other Place than that in which the two Houses shall be sitting.

Section 6. The Senators and Representatives shall receive a Compensation for their Services, to be ascertained by Law, and paid out of the Treasury of the United States. They shall in all Cases, except Treason, Felony and Breach of the Peace, be privileged from Arrest during their Attendance at the Session of their respective Houses, and in going to and returning from the same; and for any Speech or Debate in either House, they shall not be questioned in any other Place.

No Senator or Representative shall, during the Time for which he was elected, be appointed to any civil Office under the Authority of the United States, which shall have been created, or the Emoluments whereof shall have been increased during such time; and no Person holding any Office under the United States, shall be a Member of either House during his Continuance in Office.

Section 7. All Bills for raising Revenue shall originate in the House of Representatives; but the Senate may propose or concur with Amendments as on other Bills.

Every Bill which shall have passed the House of Representatives and the Senate, shall, before it become a Law, be presented to the President of the United States; If he approve he shall sign it, but if not he shall return it, with his Objections to the House in which it shall have originated, who shall enter the Objections at large on their Journal, and proceed to reconsider it. If after such Reconsideration two thirds of that House shall agree to pass the Bill, it shall be sent together with the Objections, to the other House, by which it shall likewise be reconsidered, and if approved by two thirds of that House, it shall become a Law. But in all such Cases the Votes of both Houses shall be determined by Yeas and Nays, and the Names of the Persons voting for and against the Bill shall be entered on the Journal of each House respectively. If any Bill shall not be returned by the President within ten Days (Sundays excepted) after it shall have been presented to him, the Same shall be a Law, in like Manner as if he had signed it, unless the Congress by their Adjournment prevent its Return in which Case it shall not be a Law.

Every Order, Resolution, or Vote, to which the Concurrence of the Senate and House of Representatives may be necessary (except on a question of Adjournment) shall be presented to the President of the United States; and before the Same shall take Effect, shall be approved by him, or being disapproved by him, shall be repassed by two thirds of the Senate and House of Representatives, according to the Rules and Limitations prescribed in the Case of a Bill.

Section 8. The Congress shall have Power To lay and collect Taxes, Duties, Imposts and Excises, to pay the Debts and provide for the common Defence and general Welfare of the United States; but all Duties, Imposts and Excises shall be uniform throughout the United States;

To borrow Money on the credit of the United States;

To regulate Commerce with foreign Nations, and among the several States, and with the Indian Tribes;

To establish an uniform Rule of Naturalization, and uniform Laws on the subject of Bankruptcies throughout the United States;

To coin Money, regulate the Value thereof, and of foreign Coin, and fix the Standard of Weights and Measures;

To provide for the Punishment of counterfeiting the Securities and current Coin of the United States;

To establish Post Offices and post Roads;

To promote the Progress of Science and useful Arts, by securing for limited Times to Authors and Inventors the exclusive Right to their respective Writings and Discoveries;

To constitute Tribunals inferior to the supreme Court;

To define and punish Piracies and Felonies committed on the high Seas, and Offences against the Law of Nations;

To declare War, grant Letters of Marque and Reprisal, and make Rules concerning Captures on Land and Water;

To raise and support Armies, but no Appropriation of Money to that Use shall be for a longer Term than two Years;

To provide and maintain a Navy;

To make Rules for the Government and Regulation of the land and naval Forces;

To provide for calling forth the Militia to execute the Laws of the Union, suppress Insurrections and repel Invasions;

To provide for organizing, arming, and disciplining, the Militia, and for governing such Part of them as may be employed in the Service of the United States, reserving to the States respectively, the Appointment of the Officers, and the Authority of training the Militia according to the discipline prescribed by Congress;

To exercise exclusive Legislation in all Cases whatsoever, over such District (not exceeding ten Miles square) as may, by Cession of particular States, and the Acceptance of Congress, become the Seat of the Government of the United States, and to exercise like Authority over all Places purchased by the Consent of the Legislature of the State in which the Same shall be, for the Erection of Forts, Magazines, Arsenals, dock-Yards, and other needful Buildings;—And

To make all Laws which shall be necessary and proper for carrying into Execution the foregoing Powers, and all other Powers vested by this Constitution in the Government of the United States, or in any Department or Officer thereof.

Section 9. The Migration or Importation of such Persons as any of the States now existing shall think proper to admit, shall not be prohibited by the Congress prior to the Year one thousand eight hundred and eight, but a Tax or duty may be imposed on such Importation, not exceeding ten dollars for each Person.

The privilege of the Writ of Habeas Corpus shall not be suspended, unless when in Cases of Rebellion or Invasion the public Safety may require it.

No Bill of Attainder or ex post facto Law shall be passed.

No Capitation, or other direct, Tax shall be laid, unless in Proportion to the Census or Enumeration herein before directed to be taken.

No Tax or Duty shall be laid on Articles exported from any State.

No Preference shall be given by any Regulation of Commerce or Revenue to the Ports of one State over those of another: nor shall Vessels bound to, or from, one State be obliged to enter, clear, or pay Duties in another.

No Money shall be drawn from the Treasury, but in Consequence of Appropriations made by Law; and a regular Statement and Account of the Receipts and Expenditures of all public Money shall be published from time to time.

No Title of Nobility shall be granted by the United States: And no Person holding any Office of Profit or Trust under them, shall, without the Consent of the Congress, accept of any present, Emolument, Office, or Title, of any kind whatever, from any King, Prince, or foreign State.

Section 10. No State shall enter into any Treaty, Alliance, or Confederation; grant Letters of Marque and Reprisal; coin Money; emit Bills of Credit; make any Thing but gold and silver Coin a Tender in Payment of Debts; pass any Bill of Attainder, ex post facto Law, or Law impairing the Obligation of Contracts, or grant any Title of Nobility.

No State shall, without the Consent of the Congress, lay any Imposts or Duties on Imports or Exports, except what may be absolutely necessary for executing its inspection Laws: and the net Produce of all Duties and Imposts, laid by any State on Imports or Exports, shall be for the Use of the Treasury of the United States; and all such Laws shall be subject to the Revision and Controul of the Congress.

No State shall, without the Consent of Congress, lay any Duty of Tonnage, keep Troops, or Ships of War in time of Peace, enter into any Agreement or Compact with another State, or with a foreign Power, or engage in War, unless actually invaded, or in such imminent Danger as will not admit of delay.

Article II

Section 1. The executive Power shall be vested in a President of the United States of America. He shall hold his Office during the Term of four Years, and, together with the Vice President, chosen for the same Term, be elected, as follows:

Each State shall appoint, in such Manner as the Legislature thereof may direct, a Number of Electors, equal to the whole Number of Senators and Representatives to which the State may be entitled in the Congress; but no Senator or Representative, or Person holding an Office of Trust or Profit under the United States, shall be appointed an Elector.

The Electors shall meet in their respective States, and vote by Ballot for two Persons, of whom one at least shall not be an Inhabitant of the same State with themselves. And they shall make a List of all the Persons voted for, and of the Number of Votes for each; which List they shall sign and certify, and transmit sealed to the Seat of the Government of the United States, directed to the President of the Senate. The President of the Senate shall, in the Presence of the Senate and House of Representatives, open all the Certificates, and the Votes shall then be counted. The Person having the greatest Number of Votes shall be the President, if such Number be a Majority of the whole Number of Electors appointed; and if there be more than one who have such Majority, and have an equal Number of Votes, then the House of Representatives shall immediately chuse by Ballot one of them for President; and if no Person have a Majority, then from the five highest on the List the said House shall in like Manner chuse the President. But in chusing the President, the Votes shall be taken by States, the Representation from each State having one Vote; A quorum for this Purpose shall consist of a Member or Members from two thirds of the States, and a Majority of all the States shall be necessary to a Choice. In every Case, after the Choice of the President, the Person having the greater Number of Votes of the Electors shall be the Vice President. But if there should remain two or more who have equal Votes, the Senate shall chuse from them by Ballot the Vice President.

The Congress may determine the Time of chusing the Electors, and the Day on which they shall give their Votes; which Day shall be the same throughout the United States.

No person except a natural born Citizen, or a Citizen of the United States, at the time of the Adoption of this Constitution, shall be eligible to the Office of President; neither shall any Person be eligible to that Office who shall not have attained to the Age of thirty five Years, and been fourteen Years a Resident within the United States.

In Case of the Removal of the President from Office, or of his Death, Resignation or Inability to discharge the

Powers and Duties of the said Office, the same shall devolve on the Vice President, and the Congress may by Law provide for the Case of Removal, Death, Resignation or Inability, both of the President and Vice President, declaring what Officer shall then act as President, and such Officer shall act accordingly, until the Disability be removed, or a President shall be elected.

The President shall, at stated Times, receive for his Services, a Compensation, which shall neither be increased nor diminished during the Period for which he shall have been elected, and he shall not receive within that Period any other Emolument from the United States, or any of them.

Before he enter on the Execution of his Office, he shall take the following Oath or Affirmation: "I do solemnly swear (or affirm) that I will faithfully execute the Office of President of the United States, and will to the best of my Ability, preserve, protect and defend the Constitution of the United States."

Section 2. The President shall be Commander in Chief of the Army and Navy of the United States, and of the Militia of the several States, when called into the actual Service of the United States; he may require the Opinion, in writing, of the principal Officer in each of the executive Departments, upon any Subject relating to the Duties of their respective Offices, and he shall have Power to grant Reprieves and Pardons for Offenses against the United States, except in Cases of Impeachment.

He shall have Power, by and with the Advice and Consent of the Senate to make Treaties, provided two thirds of the Senators present concur; and he shall nominate, and by and with the Advice and Consent of the Senate, shall appoint Ambassadors, other public Ministers and Consuls, Judges of the supreme Court, and all other Officers of the United States, whose Appointments are not herein otherwise provided for, and which shall be established by Law; but the Congress may by Law vest the Appointment of such inferior Officers, as they think proper, in the President alone, in the Courts of Law, or in the Heads of Departments.

The President shall have Power to fill up all Vacancies that may happen during the Recess of the Senate, by granting Commissions which shall expire at the End of their next Session.

Section 3. He shall from time to time give to the Congress Information of the State of the Union, and recommend to their Consideration such Measures as he shall judge necessary and expedient; he may, on extraordinary Occasions, convene both Houses, or either of them, and in Case of Disagreement between them, with Respect to the Time of Adjournment, he may adjourn them to such Time as he shall think proper; he shall receive Ambassadors and other public Ministers; he shall take Care that the Laws be faithfully executed, and shall Commission all the Officers of the United States.

Section 4. The President, Vice President and all civil Officers of the United States, shall be removed from Office on Impeachment for, and Conviction of, Treason, Bribery, or other high Crimes and Misdemeanors.

Article III

Section 1. The judicial Power of the United States, shall be vested in one supreme Court, and in such inferior Courts as the Congress may from time to time ordain and establish. The Judges, both of the supreme and inferior Courts, shall hold their Offices during good Behaviour, and shall, at stated Times, receive for their Services a Compensation, which shall not be diminished during their Continuance in Office.

Section 2. The judicial Power shall extend to all Cases, in Law and Equity, arising under this Constitution, the Laws of the United States, and Treaties made, or which shall be made, under their Authority;—to all Cases affecting Ambassadors, other public Ministers and Consuls;—to all Cases of admiralty and maritime Jurisdiction;—to Controversies to which the United States shall be a Party;—to Controversies between two or more States;—between a State and Citizens of another State;—between Citizens of different States;—between Citizens of the same State claiming Lands under Grants of different States, and between a State, or the Citizens thereof, and foreign States, Citizens or Subjects.

In all Cases affecting Ambassadors, other public Ministers and Consuls, and those in which a State shall be a Party, the supreme Court shall have original Jurisdiction. In all the other Cases before mentioned, the supreme Court shall have appellate Jurisdiction, both as to Law and Fact, with such Exceptions, and under such Regulations as the Congress shall make.

The Trial of all Crimes, except in Cases of Impeachment, shall be by Jury; and such Trial shall be held in the State where the said Crimes shall have been committed; but when not committed within any State, the Trial shall be at such Place or Places as the Congress may by Law have directed.

Section 3. Treason against the United States, shall consist only in levying War against them, or, in adhering to their Enemies, giving them Aid and Comfort. No Person shall be convicted of Treason unless on the Testimony of two Witnesses to the same overt Act, or on Confession in open Court.

The Congress shall have Power to declare the Punishment of Treason, but no Attainder of Treason shall work Corruption of Blood, or Forfeiture except during the Life of the Person attainted.

Article IV

Section 1. Full Faith and Credit shall be given in each State to the public Acts, Records, and judicial Proceedings of every other State. And the Congress may by general Laws prescribe the Manner in which such Acts, Records and Proceedings shall be proved, and the Effect thereof.

Section 2. The Citizens of each State shall be entitled to all Privileges and Immunities of Citizens in the several States.

A Person charged in any State with Treason, Felony, or other Crime, who shall flee from Justice, and be found in another State, shall on Demand of the executive Authority of the State from which he fled, be delivered up, to be removed to the State having Jurisdiction of the Crime.

No Person held to Service or Labour in one State, under the Laws thereof, escaping into another, shall, in Consequence of any Law or Regulation therein, be discharged from such Service or Labour, but shall be delivered up on Claim of the Party to whom such Service or Labour may be due.

Section 3. New States may be admitted by the Congress into this Union; but no new State shall be formed or erected within the Jurisdiction of any other State; nor any State be formed by the Junction of two or more States, or Parts of States, without the Consent of the Legislatures of the States concerned as well as of the Congress.

The Congress shall have Power to dispose of and make all needful Rules and Regulations respecting the Territory or other Property belonging to the United States; and nothing in this Constitution shall be so construed as to Prejudice any Claims of the United States, or of any particular State.

Section 4. The United States shall guarantee to every State in this Union a Republican Form of Government, and shall protect each of them against Invasion; and on Application of the Legislature, or of the Executive (when the Legislature cannot be convened) against domestic Violence.

Article V

The Congress, whenever two thirds of both Houses shall deem it necessary, shall propose Amendments to this Constitution, or, on the Application of the Legislatures of two thirds of the several States, shall call a Convention for proposing Amendments, which, in either Case, shall be valid to all Intents and Purposes, as part of this Constitution, when ratified by the Legislatures of three fourths of the several States, or by Conventions in three fourths thereof, as the one or the other Mode of Ratification may be proposed by the Congress; Provided that no Amendment which may be made prior to the Year One thousand eight hundred and eight shall in any Manner affect the first and fourth Clauses in the Ninth Section of the first Article; and that no State, without its Consent, shall be deprived of its equal Suffrage in the Senate.

Article VI

All Debts contracted and Engagements entered into, before the Adoption of this Constitution shall be as valid against the United States under this Constitution, as under the Confederation.

This Constitution, and the Laws of the United States which shall be made in Pursuance thereof; and all Treaties made, or which shall be made, under the Authority of the United States, shall be the supreme Law of the Land; and the Judges in every State shall be bound thereby, any Thing in the Constitution or Laws of any State to the Contrary notwithstanding.

The Senators and Representatives before mentioned, and the Members of the several State Legislatures, and all executive and judicial Officers, both of the United States and of the several States, shall be bound by Oath or Affirmation, to support this Constitution; but no religious Test shall ever be required as a Qualification to any Office or public Trust under the United States.

Article VII

The Ratification of the Conventions of nine States shall be sufficient for the Establishment of this Constitution between the States so ratifying the Same.

Amendment I [1791]

Congress shall make no law respecting an establishment of religion, or prohibiting the free exercise thereof; or abridging the freedom of speech, or of the press; or the right of the people peaceably to assembly, and to petition the Government for a redress of grievances.

Amendment II [1791]

A well regulated Militia, being necessary to the security of a free State, the right of the people to keep and bear Arms, shall not be infringed.

Amendment III [1791]

No Soldier shall, in time of peace be quartered in any house, without the consent of the Owner, nor in time of war, but in a manner to be prescribed by law.

Amendment IV [1791]

The right of the people to be secure in their persons, houses, papers, and effects, against unreasonable searches and seizures, shall not be violated, and no Warrants shall issue, but upon probable cause, supported by Oath or affirmation, and particularly describing the place to be searched, and the persons or things to be seized.

Amendment V [1791]

No person shall be held to answer for a capital, or otherwise infamous crime, unless on a presentment or indictment of a Grand Jury, except in cases arising in the land or naval forces, or in the Militia, when in actual service in time of War or public danger; nor shall any person be subject for the same offence to be twice put in jeopardy of life or limb; nor shall be compelled in any criminal case to be a witness against himself, nor be deprived of life, liberty, or property, without due process of law; nor shall private property be taken for public use, without just compensation.

Amendment VI [1791]

In all criminal prosecutions, the accused shall enjoy the right to a speedy and public trial, by an impartial jury of the State and district wherein the crime shall have been committed, which district shall have been previously ascertained by law, and to be informed of the nature and cause of the accusation; to be confronted with the witnesses against him; to have compulsory process for obtaining witnesses in his favor, and to have the Assistance of Counsel for his defence.

AMENDMENT VII [1791]

In Suits at common law, where the value in controversy shall exceed twenty dollars, the right of trial by jury shall be preserved, and no fact tried by jury, shall be otherwise re-examined in any Court of the United States, than according to the rules of the common law.

AMENDMENT VIII [1791]

Excessive bail shall not be required, nor excessive fines imposed, nor cruel and unusual punishments inflicted.

AMENDMENT IX [1791]

The enumeration in the Constitution, of certain rights, shall not be construed to deny or disparage others retained by the people.

AMENDMENT X [1791]

The powers not delegated to the United States by the Constitution, nor prohibited by it to the States, are reserved to the States respectively, or to the people.

AMENDMENT XI [1798]

The Judicial power of the United States shall not be construed to extend to any suit in law or equity, commenced or prosecuted against one of the United States by Citizens of another State, or by Citizens or Subjects of any Foreign State.

AMENDMENT XII [1804]

The Electors shall meet in their respective states, and vote by ballot for President and Vice-President, one of whom, at least, shall not be an inhabitant of the same state with themselves; they shall name in their ballots the person voted for as President, and in distinct ballots the person voted for as Vice-President, and they shall make distinct lists of all persons voted for as President, and of all persons voted for as Vice-President, and of the number of votes for each, which lists they shall sign and certify, and transmit sealed to the seat of the government of the United States, directed to the President of the Senate;—The President of the Senate shall, in the presence of the Senate and House of Representatives, open all the certificates and the votes shall then be counted;—The person having the greatest number of votes for President, shall be the President, if such number be a majority of the whole number of Electors appointed; and if no person have such majority, then from the persons having the highest numbers not exceeding three on the list of those voted for as President, the House of Representatives shall choose immediately, by ballot, the President. But in choosing the President, the votes shall be taken by states, the representation from each state having one vote; a quorum for this purpose shall consist of a member or members from two thirds of the states, and a majority of all states shall be necessary to a choice. And if the House of Representatives shall not choose a President whenever the right of choice shall devolve upon them, before the fourth day of March next following, then the Vice-President shall act as President, as in the case of the death or other constitutional disability of the President.—The person having the greatest number of votes as Vice-President, shall be the Vice-President, if such number be a majority of the whole number of Electors appointed, and if no person have a majority, then from the two highest numbers on the list, the Senate shall choose the Vice-President; a quorum for the purpose shall consist of two-thirds of the whole number of Senators, and a majority of the whole number shall be necessary to a choice. But no person constitutionally ineligible to the office of President shall be eligible to that of Vice-President of the United States.

AMENDMENT XIII [1865]

Section 1. Neither slavery nor involuntary servitude, except as a punishment for crime whereof the party shall have been duly convicted, shall exist within the United States, or any place subject to their jurisdiction.

Section 2. Congress shall have power to enforce this article by appropriate legislation.

AMENDMENT XIV [1868]

Section 1. All persons born or naturalized in the United States, and subject to the jurisdiction thereof, are citizens of the United States and of the State wherein they reside. No State shall make or enforce any law which shall abridge the privileges or immunities of citizens of the United States; nor shall any State deprive any person of life, liberty, or property, without due process of law; nor deny to any person within its jurisdiction the equal protection of the laws.

Section 2. Representatives shall be apportioned among the several States according to their respective numbers, counting the whole number of persons in each State, excluding Indians not taxed. But when the right to vote at any election for the choice of electors for President and Vice President of the United States, Representatives in Congress, the Executive and Judicial officers of a State, or the members of the Legislature thereof, is denied to any of the male inhabitants of such State, being twenty-one years of age, and citizens of the United States, or in any way abridged, except for participation in rebellion, or other crime, the basis of representation therein shall be reduced in the proportion which the number of such male citizens shall bear to the whole number of male citizens twenty-one years of age in such State.

Section 3. No person shall be a Senator or Representative in Congress, or elector of President and Vice President, or hold any office, civil or military, under the United States, or under any State, who having previously taken an oath, as a member of Congress, or as an officer of the United States, or as a member of any State legislature, or as an executive or judicial officer of any State, to support the Constitution of the United States, shall have engaged in insurrection or rebellion against the same, or given aid or comfort to the enemies thereof. But Congress may by a vote of two-thirds of each House, remove such disability.

Section 4. The validity of the public debt of the United States, authorized by law, including debts incurred for payment of pensions and bounties for services in suppressing insurrection or rebellion, shall not be questioned. But neither the United States nor any State shall assume or pay any debt or obligation incurred in aid of insurrection or rebellion against the United States, or any claim for the loss or emancipation of any slave; but all such debts, obligations and claims shall be held illegal and void.

Section 5. The Congress shall have power to enforce, by appropriate legislation, the provisions of this article.

Amendment XV [1870]

Section 1. The right of citizens of the United States to vote shall not be denied or abridged by the United States or by any State on account of race, color, or previous condition of servitude.

Section 2. The Congress shall have power to enforce this article by appropriate legislation.

Amendment XVI [1913]

The Congress shall have power to lay and collect taxes on incomes, from whatever source derived, without apportionment among the several States, and without regard to any census or enumeration.

Amendment XVII [1913]

Section 1. The Senate of the United States shall be composed of two Senators from each State, elected by the people thereof, for six years; and each Senator shall have one vote. The electors in each State shall have the qualifications requisite for electors of the most numerous branch of the State legislatures.

Section 2. When vacancies happen in the representation of any State in the Senate, the executive authority of such State shall issue writs of election to fill such vacancies: *Provided,* That the legislature of any State may empower the executive thereof to make temporary appointments until the people fill the vacancies by election as the legislature may direct.

Section 3. This amendment shall not be so construed as to affect the election or term of any Senator chosen before it becomes valid as part of the Constitution.

Amendment XVIII [1919]

Section 1. After one year from the ratification of this article the manufacture, sale, or transportation of intoxicating liquors within, the importation thereof into, or the exportation thereof from the United States and all territory subject to the jurisdiction thereof for beverage purposes is hereby prohibited.

Section 2. The Congress and the several States shall have concurrent power to enforce this article by appropriate legislation.

Section 3. This article shall be inoperative unless it shall have been ratified as an amendment to the Constitution by the legislatures of the several States, as provided in the Constitution, within seven years from the date of the submission hereof to the States by the Congress.

Amendment XIX [1920]

Section 1. The right of citizens of the United States to vote shall not be denied or abridged by the United States or by any State on account of sex.

Section 2. Congress shall have power to enforce this article by appropriate legislation.

Amendment XX [1933]

Section 1. The terms of the President and Vice President shall end at noon on the 20th day of January, and the terms of Senators and Representatives at noon on the 3d day of January, of the years in which such terms would have ended if this article had not been ratified; and the terms of their successors shall then begin.

Section 2. The Congress shall assemble at least once in every year, and such meeting shall begin at noon on the 3d day of January, unless they shall by law appoint a different day.

Section 3. If, at the time fixed for the beginning of the term of the President, the President elect shall have died, the Vice President elect shall become President. If the President shall not have been chosen before the time fixed for the beginning of his term, or if the President elect shall have failed to qualify, then the Vice President elect shall act as President until a President shall have qualified; and the Congress may by law provide for the case wherein neither a President elect nor a Vice President elect shall have qualified, declaring who shall then act as President, or the manner in which one who is to act shall be selected, and such person shall act accordingly until a President or Vice President shall have qualified.

Section 4. The Congress may by law provide for the case of the death of any of the persons from whom the House of Representatives may choose a President whenever the right of choice shall have devolved upon them, and for the case of the death of any of the persons from whom the Senate may choose a Vice President whenever the right of choice shall have devolved upon them.

Section 5. Sections 1 and 2 shall take effect on the 15th day of October following the ratification of this article.

Section 6. This article shall be inoperative unless it shall have been ratified as an amendment to the Constitution by the legislatures of three-fourths of the several States within seven years from the date of its submission.

Amendment XXI [1933]

Section 1. The eighteenth article of amendment to the Constitution of the United States is hereby repealed.

Section 2. The transportation or importation into any State, Territory, or possession of the United States for delivery or use therein of intoxicating liquors, in violation of the laws thereof, is hereby prohibited.

Section 3. This article shall be inoperative unless it shall have been ratified as an amendment to the Constitution by conventions in the several States, as provided in the Constitution, within seven years from the date of the submission hereof to the States by the Congress.

Amendment XXII [1951]

Section 1. No person shall be elected to the office of the President more than twice, and no person who has held the office of President, or acted as President, for more than two years of a term to which some other person was elected President shall be elected to the office of President more than once. But this Article shall not apply to any person holding the office of President when this Article was proposed by the Congress, and shall not prevent any person who may be holding the office of President, or acting as President, during the term within which this Article becomes operative from holding the office of President or acting as President during the remainder of such term.

Section 2. This article shall be inoperative unless it shall have been ratified as an amendment to the Constitution by the legislatures of three-fourths of the several States within seven years from the date of its submission to the States by the Congress.

Amendment XXIII [1961]

Section 1. The District constituting the seat of Government of the United States shall appoint in such manner as the Congress may direct:

A number of electors of President and Vice President equal to the whole number of Senators and Representatives in Congress to which the District would be entitled if it were a State, but in no event more than the least populous state; they shall be in addition to those appointed by the states, but they shall be considered, for the purposes of the election of President and Vice President, to be electors appointed by a state; and they shall meet in the District and perform such duties as provided by the twelfth article of amendment.

Section 2. The Congress shall have power to enforce this article by appropriate legislation.

Amendment XXIV [1964]

Section 1. The right of citizens of the United States to vote in any primary or other election for President or Vice President, for electors for President or Vice President, or for Senator or Representative in Congress, shall not be denied or abridged by the United States, or any State by reason of failure to pay any poll tax or other tax.

Section 2. The Congress shall have power to enforce this article by appropriate legislation.

Amendment XXV [1967]

Section 1. In case of the removal of the President from office or of his death or resignation, the Vice President shall become President.

Section 2. Whenever there is a vacancy in the office of the Vice President, the President shall nominate a Vice President who shall take office upon confirmation by a majority vote of both Houses of Congress.

Section 3. Whenever the President transmits to the President pro tempore of the Senate and the Speaker of the House of Representatives his written declaration that he is unable to discharge the powers and duties of his office, and until he transmits to them a written declaration to the contrary, such powers and duties shall be discharged by the Vice President as Acting President.

Section 4. Whenever the Vice President and a majority of either the principal officers of the executive departments or of such other body as Congress may by law provide, transmit to the President pro tempore of the Senate and the Speaker of the House of Representatives their written declaration that the President is unable to discharge the powers and duties of his office, the Vice President shall immediately assume the powers and duties of the office as Acting President.

Thereafter, when the President transmits to the President pro tempore of the Senate and the Speaker of the House of Representatives his written declaration that no inability exists, he shall resume the powers and duties of his office unless the Vice President and a majority of either the principal officers of the executive department or of such other body as Congress may by law provide, transmit within four days to the President pro tempore of the Senate and the Speaker of the House of Representatives their written declaration that the President is unable to discharge the powers and duties of his office. Thereupon Congress shall decide the issue, assembling within forty-eight hours for that purpose if not in session. If the Congress, within twenty-one days after receipt of the latter written declaration, or, if Congress is not in session, within twenty-one days after Congress is required to assemble, determines by two-thirds vote of both Houses that the President is unable to discharge the powers and duties of his office, the Vice President shall continue to discharge the same as Acting President; otherwise, the President shall resume the powers and duties of his office.

Amendment XXVI [1971]

Section 1. The right of citizens of the United States, who are eighteen years of age or older, to vote shall not be denied or abridged by the United States or by any State on account of age.

Section 2. The Congress shall have power to enforce this article by appropriate legislation.

Amendment XXVII [1992]

No law, varying the compensation for the services of the Senators and Representatives, shall take effect, until an election of Representatives shall have intervened.

APPENDIX C

The Uniform Commercial Code (Excerpts)

Article 2
SALES

Part 1 Short Title, General Construction and Subject Matter

§ 2–101. Short Title.

This Article shall be known and may be cited as Uniform Commercial Code—Sales.

§ 2–102. Scope; Certain Security and Other Transactions Excluded From This Article.

Unless the context otherwise requires, this Article applies to transactions in goods; it does not apply to any transaction which although in the form of an unconditional contract to sell or present sale is intended to operate only as a security transaction nor does this Article impair or repeal any statute regulating sales to consumers, farmers or other specified classes of buyers.

§ 2–103. Definitions and Index of Definitions.

(1) In this Article unless the context otherwise requires

(a) "Buyer" means a person who buys or contracts to buy goods.

(b) "Good faith" in the case of a merchant means honesty in fact and the observance of reasonable commercial standards of fair dealing in the trade.

(c) "Receipt" of goods means taking physical possession of them.

(d) "Seller" means a person who sells or contracts to sell goods.

(2) Other definitions applying to this Article or to specified Parts thereof, and the sections in which they appear are:

"Acceptance". Section 2–606.
"Banker's credit". Section 2–325.
"Between merchants". Section 2–104.
"Cancellation". Section 2–106(4).
"Commercial unit". Section 2–105.
"Confirmed credit". Section 2–325.
"Conforming to contract". Section 2–106.
"Contract for sale". Section 2–106.
"Cover". Section 2–712.
"Entrusting". Section 2–403.
"Financing agency". Section 2–104.
"Future goods". Section 2–105.
"Goods". Section 2–105.
"Identification". Section 2–501.
"Installment contract". Section 2–612.
"Letter of Credit". Section 2–325.
"Lot". Section 2–105.
"Merchant". Section 2–104.
"Overseas". Section 2–323.
"Person in position of seller". Section 2–707.
"Present sale". Section 2–106.
"Sale". Section 2–106.
"Sale on approval". Section 2–326.
"Sale or return". Section 2–326.
"Termination". Section 2–106.

(3) The following definitions in other Articles apply to this Article:

"Check". Section 3–104.
"Consignee". Section 7–102.
"Consignor". Section 7–102.
"Consumer goods". Section 9–109.
"Dishonor". Section 3–507.
"Draft". Section 3–104.

(4) In addition Article 1 contains general definitions and principles of construction and interpretation applicable throughout this Article.

As amended in 1994 and 1999.

§ 2–104. Definitions: "Merchant"; "Between Merchants"; "Financing Agency".

(1) "Merchant" means a person who deals in goods of the kind or otherwise by his occupation holds himself out as having knowledge or skill peculiar to the practices or goods involved in the transaction or to whom such knowledge or skill may be attributed by his employment of an agent or broker or other intermediary who by his occupation holds himself out as having such knowledge or skill.

(2) "Financing agency" means a bank, finance company or other person who in the ordinary course of business makes advances against goods or documents of title or who by arrangement with either the seller or the buyer intervenes in ordinary course to make or collect payment due or claimed under the contract for sale, as by purchasing or paying the seller's draft or making advances against it or by merely taking it for collection whether or not documents of title accompany the draft. "Financing agency" includes also a bank or other person who similarly intervenes between persons who are in the position of seller and buyer in respect to the goods (Section 2–707).

(3) "Between merchants" means in any transaction with respect to which both parties are chargeable with the knowledge or skill of merchants.

§ 2–105. Definitions: Transferability; "Goods"; "Future" Goods; "Lot"; "Commercial Unit".

(1) "Goods" means all things (including specially manufactured goods) which are movable at the time of identification to the contract for sale other than the money in which the price is to be paid, investment securities (Article 8) and things in action. "Goods" also includes the unborn young of animals and growing crops and other identified things attached to realty as described in the section on goods to be severed from realty (Section 2–107).

(2) Goods must be both existing and identified before any interest in them can pass. Goods which are not both existing and identified are "future" goods. A purported present sale of future goods or of any interest therein operates as a contract to sell.

(3) There may be a sale of a part interest in existing identified goods.

(4) An undivided share in an identified bulk of fungible goods is sufficiently identified to be sold although the quantity of the bulk is not determined. Any agreed proportion of such a bulk or any quantity thereof agreed upon by number, weight or other measure may to the extent of the seller's interest in the bulk be sold to the buyer who then becomes an owner in common.

(5) "Lot" means a parcel or a single article which is the subject matter of a separate sale or delivery, whether or not it is sufficient to perform the contract.

(6) "Commercial unit" means such a unit of goods as by commercial usage is a single whole for purposes of sale and division of which materially impairs its character or value on the market or in use. A commercial unit may be a single article (as a machine) or a set of articles (as a suite of furniture or an assortment of sizes) or a quantity (as a bale, gross, or carload) or any other unit treated in use or in the relevant market as a single whole.

§ 2–106. Definitions: "Contract"; "Agreement"; "Contract for Sale"; "Sale"; "Present Sale"; "Conforming" to Contract; "Termination"; "Cancellation".

(1) In this Article unless the context otherwise requires "contract" and "agreement" are limited to those relating to the present or future sale of goods. "Contract for sale" includes both a present sale of goods and a contract to sell goods at a future time. A "sale" consists in the passing of title from the seller to the buyer for a price (Section 2–401). A "present sale" means a sale which is accomplished by the making of the contract.

(2) Goods or conduct including any part of a performance are "conforming" or conform to the contract when they are in accordance with the obligations under the contract.

(3) "Termination" occurs when either party pursuant to a power created by agreement or law puts an end to the contract otherwise than for its breach. On "termination" all obligations which are still executory on both sides are discharged but any right based on prior breach or performance survives.

(4) "Cancellation" occurs when either party puts an end to the contract for breach by the other and its effect is the same as that of "termination" except that the cancelling party also retains any remedy for breach of the whole contract or any unperformed balance.

§ 2–107. Goods to Be Severed From Realty: Recording.

(1) A contract for the sale of minerals or the like (including oil and gas) or a structure or its materials to be removed from realty is a contract for the sale of goods within this Article if they are to be severed by the seller but until severance a purported present sale thereof which is not effective as a transfer of an interest in land is effective only as a contract to sell.

(2) A contract for the sale apart from the land of growing crops or other things attached to realty and capable of severance without material harm thereto but not described in subsection (1) or of timber to be cut is a contract for the sale of goods within this Article whether the subject matter is to be severed by the buyer or by the seller even though it forms part of the realty at the time of contracting, and the parties can by identification effect a present sale before severance.

(3) The provisions of this section are subject to any third party rights provided by the law relating to realty records, and the contract for sale may be executed and recorded as a document transferring an interest in land and shall

then constitute notice to third parties of the buyer's rights under the contract for sale.

As amended in 1972.

Part 2 Form, Formation and Readjustment of Contract

§ 2–201. Formal Requirements; Statute of Frauds.

(1) Except as otherwise provided in this section a contract for the sale of goods for the price of $500 or more is not enforceable by way of action or defense unless there is some writing sufficient to indicate that a contract for sale has been made between the parties and signed by the party against whom enforcement is sought or by his authorized agent or broker. A writing is not insufficient because it omits or incorrectly states a term agreed upon but the contract is not enforceable under this paragraph beyond the quantity of goods shown in such writing.

(2) Between merchants if within a reasonable time a writing in confirmation of the contract and sufficient against the sender is received and the party receiving it has reason to know its contents, its satisfies the requirements of subsection (1) against such party unless written notice of objection to its contents is given within ten days after it is received.

(3) A contract which does not satisfy the requirements of subsection (1) but which is valid in other respects is enforceable

(a) if the goods are to be specially manufactured for the buyer and are not suitable for sale to others in the ordinary course of the seller's business and the seller, before notice of repudiation is received and under circumstances which reasonably indicate that the goods are for the buyer, has made either a substantial beginning of their manufacture or commitments for their procurement; or

(b) if the party against whom enforcement is sought admits in his pleading, testimony or otherwise in court that a contract for sale was made, but the contract is not enforceable under this provision beyond the quantity of goods admitted; or

(c) with respect to goods for which payment has been made and accepted or which have been received and accepted (Sec. 2–606).

§ 2–202. Final Written Expression: Parol or Extrinsic Evidence.

Terms with respect to which the confirmatory memoranda of the parties agree or which are otherwise set forth in a writing intended by the parties as a final expression of their agreement with respect to such terms as are included therein may not be contradicted by evidence of any prior agreement or of a contemporaneous oral agreement but may be explained or supplemented

(a) by course of dealing or usage of trade (Section 1–205) or by course of performance (Section 2–208); and

(b) by evidence of consistent additional terms unless the court finds the writing to have been intended also as a complete and exclusive statement of the terms of the agreement.

§ 2–203. Seals Inoperative.

The affixing of a seal to a writing evidencing a contract for sale or an offer to buy or sell goods does not constitute the writing a sealed instrument and the law with respect to sealed instruments does not apply to such a contract or offer.

§ 2–204. Formation in General.

(1) A contract for sale of goods may be made in any manner sufficient to show agreement, including conduct by both parties which recognizes the existence of such a contract.

(2) An agreement sufficient to constitute a contract for sale may be found even though the moment of its making is undetermined.

(3) Even though one or more terms are left open a contract for sale does not fail for indefiniteness if the parties have intended to make a contract and there is a reasonably certain basis for giving an appropriate remedy.

§ 2–205. Firm Offers.

An offer by a merchant to buy or sell goods in a signed writing which by its terms gives assurance that it will be held open is not revocable, for lack of consideration, during the time stated or if no time is stated for a reasonable time, but in no event may such period of irrevocability exceed three months; but any such term of assurance on a form supplied by the offeree must be separately signed by the offeror.

§ 2–206. Offer and Acceptance in Formation of Contract.

(1) Unless other unambiguously indicated by the language or circumstances

(a) an offer to make a contract shall be construed as inviting acceptance in any manner and by any medium reasonable in the circumstances;

(b) an order or other offer to buy goods for prompt or current shipment shall be construed as inviting acceptance either by a prompt promise to ship or by the prompt or current shipment of conforming or nonconforming goods, but such a shipment of nonconforming goods does not constitute an acceptance if the seller seasonably notifies the buyer that the shipment is offered only as an accommodation to the buyer.

(2) Where the beginning of a requested performance is a reasonable mode of acceptance an offeror who is not notified of acceptance within a reasonable time may treat the offer as having lapsed before acceptance.

§ 2–207. Additional Terms in Acceptance or Confirmation.

(1) A definite and seasonable expression of acceptance or a written confirmation which is sent within a reason-

able time operates as an acceptance even though it states terms additional to or different from those offered or agreed upon, unless acceptance is expressly made conditional on assent to the additional or different terms.

(2) The additional terms are to be construed as proposals for addition to the contract. Between merchants such terms become part of the contract unless:

(a) the offer expressly limits acceptance to the terms of the offer;

(b) they materially alter it; or

(c) notification of objection to them has already been given or is given within a reasonable time after notice of them is received.

(3) Conduct by both parties which recognizes the existence of a contract is sufficient to establish a contract for sale although the writings of the parties do not otherwise establish a contract. In such case the terms of the particular contract consist of those terms on which the writings of the parties agree, together with any supplementary terms incorporated under any other provisions of this Act.

§ 2–208. Course of Performance or Practical Construction.

(1) Where the contract for sale involves repeated occasions for performance by either party with knowledge of the nature of the performance and opportunity for objection to it by the other, any course of performance accepted or acquiesced in without objection shall be relevant to determine the meaning of the agreement.

(2) The express terms of the agreement and any such course of performance, as well as any course of dealing and usage of trade, shall be construed whenever reasonable as consistent with each other; but when such construction is unreasonable, express terms shall control course of performance and course of performance shall control both course of dealing and usage of trade (Section 1–205).

(3) Subject to the provisions of the next section on modification and waiver, such course of performance shall be relevant to show a waiver or modification of any term inconsistent with such course of performance.

§ 2–209. Modification, Rescission and Waiver.

(1) An agreement modifying a contract within this Article needs no consideration to be binding.

(2) A signed agreement which excludes modification or rescission except by a signed writing cannot be otherwise modified or rescinded, but except as between merchants such a requirement on a form supplied by the merchant must be separately signed by the other party.

(3) The requirements of the statute of frauds section of this Article (Section 2–201) must be satisfied if the contract as modified is within its provisions.

(4) Although an attempt at modification or rescission does not satisfy the requirements of subsection (2) or (3) it can operate as a waiver.

(5) A party who has made a waiver affecting an executory portion of the contract may retract the waiver by reasonable notification received by the other party that strict performance will be required of any term waived, unless the retraction would be unjust in view of a material change of position in reliance on the waiver.

§ 2–210. Delegation of Performance; Assignment of Rights.

(1) A party may perform his duty through a delegate unless otherwise agreed or unless the other party has a substantial interest in having his original promisor perform or control the acts required by the contract. No delegation of performance relieves the party delegating of any duty to perform or any liability for breach.

(2) Except as otherwise provided in Section 9–406, unless otherwise agreed, all rights of either seller or buyer can be assigned except where the assignment would materially change the duty of the other party, or increase materially the burden or risk imposed on him by his contract, or impair materially his chance of obtaining return performance. A right to damages for breach of the whole contract or a right arising out of the assignor's due performance of his entire obligation can be assigned despite agreement otherwise.

(3) The creation, attachment, perfection, or enforcement of a security interest in the seller's interest under a contract is not a transfer that materially changes the duty of or increases materially the burden or risk imposed on the buyer or impairs materially the buyer's chance of obtaining return performance within the purview of subsection (2) unless, and then only to the extent that, enforcement actually results in a delegation of material performance of the seller. Even in that event, the creation, attachment, perfection, and enforcement of the security interest remain effective, but (i) the seller is liable to the buyer for damages caused by the delegation to the extent that the damages could not reasonably by prevented by the buyer, and (ii) a court having jurisdiction may grant other appropriate relief, including cancellation of the contract for sale or an injunction against enforcement of the security interest or consummation of the enforcement.

(4) Unless the circumstances indicate the contrary a prohibition of assignment of "the contract" is to be construed as barring only the delegation to the assignee of the assignor's performance.

(5) An assignment of "the contract" or of "all my rights under the contract" or an assignment in similar general terms is an assignment of rights and unless the language or the circumstances (as in an assignment for security) indicate the contrary, it is a delegation of performance of the duties of the assignor and its acceptance by the assignee constitutes a promise by him to perform those duties. This promise is enforceable by either the assignor or the other party to the original contract.

(6) The other party may treat any assignment which delegates performance as creating reasonable grounds for

insecurity and may without prejudice to his rights against the assignor demand assurances from the assignee (Section 2–609).

As amended in 1999.

Part 3 General Obligation and Construction of Contract

§ 2–301. General Obligations of Parties.

The obligation of the seller is to transfer and deliver and that of the buyer is to accept and pay in accordance with the contract.

§ 2–302. Unconscionable Contract or Clause.

(1) If the court as a matter of law finds the contract or any clause of the contract to have been unconscionable at the time it was made the court may refuse to enforce the contract, or it may enforce the remainder of the contract without the unconscionable clause, or it may so limit the application of any unconscionable clause as to avoid any unconscionable result.

(2) When it is claimed or appears to the court that the contract or any clause thereof may be unconscionable the parties shall be afforded a reasonable opportunity to present evidence as to its commercial setting, purpose and effect to aid the court in making the determination.

§ 2–303. Allocations or Division of Risks.

Where this Article allocates a risk or a burden as between the parties "unless otherwise agreed", the agreement may not only shift the allocation but may also divide the risk or burden.

§ 2–304. Price Payable in Money, Goods, Realty, or Otherwise.

(1) The price can be made payable in money or otherwise. If it is payable in whole or in part in goods each party is a seller of the goods which he is to transfer.

(2) Even though all or part of the price is payable in an interest in realty the transfer of the goods and the seller's obligations with reference to them are subject to this Article, but not the transfer of the interest in realty or the transferor's obligations in connection therewith.

§ 2–305. Open Price Term.

(1) The parties if they so intend can conclude a contract for sale even though the price is not settled. In such a case the price is a reasonable price at the time for delivery if

(a) nothing is said as to price; or

(b) the price is left to be agreed by the parties and they fail to agree; or

(c) the price is to be fixed in terms of some agreed market or other standard as set or recorded by a third person or agency and it is not so set or recorded.

(2) A price to be fixed by the seller or by the buyer means a price for him to fix in good faith.

(3) When a price left to be fixed otherwise than by agreement of the parties fails to be fixed through fault of one party the other may at his option treat the contract as cancelled or himself fix a reasonable price.

(4) Where, however, the parties intend not to be bound unless the price be fixed or agreed and it is not fixed or agreed there is no contract. In such a case the buyer must return any goods already received or if unable so to do must pay their reasonable value at the time of delivery and the seller must return any portion of the price paid on account.

§ 2–306. Output, Requirements and Exclusive Dealings.

(1) A term which measures the quantity by the output of the seller or the requirements of the buyer means such actual output or requirements as may occur in good faith, except that no quantity unreasonably disproportionate to any stated estimate or in the absence of a stated estimate to any normal or otherwise comparable prior output or requirements may be tendered or demanded.

(2) A lawful agreement by either the seller or the buyer for exclusive dealing in the kind of goods concerned imposes unless otherwise agreed an obligation by the seller to use best efforts to supply the goods and by the buyer to use best efforts to promote their sale.

§ 2–307. Delivery in Single Lot or Several Lots.

Unless otherwise agreed all goods called for by a contract for sale must be tendered in a single delivery and payment is due only on such tender but where the circumstances give either party the right to make or demand delivery in lots the price if it can be apportioned may be demanded for each lot.

§ 2–308. Absence of Specified Place for Delivery.

Unless otherwise agreed

(a) the place for delivery of goods is the seller's place of business or if he has none his residence; but

(b) in a contract for sale of identified goods which to the knowledge of the parties at the time of contracting are in some other place, that place is the place for their delivery; and

(c) documents of title may be delivered through customary banking channels.

§ 2–309. Absence of Specific Time Provisions; Notice of Termination.

(1) The time for shipment or delivery or any other action under a contract if not provided in this Article or agreed upon shall be a reasonable time.

(2) Where the contract provides for successive performances but is indefinite in duration it is valid for a reasonable time but unless otherwise agreed may be terminated at any time by either party.

(3) Termination of a contract by one party except on the happening of an agreed event requires that reasonable notification be received by the other party and an agree-

ment dispensing with notification is invalid if its operation would be unconscionable.

§ 2–310. Open Time for Payment or Running of Credit; Authority to Ship Under Reservation.

Unless otherwise agreed

(a) payment is due at the time and place at which the buyer is to receive the goods even though the place of shipment is the place of delivery; and

(b) if the seller is authorized to send the goods he may ship them under reservation, and may tender the documents of title, but the buyer may inspect the goods after their arrival before payment is due unless such inspection is inconsistent with the terms of the contract (Section 2–513); and

(c) if delivery is authorized and made by way of documents of title otherwise than by subsection (b) then payment is due at the time and place at which the buyer is to receive the documents regardless of where the goods are to be received; and

(d) where the seller is required or authorized to ship the goods on credit the credit period runs from the time of shipment but post-dating the invoice or delaying its dispatch will correspondingly delay the starting of the credit period.

§ 2–311. Options and Cooperation Respecting Performance.

(1) An agreement for sale which is otherwise sufficiently definite (subsection (3) of Section 2–204) to be a contract is not made invalid by the fact that it leaves particulars of performance to be specified by one of the parties. Any such specification must be made in good faith and within limits set by commercial reasonableness.

(2) Unless otherwise agreed specifications relating to assortment of the goods are at the buyer's option and except as otherwise provided in subsections (1)(c) and (3) of Section 2–319 specifications or arrangements relating to shipment are at the seller's option.

(3) Where such specification would materially affect the other party's performance but is not seasonably made or where one party's cooperation is necessary to the agreed performance of the other but is not seasonably forthcoming, the other party in addition to all other remedies

(a) is excused for any resulting delay in his own performance; and

(b) may also either proceed to perform in any reasonable manner or after the time for a material part of his own performance treat the failure to specify or to cooperate as a breach by failure to deliver or accept the goods.

§ 2–312. Warranty of Title and Against Infringement; Buyer's Obligation Against Infringement.

(1) Subject to subsection (2) there is in a contract for sale a warranty by the seller that

(a) the title conveyed shall be good, and its transfer rightful; and

(b) the goods shall be delivered free from any security interest or other lien or encumbrance of which the buyer at the time of contracting has no knowledge.

(2) A warranty under subsection (1) will be excluded or modified only by specific language or by circumstances which give the buyer reason to know that the person selling does not claim title in himself or that he is purporting to sell only such right or title as he or a third person may have.

(3) Unless otherwise agreed a seller who is a merchant regularly dealing in goods of the kind warrants that the goods shall be delivered free of the rightful claim of any third person by way of infringement or the like but a buyer who furnishes specifications to the seller must hold the seller harmless against any such claim which arises out of compliance with the specifications.

§ 2–313. Express Warranties by Affirmation, Promise, Description, Sample.

(1) Express warranties by the seller are created as follows:

(a) Any affirmation of fact or promise made by the seller to the buyer which relates to the goods and becomes part of the basis of the bargain creates an express warranty that the goods shall conform to the affirmation or promise.

(b) Any description of the goods which is made part of the basis of the bargain creates an express warranty that the goods shall conform to the description.

(c) Any sample or model which is made part of the basis of the bargain creates an express warranty that the whole of the goods shall conform to the sample or model.

(2) It is not necessary to the creation of an express warranty that the seller use formal words such as "warrant" or "guarantee" or that he have a specific intention to make a warranty, but an affirmation merely of the value of the goods or a statement purporting to be merely the seller's opinion or commendation of the goods does not create a warranty.

§ 2–314. Implied Warranty: Merchantability; Usage of Trade.

(1) Unless excluded or modified (Section 2–316), a warranty that the goods shall be merchantable is implied in a contract for their sale if the seller is a merchant with respect to goods of that kind. Under this section the serving for value of food or drink to be consumed either on the premises or elsewhere is a sale.

(2) Goods to be merchantable must be at least such as

(a) pass without objection in the trade under the contract description; and

(b) in the case of fungible goods, are of fair average quality within the description; and

(c) are fit for the ordinary purposes for which such goods are used; and

(d) run, within the variations permitted by the agreement, of even kind, quality and quantity within each unit and among all units involved; and

(e) are adequately contained, packaged, and labeled as the agreement may require; and

(f) conform to the promises or affirmations of fact made on the container or label if any.

(3) Unless excluded or modified (Section 2–316) other implied warranties may arise from course of dealing or usage of trade.

§ 2–315. Implied Warranty: Fitness for Particular Purpose.

Where the seller at the time of contracting has reason to know any particular purpose for which the goods are required and that the buyer is relying on the seller's skill or judgment to select or furnish suitable goods, there is unless excluded or modified under the next section an implied warranty that the goods shall be fit for such purpose.

§ 2–316. Exclusion or Modification of Warranties.

(1) Words or conduct relevant to the creation of an express warranty and words or conduct tending to negate or limit warranty shall be construed wherever reasonable as consistent with each other; but subject to the provisions of this Article on parol or extrinsic evidence (Section 2–202) negation or limitation is inoperative to the extent that such construction is unreasonable.

(2) Subject to subsection (3), to exclude or modify the implied warranty of merchantability or any part of it the language must mention merchantability and in case of a writing must be conspicuous, and to exclude or modify any implied warranty of fitness the exclusion must be by a writing and conspicuous. Language to exclude all implied warranties of fitness is sufficient if it states, for example, that "There are no warranties which extend beyond the description on the face hereof."

(3) Notwithstanding subsection (2)

(a) unless the circumstances indicate otherwise, all implied warranties are excluded by expressions like "as is", "with all faults" or other language which in common understanding calls the buyer's attention to the exclusion of warranties and makes plain that there is no implied warranty; and

(b) when the buyer before entering into the contract has examined the goods or the sample or model as fully as he desired or has refused to examine the goods there is no implied warranty with regard to defects which an examination ought in the circumstances to have revealed to him; and

(c) an implied warranty can also be excluded or modified by course of dealing or course of performance or usage of trade.

(4) Remedies for breach of warranty can be limited in accordance with the provisions of this Article on liquidation or limitation of damages and on contractual modification of remedy (Sections 2–718 and 2–719).

§ 2–317. Cumulation and Conflict of Warranties Express or Implied.

Warranties whether express or implied shall be construed as consistent with each other and as cumulative, but if such construction is unreasonable the intention of the parties shall determine which warranty is dominant. In ascertaining that intention the following rules apply:

(a) Exact or technical specifications displace an inconsistent sample or model or general language of description.

(b) A sample from an existing bulk displaces inconsistent general language of description.

(c) Express warranties displace inconsistent implied warranties other than an implied warranty of fitness for a particular purpose.

§ 2–318. Third Party Beneficiaries of Warranties Express or Implied.

Note: If this Act is introduced in the Congress of the United States this section should be omitted. (States to select one alternative.)

Alternative A

A seller's warranty whether express or implied extends to any natural person who is in the family or household of his buyer or who is a guest in his home if it is reasonable to expect that such person may use, consume or be affected by the goods and who is injured in person by breach of the warranty. A seller may not exclude or limit the operation of this section.

Alternative B

A seller's warranty whether express or implied extends to any natural person who may reasonably be expected to use, consume or be affected by the goods and who is injured in person by breach of the warranty. A seller may not exclude or limit the operation of this section.

Alternative C

A seller's warranty whether express or implied extends to any person who may reasonably be expected to use, consume or be affected by the goods and who is injured by breach of the warranty. A seller may not exclude or limit the operation of this section with respect to injury to the person of an individual to whom the warranty extends.

As amended 1966.

§ 2–319. F.O.B. and F.A.S. Terms.

(1) Unless otherwise agreed the term F.O.B. (which means "free on board") at a named place, even though used only in connection with the stated price, is a delivery term under which

(a) when the term is F.O.B. the place of shipment, the seller must at that place ship the goods in the manner provided in this Article (Section 2–504) and bear the expense and risk of putting them into the possession of the carrier; or

(b) when the term is F.O.B. the place of destination, the seller must at his own expense and risk transport the goods to that place and there tender delivery of them in the manner provided in this Article (Section 2–503);

(c) when under either (a) or (b) the term is also F.O.B. vessel, car or other vehicle, the seller must in addition at his own expense and risk load the goods on board. If the term is F.O.B. vessel the buyer must name the vessel and in an appropriate case the seller must comply with the provisions of this Article on the form of bill of lading (Section 2–323).

(2) Unless otherwise agreed the term F.A.S. vessel (which means "free alongside") at a named port, even though used only in connection with the stated price, is a delivery term under which the seller must

(a) at his own expense and risk deliver the goods alongside the vessel in the manner usual in that port or on a dock designated and provided by the buyer; and

(b) obtain and tender a receipt for the goods in exchange for which the carrier is under a duty to issue a bill of lading.

(3) Unless otherwise agreed in any case falling within subsection (1)(a) or (c) or subsection (2) the buyer must seasonably give any needed instructions for making delivery, including when the term is F.A.S. or F.O.B. the loading berth of the vessel and in an appropriate case its name and sailing date. The seller may treat the failure of needed instructions as a failure of cooperation under this Article (Section 2–311). He may also at his option move the goods in any reasonable manner preparatory to delivery or shipment.

(4) Under the term F.O.B. vessel or F.A.S. unless otherwise agreed the buyer must make payment against tender of the required documents and the seller may not tender nor the buyer demand delivery of the goods in substitution for the documents.

§ 2–320. C.I.F. and C. & F. Terms.

(1) The term C.I.F. means that the price includes in a lump sum the cost of the goods and the insurance and freight to the named destination. The term C. & F. or C.F. means that the price so includes cost and freight to the named destination.

(2) Unless otherwise agreed and even though used only in connection with the stated price and destination, the term C.I.F. destination or its equivalent requires the seller at his own expense and risk to

(a) put the goods into the possession of a carrier at the port for shipment and obtain a negotiable bill or bills of lading covering the entire transportation to the named destination; and

(b) load the goods and obtain a receipt from the carrier (which may be contained in the bill of lading) showing that the freight has been paid or provided for; and

(c) obtain a policy or certificate of insurance, including any war risk insurance, of a kind and on terms then current at the port of shipment in the usual amount, in the currency of the contract, shown to cover the same goods covered by the bill of lading and providing for payment of loss to the order of the buyer or for the account of whom it may concern; but the seller may add to the price the amount of the premium for any such war risk insurance; and

(d) prepare an invoice of the goods and procure any other documents required to effect shipment or to comply with the contract; and

(e) forward and tender with commercial promptness all the documents in due form and with any indorsement necessary to perfect the buyer's rights.

(3) Unless otherwise agreed the term C. & F. or its equivalent has the same effect and imposes upon the seller the same obligations and risks as a C.I.F. term except the obligation as to insurance.

(4) Under the term C.I.F. or C. & F. unless otherwise agreed the buyer must make payment against tender of the required documents and the seller may not tender nor the buyer demand delivery of the goods in substitution for the documents.

§ 2–321. C.I.F. or C. & F.: "Net Landed Weights"; "Payment on Arrival"; Warranty of Condition on Arrival.

Under a contract containing a term C.I.F. or C. & F.

(1) Where the price is based on or is to be adjusted according to "net landed weights", "delivered weights", "out turn" quantity or quality or the like, unless otherwise agreed the seller must reasonably estimate the price. The payment due on tender of the documents called for by the contract is the amount so estimated, but after final adjustment of the price a settlement must be made with commercial promptness.

(2) An agreement described in subsection (1) or any warranty of quality or condition of the goods on arrival places upon the seller the risk of ordinary deterioration, shrinkage and the like in transportation but has no effect on the place or time of identification to the contract for sale or delivery or on the passing of the risk of loss.

(3) Unless otherwise agreed where the contract provides for payment on or after arrival of the goods the seller must before payment allow such preliminary inspection as is feasible; but if the goods are lost delivery of the documents and payment are due when the goods should have arrived.

§ 2–322. Delivery "Ex-Ship".

(1) Unless otherwise agreed a term for delivery of goods "ex-ship" (which means from the carrying vessel) or in equivalent language is not restricted to a particular ship and requires delivery from a ship which has reached a place at the named port of destination where goods of the kind are usually discharged.

(2) Under such a term unless otherwise agreed

(a) the seller must discharge all liens arising out of the carriage and furnish the buyer with a direction which puts the carrier under a duty to deliver the goods; and

(b) the risk of loss does not pass to the buyer until the goods leave the ship's tackle or are otherwise properly unloaded.

§ 2–323. Form of Bill of Lading Required in Overseas Shipment; "Overseas".

(1) Where the contract contemplates overseas shipment and contains a term C.I.F. or C. & F. or F.O.B. vessel, the seller unless otherwise agreed must obtain a negotiable bill of lading stating that the goods have been loaded on board or, in the case of a term C.I.F. or C. & F., received for shipment.

(2) Where in a case within subsection (1) a bill of lading has been issued in a set of parts, unless otherwise agreed if the documents are not to be sent from abroad the buyer may demand tender of the full set; otherwise only one part of the bill of lading need be tendered. Even if the agreement expressly requires a full set

(a) due tender of a single part is acceptable within the provisions of this Article on cure of improper delivery (subsection (1) of Section 2–508); and

(b) even though the full set is demanded, if the documents are sent from abroad the person tendering an incomplete set may nevertheless require payment upon furnishing an indemnity which the buyer in good faith deems adequate.

(3) A shipment by water or by air or a contract contemplating such shipment is "overseas" insofar as by usage of trade or agreement it is subject to the commercial, financing or shipping practices characteristic of international deep water commerce.

§ 2–324. "No Arrival, No Sale" Term.

Under a term "no arrival, no sale" or terms of like meaning, unless otherwise agreed,

(a) the seller must properly ship conforming goods and if they arrive by any means he must tender them on arrival but he assumes no obligation that the goods will arrive unless he has caused the non-arrival; and

(b) where without fault of the seller the goods are in part lost or have so deteriorated as no longer to conform to the contract or arrive after the contract time, the buyer may proceed as if there had been casualty to identified goods (Section 2–613).

§ 2–325. "Letter of Credit" Term; "Confirmed Credit".

(1) Failure of the buyer seasonably to furnish an agreed letter of credit is a breach of the contract for sale.

(2) The delivery to seller of a proper letter of credit suspends the buyer's obligation to pay. If the letter of credit is dishonored, the seller may on seasonable notification to the buyer require payment directly from him.

(3) Unless otherwise agreed the term "letter of credit" or "banker's credit" in a contract for sale means an irrevocable credit issued by a financing agency of good repute and, where the shipment is overseas, of good international repute. The term "confirmed credit" means that the credit must also carry the direct obligation of such an agency which does business in the seller's financial market.

§ 2–326. Sale on Approval and Sale or Return; Rights of Creditors.

(1) Unless otherwise agreed, if delivered goods may be returned by the buyer even though they conform to the contract, the transaction is

(a) a "sale on approval" if the goods are delivered primarily for use, and

(b) a "sale or return" if the goods are delivered primarily for resale.

(2) Goods held on approval are not subject to the claims of the buyer's creditors until acceptance; goods held on sale or return are subject to such claims while in the buyer's possession.

(3) Any "or return" term of a contract for sale is to be treated as a separate contract for sale within the statute of frauds section of this Article (Section 2–201) and as contradicting the sale aspect of the contract within the provisions of this Article or on parol or extrinsic evidence (Section 2–202).

As amended in 1999.

§ 2–327. Special Incidents of Sale on Approval and Sale or Return.

(1) Under a sale on approval unless otherwise agreed

(a) although the goods are identified to the contract the risk of loss and the title do not pass to the buyer until acceptance; and

(b) use of the goods consistent with the purpose of trial is not acceptance but failure seasonably to notify the seller of election to return the goods is acceptance, and if the goods conform to the contract acceptance of any part is acceptance of the whole; and

(c) after due notification of election to return, the return is at the seller's risk and expense but a merchant buyer must follow any reasonable instructions.

(2) Under a sale or return unless otherwise agreed

(a) the option to return extends to the whole or any commercial unit of the goods while in substantially their original condition, but must be exercised seasonably; and

(b) the return is at the buyer's risk and expense.

§ 2–328. Sale by Auction.

(1) In a sale by auction if goods are put up in lots each lot is the subject of a separate sale.

(2) A sale by auction is complete when the auctioneer so announces by the fall of the hammer or in other customary manner. Where a bid is made while the hammer is falling in acceptance of a prior bid the auctioneer

may in his discretion reopen the bidding or declare the goods sold under the bid on which the hammer was falling.

(3) Such a sale is with reserve unless the goods are in explicit terms put up without reserve. In an auction with reserve the auctioneer may withdraw the goods at any time until he announces completion of the sale. In an auction without reserve, after the auctioneer calls for bids on an article or lot, that article or lot cannot be withdrawn unless no bid is made within a reasonable time. In either case a bidder may retract his bid until the auctioneer's announcement of completion of the sale, but a bidder's retraction does not revive any previous bid.

(4) If the auctioneer knowingly receives a bid on the seller's behalf or the seller makes or procures such as bid, and notice has not been given that liberty for such bidding is reserved, the buyer may at his option avoid the sale or take the goods at the price of the last good faith bid prior to the completion of the sale. This subsection shall not apply to any bid at a forced sale.

Part 4 Title, Creditors and Good Faith Purchasers

§ 2–401. Passing of Title; Reservation for Security; Limited Application of This Section.

Each provision of this Article with regard to the rights, obligations and remedies of the seller, the buyer, purchasers or other third parties applies irrespective of title to the goods except where the provision refers to such title. Insofar as situations are not covered by the other provisions of this Article and matters concerning title became material the following rules apply:

(1) Title to goods cannot pass under a contract for sale prior to their identification to the contract (Section 2–501), and unless otherwise explicitly agreed the buyer acquires by their identification a special property as limited by this Act. Any retention or reservation by the seller of the title (property) in goods shipped or delivered to the buyer is limited in effect to a reservation of a security interest. Subject to these provisions and to the provisions of the Article on Secured Transactions (Article 9), title to goods passes from the seller to the buyer in any manner and on any conditions explicitly agreed on by the parties.

(2) Unless otherwise explicitly agreed title passes to the buyer at the time and place at which the seller completes his performance with reference to the physical delivery of the goods, despite any reservation of a security interest and even though a document of title is to be delivered at a different time or place; and in particular and despite any reservation of a security interest by the bill of lading

(a) if the contract requires or authorizes the seller to send the goods to the buyer but does not require him to deliver them at destination, title passes to the buyer at the time and place of shipment; but

(b) if the contract requires delivery at destination, title passes on tender there.

(3) Unless otherwise explicitly agreed where delivery is to be made without moving the goods,

(a) if the seller is to deliver a document of title, title passes at the time when and the place where he delivers such documents; or

(b) if the goods are at the time of contracting already identified and no documents are to be delivered, title passes at the time and place of contracting.

(4) A rejection or other refusal by the buyer to receive or retain the goods, whether or not justified, or a justified revocation of acceptance revests title to the goods in the seller. Such revesting occurs by operation of law and is not a "sale".

§ 2–402. Rights of Seller's Creditors Against Sold Goods.

(1) Except as provided in subsections (2) and (3), rights of unsecured creditors of the seller with respect to goods which have been identified to a contract for sale are subject to the buyer's rights to recover the goods under this Article (Sections 2–502 and 2–716).

(2) A creditor of the seller may treat a sale or an identification of goods to a contract for sale as void if as against him a retention of possession by the seller is fraudulent under any rule of law of the state where the goods are situated, except that retention of possession in good faith and current course of trade by a merchant-seller for a commercially reasonable time after a sale or identification is not fraudulent.

(3) Nothing in this Article shall be deemed to impair the rights of creditors of the seller

(a) under the provisions of the Article on Secured Transactions (Article 9); or

(b) where identification to the contract or delivery is made not in current course of trade but in satisfaction of or as security for a pre-existing claim for money, security or the like and is made under circumstances which under any rule of law of the state where the goods are situated would apart from this Article constitute the transaction a fraudulent transfer or voidable preference.

§ 2–403. Power to Transfer; Good Faith Purchase of Goods; "Entrusting".

(1) A purchaser of goods acquires all title which his transferor had or had power to transfer except that a purchaser of a limited interest acquires rights only to the extent of the interest purchased. A person with voidable title has power to transfer a good title to a good faith purchaser for value. When goods have been delivered under a transaction of purchase the purchaser has such power even though

(a) the transferor was deceived as to the identity of the purchaser, or

(b) the delivery was in exchange for a check which is later dishonored, or

(c) it was agreed that the transaction was to be a "cash sale", or

(d) the delivery was procured through fraud punishable as larcenous under the criminal law.

(2) Any entrusting of possession of goods to a merchant who deals in goods of that kind gives him power to transfer all rights of the entruster to a buyer in ordinary course of business.

(3) "Entrusting" includes any delivery and any acquiescence in retention of possession regardless of any condition expressed between the parties to the delivery or acquiescence and regardless of whether the procurement of the entrusting or the possessor's disposition of the goods have been such as to be larcenous under the criminal law.

(4) The rights of other purchasers of goods and of lien creditors are governed by the Articles on Secured Transactions (Article 9), Bulk Transfers (Article 6) and Documents of Title (Article 7).

As amended in 1988.

Part 5 Performance

§ 2–501. Insurable Interest in Goods; Manner of Identification of Goods.

(1) The buyer obtains a special property and an insurable interest in goods by identification of existing goods as goods to which the contract refers even though the goods so identified are non-conforming and he has an option to return or reject them. Such identification can be made at any time and in any manner explicitly agreed to by the parties. In the absence of explicit agreement identification occurs

(a) when the contract is made if it is for the sale of goods already existing and identified;

(b) if the contract is for the sale of future goods other than those described in paragraph (c), when goods are shipped, marked or otherwise designated by the seller as goods to which the contract refers;

(c) when the crops are planted or otherwise become growing crops or the young are conceived if the contract is for the sale of unborn young to be born within twelve months after contracting or for the sale of crops to be harvested within twelve months or the next normal harvest season after contracting whichever is longer.

(2) The seller retains an insurable interest in goods so long as title to or any security interest in the goods remains in him and where the identification is by the seller alone he may until default or insolvency or notification to the buyer that the identification is final substitute other goods for those identified.

(3) Nothing in this section impairs any insurable interest recognized under any other statute or rule of law.

§ 2–502. Buyer's Right to Goods on Seller's Insolvency.

(1) Subject to subsections (2) and (3) and even though the goods have not been shipped a buyer who has paid a part or all of the price of goods in which he has a special property under the provisions of the immediately preceding section may on making and keeping good a tender of any unpaid portion of their price recover them from the seller if:

(a) in the case of goods bought for personal, family, or household purposes, the seller repudiates or fails to deliver as required by the contract; or

(b) in all cases, the seller becomes insolvent within ten days after receipt of the first installment on their price.

(2) The buyer's right to recover the goods under subsection (1)(a) vests upon acquisition of a special property, even if the seller had not then repudiated or failed to deliver.

(3) If the identification creating his special property has been made by the buyer he acquires the right to recover the goods only if they conform to the contract for sale.

As amended in 1999.

§ 2–503. Manner of Seller's Tender of Delivery.

(1) Tender of delivery requires that the seller put and hold conforming goods at the buyer's disposition and give the buyer any notification reasonably necessary to enable him to take delivery. The manner, time and place for tender are determined by the agreement and this Article, and in particular

(a) tender must be at a reasonable hour, and if it is of goods they must be kept available for the period reasonably necessary to enable the buyer to take possession; but

(b) unless otherwise agreed the buyer must furnish facilities reasonably suited to the receipt of the goods.

(2) Where the case is within the next section respecting shipment tender requires that the seller comply with its provisions.

(3) Where the seller is required to deliver at a particular destination tender requires that he comply with subsection (1) and also in any appropriate case tender documents as described in subsections (4) and (5) of this section.

(4) Where goods are in the possession of a bailee and are to be delivered without being moved

(a) tender requires that the seller either tender a negotiable document of title covering such goods or procure acknowledgment by the bailee of the buyer's right to possession of the goods; but

(b) tender to the buyer of a non-negotiable document of title or of a written direction to the bailee to deliver is sufficient tender unless the buyer seasonably objects, and receipt by the bailee of notification of the buyer's rights fixes those rights as against the bailee and all third persons; but risk of loss of the goods and of any failure by the bailee to honor the non-negotiable document of title or to obey the direction remains on the seller until the buyer has had a reasonable time to present the document or direction, and a refusal by the bailee to honor the document or to obey the direction defeats the tender.

(5) Where the contract requires the seller to deliver documents

(a) he must tender all such documents in correct form, except as provided in this Article with respect to bills of lading in a set (subsection (2) of Section 2–323); and

(b) tender through customary banking channels is sufficient and dishonor of a draft accompanying the documents constitutes non-acceptance or rejection.

§ 2–504. Shipment by Seller.

Where the seller is required or authorized to send the goods to the buyer and the contract does not require him to deliver them at a particular destination, then unless otherwise agreed he must

(a) put the goods in the possession of such a carrier and make such a contract for their transportation as may be reasonable having regard to the nature of the goods and other circumstances of the case; and

(b) obtain and promptly deliver or tender in due form any document necessary to enable the buyer to obtain possession of the goods or otherwise required by the agreement or by usage of trade; and

(c) promptly notify the buyer of the shipment.

Failure to notify the buyer under paragraph (c) or to make a proper contract under paragraph (a) is a ground for rejection only if material delay or loss ensues.

§ 2–505. Seller's Shipment under Reservation.

(1) Where the seller has identified goods to the contract by or before shipment:

(a) his procurement of a negotiable bill of lading to his own order or otherwise reserves in him a security interest in the goods. His procurement of the bill to the order of a financing agency or of the buyer indicates in addition only the seller's expectation of transferring that interest to the person named.

(b) a non-negotiable bill of lading to himself or his nominee reserves possession of the goods as security but except in a case of conditional delivery (subsection (2) of Section 2–507) a non-negotiable bill of lading naming the buyer as consignee reserves no security interest even though the seller retains possession of the bill of lading.

(2) When shipment by the seller with reservation of a security interest is in violation of the contract for sale it constitutes an improper contract for transportation within the preceding section but impairs neither the rights given to the buyer by shipment and identification of the goods to the contract nor the seller's powers as a holder of a negotiable document.

§ 2–506. Rights of Financing Agency.

(1) A financing agency by paying or purchasing for value a draft which relates to a shipment of goods acquires to the extent of the payment or purchase and in addition to its own rights under the draft and any document of title securing it any rights of the shipper in the goods including the right to stop delivery and the shipper's right to have the draft honored by the buyer.

(2) The right to reimbursement of a financing agency which has in good faith honored or purchased the draft under commitment to or authority from the buyer is not impaired by subsequent discovery of defects with reference to any relevant document which was apparently regular on its face.

§ 2–507. Effect of Seller's Tender; Delivery on Condition.

(1) Tender of delivery is a condition to the buyer's duty to accept the goods and, unless otherwise agreed, to his duty to pay for them. Tender entitles the seller to acceptance of the goods and to payment according to the contract.

(2) Where payment is due and demanded on the delivery to the buyer of goods or documents of title, his right as against the seller to retain or dispose of them is conditional upon his making the payment due.

§ 2–508. Cure by Seller of Improper Tender or Delivery; Replacement.

(1) Where any tender or delivery by the seller is rejected because non-conforming and the time for performance has not yet expired, the seller may seasonably notify the buyer of his intention to cure and may then within the contract time make a conforming delivery.

(2) Where the buyer rejects a non-conforming tender which the seller had reasonable grounds to believe would be acceptable with or without money allowance the seller may if he seasonably notifies the buyer have a further reasonable time to substitute a conforming tender.

§ 2–509. Risk of Loss in the Absence of Breach.

(1) Where the contract requires or authorizes the seller to ship the goods by carrier

(a) if it does not require him to deliver them at a particular destination, the risk of loss passes to the buyer when the goods are duly delivered to the carrier even though the shipment is under reservation (Section 2–505); but

(b) if it does require him to deliver them at a particular destination and the goods are there duly tendered while in the possession of the carrier, the risk of loss passes to the buyer when the goods are there duly so tendered as to enable the buyer to take delivery.

(2) Where the goods are held by a bailee to be delivered without being moved, the risk of loss passes to the buyer

(a) on his receipt of a negotiable document of title covering the goods; or

(b) on acknowledgment by the bailee of the buyer's right to possession of the goods; or

(c) after his receipt of a non-negotiable document of title or other written direction to deliver, as provided in subsection (4)(b) of Section 2–503.

(3) In any case not within subsection (1) or (2), the risk of loss passes to the buyer on his receipt of the goods if

the seller is a merchant; otherwise the risk passes to the buyer on tender of delivery.

(4) The provisions of this section are subject to contrary agreement of the parties and to the provisions of this Article on sale on approval (Section 2–327) and on effect of breach on risk of loss (Section 2–510).

§ 2–510. Effect of Breach on Risk of Loss.

(1) Where a tender or delivery of goods so fails to conform to the contract as to give a right of rejection the risk of their loss remains on the seller until cure or acceptance.

(2) Where the buyer rightfully revokes acceptance he may to the extent of any deficiency in his effective insurance coverage treat the risk of loss as having rested on the seller from the beginning.

(3) Where the buyer as to conforming goods already identified to the contract for sale repudiates or is otherwise in breach before risk of their loss has passed to him, the seller may to the extent of any deficiency in his effective insurance coverage treat the risk of loss as resting on the buyer for a commercially reasonable time.

§ 2–511. Tender of Payment by Buyer; Payment by Check.

(1) Unless otherwise agreed tender of payment is a condition to the seller's duty to tender and complete any delivery.

(2) Tender of payment is sufficient when made by any means or in any manner current in the ordinary course of business unless the seller demands payment in legal tender and gives any extension of time reasonably necessary to procure it.

(3) Subject to the provisions of this Act on the effect of an instrument on an obligation (Section 3–310), payment by check is conditional and is defeated as between the parties by dishonor of the check on due presentment.

As amended in 1994.

§ 2–512. Payment by Buyer Before Inspection.

(1) Where the contract requires payment before inspection non-conformity of the goods does not excuse the buyer from so making payment unless

(a) the non-conformity appears without inspection; or

(b) despite tender of the required documents the circumstances would justify injunction against honor under this Act (Section 5–109(b)).

(2) Payment pursuant to subsection (1) does not constitute an acceptance of goods or impair the buyer's right to inspect or any of his remedies.

As amended in 1995.

§ 2–513. Buyer's Right to Inspection of Goods.

(1) Unless otherwise agreed and subject to subsection (3), where goods are tendered or delivered or identified to the contract for sale, the buyer has a right before payment or acceptance to inspect them at any reasonable place and time and in any reasonable manner. When the seller is required or authorized to send the goods to the buyer, the inspection may be after their arrival.

(2) Expenses of inspection must be borne by the buyer but may be recovered from the seller if the goods do not conform and are rejected.

(3) Unless otherwise agreed and subject to the provisions of this Article on C.I.F. contracts (subsection (3) of Section 2–321), the buyer is not entitled to inspect the goods before payment of the price when the contract provides

(a) for delivery "C.O.D." or on other like terms; or

(b) for payment against documents of title, except where such payment is due only after the goods are to become available for inspection.

(4) A place or method of inspection fixed by the parties is presumed to be exclusive but unless otherwise expressly agreed it does not postpone identification or shift the place for delivery or for passing the risk of loss. If compliance becomes impossible, inspection shall be as provided in this section unless the place or method fixed was clearly intended as an indispensable condition failure of which avoids the contract.

§ 2–514. When Documents Deliverable on Acceptance; When on Payment.

Unless otherwise agreed documents against which a draft is drawn are to be delivered to the drawee on acceptance of the draft if it is payable more than three days after presentment; otherwise, only on payment.

§ 2–515. Preserving Evidence of Goods in Dispute.

In furtherance of the adjustment of any claim or dispute

(a) either party on reasonable notification to the other and for the purpose of ascertaining the facts and preserving evidence has the right to inspect, test and sample the goods including such of them as may be in the possession or control of the other; and

(b) the parties may agree to a third party inspection or survey to determine the conformity or condition of the goods and may agree that the findings shall be binding upon them in any subsequent litigation or adjustment.

Part 6 Breach, Repudiation and Excuse

§ 2–601. Buyer's Rights on Improper Delivery.

Subject to the provisions of this Article on breach in installment contracts (Section 2–612) and unless otherwise agreed under the sections on contractual limitations of remedy (Sections 2–718 and 2–719), if the goods or the tender of delivery fail in any respect to conform to the contract, the buyer may

(a) reject the whole; or

(b) accept the whole; or

(c) accept any commercial unit or units and reject the rest.

§ 2–602. Manner and Effect of Rightful Rejection.

(1) Rejection of goods must be within a reasonable time after their delivery or tender. It is ineffective unless the buyer seasonably notifies the seller.

(2) Subject to the provisions of the two following sections on rejected goods (Sections 2–603 and 2–604),

(a) after rejection any exercise of ownership by the buyer with respect to any commercial unit is wrongful as against the seller; and

(b) if the buyer has before rejection taken physical possession of goods in which he does not have a security interest under the provisions of this Article (subsection (3) of Section 2–711), he is under a duty after rejection to hold them with reasonable care at the seller's disposition for a time sufficient to permit the seller to remove them; but

(c) the buyer has no further obligations with regard to goods rightfully rejected.

(3) The seller's rights with respect to goods wrongfully rejected are governed by the provisions of this Article on Seller's remedies in general (Section 2–703).

§ 2–603. Merchant Buyer's Duties as to Rightfully Rejected Goods.

(1) Subject to any security interest in the buyer (subsection (3) of Section 2–711), when the seller has no agent or place of business at the market of rejection a merchant buyer is under a duty after rejection of goods in his possession or control to follow any reasonable instructions received from the seller with respect to the goods and in the absence of such instructions to make reasonable efforts to sell them for the seller's account if they are perishable or threaten to decline in value speedily. Instructions are not reasonable if on demand indemnity for expenses is not forthcoming.

(2) When the buyer sells goods under subsection (1), he is entitled to reimbursement from the seller or out of the proceeds for reasonable expenses of caring for and selling them, and if the expenses include no selling commission then to such commission as is usual in the trade or if there is none to a reasonable sum not exceeding ten per cent on the gross proceeds.

(3) In complying with this section the buyer is held only to good faith and good faith conduct hereunder is neither acceptance nor conversion nor the basis of an action for damages.

§ 2–604. Buyer's Options as to Salvage of Rightfully Rejected Goods.

Subject to the provisions of the immediately preceding section on perishables if the seller gives no instructions within a reasonable time after notification of rejection the buyer may store the rejected goods for the seller's account or reship them to him or resell them for the seller's account with reimbursement as provided in the preceding section. Such action is not acceptance or conversion.

§ 2–605. Waiver of Buyer's Objections by Failure to Particularize.

(1) The buyer's failure to state in connection with rejection a particular defect which is ascertainable by reasonable inspection precludes him from relying on the unstated defect to justify rejection or to establish breach

(a) where the seller could have cured it if stated seasonably; or

(b) between merchants when the seller has after rejection made a request in writing for a full and final written statement of all defects on which the buyer proposes to rely.

(2) Payment against documents made without reservation of rights precludes recovery of the payment for defects apparent on the face of the documents.

§ 2–606. What Constitutes Acceptance of Goods.

(1) Acceptance of goods occurs when the buyer

(a) after a reasonable opportunity to inspect the goods signifies to the seller that the goods are conforming or that he will take or retain them in spite of their nonconformity; or

(b) fails to make an effective rejection (subsection (1) of Section 2–602), but such acceptance does not occur until the buyer has had a reasonable opportunity to inspect them; or

(c) does any act inconsistent with the seller's ownership; but if such act is wrongful as against the seller it is an acceptance only if ratified by him.

(2) Acceptance of a part of any commercial unit is acceptance of that entire unit.

§ 2–607. Effect of Acceptance; Notice of Breach; Burden of Establishing Breach After Acceptance; Notice of Claim or Litigation to Person Answerable Over.

(1) The buyer must pay at the contract rate for any goods accepted.

(2) Acceptance of goods by the buyer precludes rejection of the goods accepted and if made with knowledge of a non-conformity cannot be revoked because of it unless the acceptance was on the reasonable assumption that the non-conformity would be seasonably cured but acceptance does not of itself impair any other remedy provided by this Article for non-conformity.

(3) Where a tender has been accepted

(a) the buyer must within a reasonable time after he discovers or should have discovered any breach notify the seller of breach or be barred from any remedy; and

(b) if the claim is one for infringement or the like (subsection (3) of Section 2–312) and the buyer is sued as a result of such a breach he must so notify the seller within a reasonable time after he receives notice of the litigation or be barred from any remedy over for liability established by the litigation.

(4) The burden is on the buyer to establish any breach with respect to the goods accepted.

(5) Where the buyer is sued for breach of a warranty or other obligation for which his seller is answerable over

(a) he may give his seller written notice of the litigation. If the notice states that the seller may come in and defend and that if the seller does not do so he will be bound in any action against him by his buyer by any determination of fact common to the two litigations, then unless the seller after seasonable receipt of the notice does come in and defend he is so bound.

(b) if the claim is one for infringement or the like (subsection (3) of Section 2–312) the original seller may demand in writing that his buyer turn over to him control of the litigation including settlement or else be barred from any remedy over and if he also agrees to bear all expense and to satisfy any adverse judgment, then unless the buyer after seasonable receipt of the demand does turn over control the buyer is so barred.

(6) The provisions of subsections (3), (4) and (5) apply to any obligation of a buyer to hold the seller harmless against infringement or the like (subsection (3) of Section 2–312).

§ 2–608. Revocation of Acceptance in Whole or in Part.

(1) The buyer may revoke his acceptance of a lot or commercial unit whose non-conformity substantially impairs its value to him if he has accepted it

(a) on the reasonable assumption that its nonconformity would be cured and it has not been seasonably cured; or

(b) without discovery of such non-conformity if his acceptance was reasonably induced either by the difficulty of discovery before acceptance or by the seller's assurances.

(2) Revocation of acceptance must occur within a reasonable time after the buyer discovers or should have discovered the ground for it and before any substantial change in condition of the goods which is not caused by their own defects. It is not effective until the buyer notifies the seller of it.

(3) A buyer who so revokes has the same rights and duties with regard to the goods involved as if he had rejected them.

§ 2–609. Right to Adequate Assurance of Performance.

(1) A contract for sale imposes an obligation on each party that the other's expectation of receiving due performance will not be impaired. When reasonable grounds for insecurity arise with respect to the performance of either party the other may in writing demand adequate assurance of due performance and until he receives such assurance may if commercially reasonable suspend any performance for which he has not already received the agreed return.

(2) Between merchants the reasonableness of grounds for insecurity and the adequacy of any assurance offered shall be determined according to commercial standards.

(3) Acceptance of any improper delivery or payment does not prejudice the party's right to demand adequate assurance of future performance.

(4) After receipt of a justified demand failure to provide within a reasonable time not exceeding thirty days such assurance of due performance as is adequate under the circumstances of the particular case is a repudiation of the contract.

§ 2–610. Anticipatory Repudiation.

When either party repudiates the contract with respect to a performance not yet due the loss of which will substantially impair the value of the contract to the other, the aggrieved party may

(a) for a commercially reasonable time await performance by the repudiating party; or

(b) resort to any remedy for breach (Section 2–703 or Section 2–711), even though he has notified the repudiating party that he would await the latter's performance and has urged retraction; and

(c) in either case suspend his own performance or proceed in accordance with the provisions of this Article on the seller's right to identify goods to the contract notwithstanding breach or to salvage unfinished goods (Section 2–704).

§ 2–611. Retraction of Anticipatory Repudiation.

(1) Until the repudiating party's next performance is due he can retract his repudiation unless the aggrieved party has since the repudiation cancelled or materially changed his position or otherwise indicated that he considers the repudiation final.

(2) Retraction may be by any method which clearly indicates to the aggrieved party that the repudiating party intends to perform, but must include any assurance justifiably demanded under the provisions of this Article (Section 2–609).

(3) Retraction reinstates the repudiating party's rights under the contract with due excuse and allowance to the aggrieved party for any delay occasioned by the repudiation.

§ 2–612. "Installment Contract"; Breach.

(1) An "installment contract" is one which requires or authorizes the delivery of goods in separate lots to be separately accepted, even though the contract contains a clause "each delivery is a separate contract" or its equivalent.

(2) The buyer may reject any installment which is non-conforming if the non-conformity substantially impairs the value of that installment and cannot be cured or if the non-conformity is a defect in the required documents; but if the non-conformity does not fall within subsection (3) and the seller gives adequate assurance of its cure the buyer must accept that installment.

(3) Whenever non-conformity or default with respect to one or more installments substantially impairs the value of the whole contract there is a breach of the whole. But

the aggrieved party reinstates the contract if he accepts a non-conforming installment without seasonably notifying of cancellation or if he brings an action with respect only to past installments or demands performance as to future installments.

§ 2–613. Casualty to Identified Goods.

Where the contract requires for its performance goods identified when the contract is made, and the goods suffer casualty without fault of either party before the risk of loss passes to the buyer, or in a proper case under a "no arrival, no sale" term (Section 2–324) then

(a) if the loss is total the contract is avoided; and

(b) if the loss is partial or the goods have so deteriorated as no longer to conform to the contract the buyer may nevertheless demand inspection and at his option either treat the contract as voided or accept the goods with due allowance from the contract price for the deterioration or the deficiency in quantity but without further right against the seller.

§ 2–614. Substituted Performance.

(1) Where without fault of either party the agreed berthing, loading, or unloading facilities fail or an agreed type of carrier becomes unavailable or the agreed manner of delivery otherwise becomes commercially impracticable but a commercially reasonable substitute is available, such substitute performance must be tendered and accepted.

(2) If the agreed means or manner of payment fails because of domestic or foreign governmental regulation, the seller may withhold or stop delivery unless the buyer provides a means or manner of payment which is commercially a substantial equivalent. If delivery has already been taken, payment by the means or in the manner provided by the regulation discharges the buyer's obligation unless the regulation is discriminatory, oppressive or predatory.

§ 2–615. Excuse by Failure of Presupposed Conditions.

Except so far as a seller may have assumed a greater obligation and subject to the preceding section on substituted performance:

(a) Delay in delivery or non-delivery in whole or in part by a seller who complies with paragraphs (b) and (c) is not a breach of his duty under a contract for sale if performance as agreed has been made impracticable by the occurrence of a contingency the nonoccurrence of which was a basic assumption on which the contract was made or by compliance in good faith with any applicable foreign or domestic governmental regulation or order whether or not it later proves to be invalid.

(b) Where the causes mentioned in paragraph (a) affect only a part of the seller's capacity to perform, he must allocate production and deliveries among his customers but may at his option include regular customers not then under contract as well as his own requirements for further manufacture. He may so allocate in any manner which is fair and reasonable.

(c) The seller must notify the buyer seasonably that there will be delay or non-delivery and, when allocation is required under paragraph (b), of the estimated quota thus made available for the buyer.

§ 2–616. Procedure on Notice Claiming Excuse.

(1) Where the buyer receives notification of a material or indefinite delay or an allocation justified under the preceding section he may by written notification to the seller as to any delivery concerned, and where the prospective deficiency substantially impairs the value of the whole contract under the provisions of this Article relating to breach of installment contracts (Section 2–612), then also as to the whole,

(a) terminate and thereby discharge any unexecuted portion of the contract; or

(b) modify the contract by agreeing to take his available quota in substitution.

(2) If after receipt of such notification from the seller the buyer fails so to modify the contract within a reasonable time not exceeding thirty days the contract lapses with respect to any deliveries affected.

(3) The provisions of this section may not be negated by agreement except in so far as the seller has assumed a greater obligation under the preceding section.

Part 7 Remedies

§ 2–701. Remedies for Breach of Collateral Contracts Not Impaired.

Remedies for breach of any obligation or promise collateral or ancillary to a contract for sale are not impaired by the provisions of this Article.

§ 2–702. Seller's Remedies on Discovery of Buyer's Insolvency.

(1) Where the seller discovers the buyer to be insolvent he may refuse delivery except for cash including payment for all goods theretofore delivered under the contract, and stop delivery under this Article (Section 2–705).

(2) Where the seller discovers that the buyer has received goods on credit while insolvent he may reclaim the goods upon demand made within ten days after the receipt, but if misrepresentation of solvency has been made to the particular seller in writing within three months before delivery the ten day limitation does not apply. Except as provided in this subsection the seller may not base a right to reclaim goods on the buyer's fraudulent or innocent misrepresentation of solvency or of intent to pay.

(3) The seller's right to reclaim under subsection (2) is subject to the rights of a buyer in ordinary course or other good faith purchaser under this Article (Section 2–403). Successful reclamation of goods excludes all other remedies with respect to them.

§ 2–703. Seller's Remedies in General.

Where the buyer wrongfully rejects or revokes acceptance of goods or fails to make a payment due on or before delivery or repudiates with respect to a part or the whole, then with respect to any goods directly affected and, if the breach is of the whole contract (Section 2–612), then also with respect to the whole undelivered balance, the aggrieved seller may

(a) withhold delivery of such goods;

(b) stop delivery by any bailee as hereafter provided (Section 2–705);

(c) proceed under the next section respecting goods still unidentified to the contract;

(d) resell and recover damages as hereafter provided (Section 2–706);

(e) recover damages for non-acceptance (Section 2–708) or in a proper case the price (Section 2–709);

(f) cancel.

§ 2–704. Seller's Right to Identify Goods to the Contract Notwithstanding Breach or to Salvage Unfinished Goods.

(1) An aggrieved seller under the preceding section may

(a) identify to the contract conforming goods not already identified if at the time he learned of the breach they are in his possession or control;

(b) treat as the subject of resale goods which have demonstrably been intended for the particular contract even though those goods are unfinished.

(2) Where the goods are unfinished an aggrieved seller may in the exercise of reasonable commercial judgment for the purposes of avoiding loss and of effective realization either complete the manufacture and wholly identify the goods to the contract or cease manufacture and resell for scrap or salvage value or proceed in any other reasonable manner.

§ 2–705. Seller's Stoppage of Delivery in Transit or Otherwise.

(1) The seller may stop delivery of goods in the possession of a carrier or other bailee when he discovers the buyer to be insolvent (Section 2–702) and may stop delivery of carload, truckload, planeload or larger shipments of express or freight when the buyer repudiates or fails to make a payment due before delivery or if for any other reason the seller has a right to withhold or reclaim the goods.

(2) As against such buyer the seller may stop delivery until

(a) receipt of the goods by the buyer; or

(b) acknowledgment to the buyer by any bailee of the goods except a carrier that the bailee holds the goods for the buyer; or

(c) such acknowledgment to the buyer by a carrier by reshipment or as warehouseman; or

(d) negotiation to the buyer of any negotiable document of title covering the goods.

(3) (a) To stop delivery the seller must so notify as to enable the bailee by reasonable diligence to prevent delivery of the goods.

(b) After such notification the bailee must hold and deliver the goods according to the directions of the seller but the seller is liable to the bailee for any ensuing charges or damages.

(c) If a negotiable document of title has been issued for goods the bailee is not obliged to obey a notification to stop until surrender of the document.

(d) A carrier who has issued a non-negotiable bill of lading is not obliged to obey a notification to stop received from a person other than the consignor.

§ 2–706. Seller's Resale Including Contract for Resale.

(1) Under the conditions stated in Section 2–703 on seller's remedies, the seller may resell the goods concerned or the undelivered balance thereof. Where the resale is made in good faith and in a commercially reasonable manner the seller may recover the difference between the resale price and the contract price together with any incidental damages allowed under the provisions of this Article (Section 2–710), but less expenses saved in consequence of the buyer's breach.

(2) Except as otherwise provided in subsection (3) or unless otherwise agreed resale may be at public or private sale including sale by way of one or more contracts to sell or of identification to an existing contract of the seller. Sale may be as a unit or in parcels and at any time and place and on any terms but every aspect of the sale including the method, manner, time, place and terms must be commercially reasonable. The resale must be reasonably identified as referring to the broken contract, but it is not necessary that the goods be in existence or that any or all of them have been identified to the contract before the breach.

(3) Where the resale is at private sale the seller must give the buyer reasonable notification of his intention to resell.

(4) Where the resale is at public sale

(a) only identified goods can be sold except where there is a recognized market for a public sale of futures in goods of the kind; and

(b) it must be made at a usual place or market for public sale if one is reasonably available and except in the case of goods which are perishable or threaten to decline in value speedily the seller must give the buyer reasonable notice of the time and place of the resale; and

(c) if the goods are not to be within the view of those attending the sale the notification of sale must state the place where the goods are located and provide for their reasonable inspection by prospective bidders; and

(d) the seller may buy.

(5) A purchaser who buys in good faith at a resale takes the goods free of any rights of the original buyer even though the seller fails to comply with one or more of the requirements of this section.

(6) The seller is not accountable to the buyer for any profit made on any resale. A person in the position of a seller (Section 2–707) or a buyer who has rightfully

rejected or justifiably revoked acceptance must account for any excess over the amount of his security interest, as hereinafter defined (subsection (3) of Section 2–711).

§ 2–707. "Person in the Position of a Seller".

(1) A "person in the position of a seller" includes as against a principal an agent who has paid or become responsible for the price of goods on behalf of his principal or anyone who otherwise holds a security interest or other right in goods similar to that of a seller.

(2) A person in the position of a seller may as provided in this Article withhold or stop delivery (Section 2–705) and resell (Section 2–706) and recover incidental damages (Section 2–710).

§ 2–708. Seller's Damages for Non-Acceptance or Repudiation.

(1) Subject to subsection (2) and to the provisions of this Article with respect to proof of market price (Section 2–723), the measure of damages for non-acceptance or repudiation by the buyer is the difference between the market price at the time and place for tender and the unpaid contract price together with any incidental damages provided in this Article (Section 2–710), but less expenses saved in consequence of the buyer's breach.

(2) If the measure of damages provided in subsection (1) is inadequate to put the seller in as good a position as performance would have done then the measure of damages is the profit (including reasonable overhead) which the seller would have made from full performance by the buyer, together with any incidental damages provided in this Article (Section 2–710), due allowance for costs reasonably incurred and due credit for payments or proceeds of resale.

§ 2–709. Action for the Price.

(1) When the buyer fails to pay the price as it becomes due the seller may recover, together with any incidental damages under the next section, the price

(a) of goods accepted or of conforming goods lost or damaged within a commercially reasonable time after risk of their loss has passed to the buyer; and

(b) of goods identified to the contract if the seller is unable after reasonable effort to resell them at a reasonable price or the circumstances reasonably indicate that such effort will be unavailing.

(2) Where the seller sues for the price he must hold for the buyer any goods which have been identified to the contract and are still in his control except that if resale becomes possible he may resell them at any time prior to the collection of the judgment. The net proceeds of any such resale must be credited to the buyer and payment of the judgment entitles him to any goods not resold.

(3) After the buyer has wrongfully rejected or revoked acceptance of the goods or has failed to make a payment due or has repudiated (Section 2–610), a seller who is held not entitled to the price under this section shall nevertheless be awarded damages for non-acceptance under the preceding section.

§ 2–710. Seller's Incidental Damages.

Incidental damages to an aggrieved seller include any commercially reasonable charges, expenses or commissions incurred in stopping delivery, in the transportation, care and custody of goods after the buyer's breach, in connection with return or resale of the goods or otherwise resulting from the breach.

§ 2–711. Buyer's Remedies in General; Buyer's Security Interest in Rejected Goods.

(1) Where the seller fails to make delivery or repudiates or the buyer rightfully rejects or justifiably revokes acceptance then with respect to any goods involved, and with respect to the whole if the breach goes to the whole contract (Section 2–612), the buyer may cancel and whether or not he has done so may in addition to recovering so much of the price as has been paid

(a) "cover" and have damages under the next section as to all the goods affected whether or not they have been identified to the contract; or

(b) recover damages for non-delivery as provided in this Article (Section 2–713).

(2) Where the seller fails to deliver or repudiates the buyer may also

(a) if the goods have been identified recover them as provided in this Article (Section 2–502); or

(b) in a proper case obtain specific performance or replevy the goods as provided in this Article (Section 2–716).

(3) On rightful rejection or justifiable revocation of acceptance a buyer has a security interest in goods in his possession or control for any payments made on their price and any expenses reasonably incurred in their inspection, receipt, transportation, care and custody and may hold such goods and resell them in like manner as an aggrieved seller (Section 2–706).

§ 2–712. "Cover"; Buyer's Procurement of Substitute Goods.

(1) After a breach within the preceding section the buyer may "cover" by making in good faith and without unreasonable delay any reasonable purchase of or contract to purchase goods in substitution for those due from the seller.

(2) The buyer may recover from the seller as damages the difference between the cost of cover and the contract price together with any incidental or consequential damages as hereinafter defined (Section 2–715), but less expenses saved in consequence of the seller's breach.

(3) Failure of the buyer to effect cover within this section does not bar him from any other remedy.

§ 2–713. Buyer's Damages for Non-Delivery or Repudiation.

(1) Subject to the provisions of this Article with respect to proof of market price (Section 2–723), the measure of

damages for non-delivery or repudiation by the seller is the difference between the market price at the time when the buyer learned of the breach and the contract price together with any incidental and consequential damages provided in this Article (Section 2–715), but less expenses saved in consequence of the seller's breach.

(2) Market price is to be determined as of the place for tender or, in cases of rejection after arrival or revocation of acceptance, as of the place of arrival.

§ 2–714. Buyer's Damages for Breach in Regard to Accepted Goods.

(1) Where the buyer has accepted goods and given notification (subsection (3) of Section 2–607) he may recover as damages for any non-conformity of tender the loss resulting in the ordinary course of events from the seller's breach as determined in any manner which is reasonable.

(2) The measure of damages for breach of warranty is the difference at the time and place of acceptance between the value of the goods accepted and the value they would have had if they had been as warranted, unless special circumstances show proximate damages of a different amount.

(3) In a proper case any incidental and consequential damages under the next section may also be recovered.

§ 2–715. Buyer's Incidental and Consequential Damages.

(1) Incidental damages resulting from the seller's breach include expenses reasonably incurred in inspection, receipt, transportation and care and custody of goods rightfully rejected, any commercially reasonable charges, expenses or commissions in connection with effecting cover and any other reasonable expense incident to the delay or other breach.

(2) Consequential damages resulting from the seller's breach include

(a) any loss resulting from general or particular requirements and needs of which the seller at the time of contracting had reason to know and which could not reasonably be prevented by cover or otherwise; and

(b) injury to person or property proximately resulting from any breach of warranty.

§ 2–716. Buyer's Right to Specific Performance or Replevin.

(1) Specific performance may be decreed where the goods are unique or in other proper circumstances.

(2) The decree for specific performance may include such terms and conditions as to payment of the price, damages, or other relief as the court may deem just.

(3) The buyer has a right of replevin for goods identified to the contract if after reasonable effort he is unable to effect cover for such goods or the circumstances reasonably indicate that such effort will be unavailing or if the goods have been shipped under reservation and satisfaction of the security interest in them has been made or tendered. In the case of goods bought for personal, family, or household purposes, the buyer's right of replevin vests upon acquisition of a special property, even if the seller had not then repudiated or failed to deliver.

As amended in 1999.

§ 2–717. Deduction of Damages From the Price.

The buyer on notifying the seller of his intention to do so may deduct all or any part of the damages resulting from any breach of the contract from any part of the price still due under the same contract.

§ 2–718. Liquidation or Limitation of Damages; Deposits.

(1) Damages for breach by either party may be liquidated in the agreement but only at an amount which is reasonable in the light of the anticipated or actual harm caused by the breach, the difficulties of proof of loss, and the inconvenience or nonfeasibility of otherwise obtaining an adequate remedy. A term fixing unreasonably large liquidated damages is void as a penalty.

(2) Where the seller justifiably withholds delivery of goods because of the buyer's breach, the buyer is entitled to restitution of any amount by which the sum of his payments exceeds

(a) the amount to which the seller is entitled by virtue of terms liquidating the seller's damages in accordance with subsection (1), or

(b) in the absence of such terms, twenty per cent of the value of the total performance for which the buyer is obligated under the contract or $500, whichever is smaller.

(3) The buyer's right to restitution under subsection (2) is subject to offset to the extent that the seller establishes

(a) a right to recover damages under the provisions of this Article other than subsection (1), and

(b) the amount or value of any benefits received by the buyer directly or indirectly by reason of the contract.

(4) Where a seller has received payment in goods their reasonable value or the proceeds of their resale shall be treated as payments for the purposes of subsection (2); but if the seller has notice of the buyer's breach before reselling goods received in part performance, his resale is subject to the conditions laid down in this Article on resale by an aggrieved seller (Section 2–706).

§ 2–719. Contractual Modification or Limitation of Remedy.

(1) Subject to the provisions of subsections (2) and (3) of this section and of the preceding section on liquidation and limitation of damages,

(a) the agreement may provide for remedies in addition to or in substitution for those provided in this Article and may limit or alter the measure of damages recoverable under this Article, as by limiting the buyer's remedies to return of the goods and repayment of the price or to repair and replacement of nonconforming goods or parts; and

(b) resort to a remedy as provided is optional unless the remedy is expressly agreed to be exclusive, in which case it is the sole remedy.

(2) Where circumstances cause an exclusive or limited remedy to fail of its essential purpose, remedy may be had as provided in this Act.

(3) Consequential damages may be limited or excluded unless the limitation or exclusion is unconscionable. Limitation of consequential damages for injury to the person in the case of consumer goods is prima facie unconscionable but limitation of damages where the loss is commercial is not.

§ 2–720. Effect of "Cancellation" or "Rescission" on Claims for Antecedent Breach.

Unless the contrary intention clearly appears, expressions of "cancellation" or "rescission" of the contract or the like shall not be construed as a renunciation or discharge of any claim in damages for an antecedent breach.

§ 2–721. Remedies for Fraud.

Remedies for material misrepresentation or fraud include all remedies available under this Article for non-fraudulent breach. Neither rescission or a claim for rescission of the contract for sale nor rejection or return of the goods shall bar or be deemed inconsistent with a claim for damages or other remedy.

§ 2–722. Who Can Sue Third Parties for Injury to Goods.

Where a third party so deals with goods which have been identified to a contract for sale as to cause actionable injury to a party to that contract

(a) a right of action against the third party is in either party to the contract for sale who has title to or a security interest or a special property or an insurable interest in the goods; and if the goods have been destroyed or converted a right of action is also in the party who either bore the risk of loss under the contract for sale or has since the injury assumed that risk as against the other;

(b) if at the time of the injury the party plaintiff did not bear the risk of loss as against the other party to the contract for sale and there is no arrangement between them for disposition of the recovery, his suit or settlement is, subject to his own interest, as a fiduciary for the other party to the contract;

(c) either party may with the consent of the other sue for the benefit of whom it may concern.

§ 2–723. Proof of Market Price: Time and Place.

(1) If an action based on anticipatory repudiation comes to trial before the time for performance with respect to some or all of the goods, any damages based on market price (Section 2–708 or Section 2–713) shall be determined according to the price of such goods prevailing at the time when the aggrieved party learned of the repudiation.

(2) If evidence of a price prevailing at the times or places described in this Article is not readily available the price prevailing within any reasonable time before or after the time described or at any other place which in commercial judgment or under usage of trade would serve as a reasonable substitute for the one described may be used, making any proper allowance for the cost of transporting the goods to or from such other place.

(3) Evidence of a relevant price prevailing at a time or place other than the one described in this Article offered by one party is not admissible unless and until he has given the other party such notice as the court finds sufficient to prevent unfair surprise.

§ 2–724. Admissibility of Market Quotations.

Whenever the prevailing price or value of any goods regularly bought and sold in any established commodity market is in issue, reports in official publications or trade journals or in newspapers or periodicals of general circulation published as the reports of such market shall be admissible in evidence. The circumstances of the preparation of such a report may be shown to affect its weight but not its admissibility.

§ 2–725. Statute of Limitations in Contracts for Sale.

(1) An action for breach of any contract for sale must be commenced within four years after the cause of action has accrued. By the original agreement the parties may reduce the period of limitation to not less than one year but may not extend it.

(2) A cause of action accrues when the breach occurs, regardless of the aggrieved party's lack of knowledge of the breach. A breach of warranty occurs when tender of delivery is made, except that where a warranty explicitly extends to future performance of the goods and discovery of the breach must await the time of such performance the cause of action accrues when the breach is or should have been discovered.

(3) Where an action commenced within the time limited by subsection (1) is so terminated as to leave available a remedy by another action for the same breach such other action may be commenced after the expiration of the time limited and within six months after the termination of the first action unless the termination resulted from voluntary discontinuance or from dismissal for failure or neglect to prosecute.

(4) This section does not alter the law on tolling of the statute of limitations nor does it apply to causes of action which have accrued before this Act becomes effective.

Article 2A LEASES

Part 1 General Provisions

§ 2A–101. Short Title.

This Article shall be known and may be cited as the Uniform Commercial Code—Leases.

§ 2A–102. Scope.

This Article applies to any transaction, regardless of form, that creates a lease.

§ 2A–103. Definitions and Index of Definitions.

(1) In this Article unless the context otherwise requires:

(a) "Buyer in ordinary course of business" means a person who in good faith and without knowledge that the sale to him [or her] is in violation of the ownership rights or security interest or leasehold interest of a third party in the goods buys in ordinary course from a person in the business of selling goods of that kind but does not include a pawnbroker. "Buying" may be for cash or by exchange of other property or on secured or unsecured credit and includes receiving goods or documents of title under a pre-existing contract for sale but does not include a transfer in bulk or as security for or in total or partial satisfaction of a money debt.

(b) "Cancellation" occurs when either party puts an end to the lease contract for default by the other party.

(c) "Commercial unit" means such a unit of goods as by commercial usage is a single whole for purposes of lease and division of which materially impairs its character or value on the market or in use. A commercial unit may be a single article, as a machine, or a set of articles, as a suite of furniture or a line of machinery, or a quantity, as a gross or carload, or any other unit treated in use or in the relevant market as a single whole.

(d) "Conforming" goods or performance under a lease contract means goods or performance that are in accordance with the obligations under the lease contract.

(e) "Consumer lease" means a lease that a lessor regularly engaged in the business of leasing or selling makes to a lessee who is an individual and who takes under the lease primarily for a personal, family, or household purpose [, if the total payments to be made under the lease contract, excluding payments for options to renew or buy, do not exceed $______].

(f) "Fault" means wrongful act, omission, breach, or default.

(g) "Finance lease" means a lease with respect to which:

(i) the lessor does not select, manufacture or supply the goods;

(ii) the lessor acquires the goods or the right to possession and use of the goods in connection with the lease; and

(iii) one of the following occurs:

(A) the lessee receives a copy of the contract by which the lessor acquired the goods or the right to possession and use of the goods before signing the lease contract;

(B) the lessee's approval of the contract by which the lessor acquired the goods or the right to possession and use of the goods is a condition to effectiveness of the lease contract;

(C) the lessee, before signing the lease contract, receives an accurate and complete statement designating the promises and warranties, and any disclaimers of warranties, limitations or modifications of remedies, or liquidated damages, including those of a third party, such as the manufacturer of the goods, provided to the lessor by the person supplying the goods in connection with or as part of the contract by which the lessor acquired the goods or the right to possession and use of the goods; or

(D) if the lease is not a consumer lease, the lessor, before the lessee signs the lease contract, informs the lessee in writing (a) of the identity of the person supplying the goods to the lessor, unless the lessee has selected that person and directed the lessor to acquire the goods or the right to possession and use of the goods from that person, (b) that the lessee is entitled under this Article to any promises and warranties, including those of any third party, provided to the lessor by the person supplying the goods in connection with or as part of the contract by which the lessor acquired the goods or the right to possession and use of the goods, and (c) that the lessee may communicate with the person supplying the goods to the lessor and receive an accurate and complete statement of those promises and warranties, including any disclaimers and limitations of them or of remedies.

(h) "Goods" means all things that are movable at the time of identification to the lease contract, or are fixtures (Section 2A–309), but the term does not include money, documents, instruments, accounts, chattel paper, general intangibles, or minerals or the like, including oil and gas, before extraction. The term also includes the unborn young of animals.

(i) "Installment lease contract" means a lease contract that authorizes or requires the delivery of goods in separate lots to be separately accepted, even though the lease contract contains a clause "each delivery is a separate lease" or its equivalent.

(j) "Lease" means a transfer of the right to possession and use of goods for a term in return for consideration, but a sale, including a sale on approval or a sale or return, or retention or creation of a security interest is not a lease. Unless the context clearly indicates otherwise, the term includes a sublease.

(k) "Lease agreement" means the bargain, with respect to the lease, of the lessor and the lessee in fact as found in their language or by implication from other circumstances including course of dealing or usage of trade or course of performance as provided in this Article. Unless the context clearly indicates otherwise, the term includes a sublease agreement.

(l) "Lease contract" means the total legal obligation that results from the lease agreement as affected by this Article and any other applicable rules of law. Unless the context clearly indicates otherwise, the term includes a sublease contract.

(m) "Leasehold interest" means the interest of the lessor or the lessee under a lease contract.

(n) "Lessee" means a person who acquires the right to possession and use of goods under a lease. Unless the context clearly indicates otherwise, the term includes a sublessee.

(o) "Lessee in ordinary course of business" means a person who in good faith and without knowledge that the lease to him [or her] is in violation of the ownership rights or security interest or leasehold interest of a third party in the goods, leases in ordinary course from a person in the business of selling or leasing goods of that kind but does not include a pawnbroker. "Leasing" may be for cash or by exchange of other property or on secured or unsecured credit and includes receiving goods or documents of title under a pre-existing lease contract but does not include a transfer in bulk or as security for or in total or partial satisfaction of a money debt.

(p) "Lessor" means a person who transfers the right to possession and use of goods under a lease. Unless the context clearly indicates otherwise, the term includes a sublessor.

(q) "Lessor's residual interest" means the lessor's interest in the goods after expiration, termination, or cancellation of the lease contract.

(r) "Lien" means a charge against or interest in goods to secure payment of a debt or performance of an obligation, but the term does not include a security interest.

(s) "Lot" means a parcel or a single article that is the subject matter of a separate lease or delivery, whether or not it is sufficient to perform the lease contract.

(t) "Merchant lessee" means a lessee that is a merchant with respect to goods of the kind subject to the lease.

(u) "Present value" means the amount as of a date certain of one or more sums payable in the future, discounted to the date certain. The discount is determined by the interest rate specified by the parties if the rate was not manifestly unreasonable at the time the transaction was entered into; otherwise, the discount is determined by a commercially reasonable rate that takes into account the facts and circumstances of each case at the time the transaction was entered into.

(v) "Purchase" includes taking by sale, lease, mortgage, security interest, pledge, gift, or any other voluntary transaction creating an interest in goods.

(w) "Sublease" means a lease of goods the right to possession and use of which was acquired by the lessor as a lessee under an existing lease.

(x) "Supplier" means a person from whom a lessor buys or leases goods to be leased under a finance lease.

(y) "Supply contract" means a contract under which a lessor buys or leases goods to be leased.

(z) "Termination" occurs when either party pursuant to a power created by agreement or law puts an end to the lease contract otherwise than for default.

(2) Other definitions applying to this Article and the sections in which they appear are:

"Accessions". Section 2A–310(1).
"Construction mortgage". Section 2A–309(1)(d).
"Encumbrance". Section 2A–309(1)(e).
"Fixtures". Section 2A–309(1)(a).
"Fixture filing". Section 2A–309(1)(b).
"Purchase money lease". Section 2A–309(1)(c).

(3) The following definitions in other Articles apply to this Article:

"Accounts". Section 9–106.
"Between merchants". Section 2–104(3).
"Buyer". Section 2–103(1)(a).
"Chattel paper". Section 9–105(1)(b).
"Consumer goods". Section 9–109(1).
"Document". Section 9–105(1)(f).
"Entrusting". Section 2–403(3).
"General intangibles". Section 9–106.
"Good faith". Section 2–103(1)(b).
"Instrument". Section 9–105(1)(i).
"Merchant". Section 2–104(1).
"Mortgage". Section 9–105(1)(j).
"Pursuant to commitment". Section 9–105(1)(k).
"Receipt". Section 2–103(1)(c).
"Sale". Section 2–106(1).
"Sale on approval". Section 2–326.
"Sale or return". Section 2–326.
"Seller". Section 2–103(1)(d).

(4) In addition Article 1 contains general definitions and principles of construction and interpretation applicable throughout this Article.

As amended in 1990 and 1999.

§ 2A–104. Leases Subject to Other Law.

(1) A lease, although subject to this Article, is also subject to any applicable:

(a) certificate of title statute of this State: (list any certificate of title statutes covering automobiles, trailers, mobile homes, boats, farm tractors, and the like);

(b) certificate of title statute of another jurisdiction (Section 2A–105); or

(c) consumer protection statute of this State, or final consumer protection decision of a court of this State existing on the effective date of this Article.

(2) In case of conflict between this Article, other than Sections 2A–105, 2A–304(3), and 2A–305(3), and a statute or decision referred to in subsection (1), the statute or decision controls.

(3) Failure to comply with an applicable law has only the effect specified therein.

As amended in 1990.

§ 2A–105. Territorial Application of Article to Goods Covered by Certificate of Title.

Subject to the provisions of Sections 2A–304(3) and 2A–305(3), with respect to goods covered by a certificate of title issued under a statute of this State or of another jurisdiction, compliance and the effect of compliance or noncompliance with a certificate of title statute are governed by the law (including the conflict of laws rules) of the jurisdiction issuing the certificate until the earlier of (a) surrender of the certificate, or (b) four months after the goods are removed from that jurisdiction and thereafter until a new certificate of title is issued by another jurisdiction.

§ 2A–106. Limitation on Power of Parties to Consumer Lease to Choose Applicable Law and Judicial Forum.

(1) If the law chosen by the parties to a consumer lease is that of a jurisdiction other than a jurisdiction in which the lessee resides at the time the lease agreement becomes enforceable or within 30 days thereafter or in which the goods are to be used, the choice is not enforceable.

(2) If the judicial forum chosen by the parties to a consumer lease is a forum that would not otherwise have jurisdiction over the lessee, the choice is not enforceable.

§ 2A–107. Waiver or Renunciation of Claim or Right After Default.

Any claim or right arising out of an alleged default or breach of warranty may be discharged in whole or in part without consideration by a written waiver or renunciation signed and delivered by the aggrieved party.

§ 2A–108. Unconscionability.

(1) If the court as a matter of law finds a lease contract or any clause of a lease contract to have been unconscionable at the time it was made the court may refuse to enforce the lease contract, or it may enforce the remainder of the lease contract without the unconscionable clause, or it may so limit the application of any unconscionable clause as to avoid any unconscionable result.

(2) With respect to a consumer lease, if the court as a matter of law finds that a lease contract or any clause of a lease contract has been induced by unconscionable conduct or that unconscionable conduct has occurred in the collection of a claim arising from a lease contract, the court may grant appropriate relief.

(3) Before making a finding of unconscionability under subsection (1) or (2), the court, on its own motion or that of a party, shall afford the parties a reasonable opportunity to present evidence as to the setting, purpose, and effect of the lease contract or clause thereof, or of the conduct.

(4) In an action in which the lessee claims unconscionability with respect to a consumer lease:

(a) If the court finds unconscionability under subsection (1) or (2), the court shall award reasonable attorney's fees to the lessee.

(b) If the court does not find unconscionability and the lessee claiming unconscionability has brought or maintained an action he [or she] knew to be groundless, the court shall award reasonable attorney's fees to the party against whom the claim is made.

(c) In determining attorney's fees, the amount of the recovery on behalf of the claimant under subsections (1) and (2) is not controlling.

§ 2A–109. Option to Accelerate at Will.

(1) A term providing that one party or his [or her] successor in interest may accelerate payment or performance or require collateral or additional collateral "at will" or "when he [or she] deems himself [or herself] insecure" or in words of similar import must be construed to mean that he [or she] has power to do so only if he [or she] in good faith believes that the prospect of payment or performance is impaired.

(2) With respect to a consumer lease, the burden of establishing good faith under subsection (1) is on the party who exercised the power; otherwise the burden of establishing lack of good faith is on the party against whom the power has been exercised.

Part 2 Formation and Construction of Lease Contract

§ 2A–201. Statute of Frauds.

(1) A lease contract is not enforceable by way of action or defense unless:

(a) the total payments to be made under the lease contract, excluding payments for options to renew or buy, are less than $1,000; or

(b) there is a writing, signed by the party against whom enforcement is sought or by that party's authorized agent, sufficient to indicate that a lease contract has been made between the parties and to describe the goods leased and the lease term.

(2) Any description of leased goods or of the lease term is sufficient and satisfies subsection (1)(b), whether or not it is specific, if it reasonably identifies what is described.

(3) A writing is not insufficient because it omits or incorrectly states a term agreed upon, but the lease contract is not enforceable under subsection (1)(b) beyond the lease term and the quantity of goods shown in the writing.

(4) A lease contract that does not satisfy the requirements of subsection (1), but which is valid in other respects, is enforceable:

(a) if the goods are to be specially manufactured or obtained for the lessee and are not suitable for lease or sale to others in the ordinary course of the lessor's business, and the lessor, before notice of repudiation is received and under circumstances that reasonably indicate that the goods are for the lessee, has made either a substantial beginning of their manufacture or commitments for their procurement;

(b) if the party against whom enforcement is sought admits in that party's pleading, testimony or otherwise in court that a lease contract was made, but the lease contract is not enforceable under this provision beyond the quantity of goods admitted; or

(c) with respect to goods that have been received and accepted by the lessee.

(5) The lease term under a lease contract referred to in subsection (4) is:

(a) if there is a writing signed by the party against whom enforcement is sought or by that party's authorized agent specifying the lease term, the term so specified;

(b) if the party against whom enforcement is sought admits in that party's pleading, testimony, or otherwise in court a lease term, the term so admitted; or

(c) a reasonable lease term.

§ 2A–202. Final Written Expression: Parol or Extrinsic Evidence.

Terms with respect to which the confirmatory memoranda of the parties agree or which are otherwise set forth in a writing intended by the parties as a final expression of their agreement with respect to such terms as are included therein may not be contradicted by evidence of any prior agreement or of a contemporaneous oral agreement but may be explained or supplemented:

(a) by course of dealing or usage of trade or by course of performance; and

(b) by evidence of consistent additional terms unless the court finds the writing to have been intended also as a complete and exclusive statement of the terms of the agreement.

§ 2A–203. Seals Inoperative.

The affixing of a seal to a writing evidencing a lease contract or an offer to enter into a lease contract does not render the writing a sealed instrument and the law with respect to sealed instruments does not apply to the lease contract or offer.

§ 2A–204. Formation in General.

(1) A lease contract may be made in any manner sufficient to show agreement, including conduct by both parties which recognizes the existence of a lease contract.

(2) An agreement sufficient to constitute a lease contract may be found although the moment of its making is undetermined.

(3) Although one or more terms are left open, a lease contract does not fail for indefiniteness if the parties have intended to make a lease contract and there is a reasonably certain basis for giving an appropriate remedy.

§ 2A–205. Firm Offers.

An offer by a merchant to lease goods to or from another person in a signed writing that by its terms gives assurance it will be held open is not revocable, for lack of consideration, during the time stated or, if no time is stated, for a reasonable time, but in no event may the period of irrevocability exceed 3 months. Any such term of assurance on a form supplied by the offeree must be separately signed by the offeror.

§ 2A–206. Offer and Acceptance in Formation of Lease Contract.

(1) Unless otherwise unambiguously indicated by the language or circumstances, an offer to make a lease contract must be construed as inviting acceptance in any manner and by any medium reasonable in the circumstances.

(2) If the beginning of a requested performance is a reasonable mode of acceptance, an offeror who is not notified of acceptance within a reasonable time may treat the offer as having lapsed before acceptance.

§ 2A–207. Course of Performance or Practical Construction.

(1) If a lease contract involves repeated occasions for performance by either party with knowledge of the nature of the performance and opportunity for objection to it by the other, any course of performance accepted or acquiesced in without objection is relevant to determine the meaning of the lease agreement.

(2) The express terms of a lease agreement and any course of performance, as well as any course of dealing and usage of trade, must be construed whenever reasonable as consistent with each other; but if that construction is unreasonable, express terms control course of performance, course of performance controls both course of dealing and usage of trade, and course of dealing controls usage of trade.

(3) Subject to the provisions of Section 2A–208 on modification and waiver, course of performance is relevant to show a waiver or modification of any term inconsistent with the course of performance.

§ 2A–208. Modification, Rescission and Waiver.

(1) An agreement modifying a lease contract needs no consideration to be binding.

(2) A signed lease agreement that excludes modification or rescission except by a signed writing may not be otherwise modified or rescinded, but, except as between merchants, such a requirement on a form supplied by a merchant must be separately signed by the other party.

(3) Although an attempt at modification or rescission does not satisfy the requirements of subsection (2), it may operate as a waiver.

(4) A party who has made a waiver affecting an executory portion of a lease contract may retract the waiver by reasonable notification received by the other party that strict performance will be required of any term waived, unless the retraction would be unjust in view of a material change of position in reliance on the waiver.

§ 2A–209. Lessee under Finance Lease as Beneficiary of Supply Contract.

(1) The benefit of the supplier's promises to the lessor under the supply contract and of all warranties, whether express or implied, including those of any third party provided in connection with or as part of the supply contract, extends to the lessee to the extent of the lessee's leasehold interest under a finance lease related to the supply contract, but is subject to the terms warranty and of the supply contract and all defenses or claims arising therefrom.

(2) The extension of the benefit of supplier's promises and of warranties to the lessee (Section 2A–209(1)) does not: (i) modify the rights and obligations of the parties to the supply contract, whether arising therefrom or otherwise, or (ii) impose any duty or liability under the supply contract on the lessee.

(3) Any modification or rescission of the supply contract by the supplier and the lessor is effective between the supplier and the lessee unless, before the modification or rescission, the supplier has received notice that the lessee has entered into a finance lease related to the supply contract. If the modification or rescission is effective between the supplier and the lessee, the lessor is deemed to have assumed, in addition to the obligations of the lessor to the lessee under the lease contract, promises of the supplier to the lessor and warranties that were so modified or rescinded as they existed and were available to the lessee before modification or rescission.

(4) In addition to the extension of the benefit of the supplier's promises and of warranties to the lessee under subsection (1), the lessee retains all rights that the lessee may have against the supplier which arise from an agreement between the lessee and the supplier or under other law.

As amended in 1990.

§ 2A–210. Express Warranties.

(1) Express warranties by the lessor are created as follows:

(a) Any affirmation of fact or promise made by the lessor to the lessee which relates to the goods and becomes part of the basis of the bargain creates an express warranty that the goods will conform to the affirmation or promise.

(b) Any description of the goods which is made part of the basis of the bargain creates an express warranty that the goods will conform to the description.

(c) Any sample or model that is made part of the basis of the bargain creates an express warranty that the whole of the goods will conform to the sample or model.

(2) It is not necessary to the creation of an express warranty that the lessor use formal words, such as "warrant" or "guarantee," or that the lessor have a specific intention to make a warranty, but an affirmation merely of the value of the goods or a statement purporting to be merely the lessor's opinion or commendation of the goods does not create a warranty.

§ 2A–211. Warranties Against Interference and Against Infringement; Lessee's Obligation Against Infringement.

(1) There is in a lease contract a warranty that for the lease term no person holds a claim to or interest in the goods that arose from an act or omission of the lessor, other than a claim by way of infringement or the like, which will interfere with the lessee's enjoyment of its leasehold interest.

(2) Except in a finance lease there is in a lease contract by a lessor who is a merchant regularly dealing in goods of the kind a warranty that the goods are delivered free of the rightful claim of any person by way of infringement or the like.

(3) A lessee who furnishes specifications to a lessor or a supplier shall hold the lessor and the supplier harmless against any claim by way of infringement or the like that arises out of compliance with the specifications.

§ 2A–212. Implied Warranty of Merchantability.

(1) Except in a finance lease, a warranty that the goods will be merchantable is implied in a lease contract if the lessor is a merchant with respect to goods of that kind.

(2) Goods to be merchantable must be at least such as

(a) pass without objection in the trade under the description in the lease agreement;

(b) in the case of fungible goods, are of fair average quality within the description;

(c) are fit for the ordinary purposes for which goods of that type are used;

(d) run, within the variation permitted by the lease agreement, of even kind, quality, and quantity within each unit and among all units involved;

(e) are adequately contained, packaged, and labeled as the lease agreement may require; and

(f) conform to any promises or affirmations of fact made on the container or label.

(3) Other implied warranties may arise from course of dealing or usage of trade.

§ 2A–213. Implied Warranty of Fitness for Particular Purpose.

Except in a finance of lease, if the lessor at the time the lease contract is made has reason to know of any particular purpose for which the goods are required and that the lessee is relying on the lessor's skill or judgment to select or furnish suitable goods, there is in the lease contract an implied warranty that the goods will be fit for that purpose.

§ 2A–214. Exclusion or Modification of Warranties.

(1) Words or conduct relevant to the creation of an express warranty and words or conduct tending to negate or limit a warranty must be construed wherever reasonable as consistent with each other; but, subject to the provisions of Section 2A–202 on parol or extrinsic evidence, negation or limitation is inoperative to the extent that the construction is unreasonable.

(2) Subject to subsection (3), to exclude or modify the implied warranty of merchantability or any part of it the language must mention "merchantability", be by a writing, and be conspicuous. Subject to subsection (3), to exclude or modify any implied warranty of fitness the exclusion must be by a writing and be conspicuous. Language to exclude all implied warranties of fitness is sufficient if it is in writing, is conspicuous and states, for example, "There is no warranty that the goods will be fit for a particular purpose".

(3) Notwithstanding subsection (2), but subject to subsection (4),

(a) unless the circumstances indicate otherwise, all implied warranties are excluded by expressions like "as is" or "with all faults" or by other language that in common understanding calls the lessee's attention to the exclusion of warranties and makes plain that there is no implied warranty, if in writing and conspicuous;

(b) if the lessee before entering into the lease contract has examined the goods or the sample or model as fully as desired or has refused to examine the goods, there is no implied warranty with regard to defects that an examination ought in the circumstances to have revealed; and

(c) an implied warranty may also be excluded or modified by course of dealing, course of performance, or usage of trade.

(4) To exclude or modify a warranty against interference or against infringement (Section 2A–211) or any part of it, the language must be specific, be by a writing, and be conspicuous, unless the circumstances, including course of performance, course of dealing, or usage of trade, give the lessee reason to know that the goods are being leased subject to a claim or interest of any person.

§ 2A–215. Cumulation and Conflict of Warranties Express or Implied.

Warranties, whether express or implied, must be construed as consistent with each other and as cumulative, but if that construction is unreasonable, the intention of the parties determines which warranty is dominant. In ascertaining that intention the following rules apply:

(a) Exact or technical specifications displace an inconsistent sample or model or general language of description.

(b) A sample from an existing bulk displaces inconsistent general language of description.

(c) Express warranties displace inconsistent implied warranties other than an implied warranty of fitness for a particular purpose.

§ 2A–216. Third-Party Beneficiaries of Express and Implied Warranties.

Alternative A

A warranty to or for the benefit of a lessee under this Article, whether express or implied, extends to any natural person who is in the family or household of the lessee or who is a guest in the lessee's home if it is reasonable to expect that such person may use, consume, or be affected by the goods and who is injured in person by breach of the warranty. This section does not displace principles of law and equity that extend a warranty to or for the benefit of a lessee to other persons. The operation of this section may not be excluded, modified, or limited, but an exclusion, modification, or limitation of the warranty, including any with respect to rights and remedies, effective against the lessee is also effective against any beneficiary designated under this section.

Alternative B

A warranty to or for the benefit of a lessee under this Article, whether express or implied, extends to any natural person who may reasonably be expected to use, consume, or be affected by the goods and who is injured in person by breach of the warranty. This section does not displace principles of law and equity that extend a warranty to or for the benefit of a lessee to other persons. The operation of this section may not be excluded, modified, or limited, but an exclusion, modification, or limitation of the warranty, including any with respect to rights and remedies, effective against the lessee is also effective against the beneficiary designated under this section.

Alternative C

A warranty to or for the benefit of a lessee under this Article, whether express or implied, extends to any person who may reasonably be expected to use, consume, or be affected by the goods and who is injured by breach of the warranty. The operation of this section may not be excluded, modified, or limited with respect to injury to the person of an individual to whom the warranty extends, but an exclusion, modification, or limitation of the warranty, including any with respect to rights and remedies, effective against the lessee is also effective against the beneficiary designated under this section.

§ 2A–217. Identification.

Identification of goods as goods to which a lease contract refers may be made at any time and in any manner explicitly agreed to by the parties. In the absence of explicit agreement, identification occurs:

(a) when the lease contract is made if the lease contract is for a lease of goods that are existing and identified;

(b) when the goods are shipped, marked, or otherwise designated by the lessor as goods to which the lease contract refers, if the lease contract is for a lease of goods that are not existing and identified; or

(c) when the young are conceived, if the lease contract is for a lease of unborn young of animals.

§ 2A–218. Insurance and Proceeds.

(1) A lessee obtains an insurable interest when existing goods are identified to the lease contract even though the goods identified are nonconforming and the lessee has an option to reject them.

(2) If a lessee has an insurable interest only by reason of the lessor's identification of the goods, the lessor, until default or insolvency or notification to the lessee that identification is final, may substitute other goods for those identified.

(3) Notwithstanding a lessee's insurable interest under subsections (1) and (2), the lessor retains an insurable interest until an option to buy has been exercised by the lessee and risk of loss has passed to the lessee.

(4) Nothing in this section impairs any insurable interest recognized under any other statute or rule of law.

(5) The parties by agreement may determine that one or more parties have an obligation to obtain and pay for insurance covering the goods and by agreement may determine the beneficiary of the proceeds of the insurance.

§ 2A–219. Risk of Loss.

(1) Except in the case of a finance lease, risk of loss is retained by the lessor and does not pass to the lessee. In the case of a finance lease, risk of loss passes to the lessee.

(2) Subject to the provisions of this Article on the effect of default on risk of loss (Section 2A–220), if risk of loss is to pass to the lessee and the time of passage is not stated, the following rules apply:

(a) If the lease contract requires or authorizes the goods to be shipped by carrier

(i) and it does not require delivery at a particular destination, the risk of loss passes to the lessee when the goods are duly delivered to the carrier; but

(ii) if it does require delivery at a particular destination and the goods are there duly tendered while in the possession of the carrier, the risk of loss passes to the lessee when the goods are there duly so tendered as to enable the lessee to take delivery.

(b) If the goods are held by a bailee to be delivered without being moved, the risk of loss passes to the lessee on acknowledgment by the bailee of the lessee's right to possession of the goods.

(c) In any case not within subsection (a) or (b), the risk of loss passes to the lessee on the lessee's receipt of the goods if the lessor, or, in the case of a finance lease, the supplier, is a merchant; otherwise the risk passes to the lessee on tender of delivery.

§ 2A–220. Effect of Default on Risk of Loss.

(1) Where risk of loss is to pass to the lessee and the time of passage is not stated:

(a) If a tender or delivery of goods so fails to conform to the lease contract as to give a right of rejection, the risk of their loss remains with the lessor, or, in the case of a finance lease, the supplier, until cure or acceptance.

(b) If the lessee rightfully revokes acceptance, he [or she], to the extent of any deficiency in his [or her] effective insurance coverage, may treat the risk of loss as having remained with the lessor from the beginning.

(2) Whether or not risk of loss is to pass to the lessee, if the lessee as to conforming goods already identified to a lease contract repudiates or is otherwise in default under the lease contract, the lessor, or, in the case of a finance lease, the supplier, to the extent of any deficiency in his [or her] effective insurance coverage may treat the risk of loss as resting on the lessee for a commercially reasonable time.

§ 2A–221. Casualty to Identified Goods.

If a lease contract requires goods identified when the lease contract is made, and the goods suffer casualty without fault of the lessee, the lessor or the supplier before delivery, or the goods suffer casualty before risk of loss passes to the lessee pursuant to the lease agreement or Section 2A–219, then:

(a) if the loss is total, the lease contract is avoided; and

(b) if the loss is partial or the goods have so deteriorated as to no longer conform to the lease contract, the lessee may nevertheless demand inspection and at his [or her] option either treat the lease contract as avoided or, except in a finance lease that is not a consumer lease, accept the goods with due allowance from the rent payable for the balance of the lease term for the deterioration or the deficiency in quantity but without further right against the lessor.

Part 3 Effect of Lease Contract

§ 2A–301. Enforceability of Lease Contract.

Except as otherwise provided in this Article, a lease contract is effective and enforceable according to its terms between the parties, against purchasers of the goods and against creditors of the parties.

§ 2A–302. Title to and Possession of Goods.

Except as otherwise provided in this Article, each provision of this Article applies whether the lessor or a third party has title to the goods, and whether the lessor, the lessee, or a third party has possession of the goods, notwithstanding any statute or rule of law that possession or the absence of possession is fraudulent.

§ 2A–303. Alienability of Party's Interest Under Lease Contract or of Lessor's Residual Interest in Goods; Delegation of Performance; Transfer of Rights.

(1) As used in this section,"creation of a security interest" includes the sale of a lease contract that is subject to Article 9, Secured Transactions, by reason of Section 9–109(a)(3).

(2) Except as provided in subsections (3) and Section 9–407, a provision in a lease agreement which (i) prohibits the voluntary or involuntary transfer, including a transfer by sale, sublease, creation or enforcement of a security interest, or attachment, levy, or other judicial process, of an interest of a party under the lease contract or of the lessor's residual interest in the goods, or (ii) makes such a transfer an event of default, gives rise to the rights and remedies provided in subsection (4), but a transfer that is prohibited or is an event of default under the lease agreement is otherwise effective.

(3) A provision in a lease agreement which (i) prohibits a transfer of a right to damages for default with respect to the whole lease contract or of a right to payment arising out of the transferor's due performance of the transferor's entire obligation, or (ii) makes such a transfer an event of default, is not enforceable, and such a transfer is not a transfer that materially impairs the propsect of obtaining return performance by, materially changes the duty of, or materially increases the burden or risk imposed on, the other party to the lease contract within the purview of subsection (4).

(4) Subject to subsection (3) and Section 9–407:

(a) if a transfer is made which is made an event of default under a lease agreement, the party to the lease contract not making the transfer, unless that party waives the default or otherwise agrees, has the rights and remedies described in Section 2A–501(2);

(b) if paragraph (a) is not applicable and if a transfer is made that (i) is prohibited under a lease agreement or (ii) materially impairs the prospect of obtaining return performance by, materially changes the duty of, or materially increases the burden or risk imposed on, the other party to the lease contract, unless the party not making the transfer agrees at any time to the transfer in the lease contract or otherwise, then, except as limited by contract, (i) the transferor is liable to the party not making the transfer for damages caused by the transfer to the extent that the damages could not reasonably be prevented by the party not making the transfer and (ii) a court having jurisdiction may grant other appropriate relief, including cancellation of the lease contract or an injunction against the transfer.

(5) A transfer of "the lease" or of "all my rights under the lease", or a transfer in similar general terms, is a transfer of rights and, unless the language or the circumstances, as in a transfer for security, indicate the contrary, the transfer is a delegation of duties by the transferor to the transferee. Acceptance by the transferee constitutes a promise by the transferee to perform those duties. The promise is enforceable by either the transferor or the other party to the lease contract.

(6) Unless otherwise agreed by the lessor and the lessee, a delegation of performance does not relieve the transferor as against the other party of any duty to perform or of any liability for default.

(7) In a consumer lease, to prohibit the transfer of an interest of a party under the lease contract or to make a transfer an event of default, the language must be specific, by a writing, and conspicuous.

As amended in 1990 and 1999.

§ 2A–304. Subsequent Lease of Goods by Lessor.

(1) Subject to Section 2A–303, a subsequent lessee from a lessor of goods under an existing lease contract obtains, to the extent of the leasehold interest transferred, the leasehold interest in the goods that the lessor had or had power to transfer, and except as provided in subsection (2) and Section 2A–527(4), takes subject to the existing lease contract. A lessor with voidable title has power to transfer a good leasehold interest to a good faith subsequent lessee for value, but only to the extent set forth in the preceding sentence. If goods have been delivered under a transaction of purchase the lessor has that power even though:

(a) the lessor's transferor was deceived as to the identity of the lessor;

(b) the delivery was in exchange for a check which is later dishonored;

(c) it was agreed that the transaction was to be a "cash sale"; or

(d) the delivery was procured through fraud punishable as larcenous under the criminal law.

(2) A subsequent lessee in the ordinary course of business from a lessor who is a merchant dealing in goods of that kind to whom the goods were entrusted by the existing lessee of that lessor before the interest of the subsequent lessee became enforceable against that lessor obtains, to the extent of the leasehold interest transferred, all of that lessor's and the existing lessee's rights to the goods, and takes free of the existing lease contract.

(3) A subsequent lessee from the lessor of goods that are subject to an existing lease contract and are covered by a certificate of title issued under a statute of this State or of another jurisdiction takes no greater rights than those provided both by this section and by the certificate of title statute.

As amended in 1990.

§ 2A–305. Sale or Sublease of Goods by Lessee.

(1) Subject to the provisions of Section 2A–303, a buyer or sublessee from the lessee of goods under an existing lease contract obtains, to the extent of the interest transferred,

the leasehold interest in the goods that the lessee had or had power to transfer, and except as provided in subsection (2) and Section 2A–511(4), takes subject to the existing lease contract. A lessee with a voidable leasehold interest has power to transfer a good leasehold interest to a good faith buyer for value or a good faith sublessee for value, but only to the extent set forth in the preceding sentence. When goods have been delivered under a transaction of lease the lessee has that power even though:

(a) the lessor was deceived as to the identity of the lessee;

(b) the delivery was in exchange for a check which is later dishonored; or

(c) the delivery was procured through fraud punishable as larcenous under the criminal law.

(2) A buyer in the ordinary course of business or a sublessee in the ordinary course of business from a lessee who is a merchant dealing in goods of that kind to whom the goods were entrusted by the lessor obtains, to the extent of the interest transferred, all of the lessor's and lessee's rights to the goods, and takes free of the existing lease contract.

(3) A buyer or sublessee from the lessee of goods that are subject to an existing lease contract and are covered by a certificate of title issued under a statute of this State or of another jurisdiction takes no greater rights than those provided both by this section and by the certificate of title statute.

§ 2A–306. Priority of Certain Liens Arising by Operation of Law.

If a person in the ordinary course of his [or her] business furnishes services or materials with respect to goods subject to a lease contract, a lien upon those goods in the possession of that person given by statute or rule of law for those materials or services takes priority over any interest of the lessor or lessee under the lease contract or this Article unless the lien is created by statute and the statute provides otherwise or unless the lien is created by rule of law and the rule of law provides otherwise.

§ 2A–307. Priority of Liens Arising by Attachment or Levy on, Security Interests in, and Other Claims to Goods.

(1) Except as otherwise provided in Section 2A–306, a creditor of a lessee takes subject to the lease contract.

(2) Except as otherwise provided in subsection (3) and in Sections 2A–306 and 2A–308, a creditor of a lessor takes subject to the lease contract unless the creditor holds a lien that attached to the goods before the lease contract became enforceable.

(3) Except as otherwise provided in Sections 9–317, 9–321, and 9–323, a lessee takes a leasehold interest subject to a security interest held by a creditor of the lessor.

As amended in 1990 and 1999.

§ 2A–308. Special Rights of Creditors.

(1) A creditor of a lessor in possession of goods subject to a lease contract may treat the lease contract as void if as against the creditor retention of possession by the lessor is fraudulent under any statute or rule of law, but retention of possession in good faith and current course of trade by the lessor for a commercially reasonable time after the lease contract becomes enforceable is not fraudulent.

(2) Nothing in this Article impairs the rights of creditors of a lessor if the lease contract (a) becomes enforceable, not in current course of trade but in satisfaction of or as security for a pre-existing claim for money, security, or the like, and (b) is made under circumstances which under any statute or rule of law apart from this Article would constitute the transaction a fraudulent transfer or voidable preference.

(3) A creditor of a seller may treat a sale or an identification of goods to a contract for sale as void if as against the creditor retention of possession by the seller is fraudulent under any statute or rule of law, but retention of possession of the goods pursuant to a lease contract entered into by the seller as lessee and the buyer as lessor in connection with the sale or identification of the goods is not fraudulent if the buyer bought for value and in good faith.

§ 2A–309. Lessor's and Lessee's Rights When Goods Become Fixtures.

(1) In this section:

(a) goods are "fixtures" when they become so related to particular real estate that an interest in them arises under real estate law;

(b) a "fixture filing" is the filing, in the office where a mortgage on the real estate would be filed or recorded, of a financing statement covering goods that are or are to become fixtures and conforming to the requirements of Section 9–502(a) and (b);

(c) a lease is a "purchase money lease" unless the lessee has possession or use of the goods or the right to possession or use of the goods before the lease agreement is enforceable;

(d) a mortgage is a "construction mortgage" to the extent it secures an obligation incurred for the construction of an improvement on land including the acquisition cost of the land, if the recorded writing so indicates; and

(e) "encumbrance" includes real estate mortgages and other liens on real estate and all other rights in real estate that are not ownership interests.

(2) Under this Article a lease may be of goods that are fixtures or may continue in goods that become fixtures, but no lease exists under this Article of ordinary building materials incorporated into an improvement on land.

(3) This Article does not prevent creation of a lease of fixtures pursuant to real estate law.

(4) The perfected interest of a lessor of fixtures has priority over a conflicting interest of an encumbrancer or owner of the real estate if:

(a) the lease is a purchase money lease, the conflicting interest of the encumbrancer or owner arises before the goods become fixtures, the interest of the lessor is perfected by a fixture filing before the goods become fixtures or within ten days thereafter, and the lessee has an interest of record in the real estate or is in possession of the real estate; or

(b) the interest of the lessor is perfected by a fixture filing before the interest of the encumbrancer or owner is of record, the lessor's interest has priority over any conflicting interest of a predecessor in title of the encumbrancer or owner, and the lessee has an interest of record in the real estate or is in possession of the real estate.

(5) The interest of a lessor of fixtures, whether or not perfected, has priority over the conflicting interest of an encumbrancer or owner of the real estate if:

(a) the fixtures are readily removable factory or office machines, readily removable equipment that is not primarily used or leased for use in the operation of the real estate, or readily removable replacements of domestic appliances that are goods subject to a consumer lease, and before the goods become fixtures the lease contract is enforceable; or

(b) the conflicting interest is a lien on the real estate obtained by legal or equitable proceedings after the lease contract is enforceable; or

(c) the encumbrancer or owner has consented in writing to the lease or has disclaimed an interest in the goods as fixtures; or

(d) the lessee has a right to remove the goods as against the encumbrancer or owner. If the lessee's right to remove terminates, the priority of the interest of the lessor continues for a reasonable time.

(6) Notwithstanding paragraph (4)(a) but otherwise subject to subsections (4) and (5), the interest of a lessor of fixtures, including the lessor's residual interest, is subordinate to the conflicting interest of an encumbrancer of the real estate under a construction mortgage recorded before the goods become fixtures if the goods become fixtures before the completion of the construction. To the extent given to refinance a construction mortgage, the conflicting interest of an encumbrancer of the real estate under a mortgage has this priority to the same extent as the encumbrancer of the real estate under the construction mortgage.

(7) In cases not within the preceding subsections, priority between the interest of a lessor of fixtures, including the lessor's residual interest, and the conflicting interest of an encumbrancer or owner of the real estate who is not the lessee is determined by the priority rules governing conflicting interests in real estate.

(8) If the interest of a lessor of fixtures, including the lessor's residual interest, has priority over all conflicting interests of all owners and encumbrancers of the real estate, the lessor or the lessee may (i) on default, expiration, termination, or cancellation of the lease agreement but subject to the agreement and this Article, or (ii) if necessary to enforce other rights and remedies of the lessor or lessee under this Article, remove the goods from the real estate, free and clear of all conflicting interests of all owners and encumbrancers of the real estate, but the lessor or lessee must reimburse any encumbrancer or owner of the real estate who is not the lessee and who has not otherwise agreed for the cost of repair of any physical injury, but not for any diminution in value of the real estate caused by the absence of the goods removed or by any necessity of replacing them. A person entitled to reimbursement may refuse permission to remove until the party seeking removal gives adequate security for the performance of this obligation.

(9) Even though the lease agreement does not create a security interest, the interest of a lessor of fixtures, including the lessor's residual interest, is perfected by filing a financing statement as a fixture filing for leased goods that are or are to become fixtures in accordance with the relevant provisions of the Article on Secured Transactions (Article 9).

As amended in 1990 and 1999.

§ 2A–310. Lessor's and Lessee's Rights When Goods Become Accessions.

(1) Goods are "accessions" when they are installed in or affixed to other goods.

(2) The interest of a lessor or a lessee under a lease contract entered into before the goods became accessions is superior to all interests in the whole except as stated in subsection (4).

(3) The interest of a lessor or a lessee under a lease contract entered into at the time or after the goods became accessions is superior to all subsequently acquired interests in the whole except as stated in subsection (4) but is subordinate to interests in the whole existing at the time the lease contract was made unless the holders of such interests in the whole have in writing consented to the lease or disclaimed an interest in the goods as part of the whole.

(4) The interest of a lessor or a lessee under a lease contract described in subsection (2) or (3) is subordinate to the interest of

(a) a buyer in the ordinary course of business or a lessee in the ordinary course of business of any interest in the whole acquired after the goods became accessions; or

(b) a creditor with a security interest in the whole perfected before the lease contract was made to the extent that the creditor makes subsequent advances without knowledge of the lease contract.

(5) When under subsections (2) or (3) and (4) a lessor or a lessee of accessions holds an interest that is superior to all interests in the whole, the lessor or the lessee may (a) on default, expiration, termination, or cancellation of the lease contract by the other party but subject to the provisions of the lease contract and this Article, or (b) if necessary to enforce his [or her] other rights and remedies under this Article, remove the goods from the whole, free and clear of all interests in the whole, but he [or she] must reimburse any holder of an interest in the whole who is not the lessee and who has not otherwise agreed for the cost of repair of any physical injury but not for any diminution in value of the whole caused by the absence of the goods removed or by any necessity for replacing them. A person entitled to reimbursement may refuse permission to remove until the party seeking removal gives adequate security for the performance of this obligation.

§ 2A–311. Priority Subject to Subordination.

Nothing in this Article prevents subordination by agreement by any person entitled to priority.

As added in 1990.

Part 4 Performance of Lease Contract: Repudiated, Substituted and Excused

§ 2A–401. Insecurity: Adequate Assurance of Performance.

(1) A lease contract imposes an obligation on each party that the other's expectation of receiving due performance will not be impaired.

(2) If reasonable grounds for insecurity arise with respect to the performance of either party, the insecure party may demand in writing adequate assurance of due performance. Until the insecure party receives that assurance, if commercially reasonable the insecure party may suspend any performance for which he [or she] has not already received the agreed return.

(3) A repudiation of the lease contract occurs if assurance of due performance adequate under the circumstances of the particular case is not provided to the insecure party within a reasonable time, not to exceed 30 days after receipt of a demand by the other party.

(4) Between merchants, the reasonableness of grounds for insecurity and the adequacy of any assurance offered must be determined according to commercial standards.

(5) Acceptance of any nonconforming delivery or payment does not prejudice the aggrieved party's right to demand adequate assurance of future performance.

§ 2A–402. Anticipatory Repudiation.

If either party repudiates a lease contract with respect to a performance not yet due under the lease contract, the loss of which performance will substantially impair the value of the lease contract to the other, the aggrieved party may:

(a) for a commercially reasonable time, await retraction of repudiation and performance by the repudiating party;

(b) make demand pursuant to Section 2A–401 and await assurance of future performance adequate under the circumstances of the particular case; or

(c) resort to any right or remedy upon default under the lease contract or this Article, even though the aggrieved party has notified the repudiating party that the aggrieved party would await the repudiating party's performance and assurance and has urged retraction. In addition, whether or not the aggrieved party is pursuing one of the foregoing remedies, the aggrieved party may suspend performance or, if the aggrieved party is the lessor, proceed in accordance with the provisions of this Article on the lessor's right to identify goods to the lease contract notwithstanding default or to salvage unfinished goods (Section 2A–524).

§ 2A–403. Retraction of Anticipatory Repudiation.

(1) Until the repudiating party's next performance is due, the repudiating party can retract the repudiation unless, since the repudiation, the aggrieved party has cancelled the lease contract or materially changed the aggrieved party's position or otherwise indicated that the aggrieved party considers the repudiation final.

(2) Retraction may be by any method that clearly indicates to the aggrieved party that the repudiating party intends to perform under the lease contract and includes any assurance demanded under Section 2A–401.

(3) Retraction reinstates a repudiating party's rights under a lease contract with due excuse and allowance to the aggrieved party for any delay occasioned by the repudiation.

§ 2A–404. Substituted Performance.

(1) If without fault of the lessee, the lessor and the supplier, the agreed berthing, loading, or unloading facilities fail or the agreed type of carrier becomes unavailable or the agreed manner of delivery otherwise becomes commercially impracticable, but a commercially reasonable substitute is available, the substitute performance must be tendered and accepted.

(2) If the agreed means or manner of payment fails because of domestic or foreign governmental regulation:

(a) the lessor may withhold or stop delivery or cause the supplier to withhold or stop delivery unless the lessee provides a means or manner of payment that is commercially a substantial equivalent; and

(b) if delivery has already been taken, payment by the means or in the manner provided by the regulation discharges the lessee's obligation unless the regulation is discriminatory, oppressive, or predatory.

§ 2A–405. Excused Performance.

Subject to Section 2A–404 on substituted performance, the following rules apply:

(a) Delay in delivery or nondelivery in whole or in part by a lessor or a supplier who complies with paragraphs (b) and (c) is not a default under the lease contract if performance as agreed has been made impracticable by the occurrence of a contingency the nonoccurrence of which was a basic assumption on which the lease contract was made or by compliance in good faith with any applicable foreign or domestic governmental regulation or order, whether or not the regulation or order later proves to be invalid.

(b) If the causes mentioned in paragraph (a) affect only part of the lessor's or the supplier's capacity to perform, he [or she] shall allocate production and deliveries among his [or her] customers but at his [or her] option may include regular customers not then under contract for sale or lease as well as his [or her] own requirements for further manufacture. He [or she] may so allocate in any manner that is fair and reasonable.

(c) The lessor seasonably shall notify the lessee and in the case of a finance lease the supplier seasonably shall notify the lessor and the lessee, if known, that there will be delay or nondelivery and, if allocation is required under paragraph (b), of the estimated quota thus made available for the lessee.

§ 2A–406. Procedure on Excused Performance.

(1) If the lessee receives notification of a material or indefinite delay or an allocation justified under Section 2A–405, the lessee may by written notification to the lessor as to any goods involved, and with respect to all of the goods if under an installment lease contract the value of the whole lease contract is substantially impaired (Section 2A–510):

(a) terminate the lease contract (Section 2A–505(2)); or

(b) except in a finance lease that is not a consumer lease, modify the lease contract by accepting the available quota in substitution, with due allowance from the rent payable for the balance of the lease term for the deficiency but without further right against the lessor.

(2) If, after receipt of a notification from the lessor under Section 2A–405, the lessee fails so to modify the lease agreement within a reasonable time not exceeding 30 days, the lease contract lapses with respect to any deliveries affected.

§ 2A–407. Irrevocable Promises: Finance Leases.

(1) In the case of a finance lease that is not a consumer lease the lessee's promises under the lease contract become irrevocable and independent upon the lessee's acceptance of the goods.

(2) A promise that has become irrevocable and independent under subsection (1):

(a) is effective and enforceable between the parties, and by or against third parties including assignees of the parties, and

(b) is not subject to cancellation, termination, modification, repudiation, excuse, or substitution without the consent of the party to whom the promise runs.

(3) This section does not affect the validity under any other law of a covenant in any lease contract making the lessee's promises irrevocable and independent upon the lessee's acceptance of the goods.

As amended in 1990.

Part 5 Default

A. In General

§ 2A–501. Default: Procedure.

(1) Whether the lessor or the lessee is in default under a lease contract is determined by the lease agreement and this Article.

(2) If the lessor or the lessee is in default under the lease contract, the party seeking enforcement has rights and remedies as provided in this Article and, except as limited by this Article, as provided in the lease agreement.

(3) If the lessor or the lessee is in default under the lease contract, the party seeking enforcement may reduce the party's claim to judgment, or otherwise enforce the lease contract by self-help or any available judicial procedure or nonjudicial procedure, including administrative proceeding, arbitration, or the like, in accordance with this Article.

(4) Except as otherwise provided in Section 1–106(1) or this Article or the lease agreement, the rights and remedies referred to in subsections (2) and (3) are cumulative.

(5) If the lease agreement covers both real property and goods, the party seeking enforcement may proceed under this Part as to the goods, or under other applicable law as to both the real property and the goods in accordance with that party's rights and remedies in respect of the real property, in which case this Part does not apply.

As amended in 1990.

§ 2A–502. Notice After Default.

Except as otherwise provided in this Article or the lease agreement, the lessor or lessee in default under the lease contract is not entitled to notice of default or notice of enforcement from the other party to the lease agreement.

§ 2A–503. Modification or Impairment of Rights and Remedies.

(1) Except as otherwise provided in this Article, the lease agreement may include rights and remedies for default in addition to or in substitution for those provided in this Article and may limit or alter the measure of damages recoverable under this Article.

(2) Resort to a remedy provided under this Article or in the lease agreement is optional unless the remedy is expressly agreed to be exclusive. If circumstances cause

an exclusive or limited remedy to fail of its essential purpose, or provision for an exclusive remedy is unconscionable, remedy may be had as provided in this Article.

(3) Consequential damages may be liquidated under Section 2A–504, or may otherwise be limited, altered, or excluded unless the limitation, alteration, or exclusion is unconscionable. Limitation, alteration, or exclusion of consequential damages for injury to the person in the case of consumer goods is prima facie unconscionable but limitation, alteration, or exclusion of damages where the loss is commercial is not prima facie unconscionable.

(4) Rights and remedies on default by the lessor or the lessee with respect to any obligation or promise collateral or ancillary to the lease contract are not impaired by this Article.

As amended in 1990.

§ 2A–504. Liquidation of Damages.

(1) Damages payable by either party for default, or any other act or omission, including indemnity for loss or diminution of anticipated tax benefits or loss or damage to lessor's residual interest, may be liquidated in the lease agreement but only at an amount or by a formula that is reasonable in light of the then anticipated harm caused by the default or other act or omission.

(2) If the lease agreement provides for liquidation of damages, and such provision does not comply with subsection (1), or such provision is an exclusive or limited remedy that circumstances cause to fail of its essential purpose, remedy may be had as provided in this Article.

(3) If the lessor justifiably withholds or stops delivery of goods because of the lessee's default or insolvency (Section 2A–525 or 2A–526), the lessee is entitled to restitution of any amount by which the sum of his [or her] payments exceeds:

(a) the amount to which the lessor is entitled by virtue of terms liquidating the lessor's damages in accordance with subsection (1); or

(b) in the absence of those terms, 20 percent of the then present value of the total rent the lessee was obligated to pay for the balance of the lease term, or, in the case of a consumer lease, the lesser of such amount or $500.

(4) A lessee's right to restitution under subsection (3) is subject to offset to the extent the lessor establishes:

(a) a right to recover damages under the provisions of this Article other than subsection (1); and

(b) the amount or value of any benefits received by the lessee directly or indirectly by reason of the lease contract.

§ 2A–505. Cancellation and Termination and Effect of Cancellation, Termination, Rescission, or Fraud on Rights and Remedies.

(1) On cancellation of the lease contract, all obligations that are still executory on both sides are discharged, but any right based on prior default or performance survives, and the cancelling party also retains any remedy for default of the whole lease contract or any unperformed balance.

(2) On termination of the lease contract, all obligations that are still executory on both sides are discharged but any right based on prior default or performance survives.

(3) Unless the contrary intention clearly appears, expressions of "cancellation," "rescission," or the like of the lease contract may not be construed as a renunciation or discharge of any claim in damages for an antecedent default.

(4) Rights and remedies for material misrepresentation or fraud include all rights and remedies available under this Article for default.

(5) Neither rescission nor a claim for rescission of the lease contract nor rejection or return of the goods may bar or be deemed inconsistent with a claim for damages or other right or remedy.

§ 2A–506. Statute of Limitations.

(1) An action for default under a lease contract, including breach of warranty or indemnity, must be commenced within 4 years after the cause of action accrued. By the original lease contract the parties may reduce the period of limitation to not less than one year.

(2) A cause of action for default accrues when the act or omission on which the default or breach of warranty is based is or should have been discovered by the aggrieved party, or when the default occurs, whichever is later. A cause of action for indemnity accrues when the act or omission on which the claim for indemnity is based is or should have been discovered by the indemnified party, whichever is later.

(3) If an action commenced within the time limited by subsection (1) is so terminated as to leave available a remedy by another action for the same default or breach of warranty or indemnity, the other action may be commenced after the expiration of the time limited and within 6 months after the termination of the first action unless the termination resulted from voluntary discontinuance or from dismissal for failure or neglect to prosecute.

(4) This section does not alter the law on tolling of the statute of limitations nor does it apply to causes of action that have accrued before this Article becomes effective.

§ 2A–507. Proof of Market Rent: Time and Place.

(1) Damages based on market rent (Section 2A–519 or 2A–528) are determined according to the rent for the use of the goods concerned for a lease term identical to the remaining lease term of the original lease agreement and prevailing at the times specified in Sections 2A–519 and 2A–528.

(2) If evidence of rent for the use of the goods concerned for a lease term identical to the remaining lease term of the original lease agreement and prevailing at the times or places described in this Article is not readily available, the rent prevailing within any reasonable time before or after the time described or at any other place or

for a different lease term which in commercial judgment or under usage of trade would serve as a reasonable substitute for the one described may be used, making any proper allowance for the difference, including the cost of transporting the goods to or from the other place.

(3) Evidence of a relevant rent prevailing at a time or place or for a lease term other than the one described in this Article offered by one party is not admissible unless and until he [or she] has given the other party notice the court finds sufficient to prevent unfair surprise.

(4) If the prevailing rent or value of any goods regularly leased in any established market is in issue, reports in official publications or trade journals or in newspapers or periodicals of general circulation published as the reports of that market are admissible in evidence. The circumstances of the preparation of the report may be shown to affect its weight but not its admissibility.

As amended in 1990.

B. Default by Lessor

§ 2A–508. Lessee's Remedies.

(1) If a lessor fails to deliver the goods in conformity to the lease contract (Section 2A–509) or repudiates the lease contract (Section 2A–402), or a lessee rightfully rejects the goods (Section 2A–509) or justifiably revokes acceptance of the goods (Section 2A–517), then with respect to any goods involved, and with respect to all of the goods if under an installment lease contract the value of the whole lease contract is substantially impaired (Section 2A–510), the lessor is in default under the lease contract and the lessee may:

(a) cancel the lease contract (Section 2A–505(1));

(b) recover so much of the rent and security as has been paid and is just under the circumstances;

(c) cover and recover damages as to all goods affected whether or not they have been identified to the lease contract (Sections 2A–518 and 2A–520), or recover damages for nondelivery (Sections 2A–519 and 2A–520);

(d) exercise any other rights or pursue any other remedies provided in the lease contract.

(2) If a lessor fails to deliver the goods in conformity to the lease contract or repudiates the lease contract, the lessee may also:

(a) if the goods have been identified, recover them (Section 2A–522); or

(b) in a proper case, obtain specific performance or replevy the goods (Section 2A–521).

(3) If a lessor is otherwise in default under a lease contract, the lessee may exercise the rights and pursue the remedies provided in the lease contract, which may include a right to cancel the lease, and in Section 2A–519(3).

(4) If a lessor has breached a warranty, whether express or implied, the lessee may recover damages (Section 2A–519(4)).

(5) On rightful rejection or justifiable revocation of acceptance, a lessee has a security interest in goods in the lessee's possession or control for any rent and security that has been paid and any expenses reasonably incurred in their inspection, receipt, transportation, and care and custody and may hold those goods and dispose of them in good faith and in a commercially reasonable manner, subject to Section 2A–527(5).

(6) Subject to the provisions of Section 2A–407, a lessee, on notifying the lessor of the lessee's intention to do so, may deduct all or any part of the damages resulting from any default under the lease contract from any part of the rent still due under the same lease contract.

As amended in 1990.

§ 2A–509. Lessee's Rights on Improper Delivery; Rightful Rejection.

(1) Subject to the provisions of Section 2A–510 on default in installment lease contracts, if the goods or the tender or delivery fail in any respect to conform to the lease contract, the lessee may reject or accept the goods or accept any commercial unit or units and reject the rest of the goods.

(2) Rejection of goods is ineffective unless it is within a reasonable time after tender or delivery of the goods and the lessee seasonably notifies the lessor.

§ 2A–510. Installment Lease Contracts: Rejection and Default.

(1) Under an installment lease contract a lessee may reject any delivery that is nonconforming if the nonconformity substantially impairs the value of that delivery and cannot be cured or the nonconformity is a defect in the required documents; but if the nonconformity does not fall within subsection (2) and the lessor or the supplier gives adequate assurance of its cure, the lessee must accept that delivery.

(2) Whenever nonconformity or default with respect to one or more deliveries substantially impairs the value of the installment lease contract as a whole there is a default with respect to the whole. But, the aggrieved party reinstates the installment lease contract as a whole if the aggrieved party accepts a nonconforming delivery without seasonably notifying of cancellation or brings an action with respect only to past deliveries or demands performance as to future deliveries.

§ 2A–511. Merchant Lessee's Duties as to Rightfully Rejected Goods.

(1) Subject to any security interest of a lessee (Section 2A–508(5)), if a lessor or a supplier has no agent or place of business at the market of rejection, a merchant lessee, after rejection of goods in his [or her] possession or control, shall follow any reasonable instructions received from the lessor or the supplier with respect to the goods. In the absence of those instructions, a merchant lessee shall make reasonable efforts to sell, lease, or otherwise dispose of the goods for the lessor's account if they

threaten to decline in value speedily. Instructions are not reasonable if on demand indemnity for expenses is not forthcoming.

(2) If a merchant lessee (subsection (1)) or any other lessee (Section 2A–512) disposes of goods, he [or she] is entitled to reimbursement either from the lessor or the supplier or out of the proceeds for reasonable expenses of caring for and disposing of the goods and, if the expenses include no disposition commission, to such commission as is usual in the trade, or if there is none, to a reasonable sum not exceeding 10 percent of the gross proceeds.

(3) In complying with this section or Section 2A–512, the lessee is held only to good faith. Good faith conduct hereunder is neither acceptance or conversion nor the basis of an action for damages.

(4) A purchaser who purchases in good faith from a lessee pursuant to this section or Section 2A–512 takes the goods free of any rights of the lessor and the supplier even though the lessee fails to comply with one or more of the requirements of this Article.

§ 2A–512. Lessee's Duties as to Rightfully Rejected Goods.

(1) Except as otherwise provided with respect to goods that threaten to decline in value speedily (Section 2A–511) and subject to any security interest of a lessee (Section 2A–508(5)):

(a) the lessee, after rejection of goods in the lessee's possession, shall hold them with reasonable care at the lessor's or the supplier's disposition for a reasonable time after the lessee's seasonable notification of rejection;

(b) if the lessor or the supplier gives no instructions within a reasonable time after notification of rejection, the lessee may store the rejected goods for the lessor's or the supplier's account or ship them to the lessor or the supplier or dispose of them for the lessor's or the supplier's account with reimbursement in the manner provided in Section 2A–511; but

(c) the lessee has no further obligations with regard to goods rightfully rejected.

(2) Action by the lessee pursuant to subsection (1) is not acceptance or conversion.

§ 2A–513. Cure by Lessor of Improper Tender or Delivery; Replacement.

(1) If any tender or delivery by the lessor or the supplier is rejected because nonconforming and the time for performance has not yet expired, the lessor or the supplier may seasonably notify the lessee of the lessor's or the supplier's intention to cure and may then make a conforming delivery within the time provided in the lease contract.

(2) If the lessee rejects a nonconforming tender that the lessor or the supplier had reasonable grounds to believe would be acceptable with or without money allowance, the lessor or the supplier may have a further reasonable time to substitute a conforming tender if he [or she] seasonably notifies the lessee.

§ 2A–514. Waiver of Lessee's Objections.

(1) In rejecting goods, a lessee's failure to state a particular defect that is ascertainable by reasonable inspection precludes the lessee from relying on the defect to justify rejection or to establish default:

(a) if, stated seasonably, the lessor or the supplier could have cured it (Section 2A–513); or

(b) between merchants if the lessor or the supplier after rejection has made a request in writing for a full and final written statement of all defects on which the lessee proposes to rely.

(2) A lessee's failure to reserve rights when paying rent or other consideration against documents precludes recovery of the payment for defects apparent on the face of the documents.

§ 2A–515. Acceptance of Goods.

(1) Acceptance of goods occurs after the lessee has had a reasonable opportunity to inspect the goods and

(a) the lessee signifies or acts with respect to the goods in a manner that signifies to the lessor or the supplier that the goods are conforming or that the lessee will take or retain them in spite of their nonconformity; or

(b) the lessee fails to make an effective rejection of the goods (Section 2A–509(2)).

(2) Acceptance of a part of any commercial unit is acceptance of that entire unit.

§ 2A–516. Effect of Acceptance of Goods; Notice of Default; Burden of Establishing Default after Acceptance; Notice of Claim or Litigation to Person Answerable Over.

(1) A lessee must pay rent for any goods accepted in accordance with the lease contract, with due allowance for goods rightfully rejected or not delivered.

(2) A lessee's acceptance of goods precludes rejection of the goods accepted. In the case of a finance lease, if made with knowledge of a nonconformity, acceptance cannot be revoked because of it. In any other case, if made with knowledge of a nonconformity, acceptance cannot be revoked because of it unless the acceptance was on the reasonable assumption that the nonconformity would be seasonably cured. Acceptance does not of itself impair any other remedy provided by this Article or the lease agreement for nonconformity.

(3) If a tender has been accepted:

(a) within a reasonable time after the lessee discovers or should have discovered any default, the lessee shall notify the lessor and the supplier, if any, or be barred from any remedy against the party notified;

(b) except in the case of a consumer lease, within a reasonable time after the lessee receives notice of litigation for infringement or the like (Section 2A–211) the lessee shall notify the lessor or be barred from any remedy over for liability established by the litigation; and

(c) the burden is on the lessee to establish any default.

(4) If a lessee is sued for breach of a warranty or other obligation for which a lessor or a supplier is answerable over the following apply:

(a) The lessee may give the lessor or the supplier, or both, written notice of the litigation. If the notice states that the person notified may come in and defend and that if the person notified does not do so that person will be bound in any action against that person by the lessee by any determination of fact common to the two litigations, then unless the person notified after seasonable receipt of the notice does come in and defend that person is so bound.

(b) The lessor or the supplier may demand in writing that the lessee turn over control of the litigation including settlement if the claim is one for infringement or the like (Section 2A–211) or else be barred from any remedy over. If the demand states that the lessor or the supplier agrees to bear all expense and to satisfy any adverse judgment, then unless the lessee after seasonable receipt of the demand does turn over control the lessee is so barred.

(5) Subsections (3) and (4) apply to any obligation of a lessee to hold the lessor or the supplier harmless against infringement or the like (Section 2A–211).

As amended in 1990.

§ 2A–517. Revocation of Acceptance of Goods.

(1) A lessee may revoke acceptance of a lot or commercial unit whose nonconformity substantially impairs its value to the lessee if the lessee has accepted it:

(a) except in the case of a finance lease, on the reasonable assumption that its nonconformity would be cured and it has not been seasonably cured; or

(b) without discovery of the nonconformity if the lessee's acceptance was reasonably induced either by the lessor's assurances or, except in the case of a finance lease, by the difficulty of discovery before acceptance.

(2) Except in the case of a finance lease that is not a consumer lease, a lessee may revoke acceptance of a lot or commercial unit if the lessor defaults under the lease contract and the default substantially impairs the value of that lot or commercial unit to the lessee.

(3) If the lease agreement so provides, the lessee may revoke acceptance of a lot or commercial unit because of other defaults by the lessor.

(4) Revocation of acceptance must occur within a reasonable time after the lessee discovers or should have discovered the ground for it and before any substantial change in condition of the goods which is not caused by the nonconformity. Revocation is not effective until the lessee notifies the lessor.

(5) A lessee who so revokes has the same rights and duties with regard to the goods involved as if the lessee had rejected them.

As amended in 1990.

§ 2A–518. Cover; Substitute Goods.

(1) After a default by a lessor under the lease contract of the type described in Section 2A–508(1), or, if agreed, after other default by the lessor, the lessee may cover by making any purchase or lease of or contract to purchase or lease goods in substitution for those due from the lessor.

(2) Except as otherwise provided with respect to damages liquidated in the lease agreement (Section 2A–504) or otherwise determined pursuant to agreement of the parties (Sections 1–102(3) and 2A–503), if a lessee's cover is by lease agreement substantially similar to the original lease agreement and the new lease agreement is made in good faith and in a commercially reasonable manner, the lessee may recover from the lessor as damages (i) the present value, as of the date of the commencement of the term of the new lease agreement, of the rent under the new lease agreement applicable to that period of the new lease term which is comparable to the then remaining term of the original lease agreement minus the present value as of the same date of the total rent for the then remaining lease term of the original lease agreement, and (ii) any incidental or consequential damages, less expenses saved in consequence of the lessor's default.

(3) If a lessee's cover is by lease agreement that for any reason does not qualify for treatment under subsection (2), or is by purchase or otherwise, the lessee may recover from the lessor as if the lessee had elected not to cover and Section 2A–519 governs.

As amended in 1990.

§ 2A–519. Lessee's Damages for Non-Delivery, Repudiation, Default, and Breach of Warranty in Regard to Accepted Goods.

(1) Except as otherwise provided with respect to damages liquidated in the lease agreement (Section 2A–504) or otherwise determined pursuant to agreement of the parties (Sections 1–102(3) and 2A–503), if a lessee elects not to cover or a lessee elects to cover and the cover is by lease agreement that for any reason does not qualify for treatment under Section 2A–518(2), or is by purchase or otherwise, the measure of damages for non-delivery or repudiation by the lessor or for rejection or revocation of acceptance by the lessee is the present value, as of the date of the default, of the then market rent minus the present value as of the same date of the original rent, computed for the remaining lease term of the original lease agreement, together with incidental and consequential damages, less expenses saved in consequence of the lessor's default.

(2) Market rent is to be determined as of the place for tender or, in cases of rejection after arrival or revocation of acceptance, as of the place of arrival.

(3) Except as otherwise agreed, if the lessee has accepted goods and given notification (Section 2A–516(3)), the measure of damages for non-conforming tender or delivery or other default by a lessor is the loss resulting in the ordinary course of events from the lessor's default as determined in any manner that is reasonable together with incidental and consequential damages, less expenses saved in consequence of the lessor's default.

(4) Except as otherwise agreed, the measure of damages for breach of warranty is the present value at the time and place of acceptance of the difference between the value of the use of the goods accepted and the value if they had been as warranted for the lease term, unless special circumstances show proximate damages of a different amount, together with incidental and consequential damages, less expenses saved in consequence of the lessor's default or breach of warranty.

As amended in 1990.

§ 2A–520. Lessee's Incidental and Consequential Damages.

(1) Incidental damages resulting from a lessor's default include expenses reasonably incurred in inspection, receipt, transportation, and care and custody of goods rightfully rejected or goods the acceptance of which is justifiably revoked, any commercially reasonable charges, expenses or commissions in connection with effecting cover, and any other reasonable expense incident to the default.

(2) Consequential damages resulting from a lessor's default include:

(a) any loss resulting from general or particular requirements and needs of which the lessor at the time of contracting had reason to know and which could not reasonably be prevented by cover or otherwise; and

(b) injury to person or property proximately resulting from any breach of warranty.

§ 2A–521. Lessee's Right to Specific Performance or Replevin.

(1) Specific performance may be decreed if the goods are unique or in other proper circumstances.

(2) A decree for specific performance may include any terms and conditions as to payment of the rent, damages, or other relief that the court deems just.

(3) A lessee has a right of replevin, detinue, sequestration, claim and delivery, or the like for goods identified to the lease contract if after reasonable effort the lessee is unable to effect cover for those goods or the circumstances reasonably indicate that the effort will be unavailing.

§ 2A–522. Lessee's Right to Goods on Lessor's Insolvency.

(1) Subject to subsection (2) and even though the goods have not been shipped, a lessee who has paid a part or all of the rent and security for goods identified to a lease contract (Section 2A–217) on making and keeping good a tender of any unpaid portion of the rent and security due under the lease contract may recover the goods identified from the lessor if the lessor becomes insolvent within 10 days after receipt of the first installment of rent and security.

(2) A lessee acquires the right to recover goods identified to a lease contract only if they conform to the lease contract.

C. Default by Lessee

§ 2A–523. Lessor's Remedies.

(1) If a lessee wrongfully rejects or revokes acceptance of goods or fails to make a payment when due or repudiates with respect to a part or the whole, then, with respect to any goods involved, and with respect to all of the goods if under an installment lease contract the value of the whole lease contract is substantially impaired (Section 2A–510), the lessee is in default under the lease contract and the lessor may:

(a) cancel the lease contract (Section 2A–505(1));

(b) proceed respecting goods not identified to the lease contract (Section 2A–524);

(c) withhold delivery of the goods and take possession of goods previously delivered (Section 2A–525);

(d) stop delivery of the goods by any bailee (Section 2A–526);

(e) dispose of the goods and recover damages (Section 2A–527), or retain the goods and recover damages (Section 2A–528), or in a proper case recover rent (Section 2A–529)

(f) exercise any other rights or pursue any other remedies provided in the lease contract.

(2) If a lessor does not fully exercise a right or obtain a remedy to which the lessor is entitled under subsection (1), the lessor may recover the loss resulting in the ordinary course of events from the lessee's default as determined in any reasonable manner, together with incidental damages, less expenses saved in consequence of the lessee's default.

(3) If a lessee is otherwise in default under a lease contract, the lessor may exercise the rights and pursue the remedies provided in the lease contract, which may include a right to cancel the lease. In addition, unless otherwise provided in the lease contract:

(a) if the default substantially impairs the value of the lease contract to the lessor, the lessor may exercise the rights and pursue the remedies provided in subsections (1) or (2); or

(b) if the default does not substantially impair the value of the lease contract to the lessor, the lessor may recover as provided in subsection (2).

As amended in 1990.

§ 2A–524. Lessor's Right to Identify Goods to Lease Contract.

(1) After default by the lessee under the lease contract of the type described in Section 2A–523(1) or 2A–523(3)(a) or, if agreed, after other default by the lessee, the lessor may:

(a) identify to the lease contract conforming goods not already identified if at the time the lessor learned of the default they were in the lessor's or the supplier's possession or control; and

(b) dispose of goods (Section 2A–527(1)) that demonstrably have been intended for the particular lease contract even though those goods are unfinished.

(2) If the goods are unfinished, in the exercise of reasonable commercial judgment for the purposes of avoiding loss and of effective realization, an aggrieved lessor or the supplier may either complete manufacture and wholly identify the goods to the lease contract or cease manufacture and lease, sell, or otherwise dispose of the goods for scrap or salvage value or proceed in any other reasonable manner.

As amended in 1990.

§ 2A–525. Lessor's Right to Possession of Goods.

(1) If a lessor discovers the lessee to be insolvent, the lessor may refuse to deliver the goods.

(2) After a default by the lessee under the lease contract of the type described in Section 2A–523(1) or 2A–523(3)(a) or, if agreed, after other default by the lessee, the lessor has the right to take possession of the goods. If the lease contract so provides, the lessor may require the lessee to assemble the goods and make them available to the lessor at a place to be designated by the lessor which is reasonably convenient to both parties. Without removal, the lessor may render unusable any goods employed in trade or business, and may dispose of goods on the lessee's premises (Section 2A–527).

(3) The lessor may proceed under subsection (2) without judicial process if that can be done without breach of the peace or the lessor may proceed by action.

As amended in 1990.

§ 2A–526. Lessor's Stoppage of Delivery in Transit or Otherwise.

(1) A lessor may stop delivery of goods in the possession of a carrier or other bailee if the lessor discovers the lessee to be insolvent and may stop delivery of carload, truckload, planeload, or larger shipments of express or freight if the lessee repudiates or fails to make a payment due before delivery, whether for rent, security or otherwise under the lease contract, or for any other reason the lessor has a right to withhold or take possession of the goods.

(2) In pursuing its remedies under subsection (1), the lessor may stop delivery until

(a) receipt of the goods by the lessee;

(b) acknowledgment to the lessee by any bailee of the goods, except a carrier, that the bailee holds the goods for the lessee; or

(c) such an acknowledgment to the lessee by a carrier via reshipment or as warehouseman.

(3) (a) To stop delivery, a lessor shall so notify as to enable the bailee by reasonable diligence to prevent delivery of the goods.

(b) After notification, the bailee shall hold and deliver the goods according to the directions of the lessor, but the lessor is liable to the bailee for any ensuing charges or damages.

(c) A carrier who has issued a nonnegotiable bill of lading is not obliged to obey a notification to stop received from a person other than the consignor.

§ 2A–527. Lessor's Rights to Dispose of Goods.

(1) After a default by a lessee under the lease contract of the type described in Section 2A–523(1) or 2A–523(3)(a) or after the lessor refuses to deliver or takes possession of goods (Section 2A–525 or 2A–526), or, if agreed, after other default by a lessee, the lessor may dispose of the goods concerned or the undelivered balance thereof by lease, sale, or otherwise.

(2) Except as otherwise provided with respect to damages liquidated in the lease agreement (Section 2A–504) or otherwise determined pursuant to agreement of the parties (Sections 1–102(3) and 2A–503), if the disposition is by lease agreement substantially similar to the original lease agreement and the new lease agreement is made in good faith and in a commercially reasonable manner, the lessor may recover from the lessee as damages (i) accrued and unpaid rent as of the date of the commencement of the term of the new lease agreement, (ii) the present value, as of the same date, of the total rent for the then remaining lease term of the original lease agreement minus the present value, as of the same date, of the rent under the new lease agreement applicable to that period of the new lease term which is comparable to the then remaining term of the original lease agreement, and (iii) any incidental damages allowed under Section 2A–530, less expenses saved in consequence of the lessee's default.

(3) If the lessor's disposition is by lease agreement that for any reason does not qualify for treatment under subsection (2), or is by sale or otherwise, the lessor may recover from the lessee as if the lessor had elected not to dispose of the goods and Section 2A–528 governs.

(4) A subsequent buyer or lessee who buys or leases from the lessor in good faith for value as a result of a disposition under this section takes the goods free of the original lease contract and any rights of the original lessee even though the lessor fails to comply with one or more of the requirements of this Article.

(5) The lessor is not accountable to the lessee for any profit made on any disposition. A lessee who has rightfully rejected or justifiably revoked acceptance shall account to the lessor for any excess over the amount of the lessee's security interest (Section 2A–508(5)).

As amended in 1990.

§ 2A–528. Lessor's Damages for Non-acceptance, Failure to Pay, Repudiation, or Other Default.

(1) Except as otherwise provided with respect to damages liquidated in the lease agreement (Section 2A–504) or otherwise determined pursuant to agreement of the parties (Section 1–102(3) and 2A–503), if a lessor elects to retain the goods or a lessor elects to dispose of the goods and the disposition is by lease agreement that for any reason does not qualify for treatment under Section 2A–527(2), or is by sale or otherwise, the lessor may recover from the lessee as damages for a default of the type described in Section 2A–523(1) or 2A–523(3)(a), or if agreed, for other default of the lessee, (i) accrued and unpaid rent as of the date of the default if the lessee has never taken possession of the goods, or, if the lessee has taken possession of the goods, as of the date the lessor repossesses the goods or an earlier date on which the lessee makes a tender of the goods to the lessor, (ii) the present value as of the date determined under clause (i) of the total rent for the then remaining lease term of the original lease agreement minus the present value as of the same date of the market rent as the place where the goods are located computed for the same lease term, and (iii) any incidental damages allowed under Section 2A–530, less expenses saved in consequence of the lessee's default.

(2) If the measure of damages provided in subsection (1) is inadequate to put a lessor in as good a position as performance would have, the measure of damages is the present value of the profit, including reasonable overhead, the lessor would have made from full performance by the lessee, together with any incidental damages allowed under Section 2A–530, due allowance for costs reasonably incurred and due credit for payments or proceeds of disposition.

As amended in 1990.

§ 2A–529. Lessor's Action for the Rent.

(1) After default by the lessee under the lease contract of the type described in Section 2A–523(1) or 2A–523(3)(a) or, if agreed, after other default by the lessee, if the lessor complies with subsection (2), the lessor may recover from the lessee as damages:

(a) for goods accepted by the lessee and not repossessed by or tendered to the lessor, and for conforming goods lost or damaged within a commercially reasonable time after risk of loss passes to the lessee (Section 2A–219), (i) accrued and unpaid rent as of the date of entry of judgment in favor of the lessor (ii) the present value as of the same date of the rent for the then remaining lease term of the lease agreement, and (iii) any incidental damages allowed under Section 2A–530, less expenses saved in consequence of the lessee's default; and

(b) for goods identified to the lease contract if the lessor is unable after reasonable effort to dispose of them at a reasonable price or the circumstances reasonably indicate that effort will be unavailing, (i) accrued and unpaid rent as of the date of entry of judgment in favor of the lessor, (ii) the present value as of the same date of the rent for the then remaining lease term of the lease agreement, and (iii) any incidental damages allowed under Section 2A–530, less expenses saved in consequence of the lessee's default.

(2) Except as provided in subsection (3), the lessor shall hold for the lessee for the remaining lease term of the lease agreement any goods that have been identified to the lease contract and are in the lessor's control.

(3) The lessor may dispose of the goods at any time before collection of the judgment for damages obtained pursuant to subsection (1). If the disposition is before the end of the remaining lease term of the lease agreement, the lessor's recovery against the lessee for damages is governed by Section 2A–527 or Section 2A–528, and the lessor will cause an appropriate credit to be provided against a judgment for damages to the extent that the amount of the judgment exceeds the recovery available pursuant to Section 2A–527 or 2A–528.

(4) Payment of the judgment for damages obtained pursuant to subsection (1) entitles the lessee to the use and possession of the goods not then disposed of for the remaining lease term of and in accordance with the lease agreement.

(5) After default by the lessee under the lease contract of the type described in Section 2A–523(1) or Section 2A–523(3)(a) or, if agreed, after other default by the lessee, a lessor who is held not entitled to rent under this section must nevertheless be awarded damages for non-acceptance under Sections 2A–527 and 2A–528.

As amended in 1990.

§ 2A–530. Lessor's Incidental Damages.

Incidental damages to an aggrieved lessor include any commercially reasonable charges, expenses, or commissions incurred in stopping delivery, in the transportation, care and custody of goods after the lessee's default, in connection with return or disposition of the goods, or otherwise resulting from the default.

§ 2A–531. Standing to Sue Third Parties for Injury to Goods.

(1) If a third party so deals with goods that have been identified to a lease contract as to cause actionable injury to a party to the lease contract (a) the lessor has a right of action against the third party, and (b) the lessee also has a right of action against the third party if the lessee:

(i) has a security interest in the goods;

(ii) has an insurable interest in the goods; or

(iii) bears the risk of loss under the lease contract or has since the injury assumed that risk as against the lessor and the goods have been converted or destroyed.

(2) If at the time of the injury the party plaintiff did not bear the risk of loss as against the other party to the lease contract and there is no arrangement between them for disposition of the recovery, his [or her] suit or settlement, subject to his [or her] own interest, is as a fiduciary for the other party to the lease contract.

(3) Either party with the consent of the other may sue for the benefit of whom it may concern.

§ 2A–532. Lessor's Rights to Residual Interest.

In addition to any other recovery permitted by this Article or other law, the lessor may recover from the lessee an amount that will fully compensate the lessor for any loss of or damage to the lessor's residual interest in the goods caused by the default of the lessee.

As added in 1990.

APPENDIX D

The United Nations Convention on Contracts for the International Sale of Goods (Excerpts)

Part I. SPHERE OF APPLICATION AND GENERAL PROVISIONS

* * * *

Chapter II—General Provisions

* * * *

Article 8

(1) For the purposes of this Convention statements made by and other conduct of a party are to be interpreted according to his intent where the other party knew or could not have been unaware what that intent was.

(2) If the preceding paragraph is not applicable, statements made by and other conduct of a party are to be interpreted according to the understanding that a reasonable person of the same kind as the other party would have had in the same circumstances.

(3) In determining the intent of a party or the understanding a reasonable person would have had, due consideration is to be given to all relevant circumstances of the case including the negotiations, any practices which the parties have established between themselves, usages and any subsequent conduct of the parties.

Article 9

(1) The parties are bound by any usage to which they have agreed and by any practices which they have established between themselves.

(2) The parties are considered, unless otherwise agreed, to have impliedly made applicable to their contract or its formation a usage of which the parties knew or ought to have known and which in international trade is widely known to, and regularly observed by, parties to contracts of the type involved in the particular trade concerned.

* * * *

Article 11

A contract of sale need not be concluded in or evidenced by writing and is not subject to any other requirement as to form. It may be proved by any means, including witnesses.

* * * *

Part II. FORMATION OF THE CONTRACT

Article 14

(1) A proposal for concluding a contract addressed to one or more specific persons constitutes an offer if it is sufficiently definite and indicates the intention of the offeror to be bound in case of acceptance. A proposal is sufficiently definite if it indicates the goods and expressly or implicitly fixes or makes provision for determining the quantity and the price.

(2) A proposal other than one addressed to one or more specific persons is to be considered merely as an invitation to make offers, unless the contrary is clearly indicated by the person making the proposal.

Article 15

(1) An offer becomes effective when it reaches the offeree.

(2) An offer, even if it is irrevocable, may be withdrawn if the withdrawal reaches the offeree before or at the same time as the offer.

Article 16

(1) Until a contract is concluded an offer may be revoked if the revocation reaches the offeree before he has dispatched an acceptance.

(2) However, an offer cannot be revoked:

(a) If it indicates, whether by stating a fixed time for acceptance or otherwise, that it is irrevocable; or

(b) If it was reasonable for the offeree to rely on the offer as being irrevocable and the offeree has acted in reliance on the offer.

Article 17

An offer, even if it is irrevocable, is terminated when a rejection reaches the offeror.

Article 18

(1) A statement made by or other conduct of the offeree indicating assent to an offer is an acceptance. Silence or inactivity does not in itself amount to acceptance.

(2) An acceptance of an offer becomes effective at the moment the indication of assent reaches the offeror. An acceptance is not effective if the indication of assent does not reach the offeror within the time he has fixed or, if no time is fixed, within a reasonable time, due account being taken of the circumstances of the transaction, including the rapidity of the means of communication employed by the offeror. An oral offer must be accepted immediately unless the circumstances indicate otherwise.

(3) However, if, by virtue of the offer or as a result of practices which the parties have established between themselves or of usage, the offeree may indicate assent by performing an act, such as one relating to the dispatch of the goods or payment of the price, without notice to the offeror, the acceptance is effective at the moment the act is performed, provided that the act is performed within the period of time laid down in the preceding paragraph.

Article 19

(1) A reply to an offer which purports to be an acceptance but contains additions, limitations or other modifications is a rejection of the offer and constitutes a counter-offer.

(2) However, a reply to an offer which purports to be an acceptance but contains additional or different terms which do not materially alter the terms of the offer constitutes an acceptance, unless the offeror, without undue delay, objects orally to the discrepancy or dispatches a notice to that effect. If he does not so object, the terms of the contract are the terms of the offer with the modifications contained in the acceptance.

(3) Additional or different terms relating, among other things, to the price, payment, quality and quantity of the goods, place and time of delivery, extent of one party's liability to the other or the settlement of disputes are considered to alter the terms of the offer materially.

* * * *

Article 22

An acceptance may be withdrawn if the withdrawal reaches the offeror before or at the same time as the acceptance would have become effective.

* * * *

Part III. SALE OF GOODS

Chapter I—General Provisions

Article 25

A breach of contract committed by one of the parties is fundamental if it results in such detriment to the other party as substantially to deprive him of what he is entitled to expect under the contract, unless the party in breach did not foresee and a reasonable person of the same kind in the same circumstances would not have foreseen such a result.

* * * *

Article 28

If, in accordance with the provisions of this Convention, one party is entitled to require performance of any obligation by the other party, a court is not bound to enter a judgment for specific performance unless the court would do so under its own law in respect of similar contracts of sale not governed by this Convention.

Article 29

(1) A contract may be modified or terminated by the mere agreement of the parties.

(2) A contract in writing which contains a provision requiring any modification or termination by agreement to be in writing may not be otherwise modified or terminated by agreement. However, a party may be precluded by his conduct from asserting such a provision to the extent that the other party has relied on that conduct.

* * * *

Chapter II—Obligations of the Seller

* * * *

Section II. Conformity of the Goods and Third Party Claims

Article 35

(1) The seller must deliver goods which are of the quantity, quality and description required by the contract and which are contained or packaged in the manner required by the contract.

(2) Except where the parties have agreed otherwise, the goods do not conform with the contract unless they:

(a) Are fit for the purposes for which goods of the same description would ordinarily be used;

(b) Are fit for any particular purpose expressly or impliedly made known to the seller at the time of the conclusion of the contract, except where the circumstances show that the buyer did not rely, or that it was unreasonable for him to rely, on the seller's skill and judgment;

(c) Possess the qualities of goods which the seller has held out to the buyer as a sample or model;

(d) Are contained or packaged in the manner usual for such goods or, where there is no such manner, in a manner adequate to preserve and protect the goods.

(3) The seller is not liable under subparagraphs (a) to (d) of the preceding paragraph for any lack of conformity of the goods if at the time of the conclusion of the contract the buyer knew or could not have been unaware of such lack of conformity.

* * * *

Article 64

(1) The seller may declare the contract avoided:

(a) If the failure by the buyer to perform any of his obligations under the contract or this Convention amounts to a fundamental breach of contract; or

(b) If the buyer does not, within the additional period of time fixed by the seller in accordance with paragraph (1) of article 63, perform his obligation to pay the price or take delivery of the goods, or if he declares that he will not do so within the period so fixed.

(2) However, in cases where the buyer has paid the price, the seller loses the right to declare the contract avoided unless he does so:

(a) In respect of late performance by the buyer, before the seller has become aware that performance has been rendered; or

(b) In respect of any breach other than late performance by the buyer, within a reasonable time:

(i) After the seller knew or ought to have known of the breach; or

(ii) After the expiration of any additional period of time fixed by the seller in accordance with paragraph (1) of article 63, or after the buyer has declared that he will not perform his obligations within such an additional period.

* * * *

Chapter IV—Passing of Risk

* * * *

Article 67

(1) If the contract of sale involves carriage of the goods and the seller is not bound to hand them over at a particular place, the risk passes to the buyer when the goods are handed over to the first carrier for transmission to the buyer in accordance with the contract of sale. If the seller is bound to hand the goods over to a carrier at a particular place, the risk does not pass to the buyer until the goods are handed over to the carrier at that place. The fact that the seller is authorized to retain documents controlling the disposition of the goods does not affect the passage of the risk.

(2) Nevertheless, the risk does not pass to the buyer until the goods are clearly identified to the contract, whether by markings on the goods, by shipping documents, by notice given to the buyer or otherwise.

* * * *

Chapter V—Provisions Common to the Obligations of the Seller and of the Buyer

Section I. Anticipatory Breach and Instalment Contracts

Article 71

(1) A party may suspend the performance of his obligations if, after the conclusion of the contract, it becomes apparent that the other party will not perform a substantial part of his obligations as a result of:

(a) A serious deficiency in his ability to perform or in his creditworthiness; or

(b) His conduct in preparing to perform or in performing the contract.

(2) If the seller has already dispatched the goods before the grounds described in the preceding paragraph become evident, he may prevent the handing over of the goods to the buyer even though the buyer holds a document which entitles him to obtain them. The present paragraph relates only to the rights in the goods as between the buyer and the seller.

(3) A party suspending performance, whether before or after dispatch of the goods, must immediately give notice of the suspension to the other party and must continue with performance if the other party provides adequate assurance of his performance.

Article 72

(1) If prior to the date for performance of the contract it is clear that one of the parties will commit a fundamental breach of contract, the other party may declare the contract avoided.

(2) If time allows, the party intending to declare the contract avoided must give reasonable notice to the other party in order to permit him to provide adequate assurance of his performance.

(3) The requirements of the preceding paragraph do not apply if the other party has declared that he will not perform his obligations.

Article 73

(1) In the case of a contract for delivery of goods by instalments, if the failure of one party to perform any of his obligations in respect of any instalment constitutes a fundamental breach of contract with respect to that instalment, the other party may declare the contract avoided with respect to that instalment.

(2) If one party's failure to perform any of his obligations in respect of any instalment gives the other party good grounds to conclude that a fundamental breach of contract will occur with respect to future instalments, he may declare the contract avoided for the future, provided that he does so within a reasonable time.

(3) A buyer who declares the contract avoided in respect of any delivery may, at the same time, declare it avoided in respect of deliveries already made or of future deliveries if, by reason of their interdependence, those deliveries could not be used for the purpose contemplated by the parties at the time of the conclusion of the contract.

Section II. Damages

Article 74

Damages for breach of contract by one party consist of a sum equal to the loss, including loss of profit, suffered by the other party as a consequence of the breach. Such damages may not exceed the loss which the party in breach foresaw or ought to have foreseen at the time of the conclusion of the contract, in the light of the facts and matters of which he then knew or ought to have known, as a possible consequence of the breach of contract.

Article 75

If the contract is avoided and if, in a reasonable manner and within a reasonable time after avoidance, the buyer has bought goods in replacement or the seller has resold the goods, the party claiming damages may recover the difference between the contract price and the price in the substitute transaction as well as any further damages recoverable under article 74.

Article 76

(1) If the contract is avoided and there is a current price for the goods, the party claiming damages may, if he has not made a purchase or resale under article 75, recover the difference between the price fixed by the contract and the current price at the time of avoidance as well as any further damages recoverable under article 74. If, however, the party claiming damages has avoided the contract after taking over the goods, the current price at the time of such taking over shall be applied instead of the current price at the time of avoidance.

(2) For the purposes of the preceding paragraph, the current price is the price prevailing at the place where delivery of the goods should have been made or, if there is no current price at that place, the price at such other place as serves as a reasonable substitute, making due allowance for differences in the cost of transporting the goods.

Article 77

A party who relies on a breach of contract must take such measures as are reasonable in the circumstances to mitigate the loss, including loss of profit, resulting from the breach. If he fails to take such measures, the party in breach may claim a reduction in the damages in the amount by which the loss should have been mitigated.

APPENDIX E

The Uniform Partnership Act (Excerpts)

(The Uniform Partnership Act was amended in 1997 to provide limited liability for partners in a limited liability partnership. Over half the states, including District of Columbia, Puerto Rico, and the U.S. Virgin Islands, have adopted this latest version of the UPA.)

Article 1 GENERAL PROVISIONS

SECTION 101. Definitions In this [Act]:

* * * *

(6) "Partnership" means an association of two or more persons to carry on as co-owners a business for profit formed under Section 202, predecessor law, or comparable law of another jurisdiction.

(7) "Partnership agreement" means the agreement, whether written, oral, or implied, among the partners concerning the partnership, including amendments to the partnership agreement.

(8) "Partnership at will" means a partnership in which the partners have not agreed to remain partners until the expiration of a definite term or the completion of a particular undertaking.

(9) "Partnership interest" or "partner's interest in the partnership" means all of a partner's interests in the partnership, including the partner's transferable interest and all management and other rights.

(10) "Person" means an individual, corporation, business trust, estate, trust, partnership, association, joint venture, government, governmental subdivision, agency, or instrumentality, or any other legal or commercial entity.

* * * *

SECTION 103. Effect of Partnership Agreement; Nonwaivable Provisions.

(a) Except as otherwise provided in subsection (b), relations among the partners and between the partners and the partnership are governed by the partnership agreement. To the extent the partnership agreement does not otherwise provide, this [Act] governs relations among the partners and between the partners and the partnership.

(b) The partnership agreement may not:

(1) vary the rights and duties under Section 105 except to eliminate the duty to provide copies of statements to all of the partners;

(2) unreasonably restrict the right of access to books and records under Section 403(b);

(3) eliminate the duty of loyalty under Section 404(b) or 603(b)(3), but:

(i) the partnership agreement may identify specific types or categories of activities that do not violate the duty of loyalty, if not manifestly unreasonable; or

(ii) all of the partners or a number or percentage specified in the partnership agreement may authorize or ratify, after full disclosure of all material facts, a specific act or transaction that otherwise would violate the duty of loyalty;

(4) unreasonably reduce the duty of care under Section 404(c) or 603(b)(3);

(5) eliminate the obligation of good faith and fair dealing under Section 404(d), but the partnership agreement may prescribe the standards by which the performance of the obligation is to be measured, if the standards are not manifestly unreasonable;

(6) vary the power to dissociate as a partner under Section 602(a), except to require the notice under Section 601(1) to be in writing;

(7) vary the right of a court to expel a partner in the events specified in Section 601(5);

* * * *

SECTION 105. Execution, Filing, and Recording of Statements.

(a) A statement may be filed in the office of [the Secretary of State]. A certified copy of a statement that is filed in an office in another State may be filed in the office of [the Secretary of State]. Either filing has the effect provided in this [Act] with respect to partnership property located in or transactions that occur in this State.

(b) A certified copy of a statement that has been filed in the office of the [Secretary of State] and recorded in the office for recording transfers of real property has the effect provided for recorded statements in this [Act]. A recorded statement that is not a certified copy of a statement filed in the office of the [Secretary of State] does not have the effect provided for recorded statements in this [Act].

* * * *

SECTION 106. Governing Law.

(a) Except as otherwise provided in subsection (b), the law of the jurisdiction in which a partnership has its chief executive office governs relations among the partners and between the partners and the partnership.

(b) The law of this State governs relations among the partners and between the partners and the partnership and the liability of partners for an obligation of a limited liability partnership.

* * * *

Article 2
NATURE OF PARTNERSHIP

SECTION 201. Partnership as Entity.

(a) A partnership is an entity distinct from its partners.

(b) A limited liability partnership continues to be the same entity that existed before the filing of a statement of qualification under Section 1001.

SECTION 202. Formation of Partnership.

* * * *

(c) In determining whether a partnership is formed, the following rules apply:

(1) Joint tenancy, tenancy in common, tenancy by the entireties, joint property, common property, or part ownership does not by itself establish a partnership, even if the co-owners share profits made by the use of the property.

(2) The sharing of gross returns does not by itself establish a partnership, even if the persons sharing them have a joint or common right or interest in property from which the returns are derived.

(3) A person who receives a share of the profits of a business is presumed to be a partner in the business, unless the profits were received in payment:

(i) of a debt by installments or otherwise;

(ii) for services as an independent contractor or of wages or other compensation to an employee;

(iii) of rent;

(iv) of an annuity or other retirement or health benefit to a beneficiary, representative, or designee of a deceased or retired partner;

(v) of interest or other charge on a loan, even if the amount of payment varies with the profits of the business, including a direct or indirect present or future ownership of the collateral, or rights to income, proceeds, or increase in value derived from the collateral; or

(vi) for the sale of the goodwill of a business or other property by installments or otherwise.

SECTION 203. Partnership Property.

Property acquired by a partnership is property of the partnership and not of the partners individually.

SECTION 204. When Property is Partnership Property.

* * * *

(d) Property acquired in the name of one or more of the partners, without an indication in the instrument transferring title to the property of the person's capacity as a partner or of the existence of a partnership and without use of partnership assets, is presumed to be separate property, even if used for partnership purposes.

Article 3
RELATIONS OF PARTNERS TO PERSONS DEALING WITH PARTNERSHIP

SECTION 301. Partner Agent of Partnership.

Subject to the effect of a statement of partnership authority under Section 303:

(1) Each partner is an agent of the partnership for the purpose of its business. An act of a partner, including the execution of an instrument in the partnership name, for apparently carrying on in the ordinary course the partnership business or business of the kind carried on by the partnership binds the partnership, unless the partner had no authority to act for the partnership in the particular matter and the person with whom the partner was dealing knew or had received a notification that the partner lacked authority.

(2) An act of a partner which is not apparently for carrying on in the ordinary course the partnership business or business of the kind carried on by the partnership binds the partnership only if the act was authorized by the other partners.

* * * *

SECTION 303. Statement of Partnership Authority.

(a) A partnership may file a statement of partnership authority, which:

(1) must include:

(i) the name of the partnership;

(ii) the street address of its chief executive office and of one office in this State, if there is one;

(iii) the names and mailing addresses of all of the partners or of an agent appointed and maintained by the partnership for the purpose of subsection (b); and

(iv) the names of the partners authorized to execute an instrument transferring real property held in the name of the partnership; and

(2) may state the authority, or limitations on the authority, of some or all of the partners to enter into other transactions on behalf of the partnership and any other matter.

* * * *

(d) Except as otherwise provided in subsection (g), a filed statement of partnership authority supplements the authority of a partner to enter into transactions on behalf of the partnership as follows:

(1) Except for transfers of real property, a grant of authority contained in a filed statement of partnership authority is conclusive in favor of a person who gives value without knowledge to the contrary, so long as and to the extent that a limitation on that authority is not then contained in another filed statement. A filed cancellation of a limitation on authority revives the previous grant of authority.

(2) A grant of authority to transfer real property held in the name of the partnership contained in a certified copy of a filed statement of partnership authority recorded in the office for recording transfers of that real property is conclusive in favor of a person who gives value without knowledge to the contrary, so long as and to the extent that a certified copy of a filed statement containing a limitation on that authority is not then of record in the office for recording transfers of that real property. The recording in the office for recording transfers of that real property of a certified copy of a filed cancellation of a limitation on authority revives the previous grant of authority.

(e) A person not a partner is deemed to know of a limitation on the authority of a partner to transfer real property held in the name of the partnership if a certified copy of the filed statement containing the limitation on authority is of record in the office for recording transfers of that real property.

(f) Except as otherwise provided in subsections (d) and (e) and Sections 704 and 805, a person not a partner is not deemed to know of a limitation on the authority of a partner merely because the limitation is contained in a filed statement.

* * * *

SECTION 305. Partnership Liable for Partner's Actionable Conduct.

(a) A partnership is liable for loss or injury caused to a person, or for a penalty incurred, as a result of a wrongful act or omission, or other actionable conduct, of a partner acting in the ordinary course of business of the partnership or with authority of the partnership.

(b) If, in the course of the partnership's business or while acting with authority of the partnership, a partner receives or causes the partnership to receive money or property of a person not a partner, and the money or property is misapplied by a partner, the partnership is liable for the loss.

SECTION 306. Partner's Liability.

(a) Except as otherwise provided in subsections (b) and (c), all partners are liable jointly and severally for all obligations of the partnership unless otherwise agreed by the claimant or provided by law.

(b) A person admitted as a partner into an existing partnership is not personally liable for any partnership obligation incurred before the person's admission as a partner.

(c) An obligation of a partnership incurred while the partnership is a limited liability partnership, whether arising in contract, tort, or otherwise, is solely the obligation of the partnership. A partner is not personally liable, directly or indirectly, by way of contribution or otherwise, for such an obligation solely by reason of being or so acting as a partner. This subsection applies notwithstanding anything inconsistent in the partnership agreement that existed immediately before the vote required to become a limited liability partnership under Section 1001(b).

SECTION 307. Actions by and Against Partnership and Partners.

(a) A partnership may sue and be sued in the name of the partnership.

* * * *

(d) A judgment creditor of a partner may not levy execution against the assets of the partner to satisfy a judgment based on a claim against the partnership unless the partner is personally liable for the claim under Section 306 and:

(1) a judgment based on the same claim has been obtained against the partnership and a writ of execution on the judgment has been returned unsatisfied in whole or in part;

(2) the partnership is a debtor in bankruptcy;

(3) the partner has agreed that the creditor need not exhaust partnership assets;

(4) a court grants permission to the judgment creditor to levy execution against the assets of a partner based on a finding that partnership assets subject to

execution are clearly insufficient to satisfy the judgment, that exhaustion of partnership assets is excessively burdensome, or that the grant of permission is an appropriate exercise of the court's equitable powers; or

(5) liability is imposed on the partner by law or contract independent of the existence of the partnership.

(e) This section applies to any partnership liability or obligation resulting from a representation by a partner or purported partner under Section 308.

SECTION 308. Liability of Purported Partner.

(a) If a person, by words or conduct, purports to be a partner, or consents to being represented by another as a partner, in a partnership or with one or more persons not partners, the purported partner is liable to a person to whom the representation is made, if that person, relying on the representation, enters into a transaction with the actual or purported partnership. If the representation, either by the purported partner or by a person with the purported partner's consent, is made in a public manner, the purported partner is liable to a person who relies upon the purported partnership even if the purported partner is not aware of being held out as a partner to the claimant. If partnership liability results, the purported partner is liable with respect to that liability as if the purported partner were a partner. If no partnership liability results, the purported partner is liable with respect to that liability jointly and severally with any other person consenting to the representation.

(b) If a person is thus represented to be a partner in an existing partnership, or with one or more persons not partners, the purported partner is an agent of persons consenting to the representation to bind them to the same extent and in the same manner as if the purported partner were a partner, with respect to persons who enter into transactions in reliance upon the representation. If all of the partners of the existing partnership consent to the representation, a partnership act or obligation results. If fewer than all of the partners of the existing partnership consent to the representation, the person acting and the partners consenting to the representation are jointly and severally liable.

* * * *

Article 4
RELATIONS OF PARTNERS TO EACH OTHER AND TO PARTNERSHIP

SECTION 401. Partner's Rights and Duties.

* * * *

(b) Each partner is entitled to an equal share of the partnership profits and is chargeable with a share of the partnership losses in proportion to the partner's share of the profits.

* * * *

(f) Each partner has equal rights in the management and conduct of the partnership business.

(g) A partner may use or possess partnership property only on behalf of the partnership.

(h) A partner is not entitled to remuneration for services performed for the partnership, except for reasonable compensation for services rendered in winding up the business of the partnership.

(i) A person may become a partner only with the consent of all of the partners.

(j) A difference arising as to a matter in the ordinary course of business of a partnership may be decided by a majority of the partners. An act outside the ordinary course of business of a partnership and an amendment to the partnership agreement may be undertaken only with the consent of all of the partners.

* * * *

SECTION 403. Partner's Rights and Duties with Respect to Information.

(a) A partnership shall keep its books and records, if any, at its chief executive office.

(b) A partnership shall provide partners and their agents and attorneys access to its books and records. It shall provide former partners and their agents and attorneys access to books and records pertaining to the period during which they were partners. The right of access provides the opportunity to inspect and copy books and records during ordinary business hours. A partnership may impose a reasonable charge, covering the costs of labor and material, for copies of documents furnished.

* * * *

SECTION 404. General Standards of Partner's Conduct.

(a) The only fiduciary duties a partner owes to the partnership and the other partners are the duty of loyalty and the duty of care set forth in subsections (b) and (c).

(b) A partner's duty of loyalty to the partnership and the other partners is limited to the following:

(1) to account to the partnership and hold as trustee for it any property, profit, or benefit derived by the partner in the conduct and winding up of the partnership business or derived from a use by the partner of partnership property, including the appropriation of a partnership opportunity;

(2) to refrain from dealing with the partnership in the conduct or winding up of the partnership business as or on behalf of a party having an interest adverse to the partnership; and

(3) to refrain from competing with the partnership in the conduct of the partnership business before the dissolution of the partnership.

(c) A partner's duty of care to the partnership and the other partners in the conduct and winding up of the partnership business is limited to refraining from engaging in grossly negligent or reckless conduct, intentional misconduct, or a knowing violation of law.

(d) A partner shall discharge the duties to the partnership and the other partners under this [Act] or under the partnership agreement and exercise any rights consistently with the obligation of good faith and fair dealing.

(e) A partner does not violate a duty or obligation under this [Act] or under the partnership agreement merely because the partner's conduct furthers the partner's own interest.

* * * *

SECTION 405. Actions by Partnership and Partners.

(a) A partnership may maintain an action against a partner for a breach of the partnership agreement, or for the violation of a duty to the partnership, causing harm to the partnership.

(b) A partner may maintain an action against the partnership or another partner for legal or equitable relief, with or without an accounting as to partnership business, to:

(1) enforce the partner's rights under the partnership agreement;

(2) enforce the partner's rights under this [Act], including:

(i) the partner's rights under Sections 401, 403, or 404;

(ii) the partner's right on dissociation to have the partner's interest in the partnership purchased pursuant to Section 701 or enforce any other right under [Article] 6 or 7; or

(iii) the partner's right to compel a dissolution and winding up of the partnership business under or enforce any other right under [Article] 8; or

(3) enforce the rights and otherwise protect the interests of the partner, including rights and interests arising independently of the partnership relationship.

* * * *

Article 5
TRANSFEREES AND CREDITORS OF PARTNER

SECTION 501. Partner Not Co-Owner of Partnership Property.

A partner is not a co-owner of partnership property and has no interest in partnership property which can be transferred, either voluntarily or involuntarily.

SECTION 502. Partner's Transferable Interest in Partnership.

The only transferable interest of a partner in the partnership is the partner's share of the profits and losses of the partnership and the partner's right to receive distributions. The interest is personal property.

SECTION 503. Transfer of Partner's Transferable Interest.

(a) A transfer, in whole or in part, of a partner's transferable interest in the partnership:

(1) is permissible;

(2) does not by itself cause the partner's dissociation or a dissolution and winding up of the partnership business; and

(3) does not, as against the other partners or the partnership, entitle the transferee, during the continuance of the partnership, to participate in the management or conduct of the partnership business, to require access to information concerning partnership transactions, or to inspect or copy the partnership books or records.

* * * *

SECTION 504. Partner's Transferable Interest Subject to Charging Order.

(a) On application by a judgment creditor of a partner or of a partner's transferee, a court having jurisdiction may charge the transferable interest of the judgment debtor to satisfy the judgment. The court may appoint a receiver of the share of the distributions due or to become due to the judgment debtor in respect of the partnership and make all other orders, directions, accounts, and inquiries the judgment debtor might have made or which the circumstances of the case may require.

* * * *

Article 6
PARTNER'S DISSOCIATION

SECTION 601. Events Causing Partner's Dissociation.

A partner is dissociated from a partnership upon the occurrence of any of the following events:

(1) the partnership's having notice of the partner's express will to withdraw as a partner or on a later date specified by the partner;

(2) an event agreed to in the partnership agreement as causing the partner's dissociation;

(3) the partner's expulsion pursuant to the partnership agreement;

(4) the partner's expulsion by the unanimous vote of the other partners if:

(i) it is unlawful to carry on the partnership business with that partner;

(ii) there has been a transfer of all or substantially all of that partner's transferable interest in the partnership, other than a transfer for security purposes, or a court order charging the partner's interest, which has not been foreclosed;

(iii) within 90 days after the partnership notifies a corporate partner that it will be expelled because it has filed a certificate of dissolution or the equivalent, its charter has been revoked, or its right to conduct business has been suspended by the jurisdiction of its incorporation, there is no revocation of the certificate of dissolution or no reinstatement of its charter or its right to conduct business; or

(iv) a partnership that is a partner has been dissolved and its business is being wound up;

(5) on application by the partnership or another partner, the partner's expulsion by judicial determination because:

(i) the partner engaged in wrongful conduct that adversely and materially affected the partnership business;

(ii) the partner willfully or persistently committed a material breach of the partnership agreement or of a duty owed to the partnership or the other partners under Section 404; or

(iii) the partner engaged in conduct relating to the partnership business which makes it not reasonably practicable to carry on the business in partnership with the partner;

(6) the partner's:

(i) becoming a debtor in bankruptcy;

(ii) executing an assignment for the benefit of creditors;

(iii) seeking, consenting to, or acquiescing in the appointment of a trustee, receiver, or liquidator of that partner or of all or substantially all of that partner's property; or

(iv) failing, within 90 days after the appointment, to have vacated or stayed the appointment of a trustee, receiver, or liquidator of the partner or of all or substantially all of the partner's property obtained without the partner's consent or acquiescence, or failing within 90 days after the expiration of a stay to have the appointment vacated;

(7) in the case of a partner who is an individual:

(i) the partner's death;

(ii) the appointment of a guardian or general conservator for the partner; or

(iii) a judicial determination that the partner has otherwise become incapable of performing the partner's duties under the partnership agreement;

* * * *

SECTION 602. Partner's Power to Dissociate; Wrongful Dissociation.

(a) A partner has the power to dissociate at any time, rightfully or wrongfully, by express will pursuant to Section 601(1).

(b) A partner's dissociation is wrongful only if:

(1) it is in breach of an express provision of the partnership agreement; or

(2) in the case of a partnership for a definite term or particular undertaking, before the expiration of the term or the completion of the undertaking:

(i) the partner withdraws by express will, unless the withdrawal follows within 90 days after another partner's dissociation by death or otherwise under Section 601(6) through (10) or wrongful dissociation under this subsection;

(ii) the partner is expelled by judicial determination under Section 601(5);

(iii) the partner is dissociated by becoming a debtor in bankruptcy; or

(iv) in the case of a partner who is not an individual, trust other than a business trust, or estate, the partner is expelled or otherwise dissociated because it willfully dissolved or terminated.

(c) A partner who wrongfully dissociates is liable to the partnership and to the other partners for damages caused by the dissociation. The liability is in addition to any other obligation of the partner to the partnership or to the other partners.

SECTION 603. Effect of Partner's Dissociation.

(a) If a partner's dissociation results in a dissolution and winding up of the partnership business, [Article] 8 applies, otherwise, [Article] 7 applies.

(b) Upon a partner's dissociation:

(1) the partner's right to participate in the management and conduct of the partnership business terminates, except as otherwise provided in Section 803;

(2) the partner's duty of loyalty under Section 404(b)(3) terminates; and

(3) the partner's duty of loyalty under Section 404(b)(1) and (2) and duty of care under Section 404(c) continue only with regard to matters arising and events occurring before the partner's dissociation, unless the partner participates in winding up the partnership's business pursuant to Section 803.

Article 7
PARTNER'S DISSOCIATION WHEN BUSINESS NOT WOUND UP

SECTION 701. Purchase of Dissociated Partner's Interest.

(a) If a partner is dissociated from a partnership without resulting in a dissolution and winding up of the partnership business under Section 801, the partnership shall cause the dissociated partner's interest in the partnership to be purchased for a buyout price determined pursuant to subsection (b).

(b) The buyout price of a dissociated partner's interest is the amount that would have been distributable to the dissociating partner under Section 807(b) if, on the date of dissociation, the assets of the partnership were sold at a price equal to the greater of the liquidation value or the value based on a sale of the entire business as a going concern without the dissociated partner and the partnership were wound up as of that date. Interest must be paid from the date of dissociation to the date of payment.

(c) Damages for wrongful dissociation under Section 602(b), and all other amounts owing, whether or not presently due, from the dissociated partner to the partnership, must be offset against the buyout price. Interest must be paid from the date the amount owed becomes due to the date of payment.

* * * *

SECTION 702. Dissociated Partner's Power to Bind and Liability to Partnership.

(a) For two years after a partner dissociates without resulting in a dissolution and winding up of the partnership business, the partnership, including a surviving partnership under [Article] 9, is bound by an act of the dissociated partner which would have bound the partnership under Section 301 before dissociation only if at the time of entering into the transaction the other party:

(1) reasonably believed that the dissociated partner was then a partner;

(2) did not have notice of the partner's dissociation; and

(3) is not deemed to have had knowledge under Section 303(e) or notice under Section 704(c).

(b) A dissociated partner is liable to the partnership for any damage caused to the partnership arising from an obligation incurred by the dissociated partner after dissociation for which the partnership is liable under subsection (a).

SECTION 703. Dissociated Partner's Liability to Other Persons.

(a) A partner's dissociation does not of itself discharge the partner's liability for a partnership obligation incurred before dissociation. A dissociated partner is not liable for a partnership obligation incurred after dissociation, except as otherwise provided in subsection (b).

(b) A partner who dissociates without resulting in a dissolution and winding up of the partnership business is liable as a partner to the other party in a transaction entered into by the partnership, or a surviving partnership under [Article] 9, within two years after the partner's dissociation, only if the partner is liable for the obligation under Section 306 and at the time of entering into the transaction the other party:

(1) reasonably believed that the dissociated partner was then a partner;

(2) did not have notice of the partner's dissociation; and

(3) is not deemed to have had knowledge under Section 303(e) or notice under Section 704(c).

* * * *

SECTION 704. Statement of Dissociation.

(a) A dissociated partner or the partnership may file a statement of dissociation stating the name of the partnership and that the partner is dissociated from the partnership.

(b) A statement of dissociation is a limitation on the authority of a dissociated partner for the purposes of Section 303(d) and (e).

(c) For the purposes of Sections 702(a)(3) and 703(b)(3), a person not a partner is deemed to have notice of the dissociation 90 days after the statement of dissociation is filed.

* * * *

Article 8
WINDING UP PARTNERSHIP BUSINESS

SECTION 801. Events Causing Dissolution and Winding Up of Partnership Business.

A partnership is dissolved, and its business must be wound up, only upon the occurrence of any of the following events:

(1) in a partnership at will, the partnership's having notice from a partner, other than a partner who is dissociated under Section 601(2) through (10), of that partner's express will to withdraw as a partner, or on a later date specified by the partner;

(2) in a partnership for a definite term or particular undertaking:

(i) within 90 days after a partner's dissociation by death or otherwise under Section 601(6) through (10) or wrongful dissociation under Section 602(b), the express will of at least half of the remaining partners to wind up the partnership business, for which purpose a partner's rightful dissociation pursuant to Section 602(b)(2)(i) constitutes the expression of that partner's will to wind up the partnership business;

(ii) the express will of all of the partners to wind up the partnership business; or

(iii) the expiration of the term or the completion of the undertaking;

(3) an event agreed to in the partnership agreement resulting in the winding up of the partnership business;

(4) an event that makes it unlawful for all or substantially all of the business of the partnership to be continued, but a cure of illegality within 90 days after notice to the partnership of the event is effective retroactively to the date of the event for purposes of this section;

(5) on application by a partner, a judicial determination that:

(i) the economic purpose of the partnership is likely to be unreasonably frustrated;

(ii) another partner has engaged in conduct relating to the partnership business which makes it not reasonably practicable to carry on the business in partnership with that partner; or

(iii) it is not otherwise reasonably practicable to carry on the partnership business in conformity with the partnership agreement; or

* * * *

SECTION 802. Partnership Continues after Dissolution.

(a) Subject to subsection (b), a partnership continues after dissolution only for the purpose of winding up its business. The partnership is terminated when the winding up of its business is completed.

(b) At any time after the dissolution of a partnership and before the winding up of its business is completed, all of the partners, including any dissociating partner other than a wrongfully dissociating partner, may waive the right to have the partnership's business wound up and the partnership terminated. In that event:

(1) the partnership resumes carrying on its business as if dissolution had never occurred, and any liability incurred by the partnership or a partner after the dissolution and before the waiver is determined as if dissolution had never occurred; and

(2) the rights of a third party accruing under Section 804(1) or arising out of conduct in reliance on the dissolution before the third party knew or received a notification of the waiver may not be adversely affected.

SECTION 803. Right to Wind Up Partnership.

(a) After dissolution, a partner who has not wrongfully dissociated may participate in winding up the partnership's business, but on application of any partner, partner's legal representative, or transferee, the [designate the appropriate court], for good cause shown, may order judicial supervision of the winding up.

(b) The legal representative of the last surviving partner may wind up a partnership's business.

(c) A person winding up a partnership's business may preserve the partnership business or property as a going concern for a reasonable time, prosecute and defend actions and proceedings, whether civil, criminal, or administrative, settle and close the partnership's business, dispose of and transfer the partnership's property, discharge the partnership's liabilities, distribute the assets of the partnership pursuant to Section 807, settle disputes by mediation or arbitration, and perform other necessary acts.

SECTION 804. Partner's Power to Bind Partnership After Dissolution.

Subject to Section 805, a partnership is bound by a partner's act after dissolution that:

(1) is appropriate for winding up the partnership business; or

(2) would have bound the partnership under Section 301 before dissolution, if the other party to the transaction did not have notice of the dissolution.

SECTION 805. Statement of Dissolution.

(a) After dissolution, a partner who has not wrongfully dissociated may file a statement of dissolution stating the name of the partnership and that the partnership has dissolved and is winding up its business.

(b) A statement of dissolution cancels a filed statement of partnership authority for the purposes of Section 303(d) and is a limitation on authority for the purposes of Section 303(e).

(c) For the purposes of Sections 301 and 804, a person not a partner is deemed to have notice of the dissolution and the limitation on the partners' authority as a result of the statement of dissolution 90 days after it is filed.

* * * *

SECTION 807. Settlement of Accounts and Contributions among Partners.

(a) In winding up a partnership's business, the assets of the partnership, including the contributions of the partners required by this section, must be applied to discharge its obligations to creditors, including, to the extent permitted by law, partners who are creditors. Any surplus must be applied to pay in cash the net amount distributable to partners in accordance with their right to distributions under subsection (b).

(b) Each partner is entitled to a settlement of all partnership accounts upon winding up the partnership business. In settling accounts among the partners, profits and losses that result from the liquidation of the partnership assets must be credited and charged to the partners' accounts. The partnership shall make a distribution to a partner in an amount equal to any excess of the credits over the charges in the partner's account. A partner shall contribute to the partnership an amount equal to any excess of the charges over the credits in the partner's account but excluding from the calculation charges attributable to an obligation for which the partner is not personally liable under Section 306.

* * * *

(d) After the settlement of accounts, each partner shall contribute, in the proportion in which the partner shares partnership losses, the amount necessary to satisfy partnership obligations that were not known at the time of the settlement and for which the partner is personally liable under Section 306.

* * * *

Article 10
LIMITED LIABILITY PARTNERSHIP

SECTION 1001. Statement of Qualification.

(a) A partnership may become a limited liability partnership pursuant to this section.

(b) The terms and conditions on which a partnership becomes a limited liability partnership must be approved by the vote necessary to amend the partnership agreement except, in the case of a partnership agreement that expressly considers obligations to contribute to the partnership, the vote necessary to amend those provisions.

(c) After the approval required by subsection (b), a partnership may become a limited liability partnership by filing a statement of qualification. The statement must contain:

(1) the name of the partnership;

(2) the street address of the partnership's chief executive office and, if different, the street address of an office in this State, if any;

(3) if the partnership does not have an office in this State, the name and street address of the partnership's agent for service of process;

(4) a statement that the partnership elects to be a limited liability partnership; and

(5) a deferred effective date, if any.

* * * *

SECTION 1002. Name.

The name of a limited liability partnership must end with "Registered Limited Liability Partnership", "Limited Liability Partnership", "R.L.L.P.", "L.L.P.", "RLLP," or "LLP".

SECTION 1003. Annual Report.

(a) A limited liability partnership, and a foreign limited liability partnership authorized to transact business in this State, shall file an annual report in the office of the [Secretary of State] which contains:

(1) the name of the limited liability partnership and the State or other jurisdiction under whose laws the foreign limited liability partnership is formed;

(2) the street address of the partnership's chief executive office and, if different, the street address of an office of the partnership in this State, if any; and

(3) if the partnership does not have an office in this State, the name and street address of the partnership's current agent for service of process.

(b) An annual report must be filed between [January 1 and April 1] of each year following the calendar year in which a partnership files a statement of qualification or a foreign partnership becomes authorized to transact business in this State.

* * * *

Article 11
FOREIGN LIMITED LIABILITY PARTNERSHIP

SECTION 1101. Law Governing Foreign Limited Liability Partnership.

(a) The law under which a foreign limited liability partnership is formed governs relations among the partners and between the partners and the partnership and the liability of partners for obligations of the partnership.

* * * *

SECTION 1102. Statement of Foreign Qualification.

(a) Before transacting business in this State, a foreign limited liability partnership must file a statement of foreign qualification. The statement must contain:

(1) the name of the foreign limited liability partnership which satisfies the requirements of the State or other jurisdiction under whose law it is formed and ends with "Registered Limited Liability Partnership", "Limited Liability Partnership", "R.L.L.P.", "L.L.P.", "RLLP," or "LLP";

(2) the street address of the partnership's chief executive office and, if different, the street address of an office of the partnership in this State, if any;

(3) if there is no office of the partnership in this State, the name and street address of the partnership's agent for service of process; and

(4) a deferred effective date, if any.

* * * *

SECTION 1104. Activities Not Constituting Transacting Business.

(a) Activities of a foreign limited liability partnership which do not constitute transacting business for the purpose of this [article] include:

(1) maintaining, defending, or settling an action or proceeding;

(2) holding meetings of its partners or carrying on any other activity concerning its internal affairs;

(3) maintaining bank accounts;

(4) maintaining offices or agencies for the transfer, exchange, and registration of the partnership's own securities or maintaining trustees or depositories with respect to those securities;

(5) selling through independent contractors;

(6) soliciting or obtaining orders, whether by mail or through employees or agents or otherwise, if the orders require acceptance outside this State before they become contracts;

(7) creating or acquiring indebtedness, with or without a mortgage, or other security interest in property;

(8) collecting debts or foreclosing mortgages or other security interests in property securing the debts, and holding, protecting, and maintaining property so acquired;

(9) conducting an isolated transaction that is completed within 30 days and is not one in the course of similar transactions; and

(10) transacting business in interstate commerce.

(b) For purposes of this [article], the ownership in this State of income-producing real property or tangible personal property, other than property excluded under subsection (a), constitutes transacting business in this State.

* * * *

APPENDIX F

The Revised Uniform Limited Partnership Act (Excerpts)

Article 1
GENERAL PROVISIONS

Section 101. Definitions.

As used in this [Act], unless the context otherwise requires:

(1) "Certificate of limited partnership" means the certificate referred to in Section 201, and the certificate as amended or restated.

(2) "Contribution" means any cash, property, services rendered, or a promissory note or other binding obligation to contribute cash or property or to perform services, which a partner contributes to a limited partnership in his capacity as a partner.

(3) "Event of withdrawal of a general partner" means an event that causes a person to cease to be a general partner as provided in Section 402.

(4) "Foreign limited partnership" means a partnership formed under the laws of any state other than this State and having as partners one or more general partners and one or more limited partners.

(5) "General partner" means a person who has been admitted to a limited partnership as a general partner in accordance with the partnership agreement and named in the certificate of limited partnership as a general partner.

(6) "Limited partner" means a person who has been admitted to a limited partnership as a limited partner in accordance with the partnership agreement.

(7) "Limited partnership" and "domestic limited partnership" mean a partnership formed by two or more persons under the laws of this State and having one or more general partners and one or more limited partners.

(8) "Partner" means a limited or general partner.

(9) "Partnership agreement" means any valid agreement, written or oral, of the partners as to the affairs of a limited partnership and the conduct of its business.

(10) "Partnership interest" means a partner's share of the profits and losses of a limited partnership and the right to receive distributions of partnership assets.

(11) "Person" means a natural person, partnership, limited partnership (domestic or foreign), trust, estate, association, or corporation.

(12) "State" means a state, territory, or possession of the United States, the District of Columbia, or the Commonwealth of Puerto Rico.

Section 102. Name.

The name of each limited partnership as set forth in its certificate of limited partnership:

(1) shall contain without abbreviation the words "limited partnership";

(2) may not contain the name of a limited partner unless (i) it is also the name of a general partner or the corporate name of a corporate general partner, or (ii) the business of the limited partnership had been carried on under that name before the admission of that limited partner;

(3) may not be the same as, or deceptively similar to, the name of any corporation or limited partnership organized under the laws of this State or licensed or registered as a foreign corporation or limited partnership in this State; and

(4) may not contain the following words [here insert prohibited words].

Section 103. Reservation of Name.

(a) The exclusive right to the use of a name may be reserved by:

(1) any person intending to organize a limited partnership under this [Act] and to adopt that name;

(2) any domestic limited partnership or any foreign limited partnership registered in this State which, in either case, intends to adopt that name;

(3) any foreign limited partnership intending to register in this State and adopt that name; and

(4) any person intending to organize a foreign limited partnership and intending to have it register in this State and adopt that name.

(b) The reservation shall be made by filing with the Secretary of State an application, executed by the applicant, to reserve a specified name. If the Secretary of State finds that the name is available for use by a domestic or foreign limited partnership, he [or she] shall reserve the name for the exclusive use of the applicant for a period of 120 days. Once having so reserved a name, the same applicant may not again reserve the same name until more than 60 days after the expiration of the last 120-day period for which that applicant reserved that name. The right to the exclusive use of a reserved name may be transferred to any other person by filing in the office of the Secretary of State a notice of the transfer, executed by the applicant for whom the name was reserved and specifying the name and address of the transferee.

Section 104. Specified Office and Agent.

Each limited partnership shall continuously maintain in this State:

(1) an office, which may but need not be a place of its business in this State, at which shall be kept the records required by Section 105 to be maintained; and

(2) an agent for service of process on the limited partnership, which agent must be an individual resident of this State, a domestic corporation, or a foreign corporation authorized to do business in this State.

Section 105. Records to Be Kept.

(a) Each limited partnership shall keep at the office referred to in Section 104(1) the following:

(1) a current list of the full name and last known business address of each partner, separately identifying the general partners (in alphabetical order) and the limited partners (in alphabetical order);

(2) a copy of the certificate of limited partnership and all certificates of amendment thereto, together with executed copies of any powers of attorney pursuant to which any certificate has been executed;

(3) copies of the limited partnership's federal, state and local income tax returns and reports, if any, for the three most recent years;

(4) copies of any then effective written partnership agreements and of any financial statements of the limited partnership for the three most recent years; and

(5) unless contained in a written partnership agreement, a writing setting out:

(i) the amount of cash and a description and statement of the agreed value of the other property or services contributed by each partner and which each partner has agreed to contribute;

(ii) the times at which or events on the happening of which any additional contributions agreed to be made by each partner are to be made;

(iii) any right of a partner to receive, or of a general partner to make, distributions to a partner which include a return of all or any part of the partner's contribution; and

(iv) any events upon the happening of which the limited partnership is to be dissolved and its affairs wound up.

(b) Records kept under this section are subject to inspection and copying at the reasonable request and at the expense of any partner during ordinary business hours.

Section 106. Nature of Business.

A limited partnership may carry on any business that a partnership without limited partners may carry on except [here designate prohibited activities].

Section 107. Business Transactions of Partners with Partnership.

Except as provided in the partnership agreement, a partner may lend money to and transact other business with the limited partnership and, subject to other applicable law, has the same rights and obligations with respect thereto as a person who is not a partner.

Article 2
FORMATION; CERTIFICATE OF LIMITED PARTNERSHIP

Section 201. Certificate of Limited Partnership.

(a) In order to form a limited partnership, a certificate of limited partnership must be executed and filed in the office of the Secretary of State. The certificate shall set forth:

(1) the name of the limited partnership;

(2) the address of the office and the name and address of the agent for service of process required to be maintained by Section 104;

(3) the name and the business address of each general partner;

(4) the latest date upon which the limited partnership is to dissolve; and

(5) any other matters the general partners determine to include therein.

(b) A limited partnership is formed at the time of the filing of the certificate of limited partnership in the office of the Secretary of State or at any later time specified in the certificate of limited partnership if, in either case, there has been substantial compliance with the requirements of this section.

Section 202. Amendment to Certificate.

(a) A certificate of limited partnership is amended by filing a certificate of amendment thereto in the office of the Secretary of State. The certificate shall set forth:

(1) the name of the limited partnership;

(2) the date of filing the certificate; and

(3) the amendment to the certificate.

(b) Within 30 days after the happening of any of the following events, an amendment to a certificate of limited partnership reflecting the occurrence of the event or events shall be filed:

(1) the admission of a new general partner;

(2) the withdrawal of a general partner; or

(3) the continuation of the business under Section 801 after an event of withdrawal of a general partner.

(c) A general partner who becomes aware that any statement in a certificate of limited partnership was false when made or that any arrangements or other facts described have changed, making the certificate inaccurate in any respect, shall promptly amend the certificate.

(d) A certificate of limited partnership may be amended at any time for any other proper purpose the general partners determine.

(e) No person has any liability because an amendment to a certificate of limited partnership has not been filed to reflect the occurrence of any event referred to in subsection (b) of this section if the amendment is filed within the 30-day period specified in subsection (b).

(f) A restated certificate of limited partnership may be executed and filed in the same manner as a certificate of amendment.

Section 203. Cancellation of Certificate.

A certificate of limited partnership shall be cancelled upon the dissolution and the commencement of winding up of the partnership or at any other time there are no limited partners. A certificate of cancellation shall be filed in the office of the Secretary of State and set forth:

(1) the name of the limited partnership;

(2) the date of filing of its certificate of limited partnership;

(3) the reason for filing the certificate of cancellation;

(4) the effective date (which shall be a date certain) of cancellation if it is not to be effective upon the filing of the certificate; and

(5) any other information the general partners filing the certificate determine.

Section 204. Execution of Certificates.

(a) Each certificate required by this Article to be filed in the office of the Secretary of State shall be executed in the following manner:

(1) an original certificate of limited partnership must be signed by all general partners;

(2) a certificate of amendment must be signed by at least one general partner and by each other general partner designated in the certificate as a new general partner; and

(3) a certificate of cancellation must be signed by all general partners.

(b) Any person may sign a certificate by an attorney-in-fact, but a power of attorney to sign a certificate relating to the admission of a general partner must specifically describe the admission.

(c) The execution of a certificate by a general partner constitutes an affirmation under the penalties of perjury that the facts stated therein are true.

Section 205. Execution by Judicial Act.

If a person required by Section 204 to execute any certificate fails or refuses to do so, any other person who is adversely affected by the failure or refusal may petition the [designate the appropriate court] to direct the execution of the certificate. If the court finds that it is proper for the certificate to be executed and that any person so designated has failed or refused to execute the certificate, it shall order the Secretary of State to record an appropriate certificate.

Section 206. Filing in Office of Secretary of State.

(a) Two signed copies of the certificate of limited partnership and of any certificates of amendment or cancellation (or of any judicial decree of amendment or cancellation) shall be delivered to the Secretary of State. A person who executes a certificate as an agent or fiduciary need not exhibit evidence of his [or her] authority as a prerequisite to filing. Unless the Secretary of State finds that any certificate does not conform to law, upon receipt of all filing fees required by law he [or she] shall:

(1) endorse on each duplicate original the word "Filed" and the day, month, and year of the filing thereof;

(2) file one duplicate original in his [or her] office; and

(3) return the other duplicate original to the person who filed it or his [or her] representative.

(b) Upon the filing of a certificate of amendment (or judicial decree of amendment) in the office of the Secretary of State, the certificate of limited partnership shall be amended as set forth therein, and upon the effective date of a certificate of cancellation (or a judicial decree thereof), the certificate of limited partnership is cancelled.

Section 207. Liability for False Statement in Certificate.

If any certificate of limited partnership or certificate of amendment or cancellation contains a false statement, one who suffers loss by reliance on the statement may recover damages for the loss from:

(1) any person who executes the certificate, or causes another to execute it on his behalf, and knew, and any general partner who knew or should have known, the statement to be false at the time the certificate was executed; and

(2) any general partner who thereafter knows or should have known that any arrangement or other fact described in the certificate has changed, making the statement inaccurate in any respect within a sufficient

time before the statement was relied upon reasonably to have enabled that general partner to cancel or amend the certificate, or to file a petition for its cancellation or amendment under Section 205.

Section 208. Scope of Notice.

The fact that a certificate of limited partnership is on file in the office of the Secretary of State is notice that the partnership is a limited partnership and the persons designated therein as general partners are general partners, but it is not notice of any other fact.

Section 209. Delivery of Certificates to Limited Partners.

Upon the return by the Secretary of State pursuant to Section 206 of a certificate marked "Filed," the general partners shall promptly deliver or mail a copy of the certificate of limited partnership and each certificate of amendment or cancellation to each limited partner unless the partnership agreement provides otherwise.

Article 3
LIMITED PARTNERS

Section 301. Admission of Additional Limited Partners.

(a) A person becomes a limited partner on the later of:

(1) the date the original certificate of limited partnership is filed; or

(2) the date stated in the records of the limited partnership as the date that person becomes a limited partner.

(b) After the filing of a limited partnership's original certificate of limited partnership, a person may be admitted as an additional limited partner:

(1) in the case of a person acquiring a partnership interest directly from the limited partnership, upon compliance with the partnership agreement or, if the partnership agreement does not so provide, upon the written consent of all partners; and

(2) in the case of an assignee of a partnership interest of a partner who has the power, as provided in Section 704, to grant the assignee the right to become a limited partner, upon the exercise of that power and compliance with any conditions limiting the grant or exercise of the power.

Section 302. Voting.

Subject to Section 303, the partnership agreement may grant to all or a specified group of the limited partners the right to vote (on a per capita or other basis) upon any matter.

Section 303. Liability to Third Parties.

(a) Except as provided in subsection (d), a limited partner is not liable for the obligations of a limited partnership unless he [or she] is also a general partner or, in addition to the exercise of his [or her] rights and powers as a limited partner, he [or she] participates in the control of the business. However, if the limited partner participates in the control of the business, he [or she] is liable only to persons who transact business with the limited partnership reasonably believing, based upon the limited partner's conduct, that the limited partner is a general partner.

(b) A limited partner does not participate in the control of the business within the meaning of subsection (a) solely by doing one or more of the following:

(1) being a contractor for or an agent or employee of the limited partnership or of a general partner or being an officer, director, or shareholder of a general partner that is a corporation;

(2) consulting with and advising a general partner with respect to the business of the limited partnership;

(3) acting as surety for the limited partnership or guaranteeing or assuming one or more specific obligations of the limited partnership;

(4) taking any action required or permitted by law to bring or pursue a derivative action in the right of the limited partnership;

(5) requesting or attending a meeting of partners;

(6) proposing, approving, or disapproving, by voting or otherwise, one or more of the following matters:

(i) the dissolution and winding up of the limited partnership;

(ii) the sale, exchange, lease, mortgage, pledge, or other transfer of all or substantially all of the assets of the limited partnership;

(iii) the incurrence of indebtedness by the limited partnership other than in the ordinary course of its business;

(iv) a change in the nature of the business;

(v) the admission or removal of a general partner;

(vi) the admission or removal of a limited partner;

(vii) a transaction involving an actual or potential conflict of interest between a general partner and the limited partnership or the limited partners;

(viii) an amendment to the partnership agreement or certificate of limited partnership; or

(ix) matters related to the business of the limited partnership not otherwise enumerated in this subsection (b), which the partnership agreement states in writing may be subject to the approval or disapproval of limited partners;

(7) winding up the limited partnership pursuant to Section 803; or

(8) exercising any right or power permitted to limited partners under this [Act] and not specifically enumerated in this subsection (b).

(c) The enumeration in subsection (b) does not mean that the possession or exercise of any other powers by a limited partner constitutes participation by him [or her] in the business of the limited partnership.

(d) A limited partner who knowingly permits his [or her] name to be used in the name of the limited partnership, except under circumstances permitted by Section 102(2), is liable to creditors who extend credit to the limited partnership without actual knowledge that the limited partner is not a general partner.

Section 304. Person Erroneously Believing Himself [or Herself] Limited Partner.

(a) Except as provided in subsection (b), a person who makes a contribution to a business enterprise and erroneously but in good faith believes that he [or she] has become a limited partner in the enterprise is not a general partner in the enterprise and is not bound by its obligations by reason of making the contribution, receiving distributions from the enterprise, or exercising any rights of a limited partner, if, on ascertaining the mistake, he [or she]:

(1) causes an appropriate certificate of limited partnership or a certificate of amendment to be executed and filed; or

(2) withdraws from future equity participation in the enterprise by executing and filing in the office of the Secretary of State a certificate declaring withdrawal under this section.

(b) A person who makes a contribution of the kind described in subsection (a) is liable as a general partner to any third party who transacts business with the enterprise (i) before the person withdraws and an appropriate certificate is filed to show withdrawal, or (ii) before an appropriate certificate is filed to show that he [or she] is not a general partner, but in either case only if the third party actually believed in good faith that the person was a general partner at the time of the transaction.

Section 305. Information.

Each limited partner has the right to:

(1) inspect and copy any of the partnership records required to be maintained by Section 105; and

(2) obtain from the general partners from time to time upon reasonable demand (i) true and full information regarding the state of the business and financial condition of the limited partnership, (ii) promptly after becoming available, a copy of the limited partnership's federal, state, and local income tax returns for each year, and (iii) other information regarding the affairs of the limited partnership as is just and reasonable.

Article 4
GENERAL PARTNERS

Section 401. Admission of Additional General Partners.

After the filing of a limited partnership's original certificate of limited partnership, additional general partners may be admitted as provided in writing in the partnership agreement or, if the partnership agreement does not provide in writing for the admission of additional general partners, with the written consent of all partners.

Section 402. Events of Withdrawal.

Except as approved by the specific written consent of all partners at the time, a person ceases to be a general partner of a limited partnership upon the happening of any of the following events:

(1) the general partner withdraws from the limited partnership as provided in Section 602;

(2) the general partner ceases to be a member of the limited partnership as provided in Section 702;

(3) the general partner is removed as a general partner in accordance with the partnership agreement;

(4) unless otherwise provided in writing in the partnership agreement, the general partner: (i) makes an assignment for the benefit of creditors; (ii) files a voluntary petition in bankruptcy; (iii) is adjudicated a bankrupt or insolvent; (iv) files a petition or answer seeking for himself [or herself] any reorganization, arrangement, composition, readjustment, liquidation, dissolution, or similar relief under any statute, law, or regulation; (v) files an answer or other pleading admitting or failing to contest the material allegations of a petition filed against him [or her] in any proceeding of this nature; or (vi) seeks, consents to, or acquiesces in the appointment of a trustee, receiver, or liquidator of the general partner or of all or any substantial part of his [or her] properties;

(5) unless otherwise provided in writing in the partnership agreement, [120] days after the commencement of any proceeding against the general partner seeking reorganization, arrangement, composition, readjustment, liquidation, dissolution, or similar relief under any statute, law, or regulation, the proceeding has not been dismissed, or if within [90] days after the appointment without his [or her] consent or acquiescence of a trustee, receiver, or liquidator of the general partner or of all or any substantial part of his [or her] properties, the appointment is not vacated or stayed or within [90] days after the expiration of any such stay, the appointment is not vacated;

(6) in the case of a general partner who is a natural person,

(i) his [or her] death; or

(ii) the entry of an order by a court of competent jurisdiction adjudicating him [or her] incompetent to manage his [or her] person or his [or her] estate;

(7) in the case of a general partner who is acting as a general partner by virtue of being a trustee of a trust, the termination of the trust (but not merely the substitution of a new trustee);

(8) in the case of a general partner that is a separate partnership, the dissolution and commencement of winding up of the separate partnership;

(9) in the case of a general partner that is a corporation, the filing of a certificate of dissolution, or its equivalent, for the corporation or the revocation of its charter; or

(10) in the case of an estate, the distribution by the fiduciary of the estate's entire interest in the partnership.

Section 403. General Powers and Liabilities.

(a) Except as provided in this [Act] or in the partnership agreement, a general partner of a limited partnership has the rights and powers and is subject to the restrictions of a partner in a partnership without limited partners.

(b) Except as provided in this [Act], a general partner of a limited partnership has the liabilities of a partner in a partnership without limited partners to persons other than the partnership and the other partners. Except as provided in this [Act] or in the partnership agreement, a general partner of a limited partnership has the liabilities of a partner in a partnership without limited partners to the partnership and to the other partners.

Section 404. Contributions by General Partner.

A general partner of a limited partnership may make contributions to the partnership and share in the profits and losses of, and in distributions from, the limited partnership as a general partner. A general partner also may make contributions to and share in profits, losses, and distributions as a limited partner. A person who is both a general partner and a limited partner has the rights and powers, and is subject to the restrictions and liabilities, of a general partner and, except as provided in the partnership agreement, also has the powers, and is subject to the restrictions, of a limited partner to the extent of his [or her] participation in the partnership as a limited partner.

Section 405. Voting.

The partnership agreement may grant to all or certain identified general partners the right to vote (on a per capita or any other basis), separately or with all or any class of the limited partners, on any matter.

Article 5
FINANCE

Section 501. Form of Contribution.

The contribution of a partner may be in cash, property, or services rendered, or a promissory note or other obligation to contribute cash or property or to perform services.

Section 502. Liability for Contribution.

(a) A promise by a limited partner to contribute to the limited partnership is not enforceable unless set out in a writing signed by the limited partner.

(b) Except as provided in the partnership agreement, a partner is obligated to the limited partnership to perform any enforceable promise to contribute cash or property or to perform services, even if he [or she] is unable to perform because of death, disability, or any other reason. If a partner does not make the required contribution of property or services, he [or she] is obligated at the option of the limited partnership to contribute cash equal to that portion of the value, as stated in the partnership records required to be kept pursuant to Section 105, of the stated contribution which has not been made.

(c) Unless otherwise provided in the partnership agreement, the obligation of a partner to make a contribution or return money or other property paid or distributed in violation of this [Act] may be compromised only by consent of all partners. Notwithstanding the compromise, a creditor of a limited partnership who extends credit, or, otherwise acts in reliance on that obligation after the partner signs a writing which reflects the obligation and before the amendment or cancellation thereof to reflect the compromise may enforce the original obligation.

Section 503. Sharing of Profits and Losses.

The profits and losses of a limited partnership shall be allocated among the partners, and among classes of partners, in the manner provided in writing in the partnership agreement. If the partnership agreement does not so provide in writing, profits and losses shall be allocated on the basis of the value, as stated in the partnership records required to be kept pursuant to Section 105, of the contributions made by each partner to the extent they have been received by the partnership and have not been returned.

Section 504. Sharing of Distributions.

Distributions of cash or other assets of a limited partnership shall be allocated among the partners and among classes of partners in the manner provided in writing in the partnership agreement. If the partnership agreement does not so provide in writing, distributions shall be made on the basis of the value, as stated in the partnership records required to be kept pursuant to Section 105, of the contributions made by each partner to the extent they have been received by the partnership and have not been returned.

Article 6
DISTRIBUTIONS AND WITHDRAWAL

Section 601. Interim Distributions.

Except as provided in this Article, a partner is entitled to receive distributions from a limited partnership before his [or her] withdrawal from the limited partnership and before the dissolution and winding up thereof to the extent and at the times or upon the happening of the events specified in the partnership agreement.

Section 602. Withdrawal of General Partner.

A general partner may withdraw from a limited partnership at any time by giving written notice to the other partners, but if the withdrawal violates the partnership agreement, the limited partnership may recover from the withdrawing general partner damages for breach of the partnership agreement and offset the damages against the amount otherwise distributable to him [or her].

Section 603. Withdrawal of Limited Partner.

A limited partner may withdraw from a limited partnership at the time or upon the happening of events specified in writing in the partnership agreement. If the agreement does not specify in writing the time or the events upon the happening of which a limited partner may withdraw or a definite time for the dissolution and winding up of the limited partnership, a limited partner may withdraw upon not less than six months' prior written notice to each general partner at his [or her] address on the books of the limited partnership at its office in this State.

Section 604. Distribution Upon Withdrawal.

Except as provided in this Article, upon withdrawal any withdrawing partner is entitled to receive any distribution to which he [or she] is entitled under the partnership agreement and, if not otherwise provided in the agreement, he [or she] is entitled to receive, within a reasonable time after withdrawal, the fair value of his [or her] interest in the limited partnership as of the date of withdrawal based upon his [or her] right to share in distributions from the limited partnership.

Section 605. Distribution in Kind.

Except as provided in writing in the partnership agreement, a partner, regardless of the nature of his [or her] contribution, has no right to demand and receive any distribution from a limited partnership in any form other than cash. Except as provided in writing in the partnership agreement, a partner may not be compelled to accept a distribution of any asset in kind from a limited partnership to the extent that the percentage of the asset distributed to him [or her] exceeds a percentage of that asset which is equal to the percentage in which he [or she] shares in distributions from the limited partnership.

Section 606. Right to Distribution.

At the time a partner becomes entitled to receive a distribution, he [or she] has the status of, and is entitled to all remedies available to, a creditor of the limited partnership with respect to the distribution.

Section 607. Limitations on Distribution.

A partner may not receive a distribution from a limited partnership to the extent that, after giving effect to the distribution, all liabilities of the limited partnership, other than liabilities to partners on account of their partnership interests, exceed the fair value of the partnership assets.

Section 608. Liability Upon Return of Contribution.

(a) If a partner has received the return of any part of his [or her] contribution without violation of the partnership agreement or this [Act], he [or she] is liable to the limited partnership for a period of one year thereafter for the amount of the returned contribution, but only to the extent necessary to discharge the limited partnership's liabilities to creditors who extended credit to the limited partnership during the period the contribution was held by the partnership.

(b) If a partner has received the return of any part of his [or her] contribution in violation of the partnership agreement or this [Act], he [or she] is liable to the limited partnership for a period of six years thereafter for the amount of the contribution wrongfully returned.

(c) A partner receives a return of his [or her] contribution to the extent that a distribution to him [or her] reduces his [or her] share of the fair value of the net assets of the limited partnership below the value, as set forth in the partnership records required to be kept pursuant to Section 105, of his [or her] contribution which has not been distributed to him [or her].

Article 7
ASSIGNMENT OF PARTNERSHIP INTERESTS

Section 701. Nature of Partnership Interest.

A partnership interest is personal property.

Section 702. Assignment of Partnership Interest.

Except as provided in the partnership agreement, a partnership interest is assignable in whole or in part. An assignment of a partnership interest does not dissolve a limited partnership or entitle the assignee to become or to exercise any rights of a partner. An assignment entitles the assignee to receive, to the extent assigned, only the distribution to which the assignor would be entitled. Except as provided in the partnership agreement, a partner ceases to be a partner upon assignment of all his [or her] partnership interest.

Section 703. Rights of Creditor.

On application to a court of competent jurisdiction by any judgment creditor of a partner, the court may charge the partnership interest of the partner with payment of the unsatisfied amount of the judgment with interest. To the extent so charged, the judgment creditor has only the rights of an assignee of the partnership interest. This [Act] does not deprive any partner of the benefit of any exemption laws applicable to his [or her] partnership interest.

Section 704. Right of Assignee to Become Limited Partner.

(a) An assignee of a partnership interest, including an assignee of a general partner, may become a limited partner if and to the extent that (i) the assignor gives the assignee that right in accordance with authority described in the partnership agreement, or (ii) all other partners consent.

(b) An assignee who has become a limited partner has, to the extent assigned, the rights and powers, and is subject to the restrictions and liabilities, of a limited partner under the partnership agreement and this [Act]. An assignee who becomes a limited partner also is liable for the obligations of his [or her] assignor to make and return contributions as provided in Articles 5 and 6. However, the assignee is not obligated for liabilities unknown to the assignee at the time he [or she] became a limited partner.

(c) If an assignee of a partnership interest becomes a limited partner, the assignor is not released from his [or her] liability to the limited partnership under Sections 207 and 502.

Section 705. Power of Estate of Deceased or Incompetent Partner.

If a partner who is an individual dies or a court of competent jurisdiction adjudges him [or her] to be incompetent to manage his [or her] person or his [or her] property, the partner's executor, administrator, guardian, conservator, or other legal representative may exercise all of the partner's rights for the purpose of settling his [or her] estate or administering his [or her] property, including any power the partner had to give an assignee the right to become a limited partner. If a partner is a corporation, trust, or other entity and is dissolved or terminated, the powers of that partner may be exercised by its legal representative or successor.

Article 8
DISSOLUTION

Section 801. Nonjudicial Dissolution.

A limited partnership is dissolved and its affairs shall be wound up upon the happening of the first to occur of the following:

(1) at the time specified in the certificate of limited partnership;

(2) upon the happening of events specified in writing in the partnership agreement;

(3) written consent of all partners;

(4) an event of withdrawal of a general partner unless at the time there is at least one other general partner and the written provisions of the partnership agreement permit the business of the limited partnership to be carried on by the remaining general partner and that partner does so, but the limited partnership is not dissolved and is not required to be wound up by reason of any event of withdrawal if, within 90 days after the withdrawal, all partners agree in writing to continue the business of the limited partnership and to the appointment of one or more additional general partners if necessary or desired; or

(5) entry of a decree of judicial dissolution under Section 802.

Section 802. Judicial Dissolution.

On application by or for a partner the [designate the appropriate court] court may decree dissolution of a limited partnership whenever it is not reasonably practicable to carry on the business in conformity with the partnership agreement.

Section 803. Winding Up.

Except as provided in the partnership agreement, the general partners who have not wrongfully dissolved a limited partnership or, if none, the limited partners, may wind up the limited partnership's affairs; but the [designate the appropriate court] court may wind up the limited partnership's affairs upon application of any partner, his [or her] legal representative, or assignee.

Section 804. Distribution of Assets.

Upon the winding up of a limited partnership, the assets shall be distributed as follows:

(1) to creditors, including partners who are creditors, to the extent permitted by law, in satisfaction of liabilities of the limited partnership other than liabilities for distributions to partners under Section 601 or 604;

(2) except as provided in the partnership agreement, to partners and former partners in satisfaction of liabilities for distributions under Section 601 or 604; and

(3) except as provided in the partnership agreement, to partners first for the return of their contributions and secondly respecting their partnership interests, in the proportions in which the partners share in distributions.

Article 9
FOREIGN LIMITED PARTNERSHIPS

Section 901. Law Governing.

Subject to the Constitution of this State, (i) the laws of the state under which a foreign limited partnership is organized govern its organization and internal affairs and the liability of its limited partners, and (ii) a foreign limited partnership may not be denied registration by reason of any difference between those laws and the laws of this State.

Section 902. Registration.

Before transacting business in this State, a foreign limited partnership shall register with the Secretary of State. In order to register, a foreign limited partnership shall submit to the Secretary of State, in duplicate, an application for registration as a foreign limited partnership, signed and sworn to by a general partner and setting forth:

(1) the name of the foreign limited partnership and, if different, the name under which it proposes to register and transact business in this State;

(2) the State and date of its formation;

(3) the name and address of any agent for service of process on the foreign limited partnership whom the foreign limited partnership elects to appoint; the agent must be an individual resident of this State, a domestic corporation, or a foreign corporation having a place of business in, and authorized to do business in, this State;

(4) a statement that the Secretary of State is appointed the agent of the foreign limited partnership for service of process if no agent has been appointed under paragraph (3) or, if appointed, the agent's authority has been revoked or if the agent cannot be found or served with the exercise of reasonable diligence;

(5) the address of the office required to be maintained in the state of its organization by the laws of that state or, if not so required, of the principal office of the foreign limited partnership;

(6) the name and business address of each general partner; and

(7) the address of the office at which is kept a list of the names and addresses of the limited partners and their capital contributions, together with an undertaking by the foreign limited partnership to keep those records until the foreign limited partnership's registration in this State is cancelled or withdrawn.

Section 903. Issuance of Registration.

(a) If the Secretary of State finds that an application for registration conforms to law and all requisite fees have been paid, he [or she] shall:

> (1) endorse on the application the word "Filed", and the month, day, and year of the filing thereof;
>
> (2) file in his [or her] office a duplicate original of the application; and
>
> (3) issue a certificate of registration to transact business in this State.

(b) The certificate of registration, together with a duplicate original of the application, shall be returned to the person who filed the application or his [or her] representative.

Section 904. Name.

A foreign limited partnership may register with the Secretary of State under any name, whether or not it is the name under which it is registered in its state of organization, that includes without abbreviation the words "limited partnership" and that could be registered by a domestic limited partnership.

Section 905. Changes and Amendments.

If any statement in the application for registration of a foreign limited partnership was false when made or any arrangements or other facts described have changed, making the application inaccurate in any respect, the foreign limited partnership shall promptly file in the office of the Secretary of State a certificate, signed and sworn to by a general partner, correcting such statement.

Section 906. Cancellation of Registration.

A foreign limited partnership may cancel its registration by filing with the Secretary of State a certificate of cancellation signed and sworn to by a general partner. A cancellation does not terminate the authority of the Secretary of State to accept service of process on the foreign limited partnership with respect to [claims for relief] [causes of action] arising out of the transactions of business in this State.

Section 907. Transaction of Business Without Registration.

(a) A foreign limited partnership transacting business in this State may not maintain any action, suit, or proceeding in any court of this State until it has registered in this State.

(b) The failure of a foreign limited partnership to register in this State does not impair the validity of any contract or act of the foreign limited partnership or prevent the foreign limited partnership from defending any action, suit, or proceeding in any court of this State.

(c) A limited partner of a foreign limited partnership is not liable as a general partner of the foreign limited partnership solely by reason of having transacted business in this State without registration.

(d) A foreign limited partnership, by transacting business in this State without registration, appoints the Secretary of State as its agent for service of process with respect to [claims for relief] [causes of action] arising out of the transaction of business in this State.

Section 908. Action by [Appropriate Official].

The [designate the appropriate official] may bring an action to restrain a foreign limited partnership from transacting business in this State in violation of this Article.

Article 10

DERIVATIVE ACTIONS

Section 1001. Right of Action.

A limited partner may bring an action in the right of a limited partnership to recover a judgment in its favor if general partners with authority to do so have refused to bring the action or if an effort to cause those general partners to bring the action is not likely to succeed.

Section 1002. Proper Plaintiff.

In a derivative action, the plaintiff must be a partner at the time of bringing the action and (i) must have been a partner at the time of the transaction of which he [or she] complains or (ii) his [or her] status as a partner must have devolved upon him by operation of law or pursuant to the terms of the partnership agreement from a person who was a partner at the time of the transaction.

Section 1003. Pleading.

In a derivative action, the complaint shall set forth with particularity the effort of the plaintiff to secure initiation of the action by a general partner or the reasons for not making the effort.

Section 1004. Expenses.

If a derivative action is successful, in whole or in part, or if anything is received by the plaintiff as a result of a judgment, compromise, or settlement of an action or claim, the court may award the plaintiff reasonable expenses, including reasonable attorney's fees, and shall direct him [or her] to remit to the limited partnership the remainder of those proceeds received by him [or her].

Article 11
MISCELLANEOUS

Section 1101. Construction and Application.

This [Act] shall be so applied and construed to effectuate its general purpose to make uniform the law with respect to the subject of this [Act] among states enacting it.

Section 1102. Short Title.

This [Act] may be cited as the Uniform Limited Partnership Act.

Section 1103. Severability.

If any provision of this [Act] or its application to any person or circumstance is held invalid, the invalidity does not affect other provisions or applications of the [Act] which can be given effect without the invalid provision or application, and to this end the provisions of this [Act] are severable.

Section 1104. Effective Date, Extended Effective Date, and Repeal.

Except as set forth below, the effective date of this [Act] is ______ and the following acts [list existing limited partnership acts] are hereby repealed:

(1) The existing provisions for execution and filing of certificates of limited partnerships and amendments thereunder and cancellations thereof continue in effect until [specify time required to create central filing system], the extended effective date, and Sections 102, 103, 104, 105, 201, 202, 203, 204 and 206 are not effective until the extended effective date.

(2) Section 402, specifying the conditions under which a general partner ceases to be a member of a limited partnership, is not effective until the extended effective date, and the applicable provisions of existing law continue to govern until the extended effective date.

(3) Sections 501, 502 and 608 apply only to contributions and distributions made after the effective date of this [Act].

(4) Section 704 applies only to assignments made after the effective date of this [Act].

(5) Article 9, dealing with registration of foreign limited partnerships, is not effective until the extended effective date.

(6) Unless otherwise agreed by the partners, the applicable provisions of existing law governing allocation of profits and losses (rather than the provisions of Section 503), distributions to a withdrawing partner (rather than the provisions of Section 604), and distributions of assets upon the winding up of a limited partnership (rather than the provisions of Section 804) govern limited partnerships formed before the effective date of this [Act].

Section 1105. Rules for Cases Not Provided For in This [Act].

In any case not provided for in this [Act] the provisions of the Uniform Partnership Act govern.

Section 1106. Savings Clause.

The repeal of any statutory provision by this [Act] does not impair, or otherwise affect, the organization or the continued existence of a limited partnership existing at the effective date of this [Act], nor does the repeal of any existing statutory provision by this [Act] impair any contract or affect any right accrued before the effective date of this [Act].

THE LEGAL ENVIRONMENT OF BUSINESS ★ CROSS AND MILLER ★ JUSTICE

APPENDIX G

The Revised Model Business Corporation Act (Excerpts)

Chapter 2. INCORPORATION

§ 2.01 Incorporators

One or more persons may act as the incorporator or incorporators of a corporation by delivering articles of incorporation to the secretary of state for filing.

§ 2.02 Articles of Incorporation

(a) The articles of incorporation must set forth:

(1) a corporate name * * * ;

(2) the number of shares the corporation is authorized to issue;

(3) the street address of the corporation's initial registered office and the name of its initial registered agent at that office; and

(4) the name and address of each incorporator.

(b) The articles of incorporation may set forth:

(1) the names and addresses of the individuals who are to serve as the initial directors;

(2) provisions not inconsistent with law regarding:

(i) the purpose or purposes for which the corporation is organized;

(ii) managing the business and regulating the affairs of the corporation;

(iii) defining, limiting, and regulating the powers of the corporation, its board of directors, and shareholders;

(iv) a par value for authorized shares or classes of shares;

(v) the imposition of personal liability on shareholders for the debts of the corporation to a specified extent and upon specified conditions;

(3) any provision that under this Act is required or permitted to be set forth in the bylaws; and

(4) a provision eliminating or limiting the liability of a director to the corporation or its shareholders for money damages for any action taken, or any failure to take any action, as a director, except liability for (A) the amount of a financial benefit received by a director to which he is not entitled; (B) an intentional infliction of harm on the corporation or the shareholders; (C) [unlawful distributions]; or (D) an intentional violation of criminal law.

(c) The articles of incorporation need not set forth any of the corporate powers enumerated in this Act.

§ 2.03 Incorporation

(a) Unless a delayed effective date is specified, the corporate existence begins when the articles of incorporation are filed.

(b) The secretary of state's filing of the articles of incorporation is conclusive proof that the incorporators satisfied all conditions precedent to incorporation except in a proceeding by the state to cancel or revoke the incorporation or involuntarily dissolve the corporation.

§ 2.04 Liability for Preincorporation Transactions

All persons purporting to act as or on behalf of a corporation, knowing there was no incorporation under this Act, are jointly and severally liable for all liabilities created while so acting.

§ 2.05 Organization of Corporation

(a) After incorporation:

(1) if initial directors are named in the articles of incorporation, the initial directors shall hold an organizational meeting, at the call of a majority of the directors, to complete the organization of the corporation by appointing officers, adopting bylaws, and carrying on any other business brought before the meeting;

(2) if initial directors are not named in the articles, the incorporator or incorporators shall hold an organizational meeting at the call of a majority of the incorporators:

(i) to elect directors and complete the organization of the corporation; or

(ii) to elect a board of directors who shall complete the organization of the corporation.

(b) Action required or permitted by this Act to be taken by incorporators at an organizational meeting may be taken without a meeting if the action taken is evidenced by one or more written consents describing the action taken and signed by each incorporator.

(c) An organizational meeting may be held in or out of this state.

* * * *

Chapter 3. PURPOSES AND POWERS

§ 3.01 Purposes

(a) Every corporation incorporated under this Act has the purpose of engaging in any lawful business unless a more limited purpose is set forth in the articles of incorporation.

(b) A corporation engaging in a business that is subject to regulation under another statute of this state may incorporate under this Act only if permitted by, and subject to all limitations of, the other statute.

§ 3.02 General Powers

Unless its articles of incorporation provide otherwise, every corporation has perpetual duration and succession in its corporate name and has the same powers as an individual to do all things necessary or convenient to carry out its business and affairs, including without limitation power:

(1) to sue and be sued, complain and defend in its corporate name;

(2) to have a corporate seal, which may be altered at will, and to use it, or a facsimile of it, by impressing or affixing it or in any other manner reproducing it;

(3) to make and amend bylaws, not inconsistent with its articles of incorporation or with the laws of this state, for managing the business and regulating the affairs of the corporation;

(4) to purchase, receive, lease, or otherwise acquire, and own, hold, improve, use, and otherwise deal with, real or personal property, or any legal or equitable interest in property, wherever located;

(5) to sell, convey, mortgage, pledge, lease, exchange, and otherwise dispose of all or any part of its property;

(6) to purchase, receive, subscribe for, or otherwise acquire; own, hold, vote, use, sell, mortgage, lend, pledge, or otherwise dispose of; and deal in and with shares or other interests in, or obligations of, any other entity;

(7) to make contracts and guarantees, incur liabilities, borrow money, issue its notes, bonds, and other obligations (which may be convertible into or include the option to purchase other securities of the corporation), and secure any of its obligations by mortgage or pledge of any of its property, franchises, or income;

(8) to lend money, invest and reinvest its funds, and receive and hold real and personal property as security for repayment;

(9) to be a promoter, partner, member, associate, or manager of any partnership, joint venture, trust, or other entity;

(10) to conduct its business, locate offices, and exercise the powers granted by this Act within or without this state;

(11) to elect directors and appoint officers, employees, and agents of the corporation, define their duties, fix their compensation, and lend them money and credit;

(12) to pay pensions and establish pension plans, pension trusts, profit sharing plans, share bonus plans, share option plans, and benefit or incentive plans for any or all of its current or former directors, officers, employees, and agents;

(13) to make donations for the public welfare or for charitable, scientific, or educational purposes;

(14) to transact any lawful business that will aid governmental policy;

(15) to make payments or donations, or do any other act, not inconsistent with law, that furthers the business and affairs of the corporation.

* * * *

Chapter 5. OFFICE AND AGENT

§ 5.01 Registered Office and Registered Agent

Each corporation must continuously maintain in this state:

(1) a registered office that may be the same as any of its places of business; and

(2) a registered agent, who may be:

(i) an individual who resides in this state and whose business office is identical with the registered office;

(ii) a domestic corporation or not-for-profit domestic corporation whose business office is identical with the registered office; or

(iii) a foreign corporation or not-for-profit foreign corporation authorized to transact business in this state whose business office is identical with the registered office.

* * * *

§ 5.04 Service on Corporation

(a) A corporation's registered agent is the corporation's agent for service of process, notice, or demand required or permitted by law to be served on the corporation.

(b) If a corporation has no registered agent, or the agent cannot with reasonable diligence be served, the corporation may be served by registered or certified mail, return receipt requested, addressed to the secretary of the corporation at its principal office. Service is perfected under this subsection at the earliest of:

(1) the date the corporation receives the mail;

(2) the date shown on the return receipt, if signed on behalf of the corporation; or

(3) five days after its deposit in the United States Mail, if mailed postpaid and correctly addressed.

(c) This section does not prescribe the only means, or necessarily the required means, of serving a corporation.

Chapter 6. SHARES AND DISTRIBUTIONS

* * * *

Subchapter B. Issuance of Shares

* * * *

§ 6.21 Issuance of Shares

(a) The powers granted in this section to the board of directors may be reserved to the shareholders by the articles of incorporation.

(b) The board of directors may authorize shares to be issued for consideration consisting of any tangible or intangible property or benefit to the corporation, including cash, promissory notes, services performed, contracts for services to be performed, or other securities of the corporation.

(c) Before the corporation issues shares, the board of directors must determine that the consideration received or to be received for shares to be issued is adequate. That determination by the board of directors is conclusive insofar as the adequacy of consideration for the issuance of shares relates to whether the shares are validly issued, fully paid, and nonassessable.

(d) When the corporation receives the consideration for which the board of directors authorized the issuance of shares, the shares issued therefor are fully paid and nonassessable.

(e) The corporation may place in escrow shares issued for a contract for future services or benefits or a promissory note, or make other arrangements to restrict the transfer of the shares, and may credit distributions in respect of the shares against their purchase price, until the services are performed, the note is paid, or the benefits received. If the services are not performed, the note is not paid, or the benefits are not received, the shares escrowed or restricted and the distributions credited may be cancelled in whole or part.

* * * *

§ 6.27 Restriction on Transfer or Registration of Shares and Other Securities

(a) The articles of incorporation, bylaws, an agreement among shareholders, or an agreement between shareholders and the corporation may impose restrictions on the transfer or registration of transfer of shares of the corporation. A restriction does not affect shares issued before the restriction was adopted unless the holders of the shares are parties to the restriction agreement or voted in favor of the restriction.

(b) A restriction on the transfer or registration of transfer of shares is valid and enforceable against the holder or a transferee of the holder if the restriction is authorized by this section and its existence is noted conspicuously on the front or back of the certificate or is contained in the information statement [sent to the shareholder]. Unless so noted, a restriction is not enforceable against a person without knowledge of the restriction.

(c) A restriction on the transfer or registration of transfer of shares is authorized:

(1) to maintain the corporation's status when it is dependent on the number or identity of its shareholders;

(2) to preserve exemptions under federal or state securities law;

(3) for any other reasonable purpose.

(d) A restriction on the transfer or registration of transfer of shares may:

(1) obligate the shareholder first to offer the corporation or other persons (separately, consecutively, or simultaneously) an opportunity to acquire the restricted shares;

(2) obligate the corporate or other persons (separately, consecutively, or simultaneously) to acquire the restricted shares;

(3) require the corporation, the holders of any class of its shares, or another person to approve the transfer of the restricted shares, if the requirement is not manifestly unreasonable;

(4) prohibit the transfer of the restricted shares to designated persons or classes of persons, if the prohibition is not manifestly unreasonable.

(e) For purposes of this section, "shares" includes a security convertible into or carrying a right to subscribe for or acquire shares.

* * * *

Chapter 7. SHAREHOLDERS

Subchapter A. Meetings

§ 7.01 Annual Meeting

(a) A corporation shall hold annually at a time stated in or fixed in accordance with the bylaws a meeting of shareholders.

(b) Annual shareholders' meetings may be held in or out of this state at the place stated in or fixed in accordance with the bylaws. If no place is stated in or fixed in accordance with the bylaws, annual meetings shall be held at the corporation's principal office.

(c) The failure to hold an annual meeting at the time stated in or fixed in accordance with a corporation's bylaws does not affect the validity of any corporate action.

* * * *

§ 7.05 Notice of Meeting

(a) A corporation shall notify shareholders of the date, time, and place of each annual and special shareholders' meeting no fewer than 10 nor more than 60 days before the meeting date. Unless this Act or the articles of incorporation require otherwise, the corporation is required to give notice only to shareholders entitled to vote at the meeting.

(b) Unless this Act or the articles of incorporation require otherwise, notice of an annual meeting need not include a description of the purpose or purposes for which the meeting is called.

(c) Notice of a special meeting must include a description of the purpose or purposes for which the meeting is called.

(d) If not otherwise fixed * * *, the record date for determining shareholders entitled to notice of and to vote at an annual or special shareholders' meeting is the day before the first notice is delivered to shareholders.

(e) Unless the bylaws require otherwise, if an annual or special shareholders' meeting is adjourned to a different date, time, or place, notice need not be given of the new date, time, or place if the new date, time, or place is announced at the meeting before adjournment. * * *

* * * *

§ 7.07 Record Date

(a) The bylaws may fix or provide the manner of fixing the record date for one or more voting groups in order to determine the shareholders entitled to notice of a shareholders' meeting, to demand a special meeting, to vote, or to take any other action. If the bylaws do not fix or provide for fixing a record date, the board of directors of the corporation may fix a future date as the record date.

(b) A record date fixed under this section may not be more than 70 days before the meeting or action requiring a determination of shareholders.

(c) A determination of shareholders entitled to notice of or to vote at a shareholders' meeting is effective for any adjournment of the meeting unless the board of directors fixes a new record date, which it must do if the meeting is adjourned to a date more than 120 days after the date fixed for the original meeting.

(d) If a court orders a meeting adjourned to a date more than 120 days after the date fixed for the original meeting, it may provide that the original record date continues in effect or it may fix a new record date.

Subchapter B. Voting

§ 7.20 Shareholders' List for Meeting

(a) After fixing a record date for a meeting, a corporation shall prepare an alphabetical list of the names of all its shareholders who are entitled to notice of a shareholders' meeting. The list must be arranged by voting group (and within each voting group by class or series of shares) and show the address of and number of shares held by each shareholder.

(b) The shareholders' list must be available for inspection by any shareholder, beginning two business days after notice of the meeting is given for which the list was prepared and continuing through the meeting, at the corporation's principal office or at a place identified in the meeting notice in the city where the meeting will be held. A shareholder, his agent, or attorney is entitled on written demand to inspect and, subject to the requirements of section 16.02(c), to copy the list, during regular business hours and at his expense, during the period it is available for inspection.

(c) The corporation shall make the shareholders' list available at the meeting, and any shareholder, his agent, or attorney is entitled to inspect the list at any time during the meeting or any adjournment.

(d) If the corporation refuses to allow a shareholder, his agent, or attorney to inspect the shareholders' list before or at the meeting (or copy the list as permitted by subsection (b)), the [name or describe] court of the county where a corporation's principal office (or, if none in this state, its registered office) is located, on application of the shareholder, may summarily order the inspection or copying at the corporation's expense and may postpone the meeting for which the list was prepared until the inspection or copying is complete.

(e) Refusal or failure to prepare or make available the shareholders' list does not affect the validity of action taken at the meeting.

* * * *

§ 7.22 Proxies

(a) A shareholder may vote his shares in person or by proxy.

(b) A shareholder may appoint a proxy to vote or otherwise act for him by signing an appointment form, either personally or by his attorney-in-fact.

(c) An appointment of a proxy is effective when received by the secretary or other officer or agent authorized to tabulate votes. An appointment is valid for 11 months unless a longer period is expressly provided in the appointment form.

* * * *

§ 7.28 Voting for Directors; Cumulative Voting

(a) Unless otherwise provided in the articles of incorporation, directors are elected by a plurality of the votes cast by the shares entitled to vote in the election at a meeting at which a quorum is present.

(b) Shareholders do not have a right to cumulate their votes for directors unless the articles of incorporation so provide.

(c) A statement included in the articles of incorporation that "[all] [a designated voting group of] shareholders are entitled to cumulate their votes for directors" (or words of similar import) means that the shareholders designated are entitled to multiply the number of votes they are entitled to cast by the number of directors for whom they are entitled to vote and cast the product for a single candidate or distribute the product among two or more candidates.

(d) Shares otherwise entitled to vote cumulatively may not be voted cumulatively at a particular meeting unless:

(1) the meeting notice or proxy statement accompanying the notice states conspicuously that cumulative voting is authorized; or

(2) a shareholder who has the right to cumulate his votes gives notice to the corporation not less than 48 hours before the time set for the meeting of his intent to cumulate his votes during the meeting, and if one shareholder gives this notice all other shareholders in the same voting group participating in the election are entitled to cumulate their votes without giving further notice.

* * * *

Subchapter D. Derivative Proceedings

* * * *

§ 7.41 Standing

A shareholder may not commence or maintain a derivative proceeding unless the shareholder:

(1) was a shareholder of the corporation at the time of the act or omission complained of or became a shareholder through transfer by operation of law from one who was a shareholder at that time; and

(2) fairly and adequately represents the interests of the corporation in enforcing the right of the corporation.

§ 7.42 Demand

No shareholder may commence a derivative proceeding until:

(1) a written demand has been made upon the corporation to take suitable action; and

(2) 90 days have expired from the date the demand was made unless the shareholder has earlier been notified that the demand has been rejected by the corporation or unless irreparable injury to the corporation would result by waiting for the expiration of the 90 day period.

* * * *

Chapter 8. DIRECTORS AND OFFICERS

Subchapter A. Board of Directors

* * * *

§ 8.02 Qualifications of Directors

The articles of incorporation or bylaws may prescribe qualifications for directors. A director need not be a resident of this state or a shareholder of the corporation unless the articles of incorporation or bylaws so prescribe.

§ 8.03 Number and Election of Directors

(a) A board of directors must consist of one or more individuals, with the number specified in or fixed in accordance with the articles of incorporation or bylaws.

(b) If a board of directors has power to fix or change the number of directors, the board may increase or decrease by 30 percent or less the number of directors last approved by the shareholders, but only the shareholders may increase or decrease by more than 30 percent the number of directors last approved by the shareholders.

(c) The articles of incorporation or bylaws may establish a variable range for the size of the board of directors by fixing a minimum and maximum number of directors. If a variable range is established, the number of directors may be fixed or changed from time to time, within the minimum and maximum, by the shareholders or the board of directors. After shares are issued, only the shareholders may change the range for the size of the board or change from a fixed to a variable-range size board or vice versa.

(d) Directors are elected at the first annual shareholders' meeting and at each annual meeting thereafter unless their terms are staggered under section 8.06.

* * * *

§ 8.08 Removal of Directors by Shareholders

(a) The shareholders may remove one or more directors with or without cause unless the articles of incorporation provide that directors may be removed only for cause.

(b) If a director is elected by a voting group of shareholders, only the shareholders of that voting group may participate in the vote to remove him.

(c) If cumulative voting is authorized, a director may not be removed if the number of votes sufficient to elect him under cumulative voting is voted against his removal. If cumulative voting is not authorized, a director may be removed only if the number of votes cast to remove him exceeds the number of votes cast not to remove him.

(d) A director may be removed by the shareholders only at a meeting called for the purpose of removing him and the meeting notice must state that the purpose, or one of the purposes, of the meeting is removal of the director.

* * * *

Subchapter B. Meetings and Action of the Board

§ 8.20 Meetings

(a) The board of directors may hold regular or special meetings in or out of this state.

(b) Unless the articles of incorporation or bylaws provide otherwise, the board of directors may permit any or all directors to participate in a regular or special meeting by, or conduct the meeting through the use of, any means of communication by which all directors participating may simultaneously hear each other during the meeting. A director participating in a meeting by this means is deemed to be present in person at the meeting.

* * * *

§ 8.22 Notice of Meeting

(a) Unless the articles of incorporation or bylaws provide otherwise, regular meetings of the board of directors may be held without notice of the date, time, place, or purpose of the meeting.

(b) Unless the articles of incorporation or bylaws provide for a longer or shorter period, special meetings of the board of directors must be preceded by at least two days' notice of the date, time, and place of the meeting. The notice need not describe the purpose of the special meeting unless required by the articles of incorporation or bylaws.

* * * *

§ 8.24 Quorum and Voting

(a) Unless the articles of incorporation or bylaws require a greater number, a quorum of a board of directors consists of:

(1) a majority of the fixed number of directors if the corporation has a fixed board size; or

(2) a majority of the number of directors prescribed, or if no number is prescribed the number in office immediately before the meeting begins, if the corporation has a variable-range size board.

(b) The articles of incorporation or bylaws may authorize a quorum of a board of directors to consist of no fewer than one-third of the fixed or prescribed number of directors determined under subsection (a).

(c) If a quorum is present when a vote is taken, the affirmative vote of a majority of directors present is the act of the board of directors unless the articles of incorporation or bylaws require the vote of a greater number of directors.

(d) A director who is present at a meeting of the board of directors or a committee of the board of directors when corporate action is taken is deemed to have assented to the action taken unless: (1) he objects at the beginning of the meeting (or promptly upon his arrival) to holding it or transacting business at the meeting; (2) his dissent or abstention from the action taken is entered in the minutes of the meeting; or (3) he delivers written notice of his dissent or abstention to the presiding officer of the meeting before its adjournment or to the corporation immediately after adjournment of the meeting. The right of dissent or abstention is not available to a director who votes in favor of the action taken.

* * * *

Subchapter C. Standards of Conduct

§ 8.30 General Standards for Directors

(a) A director shall discharge his duties as a director, including his duties as a member of a committee:

(1) in good faith;

(2) with the care an ordinarily prudent person in a like position would exercise under similar circumstances; and

(3) in a manner he reasonably believes to be in the best interests of the corporation.

(b) In discharging his duties a director is entitled to rely on information, opinions, reports, or statements, including financial statements and other financial data, if prepared or presented by:

(1) one or more officers or employees of the corporation whom the director reasonably believes to be reliable and competent in the matters presented;

(2) legal counsel, public accountants, or other persons as to matters the director reasonably believes are within the person's professional or expert competence; or

(3) a committee of the board of directors of which he is not a member if the director reasonably believes the committee merits confidence.

(c) A director is not acting in good faith if he has knowledge concerning the matter in question that makes reliance otherwise permitted by subsection (b) unwarranted.

(d) A director is not liable for any action taken as a director, or any failure to take any action, if he performed the duties of his office in compliance with this section.

* * * *

Subchapter D. Officers

* * * *

§ 8.41 Duties of Officers

Each officer has the authority and shall perform the duties set forth in the bylaws or, to the extent consistent with the bylaws, the duties prescribed by the board of directors or by direction of an officer authorized by the board of directors to prescribe the duties of other officers.

§ 8.42 Standards of Conduct for Officers

(a) An officer with discretionary authority shall discharge his duties under that authority:

(1) in good faith;

(2) with the care an ordinarily prudent person in a like position would exercise under similar circumstances; and

(3) in a manner he reasonably believes to be in the best interests of the corporation.

(b) In discharging his duties an officer is entitled to rely on information, opinions, reports, or statements, including financial statements and other financial data, if prepared or presented by:

(1) one or more officers or employees of the corporation whom the officer reasonably believes to be reliable and competent in the matters presented; or

(2) legal counsel, public accountants, or other persons as to matters the officer reasonably believes are within the person's professional or expert competence.

(c) An officer is not acting in good faith if he has knowledge concerning the matter in question that makes reliance otherwise permitted by subsection (b) unwarranted.

(d) An officer is not liable for any action taken as an officer, or any failure to take any action, if he performed the duties of his office in compliance with this section.

* * * *

Chapter 11. MERGER AND SHARE EXCHANGE

§ 11.01 Merger

(a) One or more corporations may merge into another corporation if the board of directors of each corporation adopts and its shareholders (if required * * *) approve a plan of merger.

(b) The plan of merger must set forth:

(1) the name of each corporation planning to merge and the name of the surviving corporation into which each other corporation plans to merge;

(2) the terms and conditions of the merger; and

(3) the manner and basis of converting the shares of each corporation into shares, obligations, or other securities of the surviving or any other corporation or into cash or other property in whole or part.

(c) The plan of merger may set forth:

(1) amendments to the articles of incorporation of the surviving corporation; and

(2) other provisions relating to the merger.

* * * *

§ 11.04 Merger of Subsidiary

(a) A parent corporation owning at least 90 percent of the outstanding shares of each class of a subsidiary corporation may merge the subsidiary into itself without approval of the shareholders of the parent or subsidiary.

(b) The board of directors of the parent shall adopt a plan of merger that sets forth:

(1) the names of the parent and subsidiary; and

(2) the manner and basis of converting the shares of the subsidiary into shares, obligations, or other securities of the parent or any other corporation or into cash or other property in whole or part.

(c) The parent shall mail a copy or summary of the plan of merger to each shareholder of the subsidiary who does not waive the mailing requirement in writing.

(d) The parent may not deliver articles of merger to the secretary of state for filing until at least 30 days after the date it mailed a copy of the plan of merger to each shareholder of the subsidiary who did not waive the mailing requirement.

(e) Articles of merger under this section may not contain amendments to the articles of incorporation of the parent corporation (except for amendments enumerated in section 10.02).

* * * *

§ 11.06 Effect of Merger or Share Exchange

(a) When a merger takes effect:

(1) every other corporation party to the merger merges into the surviving corporation and the separate existence of every corporation except the surviving corporation ceases;

(2) the title to all real estate and other property owned by each corporation party to the merger is vested in the surviving corporation without reversion or impairment;

(3) the surviving corporation has all liabilities of each corporation party to the merger;

(4) a proceeding pending against any corporation party to the merger may be continued as if the merger did not occur or the surviving corporation may be substituted in the proceeding for the corporation whose existence ceased;

(5) the articles of incorporation of the surviving corporation are amended to the extent provided in the plan of merger; and

(6) the shares of each corporation party to the merger that are to be converted into shares, obligations, or other securities of the surviving or any other corporation or into cash or other property are converted and the former holders of the shares are entitled only to the rights provided in the articles of merger or to their rights under chapter 13.

(b) When a share exchange takes effect, the shares of each acquired corporation are exchanged as provided in the plan, and the former holders of the shares are entitled only to the exchange rights provided in the articles of share exchange or to their rights under chapter 13.

* * * *

Chapter 13. DISSENTERS' RIGHTS

Subchapter A. Right to Dissent and Obtain Payment for Shares

* * * *

§ 13.02 Right to Dissent

(a) A shareholder is entitled to dissent from, and obtain payment of the fair value of his shares in the event of, any of the following corporate actions:

(1) consummation of a plan of merger to which the corporation is a party (i) if shareholder approval is required for the merger by [statute] or the articles of incorporation and the shareholder is entitled to vote on the merger or (ii) if the corporation is a subsidiary that is merged with its parent under section 11.04;

(2) consummation of a plan of share exchange to which the corporation is a party as the corporation whose shares will be acquired, if the shareholder is entitled to vote on the plan;

(3) consummation of a sale or exchange of all, or substantially all, of the property of the corporation other than in the usual and regular course of business, if the shareholder is entitled to vote on the sale or exchange, including a sale in dissolution, but not including a sale pursuant to court order or a sale for cash pursuant to a plan by which all or substantially all of the net proceeds of the sale will be distributed to the shareholders within one year after the date of sale;

(4) an amendment of the articles of incorporation that materially and adversely affects rights in respect of a dissenter's shares because it:

(i) alters or abolishes a preferential right of the shares;

(ii) creates, alters, or abolishes a right in respect of redemption, including a provision respecting a sinking fund for the redemption or repurchase, of the shares;

(iii) alters or abolishes a preemptive right of the holder of the shares to acquire shares or other securities;

(iv) excludes or limits the right of the shares to vote on any matter, or to cumulate votes, other than a limitation by dilution through issuance of shares or other securities with similar voting rights; or

(v) reduces the number of shares owned by the shareholder to a fraction of a share if the fractional share so created is to be acquired for cash * * * ; or

(5) any corporate action taken pursuant to a shareholder vote to the extent the articles of incorporation, bylaws, or a resolution of the board of directors provides that voting or nonvoting shareholders are entitled to dissent and obtain payment for their shares.

(b) A shareholder entitled to dissent and obtain payment for his shares under this chapter may not challenge the corporate action creating his entitlement unless the action is unlawful or fraudulent with respect to the shareholder or the corporation.

* * * *

Subchapter B. Procedure for Exercise of Dissenters' Rights

* * * *

§ 13.21 Notice of Intent to Demand Payment

(a) If proposed corporate action creating dissenters' rights under section 13.02 is submitted to a vote at a shareholders' meeting, a shareholder who wishes to assert dissenters' rights (1) must deliver to the corporation before the vote is taken written notice of his intent to demand payment for his shares if the proposed action is effectuated and (2) must not vote his shares in favor of the proposed action.

(b) A shareholder who does not satisfy the requirements of subsection (a) is not entitled to payment for his shares under this chapter.

* * * *

§ 13.25 Payment

(a) * * * [A]s soon as the proposed corporate action is taken, or upon receipt of a payment demand, the corporation shall pay each dissenter * * * the amount the corporation estimates to be the fair value of his shares, plus accrued interest.

* * * *

§ 13.28 Procedure If Shareholder Dissatisfied with Payment or Offer

(a) A dissenter may notify the corporation in writing of his own estimate of the fair value of his shares and amount of interest due, and demand payment of his estimate (less any payment under section 13.25) * * * if:

(1) the dissenter believes that the amount paid under section 13.25 * * * is less than the fair value of his shares or that the interest due is incorrectly calculated;

(2) the corporation fails to make payment under section 13.25 within 60 days after the date set for demanding payment; or

(3) the corporation, having failed to take the proposed action, does not return the deposited certificates or release the transfer restrictions imposed on uncertificated shares within 60 days after the date set for demanding payment.

(b) A dissenter waives his right to demand payment under this section unless he notifies the corporation of his demand in writing under subsection (a) within 30 days after the corporation made or offered payment for his shares.

* * * *

Chapter 14. DISSOLUTION

Subchapter A. Voluntary Dissolution

* * * *

§ 14.02 Dissolution by Board of Directors and Shareholders

(a) A corporation's board of directors may propose dissolution for submission to the shareholders.

(b) For a proposal to dissolve to be adopted:

(1) the board of directors must recommend dissolution to the shareholders unless the board of directors determines that because of conflict of interest or other special circumstances it should make no recommendation and communicates the basis for its determination to the shareholders; and

(2) the shareholders entitled to vote must approve the proposal to dissolve as provided in subsection (e).

(c) The board of directors may condition its submission of the proposal for dissolution on any basis.

(d) The corporation shall notify each shareholder, whether or not entitled to vote, of the proposed shareholders' meeting in accordance with section 7.05. The notice must also state that the purpose, or one of the purposes, of the meeting is to consider dissolving the corporation.

(e) Unless the articles of incorporation or the board of directors (acting pursuant to subsection (c)) require a greater vote or a vote by voting groups, the proposal to dissolve to be adopted must be approved by a majority of all the votes entitled to be cast on that proposal.

* * * *

§ 14.05 Effect of Dissolution

(a) A dissolved corporation continues its corporate existence but may not carry on any business except that appropriate to wind up and liquidate its business and affairs, including:

(1) collecting its assets;

(2) disposing of its properties that will not be distributed in kind to its shareholders;

(3) discharging or making provision for discharging its liabilities;

(4) distributing its remaining property among its shareholders according to their interests; and

(5) doing every other act necessary to wind up and liquidate its business and affairs.

(b) Dissolution of a corporation does not:

(1) transfer title to the corporation's property;

(2) prevent transfer of its shares or securities, although the authorization to dissolve may provide for closing the corporation's share transfer records;

(3) subject its directors or officers to standards of conduct different from those prescribed in chapter 8;

(4) change quorum or voting requirements for its board of directors or shareholders; change provisions for selection, resignation, or removal of its directors or officers or both; or change provisions for amending its bylaws;

(5) prevent commencement of a proceeding by or against the corporation in its corporate name;

(6) abate or suspend a proceeding pending by or against the corporation on the effective date of dissolution; or

(7) terminate the authority of the registered agent of the corporation.

* * * *

Subchapter C. Judicial Dissolution

§ 14.30 Grounds for Judicial Dissolution

The [name or describe court or courts] may dissolve a corporation:

(1) in a proceeding by the attorney general if it is established that:

(i) the corporation obtained its articles of incorporation through fraud; or

(ii) the corporation has continued to exceed or abuse the authority conferred upon it by law;

(2) in a proceeding by a shareholder if it is established that:

(i) the directors are deadlocked in the management of the corporate affairs, the shareholders are unable to break the deadlock, and irreparable injury to the corporation is threatened or being suffered, or the business and affairs of the corporation can no longer be conducted to the advantage of the shareholders generally, because of the deadlock;

(ii) the directors or those in control of the corporation have acted, are acting, or will act in a manner that is illegal, oppressive, or fraudulent;

(iii) the shareholders are deadlocked in voting power and have failed, for a period that includes at least two consecutive annual meeting dates, to elect successors to directors whose terms have expired; or

(iv) the corporate assets are being misapplied or wasted;

(3) in a proceeding by a creditor if it is established that:

(i) the creditor's claim has been reduced to judgment, the execution on the judgment returned unsatisfied, and the corporation is insolvent; or

(ii) the corporation has admitted in writing that the creditor's claim is due and owing and the corporation is insolvent; or

(4) in a proceeding by the corporation to have its voluntary dissolution continued under court supervision.

* * * *

Chapter 16. RECORDS AND REPORTS

Subchapter A. Records

§ 16.01 Corporate Records

(a) A corporation shall keep as permanent records minutes of all meetings of its shareholders and board of directors, a record of all actions taken by the shareholders or board of directors without a meeting, and a record of all actions taken by a committee of the board of directors in place of the board of directors on behalf of the corporation.

(b) A corporation shall maintain appropriate accounting records.

(c) A corporation or its agent shall maintain a record of its shareholders, in a form that permits preparation of a list of the names and addresses of all shareholders, in alphabetical order by class of shares showing the number and class of shares held by each.

(d) A corporation shall maintain its records in written form or in another form capable of conversion into written form within a reasonable time.

(e) A corporation shall keep a copy of the following records at its principal office:

(1) its articles or restated articles of incorporation and all amendments to them currently in effect;

(2) its bylaws or restated bylaws and all amendments to them currently in effect;

(3) resolutions adopted by its board of directors creating one or more classes or series of shares, and fixing their relative rights, preferences, and limitations, if shares issued pursuant to those resolutions are outstanding;

(4) the minutes of all shareholders' meetings, and records of all action taken by shareholders without a meeting, for the past three years;

(5) all written communications to shareholders generally within the past three years, including the financial statements furnished for the past three years * * *;

(6) a list of the names and business addresses of its current directors and officers, and

(7) its most recent annual report delivered to the secretary of state * * *.

§ 16.02 Inspection of Records by Shareholders

(a) Subject to section 16.03(c), a shareholder of a corporation is entitled to inspect and copy, during regular business hours at the corporation's principal office, any of the records of the corporation described in section 16.01(e) if he gives the corporation written notice of his demand at least five business days before the date on which he wishes to inspect and copy.

(b) A shareholder of a corporation is entitled to inspect and copy, during regular business hours at a reasonable location specified by the corporation, any of the following records of the corporation if the shareholder meets the requirements of subsection (c) and gives the corporation written notice of his demand at least five business days before the date on which he wishes to inspect and copy:

(1) excerpts from minutes of any meeting of the board of directors, records of any action of a committee of the board of directors while acting in place of the board of directors on behalf of the corporation, minutes of any meeting of the shareholders, and records of action taken by the shareholders or board of directors without a meeting, to the extent not subject to inspection under section 16.02(a);

(2) accounting records of the corporation; and

(3) the record of shareholders.

(c) A shareholder may inspect and copy the records identified in subsection (b) only if:

(1) his demand is made in good faith and for a proper purpose;

(2) he describes with reasonable particularity his purpose and the records he desires to inspect; and

(3) the records are directly connected with his purpose.

(d) The right of inspection granted by this section may not be abolished or limited by a corporation's articles of incorporation or bylaws.

(e) This section does not affect:

(1) the right of a shareholder to inspect records under section 7.20 or, if the shareholder is in litigation with the corporation, to the same extent as any other litigant;

(2) the power of a court, independently of this Act, to compel the production of corporate records for examination.

(f) For purposes of this section, "shareholder" includes a beneficial owner whose shares are held in a voting trust or by a nominee on his behalf.

APPENDIX H

The Sarbanes-Oxley Act of 2002 (Excerpts and Explanatory Comments)

Note: The author's explanatory comments appear in italics following the excerpt from each section.

SECTION 302

Corporate responsibility for financial reports[1]

(a) Regulations required

The Commission shall, by rule, require, for each company filing periodic reports under section 13(a) or 15(d) of the Securities Exchange Act of 1934 (15 U.S.C. 78m, 78o(d)), that the principal executive officer or officers and the principal financial officer or officers, or persons performing similar functions, certify in each annual or quarterly report filed or submitted under either such section of such Act that—

(1) the signing officer has reviewed the report;

(2) based on the officer's knowledge, the report does not contain any untrue statement of a material fact or omit to state a material fact necessary in order to make the statements made, in light of the circumstances under which such statements were made, not misleading;

(3) based on such officer's knowledge, the financial statements, and other financial information included in the report, fairly present in all material respects the financial condition and results of operations of the issuer as of, and for, the periods presented in the report;

(4) the signing officers—

(A) are responsible for establishing and maintaining internal controls;

(B) have designed such internal controls to ensure that material information relating to the issuer and its consolidated subsidiaries is made known to such officers by others within those entities, particularly during the period in which the periodic reports are being prepared;

(C) have evaluated the effectiveness of the issuer's internal controls as of a date within 90 days prior to the report; and

(D) have presented in the report their conclusions about the effectiveness of their internal controls based on their evaluation as of that date;

(5) the signing officers have disclosed to the issuer's auditors and the audit committee of the board of directors (or persons fulfilling the equivalent function)—

(A) all significant deficiencies in the design or operation of internal controls which could adversely affect the issuer's ability to record, process, summarize, and report financial data and have identified for the issuer's auditors any material weaknesses in internal controls; and

(B) any fraud, whether or not material, that involves management or other employees who have a significant role in the issuer's internal controls; and

(6) the signing officers have indicated in the report whether or not there were significant changes in internal controls or in other factors that could significantly affect internal controls subsequent to the date of their evaluation, including any corrective actions with regard to significant deficiencies and material weaknesses.

(b) Foreign reincorporations have no effect

Nothing in this section shall be interpreted or applied in any way to allow any issuer to lessen the legal force of the statement required under this section, by an issuer having reincorporated or having engaged in any other transaction that resulted in the transfer of the corporate domicile or offices of the issuer from inside the United States to outside of the United States.

(c) Deadline

The rules required by subsection (a) of this section shall be effective not later than 30 days after July 30, 2002.

EXPLANATORY COMMENTS: *Section 302 requires the chief executive officer (CEO) and chief financial officer (CFO) of each public company to certify that they have reviewed the company's quarterly and annual reports to be filed with the Securities and Exchange Commission (SEC). The CEO and CFO must certify that, based on their knowledge, the reports do not contain any untrue statement of a material fact or any half-truth that would make the report*

1. This section of the Sarbanes-Oxley Act is codified at 15 U.S.C. Section 7241.

misleading, and that the information contained in the reports fairly presents the company's financial condition.

In addition, this section also requires the CEO and CFO to certify that they have created and designed an internal control system for their company and have recently evaluated that system to ensure that it is effectively providing them with relevant and accurate financial information. If the signing officers have found any significant deficiencies or weaknesses in the company's system or have discovered any evidence of fraud, they must have reported the situation, and any corrective actions they have taken, to the auditors and the audit committee.

SECTION 306

Insider trades during pension fund blackout periods[2]

(a) Prohibition of insider trading during pension fund blackout periods

(1) In general

Except to the extent otherwise provided by rule of the Commission pursuant to paragraph (3), it shall be unlawful for any director or executive officer of an issuer of any equity security (other than an exempted security), directly or indirectly, to purchase, sell, or otherwise acquire or transfer any equity security of the issuer (other than an exempted security) during any blackout period with respect to such equity security if such director or officer acquires such equity security in connection with his or her service or employment as a director or executive officer.

(2) Remedy

(A) In general

Any profit realized by a director or executive officer referred to in paragraph (1) from any purchase, sale, or other acquisition or transfer in violation of this subsection shall inure to and be recoverable by the issuer, irrespective of any intention on the part of such director or executive officer in entering into the transaction.

(B) Actions to recover profits

An action to recover profits in accordance with this subsection may be instituted at law or in equity in any court of competent jurisdiction by the issuer, or by the owner of any security of the issuer in the name and in behalf of the issuer if the issuer fails or refuses to bring such action within 60 days after the date of request, or fails diligently to prosecute the action thereafter, except that no such suit shall be brought more than 2 years after the date on which such profit was realized.

(3) Rulemaking authorized

The Commission shall, in consultation with the Secretary of Labor, issue rules to clarify the application of this subsection and to prevent evasion thereof. Such rules shall provide for the application of the requirements of paragraph (1) with respect to entities treated as a single employer with respect to an issuer under section 414(b), (c), (m), or (o) of Title 26 to the extent necessary to clarify the application of such requirements and to prevent evasion thereof. Such rules may also provide for appropriate exceptions from the requirements of this subsection, including exceptions for purchases pursuant to an automatic dividend reinvestment program or purchases or sales made pursuant to an advance election.

(4) Blackout period

For purposes of this subsection, the term "blackout period", with respect to the equity securities of any issuer—

(A) means any period of more than 3 consecutive business days during which the ability of not fewer than 50 percent of the participants or beneficiaries under all individual account plans maintained by the issuer to purchase, sell, or otherwise acquire or transfer an interest in any equity of such issuer held in such an individual account plan is temporarily suspended by the issuer or by a fiduciary of the plan; and

(B) does not include, under regulations which shall be prescribed by the Commission—

(i) a regularly scheduled period in which the participants and beneficiaries may not purchase, sell, or otherwise acquire or transfer an interest in any equity of such issuer, if such period is—

(I) incorporated into the individual account plan; and

(II) timely disclosed to employees before becoming participants under the individual account plan or as a subsequent amendment to the plan; or

(ii) any suspension described in subparagraph (A) that is imposed solely in connection with persons becoming participants or beneficiaries, or ceasing to be participants or beneficiaries, in an individual account plan by reason of a corporate merger, acquisition, divestiture, or similar transaction involving the plan or plan sponsor.

(5) Individual account plan

For purposes of this subsection, the term "individual account plan" has the meaning provided in section 1002(34) of Title 29, except that such term shall not include a one-participant retirement plan (within the meaning of section 1021(i)(8)(B) of Title 29).

(6) Notice to directors, executive officers, and the Commission

2. Codified at 15 U.S.C. Section 7244.

In any case in which a director or executive officer is subject to the requirements of this subsection in connection with a blackout period (as defined in paragraph (4)) with respect to any equity securities, the issuer of such equity securities shall timely notify such director or officer and the Securities and Exchange Commission of such blackout period.

* * * *

EXPLANATORY COMMENTS: *Corporate pension funds typically prohibit employees from trading shares of the corporation during periods when the pension fund is undergoing significant change. Prior to 2002, however, these blackout periods did not affect the corporation's executives, who frequently received shares of the corporate stock as part of their compensation. During the collapse of Enron, for example, its pension plan was scheduled to change administrators at a time when Enron's stock price was falling. Enron's employees therefore could not sell their shares while the price was dropping, but its executives could and did sell their stock, consequently avoiding some of the losses. Section 306 was Congress's solution to the basic unfairness of this situation. This section of the act required the SEC to issue rules that prohibit any director or executive officer from trading during pension fund blackout periods. (The SEC later issued these rules, entitled Regulation Blackout Trading Restriction, or Reg BTR.) Section 306 also provided shareholders with a right to file a shareholder's derivative suit against officers and directors who have profited from trading during these blackout periods (provided that the corporation has failed to bring a suit). The officer or director can be forced to return to the corporation any profits received, regardless of whether the director or officer acted with bad intent.*

SECTION 402

Periodical and other reports[3]

* * * *

(i) Accuracy of financial reports

Each financial report that contains financial statements, and that is required to be prepared in accordance with (or reconciled to) generally accepted accounting principles under this chapter and filed with the Commission shall reflect all material correcting adjustments that have been identified by a registered public accounting firm in accordance with generally accepted accounting principles and the rules and regulations of the Commission.

(j) Off-balance sheet transactions

Not later than 180 days after July 30, 2002, the Commission shall issue final rules providing that each annual and quarterly financial report required to be filed with the Commission shall disclose all material off-balance sheet transactions, arrangements, obligations (including contingent obligations), and other relationships of the issuer with unconsolidated entities or other persons, that may have a material current or future effect on financial condition, changes in financial condition, results of operations, liquidity, capital expenditures, capital resources, or significant components of revenues or expenses.

(k) Prohibition on personal loans to executives

(1) In general

It shall be unlawful for any issuer (as defined in section 7201 of this title), directly or indirectly, including through any subsidiary, to extend or maintain credit, to arrange for the extension of credit, or to renew an extension of credit, in the form of a personal loan to or for any director or executive officer (or equivalent thereof) of that issuer. An extension of credit maintained by the issuer on July 30, 2002, shall not be subject to the provisions of this subsection, provided that there is no material modification to any term of any such extension of credit or any renewal of any such extension of credit on or after July 30, 2002.

(2) Limitation

Paragraph (1) does not preclude any home improvement and manufactured home loans (as that term is defined in section 1464 of Title 12), consumer credit (as defined in section 1602 of this title), or any extension of credit under an open end credit plan (as defined in section 1602 of this title), or a charge card (as defined in section 1637(c)(4)(e) of this title), or any extension of credit by a broker or dealer registered under section 78o of this title to an employee of that broker or dealer to buy, trade, or carry securities, that is permitted under rules or regulations of the Board of Governors of the Federal Reserve System pursuant to section 78g of this title (other than an extension of credit that would be used to purchase the stock of that issuer), that is—

(A) made or provided in the ordinary course of the consumer credit business of such issuer;

(B) of a type that is generally made available by such issuer to the public; and

(C) made by such issuer on market terms, or terms that are no more favorable than those offered by the issuer to the general public for such extensions of credit.

(3) Rule of construction for certain loans

Paragraph (1) does not apply to any loan made or maintained by an insured depository institution (as defined in section 1813 of Title 12), if the loan is subject to the insider lending restrictions of section 375b of Title 12.

(l) Real time issuer disclosures

Each issuer reporting under subsection (a) of this section or section 78o(d) of this title shall disclose to the public on a rapid and current basis such additional information concerning material changes in the financial condition or operations of the issuer, in plain English, which may

3. This section of the Sarbanes-Oxley Act amended some of the provisions of the 1934 Securities Exchange Act and added the paragraphs reproduced here at 15 U.S.C. Section 78m.

include trend and qualitative information and graphic presentations, as the Commission determines, by rule, is necessary or useful for the protection of investors and in the public interest.

EXPLANATORY COMMENTS: *Corporate executives during the Enron era typically received extremely large salaries, significant bonuses, and abundant stock options, even when the companies for which they worked were suffering. Executives were also routinely given personal loans from corporate funds, many of which were never paid back. The average large company during that period loaned almost $1 million a year to top executives, and some companies, including Tyco International and Adelphia Communications Corporation, loaned hundreds of millions of dollars to their executives every year. Section 402 amended the 1934 Securities Exchange Act to prohibit public companies from making personal loans to executive officers and directors. There are a few exceptions to this prohibition, such as home-improvement loans made in the ordinary course of business. Note also that while loans are forbidden, outright gifts are not. A corporation is free to give gifts to its executives, including cash, provided that these gifts are disclosed on its financial reports. The idea is that corporate directors will be deterred from making substantial gifts to their executives by the disclosure requirement—particularly if the corporation's financial condition is questionable—because making such gifts could be perceived as abusing their authority.*

SECTION 403

Directors, officers, and principal stockholders[4]

(a) Disclosures required

(1) Directors, officers, and principal stockholders required to file

Every person who is directly or indirectly the beneficial owner of more than 10 percent of any class of any equity security (other than an exempted security) which is registered pursuant to section 78l of this title, or who is a director or an officer of the issuer of such security, shall file the statements required by this subsection with the Commission (and, if such security is registered on a national securities exchange, also with the exchange).

(2) Time of filing

The statements required by this subsection shall be filed—

(A) at the time of the registration of such security on a national securities exchange or by the effective date of a registration statement filed pursuant to section 78l(g) of this title;

(B) within 10 days after he or she becomes such beneficial owner, director, or officer;

(C) if there has been a change in such ownership, or if such person shall have purchased or sold a security-based swap agreement (as defined in section 206(b) of the Gramm-Leach-Bliley Act (15 U.S.C. 78c note)) involving such equity security, before the end of the second business day following the day on which the subject transaction has been executed, or at such other time as the Commission shall establish, by rule, in any case in which the Commission determines that such 2-day period is not feasible.

(3) Contents of statements

A statement filed—

(A) under subparagraph (A) or (B) of paragraph (2) shall contain a statement of the amount of all equity securities of such issuer of which the filing person is the beneficial owner; and

(B) under subparagraph (C) of such paragraph shall indicate ownership by the filing person at the date of filing, any such changes in such ownership, and such purchases and sales of the security-based swap agreements as have occurred since the most recent such filing under such subparagraph.

(4) Electronic filing and availability

Beginning not later than 1 year after July 30, 2002—

(A) a statement filed under subparagraph (C) of paragraph (2) shall be filed electronically;

(B) the Commission shall provide each such statement on a publicly accessible Internet site not later than the end of the business day following that filing; and

(C) the issuer (if the issuer maintains a corporate website) shall provide that statement on that corporate website, not later than the end of the business day following that filing.

* * * *

EXPLANATORY COMMENTS: *This section dramatically shortens the time period provided in the Securities Exchange Act of 1934 for disclosing transactions by insiders. The prior law stated that most transactions had to be reported within ten days of the beginning of the following month, although certain transactions did not have to be reported until the following fiscal year (within the first forty-five days). Because some of the insider trading that occurred during the Enron fiasco did not have to be disclosed (and was therefore not discovered) until long after the transactions, Congress added this section to reduce the time period for making disclosures. Under Section 403, most transactions by insiders must be electronically filed with the SEC within two business days. Also, any company that maintains a Web site must post these SEC filings on its site by the end of the next business day. Congress enacted this section in the belief that if insiders are required to file reports of their transactions promptly with the SEC, companies will do more to police themselves and prevent insider trading.*

4. This section of the Sarbanes-Oxley Act amended the disclosure provisions of the 1934 Securities Exchange Act, at 15 U.S.C. Section 78p.

SECTION 404

Management assessment of internal controls[5]

(a) Rules required

The Commission shall prescribe rules requiring each annual report required by section 78m(a) or 78o(d) of this title to contain an internal control report, which shall—

(1) state the responsibility of management for establishing and maintaining an adequate internal control structure and procedures for financial reporting; and

(2) contain an assessment, as of the end of the most recent fiscal year of the issuer, of the effectiveness of the internal control structure and procedures of the issuer for financial reporting.

(b) Internal control evaluation and reporting

With respect to the internal control assessment required by subsection (a) of this section, each registered public accounting firm that prepares or issues the audit report for the issuer shall attest to, and report on, the assessment made by the management of the issuer. An attestation made under this subsection shall be made in accordance with standards for attestation engagements issued or adopted by the Board. Any such attestation shall not be the subject of a separate engagement.

EXPLANATORY COMMENTS: *This section was enacted to prevent corporate executives from claiming they were ignorant of significant errors in their companies' financial reports. For instance, several CEOs testified before Congress that they simply had no idea that the corporations' financial statements were off by billions of dollars. Congress therefore passed Section 404, which requires each annual report to contain a description and assessment of the company's internal control structure and financial reporting procedures. The section also requires that an audit be conducted of the internal control assessment, as well as the financial statements contained in the report. This section goes hand in hand with Section 302 (which, as discussed previously, requires various certifications attesting to the accuracy of the information in financial reports).*

Section 404 has been one of the more controversial and expensive provisions in the Sarbanes-Oxley Act because it requires companies to assess their own internal financial controls to make sure that their financial statements are reliable and accurate. A corporation might need to set up a disclosure committee and a coordinator, establish codes of conduct for accounting and financial personnel, create documentation procedures, provide training, and outline the individuals who are responsible for performing each of the procedures. Companies that were already well managed have not experienced substantial difficulty complying with this section. Other companies, however, have spent millions of dollars setting up, documenting, and evaluating their internal financial control systems. Although initially creating the internal financial control system is a one-time-only expense, the costs of maintaining and evaluating it are ongoing. Some corporations that spent considerable sums complying with Section 404 have been able to offset these costs by discovering and correcting inefficiencies or frauds within their systems. Nevertheless, it is unlikely that any corporation will find compliance with this section to be inexpensive.

SECTION 802 (A)

Destruction, alteration, or falsification of records in Federal investigations and bankruptcy[6]

Whoever knowingly alters, destroys, mutilates, conceals, covers up, falsifies, or makes a false entry in any record, document, or tangible object with the intent to impede, obstruct, or influence the investigation or proper administration of any matter within the jurisdiction of any department or agency of the United States or any case filed under title 11, or in relation to or contemplation of any such matter or case, shall be fined under this title, imprisoned not more than 20 years, or both.

Destruction of corporate audit records[7]

(a)(1) Any accountant who conducts an audit of an issuer of securities to which section 10A(a) of the Securities Exchange Act of 1934 (15 U.S.C. 78j-1(a)) applies, shall maintain all audit or review workpapers for a period of 5 years from the end of the fiscal period in which the audit or review was concluded.

(2) The Securities and Exchange Commission shall promulgate, within 180 days, after adequate notice and an opportunity for comment, such rules and regulations, as are reasonably necessary, relating to the retention of relevant records such as workpapers, documents that form the basis of an audit or review, memoranda, correspondence, communications, other documents, and records (including electronic records) which are created, sent, or received in connection with an audit or review and contain conclusions, opinions, analyses, or financial data relating to such an audit or review, which is conducted by any accountant who conducts an audit of an issuer of securities to which section 10A(a) of the Securities Exchange Act of 1934 (15 U.S.C. 78j-1(a)) applies. The Commission may, from time to time, amend or supplement the rules and regulations that it is required to promulgate under this section, after adequate notice and an opportunity for comment, in order to ensure that such rules and regulations adequately comport with the purposes of this section.

(b) Whoever knowingly and willfully violates subsection (a)(1), or any rule or regulation promulgated by the Securities and Exchange Commission under subsection (a)(2), shall be fined under this title, imprisoned not more than 10 years, or both.

(c) Nothing in this section shall be deemed to diminish or relieve any person of any other duty or obligation

5. Codified at 15 U.S.C. Section 7262.

6. Codified at 15 U.S.C. Section 1519.

7. Codified at 15 U.S.C. Section 1520.

imposed by Federal or State law or regulation to maintain, or refrain from destroying, any document.

EXPLANATORY COMMENTS: *Section 802(a) enacted two new statutes that punish those who alter or destroy documents. The first statute is not specifically limited to securities fraud cases. It provides that anyone who alters, destroys, or falsifies records in federal investigations or bankruptcy may be criminally prosecuted and sentenced to a fine or to up to twenty years in prison, or both. The second statute requires auditors of public companies to keep all audit or review working papers for five years but expressly allows the SEC to amend or supplement these requirements as it sees fit. The SEC has, in fact, amended this section by issuing a rule that requires auditors who audit reporting companies to retain working papers for seven years from the conclusion of the review. Section 802(a) further provides that anyone who knowingly and willfully violates this statute is subject to criminal prosecution and can be sentenced to a fine, imprisoned for up to ten years, or both if convicted.*

This portion of the Sarbanes-Oxley Act implicitly recognizes that persons who are under investigation often are tempted to respond by destroying or falsifying documents that might prove their complicity in wrongdoing. The severity of the punishment should provide a strong incentive for these individuals to resist the temptation.

SECTION 804

Time limitations on the commencement of civil actions arising under Acts of Congress[8]

(a) Except as otherwise provided by law, a civil action arising under an Act of Congress enacted after the date of the enactment of this section may not be commenced later than 4 years after the cause of action accrues.

(b) Notwithstanding subsection (a), a private right of action that involves a claim of fraud, deceit, manipulation, or contrivance in contravention of a regulatory requirement concerning the securities laws, as defined in section 3(a)(47) of the Securities Exchange Act of 1934 (15 U.S.C. 78c(a)(47)), may be brought not later than the earlier of—

(1) 2 years after the discovery of the facts constituting the violation; or

(2) 5 years after such violation.

EXPLANATORY COMMENTS: *Prior to the enactment of this section, Section 10(b) of the Securities Exchange Act of 1934 had no express statute of limitations. The courts generally required plaintiffs to have filed suit within one year from the date that they should (using due diligence) have discovered that a fraud had been committed but no later than three years after the fraud occurred. Section 804 extends this period by specifying that plaintiffs must file a lawsuit within two years after they discover (or should have discovered) a fraud but no later than five years after the fraud's occurrence. This provision has prevented the courts from dismissing numerous securities fraud lawsuits.*

SECTION 806

Civil action to protect against retaliation in fraud cases[9]

(a) Whistleblower protection for employees of publicly traded companies.—

No company with a class of securities registered under section 12 of the Securities Exchange Act of 1934 (15 U.S.C. 78l), or that is required to file reports under section 15(d) of the Securities Exchange Act of 1934 (15 U.S.C. 78o(d)), or any officer, employee, contractor, subcontractor, or agent of such company, may discharge, demote, suspend, threaten, harass, or in any other manner discriminate against an employee in the terms and conditions of employment because of any lawful act done by the employee—

(1) to provide information, cause information to be provided, or otherwise assist in an investigation regarding any conduct which the employee reasonably believes constitutes a violation of section 1341, 1343, 1344, or 1348, any rule or regulation of the Securities and Exchange Commission, or any provision of Federal law relating to fraud against shareholders, when the information or assistance is provided to or the investigation is conducted by—

(A) a Federal regulatory or law enforcement agency;

(B) any Member of Congress or any committee of Congress; or

(C) a person with supervisory authority over the employee (or such other person working for the employer who has the authority to investigate, discover, or terminate misconduct); or

(2) to file, cause to be filed, testify, participate in, or otherwise assist in a proceeding filed or about to be filed (with any knowledge of the employer) relating to an alleged violation of section 1341, 1343, 1344, or 1348, any rule or regulation of the Securities and Exchange Commission, or any provision of Federal law relating to fraud against shareholders.

(b) Enforcement action.—

(1) In general.—A person who alleges discharge or other discrimination by any person in violation of subsection (a) may seek relief under subsection (c), by—

(A) filing a complaint with the Secretary of Labor; or

(B) if the Secretary has not issued a final decision within 180 days of the filing of the complaint and there is no showing that such delay is due to the

8. Codified at 28 U.S.C. Section 1658.

9. Codified at 18 U.S.C. Section 1514A.

bad faith of the claimant, bringing an action at law or equity for de novo review in the appropriate district court of the United States, which shall have jurisdiction over such an action without regard to the amount in controversy.

(2) Procedure.—

(A) In general.—An action under paragraph (1)(A) shall be governed under the rules and procedures set forth in section 42121(b) of title 49, United States Code.

(B) Exception.—Notification made under section 42121(b)(1) of title 49, United States Code, shall be made to the person named in the complaint and to the employer.

(C) Burdens of proof.—An action brought under paragraph (1)(B) shall be governed by the legal burdens of proof set forth in section 42121(b) of title 49, United States Code.

(D) Statute of limitations.—An action under paragraph (1) shall be commenced not later than 90 days after the date on which the violation occurs.

(c) Remedies.—

(1) In general.—An employee prevailing in any action under subsection (b)(1) shall be entitled to all relief necessary to make the employee whole.

(2) Compensatory damages.—Relief for any action under paragraph (1) shall include—

(A) reinstatement with the same seniority status that the employee would have had, but for the discrimination;

(B) the amount of back pay, with interest; and

(C) compensation for any special damages sustained as a result of the discrimination, including litigation costs, expert witness fees, and reasonable attorney fees.

(d) Rights retained by employee.—Nothing in this section shall be deemed to diminish the rights, privileges, or remedies of any employee under any Federal or State law, or under any collective bargaining agreement.

EXPLANATORY COMMENTS: *Section 806 is one of several provisions that were included in the Sarbanes-Oxley Act to encourage and protect whistleblowers—that is, employees who report their employer's alleged violations of securities law to the authorities. This section applies to employees, agents, and independent contractors who work for publicly traded companies or testify about such a company during an investigation. It sets up an administrative procedure at the Department of Labor for individuals who claim that their employer retaliated against them (fired or demoted them, for example) for blowing the whistle on the employer's wrongful conduct. It also allows the award of civil damages—including back pay, reinstatement, special damages, attorneys' fees, and court costs—to employees who prove that they suffered retaliation. Since this provision was enacted, whistleblowers have filed numerous complaints with the Department of Labor under this section.*

SECTION 807

Securities fraud[10]

Whoever knowingly executes, or attempts to execute, a scheme or artifice—

(1) to defraud any person in connection with any security of an issuer with a class of securities registered under section 12 of the Securities Exchange Act of 1934 (15 U.S.C. 78l) or that is required to file reports under section 15(d) of the Securities Exchange Act of 1934 (15 U.S.C. 78o(d)); or

(2) to obtain, by means of false or fraudulent pretenses, representations, or promises, any money or property in connection with the purchase or sale of any security of an issuer with a class of securities registered under section 12 of the Securities Exchange Act of 1934 (15 U.S.C. 78l) or that is required to file reports under section 15(d) of the Securities Exchange Act of 1934 (15 U.S.C. 78o(d)); shall be fined under this title, or imprisoned not more than 25 years, or both.

EXPLANATORY COMMENTS: *Section 807 adds a new provision to the federal criminal code that addresses securities fraud. Prior to 2002, federal securities law had already made it a crime—under Section 10(b) of the Securities Exchange Act of 1934 and SEC Rule 10b-5, both of which are discussed in Chapter 41—to intentionally defraud someone in connection with a purchase or sale of securities, but the offense was not listed in the federal criminal code. Also, paragraph 2 of Section 807 goes beyond what is prohibited under securities law by making it a crime to obtain by means of false or fraudulent pretenses any money or property from the purchase or sale of securities. This new provision allows violators to be punished by up to twenty-five years in prison, a fine, or both.*

SECTION 906

Failure of corporate officers to certify financial reports[11]

(a) Certification of periodic financial reports.—Each periodic report containing financial statements filed by an issuer with the Securities Exchange Commission pursuant to section 13(a) or 15(d) of the Securities Exchange Act of 1934 (15 U.S.C. 78m(a) or 78o(d)) shall be accompanied by a written statement by the chief executive officer and chief financial officer (or equivalent thereof) of the issuer.

10. Codified at 18 U.S.C. Section 1348.
11. Codified at 18 U.S.C. Section 1350.

(b) Content.—The statement required under subsection (a) shall certify that the periodic report containing the financial statements fully complies with the requirements of section 13(a) or 15(d) of the Securities Exchange Act of 1934 (15 U.S.C. 78m or 78o(d)) and that information contained in the periodic report fairly presents, in all material respects, the financial condition and results of operations of the issuer.

(c) Criminal penalties.—Whoever—

(1) certifies any statement as set forth in subsections (a) and (b) of this section knowing that the periodic report accompanying the statement does not comport with all the requirements set forth in this section shall be fined not more than $1,000,000 or imprisoned not more than 10 years, or both; or

(2) willfully certifies any statement as set forth in subsections (a) and (b) of this section knowing that the periodic report accompanying the statement does not comport with all the requirements set forth in this section shall be fined not more than $5,000,000, or imprisoned not more than 20 years, or both.

EXPLANATORY COMMENTS: *As previously discussed, under Section 302 a corporation's CEO and CFO are required to certify that they believe the quarterly and annual reports their company files with the SEC are accurate and fairly present the company's financial condition. Section 906 adds "teeth" to these requirements by authorizing criminal penalties for those officers who intentionally certify inaccurate SEC filings. Knowing violations of the requirements are punishable by a fine of up to $1 million, ten years in prison, or both. Willful violators may be fined up to $5 million, sentenced to up to twenty years in prison, or both. Although the difference between a knowing and a willful violation is not entirely clear, the section is obviously intended to remind corporate officers of the serious consequences of certifying inaccurate reports to the SEC.*

APPENDIX I

Sample Answers for End-of-Chapter *Questions with Sample Answer*

1–2A. QUESTION WITH SAMPLE ANSWER

At the time of the Nuremberg trials, "crimes against humanity" were new international crimes. The laws criminalized such acts as murder, extermination, enslavement, deportation, and other inhumane acts committed against any civilian population. These international laws derived their legitimacy from "natural law." Natural law, which is the oldest and one of the most significant schools of jurisprudence, holds that governments and legal systems should reflect the moral and ethical ideals that are inherent in human nature. Because natural law is universal and discoverable by reason, its adherents believe that all other law is derived from natural law. Natural law therefore supersedes laws created by humans (national, or "positive," law), and in a conflict between the two, national or positive law loses its legitimacy. The Nuremberg defendants asserted that they had been acting in accordance with German law. The judges dismissed these claims, reasoning that the defendants' acts were commonly regarded as crimes and that the accused must have known that the acts would be considered criminal. The judges clearly believed the tenets of natural law and expected that the defendants, too, should have been able to realize that their acts ran afoul of it. The fact that the "positivist law" of Germany at the time required them to commit these acts is irrelevant. Under natural law theory, the international court was justified in finding the defendants guilty of crimes against humanity.

2–2A. QUESTION WITH SAMPLE ANSWER

Trial courts, as explained in the text, are responsible for settling "questions of fact." Often, when parties bring a case to court there is a dispute as to what actually happened. Different witnesses have different versions of what they saw or heard, and there may be only indirect evidence of certain issues in dispute. During the trial, the judge and the jury (if it is a jury trial) listen to the witnesses and view the evidence firsthand. Thus, the trial court is in the best position to assess the credibility (truthfulness) of the witnesses and determine the weight that should be given to various items of evidence. At the end of the trial, the judge and the jury (if it is a jury trial) decide what will be considered facts for the purposes of the case. Trial courts are best suited to this job, as they have the opportunity to observe the witnesses and evidence, and they regularly determine the reliability of certain evidence. Appellate courts, in contrast, see only the written record of the trial court proceedings and cannot evaluate the credibility of witnesses and the persuasiveness of evidence. For these reasons, appellate courts nearly always defer to trial courts' findings of fact. An appellate court can reverse a lower court's findings of fact, however, when so little evidence was presented at trial that no reasonable person could have reached the conclusion that the judge or jury reached.

3–2A. QUESTION WITH SAMPLE ANSWER

Because the joint venture in Euphratia would naturally be subject to that country's laws, company lawyers would have to look to the agreements that the joint venture had signed with the national government as well as Euphratia's laws relating to the ownership of natural resources to determine whether they would interfere with the efforts by the two companies to resolve their dispute. All countries have the right to expropriate foreign-owned property as long as they pay adequate compensation to the owners. Because the Federal Arbitration Act accords parties significant discretion in deciding where disputes should be heard and which law should govern, virtually any dispute can be the subject of arbitration. The terms of a voluntary arbitration agreement will normally be enforced by the courts if the agreement does not compel an illegal act or contravene public policy. Assuming that Euphratia's laws did not violate U.S. public policy, the dispute itself should be arbitrable.

4–2A. QUESTION WITH SAMPLE ANSWER

This question essentially asks whether good behavior can ever be unethical. The answer to this question depends on which approach to ethical reasoning you are using. Under the outcome-based approach of utilitarianism, it is simply not possible for selfish motives to be unethical if they result in good conduct. A good outcome is moral regardless of the nature of the action itself or the reason for the action. Under a duty-based approach, motive would be more relevant in assessing whether a firm's conduct was ethical. You would need to analyze the firm's conduct in terms of religious truths or to determine whether human beings were being treated with the inherent dignity that they deserve. Although a good motive would not justify a bad act to a religious ethicist, in this situation the actions were good and the motive was questionable (because the firm was simply seeking to increase its profit). Nevertheless, unless one's religion prohibited making a profit, the firm's actions would likely not be considered unethical. Applying Kantian ethics would require you to evaluate the firm's actions in light of what would happen if everyone in society acted that way (categorical imperative). Here, because the conduct was good, it would be positive for society if every firm acted that way. Hence, the profit-seeking motive would be irrelevant in a Kantian analysis. In a debate between motive and conduct, then, conduct is almost always given greater weight in evaluating ethics.

5–2A. Question with Sample Answer

As the text points out, Thomas has a constitutionally protected right to his religion and the free exercise of it. In denying his unemployment benefits, the state violated these rights. Employers are obligated to make reasonable accommodations for their employees' beliefs, right or wrong, that are openly and sincerely held. Thomas's beliefs were openly and sincerely held. By placing him in a department that made military goods, his employer effectively put him in a position of having to choose between his job and his religious principles. This unilateral decision on the part of the employer was the reason Thomas left his job and why the company was required to compensate Thomas for his resulting unemployment.

6–2A. Question with Sample Answer

The court will consider first whether the agency followed the procedures prescribed in the Administrative Procedure Act (APA). Ordinarily, courts will not require agencies to use procedures beyond those of the APA. Courts will, however, compel agencies to follow their own rules. If an agency has adopted a rule granting extra procedures, the agency must provide those extra procedures, at least until the rule is formally rescinded. Ultimately, in this case, the court will most likely rule for the food producers.

7–3A. Question with Sample Answer

As you read in the text, some torts, including assault and battery, provide a basis for criminal prosecution as well as civil liability. This question aptly demonstrates this principle. Double jeopardy is a criminal law concept and does not constitute a defense against a civil lawsuit. The Fifth Amendment prohibition against double jeopardy means that once Armington has been tried and found guilty or not guilty for this assault, he may not be tried for it again. Nevertheless, Jennings may seek damages for his injuries in a civil lawsuit because Armington's prison sentence will do nothing to reimburse him for his medical bills and disability. Armington's guilty verdict has no bearing on the civil lawsuit. The criminal conviction, however, having been proved beyond a reasonable doubt, will likely improve Jennings's chances of recovering damages from Armington in a civil case. As you will recall, in a civil suit the plaintiff merely has to prove his or her case by a preponderance of the evidence. For Jennings, this burden of proof will probably be much easier to meet, given Armington's conviction.

8–2A. Question with Sample Answer

Each system has its advantages and its disadvantages. In a common law system, the courts independently develop the rules governing certain areas of law, such as torts and contracts. This judge-made law exists in addition to the laws passed by a legislature. Judges must follow precedential decisions in their jurisdictions, but courts may modify or even overturn precedents when deemed necessary. Also, if there is no case law to guide a court, the court may create a new rule of law. In a civil law system, the only official source of law is a statutory code. Courts are required to interpret the code and apply the rules to individual cases, but courts may not depart from the code and develop their own laws. In theory, the law code will set forth all the principles needed for the legal system. Common law and civil law systems are not wholly distinct. For example, the United States has a common law system, but crimes are defined by statute as in civil law systems. Civil law systems may allow considerable room for judges to develop law: law codes cannot be so precise as to address every contested issue, so the judiciary must interpret the codes. There are also significant differences among common law countries. The judges of different common law nations have produced differing common law principles. The roles of judges and lawyers under the different systems should be taken into account. Among other factors that should be considered in establishing a business law system and in deciding what regulations to impose are the goals that the system and its regulations are intended to achieve and the expectations of those to whom both will apply, including foreign and domestic investors.

9–2A. Question with Sample Answer

According to the question, Janine was apparently unconscious or otherwise unable to agree to a contract for the nursing services she received while she was in the hospital. As you read in the chapter, however, sometimes the law will create a fictional contract in order to prevent one party from unjustly receiving a benefit at the expense of another. This is known as a quasi contract and provides a basis for Nursing Services to recover the value of the services it provided while Janine was in the hospital. As for the at-home services that were provided to Janine, because Janine was aware that those services were being provided for her, Nursing Services can recover for those services under an implied-in-fact contract. Under this type of contract, the conduct of the parties creates and defines the terms. Janine's acceptance of the services constitutes her agreement to form a contract, and she will probably be required to pay Nursing Services in full.

10–2A. Question with Sample Answer

A novation exists when a new, valid contract expressly or impliedly discharges a prior contract by the substitution of a party. Accord and satisfaction exists when the parties agree that the original obligation can be discharged by a substituted performance. In this case, Fred's agreement with Iba to pay off Junior's debt for $1,100 (as compared to the $1,000 owed) is definitely a valid contract. The terms of the contract substitute Fred as the debtor for Junior, and Junior is definitely discharged from further liability. This agreement is a novation.

11–2A. Question with Sample Answer

Anne has entered into an enforceable contract to subscribe to *E-Commerce Weekly*. In this problem, the offer to deliver, via e-mail, the newsletter was presented by the offeror with a statement of how to accept—by clicking on the "SUBSCRIBE" button. Consideration was in the promise to deliver the newsletter and in the price that the subscriber agreed to pay. The offeree had an opportunity to read the terms of the subscription agreement before making the contract. Whether she actually read those terms does not matter.

12–2A. Question with Sample Answer

To answer this question, you must first decide if there is a legal theory under which Harley may be able to recover. You may recall from your reading the intentional tort of "wrongful interference with a contractual relationship." To recover damages under this theory, Harley would need to show that he and Martha had a valid contract, that Lothar knew of this contractual relationship between Martha and Harley, and that Lothar intentionally convinced Martha to break her contract with Harley. Even though Lothar hoped that his advertisments would persuade Martha to break her contract with Harley, the question states that Martha's decision to change bakers was based solely on the advertising and not on anything else that Lothar did. Lothar's advertisements did not constitute a tort. Note, though, that while Harley cannot collect from Lothar for Martha's actions, he does have a cause of action against Martha for her breach of their contract.

13–3A. Question with Sample Answer

If Colt can prove that all due care was exercised in the manufacture of the pistol, Colt cannot be held in an action based on negligence. Under the theory of strict liability in tort, however, Colt can be held liable regardless of the degree of care exercised. The doctrine of strict liability states that a merchant-seller who sells a defective product that is unreasonably dangerous is liable for injuries caused by that product (even if all possible care in preparation and sale is exercised), provided that the product has not been substantially changed after the time of sale. Therefore, if Wayne can prove the pistol is defective, unreasonably dangerous, and caused him injury, Colt as a merchant is strictly liable, because there is no evidence that the pistol has been altered since the date of its manufacture.

14–2A. Question with Sample Answer

(a) Ursula will not be held liable for copyright infringement in this case because her photocopying pages for use in scholarly research falls squarely under the "fair use" exception to the Copyright Act.

(b) While Ursula's actions are improper, they could constitute trademark infringement, not copyright infringement. Copyrights are granted for literary and artistic productions; trademarks are distinctive marks created and used by manufacturers to differentiate their goods from those of their competitors. Trademark infringement occurs when a mark is copied to a substantial degree, intentionally or unintentionally.

(c) As with the answer to (a) above, Ursula's actions fall within the "fair use" doctrine of copyright law. Her use of the recorded television shows for teaching is the exact type of use the exception is designed to cover.

15–2A. Question with Sample Answer

A trustee is given avoidance powers by the Bankruptcy Code. One situation in which the trustee can avoid transfers of property or payments by a debtor to a creditor is when such transfer constitutes a *preference*. A preference is a transfer of property or payment that favors one creditor over another. For a preference to exist, the debtor must be insolvent and must have made payment for a preexisting debt within ninety days of the filing of the petition in bankruptcy. The Code provides that the debtor is *presumed* to be insolvent during this ninety-day period. If the payment is made to an insider (and in this case payment was made to a close relative), the preference period is extended to one year, but the presumption of insolvency still applies only to the ninety-day period. In this case, the trustee has an excellent chance of having both payments declared preferences. The payment to Cool Springs was within ninety days of the filing of the petition, and it is doubtful that Cool Springs could overcome the presumption that Peaslee was insolvent at the time the payment was made. The $5,000 payment was made to an insider, Peaslee's father, and any payment made to an insider within one year of the petition of bankruptcy is a preference—as long as the debtor was insolvent at the time of payment. The facts indicate that Peaslee probably was insolvent at the time he paid his father. If he was not, the payment is not a preference, and the trustee's avoidance of the transfer would be improper.

16–2A. Question with Sample Answer

The court would likely conclude that National Foods was responsible for the acts of harassment by the manager at the franchised restaurant, on the ground that the employees were the agents of National Foods. An agency relationship can be implied from the circumstances and conduct of the parties. The important question is the degree of control that a franchisor has over its franchisees. Whether it exercises that control is beside the point. Here, National Foods retained considerable control over the new hires and the franchisee's policies, as well as the right to terminate the franchise for violations. That its supervisors routinely approved the policies would not undercut National Foods' liability.

17–3A. Question with Sample Answer

(a) A limited partner's interest is assignable. In fact, assignment allows the assignee to become a substituted limited partner with the consent of the remaining partners. The assignment, however, does not dissolve the limited partnership.

(b) Bankruptcy of the limited partnership itself causes dissolution, but bankruptcy of one of the limited partners does not dissolve the partnership unless it causes the bankruptcy of the firm.

(c) The retirement, death, or insanity of a general partner dissolves the partnership unless the business can be continued by the remaining general partners. Because Dorinda was the only general partner, her death dissolves the limited partnership.

18–2A. Question with Sample Answer

Directors are personally answerable to the corporation and the shareholders for breach of their duty to exercise reasonable care in conducting the affairs of the corporation. Reasonable care is defined as being the degree of care that a reasonably prudent person would use in the conduct of personal business affairs. When directors delegate the running of the corporate affairs to officers, the directors are expected to use reasonable care in the selection and supervision of such officers. Failure to do so will make the directors liable for negligence or mismanagement. A director who dissents to an action by the board is not personally liable for losses resulting from that action. Unless the dissent is entered into the board meeting minutes, however, the director is presumed to have assented. Therefore, the first issue in the case of AstroStar, Inc., is whether the board members failed to use reasonable care in the selection of the president. If so, and particularly if the board failed to provide a reasonable amount of supervision (and openly embezzled funds indicate that failure), the directors will be personally liable. This liability will include Eckhart unless she can prove that she dissented and that she tried to reasonably supervise the new president. Considering the facts in this case, it is questionable that Eckhart could prove this.

19–2A. Question with Sample Answer

On creation of an agency, the agent owes certain fiduciary duties to the principal. Two such duties are the duty of loyalty and the duty to inform or notify. The duty of loyalty is a fundamental concept of the fiduciary relationship. The agent must act solely for the benefit of the principal, not in the agent's own interest or in the interest of another person. One of the principles invoked by this duty is that an agent employed to sell cannot become a purchaser without the principal's consent. When the agent is a partner, contracting to sell to another partner is equivalent to selling to oneself and is therefore a breach of the agent's duty. In addition, the agent has a duty to disclose to the principal any facts pertinent to the subject matter of the agency. Failure to disclose to Peter the knowledge of the shopping mall and the increased market value of the property also was a breach of Alice's fiduciary duties. When an agent breaches fiduciary duties owed to the principal by becoming a recipient of a contract, the contract is voidable at the election of the principal. Neither Carl nor Alice can hold Peter to the contract, and Alice's breach of fiduciary duties also allows Peter to terminate the agency relationship.

20–2A. Question with Sample Answer

The Occupational Health and Safety Act (OSHA) requires employers to provide safe working conditions for employees. The act prohibits employers from discharging or discriminating against any employee who refuses to work when the employee believes in good faith that he or she will risk death or great bodily harm by undertaking the employment activity. Denton and Carlo had sufficient reason to believe that the maintenance job required of them by their employer involved great risk, and therefore, under OSHA, their discharge was wrongful. Denton and Carlo can turn to the Occupational Safety and Health Administration, which is part of the Department of Labor, for assistance.

21–2A. Question with Sample Answer

An employer can legally impose an educational requirement if the requirement is directly related to, and necessary for, performance of the job. In this situation, the employer is requiring a high school diploma as a condition of employment for its cleaning crew. A high school diploma is not related to, or necessary for, the competent performance of a job on a cleaning crew. Chinawa obviously comes under Title VII of the 1964 Civil Rights Act, as amended. Therefore, if someone were to challenge Chinawa's practices, a court would be likely to consider the disparate impact that the educational requirement had on Chinawa's hiring of minorities. Chinawa's educational requirement resulted in its hiring an all-white cleaning crew in an area in which 75 percent of the pool of qualified applicants were minorities. Therefore, Chinawa's educational requirement would likely be considered unintentional (disparate-impact) discrimination against minorities.

22–3A. Question with Sample Answer

The NLRB has consistently been suspicious of companies that grant added benefits during election campaigns. These benefits will be considered as an unfair labor practice that biases elections, unless the employer can demonstrate that the benefits were unrelated to the unionization and would have been granted anyway.

23–3A. Question with Sample Answer

Yes. A regulation of the Federal Trade Commission (FTC) under Section 5 of the Federal Trade Commission Act makes it a violation for door-to-door sellers to fail to give consumers three days to cancel any sale. In addition, a number of state statutes require this three-day "cooling off" period to protect consumers from unscrupulous door-to-door sellers. Because the Gonchars sought to rescind the contract within the three-day period, Renowned Books was obligated to agree to cancel the contract. Its failure to allow rescission was in violation of the FTC regulation and of most state statutes.

24–2A. Question with Sample Answer

Fruitade has violated a number of federal environmental laws if such actions are being taken without a permit. First, because the dumping is in a navigable waterway, the River and Harbor Act of 1886, as amended, has been violated. Second, the Clean Water Act of 1972, as amended, has been violated. This act is designed to make the waters safe for swimming, to protect fish and wildlife, and to eliminate discharge of pollutants into the water. Both the crushed glass and the acid violate this act. Third, the Toxic Substances Control Act of 1976 was passed to regulate chemicals that are known to be toxic and could have an effect on human health and the environment. The acid in the cleaning fluid or compound could come under this act.

25–3A. Question with Sample Answer

Because all land-use regulations necessarily limit the ways in which property may be used, a regulation by itself will not generally be considered a compensable taking. Compensation will be required only if the regulation itself is found to be overly burdensome and thus subject to the requirement that just compensation be paid. Rezoning the land from industrial use to commercial use—despite the expected reduction in its market value—would probably not be considered a compensable taking because it would not prevent the owner from using the land for any reasonable income-producing or private purpose.

26–3A. Question with Sample Answer

Super-Tech's unilateral action is a violation of the Sherman Act, Section 2. Super-Tech already controls a substantial portion of the market for computers and thus has a monopoly position in this business field. Super-Tech's action is a misuse of its monopoly power in the marketplace. Any person who shall monopolize or attempt to monopolize any part of trade or commerce may be in violation of the Sherman Act. Therefore, Alcan can file a private action seeking treble damages, costs, and reasonable attorneys' fees, and the Department of Justice can institute criminal and civil proceedings.

27–3A. Question with Sample Answer

(a) Trujillo's pricing limitations are clearly an attempt at resale price maintenance and vertical price fixing which here are violations of the Sherman Act. The reasons given by the courts for holding these agreements to be illegal are that the limitations (1) tend to provide the same economic rewards to all retailers, regardless of skill, experience, and the like; (2) restrict innovation and deter a retailer from trying out new competitive techniques; and (3) may be so restrictive in the future as to fix a uniform price.

(b) Generally, whenever two or more competitors make any agreement to fix prices, it is considered a per se violation of the Sherman Act, Section 1. This is called horizontal price fixing, and generally the court will find any agreement to fix prices among competitors to be illegal. This can result in a criminal conviction. Whether this agreement will be a violation of the Sherman Act with possible criminal conviction will depend on the intent of the parties. Simply "an effect on prices, without more, will not support a criminal conviction under the Sherman Act." If this is truly a patriotic gesture and an aid to assist the unemployed, this intent could be determinative.

(c) Foam Beer's recommended or suggested prices to its distributors is not a violation of the Sherman Act, Section 1. There is no agreement, express or implied, that a distributor must resell the beer at those prices to continue to do business with Foam. All facts indicate that the price suggestions are merely a benchmark based on past attempts of distributors to make a reasonable profit. No price restrictions are imposed by Foam.

28–2A. Question with Sample Answer

No. Under federal securities law, a stock split is exempt from registration requirements. This is because no *sale* of stock is involved. The existing shares are merely being split, and no consideration is received by the corporation for the additional shares created.

Glossary

A

Abandonment In landlord-tenant law, a tenant's departure from leased premises completely, with no intention of returning before the end of the lease term.

Abus de droit A doctrine developed in the French courts. The doctrine modified employment at will and protected workers exercising their rights from wrongful discharge and other employer abuses.

Acceptance In contract law, the offeree's notification to the offeror that the offeree agrees to be bound by the terms of the offeror's proposal. Although historically the terms of acceptance had to be the mirror image of the terms of the offer, the Uniform Commercial Code provides that even modified terms of the offer in a definite expression of acceptance constitute a contract.

Accredited investors In the context of securities offerings, "sophisticated" investors, such as banks, insurance companies, investment companies, the issuer's executive officers and directors, and persons whose income or net worth exceeds certain limits.

Acquittal A certification or declaration following a trial that the individual accused of a crime is innocent, or free from guilt, and is thus absolved of the charges.

Act of state doctrine A doctrine that provides that the judicial branch of one country will not examine the validity of public acts committed by a recognized foreign government within its own territory.

Actionable Capable of serving as the basis of a lawsuit.

Actual authority Authority of an agent that is express or implied.

Actual malice A condition that exists when a person makes a statement with either knowledge of its falsity or a reckless disregard for the truth. In a defamation suit, a statement made about a public figure normally must be made with actual malice for liability to be incurred.

Actus reus (pronounced *ak*-tus *ray*-uhs) A guilty (prohibited) act. The commission of a prohibited act is one of the two essential elements required for criminal liability, the other element being the intent to commit a crime.

Adequate protection doctrine In bankruptcy law, a doctrine that protects secured creditors from losing their security as a result of an automatic stay on legal proceedings by creditors against the debtor once the debtor petitions for bankruptcy relief. In certain circumstances, the bankruptcy court may provide adequate protection by requiring the debtor or trustee to pay the creditor or provide additional guaranties to protect the creditor against the losses suffered by the creditor as a result of the stay.

Adhesion contract A "standard-form" contract, such as that between a large retailer and a consumer, in which the stronger party dictates the terms.

Adjudicate To render a judicial decision. In the administrative process, the proceeding in which an administrative law judge hears and decides on issues that arise when an administrative agency charges a person or a firm with violating a law or regulation enforced by the agency.

Adjudication The process of adjudicating. *See* Adjudicate

Administrative agency A federal or state government agency established to perform a specific function. Administrative agencies are authorized by legislative acts to make and enforce rules to administer and enforce the acts.

Administrative law The body of law created by administrative agencies (in the form of rules, regulations, orders, and decisions) in order to carry out their duties and responsibilities.

Administrative law judge (ALJ) One who presides over an administrative agency hearing and who has the power to administer oaths, take testimony, rule on questions of evidence, and make determinations of fact.

Adverse possession The acquisition of title to real property by occupying it openly, without the consent of the owner, for a period of time specified by a state statute. The occupation must be actual, open, notorious, exclusive, and in opposition to all others, including the owner.

Affidavit A written or printed voluntary statement of facts, confirmed by the oath or affirmation of the party making it and made before a person having the authority to administer the oath or affirmation.

Affirmative action Job-hiring policies that give special consideration to members of protected classes in an effort to overcome present effects of past discrimination.

Affirmative defense A response to a plaintiff's claim that does not deny the plaintiff's facts but attacks the plaintiff's legal right to bring an action. An example is the running of the statute of limitations.

After-acquired property Property of the debtor that [illegible] acquired after the execution of a security agreement.

Age of majority The age at which an individual is co[illegible]ered legally capable of conducting himself or herself re[illegible]bly. A person of this age is entitled to the full righ[illegible] citizenship, including the right to vote in elections. In [illegible] law, one who is no longer an infant and can no longer [illegible] a contract.

Agency A relationship between two parties in [illegible] party (the agent) agrees to represent or act for t[illegible] principal).

Agent A person who agrees to represent or a[illegible] called the principal.

Agreement A meeting of two or more minds i[illegible] terms of a contract; usually broken down into tw[illegible] offer by one party to form a contract, and an accep[illegible] offer by the person to whom the offer is made.

Alien corporation A designation in the United States for a corporation formed in another country but doing business in the United States.

Allegation A statement, claim, or assertion.

Allege To state, recite, assert, or charge.

Alternative dispute resolution (ADR) The resolution of disputes in ways other than those involved in the traditional judicial process. Negotiation, mediation, and arbitration are forms of ADR.

Analogy In logical reasoning, an assumption that if two things are similar in some respects, they will be similar in other respects also. Often used in legal reasoning to infer the appropriate application of legal principles in a case being decided by referring to previous cases involving different facts but considered to come within the policy underlying the rule.

Answer Procedurally, a defendant's response to the plaintiff's complaint.

Anticipatory repudiation An assertion or action by a party indicating that he or she will not perform an obligation that the party is contractually obligated to perform at a future time.

Antitrust law The body of federal and state laws and statutes protecting trade and commerce from unlawful restraints, price discrimination, price fixing, and monopolies. The principal federal antitrust statues are the Sherman Act of 1890, the Clayton Act of 1914, and the Federal Trade Commission Act of 1914.

Apparent authority Authority that is only apparent, not real. In agency law, a person may be deemed to have had the power to act as an agent for another party if the other party's manifestations to a third party led the third party to believe that an agency existed when, in fact, it did not.

Appeal Resort to a superior court, such as an appellate court, to review the decision of an inferior court, such as a trial court or an administrative agency.

Appellant The party who takes an appeal from one court to another.

Appellate jurisdiction Courts having appellate jurisdiction act as reviewing courts, or appellate courts. Generally, cases can be brought before appellate courts only on appeal from an order or a judgment of a trial court or other lower court.

Appellee The party against whom an appeal is taken—that is, the party who opposes setting aside or reversing the judgment.

Appropriate bargaining unit A designation based on job duties, skill levels, etc., of the proper entity that should be covered by collective bargaining agreement.

Appropriation In tort law, the use by one person of another person's name, likeness, or other identifying characteristic without permission and for the benefit of the user.

Arbitrary and capricious test The court reviewing an informal administrative agency action applies this test to determine [illegible]hether or not that action was in clear error. The court gives [illegible]e discretion to the expertise of the agency and decides if the [illegible]ncy had sufficient factual information on which to base its [illegible] If no clear error was made, then the agency's action [illegible]s.

[illegible]on The settling of a dispute by submitting it to a dis[illegible]d third party (other than a court), who renders a deci[illegible]e decision may or may not be legally binding.

[illegible]tion clause A clause in a contract that provides that, [illegible]of a dispute, the parties will submit the dispute to [illegible]er than litigate the dispute in court.

[illegible]A disinterested party who, by prior agreement of [illegible]bmitting their dispute to arbitration, has the power [illegible]dispute and (generally) bind the parties.

[illegible] A procedure in which an accused person is [illegible]ore the court to plead to the criminal charge in the [illegible]t or information. The charge is read to the person, and [illegible]e is asked to enter a plea—such as "guilty" or "not guilty."

Arson The malicious burning of another's dwelling. Some statutes have expanded this to include any real property regardless of ownership and the destruction of property by other means—for example, by explosion.

Articles of incorporation The document filed with the appropriate governmental agency, usually the secretary of state, when a business is incorporated; state statutes usually prescribe what kind of information must be contained in the articles of incorporation.

Articles of organization The document filed with a designated state official by which a limited liability company is formed.

Articles of partnership A written agreement that sets forth each partner's rights and obligations with respect to the partnership.

Assault Any word or action intended to make another person fearful of immediate physical harm; a reasonably believable threat.

Assignment The act of transferring to another all or part of one's rights arising under a contract.

Assumption of risk A defense against negligence that can be used when the plaintiff is aware of a danger and voluntarily assumes the risk of injury from that danger.

Attempt to monopolize Any actions by a firm to eliminate competition and gain monopoly power.

Authorization card A card signed by an employee that gives a union permission to act on his or her behalf in negotiations with management. Unions typically use authorization cards as evidence of employee support during union organization.

Automatic stay In bankruptcy proceedings, the suspension of virtually all litigation and other action by creditors against the debtor or the debtor's property; the stay is effective the moment the debtor files a petition in bankruptcy.

Award In the context of litigation, the amount of money awarded to a plaintiff in a civil lawsuit as damages. In the context of arbitration, the arbitrator's decision.

B

Bailment A situation in which the personal property of one person (a bailor) is entrusted to another (a bailee), who is obligated to return the bailed property to the bailor or dispose of it as directed.

Bailor One who entrusts goods to a bailee.

Bait-and-switch advertising Advertising a product at a very attractive price (the "bait") and then informing the consumer, once he or she is in the store, that the advertised product is either not available or is of poor quality; the customer is then urged to purchase ("switched" to) a more expensive item.

Bankruptcy court A federal court of limited jurisdiction that handles only bankruptcy proceedings. Bankruptcy proceedings are governed by federal bankruptcy law.

Battery The unprivileged, intentional touching of another.

Beyond a reasonable doubt The standard used to determine the guilt or innocence of a person criminally charged. To be guilty of a crime, one must be proved guilty "beyond and to the exclusion of every reasonable doubt." A reasonable doubt is one that would cause a prudent person to hesitate before acting in matters important to him or her.

Bilateral contract A type of contract that arises when a promise is given in exchange for a return promise.

Bill of Rights The first ten amendments to the U.S. Constitution.

Binding authority Any source of law that a court must follow when deciding a case. Binding authorities include constitutions, statutes, and regulations that govern the issue being decided, as well as court decisions that are controlling precedents within the jurisdiction.

Blue sky laws State laws that regulate the offer and sale of securities.

Bona fide Good faith. A bona fide obligation is one made in good faith—that is, sincerely and honestly.

Bona fide occupational qualification (BFOQ) Identifiable characteristics reasonably necessary to the normal operation of a particular business. These characteristics can include gender, national origin, and religion, but not race.

Boycott A concerted refusal to do business with a particular person or entity in order to obtain concessions or to express displeasure with certain acts or practices of that person or business. *See also* Secondary boycott

Breach To violate a law, by an act or an omission, or to break a legal obligation that one owes to another person or to society.

Breach of contract The failure, without legal excuse, of a promisor to perform the obligations of a contract.

Brief A formal legal document submitted by the attorney for the appellant—or the appellee (in answer to the appellant's brief)—to an appellate court when a case is appealed. The appellant's brief outlines the facts and issues of the case, the judge's rulings or jury's findings that should be reversed or modified, the applicable law, and the arguments on the client's behalf.

Browse-wrap terms Terms and conditions of use that are presented to an Internet user at the time certain products, such as software, are being downloaded but that need not be agreed to (by clicking "I agree," for example) before being able to install or use the product.

Bulk zoning Zoning regulations that restrict the amount of structural coverage on a particular parcel of land.

Bureaucracy A large organization that is structured hierarchically to carry out specific functions.

Burglary The unlawful entry into a building with the intent to commit a felony. (Some state statutes expand this to include the intent to commit any crime.)

Business ethics Ethics in a business context; a consensus of what constitutes right or wrong behavior in the world of business and the application of moral principles to situations that arise in a business setting.

Business invitees Those people, such as customers or clients, who are invited onto business premises by the owner of those premises for business purposes.

Business judgment rule A rule that immunizes corporate management from liability for actions that result in corporate losses or damages if the actions are undertaken in good faith and are within both the power of the corporation and the authority of management to make.

Business necessity A defense to allegations of employment discrimination in which the employer demonstrates that an employment practice that discriminates against members of a protected class is related to job performance.

Business tort The wrongful interference with the business rights of another.

Buyer in the ordinary course of business A buyer who, in good faith and without knowledge that the sale to him or her is in violation of the ownership rights or security interest of a third party in the goods, purchases goods in the ordinary course of business from a person in the business of selling goods of that kind.

Buyout price The amount payable to a partner on his or her dissociation from a partnership, based on the amount distributable to that partner if the firm were wound up on that date, and offset by any damages for wrongful dissociation.

Buy-sell agreement In the context of partnerships, an express agreement made at the time of partnership formation for one or more of the partners to buy out the other or others should the situation warrant—and thus provide for the smooth dissolution of the partnership.

Bylaws A set of governing rules adopted by a corporation or other association.

C

Case law The rules of law announced in court decisions. Case law includes the aggregate of reported cases that interpret judicial precedents, statutes, regulations, and constitutional provisions.

Case on point A previous case involving factual circumstances and issues that are similar to the case before the court.

Categorical imperative A concept developed by the philosopher Immanuel Kant as an ethical guideline for behavior. In deciding whether an action is right or wrong, or desirable or undesirable, a person should evaluate the action in terms of what would happen if everybody else in the same situation, or category, acted the same way.

Causation in fact An act or omission without ("but for") which an event would not have occurred.

Cease-and-desist order An administrative or judicial order prohibiting a person or business firm from conducting activities that an agency or court has deemed illegal.

Certificate of limited partnership The basic document filed with a designated state official by which a limited partnership is formed.

Certification mark A mark used by one or more persons, other than the owner, to certify the region, materials, mode of manufacture, quality, or accuracy of the owner's goods or services. When used by members of a cooperative, association, or other organization, such a mark is referred to as a collective mark. Examples of certification marks include the "Good Housekeeping Seal of Approval" and "UL Tested."

Chancellor An adviser to the king at the time of the early king's courts of England. Individuals petitioned the king for relief when they could not obtain an adequate remedy in a court of law, and these petitions were decided by the chancellor.

Charging order In partnership law, an order granted by a court to a judgment creditor that entitles the creditor to attach profits or assets of a partner on dissolution of the partnership.

Checks and balances The national government is composed of three separate branches: the executive, the legislative, and the judicial branches. Each branch of the government exercises a check on the actions of the others.

Citation A reference to a publication in which a legal authority—such as a statute or a court decision—or other source can be found.

Civil law The branch of law dealing with the definition and enforcement of all private or public rights, as opposed to criminal matters.

Civil law system A system of law derived from that of the Roman Empire and based on a code rather than case law; the predominant system of law in the nations of continental Europe and the nations that were once their colonies. In the United States, Louisiana is the only state that has a civil law system.

Click-on agreement An agreement that arises when a buyer, engaging in a transaction on a computer, indicates his or her assent to be bound by the terms of an offer by clicking on a button that says, for example, "I agree"; sometimes referred to as a *click-on license* or a *click-wrap agreement*.

Close corporation A corporation whose shareholders are limited to a small group of persons, often including only family members. The rights of shareholders of a close corporation usually are restricted regarding the transfer of shares to others.

Closed shop A firm that requires union membership by its workers as a condition of employment. The closed shop was made illegal by the Labor-Management Relations Act of 1947.

Closing The final step in the sale of real estate—also called *settlement* or *closing escrow*. The escrow agent coordinates the closing with the recording of deeds, the obtaining of title insurance, and other concurrent closing activities. A number of costs must be paid, in cash, at the time of closing, and they can range from several hundred to several thousand dollars, depending on the amount of the mortgage loan and other conditions of the sale.

Closing argument An argument made after the plaintiff and defendant have rested their cases. Closing arguments are made prior to the jury charges.

Collective bargaining The process by which labor and management negotiate the terms and conditions of employment, including working hours and workplace conditions.

Collective mark A mark used by members of a cooperative, association, or other organization to certify the region, materials, mode of manufacture, quality, or accuracy of the specific goods or services. Examples of collective marks include the labor union marks found on tags of certain products and the credits of movies, which indicate the various associations and organizations that participated in the making of the movies.

Comity A deference by which one nation gives effect to the laws and judicial decrees of another nation. This recognition is based primarily on respect.

Commerce clause The provision in Article I, Section 8, of the U.S. Constitution that gives Congress the power to regulate interstate commerce.

Commercial impracticability A doctrine under which a seller may be excused from performing a contract when (1) a contingency occurs, (2) the contingency's occurrence makes performance impracticable, and (3) the nonoccurrence of the contingency was a basic assumption on which the contract was made. Despite the fact that UCC 2–615 expressly frees only sellers under this doctrine, courts have not distinguished between buyers and sellers in applying it.

Commingle To mix together. To put funds or goods together into one mass so that the funds or goods are so mixed that they no longer have separate identities. In corporate law, if personal and corporate interests are commingled to the extent that the corporation has no separate identity, a court may "pierce the corporate veil" and expose the shareholders to personal liability.

Common law That body of law developed from custom or judicial decisions in English and U.S. courts, not attributable to a legislature.

Common situs picketing The illegal picketing of an entire construction site by workers who are involved in a labor dispute with a particular subcontractor.

Community property A form of concurrent ownership of [illegible]roperty in which each spouse technically owns an undivided one-half interest in property acquired during the marriage. This form of joint ownership occurs in only nine states and Puerto [illegible]o.

[illegible]arative law The study and comparison of legal systems [illegible]aws across nations.

[illegible]mparative negligence A theory in tort law under which [illegible]e liability for injuries resulting from negligent acts is shared by all parties who were negligent (including the injured party), on the basis of each person's proportionate negligence.

Compensatory damages A monetary award equivalent to the actual value of injuries or damages sustained by the aggrieved party.

Complaint The pleading made by a plaintiff alleging wrongdoing on the part of the defendant; the document that, when filed with a court, initiates a lawsuit.

Computer crime Any wrongful act that is directed against computers and computer parties, or wrongful use or abuse of computers or software.

Concentrated industry An industry in which a large percentage of market sales is controlled by either a single firm or a small number of firms.

Concerted action Action by employees, such as a strike or picketing, with the purpose of furthering their bargaining demands or other mutual interests.

Conciliation A form of alternative dispute resolution in which the parties reach an agreement themselves with the help of a neutral third party, called a conciliator, who facilitates the negotiations.

Concurrent jurisdiction Jurisdiction that exists when two different courts have the power to hear a case. For example, some cases can be heard in either a federal or a state court.

Concurrent ownership Joint ownership.

Condemnation The process of taking private property for public use through the government's power of eminent domain.

Condition A qualification, provision, or clause in a contractual agreement, the occurrence of which creates, suspends, or terminates the obligations of the contracting parties.

Confession of judgment The act of a debtor in permitting a judgment to be entered against him or her by a creditor, for an agreed sum, without the institution of legal proceedings.

Confiscation A government's taking of privately owned business or personal property without a proper public purpose or an award of just compensation.

Conforming goods Goods that conform to contract specifications.

Conglomerate merger A merger between firms that do not compete with each other because they are in different markets (as opposed to horizontal and vertical mergers).

Consent Voluntary agreement to a proposition or an act of another. A concurrence of wills.

Consequential damages Special damages that compensate for a loss that is not direct or immediate (for example, lost profits). The special damages must have been reasonably foreseeable at the time the breach or injury occurred in order for the plaintiff to collect them.

Consideration Generally, the value given in return for a promise. The consideration, which must be present to make the contract legally binding, must be something of legally sufficient value and bargained for and must result in a detriment to the promisee or a benefit to the promisor.

Consignment A transaction in which an owner of goods (the consignor) delivers the goods to another (the consignee) for the consignee to sell. The consignee pays the consignor for the goods when they are sold by the consignee.

Constitutional law Law that is based on the U.S. Constitution and the constitutions of the various states.

Constructive delivery An act equivalent to the actual, physical delivery of property that cannot be physically delivered because of difficulty or impossibility; for example, the transfer of a key to a safe constructively delivers the contents of the safe.

Constructive discharge A termination of employment brought about by making an employee's working conditions so intolerable that the employee reasonably feels compelled to leave.

Constructive eviction A form of eviction that occurs when a landlord fails to perform adequately any of the undertakings (such as providing heat in the winter) required by the lease, thereby making the tenant's further use and enjoyment of the property exceedingly difficult or impossible.

Consumer-debtor An individual whose debts are primarily consumer debts (debts for purchases made primarily for personal or household use).

Consumer goods Goods that are primarily for personal or household use.

Consumer law The body of statutes, agency rules, and judicial decisions protecting consumers of goods and services from dangerous manufacturing techniques, mislabeling, unfair credit practices, deceptive advertising, and so on. Consumer laws provide remedies and protections that are not ordinarily available to merchants or to businesses.

Contract An agreement that can be enforced in court; formed by two or more parties, each of whom agrees to perform or to refrain from performing some act now or in the future.

Contractual capacity The threshold mental capacity required by the law for a party who enters into a contract to be bound by that contract.

Contributory negligence A theory in tort law under which a complaining party's own negligence contributed to or caused his or her injuries. Contributory negligence is an absolute bar to recovery in a minority of jurisdictions.

Conversion The wrongful taking, using, or retaining possession of personal property that belongs to another.

Conveyance The transfer of a title to land from one person to another by deed; a document (such as a deed) by which an interest in land is transferred from one person to another.

Co-ownership Joint ownership.

Copyright The exclusive right of authors to publish, print, or sell an intellectual production for a statutory period of time. A copyright has the same monopolistic nature as a patent or trademark, but it differs in that it applies exclusively to works of art, literature, and other works of authorship, including computer programs.

Corporate governance The system by which corporations are directed and controlled and which governs the relationship of the corporation to its shareholders. The corporate governance structure specifies the distribution of rights and responsibilities among different groups within the corporation and spells out the rules and procedures for making corporate decisions.

Corporate social responsibility The concept that corporations can and should act ethically and be accountable to society for their actions.

Corporation A legal entity formed in compliance with statutory requirements. The entity is distinct from its shareholders-owners.

Cost-benefit analysis A decision-making technique that involves weighing the costs of a given action against the benefits of the action.

Co-surety A joint surety. One who assumes liability jointly with another surety for the payment of an obligation.

Counteradvertising New advertising that is undertaken pursuant to a Federal Trade Commission order for the purpose of correcting earlier false claims that were made about a product.

Counterclaim A claim made by a defendant in a civil lawsuit that in effect sues the plaintiff.

Counteroffer An offeree's response to an offer in which the offeree rejects the original offer and at the same time makes a new offer.

Court of equity A court that decides controversies and administers justice according to the rules, principles, and precedents of equity.

Court of law A court in which the only remedies that could be granted were things of value, such as money damages. In the early English king's courts, courts of law were distinct from courts of equity.

Covenant not to compete A contractual promise to refrain from competing with another party for a certain period of time (not excessive in duration) and within a reasonable geographic area. Although covenants not to compete restrain trade, they are commonly found in partnership agreements, business sale agreements, and employment contracts. If they are ancillary to such agreements, covenants not to compete will normally be enforced by the courts unless the time period or geographic area is deemed unreasonable.

Covenant of quiet enjoyment A promise by a grantor (or landlord) that the grantee (or tenant) will not be evicted or disturbed by the grantor or a person having a lien or superior title.

Covenant running with the land An executory promise made between a grantor and a grantee to which they and subsequent owners of the land are bound.

Cover Under the Uniform Commercial Code, a remedy of the buyer or lessee that allows the buyer or lessee, on the seller's or lessor's breach, to purchase the goods from another seller or lessor and substitute them for the goods due under the contract. If the cost of cover exceeds the cost of the contract goods, the breaching seller or lessor will be liable to the buyer or lessee for the difference. In obtaining cover, the buyer or lessee must act in good faith and without unreasonable delay.

Cram-down provision A provision of the Bankruptcy Code that allows a court to confirm a debtor's Chapter 11 reorganization plan even though only one class of creditors has accepted it. To exercise the court's right under this provision, the court must demonstrate that the plan does not discriminate unfairly against any creditors and is fair and equitable.

Crashworthiness doctrine A doctrine that imposes liability for defects in the design or construction of motor vehicles that increase the extent of injuries to passengers if an accident occurs. The doctrine holds even when the defects do not actually cause the accident.

Creditor A person to whom a debt is owed by another person (the debtor).

Crime A wrong against society proclaimed in a statute and, if committed, punishable by society through fines and/or imprisonment—and, in some cases, death.

Criminal law Law that defines and governs actions that constitute crimes. Generally, criminal law has to do with wrongful actions committed against society for which society demands redress.

Cross-examination The questioning of an opposing witness during a trial.

Cure Under the Uniform Commercial Code, the right of a party who tenders nonconforming performance to correct his or her performance within the contract period.

Cyber crime A crime that occurs online, in the virtual community of the Internet, as opposed to the physical world.

Cyber mark A trademark in cyberspace.

Cyber tort A tort committed in cyberspace.

Cyberlaw An informal term used to refer to all laws governing electronic communications and transactions, particularly those conducted via the Internet.

Cybersquatting The act of registering a domain name that is the same as, or confusingly similar to, the trademark of another and then offering to sell that domain name back to the trademark owner.

Cyberterrorist A hacker whose purpose is to exploit a target computer for a serious impact, such as the corruption of a program to sabotage a business.

D

Damages The monetary amount sought as a remedy for a breach of contract or for a tortious act.

De novo Anew; afresh; a second time. In a hearing *de novo*, an appellate court hears the case as a court of original jurisdiction—that is, as if the case had not previously been tried and a decision rendered.

Debtor in possession (DIP) In Chapter 11 bankruptcy proceedings, a debtor who is allowed to continue in possession of the estate in property (the business) and to continue business operations.

Deceptive advertising Advertising that misleads consumers, either by making unjustified claims concerning a product's performance or by omitting a material fact concerning the product's composition or performance.

Deed A document by which title to property (usually real property) is passed.

Defalcation The misuse of funds.

Defamation Any published or publicly spoken false statement that causes injury to another's good name, reputation, or character.

Default The failure to observe a promise or discharge an obligation. The term is commonly used to mean the failure to pay a debt when it is due.

Default judgment A judgment entered by a court against a defendant who has failed to appear in court to answer or defend against the plaintiff's claim.

Defendant One against whom a lawsuit is brought; the accused person in a criminal proceeding.

Defense That which a defendant offers and alleges in an action or suit as a reason why the plaintiff should not recover or establish what he or she seeks.

Delegation The transfer of a contractual duty to a third party. The party delegating the duty (the delegator) to the third party (the delegatee) is still obliged to perform on the contract should the delegatee fail to perform.

Delegation doctrine A doctrine based on Article I, Section 8, of the U.S. Constitution, which has been construed to allow Congress to delegate some of its power to make and implement laws to administrative agencies. The delegation is considered to be proper as long as Congress sets standards outlining the scope of the agency's authority.

Deposition The testimony of a party to a lawsuit or a witness taken under oath before a trial.

Destination contract A contract for the sale of goods in which the seller is required or authorized to ship the goods by carrier and deliver them at a particular destination. The seller assumes liability for any losses or damage to the goods until they are tendered at the destination specified in the contract.

Dilution With respect to trademarks, a doctrine under which distinctive or famous trademarks are protected from certain unauthorized uses of the marks regardless of a showing of competition or a likelihood of confusion. Congress created a federal cause of action for dilution in 1995 with the passage of the Federal Trademark Dilution Act.

Direct examination The examination of a witness by the attorney who calls the witness to the stand to testify on behalf of the attorney's client.

Discharge The termination of an obligation. (1) In contract law, discharge occurs when the parties have fully performed their contractual obligations or when events, conduct of the parties, or operation of the law releases the parties from performance. (2) In bankruptcy proceedings, the extinction of the debtor's dischargeable debts.

Disclosed principal A principal whose identity is known to a third party at the time the agent makes a contract with the third party.

Discovery A phase in the litigation process during which the opposing parties may obtain information from each other and from third parties prior to trial.

Disparagement of property An economically injurious falsehood made about another's product or property. A general term for torts that are more specifically referred to as *slander of quality* or *slander of title*.

Disparate-impact discrimination A form of employment discrimination that results from certain employer practices or procedures that, although not discriminatory on their face, have a discriminatory effect.

Disparate-treatment discrimination A form of employment discrimination that results when an employer intentionally discriminates against employees who are members of protected classes.

Dissociation Occurs when a partner ceases to be associated in the carrying on of the partnership business. The severance of the relationship between a partner and a partnership.

Dissolution The formal disbanding of a partnership or a corporation. It can take place by (1) acts of the partners or, in a corporation, of the shareholders and board of directors; (2) the death of a partner; (3) the expiration of a time period stated in a partnership agreement or a certificate of incorporation; or (4) judicial decree.

Distributed network A network that can be used by persons located (distributed) around the country or the globe to share computer files.

Distribution agreement A contract between a seller and a distributor of the seller's products setting out the terms and conditions of the distributorship.

Diversity of citizenship Under Article III, Section 2, of the Constitution, a basis for federal court jurisdiction over a lawsuit between (1) citizens of different states, (2) a foreign country and citizens of a state or of different states, or (3) citizens of a state and citizens or subjects of a foreign country. The amount in controversy must be more than $75,000 before a federal court can take jurisdiction in such cases.

Divestiture The act of selling one or more of a company's parts, such as a subsidiary or plant; often mandated by the courts in merger or monopolization cases.

Dividend A distribution to corporate shareholders of corporate profits or income, disbursed in proportion to the number of shares held.

Domain name The series of letters and symbols used to identify site operators on the Internet; Internet "addresses."

Domestic corporation In a given state, a corporation that does business in, and is organized under the law of, that state.

Double jeopardy A situation occurring when a person is tried twice for the same criminal offense; prohibited by the Fifth Amendment to the Constitution.

Dram shop act A state statute that imposes liability on the owners of bars and taverns, as well as those who serve alcoholic drinks to the public, for injuries resulting from accidents caused by intoxicated persons when the sellers or servers of alcoholic drinks contributed to the intoxication.

Due process clause The provisions of the Fifth and Fourteenth Amendments to the Constitution that guarantee that no person shall be deprived of life, liberty, or property without due process of law. Similar clauses are found in most state constitutions.

Dumping The selling of goods in a foreign country at a price below the price charged for the same goods in the domestic market.

Duress Unlawful pressure brought to bear on a person, causing the person to perform an act that he or she would not otherwise perform.

Duty of care The duty of all persons, as established by tort law, to exercise a reasonable amount of care in their dealings with others. Failure to exercise due care, which is normally determined by the "reasonable person standard," constitutes the tort of negligence.

E

E-agent A computer program, electronic, or other automated means used to perform specific tasks without review by an individual.

Early neutral case evaluation A form of alternative dispute resolution in which a neutral third party evaluates the strengths and weakness of the disputing parties' positions; the evaluator's opinion forms the basis for negotiating a settlement.

Easement A nonpossessory right to use another's property in a manner established by either express or implied agreement.

E-commerce Business transacted in cyberspace.

E-contract A contract that is entered into in cyberspace and is evidenced only by electronic impulses (such as those that make up a computer's memory), rather than, for example, a typewritten form.

E-evidence A type of evidence that consists of computer-generated or electronically recorded information, including e-mail, voice mail, spreadsheets, word processing documents, and other data.

Eight-day cooling-off period A provision of the Taft-Hartley Act that allows federal courts to issue injunctions against strikes that might create a national emergency.

Embezzlement The fraudulent appropriation of money or other property by a person to whom the money or property has been entrusted.

Eminent domain The power of a government to take land for public use from private citizens for just compensation.

Employee committee A committee created by an employer and composed of representatives of management and nonunion employees to act together to improve workplace conditions.

Employment at will A common law doctrine under which either party may terminate an employment relationship at any time for any reason, unless a contract specifies otherwise.

Employment discrimination Treating employees or job applicants unequally on the basis of race, color, national origin, religion, gender, age, or disability; prohibited by federal statutes.

Enabling legislation A statute enacted by Congress that authorizes the creation of an administrative agency and specifies the name, composition, purpose, and powers of the agency being created.

Encryption The process by which a message (plaintext) is transformed into something (ciphertext) that the sender and receiver intend third parties not to understand.

Entrapment In criminal law, a defense in which the defendant claims that he or she was induced by a public official—usually an undercover agent or police officer—to commit a crime that he or she would otherwise not have committed.

Entrepreneur One who initiates and assumes the financial risks of a new enterprise and who undertakes to provide or control its management.

Environmental impact statement (EIS) A statement required by the National Environmental Policy Act for any major federal action that will significantly affect the quality of the environment. The statement must analyze the action's impact on the environment and explore alternative actions that might be taken.

Environmental law The body of statutory, regulatory, and common law relating to the protection of the environment.

Equal dignity rule In most states, a rule stating that express authority given to an agent must be in writing if the contract to be made on behalf of the principal is required to be in writing.

Equal protection clause The provision in the Fourteenth Amendment to the Constitution that guarantees that no state will "deny to any person within its jurisdiction the equal protection of the laws." This clause mandates that state governments treat similarly situated individuals in a similar manner.

Equitable maxims General propositions or principles of law that have to do with fairness (equity).

Escrow account An account that is generally held in the name of the depositor and escrow agent; the funds in the account are paid to a third person only on fulfillment of the escrow condition.

E-signature As defined by the Uniform Electronic Transactions Act, "an electronic sound, symbol, or process attached to or logically associated with a record and executed or adopted by a person with the intent to sign the record."

Establishment clause The provision in the First Amendment to the U.S. Constitution that prohibits Congress from creating any law "respecting an establishment of religion."

Ethics Moral principles and values applied to social behavior.

Eviction A landlord's act of depriving a tenant of possession of the leased premises.

Exclusionary rule In criminal procedure, a rule under which any evidence that is obtained in violation of the accused's constitutional rights guaranteed by the Fourth, Fifth, and Sixth Amendments, as well as any evidence derived from illegally obtained evidence, will not be admissible in court.

Exclusive-dealing contract An agreement under which a seller forbids a buyer to purchase products from the seller's competitors.

Exclusive distributorship A distributorship in which the seller and the distributor of the seller's products agree that the distributor has the exclusive right to distribute the seller's products in a certain geographic area.

Exclusive jurisdiction Jurisdiction that exists when a case can be heard only in a particular court or type of court, such as a federal court or a state court.

Executive agency An administrative agency within the executive branch of government. At the federal level, executive agencies are those within the cabinet departments.

Executory contract A contract that has not as yet been fully performed.

Export To sell products to buyers located in other countries.

Express authority Authority expressly given by one party to another. In agency law, an agent has express authority to act for a principal if both parties agree, orally or in writing, that an agency relationship exists in which the agent had the power (authority) to act in the place of, and on behalf of, the principal.

Express contract A contract in which the terms of the agreement are fully and explicitly stated in words, oral or written.

Express warranty A seller's or lessor's oral or written promise, ancillary to an underlying sales or lease agreement, as to the quality, description, or performance of the goods being sold or leased.

Expropriation The seizure by a government of priv[illegible] owned business or personal property for a proper public [illegible] and with just compensation.

F

Facilitation A form of alternative dispute resolution in which the parties reach an agreement themselves with the help of a neutral third party, called a *facilitator*, who facilitates the negotiations.

Family limited liability partnership (FLLP) A limited liability partnership (LLP) in which the majority of the partners are persons related to each other, essentially as spouses, parents, grandparents, siblings, cousins, nephews, or nieces. A person acting in a fiduciary capacity for persons so related could also be a partner. All of the partners must be natural persons or persons acting in a fiduciary capacity for the benefit of natural persons.

Featherbedding A requirement that more workers be employed to do a particular job than are actually needed.

Federal form of government A system of government in which the states form a union and the sovereign power is divided between a central government and the member states.

Federal question A question that pertains to the U.S. Constitution, acts of Congress, or treaties. A federal question provides a basis for federal jurisdiction.

Federal Rules of Civil Procedure (FRCP) The rules controlling procedural matters in civil trials brought before the federal district courts.

Fee simple absolute An ownership interest in land in which the owner has the greatest possible aggregation of rights, privileges, and power. Ownership in fee simple absolute is limited absolutely to a person and his or her heirs.

Felony A crime—such as arson, murder, rape, or robbery—that carries the most severe sanctions, usually ranging from one year in a state or federal prison to the forfeiture of one's life.

Fiduciary As a noun, a person having a duty created by his or her undertaking to act primarily for another's benefit in matters connected with the undertaking. As an adjective, a relationship founded on trust and confidence.

Fiduciary duty The duty, imposed on a fiduciary by virtue of his or her position, to act primarily for another's benefit.

Filtering software A computer program that includes a pattern through which data are passed. When designed to block access to certain Web sites, the pattern blocks the retrieval of a site whose URL or key words are on a list within the program.

Final order The final decision of an administrative agency on an issue. If no appeal is taken, or if the case is not reviewed or considered anew by the agency commission, the administrative law judge's initial order becomes the final order of the agency.

Firm offer An offer (by a merchant) that is irrevocable without consideration for a period of time (not longer than three months). A firm offer by a merchant must be in writing and must be signed by the offeror.

Fixed-term tenancy A type of tenancy under which property is leased for a specified period of time, such as a month, a year, or a period of years; also called a *tenancy for years.*

Fixture A thing that was once personal property but that has become attached to real property in such a way that it takes on the characteristics of real property and becomes part of that real property.

Forbearance The act of refraining from an action that one has a legal right to undertake.

Foreign corporation In a given state, a corporation that does business in the state without being incorporated therein.

Forgery The fraudulent making or altering of any writing in a way that changes the legal rights and liabilities of another.

Forum-selection clause A provision in a contract designating the court, jurisdiction, or tribunal that will decide any dis[illegible]ising under the contract.

[illegible]ise Any arrangement in which the owner of a trade[illegible], trade name, or copyright licenses another to use that trademark, trade name, or copyright, under specified conditions or limitations, in the selling of goods and services.

Franchisee One receiving a license to use another's (the franchisor's) trademark, trade name, or copyright in the sale of goods and services.

Franchisor One licensing another (the franchisee) to use his or her trademark, trade name, or copyright in the sale of goods or services.

Fraudulent misrepresentation (fraud) Any misrepresentation, either by misstatement or omission of a material fact, knowingly made with the intention of deceiving another and on which a reasonable person would and does rely to his or her detriment.

Free exercise clause The provision in the First Amendment to the U.S. Constitution that prohibits Congress from making any law "prohibiting the free exercise" of religion.

Free-writing prospectus A free-writing prospectus is any type of written, electronic, or graphic offer that describes the issuing corporation or its securities and includes a legend indicating that the investor may obtain the prospectus at the SEC's Web site.

Frustration of purpose A court-created doctrine under which a party to a contract will be relieved of his or her duty to perform when the objective purpose for performance no longer exists (due to reasons beyond that party's control).

Full faith and credit clause A clause in Article IV, Section 1, of the Constitution that provides that "Full Faith and Credit shall be given in each State to the public Acts, Records, and Judicial Proceedings of every othere States." The clause ensures that rights established under deeds, wills, contracts, and the like in one state will be honored by the other states and that any judicial decision with respect to such property rights will be honored and enforced in all states.

G

Garnishment A legal process used by a creditor to collect a debt by seizing property of the debtor (such as wages) that is being held by a third party (such as the debtor's employer).

General partner In a limited partnership, a partner who assumes responsibility for the management of the partnership and liability for all partnership debts.

General plan A comprehensive document that local jurisdictions are often required by state law to devise and implement as a precursor to specific land-use regulations.

Genuineness of assent Knowing and voluntary assent to the terms of a contract. If a contract is formed as a result of a mistake, misrepresentation, undue influence, or duress, genuineness of assent is lacking, and the contract will be voidable.

Good faith purchaser A purchaser who buys without notice of any circumstance that would put a person of ordinary prudence on inquiry as to whether the seller has valid title to the goods being sold.

Good Samaritan statute A state statute that provides that persons who rescue or provide emergency services to others in peril—unless they do so recklessly, thus causing further harm—cannot be sued for negligence.

Grand jury A group of citizens called to decide, after hearing the state's evidence, whether a reasonable basis (probable cause) exists for believing that a crime has been committed and whether a trial ought to be held.

Grant deed A deed that simply recites words of consideration and conveyance. Under statute, a grant deed may impliedly warrant that at least the grantor has not conveyed the property's title to someone else.

Group boycott The refusal to deal with a particular person or firm by a group of competitors; prohibited by the Sherman Act.

H

Hacker A person who uses one computer to break into another. Professional computer programmers refer to such persons as "crackers."

Hirfindahl-Hirschman Index (HHI) An index of market power used to calculate whether a merger of two businesses will result in sufficient monopoly power to violate antitrust laws.

Historical school A school of legal thought that emphasizes the evolutionary process of law and that looks to the past to discover what the principles of contemporary law should be.

Holding company A company whose business activity is holding shares in another company.

Homestead exemption A law permitting a debtor to retain the family home, either in its entirety or up to a specified dollar amount, free from the claims of unsecured creditors or trustees in bankruptcy.

Horizontal market division A market division that occurs when competitors agree to divide up the market for their products or services among themselves, either geographically or by functional class of customers (such as retailers or wholesalers). Such market division constitutes a *per se* violation of the Sherman Act.

Horizontal merger A merger between two firms that are competing in the same market.

Horizontal restraint Any agreement that in some way restrains competition between rival firms competing in the same market.

Hot-cargo agreement An agreement in which employers voluntarily agree with unions not to handle, use, or deal in nonunion-produced goods of other employers; a type of secondary boycott explicitly prohibited by the Labor-Management Reporting and Disclosure Act of 1959.

I

I-9 verification All employers must verify the employment eligibility and identity of any worker hired in the U.S. To comply with the law, employers must complete an I-9 Employment Eligibility Verification Form for all new hires within three business days.

I-551 Alien Registration Receipt Commonly referred to as a "green card," the I-551 Alien Registration Receipt is proof that a foreign-born individual is lawfully admitted for permanent residence in the United States. Persons seeking employment can prove to prospective employers that they are legally within the U.S. by showing this receipt.

Identification In a sale of goods, the express designation of the goods provided for in the contract.

Identity theft The act of stealing another's identifying information—such as a name, date of birth, or Social Security number—and using that information to access the victim's financial resources.

Implied authority Authority that is created not by an explicit oral or written agreement but by implication. In agency law, implied authority (of the agent) can be conferred by custom, inferred from the position the agent occupies, or implied by virtue of being reasonably necessary to carry out express authority.

Implied-in-fact contract A contract formed in whole or in part from the conduct of the parties (as opposed to an express contract).

Implied warranty A warranty that the law derives by implication or inference from the nature of the transaction or the relative situation or circumstances of the parties.

Implied warranty of fitness for a particular purpose A warranty that goods sold or leased are fit for a particular purpose. The warranty arises when any seller or lessor knows the particular purpose for which a buyer or lessee will use the goods and knows that the buyer or lessee is relying on the skill and judgment of the seller or lessor to select suitable goods.

Implied warranty of habitability An implied promise by a landlord that rented residential premises are fit for human habitation—that is, in a condition that is safe and suitable for people to live in.

Implied warranty of merchantability A warranty that goods being sold or leased are reasonably fit for the general purpose for which they are sold or leased, are properly packaged and labeled, and are of proper quality. The warranty automatically arises in every sale or lease of goods made by a merchant who deals in goods of the kind sold or leased.

Impossibility of performance A doctrine under which a party to a contract is relieved of his or her duty to perform when performance becomes impossible or totally impracticable (through no fault of either party).

***In personam* jurisdiction** Court jurisdiction over the "person" involved in a legal action; personal jurisdiction.

***In rem* jurisdiction** Court jurisdiction over a defendant's property.

Incidental beneficiary A third party who incidentally benefits from a contract but whose benefit was not the reason the contract was formed; an incidental beneficiary has no rights in a contract and cannot sue to have the contract enforced.

Independent contractor One who works for, and receives payment from, an employer but whose working conditions and methods are not controlled by the employer. An independent contractor is not an employee but may be an agent.

Independent regulatory agency An administrative agency that is not considered part of the government's executive branch and is not subject to the authority of the president. Independent agency officials cannot be removed without cause.

Indictment (pronounced in-*dyte*-ment) A charge by a grand jury that a named person has committed a crime.

Informal contract A contract that does not require a specified form or formality in order to be valid.

Information A formal accusation or complaint (without an indictment) issued in certain types of actions (usually criminal actions involving lesser crimes) by a law officer, such as a magistrate.

Information return A tax return submitted by a partnership that only reports the income earned by the business. The partnership as an entity does not pay taxes on the income received by the partnership. A partner's profit from the partnership (whether distributed or not) is taxed as individual income to the individual partner.

Initial order In the context of administrative law, an agency's disposition in a matter other than a rulemaking. An administrative law judge's initial order becomes final unless it is appealed.

Insider A corporate director or officer, or other employee or agent, with access to confidential information and a duty not to disclose that information in violation of insider-trading laws.

Insider trading The purchase or sale of securities on the basis of "inside information" (information that has not been made available to the public) in violation of a duty owed to the company whose stock is being traded.

Insurable interest An interest either in a person's life or well-being or in property that is sufficiently substantial that insuring against injury to (or the death of) the person or against damage to the property does not amount to a mere wagering (betting) contract.

Intangible property Property that is incapable of being apprehended by the senses (such as by sight or touch); intellectual property is an example of intangible property.

Intellectual property Property resulting from intellectual, creative processes. Patents, trademarks, and copyrights are examples of intellectual property.

Intended beneficiary A third party for whose benefit a contract is formed; an intended beneficiary can sue the promisor if such a contract is breached.

Intentional tort A wrongful act knowingly committed.

International law The law that governs relations among nations. International customs and treaties are generally considered to be two of the most important sources of international law.

International organization In international law, a term that generally refers to an organization composed mainly of nations and usually established by treaty. The United States is a member of more than one hundred multilateral and bilateral organizations, including at least twenty through the United Nations.

Interpretive rule An administrative agency rule that is simply a statement or opinion issued by the agency explaining how it interprets and intends to apply the statutes it enforces. Such rules are not automatically binding on private individuals or organizations.

Investment company A company that acts on behalf of many smaller shareholder-owners by buying a large portfolio of securities and professionally managing that portfolio.

Investment contract In securities law, a transaction in which a person invests in a common enterprise reasonably expecting profits that are derived primarily from the efforts of others.

Irrevocable offer An offer that cannot be revoked or recalled by the offeror without liability. A merchant's firm offer is an example of an irrevocable offer.

J

Joint and several liability In partnership law, a doctrine under which a plaintiff may sue, and collect a judgment from, one or more of the partners separately (severally, or individually) or all of the partners together (jointly). This is true even if one of the partners sued did not participate in, ratify, or know about whatever it was that gave rise to the cause of action.

Joint liability Shared liability. In partnership law, partners incur joint liability for partnership obligations and debts. For example, if a third party sues a partner on a partnership debt, the partner has the right to insist that the other partners be sued with him or her.

Joint tenancy The joint ownership of property by two or more co-owners in which each co-owner owns an undivided portion of the property. On the death of one of the joint tenants, his or her interest automatically passes to the surviving joint tenants.

Joint venture A joint undertaking of a specific commercial enterprise by an association of persons. A joint venture is normally not a legal entity and is treated like a partnership for federal income tax purposes.

Judgment The final order or decision resulting from a legal action.

Judicial review The process by which courts decide on the constitutionality of legislative enactments and actions of the executive branch.

Jurisdiction The authority of a court to hear and decide a specific action.

Jurisprudence The science or philosophy of law.

Justiciable (pronounced jus-*tish*-a-bul) **controversy** A controversy that is not hypothetical or academic but real and substantial; a requirement that must be satisfied before a court will hear a case.

L

Laches The equitable doctrine that bars a party's right to legal action if the party has neglected for an unreasonable length of time to act on his or her rights.

Land-use control The control over the ownership and uses of real property by authorized public agencies.

Larceny The wrongful taking and carrying away of another person's personal property with the intent to permanently deprive the owner of the property. Some states classify larceny as either grand or petit, depending on the property's value.

Law A body of enforceable rules governing relationships among individuals and between individuals and their society.

Lease In real property law, a contract by which the owner of real property (the landlord, or lessor) grants to a person (the tenant, or lessee) an exclusive right to use and possess the property, usually for a specified period of time, in return for rent or some other form of payment.

Lease agreement In regard to the lease of goods, an agreement in which one person (the lessor) agrees to transfer the right to the possession and use of property to another person (the lessee) in exchange for rental payments.

Leasehold estate An estate in realty held by a tenant under a lease. In every leasehold estate, the tenant has a qualified right to possess and/or use the land.

Legal realism A school of legal thought that was popular in the 1920s and 1930s and that challenged many existing jurisprudential assumptions, particularly the assumption that subjective elements play no part in judicial reasoning. Legal realists generally advocated a less abstract and more realistic approach to the law, an approach that would take into account customary practices and the circumstances in which transactions take place. The school left a lasting imprint on American jurisprudence.

Legal reasoning The process of reasoning by which a judge harmonizes his or her decision with the judicial decisions of previous cases.

Legislative rule An administrative agency rule that carries the same weight as a congressionally enacted statute.

Lessee A person who acquires the right to the possession and use of another's property in exchange for rental payments.

Lessor A person who sells the right to the possession and use of property to another in exchange for rental payments.

Liability Any actual or potential legal obligation, duty, debt, or responsibility.

Libel Defamation in writing or other form (such as in a videotape) having the quality of permanence.

License A revocable right or privilege of a person to come on another person's land.

Licensee One who receives a license to use, or enter onto, another's property.

Lien (pronounced *leen*) An encumbrance on a property to satisfy a debt or protect a claim for payment of a debt.

Lien creditor One whose claim is secured by a lien on particular property, as distinguished from a general creditor, who has no such security.

Life estate An interest in land that exists only for the duration of the life of some person, usually the holder of the estate.

Limited jurisdiction Exists when a court's subject-matter jurisdiction is limited. Bankruptcy courts and probate courts are examples of courts with limited jurisdiction.

Limited liability Exists when the liability of the owners of a business is limited to the amount of their investments in the firm.

Limited liability company (LLC) A hybrid form of business enterprise that offers the limited liability of the corporation but the tax advantages of a partnership.

Limited liability limited partnership (LLLP) A type of limited partnership. The difference between a limited partnership and an LLLP is that the liability of the general partner in an LLLP is the same as the liability of the limited partner—that is, the liability of all partners is limited to the amount of their investments in the firm.

Limited liability partnership (LLP) A form of partnership that allows professionals to enjoy the tax benefits of a partnership while limiting their personal liability for the malpractice of other partners.

Limited partner In a limited partnership, a partner who contributes capital to the partnership but has no right to participate in the management and operation of the business. The limited partner assumes no liability for partnership debts beyond the capital contributed.

Limited partnership A partnership consisting of one or more general partners (who manage the business and are liable to the full extent of their personal assets for debts of the partnership) and one or more limited partners (who contribute only assets and are liable only to the extent of their contributions).

Liquidated damages An amount, stipulated in the contract, that the parties to a contract believe to be a reasonable estimation of the damages that will occur in the event of a breach.

Liquidated debt A debt that is due and certain in amount.
Liquidation (1) In regard to bankruptcy, the sale of all of the nonexempt assets of a debtor and the distribution of the proceeds to the debtor's creditors. Chapter 7 of the Bankruptcy Code provides for liquidation bankruptcy proceedings. (2) In regard to corporations, the process by which corporate assets are converted into cash and distributed among creditors and shareholders according to specific rules of preference.
Lockout The closing of a plant to employees by an employer to gain leverage in collective bargaining negotiations.
Long arm statute A state statute that permits a state to obtain personal jurisdiction over nonresident defendants. A defendant must have "minimum contacts" with that state for the statute to apply.

M

Mailbox rule A rule providing that an acceptance of an offer becomes effective on dispatch (on being placed in a mailbox), if mail is, expressly or impliedly, an authorized means of communication of acceptance to the offeror.
Malpractice Professional misconduct or the failure to exercise the requisite degree of skill as a professional. Negligence—the failure to exercise due care—on the part of a professional, such as a physician or an attorney, is commonly referred to as malpractice.
Mark *See* Trademark
Market concentration A situation that exists when a small number of firms share the market for a particular good or service. For example, if the four largest grocery stores in Chicago accounted for 80 percent of all retail food sales, the market clearly would be concentrated in those four firms.
Market power The power of a firm to control the market price of its product. A monopoly has the greatest degree of market power.
Market-share liability A method of sharing liability among several firms that manufactured or marketed a particular product that may have caused a plaintiff's injury. This form of liability sharing is used when the true source of the product is unidentifiable. Each firm's liability is proportionate to its respective share of the relevant market for the product. Market-share liability applies only if the injuring product is fungible, the true manufacturer is unidentifiable, and the unknown character of the manufacturer is not the plaintiff's fault.
Market-share test The primary measure of monopoly power. A firm's market share is the percentage of a market that the firm controls.
Marketable title Title to real estate that is reasonably free from encumbrances, defects in the chain of title, and other events that affect title, such as adverse possession.
Mediation A method of settling disputes outside of court by using the services of a neutral third party, called a mediator. The mediator acts as a communicating agent between the parties and suggests ways in which the parties can resolve their dispute.
Mediator A person who attempts to reconcile the differences between two or more parties.
Member The term used to designate a person who has an ownership interest in a limited liability company.
Mens rea (pronounced *mehns ray*-uh) Mental state, or intent. A wrongful mental state is as necessary as a wrongful act to establish criminal liability. What constitutes a mental state varies according to the wrongful action. Thus, for murder, the *mens rea* is the intent to take a life; for theft, the *mens rea* must involve both the knowledge that the property belongs to another and the intent to deprive the owner of it.
Merchant A person who is engaged in the purchase and sale of goods. Under the Uniform Commercial Code, a person who deals in goods of the kind involved in the sales contract; for further definitions, see UCC 2–104.
Merger A contractual and statutory process in which one corporation (the surviving corporation) acquires all of the assets and liabilities of another corporation (the merged corporation). The shareholders of the merged corporation receive either payment for their shares or shares in the surviving corporation.
Meta tags Words inserted into a Web site's key-words field to increase the site's appearance in search engine results.
Metes and bounds Metes and bounds is a system of measuring boundary lines by the distance between two points, often using physical features of the local geography, such as roads, intersections, rivers, or bridges. The legal descriptions of real property contained in deeds often are phrased in terms of metes and bounds.
Minimum-contacts requirement The requirement that before a state court can exercise jurisdiction over a foreign corporation, the foreign corporation must have sufficient contacts with the state. A foreign corporation that has its home office in the state or that has manufacturing plants in the state meets this requirement.
Minimum wage The lowest wage, either by government regulation or union contract, that an employer may pay an hourly worker.
Mini-trial A private proceeding in which each party to a dispute argues its position before the other side, and vice versa. A neutral third party may be present and act as an adviser if the parties fail to reach an agreement.
Mirror image rule A common law rule that requires, for a valid contractual agreement, that the terms of the offeree's acceptance adhere exactly to the terms of the offeror's offer.
Misdemeanor A lesser crime than a felony, punishable by a fine or imprisonment for up to one year in other than a state or federal penitentiary.
Mitigation of damages A rule requiring a plaintiff to have done whatever was reasonable to minimize the damages caused by the defendant.
Money laundering Falsely reporting income that has been obtained through criminal activity as income obtained through a legitimate business enterprise—in effect, "laundering" the "dirty money."
Monopolization The possession of monopoly power in the relevant market and the willful acquisition or maintenance of the power, as distinguished from growth or development as a consequence of a superior product, business acumen, or historic accident.
Monopoly A term generally used to describe a market in which there is a single seller or a limited number of sellers.
Monopoly power The ability of a monopoly to dictate what takes place in a given market.
Moral minimum The minimum degree of ethical behavior expected of a business firm, which is usually defined as compliance with the law.
Mortgage A written instrument giving a creditor (the mortgagee) an interest in (a lien on) the debtor's (mortgagor's) property as security for a debt.
Mortgage bond A bond that pledges specific property. If the corporation defaults on the bond, the bondholder can take the property.
Mortgagee Under a mortgage agreement, the creditor who takes a security interest in the debtor's property.
Mortgagor Under a mortgage agreement, the debtor who gives the creditor a security interest in the debtor's property in return for a mortgage loan.

Motion A procedural request or application presented by an attorney to the court on behalf of a client.
Motion for a directed verdict In a jury trial, a motion for the judge to take the decision out of the hands of the jury and direct a verdict for the moving party on the ground that the other party has not produced sufficient evidence to support his or her claim; referred to as a motion for judgment as a matter of law in the federal courts.
Motion for a new trial A motion asserting that the trial was so fundamentally flawed (because of error, newly discovered evidence, prejudice, or other reason) that a new trial is necessary to prevent a miscarriage of justice.
Motion for judgment *n.o.v.* A motion requesting the court to grant judgment in favor of the party making the motion on the ground that the jury verdict against him or her was unreasonable and erroneous.
Motion for judgment on the pleadings A motion by either party to a lawsuit at the close of the pleadings requesting the court to decide the issue solely on the pleadings without proceeding to trial. The motion will be granted only if no facts are in dispute.
Motion for summary judgment A motion requesting the court to enter a judgment without proceeding to trial. The motion can be based on evidence outside the pleadings and will be granted only if no facts are in dispute.
Motion to dismiss A pleading in which a defendant asserts that the plaintiff's claim fails to state a cause of action (that is, has no basis in law) or that there are other grounds on which a suit should be dismissed.
Multiple product order An order issued by the Federal Trade Commission to a firm that has engaged in deceptive advertising by which the firm is required to cease and desist from false advertising not only in regard to the product that was the subject of the action but also in regard to all the firm's other products.
Mutual assent The element of agreement in the formation of a contract. The manifestation of contract parties' mutual assent to the same bargain is required to establish a contract.
Mutual fund A specific type of investment company that continually buys or sells to investors shares of ownership in a portfolio.
Mutual rescission An agreement between the parties to cancel their contract, releasing the parties from further obligations under the contract. The object of the agreement is to restore the parties to the positions they would have occupied had no contract ever been formed. *See also* Rescission

N

National law Law that pertains to a particular nation (as opposed to international law).
Natural law The belief that government and the legal system should reflect universal moral and ethical principles that are inherent in human nature. The natural law school is the oldest and one of the most significant schools of legal thought.
Necessaries Necessities required for life, such as food, shelter, clothing, and medical attention; may include whatever is believed to be necessary to maintain a person's standard of living or financial and social status.
Negligence The failure to exercise the standard of care that a reasonable person would exercise in similar circumstances.
Negligence *per se* An act (or failure to act) in violation of a statutory requirement.
Negotiation In regard to dispute settlement, a process in which parties attempt to settle their dispute without going to court, with or without attorneys to represent them.
***Noerr-Pennington* doctrine** A series of cases that permits competitors to lobby for changes in the law to gain greater protection from competition.
Nominal damages A small monetary award (often one dollar) granted to a plaintiff when no actual damage was suffered.
Nonconforming goods Goods that do not conform to contract specifications.
Nonpossessory interest Interests in land, such as a right of way, that do not include any right to possess the land, but only confer the right to use the real property of another for a specified purpose. Nonpossessory interests include easements, profits, and licenses.
Normal trade relations (NTR) status A status granted through an international treaty by which each member nation must treat other members at least as well as it treats the country that receives its most favorable treatment. This status was formerly known as most-favored-nation status.
No-strike clause Provision in a collective bargaining agreement that states the employees will not strike for any reason and labor disputes will be resolved by arbitration.
Notary public A public official authorized to attest to the authenticity of signatures.
Notice-and-comment rulemaking An administrative rulemaking procedure that involves the publication of a notice of a proposed rulemaking in the *Federal Register*, a comment period for interested parties to express their views on the proposed rule, and the publication of the agency's final rule in the *Federal Register*.
Novation The substitution, by agreement, of a new contract for an old one, with the rights under the old one being terminated. Typically, there is a substitution of a new person who is responsible for the contract and the removal of an original party's rights and duties under the contract.
Nuisance A common law doctrine under which persons may be held liable for using their property in a manner that unreasonably interferes with others' rights to use or enjoy their own property.

O

Objective theory of contracts A theory under which the intent to form a contract will be judged by outward, objective facts (what the party said when entering into the contract, how the party acted or appeared, and the circumstances surrounding the transaction) as interpreted by a reasonable person, rather than by the party's own secret, subjective intentions.
Offer A promise or commitment to perform or refrain from performing some specified act in the future.
Online dispute resolution (ODR) The resolution of disputes with the assistance of organizations that offer dispute-resolution services via the Internet.
Operating agreement In a limited liability company, an agreement in which the members set forth the details of how the business will be managed and operated.
Opinion A statement by the court expressing the reasons for its decision in a case.
Order for relief A court's grant of assistance to a complainant. In bankruptcy proceedings, the order relieves the debtor of the immediate obligation to pay the debts listed in the bankruptcy petition.
Ordinance A law passed by a local governing unit, such as a municipality or a county.
Output contract An agreement in which a seller agrees to sell and a buyer agrees to buy all or up to a stated amount of what the seller produces.

P

Parent-subsidiary merger A merger of companies in which one company (the parent corporation) owns most of the stock of the other (the subsidiary corporation). A parent-subsidiary merger (short-form merger) can use a simplified procedure when the parent corporation owns at least 90 percent of the outstanding shares of each class of stock of the subsidiary corporation.

Partially disclosed principal A principal whose identity is unknown by a third person, but the third person knows that the agent is or may be acting for a principal at the time the agent and the third person form a contract.

Partner A co-owner of a partnership.

Partnership An agreement by two or more persons to carry on, as co-owners, a business for profit.

Partnership by estoppel A judicially created partnership that may, at the court's discretion, be imposed for purposes of fairness. The court can prevent those who present themselves as partners (but who are not) from escaping liability if a third person relies on an alleged partnership in good faith and is harmed as a result.

Past consideration An act done before the contract is made, which ordinarily, by itself, cannot be consideration for a later promise to pay for the act.

Patent A government grant that gives an inventor the exclusive right or privilege to make, use, or sell his or her invention for a limited time period. The word *patent* usually refers to some invention and designates either the instrument by which patent rights are evidenced or the patent itself.

Peer-to-peer (P2P) networking The sharing of resources (such as files, hard drives, and processing styles) among multiple computers without necessarily requiring a central network server.

Penalty A sum inserted into a contract, not as a measure of compensation for its breach but rather as punishment for a default. The agreement as to the amount will not be enforced, and recovery will be limited to actual damages.

Per curiam By the whole court; a court opinion written by the court as a whole instead of being authored by a judge or justice.

Per se A Latin term meaning "in itself" or "by itself."

***Per se* violation** A type of anticompetitive agreement—such as a horizontal price-fixing agreement—that is considered to be so injurious to the public that there is no need to determine whether it actually injures market competition; rather, it is in itself (*per se*) a violation of the Sherman Act.

Perfect tender rule A common law rule under which a seller was required to deliver to the buyer goods that conformed perfectly to the requirements stipulated in the sales contract. A tender of nonconforming goods would automatically constitute a breach of contract. Under the Uniform Commercial Code, the rule has been greatly modified.

Performance In contract law, the fulfillment of one's duties arising under a contract with another; the normal way of discharging one's contractual obligations.

Periodic tenancy A lease interest in land for an indefinite period involving payment of rent at fixed intervals, such as week to week, month to month, or year to year.

Personal jurisdiction *See In personam* jurisdiction

Personal property Property that is movable; any property that is not real property.

Petition in bankruptcy The document that is filed with a bankruptcy court to initiate bankruptcy proceedings. The official forms required for a petition in bankruptcy must be completed accurately, sworn to under oath, and signed by the debtor.

Petitioner In equity practice, a party that initiates a lawsuit.

Petty offense In criminal law, the least serious kind of criminal offense, such as a traffic or building-code violation.

Pierce the corporate veil To disregard the corporate entity, which limits the liability of shareholders, and hold the shareholders personally liable for a corporate obligation.

Plaintiff One who initiates a lawsuit.

Plea In criminal law, a defendant's allegation, in response to the charges brought against him or her, of guilt or innocence.

Plea bargaining The process by which a criminal defendant and the prosecutor in a criminal case work out a mutually satisfactory disposition of the case, subject to court approval; usually involves the defendant's pleading guilty to a lesser offense in return for a lighter sentence.

Pleadings Statements made by the plaintiff and the defendant in a lawsuit that detail the facts, charges, and defenses involved in the litigation; the complaint and answer are part of the pleadings.

Police powers Powers possessed by states as part of their inherent sovereignty. These powers may be exercised to protect or promote the public order, health, safety, morals, and general welfare.

Positive law The body of conventional, or written, law of a particular society at a particular point in time.

Positivist school A school of legal thought whose adherents believe that there can be no higher law than a nation's positive law—the body of conventional, or written, law of a particular society at a particular time.

Potentially responsible party (PRP) A potentially liable party under the Comprehensive Environmental Response, Compensation and Liability Act (CERCLA). Any person who generated hazardous waste, transported the hazardous waste, owned or operated a waste site at the time of disposal, or currently owns or operates a site may be responsible for some or all of the clean-up costs involved in removing the hazardous chemicals.

Power of attorney A written document, which is usually notarized, authorizing another to act as one's agent; can be special (permitting the agent to do specified acts only) or general (permitting the agent to transact all business for the principal).

Precedent A court decision that furnishes an example or authority for deciding subsequent cases involving identical or similar facts.

Predatory pricing The pricing of a product below cost with the intent to drive competitors out of the market.

Preemption A doctrine under which certain federal laws preempt, or take precedence over, conflicting state or local laws.

Preference In bankruptcy proceedings, property transfers or payments made by the debtor that favor (give preference to) one creditor over others. The bankruptcy trustee is allowed to recover payments made both voluntarily and involuntarily to one creditor in preference over another.

Preferred creditor In the context of bankruptcy, a creditor who has received a preferential transfer from a debtor.

Pretrial motion A written or oral application to a court for a ruling or order, made before trial.

Price discrimination Setting prices in such a way that two competing buyers pay two different prices for an identical product or service.

Price fixing Fixing—by means of an anticompetitive agreement between competitors—the prices of products or services.

Price-fixing agreement An agreement between competitors in which the competitors agree to fix the prices of products or services at a certain level; prohibited by the Sherman Act.

***Prima facie* case** A case in which the plaintiff has produced sufficient evidence of his or her conclusion that the case can go to to a jury; a case in which the evidence compels

the plaintiff's conclusion if the defendant produces no evidence to disprove it.
Principal In agency law, a person who agrees to have another, called the agent, act on his or her behalf.
Principle of rights The principle that human beings have certain fundamental rights (to life, freedom, and the pursuit of happiness, for example). Those who adhere to this "rights theory" believe that a key factor in determining whether a business decision is ethical is how that decision affects the rights of others. These others include the firm's owners, its employees, the consumers of its products or services, its suppliers, the community in which it does business, and society as a whole.
Privilege In tort law, the ability to act contrary to another person's right without that person's having legal redress for such acts. Privilege may be raised as a defense to defamation.
Privileges and immunities clause Special rights and exceptions provided by law. Article IV, Section 2, of the Constitution requires states not to discriminate against one another's citizens. A resident of one state cannot be treated as an alien when in another state; he or she may not be denied such privileges and immunities as legal protection, access to courts, travel rights, or property rights.
Privity of contract The relationship that exists between the promisor and the promisee of a contract.
Probable cause Reasonable grounds to believe the existence of facts warranting certain actions, such as the search or arrest of a person.
Probate court A state court of limited jurisdiction that conducts proceedings relating to the settlement of a deceased person's estate.
Procedural law Rules that define the manner in which the rights and duties of individuals may be enforced.
Product liability The legal liability of manufacturers, sellers, and lessors of goods to consumers, users, and bystanders for injuries or damages that are caused by the goods.
Product misuse A defense against product liability that may be raised when the plaintiff used a product in a manner not intended by the manufacturer. If the misuse is reasonably foreseeable, the seller will not escape liability unless measures were taken to guard against the harm that could result from the misuse.
Profit In real property law, the right to enter onto and remove things from the property of another (for example, the right to enter onto a person's land and remove sand and gravel therefrom).
Promise A declaration that something either will or will not happen in the future.
Promissory estoppel A doctrine that applies when a promisor makes a clear and definite promise on which the promisee justifiably relies; such a promise is binding if justice will be better served by the enforcement of the promise.
Prospectus A document required by federal or state securities laws that describes the financial operations of the corporation, thus allowing investors to make informed decisions.
Protected class A class of persons with identifiable characteristics who historically have been victimized by discriminatory treatment for certain purposes. Depending on the context, these characteristics include age, color, gender, national origin, race, and religion.
Proximate cause Legal cause; exists when the connection between an act and an injury is strong enough to justify imposing liability.
Proxy In corporation law, a written agreement between a stockholder and another under which the stockholder authorizes the other to vote the stockholder's shares in a certain manner.
Proxy fight A conflict between an individual, group, or firm attempting to take control of a corporation and the corporation's management for the votes of the shareholders.
Public figures Individuals who are thrust into the public limelight. Public figures include government officials and politicians, movie stars, well-known businesspersons, and generally anybody who becomes known to the public because of his or her position or activities.
Public policy A government policy based on widely held societal values and (usually) expressed or implied in laws or regulations.
Puffery A salesperson's often-exaggerated claims concerning the quality of property offered for sale. Such claims involve opinions rather than facts and are not considered to be legally binding promises or warranties.
Punitive damages Monetary damages that may be awarded to a plaintiff to punish the defendant and deter future similar conduct.

Q

Quasi contract A fictional contract imposed on parties by a court in the interests of fairness and justice; usually, quasi contracts are imposed to avoid the unjust enrichment of one party at the expense of another.
Question of fact In a lawsuit, an issue involving a factual dispute that can only be decided by a judge (or, in a jury trial, a jury).
Question of law In a lawsuit, an issue involving the application or interpretation of a law; therefore, the judge, and not the jury, decides the issue.
Quitclaim deed A deed intended to pass any title, interest, or claim that the grantor may have in the property but not warranting that such title is valid. A quitclaim deed offers the least amount of protection against defects in the title.
Quorum The number of members of a decision-making body that must be present before business may be transacted.
Quota An assigned import limit on goods.

R

Ratification The act of accepting and giving legal force to an obligation that previously was not enforceable.
Reaffirmation agreement An agreement between a debtor and a creditor in which the debtor reaffirms, or promises to pay, a debt dischargeable in bankruptcy. To be enforceable, the agreement must be made prior to the discharge of the debt by the bankruptcy court.
Real property Land and everything attached to it, such as foliage and buildings.
Reasonable person standard The standard of behavior expected of a hypothetical "reasonable person." The standard against which negligence is measured and that must be observed to avoid liability for negligence.
Recording statutes Statutes that allow deeds, mortgages, and other real property transactions to be recorded so as to provide notice to future purchasers or creditors of an existing claim on the property.
Red herring prospectus A preliminary prospectus that can be distributed to potential investors after the registration statement (for a securities offering) has been filed with the Securities and Exchange Commission. The name derives from the red legend printed across the prospectus stating that the registration has been filed but has not become effective.
Reformation A court-ordered correction of a written contract so that it reflects the true intentions of the parties.

Regulation Z A set of rules promulgated by the Federal Reserve Board to implement the provisions of the Truth in Lending Act.
Rejection In contract law, an offeree's express or implied manifestation not to accept an offer. In the law governing contracts for the sale of goods, a buyer's manifest refusal to accept goods on the ground that they do not conform to contract specifications.
Relevant evidence Evidence tending to make a fact at issue in the case more or less probable than it would be without the evidence. Only relevant evidence is admissible in court.
Remanded Sent back. If an appellate court disagrees with a lower court's judgment, the case may be remanded to the lower court for further proceedings in which the lower court's decision should be consistent with the appellate court's opinion on the matter.
Remedy The relief given to an innocent party to enforce a right or compensate for the violation of a right.
Remedy at law A remedy available in a court of law. Money damages are awarded as a remedy at law.
Remedy in equity A remedy allowed by courts in situations where remedies at law are not appropriate. Remedies in equity are based on settled rules of fairness, justice, and honesty, and include injunction, specific performance, rescission and restitution, and reformation.
Reporter A publication in which court cases are published, or reported.
Requirements contract An agreement in which a buyer agrees to purchase and the seller agrees to sell all or up to a stated amount of what the buyer needs or requires.
Res ipsa loquitur (pronounced *rehs ehp*-suh *low*-quuh-duhr) A doctrine under which negligence may be inferred simply because an event occurred, if it is the type of event that would not occur in the absence of negligence. Literally, the term means "the facts speak for themselves."
Resale price maintenance agreement An agreement between a manufacturer and a retailer in which the manufacturer specifies the minimum retail price of its products.
Rescind (pronounced reh-*sihnd*) To cancel. *See also* Rescission
Rescission (pronounced reh-*sih*-zhen) A remedy whereby a contract is canceled and the parties are returned to the positions they occupied before the contract was made; may be effected through the mutual consent of the parties, by their conduct, or by court decree.
Respondeat superior (pronounced ree-*spahn*-dee-uht soo-*peer*-ee-your) In Latin, "Let the master respond." A doctrine under which a principal or an employer is held liable for the wrongful acts committed by agents or employees while acting within the course and scope of their agency or employment.
Respondent In equity practice, the party who answers a bill or other proceeding.
Restitution An equitable remedy under which a person is restored to his or her original position prior to loss or injury, or placed in the position he or she would have been in had the breach not occurred.
Restraint of trade Any contract or combination that tends to eliminate or reduce competition, effect a monopoly, artificially maintain prices, or otherwise hamper the course of trade and commerce as it would be carried on if left to the control of natural economic forces.
Restrictive covenant A private restriction on the use of land that is binding on the party that purchases the property originally as well as on subsequent purchasers. If its benefit or obligation passes with the land's ownership, it is said to "run with the land."
Retained earnings The portion of a corporation's profits that has not been paid out as dividends to shareholders.
Revocation In contract law, the withdrawal of an offer by an offeror. Unless an offer is irrevocable, it can be revoked at any time prior to acceptance without liability.
Right-to-work law A state law providing that employees are not to be required to join a union as a condition of obtaining or retaining employment.
Robbery The act of forcefully and unlawfully taking personal property of any value from another; force or intimidation is usually necessary for an act of theft to be considered a robbery.
Rule of four A rule of the United States Supreme Court under which the Court will not issue a writ of *certiorari* unless at least four justices approve of the decision to issue the writ.
Rule of reason A test by which a court balances the positive effects (such as economic efficiency) of an agreement against its potentially anticompetitive effects. In antitrust litigation, many practices are analyzed under the rule of reason.
Rulemaking The process undertaken by an administrative agency when formally adopting a new regulation or amending an old one. Rulemaking involves notifying the public of a proposed rule or change and receiving and considering the public's comments.
Rules of evidence Rules governing the admissibility of evidence in trial courts.

S

S corporation A close business corporation that has met certain requirements as set out by the Internal Revenue Code and thus qualifies for special income tax treatment. Essentially, an S corporation is taxed the same as a partnership, but its owners enjoy the privilege of limited liability.
Sale The passing of title from the seller to the buyer for a price.
Sale on approval A type of conditional sale in which the buyer may take the goods on a trial basis. The sale becomes absolute only when the buyer approves of (or is satisfied with) the goods being sold.
Sale or return A type of conditional sale in which title and possession pass from the seller to the buyer; however, the buyer retains the option to return the goods during a specified period even though the goods conform to the contract.
Sales contract A contract for the sale of goods under which the ownership of goods is transferred from a seller to a buyer for a price.
Scienter (pronounced *sy-en*-ter) Knowledge by the misrepresenting party that material facts have been falsely represented or omitted with an intent to deceive.
Search warrant An order granted by a public authority, such as a judge, that authorizes law enforcement personnel to search particular premises or property.
Seasonably Within a specified time period, or, if no period is specified, within a reasonable time.
SEC Rule 10b-5 A rule of the Securities and Exchange Commission that makes it unlawful, in connection with the purchase or sale of any security, to make any untrue statement of a material fact or to omit a material fact if such omission causes the statement to be misleading.
Secondary boycott A union's refusal to work for, purchase from, or handle the products of a secondary employer, with whom the union has no dispute, for the purpose of forcing that employer to stop doing business with the primary employer, with whom the union has a labor dispute.
Securities Generally, corporate stocks and bonds. A security may also be a note, debenture, stock warrant, or any document given as evidence of an ownership interest in a corporation or as a promise of repayment by a corporation.

Self-defense The legally recognized privilege to protect one's self or property against injury by another. The privilege of self-defense protects only acts that are reasonably necessary to protect one's self or property.

Seniority system In regard to employment relationships, a system in which those who have worked longest for the company are first in line for promotions, salary increases, and other benefits; they are also the last to be laid off if the workforce must be reduced.

Service mark A mark used in the sale or the advertising of services, such as to distinguish the services of one person from the services of others. Titles, character names, and other distinctive features of radio and television programs may be registered as service marks.

Service of process The delivery of the complaint and summons to a defendant.

Severance pay A payment by an employer to an employee that exceeds the employee's wages due on termination.

Settlor One creating a trust.

Sexual harassment In the employment context, the granting of job promotions or other benefits in return for sexual favors or language or conduct that is so sexually offensive that it creates a hostile working environment.

Shareholder One who purchases shares of a corporation's stock, thus acquiring an equity interest in the corporation.

Sheriff's deed The deed given to the purchaser of property at a sheriff's sale as part of the foreclosure process against the owner of the property.

Shipment contract A contract for the sale of goods in which the seller is required or authorized to ship the goods by carrier. The buyer assumes liability for any losses or damage to the goods after they are delivered to the carrier.

Slander Defamation in oral form.

Slander of quality (trade libel) The publication of false information about another's product, alleging that it is not what its seller claims.

Slander of title The publication of a statement that denies or casts doubt on another's legal ownership of any property, causing financial loss to that property's owner.

Small claims courts Special courts in which parties may litigate small claims (usually, claims involving $5,000 or less). Attorneys are not required in small claims courts, and in many states attorneys are not allowed to represent the parties.

Sociological school A school of legal thought that views the law as a tool for promoting justice in society.

Sole proprietorship The simplest form of business, in which the owner is the business; the owner reports business income on his or her personal income tax return and is legally responsible for all debts and obligations incurred by the business.

Sovereign immunity A doctrine that immunizes foreign nations from the jurisdiction of U.S. courts when certain conditions are satisfied.

Spam Bulk, unsolicited ("junk") e-mail.

Special warranty deed A deed in which the grantor only covenants to warrant and defend the title against claims and demands of the grantor and all persons claiming by, through, and under the grantor.

Specific performance An equitable remedy requiring exactly the performance that was specified in a contract; usually granted only when money damages would be an inadequate remedy and the subject matter of the contract is unique (for example, real property).

Standing to sue The requirement that an individual must have a sufficient stake in a controversy before he or she can bring a lawsuit. The plaintiff must demonstrate that he or she either has been injured or threatened with injury.

Stare decisis (pronounced *ster*-ay dih-*si*-ses) A common law doctrine under which judges are obligated to follow the precedents established in prior decisions.

Statute of Frauds A state statute under which certain types of contracts must be in writing to be enforceable.

Statute of limitations A federal or state statute setting the maximum time period during which a certain action can be brought or certain rights enforced.

Statute of repose Basically, a statute of limitations that is not dependent on the happening of a cause of action. Statutes of repose generally begin to run at an earlier date and run for a longer period of time than statutes of limitations.

Statutory law The body of law enacted by legislative bodies (as opposed to constitutional law, administrative law, or case law).

Stock An equity (ownership) interest in a corporation, measured in units of shares.

Strict liability Liability regardless of fault. In tort law, strict liability may be imposed on defendants in cases involving abnormally dangerous activities, dangerous animals, or defective products.

Strike An extreme action undertaken by unionized workers when collective bargaining fails; the workers leave their jobs, refuse to work, and (typically) picket the employer's workplace.

Sublease A lease executed by the lessee of real estate to a third person, conveying the same interest that the lessee enjoys but for a shorter term than that held by the lessee.

Submission An agreement by two or more parties to refer any disputes they may have under their contract to a disinterested third party, such as an arbitrator, who has the power to render a binding decision.

Substantial performance Performance that does not vary greatly from the performance promised in a contract; the performance must create substantially the same benefits as those promised in the contract.

Substantive due process A requirement that focuses on the content, or substance, of legislation. If a law or other governmental action limits a fundamental right, such as the right to travel or to vote, it will be held to violate substantive due process unless it promotes a compelling or overriding state interest.

Substantive law Law that defines the rights and duties of individuals with respect to each other, as opposed to procedural law, which defines the manner in which these rights and duties may be enforced.

Summary jury trial (SJT) A method of settling disputes in which a trial is held, but the jury's verdict is not binding. The verdict acts only as a guide to both sides in reaching an agreement during the mandatory negotiations that immediately follow the summary jury trial.

Supremacy clause The provision in Article VI of the Constitution that provides that the Constitution, laws, and treaties of the United States are "the supreme Law of the Land." Under this clause, state and local laws that directly conflict with federal law will be rendered invalid.

Syllogism A form of deductive reasoning consisting of a major premise, a minor premise, and a conclusion.

Symbolic speech Nonverbal conduct that expresses opinions or thoughts about a subject. Symbolic speech is protected under the First Amendment's guarantee of freedom of speech.

T

Taking The taking of private property by the government for public use. Under the Fifth Amendment to the Constitution, the government may not take private property for public use without "just compensation."

Tangible employment action A significant change in employment status, such as firing or failing to promote an employee; reassigning the employee to a position with significantly different responsibilities; or effecting a significant change in employment benefits.

Tangible property Property that has physical existence and can be distinguished by the senses of touch, sight, and so on. A car is tangible property; a patent right is intangible property.

Tariff A tax on imported goods.

Tenancy at sufferance A type of tenancy under which one who, after rightfully being in possession of leased premises, continues (wrongfully) to occupy the property after the lease has been terminated. The tenant has no rights to possess the property and occupies it only because the person entitled to evict the tenant has not done so.

Tenancy at will A type of tenancy under which either party can terminate the tenancy without notice; usually arises when a tenant who has been under a tenancy for years retains possession, with the landlord's consent, after the tenancy for years has terminated.

Tenancy by the entirety The joint ownership of property by a husband and wife. Neither party can transfer his or her interest in the property without the consent of the other.

Tenancy in common Co-ownership of property in which each party owns an undivided interest that passes to his or her heirs at death.

Tender An unconditional offer to perform an obligation by a person who is ready, willing, and able to do so.

Tender of delivery Under the Uniform Commercial Code, a seller's or lessor's act of placing conforming goods at the disposal of the buyer or lessee and giving the buyer or lessee whatever notification is reasonably necessary to enable the buyer or lessee to take delivery.

Tender offer An offer to purchase made by one company directly to the shareholders of another (target) company; often referred to as a "takeover bid."

Third party beneficiary One for whose benefit a promise is made in a contract but who is not a party to the contract.

Tippee A person who receives inside information.

Title insurance Insurance commonly purchased by a purchaser of real property to protect against loss in the event that the title to the property is not free from liens or superior ownership claims.

Tombstone ad An advertisement, historically in a format resembling a tombstone, of a securities offering. The ad informs potential investors of where and how they may obtain a prospectus.

Tort A civil wrong not arising from a breach of contract. A breach of a legal duty that proximately causes harm or injury to another.

Tortfeasor One who commits a tort.

Toxic tort Failure to use or to clean up properly toxic chemicals that cause harm to a person or society.

Trade dress The image and overall appearance of a product—for example, the distinctive decor, menu, layout, and style of service of a particular restaurant. Basically, trade dress is subject to the same protection as trademarks.

Trade libel The publication of false information about another's product, alleging it is not what its seller claims; also referred to as *slander of quality.*

Trade name A term that is used to indicate part or all of a business's name and that is directly related to the business's reputation and goodwill. Trade names are protected under the common law (and under trademark law, if the name is the same as the firm's trademarked property).

Trade secret Information or a process that gives a business an advantage over competitors who do not know the information or process.

Trademark A distinctive mark, motto, device, or implement that a manufacturer stamps, prints, or otherwise affixes to the goods it produces so that they may be identified on the market and their origins made known. Once a trademark is established (under the common law or through registration), the owner is entitled to its exclusive use.

Treaty An agreement formed between two or more independent nations.

Treble damages Damages consisting of single damages determined by a jury and tripled in amount in certain cases as required by statute.

Trespass to land The entry onto, above, or below the surface of land owned by another without the owner's permission or legal authorization.

Trespass to personal property The unlawful taking or harming of another's personal property; interference with another's right to the exclusive possession of his or her personal property.

Trust An arrangement in which title to property is held by one person (a trustee) for the benefit of another (a beneficiary).

Trustee One who holds title to property for the use or benefit of another (the beneficiary).

Tying arrangement An agreement between a buyer and a seller in which the buyer of a specific product or service becomes obligated to purchase additional products or services from the seller.

U

Use zoning Zoning classifications within a particular municipality that may be distinguished based upon the uses to which the land is to be put.

U.S. trustee A government official who performs certain administrative tasks that a bankruptcy judge would otherwise have to perform.

Ultra vires (pronounced *uhl*-trah *vye*-reez) A Latin term meaning "beyond the powers"; in corporate law, acts of a corporation that are beyond its express and implied powers to undertake.

Unconscionable (pronounced un-*kon*-shun-uh-bul) **contract or clause** A contract or clause that is void on the basis of public policy because one party, as a result of his or her disproportionate bargaining power, is forced to accept terms that are unfairly burdensome and that unfairly benefit the dominating party. *See also* Procedural unconscionability; Substantive unconscionability

Undisclosed principal A principal whose identity is unknown by a third person, and the third person has no knowledge that the agent is acting for a principal at the time the agent and the third person form a contract.

Unenforceable contract A valid contract rendered unenforceable by some statute or law.

Uniform law A model law created by the National Conference of Commissioners on Uniform State Laws and/or the American Law Institute for the states to consider adopting. If the state adopts the law, it becomes statutory law in that state. Each state has the option of adopting or rejecting all or part of a uniform law.

Unilateral contract A contract that results when an offer can only be accepted by the offeree's performance.

Union shop A place of employment in which all workers, once employed, must become union members within a specified period of time as a condition of their continued employment.

Unreasonably dangerous product In product liability, a product that is defective to the point of threatening a consumer's health and safety. A product will be considered unreasonably dangerous if it is dangerous beyond the expectation of the ordinary consumer or if a less dangerous alternative was

economically feasible for the manufacturer, but the manufacturer failed to produce it.
Utilitarianism An approach to ethical reasoning in which ethically correct behavior is not related to any absolute ethical or moral values but to an evaluation of the consequences of a given action on those who will be affected by it. In utilitarian reasoning, a "good" decision is one that results in the greatest good for the greatest number of people affected by the decision.

V

Valid contract A contract that results when elements necessary for contract formation (agreement, consideration, legal purpose, and contractual capacity) are present.
Validation notice An initial notice to a debtor from a collection agency informing the debtor that he or she has thirty days to challenge the debt and request verification.
Vendee One who purchases property from another, called the vendor.
Vertical merger The acquisition by a company at one stage of production of a company at a higher or lower stage of production (such as a company merging with one of its suppliers or retailers).
Vertical restraint Any restraint on trade created by agreements between firms at different levels in the manufacturing and distribution process.
Vertically integrated firm A firm that carries out two or more functional phases—for example, manufacture, distribution, retailing—of a product.
Vesting The creation of an absolute or unconditional right or power.
Vicarious liability Legal responsibility placed on one person for the acts of another.
Void contract A contract having no legal force or binding effect.
Voidable contract A contract that may be legally avoided (canceled, or annulled) at the option of one of the parties.

W

Waiver An intentional, knowing relinquishment of a legal right.
Warehouser One in the business of operating a warehouse.
Warranty A promise that certain facts are truly as they are represented to be.
Warranty deed A deed in which the grantor guarantees to the grantee that the grantor has title to the property conveyed in the deed, that there are no encumbrances on the property other than what the grantor has represented, and that the grantee will enjoy quiet possession of the property; a deed that provides the greatest amount of protection for the grantee.
Warranty disclaimer A seller's or lessor's negation or qualification of a warranty.
Warranty of fitness *See* Implied warranty of fitness for a particular purpose
Warranty of merchantability *See* Implied warranty of merchantability
Warranty of title An implied warranty made by a seller that the seller has good and valid title to the goods sold and that the transfer of the title is rightful.
Waste The abuse or destructive use of real property by one who is in rightful possession of the property but who does not have title to it. Waste does not include ordinary depreciation due to age and normal use.
Watered stock Shares of stock issued by a corporation for which the corporation receives, as payment, less than the stated value of the shares.
Whistleblowing An employee's disclosure to government, the press, or upper-management authorities that the employer is engaged in unsafe or illegal activities.
White-collar crime Nonviolent crime committed by individuals or corporations to obtain a personal or business advantage.
Wildcat strike A strike that is not authorized by the union that ordinarily represents the striking employees.
Willful Intentional.
Winding up The second of two stages involved in the termination of a partnership or corporation. Once the firm is dissolved, it continues to exist legally until the process of winding up all business affairs (collecting and distributing the firm's assets) is complete.
Workers' compensation laws State statutes establishing an administrative procedure for compensating workers' injuries that arise out of—or in the course of—their employment, regardless of fault.
Workout An out-of-court agreement between a debtor and his or her creditors in which the parties work out a payment plan or schedule under which the debtor's debts can be discharged.
Writ of *certiorari* (pronounced sur-shee-uh-*rah*-ree) A writ from a higher court asking the lower court for the record of a case.
Wrongful discharge An employer's termination of an employee's employment in violation of an employment contract or laws that protect employees.

Z

Zoning The division of a city by legislative regulation into districts and the application in each district of regulations having to do with structural and architectural designs of buildings and prescribing the use to which buildings within designated districts may be put.
Zoning variance The granting of permission by a municipality or other public board to a landowner to use his or her property in a way that does not strictly conform with the zoning regulations so as to avoid causing the landowner undue hardship.

Table of Cases

A

B

H

I

J

K

L

M

N

O

P

THE LEGAL ENVIRONMENT OF BUSINESS
JUSTICE
CROSS AND MILLER

Index

E

G

H

I

J

O

P